# INTRODUCTION

The average English-speaker knows around 50,000 words. That represents an astonishing diversity – nearly 25 times more words than there are individual stars visible to the naked eye in the night sky. And even 50,000 seems insignificant beside the half a million recorded in the *Oxford English Dictionary*. But looked at from a historical perspective, that diversity becomes more apparent than real. Tracing a word's development back in time shows that in many cases what are now separate lexical items were formerly one and the same word. The deep prehistory of our language has nurtured little word-seeds that over the millennia have proliferated into widely differentiated families of vocabulary.

The purpose of this book is to uncover the often surprising connections between elements of the English lexicon that have become obscured by centuries of language change – the links in our word-web that join such unlikely partners as, for instance, *beef* and *cow*, *bacteria* and *imbecile*, and *bishop* and *spy*.

### The origins of the English language
The life stories of individual words, often mazy and conjectural, need a fixed backdrop if they are to make sense. So first, a little history. English is a member of the Indo-European family of languages. The precise origins of this are still a matter of some controversy, but the consensus view is that it came on the scene around 8000 years ago in the general area to the north of the Black Sea. Since then it has split up into a large number of subgroups, which today provide nearly all the languages of Europe and have also spread over large areas of the Middle East and northern India. Among them are the Indo-Iranian languages, including Hindi and ancient Sanskrit; the Slavic languages – Russian, Polish, Czech, Serbo-Croat, and so on; the Baltic languages, Latvian and Lithuanian (which of all these modern languages most closely resembles its Indo-European ancestor); the Celtic languages, such as Welsh, Gaelic, and Breton; and Greek.

But in the history of English, there are two particular groups that are of central importance. The first is the Romance languages: classical Latin, the literary language of ancient Rome; and French, Italian, Spanish, Portuguese, and Rumanian, which evolved from Vulgar Latin, the language of the common people that spread through the Western Roman empire. The role of Latin and French, in particular, in the growth of English vocabulary has been immense. We acquired a sizable proportion of our words from one or other of these sources.

The second important group, of course, is the Germanic languages: for that is the group to which English itself belongs. The existence of the Germanic peoples as a separate speech community dates back at least 3000 years. Their first northern European home has been traced to an area around the River Elbe. At this time they all spoke the same language, which is generally known as Common Germanic. Around the 2nd century BC this began to split up into three distinct dialects. One was East Germanic. The only East Germanic language of which any written evidence survives is Gothic. Now extinct, it was spoken by Germanic peoples who migrated back eastwards to the area of modern Bulgaria and the Crimea. It provides us with our closest glimpse of what prehistoric Common Germanic must have been like. The second was North Germanic, which has evolved into modern Swedish, Danish, Norwegian, and Icelandic. And lastly there was West Germanic, the ancestor of modern German, Dutch, Flemish, Frisian, and English.

The forerunners of English crossed the Channel in the 5th and 6th centuries AD. They were brought by peoples from the northeastern corner of the European mainland, around Jutland and southern Denmark – the Angles, Saxons, and Jutes. They spoke a mutually intelligible set of Germanic dialects (whose closest modern continental relative is Frisian), which formed the basis of what is now known as Old English (the alternative term 'Anglo-Saxon' is no longer much used). This was a more or less homogeneous language, but with marked geographical differences reflecting the areas into which the various Germanic peoples had moved: the Angles into the Midlands (where Mercian was spoken) and the North (whose form of Old English is now called Northumbrian); the Jutes into Kent; and the Saxons into the rest of southern and western England (their speech is known as West Saxon).

### Astonishing richness and diversity
The end of the Old English period is conventionally associated with the Norman Conquest of 1066, but in practice of course the transition into the next historical phase of the language, which we term Middle English, was a gradual process. Its crucial feature from the point of view of vocabulary was the beginning of the importation of non-native

words which over the centuries have transformed English from a parochial northeast European dialect into a lexical tapestry of astonishing richness and diversity. A smattering of Latin words entered the language following the conversion of the English to Christianity in the 7th century, but it was the Vikings who first introduced new ingredients to the lexical blend in a big way. Their forays began in the mid-8th century and lasted for several hundred years. Their impact on English was greatest in northern areas, where they settled, but the language as a whole is indebted to Old Norse for such basic words as *anger, egg, knife, law*, and *leg*.

Undoubtedly the single most significant event in the history of the English language was the Norman invasion of 1066. For it provided the impetus for a huge influx of vocabulary from across the English Channel. These new words came both via Anglo-Norman, the dialect of Old French spoken in England by the new ruling classes, which was based on the northern variety of French; and direct from Old French itself (Old French, the ancestor of modern French, was spoken from the 9th century to roughly the middle of the 16th century). It was this lexical infusion, which lasted from the 11th to the 16th centuries, which truly laid the basis for the hybrid English language of today. It would be futile to try and give a representative sample of the words it introduced, for they are so all-pervasive. From *supper* to *justice*, from *action* to *money*, from *village* to *receive*, they came in their thousands. Some were Gaulish in ultimate origin. Gaulish was the Celtic language spoken in what is now France before French killed it off. But the great majority of these French imports were descended from earlier Latin ancestors.

It was Latin itself, together with Greek, that formed the next wave of lexical innovation in English. With the Renaissance came a revival in classical scholarship, and in the 16th and 17th centuries hundreds of Latin and Greek words were naturalized into English – among them *apparatus, area, crisis, maximum, poem*, and *pollen*, to name no more than a minute fraction.

### Expanding horizons

It was around this time that English started to roam beyond its historical boundaries. As English merchant venturers sailed the world, not only did they take their language with them to distant continents, where it has since become in many cases the dominant form of speech, but they also brought back with them new and exotic terms that have found their way into the English lexicon. There is not a major language in the world that has not over the past 500 years made some contribution to English, from the bountiful donations of Italian (*aria, arcade, bandit, bust, escort, frigate, granite, madrigal, pedal, solo, umbrella*, etc) and Hindi (*bungalow, chintz, cot, juggernaut, pundit, shampoo*, etc) to the more modest gifts from the likes of Finnish (*sauna*) and Tibetan (*lama*).

English is still growing – faster probably in the late 20th century than at any previous time in its history (it has been calculated that around 800 neologisms are added to the working vocabulary of the language every year). Over half of the new items come from combinations of old ones, but there continues to be a lot of borrowing from other languages (*glasnost* and *perestroika* are notable examples from the 1980s). The formation of blends (conflations of existing words, such as *motel* formed from *motor* and *hotel*) and acronyms (words made up from initial letters, like *yuppie* – a young urban professional) is characteristic of late 20th-century English.

### Unlikely relatives

All down these centuries of evolution and acquisition runs a complex tracery of descent – often muddled, interrupted, cancelling itself out or losing itself in dead ends, but often too presenting us with breathtaking lexical fragmentation patterns that link the unlikeliest of partners. It seems scarcely plausible, for instance, that *acrobat* and *oxygen* should be related, but they are. Both go back ultimately to an Indo-European base *\*ak-*, which conveyed the notion of being 'pointed' or 'sharp.' An *acrobat* is etymologically someone who walks on the 'points' of the feet, or on tiptoe (it is based on Greek *ákros* 'terminal, topmost'), while *oxygen* means literally 'acid-producer'. It comes from Greek *oxús* 'sharp, acid,' which in turn was descended from *\*ak-*. Nor is this by any means the end of the story. For the same base is responsible for a wide range of other English words, including *acacia, acid, acme, acne, acrid, acute, eager, ear* (of corn), *edge*, and *vinegar*. Despite their common source, they have reached English along very different routes. *Ear* and *edge*, for example, come in a line of direct descent from Indo-European through Germanic, while *eager* came via Old French from Latin, and *acrobat* and *oxygen*, as we have seen, go back to Greek.

This family of English words traces its history right back to the prehistoric roots of the language, but such extreme antiquity is not a precondition for great diversity. The Latin word *gradus* 'step,' for instance, lies behind an enormous range of English vocabulary, much of it formed by prefixation: *aggression*, for example, *congress, degrade, degree, digress, egress, ingredient, ingress, progress, regress, retrograde*, and *transgress*, not to mention *grade, gradation, gradient, gradual*, and *graduate*. An even more prolific source has been Latin *cēdere* 'go, go away, give up,' which has given English *accede, ancestor, cease, cede, concede, exceed, intercede, precede, proceed, recede*, and *succeed*, plus a range of related nouns such as *concession* and *procession*.

# DICTIONARY OF
# WORD ORIGINS

# JOHN AYTO

## DICTIONARY OF
# WORD ORIGINS

Arcade Publishing • New York

Little, Brown and Company

*Library of Congress Cataloging-in-Publication Data*
Ayto, John.
    Dictionary of word origins / John Ayto. — 1st U. S. ed.
    p.  cm.

    1. English language — Etymology — Dictionaries. I. Title.
PE 1580.A97   1991
422'.03 — dc20                            91-2958

Published in the United States by Arcade Publishing, Inc., New York,
a Little, Brown company

RRD-VA

*Printed in the United States of America*

## How to use this book

The aim of this dictionary is to bring out and make explicit these sorts of historical connection between English words. It is arranged alphabetically, so that each article deals in the first instance with the origin and development of a particular word. But where appropriate the relationship of that word with other English words is described, and for quick reference a list is provided (preceded by ▶) of the words which are etymologically linked with the entry word. All the words whose story is told in the dictionary are shown with a date after them in square brackets. This denotes the century in which they are first recorded in English. Thus **cock-a-hoop** [16] indicates that *cock-a-hoop* probably entered the language in the 16th century (words that date back to the Old English period are marked simply [OE]). If, in the article about a given word, a related word is mentioned but no date is shown for it, this means that the related word has its own article, so you should look there for further information.

In all about 8000 words have their stories told here. They represent the central core of English vocabulary, plus an extensive selection of words included either because their etymology is intrinsically interesting, or because they form part of a wider lexical family. It is far from being an exhaustive account of the entire English lexicon, of course, for it is not part of the book's purpose to give a complete list of the (all too many) English words whose origins are not known for certain.

In terms of sheer numbers of years, at least half of the period which the *Dictionary of Word Origins* covers predates the emergence of writing in the West, and so much of the material in it – Indo-European forms, for instance, and prehistoric Germanic words – is not recorded from contemporary sources. That we know so much about it is due to the work of historical linguists, who have reconstructed these ancient words and word-parts from the evidence of later written sources and of the modern descendants of these prehistoric languages. It is conventional to mark such reconstructions with an asterisk, and that is what is done here. So for example the prehistoric Germanic ancestor of English *chicken* is given as *\*kiukīnam*. This means that we have no direct evidence of a word *kiukīnam*, but that *chicken* itself and its relatives in other Germanic languages, together with our knowledge of how Germanic words evolved, have enabled us to postulate its existence.

John Ayto
London, 1990

# A

---

**a, an** [OE] The indefinite article in English is ultimately identical with the word *one* (as is the case, even more obviously, in other European languages – French *un*, German *ein*, and so on). The ancestor of both *a(n)* and *one* was *ān*, with a long vowel, but in the Old English period it was chiefly used for the numeral; where we would use *a(n)*, the Anglo-Saxons tended not to use an article at all. *Ān* begins to emerge as the indefinite article in the middle of the 12th century, and it was not long before, in that relatively unemphatic linguistic environment, its vowel became weakened and shortened, giving *an*. And at about the same time the distinction between *an* and *a* began to develop, although this was a slow process; until 1300 *an* was still often used before consonants, and right up to 1600 and beyond it was common before all words beginning with *h*, such as *house*.
► one

**aardvark**   see EARTH, FARROW

**abacus** [17] *Abacus* comes originally from a Hebrew word for 'dust,' '*ābāq*. This was borrowed into Greek with the sense of 'drawing board covered with dust or sand,' on which one could draw for, among other purposes, making mathematical calculations. The Greek word, *ábax*, subsequently developed various other meanings, including 'table,' both in the literal sense and as a mathematical table. But it was as a 'dust-covered board' that its Latin descendant, *abacus*, was first used in English, in the 14th century. It was not until the 17th century that the more general sense of a counting board or frame came into use, and the more specific 'counting frame with movable balls' is later still.

**abandon** [14] The Old French verb *abandoner* is the source of *abandon*. It was based on *a bandon*, meaning literally 'under control or jurisdiction,' which was used in the phrase *mettre a bandon* 'put someone under someone else's control' – hence 'abandon them.' The word *bandon* came, in altered form, from Latin *bannum* 'proclamation,' which is circuitously related to

English *banns* 'proclamation of marriage' and is an ancestor of *contraband*.
► banns, contraband

**abash** [14] *Abash* shares a common ancestry with *abeyance* [16], although the latter underwent an about-turn in meaning in the 17th century which disguises their relationship. They go back to a Latin verb *batāre*, meaning 'yawn' or 'gape.' This was borrowed into French as *baer*, later *bayer* (it was the source of English *bay* 'recessed space'). The addition of the prefix *es-* (from Latin *ex-*) produced *esbaer*, later *e(s)bahir* 'gape with astonishment,' whence, via the present stem *e(s)bass-*, came English *abash*, which originally meant 'stand amazed' as well as 'embarass, discomfit.' (*Bashful* is a 16th-century derivative, with elision of the *a-*, which was first used by the dramatist Nicholas Udall.) Addition of the prefix *a-* to Old French *baer*, meanwhile, had given *abaer* 'aspire after,' and its noun *abeance* 'aspiration, desire.' In legal terminology, this word was used in French for the condition of a person in expectation or hope of receiving property, but in English the focus quickly became reversed to the property, and its condition of being temporarily without an owner.
► abeyance, bashful

**abbot** [OE] *Abbot* comes ultimately from *abbā*, a Syriac word meaning 'father' (which itself achieved some currency in English, particularly in reminiscence of its biblical use: 'And he said, Abba, father, all things are possible unto thee,' Mark 14:36). This came into Greek as *abbás*, and thence, via the Latin accusative *abbatem*, into Old English as *abbud* or *abbod*. The French term *abbé* (which is much less specific in meaning than English *abbot*) comes from the same source. In much the same way as *father* is used in modern English for priests, *abba* was widely current in the East for referring to monks, and hence its eventual application to the head of a monastery. A derivative of Latin *abbatem* was *abbatia*, which has given English both *abbacy* [15] and (via Old French *abbeie*) *abbey* [13]. *Abbess* is of similar antiquity (Latin had *abbatissa*).

▶ abbess, abbey

## abbreviate   see BRIEF

## abet   see BAIT

## abhor   [15]   *Abhor* comes from Latin *abhorrēre*, which literally meant 'shrink back in terror' (from the prefix *ab-* 'away' and *horrēre* 'tremble' – which also gave English *horror* and *horrid*). The word used to have this intransitive meaning 'be repelled' in English too, but the transitive usage 'loathe' (which was probably introduced from Old French in the 15th century) has completely taken its place.

▶ horrid, horror

## abide   see BIDE

## able   [14]   *Able* and *ability* both come ultimately from the Latin verb *habēre* 'have' or 'hold.' From this the Latin adjective *habilis* developed, meaning literally 'convenient or suitable for holding on to,' and hence in more general terms 'suitable' or 'apt,' and later, more positively, 'competent' or 'expert.' It came into English via Old French, bringing with it the noun *ablete* 'ability.' This was later reformed in English, on the model of its Latin source *habilitās*, to *ability*.

▶ habit

## ablution   see LAVATORY

## abode   see BIDE

## abominable   [14]   The Latin original of this word meant 'shun as an evil omen.' The prefix *ab-* 'away' was added to *ōmen* (source of English *omen*) to produce the verb *abōminārī*. From this was created the adjective *abōminābilis*, which reached English via Old French. From the 14th to the 17th century there was a general misapprehension that *abominable* was derived from Latin *ab hominem* 'away from man,' hence 'beastly, unnatural.' This piece of fanciful folk etymology not only perpetuated the erroneous spelling *abhominable* throughout this period, but also seems to have contributed significantly to making the adjective much more strongly condemnatory.

▶ omen

## abort   see ORIGIN

## abound   [14]   *Abound* has no connection with *bind* or *bound*. Its Latin source means literally 'overflow,' and its nearest relative among English words is *water*. Latin *undāre* 'flow' derived from *unda* 'wave' (as in *undulate*), which has the same ultimate root as *water*. The addition of the prefix *ab-* 'away' created *abundāre*, literally 'flow away,' hence 'overflow,' and eventually 'be plentiful.' The present participial stem of the Latin verb gave English *abundant* and *abundance*. In the 14th and 15th centuries it was erroneously

thought that *abound* had some connection with *have*, and the spelling *habound* was consequently common.

▶ inundate, surround, undulate, water

## about   [OE]   *About* in Old English times meant 'around the outside of'; it did not develop its commonest present-day meaning, 'concerning,' until the 13th century. In its earliest incarnation it was *onbūtan*, a compound made up of *on* and *būtan* 'outside' (this is the same word as modern English *but*, which was itself originally a compound, formed from the ancestors of *by* and *out* – so broken down into its ultimate constituents, *about* is *on by out*).

▶ but, by, out

## above   [OE]   As in the case of *about*, the *a-* in *above* represents *on* and the *-b-* element represents *by*; *above* (Old English *abufan*) is a compound based on Old English *ufan*. This meant both 'on top' and 'down from above'; it is related to *over*, and is probably descended from a hypothetical West Germanic ancestor *\*ufana*, whose *uf-* element eventually became modern English *up*. So in a sense, *above* means 'on by up' or 'on by over.'

▶ by, on, up

## abracadabra   [16]   This magical charm reached English, probably via French, from Greek *abrasadabra* (the *c* in the English word arose from a misinterpretation of the *c* in the original Greek word, which in the Greek alphabet stands for *s*). It seems to have originated (perhaps in the 3rd century AD) as a cabalistic word of the Basilidians, a Gnostic sect of Alexandria, and was probably based on *Abraxas*, the name of their supreme deity.

## abridge   see BRIEF

## abroad   [13]   It was only in the 15th century that *abroad* came to mean 'in foreign parts.' Earlier, it had been used for 'out of doors,' a sense still current today, if with a rather archaic air; but originally it meant 'widely' or 'about' (as in 'noise something abroad'). It was formed quite simply from *a* 'on' and the adjective *broad*, although it was probably modelled on the much earlier (Old English) phrase *on brede*, in which *brede* was a noun, meaning 'breadth.'

▶ broad

## abscess   [16]   *Abscess* comes, via French *abcès*, from Latin *abscessus*, a noun derived from *abscēdere* 'go away.' The constituent parts of this compound verb are *abs* 'away' and *cēdere* 'go,' which has given English *cede* and a whole range of other words, such as *accede* and *recede*.

The notion linking 'abscesses' and 'going away' was that impure or harmful bodily humours were eliminated, or 'went away,' via the pus that gathered in abscesses. It originated amongst the Greeks, who indeed had a word for it: *apostema*. This meant literally 'separation' (*apo* 'away' and *histánai* 'stand'), and Latin *ab-*

*scessus* was an approximate translation of it, possibly by Aulus Cornelius Celsus, the Roman writer on medical and other matters.

▶ accede, cede, recede

**absent** [14] *Absent* is based ultimately on the Latin verb 'to be,' *esse*. To this was added the prefix *ab-* 'away,' giving Latin *abesse* 'be away'; and the present participial stem of *abesse* was *absent-*. Hence, via Old French, the adjective *absent* and the noun *absence*. It has been conjectured, incidentally, that the 4nt- stem used for Latin *esse* was a descendant of Indo-European *\*sontos* 'truth,' from which English *sooth* comes.

**absolute** [14] *Absolute, absolution*, and *absolve* all come ultimately from the same source: Latin *absolvere* 'set free,' a compound verb made up from the prefix *ab-* 'away' and the verb *solvere* 'loose' (from which English gets *solve* and several other derivatives, including *dissolve* and *resolve*). From the 13th to the 16th century an alternative version of the verb, *assoil*, was in more common use than *absolve*; this came from the same Latin original, but via Old French rather than by a direct route. The *t* of *absolute* and *absolution* comes from the past participial stem of the Latin verb – *absolūt-*. The noun, the adjective, and the verb have taken very different routes from their common semantic starting point, the notion of 'setting free': *absolve* now usually refers to freeing from responsibility and *absolution* to the remitting of sins, while *absolute* now means 'free from any qualification or restriction.'

▶ dissolve, resolve, solve

**absorb** [15] *Absorb* comes, via French *absorber*, from Latin *absorbēre*, a compound verb formed from the prefix *ab-*'away' and *sorbēre* 'suck up, swallow.' Words connected with drinking and swallowing quite often contain the sounds *s* or *sh*, *r*, and *b* or *p* – Arabic, for instance, has *surāb*, which gave us *syrup* – and this noisy gulping seems to have been reflected in an Indo-European base, *\*srobh-*, which lies behind both Latin *sorbēre* and Greek *ropheín* 'suck up.'

**abstain** [14] The literal meaning of this word's ultimate source, Latin *abstinēre*, was 'hold or keep away,' and hence 'withhold' (the root verb, *tenēre*, produced many other derivatives in English, such as *contain, maintain, obtain*, and *retain*, as well as *tenacious, tenant, tenement, tenet, tenor*, and *tenure*). That is how it was used when it was first introduced into English (via Old French *abstenir*), and it was not until the 16th century that it began to be used more specifically for refraining from pleasurable activities, particularly the drinking of alcohol. The past participial stem of the Latin verb, *abstent-*, gave us *abstention*, while the present participial stem, *abstinent-*, produced *abstinent* and *abstinence*. There is no connection, incidentally, with the semantically similar *abstemious*, which comes from a Latin word for alcoholic drink, *tēmōtum*.

**abstruse** [16] It is not clear whether English borrowed *abstruse* from French *abstrus(e)* or directly from Latin *abstrūsus*, but the ultimate source is the Latin form. It is the past participle of the verb *abstrūdere*, literally 'thrust' (*trūdere*) 'away' (*ab*). (*Trūdere* contributed other derivatives to English, including *extrude* and *intrude*, and it is related to *threat*.) The original, literal meaning of *abstruse* was 'concealed,' but the metaphorical 'obscure' is just as old in English.

**abuse**   see USE

**abut**   see BUTT

**abyss** [16] English borrowed *abyss* from late Latin *abyssus*, which in turn derived from Greek *ábussos*. This was an adjective meaning 'bottomless,' from *a-* 'not' and *bussós* 'bottom,' a dialectal variant of *buthós* (which is related to *bathys* 'deep,' the source of English *bathyscape*). In Greek the adjective was used in the phrase *ábussos limnē* 'bottomless lake,' but only the adjective was borrowed into Latin, bringing with it the meaning of the noun as well. In medieval times, a variant form arose in Latin – *abysmus*. It incorporated the Greek suffix *-ismós* (English *-ism*). It is the source of French *abîme*, and was borrowed into English in the 13th century as *abysm* (whence the 19th-century derivative *abysmal*). It began to be ousted by *abyss* in the 16th century, however, and now has a distinctly archaic air.

**acacia** [16] *Acacia* comes via Latin from Greek *akakía*, a word for the shittah. This is a tree mentioned several times in the Bible (the Ark of the Covenant was made from its wood). It is not clear precisely what it was, but it was probably a species of what we now know as the acacia. The ultimate derivation of Greek *akakia* is obscure too; some hold that it is based on Greek *aké* 'point' (a distant relation of English *acid*), from the thorniness of the tree, but others suggest that it may be a loanword from Egyptian.

**academy** [16] Borrowed either from French *académie* or from Latin *acadēmia, academy* goes back ultimately to Greek *Akadēmíā*, the name of the place in Athens where the philosopher Plato (c. 428–347 BC) taught. Traditionally thought of as a grove ('the groves of Academe'), this was in fact more of an enclosed piece of ground, a garden or park; it was named after the Attic mythological hero Akadēmos or Hekadēmus. In its application to the philosophical doctrines of Plato, English *academy* goes back directly to its Latin source, but the more general meanings 'college, place of training' derive from French.

**accelerate** [16] *Accelerate* comes from Latin *accelerāre*, a compound verb formed from the intensive prefix *ad-* (*ac-* before /k/ sounds) and *celerāre* 'hurry.' *Celerāre*, in turn, derived from the adjective *celer* 'fast' (which gave English *celerity* [15] and is ultimately related to *hold*).

**accent** [14] *Accent* was originally a loan-translation from Greek into Latin (a loan-translation is when each constituent of a compound in one language is translated into its equivalent in another, and then reassembled into a new compound). Greek *prosōidíā* (whence English *prosody*) was formed from *pros* 'to' and *ōidé* 'song' (whence English *ode*); these elements were translated into Latin *ad* 'to' and *cantus* 'song' (whence English *chant, cant, cantata, canticle*), giving *accentus*. The notion underlying this combination of 'to' and 'song' was of a song added to speech – that is, the intonation of spoken language. The sense of a particular mode of pronunciation did not arise in English until the 16th century.
▶ cant, cantata, canticle, chant

**accept** [14] *Accept* comes ultimately from Latin *capere*, which meant 'take' (and was derived from the same root as English *heave*). The addition of the prefix *ad-* 'to' produced *accipere*, literally 'take to oneself,' hence 'receive.' The past participle of this, *acceptus*, formed the basis of a new verb, *acceptāre*, denoting repeated action, which made its way via Old French into English.
▶ heave

**accident** [14] Etymologically, an accident is simply 'something which happens' – 'an event.' That was what the word originally meant in English, and it was only subsequently that the senses 'something which happens by chance' and 'mishap' developed. It comes from the Latin verb *cadere* 'fall' (also the source of such diverse English words as *case, decadent,* and *deciduous*). The addition of the prefix *ad-* 'to' produced *accidere*, literally 'fall to,' hence 'happen to.' Its present participle was used as an adjective in the Latin phrase *rēs accidēns* 'thing happening,' and *accidēns* soon took on the role of a noun on its own, passing (in its stem form *accident-*) into Old French and thence into English.
▶ case, decadent, deciduous

**accolade** [17] *Accolade* goes back to an assumed Vulgar Latin verb *\*accollāre*, meaning 'put one's arms round someone's neck' (*collum* is Latin for 'neck,' and is the source of English *collar*). It put in its first recorded appearance in the Provençal noun *acolada*, which was borrowed into French as *accolade* and thence made its way into English. A memory of the original literal meaning is preserved in the use of *accolade* to refer to the ceremonial striking of a sword on a new knight's shoulders; the main current sense 'congratulatory expression of approval' is a later development.
▶ collar

**accomplice** [15] This word was borrowed into English (from French) as *complice* (and *complice* stayed in common usage until late in the 19th century).

It comes from Latin *complex*, which is related to English *complicated*, and originally meant simply 'an associate,' without any pejorative associations. The form *accomplice* first appears on the scene in the late 15th century (the first record of it is in William Caxton's *Charles the Great*), and it probably arose through a misanalysis of *complice* preceded by the indefinite article (*a complice*) as *acomplice*. It may also have been influenced by *accomplish* or *accompany*.
▶ complicated

**accomplish**   see COMPLETE

**accord** [12] In its original source, Vulgar Latin *\*accordāre, accord* meant literally 'heart-to-heart' (from Latin *ad* 'to' and *cord-*, the stem of *cor* 'heart'). It passed into Old French as *acorder*, and was borrowed comparatively early into English, turning up in the *Anglo-Saxon Chronicle* in 1123.

Its general sense of 'being in agreement' has been narrowed down in English and other languages to the notion of 'being in harmony musically,' and either Italian *accordare* or French *accorder* provided the basis for German *akkordion* (from which English got *accordion*), the musical instrument invented by Buschmann in Berlin in 1822.
▶ cordial

**account** [14] *Account* is of Old French origin. It was formed from *compter, conter* 'count' (which derived from Latin *computāre*) and the prefix *a-*. Its original meaning in English, too, was 'count' or 'count up'; this had disappeared by the end of the 18th century, but its specialized reference to the keeping of financial records is of equal antiquity. *Account for*, meaning 'explain,' arose in the mid 18th century.
▶ count

**accoutre** [16] *Accoutre* is related to both *couture* and *sew*. English borrowed it from French *accoutrer*, which meant 'equip with something, especially clothes.' A stage earlier, Old French had *acoustrer*, formed from *cousture* (whence *couture*) and the prefix *a-*. This came from Vulgar Latin *\*consūtūra*, literally 'sewn together,' from *con-* 'together' and *sūtūra* 'sewn' (whence English *suture*); *sūtūra* in turn came from the past participial stem of Latin *suere*, which derived from the same Indo-European root as English *sew*.
▶ couture, sew, suture

**accumulate** [16] *Accumulate* was borrowed from Latin *accumulāre*, a compound verb formed from the prefix *ad-*, here meaning 'in addition,' and *cumulāre* 'heap up' (the source of English *cumulative*). *Cumulāre* itself derived from *cumulus* 'heap'; English adopted this with its original Latin meaning in the 17th century, but it was not until the early 19th century that it was applied (by the meteorologist Luke Howard) to mountainous billowing cloud formations.
▶ cumulative, cumulus

**accurate** [16] 'Accuracy' is connected with 'curing,' in the sense not of 'making better' but of 'looking after' – as in 'the cure of souls.' The adjective comes from Latin *accūrātus* 'done carefully,' which in turn derived from a verb (*cūrāre* 'care for') formed from the noun *cūra* 'care' (other English words from this source are *curate, curious, procure*, and *secure*). The notion of doing something carefully led on naturally to the notion of exactness.

▶ curate, curious, procure, secure

**accuse** [13] *Accuse* comes via Old French *acuser* from the Latin verb *accūsāre*, which was based on the noun *causa* 'cause' – but cause in the sense not of 'something that produces a result,' but of 'legal action' (a meaning preserved in English *cause list*, for instance). Hence *accūsāre* was to 'call someone to account for their actions.'

The grammatical term *accusative* [15] (denoting the case of the object of a verb in Latin and other languages) is derived ultimately from *accūsāre*, but it arose originally owing to a mistranslation. The Greek term for this case was *ptôsis aitiātikê* 'case denoting causation' – a reasonable description of the function of the accusative. Unfortunately the Greek verb *aitiásthai* also meant 'accuse,' and it was this sense that Latin grammarians chose to render when adopting the term.

▶ cause, excuse

**accustom** see CUSTOM

**ace** [13] *Ace* comes from the name of a small ancient Roman coin, the *as* (which may have been of Etruscan origin). As well as denoting the coin, Latin *as* stood for 'one' or 'unity,' and it was as the 'score of one at dice' that it first entered English.

**ache** [OE] Of the noun *ache* and the verb *ache*, the verb came first. In Old English it was *acan*. From it was formed the noun, *æce* or *ece*. For many centuries, the distinction between the two was preserved in their pronunciation: in the verb, the *ch* was pronounced as it is now, with a /k/ sound, but the noun was pronounced similarly to the letter *H*, with a /ch/ sound. It was not until the early 19th century that the noun came regularly to be pronounced the same way as the verb. It is not clear what the ultimate origins of *ache* are, but related forms do exist in other Germanic languages (Low German *äken*, for instance, and Middle Dutch *akel*), and it has been conjectured that there may be some connection with the Old High German exclamation (of pain) *ah*.

**achieve** [14] *Achieve* is related to *chief*. It comes from Old French *achever* 'bring to an end,' or literally 'bring to a head,' which was based on the phrase *a chief* 'to a head' (*chief* derives ultimately from Latin *caput* 'head').

The heraldic meaning of *achievement*, 'coat of arms,' comes from the notion that the escutcheon was granted as a reward for a particular achievement. Over the centuries it has evolved an alternative form, *hatchment* [16].

▶ chief, hatchment

**acid** [17] The original notion contained in the word *acid* is 'pointedness.' In common with a wide range of other English words (for example *acute, acne, edge, oxygen*) it can be traced back ultimately to the Indo-European base *\*ak-*, which meant 'be pointed or sharp.' Among the Latin derivatives of this base was the adjective *ācer* 'sharp.' From this was formed the verb *acere* 'be sharp or sour,' and from this verb in turn the adjective *acidus* 'sour.' The scientist Francis Bacon seems to have been the first to introduce it into English, in the early 17th century (though whether directly from Latin or from French *acide* is not clear). Its use as a noun, in the strict technical sense of a class of substances that react with alkalis or bases, developed during the 18th century.

▶ acacia, acne, acrid, acute, alacrity, ear, edge, oxygen

**acknowledge** see KNOW

**acne** [19] It is ironic that *acne*, that represents a low point in many teenagers' lives, comes from *acme*, 'the highest point.' The Greeks used *akme*, which literally meant 'point,' for referring to spots on the face, but when it came to be rendered into Latin it was mistransliterated as *acnē*, and the error has stuck. (*Acme* comes, incidentally, from an Indo-European base *\*ak-*'be pointed,' and thus is related to *acid, edge*, and *oxygen*.)

▶ acid, acme, edge, oxygen

**acolyte** [14] *Acolyte* comes, via Old French and/or medieval Latin, from Greek *akólouthos* 'following.' This was formed from the prefix *a-* (which is related to *homos* 'same') and the noun *keleuthos* 'path,' and it appears again in English in *anacolouthon* [18] (literally 'not following'), a technical term for lack of grammatical sequence. The original use of *acolyte* in English was as a minor church functionary, and it did not acquire its more general meaning of 'follower' until the 19th century.

▶ anacolouthon

**acorn** [OE] *Acorn* has no etymological connection with *oak*; its nearest linguistic relative in English is probably *acre*. The Old English word was *æcern*, which may well have derived from *æcer* 'open land' (the related Middle High German *ackeran* referred to beech mast as well as acorns, and Gothic *akran* developed more widely still, to mean simply 'fruit'). There are cognate words in other, non-Germanic, Indo-European languages, such as Russian *yagoda* 'berry' and Welsh *aeron* 'fruits.' Left to develop on its own, *æcern* would have become modern English *achern*, but the accidental similarity of *oak* and *corn* have combined to reroute its pronunciation.

▶ acre

**acoustic** [17] Appropriately enough, *acoustic* may be distantly related to *hear*. It first appeared in English in Francis Bacon's *Advancement of Learning* 1605, borrowed from Greek *akoustikós*. This in turn was derived from the Greek verb for 'hear,' *akoúein*, which, it has been speculated, may have some connection with *\*khauzjan*, the original Germanic source of English *hear*, not to mention German *hören* and Dutch *horen* (as well as with Latin *cavēre* 'be on one's guard,' and hence with English *caution* and *caveat*).

▶ caution, caveat, hear

**acquaint** [13] *Acquaint* is connected with *quaint*, distant though they may seem in meaning. It comes via Old French *acointer* from medieval Latin *accognitāre*, which was based ultimately on *cognitus*, the past participle of *cognoscere* 'know.' *Cognitus* gave English *cognition*, of course, but also *quaint* (*cognitus* developed into *cointe, queinte* in Old French, and came to mean 'skilled, expert'; this led later to the notion of being skilfully made or elegant, which eventually degenerated into 'agreeably curious').

▶ cognition, quaint

**acquire** [15] The original source of *acquire*, Latin *acquīrere*, meant literally 'get something extra.' It was formed from the verb *quaerere* 'try to get or obtain' (from which English gets *query*, the derivatives *enquire* and *require*, and, via the past participial stem, *quest* and *question*) plus the prefix *ad-*, conveying the idea of being additional. English borrowed the word via Old French *acquerre*, and it was originally spelled *acquere*, but around 1600 the spelling was changed to *acquire*, supposedly to bring it more into conformity with its Latin source.

▶ query, quest, question

**acquit** [13] *Acquit* is ultimately related to *quiet*. The Latin noun *quies*, from which we get *quiet*, was the basis of a probable verb *\*quietare*, later *\*quitare*, whose original meaning, 'put to rest,' developed to 'settle,' as in 'settle a debt.' With the addition of the prefix *ad-* this passed into Old French as *a(c)quiter*, and thence into English (still with the 'settling or discharging debts' meaning). The currently most common sense, 'declare not guilty,' did not appear until the 14th century, and the most recent meaning, 'conduct oneself in a particular way,' developed from the notion of discharging one's duties.

▶ quiet

**acre** [OE] *Acre* is a word of ancient ancestry, going back probably to the Indo-European base *\*ag-*, source of words such as *agent* and *act*. This base had a range of meanings covering 'do' and 'drive,' and it is possible that the notion of driving contributed to the concept of driving animals on to land for pasture. However that may be, it gave rise to a group of words in Indo-European languages, including Latin *ager* (whence

English *agriculture*), Greek *agros*, Sanskrit *ájras*, and a hypothetical Germanic *\*akraz*. By this time, people's agricultural activities had moved on from herding animals in open country to tilling the soil in enclosed areas, and all of this group of words meant specifically 'field.' From the Germanic form developed Old English *æcer*, which as early as 1000 AD had come to be used for referring to a particular measured area of agricultural land (as much as a pair of oxen could plough in one day).

▶ act, agent, agriculture, eyrie, onager, peregrine, pilgrim

**acrid** [18] *Acrid* is related to *acid*, and probably owes its second syllable entirely to that word. It is based essentially on Latin *acer* 'sharp, pungent,' which, like *acid, acute, oxygen*, and *edge*, derives ultimately from an Indo-European base *\*ak-* meaning 'be pointed or sharp.' When this was imported into English in the 18th century, the ending *-id* was artificially grafted on to it, most likely from the semantically similar *acid*.

▶ acid, acute, edge, eglantine, oxygen, paragon

**acrobat** [19] The Greek adjective *ákros* meant 'topmost, at the tip or extremity' (it derives ultimately from the Indo-European base *\*ak-* meaning 'be pointed or sharp,' which also gave rise to *acid, acute, oxygen*, and *edge*). It crops up in *acrophobia* 'fear of heights'; in *acropolis* 'citadel,' literally 'upper city'; in *acromegaly* 'unnaturally enlarged condition of the hands, feet, and face,' literally 'large extremities'; and in *acronym*, literally 'word formed from the tips of words.' *Acrobat* itself means literally 'walking on tiptoe.' The *-bat* morpheme comes from Greek *baínein* 'walk,' which is closely related to *basis* and *base*, and is also connected with *come*. *Akrobátēs* existed as a term in Greek, and reached English via French *acrobate*.

▶ acid, acute, edge, oxygen

**across** [13] English originally borrowed *across*, or the idea for it, from Old French. French had the phrase *à croix* or *en croix*, literally 'at *or* in cross,' that is, 'in the form of a cross' or 'transversely.' This was borrowed into Middle English as *a creoix* or *o(n) croice*, and it was not until the 15th century that versions based on the native English form of the word *cross* began to appear: *in cross, on cross*, and the eventual winner, *across*.

▶ cross

**acrostic** [16] An acrostic is a piece of verse in which the first letters of each line when put together spell out a word. The term is of Greek origin (*akrostikhis*), and was formed from *ákros* 'at the extremity' (see ACROBAT) and *stíkhos* 'line of verse.' The second element crops up in several other prosodic terms, such as *distich* and *hemistich*, and comes from the Greek verb *steíkhein* 'go,' which is related ultimately to English *stair, stile*, and *stirrup*.

▶ acrobat, distich, hemistich, stair, stile, stirrup

**act** [14] *Act, action, active, actor* all go back to Latin *agere* 'do, perform' (which is the source of a host of other English derivatives, from *agent* to *prodigal*). The past participle of this verb was *āctus*, from which we get *act*, partly through French *acte*, but in the main directly from Latin. The Latin agent noun, *āctor*, came into the language at about the same time, although at first it remained a rather uncommon word in English, with technical legal uses; it was not until the end of the 16th century that it came into its own in the theatre (*player* had hitherto been the usual term).

Other Latin derivatives of the past participial stem *āct*-were the noun *āctiō*, which entered English via Old French *action*, and the adjective *āctīvus*, which gave English *active*. See also ACTUAL.

▶ action, active, agent, cogent, examine, prodigal

**actual** [14] In common with *act, action*, etc, *actual* comes ultimately from Latin *āctus*, the past participle of the verb *agere* 'do, perform.' In late Latin an adjective *āctuālis* was formed from the noun *āctus*, and this passed into Old French as *actuel*. English borrowed it in this form, and it was not until the 15th century that the spelling *actual*, based on the original Latin model, became general. At first its meaning was simply, and literally, 'relating to acts, active'; the current sense, 'genuine,' developed in the mid 16th century.

▶ act, action

**acumen** [16] *Acumen* is a direct borrowing from Latin *acūmen*, which meant both literally 'point' and figuratively 'sharpness.' It derived from the verb *acuere* 'sharpen,' which was also the source of English *acute*. The original pronunciation of *acumen* in English was /ə'kjūmen/, with the stress on the second syllable, very much on the pattern of the Latin original; it is only relatively recently that a pronunciation with the stress on the first syllable has become general.

▶ acute

**acute** [14] *Acute* derives from Latin *acūtus* 'sharp' (which was also the source of English *ague*). This was the past participle of the verb *acuere* 'sharpen,' which in turn was probably formed from the noun *acus* 'needle.' Like the related *acid, acetic*, and *acrid*, it can be traced back to an Indo-European base *ak*-'be pointed,' which was also the ultimate source of *oxygen* and *edge*.

▶ acetic, acid, acrid, ague, cute, edge, oxygen

**adage** [16] *Adage* was borrowed, via French, from Latin *adagium* 'maxim, proverb.' This seems to have been formed from a variant of *aio* 'I say' plus the prefix *ad*- 'to.' In the 16th and 17th centuries an alternative version, *adagy*, existed.

**adamant** [14] In Greek, *adamas* meant 'unbreakable, invincible.' It was formed from the verb *daman* 'subdue, break down' (which came from the same source as English *tame*) plus the negative prefix *a*-. It developed a noun usage as a 'hard substance,' specifically 'diamond' or 'very hard metal,' and this passed into Latin as *adamāns*, or, in its stem form, *adamant*-. Hence Old French *adamaunt*, and eventually English *adamant*.

▶ diamond, tame

**add** [14] Etymologically, *add* means simply 'put to.' Its source is Latin *addere*, a compound verb formed from the prefix *ad*- 'to' and the stem *-dere* 'put' (which is related to English *do*). Its original meaning in English was simply 'join one thing to another'; its specific mathematical use did not develop until the early 16th century.

▶ do

**adder** [OE] In Old English, the term for a snake (any snake, not just an adder) was *nǣddre*; there are or were related forms in many other European languages, such as Latin *natrix*, Welsh *neidr*, and German *natter* (but there does not seem to be any connection with the *natterjack* toad). Around the 14th century, however, the word began to lose its initial consonant. The noun phrase including the indefinite article, *a nadder*, became misanalysed as *an adder*, and by the 17th century *nadder* had disappeared from the mainstream language (though it survived much longer in northern dialects).

**addict** [16] Originally, *addict* was an adjective in English, meaning 'addicted.' It was borrowed from Latin *addictus*, the past participle of *addicere*, which meant 'give over or award to someone.' This in turn was formed from the prefix *ad*- 'to' and the verb *dicere*. The standard meaning of *dicere* was 'say' (as in English *diction, dictionary*, and *dictate*), but it also had the sense 'adjudge' or 'allot,' and that was its force in *addicere*.

▶ dictate, diction, dictionary

**addled** [13] *Addled* may be traceable back ultimately to a confusion between 'wind' and 'urine' in Latin. In Middle English the term was *adel eye* 'addled egg,' of which the first part derived from Old English *adela* 'foul-smelling urine or liquid manure.' It seems possible that this may be a loan-translation of the Latin term for 'addled egg,' *ōvum ūrīnae*, literally 'urine egg.' This in turn was an alteration, by folk etymology, of *ōvum ūrīnum*, a partial loan-translation of Greek *oúrion ōón*, literally 'wind egg' (a *wind egg* is an imperfect or addled egg).

**address** [14] *Address* originally meant 'straighten.' William Caxton, for example, here uses it for 'stand up straight': 'The first day that he was washed and bathed he addressed him[self] right up in the basin' *Golden Legend* 1483. This gives a clue to its ultimate source, Latin *dīrectum* 'straight, direct.' The first two syllables of this seem gradually to have merged together to produce *\*drictum*, which with the addition of the prefix *ad*- was used to produce the verb *\*addrictiāre*. Of its descendants in modern Romance languages, Italian *ad-*

*dirizzare* most clearly reveals its source. Old French changed it fairly radically, to *adresser*, and it was this form which English borrowed. The central current sense of 'where somebody lives' developed in the 17th and 18th centuries from the notion of directing something, such as a letter, to somebody.

▶ direct

**adequate**   see EQUAL

**adhere**   [16]   *Adhere* was borrowed, either directly or via French *adhérer*, from Latin *adhaerēre*. This in turn was formed from the prefix *ad-* 'to' and the verb *haerēre* 'stick.' The past participial stem of *haerēre* was *haes-* (the ultimate source of English *hesitate*), and from *adhaes-* were formed the Latin originals of *adhesion* and *adhesive*.

▶ hesitate

**adjacent**   [15]   *Adjacent* and *adjective* come from the same source, the Latin verb *jacere* 'throw.' The intransitive form of this, *jacēre*, literally 'be thrown down,' was used for 'lie.' With the addition of the prefix *ad-*, here in the sense 'near to,' was created *adjacēre*, 'lie near.' Its present participial stem, *adjacent-*, passed, perhaps via French, into English.

The ordinary Latin transitive verb *jacere*, meanwhile, was transformed into *adjicere* by the addition of the prefix *ad-*; it meant literally 'throw to,' and hence 'add' or 'attribute,' and from its past participial stem, *adject-*, was formed the adjective *adjectīvus*. This was used in the phrase *nomen adjectīvus* 'attributive noun,' which was a direct translation of Greek *ónoma épithetos*. And when it first appeared in English (in the 14th century, via Old French *adjectif*) it was in *noun adjective*, which remained the technical term for 'adjective' into the 19th century. *Adjective* was not used as a noun in its own right until the early 16th century.

▶ adjective, easy, reject

**adjourn**   [14]   *Adjourn* originally meant 'appoint a day for,' but over the centuries, such is human nature, it has come to be used for postponing, deferring, or suspending. It originated in the Old French phrase *à jour nomé* 'to an appointed day,' from which the Old French verb *ajourner* derived. *Jour* 'day' came from late Latin *diurnum*, a noun formed from the adjective *diurnus* 'daily,' which in turn was based on the noun *diēs* 'day.'

▶ diary, journal

**adjust**   see JUST

**adjutant**   [17]   An adjutant was formerly simply an 'assistant,' but the more specific military sense of an officer who acts as an aide to a more senior officer has now virtually ousted this original meaning. The word comes from a Latin verb for 'help,' and is in fact related to English *aid*. Latin *adjuvāre* 'help' developed a new form, *adjūtāre*, denoting repeated action, and the present participial stem of this, *adjutant-* 'helping,' was borrowed into English.

▶ aid, coadjutor

**admiral**   [13]   Admirals originally had nothing specifically to do with the sea. The word comes ultimately from Arabic *'amīr* 'commander' (from which English later also acquired *emir* [17]). This entered into various titles followed by the particle *-al-* 'of' (*'amīr-al-bahr* 'commander of the sea,' *'amīr-al-mūminīn* 'commander of the faithful'), and when it was borrowed into European languages, *'amīr-al-* became misconstrued as an independent, free-standing word. Moreover, the Romans, when they adopted it, smuggled in their own Latin prefix *ad-*, producing *admiral*. When this reached English (via Old French) it still meant simply 'commander,' and it was not until the time of Edward III that a strong naval link began to emerge. The Arabic title *'amīr-al-bahr* had had considerable linguistic influence in the wake of Arabic conquests around the Mediterranean seaboard (Spanish *almirante de la mar*, for instance), and specific application of the term to a naval commander spread via Spain, Italy, and France to England. Thus in the 15th century England had its *Admiral of the Sea* or *Admiral of the Navy*, who was in charge of the national fleet. By 1500 the maritime connection was firmly established, and *admiral* came to be used on its own for 'supreme naval commander.'

▶ emir

**admire**   [16]   *Admire* has rather run out of steam since it first entered the language. It comes originally from the same Latin source as *marvel* and *miracle*, and from the 16th to the 18th centuries it meant 'marvel at' or 'be astonished.' Its weaker modern connotations of 'esteem' or 'approval,' however, have been present since the beginning, and have gradually ousted the more exuberant expressions of wonderment. It is not clear whether English borrowed the word from French *admirer* or directly from its source, Latin *admīrārī*, literally 'wonder at,' a compound verb formed from *ad-* and *mīrārī* 'wonder.'

▶ marvel, miracle

**admit**   [15]   This is one of a host of words, from *mission* to *transmit*, to come down to English from Latin *mittere* 'send.' Its source, *admittere*, meant literally 'send to,' hence 'allow to enter.' In the 15th and 16th centuries the form *amit* was quite common, borrowed from French *amettre*, but learned influence saw to it that the more 'correct' Latin form prevailed.

▶ commit, mission, transmit

**admonish**   [14]   In Middle English times this verb was *amoneste*. It came, via Old French *amonester*, from an assumed Vulgar Latin verb *\*admonestāre*, an alteration of Latin *admonēre* (*monēre* meant 'warn,' and came from the same source as English *mind*). The prefix *ad-* was reintroduced from Latin in the 15th century, while the -*ish* ending arose from a mistaken analysis of -*este* as some sort of past tense inflection; the *t* was removed when producing infinitive or present tense forms, giving spellings such as *amonace* and *admonyss*, and by the 16th century this final -*is* had become identified with and transformed into the more common -*ish* ending.

▶ mind

**ado** [14] In origin, *ado* (like *affair*) means literally 'to do.' This use of the preposition *at* (*ado* = *at do*) is a direct borrowing from Old Norse, where it was used before the infinitive of verbs, where English would use *to*. *Ado* persisted in this literal sense in northern English dialects, where Old Norse influence was strong, well into the 19th century, but by the late 16th century it was already a noun with the connotations of 'activity' or 'fuss' which have preserved it (alongside the indigenous *to-do*) in modern English.

▶ do

**adobe** [18] *Adobe* is of Egyptian origin, from the time of the pharaohs. It comes from Coptic *tōbe* 'brick' (the form *t.b* appears in hieroglyphs). This was borrowed into Arabic, where the addition of the definite article *al* produced *attob* 'the brick.' From Arabic it passed into Spanish (the corridor through which so many Arabic words reached other European languages), and its use by the Spanish-speaking population of North America (for a sun-dried brick) led to its adoption into English in the mid 18th century.

**adolescent** [15] The original notion lying behind both *adolescent* and *adult* is of 'nourishment.' The Latin verb *alere* meant 'nourish' (*alimentary* and *alimony* come from it, and it is related to *old*). A derivative of this, denoting the beginning of an action, was *alēscere* 'be nourished,' hence 'grow.' The addition of the prefix *ad-* produced *adolēscere*. Its present participial stem, *adolēscent-* 'growing,' passed into English as the noun *adolescent* 'a youth' (the adjective appears not to have occurred before the end of the 18th century). Its past participle, *adultus* 'grown,' was adopted into English as *adult* in the 16th century.

▶ adult, alimentary, alimony, coalesce, coalition, proletarian, prolific

**adopt**    see OPINION
**adore**    see ORATOR
**adorn**    see ORNAMENT

**adultery** [14] Neither *adultery* nor the related *adulterate* have any connection with *adult*. Both come ultimately from the Latin verb *adulterāre* 'debauch, corrupt' (which may have been based on Latin *alter* 'other,' with the notion of pollution from some extraneous source). By the regular processes of phonetic change, *adulterāre* passed into Old French as *avoutrer*, and this was the form which first reached English, as

*avouter* (used both verbally, 'commit adultery,' and nominally, 'adulterer') and as the nouns *avoutery* 'adultery' and *avouterer* 'adulterer.' Almost from the first they coexisted in English beside *adult-* forms, deriving either from Law French or directly from Latin, and during the 15th to 17th centuries these gradually ousted the *avout-* forms. *Adulter*, the equivalent of *avouter*, clung on until the end of the 18th century, but the noun was superseded in the end by *adulterer* and the verb by a new form, *adulterate*, directly based on the past participle of Latin *adulterāre*, which continued to mean 'commit adultery' until the mid 19th century.

▶ alter

**adumbrate**    see UMBRAGE

**advance** [13] *Advance* originated in the Latin adverb *abante* 'before' (source of, among others, French *avant* and Italian *avanti*), which in turn was based on *ab* 'from' and *ante* 'before.' In post-classical times a verb, *\*abantiāre*, seems to have been formed from the adverb. It developed into Old French *avancer*, and passed into English as *avaunce*, initially with the meaning 'promote.' A new form, *advancer*, started life in Old French, on the mistaken association of *avancer* with other *av-* words, such as *aventure*, which really did derive from Latin words with the *ad-* prefix; over the 15th and 16th centuries this gradually established itself in English. The noun *advance* did not appear until the 17th century.

**advantage** [14] *Advantage* comes from Old French *avantage*, which was based on *avant* 'before'; the notion behind its formation was of being ahead of others, and hence in a superior position. As with *advance*, the intrusive -*d-* became established in the 16th century, on the analogy of words genuinely containing the Latin prefix *ad-*. The reduced form *vantage* actually predates *advantage* in English, having entered the language via Anglo-Norman in the 13th century.

**adventure** [13] *Adventure* derives ultimately from a Latin verb meaning 'arrive.' It originally meant 'what comes or happens by chance,' hence 'luck,' but it took a rather pessimistic downturn via 'risk, danger' to (in the 14th century) 'hazardous undertaking.' Its Latin source was *advenīre*, formed from the prefix *ad-* and *venīre* 'come.' Its past participial stem. *advent-*, produced English *advent* [12] and *adventitious* [17], but it was its future participle, *adventura* 'about to arrive,' which produced *adventure*. In the Romance languages in which it subsequently developed (Italian *avventura*, Spanish *aventura*, and French *aventure*, the source of Middle English *aventure*) the *d* disappeared, but it was revived in 15th–16th-century French in imitation of Latin. The reduced form *venture* first appears in the 15th century.

▶ adventitious, avent, venture

**adverb** [15] *Adverb* comes ultimately from a Latin word modelled on Greek *epírrhēma*, literally 'added word.' The elements of this compound (the prefix *epi-* and *rhēma* 'word') were translated literally into Latin (*ad-* and *verbum*), giving *adverbum*. English took the word either directly from Latin, or via French *adverbe*.

▶ verb

**advertise** [15] When it was originally borrowed into English, from French, *advertise* meant 'notice.' It comes ultimately from the Latin verb *advertere* 'turn towards' (whose past participle *adversus* 'hostile' is the source of English *adverse* [14] and *adversity* [13]). A later variant form, *advertīre*, passed into Old French as *avertir* 'warn' (not to be confused with *avertir* from which English gets *avert* [15] and *averse* [16], which came from Latin *abvertere* 'turn away'). This was later reformed into *advertir*, on the model of its Latin original, and its stem form *advertiss-* was taken into English, with its note of 'warning' already softening into 'giving notice of,' or simply 'noticing.' The modern sense of 'describing publicly in order to increase sales' had its beginnings in the mid 18th century. In the 16th and 17th centuries, the verb was pronounced with the main stress on its second syllable, like the *advertise-* in *advertisement*.

▶ adverse, adversity, verse

**advice** [13] Like modern French *avis, advice* originally meant 'opinion,' literally 'what seems to one to be the case.' In Latin, 'seem' was usually expressed by the passive of the verb *vidēre* 'see'; thus, *vīsum est*, 'it seems' (literally 'it is seen'). With the addition of the dative first person pronoun, one could express the notion of opinion: *mihi vīsum est*, 'it seems to me.' It appears either that this was partially translated into Old French as *ce m'est a vis*, or that the past participle *vīsum* was nominalized in Latin, making possible such phrases as *ad (meum) vīsum* 'in (my) view'; but either way it is certain that *a(d)-* became prefixed to *vīs(um)*, producing a new word, *a(d)vis*, for 'opinion.' It was originally borrowed into English without the *d*, but learned influence had restored the Latin spelling by the end of the 15th century. As to its meaning, 'opinion' was obsolete by the mid 17th century, but already by the late 14th century the present sense of 'counsel' was developing.

The verb *advise* [14] probably comes from Old French *aviser*, based on *avis*.

▶ vision, visit

**advocate** [14] Etymologically, *advocate* contains the notion of 'calling,' specifically of calling someone in for advice or as a witness. This was the meaning of the Latin verb *advocāre* (formed from *vocāre* 'call,' from which English also gets *vocation*). Its past participle, *advocātus*, came to be used as a noun,

originally meaning 'legal witness or adviser,' and later 'attorney.' In Old French this became *avocat*, the form in which English borrowed it; it was later relatinized to *advocate*. The verb *advocate* does not appear until the 17th century.

The word was also borrowed into Dutch, as *advocaat*, and the compound *advocaatenborrel*, literally 'lawyer's drink,' has, by shortening, given English the name for a sweetish yellow concoction of eggs and brandy.

▶ invoke, revoke, vocation

**aegis** [18] The notion of 'protection' contained in this word goes back to classical mythology, in which one of the functions or attributes of the Greek god Zeus (and later of Roman Jupiter or Minerva) was the giving of protection. This was usually represented visually as a shield, traditionally held to be made of goatskin – hence Greek *aigís*, the name of the shield, came to be associated in the popular imagination with *aix* (*aig-* in its stem form), the Greek word for 'goat.' English borrowed the word directly from Latin.

**aeolian harp** [18] Aeolus was the Greek god of the winds (the form of the name is Latin; the original Greek was *Aiolos*, deriving from the adjective *aiolos* 'quick-moving'). Hence the application of the epithet to a musical instrument whose strings are sounded by the breeze blowing over them. The term is first recorded in the writings of Erasmus Darwin, at the end of the 18th century.

**aeon** see AGE

**aeroplane** [19] The prefix *aero-* comes ultimately from Greek *āér* 'air,' but many of the terms containing it (such as *aeronaut* and *aerostat*) reached English via French. This was the case, too, with *aeroplane*, in the sense of 'heavier-than-air flying machine.' The word was first used in English in 1873 (30 years before the Wright brothers' first flight), by D S Brown in the Annual Report of the Aeronautical Society – he refers vaguely to an aeroplane invented by 'a Frenchman.' The abbreviated form *plane* followed around 1908. (An earlier, and exclusively English, use of the word *aeroplane* was in the sense 'aerofoil, wing'; this was coined in the 1860s, but did not long survive the introduction of the 'aircraft' sense.)

*Aeroplane* is restricted in use mainly to British English (and even there now has a distinctly old-fashioned air). The preferred term in American English is *airplane*, a refashioning of *aeroplane* along more 'English' lines which is first recorded from 1907.

▶ air

**aesthetic** [18] In strict etymological terms, *aesthetic* relates to perception via the senses. It comes ultimately from the Greek verb *aísthesthai* 'perceive' (which is related to Latin *audīre* 'hear'), and this meaning is preserved in *anaesthetic*, literally 'without feeling.' The derived adjective *aisthētikós* reached Western Europe via modern Latin *aesthēticus*, and was first used (in its Germanized form *ästhetisch*) in the writings of the philosopher Immanuel Kant (1724–1804). Here, it retained its original sense, 'perceptual,' but its use by A T Baumgarten as the title (*Æsthetica*) of a work on the theory of beauty in art (1750) soon led to its adoption in its now generally accepted meaning.

▶ audible, audition

## aestivate see ETHER

## affable [16] The Latin original of *affable, affābilis*, meant 'easy to speak to.' It was formed from the verb *aaffārī* 'speak to,' which in turn was derived from the prefix *ad-* 'to' and *fārī* 'speak' (the source of *fable, fame,* and *fate*). It reached English via Old French *affable*.

▶ fable, fame, fate

## affair [13] Like *ado*, and of course *to-do, affair* originally meant literally 'to do.' It was coined in Old French from the phrase *à faire* 'to do,' and entered English via Anglo-Norman *afere*. The spelling *affair* was established by Caxton, who based it on the French model. The specific sense of a 'love affair' dates from the early 18th century.

▶ fact

## affect There are two distinct verbs *affect* in English: 'simulate insincerely' [15] and 'have an effect on' [17]; but both come ultimately from the same source, Latin *afficere*. Of compound origin, from the prefix *ad-* 'to' and *facere* 'do,' this had a wide range of meanings. One set, in reflexive use, was 'apply oneself to something,' and a new verb, *affectāre*, was formed from its past participle *affectus*, meaning 'aspire or pretend to have.' Either directly or via French *affecter*, this was borrowed into English, and is now most commonly encountered in the past participial adjective *affected* and the derived noun *affectation*. Another meaning of *afficere* was 'influence,' and this first entered English in the 13th century by way of its derived noun *affectiō*, meaning 'a particular, usually unfavourable disposition' – hence *affection*. The verb itself was a much later borrowing, again either through French or directly from the Latin past participle *affectus*.

▶ fact

## affinity [14] The abstract notion of 'relationship' in *affinity* was originally a more concrete conception of a border. The word comes, via Old French *afinite*, from the Latin adjective *affīnis*, which meant literally 'bordering on something.' It was formed from the prefix *ad-* 'to' and the noun *fīnis* 'border' (from which English also gets *finish, confine,* and *define*).

▶ confine, define, finish, paraffin, refine

## affix see FIX

## afflict [14] When it originally entered English, *afflict* meant 'overthrow,' reflecting its origins in Latin *afflīgere* 'throw down,' a compound verb formed from the prefix *ad-* 'to' and *flīgere* 'strike.' English *afflict* comes either from the Latin past participle *afflictus*, from a new Latin verb formed from this, *afflictāre*, or perhaps from the now obsolete English adjective *afflict*, which was borrowed from Old French *aflit* and refashioned on the Latin model. The meaning 'torment, distress' developed in the early 16th century.

## affluent [15] The meaning 'rich' is a fairly recent development for *affluent*; it is first recorded in the mid 18th century. Originally the adjective meant simply 'flowing.' It came, via Old French, from Latin *affluent-*, the present participle of *affluere*, a compound verb formed from the prefix *ad-* 'towards' and *fluere* 'flow' (the source of English *fluid, fluent, flux, fluctuate,* and many other derivatives).

▶ fluctuate, fluent, fluid, flux

## afford [OE] This verb originally meant 'accomplish, fulfil.' In Old English times it was *geforthian*, formed from the prefix *ge-*, denoting completion of an action, and *forthian* 'advance towards completion' or literally 'further' (from the adverb *forth*). The notion of accomplishing something or managing something gradually led, by the 15th century, to the idea of being able to do something because one has enough money. Meanwhile, the original *ge-* prefix, which by Middle English times had become *i-* (*iforthien*), had been transformed into *af-* under the influence of the many Latin-based words beginning in *aff-*, and in the 16th century spellings with final *d* in place of *th* start to appear.

▶ forth

## affray [14] *Affray* is a word of mixed Germanic and Romance origin. The noun comes from the verb, 'alarm' (now obsolete, but still very much with us in the form of its past participle, *afraid*), which was borrowed into English from Anglo-Norman *afrayer* and Old French *effreer* and *esfreer*. These go back to a hypothetical Vulgar Latin verb *\*exfridāre*, which was composed of the Latin prefix *ex-* 'out' and an assumed noun *\*fridus*, which Latin took from the Frankish *\*frithuz* 'peace' (cognate with German *friede* 'peace,' and with the name *Frederick*). The underlying meaning of the word is thus 'take away someone's peace.'

▶ afraid, belfry

## affront [14] The present-day notion of 'insulting someone' has replaced the more direct action of hitting them in the face. *Affront* comes, via Old French *afronter*, from Vulgar Latin *\*affrontāre* 'strike in the face,' which was formed from the Latin phrase *ad frontem*, literally 'to the face.'

▶ front

**after**   [OE]   In the first millenium AD many Germanic languages had forms cognate with Old English *æfter* (Gothic *aftra*, for example, and Old Norse *aptr*), but, with the exception of Dutch *achter*, none survive. It is not clear what their ultimate origin is, but the suffix they share may well be a comparative one, and it is possible that they derive from a Germanic base *af- (represented in Old English *æftan* 'from behind'). It has been suggested that this goes back to Indo-European *ap- (source of Latin *ab* 'away, from' and English *of(f)*), in which case *after* would mean literally 'more off' – that is, 'further away.'

Nautical *aft* is probably a shortening of *abaft*, formed, with the prefixes *a-* 'on' and *be-* 'by,' from Old English *æftan*.

▶ of, off

**aftermath**   [16]   Originally, and literally, an aftermath was a second crop of grass or similar grazing vegetation, grown after an earlier crop in the same season had been harvested. Already by the mid 17th century it had taken on the figurative connotations of 'resulting condition' which are today its only living sense. The *-math* element comes from Old English *mǣth* 'mowing,' a noun descended from the Germanic base *mǣ, source of English *mow*.

▶ mow

**again**   [OE]   The underlying etymological sense of *again* is 'in a direct line with, facing,' hence 'opposite' and 'in the opposite direction, back' (its original meaning in Old English). It comes from a probable Germanic *gagin 'straight,' which was the source of many compounds formed with *on* or *in* in various Germanic languages, such as Old Saxon *angegin* and Old Norse *í gegn*. The Old English form was *ongēan*, which would have produced *ayen* in modern English; however, Norse-influenced forms with a hard *g* had spread over the whole country from northern areas by the 16th century. The meaning 'once more, anew' did not develop until the late 14th century. From Old English times until the late 16th century a prefix-less form *gain* was used in forming compounds. It carried a range of meanings, from 'against' to 'in return,' but today survives only in *gainsay*.

The notion of 'opposition' is carried through in *against*, which was formed in the 12th century from *again* and what was originally the genitive suffix *-es*, as in *always* and *nowadays*. The parasitic *-t* first appeared in the 14th century.

**age**   [13]   *Age* has undergone considerable transmutations and abbreviations since its beginnings in Latin. Its immediate source in English is Old French *aage*, which was the product of a hypothetical Vulgar Latin form *aetāticum* (the *t* is preserved in Provençal *atge*). This was based on Latin *aetāt-* (stem of *aetās*), which was a shortening of *aevitās*, which in turn came from

*aevum* 'lifetime.' This entered English in more recognizable form in *medieval, primeval*, etc; it is related to Greek *aión* 'age,' from which English gets *aeon* [17], and it can be traced back to the same root that produced (via Old Norse *ei*) the now archaic adverb *ay(e)* 'ever' (as in 'will aye endure').

▶ aeon, aye

**agenda**   [17]   *Agenda* is the plural of Latin *agendum*, which is the gerundive form of the verb *agere* 'do' (see AGENT); it thus means literally 'things to be done.' When the word first entered the language it was given an anglicized singular form, *agend*, with the plural *agends*, but this seems to have disappeared by the 18th century. The formal plurality of *agenda* is still often insisted on by purists, but it has been used as a singular noun since the mid 18th century.

▶ act, agent

**agent**   [15]   Latin *agere*, a verb of great semantic breadth ('drive, lead, act, do'), has been a prolific source of English words. Its past participle, *āctus*, produced *act, action, active, actor, actual, cachet*, and *exact*, while other parts of its paradigm lie behind *agile, agitate, ambiguous, coagulate, cogent, cogitate, examine, exigent, exiguous*, and *prodigal*. Its most obvious offspring, however, are *agent* (literally '(person) doing something') and *agency*, formed from the Latin present participial stem *agent-*. *Agere* itself is of considerable antiquity, being related to other Indo-European verbs such as Greek *ágein* 'drive, lead,' Old Norse *aka* 'travel in a vehicle,' and Sanskrit *ájati* 'drives.'

▶ act, agile, ambiguous, cachet, cogent, demagogue, exact, examine, prodigal

**agglutinate**   see GLUE

**aggregate**   [15]   Etymologically, *aggregate* contains the notion of a collection of animals. It comes from *greg-*, the stem of the Latin noun *grex* 'flock, herd' (also the source of *gregarious*). This formed the basis of a verb *aggregāre* 'collect together,' whose past participle *aggregātus* passed into English as *aggregate*. Latin *grex* is related to Greek *agorá* 'open space, market place,' from which English gets *agoraphobia*.

▶ agoraphobia, egregious, gregarious, segregate

**aggression**   [17]   The violent associations of *aggression* have developed from the much milder notion of 'approaching' somebody. The Latin verb *aggredī* 'attack' was based on the prefix *ad-* 'towards' and *gradī* 'walk,' a verb derived in its turn from the noun *gradus* 'step' (from which English gets, among many others, *grade, gradual*, and *degree*).

▶ degree, grade, gradual

**aghast**   [13]   *Aghast* was originally the past participle of a verb, *agasten* 'frighten,' which in turn was based on the Old English verb *gǣstan* 'torment.' The spelling with *gh* did not finally become established until the 18th century, and in fact *aghast* was the last in a series of etymologically related words in the general semantic area of 'fear' and 'horror' to undergo this transformation. It seems to have acquired its *gh* by association with *ghastly*, which in turn got it from *ghost* (probably under the ultimate influence of Flemish *gheest*).

**agiotage**  [19]  *Agiotage* is the speculative buying and selling of stocks and shares. The term was borrowed from French, where it was based on *agioter* 'speculate,' a verb formed from the noun *agio* 'premium paid on currency exchanges.' English acquired *agio* in the 17th century (as with so many other banking and financial terms, directly from Italian – *aggio*). This Italian word is thought to be an alteration of a dialectal form *lajjē*, borrowed from medieval Greek *allagion* 'exchange.' This in turn was based on Greek *allagē* 'change,' which derived ultimately from *állos* 'other' (a word distantly related to English *else*).

▶ else

**agitate**  [16]  *Agitate* is one of a host of English words descended ultimately from Latin *agere* (see AGENT). Among the many meanings of *agere* was 'drive, move,' and a verb derived from it denoting repeated action, *agitāre*, hence meant 'move to and fro.' This physical sense of shaking was present from the start in English *agitate*, but so was the more metaphorical 'perturb.' The notion of political agitation does not emerge until the early 19th century, when the Marquis of Anglesey is quoted as saying to an Irish deputation: 'If you really expect success, agitate, agitate, agitate!' In this meaning, a derivative of Latin *agitāre* has entered English via Russian in *agitprop* 'political propaganda' [20], in which *agit* is short for *agitatsiya* 'agitation.'

▶ act, agent

**agnostic**  [19]  *Agnostic* is an invented word. It was coined by the English biologist and religious sceptic T H Huxley (1825–95) to express his opposition to the views of religious gnostics of the time, who claimed that the world of the spirit (and hence God) was knowable (*gnostic* comes ultimately from Greek *gnōsis* 'knowledge'). With the addition of the Greek-derived prefix *a-* 'not' Huxley proclaimed the ultimate unknowability of God. The circumstances of the coinage, or at least of an early instance of the word's use by its coiner, were recorded by R H Hutton, who was present at a party held by the Metaphysical Society in a house on Clapham Common in 1869 when Huxley suggested *agnostic*, basing it apparently on St Paul's reference to the altar of 'the Unknown God.'

**ago**  [14]  Historically, *ago* is the past participle of a verb. Its earlier, Middle English, form – *agone* – reveals its origins more clearly. It comes from the Old English verb *āgān* 'pass away,' which was formed from *gān* 'go' and the prefix *ā-*'away, out.' At first it was used *before* expressions of time ('For it was ago five year that he was last there,' *Guy of Warwick* 1314), but this was soon superseded by the now current postnominal use.

▶ go

**agog**  [15]  *Agog* probably comes from Old French *gogue* 'merriment.' It was used in the phrase *en gogue*, meaning 'enjoying oneself' (Randle Cotgrave, in his *Dictionarie of the French and English tongues* 1611, defines *estre en ses gogues* as 'to be frolicke, lustie, lively, wanton, gamesome, all-a-hoit, in a pleasant humour; in a veine of mirth, or in a merrie mood'), and this was rendered into English as *agog*, with the substitution of the prefix *a-* (as in *asleep*) for *en* and the meaning toned down a bit to 'eager.' It is not clear where *gogue* came from (it may perhaps be imitative of noisy merrymaking), but later in its career it seems to have metamorphosed into *go-go*, either through reduplication of its first syllable (*gogue* had two syllables) or through assimilation of the second syllable to the first: hence the French phrase *à go-go* 'joyfully,' and hence too English *go-go* dancers.

**agony**  [14]  *Agony* is one of the more remote relatives of that prolific Latin verb *agere* (see AGENT). Its ultimate source is the Greek verb *ágein* 'lead,' which comes from the same Indo-European root as *agere*. Related to *ágein* was the Greek noun *agón*, originally literally 'a bringing of people together to compete for a prize,' hence 'contest, conflict' (which has been borrowed directly into English as *agon*, a technical term for the conflict between the main characters in a work of literature). Derived from *agón* was *agōníā* '(mental) struggle, anguish,' which passed into English via either late Latin *agōnia* or French *agonie*. The sense of physical suffering did not develop until the 17th century; hitherto, *agony* had been reserved for mental stress. The first mention of an *agony column* comes in the magazine *Fun* in 1863.

▶ antagonist

**agoraphobia**  [19]  *Agoraphobia* – fear of open spaces or, more generally, of simply being out of doors – is first referred to in an 1873 issue of the *Journal of Mental Science*; this attributes the term to Dr C Westphal, and gives his definition of it as 'the fear of squares or open places.' This would be literally true, since the first element in the word represents Greek *agorá* 'open space, typically a market place, used for public assemblies' (the most celebrated in the ancient world was the Agora in Athens, rivalled only by the Forum in Rome). The word *agorá* came from *ageirein* 'assemble,' which is related to Latin *grex* 'flock,' the source of English *gregarious*.

*Agoraphobia* was not the first of the *-phobias*. That honour goes to *hydrophobia* in the mid 16th century. But that was an isolated example, and the surge of compounds based on Greek *phóbos* 'fear' really starts in the 19th century. At first it was used for symptoms of physical illness (*photophobia* 'abnormal sensitivity to light' 1799), for aversions to other nationalities (*Gallophobia* 1803; the synonymous *Francophobia* does not appear until 1887), and for facetious formations (*dustophobia*, Robert Southey, 1824), and the range of specialized psychological terms familiar today does not begin to appear until the last quarter of the century (CLAUSTROPHOBIA 1879, *acrophobia* 'fear of heights' from Greek *akros* 'topmost' – see ACROBAT – 1892).

▶ aggregate, allegory, gregarious, segregate

**ague**   [14]   In its origins, *ague* is the same word as *acute*. It comes from the Latin phrase *febris acuta* 'sharp fever' (which found its way into Middle English as *fever agu*). In the Middle Ages the Latin adjective *acuta* came to be used on its own as a noun meaning 'fever'; this became *aguë* in medieval French, from which it was borrowed into English. From the end of the 14th century *ague* was used for 'malaria' (the word *malaria* itself did not enter the language until the mid 18th century).

▶ acute

**aid**   [15]   *Aid* comes ultimately from the same source as *adjutant* (which originally meant simply 'assistant'). Latin *juvāre* became, with the addition of the prefix *ad-* 'to', *adjuvāre* 'give help to'; from its past participle *adjutus* was formed a new verb, *adjūtāre*, denoting repeated action, and this passed into Old French as *aïdier*, the source of English *aid*.

▶ adjutant, jocund

**ail**   [OE]   Now virtually obsolete except in the metaphorical use of its present participial adjective *ailing*, *ail* is of long but uncertain history. The Old English verb *egl(i)an* came from the adjective *egle* 'troublesome,' which had related forms in other Germanic languages, such as Middle Low German *egelen* 'annoy' and Gothic *agls* 'disgraceful,' *aglo* 'oppression.' The derivative *ailment* did not appear until as late as the 18th century.

**aileron**   SEE AISLE

**aim**   [14]   Etymologically, *aim* is a contraction of *estimate* (see ESTEEM). The Latin verb *aestimāre* became considerably shortened as it developed in the various Romance languages (Italian has *stimare*, for instance, and Provençal *esmar*). In Old French its descendant was *esmer*, to which was added the prefix *a-* (from Latin *ad-* 'to'), producing *aesmer*; and from one or both of these English acquired *aim*. The notion of estimating or calculating was carried over into the English verb, but died out after about a hundred years. However, the derived sense of calculating, and hence directing, one's course is of equal antiquity in the language.

▶ esteem, estimate

**air**   [13]   Modern English *air* is a blend of three strands of meaning from, ultimately, two completely separate sources. In the sense of the gas we breathe it goes back via Old French *air* and Latin *āēr* to Greek *áēr* 'air' (whence the *aero*-compounds of English; see AEROPLANE). Related words in Greek were *áēmi* 'I blow' and *aúrā* 'breeze' (from which English acquired *aura* in the 18th century), and cognates in other Indo-European languages include Latin *ventus* 'wind,' English *wind*, and *nirvana* 'extinction of existence,' which in Sanskrit meant literally 'blown out.'

In the 16th century a completely new set of meanings of *air* arrived in English: 'appearance' or 'demeanour.' The first known instance comes in Shakespeare's *1 Henry IV*, IV, i: 'The quality and air of our attempt brooks no division' (1596). This *air* was borrowed from French, where it probably represents an earlier, Old French, *aire* 'nature, quality,' whose original literal meaning 'place of origin' (reflected in another derivative, *eyrie*) takes it back to Latin *ager* 'place, field,' source of English *agriculture* and related to *acre*. (The final syllable of English *debonair* [13] came from Old French *aire*, incidentally; the phrase *de bon aire* meant 'of good disposition.')

The final strand in modern English *air* comes via the Italian descendant of Latin *āēr*, *aria*. This had absorbed the 'nature, quality' meanings of Old French *aire*, and developed them further to 'melody' (perhaps on the model of German *weise*, which means both 'way, manner' and 'tune' – its English cognate *wise*, as in 'in no wise,' meant 'song' from the 11th to the 13th centuries). It seems likely that English *air* in the sense 'tune' is a direct translation of the Italian. Here again, Shakespeare got in with it first – in *A Midsummer Night's Dream*, I, i: 'Your tongue's sweet air more tunable than lark to shepherd's ear' (1590). (*Aria* itself became an English word in the 18th century.)

▶ acre, aeroplane, agriculture, aria, aura, eyrie, malaria, wind

**aisle**   [15]   The original English form of this word was *ele*. It was borrowed from Old French, which in turn took it from Latin *āla* 'wing' (the modern French form of the word, *aile*, has a diminutive form, *aileron* 'movable control surface on an aircraft's wing' [20], which has been acquired by English). Besides meaning literally 'bird's wing,' *āla* was used metaphorically for 'wing of a building,' which was the source of its original meaning in English, the 'sides of the nave of a church.' The Latin word comes from an unrecorded *\*acsla*, which is one of a complex web of 'turning' words that include Latin *axis*, Greek *axon* 'axis,' Latin *axilla* 'armpit' (whence English *axillary* and *axil*), and English *axle*.

The notion of an aisle as a detached, separate part of a building led to an association with *isle* and *island* which eventually affected Middle English *ele*'s spelling. From the 16th to the 18th century the word was usually spelled *ile* or *isle*. A further complication entered the picture in the 18th century in the form of French *aile*, which took the spelling on to today's settled form, *aisle*.

▶ aileron, axis

**ajar** [16] *Ajar* comes from Scotland and Northern England. In Middle English times it was *a char* or *on char*, literally 'on turn' (*char* comes from an Old English word *cerr* 'turn,' which in its metaphorical sense 'turn of work' has given modern English *charwoman* and *chore*). A door or window that was in the act of turning was therefore neither completely shut nor completely open. The first spellings with *j* occur in the 18th century.

▶ char, charwoman

**akimbo** [15] *Akimbo* was borrowed from Old Norse. Its original English spelling (which occurs only once, in the *Tale of Beryn* 1400) was *in kenebowe*, which suggests a probable Old Norse precursor *\*i keng boginn* (never actually discovered), meaning literally 'bent in a curve' (Old Norse *bogi* is related to English *bow*); hence the notion of the arms sticking out at the side, elbows bent. When the word next appears in English, in the early 17th century, it has become *on kenbow* or *a kenbo*, and by the 18th century *akimbo* has arrived.

▶ bow

**alabaster** [14] Chaucer was the first English author to use the word *alabaster*: in the *Knight's Tale* (1386) he writes of 'alabaster white and red coral.' It comes, via Old French and Latin, from Greek *alábast(r)os*, which may be of Egyptian origin. Scottish English used the variant form *alabast* until the 16th century (indeed, this may predate *alabaster* by a few years); and from the 16th to the 17th century the word was usually spelled *alablaster*, apparently owing to confusion with *arblaster* 'crossbowman.'

The use of alabaster for making marbles (of the sort used in children's games) gave rise to the abbreviation *alley, ally* 'marble' in the early 18th century.

**alarm** [14] *Alarm* was originally a call to arms. It comes from the Old Italian phrase *all' arme* 'to the weapons!' This was lexicalized as the noun *allarme*, which was borrowed into Old French as *alarme*, and thence into English. The archaic variant *alarum* seems to have arisen from an emphatic rolling of the *r* accompanying a prolongation of the final syllable when the word was used as an exclamation.

▶ arm

**alas** [13] In origin *alas* was an exclamation of weariness rather than grief. Latin *lassus* 'weary' (related to *let* 'allow' and source of *lassitude*) passed into Old French as *las* which, with the addition of the exclamation *a* 'ah,' became *alas*.

▶ lassitude, let

**albatross** [17] The word *albatross* has a confused history. The least uncertain thing about it is that until the late 17th century it was *alcatras*; the change of the first element to *alba*-seems to have arisen from association of the albatross's white colour with Latin *albus* 'white.' However, which particular bird the alcatras was, and where the word *alcatras* ultimately came from, are much more dubious. The term was applied variously, over the 16th to the 19th centuries, to albatrosses, frigate birds, gannets, gulls, and pelicans. Its immediate source was Spanish and Portuguese *alcatraz* 'pelican' (hence *Alcatraz*, the prison-island in San Francisco Bay, USA, once the haunt of pelicans), which was clearly of Arabic origin, and it has been speculated that it comes from Arabic *al qādūs* 'the bucket,' on the premise that the bucket of a water-wheel used for irrigation resembles a pelican's beak. Arabic *qādūs* itself comes from Greek *kádos* 'jar.'

**albino** [18] Like *album*, *albino* comes ultimately from Latin *albus* 'white.' It was borrowed into English from the Portuguese, who used it with reference to black Africans suffering from albinism (it is a derivative of *albo*, the Portuguese descendant of Latin *albus*).

▶ album

**album** [17] Latin *albus* 'white' has been the source of a variety of English words: *alb* 'ecclesiastical tunic' [OE], *albedo* 'reflective power' [19], *Albion* [13], an old word for *Britain*, probably with reference to its white cliffs, *albumen* 'white of egg' [16], and *auburn*, as well as *albino*. *Album* is a nominalization of the neuter form of the adjective, which was used in classical times for a blank, or white, tablet on which public notices were inscribed. Its original adoption in the modern era seems to have been in Germany, where scholars kept an *album amicorum* 'album of friends' in which to collect colleagues' signatures. This notion of an autograph book continues in Dr Johnson's definition of *album* in his *Dictionary* 1755: 'a book in which foreigners have long been accustomed to insert the autographs of celebrated people,' but gradually it became a repository for all sorts of souvenirs, including in due course photographs.

▶ alb, albedo, albino, albumen, auburn, daub

**alchemy** [14] *Alchemy* comes, via Old French *alkemie* and medieval Latin *alchimia*, from Arabic *alkīmīā*. Broken down into its component parts, this represents Arabic *al* 'the' and *kīmīā*, a word borrowed by Arabic from Greek *khēmīóa* 'alchemy' – that is, the art of transmuting base metals into gold. (It has been suggested that *khēmīā* is the same word as *Khēmīā*, the ancient name for Egypt, on the grounds that alchemy originated in Egypt, but it seems more likely that it derives from Greek *khūmós* 'fluid' – source of English *chyme* [17] – itself based on the verb *khein* 'pour'). Modern English *chemistry* comes not directly from

Greek *khēmīā*, but from *alchemy*, with the loss of the first syllable.

▶ chemistry, chyme

**alcohol**   [16]   Originally, alcohol was a powder, not a liquid. The word comes from Arabic *al-kuhul*, literally 'the kohl' – that is, powdered antimony used as a cosmetic for darkening the eyelids. This was borrowed into English via French or medieval Latin, and retained this 'powder' meaning for some centuries (for instance, 'They put between the eyelids and the eye a certain black powder made of a mineral brought from the kingdom of Fez, and called Alcohol,' George Sandys, *Travels* 1615). But a change was rapidly taking place: from specifically 'antimony,' *alcohol* came to mean any substance obtained by sublimation, and hence 'quintessence.' *Alcohol of wine* was thus the 'quintessence of wine,' produced by distillation or rectification, and by the middle of the 18th century *alcohol* was being used on its own for the intoxicating ingredient in strong liquor. The more precise chemical definition (a compound with a hydroxyl group bound to a hydrocarbon group) developed in the 19th century.

▶ kohl

**alcove**   [17]   *Alcove* is of Arabic origin. It reached English, via French *alcôve* and Spanish *alcoba* (where it means 'recessed area for a bed'), from Arabic *al-qobbah* 'the arch, the vault,' hence 'the vaulted room,' which was derived from the verb *qubba* 'vault.'

**alder**   [OE]   *Alder* is an ancient tree-name, represented in several other Indo-European languages, including German *erle*, Dutch *els*, Polish *olcha*, Russian *ol'khá*, and Latin *alnus* (which is the genus name of the alder in scientific classification). *Alder* is clearly the odd man out amongst all these forms in having a *d*, but it was not always so; the Old English word was *alor*, and the intrusive *d* does not begin to appear until the 14th century (it acts as a sort of connecting or glide consonant between the *l* and the following vowel, in much the same way as Old English *thunor* adopted a *d* to become *thunder*). The place-name *Aldershot* is based on the tree *alder*.

**alderman**   [OE]   *Alderman* preserves the notion that those who are old (the 'elders') are automatically in charge. In Anglo-Saxon England the *ealdor* was the chief of a family or clan, by virtue of seniority (the word is based on the adjective *eald* 'old'). *Alderman* (Old English *ealdorman*) was a political title or rank adopted probably in the early 8th century for someone who exercised in society at large an authority equivalent to that of the *ealdor*. In effect, this meant that an alderman acted as a sort of viceroy to the king in a particular district. In the 12th century the title became applied to the governor of a guild, and as the guilds gradually took over some functions of local government, an alderman

became a senior councillor. The title was officially abolished in Britain in 1974.

▶ old

**ale**   [OE]   Old English *ealu* 'ale' goes back to a Germanic root *aluth-, which also produced Old Norse *öl* (Scandinavian languages still use *ale*-related words, whereas other Germanic languages now only use *beer*-related words; English is the only one to retain both). Going beyond Germanic in time takes us back to the word's ultimate Indo-European source, a base meaning 'bitter' which is also represented in *alum* and *aluminium*. *Ale* and *beer* seem to have been virtually synonymous to the Anglo-Saxons; various distinctions in usage have developed over the centuries, such as that ale is made without hops, and is heavier (or some would say lighter) than beer, but most of the differences have depended on local usage.

The word *bridal* is intimately connected with *ale*. Nowadays used as an adjective, and therefore subconsciously associated with other adjectives ending in -al, in Old English it was a noun, literally 'bride ale,' that is, a beer-drinking session to celebrate a marriage.

**alert**   [17]   *Alert* comes, via French, from an Italian phrase *all' erta* 'on the look-out,' or literally 'at the (*alla*) watch-tower (*erta*).' *Erta* was short for *torre erta*, literally 'high tower,' in which the adjective *erta* 'high' came ultimately from Latin *ērectus*, the past participle of *ērigere* 'raise.'

▶ erect

**alexandrine**   [16]   An alexandrine is a line of verse of 12 syllables, characteristic of the classic French drama of the 17th century. The term derives from the use of this metre in *Alexandre*, a 12th-or 13th-century Old French romance about Alexander the Great.

**alfresco**   see FRESH

**algebra**   [16]   *Algebra* symbolizes the debt of Western culture to Arab mathematics, but ironically when it first entered the English language it was used as a term for the setting of broken bones, and even sometimes for the fractures themselves ('The helpes of Algebra and of dislocations,' Robert Copland, *Formulary of Guydo in surgery* 1541). This reflects the original literal meaning of the Arabic term *al jebr*, 'the reuniting of broken parts,' from the verb *jabara* 'reunite.' The anatomical connotations of this were adopted when the word was borrowed, as *algebra*, into Spanish, Italian, and medieval Latin, from one or other of which English acquired it. In Arabic, however, it had long been applied to the solving of algebraic equations (the full Arabic expression was '*ilm aljebr wa'lmuqābalah* 'the science of reunion and equation,' and the mathematician al-Khwarizmi used *aljebr* as the title of his treatise on algebra – see ALGORITHM), and by the end of the 16th century this was firmly established as the central meaning of *algebra* in English.

**algorithm**  [13]  *Algorithm* comes from the name of an Arab mathematician, in full Abu Ja'far Mohammed ibn-Musa al-Khwarizmi (c. 780–c. 850), who lived and taught in Baghdad and whose works in translation introduced Arabic numerals to the West. The last part of his name means literally 'man from Khwarizm,' a town on the borders of Turkmenistan, now called Khiva.

The Arabic system of numeration and calculation, based on 10, of which he was the chief exponent, became known in Arabic by his name – *al-khwarizmi*. This was borrowed into medieval Latin as *algorismus* (with the Arabic *-izmi* transformed into the Latin suffix *-ismus* '-ism'). In Old French *algorismus* became *augorime*, which was the basis of the earliest English form of the word, *augrim*. From the 14th century onwards, Latin influence gradually led to the adoption of the spelling *algorism* in English. This remains the standard form of the word when referring to the Arabic number system; but in the late 17th century an alternative version, *algorithm*, arose owing to association with Greek *árithmos* 'number' (source of *arithmetic* [13]), and this became established from the 1930s onwards as the term for a step-by-step mathematical procedure, as used in computing.

*Algol*, the name of a computer programming language, was coined in the late 1950s from '*algo*rithmic *l*anguage.'

▶ allegory, allergy, arithmetic

**alibi**  [18]  In Latin, *alibi* means literally 'somewhere else.' It is the locative form (that is, the form expressing place) of the pronoun *alius* 'other' (which is related to Greek *allos* 'other' and English *else*). When first introduced into English it was used in legal contexts as an adverb, meaning, as in Latin, 'elsewhere': 'The prisoner had little to say in his defence; he endeavoured to prove himself Alibi,' John Arbuthnot, *Law is a bottomless pit* 1727. But by the end of the 18th century it had become a noun, 'plea of being elsewhere at the time of a crime.' The more general sense of an 'excuse' developed in the 20th century.

Another legal offspring of Latin *alius* is *alias*. This was a direct 16th-century borrowing of Latin *aliās*, a form of *alius* meaning 'otherwise.'

▶ alias, else

**alien**  [14]  The essential notion contained in *alien* is of 'otherness.' Its ultimate source is Latin *alius* 'other' (which is related to English *else*). From this was formed a Latin adjective *aliēnus* 'belonging to another person or place,' which passed into English via Old French *alien*. In Middle English an alternative version *alient* arose (in the same way as *ancient*, *pageant*, and *tyrant* came from earlier *ancien*, *pagin*, and *tyran*), but this died out during the 17th century. The verb *alienate* 'estrange' or 'transfer to another's ownership' entered the language in the mid 16th century, eventually replacing an earlier verb *alien* (source of *alienable* and *inalienable*).

▶ alibi, else

**alike**  [OE]  *Alike* is an ancient word whose ultimate Germanic source, *\*galīkam*, meant something like 'associated form' (*\*līkam* 'form, body' produced German *leiche* 'corpse' and Old English *lic*, from which we get *lychgate*, the churchyard gate through which a funeral procession passes; and the collective prefix *\*ga-* meant literally 'with' or 'together'). In Old English, *\*galīkam* had become *gelīc*, which developed into Middle English *ilik*; and from the 14th century onwards the prefix *i-*, which was becoming progressively rarer in English, was assimilated to the more familiar *a-*.

The verb *like* is indirectly related to *alike*, and the adjective, adverb, preposition, and conjunction *like* was formed directly from it, with the elimination of the prefix.

▶ each, like

**alimony**  [17]  *Alimony* is an anglicization of Latin *alimōnia*, which is based on the verb *alere* 'nourish' (source of *alma* 'bounteous,' as in *alma mater*, and of *alumnus*). This in turn goes back to a hypothetical root *\*al-*, which is also the basis of English *adolescent*, *adult*, *altitude* (from Latin *altus* 'high'), and *old*. The original sense 'nourishment, sustenance' has now died out, but the specialized 'support for a former wife' is of equal antiquity in English.

The *-mony* element in the word represents Latin *-mōnia*, a fairly meaning-free suffix used for forming nouns from verbs (it is related to *-ment*, which coincidentally was also combined with *alere*, to form *alimentary*), but in the later 20th century it took on a newly productive role in the sense 'provision of maintenance for a former partner.' *Palimony* 'provision for a former non-married partner' was coined around 1979, and in the 1980s appeared *dallymony* 'provision for somebody one has jilted.'

▶ adult, altitude, alumnus, old

**alive**  [OE]  *Alive* comes from the Old English phrase *on līfe*, literally 'on life.' *Life* was the dative case of *līf* 'life'; between two vowels *f* was pronounced /v/ in Old English, hence the distinction in modern English pronunciation between *life* and *alive*.

▶ life

**alkali**  [14]  English acquired *alkali* via Latin from Arabic *al-qalīy* 'the ashes,' a derivative of the verb *qalay* 'fry.' The implicit reference is to the plant saltwort (Latin name *Salsola kali*), which was burnt to obtain its alkaline ashes (Chaucer's canon's yeoman, the alchemist's assistant, mentions it: 'Salt tartre, alcaly, and salt preparat, And combust matieres, and coagulat,' 1386). The modern chemical sense of a compound which combines with an acid to form a salt was first used in 1813, by the chemist Sir Humphry Davy.

**all** [OE] Words related to *all* are found throughout the Germanic languages (German *all*, Dutch *al*, Old Norse *allr*, Gothic *alls*, for instance). They can probably all be traced back to a hypothetical Germanic ancestor *\*alnaz*. Connections outside Germanic are not known, unless Lithuanian *aliai* 'completely' is a relative.

**allay** [OE] In Old English, *alecgan* meant literally 'lay aside' (*a-* 'away, aside, out,' *lecgan* 'lay'). The more recent senses 'relieve, mitigate' developed from the 13th to the 15th centuries owing to the influence of two formally similar Old French verbs: *aleger* 'lighten' (from Latin *alleviāre*, source of English *alleviate* [15]); and *al(e)ier* 'qualify, moderate' (source of English *alloy*).

▶ lay

**allege** [14] *Allege* is related to *law, legal, legislation, legation*, and *litigation*. Its original source was Vulgar Latin *\*exlitigāre*, which meant 'clear of charges in a lawsuit' (from *ex-* 'out of' and *litigāre* 'litigate'). This developed successively into Old French *esligier* and Anglo-Norman *alegier*, from where it was borrowed into English; there, its original meaning was 'make a declaration before a legal tribunal.' Early traces of the notion of making an assertion without proof can be detected within 50 years of the word's introduction into English, but it took a couple of centuries to develop fully.

The hard *g* of *allegation* suggests that though it is ultimately related to *allege*, it comes from a slightly different source: Latin *allēgātiō*, from *allēgāre* 'adduce,' a compound verb formed from *ad-* 'to' and *lēgāre* 'charge' (source of English *legate* and *legation*).

▶ law, legal, legation, legislation, litigation

**allegory** [14] Etymologically, *allegory* means 'speaking otherwise.' It comes from a Greek compound based on *allos* 'other' (which is related to Latin *alius*, as in English *alibi* and *alias*, and to English *else*) and *agoreúein* 'speak publicly' (derived from *agorá* '(place of) assembly,' which is the source of English *agoraphobia* and is related to *gregarious*). Greek *allēgorein* 'speak figuratively' produced the noun *allēgoríā*, which passed into English via Latin and French.

▶ aggregate, agoraphobia, alias, alibi, else, gregarious

**allergy** [20] *Allergy* was borrowed from German *allergie*, which was coined in 1906 by the scientist C E von Pirquet. He formed it from Greek *allos* 'other, different' and *érgon* 'work' (source of English *energy* and related to English *work*). Its original application was to a changed physiological condition caused by an injection of some foreign substance.

▶ energy, work

**alley** [14] *Alley* is related to French *aller* 'go.' Old French *aler* (which came from Latin *ambulāre* 'walk,' source of English *amble* and *ambulance*) produced the derived noun *alee* 'act of walking,' hence 'place where one walks, passage.'

▶ amble, ambulance

**alligator** [16] The Spanish, on encountering the alligator in America, called it *el lagarto* 'the lizard.' At first English adopted simply the noun ('In this river we killed a monstrous Lagarto or Crocodile,' Job Hortop, *The trauailes of an Englishman* 1568), but before the end of the 16th century the Spanish definite article *el* had been misanalysed as part of the noun – hence, *alligator*. Spanish *lagarto* derived from Latin *lacerta* 'lizard,' which, via Old French *lesard*, gave English *lizard*.

▶ lizard

**alliteration** [17] *Alliteration* is an anglicization of *alliterātiō*, a modern Latin coinage based on the prefix *ad-* 'to' and *litera* 'letter' – from the notion of an accumulation of words beginning with the same letter. The verb *alliterate* is an early 19th-century back-formation from *alliteration*.

▶ letter

**allopathy**  SEE HOMEOPATHY

**allow** [14] *Allow* comes ultimately from two completely different Latin verbs, *allaudāre* and *allocāre*, which became blended in Old French *alouer*. The first, *allaudāre*, was based on *laudāre* 'praise' (source of English *laud, laudable*, and *laudatory*); the second, *allocāre* (source of English *allocate* [17]) on *locāre* 'place.' The formal similarity of the Latin verbs gradually drew their meanings closer together. The notion of 'placing,' and hence 'allotting' or 'assigning,' developed via the now obsolete 'place to somebody's credit' to 'take into account, admit.' Meanwhile, the idea of 'praising' moved through 'commending' or 'approving' to 'accepting as true or valid,' and ultimately to 'permitting.'

▶ allocate, laudable, location

**alloy** [16] The notion of 'mixing' in *alloy* originated in the idea of 'binding' in Latin *ligāre* 'tie' (source of English *ligament, ligature*, and *lien* – via Old French *loien* from Latin *ligāmen* 'bond'). Addition of the prefix *ad-* gave *alligāre* 'bind one thing to another,' hence 'combine.' This passed into Old French as *aleier*, where it eventually became *aloier* – hence English *alloy*.

▶ ally, lien, ligament, ligature

**allusion**  SEE ILLUSION

**alluvial** [19] Alluvial material is material that has been washed down and deposited by running water. Hence the term; for its ultimate source, Latin *lavere* (a variant of *lavāre*, which produced English *latrine*, *laundry, lava, lavatory, lavish,* and *lotion*), meant 'wash.' Addition of the prefix *ad-* 'to' changed *lavere* to *luere,* giving *alluere* 'wash against.' Derived from this were the noun *alluviō* (source of the English technical term *alluvion* 'alluvium') and the adjective *alluvius,* whose neuter form *alluvium* became a noun meaning 'material deposited by running water.' English adopted *alluvium* in the 17th century, and created the adjective *alluvial* from it in the 19th century.

If Latin *alluere* meant 'wash against,' *abluere* meant 'wash away.' Its noun form was *ablūtiō,* which English acquired as *ablution* in the 14th century.

▶ ablution, latrine, laundry, lavatory, lavish, lotion

## ally   [13]

The verb *ally* was borrowed into English from Old French *alier,* an alteration of *aleier* (a different development of the Old French word was *aloier,* which English acquired as *alloy*). This came from Latin *alligāre* 'bind one thing to another,' a derivative of *ligāre* 'tie'; hence the idea etymologically contained in being 'allied' is of having a bond with somebody else.

The noun *ally* seems originally to have been independently borrowed from Old French *allié* in the 14th century, with the meaning 'relative.' The more common modern sense, 'allied person or country,' appeared in the 15th century, and is probably a direct derivative of the English verb.

▶ alloy, ligament

## alma mater   [17]

*Alma mater* literally means 'mother who fosters or nourishes.' The Latin adjective *almus* 'giving nourishment,' derives from the verb *alere* 'nourish' (source of English *alimony* and *alimentary*). The epithet *alma mater* was originally applied by the Romans to a number of goddesses whose particular province was abundance, notably Ceres and Cybele. In the 17th century it began to be used in English with reference to a person's former school or college, thought of as a place of intellectual and spiritual nourishment (Alexander Pope was amongst its earliest users, although the reference is far from kind: 'Proceed, great days! 'till Learning fly the shore . . . 'Till Isis' Elders reel, their pupils' sport, And Alma mater lie dissolv'd in Port!' *Dunciad* 1718).

If that which nourishes is *almus,* those who are nourished are *alumni* (similarly derived from the verb *alere*). *Alumnus* was first applied in English to a pupil – and more specifically a former pupil or graduate – in the 17th century; an early reference combines the notions of *alumnus* and *alma mater*: 'Lieutenant Governor . . . promised his Interposition for them, as become such an Alumnus to such an Alma Mater,' William Sewall's *Diary* 12 October 1696. The first example of the feminine form, *alumna,* comes in the 1880s.

▶ alimentary, alimony, alumnus

## almanac   [14]

One of the first recorded uses of *almanac* in English is by Chaucer in his *Treatise on the astrolabe* 1391: 'A table of the verray Moeuyng of the Mone from howre to howre, every day and in every signe, after thin Almenak.' At that time an almanac was specifically a table of the movements and positions of the sun, moon, and planets, from which astronomical calculations could be made; other refinements and additions, such as a calendar, came to be included over succeeding centuries. The earliest authenticated reference to an almanac comes in the (Latin) works of the English scientist Roger Bacon, in the mid 13th century. But the ultimate source of the word is obscure. Its first syllable, *al-,* and its general relevance to medieval science and technology, strongly suggest an Arabic origin, but no convincing candidate has been found.

## almond   [13]

The *l* in *almond* is a comparatively recent addition; its immediate source, Latin *amandula,* did not have one (and nor, correspondingly, do French *amande,* Portuguese *amendoa,* Italian *mandola,* or German *mandel*). But the relative frequency of the prefix *al-* in Latin-derived words seems to have prompted its grafting on to *amandula* in its passage from Latin to Old French, giving a hypothetical \**almandle* and eventually *al(e)mande*. French in due course dropped the *l,* but English acquired the word when it was still there.

Going further back in time, the source of *amandula* was Latin *amygdula,* of which it was an alteration, and *amygdula* in turn was borrowed from the Greek word for 'almond,' *amygdálē.* The Latin and Greek forms have been reborrowed into English at a much later date in various scientific terms: *amygdala,* for instance, an almond-shaped mass of nerve tissue in the brain; *amygdalin,* a glucoside found in bitter almonds; and *amygdaloid,* a rock with almond-shaped cavities.

## almoner   SEE ALMS

## almost   [OE]

*Almost* is simply a combination of *all* and *most.* In Anglo-Saxon times, and up until the 17th century, it meant 'mostly all' or 'nearly all' (thus one could say 'My best friends are almost men,' meaning most of them are men); but already by the 13th century the modern sense 'nearly, not quite' was well in place.

▶ all, most

## alms   [OE]

The word *alms* has become much reduced in its passage through time from its ultimate Greek source, *eleēmosúnē* 'pity, alms.' This was borrowed into post-classical (Christian) Latin as *eleēmosyna,* which subsequently became simplified in Vulgar Latin to \**alimosina* (source of the word for 'alms' in many Romance languages, such as French *aumône* and Italian *limosina*). At this stage Germanic borrowed it, and in due course dispersed it (German *almosen,* Dutch *aalmoes*). It entered Old English as *ælmesse,* which became reduced in Middle English to *almes* and finally by the 17th century to *alms* (which because of its *-s* had come to be regarded as a plural noun).

The original Greek *eleēmosúnē* is itself a derivative, of the adjective *eleēmōn* 'compassionate,' which in turn came from the noun *éleos* 'pity.'

From medieval Latin *eleēmosyna* was derived the adjective *eleēmosynarius* (borrowed into English in the 17th century as the almost unpronounceable *eleemosynary* 'giving alms'). Used as a noun, this passed into Old French as *a(u)lmonier*, and eventually, in the 13th century, became English *aumoner* 'giver of alms.' The modern sense of *almoner* as a hospital social worker did not develop until the end of the 19th century.

▶ almoner, eleemosynary

**alone**   [13]   Although partly disguised by its pronunciation, *alone* is in fact simply a compound of *all* and *one* (whose /wun/ pronunciation began to develop around the 15th century). In Old English it was a completely separate phrase, *all āna*, literally 'completely by oneself,' but by the 13th century this had coalesced into a single word. Loss of its initial *a-* in the 14th century gave rise to the adjective *lone*.

▶ all, lone, one

**along**   [OE]   The *a-* in *along* is related to the prefix *anti-*, and the original notion contained in the word is of 'extending a long way in the opposite direction.' This was the force of Old English *andlang*, a compound formed from *and-* 'against, facing' (whose original source was Greek *anti-* 'against') and *lang* 'long.' The meaning gradually changed via simply 'extending a long way,' through 'continuous' and 'the whole length of something' to 'lengthwise.' At the same time the *and-* prefix was gradually losing its identity: by the 10th century the forms *anlong* and *onlong* were becoming established, and the 14th century saw the beginnings of modern English *along*.

But there is another *along* entirely, nowadays dialectal. Used in the phrase *along of* 'with' (as in 'Come along o' me!'), it derives from Old English *gelong* 'pertaining, dependent.' This was a compound formed from the prefix *ge-*, suggesting suitability, and *long*, of which the notions of 'pertaining' and 'appropriateness' are preserved in modern English *belong*.

▶ long

**aloof**   [16]   *Aloof* was originally a nautical term, a command to steer to windward. Its second syllable is a variant of *luff* 'sail closer to the wind' [13]. This was borrowed from Old French *lof*, 'windward side of a ship,' which may itself have been, like so many maritime expressions, of Dutch origin. The modern figurative meaning 'reserved, uninvolved' developed via an intermediate physical sense 'away, at a distance.'

▶ luff

**alopecia**   [14]   This word appears to derive from the resemblance observed by the Greeks between baldness in human beings and mange in foxes. The Greek for 'fox' was *alōpēx*, hence *alōpekía*, borrowed into

Latin as *alopēcia*. *Alōpēx* is related to Latin *vulpēs* 'fox,' from which English gets *vulpine* 'foxlike' [17].

▶ vulpine

**aloud**   [14]   *Aloud* was formed in Middle English from the adjective *loud* and the prefix *a-*, as in *abroad*; it does not appear to have had a direct Old English antecedent *\*on loud*. Its opposite, *alow* 'quietly,' did not survive the 15th century.

▶ loud

**alpaca**   [18]   English gets the term *alpaca* (for a South American animal related to the llama) from Spanish, which in turn got it from *alpako*, the word for the animal in the Aymara language of Bolivia and Peru. *Alpako* was a derivative of the adjective *pako* 'reddish-brown,' a reference to the colour of the animal's hair.

**alphabet**   [15]   This word is based on the names of the first two letters of the Greek alphabet, *alpha* and *beta*, standing for the whole. It derives from Greek *alphabētos*, via Latin *alphabētum*. When it first came into English, purists tried to insist that it should be reserved for the Greek alphabet, and that the English alphabet should be referred to by the term *ABC* (which had been lexicalized in various forms, such as *abece*, *apece*, and *absee*, since the late 13th century), but, like most such prescriptive demands, this was a waste of breath and ink.

**also**   [OE]   *Also* was a late Old English compound formed from *all* 'exactly, even' and *swa* 'so'; it meant 'in just this way, thus,' and hence (recalling the meaning of German *also* 'therefore') 'similarly.' These two uses died out in, respectively, the 15th and 17th centuries, but already by the 13th century 'similarly' was developing into the current sense 'in addition.' *As* came from *also* in the 12th century.

In Old English, the notion of 'in addition' now expressed by *also* was verbalized as *eke*.

▶ as

**altar**   [OE]   The etymological notion underlying the word *altar* is that of sacrificial burning. Latin *altar*, which was borrowed directly into Old English, was a derivative of the plural noun *altāria* 'burnt offerings,' which probably came from the verb *adolēre* 'burn up.' *Adolēre* in turn appears to be a derivative of *olēre* 'smell' (the connection being the smell made by combustion), which is related to English *odour*, *olfactory*, and *redolent*. (The traditional view that *altar* derives from Latin *altus* 'high' is no longer generally accepted, although no doubt it played a part, by association, in its development.)

In Middle English, the Old French form *auter* replaced *altar*, but in the 16th century the Latin form reestablished itself.

▶ odour, olfactory, redolent

**alter**   [14]   *Alter* comes from the Latin word for 'other (of two),' *alter*. In late Latin a verb was derived from this, *alterāre*, which English acquired via French *altérer*. Latin *alter* (which also gave French *autre* and English *alternate* [16], *alternative* [17], *altercation* [14], and *altruism*, not to mention *alter ego*) was formed from the root *\*al-* (source of Latin *alius* – from which English gets *alien, alias,* and *alibi* – Greek *allos* 'other,' and English *else*) and the comparative suffix *\*-tero-*, which occurs also in English *other*. Hence the underlying meaning of Latin *alter* (and, incidentally, of English *other*) is 'more other,' with the implication of alternation between the two.

▶ alias, alien, alternative, altruism, else

## altitude    see OLD

## altruism    [19] Etymologically as well as semantically, *altruism* contains the notion of 'other people.' It was borrowed from French *altruisme*, which was apparently coined in 1830 by the philosopher Auguste Comte on the basis of Italian *altrui* 'that which belongs to other people.' This was the oblique case of *altro* 'other,' from Latin *alter*. Littré's *Dictionnaire de la langue française* suggests that the coinage was based on such French legal phrases as *le bien d'autrui* 'the welfare of others' and *le droit d'autrui* 'the rights of others' (*autrui* corresponds to Italian *altrui*).

▶ alias, alter, else

## aluminium    [19] *Aluminium* comes from a coinage by the English chemist Sir Humphry Davy, who discovered the metal. His first suggestion was *alumium*, which he put forward in Volume 98 of the *Transactions of the Royal Society* 1808: 'Had I been so fortunate as . . . to have procured the metallic substances I was in search of, I should have proposed for them the names of silicium, alumium, zirconium, and glucium.' He based it on Latin *alūmen* 'alum' (alum is a sulphate of aluminium, and the word *alum*, a 14th-century borrowing from French, derives ultimately from *alūmen*; alumina is an oxide of aluminium, and the word *alumina* is a modern Latin formation based on *alūmen*, which entered English at the end of the 18th century); and *alūmen* may be linked with Latin *alūta* 'skins dried for making leather, using alum.'

Davy soon changed his mind, however, and in 1812 put forward the term *aluminum* – which remains the word used in American English to this day. British English, though, has preferred the form *aluminium*, which was mooted contemporaneously with *aluminum* on grounds of classical 'correctness': 'Aluminium, for so we shall take the liberty of writing the word, in preference to aluminum, which has a less classical sound,' *Quarterly Review* 1812.

▶ alum

## alumnus    see ALMA MATER

## always    [13] In Old English, the expression was *alne weg*, literally 'all the way.' It seems likely that this was used originally in the physical sense of 'covering the complete distance,' but by the time it starts to appear in texts (King Alfred's is the first recorded use, in his translation of Boethius's *De consolatione philosophiae* around 888) it already meant 'perpetually.' *Alway* survived into modern English, albeit as an archaism, but began to be replaced as the main form by *always* in the 12th century. The final *-s* is genitive, not plural, and was originally added to *all* as well as *way*: *alles weis*. It has a generalizing force, much as in modern English one might say *of a morning* for 'every morning.'

▶ way

## amalgamate    [17] *Amalgamate* is a derivative of *amalgam*, a term for an alloy of mercury and another metal (now usually used for tooth fillings) borrowed into English from French or medieval Latin in the 15th century. Latin (*amalgama*) probably acquired the word from the Greek adjective *málagma* 'softening,' a derivative of the verb *malássein* 'soften,' which is a distant relative of English *malleable* (see MALLET).

## amanuensis    see MANUAL

## amaze    [OE] Old English *āmasian* meant 'stupefy' or 'stun,' with perhaps some reminiscences of an original sense 'stun by hitting on the head' still adhering to it. Some apparently related forms in Scandinavian languages, such as Swedish *masa* 'be sluggish' and Norwegian dialect *masast* 'become unconscious,' suggest that it may originally have been borrowed from Old Norse. The modern sense 'astonish' did not develop until the end of the 16th century; Shakespeare was one of its earliest exponents: 'Crystal eyes, whose full perfection all the world amazes,' *Venus and Adonis* 1592.

By the end of the 13th century both the verb and its related noun had developed a form without the initial *a-*, and in the late 14th century the word – *maze* – had begun to be applied to a deliberately confusing structure.

▶ maze

## ambassador    [14] Appropriately enough, *ambassador* is a highly cosmopolitan word. It was borrowed back and forth among several European languages before arriving in English. Its ultimate source appears to be the Indo-European root *\*ag-* 'drive, lead,' whose other numerous offspring include English *act* and *agent*. With the addition of the prefix *\*amb-* 'around' (as in *ambidextrous*), this produced in the Celtic language of Gaul the noun *ambactos*, which was borrowed by Latin as *ambactus* 'vassal.' The Latin word then found its way into the Germanic languages – Old English had *ambeht* 'servant, messenger,' Old High German *ambaht* (from which modern German gets *amt* 'official position') – from which it was later borrowed back into medieval Latin as *ambactia*. This seems to have formed the basis of a verb, *\*ambactiāre* 'go on a mission' (from which English ultimately gets *embassy*), from which in turn was derived the noun *\*ambactiātor*. This became *ambasciator* in Old Italian,

from which Old French borrowed it as *ambassadeur*. The word had a bewildering array of spellings in Middle English (such as *ambaxadour* and *inbassetour*) before finally settling down as *ambassador* in the 16th century.
► embassy

**amber** [14] *Amber* was borrowed, via Old French, from Arabic *'anbar*, which originally meant 'ambergris' (and in fact until the early 18th century *amber* was used for 'ambergris' too). A perceived resemblance between the two substances had already led in Arabic to 'amber' ousting 'ambergris' as the main meaning of *'anbar*, and this was reflected as soon as English acquired it.

In Scotland until as recently as the early 19th century *lamber* was the usual form. This arose from borrowing the French word for 'amber' complete with its definite article *le: l'ambre*.

Before the introduction of the Arabic term into European languages, the ancestor of modern English *glass* appears to have been the word used for 'amber.'
► ambergris

**ambergris** [15] The original term for ambergris (a waxy material from the stomach of the sperm whale) was *amber*. But as confusion began to arise between the two substances amber and ambergris, *amber* came to be used for both in all the languages that had borrowed it from Arabic, thus compounding the bewilderment. The French solution was to differentiate ambergris as *ambre gris*, literally 'grey amber,' and this eventually became the standard English term. (Later on, the contrastive term *ambre jaune* 'yellow amber' was coined for 'amber' in French.)

Uncertainty over the identity of the second element, *-gris*, has led to some fanciful reformulations of the word. In the 17th century, many people thought ambergris came from Greece – hence spellings such as *amber-de-grece* and *amber-greece*. And until comparatively recently its somewhat greasy consistency encouraged the spelling *ambergrease*.
► amber

**ambidextrous** [16] *Ambidextrous* means literally 'right-handed on both sides.' It was formed in Latin from the prefix *ambi-* 'both' and the adjective *dexter* 'right-handed' (source of English *dextrous*). *Ambi-* corresponds to the Latin adjective *ambo* 'both,' which derived ultimately from the Indo-European base *amb- 'around' (an element in the source of *ambassador* and *embassy*). The second element in Latin *ambo* seems to correspond to Old English *ba* 'both,' which is related to modern English *both*.

Other English words formed with the prefix *amb(i)-* include *ambient* [16] (which came, like *ambition*, from Latin *ambīre* 'go round'), *ambit* [16] (from Latin *am-*

*bitus* 'circuit'), *ambiguous*, *ambition*, *amble*, and *ambulance*.
► dextrous

**ambiguous** [16] *Ambiguous* carries the etymological notion of 'wandering around uncertainly.' It comes ultimately from the Latin compound verb *ambigere*, which was formed from the prefix *ambi-* (as in AMBIDEXTROUS) and the verb *agere* 'drive, lead' (a prodigious source of English words, including *act* and *agent*). From the verb was derived the adjective *ambiguus*, which was borrowed directly into English. The first to use it seems to have been Sir Thomas More: 'if it were now doubtful and ambiguous whether the church of Christ were in the right rule of doctrine or not' *A dialogue concerning heresies* 1528.
► act, agent

**ambition** [14] Like *ambient*, *ambition* comes ultimately from the Latin compound verb *ambīre* 'go round' (formed from the prefix *ambi-*, as in AMBIDEXTROUS, and the verb *īre* 'go,' which also gave English *exit*, *initial*, and *itinerant*). But while *ambient*, a 16th-century acquisition, remains fairly faithful to the literal meaning of the verb, *ambition* depends on a more metaphorical use. It seems that the verb's nominal derivative, *ambitiō*, developed connotations of 'going around soliciting votes' – 'canvassing,' in fact – and hence, figuratively, of 'seeking favour or honour.' When the word was first borrowed into English, via Old French *ambition*, it had distinctly negative associations of 'greed for success' (Reginald Pecock writes of 'Vices [such] as pride, ambition, vainglory,' *The repressor of overmuch blaming of the clergy* 1449), but by the 18th century it was a more respectable emotion.
► exit, initial, itinerant

**amble** [14] The ultimate source of *amble* (and of *perambulator* [17], and thus of its abbreviation *pram* [19]) is the Latin verb *ambulāre* 'walk.' This was a compound verb, formed from the prefix *ambi-* (as in AMBIDEXTROUS) and the base *el- 'go,' which also lies behind *exile* and *alacrity* [15] (from Latin *alacer* 'lively, eager,' a compound of the base *el- and *ācer* 'sharp' – source of English *acid*). Latin *ambulāre* developed into Provençal *amblar*, which eventually reached English via Old French *ambler*. At first the English word was used for referring to a particular (leisurely) gait of a horse, and it was not until the end of the 16th century that it began to be used of people.
► acid, alacrity, exile, perambulator

**ambulance** [19] Originally, *ambulance* was a French term for a field hospital – that is, one set up at a site convenient for a battlefield, and capable of being moved on to the next battlefield when the army advanced (or retreated). In other words, it was an itinerant hospital, and the ultimate source of the term is the Latin verb *ambulāre* 'walk' (as in *amble*). The earliest recorded term for such a military hospital in French was the 17th-century *hôpital ambulatoire*. This was later replaced by *hôpital ambulant*, literally 'walking hospital,' and finally, at the end of the 18th century, by *ambulance*. This sense of the word had died out by the late 19th century, but already its attributive use, in phrases such as *ambulance cart* and *ambulance wagon*, had led to its being used for a vehicle for carrying the wounded or sick.

► acid, alacrity, amble, perambulator

**ambush** [14] Originally, *ambush* meant literally 'put in a bush' – or more precisely 'hide in a wood, from where one can make a surprise attack.' The hypothetical Vulgar Latin verb *\*imboscāre* was formed from the prefix *in-* and the noun *\*boscus* 'bush, thicket' (a word of Germanic origin, related to English *bush*). In Old French this became *embuschier*, and when English acquired it its prefix gradually became transformed into *am-*.

In the 16th century, various related forms were borrowed into English – Spanish produced *ambuscado*, Italian was responsible for *imboscata*, and French *embuscade* was anglicized as *ambuscade* – but none now survives other than as an archaism.

► bush

**amen** [OE] *Amen* was originally a Hebrew noun, *āmēn* 'truth' (based on the verb *āman* 'strengthen, confirm'), which was used adverbially as an expression of confirmation or agreement. Biblical texts translated from Hebrew simply took it over unaltered (the Greek Septuagint has it, for example), and although at first Old English versions of the gospels substituted an indigenous term, 'truly,' by the 11th century *amen* had entered English too.

**amend** see MEND

**amethyst** [13] The amethyst gets its name from a supposition in the ancient world that it was capable of preventing drunkenness. The Greek word for 'intoxicate' was *methúskein*, which was based ultimately on the noun *methú* 'wine' (source of English *methyl*, and related to English *mead*). The addition of the negative prefix *a-* 'not' produced the adjective *améthustos*, used in the phrase *líthos améthustos* 'anti-intoxicant stone.' This was borrowed as a noun into Latin (*amethystus*), and ultimately into Old French as *ametiste*. English took it over and in the 16th century reintroduced the *-th-* spelling of the Latin word.

► mead, methyl

**amiable** [14] *Amiable* and *amicable* are the two English descendants of that most familiar of Latin verbs, *amo, amas, amat . . .* 'love.' It had two rather similar adjectives derived from it: *amābilis* 'lovable' and, via *amīcus* 'friend,' *amīcābilis* 'friendly' (source of English *amicable* [15]). *Amīcābilis* became in French *amiable*, and this was borrowed into English as

*amiable*, but its meaning was subsequently influenced by that of French *aimable* 'likeable, lovable,' which came from Latin *amābilis*.

► amicable

**ammonia** [18] *Ammonia* gets its name ultimately from Amon, or Amen, the Egyptian god of life and reproduction. Near the temple of Amon in Libya were found deposits of ammonium chloride, which was hence named *sal ammoniac* – 'salt of Amon.' The gas nitrogen hydride is derived from sal ammoniac, and in 1782 the Swedish chemist Torbern Bergman coined the term *ammonia* for it.

**ammonite** [18] Like *ammonia*, the *ammonite* gets its name from a supposed connection with Amon, or Amen, the Egyptian god of life and reproduction. In art he is represented as having ram's horns, and the resemblance of ammonites to such horns led to their being named in the Middle Ages *cornu Ammōnis* 'horn of Amon.' In the 18th century the modern Latin term *ammonītēs* (anglicized as *ammonite*) was coined for them. Earlier, ammonites had been called *snake stones* in English, a term which survived dialectally well into the 19th century.

**ammunition** [17] *Ammunition* is one of many words which resulted from a mistaken analysis of 'article' plus 'noun' (compare ADDER). In this case, French *la munition* 'the munitions, the supplies' was misapprehended as *l'ammunition*, and borrowed thus into English. At first it was used for military supplies in general, and it does not seem to have been until the beginning of the 18th century that its meaning became restricted to 'bullets, shells, etc.'

The word *munition* itself was borrowed into English from French in the 16th century. It originally meant 'fortification,' and came from the Latin noun *mūnītiō*; this was a derivative of the verb *munīre* 'defend, fortify,' which in turn was based on the noun *moenia* 'walls, ramparts' (related to *mūrus* 'wall,' the source of English *mural*). Also from *munīre*, via medieval Latin *mūnīmentum*, comes *muniment* [15], a legal term for 'title deed'; the semantic connection is that a title deed is a means by which someone can 'defend' his or her legal right to property.

► muniment, munition, mural

**amok** [17] *Amok* is Malayan in origin, where it is an adjective, *amoq*, meaning 'fighting frenziedly.' Its first brief brush with English actually came in the early 16th century, via Portuguese, which had adopted it as a noun, *amouco*, signifying a 'homicidally crazed Malay.' This sense persisted until the late 18th century, but by then the phrase *run amok*, with all its modern connotations, was well established, and has since taken over the field entirely. The spelling *amuck* has always been fairly common, reflecting the word's pronunciation.

**among** [OE] *Gemong* was an Old English word for 'crowd' – *ge-* was a collective prefix, signifying 'together,' and *-mong* is related to *mingle* – and so the phrase *on gemonge* meant 'in a crowd,' hence 'in the midst, surrounded.' By the 12th century, the *ge-* element had dropped out, giving *onmong* and eventually *among*. A parallel *bimong* existed in the 13th century.

▶ mingle

**amount** see MOUNTAIN

**ampere** [19] This international term for a unit of electrical current derives from the name of André-Marie Ampère (1775–1836), the French physicist and mathematician. It was officially adopted by the Congrès Électrique in Paris in 1881. Ampère himself is best remembered for first making the distinction between electrical current and voltage, and for explaining magnetism in terms of electrical currents. The term *ammeter* 'current-measuring device' [19] was based on *ampere*.

**ampersand** [19] This word for the printed character & is a conflation of the phrase *and per se and*, literally 'and by it self and.' This has been variously explained as either 'the single character "&" signifies *and*,' or 'and on its own [that is, as the final character in a list of the letters of the alphabet given in old grammar books and primers], &.' The character & itself is a conventionalized printed version of an abbreviation used in manuscripts for Latin *et* 'and.'

▶ and

**amphibious** [17] The Greek prefix *amphi-* meant 'both, on both sides' (hence an *amphitheatre* [14]: Greek and Roman theatres were semicircular, so two joined together, completely surrounding the arena, formed an amphitheatre). Combination with *bios* 'life' (as in *biology*) produced the Greek adjective *amphibios*, literally 'leading a double life.' From the beginning of its career as an English word it was used in a very wide, general sense of 'combining two completely distinct or opposite conditions or qualities' (Joseph Addison, for example, used it as an 18th-century equivalent of modern *unisex*), but that meaning has now almost entirely given way to the word's zoological application. At first, *amphibious* meant broadly 'living on both land and water,' and so was applied by some scientists to, for example, seals; but around 1819 the zoologist William Macleay proposed the more precise application, since generally accepted, to frogs, newts, and other members of the class Amphibia whose larvae have gills but whose adults breathe with lungs.

▶ biology

**amuse** [15] *Amuse* is probably a French creation, formed with the prefix *a-* from the verb *muser* (from which English gets *muse* 'ponder' [14]). The current meaning 'divert, entertain' did not begin to emerge until the 17th century, and even so the commonest application of the verb in the 17th and 18th centuries was

'deceive, cheat.' This seems to have developed from an earlier 'bewilder, puzzle,' pointing back to an original sense 'make someone stare open-mouthed.' This links with the probable source of *muser*, namely *muse* 'animal's mouth,' from medieval Latin *mūsum* (which gave English *muzzle* [15]). There is no connection with the inspirational muse, responsible for *music* and *museums*.

▶ muse, muzzle

**anachronism** [17] The Greek prefix *ana-* meant 'up,' and hence, in terms of time, 'back'; Greek *khrónos* meant 'time' (as in English *chronicle*): hence Greek *anakhronismós* 'reference to a wrong time.' From the point of view of its derivation it should strictly be applied to the representation of something as happening earlier than it really did (as if Christ were painted wearing a wristwatch), but in practice, ever since the Greek term's adoption into English, it has also been used for things surviving beyond their due time.

▶ chronicle

**anacolouthon** see ACOLYTE

**anaconda** [18] The term *anaconda* has a confused history. It appears to come from Sinhalese *henakandayā*, literally 'lightning-stem,' which referred to a type of slender green snake. This was anglicized as *anaconda* by the British naturalist John Ray, who in a *List of Indian serpents* 1693 described it as a snake which 'crushed the limbs of buffaloes and yoke beasts.' And the 1797 edition of the *Encyclopedia Britannica* notes it as a 'very large and terrible snake [from Ceylon] which often devours the unfortunate traveller alive.' However, in the early 19th century the French zoologist François Marie Daudin for no known reason transferred the name to a large South American snake of the boa family, and that application has since stuck.

**analysis** [16] The underlying etymological notion contained in *analysis* is of 'undoing' or 'loosening,' so that the component parts are separated and revealed. The word comes ultimately from Greek *análusis*, a derivative of the compound verb *analúein* 'undo,' which was formed from the prefix *ana-* 'up, back' and the verb *lúein* 'loosen, free' (related to English *less, loose, lose,* and *loss*). It entered English via medieval Latin, and in the 17th century was anglicized to *analyse*: 'The Analyse I gave of the contents of this Verse,' Daniel Rogers, *Naaman the Syrian* 1642. This did not last long, but it may have provided the impetus for the introduction of the verb *analyse*, which first appeared around 1600; its later development was supported by French *analyser*.

▶ dialysis, less, loose, lose, loss

**anathema** [16] Originally in Greek *anáthēma* was a 'votive offering' (it was a derivative of the compound verb *anatithénai* 'set up, dedicate,' formed from the prefix *ana-* 'up' and the verb *tithénai* 'place,' source of English *theme* and related to English *do*). But from being broadly 'anything offered up for religious purposes,' the word gradually developed negative associations of 'something dedicated to evil'; and by the time it reached Latin it meant 'curse' or 'accursed person.'

▶ do, theme

**anatomy** [14] Etymologically, *anatomy* means 'cutting up' (the Greek noun *anatomía* was compounded from the prefix *ana-*'up' and the base *\*tom-*, which figures in several English surgical terms, such as *tonsillectomy* [19], as well as in *atom* and *tome*), and when it first came into English it meant literally 'dissection' as well as 'science of bodily structure.' From the 16th century to the early 19th century it was also used for 'skeleton,' and in this sense it was often misanalysed as *an atomy*, as if the initial *an-* were the indefinite article: 'My bones . . . will be taken up smooth, and white, and bare as an atomy,' Tobias Smollett, *Don Quixote* 1755.

▶ atom, tome

**ancestor** [13] Ultimately, *ancestor* is the same word as *antecedent* [14]: both come from the Latin compound verb *antecēdere* 'precede,' formed from the prefix *ante-* 'before' and the verb *cēdere* 'go' (source of English *cede* and a host of related words, such as *proceed* and *access*). Derived from this was the agent noun *antecessor* 'one who precedes,' which was borrowed into Old French at two distinct times: first as *ancessour*, and later as *ancestre*, which subsequently developed to *ancêtre*. Middle English had examples of all three of these forms. The modern spelling, *ancestor*, developed in the 16th century.

▶ access, antecedent, cede, precede, proceed

**anchor** [OE] English borrowed this word from Latin in the 9th century, but its ultimate source is Greek *ágkūra* (which goes back to an Indo-European base *\*angg-* 'bent,' also the source of *angle* and *ankle*). Originally it was spelled *ancor*, reflecting Latin *ancora*; the inauthentic *h* began to creep in in the 16th century, in imitation of the learned-looking but misguided Latin spelling *anchora*.

▶ angle, ankle

**anchovy** [16] English acquired *anchovy* from Spanish *anchova* (the word first turns up as an item on Falstaff's bill at the Boar's Head: 'Anchovies and sack after supper . . . 2s 6d,' *1 Henry IV* 1596), but before that its history is disputed. One school of thought holds that it comes via Italian dialect *ancioa* from Vulgar Latin *\*apjua*, which in turn was derived from Greek *aphúē* 'small fry'; but another connects it with Basque *anchu*, which may mean literally 'dried fish.'

**ancient** [14] Like *antique*, *ancient* was originally, in Latin, an adjectivized version of the adverb and preposition 'before': to *ante* 'before' was added the adjective suffix *-ānus*, to produce the adjective *\*ante-*

*ānus* 'going before.' In Old French this became *ancien*, and it passed into English via Anglo-Norman *auncien*. The final *-t* began to appear in the 15th century, by the same phonetic process as produced it in *pageant* and *tyrant*.

The now archaic use of *ancient* as 'standard, flag' and as 'standard-bearer' (as most famously in Shakespeare's 'ancient Pistol') arose from an alteration of *ensign*.

▶ antique

**and** [OE] A word as ancient as the English language itself, which has persisted virtually unchanged since at least 700AD, *and* has cognates in other Germanic languages (German *und*, Dutch *en*), but no convincing ultimate ancestor for it has been identified.

**anecdote** [17] In Greek, *anékdotos* meant 'unpublished.' It was formed from the negative prefix *an-* and *ékdotos*, which in turn came from the verb *didónai* 'give' (a distant cousin of English *donation* and *date*) plus the prefix *ek-* 'out' – hence 'give out, publish.' The use of the plural *anékdota* by the 6th-century Byzantine historian Procopius as the title of his unpublished memoirs of the life of the Emperor Justinian, which revealed juicy details of court life, played a major part in the subsequent use of Latin *anecdota* for 'revelations of secrets,' the sense which *anecdote* had when it first came into English. The meaning 'brief amusing story' did not develop until the mid 18th century.

▶ date, donation

**anemone** [16] The wild' wood anemone is sometimes called the *wind flower*, and this idea may be reflected in its standard name too. For it comes from Greek *anemónē*, which appears to be a derivative of *ánemos* 'wind' (also the source of English *animal* and *animate*). However, it has also been speculated that the Greek word may be an alteration of Hebrew *Na'amān*, which was an epithet applied to Adonis, the beautiful youth beloved of Aphrodite from whose blood, according to Greek legend, the anemone sprang after he was killed while boar hunting. According to this view, *anemónē* arose from a folk-etymological reformulation of the Hebrew word to make it approximate more closely to the Greek for 'wind.'

The application to *sea anemone* began in the late 18th century.

▶ animal, animate

**angel** [12] In a sense, English already had this word in Anglo-Saxon times; texts of around 950 mention *englas* 'angels.' But in that form (which had a hard *g*) it came directly from Latin *angelus*. The word we use today, with its soft *g*, came from Old French *angele* (the 'hard *g*' form survived until the 13th century). The French word was in its turn, of course, acquired from Latin, which adopted it from Greek *ángelos* or *ággelos*. This meant literally 'messenger,' and its use in religious contexts arises from its being used as a direct translation of Hebrew *mal'ākh* 'messenger,' the term used in the scriptures for God's intermediaries. The Greek word itself may be of Persian origin.

► evangelist

**anger** [12] The original notion contained in this word was of 'distress' or 'affliction'; 'rage' did not begin to enter the picture until the 13th century. English acquired it from Old Norse *angr* 'grief,' and it is connected with a group of words which contain connotations of 'constriction': German and Dutch *eng* (and Old English *enge*) mean 'narrow,' Greek *ánkhein* meant 'squeeze, strangle' (English gets *angina* from it), and Latin *angustus* (source of English *anguish*) also meant 'narrow.' All these forms point back to an Indo-European base *\*angg-* 'narrow.'

► angina, anguish

**angina**   see ANGUISH

**angle** There have been two distinct words *angle* in English. The older is now encountered virtually only in its derivatives, *angler* and *angling*, but until the early 19th century an *angle* was a 'fishing hook' (or, by extension, 'fishing tackle'). It entered the language in the Old English period, and was based on Germanic *\*angg-* (source also of German *angel* 'fishing tackle'). An earlier form of the word appears to have been applied by its former inhabitants to a fishhook-shaped area of Schleswig, in the Jutland peninsula; now *Angeln*, they called it *Angul*, and so they themselves came to be referred to as *Angles*. They brought their words with them to England, of course, and so both the country and the language, *English*, now contain a reminiscence of their fishhooks.

Angle in the sense of a 'figure formed by two intersecting lines' entered the language in the 14th century (Chaucer is its first recorded user). It came from Latin *angulus* 'corner,' either directly or via French *angle*. The Latin word was originally a diminutive of *\*angus*, which is related to other words that contain the notion of 'bending,' such as Greek *ágkūra* (ultimate source of English *anchor*) and English *ankle*. They all go back to Indo-European *\*angg-* 'bent,' and it has been speculated that the fishhook *angle*, with its temptingly bent shape, may derive from the same source.

► English / anchor, ankle

**anguish** [13] English acquired *anguish* from Old French *anguisse*, changing its ending to -*ish* in the 14th century. Its central notion of 'distress' or 'suffering' goes back ultimately (as in the case of the related *anger*) to a set of words meaning 'constriction' (for the sense development, compare the phrase *in dire straits*, where *strait* originally meant 'narrow'). Old French *anguisse* came from Latin *angustia* 'distress,' which was derived from the adjective *angustus* 'narrow.' Like Greek *ánkhein* 'squeeze, strangle' (ultimate source of

English *angina* [16]) and Latin *angere* 'strangle,' this came originally from an Indo-European base *\*angg-* 'narrow.'

► anger, angina

**animal** [14] Etymologically, an *animal* is a being which breathes (compare DEER). Its immediate source was the Latin adjective *animālis* 'having a soul,' a derivative of the noun *anima* 'breath, soul' (which also gave English the verb and adjective *animate* [15]). *Anima* is a member of a set of related words in which the notions of 'breath, wind' and 'spirit, life' are intimately connected: for instance, Greek *ánemos* 'wind' (possible source of English *anemone*), Latin *animus* 'spirit, mind, courage, anger' (source of English *animosity* [15] and *animus* [19]), Sanskrit *ániti* 'breathe,' Old English *ōthian* 'breathe,' Swedish *anda* 'breath, spirit,' and Gothic *usanan* 'breathe out.' The 'breath' sense is presumably primary, the 'spirit, life' sense a metaphorical extension of it.

► anemone, animate, animosity, animus

**ankle** [14] *Ankle* comes from a probable Old Norse word *\*ankula*. It has several relatives in other Germanic languages (German and Dutch *enkel*, for instance, and Swedish and Danish *ankel*) and can be traced back to an Indo-European base *\*angg-* 'bent' (ultimate source also of *anchor* and *angle*). Before the Old Norse form spread through the language, English had its own native version of the word: *anclēow*. This survived until the 15th century in mainstream English, and for much longer in local dialects.

► anchor, angle

**annals**   see ANNUAL

**annex** [14] The verb *annex* entered English about a century and a half before the noun. It came from French *annexer*, which was formed from the past participial stem of Latin *annectere* 'tie together' (a verb *annect*, borrowed directly from this, was in learned use in English from the 16th to the 18th centuries). *Annectere* itself was based on the verb *nectere* 'tie,' from which English also gets *nexus* and *connect*. The noun was borrowed from French *annexe*, and in the sense 'extra building' retains its -*e*.

► connect, nexus

**annihilate** [16] *Annihilate* comes from the past participle of the late Latin verb *annihilāre*, meaning literally 'reduce to nothing' (a formation based on the noun *nihil* 'nothing,' source of English *nihilism* and *nil*). There was actually an earlier English verb, *annihil*, based on French *annihiler*, which appeared at the end of the 15th century, but it did not long survive the introduction of *annihilate*.

► nihilism, nil

**anniversary** [13] Like *annual*, *anniversary* is based ultimately on Latin *annus* 'year.' The underlying idea it contains is of 'yearly turning' or 'returning';

the Latin adjective *anniversārius* was based on *annus* and *versus* 'turning' (related to a wide range of English words, from *verse* and *convert* to *vertebra* and *vertigo*). This was used in phrases such as *diēs anniversāria* 'day returning every year,' and eventually became a noun in its own right.

▶ annual, convert, verse

**announce** SEE PRONOUNCE

**annoy** [13] *Annoy* comes ultimately from the Latin phrase *in odiō*, literally 'in hatred,' hence 'odious' (*odiō* was the ablative sense of *odium*, from which English got *odious* [14] and *odium* [17]). The phrase was turned into a verb in later Latin – *inodiāre* 'make loathsome' – which transferred to Old French as *anuier* or *anoier* (in modern French this has become *ennuyer*, whose noun *ennui* was borrowed into English in the mid 18th century in the sense 'boredom').

▶ ennui, noisome, odious

**annual** [14] *Annual* comes, via Old French *annuel*, from *annuālis*, a late Latin adjective based on *annus* 'year' (perhaps as a blend of two earlier, classical Latin adjectives, *annuus* and *annālis* – ultimate source of English *annals* [16]). *Annus* itself may go back to an earlier, unrecorded *\*atnos*, probably borrowed from an ancient Indo-European language of the Italian peninsula, such as Oscan or Umbrian. It appears to be related to Gothic *athnam* 'years' and Sanskrit *átati* 'go, wander.'

The medieval Latin noun *annuitās*, formed from the adjective *annuus*, produced French *annuité*, which was borrowed into English as *annuity* in the 15th century.

▶ annals, anniversary, annuity

**anode** [19] The term *anode*, meaning 'positive electrode,' appears to have been introduced by the English philosopher William Whewell around 1834. It was based on Greek *ánodos* 'way up,' a compound noun formed from *aná-* 'up' and *hodós* 'way' (also represented in *exodus* 'way out' and *odometer* 'instrument for measuring distance travelled,' and possibly related to Latin *cēdere*, source of English *cede* and a host of derived words). It specifically contrasts with *cathode*, which means literally 'way down.'

▶ exodus, odometer

**anonymous** SEE NAME

**answer** [OE] Etymologically, the word *answer* contains the notion of making a sworn statement rebutting a charge. It comes from a prehistoric West and North Germanic compound *\*andswarō*; the first element of this was the prefix *\*and-* 'against,' related to German *ent-* 'away, un-' and to Greek *anti-*, source of English *anti-*; and the second element came from the same source as English *swear*. In Old English, the Germanic compound became *andswaru* (noun) and *andswarian* (verb) 'reply,' which by the 14th century had been reduced to *answer*.

The synonymous *respond* has a similar semantic his-

tory: Latin *respondēre* meant 'make a solemn promise in return,' hence 'reply.' And, as another element in the jigsaw, Swedish *ansvar* means 'responsibility' – a sense echoed by English *answerable*.

▶ swear

**ant** [OE] The word *ant* appears to carry the etymological sense 'creature that cuts off or bites off.' Its Old English form, *æmette*, was derived from a hypothetical Germanic compound *\*aimaitjōn*, formed from the prefix *\*ai-* 'off, away' and the root *\*mait-*'cut' (modern German has the verb *meissen* 'chisel, carve'): thus, 'the biter.' The Old English word later developed along two distinct strands: in one, it became *emmet*, which survived into the 20th century as a dialectal form; while in the other it progressed through *amete* and *ampte* to modern English *ant*.

If the notion of 'biting' in the naming of the ant is restricted to the Germanic languages (German has *ameise*), the observation that it and its nest smell of urine has been brought into play far more widely. The Indo-European root *\*meigh-*, from which ultimately we get *micturate* 'urinate' [18], was also the source of several words for 'ant,' including Greek *múrmēx* (origin of English *myrmecology* 'study of ants,' and also perhaps of *myrmidon* [14] 'faithful follower,' from the *Myrmidons*, a legendary Greek people who loyally followed their king Achilles in the Trojan war, and who were said originally to have been created from ants), Latin *formīca* (hence English *formic acid* [18], produced by ants, and *formaldehyde* [19]), and Danish *myre*. It also produced Middle English *mire* 'ant,' the underlying meaning of which was subsequently reinforced by the addition of *piss* to give *pismire*, which again survived dialectally into the 20th century.

**antagonist** [16] Greek *agón* (source of English *agony*) meant 'contest, conflict.' Hence the concept of 'struggling against (*anti-*) someone' was conveyed in Greek by the verb *antagōnízesthai*. The derived noun *antagōnistés* entered English via French or late Latin.

▶ agony

**antecedent** SEE ANCESTOR

**antelope** [15] *Antelope* comes from medieval Greek *antholops*. In the Middle Ages it was applied to an outlandish but figmentary beast, in the words of the *Oxford English Dictionary*, 'haunting the banks of the Euphrates, very savage, hard to catch, having long saw-like horns with which they cut in pieces and broke all 'engines' and even cut down trees.' The term was subsequently used for a heraldic animal, but it was not until the early 17th century that it was applied, by the naturalist Edward Topsell, to the swift-running deerlike animal for which it is now used.

**anthem** [OE] *Anthem* is ultimately an alteration of *antiphon* 'scriptural verse said or sung as a response' (which was independently reborrowed into English from ecclesiastical Latin in the 15th century). It comes from Greek *antíphōnos* 'responsive,' a compound formed from *anti-* 'against' and *phōné* 'sound' (source of English *phonetic, telephone*, etc). By the time it had become established in Old English, *antiphon* had already developed to *antefn*, and gradually the /v/ sound of the *f* became assimilated to the following *n*, producing *antemne* and eventually *antem*. The spelling with *th* begins to appear in the 15th century, perhaps influenced by Old French *anthaine*; it gradually altered the pronunciation.

The meaning 'antiphon' died out in the 18th century, having been succeeded by 'piece of choral church music' and more generally 'song of praise.' The specific application to a 'national song' began in the 19th century.

▶ antiphon, phonetic, telephone

**anther** [18] Greek *ánthos* originally meant 'part of a plant which grows above ground' (this was the basis of the Homeric 'metaphor' translated as 'flower of youth,' which originally referred to the first growth of beard on young men's faces). Later it narrowed somewhat to 'flower.' The adjective derived from it was *anthērós*, which was borrowed into Latin as *anthēra*, a noun meaning 'medicine made from flowers.' In practice, herbalists often made such medicines from the reproductive part of the flower, and so *anther* came to be applied to the pollen-bearing part of the stamen.

More remote semantically, but also derived from Greek *ánthos*, is *anthology* [17]. The second element represents Greek *logíā* 'collecting,' a derivative of the verb *legein* 'gather' (which is related to *legend* and *logic*). The notion of a collection of flowers, *anthologíā*, was applied metaphorically to a selection of choice epigrams or brief poems; borrowed into English, via French *anthologie* or medieval Latin *anthologia*, it was originally restricted to collections of Greek verse, but by the mid 19th century its application had broadened out considerably. The parallel Latin formation, *florilegium*, also literally 'collection of flowers,' has occasionally been used in English for 'anthology.'

▶ anthology

**anthrax** [14] In Greek, *anthrax* means 'coal' (hence English *anthracite* [19]). The notion of a burning coal led to its being applied metaphorically to a very severe boil or carbuncle, and that is how it was first used in English. It was not until the late 19th century that the word came into general use, when it was applied to the bacterial disease of animals that had been described by Louis Pasteur (which produces large ulcers on the body).

▶ anthracite

**antic** see ANTIQUE

**antidote** see DATE

**antimacassar** [19] An antimacassar was a cloth spread over chairbacks in the 19th and early 20th centuries to protect them from greasy hair. It took its name from Macassar oil, a proprietary brand of hair oil made by Rowland and Son, allegedly from ingredients obtained from Makassar, a region of the island of Sulawesi (formerly Celebes) in Indonesia.

**antimony** [15] *Antimony*, from medieval Latin *antimōnium*, was used by alchemists of the Middle Ages for 'stibnite,' the mineral from which antimony is obtained, and for 'stibium,' or 'black antimony,' a heated and powdered version of the mineral used for eye make-up. The element antimony itself was first described in the late 18th century, when it was called *regulus of antimony*; the British chemist Humphry Davy appears to have been the first to apply the simple term *antimony* to it, in 1812.

The ultimate origins of the word *antimony* are obscure, but attempts have been made to link it with Latin *stibium* (source of *Sb*, the chemical symbol for antimony). It has been speculated that Latin *antimōnium* may have been a modification of Arabic *ithmid*, which was perhaps borrowed from Greek *stímmi* or *stíbi* (source of Latin *stibium*). This in turn has been conjecturally traced back to an Egyptian word *stm*, which was used for a sort of powder applied to the eyelids as make-up.

**antiphon** see ANTHEM

**antipodes** [16] Greek *antípodes* meant literally 'people who have their feet opposite' – that is, people who live on the other side of the world, and therefore have the soles of their feet 'facing' those of people on this side of the world. It was formed from the prefix *anti-* 'against, opposite' and *poús* 'foot' (related to English *foot* and *pedal*). English *antipodes*, borrowed via either French *antipodes* or late Latin *antipodes*, originally meant 'people on the other side of the world' too, but by the mid 16th century it had come to be used simply for the 'opposite side of the globe.'

▶ foot, pedal

**antique** [16] Originally, in Latin, *antique* was an adjectivized version of the adverb and preposition 'before': to *ante* 'before' was added the adjective suffix *-īcus*, to produce the adjective *antīquus* (somewhat later an exactly parallel formation, using the suffix *-ānus* rather than *-īcus*, produced the adjective which became English *ancient*). English acquired the word either via French *antique* or directly from Latin. To begin with, and until relatively recently, it meant simply 'ancient,' or specifically 'of the ancient world'; it was only towards the end of the 18th century that the modern sense 'made long ago and therefore collectable' began to become established.

In Italian, *antico* (from Latin *antīquus*) was often applied to grotesque carvings found in ancient remains. It was borrowed into English in the 16th century as an adjective, *antic*, meaning 'bizarre,' but also as a noun, usually used in the plural, in the sense 'absurd behaviour.'

▶ ancient, antic

## antirrhinum
[16] *Antirrhinum* means literally 'similar to a nose.' The Greek compound *antírrhīnon* was formed from the prefix *anti-* 'against, simulating' and *rhīn-*, the stem of *rhīs* 'nose' (also found in English *rhinoceros*). The English word was borrowed from the latinized form, *antirrhinum*. The name comes, of course, from the snapdragon flower's supposed resemblance to an animal's nose or muzzle (another early name for the plant was *calf's snout*).

▶ rhinoceros

## antler
[14] English acquired *antler* via Anglo-Norman *auntelere* from Old French *antoillier* (modern French has *andouiller*). Its previous history is not altogether clear; it has been speculated that it comes originally from Latin *\*anteoculāris*, which would have meant literally 'positioned before (*ante*) the eye (*oculus*),' but this derivation is rather dubious.

## anvil
[OE] Etymologically, an anvil is 'something on which you hit something else.' The Old English word was *anfilte*, which came from a prehistoric West Germanic compound formed from *\*ana* 'on' and a verbal component meaning 'hit' (which was also the source of English *felt*, Latin *pellere* 'hit,' and Swedish dialect *filta* 'hit'). It is possible that the word may originally have been a loan-translation based on the Latin for 'anvil,' *incūs*; for this too was a compound, based on *in* 'in' and the stem of the verb *cūdere* 'hit' (related to English *hew*).

▶ appeal

## any
[OE] *Any* is descended from a prehistoric Germanic compound meaning literally 'one-y' (a formation duplicated in *unique*, whose Latin source *ūnicus* was compounded of *ūnus* 'one' and the adjective suffix *-icus*). Germanic *\*ainigaz* was formed from *\*ain-* (source of English *one*) and the stem *\*-ig-*, from which the English adjective suffix *-y* is ultimately derived. In Old English this had become *ǣnig*, which diversified in Middle English to *any* and *eny*; modern English *any* preserves the spelling of the former and the pronunciation of the latter.

▶ one

## aorta
SEE ARTERY

## apart
[14] English acquired *apart* from Old French *apart*, where it was based on the Latin phrase *ā parte* 'at *or* to the side' (Latin *pars, part-* is the source of English *part*). By the time it came into English it already contained the notion of separation.

▶ part

## apartheid
[20] *Apartheid* is a direct borrowing from Afrikaans *apartheid*, literally 'separateness,' which is a compound based on Dutch *apart* and the suffix *-heid* (related to English *-hood*). The first record of its use in Afrikaans is in 1929, but it does not appear in English-language contexts until 1947.

## ape
[OE] *Ape* (in Old English *apa*) has cognates in several Germanic languages (German *affe*, Dutch *aap*, Swedish *apa*), and comes from a prehistoric West and North Germanic *\*apan* (perhaps originally borrowed from Celtic). Until the early 16th century, when English acquired the word *monkey*, it was the only term available for any of the non-human primates, but from around 1700 it began to be restricted in use to the large primates of the family Pongidae.

## aphorism
SEE HORIZON

## aplomb
[18] Originally, *aplomb* meant literally 'quality of being perpendicular.' It was borrowed from French, where it was a lexicalization of the phrase *à plomb* 'according to the plumb line' (*plomb* came from Latin *plumbum* 'lead,' also the ultimate source of English *plumb, plumber, plumbago*, and *plummet*). The notion of 'uprightness' gave rise in the 19th century to the metaphorical sense 'composure.'

▶ plumb, plumber, plummet

## apocalypse
[13] A 'catastrophic event, such as the end of the world' is a relatively recent, 20th-century development in the meaning of *apocalypse*. Originally it was an alternative name for the book of the Bible known as the 'Revelation of St John the divine,' which describes a vision of the future granted to St John on the island of Patmos. And in fact, the underlying etymological meaning of *apocalypse* is literally 'revelation.' It comes, via Old French and ecclesiastical Latin, from Greek *apokálupsis*, a derivative of the verb *apokalúptein* 'uncover, reveal,' which was formed from the prefix *apo-* 'away, off' and the verb *kalúptein* 'cover' (related to English *conceal*).

▶ conceal

## apocrypha
SEE CRYPT

## apocryphal
[16] *Apocryphal* is a 'second-generation' adjective; the original adjective form in English was *apocrypha* ('The writing is apocrypha when the author thereof is unknown,' John de Trevisa 1387). This came, via ecclesiastical Latin, from Greek *apókruphos* 'hidden,' a derivative of the compound verb *apokrúptein* 'hide away,' which was formed from the prefix *apo-* 'away, off' and the verb *krúptein* 'hide' (source of English *crypt* and *cryptic*). It was applied as a noun to writings in general that were of unknown authorship, and in the 16th century came to be used specifically as the collective term for the uncanonical books of the Old Testament. It was perhaps confusion between the adjectival and nominal roles of *apocrypha* that led to

the formation of the new adjective *apocryphal* towards the end of the 16th century.
▶ crypt, cryptic

**apogee** [17] In its original, literal sense, a planet's or satellite's apogee is the point in its orbit at which it is furthest away from the Earth; and this is reflected in the word's ultimate source, Greek *apógaios* or *apógeios* 'far from the Earth,' formed from the prefix *apo-* 'away' and *gē* 'earth' (source of English *geography*, *geology*, and *geometry*). From this was derived a noun, *apógaion*, which passed into English via Latin *apogeum* or French *apogée*. The metaphorical sense 'culmination' developed in the later 17th century.

The opposite of *apogee*, *perigee* [16], contains the Greek prefix *peri-* 'around,' in the sense 'close around,' and entered English at about the same time as *apogee*.
▶ geography, perigee

**apology** [16] The original meaning of *apology* was 'formal self-justification,' often used as the title of a piece of writing rebutting criticism (as in the *Apology of Sir Thomas More, knight* 1533). This is indicative of the word's origins in Greek *apología*, a derivative of the verb *apologeisthai* 'speak in one's defence,' formed from the prefix *apo-* 'away, off' and *logos* 'speech' (source of English *logic*). It entered English through either French *apologie* or Latin *apologia* (which was separately borrowed into English as a Latinism in the late 18th century). The meaning 'expression of regret for offence given' developed in the late 16th century.
▶ logic

**apoplexy** [14] The Greek verb *apopléssein* meant 'incapacitate by means of a stroke.' It was formed from the prefix *apo-* 'away, off' (here used as an intensive) and the verb *pléssein* 'hit' (source of English *plectrum* [17] and related to English *complain*, *plangent*, *plankton*, and *plague*). The derived noun, *apoplēxía*, entered English via Latin and Old French.
▶ complain, plague, plangent, plankton, plectrum

**apostle** [OE] *Apostle* was an early borrowing into Old English from Latin, and like *angel* it originally meant 'messenger.' Latin *apostolus* came from Greek *apóstolos* 'messenger,' or literally 'someone sent out'; this was a compound formed from the prefix *apo-* 'away' and the verb *stéllein* 'send' (related to English *stall* and *local*). The Old English form, *apostol*, was gradually replaced from the 12th century by *apostle*, from Old French *apostle*.
▶ epistle, local, stall

**apostrophe** [17] *Apostrophe* comes originally from the Greek phrase *prosōidiā apóstrophos*, literally 'accent of turning away,' hence, a mark showing where a letter or sound has been omitted. *Apóstrophos* itself was derived from the compound verb *apostréphein*, formed from the prefix *apo-* 'away' and the verb *stréphein* 'turn' (related to the second element of

*catastrophe* [16], whose Greek original meant literally 'overturning'). English acquired the word via French and Latin.
▶ catastrophe

**apothecary** [14] Originally, an apothecary was simply a shopkeeper – the word comes via Old French from late Latin *apothēcārius*, which was based on Greek *apothḗkē* 'storehouse' (source, via French, of *boutique* [18] and via Spanish of *bodega* [19]), a derivative of the verb *apotithénai* 'put away' (formed from the prefix *apo-* 'away' and the verb *tithénai* 'put' – source of *thesis*). By the time the word entered English it was reserved to shopkeepers who sold non-perishable groceries, such as spices – and herbal and other remedies. Gradually, apothecaries began to specialize more and more in drugs, so that in 1617 a formal separation took place between the Apothecaries' Company of London and the Grocers' Company. *Apothecary* remained the general term for a 'druggist' until about 1800, when *chemist* began to take over.
▶ bodega, boutique, thesis

**apotheosis** see THEOLOGY

**apparatus** [17] Etymologically, *apparatus* is 'equipment that has been prepared for a particular use.' The word is borrowed from Latin *apparātus*, the past participle of the compound verb *apparāre*, formed from the prefix *ad-* and *parāre* 'make ready' (source of *prepare* 'make ready in advance,' and related to *parent*). At the beginning of the 17th century, the related but anglicized form *apparate* put in a brief appearance in the language (possibly borrowed from French *apparat*), but within 20 years *apparatus* had supplanted it.
▶ parent, prepare

**apparel** [13] *Apparel* has the same source as *apparatus*, and originally it had the same meaning, too: until as late as the start of the 18th century, it was used for 'equipment needed for performing a particular function.' But the sense 'clothing' is of equal antiquity in English, and by the 16th century it had become established as the central meaning of the word. Its immediate source was Old French *apareil* (modern French *appareil* means chiefly 'apparatus'), which came from a hypothetical Vulgar Latin verb *\*appariculāre*, an irregular formation based on Latin *apparāre* 'make ready' (see APPARATUS).
▶ parent, prepare

**apparent** see APPEAR

**apparition** see APPEAR

**appeal** [14] The ultimate Latin source of *appeal*, the verb *adpellere* (formed from the prefix *ad-* 'to' and *pellere* 'drive' – related to *anvil*, *felt*, and *pulse*), seems to have been used in nautical contexts in the sense 'direct a ship towards a particular landing.' It was extended metaphorically (with a modification in form to *appellāre*) to mean 'address' or 'accost,' and from these came two specific, legal, applications: 'accuse' and 'call for the reversal of a judgment.' *Appeal* had both these meanings when it was first adopted into English from Old French *apeler*. The former had more or less died out by the beginning of the 19th century, but the second has flourished and led to the more general sense 'make an earnest request.'

*Peal* [14], as in 'peal of bells,' is an abbreviated form of *appeal*, and *repeal* [14] comes from the Old French derivative *rapeler*.

▶ anvil, felt, peal, pulse, repeal

**appear** [13] *Appear* comes via Old French *apareir* from Latin *appārēre*, a compound verb formed from the prefix *ad-* and *pārēre* 'show, become visible' (related to Greek *peparein* 'display'). *Appārēre* was also the ultimate source of *apparent* [14], via its present participial stem *appārent-*, and of *apparition* [15], via its noun derivative *appāritiō*.

▶ apparent, apparition

**appease** SEE PEACE

**appendix** SEE PENTHOUSE

**appetite** [14] In its origins, *appetite* referred to a very generalized desire or inclination; the wish for food is a secondary development. The Latin noun was *appetītus*, a derivative of the compound verb *appetere* 'strive after, desire eagerly,' which was based on *petere* 'go to, seek out' (source also of English *compete, impetus, petition,* and *repeat,* and related to *feather*).

▶ compete, impetus, petition, repeat

**applaud** [15] English probably acquired this word directly from Latin *applaudere*, which meant literally 'clap at.' It was a compound formed from the prefix *ad-* 'to' and the verb *plaudere* 'clap,' source also of *plaudit* [17] and of *explode*, whose original sense seems to have been 'drive from the stage by clapping' (or, presumably, by any other signals of disapproval favoured by Roman audiences).

▶ explode, plaudit

**apple** [OE] Words related to *apple* are found all over Europe; not just in Germanic languages (German *apfel*, Dutch *appel*, Swedish *äpple*), but also in Balto-Slavonic (Lithuanian *óbuolas*, Polish *jabłko*), and Celtic (Irish *ubhall*, Welsh *afal*) languages. The Old English version was *æppel*, which developed to modern English *apple*. Apparently from earliest times the word was applied not just to the fruit we now know as the apple, but to any fruit in general. For example, John de Trevisa, in his translation of *De proprietatibus rerum* 1398 wrote 'All manner apples [that is, 'fruit'] that are enclosed in a hard skin, rind, or shell, are called Nuces [nuts].' The term *earth-apple* has been applied to several vegetables, including the cucumber and the potato (compare French *pomme de terre*), and *pineapple* (which originally meant 'pinecone,' with particular reference to the edible pinenuts) was applied to the tropical fruit in the 17th century, because of its supposed resemblance to a pinecone.

**apple-pie bed** SEE PLY

**apply** SEE PLY

**appoint** [14] *Appoint* came from the Old French verb *apointier* 'arrange,' which was based on the phrase *a point*, literally 'to a point.' Hints of the original meaning can still be found in some of the verb's early uses in English, in the sense 'settle a matter decisively,' but its main modern meanings, 'fix by prior arrangement' and 'select for a post,' had become established by the mid 15th century.

▶ point

**appraise** [15] Originally, *appraise* meant simply 'fix the price of.' It came from the Old French verb *aprisier* 'value,' which is ultimately a parallel formation with *appreciate*; it is not clear whether it came directly from late Latin *appretiāre*, or whether it was a newly formed compound in Old French, based on *pris* 'price.' Its earliest spellings in English were thus *apprize* and *apprise*, and these continued in use down to the 19th century, with the more metaphorical meaning 'estimate the worth of' gradually coming to the fore. From the 16th century onwards, however, it seems that association with the word *praise* (which is quite closely related etymologically) has been at work, and by the 19th century the form *appraise* was firmly established.

*Apprise* 'inform,' with which *appraise* is often confused (and which appears superficially to be far closer to the source *pris* or *pretium* 'price'), in fact has no etymological connection with it. It comes from *appris*, the past participle of French *apprendre* 'teach' (closely related to English *apprehend*).

▶ appreciate, price

**appreciate** [17] Like *appraise*, *appreciate* originally comes from the notion of setting a price on something. It comes from late Latin *appretiāre*, a compound verb formed from *ad-* 'to' and *pretium* 'price.' The neutral sense of 'estimating worth' was already accompanied by the more positive 'esteem highly' when the word began to be used in English, and by the late 18th century the meaning 'rise in value' (apparently an American development) was well in place.

▶ appraise, price

**apprehend** [14] The underlying notion in *apprehend* is of 'seizing' or 'grasping'; it comes ultimately from the Latin verb *prehendere* 'seize' (source also of *comprehend, predatory,* and *prehensile*). Latin *apprehendere* 'lay hold of,' formed with the prefix *ad-*, developed the metaphorical meaning 'seize with the mind' – that is, 'learn'; and that was the earliest meaning *apprehend* had in English when it was borrowed either directly from Latin or via French *appréhender*: John de Trevisa, for instance, in his translation of *De*

*proprietatibus rerum* 1398 writes 'he holds in mind
. . . without forgetting, all that he apprehends.' More
familiar modern senses, such as 'arrest' and 'understand,' followed in the 16th century.

A contracted form of the Latin verb, *apprendere*, became Old French *aprendre*, modern French *apprendre*
'learn.' This provided the basis for the derivative *apren-
tis* 'someone learning,' from which English gets *apprentice* [14]; and its past participle *appris*, in the
causative sense 'taught,' was the source of English *apprise* [17].

The chief modern meaning of the derived noun *apprehension*, 'fear,' arose via the notion of 'grasping
something with the mind,' then 'forming an idea of
what will happen in the future,' and finally 'anticipation
of something unpleasant.'
▸ apprentice, comprehend, impregnable, predatory,
prehensile

**approach** [14] *Approach* is etymologically
connected with *propinquity* 'nearness'; they both go
back ultimately to Latin *prope* 'near.' *Propinquity* [14]
comes from a derived Latin adjective *propinquus*
'neighbouring,' while *approach* is based on the comparative form *propius* 'nearer.' From this was formed
the late Latin verb *appropiāre* 'go nearer to,' which
came to English via Old French *aprochier*. Latin *prope*,
incidentally, may be connected in some way with the
preposition *prō* (a relative of English *for*), and a hypothetical variant of it, *proqe*, may be the source, via its
superlative *proximus*, of English *proximity* and
*approximate*.
▸ approximate, propinquity, proximity

**appropriate**   see PROPER

**approve** [14] The Latin source of *approve*, *approbāre*, was a derivative of *probāre*, source of English
*prove*. *Probāre* originally meant 'test something to find
if it is good' (it was based on Latin *probus* 'good') and
this became extended to 'show something to be good or
valid.' It was this sense that was taken up by *approbāre*
and carried further to 'assent to as good.' When English
acquired the word, via Old French *aprover*, it still carried the notion of 'demonstrating,' but this was gradually taken over exclusively by *prove*, and the senses
'sanction' and 'commend,' present since the beginning,
established their primacy.
▸ probity, prove

**approximate**   see PROXIMITY

**apricot** [16] The word *apricot* reached English
by a peculiarly circuitous route from Latin. The original
term used by the Romans for the apricot, a fruit which
came ultimately from China, was *prūnum Arminiacum*
or *mālum Arminiacum* 'Armenian plum *or* apple' (Ar-
menia was an early source of choice apricots). But a
new term gradually replaced these: *mālum praecocum*

'early-ripening apple' (*praecocus* was a variant of *praecox*, from which English gets *precocious*). *Praecocum*
was borrowed by a succession of languages, making its
way via Byzantine Greek *beríkokkon* and Arabic *al bir-
qūq* 'the apricot' to Spanish *albaricoque* and Portuguese *albricoque*. This was the source of the English
word, but its earliest form, *abrecock*, shows that it had
already acquired the initial *abr-* of French *abricot*, and
the final *-t* followed almost immediately. Spellings with
*p* instead of *b* are also found in the 16th century.
▸ precocious

**April** [14] *Aprīlis* was the name given by the Romans to the fourth month of the year. It is thought that
the word may be based on *Apru*, an Etruscan borrowing
of Greek *Aphrō*, a shortened version of *Aphroditē*, the
name of the Greek goddess of love. In that case *Aprīlis*
would have signified for the Romans 'the month of Venus.' English acquired the word direct from Latin, but
earlier, in the 13th century, it had borrowed the French
version, *avril*; this survived, as *averil*, until the 15th
century in England, and for longer in Scotland. The
term *April fool* goes back at least to the late 17th
century.
▸ Aphrodite

**apron** [14] As in the case of *adder, umpire*, and
many others, *apron* arose from a mistaken analysis of
the combination 'indefinite article + noun.' The original Middle English word was *napron*, but as early as the
15th century *a napron* had turned into *an apron*.
*Napron* itself had been borrowed from Old French
*naperon*, a derivative of *nape* 'cloth' (source of English
*napery* and *napkin*); and *nape* came from Latin *mappa*
'napkin, towel' (source of English *map*).
▸ map, mat, napkin

**apse** [19] *Apse* 'vaulted recess in a church' is an
anglicization of Latin *apsis*. This was a borrowing of
Greek *apsís* or *hapsís*, which meant literally 'a fastening together' (it was derived from the verb *háptein*
'join'). The notion that underlies its application to a
vaulted space seems to be the joining together of arcs to
form a circle; an early Greek use was as a 'felloe,' part
of the rim of a wheel, and this later came to mean, by
extension, the wheel itself. Further metaphoricization
led to the sense 'orbit,' and, more semicircularly, 'arch'
or 'vault.'

The Latin/Greek form *apsis* itself was borrowed into
English at the beginning of the 17th century, and remains in use as a technical term in astronomy, 'extreme
point of an orbit.'

**apt** [14] *Apt* comes from Latin *aptus* 'fit, suited,'
the past participle of the verb *apere* 'fasten.' Other English words from this source are *adapt, adept, inept*, and
(with the Latin prefix *com-*) *couple* and *copulation*. Related words are found in Indo-European languages of

the Indian subcontinent: for instance, Sanskrit *āpta* 'fit.'

▶ adapt, adept, attitude, couple, inept

**aquamarine** [19] *Aquamarine* means literally 'sea water' – from Latin *aqua marīna*. Its first application in English was to the precious stone, a variety of beryl, so named because of its bluish-green colour. The art critic John Ruskin seems to have been the first to use it with reference to the colour itself, in *Modern Painters* 1846. (The French version of the word, *aiguemarine*, was actually used in English somewhat earlier, in the mid 18th century, but it did not long survive the introduction of the Latin version.)

Latin *aqua* 'water' has of course contributed a number of other words to English, notably *aquatic* [15] (from Latin *aquāticus*), *aqualung* (coined around 1950), *aquarelle* [19] (via Italian *acquerella* 'water colour'), *aquatint* [18] (literally 'dyed water'), *aqueduct* [16] (from Latin *aquaeductus*), and *aqueous* [17] (a medieval Latin formation); it is related to Old English *ēa* 'water' and *īg* 'island,' and is of course the source of French *eau*, Italian *acqua*, and Spanish *agua*.

**aquarium** [19] *Aquarium* is a modern adaptation of the neuter form of the Latin adjective *aquārius* 'watery' (a noun *aquārium* existed in Roman times, but it meant 'place where cattle drink'). Its model was *vivarium*, a 16th-century word for a 'place for keeping live animals.' This was the term first pressed into service to describe such a place used for displaying fish and other aquatic life: in 1853 the magazine *Athenaeum* reported that 'the new Fish house [at the London Zoo] has received the somewhat curious title of the 'Marine Vivarium''; and in the following year the guidebook to the Zoological Gardens called it the 'Aquatic Vivarium.' Within a year or two of this, however, the term *aquarium* had been coined and apparently established.

**aquiline** see EAGLE

**arbitrary** [15] *Arbitrary* comes ultimately from Latin *arbiter* 'judge,' via the derived adjective *arbitrārius*. It originally meant 'decided by one's own discretion or judgment,' and has since broadened, and 'worsened,' in meaning to 'capricious.' The Latin noun has of course contributed a large number of other words to English, including *arbiter* [15] itself, *arbitrate* [16] (via the Latin verb *arbitrārī*), and *arbitrament* [14]. *Arbitrage* in the sense 'buying and selling shares to make a profit' is a 19th-century borrowing from French, where it means literally 'arbitration.'

▶ arbitrate

**arbour** [14] Despite its formal resemblance to, and semantic connections with, Latin *arbor* 'tree,' *arbour* is not etymologically related to it. In fact, its nearest English relative is *herb*. When it first came into English it was *erber*, which meant 'lawn' or 'herb/flower garden.' This was borrowed, via Anglo-Norman, from Old French *erbier*, a derivative of *erbe* 'herb.' This in turn goes back to Latin *herba* 'grass, herb' (in the 16th century a spelling with initial *h* was common in England). Gradually, it seems that the sense 'grassy plot' evolved to 'separate, secluded nook in a garden'; at first, the characteristic feature of such shady retreats was their patch of grass, but their seclusion was achieved by surrounding trees or bushes, and eventually the criterion for an arbour shifted to 'being shaded by trees.' Training on a trellis soon followed, and the modern *arbour* as 'bower' was born. The shift from grass and herbaceous plants to trees no doubt prompted the alteration in spelling from *erber* to *arbour*, after Latin *arbor*; this happened in the 15th and 16th centuries.

▶ herb

**arc** see ARCH

**arcane** [16] *Arcane* comes from the Latin adjective *arcānus* 'hidden, secret.' This was formed from the verb *arcēre* 'close up,' which in turn came from *arca* 'chest, box' (source of English *ark*). The neuter form of the adjective, *arcānum*, was used to form a noun, usually used in the plural, *arcāna* 'mysterious secrets.'

▶ ark

**arch** [14] English acquired *arch* via Old French *arche* and a hypothetical Vulgar Latin *\*arca* from Latin *arcus* 'curve, arch, bow' (from which English also got *arc* [14]). When it first came into the language it was still used in the general sense of 'curve, arc' as well as 'curved structure' (Chaucer in his *Treatise on the astrolabe* 1391 wrote of 'the arch of the day ... from the sun arising till it go to rest'), but this had died out by the mid 19th century. Vulgar Latin *\*arca* also produced Italian *arcata*, which entered English via French as *arcade* in the 18th century.

*Arch* meaning 'saucy' is an adjectival use of the prefix *arch-* (as in *archetype*).

▶ arc

**archaic** see ARCHIVES

**archer** [13] Like *arch*, *archer* comes from Latin *arcus* 'curve, bow.' Its hypothetical Vulgar Latin derivative *\*arcārius* 'bowman' passed via Old French *archier* and Anglo-Norman *archer* into English. The ultimate source of *arcus* was the Indo-European base *\*arkw-*, from which English *arrow* eventually developed.

▶ arc, arch, arrow

**archetype** [17] *Archetype* comes, via Latin *archetypum*, from Greek *arkhétupon*, a nominal use of the adjective *arkhétupos*, literally 'first-moulded,' from *túpos* 'mould, model, type.'

The Greek prefix *arkhe-* was based on the noun *arkhos* 'chief, ruler,' a derivative of the verb *arkhein* 'begin, rule' (see ARCHIVES). It first entered our language (via Latin *archi-*) in the Old English period, as *arce-* (*archbishop* was an early compound formed with it); and it was reborrowed in the Middle English period from Old French *arche-*. Its use has gradually extended from 'highest in status' and 'first of its kind' to 'the ultimate – and usually the worst – of its kind,' as in *architraitor*. Its negative connotations lie behind its eventual development, in the 17th century, into an independent adjective, first as 'cunning, crafty,' later as 'saucy, mischievous.'

The same Greek root has provided English with the suffixes *-arch* and *-archy* (as in *monarch, oligarchy*); but here the original meaning of 'ruling' has been preserved much more stably.

▶ archaic, archives

**archipelago**   [16]   Originally,   *archipelago* was a quite specific term – it was the name of the Aegean Sea, the sea between Greece and Turkey. Derivationally, it is a compound formed in Greek from *arkhi-* 'chief' and *pélagos* 'sea' (source of English *pelagic* [17] and probably related to *plain, placate,* and *please*). The term 'chief sea' identified the Aegean, as contrasted with all the smaller lagoons, lakes, and inlets to which the word *pélagos* was also applied. An 'Englished' form of the word, *Arch-sea*, was in use in the 17th century, and in sailors' jargon it was often abbreviated to *Arches*: 'An island called Augusto near Paros, in the Arches,' Sir T Roe, *Negotiations* 1626. A leading characteristic of the Aegean Sea is of course that it contains a large number of islands, and from the 16th century onwards we see a strong and steady move towards what is now the word's main meaning, 'large group of islands.'

The immediate source of the English word was Italian *arcipelago*, and some etymologists have speculated that rather than coming directly from Greek *arkhipélagos*, this may have been a sort of folk-etymological resuscitation of it based on a misunderstanding of Greek *Aigaion pelagos* 'Aegean Sea.'

▶ pelagic

**architect**   [16]   Etymologically, an *architect* is a 'master builder.' The word comes, via French *architecte*, Italian *architetto*, and Latin *architectus*, from Greek *arkhitéktōn*, a compound formed from the prefix *arkhi-* 'leading' and *téktōn* 'builder' (source of English *tectonic* and related, via Greek *tékhnē*, to English *technical*).

▶ technical

**archives**   [17]   The Greek verb *arkhein* meant originally 'begin' – and hence 'be in first place, rule.' This sense development lies behind the diversity in meaning of the words ultimately derived from it in English. Greek *arkheion* was the official residence of a ruler, a 'public office,' and its plural, *arkheia*, was used for 'public records'; it passed into English via Latin *archīa*, later *archīva*, and French *archives*. Greek *arkhē*, on the other hand, had the sense 'beginning,' and the adjective formed from it, *archaios*, later *arkhaikós*,

'ancient,' came through French *archaïque* into English as *archaic* [19] (*arkhaios* is also the source of *archaeology* [17]). The same split in meaning is evident in the prefix *arch-*, which comes from the same source: in *archetype*, for instance, it signifies 'first,' whereas in *archduke* it implies 'highest in rank.'

▶ archaic, archetype

**arduous**   [16]   Latin *arduus*, the source of English *arduous*, originally meant 'high, steep' (it is related to Greek *orthós* 'straight, upright, correct,' as in English *orthodox*); the sense 'difficult, laborious' was a later metaphorical development. (The word has no connection with *ardour*, which comes ultimately from Latin *ardēre* 'burn'; see ARSON.)

▶ orthodox

**area**   [16]   *Area* is a direct borrowing from Latin *ārea*, which simply meant 'level piece of open ground, particularly one not built on in a city.' An alternative sense of the Latin word, 'place where grain is threshed,' has suggested to some etymologists a derivation from the Latin verb *ārēre* 'be dry' (related to *ardor* and *aridus*, sources of English *ardour* and *arid*).

▶ ardour, arid

**arena**   [17]   The original sense of Latin *(h)arēna* was 'sand' (hence the English technical term *arenaceous* 'sandy' [17]). The central, 'stage' area of classical amphitheatres, where contests were held, was covered with sand (to soak up the contestants' blood) and so by metaphorical extension *arēna* became the term for this central area, and hence for any enclosed place used for contests. The word may ultimately be of Etruscan origin.

**argosy**   [16]   On the face of it *argosy*, an archaic term for 'large merchant ship,' gives every appearance of being connected with the Argonauts, members of the crew of the ship Argo who sailed with Jason in quest of the Golden Fleece; but in fact the words are completely unrelated. When English first acquired *argosy*, from Italian, it was *ragusea*, which meant literally 'vessel from Ragusa' (an important city and seaport on the Dalmatian coast, now known as Dubrovnik). From the hotchpotch of spellings used in English in the 16th and 17th centuries (including *ragusye, rhaguse, argosea,* and *arguze*), *argosy* finally emerged as victor.

**argue**   [14]   English acquired *argue* and its various meanings via rather complex paths, but its ultimate origin is straightforward: the Latin verb *arguere* derived from a prehistoric Indo-European base *arg-* 'be white, bright, or clear' (source also of Latin *argentum* 'silver,' and thus of French *argent* 'money'); it therefore meant primarily 'make clear,' but this subsequently developed into 'assert, prove.' A frequentative form (that is, one denoting repeated action) evolved, *argūtāre*; this signified 'make repeated assertions or accusations.' This passed into medieval French as *arguer* 'accuse, blame,' and also 'bring forward reasons for an assertion,' and thence into English. The meaning 'accuse' died out in English in the late 17th century, leaving 'reasoning, discussing' as the main sense of *argue*. Meanwhile, original Latin *arguere* had made its presence felt in establishing the sense 'prove' in English, now somewhat weakened to 'imply, indicate' (as in 'Their lack of involvement argues indifference'). The sense 'quarrel' seems to have developed from 'discuss' in the 17th century.

**aria**  see AIR

**arid**  [17] English acquired *arid* from Latin *aridus*, either directly or via French *aride*. The Latin adjective is part of a web of related words denoting 'dryness' or 'burning': it came from the verb *ārēre* 'be dry,' which may be the source of *area*; it seems to have connections with a prehistoric Germanic *azgon, source of English *ash* 'burnt matter,' and with Greek *azaléos* 'dry,' source of English *azalea* [18] (so named from its favouring dry soil); and the Latin verb *ardēre* 'burn' was derived from it, from which English gets *ardour* [14], *ardent* [14], and *arson*.
▶ ardour, area, arson, ash, azalea

**arise**  [OE] *Arise* is a compound verb with cognate forms in many other Germanic languages (Gothic, for instance, had *urreisan*). The prefix *a-* originally meant 'away, out,' and hence was used as an intensive; *rise* comes from an unidentified Germanic source which some etymologists have connected with Latin *rīvus* 'stream' (source of English *rivulet*), on the basis of the notion of a stream 'rising' from a particular source. The compound *arise* was in fact far commoner than the simple form *rise* in the Old English period, and it was only in early Middle English that *rise* began to take its place. This happened first in northern dialects, and may have been precipitated by Old Norse *rísa*. Today, it is only in the sense 'come into existence' that *arise* is commoner.
▶ raise, rear, rise, rivulet

**aristocracy**  [16] Greek *áristos* meant 'best'; hence *aristocracy* signifies, etymologically, 'rule by the best' (the suffix *-cracy* derives ultimately from Greek *krátos* 'strength, power,' a relative of English *hard*). The term *aristokratíā* was used by Aristotle and Plato in their political writings, denoting 'government of a state by those best fitted for the task,' and English writers perpetuated the usage when the word was borrowed from French *aristocratie*: Thomas Hobbes, for instance, wrote 'Aristocracy is that, wherein the highest magistrate is chosen out of those that have had the best education,' *Art of Rhetoric* 1679. But from the first the term was also used in English for 'rule by a privileged class,' and by the mid 17th century this had begun to pass into 'the privileged class' itself, 'the nobility.' The derived *aristocrat* appeared at the end of the 18th cen-

tury; it was a direct borrowing of French *aristocrate*, a coinage inspired by the French Revolution.
▶ hard

**arithmetic**  see ALGORITHM

**ark**  [OE] The notion underlying *ark* seems to be that of 'enclosing or defending a space.' Its ultimate Latin source, *arca* 'large box or chest,' was related to *arx* 'citadel' and to *arcēre* 'close up' (from which English gets *arcane*). *Arca* was borrowed into prehistoric Germanic, and came into English as *ærc*. In addition to meaning 'chest' (a sense which had largely died out by the 18th century), it signified the 'coffer in which the ancient Hebrews kept the tablets of the Ten Commandments' – the Ark of the Covenant – and by extension, the large commodious vessel in which Noah escaped the Flood.
▶ arcane, exercise

**arm**  [OE] The two distinct senses of *arm*, 'limb' and 'weapon,' both go back ultimately to the same source, the Indo-European base *ar- 'fit, join' (which also produced *art* and *article*). One derivative of this was Latin *arma* 'weapons, tools,' which entered English via Old French *armes* in the 13th century (the singular form was virtually unknown before the 19th century, but the verb *arm*, from Latin *armāre* via Old French *armer*, came into the language in the 13th century). The other strand is represented in several European languages, meaning variously 'joint,' 'shoulder,' and 'arm': Latin *armus* 'shoulder,' for example, and Greek *harmos* 'joint.' The prehistoric Germanic form was *armaz, from which developed, among others, German, Dutch, Swedish, and English *arm*.
▶ art, article

**armour**  [13] *Armour* comes ultimately from Latin *armātūra* 'armour, equipment,' a derivative of the verb *armāre* 'arm' (the direct English borrowing *armature* [15] originally meant 'armour' or 'weapons,' but the 'protective' notion of armour led to its application in the 18th century to 'metal covering the poles of a magnet'). In Old French *armātūra* became *armeure*, and subsequently *armure*, the form in which it was borrowed into English (the *-our* ending was artificially grafted on in the 14th century on the model of other Latin-based words such as *colour* and *odour*). *Armoury* is French in origin: Old French *armoier* 'coat of arms' was a derivative of *arme* 'weapon'; this became *armoirie*, which was borrowed into English in the 15th century as *armory*, meaning 'heraldry,' but also, owing to their formal similarity, came to be used with the same sense as *armour* – 'protective metal suit' or 'weapons.' This was what *armoury* meant when it came into English in the 14th century (and the sense survived long enough to be used by Wordsworth in a sonnet to 'Liberty' 1802: 'In our halls is hung armoury of invincible knights of old'). The meaning 'place for keeping weapons' developed in the 16th century.

▶ armature

**army**    [14]    Latin *armāta* 'armed,' the past participle of the verb *armāre*, was used in post-classical times as a noun, meaning 'armed force.' Descendants of *armāta* in the Romance languages include Spanish *armada* and French *armée*, from which English borrowed *army*. In early usage it could (like Spanish *armada*) mean a naval force as well as a land force ('The King commanded that £21,000 should be paid to his army (for so that fleet is called everywhere in English Saxon) which rode at Greenwich,' Marchamont Needham's translation of Selden's *Mare clausum* 1652), but this had virtually died out by the end of the 18th century.

▶ arm, armada

**around**    [14]    *Around* was formed in Middle English from the prefix *a-* 'on' and the noun *round* (perhaps influenced by the Old French phrase *a la reonde* 'in the round, roundabout'). It was slow to usurp existing forms such as *about* – it does not occur in Shakespeare or the 1611 translation of the Bible – and it does not seem to have become strongly established before the end of the 17th century. The adverb and preposition *round* may be a shortening of *around*.

▶ round

**arouse**    [16]    Shakespeare is the first writer on record to use *arouse*, in *2 Henry VI*, 1593: 'Loud howling wolves arouse the jades that drag the tragic melancholy night.' It was formed, with the intensive prefix *a-*, from *rouse*, a word of unknown origin which was first used in English in the 15th century as a technical term in falconry, meaning 'plump up the feathers.'

▶ rouse

**arpeggio**    SEE HARPSICHORD

**arrack**    [17]    *Arrack* is an Asian alcoholic drink distilled from rice or molasses. The word comes ultimately from Arabic *'araq* 'sweat, juice, liquor,' which was borrowed in a variety of forms into several Asiatic languages. The immediate source of English *arrack* seems to have been an Indian language.

**arrange**    [14]    *Arrange* is a French formation: Old French *arangier* was a compound verb formed from the prefix *a-* and the verb *rangier* 'set in a row' (related to English *range* and *rank*). In English its first, and for a long time its only meaning was 'array in a line of battle.' Shakespeare does not use it, and it does not occur in the 1611 translation of the Bible. It is not until the 18th century that it becomes at all common, in the current sense 'put in order,' and it has been speculated that this is a reborrowing from modern French *arranger*.

▶ range, rank

**arrant**    [16]    *Arrant* is an alteration of *errant*, as in *knight errant*. This originally meant 'roaming, wandering,' but its persistent application to nouns with negative connotations, such as *rogue* and *thief*, gradually drove its meaning downwards by association, to 'notorious.'

▶ errant

**arras**    [15]    An *arras* is a tapestry hanging, immortalized by Shakespeare in *Hamlet* when he conceals Polonius behind one, there to be killed by Hamlet. The word comes from the Anglo-Norman phrase *draps d'arras*, literally 'cloth of Arras': Arras is a city in the Pas-de-Calais, northern France, famous in the Middle Ages as a centre for the manufacture of woollens and tapestry.

**arrear**    SEE REAR

**arrest**    [14]    The Latin verb *restāre* meant 'stand back, remain behind' or 'stop' (it is the source of English *rest* in the sense 'remainder'). The compound verb *arrestāre*, formed in post-classical times from the prefix *ad-* and *restāre*, had a causative function: 'cause to remain behind or stop,' hence 'capture, seize.' These meanings were carried over via Old French *arester* into English.

▶ rest

**arrive**    [13]    When speakers of early Middle English 'arrived,' what they were literally doing was coming to shore after a voyage. For *arrive* was originally a Vulgar Latin compound verb based on the Latin noun *rīpa* 'shore, river bank' (as in the English technical term *riparian* 'of a river bank'; and *river* comes from the same source). From the phrase *ad rīpam* 'to the shore' came the verb *\*arripāre* 'come to land,' which passed into English via Old French *ariver*. It does not seem to have been until the early 14th century that the more general sense of 'reaching a destination' started to establish itself in English.

▶ riparian, river

**arrogant**    [14]    Etymologically, to be *arrogant* is to make great claims about oneself. It originated in the Latin compound verb *arrogāre* 'claim for oneself,' formed from the prefix *ad-*'to' and *rogāre* 'ask' (as in English *interrogate*). Already in Latin the present participle *arrogāns* was being used adjectivally, for 'overbearing,' and this passed via Old French into English.

▶ interrogate, prerogative

**arrow**    [OE]    Appropriately enough, the word *arrow* comes from the same ultimate Indo-European source that produced the Latin word for 'bow' – *\*arkw-*. The Latin descendant of this was *arcus* (whence English *arc* and *arch*), but in Germanic it became *\*arkhw-*. From this basic 'bow' word were formed derivatives in various Germanic languages meaning literally 'that which belongs to the bow' – that is, 'arrow' (Gothic, for instance, had *arhwazna*). The Old English version of this was *earh*, but it is recorded only once, and the commonest words for 'arrow' in Old

English were *strǣl* (still apparently in use in Sussex in the 19th century, and related to German *strahl* 'ray') and *flān* (which remained in Scottish English until around 1500). Modern English *arrow* seems to be a 9th-century reborrowing from Old Norse *\*arw-*.

▶ arc, arch

**arrowroot** [17] Arrowroot, a tropical American plant with starchy tubers, gets its name by folk etymology, the process whereby an unfamiliar foreign word is reformulated along lines more accessible to the speakers of a language. In this case the word in question was *aru-aru*, the term used by the Arawak Indians of South America for the plant (meaning literally 'meal of meals'). English-speakers adapted this to *arrowroot* because the root of the plant was used by the Indians to heal wounds caused by poisoned arrows.

**arse** [OE] *Arse* is a word of considerable antiquity, and its relatives are found practically from end to end of the geographical range of the Indo-European language family, from Old Irish *err* 'tail' in the west to Armenian *or* 'rump.' Its Indo-European source was *\*órsos*, which produced the Germanic form *\*arsaz*: hence German *arsch*, Dutch *aars*, and, via Old English *ærs*, English *arse*. The euphemistic American spelling *ass* appears to be as recent as the 1930s, although there is one isolated (British) record of it from 1860.

The term *wheatear*, for a thrushlike European bird, is an alteration over time of a Middle English epithet 'white arse,' after its white rump feathers.

**arsenal** [16] The word *arsenal* has a complicated history, stretching back through Italian to Arabic. The Arabic original was *dār-as-sinā'ah*, literally 'house of the manufacture.' This seems to have been borrowed into Venetian Italian, somehow losing its initial *d*, as *arzaná*, and been applied specifically to the large naval dockyard in Venice (which in the 15th century was the leading naval power in the Mediterranean). The dockyard is known to this day as the Arzenale, showing the subsequent addition of the *-al* ending. English acquired the word either from Italian or from French *arsenal*, and at first used it only for dockyards ('making the Arsenal at Athens, able to receive 1000 ships,' Philemon Holland's translation of Pliny's *Natural history* 1601); but by the end of the 16th century it was coming into more general use as a 'military storehouse.' The English soccer club Arsenal gets its name from its original home in Woolwich, south London, where there used to be a British government arsenal.

**arsenic** [14] The term *arsenic* was originally applied to the lemon-yellow mineral arsenic trisulphide, and its history reveals the reason: for it appears to be based ultimately on Persian *zar* 'gold' (related forms include Sanskrit *hari* 'yellowish,' Greek *khlōros* 'greenish-yellow,' and English *yellow* itself). The derivative *zarnīk* was borrowed into Arabic as *zernīkh*, which, as usual with Arabic words, was perceived by foreign listeners as constituting an indivisible unit with its definite article *al* 'the' – hence *azzernīkh*, literally 'the arsenic trisulphide.' This was borrowed into Greek, where the substance's supposed beneficial effects on virility led, through association with Greek *árrēn* 'male, virile,' to the new forms *arrenikón* and *arsenikón*, source of Latin *arsenicum* and, through Old French, of English *arsenic*. The original English application was still to arsenic trisulphide (*orpiment* was its other current name), and it is not until the early 17th century that we find the term used for white arsenic or arsenic trioxide. The element arsenic itself was isolated and so named at the start of the 19th century.

▶ chlorine, yellow

**arson** [17] Like *ardour* and *ardent*, *arson* comes from the Latin verb *ardēre* 'burn.' Its past participle was *arsus*, from which was formed the noun *arsiō* 'act of burning.' This passed via Old French into Anglo-Norman as *arson*, and in fact was in use in the Anglo-Norman legal language of England from the 13th century onwards (it occurs in the Statute of Westminster 1275). The jurist Sir Matthew Hale was the first to use the word in a vernacular text, in 1680. Other words in English ultimately related to it include *arid* and probably *ash*, *area*, and *azalea*.

▶ ardour, area, ash, azalea

**art** [13] Like *arm*, *arthritis*, and *article*, *art* goes back to an Indo-European root *\*ar-*, which meant 'put things together, join.' Putting things together implies some skill: hence Latin *ars* 'skill.' Its stem *art-* produced Old French *art*, the source of the English word. It brought with it the notion of 'skill,' which it still retains; the modern association with painting, sculpture, etc did not begin until the mid 17th century. Latin derivatives of *ars* include the verb *artīre* 'instruct in various skills,' from which ultimately English gets *artisan* [16]; and *artificium*, a compound formed with a variant of *facere* 'do, make,' from which we get *artificial* [14].

▶ arm, arthritis, article, artificial, artisan, inert

**artery** [14] *Artery* is a direct borrowing from Latin *artēria*, which in turn came from Greek *artēría*. This appears to have been based on the root *\*ar-* 'lift.' A parallel formation is thus *aorta* 'main coronary artery' [16], which comes from Greek *aortē*, a derivative of *aeírein* 'lift' – again ultimately from the root *\*ar-*. The notion underlying *aortē* seems to be that the heart was thought of by the ancients as in some sense suspended from it, as if from a strap (Greek *aortēs* 'strap'), so that it was 'held up' or 'raised' by the *aortē* (the aorta emerges from the top of the heart). The Greeks, of course, did not know about the circulation of the blood, and since arteries contain no blood after death it was supposed that their function was conveying air. Hence Hippocrates' application of the term *aorta* to branches of the windpipe, and the use of *artery* for 'windpipe' in English up until as late as the mid 17th century: '[The lungs] expel the air: which through the artery, throat and mouth, makes the voice,' Francis Bacon, *Sylva sylvarum* 1626.

▶ aorta

**artesian** [19] In the 18th century drillings made in Artois (a former northern French province roughly corresponding to the modern Pas-de-Calais) produced springs of water which rose spontaneously to the surface, without having to be pumped. The name of the province, in its erstwhile form *Arteis*, was bestowed on the phenomenon, and has been so used ever since.

**arthritis** [16] Greek *árthron* meant 'joint' (it is used in various technical terms in biology, such as *arthropod* 'creature, such as an insect, with jointed limbs'). It came from the Indo-European root *\*ar-* 'put things together, join, fit,' which also produced Latin *artus* 'limb' (source of English *article*) and English *arm*, as well as *art*. The compound *arthritis* is a Greek formation (*-itis* was originally simply an adjectival suffix, so *arthritis* meant 'of the joints' – with 'disease' understood; its application to 'inflammatory diseases' is a relatively modern development); it reached English via Latin.

▶ arm, art, article

**artichoke** [16] The word *artichoke* is of Arabic origin; it comes from *al kharshōf* 'the artichoke,' which was the Arabic term for a plant of the thistle family with edible flower-parts. This was borrowed into Spanish as *alcarchofa*, and passed from there into Italian as *arciciofo*. In northern dialects this became *articiocco*, the form in which the word was borrowed into other European languages, including English.

The term was first applied to the Jerusalem artichoke, a plant with edible tuberous roots, early in the 17th century. The epithet *Jerusalem* has no connection with the holy city; it arose by folk etymology, that is, the adaptation of an unfamiliar foreign word to the lexical system of one's own language. In this case the word was *girasole*, Italian for 'sunflower' (the Jerusalem artichoke is of the sunflower family).

**article** [13] Like *art*, *arm*, and *arthritis*, *article* goes back to an Indo-European root *\*ar-*, which meant 'put things together, join, fit.' Amongst its derivatives was Latin *artus* 'joint' (a form parallel to Greek *árthron*, source of *arthritis*), of which the diminutive was *articulus* 'small joint.' This was extended metaphorically to mean 'division, part,' and when the word first entered English, via Old French *article*, it was used for a particular clause of a treaty, of a contract, or specifically of the Creed. Its application to an 'item, thing' is a comparatively late development, from the start of the 19th century.

A Latin derivative of *articulus*, the verb *articulāre* 'divide into joints,' hence 'speak distinctly,' gave rise to English *articulate* [16].

▶ arm, art, arthritis

**artillery** [14] Originally *artillery* meant 'military supplies, munitions' (Chaucer used it thus); it was not until the late 15th century that it came to be used for 'weapons for firing missiles' – originally catapults, bows, etc. The source of the English word was Old French *artillerie*, a derivative of the verb *artiller* 'equip, arm.' This was an alteration of an earlier form *atillier*, probably influenced by *art*, but the ultimate provenance of *atillier* is not clear. Some etymologists trace it back to a hypothetical Latin verb *\*apticulāre* 'make fit, adapt,' a derivative of *aptus* 'fitting' (source of English *apt* and *adapt*); others regard it as a variant of Old French *atirier* 'arrange, equip' (source of English *attire* [13]), which was based on *tire* 'order, rank,' a noun of Germanic origin, related to Latin *deus* 'god.'

**as** [12] Ultimately, *as* is the same word as *also*. Old English *alswā* 'in just this way' was used in some contexts in which modern English would use *as*, and as it was weakly stressed in such contexts it gradually dwindled to *als* or *ase* and finally to *as*.

▶ also

**asbestos** [14] Originally, the word we now know as *asbestos* was applied in the Middle Ages to a mythical stone which, once set alight, could never be put out; it came from the Greek compound *ásbestos*, literally 'inextinguishable,' which was formed from the prefix *a-*'not' and *sbestós*, a derivative of the verb *sbennúnai* 'extinguish.' However, by the time it first came into English, its form was not quite what it is today. To begin with, it was the Greek accusative form, *ásbeston*, that was borrowed, and in its passage from Latin through Old French it developed several variants, including *asbeston* and *albeston*, most of which turned up in English. Then, in the early 17th century, the word was reborrowed from the original Greek source, *ásbestos*, and applied to a noncombustible silicate mineral.

**ascend** see DESCEND

**ascribe** see SCRIBE

**ash** [OE] There are two distinct words *ash* in English: *ash* the tree and *ash* 'burnt material.' The tree (Old English *æsc*) comes from a prehistoric Germanic *\*askiz*, which in turn derived from the Indo-European base *\*os-*; this was the source of several tree-names in other Indo-European languages, not all of them by any means corresponding to the ash: Latin *ornus*, for instance, meant 'elm,' and Albanian *ah* is 'beech.' *Ash* as in 'cigarette ash' is a descendant of Old English *æsce*. It has cognate forms in other Germanic languages (German *asche*, Dutch *asch*, Swedish *aska*), pointing to a prehistoric Germanic *\*azgon*, which may be related to the Latin verbs *ārēre* 'be dry' (source of English *arid*) and *ārdēre* 'burn' (source of English *ardent, ardour*, and *arson*).

► ardent, arid, arson

**ashamed**   [OE]   *Ashamed* is an Old English compound, formed ultimately from the noun *scamu* 'shame.' The verb derived from this, *scamian*, meant 'feel shame' as well as (as in modern English) 'put to shame,' and in this sense the intensive prefix *ā-* was added to it. The resulting verb *ashame* died out in the 16th century, but its past participle *ashamed* has survived.

► shame

**aside**   [14]   *Aside* is a reduced form of the Middle English phrase *on syde*, literally 'on side,' meaning 'to one side.'

► side

**ask**   [OE]   The Old English ancestor of *ask* existed in two main forms: *āscian* and *ācsian*. The first produced descendants such as *asshe*, which died out in the 16th century; the second resulted in *axe* (still extant in some dialects), which by metathesis – the reversal of the consonant sounds *k* and *s* – became modern English *ask*. Ultimately the word comes from a prehistoric West Germanic verb *\*aiskōjan* (source of German *heischen*, a poetical term for 'ask'); cognates in other, non-Germanic, Indo-European languages include Latin *aeruscāre* 'beg' and Sanskrit *icchāti* 'seek.'

**askance**   [16]   The origins of *askance* remain obscure. When it first entered the language it meant literally 'obliquely, sideways' ('He bid his angels turn askance the poles of Earth,' John Milton, *Paradise Lost* 1667), so a possible source is Italian *a scancio* 'obliquely, slantingly,' but this has never been firmly established. Its metaphorical use in the phrase *look askance* dates from the 17th century.

**asp**   see ASPIC

**asparagus**   [15]   *Asparagus* comes ultimately from Greek *aspáragos* (a word related to the Greek verb *spargan* 'swell,' to the Latin verb *spargere* 'scatter' – ultimate source of English *sparse, disperse*, and *aspersions* – and also to English *spark*), and has over the past 150 years or so returned to the full Latin form, *asparagus*, in which it was originally borrowed by English. In the intervening centuries, however, it went through several metamorphoses: in the 16th century, the truncated medieval Latin variant *sparagus* was current (it also occurs in one isolated example from a book of Anglo-Saxon remedies of around 1000AD); from then until the 18th century an anglicized version, *sperage*, was used; and in the 17th century folk etymology (the process by which an unfamiliar word is assimilated to one more familiar) turned *asparagus* into *sparrowgrass*. This gradually died out during the 19th century, but the abbreviation *grass* remains current in the jargon of the grocery trade.

► aspersion, spark

**aspersion**   see SPREAD

**asphalt**   [14]   The ultimate source of *asphalt* is Greek *ásphalton*, but when it first came into English it was with the *p* that had developed in late Latin *aspaltus: aspalte*. The *ph* of the original Greek form began to be reintroduced in the 18th century.

**aspic**   [18]   *Aspic* was borrowed from French, where, like the archaic English *asp* which reputedly bit Cleopatra, it also means 'snake' (ultimately from Greek *aspís*). This has led to speculation that *aspic* the jelly was named from *aspic* the snake on the basis that the colours and patterns in which moulds of aspic were made in the 18th and 19th centuries resembled a snake's coloration. There does not appear to be any watertight evidence for this rather far-fetched theory, and perhaps more plausible is some connection with French *aspic* 'lavender, spikenard,' formerly used for flavouring aspic, or with Greek *aspís* 'shield' (source of *aspidistra* [19]), on the basis that the earliest aspic moulds were shield-shaped.

**aspire**   see SPIRIT

**aspirin**   [19]   The word *aspirin* was coined in German towards the end of the 19th century. It is a condensed version of the term *acetylierte spirsäure* 'acetylated spiraeic acid.' *Spiraeic acid* is a former term for 'salicylic acid,' from which aspirin is derived; its name comes from the *spiraea*, a plant of the rose family.

► spiraea

**ass**   [OE]   *Ass* comes ultimately from Latin *asinus* 'donkey' (whence English *asinine* [16]), and English probably acquired it via a Celtic route, from a prehistoric Old Celtic *\*as(s)in* (source of Welsh *asyn*). As borrowed directly into the Germanic languages, by contrast, the *n* of Latin *asinus* changed to *l*; from this branch of the word's travels Old English had *esol*, long defunct, and Dutch has *ezel*, which English has appropriated as *easel*. Further back in time the word's antecedents are unclear, but some would trace it to Sumerian *ansu*, which could also be the source of Greek *ónos* (whence English *onager* 'wild ass' [14]) and Armenian *eš*.

► easel, onager

**assassin**   [17]   Etymologically, an assassin is an 'eater or smoker of hashish,' the drug cannabis. At the time of the Crusades there was a sect of fanatical Ismaili Muslims who pledged themselves to kill Christians and other enemies. They committed their murders under the influence of cannabis. Hence the *hashshāshīn* (plural of *hashshāsh*, Arabic for 'hashish-eater') came to have a reputation as murderers. In English the Arabic plural form was perceived as singular. The word has retained its connotation of one who kills for political or religious rather than personal motives.

▶ hashish

**assault** [13] To assault somebody was originally to 'jump on' them. The word comes from a Vulgar Latin compound verb *assaltāre*, formed from the prefix *ad-* 'to' and *saltāre* 'jump,' a frequentative form (denoting repeated action) of the verb *salīre* 'jump' (which is the source of English *salient*, and by a similar compounding process produced *assail* [13]). In Old French this became *asauter*, and English originally borrowed it as *asaute*, but in the 16th century the *l* was reintroduced.

▶ assail, somersault

**assay**    see ESSAY

**assemble**    see SIMILAR

**assent**    see SENSE

**assert** [17]    *Assert* comes ultimately from Latin *asserere*, which meant literally 'join oneself to something.' It was a compound verb formed from the prefix *ad-* 'to' and *serere* 'join' (source of English *series* and *serial*), and it came to take on various metaphorical connotations: if one 'joined oneself to' a particular thing, one 'declared one's right to' it, and if one 'joined oneself to' a particular point of view, one 'maintained' it, or 'claimed' it. The verb was used in all these senses when English acquired it, from the Latin past participial stem *assert-*, but the former had more or less died out by the end of the 18th century.

▶ serial, series

**assess** [15]    The literal meaning of Latin *assidēre*, ultimate source of *assess*, was 'sit beside someone' (it was a compound verb formed from the prefix *ad-* 'near' and *sedēre* 'sit,' a relative of English *sit*). This developed the secondary meaning 'sit next to a judge and assist him in his deliberations' (which lies behind English *assize*), and in medieval Latin the sense passed from helping the judge to performing his functions, particularly in fixing the amount of a fine or tax to be paid. Hence English *assess*, which came via Old French *assesser* from Latin *assess-*, the past participial stem of *assidēre*. (The Latin adjective *assiduus*, formed from *assidēre* in the sense 'apply oneself to something,' gave English *assiduous* [16].)

▶ assiduous, assize, session, sit, size

**asset** [16]    Originally, to have *assets* was simply to have 'enough' – as in French *assez*. The Anglo-Norman legal phrase *aver asetz* signified 'have enough money to meet one's debts,' and eventually *asetz*, later *assets*, passed from the general meaning 'enough' to the particular 'financial resources' (the final *-s* caused it to be regarded as a plural noun, but the analogical singular *asset* does not appear until the 19th century). Anglo-Norman *asetz* itself goes back via Old French *asez* to Vulgar Latin *\*assatis*, formed from the Latin phrase *ad*

*satis* 'to enough' (*satis* is the source of English *satisfy* and *satiate*, and is related to *sad*).

▶ sad, satiate, satisfy

**asseveration**    see SEVERE

**assiduous**    see ASSESS

**assign**    see SIGN

**assist** [15]    Etymologically, *assist* means 'stand by.' It comes, via French *assister*, from Latin *assistere*, a compound verb formed from the prefix *ad-* 'near' and *sistere* 'stand' (related to Latin *stāre* 'stand,' from which English gets *state*, *station*, *status*, *statue*, etc). A remnant of this original meaning survives in the sense 'be present without actually participating,' but the main use of the word in English has always been that which came from the metaphorical sense of the Latin verb – 'help.'

▶ state, station, statue, status

**assize** [13]    Like *assess*, *assize* comes ultimately from Latin *assidēre*, which meant literally 'sit beside someone' (it was a compound verb formed from the prefix *ad-* 'near' and *sedēre* 'sit,' related to English *sit*). In Old French this became *asseeir* (modern French has *asseoir*), of which the past participle was *assis*. The feminine form of this, *assise*, came to be used as a noun ranging in meaning from the very general 'act of sitting' or 'seat' to the more specific legal senses 'sitting in judgement' and 'session of a court' (English *session* comes ultimately from Latin *sedēre* too). It was the legal usages which passed into English.

▶ session, sit, size

**associate** [14]    Latin *socius* meant 'companion' (it is related to English *sequal* and *sue*), and has spawned a host of English words, including *social*, *sociable*, *society*, and *socialism*. In Latin, a verb was formed from it, using the prefix *ad-* 'to': *associāre* 'unite.' Its past participle, *associātus*, was borrowed into English as an adjective, *associate*; its use as a verb followed in the 15th century, and as a noun in the 16th century.

▶ sequal, social, society, sue

**assort**    see SORT

**assuage**    see PERSUADE

**assume**    see PROMPT

**assure**    see INSURE

**asthma** [14]    The original idea contained in *asthma* is that of 'breathing hard.' The Greek noun *asthma* was derived from the verb *ázein* 'breathe hard' (related to *áein* 'blow,' from which English gets *air*). In its earliest form in English it was *asma*, reflecting its immediate source in medieval Latin, and though the Greek spelling was restored in the 16th century, the word's pronunciation has for the most part stuck with *asma*.

▶ air

**astound** [17] *Astound, astonish,* and *stun* all come ultimately from the same origin: a Vulgar Latin verb *\*extonāre,* which literally meant something like 'leave someone thunderstruck' (it was formed from the Latin verb *tonāre* 'thunder'). This became Old French *estoner,* which had three offshoots in English: it was borrowed into Middle English in the 13th century as *astone* or *astun,* and immediately lost its initial *a,* producing a form *stun*; then in the 15th century, in Scotland originally, it had the suffix *-ish* grafted on to it, producing *astonish*; and finally in the 17th century its past participle, *astoned* or, as it was also spelled, *astound,* formed the basis of a new verb.

▶ astonish, stun

**astronomy** [13] *Astronomy* comes via Old French and Latin from Greek *astronomíā,* a derivative of the verb *astronomein,* literally 'watch the stars.' Greek *ástron* and *astér* 'star' (whence English *astral* [17] and *asterisk* [17]) came ultimately from the Indo-European base *\*ster-,* which also produced Latin *stella* 'star,' German *stern* 'star,' and English *star*. The second element of the compound, which came from the verb *némein,* meant originally 'arrange, distribute.'

At first, no distinction was made between astronomy and astrology. Indeed, in Latin *astrologia* was the standard term for the study of the stars until Seneca introduced the Greek term *astronomia*. When the two terms first coexisted in English (*astrology* entered the language about a century later than *astronomy*) they were used interchangeably, and in fact when a distinction first began to be recognized between the two it was the opposite of that now accepted: *astrology* meant simply 'observation,' whereas *astronomy* signified 'divination.' The current assignment of sense was not fully established until the 17th century.

▶ asterisk, astral, star

**asylum** [15] Greek *sulon* meant 'right of seizure.' With the addition of the negative prefix *a-* 'not' this was turned into the adjective *ásūlos* 'inviolable,' which in turn was nominalized as *āsūlon* 'refuge.' When it first entered English, via Latin *asȳlum,* it was used specifically for 'place of sanctuary for hunted criminals and others' (a meaning reflected in modern English 'political asylum'), and it was not until the mid 18th century that it came to be applied to mental hospitals.

**at** [OE] The preposition *at* was originally found throughout the Germanic languages: Old English had *æt,* Old High German *az,* Gothic and Old Norse *at*. It survives in the Scandinavian languages (Swedish *att,* for instance) as well as English, but has been lost from German and Dutch. Cognates in other Indo-European languages, including Latin *ad* 'to, at,' suggest an ultimate common source.

**athlete** [18] The etymological idea underlying *athlete* is 'competing for a prize.' Greek *áthlon* meant 'award, prize,' whence the verb *athlein* 'compete for a prize.' Derived from this was the noun *athlētḗs* 'competitor.' The context in which the word was most commonly used in Greek was that of the public games, where competitors took part in races, boxing matches, etc. Hence the gradual narrowing down of the meaning of *athlete* to 'one who takes part in sports involving physical exercise,' and even further to 'participant in track and field events.'

**atlas** [16] In Greek mythology, *Atlas* was a Titan who as a punishment for rebelling against the gods was forced to carry the heavens on his shoulders. Hence when the term was first used in English it was applied to a 'supporter': 'I dare commend him to all that know him, as the Atlas of Poetry,' Thomas Nashe on Robert Greene's *Menaphon* 1589. In the 16th century it was common to include a picture of Atlas with his onerous burden as a frontispiece in books of maps, and from this arose the habit of referring to such books as *atlases* (the application is sometimes said to have arisen specifically from such a book produced in the late 16th century by the Flemish cartographer Gerardus Mercator (1512–94), published in England in 1636 under the title *Atlas*).

Atlas also gave his name to the Atlantic ocean. In ancient myth, the heavens were said to be supported on a high mountain in northwestern Africa, represented as, and now named after, the Titan Atlas. In its Greek adjectival form *Atlantikós* (later Latin *Atlanticus*) it was applied to the seas immediately to the west of Africa, and gradually to the rest of the ocean as it came within the boundaries of the known world.

▶ Atlantic

**atmosphere** [17] Etymologically, *atmosphere* means 'ball of vapour.' It was coined as modern Latin *atmosphaera* from Greek *atmós* 'vapour' (related to *áein* 'blow,' ultimate source of English *air*) and *sphaira* 'sphere.' Its original application was not, as we would now understand it, to the envelope of air encompassing the Earth, but to a mass of gas exhaled from and thus surrounding a planet; indeed, in the first record of the word's use in English, in 1638, it was applied to the Moon, which of course is now known to have no atmosphere. The denotation of the word moved forward with the development of meteorological knowledge.

▶ air, sphere

**atoll** [17] *Atoll* was borrowed from Malayalam *atolu* 'reef,' the name used by Maldive Islanders for their islands, many of which are coral atolls.

**atom** [16] Etymologically, *atom* means 'not cut, indivisible.' Greek *átomos* 'that which cannot be divided up any further' was formed from the negative prefix *a-* 'not' and the base *\*tom-* 'cut' (source also of English *anatomy* and *tome*), and was applied in the Middle Ages not just to the smallest imaginable particle of matter, but also to the smallest imaginable division of time; an hour contained 22,560 atoms. Its use by classical writers on physics and philosophy, such as Democritus and Epicurus, was sustained by medieval philosophers, and the word was ready and waiting for 19th-century chemists when they came to describe and name the smallest unit of an element, composed of a nucleus surrounded by electrons.

▶ anatomy, tome

**atone** [16] As its spelling suggests, but its pronunciation disguises, *atone* comes from the phrase *at one* 'united, in harmony,' lexicalized as *atone* in early modern English. It may have been modelled on Latin *adūnāre* 'unite,' which was similarly compounded from *ad* 'to, at' and *ūnum* 'one.'

▶ at, one

**atrocious** [17] Traced back to its ultimate source, *atrocious* meant something not too dissimilar to 'having a black eye.' Latin *āter* was 'black, dark' (it occurs also in English *atrabilious* 'melancholic' [17] – Greek *mélās* meant 'black'), and the stem *-oc-, *-ox* meant 'looking, appearing' (Latin *oculus* 'eye' and *ferox* 'fierce' – based on *ferus* 'wild,' and source of English *ferocious* – were formed from it, and it goes back to an earlier Indo-European base which also produced Greek *ōps* 'eye' and English *eye*). Combined, they formed *atrox*, literally 'of a dark or threatening appearance,' hence 'gloomy, cruel.' English borrowed it (in the stem form *atrōci-*) originally in the sense 'wantonly cruel.'

▶ eye, ferocious, inoculate, ocular

**attach** [14] When English first acquired it, *attach* meant 'seize' or 'arrest.' It is Germanic in origin, but reached us via Old French *atachier*. This was an alteration of earlier Old French *estachier* 'fasten (with a stake),' which was based on a hypothetical Germanic *\*stakōn*. The metaphorical meaning 'arrest' appears to have arisen in Anglo-Norman, the route by which the word reached English from Old French; the original, literal sense 'fasten, join' did not arrive in English until as late as the 18th century, as a reborrowing from modern French *attacher*.

A similar borrowing of Germanic *\*stakōn* into Italian produced the ancestor of English *attack*.

▶ attack, stake

**attack** [16] *Attack* reached English via French *attaquer* from Italian *attaccare* 'attach, join,' which, like Old French *atachier* (source of English *attach*) was based on a hypothetical Germanic *\*stakōn* (from which English gets *stake*). Phrases such as *attaccare battaglia* 'join battle' led to *attaccare* being used on its own to mean 'attack.' *Attach* and *attack* are thus 'doublets' –

that is, words with the same ultimate derivation but different meanings.

▶ attach, stake

**attain** [14] Unlike *contain, maintain, obtain*, and the rest of a very long list of English words ending in *-tain*, *attain* does not come from Latin *tenēre* 'hold.' Its source is Latin *tangere* 'touch' (as in English *tangible* and *tangent*). The addition of the prefix *ad-* 'to' produced *attingere* 'reach,' which passed via Vulgar Latin *\*attangere* and Old French *ataindre* into English.

▶ tangent, tangible

**attempt** [14] *Attempting* is etymologically related to *tempting*. The Latin verb *attemptāre* was formed with the prefix *ad-* from *temptāre*, which meant 'try' as well as 'tempt' (the semantic connection is preserved in modern English *try*, with the contrasting senses 'attempt' and 'put to the test'). The Latin form passed into Old French as *atenter* (hence modern French *attenter*), but was later latinized back to *attempter*, the form in which English acquired it.

▶ tempt

**attend** [13] Etymologically, *attend* means 'stretch to.' It comes originally from Latin *attendere*, a compound verb formed from the prefix *ad-* 'to' and *tendere* 'stretch' (a descendant of an Indo-European base *\*ten-, *ton-* 'stretch' which also produced, among others, Latin *tenēre* 'hold' – source of English *contain, maintain, obtain*, etc – and English *tendon, thin*, and *tone*). By metaphorical extension 'stretch to' became 'direct one's attention to,' which was the original meaning of the verb in Old French *atendre* and subsequently in English. The sense 'take care of' developed in the 15th century, 'be present' much later, in the 17th century. The noun derivative *attention* [14] comes from Latin *attentiō*.

*Tend* meaning 'look after' comes mainly from *attend*, but also partly from *intend*, in both cases with loss of the first syllable.

▶ contain, maintain, obtain, tendon, thin, tone

**attest** see TESTAMENT

**attic** [18] In classical architecture, an Attic order was a pilaster, or square column (the name comes from Attica, a region of ancient Greece of which Athens was the capital). This type of column was often used in a relatively low storey placed above the much higher main façade of a building, which hence became known in the 18th century as an *attic storey*. It was a short step to applying the word *attic* itself to an 'upper storey'; the first record of it in this sense comes in Byron's *Beppo* 1817: 'His wife would mount, at times, her highest attic.'

**attire** see TYRE

**attitude** [17] In origin, *attitude* is the same word as *aptitude*. Both come ultimately from late Latin *aptitūdō*. In Old French this became *aptitude*, which

English acquired in the 15th century, but in Italian it became *attitudine*, which meant 'disposition' or 'posture.' This was transmitted via French *attitude* to English, where at first it was used as a technical term in art criticism, meaning the 'disposition of a figure in a painting.' The metaphorical sense 'mental position with regard to something' developed in the early 19th century.

▶ aptitude

**attorney** [14] *Attorney* was formed in Old French from the prefix *a-* 'to' and the verb *torner* 'turn.' This produced the verb *atorner*, literally 'turn to,' hence 'assign to' or 'appoint to.' Its past participle, *atorne*, was used as a noun with much the same signification as *appointee* – 'someone appointed' – and hence 'someone appointed to act as someone else's agent,' and ultimately 'legal agent.' Borrowed into English, over the centuries the term came to mean 'lawyer practising in the courts of Common Law' (as contrasted with a *solicitor*, who practised in the Equity Courts); but it was officially abolished in that sense by the Judicature Act of 1873, and now survives only in American English, meaning 'lawyer,' and in the title *Attorney-General*, the chief law officer of a government.

▶ turn

**attract** [15] Etymologically, *attract* means literally 'pull something towards one.' It comes from *attract-*, the past participial stem of the Latin verb *attrahere*, a compound formed from the prefix *ad-* 'to' and the verb *trahere* 'pull.' It was quite a late formation, of around the mid 15th century, coined on the model of other English verbs, such as *abstract* and *contract*, deriving ultimately from Latin *trahere*.

▶ abstract, contract, retract, subtract

**attrition**    see THROW

**attune**    see TUNE

**aubergine** [18] Etymologically, the aubergine is the 'anti-fart vegetable.' That was the meaning of its ultimate source, Sanskrit *vātinganah*, so named because it did not produce intestinal gas. This was borrowed into Persian as *bādingān*, and reached Arabic as (with the definite article *al*) *al-bādindjān*. It then made its way with the Moors into the Iberian peninsula: here it produced Portuguese *beringela* (source of *brinjal* [18], an Indian and African English term for 'aubergine') and, with the definite article retained, Catalan *alberginia*. French turned this into *aubergine* and passed it on to English. In British English it has gradually replaced the earlier *eggplant*, named after the vegetable's shape, which American English has retained.

**auburn** [15] The colour of *auburn* has changed over the centuries. The word comes originally from Latin *albus* 'white' (whence English *album*, *albino*, *alb*, *albedo*, and *albion*), from which was derived in medi-

eval Latin *alburnus* 'off-white.' This passed via Old French *alborne*, *auborne* into English, still meaning 'yellowish-white.' From the 15th to the 17th century it was often spelled *abrun* or *abrown*, and it seems likely that its similarity to *brown* led to its gradual shift in meaning to 'golden-brown' or 'reddish-brown' over the centuries.

▶ albino, album

**auction** [16] The etymological idea underlying *auction* is that of 'increasing' – as the sale proceeds, the price offered goes up. The word comes from Latin *auctiō* 'increase,' a noun derived from *auct-*, the past participial stem of the verb *augēre* 'increase' (source of English *augment* [15] and *author*, and related to *auxiliary* [17] and *eke*). The sense 'auction sale' was already present in Latin.

▶ augment, August, author, auxiliary, eke, wax

**audible** [16] *Audible* is one of a wide range of English words based ultimately on the Latin verb *audīre* 'hear' (which came from the Indo-European root *\*awiz-*, source also of Greek *aithánesthai* 'perceive' and Sanskrit *āvis* 'evidently'). Others include *audience* [14], *audio-* [20], *audit* [15] (from Latin *audītus* 'hearing'; audits were originally done by reading the accounts out loud), *audition* [16], and *auditorium* [17].

▶ obey, oyez

**augur** [14] In Roman times, an augur was someone who foretold the future by observing the flight of birds (or by examining their entrails). His method of divination was reflected in his title, for the Latin word *augur*, earlier *auger*, seems to have meant literally 'one who performs with birds,' from *avis* 'bird' (as in English *aviary* [16] and *aviation* [19]) and *gerere* 'do, perform' (as in English *gestation, gesture, gerund, digest,* and *suggest*). (A parallel formation is *auspice* [16], whose Latin antecedent *auspex* meant 'one who observed the flight of birds'; it was compounded from *avis* and the verb *specere* 'look,' which is related to English *species* and *spy*.) A Latin derivative was the verb *inaugurāre* 'foretell the future from the flight of birds,' which was applied to the installation of someone in office after the appropriate omens had been determined; by the time it reached English as *inaugurate* [17], association with divination had been left far behind.

▶ aviary, aviation, inaugurate

**August** [OE] The month of August was named by the Romans after their emperor Augustus (63BC–14AD). His name was Caius Julius Caesar Octavian, but the Senate granted him the honorary title *Augustus* in 27BC. This connoted 'imperial majesty,' and was a specific use of the adjective *augustus* 'magnificent, majestic' (source of English *august* [17]); it may derive ultimately from the verb *augēre* 'increase' (from which English gets *auction* and *augment*).

▶ auction, augment

**aunt** [13] *Aunt* appears to come ultimately from *\*amma*, a hypothetical non-Indo-European word for 'mot'er' (parallel to Indo-European *\*mammā*, and like it reproducing syllables perceived to be uttered by babies), which at some point was borrowed into Latin. It first appears in the derived form *amita* 'paternal aunt,' which passed into English via Old French *ante* (of which modern French *tante* is an alteration) and Anglo-Norman *aunte*.

**aura** see AIR

**aurochs** see OX

**auspice** see AUGUR

**authentic** [14] Etymologically, something that is authentic is something that has the authority of its original creator. Greek *authentikós* was a derivative of the noun *authéntēs* 'doer, master,' which was formed from *autós* 'self' and the base *-hentēs* 'worker, doer' (related to Sanskrit *sanoti* 'he gains'). The adjective's original meaning in English was 'authoritative'; the modern sense 'genuine' did not develop fully until the late 18th century. (Greek *authéntēs*, incidentally, was pronounced /afthendis/, and was borrowed into Turkish as *efendī*, source of English *effendi* [17].)

► effendi

**author** [14] Latin *auctor* originally meant 'creator, originator'; it came from *auct-*, the past participial stem of *augēre*, which as well as 'increase' (as in English *augment*) meant 'originate.' But it also developed the specific sense 'creator of a text, writer,' and brought both these meanings with it into English via Old French *autor*. Forms with *-th-* began to appear in the mid 16th century (from French), and originally the *-th-* was just a spelling variant of *-t-*, but eventually it affected the pronunciation.

While the 'writing' sense has largely taken over *author*, *authority* [13] (ultimately from Latin *auctōritās*) and its derivatives *authoritative* and *authorize* have developed along the lines of the creator's power to command or make decisions.

► auction, augment

**autograph** [17] Greek *auto-* was a prefixal use of the adjective *autós*, meaning 'same, self.' Many of the commonest *auto-*words in English, including *autograph* itself and also *autocrat* [19], *automatic* [18] (a derivative of *automaton* [17], which was formed from a hypothetical base *\*men-* 'think' related to *mental* and *mind*), *autonomy* [17], and *autopsy* [17] (originally meaning 'eye-witness', and derived from Greek *optós* 'seen,' source of English *optic*), are original Greek formations. But the 19th and particularly the 20th century have seen a mass of new coinages, notably in scientific and technical terminology, including such familiar words as *autism*, *autobiography*, *autoerotic*, *autofocus*, *autogiro*, *autoimmune*, *automotive*, *auto-*

*suggestion*, and of course *automobile* (originally a French formation of the 1870s). *Automobile* has itself, of course, given rise to a completely new use for the *auto-* prefix, with the general connotation of 'motorized transport,' as in *autobus*, *autocar*, *autocycle*, and the German *autobahn*.

**autumn** [14] English acquired *autumn* from Latin *autumnus*, partly via Old French *autompne*. Where Latin got the word from is a mystery; it may have been a borrowing from Etruscan, a long-extinct pre-Roman language of the Italian peninsula. In Old English, the term for 'autumn' was *harvest*, and this remained in common use throughout the Middle Ages; it was not until the 16th century that *autumn* really began to replace it (at the same time as *harvest* began to be applied more commonly to the gathering of crops). *Fall*, now the main US term for 'autumn,' is 16th-century too.

**avail** see VALUE

**available** see VALUE

**avalanche** [18] Not surprisingly, *avalanche* originated in the Alps. The French dialect of Savoy, an area near the Italian border in the western Alps, had a term *lavantse*, apparently derived from a Vulgar Latin *\*labanca* (whence Provençal *lavanca*). Through association with the verb *avale* 'descend' (see DOWN), this underwent metathesis (transposition of *l* and *v*) to produce in the Romansh language of Switzerland *avalantze*, which was borrowed into French as *avalanche*.

**avant-garde** see VANGUARD

**avarice** [13] The Latin verb *avēre* meant 'covet.' One of its derivatives was the adjective *avārus* 'greedy,' from which the noun *avāritia* was formed. This entered English via Old French *avarice*. Another of its derivatives was the adjective *avidus* 'greedy' which, as well as being the source of English *avid* [18], produced, via a hypothetical contracted form *\*audus*, the adjective *audax* 'bold,' source of English *audacity* [15].

► audacity, avid

**avenge** see VINDICATE

**average** [15] The word *average* has a devious history. It began in Arabic, as *'awārīya*, the plural of *'awār*, a noun derived from the verb *'āra* 'mutilate;' this was used as a commercial term, denoting 'damaged merchandise.' The first European language to adopt it was Italian, as *avaria*, and it passed via Old French *avarie* into English (where in the 16th century it acquired its *-age* ending, probably by association with the then semantically similar *damage*). Already by this time it had come to signify the 'financial loss incurred through damage to goods in transit,' and this passed in the 17th century to the 'equal sharing of such loss by those with a financial interest in the goods,' and eventually, in the 18th century, to the current (mathematical and general) sense of 'mean.'

**aviary**   see AUGUR

**aviation**   see AUGUR

**avocado**   [17]   Anyone tucking into an avocado could well be taken aback to learn that in the South American Indian language from which the word originally came, it meant literally 'testicle.' The Nahuatl Indians named the fruit *ahuacatl* 'testicle' on account of its shape. The Spanish conquistadors took the word over as *aguacate*, but before long this became altered by folk etymology (the substitution of familiar for unfamiliar forms) to *avocado* (literally 'advocate' in Spanish). When English borrowed the word, folk etymology took a hand yet again, for in the late 17th century it became known as the *alligator pear*, a name which survived into the 20th century.

**avoid**   [14]   *Avoid* at first meant literally 'make void, empty.' It was formed in Old French from the adjective *vuide* 'empty' (source of English *void* [13], and derived from a hypothetical Vulgar Latin *\*vocitus*, which is related ultimately to *vacant*). With the addition of the prefix *es-* 'out,' a verb *evuider* was formed, which passed into English via Anglo-Norman *avoider*. The original sense 'empty' barely survived into the 17th century, but meanwhile it had progressed through 'withdrawing, so as to leave someone alone or leave a place empty' to 'deliberately staying away from someone or something.'

▶ vacant, void

**awake**   [OE]   *Awake* was formed by adding the intensive prefix *ā-* to the verb *wake* (in Old English *wacan* or *wacian*, related to *watch*, and also ultimately to *vegetable, vigil*, and *vigour*). The adjective *awake* arose in the 13th century; it was originally a variant form of the past participle of the verb.

▶ vigil, wake, watch

**aware**   see WARE

**away**   [OE]   *Away* was formed in the late Old English period by conflating the phrase *on weg*, literally 'on way,' that is, 'on one's way, departing.' This soon became reduced to *aweg*, hence *away*.

▶ way

**awe**   [13]   Old English had the word *ege*, meaning 'awe,' but modern English *awe* is a Scandinavian borrowing; the related Old Norse *agi* steadily infiltrated the language from the northeast southwards during the Middle Ages. *Agi* came, like *ege*, from a hypothetical Germanic form *\*agon*, which in turn goes back to an Indo-European base *\*agh-* (whence also Greek *ákhos* 'pain'). The guttural *g* sound of the 13th-century English word (technically a voiced velar spirant) was changed to *w* during the Middle English period. This was a general change, but it is not always reflected in

spelling – as in *owe* and *ought*, for instance, which were originally the same word.

**awkward**   [14]   When *awkward* was coined, in Scotland and northern England, it meant 'turned in the wrong direction.' Middle English had an adjective *awk*, which meant 'the wrong way round, backhanded,' and hence 'perverse,' and with the addition of the suffix *-ward* this became *awkward*. *Awk* itself was adopted from Old Norse *afugr*, which is related to German *ab* 'away' and English *off*. *Awkward* followed a similar semantic path to *awk*, via 'perverse, ill-adapted' to 'clumsy.'

▶ off

**awl**   [OE]   The Old English form, *æl*, came from a hypothetical Germanic base *\*āl-*, which had a probable relative in Sanskrit *ārā*. The compound *bradawl* was formed in the 19th century using the term *brad* 'thin flat nail,' which came originally from Old Norse *broddr* 'spike.' Awls, tools for making holes to take nails, are part of the shoemaker's traditional set of implements: hence the apparently quite recent, early 20th-century rhyming slang *cobbler's awls* (*cobblers* for short) for 'balls.'

**axe**   [OE]   Relatives of the word *axe* are widespread throughout the Indo-European languages, from German *axt* and Dutch *aaks* to Latin *ascia* and Greek *axínē*. These point back to a hypothetical Indo-European *\*agwesī* or *\*akusī*, which denoted some sort of cutting or hewing tool. The Old English form was *æx*, and there is actually no historical justification for the modern British spelling *axe*, which first appeared in the late 14th century; as late as 1885 the *Oxford English Dictionary* made *ax* its main form, and it remains so in the USA.

**axis**   [14]   *Axis* is at the centre of a complex web of 'turning' words. Besides its immediate source, Latin *axis*, there were Greek *áxōn*, Sanskrit *ákshas*, and a hypothetical Germanic *\*akhsō* which produced Old English *eax* 'axle' as well as modern German *achse* 'axle, shaft' and Dutch *as*; and there could well be a connection with Latin *agere* (source of English *act, agent*, etc) in the sense 'drive.' Also related is an unrecorded Latin form *\*acslā*, which produced *āla* 'wing' (source of English *aileron* and *aisle*); its diminutive was *axilla* 'armpit,' from which English gets the adjective *axillary* [17] and the botanical term *axil* [18].

▶ aileron, aisle, axil

**axle**   [17]   The word *axle* emerges surprisingly late considering the antiquity of axles, but related terms had existed in the language for perhaps a thousand years. Old English had *eax*, which came from a hypothetical Germanic *\*akhsō*, related to Latin *axis*. This survived in the compound *ax-tree* until the 17th century (later in Scotland); *tree* in this context meant 'beam.' But from the early 14th century the native *ax-tree* began to be ousted by Old Norse *öxultré* (or as it became in English *axle-tree*); the element *öxull* came from a prehistoric Germanic *\*akhsulaz*, a derivative of *\*akhsō*. *Axle* first appeared on its own in the last decade of the 16th century (meaning 'axis,' a sense it has since lost), and became firmly established in the early 17th century.

**aye** see EVER, I

**azalea** see ARID

**azimuth** see ZENITH

**azure** [14] *Azure* is of Persian origin. It comes ultimately from Persian *lāzhuward*, source also of the *lazuli* in *lapis lazuli*, a blue semiprecious stone (and *azure* originally meant 'lapis lazuli' in English). The Arabs borrowed the Persian term as (with the definite article *al*) *allazward*, which passed into Old Spanish as *azur* or *azul*. Old French borrowed *azur* and handed it on to English.

▶ lapis lazuli

# B

----

**babel** [14] According to Genesis 11: 1–9, the tower of Babel was built in Shinar by the descendants of Noah in an attempt to reach heaven. Angered at their presumption, God punished the builders by making them unable to understand each other's speech: hence, according to legend, the various languages of the world. Hence, too, the metaphorical application of *babel* to a 'confused medley of sounds,' which began in English in the 16th century. The word has no etymological connection with 'language' or 'noise,' however. The original Assyrian *bāb-ilu* meant 'gate of god,' and this was borrowed into Hebrew as *bābel* (from which English acquired the word). The later Greek version is *Babylon*.
▶ Babylon

**baboon** [14] The origins of *baboon* are obscure, but it seems that the notion underlying it may be that of 'grimacing.' Baboons characteristically draw back their lips in snarling, revealing their teeth, and it has been speculated that there may be a connection with Old French *baboue* 'grimace.' However that may be, it was certainly in Old French that the word first surfaced, as *babuin*, and originally it meant 'gaping figure' (as in a gargoyle) as well as 'ape.' This alternative meaning was carried over when the Old French word was borrowed into English, where it remained a live sense of *baboon* until the 16th century.

**baby** [14] Like *mama* and *papa*, *baby* and the contemporaneous *babe* are probably imitative of the burbling noises made by an infant that has not yet learned to talk. In Old English, the term for what we would now call a 'baby' was *child*, and it seems only to have been from about the 11th century that *child* began to extend its range to the slightly more mature age which it now covers. Then when the word *baby* came into the language, it was used synonymously with this developed sense of *child*, and only gradually came to refer to infants not yet capable of speech or walking.

**bacchanalian** [16] *Bákkhos* was the Greek god of wine. Son of Zeus and Semele, he was also known as *Diónūsos*. The Romans adopted him, amend-

ing his name to *Bacchus*, and his worshippers went in for a brand of licentious revelry, in his honour, known as *Bacchanalia*. Hence the metaphorical application of the English adjective to anything drunkenly orgiastic.

**bachelor** [13] The ultimate origins of *bachelor* are obscure, but by the time it first turned up, in Old French *bacheler* (from a hypothetical Vulgar Latin *\*baccalāris*), it meant 'squire' or 'young knight in the service of an older knight.' This was the sense it had when borrowed into English, and it is preserved, in fossilized form, in *knight bachelor*. Subsequent semantic development was via 'university graduate' to, in the late 14th century, 'unmarried man.' A resemblance to Old Irish *bachlach* 'shepherd, peasant' (a derivative of Old Irish *bachall* 'staff,' from Latin *baculum*, source of English *bacillus* and related to English *bacteria*) has led some to speculate that the two may be connected.

English *baccalaureate* [17] comes via French *baccalauréat* or medieval Latin *baccalaureātus* from medieval Latin *baccalaureus* 'bachelor,' which was an alteration of an earlier *baccalārius*, perhaps owing to an association with the 'laurels' awarded for academic success (Latin *bacca lauri* meant literally 'laurel berry').

**back** [OE] *Back* goes back to a prehistoric West and North Germanic *\*bakam*, which was represented in several pre-medieval and medieval Germanic languages: Old High German *bah*, for example, and Old Norse *bak*. In most of them, however, it has been ousted by relatives of English *ridge*, originally 'spine' (such as German *rücken* and Swedish *rygg*), and only English retains *back*.
▶ bacon

**backgammon** [17] *Backgammon* appears to mean literally 'back game,' although the reason for the name is far from clear (*gammon* has been used since at least the early 18th century for a particular type of victory in the game, but it is hard to say whether the term for the victory came from the term for the game, or vice versa). Either way, *gammon* represents Old English *gamen*, the ancestor of modern English *game*. The game backgammon goes back far further than the 17th century, of course, but before that it was called *tables* in English.

▶ game

**bacon**  [12]  Originally, *bacon* meant literally 'meat from a pig's back.' It comes ultimately from a prehistoric Germanic *\*bakkon*, which was related to *\*bakam*, the source of English *back*. It reached English via Frankish *báko* and Old French *bacon*, and at first meant 'a side of pig meat (fresh or cured).' Gradually it narrowed down to 'a side of cured pig meat' (bringing it into competition with the Old English word *flitch*, now virtually obsolete), and finally to simply 'cured pig meat.'

▶ back

**bacterium**  [19]  *Bacterium* was coined in the 1840s from Greek *baktērion*, a diminutive of *báktron* 'stick,' on the basis that the originally discovered bacteria were rod-shaped. At first it was sometimes anglicized to *bactery*, but the Latin form has prevailed. Related, but a later introduction, is *bacillus* [19]: this is a diminutive of Latin *baculum* 'stick,' and the term was again inspired by the microorganism's shape. Latin *baculum* is also responsible, via Italian *bacchio* and its diminutive form *bacchetta*, for the long French loaf, the *baguette*.

▶ bacillus, baguette, débacle, imbecile

**bad**  [13]  For such a common word, *bad* has a remarkably clouded history. It does not begin to appear in English until the end of the 13th century, and has no apparent relatives in other languages. The few clues we have suggest a regrettably homophobic origin. Old English had a pair of words, *bæddel* and *bædling*, which appear to have been derogatory terms for homosexuals, with overtones of sodomy. The fact that the first examples we have of *bad*, from the late 13th and early 14th centuries, are in the sense 'contemptible, worthless' as applied to people indicates that the connotations of moral depravity may have become generalized from an earlier, specifically anti-homosexual sense.

**badger**  [16]  The Old English term for a 'badger' was *brock*, a word of Celtic origin, and *badger* does not begin to appear, somewhat mysteriously, until the early 16th century. The name has never been satisfactorily explained, but perhaps the least implausible explanation is from the word *badge*, in reference to the white stripes on the animal's forehead, as if it were wearing a badge (a term originally applied to a distinctive device worn by a knight for purposes of recognition); the early spelling *bageard* suggests that it may have been formed with the suffix *-ard*, as in *dullard* and *sluggard*. (*Badge* itself is of even more obscure origin; it first turns up in Middle English, in the mid 14th century.) Other early terms for the badger were *bauson* (14th–18th centu-

ries), from Old French *bausen*, and *grey* (15th–17th centuries).

**badminton**  [19]  The game of 'battledore and shuttlecock' has been around for some time (it appears to go back to the 16th century; the word *battledore*, which may come ultimately from Portuguese *batedor* 'beater,' first turns up in the 15th century, meaning 'implement for beating clothes when washing them,' but by the 16th century is being used for a 'small racket'; while *shuttlecock*, so named because it is hit back and forth, first appears in the early 16th century, in a poem of John Skelton's). This was usually a fairly informal, improvised affair, however, and latterly played mainly by children; the modern, codified game of badminton did not begin until the 1860s or 1870s, and takes its name from the place where it was apparently first played, Badminton House, Avon, country seat of the dukes of Beaufort. (A slightly earlier application of the word *badminton* had been to a cooling summer drink, a species of claret cup.)

**baffle**  [16]  The etymology of *baffle* is appropriately baffling. Two main candidates have been proposed as a source. The first is the medieval Scots verb *bawchill* or *bauchle*, meaning 'discredit publicly.' This fits in with the way *baffle* was first used: 'I will baffull your good name, sound with the trumpet your dishonour, and paint your pictor with the heeles vpward, and beate it in despight of yourselfe,' *Churchyardes chippes* 1570. The other strand is represented by French *bafouer* 'hoodwink, deceive,' which perhaps comes from Old French *beffer*. This corresponds more closely to the present-day meaning of *baffle*, and it may well be that there are two distinct words here.

**bag**  [13]  English acquired *bag* from Old Norse *baggi* 'bag, bundle,' but it does not appear in any other Germanic language, which suggests that it may have been borrowed at some point from a non-Germanic language. Forms such as Old French *bague*, Italian *baga*, and Portuguese *bagua* show that it existed elsewhere. A derivative of the Old French word was *bagage*, from which in the 15th century English got *baggage*; and Italian *baga* may have led, by a doubling of diminutive suffixes, to *bagatella* 'insignificant property, trifle,' which entered English in the 17th century via French *bagatelle* (although this has also been referred to Latin *bacca* 'berry' – see BACHELOR).

▶ bagatelle, baggage

**bail**  There are now three distinct words *bail* in English, although they may all be related. *Bail* 'money deposited as a guarantee when released' [14] comes from Old French *bail*, a derivative of the verb *baillier* 'take charge of, carry,' whose source was Latin *bājulāre* 'carry,' from *bājulus* 'carrier.' *Bail* 'remove water' [13], also spelled *bale*, probably comes ultimately from the same source; its immediate antecedent was Old

French *baille* 'bucket,' which perhaps went back to a hypothetical Vulgar Latin *\*bājula*, a feminine form of *bājulus*. The *bail* on top of cricket stumps [18] has been connected with Latin *bājulus* too – this could have been the source of Old French *bail* 'cross-beam' ('load-carrying beam'), which could quite plausibly have been applied to cricket bails; on the other hand it may go back to Old French *bail*, *baille* 'enclosed court' (source of English *bailey* [13]), which originally in English meant the 'encircling walls of a castle' but by the 19th century at the latest had developed the sense 'bar for separating animals in a stable.'

▶ bailey

**bailiff** [13] Latin *bājulus* meant literally 'carrier' (it is probably the ultimate source of English *bail* in some if not all of its uses). It developed the metaphorical meaning 'person in charge, administrator,' which passed, via the hypothetical medieval adjectival form *\*bājulīvus*, into Old French as *bailiif*, and hence into English.

▶ bail

**bain-marie** [19] In its origins, the bain-marie was far from today's innocuous domestic utensil for heating food over boiling water. It takes its name from Mary, or Miriam, the sister of Moses, who according to medieval legend was an adept alchemist – so much so that she had a piece of alchemical equipment named after her, 'Mary's furnace' (medieval Greek *kaminos Marias*). This was mistranslated into medieval Latin as *balneum Mariae* 'Mary's bath,' from which it passed into French as *bain-marie*. English originally borrowed the word in the 15th century, in semi-anglicized form, as *balneo of Mary*. At this time it still retained its original alchemical meaning, but by the early 19th century, when English adopted the French term, it had developed its present-day use.

**bairn** see BEAR

**bait** [13] Etymologically, the verb *bait* means 'cause to bite.' It comes from Old Norse *beita*, a causative version of *bíta* 'bite' (related to English *bite*). This took two semantic paths in English. In its aggressive mode, it meant literally 'set dogs on someone,' and hence by figurative extension 'harrass, persecute.' More peaceably, it signified 'feed an animal.' And this sense of 'food provided' is reflected in the noun *bait*, which comes partly from the verb, partly from the related Old Norse nouns *beit* 'pasturage' and *beita* 'fish bait.'

Old Norse *beita* was probably borrowed into Old French as *beter*, which with the prefix *a-* produced *abeter*, source of English *abet* [14], originally meaning 'urge on, incite.'

▶ abet, bite

**bake** [OE] The Old English verb *bacan* goes back to a prehistoric Germanic base *\*bak-*, which also

produced German *backen*, Dutch *bakken*, and Swedish *baka*; its ultimate source was the Indo-European base *\*bhog-*, another descendant of which was Greek *phógein* 'roast.' Derivatives of the English verb include *batch* [15], which comes from Old English *\*bæcce*, literally 'something baked,' and the name *Baxter*, which originally meant 'female baker.'

▶ batch

**balance** [13] The underlying etymological meaning of *balance* is of a weighing apparatus with 'two pans' for holding things. In Latin this was a *lībra bilanx*, literally 'scales with two pans' – *bilanx* being compounded from *bi-* 'two' and *lanx* 'plate, pan.' *Bilanx* passed, in its stem form *bilanc-*, via Vulgar Latin *\*bilancia* into Old French *balance*, the source of the English word.

**balcony** [17] *Balcony* entered English from Italian *balcone*, but it seems to be ultimately of Germanic origin. It was probably borrowed into Old Italian, with the meaning 'scaffold,' from Germanic *\*balkon* 'beam,' source of English *balk* – perhaps from the notion of a platform or scaffold being built from beams of timber, although the connection is not altogether clear.

▶ balk

**bald** [14] In Middle English times, *bald* was *ballede*, which suggests that it may have been a compound formed in Old English with the suffix *-ede* 'characterized by, having.' It has been conjectured that the first element in the compound was Old English *\*ball-*, meaning 'white patch' or 'blaze' on an animal's head; this may be supported by isolated examples of the use of the adjective to mean (of a horse) 'white-faced' from the 16th to the 18th centuries, and by the obsolete dialectal *ball* meaning both 'white patch on the head' and 'white-faced horse.' This would have produced the Old English adjective *\*bællede* or *\*beallede*, which, from 'having a white blaze,' progressed naturally in meaning to 'hairless.'

The compounds *piebald* [16] and *skewbald* [17] are both based on *bald*: *piebald* means 'having black and white patches like a magpie,' while *skewbald* may be based on Middle English *skew* '(cloudy) skies' or on Old French *escu* 'shield.'

▶ piebald, skewbald

**balk** [OE] There are two separate strands of meaning in *balk*, or *baulk*, as it is also spelled. When it first entered English in the 9th century, from Old Norse *bálkr*, it meant a 'ridge of land, especially one between ploughed furrows,' from which the modern sense 'stumbling block, obstruction' developed. It is not until about 1300 that the meaning 'beam of timber' appears in English, although it was an established sense of the Old Norse word's Germanic ancestor *\*balkon* (source also of English *balcony*). The common element of meaning in these two strands is something like 'bar,' which may have been present in the word's ultimate Indo-European base *bhalg- (possible source of Greek *phálagx* 'log, phalanx').

▶ balcony, phalanx

**ball**   There are two distinct words *ball* in English. The 'round object' [13] comes via Old Norse *böllr* from a prehistoric Germanic *balluz* (source also of *bollock* [OE], originally a diminutive form). A related form was Germanic *ballón*, which was borrowed into Italian to give *palla* 'ball,' from which French probably acquired *balle*. Derivatives of this branch of the family to have reached English are *balloon* [16], from French *ballon* or Italian *ballone*, and *ballot* [16], from the Italian diminutive form *ballotta* (originally from the use of small balls as counters in secret voting). The Germanic stem form *bal-, *bul- was also the ultimate source of English *bowl* 'receptacle.'

The 'dancing' *ball* [17] comes from French *bal*, a derivative of the now obsolete verb *bal(l)er* 'dance,' which was descended via late Latin *ballāre* from Greek *ballízein* 'dance.' Related words in English include *ballad(e)* [14], which came via Old French from Provençal *balada* 'song or poem to dance to,' and *ballet*.

▶ ballon, ballot, bollock / ballad, ballet

**ballast**   [16]   Originally, *ballast* appears to have meant literally 'bare load' – that is, a load carried by a ship simply for the sake of its weight, and without any commercial value. English probably acquired it, via Low German, from a Scandinavian language; Old Swedish and Old Danish had not only *ballast* but also *barlast*, which appears to betray the word's component parts: *bar*, related to English *bare*, and *last* 'burden' (Old English had *hlæst* 'burden,' related to *lade*, which survived into the 20th century as a measure of weight for various commodities).

▶ bare, lade

**ballet**   [17]   Etymologically, a *ballet* is a 'little dance.' English acquired the word, via French *ballet*, from Italian *balletto*, a diminutive of *ballo* 'dance,' related to English *ball* (the diminutive of Italian *balla* 'spherical ball' is *ballotta*, whence English *ballot*). The noun *ballo* came from the verb *ballare* (a descendant via late Latin *ballāre* of Greek *ballízein* 'dance'), of which another derivative was *ballerino* 'dancing master.' The feminine form, *ballerina*, entered English in the late 18th century. *Balletomane* 'ballet enthusiast' is a creation of the 1930s.

Another word *ballet*, also a diminutive, exists, or at least existed, in English. It meant 'little [spherical] ball,' and was used in the 18th century as a technical term in heraldry.

▶ ball

**ballistic**   see PARABLE
**balloon**   see BALL
**ballot**   see BALL

**balm**   [13]   In origin, *balm* and *balsam* are the same word. Both come via Latin *balsamum* from Greek *bálsamon*, an 'aromatic oily resin exuded from certain trees.' Its ultimate source may have been Hebrew *bāśām* 'spice.' Latin *balsamum* passed into Old French, and thence into English, as *basme* or *baume* (hence the modern English pronunciation), and in the 15th to 16th centuries the Latin *l* was restored to the written form of the word. The new borrowing *balsam*, direct from Latin, was made in the 15th century.

▶ balsam

**baluster**   [17]   Etymologically, *baluster* and *banister* are the same word. Both come ultimately from Greek *balāustion* 'pomegranate flower,' which reached English via Latin *balaustium*, Italian *balaustro*, and French *balustre*. The reason for the application of the term to the uprights supporting a staircase handrail is that the lower part of a pomegranate flower has a double curve, inwards at the top and then bulging outwards at the bottom, similar to the design of some early balusters. A *balustrade* [17], from Italian *balaustrata* via French, is a row of balusters. Already by the mid 17th century a transformation of the *l* to an *n* had taken place, producing the parallel *banister*.

▶ balustrade, banister

**bamboo**   [16]   *Bamboo* appears to come from a Malay word *mambu*. This was brought back to Europe by the Portuguese explorers, and enjoyed a brief currency in English from the 17th to the 18th century. However, for reasons no one can explain, the initial *m* of this word became changed to *b*, and it acquired an *s* at the end, producing a form found in Latin texts of the time as *bambusa*. This appears to have passed into English via Dutch *bamboes*, so the earliest English version of the word was *bambos*. As so often happens in such cases, the final *s* was misinterpreted as a plural ending, so it dropped off to give the new 'singular' *bamboo*.

**bamboozle**   [18]   *Bamboozle* is a mystery word. It first appears in 1703, in the writings of the dramatist Colly Cibber, and seven years later it was one of a list of the latest buzzwords cited by Jonathan Swift in the *Tatler* (others included *bully, mob*, and *sham*). It is probably a 'cant' term (a sort of low-life argot), and may perhaps be of Scottish origin; there was a 17th-century Scottish verb *bombaze* 'perplex,' which may be the same word as *bombace*, literally 'padding, stuffing,' but metaphorically 'inflated language' (the variant form *bombast* has survived into modern English).

▶ bombast

**ban**   [OE]   *Ban* is one of a widespread group of words in the European languages. Its ultimate source is the Indo-European base *bha-*, which also gave English *fame* (from a derivative of Latin *fārī* 'speak') and *phase* (from Greek *phāsis*). The Germanic offshoot of the Indo-European base, and source of the English word, was *bannan*, which originally probably meant simply 'speak, proclaim.' This gradually developed through 'proclaim with threats' to 'put a curse on,' but the sense 'prohibit' does not seem to have arisen until as late as the 19th century.

The Germanic base *bann-* was borrowed into Old French as the noun *ban* 'proclamation.' From there it crossed into English and probably mingled with the cognate English noun, Middle English *iban* (the descendant of Old English *gebann*). It survives today in the plural form *banns* 'proclamation of marriage.' The adjective derived from Old French *ban* was *banal*, acquired by English in the 18th century. It originally meant 'of compulsory military service' (from the word's basic sense of 'summoning by proclamation'); this was gradually generalized through 'open to everyone' to 'commonplace.'

▶ banal, bandit, banish, contraband, fame, phase

**banana** [16] *Banana* comes from a West African language – possibly Wolof, a language of the Niger-Congo family, spoken in Senegal and the Gambia. The original European discoverers of the word – and the fruit – were the Spanish and Portuguese, who passed them on to England. The term *bananas* 'mad' is 20th-century, but its origins are obscure; some have compared *banana oil*, a 20th-century slang term for 'mad talk, nonsense.'

**band** There are two distinct words *band* in English, but neither of them goes back as far as Old English. The one meaning 'group of people' [15] comes from Old French *bande*, but is probably Germanic in ultimate origin; the specific sense 'group of musicians' developed in the 17th century. *Band* 'strip' [13] comes from Germanic *bindan*, source of English *bind*, but reached English in two quite separate phases. It first came via Old Norse *band*, in the sense 'something that ties or constrains'; this replaced Old English *bend*, also from Germanic *bindan* (which now survives only as a heraldic term, as in *bend sinister*), but is now itself more or less obsolete, having been superseded by *bond*, a variant form. But then in the 15th century it arrived again, by a different route: Old French had *bande* 'strip, stripe,' which can be traced back, perhaps via a Vulgar Latin *binda*, to the same ultimate source, Germanic *bindan*.

▶ bend, bind, bond, bundle, ribbon

**bandit** [16] Etymologically, a *bandit* is someone who has been 'banished' or outlawed. The word was borrowed from Italian *bandito*, which was a nominal use of the past participle of the verb *bandire* 'ban.' The source of this was Vulgar Latin *bannīre*, which

was formed from the borrowed Germanic base *bann-* 'proclaim' (from which English gets *ban*). Meanwhile, in Old French, *bannīre* had produced *banir*, whose lengthened stem form *baniss-* gave English *banish* [14].

▶ ban, banish

**bandy** [16] To 'bandy words with someone' may go back to an original idea of 'banding together to oppose others.' The word comes from French *bander* 'oppose,' which is possibly a derivative of *bande* 'group, company' (source of English *band*). The rather complex semantic development goes from 'taking sides,' through 'opposing a third party,' 'exchanging blows,' 'exchanging hits' (in the 16th and 17th centuries it was a term in tennis), to 'exchanging hostile words.'

The adjective *bandy* [17], as in 'bandy legs,' probably comes from the noun *bandy* 'curved stick used in an early form of hockey' (the game was also known as *bandy*). It may ultimately be related to the verb *bandy*, the connection being the notion of knocking a ball to and fro.

▶ band

**banish**   see BANDIT
**banister**   see BALUSTER
**banjo** [18] The origins of *banjo* are uncertain, but its likeliest source seems to be *bandore*, the name of a 16th-century stringed instrument similar to the lute. It has been argued that in the speech of Southern US blacks, amongst whom the banjo originated, *bandore* became *banjo*, perhaps under the influence of *mbanza*, a term for a similar instrument in the Kimbundu language of Northern Angola (although it might be more plausible to suggest that *mbanza* is the immediate source, altered by English-speakers more familiar with *bandore*).

*Bandore* itself appears to be a variant of *pandore* or *pandora*, which comes from Greek *pandoura* 'three-stringed lute.' A more far-reaching modification produced *mandore*, likewise a term for a lutelike instrument. The Italian version of the word, *mandola*, is familiar in English from its diminutive form, which has given us *mandolin* [18].

▶ mandolin

**bank** [12] The various disparate meanings of modern English *bank* all come ultimately from the same source, Germanic *bangk-*, but they have taken different routes to reach us. Earliest to arrive was 'ridge, mound, bordering slope,' which came via a hypothetical Old Norse *banki*. Then came 'bench' [13] (now obsolete except in the sense 'series of rows or tiers' – as in a typewriter's *bank* of keys); this arrived from Old French *banc*, which was originally borrowed from Germanic *bangk-* (also the source of English *bench*). Finally came 'moneylender's counter' [15], whose source was either French *banque* or Italian *banca* – both in any case deriving ultimately once again from Germanic *bangk-. The current sense, 'place where money is kept,' developed in the 17th century.

The derived *bankrupt* [16] comes originally from Italian *banca rotta*, literally 'broken counter' (*rotta* is related to English *bereave* and *rupture*); in early times a broken counter or bench was symbolic of an insolvent moneylender.

The diminutive of Old French *banc* was *banquet* 'little bench' (perhaps modelled on Italian *banchetto*), from which English gets *banquet* [15]. It has undergone a complete reversal in meaning over the centuries; originally it signified a 'small snack eaten while seated on a bench (rather than at table).'

▶ bench

**banner** [13] *Banner* is of Germanic origin, but it reached English via Latin. Early forms which show its Germanic antecedents are Gothic *bandwo* 'sign' and the related Old Norse *benda* 'give a sign,' but at some stage it was acquired by Latin, as *bandum* 'standard.' This passed via Vulgar Latin *bandāria* into various Romance languages, in some of which the influence of derivatives of Germanic *bann-* (source of English *ban*) led to the elimination of the *d*. Hence Old French *baniere* and Anglo-Norman *banere*, source of English *banner*.

▶ ban

**banyan** [17] *Banyan* originally meant 'Hindu trader.' It is an arabization of Gujerati *vāniyān* 'traders,' which comes ultimately from Sanskrit *vanija* 'merchant' (the Portuguese version, *banian*, produced an alternative English spelling). When European travellers first visited Bandar Abbas, a port on the Persian Gulf, they found there a pagoda which the banyans had built in the shade of a large Indian fig tree. They immediately applied the name *banyan* to this particular tree, and the term later widened to include all such trees.

**baptize** [13] The underlying notion of *baptize* is of 'dipping,' as those baptized were originally (and sometimes still are) immersed in water. It comes from Greek *báptein* 'dip,' whose derivative *baptízein* 'baptize' passed via Latin *baptizāre* and Old French *baptiser* into English. Old Norse *kafa* 'dive' is a Germanic relative.

**bar** [12] The history of *bar* cannot be traced back very far. Forms in various Romance languages, such as French *barre* (source of the English verb) and Italian and Spanish *barra*, point to a Vulgar Latin *barra*, but beyond that nothing is known. The original sense of a 'rail' or 'barrier' has developed various figurative applications over the centuries: in the 14th century to the 'rail in a court before which a prisoner was arraigned' (as in 'prisoner at the bar'); in the 16th century to a 'partition separating qualified from unqualified lawyers in

hall' (as in 'call to the bar'); and also in the 16th century to a 'counter at which drink is served.'

Related nouns include *barrage* [19], originally an 'artificial obstruction in a waterway,' and *barrier* [14], from Anglo-Norman *barrere*.

▶ barrage, barrel, barrier, barrister, embargo

**barb** see BEARD

**barbarous** [15] Originally, a *barbarous* person was a 'foreigner,' anyone who did not speak your own language. Greek *bárbaros* meant 'foreign, ignorant,' and it has been speculated that its ultimate signification was 'unable to speak intelligibly' (the related Sanskrit *barbaras* meant 'stammering'). English acquired the word from Latin *barbarus*, a modified Vulgar Latin version of which, *brabus*, produced Italian *bravo* and hence, via French, English *brave*.

▶ brave

**barbecue** [17] *Barbecue* originated in the language of the now extinct Taino people of the West Indies. It first emerges in the Haitian creole term *barbacoa*, which meant simply 'wooden framework' (used for other purposes than roasting meat – for example, as a bed). American Spanish adopted the word, and passed it on to English. Compare BUCCANEER.

**barbel** see BEARD

**barber** see BEARD

**bard** [14] *Bard* is of Celtic origin. A prehistoric Old Celtic *bardos* produced Scottish and Irish Gaelic *bárd* and Welsh *bardd*, which meant 'poet-singer.' It appears to have been the Scottish form which introduced the word into English, in the sense 'strolling minstrel.' The modern, more elevated meaning 'poet' is 17th-century.

**bare** [OE] *Bare* is an ancient word, traceable back to an Indo-European *bhosos*. Descendants of this in non-Germanic languages include Lithuanian *basas* 'barefoot,' but for the most part it is the Germanic languages that have adopted the word. Germanic *bazaz* produced German and Swedish *bar*, Dutch *baar*, and, via Old English *bær*, modern English *bare*.

**bargain** [14] *Bargain* appears to be distantly related to *borrow*. Its immediate source was Old French *bargaignier* 'haggle,' but this was probably borrowed from Germanic *borganjan*, a derivative of *borgan* (from which ultimately we get *borrow*). The sense development may have been as follows: originally 'look after, protect' (the related Germanic *burg-* produced English *borough*, which to begin with meant 'fortress,' and *bury*); then 'take on loan, borrow'; then 'take or give'; and hence 'trade, haggle, bargain.'

▶ belfrey, borough, borrow, bury

**barge** [13] *Barge* comes in the first instance from Old French *barge*, but speculation has pushed it further back to medieval Latin *barica*, which would have derived from *báris*, a Greek word for an Egyptian boat. This hypothetical *\*barica* would have been a by-form of late Latin *barca*, which came into English via Old French as *barque*, also spelled *bark*, 'sailing vessel' [15] (source of *embark*). The metaphorical use of the verb *barge*, 'move clumsily or rudely,' is barely a hundred years old; it comes from the ponderous way made by barges.

▶ bark, barque, embark

**baritone**    see GRAVITY

**barium**    see GRAVITY

**barley**    [OE]    The Old English word for 'barley' was *bære* or *bere*. It came from an Indo-European base *\*bhar-* which also gave Latin *farīna* 'flour' (from which English gets *farinaceous* [17]) and Old Norse *farr* 'barley.' *Barley* (Old English *bærlic*) was in fact originally an adjective formed from this (like *princely* based on *prince*), and it was not until the early twelfth century that it came to be used as a noun.

A *barn* [OE] was originally a building for storing barley. The Old English word *ber(e)n* was a compound formed from *bere* and *ern* or *ærn* 'house' (which may be related to English *rest*).

▶ barn, farinaceous, farrago

**barnacle**    [12]    The term *barnacle* was originally applied to a type of goose, *Branta leucopsis*, which according to medieval legend grew on trees or on logs of wood. Various fanciful versions of its reproductive cycle existed, among them that it emerged from a fruit or that it grew attached to a tree by its beak, but the most tenacious was that it developed inside small shellfish attached to wood, rocks, etc by the seashore. Hence by the end of the 16th century the term had come to be applied to these shellfish, and today that is its main sense. The word was originally *bernak* (it gained its *-le* ending in the 15th century) and came from medieval Latin *bernaca*, but its ultimate source is unknown.

**baron**    [12]    The earliest historical sense of *baron*, 'tenant under the feudal system who held his land and title directly from the king,' can be traced back to its probable source, medieval Latin *barō*, which originally meant simply 'man,' and hence 'vassal' or 'retainer.' The word was of course brought into English by the Normans, as Anglo-Norman *barun*, and from earliest times was used as a title for someone belonging to the lowest order of peerage. Some have suggested an ultimate Germanic origin, and compared Old High German *baro* 'freeman.'

**barque**    see EMBARK

**barrage**    see BAR

**barricade**    [17]    May 12, 1588 was known as *la journée des barricades* 'the day of the barricades,' because in the course of disturbances in Paris during the Huguenot wars, large barrels (French *barriques*) filled with earth, cobblestones, etc were hauled into the street on that day to form barricades – and the term has stuck ever since. *Barrique* itself was borrowed from Spanish *barrica* 'cask,' which was formed from the same stem as that from which English gets *barrel* [14]. It has been speculated that this was Vulgar Latin *\*barra* 'bar,' on the basis that barrels are made of 'bars' or 'staves.'

▶ bar, barrel

**barrier**    see BAR

**barrister**    [16]    A barrister is a lawyer who has been 'called to the bar' – that is, admitted to plead as an advocate in the superior courts of England and Wales. This notion derives from the ancient practice of having in the inns of court a partition separating senior members from students, which barrier the students metaphorically passed when they qualified. The ending *-ister* was probably added on the analogy of such words as *minister* and *chorister*.

▶ bar

**barrow**    [OE]    *Barrow* for carrying things and *barrow* the burial mound are two distinct words in English. The *barrow* of *wheelbarrow* is related to *bear* 'carry.' The Old English word, *bearwe*, came from the same Germanic base, *\*ber-* or *\*bar-*, as produced *bear*, and also *bier*. *Barrow* the burial mound, as erected by ancient peoples over a grave site, is related to German *berg* 'mountain, hill.' The Old English word, *beorg*, came from prehistoric Germanic *\*bergaz*.

▶ bear, bier

**base**    There are two distinct words *base* in English. *Base* meaning 'lower part, foundation' [14] came either via Old French *base* or was a direct anglicization of Latin *basis* (acquired by English in its unaltered form at around the same time). The Latin word in its turn came from Greek *básis*, which meant originally 'step' and came ultimately from the Indo-European base *\*gwm-*, from which English gets *come*; the semantic progression involved was 'going, stepping' to 'that on which one walks or stands' to 'pedestal.' The derivative *basement* [18] is Italian in origin (Italian *basamento* means 'base of a column'), but probably reached English via early modern Dutch *basement* 'foundation.'

*Base* meaning 'low' [14] comes via Old French *bas* from medieval Latin *bassus* 'short, low.' The ultimate antecedents of this are uncertain, although some have suggested a connection with *básson*, the comparative form of Greek *bathús* 'deep.' The adjective *bass* is historically the same word as *base*, but since the 16th century has been distinguished from it by spelling.

▶ basis / bass

**bashful**    see ABASH

**basilisk**    [14]    Greek *basilískos* meant literally 'little king' – it was a diminutive of *basiléus* 'king,' source also of English *basil* [15] (probably from the herb's use by the Greeks in certain royal potions) and of

English *basilica* [16] (a church built originally on the plan of a royal palace). The Greeks used it for a 'gold-crested wren,' but also for a type of serpent, and it is this latter use which developed into the fabulous monster of classical and medieval times, whose breath and glance could kill. The name was said by Pliny to be based on the fact that the basilisk had a crown-shaped mark on its head.

▶ basil, basilica

**basin** [13] *Basin* comes via Old French *bacin* from medieval Latin *\*bacchinus*, a derivative of Vulgar Latin *\*bacca* 'water vessel,' which may originally have been borrowed from Gaulish. The Old French diminutive *bacinet* produced English *basinet* 'helmet' [14] and, with a modification of the spelling, *bassinette* 'cradle' [19], which was originally applied in French to any vaguely basin-shaped object.

▶ basinet, bassinette

**bask** [14] When English first acquired this word, probably from Old Norse *bathask*, it was in the sense 'wallow in blood': 'seeing his brother basking in his blood,' John Lydgate, *Chronicles of Troy* 1430. It was not until the 17th century that the modern sense 'lie in pleasant warmth' became established: 'a fool, who laid him down, and basked him in the sun,' Shakespeare, *As You Like It* 1600. The word retains connotations of its earliest literal sense 'bathe' – Old Norse *bathask* was the reflexive form of *batha* 'bathe.'

▶ bathe

**basket** [13] *Basket* is something of a mystery word. It turns up in the 13th century in Old French and Anglo-Norman as *basket* and in Anglo-Latin as *baskettum*, but how it got there is far from clear. Some have suggested that Latin *bascauda* 'washing tub,' said by the Roman writer Martial to be of British origin (and thought by some etymologists to be possibly of Celtic origin), may be connected with it in some way, but no conclusive proof of this has ever been found.

**bass** *Bass* the fish [15] and *bass* the musical term [15] are of course completely unrelated words, with different pronunciations. *Bass* meaning 'of the lowest register' is simply a modified spelling of the adjective *base*, under the influence of Italian *basso*. Related words are *bassoon* [18], from French *basson*, and *basset-horn* [19], a partial translation of Italian *corno di bassetto*, literally 'bass horn.'

The bass is a spiny-finned fish, and it may be that its name is related to Old English *byrst* 'bristle.' The Old English term for the fish was *bærs*, which survived dialectally until the 19th century in the form *barse*, and it is thought that it goes back to a Germanic base *\*bars-* (source of German *barsch*); this may be cognate with *\*bors-*, from which Old English *byrst* came. In the 15th

century, *barse* underwent some sort of phonetic mutation to produce *bass*.

▶ base, bassoon

**bassinette** see BASIN

**bastard** [13] The idea underlying the word *bastard* appears to be that of a child born of an impromptu sexual encounter on an improvised bed, for it seems to echo Old French *fils de bast*, literally 'packsaddle son,' that is, one conceived on a packsaddle pillow. If this is the case, the word goes back to medieval Latin *bastum* 'packsaddle,' whose ultimate source was Greek *bastázein* 'carry'; this passed via Old French *bast*, later *bat*, into late Middle English as *bat*, which now survives only in *batman* [18]. The derived form is first found in medieval Latin as *bastardus*, and this reached English via Old French *bastard*. Its modern usage as a general term of abuse dates from the early 19th century.

▶ batman

**baste** There are two separate verbs *baste* in English, one meaning 'sew loosely' [14], the other 'moisten roasting meat with fat' [15]. The first comes from Old French *bastir*, which was acquired from a hypothetical Germanic *\*bastjan* 'join together with bast.' This was a derivative of *\*bastaz*, from which English gets *bast* 'plant fibre' [OE]. The origin of the second is far more obscure. It may come from an earlier *base*, with the past form *based* being interpreted as the present tense or infinitive.

**bat** *Bat* as in 'cricket bat' [OE] and *bat* the animal [16] come from entirely different sources. *Bat* the wooden implement first appears in late Old English as *batt* 'cudgel,' but it is not clear where it ultimately came from. Some have postulated a Celtic source, citing Gaulish *andabata* 'gladiator,' which may be related to English *battle* and Russian *bat* 'cudgel,' but whatever the word's origins, it seems likely that at some point it was influenced by Old French *batte*, from *battre* 'beat.'

The flying *bat* is an alteration of Middle English *backe*, which was borrowed from a Scandinavian language. The word is represented in Old Swedish *natbakka* 'night bat,' and appears to be an alteration of an earlier *-blaka*, as in Old Norse *lethrblaka*, literally 'leather-flapper.' If this is so, *bat* would mean etymologically 'flapper,' which would be of a piece with other names for the animal, particularly German *fledermaus* 'fluttermouse' and English *flittermouse*, which remained a dialectal word for 'bat' into the 20th century. It is unusual for the name of such a common animal not to go right back to Old English; in this case the Old English word was *hrēremūs*, which survived dialectally into the 20th century as *rearmouse*.

▶ battle

**batch** see BAKE

**bath** [OE] *Bath* is a word widely dispersed among the Germanic languages (German has *bad*, as does Swedish). Like the others, Old English *bæth* goes back to a hypothetical Germanic *batham*, which perhaps derives from the base *ba-* (on the suffix *-th* see BIRTH). If this is so, it would be an indication (backed up by other derivatives of the same base, such as *bake*, and cognate words such as Latin *fovēre* 'heat,' source of English *foment*) that the original notion contained in the word was of 'heat' rather than 'washing.' This is preserved in the *steam bath* and the *Turkish bath*. The original verbal derivative was *bathe*, which goes back to Germanic *bathōn* (another derivative of which, Old Norse *batha*, had a reflexive form *bathask*, which probably lies behind English *bask*); use of *bath* as a verb dates from the 15th century.

► bask, bathe

**bathos** [18] *Bathos*, the descent from the sublime to the commonplace, means etymologically 'depth.' It represents Greek *báthos*, a derivative of the adjective *bathús* 'deep' (which has also given English such technical terms as *bathyal* 'of the deep sea,' *bathymetry*, *bathyscaphe*, and *bathysphere*). The use of the word in English seems to have been initiated by the poet Alexander Pope (1688–1744), in his *Bathos*.

**batman**   see BASTARD

**battalion**   see BATTLE

**battery** [16] The original meaning of *battery* in English was literally 'hitting,' as in *assault and battery*. It came from Old French *batterie*, a derivative of *batre*, *battre* 'beat' (from which English also gets *batter* [14]). The ultimate source of this, and of English *battle*, was Latin *battuere* 'beat.' The development of the word's modern diversity of senses was via 'bombardment by artillery,' to 'unit of artillery,' to 'electric cell': it seems that this last meaning was inspired by the notion of 'discharge of electricity' rather than 'connected series of cells.'

► batter, battle

**battle** [13] English acquired *battle* via Old French *bataille* and Vulgar Latin *\*battālia* from late Latin *battuālia* 'fencing exercises.' This was a derivative of the verb *battuere* 'beat' (source also of English *batter* and *battery*), which some have viewed as of Celtic origin, citing Gaulish *andabata* 'gladiator,' a possible relative of English *bat*. Related words include *battalion* [16], ultimately from Italian *battaglione*, a derivative of *battaglia* 'battle'; *battlements* [14], from Old French *batailler* 'provide with *batailles* – fortifications or battlements'; and derivatives such as *abate*, *combat*, and *debate*.

► abate, bat, battalion, battery, combat, debate

**bawdy** [15] The adjective *bawdy* appears on the scene relatively late, but it is a derivative of *bawd* 'prostitute' or 'madam,' which entered English in the 14th century. Its origins are not altogether clear, but it appears to have come from the Old French adjective *baud*

'lively, merry, bold,' which in turn was probably acquired from Germanic *\*bald-*, source of English *bold*.

► bold

**bay** There are no fewer than six distinct words *bay* in English. The 'sea inlet' [14] comes via Old French *baie* from Old Spanish *bahia*. *Bay* as in *bay leaf* [14] comes from a different Old French word *baie*, whose source was Latin *bāca* 'berry.' The 'reddish-brown colour of a horse' [14] comes via Old French *bai* from Latin *badius*, which is related to Old Irish *buide* 'yellow.' The 'recessed area or compartment' [14] comes from yet another Old French *baie*, a derivative of the verb *bayer* 'gape, yawn,' from medieval Latin *batāre* (English acquired *abash* and *abeyance* from the same source, and it may also be represented in the first syllable of *beagle*). *Bay* 'bark' [14] comes from Old French *abaiier*, in which the element *-bai-* probably originated as an imitation of a dog howling. And it is the source of *bay* as in *at bay* [13] (from Old French *abai*), the underlying idea of which is that of a hunted animal finally turning and facing its barking pursuers.

► abash, abeyance, beagle

**bayonet** [17] *Bayonet* comes from French *bayonette*, an early spelling of what is now *baïonette*. The French term is traditionally derived from *Bayonne*, the name of a town and port on the southwest coast of France, near Biarritz, where bayonets were supposedly first used by Basques of the area, in the 17th century. But this etymology is not universally accepted, and some have noted the resemblance to Old French *bayon* 'crossbow bolt.'

**bazaar** [16] *Bazaar* is a word of Persian origin; it comes from Persian *bāzār* 'market' (whose ultimate source was a prehistoric Old Persian *\*abēcharish*), and reached English via Turkish and Italian (whence the early English form *bazarro*). Many fanciful spellings competed in 16th- and 17th-century English, including *buzzard*.

**be** [OE] There are four distinct components that go to make up the modern English verb *be*. The infinitive form *be* comes ultimately from an Indo-European base *\*bheu-*, *\*bhu-*, which also produced, by other routes, *future* and *physical*. Its Germanic descendent was *\*bu-*, which signified on the one hand 'dwell' (from which we get *booth*, *bower*, *byre*, *build*, *burly*, *byelaw*, and the final element of *neighbour*), and on the other hand 'grow, become,' which led to its adoption as part of the verb expressing 'being' (in Old English particularly with the future sense of 'coming to be').

*Am* and *is* go back to the ancient Indo-European verb 'be,' *\*es-* or *\*s-*, which has contributed massively to 'be' verbs throughout all Indo-European languages (third person present singulars Greek *esti*, Latin *est*, French *est*, German *ist*, Sanskrit *ásti*, Welsh *ys*, for example). The Indo-European first and third person singular forms were, respectively, *ésmi* and *ésti*.

For the present plural Old English used the related *sind(on)* (as found in Latin *sunt*, French *sont*, and German *sind*), but this died out in the 12th century, to be replaced by *are*, which comes from a Germanic base *\*ar-* of unknown origin. From the same source is the now archaic second person singular *art*.

The past tense forms *was*, *were* come ultimately from an Indo-European base *\*wes-* which meant 'dwell, remain.' Related words in other Indo-European languages include Sanskrit *vásati* 'dwell, remain' and Gothic *wisan* 'remain, continue.'

▶ booth, bower, build, burly, byelaw, byre

**beach**   [16]   *Beach* is a mystery word. When it first turns up, in the dialect of the southeast corner of England, it means 'shingle'; and since long stretches of the seashore in Sussex and Kent are pebbly, it is a natural extension that the word for 'shingle' should come to be used for 'shore.' Its ultimate source is obscure, but some etymologists have suggested a connection with Old English *bæce* or *bece* 'stream' (a relative of English *beck* [14]), on the grounds that the new meaning could have developed from the notion of the 'pebbly bed of a stream.'

▶ beck

**beacon**   [OE]   In Old English, *bēacen* meant simply 'sign'; it did not develop its modern senses 'signal fire' and 'lighthouse' until the 14th century. Its source is West Germanic *\*baukna*, from which English also gets *beckon* [OE].

▶ beckon

**bead**   [13]   The word *bead* originally meant 'prayer.' It comes ultimately from Germanic *\*beth-*, source also of English *bid*. This passed into Old English as *gebed*, which by the 13th century had lost its prefix to become *bede*. (German has the parallel *gebet* 'prayer.') The modern sense 'small pierced decorative ball' developed in the 14th century, from the use of a string of rosary beads for counting while saying one's prayers.

▶ bid

**beadle**   see BID

**beagle**   [15]   The likeliest source of *beagle* appears to be Old French *becgueule* 'noisy person' (the supposition is that the dog had the term applied to it because of its loud bark). *Becgueule* itself was probably a compound formed from *beer* 'gape, yawn' (source also of English *abash* and *abeyance* and, in its later form *bayer*, of English *bay* 'recessed area') and *gueule* 'throat' (related to English *gullet*).

▶ abash, abeyance, bay, bullet

**beak**   [13]   English acquired *beak* via Old French *bec* from Latin *beccus*, which was probably borrowed from some Gaulish word (the original Latin word for 'beak' was *rostrum*). The Roman historian Suetonius

(c. 69–140AD) tells of one Antonius Primus, a native of Toulouse, who was nicknamed as a boy *Beccus*, 'that is, hen's beak.' The Old English term for 'beak' was *bile* 'bill.'

▶ soubriquet

**beaker**   [14]   The immediate source of *beaker* was Old Norse *bikarr*. It is widespread in the West Germanic languages (German has *becher*, for instance), and it seems likely that Old Norse acquired it from Old Saxon *bikeri*. But it was borrowed into prehistoric West Germanic from medieval Latin *bicarius*, which in turn goes back to Greek *bikos* 'earthenware jug' (ultimate source of English *pitcher* [13]).

▶ pitcher

**beam**   [OE]   In Old English times the word *bēam* (like modern German *baum*) meant 'tree' – a signification preserved in tree-names such as *hornbeam* and *whitebeam*. But already before the year 1000 the extended meanings we are familiar with today – 'piece of timber' and 'ray of light' – had started to develop. Related forms in other Germanic languages (which include, as well as German *baum*, Dutch *boom*, from which English gets *boom* 'spar' [16]) suggest a West Germanic ancestor *\*bauma*, but beyond that all is obscure.

▶ boom

**bean**   [OE]   The word *bean* (Old English *bēan*) has relatives in several Germanic languages (German *bohne*, Dutch *boon*, Swedish *böna*), pointing to a common West and North Germanic source *\*baunō*, but that is as far back in history as we can pursue it.

*Beanfeast* [19] apparently derived from the practice of serving bacon and beans (or, according to some, bean geese, a species of goose) at the annual dinners given by firms to their employees in the 19th century. *Beano*, originally a printers' abbreviation, appears towards the end of the 19th century.

**bear**   [OE]   The two English words *bear* 'carry' and *bear* the animal come from completely different sources. The verb, Old English *beran*, goes back via Germanic *\*ber-* to Indo-European *\*bher-*, which already contained the two central meaning elements that have remained with its offspring ever since, 'carry' and 'give birth.' It is the source of a very large number of words in the Indo-European languages, including both Germanic (German *gebären* 'give birth,' Swedish *börd* 'birth') and non-Germanic (Latin *ferre* and Greek *phérein* 'bear,' source of English *fertile* and *amphora* [17], and Russian *brat* 'seize'). And a very large number of other English words are related to it: on the 'carrying' side, *barrow*, *berth*, *bier*, *burden*, and possibly *brim*; and on the 'giving birth' side, *birth* itself and *bairn* 'child' [16]. *Borne* and *born* come from *boren*, the Old English past participle of *bear*; the distinction in usage between the two (*borne* for 'carried,' *born* for 'given birth') arose in the early 17th century.

Etymologically, the bear is a 'brown animal.' Old 'English *bera* came from West Germanic *\*bero* (whence also German *bär* and Dutch *beer*), which may in turn go back to Indo-European *\*bheros*, related to English *brown*. The poetic name for the bear, *bruin* [17], follows the same semantic pattern (it comes from Dutch *bruin* 'brown'), and *beaver* means etymologically 'brown animal' too.

▶ amphora, bairn, barrow, berth, bier, born, burden, fertile, fortune, paraphernalia, suffer / brown

**beard** [OE] Old English *beard* came from West Germanic *\*bartha*, which was also the source of German *bart* and Dutch *baard*. A close relative of this was Latin *barba* 'beard,' which gave English *barb* [14] (via Old French *barbe*), *barber* [13] (ultimately from medieval Latin *barbātor*, originally a 'beard-trimmer'), and *barbel* [14], a fish with sensitive whisker-like projections round its mouth (from late Latin *barbellus*, a diminutive form of *barbus* 'barbel,' which was derived from *barba*).

▶ barb, barber

**beast** [13] *Beast* replaced *deer* as the general word for 'animal' in the 13th century (*deer* of course remained in use for antlered animals of the family Cervidae), and was itself replaced by *animal* in the 17th century. It entered English via Old French *beste* from Latin *bēstia* (source of English *bestial* [14]).

▶ bestial

**beat** [OE] Old English *bēatan* and the related Old Norse *bauta* may be traced back to a prehistoric Germanic *\*bautan*. It has been conjectured that this could be connected with *\*fu-*, the base of Latin *confūtāre* and *refūtāre* (source respectively of English *confute* [16] and *refute* [16]) and of Latin *fustis* 'club' (from which English gets *fusty* [14]).

▶ beetle, confute, fusty, refute

**beauty** [13] *Beauty* came via Anglo-Norman *beute* and Old French *bealte* from Vulgar Latin *\*bellitas*, a derivative of Latin *bellus* 'beautiful' (this developed from an earlier, unrecorded *\*dwenolos*, a diminutive form of Old Latin *\*duenos*, *\*duonos*, which is related to Latin *bonus* 'good' – source of English *bonus* [18], *bounty* [13], and *bounteous* [14]). Other English words from the same ultimate source are *beau* [17] and its feminine form *belle* [17]; *beatific* [17], which comes from Latin *beātus* 'blessed, happy,' the past participle of the verb *beāre*, a relative of *bellus*; *embellish*; and *bibelot* 'small ornament' [19], originally a French word based ultimately on *\*belbel*, a reduplication of Old French *bel* 'beautiful.' English *beautiful* is 15th century.

▶ beau, belle, beatific, bibelot, bonus, bounty, embellish

**beaver** [OE] Like *bear*, *beaver* appears to mean etymologically 'brown animal.' Old English *beofor* or *befor* came from a prehistoric West and North Germanic *\*bebruz*, which in turn went back to an Indo-European *\*bhebhrús*, a derivative of the base *\*bhru-* 'brown.' Other words for 'beaver' from the same source include Czech *bobr*, Lithuanian *bebrùs*, and Latin *fiber*.

**because** [14] *Because* originated in the phrase *by cause*, which was directly modelled on French *par cause*. At first it was always followed by *of* or by a subordinate clause introduced by *that* or *why*: 'The Holy Ghost was not yet given; because that Jesus was not yet glorified,' *St John's Gospel*, 7:39, 1611. But already by the end of the 14th century *that* and *why* were beginning to be omitted, leaving *because* to function as a conjunction, a move which would perhaps have exercised contemporary linguistic purists as much as 'The reason is because . . . ' does today. The abbreviated form '*cause* first appears in print in the 16th century.

▶ cause

**beckon** see BEACON

**become** [OE] *Become* is a compound verb found in other Germanic languages (German *bekommen*, for instance, and Dutch *bekomen*), which points to a prehistoric Germanic source *\*bikweman*, based on *\*kweman*, source of English *come*. Originally it meant simply 'come, arrive,' but the modern senses 'come to be' and 'be suitable' had developed by the 12th century. A parallel semantic development occurred in French: Latin *dēvenīre* meant 'come,' but its modern French descendant *devenir* means 'become.'

▶ come

**bed** [OE] *Bed* is common throughout the Germanic languages (German *bett*, Dutch *bed*), and comes from a prehistoric Germanic *\*bathjam*. Already in Old English times the word meant both 'place for sleeping' and 'area for growing plants,' and if the latter is primary, it could mean that the word comes ultimately from the Indo-European base *\*bhodh-*, source of Latin *fodere* 'dig' (from which English gets *fosse* and *fossil*), and that the underlying notion of a bed was therefore originally of a sleeping place dug or scraped in the ground, like an animal's lair.

▶ fosse, fossil

**bedizen** see DISTAFF

**bedlam** [15] The word *bedlam* is a contraction of *Bethlehem*. It comes from the Hospital of St Mary of Bethlehem founded in 1247 by Simon FitzMary, Sheriff of London, as the Priory of St Mary Bethlehem. Situated outside Bishopsgate, in the City of London, the hospital began to admit mental patients in the late 14th century. In the 16th century it officially became a lunatic asylum. The word *bedlam* came to be used for any 'madhouse,' and by extension for a 'scene of noisy confusion,' in the 17th century.

**bee** [OE]  Old English *bēo* 'bee' came from a prehistoric West and North Germanic *\*bīōn*, source also of German *biene*, Dutch *bij*, and Swedish *bi*, which may all be traceable back to an Indo-European base *\*bhi-* 'quiver.' This, if it is true, means that the *bee* was originally named as the 'quivering,' or perhaps 'humming' insect. Latin *fucus* 'drone' appears to be related.

**beech** [OE]  Like many other tree-names, *beech* goes back a long way into the past, and is not always what it seems. Among early relatives Latin *fāgus* meant 'beech' (whence the tree's modern scientific name), but Greek *phāgós*, for example, referred to an 'edible oak.' Both come from a hypothetical Indo-European *\*bhagos*, which may be related to Greek *phagein* 'eat' (which enters into a number of English compounds, such as *phagocyte* [19], literally 'eating-cell,' *geophagy* [19], 'earth-eating,' and *sarcophagus*). If this is so, the name may signify etymologically 'edible tree,' with reference to its nuts, 'beech mast.' The Old English word *bēce*'s immediate source was Germanic *\*bōkjōn*, but this was a derivative; the main form *bōkō* produced words for 'beech' in other Germanic languages, such as German *buche* and Dutch *beuk*, and it survives in English as the first element of *buckwheat* [16], so named from its three-sided seeds which look like beech nuts. It is thought that *book* may come ultimately from *bōk-* 'beech,' on the grounds that early runic inscriptions were carved on beechwood tablets.

▶ book, buckwheat, phagocyte, sarcophagus

**beef** [13]  Like *mutton, pork,* and *veal, beef* was introduced by the Normans to provide a dainty alternative to the bare animal names *ox, cow,* etc when referring to their meat. Anglo-Norman and Old French *boef* or *buef* (which of course became modern French *boeuf*) came from Latin *bov-*, the stem of *bōs* 'ox,' from which English gets *bovine* [19] and *Bovril* [19]. *Bōs* itself is actually related etymologically to *cow*.

The compound *beefeater* 'yeoman warder of the Tower of London' was coined in the 17th century; it was originally a contemptuous term for a 'well-fed servant.'

▶ bovine, cow

**beer** [OE]  Originally, *beer* was probably simply a general term for a 'drink': it seems to have come from late Latin *biber* 'drink,' which was a derivative of the verb *bibere* 'drink' (from which English gets *beverage, bibulous, imbibe,* and possibly also *bibber*). The main Old English word for 'beer' was *ale*, and *beer* (Old English *bēor*) is not very common until the 15th century. A distinction between hopped *beer* and unhopped *ale* arose in the 16th century.

▶ beverage, bibulous, imbibe

**beetle** English has three separate words *beetle*. The commonest, *beetle* the insect, comes from Old

English *bitula*, which was a derivative of the verb *bītan* 'bite': *beetle* hence means etymologically 'the biter.' *Beetle* 'hammer,' now largely restricted to various technical contexts, is also Old English: the earliest English form, *bētel*, goes back to a prehistoric Germanic *\*bautilaz*, a derivative of the verb *\*bautan*, from which English gets *beat* (the cognate Old Norse *beytill* meant 'penis'). The adjective *beetle* [14], as in 'beetle brows,' and its related verb are of unknown origin, although it has been speculated that there is some connection with the tufted antennae of certain species of beetle, which may suggest eyebrows.

▶ bite / beat

**before** [OE]  *Before* is a Germanic compound, made up of *\*bi-* 'by' and *\*forana* 'from the front' (the resulting *\*biforana* entered Old English as *beforan*). The second element, *\*forana*, is a derivative of *\*fora*, source of English *for*; this originally meant 'before,' and only gradually developed the senses we are familiar with today.

▶ for

**beg** [OE]  *Beg* first turns up in immediately recognizable form in the 13th century, as *beggen*, but it seems likely that it goes back ultimately to an Old English verb *bedecian* 'beg.' This came from the Germanic base *\*beth-*, from which English also gets *bid*.

▶ bid

**begin** [OE]  *Begin* comes from a prehistoric West Germanic compound verb *\*biginnan*, which also produced German and Dutch *beginnen*; the origin of the second element, *\*ginnan*, is not known for certain. The form *gin* was common in the Middle Ages and up until about 1600; this was a shortening, perhaps not so much of *begin* as of the now obsolete *ongin* 'begin,' which was far more widespread than *begin* in Old English.

**behalf** [14]  *Behalf* was compounded from the prefix *be-* 'by' and the noun *half*, in the sense 'side.' The latter had been used in such phrases as *on my half*, that is, 'on my side, for my part,' since late Old English times, and the new compound began to replace it in the 14th century. (That particular use of *half* had died out by the end of the 16th century.) The modern sense of 'representing or in the interests of someone' was present from the beginning.

▶ half

**behave** [15]  To 'behave oneself' originally meant literally to 'have oneself in a particular way' – *have* being used here in the sense 'hold' or 'comport.' The *be-* is an intensive prefix. Of particular interest is the way in which the word preserves in aspic the 15th-century pronunciation of *have* in stressed contexts. For much of its history *behave* has been used with reference to a person's bearing and public dignity ('He was some years a Captain, and behaved himself with great gallantry in several engagements,' Richard Steele, *Spectator*

Number 2, 1711), and the modern connotations of propriety, of 'goodness' versus 'naughtiness,' are a relatively recent, 19th-century development.

The noun *behaviour* [15] was formed on analogy with the verb from an earlier *haviour*, a variant of *aver* 'possession' [14], from the nominal use of the Old French verb *aveir* 'have.'

▶ have

**behind** [OE] *Behind* was compounded in Old English times from the prefix *bi-* 'by' and *hindan* 'from behind.' This second element, and the related Old English *hinder* 'below,' have relatives in other Germanic languages (German *hinten* and *hinter* 'behind,' for example), and are connected with the English verb *hinder*, but their ultimate history is unclear. Modern English *hind* 'rear' may come mainly from *behind*.

▶ hind, hinder

**behold** see HOLD

**belch** [OE] *Belch* first appears in recognizable form in the 15th century, but it can scarcely not be related to *belk* 'eructate,' which goes back to Old English *bealcan* and survived dialectally into the modern English period. *Belch* itself may derive either from an unrecorded variant of *bealcan*, *\*belcan* (with the *c* here representing a /ch/ sound), or from a related Old English verb *belcettan* 'eructate.' But whichever route it took, its ultimate source was probably a Germanic base *\*balk-* or *\*belk-*, from which German got *bölken* 'bleat, low, belch.' *Belch* was originally a perfectly inoffensive word; it does not seem to have been until the 17th century that its associations began to drag it down towards vulgarity.

**beleaguer** see LAIR

**belfry** [13] Etymologically, *belfry* has nothing to do with *bells*; it was a chance similarity between the two words that led to *belfry* being used from the 15th century onwards for 'bell-tower.' The original English form was *berfrey*, and it meant 'movable seige-tower.' It came from Old French *berfrei*, which in turn was borrowed from a hypothetical Frankish *\*bergfrith*, a compound whose two elements mean respectively 'protect' (English gets *bargain, borough, borrow,* and *bury* from the same root) and 'peace, shelter' (hence German *friede* 'peace'); the underlying sense of the word is thus the rather tautological 'protective shelter.' A tendency to break down the symmetry between the two *r*s in the word led in the 15th century to the formation of *belfrey* in both English and French (*l* is phonetically close to *r*), and at around the same time we find the first reference to it meaning 'bell-tower,' in *Promptorium parvulorum* 1440, an early English-Latin dictionary: 'Bellfray, *campanarium*.'

▶ affray, bargain, borrow, borough, bury, neighbour

**believe** [OE] *Believing* and *loving* are closely allied. Late Old English *beléfan* took the place of an earlier *geléfan* 'believe' (with the associative prefix *ge-*), which can be traced back to a prehistoric West and North Germanic *\*galaubjan* (source also of German *glauben* 'believe'). This meant 'hold dear, love,' and hence 'trust in, believe,' and it was formed on a base, *\*laub-*, which also produced, by various routes, English *love, lief* 'dear,' *leave* 'permission,' and the second element of *furlough*.

▶ furlough, leave, lief, love

**bell** [OE] The Old English word was *belle*. Apart from Dutch *bel* it has no relatives in the other main European languages (many of them use words related to English *clock* for 'bell': French *cloche*, for instance, and German *glocke*). It has been speculated that it may be connected with the verb *bell*, used of the baying call made by a hound or stag, which itself is perhaps related to *bellow*, a descendant of a hypothetical Old English *\*belgan*. The ultimate source may possibly be the same as for *bellows*.

▶ bellow

**belle** see BEAUTY

**bellicose** see REBEL

**belligerent** see REBEL

**bellows** [OE] *Bellows* and *belly* were originally the same word, Old English *belig*, which meant 'bag.' This was used in the compound *blǣstbelig*, literally 'blowing bag,' a device for blowing a fire, which was replaced in the late Old English period by the plural form of the noun, *belga* or *belgum*, from which we get *bellows*. Meanwhile the meaning of *belly* developed from 'bag' to, in the 13th century, 'body' and, in the 14th century, 'abdomen.' Ultimately the word goes back to Germanic *\*balgiz* 'bag,' from the base *\*balg-* or *\*belg-* (itself a descendant of Indo-European *\*bhel-* 'swell'), which also lies behind *billow* [16], *bolster*, and possibly *bellow* and *bell*.

▶ bell, bellow, belly, billow, bold, bolster

**belong** [14] Old English had a verb *langian*, meaning 'pertain to.' It had no immediate connection with the other Old English verb *langian*, modern English *long*, 'desire,' but came from the Old English adjective *gelang* 'pertaining, belonging' (although ultimately this *gelang* and the modern English adjective and verb *long* come from the same Germanic source, *\*langgaz*). The intensive prefix *be-* was added in the 14th century.

▶ long

**below** [14] *Below* is a lexicalization of the phrase *by low*, replacing an earlier *on low*, the opposite of *on high*. It was perhaps modelled on *beneath*.

▶ low

**belt** [OE] Old English *belt* and related Germanic forms such as Swedish *bälte* point to a source in Germanic *\*baltjaz*, which was borrowed from Latin *balteus*, possibly a word of Etruscan origin. The verbal idiom *belt up* 'be quiet' appears to date from just before World War II.

**bench**   [OE]   Old English *benc* goes back to Germanic *\*bangk-*, also the source of English *bank* (the related German *bank* means 'bench'). The Northern and Scottish English versions of the word were *benk* and *bink*. The specific application to the seat on which a judge sits arose in the 13th century.

▸bank

**bend**   [OE]   English *band, bend, bind, bond*, and *bundle* are closely allied: all go back to a prehistoric Germanic base *\*band-*. The relationship in meaning was, in the case of *bend*, more obvious in Old English times, when *bendan* meant 'tie up' as well as 'curve' (a sense preserved in the modern English noun *bend* 'knot,' as in *carrick bend*). The rather strange-seeming meaning development appears to have come about as follows: *bend* in the sense 'tie, constrain' was used for the pulling of bow-strings, with reference to the strain or tension thereby applied to the bow; the natural consequence of this was of course that the bow curved, and hence (although not until the late 13th century) *bend* came to be used for 'curve.'

▸band, bind, bond, bundle

**beneath**   [OE]   *Beneath* is a compound adverb and preposition, formed in Old English from *bi* 'by' and *nithan* or *neothan* 'below.' This came originally from Germanic *\*nith-* (also the source of *nether* [OE]), a derivative of the base *\*ni-* 'down.'

▸nether

**benefit**   [14]   The element *bene-* occurs in a wide variety of English words. It comes from Latin *bene* 'well,' a close relative of Latin *bonus* 'good.' Amongst its combinations are *benediction* [15], literally 'saying well,' hence 'blessing,' *benefaction* 'doing well' [17], and *benevolent* 'wishing well' [15]. *Benefit* is related to *benefaction*, since it too comes ultimately from Latin *bene facere*, but it took a more indirect route to English, from Latin *benefactum* 'good deed' via Old French *bienfait* and Anglo-Norman *benfet*.

**benzene**   [19]   The original name given to this hydrocarbon, by the German chemist Eilhardt Mitscherlich in 1833, was *benzine*. He based it on the term *benzoic acid*, a derivative of *benzoin*, the name of a resinous substance exuded by trees of the genus *Styrax*. This came ultimately from Arabic *lubān-jāwī*, literally 'frankincense of Java' (the trees grow in Southeast Asia). When the expression was borrowed into the Romance languages, the initial *lu-*was apprehended as the definite article, and dropped (ironically, since in so many Arabic words which *do* contain the article *al*, it has been retained as part and parcel of the word – see ALGEBRA). This produced a variety of forms, including French *benjoin*, Portuguese *beijoim*, and Italian *benzoi*.

English probably acquired the word mainly from French (a supposition supported by the folk-etymological alteration *benjamin* which was in common use in English from the end of the 16th century), but took the *z* from the Italian form.

Meanwhile, back with *benzine*, in the following year, 1834, the German chemist Justus von Liebig proposed the alternative name *benzol*; and finally, in the 1870s, the chemist A W Hofmann regularized the form to currently accepted chemical nomenclature as *benzene*.

▸benzol

**bequeath**   [OE]   Etymologically, what you bequeath is what you 'say' you will leave someone in your will. The word comes from Old English *becwethan*, a derivative of *cwethan* 'say,' whose past tense *cwæth* gives us *quoth* (it is no relation to *quote*, by the way). The original sense 'say, utter' died out in the 13th century, leaving the legal sense of 'transferring by will' (first recorded in 1066).

The noun derivative of Old English *cwethan* in compounds was *-cwiss*. Hence we can assume there was an Old English noun *\*becwiss*, although none is recorded. The first we hear of it is at the beginning of the 14th century, when it had unaccountably had a *t* added to it, producing what we now know as *bequest*.

▸bequest, quoth

**berate**   see RATE

**bereave**   see ROB

**beret**   [19]   The beret originated in the southwestern corner of France, worn by the farmers and peasants of Gascony, and the word for it comes from the southwestern dialect term *berret* (it reached English via mainstream French *béret*). It derives from Latin *birrus* 'hooded cloak,' which is probably of Celtic origin (Middle Irish *berr* 'short' has been compared), and is thus a relative of *biretta* [16], the term for the square cap worn by Roman Catholic clergy, formed as a diminutive of *birrus* in Italian (*berretta*) and Spanish (*birreta*).

▸biretta

**berry**   [OE]   *Berry* is a strictly Germanic word, not found in other branches of Indo-European (German has *beere*, Dutch *bes*, and Danish *bær*). Its earliest application seems to have been specifically to grapes: the only record of it in Old Saxon and Gothic is in the compound 'wineberry,' and around 1000 Aelfric translated *Deuteronomy* 23:24 into Old English as 'If you go into your friend's vineyard, eat the berries.' But by the Middle Ages the term had broadened out to encompass the sorts of fruit we would recognize today as *berries*. The word goes back ultimately to a prehistoric Germanic *\*basj-*, which it has been speculated may be related to Old English *basu* 'red.'

**berserk**   [19]   Sir Walter Scott appears to be responsible for introducing this word to the English language. He mentions it in a footnote to his novel *The pirate* 1822, adopting it (in the form *berserkar*) from the Icelandic *berserkr* 'frenzied Norse warrior.' Its etymology is not altogether clear. Its second syllable represents *serkr* 'coat, shirt' (a word English used to have, as *sark*: *cutty sark* meant 'short shirt'), but the first is disputed. Scott took it to mean 'bare' (which would have been Icelandic *berr*), and in fact the anglicized form *baresark* was quite commonly used in the mid 19th century; the plausible-sounding notion underlying this is that the original *berserkr* was so called because in his battle-crazed frenzy he tore off his armour and fought in his shirt-sleeves – 'bare-shirted.' However, 20th-century etymologists have tended to prefer the theory that *ber-* is 'bear,' representing Icelandic *bern-*, a by-form of *bjorn* 'bear.' The concept of warriors dressing themselves in animals' skins is an ancient one, found in many mythologies.

The modern use of the word as an adjective, meaning 'in a violent frenzy,' appears to date from the third quarter of the 19th century.

**berth** [17] Like *birth*, *berth* appears to be based on the verb *bear*, although it is a separate and much later formation. At first it meant 'safe manoeuvring distance at sea' (from which we get the metaphorical 'give a wide berth to'); this seems to have come from the nautical sense of *bear* 'steer in a particular direction' as in *bear away* (from which we get *bear down on*, as well as more general applications, such as 'bear left'). This led, via 'convenient space for a ship to moor,' to, in the 18th century, the more familiar modern senses 'sleeping place on a ship' and 'job, situation (originally on board ship).'
▶ bear, birth

**beseech** see SEEK

**beside** [13] *Beside* was a Middle English lexicalization of the Old English phrase *be sīdan*, literally 'by the side of.' The *-s* of *besides* is a survival of the genitive ending added to certain adverbs in the Old English and early Middle English period (such as *always*). The metaphorical *beside oneself* originated in the 15th century.
▶ side

**best** [OE] *Best* and *better*, the anomalous superlative and comparative of *good*, go back to a prehistoric Germanic base *\*bat-*, which is related to the archaic English *boot* 'remedy' (as in *to boot*) and meant generally 'advantage, improvement.' Its comparative and superlative were *\*batizon* and *\*batistaz*, which came into Old English as respectively *betera* and *betest* (gradually reduced via *betst* to *best*).

The term *best man* originated in Scotland; it has gradually replaced the earlier *bride(s)man* and *groomsman*.
▶ better, boot

**bestial** see BEAST

**bet** [16] Since its comparatively late arrival, *bet* has ousted the earlier *lay, wager*, and *game* as the main term for 'risking money on an uncertain outcome' (*gamble* is later still). It is by no means clear where it came from; the usual explanation is that it is short for the noun *abet*, in the sense 'instigation, encouragement, support' – that is, one is giving one's 'support' to that which one thinks, or hopes, may happen in the future (*abet* itself comes from the Old French verb *abeter*, and is related to English *bait*). It first appears in Robert Greene's *Art of Cony Catching* 1592, which suggests an origin in the argot of small-time Elizabethan criminals.
▶ abet, bait, bite

**betray** [13] *Betray* is an English formation based on the Old French verb *traïr* 'betray,' which came from Latin *tradere* 'hand over, deliver up' (originally a compound formed from *trans-* 'across' and *dāre* 'give'). The noun formed from *tradere* was *trāditiō*, from which English gets, directly, *tradition*, and indirectly, via Old French and Anglo-Norman, the appropriate *treason*.
▶ tradition, treason

**betroth** see TRUE

**between** [OE] The second syllable of *between* is related to *two* and *twin*; the word as a whole seems to represent an original phrase meaning something like 'by two each.' Old English *betwēonum* reflects a Germanic *\*twēon*, reduced from an earlier *\*twikhnai*; this represents the base *\*twīkh-* (from which we get *two*) plus an *-n* suffix with apparently some sort of distributive function. The related *betwixt* comes ultimately from Germanic *\*twa* 'two' and the element *\*-isk-* '-ish.'
▶ twin, two

**beverage** [13] *Beverage* goes back to Latin *bibere* 'drink,' from which English also gets *imbibe* [14], *bibulous* [17], *beer*, and probably *bibber*. From the verb was formed the Vulgar Latin noun *\*biberāticum* 'something to drink,' and hence, via Old French *bevrage*, English *beverage*. The colloquial abbreviation *bevvy* is at least 100 years old (it has been speculated, but never proved, that *bevy* 'large group' [15] comes from the same source).
▶ beer, bevy, bib, bibulous, imbibe

**beware** see WARE

**bewilder** see WILD

**beyond** [OE] *Beyond* is a lexicalization of the Old English phrase *be geondan* 'from the farther side.' The second element comes from a prehistoric Germanic *\*jandana*, formed on a base *\*jan-* which also gave English the now largely dialectal *yon* [OE] and *yonder* [13]. To German it contributed the demonstrative adjective and pronoun *jener* 'that,' and there are related demonstrative forms without the initial *j-* in other Indo-European languages, including non-Germanic ones (Old Slavonic *onu* 'that,' for instance, and Sanskrit *āna-* 'this one').

▶ yon, yonder

**bias**   [16]   English acquired *bias* from Old French *biais*, but its previous history is uncertain. It probably came via Old Provençal, but where from? Speculations include Latin *bifacem* 'looking two ways,' from *bi-* 'two' and *faciēs* 'face,' and Greek *epikársios* 'oblique.' When the word first entered English it meant simply 'oblique line,' but by the end of the 16th century it was being applied more specifically to the game of bowls, in the sense of the 'bowl's curved path,' and also the 'unequal weighting given to the bowl in order to achieve such a path.' The modern figurative senses 'inclination' and 'prejudice' derive from this.

**bib**   [16]   The word *bib* is first mentioned in John Baret's *Quadruple dictionarie* 1580, where it is described as being 'for a child's breast.' It appears to come from the now archaic verb *bib* (as in *wine-bibber*), perhaps from the notion that the bib protects the baby's clothes as it drinks. The verb itself is possibly from Latin *bibere* 'drink,' source of *beer, beverage, bibulous,* and *imbibe*.

▶ beer, bibulous, imbibe

**bibelot**   see BEAUTY

**bible**   [13]   Greek *ta biblía* meant literally 'the books.' This was borrowed into ecclesiastical Latin as *biblia*, where the plural form came to be misanalysed as a feminine singular; hence Old French, and through it English, received *bible* as a singular noun. Greek *biblía* itself was the plural of *biblíon* 'book' (whence English *bibliography* [17]), which was originally a diminutive form of *bíblos* or *búblos*. This was used for 'book,' and for the book's forerunners, such as scrolls and papyri. It may come from *Bublos*, an ancient Phoenician port from which papyrus was exported to Greece.

▶ bibliography

**bicycle**   [19]   The word *bicycle*, literally 'two-wheeled' (from Greek *kúklos* 'circle, wheel'), was originally coined in French, and first appeared in English in 1868, in the 7 September edition of the *Daily News*: 'bysicles and trysicles which we saw in the Champs Élysées and the Bois de Boulogne this summer.' This reflects the fact that it was in the 1860s that the bicycle first assumed the form we know it in today, with pedals and cranks driving the front wheel. (Slightly earlier was the now obsolete *velocipede*, literally 'swift foot,' first applied to pedal bicycles and tricycles around 1850. Until the introduction of pneumatic tyres in the 1880s, the new cycles were known as *bone-shakers* – a term first encountered in 1874.)

▶ cycle, wheel

**bid**   [OE]   *Bid* has a complicated history, for it comes from what were originally two completely dis-

tinct Old English verbs. The main one was *biddan* (past tense *bæd*) 'ask, demand,' from which we get such modern English usages as 'I bade him come in.' It goes back to a prehistoric Germanic *\*bithjan* (source of German *bitten* 'ask'), which was formed from the base *\*beth-* (from which modern English gets *bead*). But a contribution to the present nexus of meanings was also made by Old English *bēodan* (past tense *bēad*) 'offer, proclaim' (whence 'bid at an auction' and so on). This can be traced ultimately to an Indo-European base *\*bh(e)udh-*, which gave Germanic *\*buth-*, source also of German *bieten* 'offer' and perhaps of English *beadle* [13], originally 'one who proclaims.'

▶ bead, beadle

**bide**   [OE]   *Bide* appears to be related ultimately to Old English *bēodan*, partial source of modern English *bid*, but exactly how is not clear. It comes from a lengthened version of the same stem, producing a hypothetical Germanic *\*bīthan*, and to all outward appearances is connected with such non-Germanic forms as Latin *fīdere* and Greek *peithésthai*; but as these mean 'believe, trust,' it is not easy to reconstruct a semantic connection with *bide* 'remain.' *Bide* itself is now little used, except in 'bide one's time,' but the derived *abide* [OE] remains current, especially in the sense 'endure,' as does the noun formed from it, *abode* [13].

▶ abide, abode, bid

**bier**   [OE]   Etymologically, a *bier* is 'something used for carrying.' It comes from West Germanic *\*bērō*, a derivative of the same base (*\*ber-*) as produced the verb *bear*. Its Old English form was *bēr*, and it was not spelled with an *i* until the 16th century. The original general sense 'framework for carrying something' (which it shares with the etymologically related *barrow*) died out around 1600, but already by about 1000 the modern specific meaning 'stand for a coffin' had developed.

▶ barrow, bear

**bifurcate**   see FORK

**big**   [13]   *Big* is one of the notorious mystery words of English etymology – extremely common in the modern language, but of highly dubious origin. In its earliest use in English it meant 'powerful, strong,' and it is not really until the 16th century that we get unequivocal examples of it in the modern sense 'large.' It occurs originally in northern texts, only slowly spreading south, which suggests that it may be of Scandinavian origin; some have compared Norwegian dialect *bugge* 'important man.'

**bight**   see BOW

**bigot**   [16]   According to the 12th-century Anglo-Norman chronicler Wace, *bigot* was a contemptuous term applied by the French to the Normans, but it is far from clear where this came from, whether it is the same word as present-day *bigot*, and, if it is, how it came to mean 'narrow-minded person.' All that can be said for certain is that the word first turned up in its modern form in the 15th century as French *bigot*, from which English borrowed it.

**bigwig**   see WIG

**bikini**   [20]   For Frenchmen, the sight of the first minimal two-piece swimming costumes for women produced by fashion designers in 1947 was as explosive as the test detonation of an atom bomb by the USA at Bikini Atoll in the Marshall Islands, in the western Pacific Ocean, in July 1946. Hence their naming it the 'Bikini,' the first record of which is in the August 1947 issue of *Le Monde Illustré*. English acquired the word in 1948. The *monokini*, essentially a bra-less bikini, first appeared in 1964, the inspiration for its name being the accidental resemblance of the element *bi-* in *bikini* to the prefix *bi-* 'two.'

**bilge**   see BULGE

**bill**   There are three distinct words *bill* in English (not counting the proper name), and of them all, the most recent is the commonest. *Bill* 'note of charges' [14] comes from Anglo-Latin *billa*, which is probably a variant of Latin *bulla* 'document, seal' (as in 'papal bull'). English *billet* [15], as in 'billeting soldiers on a house,' was originally a diminutive form of *billa* (French *billet* 'letter' comes from the same source). *Bill* 'hook-bladed weapon' [OE], now found mainly in *bill-hook*, comes from a prehistoric West Germanic *bilja*, which may be based ultimately on Indo-European *bhid-*, source of English *bite*. *Bill* 'beak' [OE] may be related to *bill* 'weapon,' but this is not clear. The verbal sense 'caress,' as in 'bill and coo,' is 16th-century; it arose from the courting behaviour of doves stroking each other's beaks.

▶ billet

**billiards**   [16]   *Billiard* comes from French *billard*, which is the name not only of the game, but also of the cue it is played with. And the cue is the clue to the word's history, for it comes from French *bille* 'tree trunk,' hence 'long cylindrical bit of wood.' The import of the *-ard* suffix is not altogether clear, but another suffix used with *bille* was the diminutive *-ette*, from which English got *billet* 'piece of wood' [15] (not to be confused with *billet* 'assignment to lodgings'; see BILL). *Bille* itself came from medieval Latin *billa* or *billus*, which may have been of Celtic origin.

▶ billet

**biltong**   [19]   *Biltong*, strips of sun-dried meat – anything from beef to ostrich – used as iron rations in southern Africa, has the unpromising literal meaning 'buttock-tongue' (Afrikaans *bil* is 'buttock,' *tong* is 'tongue'). The reason for the name is supposedly that the meat for biltong was customarily cut from the hind quarters of the animal, and that the coiner found in it, perhaps rather optimistically, a resemblance to the taste of smoked ox tongue.

**bin**   [OE]   Old English had the word *bin* or *binne* (it meant 'manger'), but it is not clear where it got it from. Perhaps the most likely source is a word, *benna*, in the Celtic language of the pre-Anglo-Saxon inhabitants of Britain (Welsh has *ben* 'cart'). But it may also have come from medieval Latin *benna*, which gave French *benne* 'large basket.' In English, the modern sense 'storage container' does not fully emerge until the 14th century.

**bind**   [OE]   *Band, bend, bind, bond*, and *bundle* can all be traced back ultimately to an Indo-European base *bhendh-*, which was also the source of Sanskrit *bandh* 'bind' and Greek *peisma* 'cable.' In the case of *bind*, the immediate precursor of Old English *bindan* was the Germanic stem with an *i* vowel, *bind-*. In the 14th century the verb came to be used as a noun, for the 'stem of a climbing plant,' from which we get *bine* (as in *woodbine* 'honeysuckle').

▶ band, bend, bond, bundle

**binnacle**   [15]   *Binnacle* 'ship's compass housing' has a curious history: etymologically it means 'place where something lives,' and it is related to *habitation* and *inhabit*. Forms with *-nn-* do not begin to appear before the 18th century. Until then the word had been *bittacle*, which came from Spanish *bitácula*. A close relative of the Spanish word, French *habitacle*, gives a clue to its ultimate provenance in Latin *habitāculum*, a derivative of *habitāre* 'inhabit.'

**biology**   [19]   The modern European languages have made prolific use of Greek *bíos* 'life' as a prefix, particularly in the 20th century. The first compound into which it entered in English seems to have been *biotic*, in the now obsolete sense 'of secular life' (around 1600), but the trend was really set by *biography*, first recorded as being used by John Dryden in his *Life of Plutarch* 1683. *Biology* itself came along at the beginning of the 19th century, via French, having been coined in German by Gottfried Reinhold in 1802. Twentieth-century contributions have included *bio-engineering, biometric, bionic, biorhythm*, and *biotechnology*. Greek *bíos* itself goes back to an Indo-European base *gwej-*, from which English also ultimately gets *quick, vital, vivid*, and *zoo*.

▶ quick, vital, vivid, zoo

**birch**   [OE]   Old English *bi(e)rce* came from a prehistoric Germanic *berkjōn*, source also of German *birke*. The word goes back ultimately to an Indo-European *bhergo*, but as is often the case with ancient tree-names, it does not denote the same type of tree in every language in which it has descendants: Latin *fraxinus*, for example, means 'ash tree.' It has been speculated that the word is related to *bright* (whose Indo-European source was *bhereg-*), with reference to the tree's light-coloured bark. It could also be that the word *bark* [13] itself is related. The verb *birch* 'flog' (originally with a birch rod or bunch of birch twigs) is early 19th-century.

▶ bark, bright

**bird**   [OE]   *Bird* is something of a mystery word. It was not the ordinary Old English word for 'feathered flying animal'; that was *fowl*. In Old English, *bird* meant specifically 'young bird, nestling.' It did not begin to replace *fowl* as the general term until the 14th century, and the process took many hundreds of years to complete. Its source is quite unknown; it has no obvious relatives in the Germanic languages, or in any other Indo-European language.

The connotations of its original meaning have led to speculation that it is connected with *breed* and *brood* (the usual Old English form was *brid*, but the *r* and *i* subsequently became transposed in a process known as metathesis), but no convincing evidence for this has ever been advanced.

As early as 1300, *bird* was used for 'girl,' but this was probably owing to confusion with another similar Middle English word, *burde*, which also meant 'young woman.' The usage crops up from time to time in later centuries, clearly as an independent metaphorical application, but there does not really seem to be an unbroken chain of occurrences leading up to the sudden explosion in the use of *bird* for 'young woman' in the 20th century.

Of other figurative applications of the word, 'audience disapproval' (as in 'get the bird') comes from the hissing of geese, and in 'prison sentence' *bird* is short for *bird lime*, rhyming slang for *time*.

**birth**   [12]   Old English had a word *gebyrd* 'birth' which survived until the end of the 13th century as *birde*, but it was quite distinct from (though related to) modern English *birth*, which was borrowed from Old Norse *byrth*. This came from the same Germanic stem (*\*ber-*, *\*bur-*) as produced *bear, bairn*, and indeed Old English *gebyrd*. The suffix *-th* denotes a process, or the result of a process: hence *birth* is '(the result of) the process of bearing a child.' Along with *bath* and *death* it is one of the most ancient words formed with *-th*.

▶ bairn, bear, berth

**biscuit**   [14]   *Biscuit* means literally 'twice-cooked' – from the method of cooking, in which the biscuits are returned to the oven after the initial period of baking in order to become dry or crisp. The original source of the word was probably a medieval Latin *\*biscoctus*, from *bis* 'twice' and *coctus* 'cooked,' the past participle of *coquere* (which is related to English *cook*). It reached English via Old French *biscut*.

▶ cook

**bisect**   SEE SECTION

**bishop**   [OE]   *Bishop* originally had no ecclesiastical connections; its Greek source, *epískopos*, at first

meant simply 'overseer,' from *epi-* 'around' and *skopein* 'look' (antecedent of English *scope*, and related to *spy*). From the general sense, it came to be applied as the term for various government officials, and was waiting to be called into service for a 'church officer' as Christianity came into being and grew. The Greek word was borrowed into ecclesiastical Latin as *episcopus* (source of French *évêque*), and in more popular parlance lost its *e-*, giving *\*biscopus*, which was acquired by English in the 9th century.

▶ scope, spy

**bison**   [14]   *Bison* appears to be of Germanic origin, from a stem *\*wisand-* or *\*wisund-*. This became Old English *wesand*, which did not survive; and it was acquired again in the 19th century as *wisent*, borrowed from German *wisent*, applied to the 'aurochs,' an extinct species of European wild ox. The *b*-form came into English via Latin *bison*, a borrowing from the Germanic. Originally of course referring to the European bison, the term was first applied to the North American species at the end of the 17th century.

**bit**   There are three distinct nouns *bit* in English, but the two most ancient ones are probably both related ultimately to the verb *bite*. *Bit* as in 'drill bit' [OE] originally meant simply 'bite' or 'biting.' The Old English word, *bite*, came from Germanic *\*bitiz*, a derivative of the verb *\*bītan* 'bite.' The 'drill bit' sense did not develop until the 16th century. The *bit* placed in a horse's mouth is probably the same word. *Bit* meaning 'small piece' [OE] also comes from a Germanic derivative of *\*bītan*, in this case *\*biton*; this gave Old English *bita* 'piece bitten off.' The more general sense, 'small piece,' developed in the 16th century. The third *bit*, 'unit of computer information' [20], is a blend formed from '*bi*nary dig*it*.'

▶ bite

**bitch**   [OE]   The antecedents of Old English *bicce* 'female dog' are obscure. It may come from a prehistoric Germanic *\*bekjōn-*, but the only related form among other Germanic languages appears to be Old Norse *bikkja*. The superficially similar French *biche* means 'female deer,' and is probably not related. The use of the word as a derogatory term for 'woman' seems to have originated in the 14th century.

**bite**   [OE]   The Old English verb *bītan* came from prehistoric Germanic *\*bītan*, which also produced German *beissen* and Dutch *bijten*. The short-vowel version of the base, *\*bit-*, was the source of *bit, beetle*, and probably *bitter*, and is also represented in various non-Germanic forms, such as Latin *fidere* 'split' (from which English gets *fission*). *Bait* came via Old Norse from a causal usage, 'cause to bite,' and passed via Old French into *abet* (the possible source of *bet*).

▶ beetle, bit, bitter, fission

**bitter** [OE] Old English *biter* appears to have come from *\*bit-*, the short-vowel version of *\*bīt-*, source of *bite*. Its original meaning would thus have been 'biting,' and although there do not seem to be any traces of this left in the historical record, the sense development to 'acrid-tasting' is fairly straightforward (compare the similar case of *sharp*).

It seems likely that the *bitter* of 'bitter end' comes from a different source altogether, although in its current meaning it appears to have been influenced by the adjective *bitter*. A *bitter* was originally a 'turn of a cable round the bitts,' and a *bitt* was a 'post on the deck of a ship for fastening cables to.' It is not clear where *bitt* came from, although it was probably originally a seafarer's term from the north German coast, and it may be related to English *boat*. Thus in the first instance 'to the bitter end' probably meant 'to the very end, as far as it is possible to go.'

▸ bite

**bittern** [14] The Latin word for 'bittern' (a marsh bird) was *būtiō*, but by the time it reached Old French it had become *butor*. The discrepancy has been accounted for by proposing a Vulgar Latin intermediate *\*būtitaurus*, literally 'bittern-bull' (Latin *taurus* is 'bull'), coined on the basis of the bittern's loud booming call, supposedly reminiscent of a bull's. The original English forms, as borrowed from Old French, were *botor* and *bitoure*; the final *-n* first appeared in the 16th century, perhaps on the analogy of *heron*.

**bitumen** see CUD

**bivouac** [18] *Bivouac* appears to be of Swiss-German origin. The early 19th-century writer Stalder noted that the term *beiwacht* (*bei* 'additional' + *wacht* 'guard' – a relative of English *watch* and *wake*) was used in Aargau and Zürich for a sort of band of vigilantes who assisted the regular town guard. *Beiwacht* was borrowed into French as *bivac*, and came to English in a later form *bivouac*. Its original application in English was to an army remaining on the alert during the night, to guard against surprise attack; in so doing, of course, the soldiers did not go to sleep in their tents, and from this the term *bivouac* spread to 'improvised, temporary camp,' without the luxury of regular tents.

▸ wake, watch

**bizarre** [17] *Bizarre* is probably of Basque origin. *Bizarra* is the Basque word for 'beard,' and it seems to have been borrowed into Spanish and Portuguese as *bizarro*, meaning 'handsome' or 'brave' (apparently on the grounds that someone with a beard was thought of as no end of a dashing fellow). The Spanish word was acquired by French as *bizarre* (source of the English term), and in due course developed in meaning (for unexplained reasons) to 'odd.'

**black** [OE] The usual Old English word for 'black' was *sweart* (source of modern English *swart* and

swarthy, and related to German *schwarz* 'black'), but *black* already existed (Old English *blæc*), and since the Middle English period it has replaced *swart*. Related but now extinct forms existed in other Germanic languages (including Old Norse *blakkr* 'dark' and Old Saxon *blac* 'ink'), but the word's ultimate source is not clear. Some have compared it with Latin *flagrāre* and Greek *phlégein*, both meaning 'burn,' which go back to an Indo-European base *\*phleg-*, a variant of *\*bhleg-*.

**blackmail** see MAIL

**bladder** [OE] Old English *blǣdre* came from a hypothetical West and North Germanic *\*blǣdrōn*, a derivative of the stem *\*blǣ-*, from which we get *blow*. The name perhaps comes from the bladder's capacity for inflation. It was originally, and for a long time exclusively, applied to the urinary bladder.

▸ blow

**blade** [OE] The primary sense of *blade* appears to be 'leaf' (as in 'blades of grass,' and German *blatt* 'leaf'). This points back to the ultimate source of the word, the Germanic stem *\*bhlō-*, from which English also gets *bloom*, *blossom*, and the now archaic *blow* 'come into flower.' However, the earliest sense recorded for Old English *blæd* was the metaphorical 'flattened, leaflike part,' as of an oar, spade, etc. The specific application to the sharp, cutting part of a sword or knife developed in the 14th century.

▸ bloom, blossom, blow

**blame** [12] *Blame* and *blaspheme* are ultimately the same word. Both come from Greek *blasphēmein* 'say profane things about,' but whereas *blaspheme* has stuck to the path of 'profanity,' *blame* has developed the more down-to-earth sense 'reproach, censure.' The radical change of form seems to have come via *blastēmāre*, a demotic offshoot of late Latin *blasphēmāre*, which passed into Old French as *blasmer*, later *blamer* (whence English *blame*).

▸ blaspheme

**blanch** see BLANK

**blancmange** [14] *Blancmange* means literally simply 'white food.' It comes from a French compound made up of *blanc* 'white' and *manger*, a noun derived from the verb *manger* 'eat' (related to English *manger*). Originally it was a savoury dish, of chicken or similar white meat in a sauce made with cream, eggs, rice, etc and often sugar and almonds. Gradually the meat content came to be omitted, and blancmange turned into a sweet dish, typically containing gelatine.

▸ manger

**blank** [15] Although English got *blank* from French *blanc* 'white,' its ultimate source is Germanic. Forms such as Old High German *blanc* 'white' suggest a prehistoric Germanic *\*blangkaz*, which could have been borrowed into Romanic, the undifferentiated precursor of the Romance languages, as *blancus* – hence French *blanc*, Italian *bianco*, Spanish *blanco*, and Portuguese *branco*. The word originally meant simply 'white' in English, but this sense had all but died out by the early 18th century, by which time the present-day 'unmarked' was well established.

Other derivatives of French *blanc* include the verb *blanch* [14], from French *blanchier*, and *blanket* [13], from Old French *blancquet*. *Blanco* is a trade name (based on *blanc*) coined in the 1890s for a whitening preparation for military webbing (subsequently applied to the khaki-coloured version as well).

► blanch, blanket

## blaspheme
[14] *Blaspheme* has maintained a remarkable semantic and formal stability since its origins in Greek *blásphēmos*, which meant 'speaking evil or profane things' (*blas-* is related to *blaptikós* 'hurtful'; the *-phēmos* element denotes 'speaking,' and is related to *phēmí* 'I say'). The derived Greek verb *blasphēmein* was transmitted via ecclesiastical Latin *blasphēmāre* to Old French and thence to English. *Blastēmāre*, an altered version of *blasphēmāre*, produced *blame*.

► blame

## blatant
[16] *Blatant* appears to have been coined, or at least introduced, by the poet Edmund Spenser. In the *Faerie Queene* 1596 he describes how 'unto themselves they [Envy and Detraction] gotten had a monster which the blatant beast men call, a dreadful fiend of gods and men ydrad [dreaded].' This 'blatant beast' was an allegorical representation of calumny. In the 17th century the word came to be applied to offensively voluble people, but the main modern sense, 'offensively conspicuous,' does not seem to have developed until the late 19th century. If the word was Spenser's own introduction, it is not clear where he got it from. The likeliest candidate seems to be Latin *blatīre* 'babble, gossip,' of imitative origin.

## blaze
There are three distinct words *blaze* in English. The commonest, meaning 'fire, flame' [OE], comes from a prehistoric Germanic *blasōn*. Its original signification was 'torch' (in the sense, of course, of a burning piece of wood or bunch of sticks), but by the year 1000 the main current meaning was established. The precise source of *blaze* 'light-coloured mark or spot' [17] is not known for certain, but there are several cognate forms in other Germanic languages, including Old Norse *blesi* and German *blässe*; perhaps the likeliest candidate as far as *blaze* is concerned is Middle Low German *bles*. The verbal usage, as in 'blaze a trail' (that is, by making conspicuous marks on trees) originated in the mid 18th century. The related German adjective *blass* 'pale,' which originally meant 'shining,' points up the fact that ultimately these two words *blaze* are related, the primeval sense 'shining' having diverged on

the one hand through 'pale,' on the other through 'glowing, burning.'

The third *blaze*, 'proclaim' [14], as in 'blaze abroad,' is now seldom encountered. It originally meant 'blow a trumpet,' and comes ultimately from the Indo-European base *bhlā-* (source of *blow*). Its immediate source in English was Middle Dutch *blāsen*. Despite its formal and semantic similarity, it does not appear to have any connection with *blazon* [13], which comes from Old French *blason* 'shield,' a word of unknown origin.

A *blazer* [19] got its name from being a brightly coloured jacket (from *blaze* meaning 'fire, flame'). It originated among English university students in the late 19th century. According to a correspondent in the *Daily News* 22 August 1889, the word was originally applied specifically to the red jackets worn by members of the 'Lady Margaret, St John's College, Cambridge, Boat Club.' But by the 1880s its more general application had become widely established: in the *Durham University Journal* of 21 February 1885 we read that 'the latest novelty . . . for the river is flannels, a blazer, and spats.'

► blow

## bleak
[16] *Bleak* originally meant 'pale,' and comes ultimately from an Indo-European base *bhleg-*, possible source of *black* and a variant of *phleg-*, which produced Greek *phlégein* 'burn' and Latin *flagrāre* 'burn' (whence English *conflagration* and *flagrant*; *flame*, *fulminate*, and *refulgent* are also closely related). From *bhleg-* came the prehistoric Germanic adjective *blaikos* 'white,' from which Old English got *blāc* 'pale' (the sense relationship, as with the possibly related *blaze*, is between 'burning,' 'shining brightly,' 'white,' and 'pale'). This survived until the 15th century in southern English dialects as *bloke*, and until the 16th century in the North as *blake*. Its disappearance was no doubt hastened by its resemblance to *black*, both formally and semantically, since both 'pale' and 'dark' carry implications of colourlessness. *Blake* did however persist in Northern dialects until modern times in the sense 'yellow.' Meanwhile, around the middle of the 16th century *bleak* had begun to put in an appearance, borrowed from a close relative of *bloke/blake*, Old Norse *bleikr* 'shining, white.' The modern sense 'bare' is recorded from very early on.

A derivative of the Germanic base *blaik-* was the verb *blaikjōn*, source of Old English *blǣcan* 'whiten,' the ancestor of modern English *bleach* (which may be related to *blight*). And a nasalized version of the stem may have produced *blink* [14].

► bleach, blight, blink, conflagration, flagrant, flame, fulminate

## bleed
[OE] As its form suggests, *bleed* is a derivative of *blood*, but a very ancient one. From Germanic *blōtham* 'blood' was formed the verb *blōthjan* 'emit

blood,' which came into Old English as *blēdan*, ancestor of *bleed*.

▶blood

**blend** [13] Old English had a verb *blendan*, but it meant 'make blind' or 'dazzle.' Modern English *blend* appears to come from *blend-*, the present stem of Old Norse *blanda* 'mix' (a relative of Old English *blandan* 'mix'). The ultimate source of this is not clear, but it does not seem to be restricted to Germanic (Lithuanian has the adjective *blandus* 'thick' in relation to soup), so it may not be too far-fetched to suggest a link with *blind*, whose Indo-European ancestor *\*bhlendhos* meant among other things 'confused.'

**bless** [OE] *Bless* occurs in no other language than English, and originally meant 'mark with blood,' from some sort of religious rite in which such marking conferred sanctity. It probably goes back to a prehistoric Germanic formation *\*blōthisōjan*, a derivative of *\*blōtham* 'blood,' which was taken up by no Germanic language other than Old English. Here it produced *blētsian*, which by the 13th century had become *blesse*. The word's connotations of 'happiness' and 'well-being,' which go back at least to the year 1000, were probably influenced by the etymologically unrelated *bliss*.

▶blood

**blight** [17] *Blight* appeared out of the blue in the early 17th century in agricultural and horticultural texts, and its origins are far from clear. It has, however, been speculated that it may be connected with the Old English words *blǣce* and *blǣcthu*, both terms for some sort of itchy skin condition such as scabies. These in turn are probably related to Old English *blǣcan* 'bleach,' the link being the flaky whiteness of the infected skin. In Middle English, *blǣcthu* would have become *\*bleht*, which could plausibly have been the source of *blight*. A related piece in the jigsaw is *blichening* 'blight or rust in corn,' found once in Middle English, which may have come ultimately from Old Norse *blikna* 'become pale.'

▶bleach

**blighty** [20] *Blighty* is a legacy of British rule in India. Originally a term used by British soldiers serving in India for 'home, Britain,' it is an anglicization of Hindi *bilāyatī*, which meant 'foreign,' and particularly 'European.' This was actually a borrowing from Arabic *wilāyat* 'district, country,' which was independently acquired by English in the 19th century in its Turkish form *vilayet*. It was a derivative of the Arabic verb *waliya* 'rule,' and is related to *walī* 'ruler.'

**blind** [OE] The connotations of the ultimate ancestor of *blind*, Indo-European *\*bhlendhos*, seem to have been not so much 'sightlessness' as 'confusion' and 'obscurity.' The notion of someone wandering around in actual or mental darkness, not knowing where to go, naturally progressed to the 'inability to see.' Re-

lated words that fit this pattern are *blunder*, possibly from Old Norse *blunda* 'shut one's eyes,' *blunt*, and maybe also *blend*. By the time the word entered Old English, as *blind*, it already meant 'sightless,' but ancestral associations of darkness and obscurity were retained (Pepys in his diary, for instance, writes of a 'little blind [that is, dark] bed-chamber' 1666), and traces of them remain in such usages as 'blind entrance.'

▶blend, blunder, blunt

**blindfold** [16] The original term for covering someone's eyes with a bandage was *blindfell* [OE], which survived until the 16th century. This meant literally 'strike someone blind,' the second element being the *fell* of 'felling trees.' It appears that its past form, *blindfelled*, came to be mistaken for a present form, and this, together with some perceived connection with *fold* (presumably the 'folding' of the bandage round somebody's head), conspired to produce the new verb *blindfold*.

**bliss** [OE] Despite its formal and semantic similarity, *bliss* has no connection with *bless*. It comes ultimately from Germanic *\*blīthiz* 'gentle, kind,' which is the source of English *blithe* 'happy' [OE]. The addition of the noun suffix *\*-tjō* produced the derivative *\*blīthsjō*, which entered Old English as *blīths* 'happiness,' later reduced to *bliss*.

▶blithe

**blister** [13] *Blister* and its now extinct variant *blester* first appear in English at the end of the 13th century, possibly borrowed from Old French *blestre, blostre*. It seems that this in turn may have come from Middle Dutch *bluyster* 'swelling,' but further back than that it has not proved possible to trace the word.

**bloat** [13] *Bloat* has a confused and uncertain history. It seems first to have appeared on the scene in the 13th century as an adjective, *blout*, meaning 'soft, flabby,' a probable borrowing from Old Norse *blautr* 'soft from being cooked with liquid.' This occurs only once, and does not resurface until the early 17th century, in *Hamlet* as it happens, as *blowt*: 'Let the blowt king tempt you again to bed.' This appears to be the same word as turns up slightly later in the century as *bloat*, its meaning showing signs of changing from 'flabby' to 'puffed up.' Then in the 1660s we encounter *bloated* 'puffed up, swollen,' which paved the way for the verb *bloat*, first recorded in the 1670s.

It is not clear whether *bloater* [19] comes from the same source. Its linguistic ancestor is the *bloat herring* [16], which may perhaps have been given its name on the grounds that herrings preserved by light smoking are plumper than those fully dried.

**block** [14] English borrowed *block* from Old French *bloc*, but its ultimate origin appears to be Germanic; French acquired it from Middle Dutch *blok* 'tree trunk.' The derived verb *block* 'impede' first crops up in the early 15th century, but was not established until the later 16th century; it originally meant 'put blocks [of wood] or obstacles in the way of.' *Blockade* was coined in the 17th century, perhaps on the model of *ambuscade*, a contemporary synonym of *ambush*.

▶ blockade

**blood** [OE] *Blood* is a Germanic word, occurring as German *blut*, Dutch *bloed*, Swedish *blod*, etc, as well as in English (the Romance languages take their words from Latin *sanguis*, whence English *sanguine* [14], while Greek had *haima*, as in English *haemorrhage*, *haemoglobin*, etc). The ultimate source of all these was Germanic *\*blōtham*, a derivative of which, *\*blōthjan*, produced English *bleed*. Old English had the adjective *blōdig*, from which we get *bloody*; its use as an expletive dates from the 17th century.

▶ bleed, bless

**bloom** [13] The Old English word for 'flower' was the probably related *blossom*, and English did not acquire *bloom* until the 13th century, when it borrowed it from Old Norse *blómi*. This came from Germanic *\*blōmon*, a derivative of the Indo-European *\*bhlō-* which also produced Latin *flōs* (whence English *flower*), the now archaic English verb *blow* 'come into flower,' and English *blade*.

▶ blade, blossom, blow, flower

**bloomer** [19] *Bloomers*, long loose trousers worn by women, were not actually invented by someone called Bloomer – the credit for that seems to go to a Mrs Elizabeth Smith Miller of New York – but their first advocate was Amelia Jenks Bloomer (1818–94), a US feminist who strongly promoted their use in the early 1850s as a liberated garment for women. The extent to which this became a cause celebre can be gauged by the fact that it gave rise to so-called *Bloomerism*, a movement for 'rationalizing' women's dress; in 1882 Lady Harberton wrote in *Macmillan's Magazine* "Bloomerism" still lurks in many a memory.'

*Bloomer* 'mistake' is late 19th-century, and apparently originally Australian. Early commentators derived it, not altogether convincingly, from 'blooming error.'

**blossom** [OE] *Blossom* probably comes ultimately from an Indo-European base *\*bhlōs-*, which was also the source of Latin *flōs*, from which English gets *flower*. It seems reasonable to suppose, in view of the semantic connections, that this *\*bhlōs-* was an extended form of *\*bhlō-*, from which English gets *blade*, *bloom*, and the now archaic verb *blow* 'come into flower.'

▶ blade, bloom, blow, flower

**blow** There are three distinct *blows* in English. The commonest, the verb 'send out air' [OE] , can be traced back to an Indo-European base *\*bhlā-*. It came into English (as Old English *blāwan*) via Germanic *\*blæ-*,

source also of *bladder*. The Indo-European base also produced Latin *flāre* 'blow,' from which English gets *flatulent* and *inflate*. The other verb *blow*, 'come into flower' [OE], now archaic, comes ultimately from Indo-European *\*bhlō-*. It entered English (as Old English *blōwan*) via Germanic *\*blo-*, from which English also gets *bloom* and probably *blade*. A variant form of the Indo-European base with *-s-* produced Latin *flōs* (source of English *flower*) and English *blossom*. The noun *blow* 'hard hit' [15] is altogether more mysterious. It first appears, in the form *blaw*, in northern and Scottish texts, and it has been connected with a hypothetical Germanic *\*bleuwan* 'strike.'

▶ bladder, flatulent, inflate / blade, bloom, blossom, flower

**blubber** [14] The original notion underlying *blubber* is of 'bubbling' or 'foaming,' particularly in relation to the sea, and it may, like *bubble* itself, be an onomatopoeic creation, imitative of the sound of spluttering or popping water. This sense died out in the mainstream language in the 16th century (though it survived longer dialectally), but it lies behind the verbal sense 'cry copiously.' The development of the noun to its present meaning 'whale fat' is not altogether clear, but it may have been via an intermediate 15th-century application to 'fish's entrails,' which perhaps bubbled or appeared pustular when ripped open by the fishermen.

**blue** [13] Colour terms are notoriously slippery things, and *blue* is a prime example. Its ultimate ancestor, Indo-European *\*bhlēwos*, seems originally to have meant 'yellow' (it is the source of Latin *flāvus* 'yellow,' from which English gets *flavine* 'yellow dye' [19]). But it later evolved via 'white' (Greek *phalós* 'white' is related) and 'pale' to 'livid, the colour of bruised skin' (Old Norse has *blá* 'livid'). English had the related *blāw*, but it did not survive, and the modern English word was borrowed from Old French *bleu*. This was descended from a Common Romance *\*blāvus*, which in turn was acquired from prehistoric Germanic *\*blǣwaz* (source also of German *blau* 'blue').

▶ flavine

**bluestocking** [18] The term *bluestocking* 'female intellectual' derives from the gatherings held at the houses of fashionable mid-18th-century hostesses to discuss literary and related topics. It became the custom at these not to put on full formal dress, which for gentlemen included black silk stockings. One habitué in particular, Mr Benjamin Stillingfleet, used to wear greyish worsted stockings, conventionally called 'blue.' This lack of decorum was looked on with scorn in some quarters, and Admiral Boscawan dubbed the participants the 'Blue Stocking Society.' Women who attended their highbrow meetings thus became known as 'Blue Stocking Ladies' (even though it was a man who had worn the stockings), and towards the end of the century this was abbreviated to simply *bluestockings*.

**bluff**   English has two words *bluff*, one or perhaps both of them of Dutch origin. The older, 'hearty' [17], originally referred to ships, and meant 'having a flat vertical bow.' This nautical association suggests a Dutch provenance, though no thoroughly convincing source has been found. The sense 'flat, vertical, (and broad)' came to be applied to land features, such as cliffs (hence the noun *bluff* 'high steep bank,' which emerged in America in the 18th century). The word's metaphorical extension to people was at first derogatory – 'rough, blunt' – but the more favourable 'hearty' had developed by the early 19th century.

*Bluff* 'deceive' [19] was originally a US poker term. It comes from Dutch *bluffen* 'boast,' the descendant of Middle Dutch *bluffen* 'swell up.'

**blunder**   [14]   When *blunder* first entered the language, it meant 'stumble around blindly, bumping into things,' which gives a clue to its possible ultimate connection with *blind*. Its probable source was Old Norse *blundra* 'shut one's eyes,' forerunner of Swedish *blunda* and Norwegian *blunda* (*Jon Blund* is the Swedish equivalent of 'the sandman'), and very likely a descendant of Indo-European *\*bhlendhos*, from which *blind* comes. The first record of the modern sense 'foolish mistake' comes in Edward Phillips's *The new world of English words* 1706.

▶blind

**blunderbus**   [17]   *Blunderbus* was originally Dutch *donderbus* (literally 'thundergun'), and its transformation is due to folk etymology: the unfamiliar *donder* was replaced by the English word *blunder*, perhaps with some reference to the fact that, with its wide muzzle, it is capable only of fairly random firing. The second part of the word (which also occurs in *arquebus*) is ultimately related to *box*, Dutch *bus* or *buis* being not just a 'box' but also a 'tube,' and hence a 'gun.' There is no connection with the 20th-century *thunderbox*, a colloquial term for a 'portable loo.'

**blunt**   [12]   *Blunt* originally meant 'dull, obtuse, foolish' in English, and it has been speculated that behind it there lay an earlier 'dull of sight,' linking the word with *blind*. A possible source would be a derivative of Old Norse *blunda* 'shut one's eyes' (whence probably also *blunder*). The application of *blunt* to dull, non-sharp edges or blades developed in the 14th century.

▶blind, blunder

**blush**   [OE]   Modern English *blush* is a descendant of Old English *blyscan* 'turn red, blush,' which was related to and perhaps derived from Old English *blȳsa* 'firebrand, torch.' Similarities of form and meaning make it tempting to compare *blaze*, which meant 'torch' in Old English and came from a prehistoric Germanic *\*blasōn*, but no connection has ever been established. Middle Dutch *blosen* 'glow' may be an intermediate form.

**board**   [OE]   Old English *bord* had a wide range of meanings, whose two main strands ('plank' and 'border, side of a ship') reveal that it came from two distinct sources: Germanic *\*bortham* and *\*borthaz* respectively (despite their similarity, they have not been shown to be the same word). Related forms in other Germanic languages that point up the dichotomy are Dutch *bord* 'shelf' and *boord* 'border, side of a ship.' The second, 'edge' element of *board* (which is probably related to *border*) now survives in English only in *seaboard* (literally the 'edge of the sea') and in variations on the phrase *on board ship* (whose original reference to the ship's sides is nowadays perceived as relating to the deck).

*Board* 'food' (as in 'board and lodging'), and hence *boarder*, are metaphorical applications of *board* 'table.'

▶border

**boast**   [13]   The immediate source of *boast* appears to be Anglo-Norman *bost*, but where it came from before that is far from clear; German dialect *bauste(r)n* 'swell' has been compared, suggesting that it could be of Germanic origin. To begin with it meant 'loud or threatening talk' as well as 'bragging.'

**boat**   [OE]   In origin, the word *boat* seems to be restricted to northern parts of Europe: Old English *bāt* and Old Norse *beit* are the only early examples (German *boot* was borrowed from them, and French *bateau* comes from the English word). They point to a common Germanic origin in *\*bait-*. It has been speculated that this may be related to *bitt* 'post for fastening ship's cables.' If true, this could mean that *boat* originally referred to one or other of the structural members of a wooden vessel.

**bobby**   [19]   The British *bobby* 'policeman' gets his name from the English statesman Sir Robert Peel (1788–1850) – *Bobby* or *Bob* being the pet form of *Robert*. Peel was Home Secretary when the Metropolitan Police Force was formed in 1828, but the term *bobby* is not actually recorded until 1844. A much earlier application of his name was the now obsolete *Peeler*, used from 1817 for members of the Irish Constabulary, founded under Peel's auspices, and later for English policemen.

**Boche**   see CABBAGE

**bodice**   [16]   Originally, *bodice* was identical with *bodies* – that is, the plural of *body*. This use of *body* began early in the 16th century, when it referred to the part of a woman's dress that covered the trunk, as opposed to the arms; and it soon became restricted specifically to the part above the waist. The reason for the adoption of the plural form (which was often used originally in the phrase *pair of bodies*) was that the upper portion of women's dresses was usually in two parts, which fastened down the middle. In the 17th and 18th centuries the term *bodice* was frequently applied to 'corsets.'

▶ body

**bodkin**  [14]  A bodkin was originally a small dagger, and only in the 18th century did it develop the perhaps more familiar sense 'long blunt needle.' Initially it was a three-syllable word, spelled *boidekyn*, and its origins are mysterious. Most speculation has centred on Celtic as a source, Welsh *bidog* 'dagger' being cited (the *-kin* is no doubt a diminutive suffix).

**body**  [OE]  For a word so central to people's perception of themselves, *body* is remarkably isolated linguistically. Old High German had *potah* 'body,' traces of which survived dialectally into modern times, but otherwise it is without known relatives in any other Indo-European language. Attempts have been made, not altogether convincingly, to link it with words for 'container' or 'barrel,' such as medieval Latin *butica*. The use of *body* to mean 'person in general,' as in *somebody, nobody*, got fully under way in the 14th century.

**bog**  [13]  *Bog* is of Gaelic origin. It comes from *bogach* 'bog,' which was a derivative of the adjective *bog* 'soft.' A possible link between Gaelic *bog* and Old English *būgan* 'bend' (source of modern English *bow*) has been suggested. The British slang use 'lavatory,' which dates from the 18th century, appears to be short for the slightly earlier *bog-house*, which may have been an alteration of the 16th-century *boggard* – quite possibly completely unrelated to *bog* 'swamp.'

**bogey**  [19]  *Bogey* is one of a set of words relating to alarming or annoying manifestations of the supernatural (others are *bogle, bug, bugbear*, and possibly *boggle* and *bugaboo*) whose interconnections are difficult to sort out. A strand common to most of them is a northern origin, which has led some to suggest an ultimate source in Scandinavia – perhaps an ancestor of Norwegian dialect *bugge* 'important man' (which has also been linked with English *big*) might lie behind Middle English *bugge*, originally 'scarecrow' but later used for more spectral objects of terror. Others, however, noting Welsh *bwg, bwgan* 'ghost,' have gone with a Celtic origin.

Of more recent uses of *bogey*, 'policeman' and 'nasal mucus' seem to have appeared between the two World Wars, while 'golf score of one stroke over par' is said to have originated at the Great Yarmouth Golf Club in the 1890s, when a certain Major Wellman exclaimed, during the course of a particularly trying round, that he must be playing against the 'bogey-man' (a figure in a popular song of the time). *Bogie* 'undercarriage' [19] is a different word (of if anything obscurer origin than *bogey*).

**boil**  *Boil* 'large spot' [OE] and *boil* 'vaporize with heat' [13] are distinct words. The former comes from Old English *bȳl* or *bȳle*, which became *bile* in Middle English; the change to *boil* started in the 15th century, perhaps from association with the verb. The Old English word goes back ultimately to a West Germanic *\*būlja*, whose central meaning element was 'swelling'; from it also comes German *beule* 'lump, boil.' The verb's source, via Anglo-Norman *boiller*, is Latin *bullīre*, a derivative of *bulla* 'bubble,' a word which also gave us *bull* (as in 'Papal bull'), *bullion, bowl* (as in the game of 'bowls'), *budge, bullet, bulletin*, and *bully* (as in 'bully beef'), as well, perhaps, as *bill*.

▶ bill, bowl, budge, bull, bullet, bulletin, bullion, bully, ebullient

**bold**  [OE]  In Old English, *bold* meant simply 'brave'; the modern connotations of immodesty or presumptuousness do not seem to have developed until the 12th century. The word goes back to a prehistoric Germanic *\*balthaz*, based ultimately, it has been speculated, on Indo-European *\*bhel-* 'swell' (the psychological link through 'being puffed up' via 'adventurous courage' to 'audacity' is scarcely far-fetched). If this is so it would mean *bold* is related to *bellows, belly, billow, bolster*, and possibly *bellow* and *bell*. The notion of impetuosity is perhaps retained in the related German *bald* 'soon.'

▶ bell, bellows, belly, billow, bolster

**bollock**  see BALL

**bolshevik**  [20]  Russian *bol'shévik* is a derivative of *ból'shiy*, the comparative form of the adjective *ból'shoy* 'big.' It was originally applied, at the 1903 congress of the Russian Social Democratic Party, to those party members who wished to go for a 'big,' or extreme, socialist programme (in contrast with the more moderate *Mensheviks* – from Russian *mén'shij* 'less'); but since the Bolsheviks outnumbered the Mensheviks, the word soon became interpreted as 'those in the majority in the party.' The transferred use of the English abbreviation *bolshy* to mean 'stubbornly uncooperative' dates from around 1918.

▶ debility

**bolster**  [OE]  The idea underlying *bolster* 'long pillow' is of something stuffed, so that it swells up. It comes from a prehistoric Germanic *\*bolstraz*, which was a derivative of *\*bolg-, \*bulg-*(source also of *bellows, belly, billow* and possibly *bell, bellow*, and *bold*). German has the related *polster* 'cushion, pillow.'

▶ bell, bellow, belly, billow, bold

**bolt**  [OE]  In Old English, a bolt was an arrow, particularly of the short stout variety used in crossbows (hence the phrase *shoot one's bolt*). The more familiar modern sense 'fastening pin' developed in the 13th century. The verbal sense 'make a quick escape' comes from the notion of firing a projectile. The word appears in other Germanic languages (for instance German *bolz* 'bolt'), but its ultimate origin is unknown.

**bomb** [17] *Bomb* is ultimately of onomatopoeic origin, and can probably be traced back to Greek *bómbos*, a word for a booming or buzzing sound. This passed into Latin as *bombus*, the probable source of Italian *bomba*, which acquired more explosive connotations. English got the word via French *bombe*. The derivative *bombard* preceded *bomb* into English, in the 15th century.

▶ bound

**bombast** [16] *Bombast* originally meant 'cotton-wool,' especially as used for stuffing or padding clothes, upholstery, etc; hence, before the end of the 16th century, it had been transferred metaphorically to 'pompous or turgid language.' The ultimate source of the word was Greek *bómbux* 'silk, silkworm,' which came into English via Latin *bombyx, bombax* (source also of English *bombazine* [16]) and Old French *bombace*. The earliest English form was *bombace*, but it soon developed an additional final -*t*.

▶ bombazine

**bonanza** [19] *Bonanza* entered the language via American English from Spanish, where *bonanza* means 'prosperity,' or literally 'good weather.' It came from an unrecorded general Romance *\*bonacia*, a derivative of Latin *bonus* 'good.' (Other English words acquired ultimately from *bonus* – a descendant of Old Latin *duenos* – include *bonbon* [19], *bonus* [18], *boon* [14] (as in 'boon companion'), *bounty* [13] (from Latin *bonitas* 'goodness'), and perhaps *bonny* [15].) It appears to have been formed on the analogy of Latin *malacia*, as if this meant 'bad weather,' from *malus* 'bad,' although it in fact originally meant 'calm at sea,' from Greek *malakós*.

▶ bonbon, bonny, bonus, boon, bounty

**bond** English has two distinct words *bond*, which started life very differently but have gradually grown together. *Bond* 'something that binds' [13] was originally the same word as *band* (from Old Norse *band*), and only gradually diverged from it in pronunciation, spelling, and meaning. The key modern legal and financial senses began to develop in the 16th century, the underlying notion being of something one is 'bound' or 'tied' to by a promise. *Bond* 'bound in slavery' [14], as in *bondservant*, is an adjectival use of the late Old English noun *bonda* 'householder,' which came from Old Norse *bóndi* (the second element of *húsbóndi*, from which English gets *husband*). This represented an earlier *bóandi*, which was originally the present participle of east Norse *bóa* 'dwell,' a derivative of the Germanic base *\*bū-* 'dwell' (from which English also gets *be, boor, booth, bower, build, burly, byelaw*, and *byre*). The semantic association of 'tying up' and 'servitude'

has led to the merging of the two words, as shown in the derivative *bondage*.

▶ band / be, boor, booth, build, byelaw, neighbour

**bone** [OE] Somewhat unusually for a basic body-part term, *bone* is a strictly Germanic word; it has no relatives in other Indo-European languages. It comes from a presumed Germanic *\*bainam*, which also produced for example German *bein* and Swedish *ben*. These both mean 'leg' as well as 'bone,' suggesting that the original connotation of *\*bainam* may have been 'long bone.'

**bonfire** [14] A bonfire was originally a fire in which bones were burned. References to such (presumably rather evil-smelling) fires, which were large openair affairs, continue down to the 18th century, but latterly they have a distinctly antiquarian air, as if such things were a thing of the past. By the later 15th century the word was already passing to the more general modern meaning 'large outdoor fire,' either celebratory (as in Bonfire Night, 5 November) or for destroying refuse.

▶ bone

**bonus** SEE BEAUTY

**book** [OE] *Book* is widespread throughout the Germanic languages. German has *buch*, for example, Dutch *bock*, and Swedish *bok*. These point to a prehistoric Germanic *\*bōks*, which was probably related to *\*bōkā* 'beech,' the connection being that the early Germanic peoples used beechwood tablets for writing runic inscriptions on. The original meaning of the word in Old English (*bōc*) was simply 'written document or record,' but by the 9th century it had been applied to a collection of written sheets fastened together.

▶ beech

**boom** SEE BEAM

**boor** [15] *Boor* was borrowed into English either from Low German *būr* or from Dutch *boer* (*Boer* 'Dutch colonist in South Africa' is a later, 19th-century borrowing). When first acquired it meant 'peasant farmer,' and did not develop its modern explicit connotations of coarseness and rudeness until the 16th century. Its ultimate source was the Germanic base *\*bū-* 'dwell,' so its original meaning was something like 'person who lives in a particular place' (the related *neighbour* was literally 'someone who lives nearby'). Other English words from the same source include *be, booth, bound* 'intending to go,' *bower, build, burly, byelaw, byre*, and the -*band* of *husband*.

▶ be, boer, booth, bower, build, burly, byelaw, byre, husband, neighbour

**boot** [14] *Boot* is a comparatively late acquisition by English. It came, either directly or via Old Norse *bóti*, from Old French *bote*, whose source is unknown. The modern British sense 'car's luggage compartment' goes back to a 17th-century term for an outside compartment for attendants on a coach, which may have come directly from modern French *botte*.

The *boot* of 'to boot' is a completely different word. It comes from Old English *bōt* 'advantage, remedy,' which can be traced back to a prehistoric Germanic base *bat-*, source also of *better* and *best*.

▶ best, better

**booth** [12] In common with a wide range of other English words, including *bower* and the *-bour* of *neighbour*, *booth* comes ultimately from the Germanic base *bū-* 'dwell.' From this source came the East Norse verb *bóa* 'dwell' (whose present participle produced English *bond* and the *-band* of *husband*); addition of the suffix *-th* produced the unrecorded noun *bóth* 'dwelling,' which came into Middle English as *bōth*.

▶ be, boor, bower, husband, neighbour

**booty** [15] *Booty* has no connection with *boots*. It came into English as *butin* (it did not finally lose its *n* until the 18th century), a borrowing from Old French *butin*, but Old French had got it from Middle Low German *būte* 'exchange' (whence German *beute* and Dutch *buit* 'loot'), pointing to a prehistoric Germanic source *būtiōn*.

▶ filibuster, freebooter

**booze** [13] This word seems to have been borrowed on two distinct and widely separate occasions from Middle Dutch *būsen* 'drink much alcohol' (which some have connected with Middle High German *būs* 'swelling'). In the 13th century this gave Middle English *bouse*, which if it had continued to the present day would have rhymed with the verb *house*. However, in the 16th century the Middle Dutch word was reborrowed, giving modern English *booze*.

**borage** [13] The plant-name *borage* comes via Old French *bourrache* from Latin *borrāgo*. Various words have been advanced as an ultimate source, including late Latin *burra* 'shaggy cloth,' on account of its hairy leaves, but in view of the fact that the Arabs used the plant medicinally to induce sweating, the likeliest contender is Arabic *abū 'āraq*, literally 'father of sweat.'

**border** [14] English acquired *border* from Old French *bordure*. This came from the common Romance verb *bordāre* 'border,' which was based on *bordus* 'edge,' a word of Germanic origin whose source, *borthaz*, was the same as that of English *board* in the sense 'side of a ship.'

▶ board

**bore** *Bore* 'make a hole' [OE] and *bore* 'be tiresome' [18] are almost certainly two distinct words. The former comes ultimately from an Indo-European base *bhor-*, *bhr-*, which produced Latin *forāre* 'bore' (whence English *foramen* 'small anatomical opening'), Greek *phárynx*, and prehistoric Germanic *borōn*, from which we get *bore* (and German gets *bohren*). *Bore*

connoting 'tiresomeness' suddenly appears on the scene as a sort of buzzword of the 1760s, from no known source; the explanation most commonly offered for its origin is that it is a figurative application of *bore* in the sense 'pierce someone with ennui,' but that is not terribly convincing. In its early noun use it meant what we would now call a 'fit of boredom.'

There is one other, rather rare English word *bore* – meaning 'tidal wave in an estuary or river' [17]. It may have come from Old Norse *bára* 'wave.'

▶ perforate, pharynx

**born** [OE] The Old English past participle of the verb meaning 'bear' was *boren*. By Middle English times this had become contracted to *born(e)*, but no distinction in meaning was made on the basis of spelling. This did not come about until around 1600, since when *born* has become established as the obstetric orthography, while *borne* remains the straightforward past participle of *bear* 'carry.'

▶ bear

**borough** [OE] *Borough* (Old English *burg* or *burh*) comes from Germanic *burgs* 'fortress' (whence also German *burg* 'castle, stronghold'). It was a derivative of the base *burg-* 'protect' (whence also *bury*), a variant of *berg-* (source of English *barrow* 'mound' and German *berg* 'mountain') and *borg-* (source of English *borrow*). At some time during the prehistoric Germanic period a progression in meaning began to take place from 'fortress' (which had largely died out in English by 1000), through 'fortified town,' to simply 'town.' Romance languages borrowed the word, giving for instance French *bourg*, from which English gets *burgess* [13] and *bourgeois* [16]. *Burrow* [13] is probably a variant form.

▶ bourgeois, burgess, burrow, bury

**borrow** [OE] Modern English *borrow* is a descendant of Old English *borgian*, which came from the Germanic base *borg-*. This was a variant of *berg-* (source of English *barrow* 'mound') and *burg-* (source of English *borough* and *bury*). The underlying sense of the Germanic base was 'protection, shelter,' and the development of meaning in the case of *borrow* seems to have been like this: originally, to *borrow* something from somebody was to receive it temporarily from them in return for some sort of security, which would be forfeited if the thing borrowed were not kept safe and eventually returned. Gradually, the notion of giving some sort of concrete security, such as money, weakened into a spoken pledge, which by modern times had become simply the unspoken assumption that anything that has been borrowed must by definition be returned.

▶ barrow, borough, bury

**bosom** [OE] The immediate source of Old English *bōsm* was West Germanic *bōsm-*, which also produced German *busen* and Dutch *boezem*. It has been conjectured that it may come ultimately from Indo-European *bhāghús*, which perhaps meant 'arm' (source of English *bough* and possibly *bow*, as in 'ship's bow'); the early occurrence of phrases like 'in someone's bosom' meaning 'clasped to someone's chest, in someone's arms' may support this.

▶ bough, bow

**boss** English has two words *boss*, of which the more familiar is far more recent; both are fairly obscure in origin. We know that *boss* 'chief' [19] comes from Dutch *baas* 'master' (it was introduced to American English by Dutch settlers), but where Dutch got the word from we do not know for certain. *Boss* 'protuberance' [13] was borrowed from Old French *boce*, which comes from an assumed general Romance *botja*, but there the trail goes cold.

*Boss-eyed* [19] and *boss shot* 'bungled attempt' [19] are both usually assumed to come from, or at least be connected with a 19th-century English dialect verb *boss* 'bungle,' of unknown origin.

**botany** [17] *Botany* was derived from *botanic*, a borrowing, either directly or via French *botanique*, of Latin *botanicus*. The ultimate source of the word was Greek *botánē* 'plant, pasture,' a derivative of the verb *boskein* 'feed.'

**both** [12] The Old English word for 'both' was *bēgen* (masculine; the feminine and neuter form was *bā*), a relative of a wide range of Indo-European words denoting 'each of two,' including the second syllables of Old Slavic *oba* and Latin *ambō* (represented in English *ambidextrous*). Most Germanic languages extended the base form by adding *-d* or *-th* (as in German *beide* 'both'). In the case of Old Norse, this produced *bāthir*, the form from which English acquired *both*.

▶ ambidextrous

**bother** [18] When the word *bother* first turns up in English in the first half of the 18th century, it is largely in the writings of Irishmen, such as Thomas Sheridan and Jonathan Swift. This has naturally led to speculation that the word may be of Irish origin, but no thoroughly convincing candidate has been found. The superficially similar Irish Gaelic *bodhar* 'deaf, afflicted' is more alike in spelling than pronunciation. Another suggestion is that it may represent an Irish way of saying *pother* [16], an archaic word for 'commotion' which is itself of unknown origin.

**bottle** [14] Etymologically, a *bottle* is a small butt, or barrel. The word comes ultimately from medieval Latin *butticula*, a diminutive form of late Latin *buttis* 'cask' (whence English *butt* 'barrel'). It reached English via Old French *botele*. The 20th-century British colloquial meaning 'nerve, courage' comes from rhyming slang *bottle and glass* 'class.'

In medieval Latin, a servant who handed wine round at meals and looked after the wine cellar was a *buticu-*

*lārius*: hence, via Old French *bouteillier* and Anglo-Norman *buteler*, English *butler* [13].

▶ butler

**bottom** [OE] *Bottom* is a word with cognates widely represented in other Indo-European languages. It comes ultimately from the Indo-European base *bhudh-* or *bhundh-* 'base, foundation,' source of Latin *fundus*, from which English gets *fund, fundamental, foundation*, and *founder* 'sink.' An extended form of the base passed into Germanic as *buthm-* or *buthn-*, which produced German *boden* 'ground, earth' and English *bottom*. The application of the word to the 'buttocks' seems to have arisen towards the end of the 18th century.

▶ foundation, fund, fundamental

**botulism** [19] The fact that Latin *botulus* was used metaphorically for 'intestine' is in this case just a red herring; its principal meaning was 'sausage,' and it was the discovery of the food-poisoning germ in cooked meats, such as sausages, which led to the term *botulism*. Early work on unmasking the bacterium responsible (now known as *Clostridium botulinum*) was done in Germany, and at first the German form of the word, *botulismus*, was used in English, but by the late 1880s we find the naturalized *botulism* fairly well established.

**bouclé** see BUCKLE

**bough** [OE] *Bough* is a word of some antiquity, dispersed far and wide throughout the Indo-European languages, but it is only in English that it has come to mean 'branch.' It comes ultimately from an Indo-European *bhāghūs*; the meaning this had is not altogether clear, but many of its descendants, such as Greek *pakhus* and Sanskrit *bāhús*, centre semantically round 'arm' or 'forearm' (a meaning element which can be discerned in the possibly related *bosom*). Germanic adopted the Indo-European form as *bōgus*, with apparently a shift in signification up the arms towards the shoulders (Old English *bōg, bōh*, Old Norse *bógr*, and Middle Dutch *boech* all meant 'shoulder,' and the Dutch word later came to be applied to the front of a ship – possibly the source of English *bow*).

▶ bosom, bow

**boulder** [13] *Boulder* is an abbreviated form of the original compound noun *boulder-stone*, which was a partial translation of a Scandinavian word which survives in Swedish dialect *bullersten* 'large stone in a stream.' *Sten* is 'stone,' of course, and *buller* is usually identified with Swedish *buller* 'rumbling noise,' on the basis presumably of the sound of a stream gurgling over rocks. *Boulder* first appears on its own, outside the compound *boulder-stone*, in the 17th century.

**boulevard** [18] *Boulevard* is a frenchified version of German *bollwerk* 'fortification' (the corresponding anglicized version is *bulwark*). The meaning of the French word, apparently quite divergent from that of *bulwark*, comes originally from the practice of constructing walkways along the top of demolished ramparts.

▶ bulwark

**bounce** [13] *Bounce* is something of a mystery word. When it first appears in Middle English it means 'hit,' and it does not acquire its modern sense 'rebound' until the late 16th century. There are similar words in other Germanic languages, such as Dutch *bons* 'thump,' but there is no reason to suppose that any of them is actually the source of the English word. Many etymologists incline to the view that *bounce* is an independent onomatopoeic formation.

**bound** English has no fewer than four separate words *bound*. The only one which goes back to Old English is the adjective, meaning 'obliged' or 'destined,' which comes from the past participle of *bind* (in Old English this was *bunden*, which survives partially in 'bounden duty'). Next oldest is the adjective meaning 'going or intending to go' [13] . Originally meaning 'ready,' this was borrowed from Old Norse *búinn*, the past participle of *búa* 'prepare,' which derived from the same ultimate source (the Germanic base *\*bū-* 'dwell, cultivate') as *be, boor, booth, bower, build, burly, bye-law*, and *byre*. The final *-d* of *bound*, which appeared in the 16th century, is probably due to association with *bound* 'obliged.' Virtually contemporary is the noun *bound* 'border, limit' [13]. It originally meant 'landmark,' and came via Anglo-Norman *bounde* from early Old French *bodne* (source also of Old French *borne*, from which English got *bourn*, as in Hamlet's 'undiscovered country from whose bourn no traveller returns'). Its ultimate source was medieval Latin *bodina*, perhaps from a prehistoric Gaulish *\*bodina*. *Boundary* [17] seems to have been formed from the dialectal *bounder*, an agent noun derived from the verb *bound* 'form the edge or limit of.' Finally, *bound* 'leap' [16] comes from Old French *bondir*. It originally meant 'rebound' in English (*rebound* [14] began as an Old French derivative of *bondir*), but this physical sense was a metaphorical transference from an earlier sense related to sound. Old French *bondir* 'resound' came from Vulgar Latin *\*bombitīre* 'hum,' which itself was a derivative of Latin *bombus* 'booming sound' (source of English *bomb*).

▶ band, bend, bind, bond, bundle / be, boor, booth, bower, build, burly, byre, neighbour / boundary, bourn / bomb, rebound

**bounty**   see BEAUTY
**bouquet**   see BUSH
**bourgeois**   see BOROUGH
**bout**   see BOW
**boutique**   see APOTHECARY
**bovine**   see BEEF

**bow** There are three distinct words *bow* in English, although two of them, 'arrow-shooter' [OE] and 'bend the body' [OE], are ultimately related. *Bow* for arrows comes from Old English *boga*, which also meant more generally 'arch'; its source was Germanic *\*bugon*, a derivative of *\*bug-*, the short stem of *\*beugan*. This *\*beugan* was also the source of Old English *bōgan*, antecedent of modern English *bow* 'bend the body,' while the short stem lies additionally behind *bight* [OE] and *bout* [16]. *Buxom*, which originally meant 'flexible' and 'obedient,' derived from *bow* 'bend the body.'

The other *bow* 'front of a boat' [15] was probably borrowed from Dutch *boeg*, a word related to English *bough*.

▶ bight, bout, buxom / bough

**bowdlerize** [19] In 1818 Dr Thomas Bowdler (1754–1825), an English editor, published his *Family Shakespeare*, an expurgated edition of the plays 'in which those words and expressions are omitted which cannot with propriety be read aloud in a family.' This and other similarly censored versions of the English classics led to Bowdler's name being cast as the epitome of Whitehousian suppression. The first recorded use of the verb was in a letter by General P Thompson in 1836.

**bowel** [13] *Bowel* comes via Old French *buel* or *bouel* from Latin *botellus* 'small intestine, sausage,' a diminutive form of *botulus* 'sausage.' The term *botulism* 'food poisoning' was coined on the basis that the toxin responsible for it was originally found in sausages and other preserved meats.

▶ botulism

**bower** [OE] A bower was originally simply a place where one lived; the modern connotation of a 'secluded arbour' did not become fully established until the 16th century. Old English *būr* came from West and North Germanic *\*būraz* or *\*būram*, a derivative of the prolific base *\*bū-* 'dwell,' which also produced *be, boor, booth, bound* 'intending to go,' *build, burly, bye-law, byre*, and the *-bour* of *neighbour*.

▶ be, boor, booth, build, burly, byre, neighbour

**bowl** *Bowl* 'round receptacle' [OE] and *bowl* 'ball used in bowls' [15] come from different sources. The former (Old English *bolle* or *bolla*) comes ultimately from the Germanic base *\*bul-*, *\*bal-*, which was also the source of English *ball, balloon*, and *ballot*. The Middle Dutch form corresponding to Old English *bolle* was *bolle*, which was borrowed into English in the 13th century as *boll*, initially meaning 'bubble' but latterly 'round seed-head.'

The other *bowl* was originally simply a synonym for *ball*, but its modern specialized uses in the game of *bowls*, and the verbal usage 'deliver the ball' in cricket and other games, had already begun their development in the 15th century. The word came via Old French *boule* from Latin *bulla* 'bubble,' which also lies behind English *boil, bull* (as in 'papal bull'), *bullion, bullet, bulletin,* and *bully* (as in 'bully beef'), as well, perhaps, as *bill.*

▶ball, balloon, ballot / boil, bull, bullet, bulletin, bully

**bowler** [19] The bowler hat was apparently named after the Bowlers, a family of 19th-century London hatters who specialized in its manufacture. The first known reference to it comes in the *Saturday Review* 21 September 1861: 'We are informed that he . . . wore . . . a white bowler hat.'

**box** English has two distinct words *box*. The 'receptacle' [OE] probably comes from late Latin *buxis,* a variant of Latin *pyxis* (whence English *pyx* 'container for Communion bread' [14]). This was borrowed from Greek *puxís,* which originally meant not simply 'box,' but specifically 'box made of wood'; for it was a derivative of Greek *púxos,* which via Latin *buxus* has given English *box* the tree [OE].

*Box* 'fight with the fists' is of unknown origin. It first appeared in English as a noun, meaning 'blow' [14], now preserved mainly in 'a box round the ears.'

▶pyx

**boy** [13] The etymology of *boy* has long been problematical, but the now most generally accepted view is that it is probably a reduced form of an unrecorded Anglo-Norman *\*abuie* or *\*embuie* 'fettered,' from the Old French verb *embuier* 'fetter.' This came from Vulgar Latin *\*imboiāre,* a compound verb based on Latin *boiae* 'leather collar, fetter,' which was adapted from Greek *boeiai doraí* 'ox-hides' (hence 'ox-leather thongs'), from *bous* 'ox' (related to English *bovine* and *cow*). The apparently implausible semantic connection is elucidated by the early meaning of *boy* in English, which was 'male servant'; according to this view, a boy was etymologically someone kept in leather fetters, and hence a 'slave' or 'servant.' The current main sense, 'young male,' developed in the 14th century.

▶cow

**boycott** [19] The word *boycott* sprang into general use in the year 1880, to describe the activities of the Irish Land League. This was an organization set up in 1879 by the Irish nationalist Michael Davitt to press for agrarian reforms, rent reductions, etc. Those who did not agree with its aims, it subjected to an organized campaign of ostracism. One of the first to suffer from this was one Captain Charles Cunningham Boycott (1832–97), a British estate manager in County Mayo. Hence 'to boycott,' which became a buzzword of the early 1880s, was quickly adopted by other European languages, and has remained in current use ever since.

**bra** [20] The word *bra* made its first appearance in English in the mid 1930s. It is of course an abbreviation of *brassiere* (an early alternative abbreviated form was *bras*), which was borrowed from French around 1910.

The French term originated in the 17th century, when it meant simply 'bodice'; it appears to have been an alteration of an earlier, Old French *braciere* 'piece of armour for the arm or wrist' (borrowed into English as *bracer* in the 14th century), a derivative of *bras* 'arm.'

**brace** [14] English borrowed *brace* from Old French *brace,* which meant simply '(the length measured by) two arms.' It came from Latin *bracchia,* the plural of *bracchium* 'arm' (source of French *bras* 'arm,' and also of various English technical terms, such as *brachiopod* [19], a type of shellfish, literally 'armfoot'). The word's ultimate source was Greek *brakhíōn* 'arm,' originally 'upper arm,' which was formed from the comparative of *brakhús* 'short,' a relative of English *brief* (the sense development is probably that the upper arm was named from being 'shorter' than the forearm). Of the rather diverse range of meanings the word has in modern English, 'pair' derives from the original notion of 'twoness,' while 'strengthening or supporting structure' owes much to the idea of 'clasping,' mainly contained originally in the verb *brace* [14], from Old French *bracier* 'put one's arms around' (a derivative of Old French *brace*). In English it now only means 'support, strengthen,' the sense 'clasp with the arms' being reserved to *embrace* [14], from Old French *embracer.*

▶brief, embrace

**bracelet** [15] The Latin word for 'bracelet' was *bracchiāle,* a derivative of *bracchium* 'arm' – thus, 'something worn on or round the arm.' This passed into Old French as *bracel,* which made a brief and unconvincing appearance in English in the early 16th century. It was the French diminutive form, *bracelet,* which caught on in English. Its colloquial use as a term for 'handcuffs' goes back to the early 19th century.

**bracket** [16] The word *bracket* appears to have come from medieval French *braguette,* which meant 'codpiece,' a resemblance evidently having been perceived between the codpiece of a pair of men's breeches and the 'projecting architectural support' which was the original meaning of *bracket* in English. Before the word even arrived in English, it had quite an eventful career. The French word was a diminutive form of *brague,* which in the plural meant 'breeches.' It was borrowed from Old Provençal *braga,* which got it from Latin *brāca*; Latin in turn acquired it from Gaulish *brāca,* but the Gaulish word seems ultimately to have been of Germanic origin, and to be related to English *breeches.*

▶breeches

**brag** [13] *Brag* first turned up in English as an adjective, meaning 'spirited' or 'boastful'; the verb and noun did not appear until the 14th century. Where English got the word from, however, remains a mystery. French has *braguer* 'brag,' but it is not clear whether English borrowed from French, or vice versa; French did, however, contribute the derivative *bragard,* which

English adopted as *braggart* [16]. This probably also formed the basis of *braggadocio*, an Italianate coinage first used by the poet Edmund Spenser as a personification of 'boastfulness' in his *Faerie Queene* 1590.

**braid** [OE] The ultimate source of *braid* was West and North Germanic *\*bregthan*, whose underlying meaning was probably 'make sudden jerky movements from side to side.' This was carried through into Old English *bregdan*, but had largely died out by the 16th century. However, 'making swift side-to-side movements' had early developed a special application to the intertwining of strands or threads, and it is this 'plaiting' sense which has survived. The Germanic base *\*bregth-* was also the ultimate source of *bridle*, but the superficially similar *embroider* had a different origin.

▶ bridle, upbraid

**braille** [19] Braille, the system of printing in raised dots for the blind, was named after its inventor, the French teacher Louis Braille (1809–52), himself blind from the age of three. He perfected his set of letter and number signs in 1834, but the term did not appear in English until the early 1850s.

**brain** [OE] Old English *brægen* came from a Germanic *\*bragnam*. Its rather restricted distribution in modern Germanic languages (apart from English *brain* there is only Dutch and Frisian *brein*) suggests that in prehistoric times it may have been limited to the area of North Germany where the Low German dialects were spoken, but it may well have some connection with Greek *brekhmós* 'forehead.'

**braise** [18] *Braise* has a wide range of rather surprising living relatives. Its immediate source is French *braiser*, a derivative of *braise* 'live coals' (from which English gets *brazier* [17] and the *breeze* of *breezeblock*). In Old French this was *brese*, a borrowing from Germanic *\*brasa*, which came from the same base as produced German *braten* 'roast' (as in *bratwurst*) and Old English *brǣdan* 'roast.' The ultimate source of this base was Indo-European *\*bhrē-* 'burn, heat,' which produced such other diverse offspring as English *breath*, *breed*, *brood*, and probably *brawn*.

▶ brawn, brazier, breath, breed, brood

**brake** There are two distinct words *brake* in English. By far the older is that meaning 'overgrown area, thicket' [OE] . Its source is uncertain, but it has been speculated that it is ultimately related to *break*, its original meaning perhaps having been something like 'broken wood.' *Brake* 'decelerating mechanism' [15] meant 'bridle' for stopping a horse's progress, and may have been borrowed from Middle Dutch *braeke*, a word which was used for a wide variety of crushing implements but also apparently for a ring put through the nose

of a draught ox. There may well be some ultimate connection with *break* here too.

▶ break

**bramble** [OE] *Bramble* has several cognates in other Germanic languages, but as with many plant-names it does not always refer to the same plant. Old High German *brāmma*, for instance, is a 'wild rose'; Old Saxon *hiopbrāmio* is a 'hawthorn bush'; and then there is English *broom*. All come from a prehistoric Germanic *\*brǣmoz* 'thorny bush.' In the case of *bramble*, Old English originally had *brēmel*, but the medial -*b*- had developed before the end of the Old English period. The bird-name *brambling* [16] is probably derived from it.

▶ broom

**bran** [13] English borrowed *bran* from Old French *bran*, but its ultimate source is unclear. Modern French *bran* means 'excrement,' and if this had always been a part of the word's make-up it might have been possible to suggest a Celtic origin, perhaps a Gaulish *\*brenno-* (Welsh *braen* and Irish *brean* both mean 'manure'), but English *bran* appears never to have meant anything but 'cereal husks.' It may ultimately be connected with *burn*.

▶ burn

**branch** [13] *Branch* comes via Old French *branche* from late Latin *branca* 'paw,' but its ultimate origins are not known. In other Romance languages it retains more of its original Latin sense (Spanish *branca* 'claw,' for example, and Rumanian *brinca* 'hand, paw'). The semantic connection between 'limb of a tree' and 'appendage of a person or animal' is fairly straightforward (compare BOUGH).

**brand** [OE] A *brand* was originally a 'piece of burning wood'; the word comes from West and North Germanic *\*brandaz*, a derivative of the same base (*\*bran-*, *\*bren-*) as produced *burn*, *brandy*, and perhaps *broil*. In the 16th century it came to be applied to an '(identifying) mark made with a hot iron,' which provided the basis for the modern sense 'particular make of goods,' a 19th-century development. A specialized (now archaic) sense of the word in English and other Germanic languages was 'sword' (perhaps from the flashing sword blade's resemblance to a burning stick). This was borrowed into Vulgar Latin as *\*brando*, and its derived verb *\*brandīre* came into English via Old French as *brandish* [14].

*Brand-new* [16] may be from the notion of emerging pristine from the furnace.

▶ brandish, brandy, broil, burn

**brandy** [17] English acquired the word for this distilled spirit from Dutch *brandewijn*, and at first altered and translated it minimally to *brandewine*. Soon however this became *brandy wine*, and by the mid-17th century the abbreviated *brandy* was in common use.

The Dutch compound meant 'distilled wine,' from *branden*, which denoted 'distil' as well as 'burn' (it was a derivative of *brand* 'fire,' cognate with English *brand*).

▶ brand

**brass** [OE] Related forms occur in one or two other Germanic languages (such as Middle Low German *bras*, which meant simply 'metal'), but essentially *brass* is a mystery word, of unknown ancestry. Its association with 'effrontery' begins in the late 16th century, prefigured by Shakespeare's 'face of brass' in *Love's Labours Lost* 1580, and by the first instances of the use of the derived adjective *brazen* to mean 'shameless' (the underlying notion is probably of a face as hard as brass, and therefore unable to show shame). *Brass* 'high-ranking people,' as in *top brass*, comes from *brass hat* [19], a derogatory slang term for a senior military officer with golden insignia on his cap.

**brat** [16] The origins of *brat* are not altogether clear, but it has plausibly been connected with the English dialect *brat* 'makeshift or ragged garment,' as being the sort of apparel a rough or ill-mannered child might wear. This *brat* first appeared in late Old English as *bratt*, meaning 'cloak,' a borrowing from Old Irish *bratt* 'covering, mantle.'

**brave** [15] The word which today means 'courageous' comes from one which meant 'uncivilized, savage, wild.' English acquired *brave* via French *brave*, Italian *bravo*, and Vulgar Latin *\*brabus* from Latin *barbarus*, source, via a different route, of English *barbarous*. Also from the Italian form come the exclamation *bravo* [18] and its derivative *bravura* [18], while Spanish *bravada* has contributed *bravado* [16].

▶ bravado, bravo, bravura

**brawn** [14] English acquired *brawn* from Anglo-Norman *braun* or Old French *braon*, which meant 'flesh, muscle,' but the word's ultimate origins are not so much a matter of physiological substance as of suitability for cooking and eating. For the source of the French word was Germanic *\*brādon* 'roast,' which can probably be traced back to Indo-European *\*bhrē-* 'burn, heat' (ancestor also of English *braise*, *breath*, *breed*, and *brood*). *Brawn* was thus originally a 'piece of meat suitable for roasting.'

▶ braise, breath, breed, brood

**breach** see BREAK

**bread** [OE] The general Germanic word for 'bread' in prehistoric times was what we now know as *loaf*; *bread* probably originally meant simply '(piece of) food,' but as bread was among the commonest foods, the word *bread* gradually became more specialized, passing via 'piece of bread,' 'broken bread,' to simply 'bread.' Old English *brēad* and related Germanic forms such as German *brot* and Swedish *bröd* point to a hypothetical Germanic precursor *\*brautham*, but the word's

ultimate origins are unknown. Some etymologists have derived it from Indo-European *\*bhreu-*, source of English *brew*.

**breadth** [16] *Breadth* was formed in the 16th century by adding the suffix *-th* (as in *length*) to the already existing noun *brede* 'breadth.' This was an ancient formation, directly derived in prehistoric Germanic times from *\*braid-*, the stem of *broad*. It came into Old English as *brǣdu*.

▶ broad

**break** [OE] *Break* comes via prehistoric Germanic *\*brekan* from the Indo-European base *\*bhreg-*, which also produced Latin *frangere* 'break' (source of English *fraction* and *fracture*). Possibly related words include *brake*, *bark* 'sound made by a dog,' and *brigade*, while the Germanic derived noun *\*brecho* passed into English via Old French as *breach* [14] (Old English had the parallel form *bryce*, which died out). The application of *broke* (originally a variant of the past participle *broken*) to 'insolvency' dates from the 18th century.

▶ bark, brake, breach, brigade, fraction, fracture

**breakfast** [15] Breakfast is the first food one eats in the morning, thereby literally 'breaking' the night's 'fast.' The word is first recorded in a text of 1463: 'Expenses in breakfast, xj d.' It is a lexicalization of the phrase 'break one's fast,' which itself seems to have originated in the 14th century.

**breast** [OE] *Breast* can be traced back via prehistoric Germanic *\*breustam* to an Indo-European base *\*bhrus-* or *\*bhreus-*, whose other descendants, including Old Saxon *brustian* 'bud,' Middle High German *briustern* 'swell,' and Irish *brú* 'abdomen, womb,' suggest that the underlying reference contained in the word may be to the growth and swelling of the female breasts. By the time it reached Old English, as *brēost*, it had already developed a more general, non-sex-specific sense 'chest,' but the meaning element 'mammary gland' has remained throughout, and indeed over the past two hundred years 'chest' has grown steadily more archaic.

**breath** [OE] *Breath* comes ultimately from the Indo-European base *\*bhrē-* 'burn, heat' (source also of *braise*, *breed*, *brood*, and probably *brawn*), and in its original Indo-European form *\*bhrētos* appears to have meant something like the 'steam, vapour, etc given off by something burning or cooking.' When it reached Old English, via Germanic *\*brǣthaz*, it still meant 'smell' or 'exhalation,' and it was not in fact until as late as the 14th century that this notion of 'exhalation' came to be applied to human or animal respiration (the main Old English word for 'breath' had been *ǣthm*, which German still has in the form *atem*). The verb *breathe* is 13th-century.

▶ braise, brawn, breed, brood

**breeches** [OE] The theoretical singular of this word, *breech*, comes from a form which in Old English was plural – *brēc*. Its unrecorded singular, which would have been *\*brōc*, came from a prehistoric West and North Germanic *\*brōks*. The word's ultimate origin is not known, although some connect it with *break*; and it is possible that it was borrowed early on into Gaulish as *brāca*, the probable source of English *bracket*.

The Old Norse descendant of the Germanic form, *brók*, was not only partly responsible for the Scottish version of *breeches, breeks*, but is also the source of *brogue*.

▶ brogue

**breed** [OE] The Old English verb *brēdan* came from West Germanic *\*brōdjan*, a derivative of *\*brōd-*, which produced *brood*. This in turn was based on *\*brō-*, whose ultimate source was the Indo-European base *\*bhrē-* 'burn, heat' (its other English descendants include *braise, breath*, and probably *brawn*). The underlying notion of *breed* is thus not 'reproduction' so much as 'incubation, the warmth which promotes hatching.'

▶ braise, brawn, breath, brood

**breeze** [16] *Breeze* has not always connoted 'lightness' or 'gentleness.' Old Spanish *briza*, its probable source, meant 'cold northeast wind,' and that is the meaning it originally had in English. The word was picked up through English-Spanish contact in Central and South America, and the fact that on the Atlantic coast of the area the onshore winds were from the east and northeast led in the 17th century to *breeze* being applied to any cool wind from the sea (as in 'sea breezes'), and gradually to any light wind. The adjective *breezy* perhaps retains more of the word's earlier 'cold' connotations.

The *breeze* [18] of *breezeblock* is a completely different word, meaning 'cinders,' and comes from French *braise* 'live coals,' source also of English *braise* and *brazier*.

**breviary**     see BRIEF
**brevity**     see BRIEF

**brew** [OE] The ancestral meaning of *brew* has basically to do with 'heat.' It comes from an Indo-European base *\*bhreu-*or *\*bhru-*, which is also the source of Latin *fervēre* 'boil,' from which we get *fervent, ferment*, and the second syllable of *comfrey*. *Broth* and possibly *bread* can be traced back to the same Indo-European base, and some etymologists have linked it with *burn*. To 'brew' was thus originally something like 'make a drink by boiling,' 'fermentation' being a secondary but connected connotation.

▶ broth, comfrey, ferment, fervent

**briar** There are two distinct words *briar* in English, both of which can also be spelled *brier*, and as their meanings are fairly similar, they are often confused. The older [OE] is a name given to the wild rose, although in fact this usage is as recent as the 16th century, and in Old English times the word was used generally

for any prickly bush, including particularly the bramble. The Old English form was *brēr*, but it is not known where this came from. The other *briar*, 'wild heather' [19], is the one whose root is used for making briar pipes. The word comes from French *bruyère*, and was spelled *bruyer* when first introduced into English in the third quarter of the 19th century; the current spelling is due to assimilation to the other *briar*. The French form comes from Gallo-Roman *\*brūcaria*, a derivative of *\*brūcus*, which was borrowed from Gaulish *brūko*. It appears to be related to the Greek word for 'heather,' *ereikē*, from which English gets the technical botanical term *ericaceous* [19].

**bribe** [14] The origin of *bribe* is obscure, and its semantic history is particularly involved. The word first turns up in Old French, as a noun meaning 'piece of bread, especially one given to a beggar.' From this, the progression of senses seems to have been to a more general 'alms'; then to the 'practice of living on alms'; then, pejoratively, to simple 'begging.' From there it was a short step to 'stealing,' and that was the meaning the verb had when first recorded in English. The shift to the current application to financial corruption occurred in the 16th century, originally, it seems, in the context of judges and others in authority who exacted, or 'stole,' money in exchange for favours such as lenient sentences.

**bric-a-brac** [19] *Bric-a-brac* first appears in English in William Thackeray's *The adventures of Philip* 1862: 'all the valuables of the house, including, perhaps, JJ's bricabrac, cabinets, china, and so forth.' It comes from the obsolete French phrase *à bric et à brac* 'at random'; the *brac* element is a fanciful alteration of *bric* 'piece.'

**brick** [15] For what is today such a common phenomenon, the word *brick* made a surprisingly late entry into the English language. But of course until the later Middle Ages, bricks were very little used in Britain. It was not until the mid-15th century that they were introduced by Flemish builders, and they appear to have brought the word, Middle Dutch *bricke*, with them. The ultimate source of the word is not clear, although some have tried to link it with *break*.

**bride** [OE] *Bride* goes back via Old English *brȳd* to Germanic *\*brūthiz*, and has a wide range of relations in other Germanic languages (including German *braut*, Dutch *bruid*, and Swedish *brud*). All mean 'woman being married,' so the word has shown remarkable semantic stability; but where it came from originally is not known. In modern English *bridal* is purely adjectival, but it originated in the Old English noun *brȳdealu* 'wedding feast,' literally 'bride ale.'

**bridegroom**     see GROOM

**bridge** [OE] A distant relative of *bridge*, Old Slavic *bruvino* 'beam,' coupled with the meaning of the cognate Old Norse *bryggja* 'gangway,' suggest that the underlying etymological meaning of the word is not 'spanning structure' but 'road or structure made of logs.' The Norse word, incidentally, produced the Scottish and northern English *brig* 'bridge.'

The card game *bridge* is first unambiguously mentioned in English in the 1880s, and its name has no connection with the 'spanning' *bridge*. The earliest recorded form of the word is *biritch*. Its source has never been satisfactorily explained, but since a game resembling bridge is known to have been played for many centuries in the Middle East, it could well be that the name originated in that area. One suggestion put forward is that it came from an unrecorded Turkish *\*bir-ü*, literally 'one-three' (one hand being exposed during the game while the other three are concealed).

**bridle** [OE] The Old English word was *brīdel*, which came from the same source (Germanic *\*bregd-*) as *braid*. The basic meaning element of this was something like 'pull or twitch jerkily from side to side,' so the application to *bridle*, which one pulls on with reins to one side or the other to control the horse's direction, is fairly clear. The metaphorical verbal sense 'take offence' dates from the 18th century.

▶ braid

**brief** [14] *Brief* comes via Old French *bref* from Latin *brevis* 'short,' which is probably related to Greek *brakhús* 'short,' from which English gets the combining form *brachy-*, as in *brachycephalic*. Latin produced the nominal derivative *breve* 'letter,' later 'summary,' which came into English in the 14th century in the sense 'letter of authority' (German has *brief* simply meaning 'letter'). The notion of an 'abbreviation' or 'summary' followed in the next century, and the modern legal sense 'summary of the facts of a case' developed in the 17th century. This formed the basis of the verbal sense 'inform and instruct,' which is 19th-century. *Briefs* 'underpants' are 20th-century.

The musical use of the noun *breve* began in the 15th century when, logically enough, it meant 'short note.' Modern usage, in which it denotes the longest note, comes from Italian *breve*. Other derivatives of *brief* include *brevity* [16], introduced into English via Anglo-Norman *brevete*; *abbreviate* [15], from late Latin *abbreviāre* (which is also the source, via Old French *abregier*, of *abridge* [14]); and *breviary* 'book of church services' [16], from Latin *breviārium*.

▶ abbreviate, abridge, brevity

**brigade** [17] *Brigade* is one of a small set of words (others are *brigand* and *brigantine*) which go back to Italian *briga* 'strife.' It is not clear where this came from; theories have centered either on a Celtic origin, comparing Old Irish *brig* 'strength,' or on a derivation from the Indo-European base *\*bhreg-*, which produced English *break*. Either way, the noun *briga*

produced the verb *brigare* 'contend, brawl,' from which in turn came the noun *brigata*. This originally meant simply 'crowd or gang of people,' but soon developed the special sense 'military company.' English acquired the word via French *brigade*. Meanwhile, the present participle of the Italian verb had given *brigante*, which English borrowed via Old French as *brigand* [14], and the diminutive *brigantino* 'fighting ship,' source of English *brigantine* [16] (abbreviated in the 18th century to *brig*). *Brigadier* is a 17th-century adoption, from French.

▶ brig, brigand, brigantine

**bright** [OE] *Bright* is a word of ancient origins, going back to Indo-European *\*bhereg-*, which has produced a range of words with the same general meaning in a range of Indo-European languages (for example Sanskrit *bhrājate* 'shine'). The Germanic derivative was *\*berkhtaz*, which produced a number of offspring amongst the early Germanic languages, including Old English *beorht*, Old High German *beraht*, and Old Norse *bjartr*, all now lost except English *bright*.

**brilliant** [17] *Brilliant* comes from French *brillant*, the present participle of *briller* 'shine.' French borrowed the verb from Italian *brillare*, but it is not altogether clear where Italian got it from. One theory is that it came from Vulgar Latin *\*bērillāre*, a derivative of *bērillus* 'precious stone' (whence English *beryl* [13]). The source of the Latin noun was Greek *bérullos*, which may have come from one of the Indo-European languages of India (Sanskrit *vaidūrya* 'cat's-eye' has been compared).

**brim** [13] *Brim* appears out of the blue at the beginning of the 13th century, meaning 'edge, border,' with no apparent ancestor in Old English. It is usually connected with Middle High German *brem* and Old Norse *barmr*, both 'edge,' which would point to a prehistoric Germanic source *\*berm-* or *\*barm-*. It has been conjectured that this could derive from the stem *\*ber-* (source of English *bear* 'carry'), and that the etymological meaning of *brim* is thus 'raised border.' The modern sense 'rim of a hat' is first recorded in Shakespeare.

▶ bear

**brimstone** see SULPHUR

**bring** [OE] *Bring* is an ancient verb, which has come down to us, with great semantic stability, from its Indo-European source *\*bhrengk-*. It is widespread in the Germanic languages, apart from the Scandinavian ones (German has *bringen*, Dutch *brengen*), but outside Germanic it seems to have flourished only in the Celtic languages (Welsh has *hebrwng* 'accompany').

**brisk** see BRUSQUE

**brittle** [14] *Brittle* probably comes from a Germanic stem *\*brut-* 'break,' which had several descendants in Old English (including the verbs *brēotan* and *gebryttan* 'break') that did not survive the Norman Conquest. It came in a more than usual profusion of spellings in Middle English (*bretil, brutil*, etc), not all of which may be the same word; *brottle*, for instance, current from the 14th to the 16th century, may well have come from the aforementioned Old English *brēotan*. There is also the synonymous *brickle* [15], which survived dialectally into the 20th century; this is related ultimately to *break*.

**broach** [14] The original meaning of *broach* was 'pierce,' and it came from a noun meaning 'spike.' The word's ultimate source was the Latin adjective *brocchus* 'pointed, projecting,' which in Vulgar Latin came to be used as a noun, *\*broca* 'spike.' This passed into Old French as *broche*, meaning 'long needle' and also 'spit for roasting.' English first borrowed the word in the 13th century, as *brooch*, and then took it over again in the 14th century in the above quoted French meanings. The nominal senses have now either died out or are restricted to technical contexts, but the verb, from the Vulgar Latin derivative *\*broccare*, remains. From 'pierce,' its meaning became specifically 'tap a barrel,' which in the 16th century was applied metaphorically to 'introduce a subject.'

In French, the noun *broche* has produced a diminutive *brochette* 'skewer,' borrowed into English in the 18th century; while a derivative of the verb *brocher* 'stitch' has been *brochure*, literally 'a few pages stitched together,' also acquired by English in the 18th century. A further relative is *broccoli* [17], plural of Italian *broccolo* 'cabbage sprout,' a diminutive of *brocco* 'shoot,' from Vulgar Latin *\*brocca*.

▶ broccoli, brochure, brooch

**broad** [OE] *Broad*'s close relatives are widespread in the Germanic languages (German *breit*, for example, Dutch *breed*, and Swedish *bred*), pointing to a prehistoric Germanic ancestor *\*braithaz*, but no trace of the word is found in any non-Germanic Indo-European language. The original derived noun was *brede*, which was superseded in the 16th century by *breadth*.

The 20th-century American slang noun use 'woman' may come from an obsolete American compound *broadwife*, short for *abroadwife*, meaning 'woman away from her husband'; this was a term applied to female slaves in relation to their new 'masters.'

▶ breadth

**broadcast** [18] *Broadcast* was originally an adjective and adverb, and meant literally 'scattered widely,' particularly in the context of sowing seeds. A metaphorical sense developed in the late 18th and 19th centuries (William Stubbs, in his *Constitutional History of England* 1875 writes of 'broadcast accusations'), and the word was ready in the early 1920s for application to the transmission of radio signals (the first actual

record of such a use is as a verb, in the April 1921 issue of *Discovery*: 'The [radio] station at Poldhu is used partly for broadcasting Press and other messages to ships').

**broccoli**  see BROACH

**brochure**  see BROACH

**brogue** [16] A brogue was originally a rudimentary sort of shoe worn in the more wild and woolly Celtic corners of the British Isles; the term does not seem to have been applied to today's 'stout country walking shoe' until the early 20th century. The word, Irish and Scots Gaelic *brōg*, comes from Old Norse *brók* 'leg covering,' which is related to English *breeches*; the relationship between 'leg covering' and 'foot covering' is fairly close, and indeed from the 17th to the 19th century *brogue* was used for 'leggings.'

It is not clear whether *brogue* 'Irish accent' [18] is the same word; if it is, it presumably comes from some such notion as 'the speech of those who wear brogues.'

▶ breeches

**broker** [14] *Broker* has no connection with the past tense of *break*. It comes from Anglo-Norman *brocour* 'small trader,' but its ultimate origin is not clear. A variant Anglo-Norman form *abrocour* has fuelled speculation as to a link with Spanish *alboroque* 'sealing of a bargain' and Portuguese *alborcar* 'barter,' which are presumably of Arabic origin (the *al-* representing the Arabic definite article); but other etymologists have sought to link the word with *broach*, as if the underlying sense were 'someone who sells wine from [that is, by broaching] the cask,' and hence any 'retailer.'

**bronze** [18] Until the 18th century, copper alloys were lumped together under the general term *brass*. *Bronze* seems originally to have been introduced as a specialist term for ancient artefacts made from the metal, but the modern distinction tends to be between *brass* (alloy of copper and zinc) and *bronze* (copper and tin). The word comes via French from Italian *bronzo*, but its ultimate source is not clear. Perhaps the likeliest candidate is Persian *birinj, pirinj* 'copper,' but it has also been speculated that it comes via medieval Greek *brontésion* from medieval Latin *aes brundisium*, literally 'brass of Brindisi,' a port on the Adriatic coast of Italy where in antiquity bronze mirrors were made.

**brooch** [13] English acquired *brooch* from Old French *broche*, a source it returned to a century later to borrow *broach*. The French word meant 'long needle,' and at first a *brooch* was simply a decorative pin whose main function was to fasten a garment. Over the centuries the decorative role has replaced the practical one.

▶ broach

**brood** [OE] Like *breed*, *brood* came from a prehistoric Germanic base *\*brōd-*, whose ultimate source was Indo-European *\*bhrē-* 'burn, heat' (its other English descendants include *braise, breath*, and probably *brawn*). The underlying notion of *brood* is thus not so much 'reproduction' as 'incubation, the warmth that promotes hatching.' The verbal sense 'worry' developed in the 18th century.

▶ braise, brawn, breath, breed

**brook** [OE] There are two distinct words *brook* in English. The one meaning 'stream' is comparatively isolated; it apparently has relatives in other Germanic languages (such as German *bruch*), but they mean 'swamp,' and there the story ends. The now rather archaic verb *brook*, however, meaning 'stand for, tolerate,' can be traced right back to an Indo-European base *\*bhrug-*, from which English also gets *fruit* and *frugal*. Its Germanic descendant was *\*brūk-*'use,' which has given rise to a range of current verbs in the Germanic languages, including German *brauchen* 'use, need.' The Old English version was *brūcan*, which also meant 'use.' A particular application to food ('use' in the sense 'eat,' and later 'be able to digest') started to develop in the late Old English period, and by the 16th century this had come to be used more generally (rather like *stomach*) for 'tolerate.'

▶ frugal, fruit

**broom** [OE] *Broom* was originally the name of the yellow-flowered bush; its application to the long-handled brush did not come about until the 15th century (the underlying notion is of a brush made from broom twigs tied to a handle). The plant-name occurs throughout the Germanic languages, but it is applied to quite a wide range of plants: Old High German *brāmma*, for instance, is a 'wild rose'; Old Saxon *hiopbrāmio* is a 'hawthorn bush'; and English *bramble* probably comes from the same source.

▶ bramble

**broth** [OE] *Broth* comes ultimately from the Indo-European base *\*bhreu-* or *\*bhru-* 'heat, boil,' which also produced *brew* and *fervent*. Etymologically, therefore, it means 'liquid in which something has been boiled.' The notion of 'heating' has now disappeared, but it seems to have survived into the modern English period, as is shown by such compounds as *snow-broth* 'melted snow,' first recorded at the end of the 16th century.

The Germanic form *\*brotham* was borrowed into Vulgar Latin as *\*brodo*, which came via Old French *broez* into 13th-century English as *broys* or *browes*. This survives in Scottish English as *brose* 'type of porridge,' as in *Atholl brose*.

▶ brew, fervent, imbrue

**brothel** [14] Originally, *brothel* was a general term of abuse for any worthless or despised person (John Gower, in his *Confessio Amantis* 1393, writes: 'Quoth Achab then, there is one, a brothel, which Micheas hight [who is called Micheas]'); it was a deriv-

ative of the Old English adjective *brothen* 'ruined, degenerate,' which was originally the past participle of the verb *brēothan* 'deteriorate' (possibly a relative of *brēotan* 'break,' which may be connected with *brittle*). In the late 15th century we have the first evidence of its being applied specifically to a 'prostitute.' Thence came the compound *brothel-house*, and by the late 16th century this had been abbreviated to *brothel* in its current sense.

**brother** [OE] The word *brother* is widespread throughout the Indo-European languages. The Indo-European form was *\*bhrāter*, from which are descended, among many others, Latin *frāter* (as in English *fraternal*), Greek *phrātēr*, Sanskrit *bhrātr*, and Breton *breur*. Its Germanic descendant was *\*brōthar*, which, as well as English *brother*, has produced German *bruder*, Dutch *broeder*, and Swedish *broder*.

▶ buddy, fraternal, pal

**brougham** [19] A brougham was a four-wheeled one-horse carriage. It was named after Henry Peter Brougham, first Baron Brougham and Vaux (1778–1868), British Whig politician, jurist, and educational reformer, who designed the original brougham in 1838.

**brow** [OE] In Old English, *brow* meant 'eyelash,' but there seems little doubt, from related words in other languages (such as Sanskrit *bhrūs* and Greek *ophrus*), that the original underlying sense of the word is 'eyebrow,' and this resurfaced, or was recreated, in English in the 11th century. Its ultimate source is Indo-European *\*bhrūs*, which passed via Germanic *brūs* into Old English as *brū*.

**brown** [OE] In Old English, *brown* meant, rather vaguely, 'dark'; it does not seem to have become a definite colour word until the 13th century. It comes from West and North Germanic *\*brūnaz*, which probably goes back ultimately to the same Indo-European source (*\*bheros*) as *bear*, etymologically the 'brown [that is, dark] animal.' An additional meaning of *brown* in Old and Middle English, shared also by related words such as Old High German *brūn*, was 'shining, glistening,' particularly as applied to weapons (it survives in fossilized form in the old ballad *Cospatrick*, recorded in 1802: 'my bonny brown sword'); Old French took it over when it borrowed *brun* from Germanic, and it is the basis of the verb *burnir* 'polish,' from which English gets *burnish* [14]. Another contribution made by French *brun* to English is the feminine diminutive form *brunette* [17]. An earlier Old French variant *burnete* had previously been borrowed by English in the 12th century as *burnet*, and since the 14th century has been applied to a genus of plants of the rose family. The term *burnet moth* is first recorded in 1842.

▶ bear, brunette, burnish

**browse** [16] Although the noun has now largely died out, *browse* was origianlly both a verb and a noun, and appears to come from Old French *broust, brost* 'young shoots, twigs' (hence the verb meant originally 'feed on such shoots'). The source of the French word is not clear, but it is probably ultimately Germanic; a certain similarity in form and meaning has suggested a connection with the Old Saxon verb *brustian* 'bud' which, if it were so, would mean that *browse* is related to *breast*. The modern figurative sense, applied to shops, libraries, etc seems to be 19th-century.

**bruin** see BEAR

**bruise** [OE] Modern English *bruise* is a blend of words from two sources. The main contributor is Old English *brȳsan*, which as well as 'bruise' meant 'crush to pieces,' and is related to Latin *frustum* 'piece broken or cut off.' But then in the early Middle English period we begin to see the influence of the unrelated Old French verb *bruisier* 'break' and its Anglo-Norman form *bruser* (which in modern French has become *briser*). Their main effect has been on the spelling of the word, although the use of *bruise* for 'break' from the 14th to the 17th century seems to have been due to French influence too, rather than a survival of the Old English meaning: 'Had his foot once slipped . . . he would have been bruised in pieces,' *The most dangerous and memorable adventure of Richard Ferris* 1590. *Bruiser* 'large rough man' originated in an 18th-century term for a prize-fighter.

▶ débris

**brunette** see BROWN

**brush** [14] It is not clear whether *brush* for sweeping and *brush* as in *brushwood* are the same word, although both appeared in the language at about the same time, from a French source. *Brush* 'broken branches' comes from *brousse*, the Anglo-Norman version of Old French *broce*, which goes back to an unrecorded Vulgar Latin *\*bruscia*. *Brush* for sweeping, on the other hand, comes from Old French *broisse* or *brosse*. It is tempting to conclude that this is a variant of Old French *broce*, particularly in view of the plausible semantic link that brushwood (cut twigs, etc) bundled together and tied to a handle makes a serviceable brush (that is how *broom* came to mean 'brush'). The verb *brush* 'move fast or heedlessly' comes from Old French *brosser* 'dash through undergrowth,' a derivative of *broce*; its frequent modern connotation of 'touching in passing' comes from the other *brush*.

**brusque** [17] *Brusque* comes ultimately from the name of an unpleasant spiky shrub, the butcher's broom, which instead of normal branches and leaves has twigs flattened into a leaflike shape, with at their ends stiff spines. The term for this in Vulgar Latin was *\*bruscum*, which, passing into Italian as *brusco*, came to be used as an adjective, meaning 'sharp, tart.' French

borrowed it as *brusque* 'lively, fierce,' and passed it on to English. It seems likely that English *brisk* [16] is derived from it.

▶ brisk

**brute** [15] The primordial meaning of *brute* appears to be 'heavy.' It comes from Latin *brūtus* 'heavy,' and it has been speculated that it is related to Latin *grāvis* 'heavy' (from which English gets *grave, gravity*, and *grieve*). In Latin the sense 'heavy' had already progressed to 'stupid,' and it later developed to 'of the lower animals.' It was with this meaning that the word reached English via French. Connotations of 'cruelty' do not begin to appear until the 17th century. *Brut* meaning 'very dry' in relation to champagne is a late 19th-century borrowing of the French adjectival form *brut*, literally 'rough.'

**bubble** [14] Several Germanic languages have words that sound like, and mean the same as, *bubble* – Swedish *bubla*, for instance, and Dutch *bobbel* – but all are relatively modern, and there is no evidence to link them to a common source. As likely as not, the whole family of *bubble* words represents ultimately an attempt to lexicalize the sound of bubbling, by blowing through nearly closed lips.

**buccaneer** [17] A buccaneer was originally 'someone who dried meat on a wooden frame over a fire.' The word comes ultimately from *mukem*, the term for such a frame in the Tupi language of the Caribbean islands, which in the mouths of early French settlers became *boucan* (the Haitian term was *barbacoa*, from which we get *barbecue*). French *boucanier* thus came to be applied in the 17th century to a woodsman in the West Indies who prepared his food in such a way; such men were fairly lawless, and took to piratical ways, bringing their name with them in the late 17th century.

**buck** [OE] Old English had two related words which have coalesced into modern English *buck*: *bucca* 'male goat' and *buc* 'male deer.' Both go back to a prehistoric Germanic stem *\*buk-*, and beyond that probably to an Indo-European source. The 18th-century meaning 'dashing fellow' probably comes ultimately from the related Old Norse *bokki*, a friendly term for a male colleague, which was originally adopted in English in the 14th century meaning simply 'fellow.' The colloquial American sense 'dollar' comes from an abbreviation of *buckskin*, which was used as a unit of trade with the Native Americans in Frontier days.

▶ butcher

**bucket** [13] We first encounter *bucket* in the Anglo-Norman forms *buket* and *buquet*. It is not entirely clear where this came from, but it may be a derivative of Old English *būc*. The primary underlying sense of this was 'something bulging or swelling,' and hence it meant not only 'jug' but also 'belly' (related are German *bauch* and Swedish *buk* 'paunch'). It survived dialectally into modern English as *bowk*, meaning 'milk-pail' and 'large tub used in coal mines.' The *bucket* of 'kick the bucket' was originally a beam from from which slaughtered animals were hung; it is probably a separate word, from Old French *buquet* 'balance.'

**buckle** [14] English acquired *buckle* via Old French *boucla* from Latin *buccula* 'cheek strap of a helmet.' This was a diminutive form of Latin *bucca* 'cheek' (source of French *bouche* 'mouth'), which gave English the anatomical term *buccal* 'of the cheeks' [19], and some have speculated is related to English *pock*. The notion of 'fastening' implicit in the Latin word carried through into English.

As well as 'cheek strap,' Latin *buccula* meant 'boss in the middle of a shield.' Old French *boucle* adopted this sense too, and created the derivative *boucler*, originally an adjective, meaning (of a shield) 'having a central boss.' English borrowed this as *buckler* 'small round shield' [13].

The verb *buckle* was created from the English noun in the late 14th century, but the sense 'distort,' which developed in the 16th century, comes from French *boucler*, which had come to mean 'curl, bulge.' Also from the French verb is *bouclé* 'yarn with irregular loops' [19].

▶ bouclé, buckler

**buckram** [14] Etymologically, *buckram* 'stiffened cloth' is cloth from Bokhara, a city in central Asia (now the Soviet city of Bukhara), from where in the Middle Ages cloth was exported to Europe. And not just any cloth: originally *buckram* denoted a high-quality cotton or linen fabric, and it was only in the 15th century that the word came to be applied to a coarser textile. It came into English from Old French *boquerant*.

**buckwheat** [16] Buckwheat has no connection with male deer. The *buck-* element is related to the English word *beech*, and the name comes from the resemblance of buckwheat (the seeds of a plant of the dock family) to the three-sided seeds of the beech tree. The word was actually borrowed from Middle Dutch *boecweite*, meaning literally 'beechwheat.'

▶ beech

**bud** [14] *Bud* is something of a mystery word. It appears in the late 14th century, with no apparent English ancestors. Various suggestions have been put forward as to its origin, including Old French *boter* 'push forward, thrust' (a distant relative of English *button*). Similarities have also been noted to Old English *budd* 'beetle' and Sanskrit *bhūri* 'abundant.' But the question remains open. The American colloquial form of address *bud* is short for *buddy* [19], probably itself an alteration of *brother*.

**budge** see BULL

**budgerigar** [19] When the first English settlers arrived at Port Jackson (now Sydney Harbour) in the late 18th century, they heard the local Aborigines referring to a small green parrot-like bird as *budgerigar*. In the local language, this meant literally 'good' (*budgeri*) 'cockatoo' (*gar*). The English language had acquired a new word, but to begin with it was not too sure how to spell it; the first recorded attempt, in Leichhardt's *Overland Expedition* 1847, was *betshiregah*. The abbreviated *budgie* is 1930s.

**budget** [15] Originally, a budget was a 'pouch.' English got the word from Old French *bougette*, which was a diminutive form of *bouge* 'leather bag' (from which we get *bulge*). This came from Latin *bulga*, which may have been of Gaulish origin (medieval Irish *bolg* 'bag' has been compared). The word's financial connotations arose in the 18th century, the original notion being that the government minister concerned with treasury affairs opened his budget, or wallet, to reveal what fiscal measures he had in mind. The first reference to the expression occurs in a pamphlet called *The budget opened* 1733 directed against Sir Robert Walpole: 'And how is this to be done? Why by an Alteration only of the present Method of collecting the publick Revenues . . . So then, out it comes at last. The Budget is opened; and our State Empirick hath dispensed his packets by his Zany Couriers through all parts of the Kingdom . . . I do not pretend to understand this Art of political Legerdemain.' The earliest recorded use of the word non-satirically in this sense seems to be from 1764.

▶ bulge

**buff** [16] *Buff* originally meant 'buffalo'; it was presumably an alteration of the French word *buffe* 'buffalo.' That sense had died out by the early 18th century, but since then the word has undergone a bizarre series of semantic changes. First, it came to mean 'leather,' originally from buffalo hides, but later from ox hides. This was commonly used in the 16th and 17th centuries for making military uniforms, so *be in buff* came to mean 'be in the army.' Then in the 17th century the associations of 'hide' and 'skin' led to the expression *in the buff* 'naked.' The colour of buff leather, a sort of dull yellowish-brown, led to the word's adoption in the 18th century as a colour term. In the 19th century, soft buff or suede leather was used for the small pads or wheels used by silversmiths, watchmakers, etc for polishing: hence the verb *buff* 'polish.' And finally, in the 1820s New York City volunteer firemen were known as 'buffs,' from the colour of their uniforms; thus anyone who was a volunteer or enthusiastic for something became known as a *buff* (as in 'film buff').

The *buff* of *blind-man's buff* is a different word. It meant 'blow, punch,' and was borrowed in the 15th century from Old French *buffe*, source also of English *buffet* 'blow' [13]. The term *blind-man's buff* is first recorded around 1600, somewhat later than its now obsolete synonym *hoodman blind*.

▶ buffalo, buffet

**buffalo** [16] English probably acquired *buffalo* from Portuguese *bufalo*, originally naming the 'water buffalo,' *Bubalis bubalis*, a large oxlike animal of Asia and Africa, and subsequently extended to the 'Cape buffalo' of South Africa, *Syncerus caffer*. The Portuguese word came from late Latin *bufalus*, an alteration of Latin *bubalus*, which was borrowed from Greek *boúbalos*. The Greek word, which seems to have named a type of African gazelle, may have been formed from *bous* 'ox.'

The application of the word to the North American bison, which is still regarded as 'incorrect,' dates from the late 18th century.

▶ buff

**buffer** Neither *buffer* 'fellow' [18] nor *buffer* 'shock absorber' [19] can be traced back with any certainty to a source, but the likeliest conjecture is that they both come (independently) from an obsolete English verb *buff*, which was probably originally (like *puff*) imitative of the sound of blowing or breathing out. The earliest recorded sense of this, in the late 13th century, was 'stammer,' and so the human *buffer* may originally have been a 'stammerer.' By the 16th century we find the verb being used in the sense 'make the sound of something soft being hit,' which is a likely source of *buffer* 'shock absorber.'

**bug** [14] Originally, *bug* meant 'something frightening' – and in fact one of the earliest known uses of the word was for what we would now call a 'scarecrow.' It is one of a set of words (others are *bogle* and perhaps *bugaboo*) for alarming or annoying phenomena, usually supernatural, whose interrelationship and ultimate source have never been adequately explained (see BOGEY).

*Bug* 'insect' [16] is probably the same word, although it has also been connected with Old English *budd* 'beetle.' The meanings 'defect' (from the 19th century) and 'germ' and 'hidden microphone' (both 20th-century) all developed from 'insect.'

**bugbear** [16] Early references to *bugbear* suggest that it was a sort of *bug* – 'frightening creature' – conjured up to frighten naughty children. It is usually assumed that the second element of the word simply represents the animal 'bear,' and that the frightening creature was represented as being in the shape of a bear. The modern sense 'source of annoyance' developed in the late 19th century.

**bugger** [16] The Bulgarians, belonging from the early Christian era to the Eastern Orthodox Church, were regarded by Western Europeans as heretics. Thus it was that the Latin word *Bulgarus* came to be applied generically to any heretic, and eventually specifically to

the Albigenses, a Catharistic sect in southern France in the 11th to 13th centuries. It passed via Old French *bougre* and Middle Dutch *bugger* into English, acquiring along the way bigoted associations of heresy with anal intercourse. The weakened use of the word as a general term of abuse dates from the early 18th century.

**bugle** [14] *Bugle* originally meant 'buffalo' or 'bull.' It comes via Old French *bugle* from Latin *būculus*, a diminutive form of *bos* 'ox' (a relative of English *cow*). It was used from the early 14th century in the compound *bugle-horn*, denoting a bull's horn used either as a drinking vessel or as a hunting horn, and it was not long before *bugle* took on a separate life of its own in the 'musical horn' sense.

▶ cow

**build** [OE] In common with a wide range of other English words, including *bower*, *booth*, and the *-bour* of *neighbour*, *build* comes ultimately from the Germanic base *bū-* 'dwell.' A derivative of this, Germanic *buthlam*, passed into Old English as *bold*, which meant 'house'; the verb formed from this, *byldan*, thus originally meant 'construct a house,' and only gradually broadened out in meaning to encompass any sort of structure.

▶ boor, booth, bower, build, byre, neighbour

**bulb** [16] *Bulb* can be traced back to Greek *bólbos*, which was a name for various plants with a rounded swelling underground stem. In its passage via Latin *bulbus* to English it was often applied specifically to the 'onion,' and that was its original meaning in English. Its application to the light bulb, dating from the 1850s, is an extension of an earlier 19th-century sense 'bulb-shaped swelling in a glass tube,' used from the 1830s for thermometer bulbs.

**bulge** [13] Etymologically, *bulge* and *budget* are the same word, and indeed when English first acquired *bulge* it was as a noun, with, like *budget*, the sense 'pouch.' It came from Old French *bouge* 'leather bag,' a descendant of Latin *bulga*, which may have been of Gaulish origin (medieval Irish *bolg* 'bag' has been compared). The word's present-day connotations of 'swelling' and 'protruding' presumably go back to an early association of 'pouches' with 'swelling up when filled' (compare the case of *bellows* and *belly*, which originally meant 'bag,' and came from a source which meant 'swell'), but curiously, apart from an isolated instance around 1400 when *bulge* is used for a 'hump on someone's back,' there is no evidence for this meaning in English before the 17th century. Additionally, from the 17th to the 19th centuries *bulge* was used for the 'bottom of a ship's hull'; it has now been superseded in this sense by *bilge* [15], which may well be a variant form.

▶ bilge, budget

**bulk** [14] Formally, *bulk* comes from Old Norse *búlki*, which meant 'cargo' or 'heap': the original connotation of the English word in this sense was thus of goods loaded loose, in heaps, rather than neatly packed up. That is the source of the phrase *in bulk*. However, a certain similarity in form and meaning to the English word *bouk* 'belly' (from Old English *būc*, and ultimately a descendant of West and North Germanic *\*būkaz*) led to the two being confused, so that *bulk* was used for 'belly,' or more generally 'body.' Modern connotations of 'great size' seem to be a blend of these two.

The *bulk* of *bulkhead* [15] is a different word; it may come from Old Norse *bálkr* 'partition.'

**bull** There are three distinct words *bull* in English. The oldest is the animal name, which first appears in late Old English as *bula*. Related forms occur in other Germanic languages, including German *bulle* and Dutch *bul*. The diminutive *bullock* is also recorded in late Old English. The second *bull* is 'edict' [13], as in 'papal bull.' This comes from medieval Latin *bulla* 'sealed document,' a development of an earlier sense 'seal,' which can be traced back to classical Latin *bulla* 'bubble' (source also of English *bowl*, as in the game of bowls; of *boil* 'heat liquid'; of *budge* [16], via Old French *bouger* and Vulgar Latin *\*bullicāre* 'bubble up, boil'; and probably of *bill* 'statement of charges'). And finally there is 'ludicrous or self-contradictory statement' [17], usually now in the phrase *Irish bull*, whose origins are mysterious; there may be a connection with the Middle English noun *bul* 'falsehood' and the 15th- to 17th-century verb *bull* 'mock, cheat,' which has been linked with Old French *boler* or *bouller* 'deceive.'

The source of the modern colloquial senses 'nonsense' and 'excessive discipline' is not clear. Both are early 20th-century, and closely associated with the synonymous and contemporary *bullshit*, suggesting a conscious link with *bull* the animal. In meaning, however, the first at least is closer to *bull* 'ludicrous statement.'

*Bull's-eye* 'centre of a target' and 'large sweet' are both early 19th-century. *Bulldoze* is from 1870s America, and was apparently originally applied to the punishment of recalcitrant black slaves; it has been conjectured that the underlying connotation was of 'giving someone a dose fit for a bull.' The term *bulldozer* was applied to the vehicle in the 1930s.
▶ phallic / bill, bowl, budge

**bullet** [16] Etymologically, a *bullet* is a 'little ball.' It comes from French *boulette*, a diminutive form of *boule* 'ball', from which English also gets *bowl*, as in the game of bowls. It originally meant 'cannon-ball' as well as 'rifle or pistol projectile,' but this sense had effectively died out by the mid-18th century.
▶ bowl

**bulletin** [17] If a bullet is etymologically a 'little ball,' a *bulletin* is a 'little little edict.' It comes via French *bulletin* from Italian *bulletino*, which was a di-

minutive form of *bulletta* 'document, voting slip' (briefly introduced into English in the 17th century as *bullet*: 'Elected by the Great Master and his Knights, who give their voices by bullets,' George Sandys, *Travels* 1615); French *billet* 'letter,' and indeed English *billet*, as in 'billeting' soldiers on a house, are parallel formations on a variant of the root of *bulletta*. And to return to *bulletta*, this was itself a diminutive form of *bulla*, from medieval Latin *bulla* 'sealed document,' which is the source of English *bull*, as in 'papal bull.'
▶ billet, bull

**bullion** [14] The immediate source of *bullion* was Anglo-Norman *bullion*, which meant 'place where coins are made, mint,' so presumably the underlying connotation is of melting, or 'boiling,' metal down and then turning it into coins. On this reasoning it would come ultimately from Vulgar Latin *\*bulliōnem*, a nominal derivative of Latin *bullīre* 'boil,' from *bulla* 'bubble' (source of English *boil*). The present-day meaning 'gold and silver in bulk' had developed by the mid-15th century.
▶ boil

**bully** [16] *Bullies* have undergone a sad decline in status. In the 16th century the word meant 'sweetheart': 'Though she be somewhat old, it is my own sweet bully,' John Bale, *Three laws* 1538. But gradually the rot set in, its meaning passing through 'fine fellow' to 'blusterer' to the present-day harasser of inferiors. In the 18th and 19th centuries it also meant 'pimp.' It is probably a modification of Dutch *boele* 'lover' which, as a term of endearment, may have originated as baby-talk.

This *bully* has no connection with the *bully* of *bully beef* [18], which comes from French *bouilli*, the past participle of *bouillir* 'boil.' The *bully* of *bully off* [19], a now discontinued way of starting play in hockey, appears to come from a term for 'scrummage' in Eton football, but whether that is related to the cruel *bully* is not clear.

**bulwark** [15] *Bulwark* comes from Middle High German *bolwerc* 'fortification,' a compound formed from *bole* 'plank' (the same word as English *bole* 'tree trunk') and *werc*, equivalent to English *work*. It thus originally meant 'rampart constructed out of planks or tree trunks.' The word was shared by other Germanic languages, including Swedish *bolverk*, and French borrowed it as *boullewerc*, which has since become *boulevard*.
▶ bole, boulevard, work

**bum** There are two distinct words *bum* in English. By far the older, 'buttocks,' is first recorded in John de Trevisa's translation of Ranulph Higden's *Polychronicon* 1387: 'It seemeth that his bum is out that hath that evil [piles] .' It is not clear where it comes from. The other, 'tramp, loafer,' and its associated verb 'spend time aimlessly' [19], chiefly American, probably come from an earlier *bummer*, derived from the German verb *bummeln* 'loaf around, saunter' (familiar to English speakers from the title of Jerome K Jerome's novel *Three Men on the Bummel* 1900, about a jaunt around Germany).

**bump** [16] The earliest recorded sense of *bump* is 'swelling, lump,' but the evidence suggests that the primary meaning is 'knock,' and that this led on to 'swelling' as the result of being hit. It is not clear where the word came from, although it may be of Scandinavian origin; no doubt ultimately it imitates the sound of somebody being hit. The verbal sense 'swell,' now obsolete, is probably responsible for *bumper*, which originally meant 'full glass or cup,' and in the 19th century was extended to anything large or abundant (as in 'bumper crop').

**bumpkin** [16] Originally, *bumpkin* seems to have been a humourously disparaging epithet for a Dutch person: in the first known record of the word, in Peter Levins's *Dictionary of English and Latin words* 1570, it is glossed *batavus* (*Batavia* was the name of an island at the mouth of the Rhine in ancient times, and was henceforth associated with the Netherlands). It was probably a Dutch word, *boomken* 'little tree' (from *boom* 'tree,' related to German *baum* 'tree' and English *beam*), used with reference to Netherlanders' supposedly dumpy stature. The phrase 'country bumpkin' is first recorded from the later 18th century.

▶ beam

**bun** [14] The word *bun* first crops up in 1371, in an Anglo-Latin document relating to different types of bread. Its origins, however, are completely shrouded in mystery. Equally obscure, but presumably unrelated, is another word *bun*, which in the 16th century meant 'squirrel.' By the 19th century we find it being used for 'rabbit,' and it survives in its familiar form *bunny*.

**bunch** [14] *Bunch* originally meant 'swelling' (the first text recorded as containing the word, the Middle English poem *Body and Soul* 1325, speaks of ragged folk 'with broad bunches on their back'), but we have no real clues as to its source. Perhaps, like *bump*, it was ultimately imitative of the sound of hitting something, the sense 'swelling' being the result of the blows. The first hints of the modern sense 'cluster, collection' come in the mid-15th century in the phrase *bunch of straw*, although how this derived from 'swelling' is not clear.

**bundle** [14] Etymologically, *bundle* is 'that which binds or is bound.' Like *band, bend, bind,* and *bond*, it can be traced back ultimately to an Indo-European base *\*bhendh-* 'tie.' The Germanic base *\*bund-*, derived from this, produced Old English *byndelle* 'binding.' There is no direct evidence to link this with the much later *bundle*, although the similarities are striking. Alternatively, the source may be the related Middle Dutch *bundel* 'collection of things tied together.'

▶ band, bend, bind, bond

**bungalow** [17] Etymologically, *bungalow* means simply 'Bengali.' *Banglā* is the Hindi word for 'of Bengal' (as in *Bangladesh*), and English borrowed it (probably in the Gujarati version *bangalo*) in the sense 'house in the Bengal style.' Originally this signified any simple, lightly-built, usually temporary structure, which by definition had only one storey, but it is the one-storeyedness that has come to be the identifying characteristic.

**bunion** [18] *Bunion* is probably a modification of the East Anglian dialect word *bunny* 'lump, swelling,' representing a 15th-century form *bony*, glossed in a contemporary English-Latin dictionary as 'great knob.' This was apparently borrowed from Old French *bugne* 'bump on the head.'

**bunkum** [19] Buncombe is a county of North Carolina, USA. Around 1820, during a debate in the US Congress, its representative Felix Walker rose to make a speech. He spoke on – and on – and on. Fellow congressmen pleaded with him to sit down, but he refused to be deflected, declaring that he had to make a speech 'for Buncombe.' Most of what he said was fatuous and irrelevant, and henceforth *bunkum* (or *buncombe*, as it was at first spelled) became a term for political windbagging intended to ingratiate the speaker with the voters rather than address the real issues. It early passed into the more general sense 'nonsense, claptrap.'

Its abbreviated form, *bunk*, is 20th-century; it was popularized by Henry Ford's remark 'History is more or less bunk,' made in 1916. Of the other English words *bunk*, 'bed' [19] is probably short for *bunker*, which first appeared in 16th-century Scottish English, meaning 'chest, box'; while *bunk* as in *do a bunk* and *bunk off* [19] is of unknown origin.

**bunt** see PUNT

**bunting** *Bunting* 'bird' [13] and *bunting* 'flags' [18] are presumably two distinct words, although in neither case do we really know where they come from. There was a now obsolete English adjective *bunting*, first recorded in the 16th century, which meant 'plump, rounded, short and thick' (could a subliminal memory of it have been in Frank Richards's mind when he named Billy Bunter?). Perhaps the small plump bird, the *bunting*, was called after this. The adjective probably came from an obsolete verb *bunt*, which meant (of a sail) 'swell, billow,' but since we do not know where that came from, it does not get us very much further. As for *bunting* 'flags,' the word originally referred to a loosely woven fabric from which they were made, and it has been conjectured that it came from the English dialect verb *bunt* 'sift,' such cloth having perhaps once been used for sifting flour.

**buoy** [13]   Buoy is of disputed origin, as to both its immediate source and its ultimate derivation. One school of thought holds that English borrowed it directly from Old French *boie* 'chain,' while another views Middle Dutch *boeye* as an intermediate stage. Again some etymologists maintain that its beginnings were amongst the Germanic languages, and have connected it with English *beacon*, while others would trace it via Latin *boia* 'strap' to Greek *boeiai* 'ox-leather straps,' a derivative of *bous* 'ox' (which is related to English *cow*). The meaning of Old French *boie* favours the latter explanation, the semantic link being that buoys are held in place by chains.

Buoyant [16] comes from Spanish *boyante*, the present participle of *boyar* 'float,' which was derived from *boya* 'buoy,' a borrowing from Old French *boie*.

**burden**   There are two distinct words *burden* in English. By far the older, 'load,' comes from Old English *byrthen*. Like *bear, birth, bairn, bier, barrow,* and *berth* it goes back ultimately to an Indo-European base *bher-*, which signified both 'carry' and 'give birth.' Its immediate Germanic ancestor was *burthi-*, which also gave German *bürde* 'load.' The other *burden*, 'refrain,' and hence 'main theme,' is an alteration of an earlier *bourdon* [14] , which was borrowed from Old French *bourdon* 'bass pipe.'

▶ bairn, barrow, bear, berth, bier, birth

**bureau** [17]   Etymologically, *bureau* seems to mean 'red.' Its ultimate source is probably Greek *purrhós* 'red,' a derivative of *pur* 'fire' (as in English *pyre* and *pyrotechnic*), which is related to English *fire*. This was borrowed into Latin as *burrus*, which developed into Old French *bure* 'dark brown.' This seems to have formed the basis of a derivative *burel*, later *bureau*, meaning 'dark brown cloth.' This cloth was used for covering the writing surface of desks, and so eventually *bureau* came to mean 'writing desk' itself. Offices being the natural habitat of writing desks, *bureau* was later applied to them too. The derivative *bureaucracy* is 19th-century, of French origin.

▶ pyre, pyrotechnic

**burgess**   see BOROUGH

**burglar** [15]   The first trace we have of *burglar* is as *burgulator* in 13th-century Anglo-Latin texts, and it appears in Anglo-Norman legal documents of the 15th century as *burgler*. These point to an unrecorded medieval Latin base *burg-* 'plunder,' which appears in Old French *burgur* 'robber.' The verb *burgle* is a 19th-century back-formation from *burglar*.

**burk** [20]   Although *burk* is now the commoner spelling, presumably under the influence of the proper name *Burk*, the original form of the word was *berk*. It is short for *Berkeley* (or perhaps *Berkshire*) *hunt*, rhyming slang for *cunt*. (The Berkeley hunt chases foxes in Gloucestershire.) The pronunciation of the word repre-

sents, of course, the dialectal or nonstandard version of *Berkeley/Berkshire*, rather than the /baːk/ which became standard in southern British English from the 15th century.

**burke** [19]   In present-day English *burke* means 'avoid,' as in 'burke an issue,' but it can be traced back semantically via 'suppress, hush up' to 'suffocate so as to provide a body for surgical dissection.' In this sense it was a macabre adoption of the name of William Burke (1792–1829), an Irishman who with his colleague William Hare set up a profitable but nefarious business in early 19th-century Edinburgh providing cadavers for surgeons to dissect. To begin with they obtained their supplies by robbing graves, but eventually, in order to get higher-quality material, they took to murdering people, generally by suffocation or strangling. Burke was executed.

**burlesque** [17]   French is the immediate source of English *burlesque*, but French got it from Italian *burlesco*, a derivative of *burla* 'joke, fun.' This may come from Vulgar Latin *burrula*, a derivative of late Latin *burra* 'trifle,' perhaps the same word as late Latin *burra* 'wool, shaggy cloth.'

**burly** [13]   Burly has come down in the world over the centuries. Originally it meant 'excellent, noble, stately,' and it appears to come from an unrecorded Old English adjective *burlic*, literally 'bowerly' – that is, 'fit to frequent a lady's apartment.' Gradually, connotations of 'stoutness' and 'sturdiness' began to take over, and by the 15th century the modern 'heavily built' had become well established.

▶ boor, booth, bower

**burn** [OE]   English has two separate words *burn*. The commoner, relating to 'fire,' is actually a conflation of two Old English verbs: *birnan*, which was intransitive, and *bærnan*, which was transitive. Both come ultimately from the Germanic base *bren-*, *bran-*, which also produced *brand* and possibly *broil*, and was the source of German *brennen* and Swedish *brinna* 'burn' (another variant of the base, *brun-*, lies behind the *brim-* of *brimstone*). It has been conjectured that Latin *fervēre* 'boil' (source of English *fervent* and *ferment*) may be connected.

Burn 'stream' comes from Old English *burn(e)*, *burna*, which was a descendant of a Germanic base *brun-*, source also of German *brunne* 'stream.' This too has been linked with Latin *fervēre* (from the notion of fast-running water 'boiling' over rocks).

▶ brand, brimstone, broil, ferment, fervent

**burnish**   see BROWN

**burrow**   see BOROUGH

**bursar**   see PURSE

**burst** [OE]   In Old English, *burst* meant simply 'break suddenly and sharply'; the modern connotation of 'breaking open owing to internal pressure' developed in the 16th century. The word comes from a prehistoric West and North Germanic *brestan, which can be traced back to an Indo-European base *bhrest- (this has been linked with medieval Irish brosc 'noise').

**bury** [OE] Modern English bury is a decendant of Old English byrgan, which came from the Germanic base *burg- (source also of English borough). The underlying meaning of the base was 'protection, shelter,' and in the case of bury this referred to 'covering a dead body with earth' (in Old English, bury applied only to interment; the general sense 'put underground' did not develop until the 14th century). The derived burial goes back to Old English byrgels, which in Middle English times was mistaken for a plural.
▶ borough

**bus** [19] Bus is, of course, short for omnibus. The first person on record as using it was the British writer Harriet Martineau, who spelled it buss: 'if the station offers me a place in the buss,' Weal and woe in Garveloch 1832. Omnibus itself was borrowed from French, where it was first applied in 1828 to a voiture omnibus, literally 'carriage for everyone' (omnibus is the dative plural of Latin omnis 'all').

**busby** [18] Busby originally meant 'large bushy wig,' and so may be related to buzz wig, a term with similar meaning current during the 19th century (and perhaps the inspiration for Sergeant Buzfuz, the lawyer in Dickens's Pickwick Papers). The application to the full-dress fur hat worn by hussars in the British army dates from the early 19th century, but its extension to the Guards' bearskin (still regarded as a solecism in some quarters) seems to have been a 20th-century development.

**bush** [13] Bush comes ultimately from a prehistoric Germanic *busk-, which also produced German busch 'bush.' There is no actual record of the word in Old English, but it probably existed as *bysc. The Germanic base was also borrowed into the Romance languages, where in French it eventually produced bois 'wood.' A diminutive form of this gave English bouquet [18], while a variant bosc may have been at least partly responsible for the now archaic English bosky 'wooded' [16]. A derived Vulgar Latin verb *imboscāre gave English ambush.
▶ ambush, bouquet, oboe

**bust** There are two different words bust in English. The one meaning 'break' [18] is simply an alteration of burst. Bust 'sculpture of head and chest' [17] comes via French buste from Italian busto 'upper body,' of uncertain origin (Latin had the temptingly similar bustum 'monument on a tomb,' but this does not seem to fit in with the word's primary sense 'upper body'). In English, application of the word to the human chest probably developed in the 18th century (one of the earliest

examples is from Byron's Don Juan 1819: 'There was an Irish lady, to whose bust I ne'er saw justice done'), although as late as the early 19th century it could still be used with reference to men's chests, and had not become particularized to female breasts: 'His naked bust would have furnished a model for a statuary,' Washington Irving, A tour on the prairies 1835.

**bustard** [15] Bustard (the name of a large game bird now extinct in Britain) is something of a mystery word. Old French had two terms for the bird, bistarde and oustarde, both of which come from Latin avis tarda, literally 'slow bird' (Latin tardus gave English tardy [15]). This, according to the Roman writer Pliny, was what the bird was called in Spain. It has been objected that the bustard can run quite fast, and that the name avis tarda must be some sort of folk-etymological alteration of a non-Latin word; but in fact the bird's normal gait is a fairly slow and stately walk, so the term is not so far-fetched. The English word is presumably a blend of the two Old French ones, perhaps via an Anglo-Norman *bustarde.
▶ tardy

**busy** [OE] Busy goes back to an Old English bisig, which also meant 'occupied.' Apart from Dutch bezig, it has no apparent relatives in any Indo-European language, and it is not known where it came from. The sense 'inquisitive,' from which we get busybody [16], developed in the late 14th century. Business was originally simply a derivative formed from busy by adding the suffix -ness. In Old English it meant 'anxiety, uneasiness,' reflecting a sense not recorded for the adjective itself until the 14th century. The modern commercial sense seems to have originated in the 15th century. (The modern formation busyness, reflecting the fact that business can no longer be used simply for the 'state of being busy,' is 19th-century.)
▶ pidgin

**but** [OE] But originally meant 'outside.' It was a compound word formed in prehistoric West Germanic from *be (source of English by) and *ūtana (related to English out). This gave Old English būtan, which quickly developed in meaning from 'outside' to 'without, except,' as in 'all but me' (the sense 'outside' survived longer in Scotland than elsewhere). The modern conjunctive use of but did not develop until the late 13th century.
▶ by, out

**butcher** [13] Butcher comes via Anglo-Norman boucher from Old French bouchier, a derivative of boc 'male goat' (this was probably borrowed from a Celtic word which came ultimately from the same Indo-European base as produced English buck). The original sense of the word was thus 'dealer in goat's flesh.'
▶ buck

**butler**   see BOTTLE

**butt**   There are no fewer than four distinct words *butt* in English. The oldest, 'hit with the head' [12], comes via Anglo-Norman *buter* from Old French *boter*. This can be traced back through Vulgar Latin *\*bottāre* 'thrust' (source of English *button*) to a prehistoric Germanic *\*buttan*. Old French *boter* produced a derivative *boteret* 'thrusting,' whose use in the phrase *ars boterez* 'thrusting arch' was the basis of English *buttress* [13].

Butt 'barrel' [14] comes via Anglo-Norman *but* and Old French *bot* or *bout* from late Latin *buttis* 'cask' (a diminutive form of which was the basis of English *bottle*). A derivative of the Anglo-Norman form was *buterie* 'storeroom for casks of alcohol,' from which English gets *buttery* 'food shop in a college' [14]. *Butt* 'target' [14] probably comes from Old French *but* 'goal, shooting target,' but the early English sense 'mound on which a target is set up' suggests association also with French *butte* 'mound, knoll' (which was independently borrowed into English in the 19th century as a term for the isolated steep-sided hills found in the Western states of the USA).

Butt 'thick end' [15], as in 'rifle butt' and 'cigarette butt,' appears to be related to other Germanic words in the same general semantic area, such as Low German *butt* 'blunt' and Middle Dutch *bot* 'stumpy,' and may well come ultimately from the same base as produced *buttock* [13]. (The colloquial American sense of *butt*, 'buttocks,' originated in the 15th century.)

The verb *abut* [15] comes partly from Anglo-Latin *abuttāre*, a derivative of *butta* 'ridge or strip of land,' which may be related to English *butt* 'thick end,' and partly from Old French *aboter*, a derivative of *boter*, from which English gets *butt* 'hit with the head.'

▶ button, buttress / bottle, butler, butte, début / buttock / abut

**butter**   [OE]   The ultimate source of *butter* is Greek *boútūron*. This is usually said to be a compound noun, formed from *boús* 'cow' and *tūros* 'cheese,' but not all etymologists accept the admittedly attractive hypothesis that *butter* was once 'cow-cheese,' preferring to see the Greek word as a foreign borrowing. In Latin it became *būtȳrum* (from which came French *beurre*), which was borrowed into the West Germanic languages, producing English and German *butter* and Dutch *boter*.

▶ cow

**butterfly**   [OE]   A number of theories have been put forward as to how the butterfly got its name. Perhaps the most generally accepted is that it is a reflection of a once-held notion that butterflies land on and consume butter or milk left uncovered in kitchen or dairy (an idea perhaps supported by the German name for the 'butterfly,' *milchdieb*, literally 'milk-thief').

Other suggestions are that the word is a reference to the yellow wings of certain species of the insect, or to the colour of butterflies' excrement.

**button**   [14]   *Button* comes via Old French *bouton* from Vulgar Latin *\*botōne*, a word connected with the verb *\*bottāre* 'thrust' (from which ultimately English gets *butt* 'hit with the head'). The underlying notion contained in *button* is thus of something which pushes up, thrusts itself outwards, rather like a bud growing on a plant; the fact that the resulting round knob is used for fastening is, from the point of view of the word's semantic history, secondary. (Inconclusive attempts have in fact been made to link *bud* with Old French *boter*, a descendant of Vulgar Latin *\*bottāre*, and from the 15th century the word *button* has been applied in English to 'buds.')

▶ butt

**buxom**   [12]   Originally, *buxom* meant 'obedient.' It goes back to an unrecorded *\*būhsum*, which meant literally 'capable of being bent,' and was formed from the verb *būgan* 'bend,' from which modern English gets *bow*. The sequence by which the word's present-day sense developed seems to have been 'compliant, obliging,' 'lively, jolly,' 'healthily plump and vigorous,' and finally (of a woman) 'large-breasted.'

▶ bow

**buy**   [OE]   *Buy* has relatives in most other Germanic languages, with the exception of German, and can be traced back to a prehistoric Germanic *\*bugjan* (the Old English form was *bycgan*), but no non-Germanic connections have ever been identified.

**by**   [OE]   *By* comes from a prehistoric Germanic *\*bi*, which appears ultimately to be the same form as the second syllable of Latin *ambi-* (as in *ambidextrous*), Greek *amphí* (as in *amphitheatre*), and Old English *ymbe*, all of which meant 'on both sides, round.' The original meaning of *by* thus seems to be 'close to, near.' *By* is the basis of the prefix *be-*, as in *befall* and *belong*.

**byelaw**   [13]   Although nowadays often subconsciously thought of as being a 'secondary or additional law,' in fact *byelaw* has no connection with *by*. The closest English relatives of its first syllable are *be, boor, bower, booth, bound* 'about to go,' *build, burly, byre*, and the second syllable of *neighbour*. It comes ultimately from the Germanic base *\*bu-* 'dwell,' and is assumed to have reached English via an unrecorded Old Norse *\*býlagu* 'town law,' a compound of *býr* 'place where people dwell, town, village,' and *lagu*, source of English *law*. It thus originally meant 'law or regulation which applied only to a particular local community,' rather than the whole country.

▶ be, boor, booth, bower, build, burly, byre, neighbour

# C

**cab** [19] *Cab* is short for *cabriolet*, a term, borrowed from French, for a light horse-drawn carriage. It comes, via the French verb *cabrioler*, from Italian *capriolare* 'jump in the air,' a derivative of *capriolo* 'roebuck,' from Latin *capreolus*, a diminutive form of *caper* 'goat' (source of English *caper* 'leap' and *Capricorn*). The reason for its application to the carriage was that the vehicle's suspension was so springy that it appeared to jump up and down as it went along. From the same source comes the *cabriole leg* 'curved furniture leg' [18], from its resemblance to the front leg of a capering animal.
► cabriole, cabriolet, caper, Capricorn

**cabbage** [14] The shape of a cabbage, reminiscent of someone's head, led to its being named in Old French *caboce*, which meant literally 'head.' English acquired the word via the Old Northern French variant *caboche* (whose modern French descendant *caboche*, in the sense 'head,' is said to provide the basis for *Boche*, the contemptuous term for 'Germans'). It is not known where it comes from ultimately; etymologists used to link it with Latin *caput* 'head,' but that theory is no longer generally accepted. The Old English word for 'cabbage' was *cāwel*, which remains with us in the form of various Germanic relatives such as *kohl-rabi, cauliflower*, and Scottish *kale*.
► Boche

**cabin** [14] English acquired *cabin* from Old French *cabane*, which had it via Provençal *cabana* from late Latin *capanna* or *cavanna* 'hut, cabin.' Surprisingly, despite their formal and semantic similarity, which has grown closer together over the centuries, *cabin* has no ultimate connection with *cabinet* [16], whose immediate source is French *cabinet* 'small room.' The etymology of the French word is disputed; some consider it to be a diminutive form of Old Northern French *cabine* 'gambling house,' while others take it as a borrowing from Italian *gabbinetto*, which perhaps ultimately comes from Latin *cavea* 'stall, coop, cage' (from which English gets *cage*). Its modern political sense derives from a 17th-century usage 'private room in which the sovereign's advisors or council meet'; the body that met there was thus called the *Cabinet Council*, which quickly became simply *Cabinet*.

**cable** [13] The ultimate source of *cable* is late Latin *capulum* 'lasso,' a derivative of the verb *capere* 'take, seize,' either directly or perhaps via Arabic *habl*. In Provençal, *capulum* became *cable*, which produced the Old French form *chable*: so English must either have borrowed the word straight from Provençal, or from *\*cable*, an unrecorded Anglo-Norman variant of the Old French word.
► capture, heave

**cabriole** see CAB

**cachet** [17] *Cachet* was a Scottish borrowing of a French word which originally meant 'seal affixed to a letter or document.' In the 19th century this developed into the figurative 'personal stamp, distinguishing characteristic,' which, through its use in the context of distinguished or fashionable people or things, has come to mean 'prestige.' The original notion contained in the word is of 'pressing.' It comes via the medieval French verb *cacher* 'press' from Latin *coactāre* 'constrain.' This was a derivative of *coact-*, the past participial stem of *cōgere* 'drive together' (source of English *cogent*), a compound verb formed from *con-* 'together' and *agere* 'drive' (source of English *act* and a host of other derivatives from *agent* to *prodigal*).

Modern French *cacher* means 'hide,' which is the source of *cache* 'hoard,' borrowed by English in the 19th century.
► cache, cogent

**cack-handed** [19] *Cack* comes from a 15th-century dialect verb meaning 'defecate,' which probably came from Middle Dutch *cacken*. It goes back via Latin *cacāre* to an ultimate Indo-European base *\*kak-*, from which a lot of other Indo-European languages get words connected with 'excrement.' The connection with *cack-handed* is usually explained as being that clumsy people make a mess; on this view 'left-handed,' which *cack-handed* also means, is a secondary sense derived from 'clumsy.' It may be nearer the mark to place 'left-handed' first, however, bearing in mind the traditional role of the left hand in many cultures for wiping the anus.

**cackle**   see CHEEK

**cactus**   [17]   *Cactus* comes via Latin from Greek *káktos*, which was the name of the cardoon, a plant of the thistle family with edible leafstalks. *Cactus* originally had that meaning in English too, and it was not until the 18th century that the Swedish botanist Linnaeus applied the term to a family of similarly prickly plants.

**cad**   see CADET

**cadaver**   [16]   *Cadaver* literally means 'something that has fallen over.' It is a derivative of the Latin verb *cadere* 'fall' (from which English gets a wide range of other words, from *case* to *accident*). Its application to 'dead body' arises from the metaphorical use of the Latin verb for 'die.'

▶ accident, cadence, case

**caddy**   [18]   *Caddy* comes ultimately from Malay *katī*, which was a measure of weight equal to about 0.6 kilos or 1½ pounds: it was thus originally 'container which holds one caddy of tea.' English acquired the word in the 16th century as *catty*, and it is not altogether clear where the *-dd-* spelling came from. It has no connection with the golfer's *caddie* (see CADET).

**cadet**   [17]   Etymologically, a *cadet* is a 'little head.' Its original meaning in English was 'younger son or brother,' and it came from French *cadet*, an alteration of a Gascon dialect term *capdet* 'chief.' This in turn derived from Vulgar Latin *\*capitellus* 'little head,' a diminutive form of Latin *caput* 'head' (from which English also gets *captain* and *chief*). The reason for its apparently rather strange change in meaning from 'chief' to 'younger son' seems to be that the younger sons of Gascon families were in former times sent to the French court to fulfil the role of officers.

When English borrowed French *cadet*, it did so not only in a form that retained the original spelling, but also as *caddie* or *cadee*, which originally meant 'young officer.' The Scottish version, *caddie*, gradually developed in meaning over the centuries through 'person who runs errands' to, in the 19th century, 'golfer's assistant.' *Cad*, originally 'unskilled assistant' [18], is an abbreviation of *caddie* or *cadee*.

▶ captain, chief

**cadre**   see QUARTER

**caesarian**   [17]   The application of the adjective *caesarian* to the delivery of a baby by surgical incision through the abdomen and womb arises from the legend that Julius Caesar (c100–44BC) himself or an earlier ancestor of his was born in this way. The name *Caesar* comes from the Latin phrase *a caeso mātris*

*ūtere*, literally 'from the mother's cut womb' (*caesus* was the past participle of the Latin verb *caedere* 'cut,' from which English gets *concise*, *incise*, *precise*, etc). The abbreviation *caesar* for 'caesarian section' is mid 20th-century.

▶ concise, incise, precise

**café**   see COFFEE

**cafeteria**   see COFFEE

**caffeine**   see COFFEE

**cage**   [13]   English acquired *cage* via Old French *cage* from Latin *cavea*, which meant 'enclosure for animals, such as a coop, hive, or stall,' and also 'dungeon.' This is usually referred to Latin *cavus* 'hollow,' from which English gets *cave* and *cavern*, although not all etymologists agree with this derivation. A Vulgar Latin derivative of *cavea*, *\*caveola*, was the ancestor of English *gaol*, and *cavea* has also been postulated as the ultimate source of *cabinet*.

▶ cabinet, cave, decoy, gaol, jail

**cainozoic**   see RECENT

**cajun**   [19]   *Cajun*, denoting a French-speaking culture of Louisiana, USA, is an alteration of *Acadian*. Acadia was the name of a French colony in Canada (now Nova Scotia, New Brunswick, and Prince Edward Island) whose inhabitants were driven out by the British in the 18th century and migrated to the southern states of the USA (the source of the original French *Acadie* is not known). The word became much more widely known in the 1980s following a sudden fashion for Cajun food and dance music.

**cake**   [13]   Originally, *cake* was a term for a flat round loaf of bread (it is this 'shape' element in its meaning that lies behind more modern usages such as 'cake of soap'). It is not until the 15th century that we find it being applied to foodstuffs we would now recognize as cakes, made with butter, eggs, and some sort of sweetening agent. English borrowed the word from Old Norse *kaka*; it is related to *cookie* (from Dutch *koekje*), but not, despite the similarity, to *cook*. The expression *piece of cake* 'something easy' seems to have originated in the 1930s.

▶ cookie

**calcium**   [19]   *Calcium* was coined by the English chemist Sir Humphry Davy in 1808 on the basis of Latin *calx* 'limestone' (which is also the ancestor of English *calcareous*, *calculate*, *calculus*, *causeway*, and *chalk*). The Latin word probably came from Greek *khálix*, which meant 'pebble' as well as 'limestone.'

▶ calcarious, calculate, causeway, chalk

**calculate**   [16]   *Calculate* comes from the past participial stem of the Latin verb *calculāre*, a derivative of the noun *calculus*, which meant 'pebble.' This was almost certainly a diminutive form of Latin *calx*, from which English gets *calcium* and *chalk*. The notion of 'counting' was present in the word from ancient times, for a specialized sense of Latin *calculus* was 'stone used in counting, counter' (its modern mathematical application to differential and integral calculus dates from the 18th century). Another sense of Latin *calculus* was 'stone in the bladder or kidney,' which was its meaning when originally borrowed into English in the 17th century.

▶ calcarious, calcium, calculus, causeway, chalk

**calendar** [13] English acquired *calendar* via Anglo-Norman *calender* and Old French *calendier* from Latin *calendārium*, which was a 'moneylender's account book.' It got its name from the *calends* (Latin *calendae*), the first day of the Roman month, when debts fell due. Latin *calendae* in turn came from a base *kal-* 'call, proclaim,' the underlying notion being that in ancient Rome the order of days was publicly announced at the beginning of the month.

The *calendula* [19], a plant of the daisy family, gets its name from Latin *calendae*, perhaps owing to its once having been used for curing menstrual disorders. *Calender* 'press cloth or paper between rollers' [15], however, has no connection with *calendar*; it probably comes from Greek *kúlindros* 'roller,' source of English *cylinder*.

**calf** English has two distinct words *calf*, both of Germanic origin. *Calf* 'young cow' goes back to Old English *cealf*, descendant of a prehistoric West Germanic *kalbam*, which also produced German *kalb* and Dutch *kalf*. *Calf* of the leg [14] was borrowed from Old Norse *kálfi*, of unknown origin.

**calibre** [16] *Calibre*, and the related *calliper*, are of Arabic origin. They come ultimately from Arabic *qālib* 'shoemaker's last, mould' (there is some dispute over the source of this: some etymologists simply derive it from the Arabic verb *qalaba* 'turn, convert,' while others trace it back to Greek *kalapoús*, literally 'wooden foot,' a compound formed from *kalon* 'wood,' originally 'firewood,' a derivative of *kaiein* 'burn,' and *poús* 'foot'). English acquired the Arabic word via Italian *calibro* and French *calibre*. The original Western meaning, 'diameter of a bullet, cannon-ball, etc,' derives from the Arabic sense 'mould for casting metal.'

*Calliper* [16], which originally meant 'instrument for measuring diameters,' is generally taken to be an alteration of *calibre*.

▶ calliper

**calico** [16] *Calico*, a plain cotton cloth, was originally *Calicut-cloth*. In the 16th and 17th centuries it was the main export of Calicut, now known as Kozhikode, a city and port on the southwest coast of India whose first European visitor was the Portuguese explorer Vasco da Gama (c1469–1524). In the 19th century Calicut was South India's major port. (It has no connection with Calcutta.)

**call** [OE] Essentially, *call* is a Scandinavian word, although it does occur once in an Old English text, the late 10th-century *Battle of Maldon*. It was borrowed from Old Norse *kalla*, which can be traced back via West and North Germanic *kal-* to an Indo-European base *gol-* (among other derivatives of this is Serbo-Croat *glagól* 'word,' source of *Glagolitic*, a term for an early Slavic alphabet).

**calligraphy**　　see KALEIDOSCOPE
**calliper**　　see CALIBRE
**callisthenics**　　see KALEIDOSCOPE
**callow** [OE] Old English *calu* meant 'bald.' Eventually, the word came to be applied to young birds which as yet had no feathers, and by the late 16th century it had been extended metaphorically to any young inexperienced person or creature. It probably came, via West Germanic *kalwaz*, from Latin *calvus* 'bald.'

▶ calvary

**calm** [14] The underlying meaning of *calm* seems to be not far removed from 'siesta.' It comes ultimately from Greek *kauma* 'heat,' which was borrowed into late Latin as *cauma*. This appears to have been applied progressively to the 'great heat of the midday sun,' to 'rest taken during this period,' and finally to simply 'quietness, absence of activity.' *Cauma* passed into Old Italian as *calma*, and English seems to have got the word from Italian.

**calorie**　　see CAULDRON
**calumny**　　see CHALLENGE
**calvary** [18] Latin *calvāria* meant literally 'skull' (it was a derivative of *calva* 'scalp,' which in turn came from *calvus* 'bald,' source of English *callow*). It was therefore used to translate Aramaic *gulgūtha*, also 'skull,' which was the name of the hill outside Jerusalem on which Christ was crucified (applied to it because of its shape).

▶ callow

**cambium**　　see CHANGE
**camel** [OE] Naturally enough, *camel* is of Semitic origin: Hebrew has *gāmāl*, for example, and Arabic *jamal*. It was a relative of these that was the source of Greek *kámēlos*, which passed via Latin *camēlus* into English as early as the mid 10th century. (It replaced a previous Old English *olfend*, a word – shared by other early Germanic languages – apparently based on the misconception that a camel was an elephant.)

**cameo** [15] The immediate source of modern English *cameo* was Italian *cameo* or *cammeo*. No one is too sure where it ultimately came from, but it has always been assumed that it had some sort of Oriental source – perhaps Arabic *qamaā'īl* 'flower buds.' The original form of the word in English was *cameu*, which came from Old French *camahieu*; the Italianate *cameo* does not appear until the late 17th century.

**camera** [18] Latin *camera* originally meant 'vaulted room' (a sense preserved in the *Radcliffe Camera*, an 18th-century building housing part of Oxford University library, which has a vaulted roof). It came from Greek *kamárā* 'vault, arch,' which is ultimately related to English *chimney*. In due course the meaning 'vaulted room' became weakened to simply 'room,' which reached English, via Old French *chambre*, as *chamber*, and is preserved in the legal Latin phrase *in camera* 'privately, in judge's chambers.'

In the 17th century, an optical instrument was invented consisting of a small closed box with a lens fixed in one side which produced an image of external objects on the inside of the box. The same effect could be got in a small darkened room, and so the device was called a *camera obscura* 'dark chamber.' When the new science of photography developed in the 19th century, using the basic principle of the *camera obscura*, *camera* was applied to the picture-forming box.

▶ chamber, chimney

**camouflage** [20] *Camouflage* reached the English language during World War I, when the art of concealing objects from the enemy was considerably developed. It is of French origin, a derivative of the verb *camoufler* 'disguise,' which came from Italian *camuffare* 'disguise, trick.'

**camp** [16] Latin *campus* meant 'open field.' It branched out into various more specialized meanings. One of them, for example, was 'battle field': this was borrowed into the Germanic languages as 'battle' (German has *kampf*, for instance, as in the title of Adolf Hitler's book *Mein Kampf* 'My struggle'). Another was 'place for military exercises,' and this seems to have developed, in the word's passage via Italian *campo* and French *camp*, to 'place where troops are housed.' English got the word from French.

*Camp* 'mannered, effeminate' [20] is presumably a different word, but its origins are obscure.

Latin *campus* itself was adopted in English in the 18th century for the 'grounds of a college.' It was originally applied to Princeton university in the USA.

▶ campaign, champion, decamp, scamp

**campaign** [17] Ultimately, *campaign* and *champagne* are the same word. Both go back to late Latin *campānia*, a derivative of Latin *campus* 'open field' (source of English *camp*). This passed into Old French as *champagne* and into Italian as *campagna* 'open country,' and both words have subsequently come to be used as the designation of regions in France and Italy (whence English *champagne* [17], wine made in the Champagne area of eastern France). The French word was also borrowed into English much earlier, as the now archaic *champaign* 'open country' [14]. Meanwhile, in Italian a particular military application of *campagna* had arisen: armies disliked fighting in winter because of the bad weather, so they stayed in camp, not emerging to do battle in the open countryside (the *campagna*) until summer. Hence *campagna* came to mean 'military operations'; it was borrowed into French as *campagne*, and thence into English.

▶ camp, champagne

**camphor** [15] *Camphor* is probably of Indian origin. It has been traced back to Sanskrit *karpūram*, which appears to have reached English via Arabic *kāfūr* and then either Old French *camphre* or medieval Latin *camphora*. European forms replaced the long Arabic *ā* with a nasalized vowel.

**can** [OE] English has two distinct words *can*. The verb 'be able to' goes back via Old English *cunnan* and Germanic *\*kunnan* to an Indo-European base *\*gn-*, which also produced *know*. The underlying etymological meaning of *can* is thus 'know' or more specifically 'come to know,' which survived in English until comparatively recently (in Ben Jonson's *The Magnetick Lady* 1632, for example, we find 'She could the Bible in the holy tongue'). This developed into 'know how to do something,' from which we get the current 'be able to do something.' The past tense *could* comes ultimately from prehistoric Germanic *\*kuntha*, via Old English *cūthe* (related to English *uncouth*) and late Middle English *coude*; the *l* is a 16th-century intrusion, based on the model of *should* and *would*. (*Canny* [16] is probably a derivative of the verb *can*, mirroring a much earlier but parallel formation *cunning*.)

*Can* 'container' appears to come from a prehistoric Germanic *\*kannōn-*.

▶ canny, cunning, ken, know, uncouth

**canary** [16] Small green finches (*Serinus canarius*) native to the Canary Islands were introduced as cage birds in England in the 16th century (the domestic breed is now for the most part yellow). They were called, naturally enough, *canary birds*, and by the mid 17th century this had become simply *canary*. The Canaries, a group of Spanish islands in the Atlantic off the northwest coast of Africa, got their name because one of them was famous in Roman times for a large breed of dog found there (Latin *canārius* 'of dogs' was a derivative of *canis*, source of English *canine*, *chenille*, and *kennel* and related to English *hound*).

▶ canine, chenille, hound, kennel

**cancan** [19] The English word was borrowed from French, where it originally, in the 16th century, meant 'noise, uproar.' Its ultimate source is unknown, although it has traditionally been associated with Latin *quanquam* 'although,' taken to be the prelude to a noisy scholastic argument. Its application to the uproarious dance began in the 19th century, in French as well as English; however, its present-day association with high-kicking chorus girls (with, according to the *Oxford English Dictionary*, 'extravagant and indecent gestures') seems to be a slightly later development, since the earliest examples of its use quoted by the *OED* apparently refer to men: 'He usually compromises by dancing the Can-can,' A E Sweet, *Texas Siftings* 1882.

**cancel** see CHANCELLOR

**cancer** [14] *Cancer* comes from Latin *cancer*, which meant literally 'crab.' It was a translation of Greek *karkínos* 'crab,' which, together with its derivative *karkínōma* (source of English *carcinoma* [18]) was, according to the ancient Greek physician Galen, applied to tumours on account of the crablike pattern formed by the distended blood vessels around the affected part. Until the 17th century, the term generally used for the condition in English was *canker*, which arose from an earlier borrowing of Latin *cancer* in Old English times; before then, *cancer* had been used exclusively in the astrological sense. The French derivative of Latin *cancer*, *chancre*, was borrowed into English in the 16th century for 'syphilitic ulcer.'

▶ canker, carcinoma

**candelabrum** see CANDLE

**candid** [17] Originally, *candid* meant simply 'white'; its current sense 'frank' developed metaphorically via 'pure' and 'unbiased.' English acquired the word, probably through French *candide*, from Latin *candidum*, a derivative of the verb *candēre* 'be white, glow' (which is related to English *candle*, *incandescent*, and *incense*). The derived noun *candour* is 18th-century in English. *Candida*, the fungus which causes the disease *thrush*, got its name from being 'white.' And in ancient Rome, people who were standing for election wore white togas; they were thus called *candidāti*, whence English *candidate* [17].

▶ candidate, candle, incandescent, incense

**candle** [OE] *Candle* is one of the earliest English borrowings from Latin. It probably arrived with Christianity at the end of the 6th century, and is first recorded in a gloss from around the year 700. Latin *candēla* was a derivative of the verb *candēre* 'be white, glow,' also the source of English *candid* and related to *incandescent* and *incense*. *Candelabrum* [19] is a Latin derivative.

The Christian feast of *Candlemas* [OE] (February 2) gets its name from the blessing of church candles on that day.

▶ candelabrum, candid, incandescent, incense

**cane** [14] *Cane* is a word of ancient ancestry. It can be traced back to Sumerian *gin* 'reed,' and has come down to us via Assyrian *kanū* and Greek *kánna* (a derivative of which, *kánastron* 'wicker basket,' was the ultimate source of English *canister* [17]). Latin borrowed the word as *canna*, and broadened its meaning out from 'reed, cane' to 'pipe,' which is the basis of English *ca-*

*nal, channel, cannon,* and *canyon*. From Latin came Old French *cane*, source of the English word.

▶ canal, canister, cannon, canyon, channel

**canine** see KENNEL

**cannibal** [16] *Cannibal* was originally a proper name, applied by the Spaniards to the Carib people of the West Indies (whom they regarded as eaters of human flesh). It is a variant, originally used by Christopher Columbus, of *Caribes*, which comes from *Carib*, a word of Carib origin in the Arawakan language of northern South America and the Caribbean. It is related to the Caribs' name for themselves, *Galibi*, literally 'strong men.'

**cannon** English has two different words *cannon*, neither of which can for certain be connected with *canon*. The earlier, 'large gun' [16] , comes via French *canon* from Italian *cannone* 'large tube,' which was a derivative of *canna* 'tube, pipe,' from Latin *canna* (source of English *cane*). *Cannon* as in 'cannon off something' [19] is originally a billiards term, and was an alteration (by association with *cannon* the gun) of an earlier *carom* (the form still used in American English). This came from Spanish *carombola*, a kind of fruit fancifully held to resemble a billiard ball, whose ultimate source was probably an unrecorded *\*karambal* in the Marathi language of south central India.

▶ cane / carom

**canny** see CAN

**canoe** [16] Like *cannibal*, *canoe* is a word of Caribbean origin. In the language of the local Carib people it was *canaoua*, and it passed via Arawakan into Spanish (recorded by Christopher Columbus) as *canoa*. That was the form in which it first came into English; modern *canoe* is due to the influence of French *canoe*. Originally, the word was used for referring to any simple boat used by 'primitive' tribes; it was not until the late 18th century that a more settled idea of what we would today recognize as a canoe began to emerge.

**canon** There are today two distinct words *canon* in English, although ultimately they are related. The older, '(ecclesiastical) rule' [OE] , comes via Latin *canōn* from Greek *kanōn* 'rule,' which some have speculated may be related to Greek *kánnā* 'reed,' source of English *cane* (the semantic link is said to be 'reed' – 'rod' – 'measuring rod' – 'rule'). The derived adjective, *kanonikós*, passed into ecclesiastical Latin as *canonicus*, which was used as a noun, 'clergyman'; in Old French this became *canonie* or *chanonie*, and as it crossed into English its last syllable dropped off (owing to the influence of *canon* 'rule'). The underlying sense of *canon* 'clergyman' [13] is thus 'one living according to the rules of religious life.'

**canopy** [14] Etymologically, a *canopy* is a 'mosquito net.' The word comes ultimately from Greek *kōnōpeion*, a derivative of *kónops* 'mosquito.' This passed via Latin *cōnōpūum* into medieval Latin as *canopeum*, which meant both 'mosquito net' and 'couch with such a net.' English adopted it directly from Latin as *canope* or *canape*, meaning 'covering suspended over a throne, bed, etc.' The French version of the word, however, concentrated on other aspects of *canopeum*'s meaning; French *canapé* means 'couch, sofa.' Its metaphorical extension, 'piece of bread or biscuit with a savoury topping,' was borrowed into English towards the end of the 19th century.

► canapé

**cant**   English has two separate words *cant*. The older, 'oblique angle' [14], originally meant 'edge,' and appears to have come via Middle Low German *kant* or Middle Dutch *cant*, both meaning 'edge' or 'corner,' from Vulgar Latin *\*canto*, a descendant of Latin *cantus* 'iron tyre,' which was probably of Celtic origin (Welsh *cant* means 'rim'). The accusative case of the Vulgar Latin word, *\*cantōnem*, was the source of English *canton* [16], originally 'corner, section,' now 'territorial division'; while its Italian descendant, *canto*, may be the source of Italian *cantina* 'cellar,' from which English got *canteen* [18]. *Cant* 'thieves' jargon' or 'hypocritical talk' [16] was probably originally a specific application of the Latin verb *cantāre* 'sing' (source also of English *chant*, *canto*, *cantor*, *cantata*, and *canticle*). It is usually assumed that the usage derives from an ironic transference of the singing of church congregations or choirs to the wheedling 'song' of beggars and (by association) thieves.

► canteen, canton / cantata, cantor, chant

**cantankerous**   [18]   *Cantankerous* is a rather mysterious word. It first appears in the 1770s, and the earliest known reference to it is in Oliver Goldsmith's *She Stoops to Conquer* 1772: 'There's not a more bitter cantanckerous road in all christendom.' Its origin is disputed: perhaps the likeliest source is Middle English *contekour* 'brawler,' from *contek* 'strife,' a borrowing from an unrecorded Anglo-Norman *\*contek*, but an Irish origin has also been suggested, perhaps from Irish *cannrán* 'strife, grumbling' (another early user of the word was the Irish playwright Thomas Sheridan).

**cantata**   see CHANT

**canteen**   see CANT

**canter**   [18]   *Canter* comes from phrases such as *Canterbury trot*, *Canterbury pace*, etc, which were terms applied to the pace at which medieval pilgrims rode on their way by horse to the shrine of Thomas a'Beckett at Canterbury in Kent (earliest references to it are from the 17th century, much later than the time of Chaucer's pilgrims in the Middle Ages). The abbreviated form *canter* appeared in the 18th century, initially as a verb, and Samuel Johnson in his *Dictionary* 1755 de-

fined *Canterbury gallop* as 'the hand gallop of an ambling horse, commonly called a canter.'

**canticle**   see CHANT

**canto**   see CHANT

**canton**   see CANT

**canvas**   [14]   *Canvas* is related ultimately to *hemp*, for originally canvas was a cloth made from hemp. Latin *cannabis* (from the same source as English *hemp*) produced the Vulgar Latin derivative *\*cannapāceum*, which passed into English via Old Northern French *canevas*. The verb *canvass* [16] appears to come from the noun: it originally meant 'toss in a canvas sheet,' and this was perhaps the basis, via an intermediate 'criticize roughly,' of the metaphorical sense 'discuss thoroughly.' It is not clear where the political meaning 'solicit votes' came from.

► cannabis, hemp

**cap**   [OE]   Old English *cæppa* came from late Latin *cappa* 'hood,' source also of English *cape* 'cloak.' The late Latin word may well have come from Latin *caput* 'head,' its underlying meaning thus being 'head-covering.'

► chapel, chaperone, képi

**capable**   [16]   In common with a wide range of other English words, from *capture* to *recuperate*, *capable* comes from Latin *capere* 'take,' a relative of English *heave*. An adjective derived from the verb was Latin *capāx* 'able to hold much,' from which English gets *capacious* [17] and *capacity* [15]. From its stem *capāci-* was formed the late Latin adjective *capābilis*, also originally 'able to contain things.' This meaning still survived when the word passed, via French *capable*, into English ('They are almost capable of a bushel of wheat,' Thomas Wright, *The Passions of the Mind* 1601), but by the end of the 18th century it had died out, having passed into the current 'able to, susceptible of.'

► capacious, capacity, capture, chase, heave, recuperate

**cape**   There are two distinct words *cape* in English, but they may come from the same ultimate source. The earlier, 'promomtory, headland' [14], comes via Old French *cap* and Provençal *cap* from Vulgar Latin *\*capo*, a derivative of Latin *caput* 'head.' *Cape* 'cloak' [16] comes via French *cape* and Provençal *capa* from late Latin *cappa* 'hood,' source of English *cap*; this too may be traceable back to Latin *caput*. (Other English descendants of *caput* include *achieve*, *cadet*, *capital*, *captain*, *chapter*, and *chief*; and *cappa* was also the precursor of *chapel*, *chaperone*, and *cope*).

► achieve, cadet, capital, captain, chapel, chaperon, chapter, chief, escape

**caper**   *Caper* 'jump about' [16] and the edible *caper* [15] are two different words. The former is a shortening of *capriole* 'leap,' now obsolete except as a technical term in horsemanship, which comes via early

French *capriole* from Italian *capriola*, a derivative of the verb *capriolare* 'leap,' which in turn was formed from *capriolo* 'roebuck'; its ultimate source was Latin *capreolus*, a diminutive form of *caper* 'goat' (whence the English astrological term *Capricorn*, literally 'goat's horn'). (The French by-form *cabrioler* was the source of English *cab*.) *Caper* 'edible bud' came via French *câpres* and Latin *capparis* from Greek *kápparis*; the earliest English form was *capres*, but this came to be misinterpreted as a plural, and the *-s* was dropped from the singular in the 16th century.

▶ cab, Capricorn, capriole

**capercaillie**    [16]    The name of the capercaillie, a very large species of grouse, means literally 'horse of the woods' in Scots Gaelic. The Gaelic form of the word is *capalcoille*, a compound formed from *capall* 'horse' (probably borrowed from Latin *caballus* 'horse,' source of English *cavalier*) and *coille* 'woods.'

▶ cavalier

**capillary**    see DISHEVELLED

**capital**    [13]    Etymologically, *capital* is something that is at the top or 'head'; it comes from Latin *caput* 'head.' The various current English uses of the word reached us, however, by differing routes. The first to come was the adjective, which originally meant simply 'of the head' (Milton in *Paradise lost* wrote of the Serpent's 'capital bruise,' meaning the bruise to its head); this came via Old French *capital* from Latin *capitālis*, a derivative of *caput*. The other senses of the adjective have derived from this: 'capital punishment,' for instance, comes from the notion of a crime which, figuratively speaking, affects the head, or life. Its use as a noun dates from the 17th century: the immediate source of the financial sense is Italian *capitale*. The architectural *capital* 'top of a column' (as in 'Corinthian capitals') also comes from Latin *caput*, but in this case the intermediate form was the diminutive *capitellum* 'little head,' which reached English in the 14th century via Old French *capitel*.

▶ cattle, chapter, head

**capitulate**    see CHAPTER

**capon**    [OE]    *Capon*, a 'castrated male chicken,' is probably literally a 'cut cockerel.' The word comes via Anglo-Norman *capun* from Latin *capō*, which is probably ultimately derived from a word for 'cut' – Greek *kóptein*, for example – the underlying reference of course being to the cutting off of the unfortunate bird's testicles.

**caprice**    [17]    Etymologically, *caprice* means 'hedgehog-head.' It comes, via French *caprice*, from an Italian noun *capriccio*, formed from *capo* 'head' (from Latin *caput*) and *riccio* 'hedgehog' (from Latin *ericeus*, source of English *urchin*). Originally this meant 'horror, shuddering,' the reference being to the hair of a terror-stricken person standing on end. The

word's present-day meaning 'whim, fickleness' seems to be partly due to association with Italian *capra* 'goat,' from the animal's frisky behaviour.

▶ urchin

**capsicum**    see CASE

**capstan**    [14]    *Capstan* is a borrowing from Old Provençal. There the word was *cabestan*. Its earlier form *capestran* was a derivative of *capestre* 'rope, noose,' which came from Latin *capistrum* 'halter.' This in turn came from *capere* 'take,' a prolific source of English words, and related to English *heave*.

▶ capture, heave

**capsule**    see CASE

**captain**    [14]    Etymologically, a *captain* is someone who is at the 'head' of an organization, team, etc. It derives ultimately from late Latin *capitāneus* 'chief,' a derivative of *caput* 'head,' which came to English via Old French *capitain*. A parallel but earlier formation was *chieftain*, which also came from late Latin *capitāneus*, but along a different route, by way of Old French *chevetaine*.

▶ chieftain

**capture**    [16]    Along with its relatives *captive, captivity, captivate*, and *captor*, *capture* is the English language's most direct lineal descendant of Latin *capere* 'take, seize' (others include *capable*, *case* for carrying things, *cater*, and *chase*, and *heave* is distantly connected). First to arrive was *captive* [14], which was originally a verb, meaning 'capture'; it came via Old French *captiver* from Latin *captīvus*, the past participle of *capere*. Contemporary in English was the adjectival use of *captive*, from which the noun developed. (The now archaic *caitiff* [13] comes from the same ultimate source, via an altered Vulgar Latin *\*cactivus* and Old French *caitif* 'captive.') Next on the scene was *capture*, in the 16th century; originally it was only a noun, and it was not converted to verbal use until the late 18th century, when it replaced *captive* in this role. Also 16th-century is *captivate*, from the past participle of late Latin *captivāre*, a derivative of *captīvus*; this too originally meant 'capture,' a sense which did not die out until the 19th century: 'The British ... captivated four successive patrols,' John Neal, *Brother Jonathan* 1825.

▶ captive, cater, chase, cop, heave

**car**    [14]    *Car* seems first to have been used as an independent term for a road vehicle powered by an internal-combustion engine in 1896, in the publication *Farman's Auto-Cars* (the compounds *autocar* and *motorcar* are a year earlier). But the word is of course of far longer standing as a general term for a wheeled conveyance. It comes ultimately from an unrecorded Celtic *\*karros*, via Latin *carrus* 'two-wheeled wagon,' Vulgar Latin *\*carra*, and Anglo-Norman *carre* or *car*; it is probably linked with *current* and *course*, giving an underlying meaning 'move swiftly.' English words derived at some point or other from the same source include *career, carriage, carry, charge,* and *chariot.*

► career, caricature, carriage, carry, charge, chariot, course, current

**carat** [16] The *carat* gets its name from the use of carob beans as standard weights for measuring the heaviness of small quantities. The Greek name for the elongated seed pod of the carob tree was *kerátion,* a derivative of *kéras* 'horn' (related to English *horn*). This passed into Arabic as *qīrāt,* where it became formalized in a system of weights and measures as 'four grains'. It passed into English via Italian *carato* and French *carat.*

► horn

**caravan** [16] *Caravans* have no etymological connection with cars, nor with char-a-bancs. The word comes ultimately from Persian *kārwān* 'group of desert travellers,' and came into English via French *caravane.* Its use in English for 'vehicle' dates from the 17th century, but to begin with it referred to a covered cart for carrying passengers and goods (basis of the shortened form *van* [19]), and in the 19th century it was used for the basic type of third-class railway carriage; its modern sense of 'mobile home' did not develop until the late 19th century. *Caravanserai* 'inn for accommodating desert caravans' [16] comes from Persian *kārwānserāī: serāī* means 'palace, inn,' and was the source, via Italian, of *seraglio* 'harem' [16].

► caravanserai, van

**caraway** [14] The ultimate source of *caraway* is probably Greek *káron* 'cumin' (caraway and cumin seeds are very similar). Arabic borrowed the word as *al-karāwiyā* 'the cumin,' and it subsequently diverged along different branches. Borrowed into medieval Latin it became *carvi,* which was the source of *carvy,* the Scottish word for 'caraway' since the 17th century. The source of English *caraway,* however, was most likely Old Spanish *alcarahueya.*

**carbon** [18] The notion underlying *carbon* is probably that of 'burning'; it has been tentatively traced back to a base *kar-* 'fire.' The word's immediate source was French *carbone,* coined in the 1780s on the basis of Latin *carbō* 'coal, charcoal' (supplementing an earlier borrowing *charbon* 'coal, charcoal'). It is not certain whether *char* and *charcoal* are related to it.

**carbuncle** [13] Etymologically, a *carbuncle* is a 'small piece of coal.' It comes ultimately from Latin *carbunculus,* a diminutive form of *carbō* 'coal' (source of English *carbon*). This reached English via Old French *carbuncle.* The Latin word had two main metaphorical meanings, based on the idea of a glowing coal: 'red gem' and 'red inflamed spot,' both of which passed into English. The latter achieved some notoriety in British English in the 1980s following a remark by the Prince of Wales in 1984 comparing a piece of modern architecture unfavourably to a 'carbuncle,' although ironically from the 15th to the 17th centuries the word was used for 'something of great splendour.'

► carbon

**carburettor** [19] *Carburettor* is a derivative of *carburet,* an obsolete term for what is now known as *carbide* 'a carbon compound.' It was originally used for a device for adding carbon to a gas for enhancing its power of illumination; the current application to a device for producing air/fuel vapour in an engine dates from the 1890s. *Carburet* itself was a later form of *carbure,* borrowed in the 1790s from French; its ultimate origin was in Latin *carbō,* source of English *carbon.*

► carbon

**carcass** [14] English first acquired this word from Anglo-Norman *carcois,* and early forms were *carcays* and *carcoys.* Spellings similar to modern English *carcass* begin to emerge in the 16th century, and may be due to reborrowing from French *carcasse,* to association with the noun *case* 'container,' which meant 'body' in the 16th century, or to a combination of both. The usual current spelling throughout the English-speaking world is *carcass,* but British English also uses *carcase.* The word's ultimate origin is unknown.

**carcinoma** SEE CANCER

**card** [16] English borrowed *card* from French *carte,* for some unknown reason changing *t* to *d* in the process. The French word (source also of English *carton*) came from Latin *charta,* which originally denoted 'leaf of the papyrus plant'; and since papyrus leaves were used for making paper, the word in due course came to mean 'paper' (Latin *charta* also gave English *chart* and *charter*). The Latin word in turn came from Greek *khártēs,* which is probably of Egyptian origin.

► carton, chart, charter, discard

**cardiac** SEE HEART

**cardigan** [19] The cardigan was named after James Thomas Brudenell, 7th earl of Cardigan (1797– 1868), an early sporter of button-through woollen jackets. His other, but less successful, claim to fame was that he led the Charge of the Light Brigade (1854) at Balaclava during the Crimean War.

**cardinal** [12] The ultimate source of *cardinal* is Latin *cardō* 'hinge,' and its underlying idea is that something of particular, or 'cardinal,' importance is like the hinge on which all else depends. English first acquired it as a noun, direct from ecclesiastical Latin *cardinālis* (originally an adjective derived from *cardō*), which in the early church denoted simply a clergyman attached to a church, as a door is attached by hinges; it only gradually rose in dignity to refer to princes of the Roman Catholic church. The adjective reached English in the 13th century, via Old French *cardinal* or Latin *cardinālis*.

**care** [OE]   Care goes back ultimately to a prehistoric Indo-European *\*gar-*, source of a wide range of words in other Indo-European languages, two of which, *garrulous* and *slogan*, have also reached English. In the case of *care*, the route was via Germanic *\*karō*, which reached Old English as *caru*. The related adjective from the same source is *chary* [OE], which originally meant 'sad.'

▶ chary, garrulous, slogan

**careen** [16]   *Careen* comes ultimately from *carīna*, the Latin word for a 'nutshell,' which is related to Greek *káruon* 'nut' and Sanskrit *kárakas* 'coconut.' The idea of a 'nut' as a metaphor for a 'boat' is a fairly obvious one (*shell* is similarly used for a 'rowing boat'), and the Latin word came to be used for a 'ship's keel,' the raised seam of a walnut perhaps suggesting the line of the timber along the ship's bottom. It passed via the Genoese dialect *carena* into French, where a vessel *en carène* was turned over on its side so that its keel was exposed; hence the verb. The equation of *careen* with *career* 'go wildly' is 20th-century and of American origin.

**career** [16]   Originally, a *career* was a 'road or racetrack for vehicles.' Its ultimate source was Latin *carrus* 'wheeled vehicle' (from which we get *car*), which produced the Vulgar Latin derivative *\*carāria* 'track for wheeled vehicles.' This passed into English via Provençal *carreira*, Italian *carriera*, and French *carrière*. Its earliest meaning was 'racecourse,' and hence, by extension, 'swift course'; the main present-day sense 'course of someone's working life' did not develop until the 19th century, probably owing to renewed influence of French *carrière*.

▶ car

**carfax**    see QUARTER

**cargo**    see CHARGE

**carillon**    see QUARTER

**carmine**    see CRIMSON

**carnal** [15]   *Carnal* means literally 'of the flesh'; it comes from late Latin *carnālis*, a derivative of Latin *carō* 'flesh, meat.' Other English words from the same source are *carnivorous* 'meat-eating' [17]; *carnage* [16], which came via French *carnage* and Italian *carnaggio* from medieval Latin *carnāticum* 'slaughter of animals'; *carnation* [16], which originally meant 'pink, colour of flesh' and came via French *carnation* and Italian *carnagione* from late Latin *carnātiō* 'fleshiness, fatness'; *charnel* [14], as in *charnel house*, from Old French *charnel*; and also *carnival* and *carrion*.

▶ carnage, carnation, carnival, carnivorous, carrion, charnel

**carnival** [16]   Etymologically, *carnival* means 'raising flesh' – that is, the 'removal of meat' from the diet during Lent (*carnival* was originally a period of merrymaking preceding Lent). It comes from medieval Latin *carnelevāmen*, a compound noun made up of *carō* 'flesh' (source of English *carnal*) and *levāmen*, a derivative of the verb *levāre* 'lighten, raise' (source of English *lever*, *levity*, and *levy*).

▶ carnal, carrion, lever, levy

**carol** [13]   English acquired *carol* from Old French *carole*, and the similarity of form and meaning naturally suggests that this in turn came from late Latin *choraula* 'choral song.' In classical Latin times this had meant 'person who accompanies a choir on a flute or reed instrument,' and it came from Greek *khoraúlēs*, a compound formed from *khorós* 'choir' (source of English *chorus* and *choir*) and *aulos* 'reed instrument.' However, the fact that the earliest recorded use of the word is for a dance in a ring, accompanied by singing, has led some etymologists to speculate that the underlying notion contained in it may be not 'song' but 'circle' (perhaps from Latin *corolla* 'little crown, garland').

▶ choir, chorus

**carouse** [16]   Etymologically, *carouse* means to drink something up 'completely.' Originally it was an adverb, used in phrases such as *drink carouse* ('the tiplinge sottes at midnight which to quaffe carouse do use,' Thomas Drant, *Horace's Epigrams* 1567). These were a partial translation of German *trinken garaus*, in which *garaus* is a compound adverb made up of *gar* 'completely, all' and *aus* 'out.'

**carp**   *Carp* the fish [14] and *carp* 'criticize' [13] are distinct words in English. The former comes from medieval Latin *carpa*, probably via Old French *carpe*, but the word is probably ultimately of Germanic origin. The verb, which originally simply meant 'talk,' was a borrowing from Old Norse *karpa*. The present-day sense 'criticize' did not develop until the 16th century, probably under the influence of Latin *carpere* 'pluck' (related to English *harvest*), which had the metaphorical meaning 'slander.'

▶ harvest

**carpenter** [14]   Etymologically, a carpenter is a 'maker of carriages.' The word comes, via Anglo-Norman *carpenter*, from late Latin *carpentārius*, originally an adjective derived from *carpentum* 'two-wheeled vehicle.' This, like the similar and perhaps related Latin *carrus*, source of English *car*, was of Celtic origin. The generalization in meaning to 'worker in wood' took place before the word was borrowed into English.

**carpet** [14]   Originally, *carpet* was simply a sort of rough cloth, and medieval Latin *carpīta*, for example, was sometimes used for a garment made from it. In earliest English use it was a 'table-cloth' or 'bedspread,' and it was not until the 15th century that the specialized 'floor-covering' began to establish itself. The word itself entered English via either Old French *carpite* or medieval Latin *carpīta*, which was derived from *carpīre*, an alteration of Latin *carpere* 'pluck' (related to English *harvest*). The underlying notion seems to be that such cloth was originally made from 'plucked' fabric, that is, fabric which had been unravelled or shredded.

**carriage** [14] *Carriage* is literally 'carrying.' It is an Old Northern French derivative of the verb *carier*, in the sense 'transport in a vehicle.' At first it meant simply 'conveyance' in the abstract sense, but in the 15th century more concrete meanings began to emerge: 'load, luggage' (now obsolete) and 'means of conveyance, vehicle.' By the 18th century the latter had become further specialized to 'horse-drawn wheeled vehicle for carrying people' (as opposed to goods).

▶ carry

**carrion** [13] Ultimately, *carrion* is a derivative of Latin *carō* 'flesh' (source also of English *carnal*). This appears to have had a Vulgar Latin offshoot *\*carōnia*, which entered English via Anglo-Norman *caroine*. At first it was used in English for 'dead body,' but before the end of the 13th century the current sense 'flesh unfit for human consumption' had begun to establish itself.

▶ carnal, crone

**carry** [14] For such a basic and common word, *carry* has a surprisingly brief history. It does not go back to some prehistoric Indo-European root, but was formed less than 1000 years ago in Anglo-Norman or Old Northern French, on the basis of *carre* or *car* (immediate source of English *car*). The verb *carier* thus meant literally 'transport in a wheeled vehicle.' This sense was carried over into English, and though it has since largely given way to the more general 'convey,' it is preserved in the derivative *carriage*, in such expressions as 'carriage paid.'

▶ car, carriage

**cart** [13] Old English had a word *cræt* 'carriage,' which may, by the process known as metathesis (reversal of speech sounds), have produced the word which first appeared at the beginning of the 13th century as *karte* or *carte*. But a part must certainly also have been played by Old Norse *kartr* 'cart,' and some have also detected the influence of Anglo-Norman *carete*, a diminutive form of *car* (source of English *car*).

▶ car

**cartel** see CHART
**carton** see CHART
**cartoon** [17] *Cartoon* comes via French *carton* from Italian *cartone*, which meant literally 'strong heavy paper, pasteboard' (it was a derivative of *carta*

'paper,' which came from Latin *charta*, source also of English *card, carton, chart*, and *charter*). Its meaning was in due course transferred to the preliminary sketches made by artists on such paper, the original and for nearly two centuries the only sense of the word in English: 'But the sight best pleased me was the cartoons by Raphael, which are far beyond all the paintings I ever saw,' Hatton family correspondence, 1697. Its application to comic drawings in newspapers and magazines began in the 1840s.

▶ card, carton, chart, charter

**cartouche** see CHART
**cartridge** see CHART
**carve** [OE] Originally, *carve* meant simply 'cut.' That sense died out in the 16th century, leaving the more specialized 'cut or incise decoratively' and later 'cut up meat at table.' Related words in other Germanic languages, such as Dutch *kerven*, point to a prehistoric West Germanic *\*kerfan*, which is probably ultimately linked to Greek *gráphein* 'write' (source of English *graphic*), whose original notion was 'scratch or incise on a surface.'

▶ graphic

**cascara** see CONCUSSION
**case** [13] There are two distinct words *case* in English, both acquired via Old French from Latin and both members of very large families. *Case* 'circumstance' was borrowed from Old French *cas*, which in turn came from Latin *cāsus* 'fall, chance.' This was formed from the base of the verb *cadere* 'fall.' The progression of senses is from the concrete 'that which falls' to the metaphorical 'that which befalls, that which happens (by chance)' (and English *chance* is also derived ultimately from Latin *cadere*). Other related words in English include *accident, cadence, cadaver, cheat, chute, coincide, decadent, decay, deciduous*, and *occasion*. *Case* 'container' comes via Old French *casse* from Latin *capsa* 'box,' a derivative of the verb *capere* 'hold' (which is related to English *heave*). At various points during its history it has produced offshoots which in English have become *capsule* [17], a diminutive form, *cash, chassis*, and perhaps *capsicum* [18] and *chase* 'engrave.'

▶ accident, cadaver, cheat, chute, decay, deciduous, occasion, occident / capsicum, capsule, cash, chassis

**cash** [16] *Cash* originally meant 'money-box.' English acquired it via French *casse* or Italian *cassa* from Latin *capsa* 'box' (source of English *case*). It was not until the mid 18th century that this underlying sense died out, leaving the secondary 'money' (which had already developed before the word entered English). *Cashier* 'person in charge of money' [16] is a derivative, coming from French *caissier* or perhaps from Dutch *cassier*, but the verb *cashier* 'dismiss' [16] is completely unrelated. It comes from Dutch *casseren*, a borrowing from Old French *casser* 'discharge, annul.' This in turn goes back to Latin *quassāre* 'break up,' source of English *quash*.

▶ case

**cassock** [16] Etymologically, a *cassock* is probably a cloak worn by a *Cossack*; the two words appear to be ultimately identical. *Cassock*, which originally meant simply 'cloak' or 'long coat' (its current application to clergymen's tunics arose in the 17th century), comes via French *casaque* from Italian *casacca*. It has been conjectured that this was a descendant of Turkish *quzzāk* 'nomad' (a derivative of the verb *qaz* 'wander'), which also, via Russian *kozak*, gave English *Cossack* [16]. However, another theory is that *cassock* comes ultimately from Persian *kazhāghand* 'padded jacket,' a compound formed from *kazh* 'raw silk' and *āghand* 'stuffed.'

▶ Cossack

**cast** [31] *Cast* comes from Old Norse *kasta* 'throw.' It has gradually been replaced since Middle English times as the ordinary word for 'propelling with the arm' by *throw*. Of the various metaphorical senses of the noun, 'set of performers in a play' developed in the 17th century, apparently from an earlier 'plan, design.'

**castanet** [17] *Castanets* were originally named in Spanish from their resemblance to the shells of chestnuts, Spanish *castañeta* being a diminutive form of *castaña* 'chestnut,' from Latin *castanea* (itself the ultimate source of English *chestnut*). Another name for them in 17th-century English was *knackers*: 'Castinettas: knackers of the form of chestnuts, used to this day by the Spaniards in their dances,' Robert Stapylton, *Juvenal's sixteen satires* 1647.

▶ chestnut

**caste** [16] *Caste* has no etymological connection with *cast*. It is borrowed from Spanish and Portuguese *casta* 'race, breed,' a nominal use of the adjective *casta* 'pure,' from Latin *castus* (source of English *chaste*). The notion underlying the word thus appears to be 'racial purity.' Use of *casta* by the Portuguese in India with reference to the Hindu social groupings led to its being adopted in this sense by English in the 17th century.

▶ chaste, incest

**castle** [11] *Castle* was one of the first words borrowed by the English from their Norman conquerors: it is mentioned in the *Anglo-Saxon chronicle* only nine years after the battle of Hastings. It comes via Anglo-Norman *castel* from Latin *castellum*, a diminutive form of *castrum* 'fort' (which was acquired by Old English as *ceaster*, and now appears in English place-names as -*caster* or -*chester*). The Old French version of *castel*, *chastel*, produced modern French *château*, and also its

derivative *châtelaine*, borrowed into English in the 19th century.

▶ château

**castor** There are two distinct words *castor* in English. The older originally meant 'beaver' [14], and was early used with reference to a bitter pungent substance secreted by glands near the beaver's anus, employed in medicine and perfumery. The term *castor oil* [18] probably comes from the use of this oil, derived from the seed of a tropical plant, as a substitute for castor in medicine. The more recent *castor* [17] is simply a derivative of the verb *cast*; it was originally (and still often is) spelled *caster*. Its use for sprinkling or 'throwing' sugar is obvious (the term *castor sugar* dates back to the mid 19th century), but its application to a 'small swivelling wheel' is less immediately clear: it comes from a now obsolete sense of the verb, mainly nautical, 'veer, turn': 'Prepare for casting to port,' George Nares, *Seamanship* 1882.

▶ cast

**cat** [OE] The word *cat* seems to have appeared on the European scene, in the form of Latin *catta* or *cattus*, around 1000 AD (the previous Latin word was *fēlēs*, source of English *feline*). No one is completely sure where it came from (although given the domestic cat's origins in Egypt, it is likely to have been an Egyptian word), but it soon spread north and west through Europe. The Latin word reached English via Germanic *\*kattuz*, later backed up by Anglo-Norman *cat*, a variant of Old French *chat*.

**catacomb** [17] *Catacomb* derives from the name of an underground cemetary in ancient Rome, the *Coemetērium Catacumbas*, beneath the Basilica of St Sebastian near the Appian Way. It is said that the bodies of St Peter and St Paul were deposited in or near its subterranean passages. The word's more general application to any underground labyrinth dates from the 17th century. The original significance of Latin *Catacumbas* is not known.

**catafalque**   see SCAFFOLD

**catamaran** [17] *Catamaran* is a word borrowed from the Tamil language of the southeast coast of India. It is a compound meaning literally 'tied wood,' made up of *kattu* 'tie' and *maram* 'wood, tree.' It was first recorded in English in William Dampier's *Voyages* 1697: 'The smaller sort of Bark-logs are more governable than the others . . . This sort of Floats are used in many places both in the East and West Indies. On the Coast of Coromandel . . . they call them Catamarans.'

**cataract** [15] Greek *kataráktēs* meant literally 'swooping down, rushing down'; it was a derivative of the verb *katarássein*, a compound formed from the prefix *katá-* 'down' (which appears in a wide range of English words, including *cataclysm*, *catalepsy*, *catalogue*, *catapult* – literally 'hurl down' – and *catastrophe*) and the verb *rássein* 'strike.' Hence it was applied metaphorically to various things that 'rush down,' including waterfalls and portcullises. The word passed into English via Latin *cataracta*, and the sense 'opacity of the eye's lens' developed in the 16th century, probably as a metaphorical extension of the now obsolete 'portcullis.'

**catarrh** [16] Etymologically, *catarrh* is 'something that flows down.' It comes via French *catarrhe* and late Latin *catarrhus* from Greek *katárrhous*, a derivative of the verb *katarrhein*, a compound formed from the prefix *katá-* 'down' (as in *cataract*) and the verb *rhein* 'flow' (a relative of English *rheumatism* and *stream*).

▶ diarrhoea, rheumatism, stream

**catastrophe**   see APOSTROPHE

**catch** [13] Originally *catch* meant 'chase, hunt' (and in fact it is etymologically related to the English word *chase*). However, it remarkably quickly moved on to be applied to the next logical step in the procedure, 'capture,' and by the early 16th century 'chase' was becoming obsolete (although it remains the only sense of related words in other languages, such as French *chasser* and Italian *cacciare*). Looked at from another point of view, however, *catch* might be said to be harking back to its ultimate roots in Latin *capere* 'take,' source of English *capture*. Its past participle, *captus*, provided the basis for a new verb *captāre* 'try to seize, chase.' In Vulgar Latin this became altered to *\*captiāre*, source of Old French *chacier* (whence English *chase*) and the corresponding Anglo-Norman *cachier* (whence English *catch*).

▶ capture, chase

**catechism** [16] Etymologically, *catechism* is 'teaching by the spoken word.' It is a derivative of *catechize* [15], which comes ultimately from the Greek verb *katēkhein*, a compound formed from the prefix *katá-* 'thoroughly' and the verb *ēkhein* 'sound, resound' (related to English *echo*). Thus originally to 'catechize' someone was literally to 'din' instruction into them, hence 'instruct orally.' The word came into English via a later ecclesiastical Greek derivative *katēkhízein* and Latin *catēchīzāre*.

▶ echo

**category** [15] The word *category* has a rather complicated semantic history. It comes ultimately from Greek *katēgorein* 'accuse,' a compound formed from the prefix *katá-* 'against' and *agorá* 'public assembly' (source of English *agoraphobia* and related to *gregarious*) – hence 'speak against publicly.' 'Accuse' gradually became weakened in meaning to 'assert, name,' and the derived noun *katēgoríā* was applied by Aristotle to the enumeration of all classes of things that can be named – hence 'category.' The word reached English via late Latin *catēgoria* or French *catégorie*.

▶ agoraphobia, gregarious, panegyric

**cater** [16] *Cater* is related to French *acheter* 'buy,' and originally meant 'buy provisions.' It comes ultimately from Vulgar Latin *\*accaptāre*, a compound verb formed from the Latin prefix *ad-* 'to' and the verb *captāre* 'try to seize' (source of English *catch* and *chase*). This provided the basis for the Anglo-Norman agent noun *acatour* 'buyer, purveyor,' which gave English the now obsolete *acater*. Losing its *a-*, this became *cater*, which until the early 17th century was the word for what we would now call a 'caterer.' At around the same time *cater* began to be used as a verb; the first known example of this is in Shakespeare's *As You Like It* II, iii: 'He that doth the ravens feed, yea providently caters for the sparrow.'

▶ capture, catch, chase

**caterpillar** [15] Etymologically, a *caterpillar* is a 'hairy cat.' The word comes ultimately from late Latin *\*catta pilōsa*: *catta* is the source of English *cat*, while *pilōsus* 'hairy' is a derivative of Latin *pilus* 'hair,' from which English gets *pile* of a carpet. In Old French *\*catta pilōsa* became *chatepelose*, which passed into English as *catyrpel*. The present-day form arose in the 16th century, probably from association with the now obsolete *piller* 'plunderer' (related to English *pillage*) – caterpillars being regarded, of course, as plunderers of leaves. The notion that caterpillars resemble small furry mammals is also reflected in such names as *pussmoth* and *woolly bear*.

▶ cat, pile

**caterwaul** [14] The earliest known use of this word comes in Chaucer's *Wife of Bath's Prologue* 1386: 'If the cat's skin be slick and grey, forth she will, ere any day be dawned, to show her skin, and go a-caterwauling.' The first element of the word is generally accepted to be *cat*, while the second (in Middle English it was usually *-wawe* or *-wrawe*) is presumably onomatopoeic, imitating the sound of a cat wailing or yowling. It is not clear whether it was a purely native creation, or whether English borrowed it from Low German *katerwaulen* (where *kater* means 'tom cat').

**cathedral** [13] *Cathedral* is a shortening of *cathedral church*, which was originally the 'church housing the bishop's throne.' For ultimately *cathedral* comes from Greek *kathédrā* (source also of English *chair*), a compound noun meaning 'seat,' formed from *katá-* 'down' and *\*hed-* 'sit.' The adjectival form was created in late Latin as *cathedrālis*, and reached English via Old French. The notion of the bishop's authority residing in his throne recurs in *see*, which comes from Latin *sēdem* 'seat,' a relative of English *sit*.

▶ chair

**cathode** [19] The term *cathode*, meaning 'negative electrode,' appears to have been introduced by the English philosopher William Whewell around 1834. It was based on Greek *káthodos* 'way down,' a compound formed from *katá-* 'down' and *hodós* 'way' (also represented in *exodus* 'way out' and *odometer* 'instrument for measuring distance travelled,' and possibly related to Latin *cēdere*, source of English *cede* and a host of derived words). It specifically contrasts with *anode*, which means literally 'way up.'
▶ exodus, odometer

**catholic** [14] Etymologically, the Catholic Church is the universal church, comprising all Christians. For *catholic* comes ultimately from a Greek word, *katholikós*, meaning 'relating to all, general.' It was a derivative of *kathólou*, a compound formed from *katá* 'relating to' and *hólos* 'whole' (source of English *holism* and *holistic*). It passed into English via Old French *catholique* or ecclesiastical Latin *catholicus*. Its original meaning is preserved today in such contexts as 'catholic tastes' – that is, 'wide-ranging tastes.'
▶ holistic

**cattle** [13] Ultimately, *cattle* is the same word as *chattel* [13], and when it first entered English it had the same meaning, 'property.' From earliest times, however, it was applied specifically to livestock thought of as property. In the Middle Ages it was a wide-ranging term in animal husbandry, being used for horses, sheep, pigs, and even poultry and bees, as well as cows, and such usages survived dialectally until comparatively recently, but from the mid 16th century onwards there is increasing evidence of the word's being restricted solely to cows. Its ultimate source is medieval Latin *capitāle* 'property,' which came to English via Old French *chatel* as *chattel* and via Anglo-Norman *catel* as *cattle*. *Capitāle* itself goes back to classical Latin *capitālis* (from *caput* 'head'), from which English gets *capital*.
▶ capital, chattel

**caucus** [18] *Caucus* 'closed party meeting' is believed to be of native American origin. Certainly its early usage was restricted to the USA (it did not reach British English until the 1870s, when it became something of a political buzzword for a time). In form and meaning it stongly resembles *caucauasu*, a word meaning 'counsellor' in the Algonquian languages of eastern Canada and the USA which was recorded in print by Captain John Smith (1580–1631), an early English colonist in America.

**caudal** see QUEUE

**cauldron** [13] Etymologically, *cauldrons* are for heating not food but people. The word comes ultimately from Latin *calidārium* 'hot bath,' which was a derivative of the adjective *calidus* 'warm' (related to English *calorie*, and, by a much more circuitous route,

*lee* 'sheltered area' and probably *lukewarm*). Among the descendants of *calidārium* were late Latin *caldāria* 'pot,' which produced French *chaudière* (possible source of English *chowder*) and Vulgar Latin *\*caldario*, which passed into Anglo-Norman, with a suffix indicating great size, as *caudron* 'large cooking pot.' In English, the *l* was reintroduced from Latin in the 15th century.
▶ calorie, chowder, nonchalent

**cauliflower** [16] *Cauliflower* is literally 'flowered cabbage.' English probably borrowed and adapted the word from Italian *cavoli fiori*, plural of *cavolo fiore* 'cabbage flower.' *Cavolo* came from late Latin *caulus*, a variant of Latin *caulis* 'cabbage.' This word originally meant 'stem,' but the notion ultimately underlying it is 'hollow stem,' for it can be traced back to an Indo-European base which also produced *hole* and *hollow*. It was borrowed early on into the Germanic languages, and via this route has produced in English the now rare *cole* 'cabbage, rape' [14] (more familiar in the Dutch borrowing *coleslaw*); the Scots version *kale* [13], from Old Norse *kál*, best known south of the border in the form *curly kale*; and via German *kohlrabi* [19], the last element of which is related to English *rape* the plant.
▶ cole, coleslaw, hole, hollow, kale, kohlrabi

**cause** [13] *Cause* comes via Old French *cause* from Latin *causa*, which as well as 'reason' meant 'lawsuit'; this was carried over into English legal language (it survives in terms such as *cause-list* 'list of cases to be tried') and its use in expressions like 'plead someone's cause' led in the late 16th century to a more general application 'goal or principle pursued or supported.' French *chose* 'thing' also comes from Latin *causa*, in the weakened sense 'matter, subject.'
▶ excuse

**causeway** [15] Etymologically, a *causeway* is a road paved with limestone. In late Middle English, the word was *causey way*, *causey* coming via Anglo-Norman *\*cauce* from Vulgar Latin *\*calciāta*, an adjective derived from Latin *calx* 'limestone' (source also of English *chalk*, *calcium*, and *calculate*). The simple form *causey* 'causeway, path' survived dialectally well into the 20th century, and its French relative *chausée* 'road' is still very much alive.
▶ calcium, calculate, chalk

**caustic** see HOLOCAUST

**cauterize** see HOLOCAUST

**caution** see SHOW

**cavalcade** [16] Originally, a *cavalcade* was simply a ride on horseback, often for the purpose of attack: in James I's *Counterblast to tobacco* 1604, for example, we find 'to make some sudden cavalcade upon your enemies.' By the 17th century this had developed to 'procession on horseback,' and it was not long after that that the present-day, more general 'procession' emerged. The word comes via French *cavalcade* from Italian *cavalcata*, a derivative of the verb *cavalcare* 'ride on horseback.' This in turn came from Vulgar Latin *\*caballicāre*, which was based on Latin *caballus* 'horse' (source also of English *cavalier* and French *cheval* 'horse'). In the 20th century, *-cade* has come to be regarded as a suffix in its own right, meaning 'procession, show,' and producing such forms as *motorcade*, *aquacade*, and even *camelcade*.

▶ cavalier

**cavalier** [16] Etymologically, a *cavalier* is a 'horseman.' The word comes via French *cavalier* from Italian *cavaliere*, which was derived from Latin *caballus* 'horse,' either directly or via late Latin *caballārius* 'horseman, rider.' From the beginning in English its connotations were not those of any old horse-rider, but of a mounted soldier or even a knight, and before the end of the 16th century the more general meaning 'courtly gentleman' was establishing itself. This led in the mid-17th century to its being applied on the one hand to the supporters of Charles I, and on the other as an adjective meaning 'disdainful.' Italian *cavaliere* was also the source of *cavalleria* 'body of horse-soldiers,' which was borrowed into English in the 16th century, via French *cavallerie*, as *cavalry*. (The parallel form routed directly through French rather than via Italian was *chivalry*.)

▶ cavalry, chivalry

**cave** There are two English words *cave* which, despite their apparent similarity, are probably unrelated. The earlier, 'underground chamber' [13], comes via Old French *cave* from Latin *cavea*, a nominal use of the adjective *cavus* 'hollow' (source also of *cavern* [14], via Old French *caverne* or Latin *caverna*, and of *cavity* [16], from the late Latin derivative *cavitās*). The verb *cave* [18], however, as in 'cave in,' seems to come from an earlier dialectal *calve* 'collapse, fall in,' once widespread in the eastern counties of England; it has been speculated that this was borrowed from a Low German source, such as Flemish *inkalven*. It has subsequently, of course, been much influenced by the noun *cave*.

▶ cavern, cavity, decoy

**caveat** see SHOW

**caviare** [16] *Caviare* is of Turkish origin; it comes from Turkish *khāvyār*. It spread from there to a number of European languages, including Italian *caviale* and French *caviar*, many of which contributed to the rather confusing diversity of forms in 16th-, 17th-, and early 18th-century English: *cavialy*, *cavery*, *caveer*, *gaveare*, etc. By the mid-18th century *caviare* or *caviar* had become the established spellings. Ironically, although caviare is quintessentially a Russian delicacy, Russian does not have the word *caviare*; it uses *ikrá*.

**cavil** see CHALLENGE

**cavity** see CAVE

**cay** see QUAY

**cease** [14] *Cease* comes via Old French *cesser* from Latin *cessāre* 'delay, stop.' This was derived from *cessus*, the past participle of *cēdere* 'go away, withdraw, yield,' which was also the basis of *cessation* [14], from Latin *cessātiō*.

▶ cessation

**cede** [17] *Cede* comes, either directly or via French *céder*, from Latin *cēdere* 'go away, withdraw, yield.' The Latin verb provided the basis for a surprisingly wide range of English words: the infinitive form produced, for instance, *accede*, *concede*, *precede*, *proceed*, and *succeed*, while the past participle *cessus* has given *ancestor*, *cease*, *excess*, *recession*, etc.

▶ accede, ancestor, cease, concession, excess, necessary, proceed, recession, succeed

**ceiling** [14] *Ceiling* is something of a mystery word. It originally signified the internal lining of any part of a building, including walls as well as roof (the modern sense 'overhead inside surface of a room' began to crystallize out in the 16th century), and the material of which it was made took in wooden planks and even tapestry hangings, as well as plaster. But where it comes from is not at all clear. It has no apparent relations in other modern European languages, and the likeliest candidate as a source may be Latin *caelāre* 'carve, engrave.' This is perhaps endorsed by an item in the accounts of the Lord High Treasurer of Scotland, 1497, revealing how a 'carver' was paid £2 14s for 'the cieling of the chapel' – an indication that the underlying notion of *ceiling* may be 'carved internal surface of a room.'

**celerity** see ACCELERATE

**celery** [17] *Celery* comes ultimately from Greek *sélīnon*, which signified 'parsley' – like the celery, a plant of the group Umbelliferae (the English word *parsley* comes from Greek *petrōselīnon*, literally 'rock parsley'). It came into English via Latin *selīnon*, Italian dialect *selleri*, and French *céleri*. The term *celeriac* was formed from *celery* in the early 18th century; it first appears in an advertisement in the *London and country brewer* 1743.

▶ parsley

**cell** [12] *Cell* has branched out a lot over the centuries, but its original meaning seems to be 'small secluded room,' for it comes ultimately from an Indo-European base *\*kel-*, which is also the source of English *conceal*, *clandestine*, and *occult*. It came into English either via Old French *celle* or directly from Latin *cella* 'small room, storeroom, inner room of a temple,' and at first was used mainly in the sense 'small subsidiary monastery.' It is not until the 14th century that we find it being used for small individual apartments within a monastic building, and the development from this to 'room in a prison' came as late as the 18th century. In medieval biology the term was applied metaphorically to bodily cavities, and from the 17th century onwards it began to be used in the more modern sense 'smallest structural unit of an organism' (the botanist Nehemiah Grew was apparently the first so to use it, in the 1670s). A late Latin derivative of *cella* was *cellārium* 'group of cells, storeroom'; this was the source of English *cellar* [13], via Anglo-Norman *celer*.

▶ apocalypse, cellar, clandestine, conceal, hall, hell, hull, occult

**cement** [13] Latin *caementa* meant 'stone chips used for making mortar'; etymologically, the notion behind it was of 'hewing for a quarry,' for it was originally *\*caedmenta*, a derivative of *caedere* 'cut' (from which English gets *concise* and *decide*). In due course the signification of the Latin word passed from 'small broken stones' to 'powdered stone (used for mortar),' and it was in this sense that it passed via Old French *ciment* into English.

▶ concise, decide

**cemetery** [14] Not surprisingly for a word having associations with death, *cemetery*'s origins are euphemistic. It comes via late Latin *coemētērium* from Greek *koimētérion*, which originally meant 'dormitory' (it was a derivative of the verb *koiman* 'put to sleep'); it was apparently early Greek Christian writers who first applied the word to burial grounds.

**censer**    see INCENSE

**census**    see EXCISE

**cent** [16] *Centum* is the Latin word for 'hundred' – indeed both come ultimately from the same Indo-European source, *\*kmtóm*. It first appeared in English in the form *cent* in the phrase *per cent* (originally used apparently by the financier Sir Thomas Gresham in a letter of 1568: 'the interest of xij per cent by the year'); this was probably borrowed from Italian *per cento* (it is not a genuine Latin phrase). The use of *cent* for a unit of currency dates from the 1780s, when it was adopted by the newly founded USA; its status as one hundredth of a dollar was officially ordained by the Continental Congress on 8 August 1786.

▶ century

**centre** [14] The word *centre* came originally from the spike of a pair of compasses which is stuck into a surface while the other arm describes a circle round it. Greek *kéntron* meant 'sharp point,' or more specifically 'goad for oxen' (it was a derivative of the verb *kentein* 'prick'), and hence was applied to a compass spike; and it was not long before this spread metaphorically to 'mid-point of a circle.' The word reached English either via Old French *centre* or directly from Latin *centrum*. The derived adjective *central* is 16th-century.

▶ eccentric

**century** [16] Latin *centuria* meant 'group of one hundred' (it was a derivative of *centum* 'hundred'). Among the specialized applications of this general sense, the most familiar to us today is that of a division of the Roman army consisting originally of a hundred soldiers (the title of its commander, *centurion* [14] – Latin *centuriō* – derives from *centuria*). When English took the word over, however, it put it to other uses: it was first applied to 'period of 100 years' in the early 17th century, while 'score of 100 or more in cricket' comes from the mid 19th century.

▶ cent, centurion

**cereal** [19] *Cereal* is a comparatively modern introduction of the Latin adjective *cereālis* 'of grain,' which was derived from the name of *Cerēs*, the Roman goddess of agriculture (identified with Greek *Demeter*). It has, needless to say, no connection with *serial* (see SERIES).

**cerebellum**    see SAVELOY

**cerebral**    see SAVELOY

**ceremony** [14] The antecedents of *ceremony* are obscure. We can trace it back to Latin *caerimōnia* 'religious rites,' but there the trail stops. It probably arrived in English via Old French *ceremonie*.

**certain** [13] *Certain* comes ultimately from Latin *certus* 'sure, fixed,' which derived from the past participle of the verb *cernere* 'decide.' The Latin adjective was extended in Vulgar Latin to *\*certānus*, which passed into English via Old French *certain*. Other English words based on *certus* include *certify* [14] (from late Latin *certificāre*) and its derivative *certificate*, and *certitude* [15] (from late Latin *certitūdō*).

▶ crime, crisis, decree, discern, discrete, discriminate, excrement, riddle, secret

**cessation**    see CEASE

**cesspool** [17] *Cesspool* has no direct etymological connection with *pool*. It comes from Old French *suspirail* 'ventilator, breathing hole,' a derivative of *souspirer* 'breathe' (this goes back to Latin *suspīrāre*, source of the archaic English *suspire* 'sigh'). This was borrowed into English in the early 15th century as *suspiral* 'drainpipe,' which in the subsequent two hundred years appeared in a variety of spellings, including *cesperalle*. By the early 16th century we find evidence of its being used not just for a pipe to drain matter away, but also for a well or tank to receive matter thus drained (originally any effluent, not just sewage). The way was thus open for a 'reinterpretation' of the word's final element as *pool* (by the process known as folk etymology), and in the late 17th century the form *cesspool* emerged. By analogy, as if there were really a word *cess* 'sewage,' the term *cesspit* was coined in the mid-19th century.

▶ suspire

**cha** see TEA

**chaffinch** [OE] Etymologically, a chaffinch is a finch which gets its food by pecking amongst the chaff and other grain debris in the barnyard. The word *chaff* itself (Old English *ceaf*) probably goes back to a prehistoric Germanic base *\*kaf-*, *\*kef-* 'chew,' which was also the source of *chafer* 'beetle' [OE] (literally the 'chewing creature') and *jowl*. (The verb *chaff* 'make fun of' [19], on the other hand, is probably an alteration of *chafe*, which came via Old French *chaufer* and Vulgar Latin *\*califāre* from Latin *calefacere* 'make warm,' a relative of English *cauldron* and *calorie*.)
▶ chafer, jowl

**chagrin** [17] The word *chagrin* first appeared in French in the 14th century as an adjective, meaning 'sad, vexed,' a usage at first adopted into English: 'My wife is in a chagrin humour, she not being pleased with my kindness to either of them,' Samuel Pepys's *Diary* 6 August 1666. It died out in English in the early 18th century, but the subsequently developed noun and verb have persisted. Etymologists now discount any connection with French *chagrin* 'untanned leather' (source of English *shagreen* [17]), which came from Turkish *sagri*.

**chain** [13] *Chain* is a direct descendant of Latin *catēna* 'chain,' source also of English *concatenate* [16], literally 'link together in a chain.' This passed into Old French as *chaeine*, a later form of which, *chaine*, was adopted by English. The Latin word's antecedents are not known.
▶ concatenate

**chair** [13] *Chair* comes ultimately from Greek *kathédrā* 'seat' (source also of *cathedral*, of course), which was a compound originally meaning literally 'something for sitting down on' – it was formed from *katá-* 'down' and *\*hed-* 'sit.' It produced Latin *cathedra*, which in Old French became *chaiere*, the source of the English word. The use of *chair* specifically for the seat occupied by someone presiding at a meeting dates from the mid 17th century, and its metaphorical extension to the person sitting *in* it, as symbolizing his or her office – as in 'address one's remarks to the chair' – is virtually contemporary ('The Chair behaves himself like a Busby amongst so many schoolboys,' Thomas Burton's *Diary*, 23 March 1658); but its use as a synonym for *chairperson*, to avoid a distinction on grounds of sex, is a late 20th-century development.
▶ cathedral

**chalice** [13] Latin *calix* 'cup' and its relative, Greek *kálux* 'pod,' perhaps hold the record for the words most often borrowed into English. *Calix* first made its appearance as part of the original West Germanic stratum of English, into which it had been borrowed from Latin; this was as Old English *cælc*. Then came *cælic*, which Old English independently acquired

from Latin after the conversion of the English to Christianity. Next was *calice*, whose source was an Old French dialectal form descended from Latin *calix*. And finally, at the end of the 13th century, the main Old French form *chalice* was adopted. The final twist in the story is that in the 17th century Latin *calyx* (a descendant of the related Greek *kálux*) was borrowed into English as a botanical term, 'outer covering of a flower.'

**chalk** [OE] Latin *calx* meant broadly 'lime, limestone' (it probably came from Greek *khálix* 'pebble'). This was borrowed in early times into the Germanic languages, and in most of them it retains this meaning (German *kalk*, for instance, means 'limestone'). In English, however, it fairly soon came to be applied to a particular soft white form of limestone, namely chalk (the Old English word was *cealc*). The Latin word is also the source of English *calculate*, *calcium*, and *causeway*.
▶ calcium, calculate, causeway

**challenge** [13] The original notion contained in *challenge* in English was of 'accusation.' The word comes, via Old French *chalenge* or *calenge*, from Latin *calumnia* 'false charge, deception' (source of English *calumny* [15]). By the early 14th century, the modern, more neutral sense of 'inviting to a contest' had emerged, however, and before the end of the 17th century the word's accusatory connotations had virtually died out. Latin *calumnia* probably came from the verb *calvī* 'deceive.' This may, via an unrecorded intermediary *\*calvilla*, be related to Latin *cavilla* 'raillery,' whose derived verb *cavillārī* was the source of English *cavil* [16].
▶ calumny

**chamber** [13] The ultimate source of *chamber* is Greek *kamárā* 'something with an arched cover, room with a vaulted roof.' This passed into Latin as *camara* or *camera* (source of English *camera*), and in Old French became transformed into *chambre*, the immediate source of the English word. Related forms in English include *comrade* (from Spanish *camarada*), originally 'someone sharing a room'; *chamberlain* [13], which was originally coined in the West Germanic language of the Franks as *\*kamerling* using the diminutive suffix *-ling*, and came into English via Old French *chamberlenc*; and *chimney*.
▶ camera, chamberlain, chimney

**chamelion** [14] Etymologically, a *chamelion* is a 'ground lion.' The word comes from Greek *khamailéōn*, a compound formed from *khamaí* 'on the ground' (English *humus* and *humble* are related to it) and *léōn* 'lion.' Until the 19th century the word was usually spelled *camelion*, which led to popular association of the first element with *camel*; this in turn encouraged an identification with *camelopard*, a now obsolete word for 'giraffe,' and in the 14th and 15th centuries *camelion* was used for 'giraffe.'

▶ humble, humus, lion

**chamois** [16]   The word *chamois* (the name of a species of Alpine antelope) probably goes back to a language spoken in the Alps before the Romans penetrated northwards. They adopted it as late Latin *camox*, and in the local Romansch language it is *kamuotsch*, but the source of the English word is the related French *chamois*. Its use in the sense 'soft wash-leather,' as originally made from the skin of the chamois, dates from the 16th century, although the spelling *shammy* is not recorded before the 17th century.

**champagne** [17]   *Champagne* comes (as does *campaign*) from late Latin *campānia*, a derivative of Latin *campus* 'open field' (source of English *camp*). This passed into Old French as *champagne* 'open country,' a word borrowed into English in the 14th century as *champaign* (now archaic). It came to be applied specifically to a province of northeastern France (an area largely of open rolling countryside) and hence to the wine produced in that area. There are references to 'brisk Champagne' and 'sparkling Champagne' in English from the 1660s and 1670s, but it was not until about two hundred years ago that modern champagne, produced by secondary fermentation in bottle, was invented (according to legend, by the monk Dom Perignon).

▶ camp, campaign, champion

**champion** [13]   Etymologically, a *champion* is someone who fought in the *campus* or arena. Latin *campus* (source of English *camp*) meant, among other things, 'field of battle' – both a full-scale military battlefield and an area for staged battles between gladiators. Those who fought in such battles – the gladiators – were called in medieval Latin *campiones*. The word passed into English via Old French *champion*. The word's original meaning survives historically in such phrases as 'king's champion,' someone who will fight on behalf of the king, and by extension in 'supporter,' as in 'a champion of prisoners' rights.' The modern sense 'winner' did not develop until the early 19th century. The abbreviated form *champ* is 19th-century American.

An alternative and now obsolete form of the word is *campion*, from Old Northern French, and it has been speculated that this is the origin of the plant-name *campion* [16], on the basis that it was used to make garlands for fighters.

▶ camp, campion, champagne, champion

**chance** [13]   Like the related *case, chance* originally meant 'that which befalls (by *accident*, also a relative).' It comes ultimately from Vulgar Latin *\*cadēre*, a descendant of Latin *cadere* 'fall' (source of English *cadence* and *cadenza*). This passed into Old French as *cheoir*, whose noun derivatives included *cheoite*

(source of English *chute*) and *cheance*, acquired by English via Anglo-Norman *chaunce*.

▶ accident, cadence, case, chute

**chancellor** [11]   Etymologically, a *chancellor* was an attendant or porter who stood at the *cancellī*, or 'lattice-work bar,' of a court in Roman times – hence the Latin term *cancellārius*. Over the centuries the *cancellārius*'s status rose to court secretary, in due course with certain legal functions. The word came into English, via Anglo-Norman *canceler* or *chanceler*, in the time of Edward the Confessor, denoting the king's official secretary, a post which developed into that of Lord Chancellor, head of the English judiciary. The court over which he presides, *Chancery*, gets its name by alteration from Middle English *chancellerie*, which came from an Old French derivative of *chancelier* 'chancellor.'

The word's ultimate source, Latin *cancellī* 'crossbars, lattice, grating' (a diminutive form of *cancer* 'lattice'), came to be applied to the part of a church or other building separated off by such a screen: hence, via Old French, English *chancel* 'part of a church containing the altar and choir' [14]. And a metaphorical application of the notion of a lattice or bars crossing each other has given English *cancel* [14], via Latin *cancellāre* and Old French *canceller*, which originally meant 'cross something out.'

▶ cancel, chancel

**change** [13]   *Change* goes back ultimately to Latin *cambīre* 'barter,' which is probably of Celtic ancestry. A later form of the verb was *cambiāre*, whose most readily recognizable descendants are probably Italian *cambio*, which appears outside currency-exchange shops, and English *cambium* 'layer of plant tissue' [17], coined from the notion that it 'changes' into new layers. Another branch of development, however, was to Old French *changier*, source of English *change*.

▶ cambium

**channel** [13]   *Channel* and *canal* are ultimately the same word. Their common ancestor was Latin *canālis* 'groove, channel,' a derivative of *canna* 'pipe' (source of English *cane*). This passed into Old French as *chanel*, which English took over as *channel*. But then in the 15th century English acquired *canal*, either directly from Latin, or from French *canal*, which was itself remodelled on the Latin form – it is not clear which.

▶ canal, cane

**chant** [14]   The Latin verb for 'sing' was *canere* (possibly related to English *hen*). A form derived from it to denote repeated action was *cantāre* 'keep on singing,' a rich source of English words. From its French descendant *chanter* we have *chant* and the derived *chantry* [14]; from Italian, *cantata* [18], originally a past participle; and from the Latin noun *cantus* 'song' the derivatives *accent, descant*, and *canticle* [13], as well as (via Italian) *canto* [16]. *Cant* 'hypocritical talk' is probably from the same source, and *shanty* or *chanty* 'sailor's song' is also related.

▶ accent, cant, cantata, canto, chanty, descant, hen, incantation, recant

## chaos see GAS

## chap
There are four distinct words *chap* in English. The oldest, 'sore on the skin' [14], originally meant more generally 'crack, split,' and may be related to Middle Low German *kappen* 'chop off'; it seems ultimately to be the same word as *chop* 'cut.' *Chap* 'jaw' [16] (as in *Bath chaps*) is probably a variant of *chop* (as in 'lick one's chops'). *Chap* 'fellow' [16] originally meant 'customer'; it is an abbreviation of *chapman* 'trader' [OE] (source of the common surname, but now obsolete as an ordinary noun), whose first element is related to English *cheap*. *Chaps* 'leggings' [19] is short for Mexican Spanish *chaparreras*, a derivative of Spanish *chaparro* 'evergreen oak'; they were named from their use in protecting the legs of riders from the low thick scrub that grows in Mexico and Texas (named with another derivative of *chaparro, chaparral*). *Chaparro* itself probably comes from Basque *txapar*, a diminutive of *saphar* 'thicket.'

▶ chop / cheap / chaparral

## chapel
[13] *Chapel* has a very specific source: it was originally applied to the shrine built to preserve the cloak (late Latin *cappa*) of St Martin of Tours as a holy relic. The diminutive form of *cappa* was *cappella*, and this came to be applied to the building itself, gradually being broadened out subsequently to any moderately sized place of worship. The word reached English via Old French *chapele*. The church functionary who guarded St Martin's cloak was known by the derivative term *cappellānus*, source of English *chaplain* [12].

▶ chaplain

## chaperon
[14] A *chaperon* was originally a 'hood.' The word comes from Old French *chaperon*, a derivative of *chape*, whose variant *cape* was the source of English *cape*, and goes back ultimately to late Latin *cappa* 'hood, cloak.' The word's modern sense, 'companion safeguarding propriety,' which first appears in English in the 18th century, arose from the general notion of a 'hood' as something that gives protection.

▶ cape

## chaplain see CHAPEL

## chapter
[13] Ultimately, *chapter* is the same word as *capital*. Both came via Old French from Latin *capitulum* 'small head,' a diminutive form of *caput* 'head,' but whereas *capital* represents a late, 12th-century borrowing into French in ecclesiastical and legal contexts, *chapter* is far earlier and therefore shows more differences: in Old French, *capitulum* became *chapitle*, later *chapitre*. Already in Latin the word was

used for 'section of a book'; the semantic development seems to parallel English *head* 'category, section' (as in 'heads of agreement') and the derived *heading*. The ecclesiastical use of *chapter*, as a collective term for the canons of a cathedral, originated in the canons' practice of meeting to read a chapter of Scripture.

Latin *capitulum* in the sense 'head of a discourse, chapter' produced the derivative *capitulāre* 'draw up under separate headings.' When its past participle passed into English in the 16th century as the verb *capitulate*, it was still with this meaning, and it did not narrow down to the more specific 'make terms of surrender' until the 17th century.

▶ capital, capitulate, cattle, recapitulate

## char see CHARCOAL

## character
[14] The ultimate source of *character* is Greek *kharaktḗr*, a derivative of the verb *kharássein* 'sharpen, engrave, cut,' which in turn came from *kharax* 'pointed stake.' *Kharaktḗr* meant 'engraved mark,' and hence was applied metaphorically to the particular impress or stamp which marked one thing as different from another – its 'character.' The word came into English via Latin *charactēr* and Old French *caractere*. *Characteristic* followed in the 17th century.

▶ gash

## charcoal
[14] The words *char* and *charcoal* are related, but not in the way commonsense might lead one to suppose: for the verb *char* [17], originally apparently a charcoal-burner's term, appears to derive from *charcoal*. So etymologically, the element *char* has nothing to do with 'burning.' There are two main suggestions as to *charcoal*'s origins: firstly that it comes from Old French *charbon* 'charcoal' (related to English *carbon*); and secondly that it represents the now obsolete English verb *chare* (see CHARWOMAN), which in Old English times (*cerran*) meant 'turn.' On the basis of this theory, the etymological meaning of the word would be 'turning into charcoal' (for in Old English, *coal* meant 'charcoal' as well as 'coal').

## charge
[13] The notion underlying the word *charge* is of a 'load' or 'burden' – and this can still be detected in many of its modern meanings, as of a duty laid on one like a load, or of the burden of an expense, which began as metaphors. It comes ultimately from Latin *carrus* 'two-wheeled wagon' (source also of English *car*). From this was derived the late Latin verb *carricāre* 'load,' which produced the Old French verb *charger* and, via the intermediate Vulgar Latin \**carrica*, the Old French noun *charge*, antecedents of the English words. The literal sense of 'loading' or 'bearing' has now virtually died out, except in such phrases as 'charge your glasses,' but there are reminders of it in *cargo* [17], which comes from the Spanish equivalent of the French noun *charge*, and indeed in *carry*, descended from the same ultimate source.

The origins of the verb sense 'rush in attack' are not altogether clear, but it may have some connection with the sense 'put a weapon in readiness.' This is now familiar in the context of firearms, but it seems to have been used as long ago as the 13th century with reference to arrows.

The Italian descendant of late Latin *carricāre* was *caricare*, which meant not only 'load' but also, metaphorically, 'exaggerate.' From this was derived the noun *caricatura*, which reached English via French in the 18th century as *caricature*.

▶ car, cargo, caricature

**charlatan** [17] *Charlatan* is of Italian origin. It comes from the verb *cialare* 'chatter, prattle.' Its original application was to the patter of salesmen trying to sell quack remedies, and hence Italian *ciarlatano* at first referred to such vendors, and then by extension to any dispenser of impostures. Some etymologists have sought to connect the word with Italian *Cerretano*, literally 'inhabitant of Cerreto,' an Italian village supposedly noted for exaggeration, alleging that it may have contributed its suffix to *ciarlatano* and reinforced its meaning. However that may be, the word reached English in its current form via French *charlatan*.

**charm** [13] Although now largely weakened to mere 'attractiveness,' the origins of *charm* are in magic spells and incantations. It comes via Old French *charme* from Latin *carmen* 'song,' which was also used for the chanting or reciting of verses with supposedly magic powers. Thus in the Middle Ages, charms were synonymous with enchantment – either spoken or, in more concrete form, carried as talismans. The latter have degenerated in modern times to small trinkets worn on bracelets, an application first recorded in the mid 19th century.

**charnel** see CARNAL

**chart** [16] English *card* and *chart* are related. Both come from Latin *charta* 'paper,' but whereas *card* was routed via French *carte*, and for some reason changed its *t* to a *d*, *chart* was borrowed directly from the Latin word, in which the meaning 'map' had already developed.

Latin *charta* originally denoted 'leaf of the papyrus plant,' and developed the sense 'paper' because paper was originally made from papyrus (indeed the English word *paper* comes from *papyrus*). It came from Greek *khártēs*, which is probably of Egyptian origin. It has provided the basis of a number of other English words besides *card* and *chart*, including *charter* [13], which comes via Old French from Latin *chartula*, a diminutive form of *charta*; *carton* [19], which comes from a French derivative, and was originally used in English for the 'white disc at the centre of a target'; and, via Italian *carta*, *cartel*, *cartoon*, *cartouche*, and *cartridge*. *Cartel* [16] comes via French from the Italian diminutive

form *cartello*, which meant literally 'placard.' It was used metaphorically for 'letter of defiance,' and entered English with the sense 'written challenge.' The modern commercial sense comes from German *kartell*. *Cartouche* [17] comes via French from Italian *cartoccio*. It originally signified a 'cartridge,' made from a roll or twist of paper; the modern architectural sense of 'ornamental tablet' arose from its original scroll-like shape. *Cartridge* [16] is an English modification of *cartouche*; an intermediate form was *cartage*.

▶ card, cartel, carton, cartoon, cartouche, cartridge, charter

**charwoman** [16] A *charwoman* is, quite literally, a woman who does 'chores.' *Chore* is a variant of the now obsolete noun *chare* or *char*, which meant literally 'turn' (it derived from the Old English verb *cerran*, which may be the source of *charcoal*). Hence 'doing one's turn,' 'one's turn at work' in due course advanced its meaning to 'job.' Already by the 15th century it had connotations of menial or household jobs: 'making the beds and such other chares,' Nicholas Love, *Bonaventura's Mirror* 1410.

▶ ajar, chore

**chary** see CARE

**chase** There are two distinct words *chase* in English, although they may come from the same ultimate source. The commoner, and older, 'pursue' [13] , comes via Old French *chacier* from Vulgar Latin *\*captiāre* (which also produced Anglo-Norman *cachier*, source of English *catch*). This was an alteration of Latin *captāre* 'try to seize,' which was formed from *captus*, the past participle of *capere* 'take' (source of a wide range of English words, including *capture, capable*, and *cater*, and distantly related to *heave*). The other, 'engrave' [14], may come from Old French *chas* 'enclosure,' which in turn came from Latin *capsa* 'box' (source of English *case* and related ultimately to Latin *capere*). The semantic connection would seem to be between putting a jewel in its setting, or 'enclosure,' and decorating jewellery or precious metal by other means such as engraving or embossing.

▶ capable, capture, case, catch, cater, heave, purchase

**chasm** see YAWN

**chassis** see SASH

**chaste** [13] *Chaste* comes via Old French from Latin *castus* 'pure.' The notion of making someone pure, by correcting or reproving them, was expressed in Latin by the derived verb *castīgāre*, which passed into English in the 17th century as *castigate*. Old French, however, had already adopted it as *chastier*, which in the 12th century produced the now obsolete English verb *chaste* 'discipline.' From it were formed the derivatives *chastise* [14] and *chasten* [16]. Also ultimately from Latin *castus* is English *caste*.

▶ caste, chasten, chastise, incest

**chattel** see CATTLE

**chauvinism** [19] *Chauvinism* in its original sense of 'blind patriotism' was coined in French from the name of one Nicholas Chauvin of Rochefort, a (possibly legendary) French soldier and veteran of Napoleon's campaigns noted for his patriotic zeal. He was taken up and ridiculed as the type of the old soldier forever harking back to the glories of Napoleon's times, and became widely known particularly through the play *La cocarde tricolore* 1831 by the brothers Cogniard, in which there occurs the line 'Je suis français, je suis Chauvin.' Hence French *chauvinisme*, which first appeared in English in 1870.

The word's more general application to an unreasoning belief in the superiority of one's own group (particularly in the context *male chauvinism*) arose around 1970.

**cheap** [16] The adjectival use of *cheap* in English is quite recent, but the word itself goes back a long way. Its ultimate source is the Latin noun *caupō* 'tradesman,' which was borrowed into Germanic in prehistoric times. Among its descendants were German *kaufen* 'buy,' Old English *cēapian* 'trade' (the possible source of *chop*, as in 'chop and change'), and the Old English noun *cēap* 'trade.' In Middle English times this came to be used in such phrases as *good chepe*, meaning 'good bargain,' and by the 16th century an adjectival sense 'inexpensive' had developed. The original sense 'trade' is preserved in the personal name *Chapman*, which until the 19th century was an ordinary noun meaning 'trader' (it is the source of *chap* 'fellow').

▶ chap, chop

**cheat** [14] *Cheat* is a reduced form of *escheat*, a legal term for the reversion of property to the state on the death of the owner without heirs. This came from Old French *escheoite*, a derivative of the past participle of the verb *escheoir* 'befall by chance, happen, devolve,' from Vulgar Latin *\*excadēre* 'fall away,' a compound veb formed from the prefix *ex-* 'out' and Latin *cadere* 'fall' (source of a wide range of English words from *case* 'circumstance' to *occasion*). The semantic steps leading to the modern English sense of *cheat* seem to be 'confiscate'; 'deprive of something dishonestly'; 'deceive.'

▶ cadence, case, escheat, occasion, occident

**check** There are two distinct words *check* in English, although by very involved pathways they are related. *Check* 'verify' [14] is originally a chess term meaning 'threaten the king.' It comes from Old French *eschequier*, a derivative of the noun *eschec* (source also of English *chess*), which goes back via Vulgar Latin *\*scaccus* and Arabic *shāh* to Persian *shāh* 'king' (whence also, of course, English *shah*). (*Checkmate* [14] comes via Old French *eschec mat* from Persian *shāh māt* 'the king is left helpless'; the second element

turns up again in *mat* or *matt* 'lustreless.') From the very specific chess sense there developed more general applications such as 'attack,' 'arrest,' 'stop,' 'restrict,' and 'verify.' Among these in the 18th century was 'token used as a counterfoil for verifying something, such as an amount.' As *check* this survives mainly in American English (as in 'hat-check'), but in the specific financial sense of 'written money order' it was transformed in British English into *cheque*, perhaps under the influence of *exchequer*. *Check* 'pattern of squares' [14] is probably short for *chequer*, which in turn is a reduced form of *exchequer*, a word derived ultimately from Vulgar Latin *\*scaccus* 'check.'

▶ cheque, chess, exchequer

**cheek** [OE] Old English *cēace* and *cēoce* go back respectively to prehistoric West Germanic *\*kēkōn* and *\*keukōn*, but beyond that the word has no known relatives in other Indo-European languages. It has, however, produced one or two interesting offshoots. It forms the basis of the verb *choke*, and may be the source of *chock-full* (literally, 'full up to the cheeks'); and Middle Dutch *kākelen*, source of English *cackle* [13], may be partly based on the related Middle Dutch *kāke* 'jaw.' The metaphorical sense 'impudence' (whence *cheeky*) arose in the 19th century, originally as 'insolent talk.'

▶ cackle, chock-full, choke

**cheer** [13] Originally, *cheer* meant 'face.' It came via Anglo-Norman *chere* 'face' and late Latin *cara* 'face' from Greek *kárā* 'head.' As often happens, 'face' was taken as a metaphor of the mental condition causing the expression on it, so 'be of good cheer' came to mean 'be in a good mood'; and gradually *cheer* grew to be used on its own for 'happy frame of mind, cheerfulness.' It first appears in the sense 'shout of applause or encouragement' at the start of the 18th century, when Daniel Defoe identifies it as a nautical usage.

**cheese** [OE] *Cheese* is of Latin origin, but was borrowed into the West Germanic languages in prehistoric times, producing German *käse* and Dutch *kaas* as well as *cheese*. The Latin word was *cāseus* (source also of Spanish *queso* 'cheese'), whose possible distant relative Sanskrit *kvathati* 'he boils' suggests an underlying idea of froth or bubbles in the milk from which the cheese is made.

**chemical** [16] Essentially *chemical*, and the related *chemistry* and *chemist*, come from *alchemy* with the initial *al-* dropped. *Alchemy* itself is of Arabic origin; *al* represents the Arabic definite article 'the,' while the second element was borrowed from Greek *khēmíā* 'alchemy.' Loss of *al-* seems to have taken place originally in French, so the immediate source of the English words was French *chimiste* and *chimique* (whence the now obsolete English *chemic*, on which *chemical* was based). At first this whole group of words continued to be used in the same sense as its progenitor *alchemy*; it is not really until the 17th century that we find it being consistently applied to what we would now recognize as the scientific discipline of chemistry.

► alchemy

**chenille**    SEE KENNEL

**chequer**    SEE EXCHEQUER

**cherry**    [14]    Cherry comes ultimately from Greek kerasós 'cherry tree,' which in Latin became cerasus. This was borrowed into the Germanic languages in prehistoric times, producing, as well as German kirsche, Old English ciris 'cherry,' which died out in the 11th century. In Vulgar Latin, meanwhile, cerasus had become ceresia, which passed into Old Northern French as cherise (source of modern French cerise). When it was borrowed into English, its -s ending was misinterpreted as indicating plurality, so a 'new' singular cherry was created.

**cherub**    [OE]    Cherub is of Akkadian origin (Akkad was the northern region of ancient Babylonia). Akkadian karūbu meant 'gracious.' This was borrowed into Hebrew as kerūbh (plural kerūbhīm), which was used in the Old Testament to signify a certain class of winged divine being. It passed into English via Greek kheroúb and Latin cherūb.

**chess**    [13]    The game of chess was named after its key move, in which the king is put in check. The plural of Old French eschec (from which we get check) was esches, which in Middle English became chess. (A roughly contemporary English term for the game was chequer, but this died out in the 15th century.)

Old French eschec came ultimately from Persian shāh 'king,' the game's eastern origins. However, the terms for the game in Persian (chatrang) and Sanskrit (chaturanga) signify 'four members of an army' – namely, elephants, horses, chariots, and foot-soldiers.

► check, cheque, exchequer

**chest**    [OE]    Chest comes ultimately from Greek kístē 'box, basket.' In Latin this became cista (source of English cistern [13]). In prehistoric times the word was borrowed into Germanic as *kistā, which was the source of Old English cest. This still meant 'box,' a sense which continued in isolation until the 16th century, when it was first applied to the 'thorax' – the basis of the metaphor presumably being that the ribs enclose the heart and lungs like a box. It has since replaced breast as the main term for the concept.

► cistern

**chestnut**    [16]    The Greek word for 'chestnut' was kastanéā, which appears to have meant originally 'nut from Castanea' (in Pontus, Asia Minor) or 'nut from Castana' (in Thessaly, Greece). It came into English via Latin castanea and Old French chastaine, which in the 14th century produced the Middle English

form chasteine or chesteine. Over the next two hundred years this developed to chesten, and in due course had nut added to it to produce the modern English form. Castaña, the Spanish descendant of Latin castanea, is the source of castanet.

► castanet

**chew**    [OE]    Chew, and its Germanic relatives German kauen and Dutch kauwen, can be traced back to a prehistoric West Germanic *kewwan. It has relatives in other Indo-European languages, including Latin gingīva 'gum' (source of English gingivitis).

► gingivitis

**chicken**    [OE]    Chicken is a widespread Germanic word (Dutch has kuiken, for instance, and Danish kylling), whose ancestor has been reconstructed as *kiukīnam. This was formed, with a diminutive suffix, on a base *keuk-, which some have claimed is a variant of a base which lies behind cock; if that is so, a chicken would amount etymologically to a 'little cock' (and historically the term has been applied to young fowl, although nowadays it tends to be the general word, regardless of age). Chick is a 14th-century abbreviation. The modern adjectival sense 'scared' is a 20th-century revival of a 17th- and 18th-century noun sense 'coward,' based no doubt on chicken-hearted.

► cock

**chickenpox**    SEE POX

**chief**    [13]    Etymologically, the chief is the 'head.' The word comes via Old French chef or chief and Vulgar Latin *capum from Latin caput 'head.' The adjectival use is equally as old as the noun use in English. Other English offshoots of *capum are cape and, via the diminutive form *capitellus, cadet, and it also forms the basis of achieve. The form which has come through into modern French is, of course, chef, which entered English in the sense 'cook' (short for chef de cuisine 'head of the kitchen') in the 19th century.

Chieftain [14] comes via Old French chevetaine from late Latin capitāneus (a derivative of caput 'head'), which was later reborrowed as captain.

► achieve, cadet, cape, captain, chef

**chiffon**    SEE CHIP

**child**    [OE]    For a word of so central importance, child is surprisingly isolated, having no known living relatives in other Germanic languages. Its prehistoric Germanic ancestor has been reconstructed as *kiltham, which some have linked with Gothic kilthei 'womb' and even with Sanskrit jathara 'belly.' The plural children is not an original feature; it developed in the 12th century. In earliest Old English times the plural was unchanged, like sheep.

**chill**    [14]    Old English had a noun cele or ciele 'cold' (from the same Germanic base as cold) which developed into Middle English chile 'cold, frost.' Gaps in the record, however, cast doubt on whether this was the direct ancestor of the modern English noun, which may more plausibly be derived from the verb *chill*. This has been tentatively traced back to a hypothetical Old English verb *\*cieldan* (also from the same Germanic base as *cold*), whose later form *child* may have been misinterpreted as a past participle, giving the new base form *chill*. *Chilblain* [16] is a compound formed from *chill* and *blain* 'blister,' which comes from Old English *blegen*.

▶ cold

**chime** [13] Etymologically, *chime* is the same word as *cymbal* – indeed it originally meant 'cymbal' in English – but the route by which it reached English is not altogether clear. Latin *cymbalum* was borrowed into Old French as *chimbe*, which is perhaps the most likely source of the English word, whose earliest forms include *chimbe*. However, Old English also acquired the Latin word, as *cimbal*, and it has been speculated that this may have survived into the Middle English period as *\*chimbel*, whose last syllable was misinterpreted as *bell*. This would have opened the way to a misanalysis of the word as *chime bell*, a term which does actually occur from the 13th to the 15th centuries. This theory has the advantage of explaining the transference of the word's meaning from 'cymbals' to 'bells,' which occurred between the 14th and 15th centuries.

▶ cymbal

**chimney** [14] Greek *kámīnos* meant 'furnace' (it was related to *kamárā* 'vaulted room,' source of English *camera* and *chamber*). It was borrowed into Latin as *camīnus*, from which the adjective *camīnātus* 'having a furnace, oven, etc' was derived. By late Latin times this had become a noun, *camīnāta*, which passed into Old French as *cheminee*, and thence into English. The original meanings 'fireplace' and 'stove' persisted until the 19th century, but already in Old French the sense 'flue' had developed, which was finally to win out.

▶ camera, chamber

**chin** [OE] *Chin* has relatives throughout the Germanic languages (German has *kinn*, for instance, and Dutch *kin*) and is also represented in words for 'lower jaw,' 'mouth,' 'cheek,' etc in other Indo-European languages (Greek *gnáthos* 'jaw,' for example, which gave English *prognathous* 'having projecting jaws'). All go back to a prehistoric Indo-European source *\*genw-*.

▶ prognathous

**chintz** [17] *Chintz* is originally an Indian word. English borrowed it from Hindi *chīnt*, and at first used it unaltered: Samuel Pepys, for instance, writing in his diary for 5 September 1663, notes 'Bought my wife a chint, that is, a painted Indian calico, for to line her new study.' However, since in commercial use the plural form, *chints*, was so much commoner than the singular,

it eventually came to be regarded as a singular itself, and the *s*-less form dropped out of the language. In the 18th century, for some unexplained reason (perhaps on the analogy of such words as *quartz*) *chints* began to be spelled *chintz*. The Hindi word itself was originally an adjective, which came from Sanskrit *chitra* 'many-coloured, bright' (ultimate source of English *chit* 'small piece of paper containing some sort of official notification' [18]).

▶ chit

**chip** [OE] Old English *cipp* meant 'share-beam of a plough' (a sense paralleled in related forms in other Germanic languages, such as Dutch *kip* 'plough-beam' and Old Norse *keppr* 'stick'). This seems a far cry from the modern use of *chip*, for which there is no evidence before the 14th century, and in fact our noun *chip* may be a new formation based on the verb *chip*, which goes back to Old English *-cippian* 'cut' (found only in compounds). Here again, though, the record is incomplete; for the post-Old English verb does not turn up until the late 15th century, and then in the very specialized sense 'cut the crust off bread.' The more general meaning 'cut' appears in the 17th century, but the modern 'break off a small fragment' is as late as the 18th century. All in all, a picture confused by lack of evidence. But probably the basic etymological sense that underlies all later usage is 'cut off' or 'piece cut off' (the early noun senses representing 'branch or bough cut off a tree'). 'Small piece of fried potato' dates from the 1860s. (Old French borrowed the word as *chipe*, and a variant of this, *chiffe* 'rag,' is the ultimate source of English *chiffon* [18].)

▶ chiffon

**chipolata** see CHIVES

**chiropodist** see SURGEON

**chisel** [14] *Chisel* and *scissors* are related, for both come ultimately from Latin *caedere* 'cut' (source of a range of other English words from *cement* to *concise* and *decide*). From its past participle *caesus* was formed an unrecorded Vulgar Latin term for a cutting tool, probably *\*caesellus*. This must have become changed at some point to *\*cīsellus*, probably under the influence of late Latin *cīsōrium* (source of English *scissors*), itself derived from *caedere*. This passed into Old Northern French as *chisel*, and thence into English. (The modern French equivalent, in the plural, is *ciseaux* 'scissors.')

▶ cement, concise, decide, precise, scissors

**chit** see CHINTZ

**chivalry** [13] Etymologically, *chivalry* is the practice of riding horses. It comes from Old French *chivalerie*, a derivative of medieval Latin *caballārius* (related to, and perhaps direct source of, English *cavalier*). This meant 'horseman,' and was formed from Latin *caballus* 'horse' (whence French *cheval*). The meaning of *chivalerie* had two main strands, both of them adopted into English: on the one hand 'mounted soldiery' (a sense superseded by the related *cavalry*), and on the other 'knightly behaviour.'

▶ cavalier, cavalry

**chives**   [14]   The Latin for 'onion' was *cēpa*. The only member of the onion family to carry a reminiscence of that name in English is *chives* (although it crops up too in *chipolata* [19], which comes from Italian *cipolata* 'with onions,' a derivative of Italian *cipolla* 'onion,' ultimately from Latin *cēpa*). The Latin word entered Old French as *cive* (the term *civet* 'game stew' derives from *cive*, such stews originally having been flavoured with green onions). It must, however, have been a northern dialect version of this, *\*chive*, which English borrowed.

▶ chipolata

**chlorine**   [19]   Chlorine is a greenish-yellow gas, and was named for its colour. The term was coined by the British chemist Sir Humphry Davy in 1810, from the Greek *khlōrós* 'greenish-yellow.' Of other words containing this element, *chlorophyll* [19] too was based on the notion of colour (in reference to the green colouring matter of leaves: the Greek elements literally mean 'green leaf'), but *chloroform* [19], originally French, is a secondary formation based ultimately on *chlorine* (since it was originally regarded as a trichloride of formyl).

▶ yellow

**chock-full**   [14]   There is more than one theory to account for this word. It occurs in a couple of isolated instances around 1400, as *chokkefulle* and *chekeful*, prompting speculation that the first element may be either *chock* 'wooden block,' which came from an assumed Old Northern French *\*choque* (thus 'stuffed full with lumps of wood') or *cheek* (thus 'full up as far as the cheeks'). It resurfaces in the 17th century as *choke-ful*, which has given rise to the idea that it may originally have meant 'so full as to choke.' The available evidence seems too scanty to come to a firm conclusion.

**chocolate**   [17]   *Chocolate* is one of the contributions made to English by the Nahuatl language of the Aztec people. Their *xocolatl* was a compound noun formed from *xococ* 'bitter' and *atl* 'water,' and therefore when first adopted by European languages (via Spanish) it was used for the drink 'chocolate.' This was its original sense in English, and it was not for half a century or more that it came to be applied to solid, edible 'chocolate.'

**choice**   [13]   *Choice* is a French formation, although like the verb with which it is linked, *choose*, its ancestry is Germanic. The source of the English word was Old French *chois*, a derivative of the verb *choisir* 'choose,' which came ultimately from the same Germanic base, *\*kaus-* or *\*keus-*, as produced *choose*. English had its own native formation, Old English *cyre*

'choice,' which died out in Middle English times; had it survived to the present day, it might have been something like *kire*.

▶ choose

**choir**   [13]   Modern choirs merely sing, but far back in time they danced too. The word comes ultimately from Greek *khorós*, which in ancient Greek drama signified a group of singers and dancers who commented on the action of the play (the element of dance is preserved in *choreography*). In Latin, *khorós* became *chorus* – whence English *chorus* [16], *choral*, and probably also *carol*. The Latin form in turn developed to Old French *quer*, in which form it was borrowed into English; the spelling *choir*, modelled on Latin and the modern French form *choeur*, was introduced in the 17th century.

▶ carol, choreography, chorus

**choke**   [14]   Etymologically, to *choke* is to cut off air by constricting the 'cheeks,' for it is a derivative of *cēoce*, the Old English word for 'cheek.' There is actually such a verb recorded, just once, from Old English: the compound *ācēocian*, with the intensive prefix *ā-*; so probably the simple verb existed too, though evidence for it has not survived. The noun sense 'valve controlling the flow of air to an engine' dates from the 1920s, but it was a natural development from an earlier (18th-century), more general sense 'constriction in a tube'; its parallelism with *throttle*, both being applied to constriction of the air passage and hence to control valves in an engine tube, is striking. (The *choke* of *artichoke* has no etymological connection with *choke* 'deprive of air.')

**cholera**   [14]   Greek *kholéra* originally meant 'illness caused by choler, bilious attack'; it was a derivative of *kholé* 'bile' (which is related to English *gall*). Passing into Latin as *cholera*, it began to be used for 'bile' itself, both in the physiological sense and as representing one of the four ancient humours, 'anger.' It had that sense when first adopted into English, and into French, where it became *colère* (source of English *choler* [14]). It was revived as a term for a severe digestive disorder, involving vomiting, diarrhoea, etc, in the 17th century, and in the 19th century was applied (from the similarity of the symptoms) to the often fatal infectious disease caused by the bacterium *Vibrio comma*.

▶ gall, melancholy

**choose**   [OE]   *Choose* is a verb of ancient pedigree. It can be traced back to the prehistoric Indo-European base *\*geus-*, whose descendants in other Indo-European languages include Latin *gustus* 'taste,' source of English *gusto* and *gustatory* and French *goût*. Its Germanic offshoot, *\*kiusan*, produced a diversity of forms in the early Middle Ages, including Old English *cēosan*, but most of them, apart from English *choose* and Dutch *kiezen*, have now died out. Germanic had an alternative version of the verb, however, *\*kausjan*, and this was borrowed into Gallo-Roman as *causīre*, which provided the basis of Old French *choisir* 'choose,' and hence of *chois*, source of English *choice*.

► choice, gusto

**chop** There are three distinct words *chop* in English. The oldest [14] originally meant 'trade, barter,' but it is now found only in the phrase *chop and change*. It appears to come from Old English *cēapian* 'trade,' which is related to English *cheap*. *Chop* 'jaw, jowl' [15] (now usually in the plural form *chops*) is of unknown origin; the now archaic *chap* is a variant. *Chop* 'cut' [16] seems ultimately to be the same word as *chap* (as in 'chapped lips'), and may be related to Middle Low German *kappen* 'chop off.' The specific noun sense 'meat cutlet' dates from the 15th century.

► chap, cheap

**chopstick** [17] A *chopstick* is literally a 'quick stick.' The element *chop* occurs more recognizably in *chop-chop* 'quickly'; it is a Pidgin English modification of Cantonese Chinese *gap* 'urgent.' 'Quick stick' is a rather free translation of the Chinese term for 'chopsticks,' Cantonese *kuàizi*, literally 'fast ones, nimble ones.'

► chop-chop

**chord** see CORD

**choreography** [18] *Choreography* 'arrangement of dances' comes from French *choré-ographie*, which was based on Greek *khoreíā* 'dance,' a derivative of *khorós*. (Source of English *chorus, choir*, and possibly also *carol*, this originally encompassed dancing as well as singing.) *Khoreíā* passed into Latin as *chorea*, applied in English to various muscular disorders (such as *Huntington's chorea*); the usage probably originated in the Latin phrase *chorea sancti Viti* 'St Vitus's dance.'

► carol, choir, chorea, chorus

**chorus** see CHOIR

**chowder** [18] *Chowder*, a North American seafood soup, probably takes its name from the pot in which it was originally cooked – French *chaudière* 'stew pot.' This came from late Latin *caldāria* 'pot,' a descendant of Latin *calidārium* 'hot bath' (which lies behind English *cauldron*); this in turn was a derivative of the adjective *calidus* 'warm.'

► calorie, cauldron

**chrism** see CREAM

**Christian** [16] *Christian* is derived, of course, from the name of Christ. It is a surprisingly recent word, having been introduced in the 16th century from Latin *Chrīstiānus*, replacing the existing English adjective *christen*, which came from Old English *crīsten*. The latter was the basis of the Old English verb *crīstnian*, from which we get modern English *christen*. The name *Christ* itself was borrowed into Old English

from Latin *Chrīstus*, which in turn came from Greek *Khrīstós*. This meant literally 'anointed,' and came from the verb *khríein* 'anoint.' It was a direct translation of Hebrew *māshīah* (source of English *messiah*), which also meant literally 'anointed.' *Christmas* comes from late Old English *crīstes mæsse*, literally 'Christ's mass.'

► cretin

**chrome** [19] Compounds formed from the element chromium are brilliantly coloured green, red, and yellow. Hence, when it was first described by the French chemist Vauquelin in 1797, he named it *chrome*, after Greek *khrōma* 'colour.' This was soon latinized to *chromium*, and *chrome* was henceforth used for chromium pigments or chromium plating.

The Greek adjective derived from *khrōma* was *khrōmatikós*, which as well as referring to colour, denoted the gradations of notes in a musical scale; and it was in this musical sense that it was first borrowed into English in the 17th century.

**chronicle** [14] English has a number of words derived from Greek *khrónos* 'time,' among them *chronology* [16], *chronometer* 'timepiece' [18], and *crony*. And from its adjective *kronikós* 'of time' comes English *chronic* [15], by way of Latin *chronicus*, which in medieval times picked up the medical connotations which characterize the word today. Greek *bíblia khroniká* meant 'books about time'; hence *khroniká* came to be used on its own for 'historical records,' passing via Latin *chronica* and Old French *chronique* to Anglo-Norman, where it acquired a new ending, *cronicle*. English took it over, and restored the Latin *ch-* spelling in the 16th century.

► anachronism, chronic, chronology

**chrysalis** [17] Etymologically, a *chrysalis* is a 'gold'-coloured pupa, for the word derives ultimately from Greek *khrūsós* 'gold.' Many butterflies do have pupae that, at least to start with, have a metallic sheen of gold, so the Greeks applied to them the term *khrūsallís*, in which the final element seems to mean something like 'sheath.' This passed into English via Latin *chrȳsalis*.

Also formed from Greek *khrūsós* (which is of Semitic origin) is *chrysanthemum* [16], which means literally 'gold flower.'

**chukker** see CYCLE

**church** [OE] Etymologically, a *church* is the 'Lord's house.' Its ultimate source is Greek *kūrios* 'lord, master' (perhaps most familiar nowadays from the words of the choral mass *kyrie eleison* 'lord have mercy'). The adjective derived from this was *kūriakós*, whose use in the phrase 'house of the lord' led to its use as a noun, *kūrikón*. The medieval Greek form, *kūrkón* 'house of worship' was borrowed into West Germanic as *\*kirika*, producing eventually German *kirche* and

English *church*. The Scots form *kirk* comes from Old Norse *kirkja*, which in turn was borrowed from Old English.

▶ kirk, kyrie

**churn** [OE] It has been speculated that the term *churn* is based on the granular appearance cream takes on as it is stirred or agitated. The Old English noun *cyrin* comes from a prehistoric Germanic *\*kernjōn*, which may be related to English *corn* and *kernel* and Latin *grānum* 'grain.' The derived verb *churn* is a comparatively late creation, not appearing until the 15th century.

▶ corn, grain, kernel

**chyme** see GUT

**cider** [14] Despite its seeming roots in the apple-producing English countryside, *cider* is a very ancient word, which has come a long way to reach us. Hebrew *shēkhār* meant 'any strong drink in general.' It crops up in several places in the Bible, and was adopted by Greek and Latin translators as, respectively, *sīkéra* and *sīcera*. The Latin form was borrowed into Old French, where it became *sisdre* and eventually *sidre*. By now it was being applied more specifically to drink made from apples, and it had that meaning when it was borrowed into English.

However, its biblical associations were still sufficiently strong for it to retain its original meaning in certain contexts: for example, in 1382 John Wyclif translated Luke 1:15 ('he shall drink neither wine nor strong drink') as 'he shall not drink wine and cider.' Its original form survived for a while, too, as *sicar*, which did not disappear from English until the 17th century.

**cigar** [18] *Cigar* comes from Spanish *cigarro*, whose origin is disputed. One story, perhaps more picturesque than accurate, is that it is an adaptation of *cigarra*, the Spanish word for 'cicada'; supposedly this insect, with its stout body round which are wrapped large transparent leaflike wings, was held to resemble a cigar. Others have preferred to see as the source *sicar*, the verb for 'smoke' in the language of the ancient Maya of Central America. *Cigarette* is a French derivative, with the diminutive suffix *-ette*, apparently coined in the early 1840s.

**cilium** see SUPERCILIOUS

**cincture** see PRECINCT

**cinder** [OE] Despite the similarity of form and meaning, *cinder* has no etymological connection with French *cendre* (which comes from Latin *cinis* 'ashes,' and is thus related to English *incinerate* and *cineraria*, a plant so named because of the grey down on its leaves). It is a Germanic word, related to German *sinter* 'deposit formed by evaporation' (itself borrowed into English in the 18th century), and from Old English times until the 16th century was usually spelled with an initial *s-*; the *c-*

is an adoption from French *cendre*. The name of the fairy-tale character *Cinderella* is a translation and adaptation of French *cendrillon*, originally a generic term for any downtrodden kitchen maid who spent much of her time among the *cendres* of the hearth.

**cinema** [20] The *cinema* is so named because it shows moving pictures. The Greek verb for 'move' was *kīnein* (source of English *kinetic* and, via the related Latin *cīre*, a range of *-cite* words, including *excite*, *incite*, and *recite*). Its noun derivative was *kínēma* 'movement,' from which in 1896 Auguste and Louis Jean Lumière coined the French term *cinématographe* for their new invention for recording and showing moving pictures. This and its abbreviated form *cinéma* soon entered English, the latter in 1909. In early years the graecized form *kinema* had some currency in English, but this had virtually died out by the 1940s.

▶ cite, excite, kinetic, incite, recite

**cipher** [14] The central meaning of *cipher* is 'zero' (a word to which it is related); its use since the 16th century in connection with encrypted communications derives from the fact that in their earliest forms such codes usually consisted of numbers representing letters, and *cipher* had by then broadened in use from 'nought' to 'any numeral.' It entered English through Old French *cifre*, which came via medieval Latin *cifra* from Arabic *sifr* (source of English *zero*); this was a nominal use of an adjective meaning 'empty.'

▶ zero

**circle** [14] Etymologically, a *circle* is a 'small ring.' The word comes ultimately from Latin *circus* (source of course of English *circus* and of a host of *circle*-related words), whose diminutive form was *circulus*. This was actually borrowed into English in Old English times, as *circul*, but this died out. Modern English *circle* came via Old French *cercle*, and to begin with was thus spelled in English, but in the 16th century the Latin *i* was reintroduced. Latin derivatives include the adjective *circulāris*, source of English *circular* [15], and the verb *circulāre*, whose past participle gave English *circulate* [15].

▶ circulate, circus, search

**circumstance** see STATUE

**circus** [16] Latin *circus* meant literally 'ring, circle,' but it was applied metaphorically by the Romans to the circular arena in which performances and contests were held. That was the original signification of the word in English, applied in a strictly antiquarian sense to the ancient world, and it was not until the late 18th century that it began to be used for any circular arena and the entertainment staged therein.

The Latin word is related to, and may have come from, Greek *kírkos*; and it is also connected with Latin *curvus*, source of English *curve*. It has additionally been linked with Latin *corōna* 'circlet,' from which

English gets *crown*. And it is of course, via its accusative form *circum*, the starting point of a wide range of English words with the prefix *circum-*, from *circumference* to *circumvent* (in this category is *circuit* [14], which goes back to an original Latin compound verb *circumīre*, literally 'go round').

▶ circle, circuit, circulate, crown, curve, search

## cistern   see CHEST

## citadel   see CITY

## cite   [15]   Latin *ciēre* or *cīre* meant 'move' (it was related to Greek *kīnein* 'move,' source of English *kinetic* and *cinema*). From its past participle, *citus*, was formed the verb *citāre*, meaning 'cause to move,' and hence 'call, summon.' This passed into English (via Old French *citer*), as *cite* 'summon officially.' In the 16th century this came to be applied metaphorically to the 'calling forth' of a particular passage of writing, author, etc as an example or proof of what one is saying – hence the modern sense 'quote.' The same Latin verb lies behind a range of other English verbs, including *excite*, *incite*, *recite*, and *solicit*.

▶ cinema, excite, incite, kinetic, recite, solicit

## citizen   [14]   The Latin word for 'citizen' was *cīvis*. From it was formed the derivative *cīvitās* 'citizenship, city state,' from which English gets *city*. From this in turn a new derivative was formed in Vulgar Latin, *\*cīvitātānus* 'citizen,' replacing the original *cīvis*. This found its way, much changed, into Old French as *citeain* (whence modern French *citoyen*). Anglo-Norman altered the Old French form to *citezein*, possibly on analogy with Anglo-Norman *deinzein* 'denizen.'

## citrus   [19]   Latin *citrus* signified the 'citron,' a tree (*Citrus medica*) of Asian origin with a lemon-like fruit which was the earliest of the citrus fruits to become known in the West. Like the fruit itself, the name is presumably of Eastern origin – perhaps from a non-Indo-European language from around the eastern end of the Himalayas. *Citron* is a French derivative of *citrus*, coined on the model of French *limon* 'lemon'; it was borrowed into English in the 16th century.

## cittern   see GUITAR

## city   [13]   The Latin word for 'city' was *urbs* (whence English *urban*), but a 'citizen' was *cīvis*. From this was derived the noun *cīvitās*, which originally had the abstract sense 'citizenship.' Gradually it acquired more concrete connotations, eventually coming to be used as a synonym of *urbs*. It passed into English via Old French *cite*, and at first was used for any settlement, regardless of size (although it was evidently felt to be a grander term than the native *borough*); the modern distinction between *towns* and *cities* developed during the 14th century.

The Italian descendant of Latin *cīvitās* is *città*. A now

obsolete variant of this was *cittade*, whose diminutive form is the source of English *citadel* [16].

▶ citadel, citizen, civil

## civil   [14]   Latin *cīvis* 'citizen' had two adjectival derivatives which have passed into English: *cīvicus*, source of *civic* [16], and *cīvīlis*, from which, via Old French, we get *civil*. Of *its* derivatives, *civility* [14] comes from Latin *cīvīlitās*, but *civilize* [17] and *civilian* [14] are French creations.

▶ civilize, city

## claim   [13]   The etymological notion behind *claim* is of 'calling out.' It comes from *claim-*, the present stem of Old French *clamer*, which goes back to Latin *clāmāre* 'cry out, shout' (whose derived noun *clāmor* is the source of English *clamour* [14]). Relatives of *clāmāre* include *clārus* (source of English *clear*) and possibly *callāre* 'call out' (whence English *council*); and it formed the basis of the English verbs *acclaim*, *exclaim*, and *proclaim* (their spelling was altered through association with *claim*). These words' ultimate source was the onomatopoeic Indo-European base *\*klā-*, which also produced *low* 'make the noise characteristic of cattle.'

▶ acclaim, clamour, clear, council, exclaim, low, proclaim

## clam   [OE]   Old English *clam* meant 'something for tying up or fastening, fetter'; it can be traced back to a prehistoric Germanic base *\*klam-*, which also produced *clamp* [14] and is related to *climb*. There is a gap in the word's history in early Middle English times, but it reappears at the end of the 14th century in the sense 'clamp,' and in the 16th century it was applied, originally in Scotland, to the mollusc which now bears the name, apparently on the grounds that its two shells close like the jaws of a clamp or vice.

▶ clamp, climb

## clammy   [14]   Etymologically, *clammy* means 'sticky as if smeared with clay.' It comes from the now obsolete verb *clam* 'smear, stick.' This goes back to Old English *clǣman*, a word of ancient ancestry: its prehistoric Germanic source was *\*klaimjan*, a verb derived from *\*klaimaz* 'clay'; this was formed from the base *\*klai-*, which is also the ultimate source of English *clay* and can be traced back to the Indo-European base *\*gloi-*, *\*glei-*, *\*gli-*, from which English gets *glue* and *gluten*.

▶ clay, glue

## clamour   see CLAIM

## clamp   see CLIMB

## clan   [14]   The immediate source of *clan* is naturally enough Gaelic, but ultimately it comes, somewhat unexpectedly, from Latin, for etymologically it is the same word as *plant*. Scots Gaelic *clann* originally meant 'offspring' (hence the modern meaning 'family

group'), and it came from Old Irish *cland*, a direct borrowing from Latin *planta* (the Celtic languages of the British Isles tended to change Latin /p/ to /k/). This was the source of English *plant*, but it did not then have nearly such a broad application; it meant specifically 'shoot suitable for planting out,' and the connotations of 'new growth' and 'offspring' show up in the Gaelic borrowing.

▶ plant

**clandestine**   see CONCEAL

**clangor**   see LAUGH

**claret**   [14]   *Claret* was originally a 'light-coloured wine' – pale red (virtually what we would now call rosé), but also apparently yellowish. The word comes ultimately from Latin *clārus* 'clear'; from this was derived the verb *clārāre*, whose past participle was used in the phrase *vīnum clārātum* 'clarified wine.' This passed into Old French as *vin claret*. Modern French *clairet* preserves the word's early sense 'pale wine, rosé,' but in English by the later 17th century seems to have been transferred to red wine, and since in those days the vast majority of red wine imported into Britain came from Southwest France, and Bordeaux in particular, it was not long before *claret* came to mean specifically 'red Bordeaux.'

▶ clear

**clarion**   see CLEAR

**class**   [16]   Latin *classis* originally denoted 'the people of Rome under arms, the ancient Roman army'; it appears to come from an earlier unrecorded *\*qladtis*, a derivative of the base *\*qel-* 'call,' which points to an underlying sense 'call to arms.' Under the terms of the constitution attributed to Servius Tullius, a 6th-century BC king of Rome, the army, and hence the people, was divided into six such *classes*, membership of each based originally on the amount of land held, and latterly on wealth in money terms. English first adopted the word in this antiquarian sense (which provided the basis for the modern application to social class), but its widespread use in the language probably began in the sense 'group of pupils.' The derivatives *classic* [17] and *classical* [16] come from Latin *classicus*, probably via French *classique*; in Latin, the adjective signified 'of the highest class of Roman citizen,' whence the word's present-day approbatory connotations.

**clause**   [13]   The etymological notion underlying *clause* is of 'closing' or 'termination.' The word derives ultimately from Latin *claudere* (source of English *close*) and was originally applied either as a rhetorical term to the conclusion of a sentence, or as a legal term to the termination of a legal argument. Gradually, in both cases, the element of finality fell away, leaving the senses 'short sentence' and 'section of a legal document,' which passed into English. The past participle of Latin *claudere*, *clausus*, probably produced an unrecorded noun *\*clausa* (known only in its diminutive form *clausula*), which passed into English via Old French *clause*.

▶ clavier, close

**claustrophobia**   see CLOISTER

**clavier**   [18]   The Latin word for 'key' was *clāvis* (it was related to *claudere* 'close'). Its application to the keys of a musical instrument has contributed two words to English: *clavier*, which came via French or German from an unrecorded Latin *\*clāviārius* 'key-bearer'; and *clavichord* [15], from medieval Latin *clāvichordium*, a compound of Latin *clāvis* and Latin *chorda*, source of English *chord*. Its diminutive form *clāvicula* was aplied metaphorically to the collar-bone (hence English *clavicle* [17]) on account of the bone's resemblance to a small key. And in Latin, a room that could be locked 'with a key' was a *conclāve* – whence (via Old French) English *conclave* [14]. Also related to *clāvis* is *cloy*.

▶ clavicle, close, cloy, conclave

**clay**   [OE]   Clay is named from its consistency – its stickiness, its squidginess, its capacity for being smeared. Its ultimate source is the Indo-European base *\*gloi-*, *\*glei-*, *\*gli-*, from which English also gets *glue* and *gluten*. From it was descended the Germanic base *\*klai-*, on which was formed West Germanic *\*klaijō-*. This passed into Old English as *clæg* – hence modern English *clay*. (*Clammy* comes from the same Germanic source, and *clag*, from which we get *claggy* 'muddy,' is essentially the same word as *clay*, although it reached English via a Scandinavian route.)

▶ clammy, clean

**claymore**   see GLADIATOR

**clean**   [OE]   Etymologically, *clean* and German *klein* 'small' are the same word. Both go back to West Germanic *\*klainoz*, which meant 'clear, pure,' but whereas the English adjective has stayed fairly close to the original meaning, the German one has passed via 'clean,' 'neat,' 'dainty,' and 'delicate' to 'small.' It has been speculated that *\*klainiz* was based on *\*klai-*, which connoted 'stickiness' (it was the source of English *clay* and *clammy*). The reasoning is that something sticky, perhaps from a coating of oil, would have been perceived as having a clear or shiny surface, and there may also have been a suggestion of the purity conferred by a ceremonial anointing with oil. The derivatives *cleanse* and *cleanly* (whence *cleanliness*) are both Old English formations.

▶ clammy, clay, cleanse

**clear**   [13]   *Clear* comes via Old French *cler* from Latin *clārus* (source also of English *claret* and *clarion* [14]). It has been suggested that *clārus* is related to *calāre* 'call out' (whence English *council*). Latin derivatives that have come down to English are *clārificāre*, from which English gets *clarify* [14], and *clāritās*, whence English *clarity* [16]. The Middle English spelling of the adjective is preserved in *clerestory* 'upper sto-rey of a church' [15] (so named from its being 'bright' or 'lighted' with numerous windows).

▶ claim, claret, clarion, clarity, clerestory, declare, low

**cleave**   [OE]   There are two distinct verbs *cleave* in English, both of Germanic origin. *Cleave* 'cut' comes from Germanic *\*kleuban*, which goes back to an Indo-European base *\*gleubh-* (this also produced Greek *glúphein* 'carve,' source of English *hieroglyphics*). *Cleave* 'adhere' can be traced back ultimately to an Indo-European base *\*gloi-*, *\*glei-*, *\*gli-* 'stick,' from which English also gets *glue* and *gluten*. Its Germanic descendant *\*klai-* produced English *clay* and *clammy*, and *\*kli-* developed into *cleave*.

▶ clammy, clay, climb, glue, hieroglyphics

**clench**   see CLING

**clerestory**   see CLEAR

**clerk**   [11]   *Clerk* and its relatives *cleric* and *cler-gy* owe their existence ultimately to a Biblical refer-ence, in Deuteronomy xviii 2, to the Levites, members of an Israelite tribe whose men were assistants to the Temple priests: 'Therefore shall they have no inheri-tance among their brethren: the Lord is their inheri-tance.' Greek for 'inheritance' is *klēros*, and so it came about that matters relating to the Christian ministry were denoted in late Greek by the derived adjective *klērikós*. This passed into ecclesiastical Latin as *clēr-icus*, which was originally borrowed into late Old Eng-lish as *cleric* or *clerc*, later reinforced by Old French *clerc* to give modern English *clerk*. Its present-day bureaucratic connotations, which emerged in the 16th century, go back to an earlier time when members of the clergy were virtually the only people who could read or write. However, religious associations have of course been preserved in *cleric* [17], from ecclesiastical Latin *clēricus*, and *clergy* [13], a blend of Old French *clergie* (a derivative of *clerc*) and *clerge* (from the ecclestiasti-cal Latin derivative *clēricātus*). The compound *clergy-man* is 16th century.

▶ cleric, clergy

**clever**   [13]   *Clever* is rather a mystery word. There is one isolated instance of what appears to be the word in an early 13th-century bestiary, where it means 'dextrous,' and the connotations of 'clutching some-thing' have led to speculation that it may be connected with *claw*. It does not appear on the scene again until the late 16th century, when its associations with 'agility' and 'sprightliness' may point to a link with Middle Dutch *klever*, of similar meaning. The modern sense 'intelligent' did not develop until the 18th century.

**cliché**   [19]   Originally, French *clicher* meant lit-erally 'stereotype' – that is, 'print from a plate made by making a type-metal cast from a mould of a printing sur-face.' The word was supposedly imitative of the sound made when the mould was dropped into the molten type

metal. Hence a word or phrase that was *cliché* – had lit-erally been repeated time and time again in identical form from a single printing plate – had become hackneyed.

**client**   [14]   The original status of a client was rather lowly: he was someone who was at another's beck and call, and dependent on them. The word comes from Latin *cliēns*, an alteration of an earlier *cluēns*, the present participle of the verb *cluēre* 'listen, follow, obey'; hence someone who was *cliēns* was always lis-tening out for another's orders, unable to take indepen-dent action (in ancient Rome it meant specifically a plebeian under the protection of a nobleman). That sense is preserved in such English expressions as 'client state.' The word's more modern senses have developed through 'person on whose behalf a lawyer acts' in the 15th century to simply 'customer' in the 17th century.

**cliff**   [OE]   *Cliff* comes from a prehistoric German-ic *\*kliban*, of unknown origin (German *klippe* 'crag' is a collateral relative). The compound *cliffhanger* seems to have originated in the USA in the 1930s; it comes from the serial movies then popular, in which at the end of each episode the hero or heroine was left in some per-ilous situation, such as hanging off the edge of a cliff, not resolved until the next instalment.

**climate**   [14]   The notion underlying *climate* is of 'sloping' or 'leaning.' It comes, via Old French *cli-mat* or late Latin *clīma* (whence English *clime* [16]), from Greek *klīma* 'sloping surface of the earth,' which came ultimately from the same source (the Indo-European base *\*kli-*) as produced English *lean*. Greek geographers assigned the earth's surface to various zones according to the angle which their 'slope' made with the rays of the sun (originally there were seven of these, ranging from 17 degrees of latitude North to 48 degrees, but later the system was elaborated so that each hemisphere was divided into 24 bands or 'climates' of latitude). This was the sense in which the word passed into Latin, where it broadened out into simply 'region,' and hence 'weather associated with a particular area.'

▶ ladder, lean

**climax**   [16]   Etymologically, a *climax* is a series of steps by which a goal is achieved, but in the late 18th century English, anticipating the culmination, started using it for the goal itself. It comes, via late Latin, from Greek *klīmax* 'ladder,' which was ultimately from the same source (the Indo-European base *\*kli-*) as produced English *lean*. This came to be used metaphorically as a rhetorical term for a figure of speech in which a series of statements is arranged in order of increasing forceful-ness, and hence for any escalating progression: 'the top of the climax of their wickedness,' Edmund Burke 1793. Whence modern English 'high point.'

▶ ladder, lean

**climb** [OE] The original notion contained in *climb* seems not to have been so much 'ascent' as 'holding on.' Old English *climban* came from a prehistoric West Germanic *\*klimban*, a nasalized variant of the base which produced English *cleave* 'adhere.' To begin with this must have meant strictly 'go up by clinging on with the hands and feet' – to 'swarm up,' in fact – but already by the late Old English period we find it being used for 'rising' in general. The original past tense *clamb*, which died out in most areas in the 16th century, is probably related to *clamp* 'fastening' [14].

▶ clamp, cleave

**cling** [OE] The basic underlying sense of *cling* seems to be 'stick, adhere,' but surviving records of the word in Old English reveal it only in the more specialized senses 'congeal' or 'shrivel' (the notion being that loss of moisture causes something to contract upon itself or adhere more closely to a surface). It is not really until the late 13th century that the more familiar 'adhere' (as in 'a wet shirt clinging to someone's back') begins to show itself, and no hint that 'clinging' is something a human being can do with his or her arms emerges before the early 17th century. The word goes back to a prehistoric Germanic base *\*klingg-*, whose variant *\*klengk-*is the source of English *clench* [13] and *clinch* [16].

▶ clench, clinch

**clinic** [17] Etymologically, a *clinic* is a place with 'beds.' It comes ultimately from Greek *klínē* 'bed,' which goes back to the Indo-European base *\*kli-* 'lean, slope' (source also of English *lean*) and hence was originally 'something on which one reclines.' The adjective derived from this, *klīnikós*, reached English via Latin *clīnicus*, having become specialized in meaning from 'bed' in general to 'sick-bed.' *Clinic* was replaced as an adjective by *clinical* in the 18th century, but it continued on as a noun, originally in the sense 'sick or bedridden person.' This survived into the 19th century ('You are free to roam at large over the bodies of my clinics,' E Berdoe, *St Bernard's* 1887), and the modern sense 'hospital' did not arrive until the late 19th century, borrowed from French *clinique* or German *klinik*.

▶ decline, lean

**clock** [14] The *clock* appears to have been so named because it told the hours by the chiming of a 'bell,' medieval Latin *clocca*. The Latin word, which emerged in the 7th century and may have been of Irish origin, probably reached English via Middle Dutch *klocke*. Besides being applied to time-pieces, it has also lent its name to two garments on account of their supposedly bell-like shape: *cloak* [13], which comes from the Old French dialect *cloke* or *cloque*, and *cloche* hat [20], from French *cloche* 'bell.'

▶ cloak, cloche

**cloister** [13] A *cloister* was originally simply an enclosed place, a 'close.' The word comes from Old French *cloistre*, a descendant of Latin *claustrum* 'bar, bolt, enclosure,' which was formed from the past participial stem of Latin *claudere* 'close' (source of English *close*). The notion of 'enclosure' led to the word's being applied to a place of religious seclusion, such as a monastery or convent, and hence to a covered walkway within a monastic building. It also lies behind *claustrophobia* [19], which was formed from Latin *claustrum*.

▶ claustrophobia, close

**close** [13] *Close* originally entered English as a verb. It came from *clos-*, the past participial stem of Old French *clore* 'shut,' which was a descendant of Latin *claudere* (related to Latin *clāvis* 'key,' from which English gets *clavier, clavichord, clavicle, clef*, and *conclave*, and to Latin *clāvus* 'nail,' from which French gets *clou* 'nail' – whence English *clove* – and English gets *cloy*). The adjective was quick to follow, via Old French *clos*, but in this case the intermediate source was the Latin past participial stem *claus-* rather than the Old French *clos-*. It originally meant simply 'shut, enclosed, confined,' and did not evolve the sense 'near' until the late 15th century; it arose from the notion of the gap between two things being brought together by being closed off. Related forms in English include *clause, cloister, closet* [14] (from Old French, 'small private room,' a diminutive form of *clos*) and the various verbs ending in *-clude*, including *conclude, include*, and *preclude*.

▶ clause, clavier, clef, cloister, closet, clove, cloy, conclave, conclude, enclave, include, preclude

**cloth** [OE] The history of the word *cloth* is not known, beyond the fact that its immediate source is Germanic (German has the related *kleid* 'garment'). In Old English it meant both 'piece of fabric' and 'fabric in general,' and in the plural it was applied to 'garments' (hence modern English *clothes*). The verb *clothe*, too, probably goes back to Old English times, although it is not recorded before the 12th century.

**cloud** [OE] In Old English the word for 'cloud' was *weolcen* (whence modern English *welkin*, a poetical term for 'sky'), which is related to German *wolke* 'cloud.' At that time Old English *clūd*, the ancestor of *cloud*, meant 'mass of rock, hill' (it is probably related to *clod*). As applied to 'clouds,' presumably from a supposed resemblance between cumulus clouds and lumps of earth or rock, it dates from the 13th century.

▶ clod

**clout** [OE] In Old English, a *clout* was a patch of cloth put over a hole to mend it. Hence in due course it came to be used simply for a 'piece of cloth,' and by further extension for a 'garment' (as in 'Ne'er cast a clout till May be out'). However, the reason for its colloquial application to 'hit, blow,' which dates from the 14th century, is not known, and indeed this may be an entirely different word. As for the word's ultimate antecedents, it probably comes, along with *cleat, clot, cluster*, and *clutter*, from a prehistoric Germanic base *\*klut-*, *\*kleut-*, *\*klaut-*.

▶ cleat, clot, cluster, clutter

**clove**   There are two distinct words *clove* in English. In *clove* of garlic [OE] the underlying notion is of 'cutting'; the head of garlic is as it were 'divided up' into separate sections. The word goes back ultimately to the Indo-European base *\*gleubh-* 'cut, carve,' which also produced English *cleave* and its now archaic past tense *clove*.

Clove the spice [14] originated in the Old French phrase *clou de girofle*, which meant literally 'nail of the clove-tree.' The term 'nail' was applied to the tree's dried unopened flower bud because of a perceived resemblance in shape. (French *clou* 'nail' comes from Latin *clāvus*, source of English *cloy*, and French *girofle* – whence English *gillyflower* [14], which originally meant 'clove' – goes back via medieval Latin *caryophyllum* to Greek *karuóphullon*, which literally meant 'nut leaf.')

▶ cleave / cloy, gillyflower

**clown**   [16]   *Clown*'s antecedents are obscure. Its earliest recorded sense is 'unsophisticated or boorish country fellow,' which has led to speculation that it may come ultimately from Latin *colonus* 'colonist, farmer' (residence in the country often being associated with backwardness or lack of sophistication, as in the case *heathen* and *pagan*). Others, however, see a more direct source in a Germanic language from the Low Countries or Scandinavia: North Frisian *klönne* and Icelandic *klunni*, both meaning 'clumsy person', have been compared.

**cloy**   [14]   *Cloy* originally meant 'fasten with a nail.' It is a reduced form of the long obsolete *acloy*, which came from Anglo-Norman *acloyer*. This was a variant of Old French *encloyer*, a descendant of the Vulgar Latin compound verb *inclāvāre*, based on Latin *clāvus* 'nail' (source of Latin *claudere* 'shut,' from which English gets *close*).

▶ close

**club**   [13]   The original meaning of *club* is 'thick heavy stick for hitting people'; it was borrowed from Old Norse *klubba*. The sense 'association' developed in the 17th century, apparently originally as a verb. To *club together* seems to have been based on the notion of 'forming into a mass like the thickened end of a club': 'Two such worlds must club together and become one,' Nathaniel Fairfax, *The bulk and selvedge of the world* 1674. Hence the noun *club*, which originally signified simply a 'get-together,' typically in a tavern, but by the end of the 17th century seems to have become more of a formalized concept, with members and rules.

**clue**   [15]   *Clue* is a variant spelling of the now obsolete *clew* 'ball of thread,' and its current application to 'that which helps to solve a problem,' which originated in the early 17th century, is based on the notion of using (like Theseus in the Minotaur's labyrinth) a ball of thread to show one the way out of an intricate maze one has entered. *Clew* itself goes back to Old English *cliwan* or *cleowan*, which may be related to *claw*.

▶ claw

**clumsy**   [16]   When *clumsy* first appeared on the scene around 1600, both it and the presumably related but now obsolete *clumse* were used not only for 'awkward' but also for 'numb with cold.' This, and the fact that the word's nearest apparent relatives are Scandinavian (such as Swedish dialect *klumsig* 'numb, clumsy'), suggests that the notion originally contained in them was of being torpid from cold – so cold that one is sluggish and cannot coordinate one's actions.

**clutch**   *Clutch* 'seize' [14] and *clutch* of eggs [18] are separate words, although they may ultimately be related. The verb arose in Middle English as a variant of the now obsolete *clitch*, which came from Old English *clyccan* 'bend, clench.' The modern sense of the noun, 'device for engaging a motor vehicle's gears,' which was introduced at the end of the 19th century, developed from a more general early 19th-century meaning 'coupling for bringing working parts together,' based no doubt on the notion of 'seizing' and 'grasping.' *Clutch* of eggs is a variant of the now obsolete dialectal form *cletch* [17]. This was a derivative of the Middle English verb *clecken* 'give birth,' which was borrowed from Old Norse *klekja* (probably a distant relative of *clutch* 'seize').

**coach**   [16]   *Coach* is one of the few English words borrowed from Hungarian. It comes (via French *coche* and German *kutsche*) from Hungarian *kocsi*, an adjective meaning 'of Kocs' (Kocs is a village in northeast Hungary, between Budapest and Györ, where carriages, carts, etc were made). In Hungarian the original full form was *kocsi szeker* 'cart from Kocs.' The modern sense 'instructor, trainer' originated in 19th-century university slang, the notion being that the student was conveyed through the exam by the tutor as if he were riding in a carriage.

**coal**   [OE]   In Old English, *col* meant 'glowing ember.' It came from a prehistoric Germanic *\*kolam* (source also of German *kohle* and Dutch *kool*), which may be related to Irish Gaelic *gual* 'coal.' By the 12th century at the latest it was also being used for 'charcoal' (the word *charcoal* is based on it), but it was not until the mid 13th century that the modern application to the black solid fossil fuel appears. It seems quite likely that the word's underlying etymological meaning is 'glow.' Derived from *coal* are *collier* [14], which originally meant 'charcoal-burner,' *colliery* [17], and possibly *collie* [17], on the basis of its dark colour.

▶charcoal, collier

**coarse** [14] For such an everyday word, the origins of *coarse* are surprisingly clouded. It first appears in the forms *corse* or *course*, and meaning 'ordinary, everyday,' which has led to speculation that it is an application of the noun *course*, in the sense 'the ordinary run of things, the usual practice'; however, not all etymologists accept this. The modern spelling *coarse* became established in the 18th century.

**coast** [13] Latin *costa* meant 'rib' (hence the English medical term *intercostal* 'between the ribs'), but also more generally 'flank, side.' It was in this sense that it passed into Old French as *coste*, and subsequently into English. The modern meaning 'seashore' (which had already developed in Old French) arises from the shore being thought of as the 'side' or 'edge' of the land (compare *seaside*). Amongst the senses of the French word little represented in English is 'hillside, slope'; it was however adopted in North America for a 'slope down which one slides on a sledge,' and came to be used in the mid 19th century as a verb meaning 'sledge down such a slope.' That was the source of the modern verbal sense 'freewheel.'

The *coster* of *costermonger* [16] was originally *costard*, a variety of apple named from its prominent 'ribs.' And another hidden relative is *cutlet* [18], borrowed from French *côtelette*, literally 'little rib.'

▶costermonger, cutlet, intercostal

**coat** [13] *Coat* seems originally to have signified a sort of short close-fitting cloth tunic with sleeves, worn by men. Over the centuries fashion has lengthened the garment, and its male exclusivity has disappeared (originally, as a woman's garment a *coat* was a skirt, a sense preserved in *petticoat*). The word is of Germanic origin (it has been traced back to Frankish *\*kotta*), but it reached English via Old French *cote*.

**coax** [16] In the 16th and 17th century a *cokes* was a 'simpleton, someone easily duped' (it is not known where the word came from, although it might perhaps be related to *cockney*). To *cokes* someone was thus to 'make a cokes of them, fool them.' This spelling survived until the 18th century, when it was supplanted by *coax*. The word's meaning, meanwhile, had passed via 'treat as a simpleton or pet' and 'fondle' to 'wheedle.'

**cob** [15] *Cob* has a bizarre range of meanings – 'nut,' 'horse,' 'male swan,' 'loaf,' 'ear of maize' – but a distillation of them points back to an original 'head, or something similarly rounded' (cobnuts and cobloaves, for example, are spherical, and the male swan is the 'chief' or 'leader'). It is therefore tempting to see a connection with the now obsolete *cop* 'top, head' (probably

represented in *cobweb*), and even with Latin *caput* 'head.'

▶cobble

**cobalt** [17] German *kobold* means 'goblin': and in former times it was believed by German silver miners that impurities in the ore they were extracting, which lessened the value of the silver and even made them ill, were put there by these mischievous creatures. In fact these impurities were a silver-white metallic element, which was named *kobalt* after a Middle High German variant of *kobold* (the miners' sickness was probably caused by the arsenic with which it occurred).

**cobble** *Cobble* as in *cobblestone* [15] and *cobble* 'mend' [15] are two distinct words. The former was derived from *cob* 'rounded lump,' with the diminutive suffix *-le*. The earliest evidence of it is in the compound *cobblestone*, and it is not recorded on its own until about 1600. The verb *cobble* is a back-formation from *cobbler* 'shoemaker' [14], of unknown origin. The derivative *cobblers* 'nonsense' [20] is short for *cobbler's awls*, rhyming slang for 'balls.'

▶cob

**cobweb** [14] A *cobweb* was originally literally a web woven by a *cop*, a Middle English word for 'spider.' It was short for *attercop* 'spider,' a compound of Old English origin which had largely died out by the 17th century. This seems to have meant literally 'poison head,' from Old English *ātōr* 'poison' and *coppe* 'head, top' (a possible relative of English *cob*). It was revived by J R R Tolkien in *The Hobbit* 1937.

**coccyx** [17] The Greek physician Galen considered that the small tapering bone at the base of the human spine resembled a cuckoo's beak. He therefore named it *kókkux*, which was Greek for 'cuckoo.' It reached English via the Latin form *coccyx*.

**cochineal** [16] *Cochineal* 'red dye' comes via French *cochenille* from Old Spanish *cochinilla*, a term appled both to the dye and to the small insect related to the mealybugs, from whose dried body it is made. It is generally thought to be a derivative of Latin *coccinus* 'scarlet,' which in turn came from Greek *kokkinos*, a derivative of *kókkos*, the Greek term for the cochineal insect (the word originally meant 'berry, seed' – it was applied to various bacteria, such as *streptococcus* and *staphylococcus*, because of their spherical seedlike shape – and it was thought in ancient times that the dried body of the insect was a berry).

▶staphylococcus, streptococcus

**cock** [OE] The word *cock* is probably ultimately of onomatopoeic origin, imitative of the male fowl's call (like the lengthier English *cockadoodledoo* [16], French *coquerico*, and German *kikeriki*). Beyond that it is difficult to go with any certainty; it reflects similar words in other languages, such as medieval Latin *coccus* and Old Norse *kokkr*, but which if any the English word was borrowed from is not clear. It has been suggested that it goes back to a Germanic base *kuk-, of which a variant was the source of *chicken*, but typical Old English spellings, such as *kok* and *kokke*, suggest that it may have been a foreign borrowing rather than a native Germanic word – perhaps pointing to Germanic *coccus*. The origin of the interconnected set of senses 'spout, tap,' 'hammer of a firearm,' and 'penis' is not known; it is possible that it represents an entirely different word, but the fact that German *hahn* 'hen' has the same meanings suggests otherwise.

Of derived words, *cocker* [19], as in 'cocker spaniel,' comes from *cocking*, the sport of shooting woodcock, and *cocky* [18] is probably based on the notion of the cock as a spirited or swaggering bird, lording it over his hens (there may well be some connection with *cock* 'penis,' too, for there is an isolated record of *cocky* meaning 'lecherous' in the 16th century). *Cockerel* [15] was originally a diminutive form.

▶ chicken, cocky

## cock-a-hoop  [16]  *Cock-a-hoop* comes from a 16th- and 17th-century expression *set the cock on the hoop* 'make merry' – but exactly how the expression arose is not clear. One obvious interpretation is that it meant 'put the tap on the barrel' – that is, let the wine or beer flow freely – but it has also been suggested that *hoop* here means 'measure of grain' (a sense which originated in the 16th century), the notion being that to put a cockerel on a heap of grain implied prodigality.

## cockatoo  [17]  *Cockatoo* was originally a Malay word, although it has changed somewhat under the influence of English *cock*. It comes via Dutch *kaketoe* from Malay *kakatua*, a compound formed from *kakak* 'elder brother or sister' and *tua* 'old.' A related word is *cockatiel* 'small Australian parrot' [19]; it comes ultimately from Portuguese *cacatilha*, formed from Malay *kakatua* with the Portuguese diminutive suffix *-ilha*, and it reached English via Dutch *kaketielje*.

## cockatrice  [14]  The name of the cockatrice, a mythical serpent whose glance could kill, has a bizarre history. It started life as medieval Latin *calcātrix*, which meant literally 'tracker, hunter' (it was formed from the verb *calcāre* 'tread, track,' a derivative of *calx* 'heel'). This was a direct translation of Greek *ikhneúmōn* (a derivative of *ikhneúein* 'track'), a name given to a mysterious Egyptian creature in ancient times which was said to prey on crocodiles. At one point Latin *calcātrix*, later *caucātrix*, came to be used for the crocodile itself, but this application never gained much currency in English (which adopted the word via Old French *cocatris*). Instead, it was adopted as another name for the basilisk, a mythical serpent. The accidental similarity of the first syllable to *cock* led both to the embroidering of the basilisk/cockatrice legend, so that it was said to have been born from a cock's egg, and to

the word's 16th-century rerouteing as a heraldic term for a beast with the head, wings, and body of a cock and the tail of a serpent.

## cockchafer  [18]  Etymologically, *cockchafer* (a medium-sized beetle) is probably a 'large gnawer.' The second part of the word, which goes back to Old English times (*ceafor*), can be traced to a prehistoric base *kab- 'gnaw,' source also of English *jowl*. The first element, *cock*, may be an allusion to the species' greater size in relation to other *chafers*.

▶ jowl

## cockle  [14]  The *cockle* is related etymologically to another mollusc, the *conch*: they both began life in Greek *kónkhē* – which meant 'mussel' as well as 'conch.' From this was formed the diminutive *konkhúlion* 'small variety of conch' – hence 'cockle.' The Greek word subsequently became reduced to *kokhúlion*, whose plural passed into medieval Latin as *\*cochilia*. Next in the chain was Old French *coquille*, source of the English word. The origin of the phrase *cockles of one's heart* (first recorded in the mid 17th century) are not clear: some have claimed that the heart resembles a cockle shell, or more specifically that the fibres of the heart muscle spiral like the lines on a cockle shell, while others note a supposed resemblance of *cockle* to *corculum*, a Latin diminutive of *cor* 'heart,' and others again point out that the scientific name for the cockle is *Cardium*, from Greek *kardía* 'heart,' but none of these explanations really carries conviction.

▶ conch

## cockney  [14]  Etymologically, a *cockney* is a 'cock's egg' (it comes from *cokene*, the old genitive plural of *cock*, and *ey*, the Middle English word for 'egg'). This was a medieval term for a small or misshapen egg, the 'runt' of the clutch, supposedly laid by a cock, and it came to be applied (probably egged on by Middle English *cocker* 'pamper') to a 'pampered child' or 'mother's boy.' In the 16th century we find that it has passed on to 'town dweller' (the notion being that people who lived in towns were soft and effete compared with countrymen), and by around 1600 it had started to mean more specifically 'someone born in the city of London.' The popular definition 'someone born within the sound of Bow bells' is first reported by the lexicographer John Minsheu in 1617.

▶ cock, egg

## cockroach  [17]  *Cockroach* is a product of folk etymology, the process by which a 'foreign'-sounding is adapted by speakers of a language so as to seem more familiar. In this case the foreign word was Spanish *cucaracha*. This was evidently too much for 17th-century English tongues, so the first element was transformed into *cock* and the second to *roach* (presumably after the freshwater fish of that name). Modern English *roach* 'butt of a marijuana cigarette' [20] is

probably an abbreviation of *cockroach*, but this is not certain.

**cocktail**   [19]   The origins of the word *cocktail* are mysterious. It first appeared (in America) in the first decade of the 19th century, roughly contemporary with *cocktail* meaning 'horse with a cocked tail' – that is, one cut short and so made to stick up like a cock's tail – but whether the two words are connected, and if so, how the drink came to be named after such a horse, are not at all clear.

**cocoa**   [18]   Like *chocolate, cocoa* came to English from the Nahuatl language of the Aztec people. Their *cacahuatl* meant 'beans of the cocoa tree.' Its first element was borrowed into Spanish as *cacao*. This was adopted by English in the 16th century, and remained the standard form until the 18th century, when it was modified to *cocoa*. Originally it was pronounced with three syllables (/ko-ko-a/), but confusion with the *coco* of *coconut* (which was also sometimes spelled *cocoa*) led to the current two-syllable pronunciation.

**coconut**   [17]   Despite its tropical origins, the coconut has a European name. The base of the coconut's shell, with its three small holes, apparently reminded early Spanish and Portuguese explorers of a human face, so they called it *coco*; this was the Portuguese word for a grinning or grimacing face, as of a scarecrow. English adopted it in the 16th century, and it formed the basis of the compound *coconut*, first recorded in 1613. (Before then the fruit of the coconut palm had been known as the *Indian nut*.)

**cod**   [13]   Like most fish-names, the origins of *cod* are obscure. It has been suggested, not all that convincingly, that it comes from another word *cod* [OE], now obsolete, which meant broadly 'pouch' – the idea being that the fish supposedly has a 'baglike' appearance. Among the specific applications of this other *cod*, which was of Germanic origin, were 'seedcase' (which survived into the twentieth century in the archaic compound *peascod* 'pea pod') and 'scrotum.' By transference the latter came to mean 'testicles,' whence *codpiece*, a 15th- to 17th-century garment somewhat analogous to the jockstrap. The *cuttle* of *cuttlefish* comes from the same source.

▶ cuttlefish

**coda**   see QUEUE

**code**   [14]   'System of secret communication signs' is a relatively recent semantic development of the word *code*, which emerged in the early 19th century. It derived from an earlier sense 'system of laws,' which was based on a specific application to various sets of statutes introduced by the Roman emperors. The word itself came from Old French *code*, a descendant of Latin *cōdex*, whose meaning 'set of statutes, book of laws' derived from a broader sense 'book.' This in turn came from an earlier 'piece of wood coated with wax for writ-

ing on,' which was based ultimately on 'tree trunk,' the word's original meaning. *Codex* itself was borrowed into English in the 16th century. Its Latin diminutive form, *cōdicillus*, produced English *codicil* [15].

▶ codex, codicil

**coerce**   [17]   The underlying etymological meaning of *coerce* is 'restraining' or 'confining.' It comes from the Latin compound verb *coercēre* 'constrain,' which was formed from the prefix *co*-'together' and the verb *arcēre* 'shut up, ward off' (possibly a relative of Latin *arca* 'chest, box,' from which English gets *ark*). An earlier, 15th-century, form of the English word was *coherce*, which came via Old French *cohercier*.

▶ ark

**coffee**   [16]   The word *coffee* first reached us in a form which we would now recognize in the 17th century, probably via Italian *caffè*. It is ultimately, however, of Middle Eastern origin, and the earliest spellings recorded in English reflect this: *chaoua, cauwa, kahue, cahve*, etc are modelled closely on Turkish *kahveh* and its source, Arabic *qahwah*. Where the Arabic word came from is not known for certain: probably it is based in some way on *Kaffa*, the name of an area in the south Abyssinian highlands from which the coffee tree is said to originate, but it has also been claimed to have signified originally some sort of wine. *Café* [19] comes of course from French *café*, whose source was Italian *caffè*. From the French word was derived *caféine*, from which English gets *caffeine* [19], while Spanish *café* produced *cafetero* 'coffee-seller,' source of English *cafeteria* [20].

▶ café, caffeine, cafeteria

**coffin**   [14]   Greek *kóphinus* meant 'basket.' It passed via Latin *cophinus* into Old French, where it split into two words. *Cofin* came to mean 'box, chest' as well as 'basket,' and it was with these senses that it was borrowed into English. The specific application to boxes for burial is not recorded before the early 16th century. The other Old French descendant of Latin *cophinus* was *coffre*, which gave English *coffer* [13].

▶ coffer

**cogent**   see SQUAT

**cognate**   see NATIVE

**cognizance**   [14]   Latin *gnōscere* meant 'know' (it is related to *know* and *notion*). From it was derived the compound verb *cognōscere* 'get to know, recognize, acknowledge.' Its present participial stem *cognōscent*- formed the basis of a Vulgar Latin noun *\*connōscentia*, which passed into Old French as *connoissance*. English borrowed this as *conisance*, restoring the Latin *g* to the spelling in the 15th century, which eventually affected the word's pronunciation. Also from the Latin present participle came Italian *conoscente*, which in its latinized form was borrowed into English as *cognoscente* in the 18th century. Meanwhile, the past participial stem of the Latin verb, *cognit-*, produced the noun *cognitiō*, source of English *cognition* [15].

The infinitive form of the Latin verb passed into Old French as *connoître*, from which was derived the agent noun *connoisseur*, borrowed into English in the 18th century (modern French has *connaisseur*).

► cognition, connoisseur, know, notion, recognize, reconnaissance, reconnoitre

**cohort** [15] Etymologically, *cohort* is an 'enclosed yard.' It comes via Old French *cohorte* from Latin *cohors*, a compound noun formed from the prefix *com-* 'with' and an element *hort-*which also appears in Latin *hortus* 'garden' (source of English *horticulture*) and is related to English *garden, yard*, and the second element of *orchard*. From the underlying sense of 'enclosed place' it came to be applied to a crowd of people in such a place, and then more specifically to an infantry company in the Roman army. Its meaning has spread figuratively in English to 'band of associates or accomplices,' whose frequent use in the plural led to the misapprehension that a single cohort was an 'associate' or 'accomplice' – a usage which emerged in American English in the mid 20th century.

The original form of the Latin word is well preserved in *cohort*, but it has also reached us, more thickly disguised, as *court*.

► court, garden, horticulture, orchard, yard

**coil** [16] Ultimately, *coil, cull*, and *collect* are the same word. All come from Latin *colligere* 'gather together.' Its past participial stem produced *collect*, but the infinitive form passed into Old French as *coillir, culler*, etc, and thence into English. In the case of *coil*, its original general sense 'gather, collect' (of which there is no trace in English) was specialized, no doubt originally in nautical use, to the gathering up of ropes into tidy shapes (concentric rings) for stowage.

► collect, cull

**coin** [14] Latin *cuneus* meant 'wedge' (from it we get *cuneiform* 'wedge-shaped script'). It passed into Old French as *coing* or *coin*, where it developed a variety of new meanings. Primary amongst these was 'corner-stone' or 'corner,' a sense preserved in English mainly in the now archaic spelling *quoin*. But also, since the die for stamping out money was often wedge-shaped, or operated in the manner of a wedge, it came to be referred to as a *coin*, and the term soon came to be transferred to the pieces of money themselves.

► quoin

**coitus** see EXIT

**colander** [14] *Colander* probably comes ultimately from Latin *colum* 'seive.' From this was derived the verb *cōlāre* 'strain,' which produced a Vulgar Latin noun *\*cōlātor*. This is assumed to have passed into Old Provençal as *colador*, which appears to have been the source of early English forms such as *culdor* and *culatre*. The *n* is a purely English innovation.

► percolate, portcullis

**cold** [OE] *Cold* is a word of ancient roots. It can be traced back to the Indo-European base *\*gel-, \*gol-*, which also produced Latin *gelu* 'frost,' ultimate source of English *congeal, gel*, and *jelly*. Its prehistoric Germanic descendant was *\*kal-, \*kōl-*, from which English gets *cool*, probably *chill*, and, via a past participial adjective *\*kaldaz, cold*. The noun use of the adjective dates back to Old English times, but the sense 'viral infection of the nose, throat, etc' is a 16th- century development.

► chill, congeal, cool, gel, jelly

**coleslaw** [18] *Cole* is an ancient and now little used English word for plants of the cabbage family, such as cabbage or rape (it comes ultmately from Latin *caulis* 'cabbage,' whose underlying meaning was 'hollow stem' – see CAULIFLOWER). It was used in the partial translation of Dutch *koolsla* when that word was borrowed into English in the late 18th century. *Kool*, Dutch for 'cabbage,' became *cole*, but *sla* presented more of a problem (it represents a phonetically reduced form of *salade* 'salad'), and it was rendered variously as *-slaugh* (now defunct) and *-slaw*. (Interestingly enough, the earliest record of the word we have, from America in the 1790s – it was presumably borrowed from Dutch settlers – is in the form *cold slaw*, indicating that even then in some quarters English *cole* was not a sufficiently familiar word to be used for Dutch *kool*. *Coldslaw* is stll heard, nowadays as a folk-etymological alteration of *coleslaw*.)

► cauliflower, cole, salad

**collar** [13] Etymologically, a *collar* is simply something worn round one's 'neck.' The word comes via Anglo-Norman *coler* from Latin *collāre*, which meant 'necklace' as well as 'part of a garment that encircles the neck' (both senses have come through into English, although the latter has predominated). *Collāre* was a derivative of *collum* 'neck,' which came from an earlier base *\*kols-* that also produced German and Swedish *hals* 'neck.' It has been speculated that it goes back ultimately to Indo-European *\*qwelo-* 'go round,' the root from which we get English *wheel* – the underlying notion being that the neck is that on which the head turns.

► décolleté, hauberk, wheel

**colleague** [16] A *colleague* is literally 'one chosen or delegated to be or work with another.' It comes via French *collègue* from Latin *collēga*, a compound noun formed from *com-* 'with' and *lēg-*, the stem of *lēgāre* 'choose' (whence also English *legation* and *delegate*) and *lēx* 'law' (source of English *legal, legitimate*, etc). Despite the similarity in spelling, it is not related to English *league*.

► college, delegate, legal, legitimate

**collect**   [16]   *Collect* comes via French *collecter* or medieval Latin *collēctāre* from *collēct-*, the past participial stem of Latin *colligere* 'gather together,' a compound verb formed from *com-* 'together' and *legere* 'gather' (source also of English *elect, neglect*, and *select* and, from its secondary meaning 'read,' *lecture* and *legible*). The specialized noun use of *collect*, 'short prayer,' pronounced with its main stress on the first syllable, antedates the verb in English, having arrived via Old French in the 13th century. It comes from late Latin *collēcta* 'assembly,' a nominalization of the past participle of *colligere*, which was used in medieval times in the phrase *ōrātiō ad collēctam* 'prayer to the congregation.'

*Collect* comes from the past participle of Latin *colligere*, but its infinitive form is the source of English *coil* and *cull*.

▶ coil, cull, elect, lecture, legible, ligneous, neglect, select

**college**   [14]   *College* comes from the same source as *colleague*, Latin *collēga*, literally 'one chosen to work with another,' a compound based on the stem of *lēgāre* 'choose.' An 'association of *collēgae*, partnership' was thus a *collēgium*, whence (possibly via Old French *college*) English *college*. For many hundreds of years this concept of a 'corporate group' was the main semantic feature of the word, and it was not really until the 19th century that, via the colleges of Oxford and Cambridge universities, the notion of 'academic institution' overtook it.

▶ colleague, delegate, legal, legitimate

**collide**   [17]   *Collide* comes from Latin *collīdere*, a compound verb formed from *com-* 'together' and *laedere* 'injure by striking.' Other English descendants of *laedere* are *elide* and *lesion*.

▶ elide, lesion

**collie**   see COAL

**colliery**   see COAL

**colloquial**   see VENTRILOQUIST

**colon**   There are two distinct words *colon* in English. *Colon* 'part of the large intestine' [16] comes via Latin from Greek *kólon*, which meant 'food, meat' as well as 'large intestine.' *Colon* the punctuation mark [16] comes via Latin from Greek *kōlon*, which originally meant literally 'limb.' It was applied metaphorically (rather like *foot*) to a 'unit of verse,' and hence to a 'clause' in general, meanings which survive in English as technical terms. From there it was a short step to the main present-day meaning, 'punctuation mark'.

**colonel**   [17]   Historically, a colonel was so called because he commanded the company at the head of a regiment, known in Italian as the *compagna colonnella*, literally the 'little-column company'; hence the commander himself took the title *colonnella*. The word

*colonnella* is a diminutive form of *colonna*, which is descended from Latin *columna* 'pillar' (source of English *column*). It appears first to have entered English via French in the form *coronel*, in which the first *l* had mutated to *r*. Spellings with this *r* occur in English from the 17th and 18th centuries, and it is the source of the word's modern pronunciation. *Colonel* represents a return to the original Italian spelling.

▶ column

**colony**   [16]   Etymologically, a *colony* is a 'settled land.' The word goes back ultimately to the Indo-European base *qwel-, *qwol-*, which signified 'move around' (it is the source of English *cycle* and *wheel*) and hence 'move habitually in, settle in, inhabit.' One of the descendants of this base was Latin *colere* 'inhabit, cultivate.' Thus someone who settled on a new piece of land and cultivated it was a *colōnus*, and the land he settled was his *colōnia*. (The German city of Cologne gets its name from Latin *colōnia*; in Roman times it was called *Colōnia Agrippīna*, the 'settlement or colony of Agrippa.')

▶ cycle, wheel

**colossal**   [18]   *Colossal* comes ultimately from Greek *kolossós*, a word of unknown origin which was first used by the historian Herodotus as a name for certain gigantic statues in Egypt. It became much better known, of course, when applied to the Colossus of Rhodes, a 36-metre-high statue of Apollo that stood at the entrance to Rhodes harbour, built around 280BC. Various adjectives meaning 'huge' have since been derived from it: Latin had *colossēus* and *colossicus*, and in the 17th century English tried *colossean* and *colossic*, but in the 18th century the choice fell on *colossal*, borrowed from French. The amphitheatre built in Rome by Vespasian and Titus around 80–75BC was named *Colossēum* after its great size.

**colour**   [13]   The Old English words for 'colour' were *hīw* 'hue' and *blēo*, but from the 13th century onwards they were gradually replaced by Old French *colur*. This came from Latin *color*, which appears to have come ultimately from an Indo-European base *kel-* 'hide' (source also of *apocalypse, cell, clandestine, conceal*, and *occult*). This suggests that its original underlying meaning was 'outward appearance, hiding what is inside,' a supposition supported by the long history of such senses of English *colour* as 'outward (deceptive) appearance' and '(specious) plausibility' (as in 'lend colour to a notion').

▶ apocalypse, cell, conceal, hell, occult

**column**   [15]   The notion underlying *column* is of 'height, command, extremity.' It comes, via Old French *colomne*, from Latin *columna* 'pillar,' which was probably a derivative of *columen, culmen* 'top, summit' (from which English also gets *culminate*). It goes back ultimately to a base *kol-, *kel-, distant ancestor of English *excel* and *hill*.

The word's application to vertical sections of printed matter dates from the 15th century, but its transference to that which is written (as in 'write a weekly newspaper column') is a 20th-century development.

▶ culminate, excel, hill

**comb** [OE]   *Comb* is an ancient word, which has been traced back to an Indo-European *gombhos*. This appears to have signified 'tooth,' for among its other descendants were Sanskrit *jámbhas* 'tooth' and Greek *góphos* 'pin, tooth.' In prehistoric West and North Germanic it became *kambaz*, which produced English *comb*, German *kamm*, and Dutch *kam* (probably borrowed into English in the 18th century as *cam*, originally 'projecting cog-like part on a wheel for transferring motion'). The Old English verb formed from *comb* lasted dialectally as *kemb* until the 19th century, but today it survives only in *unkempt*.

The origin of the word's application to *honeycomb*, first recorded in the 13th century, is not known.

▶ oakum, unkempt

**combat** [16]   *Combat* means literally 'fight with.' It comes via French *combattre* from late Latin *combattere*, a compound verb formed from Latin *com-* 'with' and *battere*, an assumed variant of Latin *battuere* 'fight, beat' (ultimate source of English *abate, battle*, and *debate*).

▶ abate, battle, debate

**combine** [15]   The notion underlying *combine* is simply 'two together.' It comes, perhaps via French *combiner*, from late Latin *combīnāre*, a compound verb formed from Latin *com-* 'together' and *bīnī* 'two at a time'; this Latin adverb was formed from the prefix *bi-* 'twice,' and is the basis of English *binary*.

▶ binary

**come** [OE]   *Come* is of course one of the basic words of English, and its history goes back to the language's Indo-European roots. Here its distant ancestor was the base *gwem-*, which also produced Greek *baínein* 'go, walk' (related to English *base* and *basis*) and Latin *venīre* 'come' (source of a whole range of English words from *adventure* to *venue*). The prehistoric Germanic descendant of *gwem-* was *kweman* or *kuman*, which has produced German *kommen*, Dutch *komen*, Swedish *komma*, and English *come*. The compound *become* (source of *comely*) was formed in Germanic in prehistoric times.

▶ adventure, base, basis, become, venue

**comedy** [14]   *Comedy* is of Greek origin. It comes ultimately from Greek *kōmos* 'revelry.' This appears to have been combined with *ōidós* 'singer, poet' (a derivative of *aeídein* 'sing,' source of English *ode* and *odeon*) to produce *kōmōidós*, literally 'singer in the revels,' hence 'actor in a light amusing play.' From this

was derived *kōmōidíā*, which came to English via Latin *cōmoedia* and Old French *comedie*.

▶ encomium, ode

**comely** [13]   Old English had an adjective *cȳmlic* 'beautiful' (no relation at all to *come*), but this seems to have died out around the year 1000, and it is likely that *comely*, which first appears in the early 13th century, represents a reduced version of *becomely*, an adjective long since defunct of which there are a few records towards the end of the 12th century. This meant 'suitable, becoming' (it was formed, of course, from the verb *become*), an early meaning of *comely*; its other semantic strand, 'beautiful,' is probably a memory of Old English *cȳmlic*.

▶ become

**comestible**   see EAT

**comet** [13]   *Comet* means literally 'the long-haired one.' Greek *kómē* meant 'hair,' but it was also applied metaphorically to the tail of a comet, which was thought of as streaming out behind like a luxuriant head of hair being blown by the wind. Hence an *astēr kométēs* 'long-haired star' was the name given to a comet. Eventually the adjective *kométēs* came to stand for the whole phrase, and it passed via Latin *comēta* and Old French *comete* into English.

**comfit**   see CONFETTI

**comfort** [13]   *Comfort* did not always have its present 'soft' connotations of physical ease, contentment, and well-being. Etymologically it means 'make someone stronger,' and its original English sense was 'encourage, support' (this survives in such contexts as 'give aid and comfort to the enemy'). It comes via Old French *conforter* from late Latin *confortāre* 'strengthen greatly,' a compound verb formed from the prefix *com-* 'with' used as an intensive and the adjective *fortis* 'strong' (source of English *force, fort*, and *effort*).

The antonym *discomfort* is not etymologically related to *discomfit*, a word with which it is often confused.

▶ effort, force, fort

**comfrey**   see FERVENT

**comma** [16]   Greek *kómma* meant literally 'piece cut off, segment.' It derived from the verb *kóptein* 'cut,' relatives of which include Russian *kopje* 'lance,' source of the coin-name *kopeck*, and probably English *capon*. *Kómma* came to be applied metaphorically, as a technical term in prosody, to a small piece of a sentence, a 'short clause,' a sense which it retained when it reached English via Latin *comma*. It was not long before, like *colon*, it was applied to the punctuation mark signifying the end of such a clause.

▶ capon, kopeck

**command** [13]   Ultimately, *command* and *commend* are the same word. Both come from Latin compound verbs formed from the intensive prefix *com-*

and the verb *mandāre* 'entrust, commit to someone's charge' (from which we get *mandate*). In the classical period this combination produced *commendāre* 'commit to someone's charge, commend, recommend,' which passed into English in the 14th century (*recommend*, a medieval formation, was acquired by English from medieval Latin in the 14th century). Later on, the compounding process was repeated, giving late Latin *commandāre*. By this time, *mandāre* had come to mean 'order' as well as 'entrust' (a change reflected in English *mandatory*). *Commandāre* inherited both these senses, and they coexisted through Old French *comander* and Anglo-Norman *comaunder* into Middle English *commande*. But 'entrust' was gradually taken over from the 14th century by *commend*, and by the end of the 15th century *command* meant simply 'order.'

*Commandeer* and *commando* are both of Afrikaans origin, and became established in English at the end of the 19th century largely as a result of the Boer War. *Commodore* [17] is probably a modification of Dutch *komandeur*, from French *commandeur* 'commander.'

▶ commend, commodore, demand, mandatory, recommend, remand

## commensurate　SEE MEASURE

## comment
[15] In Latin, a *commentum* was originally 'something invented or devised.' It was derived from the verb *comminiscī* 'devise, contrive by thought,' a compound formed from the prefix *com-* 'with' and a base *\*men-* (this also produced Latin *mens* and *mentiō*, source respectively of English *mental* and *mention*). It was used in the 7th century by the Spanish theologian Isidore in the sense 'interpretation, annotation,' and it was with that meaning rather than the original 'contrivance' that the word passed eventually into English.

▶ mental, mention, mind

## commerce
[16] *Commerce* is etymologically related to *market, merchandise, merchant,* and *mercury*. It comes, perhaps via French *commerce*, from Latin *commercium* 'trade,' a compound noun formed from the collective prefix *com-* 'together' and *merx* 'merchandise.' The adjective *commercial* is 17th-century, its nominal use for 'broadcast advertisement' 20th-century.

▶ market, merchant, mercury

## commit
[14] Etymologically, *commit* simply means 'put together.' It comes from Latin *committere*, a compound verb formed from the prefix *com-* 'together' and the verb *mittere* 'put, send' (whence English *missile* and *mission*). It originally meant literally 'join, connect,' but then branched out along the lines of 'put for safety, entrust' (the force of *com-* here being more intensive than collective) and 'perpetrate' (exactly how this sense evolved is not clear). The whole range of meanings followed the Latin verb into English, although 'put together' was never more than an archaism, and died out in the 17th century. Of derivatives based on the Latin verb's past participial stem *commiss-*, *commission* entered English in the 14th century and *commissionaire* (via French) in the 18th century. Medieval Latin *commissārius* produced English *commissary* [14] and, via French, Russian *commissar*, borrowed into English in the 20th century.

▶ commissar, committee, missile, mission

## committee
[15]　*Committee* was formed from the verb *commit* by adding the suffix *-ee*. Following the pattern of all such formations, it originally meant 'person to whom something is committed'; it was not until the 17th century that the sense 'body of people delegated to perform a particular function' developed.

## commodious
[15]　Latin *commodus* meant 'convenient.' It was a compound adjective formed from *com-* 'with' and *modus* 'measure,' and thus meaning literally 'conforming with due measure.' From it was derived the medieval Latin adjective *commodiōsus*, which passed, probably via French *commodieux*, into English. This originally meant 'advantageous, useful, convenient,' and it was not really until the 16th century that it developed the meaning 'affording a conveniently large amount of space.' The noun derivative *commodity* entered English in the 14th century, and from earliest times had the concrete meaning 'article of commerce,' deriving from the more general sense 'something useful.'

*Commodus* was borrowed into French as *commode* 'convenient,' which came to be used as a noun meaning both 'tall headdress for women' and 'chest of drawers.' English adopted the word in the 17th century, and in the 19th century added the new sense 'chair housing a chamber pot' (a semantic development paralleling the euphemistic use of *convenience* for *lavatory*).

▶ commode, commodity

## commodore　SEE COMMAND

## common
[13]　*Common* comes ultimately from an Indo-European base *\*moi-*, *\*mei-*, signifying 'change, exchange,' which also produced English *immune, mutate, mutual,* and *remunerate*. A derivative of this base, *\*moin-*, *\*mein-* seems to have joined up with the Indo-European collective *\*kom-* to produce *\*komoin-*, *\*komein-* 'shared by all.' In Germanic this became *\*gamainiz*, source of English *mean* 'despicable,' while in Latin it gave *commūnis*, source, via Old French *comun*, of English *common*. Both the Latin and French forms have given English a number of derivatives: from the former we have *community* [14] (Latin *commūnitātis*), *communion* [14] (Latin *commūniō*), and *communicate* [16] (Latin *commūnicāre*), while the latter has yielded *commune* [13] (Old French *comuner*)

and *communism* [19] (French *communisme*, coined around 1840).

▶ communicate, communism, community, immune, mean, mutual, mutate, remunerate

**commonwealth** see WEALTH

**commotion** see MOTOR

**compact** There are two distinct words *compact* in English; both are of Latin origin, but they come from completely different sources. The adjective, 'compressed' [14], comes from Latin *compactus*, the past participle of *compingere*, a compound verb formed from *com-* 'together' and *pangere* 'fasten.' The noun use 'small case for face powder' is 20th-century and based on the notion of firmly compacted powder. *Compact* 'agreement' [16] comes from Latin *compactum*, a noun based on the past participle of the verb *compacīscī* 'come to an agreement.' The unprefixed form *pacīscī*, a relative of Latin *pax* 'peace,' gave English *pact* [15].

▶ pact, peace

**companion** [13] Etymologically, your *companion* is someone who shares your 'bread' with you. It comes, via Old French *compaignon*, from Vulgar Latin *\*compāniō*, a compound noun formed from Latin *com-* 'with' and *pānis* 'bread.' The Old French stem *compaign-* also formed the basis of *compaignie*, from which English gets *company* [13]. Compare MATE.

The *companion* of *companionway* 'stairway on a ship' [18] is of similar but distinct origin. It comes ultimately from Vulgar Latin *\*compānia*, a compound noun meaning 'what one eats with bread,' formed from Latin *com-* 'with' and *pānis* 'bread.' In Italian this became *campagna* 'provisions,' which was used in the phrase *camera della campagna* '(ship's) storeroom.' The meaning of the phrase eventually passed to *campagna* on its own, and was carried via Old French *compagne* to Dutch *kompanje*, which meant 'quarterdeck.' English borrowed this, and adapted it to the more familiar English pattern *companion*.

▶ company, pannier

**compare** [15] *Compare* comes via Old French *comparer* from Latin *comparāre* 'couple, match,' a verb based on the adjective *compar* 'equal,' a compound formed from the prefix *com-* 'mutually' and *pār* 'equal' (source of English *pair, peer,* and *parity*). The Latin derivative noun *comparātiō* gave Old French *comparesoun* and hence English *comparison* [14].

▶ pair, par, parity, peer

**compass** [13] The notion underlying *compass* is of 'measuring out with paces.' It originated as a verb, Vulgar Latin *\*compassāre* 'pace out,' a compound formed from the Latin intensive prefix *com-* and *passus* (source of English *pace*). This passed into Old French as *compasser* 'measure,' and thence into English. The derived Old French noun *compas* was early applied to a pivoted two-armed measuring and drawing instrument,

presumably inspired equally by the ideas 'stepping' and 'measuring,' and English acquired this sense in the 14th century. The use of the word for a magnetic direction indicator, which dates from the 16th century, may be due to the device's circular container.

▶ pace

**compel** see PULSE

**compendium** see PONDER

**compensate** see PONDER

**compete** [17] *Compete* comes from Latin *competere*. This was a compound verb formed from *com-* 'together' and *petere* 'seek, strive' (source of English *petition, appetite, impetus,* and *repeat*). At first this meant 'come together, agree, be fit or suitable,' and the last of these meanings was taken up in the present participial adjective *competēns*, source of English *competent* [14]. In later Latin, however, *competere* developed the sense 'strive together,' and this formed the basis of English *compete*.

▶ appetite, competent, impetus, petition, repeat

**compile** see PILE

**complacent** see COMPLAISANT

**complain** [14] *Complain* goes back to the Latin verb *plangere*, source also of English *plangent*. This was formed on a prehistoric base *\*plak-* (from which we also get *plankton*), and it originally meant 'hit.' Its meaning developed metaphorically through 'beat one's breast' to 'lament,' and in medieval Latin it was combined with the intensive prefix *com-* to produce *complangere*. When it entered English via Old French *complaindre* it still meant 'lament,' and although this sense had died out by about 1700, traces of it remain in 'complain of' a particular illness. *Complaint* [14] came from Old French *complainte*.

▶ plangent, plankton

**complaisant** [17] *Complaisant* and *complacent* [17] are virtual doublets. Both come from Latin *complacēre* 'please greatly' (a compound verb formed from *placēre*, source of English *please*), but they reached English along different routes. *Complaisant* came via French, from *complaisant*, the present participle of *complaire* 'gratify,' but *complacent* was a direct borrowing from the Latin present participle. It originally meant simply 'pleasant, delightful,' and did not take on its present derogatory connotations (at first expressed by the now obsolete *complacential*) until the mid 18th century.

▶ complacent, please

**complete** [14] *Complete* first reached English as an adjective, either via Old French *complet* or direct from Latin *complētus*. This was the past participle of *complēre* 'fill up, finish,' a compound verb formed from the intensive prefix *com-* and *plēre* 'fill,' a word related to Latin *plēnus* 'full' (whence *plenary, plenitude, plenty,* etc) and indeed to English *full.*

The verb *complēre* itself came into Old French as the now obsolete *complir* (*complete* as a verb is a later formation from the adjective), and was prefixed with *a-* to produce *accomplir.* From its stem *accompliss-* English got *accomplish* [14].

▶ accomplish, compliment, comply, expletive, plenary, plenty

**compliant**     see COMPLY

**complicate**     see PLY

**compliment**     [17] *Compliment* and *complement,* so often confused, are in effect doublets. They come from the same ultimate source, Latin *complēmentum,* a noun derived from *complēre* 'fill up, finish' (source of English *complete* and *accomplish*). English borrowed *complement* direct from Latin in the 14th century in the sense 'fulfilment, accomplishment,' and by the 16th century this had developed the more specific metaphorical meaning 'fulfilment of the obligation of politeness' – hence 'polite words of praise.' But then in the 17th century came competition in the form of *compliment,* also meaning 'polite words of praise.' This also came from Latin *complēmentum,* but along a circuitous route via Vulgar Latin *\*complimentum,* Spanish *cumplimiento,* and French *compliment.* It gradually took over from *complement* in this 'flattering' sense, while *complement* went on to develop its leading current meaning, 'counterpart,' in the 19th century.

▶ accomplish, complement, complete, comply, expletive, plenary, plenty

**comply**     [17] Like *accomplish, complete, complement,* and *compliment, comply* comes from Latin *complēre* 'fill up, finish.' It was originally acquired in the 14th century, via Old French *complire,* but does not seem to have survived, and the sudden explosion in its use in the early 17th century represents a new borrowing, from Italian *complire.* Italian had the word from Spanish *cumplir,* in which the meaning 'be courteous' had developed. This passed into English, and though long defunct, seems to have been the basis of the modern English sense 'be amenable or obedient.' *Compliant* [17] is an English development.

▶ complete, compliant, compliment

**compose**     [15] Etymologically, *compose* means simply 'put together'; it comes, via Old French *composer,* from *compos-,* the perfect stem of Latin *compōnere,* a compound verb formed from the prefix *com-* 'with' and *pōnere* 'place, put,' source of English *position.* Amongst its many descendants and derivatives are *compound, component* [17] (from the Latin present participle *compōnent-*), *composite* [16] (from the Latin past participle *compositus*), and *compost* [14] (which originally meant 'stewed fruit,' like the later-borrowed *compote* [17]).

▶ component, composite, compost, compote, compound, position

**compound**     There are two disinct words *compound* in English. The one meaning 'combine' [14] comes ultimately from Latin *compōnere* 'put together.' Old French took two verbs from this: the perfect stem *compos-*produced *composer* (whence English *compose*) while the infinitive became *compondre,* source of English *compound.* Its original Middle English form was *compoune*; the final *d* came from the adjectival use of the past participle *compouned. Compound* 'enclosure' [17] is of Eastern origin: it comes from Malay *kampong* 'group of buildings, village,' and was borrowed via Portuguese *campon* or Dutch *campoeng.* The English form was no doubt remodelled on the basis of *compound* 'combine.'

▶ compose, composite, position

**comprehend**     see PREY

**compress**     see PRESS

**comprise**     see PREY

**compunction**     [14] Etymologically, to do something 'without compunction' means literally to do it without one's conscience pricking. The word comes via Old French *componction* from late Latin *compunctiō,* a derivative of *compungere* 'prick hard,' a compound verb formed from the intensive prefix *com-* and *pungere* 'prick' (source of English *puncture* and *pungent*).

▶ puncture, pungent

**compute**     [17] Latin *computāre* meant 'reckon together.' It was a compound verb formed from the prefix *com-* 'together' and *putāre* 'reckon, think' (source of English *putative* and various derived forms such as *amputate, deputy, dispute, impute,* and *reputation*). It was borrowed into Old French as *compter,* from which English got *count,* but English *compute* was a direct borrowing from Latin. The derivative *computer* was coined in the mid-17th century, and originally meant simply 'person who computes'; the modern meaning developed via 'device for calculating' at the end of the 19th century and 'electronic brain' in the 1940s.

▶ amputate, count, deputy, dispute, impute, putative, reputation

**comrade**     [16] Etymologically, one's *comrade* is someone with whom one shares a room. The word came via French *camerade* from Spanish *camarada* 'room-sharer,' a derivative of *camara* 'room,' from Latin *camera. Cameraderie* is a 19th-century borrowing from French.

▶ camaraderie, camera, chamber, chamberlain, chimney

**concatenation**     [17] A *concatenation* is literally a 'chain' of events or occurrences. It is a derivative of the seldom-encountered verb *concatenate* [16], which comes from Latin *concatēnāre* 'chain together, link,' a compound verb formed from the prefix *com-* 'together' and *catēna* 'chain' (source of English *chain*).

▶ chain

**conceal** [14] *Conceal* can be traced back to the Indo-European base *\*kel-* 'hide,' which was also the source of English *apocalypse, cell, occult*, and probably *colour*. It formed the basis of the Latin verb *cēlāre* 'hide,' which was strengthened by the intensive prefix *com-* to produce *concēlāre*. This reached English via Old French *conceler*. Another offshoot of the Latin verb was the adverb *clam* 'secretly'; from this was formed the adjective *clandestīnus*, acquired by English as *clandestine* in the 16th century.

▶ apocalypse, cell, clandestine, hole, holster, occult, supercilious

**conceive** [13] *Conceive* is one of a number of English words (*deceive, perceive*, and *receive* are others) whose immediate source is the Old French morpheme *-ceiv-*. This goes back ultimately to Latin *capere* 'take' (source of English *capture*), which when prefixed became *-cipere*. In the case of *conceive*, the compound verb was *concipere*, where the prefix *com-* had an intensive force; it meant generally 'take to oneself,' and hence either 'take into the mind, absorb mentally' or 'become pregnant' – meanings transmitted via Old French *conceivre* to English *conceive*. The noun *conceit* [14] is an English formation, based on the models of *deceit* and *receipt*. *Conception* [13], however, goes back to the Latin derivative *conceptiō*.

▶ capture, conceit, conception, deceive, perceive, receive

**concern** [15] In earliest use, English *concern* meant 'distinguish, discern.' This was a reflection of its ultimate source, Latin *cernere* 'sift, separate.' In combination with the prefix *com-* 'together' it produced *concernere*, which in classical times meant specifically 'mix together preparatory to sifting.' Later, however, the prefix seems to have taken on a more intensive role, with *concernere* reverting to the same range of senses as *cernere*. By the Middle Ages these not only included 'discern, perceive' and 'decide' (whence English *certain*, from the past participle of *cernere*), but had widened considerably to 'relate to' – a meaning which emerged in English *concern* in the 16th century. Connotations of distress or worry began to develop in the late 17th century.

▶ certain, discern

**concert** [16] *Concert* probably comes ultimately from Latin *concertāre*, a compound verb formed from the prefix *com-* 'with' and *certāre* 'strive, contend,' a verb derived from *certus* 'sure, fixed' (source of English *certain*), which in turn came from *cernere* (source of English *concern*). Some etymologists have

rejected *concertāre* as the origin of *concert*, on the grounds that its meaning – 'dispute, debate' – was completely opposite, but it seems that in post-classical times the Latin verb came to mean 'strive together (in cooperation)' – a much more plausible sense relationship. It passed into Italian as *concertare* 'bring into agreement,' and developed specific musical connotations of 'harmony.' English acquired it via French *concerter*. The noun *concerto* [18] was an Italian derivative of the verb; French borrowed it as *concert*, and passed it on to English as the noun *concert* [17]. *Concertina* was coined in the 1830s, from the noun *concert*.

▶ certain, concern, concertina, concerto, disconcert

**conciliate** see COUNCIL

**conclave** see CLAVIER

**concoct** [16] To *concoct* an excuse is the same, etymologically, as to 'cook' one up. The word *concoct* comes from the past participle of Latin *concoquere*, a compound verb formed from the prefix *com-* 'together' and *coquere* 'cook.' This was a derivative of the noun *coquus* 'cook,' which was the source of English *cook*. The Latin verb developed several figurative senses, including 'digest food' and 'reflect on something in the mind,' but 'fabricate' seems to be an English creation (first recorded in the late 18th century), developed from an earlier 'make by mixing ingredients.'

▶ cook

**concomitant** see COUNT

**concord** [13] Etymologically, *concord* signifies that two people's hearts are together, as one. The word comes, via Old French *concorde*, from Latin *concordia*, a derivative of the adjective *concors*. This meant literally 'hearts together,' and thus 'of one mind, in harmony.' It was formed from the prefix *com-* 'together' and the noun *cors* 'heart' (source of English *cordial* and French *coeur*). *Concordat* [17] comes from the past participle of the Latin verb *concordāre* 'agree.'

*Discord* [13], the antonym of *concord*, has a parallel origin, coming ultimately from Latin *discors* 'disagreeing.'

▶ concordat, cordial, discord

**concourse** see COURSE

**concrete** [14] In origin, something *concrete* is something that has 'grown together.' The word comes, via Old French *concret*, from Latin *concrētus*, the past participle of *concrēscere* 'grow together,' hence 'harden.' This was a compound verb formed from the prefix *com-* 'together' and *crēscere* 'grow' (source also of English *crescent, increase*, and *accrue*). Its original application in English was fairly general – referring to that which is solid or material; its use for the building material did not emerge until the early 19th century.

▶ accrue, crescent, decrease, increase

**concubine** [13] A *concubine* is etymologically a person with whom one goes to bed. It comes via Old French *concubine* from Latin *concubīna*, a compound noun formed from the prefix *com-*'with' and *cub-*, the stem of the verb *cubāre* 'lie down, go to bed.' Another derivative of this verb was Latin *cubiculum*, whose meaning 'bedroom' was carried through into English *cubicle* [15]; the more general 'partitioned-off area' did not emerge fully until the 20th century.

▶ cubicle

**concupiscence** see CUPIDITY

**concussion** [15] The etymological notion underlying *concussion* is of 'violent shaking'; the modern connotation of a 'jarring injury to the brain' did not emerge until the 16th century. The word comes from late Latin *concussiō*, a noun derived from the past participial stem of *concutere* 'shake violently.' This was a compound verb formed from the intensive prefix *com-* and *-cutere*, an alteration of *quatere* 'shake, strike' (its variant *quassāre* was the source of English *quash* and *cashier* 'dismiss,' and probably lies behind *cascara* [19], etymologically 'bark broken off the tree'). The verb *concuss* is 17th-century.

The related *percussion* [16] comes ultimately from Latin *percutere* 'strike through.'

▶ cascara, cashier, percussion, quash, rescue

**condign** [15] From its virtually exclusive modern use in the phrase *condign punishment*, *condign* has come to be regarded frequently as meaning 'severe,' but etymologically it signifies 'fully deserved.' It comes via Old French *condigne* from Latin *condignus*, a compound adjective formed from the intensive prefix *com-* and *dignus* 'worthy' (source of English *dainty, deign, dignity, disdain*, and *indignant*, and related to *decent*). The collocation with *punishment* arises from the frequent use of the phrase in Tudor acts of parliament.

▶ dainty, decent, deign, dignity, disdain, indignant

**condiment** see RECONDITE

**condition** [14] Latin *condīcere* originally meant literally 'talk together' – it was a compound verb formed from the prefix *com-* 'together' and *dīcere* 'talk' (whose base *dic-* forms the basis of a wide range of English words from *abdicate* to *vindicate*, including *diction* and *dictionary*). Gradually the idea of 'talking together, discussing' passed to 'agreeing,' and the derived Latin noun *conditiō* originally meant 'agreement.' From this came 'stipulation, provision,' and hence 'situation, mode of being,' all of them senses which passed via Old French *condicion* into English *condition*.

▶ abdicate, diction, dictionary, predict, vindicate

**condolence** [17] *Condolence* and *sympathy* are parallel formations: both go back to classical originals (late Latin *condolēre* and Greek *sumpátheia* respectively) which meant literally 'together-suffering.'

Latin *condolēre* was a compound verb formed from the prefix *com-*'together' and *dolēre* 'suffer pain' (source of English *dolour* and *doleful*). This entered English in the 16th century as the now seldom encountered verb *condole*, but the comparative frequency of the noun *condolence* is probably due to the early 17th-century adoption of French *condoléance* (the spelling *condoleance* was common in English in the 17th and 18th centuries).

▶ doleful, dolour

**condone** see DATE

**cone** [16] Greek *kōnos* originally meant 'pine-cone' – it was the pine-cone's typical shape which suggested the application of the word to a conical geometrical figure. The word passed into English via Latin *cōnus* and French *cône*. *Coniferous* [17] was formed from Latin *cōnifer*, literally 'cone-bearing' (*-ifer* goes back to Latin *ferre* 'carry,' a relative of English *bear*).

▶ hone

**confess** [14] *Confess* comes from Latin *confitērī* 'acknowledge.' This was a compound verb formed from the intensive prefix *com-* and *fatērī* 'admit' (a relative of English *fable, fame*, and *fate*). Its past participle was *confessus*, and this was taken as the basis of a new Vulgar Latin verb *\*confessāre*, which passed into English via Old French *confesser*.

▶ fable, fame, fate

**confetti** [19] The Latin compound verb *conficere* meant 'put together, make, prepare' (it was formed from the prefix *com-* and *facere* 'do, make,' source of English *fact, factory, fashion*, etc and related to English *do*). From its past participial stem was formed the noun *confectiō*, which passed into English, via Old French, as *confection* in the 14th century (by which time it already had its present-day association with sweets). But the past participle *confectum* also produced Old French *confit*, whence English *comfit* [15], and Italian *confetto*, which was a small sweet traditionally thrown during carnivals. The British adapted the missiles to weddings (displacing the traditional rice) at the end of the 19th century, using symbolic shreds of coloured paper rather than real sweets.

▶ comfit, confection, discomfit, do, fact, factory, fashion

**confide** [15] To *confide* in somebody is literally to 'put one's trust or faith' in them. The word comes from the Latin compound verb *confīdere*, which was formed from the intensive prefix *com-* and *fīdere* 'trust.' This was a derivative of *fīdes* 'trust' (whence English *faith*). *Confidant* [16] and *confidence* [15] come from the Latin verb's present participle, *confīdēns*, in which the secondary notion of 'self-assurance' was already present. The abbreviation *con* for *confidence man, confidence trick*, etc originated in the USA in the late 19th century.

▶ confident, faith

**confine**   see FINE

**confiscate** [16] *Confiscate*'s etymological connotations are financial: the Latin verb *confiscāre* meant 'appropriate to the public treasury.' It was formed from the collective prefix *com-* and *fiscus*. This meant originally 'rush-basket'; it was applied to the baskets used by tax collectors, and hence came to mean 'public treasury' (English gets *fiscal* from it). The looser sense of *confiscate*, 'seize by authority,' dates from the early 19th century.

▶ fiscal

**conflagration**   see FLAGRANT

**conflict**   see PROFLIGATE

**confound** [13] Latin *confundere* literally meant 'pour together'; it was a compound verb formed from the prefix *com-* 'together' and *fundere* 'pour' (source of English *found* 'melt' and *fuse*). This sense was later extended figuratively to 'mix up, fail to distinguish,' a meaning which passed via Old French *confondre* into English. Meanwhile, the Latin verb's past participle, *confusus*, came to be used as an adjective; in Old French this became *confus*, which English acquired in the 14th century as *confuse*. This was soon assimilated to the normal pattern of English past participial adjectives as *confused*, from which the new verb *confuse* was coined.

▶ confuse, found, fuse

**confute**   see BEAT

**congratulate**   see GRATEFUL

**congregation** [14] Etymologically, a church's *congregation* is comparable to a pastor's flock. The word comes from Latin *congregātiō*, a noun derivative of *congregāre* 'flock together.' This was a compound verb formed from the collective prefix *com-* and *grex* 'flock, herd' (source of English *egregious* and *gregarious*). *Congregation* was thus originally simply a 'meeting, assembly'; its religious connotations arose from its frequent use in the 1611 translation of the Bible to render 'solemn public assembly.' The verb *congregate* was independently borrowed in the 15th century.

▶ aggregate, egregious, gregarious, segregate

**congress** [16] A *congress* is literally a 'coming together' – hence, a 'meeting.' The word comes from Latin *congessus*, which was based on the past participial stem of *congredī* 'come together.' This was a compound verb formed from the prefix *com-* 'together' and *gradī* 'go, walk' (a derivative of *gradus* 'step,' from which English gets *grade*, *gradual*, and *graduate*). The application of the word to the US legislature dates from the 1770s.

▶ grade, gradual, graduate, progress, transgress

**congruent** [15] Etymologically, triangles that are *congruent* 'come together' or 'agree' – that is, are similar. The word comes from *congruēns*, the pres-

ent participle of Latin *congruere* 'come together, meet, agree.' This was a compound verb formed from the prefix *com-* 'together' and a verb, *\*gruere*, not found elsewhere (some have linked it with Latin *ruere* 'fall' – ultimate source of English *ruin* – in which case *congruere* would have meant literally 'fall together,' but others have seen a connection with Greek *zakhrēēs* 'attacking violently'). *Incongruous* is a 17th-century adoption from Latin *incongruus*.

**coniferous**   see CONE

**conjecture** [14] A *conjecture* is, etymologically speaking, simply something 'thrown together.' The word comes, perhaps via Old French, from Latin *conjectūra* 'conclusion, interpretation,' a noun derived from the past participle of *conicere* 'throw together.' This was a compound verb formed from the prefix *com-* 'together' and *jacere* 'throw' (source of English *jet*, *jettison*, and *jetty*). The notion behind the word's semantic development is that facts are 'thrown together' in the mind and (provisional) conclusions drawn.

▶ jet, jettison, jetty

**conjugal** [16] The notion underlying *conjugal* is of 'joining together.' It comes from Latin *conjugālis*, an adjective derived from *conjux* 'spouse.' This in turn was derived from *conjugāre* 'join together (in marriage),' a compound verb formed from the prefix *com-* 'together' and *jugāre* 'yoke' (a derivative of *jugum* 'yoke,' which is related to English *yoke* and *yoga*). (The grammatical connotations of English *conjugate* [16] arise from the notion of a 'connected' set of verb forms.) The base of *jugum*, *\*jug-*, also produced *jungere* 'join,' whose derivative *conjungere* 'join together' is responsible for the parallel set of English words *conjoin* [14], *conjunct* [15], and *conjunction* [14].

▶ conjugate, conjunction, join, yoga, yoke

**conker** [19] A *conker* was originally a 'snail shell.' Small boys tied them on to pieces of string and played a game involving trying to break their opponent's shell (another method of playing was simply to press two shells together and see which one broke). The first record of the use of horse chestnuts instead of snail shells is from the 1880s, but in the succeeding century this has established itself as the word's sole application. It is not entirely clear where it originally came from. The connection with molluscs has inevitably suggested a derivation from *conch* (itself ultimately from Greek *kónkhē*), but early 19th-century spellings of the game as *conquering*, and of *conker* as *conqueror*, point to a simpler explanation, that the stronger snail shell defeated, or 'conquered,' the weaker.

**connect** [17] Etymologically, *connect* means 'tie together.' It comes from Latin *connectere*, a compound verb formed from the prefix *com-* 'together' and *nectere* 'bind, tie' (whose past participial stem, *nex-*, is the ultmate source of English *nexus* [17]). The derived noun *connection* first appeared, in the spelling *connexion*, in the 14th century.

▶nexus

## connubial  see NUBILE

## conquer
[13] Latin *conquīrere* originally meant 'seek something out.' It was a compound verb formed from the intensive prefix *com-* and *quaerere* 'seek' (source of English *query, quest, question, inquire,* and *require*). Bit by bit, 'searching for something' slid into 'acquiring it,' including by force of arms: hence the sense 'vanquish,' already current in the 13th century. The term *Conqueror* appears first to have been applied to William I of England around 1300.

▶enquire, inquest, query, quest, question, require

## conscience
[13] Latin *conscīre* meant 'be mutually aware.' It was a compound verb formed from the prefix *com-* 'with, together' and *scīre* 'know' (source of English *science*). To 'know something with oneself' implied, in a neutral sense, 'consciousness,' but also a moral awareness, a mental differentiation between right and wrong, and hence the derived noun *conscientia* carried both these meanings, via Old French, into English (the more general, amoral, 'consciousness' died out in the 18th century). A parallel Latin formation, using *\*sci-*, the base of *scīre*, was *conscius* 'aware,' acquired by English in the 17th century as *conscious*. *Conscientious* is also a 17th-century borrowing, ultimately from Latin *conscientiōsus*.

▶science

## consecutive  see SEQUENCE

## consent
[13] The notion underlying 'giving one's consent' is 'feeling together' – that is, 'agreeing,' and hence 'giving approval or permission.' The word comes from Old French *consente*, a derivative of the verb *consentir*. This was a descendant of Latin *consentīre* 'agree,' a compound verb formed from the prefix *com-* 'together' and *sentīre* 'feel' (source of English *sense, sentence, sentiment,* etc). *Consensus*, originally the past participle of Latin *consentīre*, was borrowed into English in the 19th century.

▶consensus, sense, sentence, sentiment

## consequence  see SEQUENCE

## conserve
[14] Latin *servāre* meant 'keep, preserve' (it was not related to *servus* 'slave,' source of English *serve* and *servant*). Among the compounds formed from it were *praeservāre* 'guard in advance' and, using the intensive prefix *com-*, *conservāre*. This passed into English via Old French *conserver*. Amongst its derivatives are *conservation* [14], *conservative* [14] (first used in the modern political sense by J Wilson Croker in 1830), and *conservatory* [16] (whose French

original, *conservatoire*, was reborrowed in the 18th century in the sense 'musical academy').

▶observe, preserve, reserve

## consider
[14] Etymologically, *consider* means 'observe the stars.' Amongst the most popular of ancient Roman methods of divination was astrology, and so the Latin verb *consīderāre* was coined (from the intensive prefix *com-* and *sīdus* 'star,' source of English *sidereal*) to describe the activity of carefully noting the stars' courses for the purpose of drawing auguries. From 'observing stars' it soon broadened out in meaning to simply 'observe,' and hence figuratively 'think over something,' but the sense 'have an opinion' seems to be an English development of the 16th century. English acquired the word via Old French *considerer*, but borrowed *considerable* directly from Latin *consīderābilis*; the modern sense 'large in amount' arose in the mid-17th century, on the basis of an earlier 'worthy of consideration because of great quantity.'

▶desire, sidereal

## consign  see SIGN

## consist
[16] Latin *consistere* meant originally 'stand still, be firmly in place.' It was a compound verb formed from the intensive prefix *com-* and *sistere* 'place' (a relative of Latin *stāre*, which entered into a parallel compound to form *constāre* 'stand firm,' source of English *constant* [14]). The concrete concept of 'standing firm' passed into the more abstract 'exist,' and hence 'have a particular kind of existence, have particular inherent qualities.' By the time English borrowed the verb it had come to mean 'be composed of.'

▶constant, constitute

## console
[14] *Console* means literally 'offer solace.' It comes from Latin *consōlārī*, a compound verb formed from the intensive prefix *com-* and *sōlārī* 'comfort' (source of the Latin noun *sōlātium*, from which English gets *solace* [13]). English acquired it either directly, or via French *consoler*. The Latin agent noun derived from *consōlārī* was *consōlātor* 'comforter,' which passed into French as *consolateur*. This came to be used as an architectural term for a carved human figure supporting a cornice, shelf, etc, and was eventually shortened to *console*; this was borrowed into English in the 18th century.

▶solace

## consonant
[14] Etymologically, *consonant* means 'sounding together.' It comes via Old French *consonant* from Latin *consonāns*, the present particple of *consonāre*, a compound verb formed from the prefix *com-* 'together' and *sonāre* 'sound.' Its application to particular speech sounds, contrasted with 'vowels,' comes from the notion that they were 'pronounced together with' vowels, rather than independently.

▶sonorous, sound

**consort** see SORT

**conspire** see SPIRIT

**constable** [13] The late Latin *comes stabulī* was an officer in charge of the stables (*comes* is the source of the English title *count*, and *stabulum* is the ancestor of English *stable*). From the comparatively lowly status of head groom, the job gradually grew in importance until Old French *conestable* was used for the principal officer of the household of the early French kings. In the 14th century the title was adopted for the Constable of England. On a less exalted level, the word has also been used since the 14th century for someone appointed to uphold law and order, and was applied to police officers when they were called into being in the 1830s.

▶ count, stable

**constant** see CONSIST

**consternation** see STRATA

**constipation** [15] Latin *constīpātiō* originally meant 'condition of being closely packed or compressed.' Its English descendant *constipation* was briefly used in that literal sense in the 17th and 18th centuries, but for the most part it has been a medical term: at first for constriction of some internal organ, blood vessel, etc, and from the mid-16th century for impaired bowel function. The Latin past participle *constīpātus* passed into Old French as *costive*, which English acquired, via an unrecorded Anglo-Norman *\*costif* 'constipated' [14].

▶ costive, stevedore, stiff

**constitute** [15] Etymologically, that which is *constituted* is that which is 'caused to stand' or 'set up.' The word comes from the past participle of Latin *constituere* 'fix, establish,' a compound verb formed from the intensive prefix *com-* and *statuere* 'set up' (source of English *statute*). This was a derivative of Latin *status* (whence English *state* and *status*), which itself began life as the past participle of *stāre* 'stand' (a relative of English *stand*). The derivative *constituent* [17] comes (partly via French) from the Latin present participle *constituēns*.

▶ stand, statue, status, statute

**constrain** see STRAIN

**construct** [17] *Construct* comes from the present participle of Latin *construere* 'pile up together, build,' a compound verb formed from the prefix *com-* and *struere* 'pile up' (source of English *destroy* and *structure*). English acquired the same verb somewhat earlier, in the 14th century, in the form *construe*.

▶ construe, destroy, structure

**consult** [17] The *-sult* element of *consult* represents a prehistoric Indo-European *\*sal-*, which may be related to Sanskrit *sar-* 'go.' It was used with the prefix *com-* 'together' to form the Latin verb *consulere* 'dis-

cuss, consult.' An altered form developed, *consultāre* denoting repeated action, and this was the source, via French *consulter*, of the English verb. Related to Latin *consulere* were the nouns *consul*, borrowed into English in the 14th century, and *consilium*, ultimate source of English *counsel* [13].

▶ consul, counsel

**consummate** see SUM

**contact** [17] The underlying notion of *contact* is not surprisingly one of 'touching.' It comes ultimately from Latin *tangere* 'touch,' source of English *tactile*, *tangent*, and *tangible*. Using the prefix *com-* 'together' this was formed into a compound verb *contangere* 'touch, border on,' whose past participle *contāctus* was borrowed into English, originally as a noun (its use as a verb is a surprisingly late development, which did not happen until the late 19th century). Also derived from Latin *contangere* is *contagion* [14], and *contaminate* is probably related.

▶ contagion, contaminate, tactile, tangent, tangible

**contain** [13] *Contain* comes ultimately from Latin *tenēre* 'hold,' source of a wide range of English words from *abstain* to *tenor*. In the case of *contain* the immediate ancestor, via Old French *contenir*, is Latin *continēre* 'hold together, enclose, contain,' a compound formed with the prefix *com-* 'together.' *Contain* still adheres fairly closely to the meaning of its Latin original, but other descendants, such as *content, continent, continue,* and *countenance,* have branched out a lot semantically.

▶ abstain, content, continent, continue, countenance, retain, sustain, tenor

**contaminate** [15] *Contaminate* appears to come from the same ultimate source as *contact*, a base *\*tag-* 'touch,' which produced the Latin verb *tangere* 'touch' (whence English *tactile, tangent,* and *tangible*). It seems also to have formed the basis of a compound Latin noun *\*contagmen* 'contact, pollution,' which became altered to *contāmen*. From this was derived the verb *contamināre*, whose past participle gave English *contaminate*.

▶ contact, tactile, tangible

**contemplate** [16] Etymologically, to *contemplate* something is to observe it in a 'temple.' The word comes from the past participle of Latin *contemplārī*, a compound verb formed from the intensive prefix *com-* and *templum*. This word, source of course of English *temple*, originally signified a space marked out by augurs (priests in ancient Rome who interpreted omens) for making observations. Hence *contemplārī* originally meant 'observe omens carefully,' but its application soon became more general.

▶ temple

**contend**   see TEND

**content**   The adjective and noun *content* come ultimately from the same source, but as their divergent pronunciations suggest, they reached English via different routes. Their common original is Latin *contentus*, past participle of *continēre* 'hold together, enclose, contain' (source of English *contain, continent, continue*, and *countenance*). The more recent borrowing, the noun *content* [15], comes directly from medieval Latin *contentum*, and retains the original meaning of the Latin verb. The adjective *content* [14], however, comes via Old French *content*, and reflects a metaphorical change in the Latin past participle from 'contained' via 'restrained' and 'self-restrained' to 'satisfied.'

▶ contain, continent, continue, countenance, retentive

**contest**   [16]   The idea underlying *contest*, unlikely as it may seem, is of 'bearing witness.' It goes back to Latin *contestārī*, a compound verb formed from the prefix *com-* 'together' and *testārī* 'bear witness,' which in turn was derived from *testis* 'witness' (whence English *testament, testicle*, and *testimony*). This verb signified the bringing of a lawsuit by 'calling witnesses together' from both sides. Hence was introduced the adversarial or competitive notion that passed into English, probably via Old French *contester* (although in the 16th and 17th centuries traces of the original Latin sense 'bear joint witness, attest' survived in English, presumably as a scholarly reintroduction).

▶ testament, testicle, testimony

**context**   see TEXT

**continent**   [14]   *Continent* comes via Old French from Latin *continēns*, the present participle of *continēre* 'hold together, enclose, contain' (source of English *contain*). From the beginning it meant in general 'exercising self-restraint'; of the more specific senses, 'chaste' developed in the 14th century and 'able to retain urine and faeces' apparently in the early 19th century. The word's noun use developed from the Latin phrase *terra continēns* 'continuous land' (for this sense of Latin *continēre* see CONTINUE). It was at first applied in the 16th century to any large continuous expanse of territory, and from the early 17th century specifically to any of the Earth's major landmasses (the English use of 'the Continent' for mainland Europe is roughly contemporary with this).

▶ contain, content, continue, countenance

**continue**   [14]   Latin *continēre* in its transitive sense (with an object) meant 'hold together, contain,' and led to English *contain*. However, it was also used intransitively in the sense 'hang together.' From it was derived the adjective *continuus* 'uninterrupted' (source of English *continuous* [17]), which formed the basis of a new verb *continuāre* 'make or be continuous.' English

acquired this via Old French *continuer*. (The derivative *continual* entered English in the 14th century.)

▶ contain, content, continent, countenance

**contort**   see TORMENT

**contraband**   [16]   *Contraband* means literally 'proclamation against' – hence 'prohibition.' It comes via French *contebande* from Italian *contrabbando*, a compound formed from *contra* 'against' (see CONTRARY) and *bando* 'proclamation' (whose source was late Latin *bannus, bannum*, a relative of English *ban*). The sense 'dealing in prohibited goods' had already developed before English acquired the word, and rapidly developed through 'smuggling' to 'smuggled goods.'

▶ ban, contrary

**contract**   [14]   English acquired the word *contract* in stages, although in all cases the ultimate source was *contractus*, the past participle of Latin *contrahere*, a compound verb formed from the prefix *com-* 'together' and *trahere* 'pull, draw' (source of English *traction* and *tractor*). This meant literally 'pull together,' but it had a variety of metaphorical senses, including 'bring about' and 'enter into an agreement,' and it was the latter which first passed into English via Old French as a noun meaning 'mutual agreement.' The arrival of the verb *contract* did not happen until the 16th century; it developed from an earlier adjective *contract*, which came again from Old French *contract*. This introduced a further sense of Latin *contrahere*: 'become narrowed, get smaller.'

▶ distract, retract, traction, tractor

**contrary**   [14]   *Contrary* originated as a Latin adjectival formation based on the preposition *contrā* 'against,' which historically was a derivative of *com* or *cum* 'with.' Latin *contrārius* passed into English via Old French *contraire* and Anglo-Norman *contrarie*. Originally *contrary* was pronounced with the main stress on its middle syllable, but this survives only in the sense 'obstinately self-willed'; from the 18th century onwards, the stress has usually been placed on the first syllable.

**contrast**   see STATUE

**contribute**   see TRIBE

**contrition**   see THROW

**contrive**   [14]   In Middle English, *contrive* was *controve*; it was not transformed into *contrive* (perhaps under the influence of Scottish pronunciation) until the 15th century. It came via Old French *controver* from Latin *contropāre* 'represent metaphorically, compare,' a compound verb based on the prefix *com-* 'too' and *tropus* 'figure of speech' (source of English *trope*). The word's meaning has progressed through 'compare via a figure of speech' and Old French 'imagine' to 'devise.'

▶ trope

**control** [15] Implausible as it may seem, *control*'s closest relative in English is *contra-rotating*. It has its origins in a medieval method of checking accounts which involved a duplicate register, or 'counter-roll,' as it was known (*contrārotulus* in medieval Latin, *contrā* meaning 'opposite' and *rotulus* being the diminutive of *rota* 'wheel'). From the medieval Latin noun a verb was formed, *contrārotulāre*, meaning 'check accounts by such means,' and hence 'exert authority.' This passed into English via Anglo-Norman *contreroller*. The spelling of the agent noun *controller* as *comptroller*, still encountered in certain official designations, arises from an erroneous 16th-century association of the first syllable with *count*, from late Latin *computus*.

▶ rota, rotate

**controversy**   see VERSE

**contumely** [14] The idea underlying *contumely* 'insolence' is 'swelling up.' It comes, via Old French *contumelie*, from Latin *contumēlia* 'insult, reproach,' a compound noun formed from the intensive prefix *com-* and (probably) *tumēre* 'swell' (source of English *tumour*). The sense development – from being 'puffed up' and 'angry,' 'proud,' or 'stubborn' through 'overbearing' to 'insulting' – appears also to be reflected in *contumacy* 'insubordination' [14], whose Latin source *contumācia* likewise probably came from *tumēre*.

▶ contumacy, tumour

**contusion** [14] Latin *tundere* meant 'beat, hit' (it may be related to English *stint* and *stunt*). Addition of the intensive prefix *com-* produced *contundere* 'beat hard, pound,' and from its past participle *contūsus* was formed the noun *contūsiō*, which passed into English via Old French *contusion*. Apart from isolated instances in the 17th and 18th centuries when it was used for 'beating' generally (probably scholarly archaisms), *contusion* has always had the physiological connotation of 'bruising' in English.

▶ stint, stunt, toil

**conundrum** [16] *Conundrum* originally appeared in all manner of weird and wonderful guises – *conimbrum, conuncrum, quonundrum, connunder*, etc – before settling down to *conundrum* in the late 18th century. It bears all the marks of one of the rather heavy-handed quasi-Latin joke words beloved of scholars in the 16th and 17th centuries, and a mid-17th-century commentator attributed it to Oxford university. At first it meant 'whim' and then 'pun'; the current sense 'puzzling problem' did not develop until the end of the 18th century.

**convalesce** [15] Latin *valēre* meant 'be strong or healthy' (from it English gets *valiant, valid, valour*, and *value*). Derived from it was *valēscere* 'grow strong,' which, with the addition of the intensive

prefix *com-* produced *convalēscere*, source of English *convalesce*. It was quite a commonly used word in Scottish English from earliest times, but does not seem to have established itself south of the border until the 19th century.

▶ valiant, valid, valour, value

**convenient** [14] *Convenient* comes from Latin *conveniēns*, the present participle of *convenire* 'come together, be suitable, agree,' a compound verb formed from the prefix *com-* 'together' and *venire* 'come' (a distant relative of English *come*). *Convenient* reflects the more figurative of *convenire*'s meanings, as ultimately does *covenant*, but its original literal sense 'assemble' is preserved in *convene* [15], *convention* [15], *convent*, and *coven*.

▶ convent, convention, coven, covenant, venue

**convent** [13] Latin *conventus* meant 'assembly' (it was the past participle of *convenire* 'come together,' source of English *convenient*), but as it passed via Anglo-Norman *covent* into English it acquired the specialized sense 'religious community' (in early use it was applied to communities of either sex, but since the end of the 18th century it has come to be used exclusively for a 'house of nuns'). Until the mid-15th century the Anglo-Norman spelling *covent* was retained in English (it survives in *Covent Garden*, which was formerly a vegetable garden belonging to the monks of Westminster Abbey, and may also the the source of *coven* [16]).

▶ convenient, coven, venue

**converge**   see VERGE

**conversation** [14] Latin *convertere* meant 'turn round, transform.' It was a compound verb formed from the intensive prefix *com-* and *vertere* 'turn' (source of English *verse, version*, and *vertigo*). It has spawned a variety of English words, its most direct descendant being *convert* [13]. Its past participle *conversus* produced the noun *converse* 'opposite' [16], but this should not be confused with the verb *converse* 'talk' [14], which came via quite a different route. Latin *vertere* had a specialized form, *vertāre*, denoting repeated action. From it came *versārī* 'live, occupy oneself,' which, with the addition of the *com-* prefix, produced *conversārī* 'live, dwell, associate or communicate with others.' This passed via Old French *converser* into English, but at first both it and its derivative *conversation* were limited semantically to the notion of 'dwelling' and 'social life'; the specific modern sense 'talk' was not brought into play until the late 16th century.

▶ convert, verse, version

**convex** [16] *Convex* was borrowed from Latin *convexus*, mainly an architectural term meaning 'arched, vaulted.' The element *-vexus* probably came from *vehere* 'carry' (source of English *vehicle*), the notion being that vaults are 'carried together' (Latin *com*-'together') to meet at a point at the centre of a roof, although some have speculated that it is related to Latin *vārus* 'bent, knock-kneed' (source of English *prevaricate*).

▶ vehicle, vex

**convey** [13] Etymologically, to *convey* something is to go with it on its way. It comes via Old French *conveier* from medieval Latin *conviāre* 'accompany, escort,' a compound verb formed from the prefix *com*-'with' and *via* 'way.' The verb's Latin meaning was carried through into English, and though it died out in *convey* in the 18th century it survives in *convoy* [14], borrowed from a later French version of the word.

▶ convoy, via

**convince** [16] Latin *convincere* meant originally 'overcome decisively' (it was a compound verb formed from the intensive prefix *com*- and *vincere* 'defeat,' source of English *victory*). It branched out semantically to 'overcome in argument,' 'prove to be false or guilty'; and when borrowed into English it brought these meanings with it. Before long they died out, leaving 'cause to believe,' which developed in the 17th century, as the only current sense, but 'find or prove guilty' survives in *convict* [14], acquired from the Latin past participle *convictus*.

▶ convict, victory

**convivial**    see VIVID

**convoke**    see VOCATION

**convolution**    see VOLUME

**convolvulus**    see VOLUME

**convoy**    see CONVEY

**cony** [13] The rabbit was not originally native to northern Europe, so there is no Germanic word for it. *Cony* was introduced into English (originally in the sense 'rabbit fur,' not until a century later for the animal itself) from Anglo-Norman *conis*, which was the plural of *conil*. This in turn came from Latin *cunīculus*, which is thought to have been borrowed from an ancient language of Spain or Portugal. The word *rabbit* was introduced in the 14th century, originally denoting the 'young of a rabbit,' but gradually replacing *cony* as the general term for the animal.

**cook** [OE] The noun *cook* is a lot more ancient than the verb, which in English was a 14th-century development from the noun. The noun itself was borrowed in Old English times from Vulgar Latin *cōcus*, a descendant of classical Latin *coquus*. This is of Indo-European origin, and has been linked with Greek *péssein* 'cook, boil.' Also from Latin *coquus* English gets *concoct* and *biscuit*, but *cookie* [18], a borrowing from

Dutch *koekje*, is, despite its similarity, related not to *cook* but to *cake*.

▶ apricot, concoct, cuisine, culinary, kiln, kitchen, pepsin, precocious

**cool** [OE] *Cool* comes from the same source as *cold*, namely Indo-European *\*gel-*, *\*gol-* (from which English also gets *congeal, gel*, and *jelly*). The Germanic descendants of this Indo-European base were *\*kal-*, *\*kōl-*. From these were derived the Germanic adjective *\*kōluz*, which passed into Old English as *cōl*. Its use for 'fashionable, hip' is mid-20th-century, but its nonchalant application to large sums of money is of surprisingly long standing: 'I just made a couple of bets with him, took up a cool hundred, and so went to the King's Arms,' John Vanbrugh and Colly Cibber, *The Provok'd Husband* 1728.

▶ cold, congeal, gel, jelly

**coolie** [17] *Coolie* is not etymologically related to *cool*. It comes from Hindi *kulī*, which may be the same word as *Kulī*, the name of an aboriginal tribe of Gujarat in western India. It has been speculated that the word was transported by the Portuguese from there to southern India and thence to China (it is now mainly applied to Far Easten labourers), its meaning perhaps influenced by Tamil *kūli* 'hire.'

**coop**    see CUP

**cooperate**    see OPERATE

**co-opt**    see OPINION

**cope** There are two distinct words *cope* in English. The now more familiar one, 'deal with' [14], comes from Old French *coper*, and originally meant 'hit, punch.' The Old French verb was a derivative of the noun *cop* 'blow,' which in turn was a variant of *colp* (from which modern French gets *coup*, borrowed into English in the 18th century). This came via medieval Latin *colpus* (ultimate source of English *coppice*) and Latin *colaphus* from Greek *kólaphos* 'blow, punch.' The modern English sense of the verb developed via 'come to blows with' and 'contend with' to 'handle successfully.'

*Cope* 'cloak' [13] was borrowed from medieval Latin *cāpa*, a variant of *cappa*, which produced English *cap* and *cape* as well as *chapel* and *chaperone*. It may ultimately be descended from Latin *caput* 'head.'

▶ coppice, coup / cap, cape, chapel, chaperon

**copious** [14] *Copious* comes, either directly or via Old French *copieux*, from Latin *copiōsus*, a derivative of *copia* 'abundance' (from which English also gets *copy*). *Copia* itself was originally a compound noun, formed from the intensive prefix *com*- and *ops* 'wealth, power.'

▶ copy, opulent

**copper** [OE] A major source of copper in the ancient world was the Mediterranean island of Cyprus, so the Romans called it *cyprium aes* 'metal of Cyprus.' This became *cuprum* in late Latin, from which it was borrowed into prehistoric West and North Germanic as *\*kupar*, source of Old English *coper*. (*Copper* the slang term for 'policeman' [19] is simply the agent noun formed from the verb *cop* 'seize,' which probably comes via Old French *caper* from Latin *capere* 'seize, take,' source of English *capture*.)

**coppice**   [14]   The notion underlying *coppice* is of 'cutting.' Its ultimate source is the Greek noun *kólaphos* 'blow,' which passed via Latin *colaphus* into medieval Latin as *colpus* (source of English *cope* and *coup*). From *colpus* was derived a verb *colpāre* 'cut,' which formed the basis of Vulgar Latin *colpātīcium* 'having the quality of being cut.' Its Old French descendant *copeïz* came to be applied to an area of small trees regularly cut back. English borrowed this as *coppice* (and in the 16th century spawned a new contracted form *copse*).

► cope, copse, coup

**copulate**   see COUPLE

**copy**   [14]   *Copy* has a very devious semantic history. It comes from Latin *copia* 'abundance' (source also of English *copious*), and came into English via Old French *copie*. In addition to its central sense 'abundance,' Latin *copia* could also mean 'power, right,' and it appears that its use in such phrases as 'give someone the right to transcribe' led to its application to 'right of reproduction' and ultimately to simply 'reproduction.'

► copious

**coral**   [14]   *Coral* may ultimately be of Semitic origin (Hebrew *gōrāl* 'pebble' has been compared), but the first record we have of it is as Greek *korállion*, which came to English via Latin *corallum* or *corallium* and Old French *coral*. Until the 17th century, the word was applied exclusively to the red coral (*Corallium nobile*); hence its use, since the early 16th century, for a 'rich red colour.'

**cord**   [13]   *Cord* 'string' and *chord* 'straight line' were originally the same word. They go back to Greek *khordē* 'string,' which came into English via Latin *chorda* and Old French *corde*. In English it was originally written *cord*, a spelling which included the sense 'string of a musical instrument.' But in the 16th century the spelling of this latter sense was remodelled to *chord*, on the basis of Latin *chorda*, and it has been retained for its semantic descendants 'straight line joining two points on a curve' and 'straight line joining the front and rear edges of a wing.' (*Chord* 'combination of musical notes' [15] is no relation: it is a reduced version of *accord*, which comes via Old French *acorder* from Vulgar Latin *\*accordāre*, a compound verb based on Latin *cors* 'heart,' and ironically was originally spelled *cord*.) Related words include *cordon* [16], from the French diminutive form *cordon*, and *cordite* [19], so named from

its often being shaped into cords resembling brown twine.

► chord, cordite, cordon, yarn

**corduroy**   [18]   Popular etymology usually associates *corduroy* with a supposed French *corde du roy* 'cord of the king' or even *couleur du roy* 'king's colour' (the original corduroy having according to this theory been purple), but in fact there is no concrete evidence to substantiate this. A more likely explanation is that the word's first syllable represents *cord* in the sense 'ribbed fabric,' and that the second element is the now obsolete noun *duroy* 'coarse woollen fabric' [17], of unknown origin.

**core**   [14]   The origins of *core* are a mystery, over which etymologists disagree. Several candidates have been put forward, including Old French *cor* 'horn,' on the grounds that two of *core*'s earliest applications were to the horny central part of apples and pears and to corns on the foot, and Latin *cor* 'heart,' on the grounds that an apple's *core* is its 'heart.'

**corgi**   see HOUND

**cork**   [14]   The earliest ascertainable ancestor of *cork* is Spanish *alcorque* 'cork sole,' which passed into English via Dutch *kork*. The initial *al-*, of course, suggests that this was of Arabic origin (*al* being the Arabic definite article), and it seems likely that it represents Arabic *al-qūrq*, which some have suggested came from Latin *cortex* 'bark,' source of English *cortex* [17]. The use of *cork* for a bottle-stopper made from cork dates from the early 16th century.

► cortex

**cormorant**   [13]   In early medieval times the cormorant was named 'sea raven' – that is, in Latin, *corvus marīnus*. This passed into Old French first as *cormareng*, which later became *cormaran*. English adopted it and added a final *t*. The word's origins are still evident in Portuguese *corvo marinho* 'cormorant.'

► marine

**corn**   [OE]   The underlying sense of *corn* is of grinding down into small particles. The word comes ultimately from the Indo-European base *\*ger-*, which meant 'wear away.' From it was derived *\*grnóm* 'worn-down particle,' which in Latin produced *grānum* (source of English *grain*) and in prehistoric Germanic produced *\*kurnam*, which developed into Old English *corn*. Already in Germanic times the word had developed in meaning from simply 'particle' to 'small seed' and specifically 'cereal grain,' but English *corn* was not of course applied to 'maize' before that plant came to Europe from America in the 16th century. The original sense 'particle' survives in *corned beef*, where *corned* refers to the grains of salt with which the meat is preserved. The meaning 'hackneyed or sentimental matter' is a 20th-century development, based on the supposedly unsophisticated life of country areas. *Kernel* comes from an Old English diminutive form of *corn*.

*Corn* 'hardening of the skin' [15] is a completely different word, coming via Anglo-Norman *corn* from Latin *cornū* 'horn.'

▶ grain / horn

**corner** [13] The idea underlying *corner* is of a 'projecting part' or 'point.' It came via Anglo-Norman *corner* from Vulgar Latin *\*cornārium*, a derivative of Latin *cornū* 'point' ('point' was in fact a secondary sense, developed from an original 'horn' – and Latin *cornū* is related to English *horn*). Other English descendants of *cornū* are *corn* 'hard skin,' *cornea* [14], *cornet* [14], originally a diminutive form, and *cornucopia* [16], literally 'horn of plenty.'

▶ cornea, cornet, horn

**corollary** [14] Latin *corolla* was a 'little crown or garland,' typically made from flowers (the word was a diminutive form of *corōna* 'crown,' source of English *crown*). Hence a *corollārium* was 'money paid for such a garland,' and by extension 'gratuity.' Later it developed the meaning 'deduction,' applied in geometry to a subsidiary proposition dependent on a previous proof, the sense in which it was first borrowed into English. (English acquired *corolla* itself in the 17th century.)

▶ coronary, crown

**coronary** [17] *Coronary* comes from Latin *coronārius*, an adjectival derivative of *corōna* 'garland, crown.' It was applied in the later 17th century to any anatomical structure, such as an artery, nerve, or ligament, that encircles another like a crown. A leading example of such a conformation is the heart, with its encircling blood vessels, and gradually *coronary* came to be used for 'of the heart.' Its application as a noun to 'heart attack' appears to be post-World War II. Other English descendants of Latin *corōna* (which came from Greek *korōnē* 'something curved') include *coronation* [14], the diminutive *coronet* [15], *coroner* [14], originally an 'officer of the crown,' *crown*, and of course *corona* [16] itself.

▶ corollary, coronation, coroner, crown

**corporal** [14] *Corporal* comes via Old French *corporal* from Latin *corporālis* 'bodily,' an adjective derived from *corpus* 'body.' The noun *corporal* 'non-commissioned officer' [16] was probably originally a completely different word. It was borrowed from French *corporal*, which appears to have been an alteration of *caporal*; this in turn came from Italian *caporale*, a derivative of *capo* 'head' (the change to *corporal* seems to have been based on the notion of the corporal as being in charge of a 'body' of troops).

▶ corpse

**corpse** [14] Latin *corpus* 'body' has two direct descendants in English: *corpse*, which came via Old French *cors*, and *corps* [18], which came via modern

French *corps*. The former first entered English in the 13th century as *cors*, and during the 14th century it had its original Latin *p* reinserted. At first it meant simply 'body,' but by the end of the 14th century the current sense 'dead body' was becoming firmly established. The idea originally underlying *corps*, on the other hand, was of a small 'body' of troops.

Other English derivatives of *corpus* include *corporal, corporate* [15], from the past participle of Latin *corporāre* 'make into a body,' *corpulent* [14], two diminutives *corpuscle* [17] and *corset* [14], and *corsage* [15]. *Corpus* itself was acquired in the 14th century.

▶ corporal, corporate, corpulent, corset

**corral** [16] English acquired *corral* from Spanish *corral*, but its previous history is disputed. Some etymologists consider that it is of southern African origin, from the language of the Hottentot people, but others derive it from Vulgar Latin *\*currale* 'enclosure for vehicles,' which would have been based on Latin *currus* 'two-wheeled wagon' (source of English *car* and *carry*). *Kraal* [18] originated as an Afrikaans adaptation of Portuguese *curral*, corresponding to Spanish *corral*.

▶ kraal

**correct** [14] *Correct* is etymologically related to *rectitude* and *rightness*. It comes from the past participle of Latin *corrigere* 'make straight, put right,' a compound verb formed from the intensive prefix *com-* and *regere* 'lead straight, rule.' This *regere* (source of English *regent, régime, regiment*, and *region*) goes back to an Indo-European base *\*reg-* 'move in a straight line,' which also produced English *right, rectitude, regal, royal*, and *rule*. In English the verb *correct* by a long time predates the adjective, which first appeared (via French) in the 17th century.

▶ escort, regal, region, right, royal, rule

**corridor**   see CURRENT

**corroborate**   see ROBUST

**corrode**   see ROSTRUM

**corrupt** [14] The Latin verb *rumpere* meant 'break' (it is etymologically related to English *bereave* and *rob*). It (or rather its past participial stem *rup-*) was the source of English *rupture* [15], and it entered into partnership with the intensive prefix *com-* to produce *corrumpere* 'destroy completely.' This was the ancestor (either directly or via Old French) of English *corrupt*, both adjective and verb.

▶ bereave, curse, rob, rupture

**corsage**   see CORPSE

**corsair** [15] Etymologically, a *corsair* is someone who goes on a 'course.' Latin *cursus* (source of English *course*) was a derivative of Latin *currere* 'run,' and meant originally a 'run.' From this it developed to 'journey' and 'expedition' to 'hostile or predatory expedition,' and eventually to the proceeds of such a raid, the 'plunder' or 'booty.' In medieval Latin the term *cursārius* was derived from it to denote someone who took part in such raids, and this passed into English via Old Italian *corsaro*, Provençal *corsari*, and Old French *corsaire*.

▶ course, hussar

**corset** see CORPSE

**cortege** see COURT

**cortex** see CORK

**cosmos** [17] *Cosmos* is a learned borrowing from Greek *kósmos*. The underlying meaning of this was 'order,' and it appears originally to have been applied to the world and the universe by Pythagoras and his school in reference to the orderliness of creation. In the mid 20th century the word provided a useful linguistic distinction between Western and Soviet activities in space, *cosmonaut* (from Russian *kosmonavt*) contrasting with *astronaut*. Somebody who is *cosmopolitan* [19] is literally a 'citizen of the world,' from Greek *kosmopolitēs*, a compound of *kósmos* and *polítēs*.

From Greek *kósmos* 'order' was derived the verb *kosmein* 'arrange, adorn.' This in turn provided the basis of the adjective *kosmētikós* 'skilled in adornment,' which passed into English as *cosmetic* [17].

▶ cosmetic, cosmopolitan

**Cossack** see CASSOCK

**cosset** [17] *Cosset* may originally have meant 'someone who lives in a cottage.' Old English had a word *cotsǣta* 'cottager,' which was formed from *cot* 'cottage' and *\*sǣt-*, an element related to the verb *sit*. This disappeared from the language after the Old English period, but not before it was adopted into Anglo-Norman as *cozet* or *coscet* (forms which appear in Domesday Book). It has been suggested that this is the same word as turns up in local dialects from the 16th century meaning 'lamb reared by hand, pet lamb' (that is, a lamb kept by a cottager rather than at liberty with the flock), and further that the notion of pampering a pet lamb gave rise to the verb *cosset*.

**cost** [13] In Latin, something that *cost* a particular price literally 'stood at or with' that price. The Latin verb *constāre* was formed from the prefix *com-* 'with' and *stāre* 'stand' (a relative of English *stand*). In Vulgar Latin this became *\*costāre*, which passed into English via Old French *coster* (the derived noun arrived first, the verb a couple of decades later). The adjective *costly* is a 14th century formation.

▶ stand, statue

**coster** [19] *Coster* is short for *costermonger*, a term dating from the 16th century. Since the 19th century, and perhaps before, it has been a general term in Britain, and particularly in London, for a street trader with a barrow or stall, but further back in time it meant

'fruiterer,' and originally, more specifically still, a 'seller of apples.' The first element, *coster*, was an alteration of *costard*, a word of Anglo-Norman origin for a type of large apple. This was derived from *coste* 'rib' (a descendant of Latin *costa*, source of English *coast*), and the costard was apparently so called because of its prominent 'ribs.' (*Monger* 'dealer' [OE], now used in English only in compounds, comes from a prehistoric Germanic *\*manggōjan*, a borrowing from Latin *mangō* 'dealer.')

▶ coast

**costive** see CONSTIPATION

**costume** [18] Ultimately, *costume* and *custom* are the same word. Both come from Latin *consuētūdō* 'custom.' But whereas *custom* was an early borrowing, from Old French, *costume* took a lengthier and more circuitous route via Italian *costume* 'custom, fashion, dress' and French *costume*. In the early 18th century the word referred to the custom or fashion of a particular period as it related to the representation of the clothes, furniture, etc of that period in art. In the 19th century this passed into 'mode of dress appropriate to a particular time or place,' and thence (completing a semantic development rather similar to that of *habit*) into simply 'garments, outfit.'

▶ custom

**coterie** [18] In Old French, *coterie* was a term for an association of peasant tenants under the feudal system. It was probably derived from an unrecorded *\*cote* 'hut.' This would have been borrowed from Middle Low German *kote*, a relative of English *cote* and *cot*. In French the word gradually broadened out in meaning to 'group of people sharing a common interest,' the sense in which English borrowed it in the mid-18th century.

**cottage** [14] The Old English words for a small house or hut were *cot* and *cote*, both of which survive – just: *cot* as an archaic term for 'cottage' and *cote* in *dovecote* and *sheepcote*. (*Cot* 'child's bed' [17], incidentally, is of Hindi origin.) They both derive ultimately from a Germanic base *\*kut-*. Then, probably in the 12th century, one or both of them seem to have been taken up by the language of the gentry, Anglo-Norman, and had the suffix *-age* added, giving *\*cotage*, which was eventually adopted by English as *cottage*. Originally this simply denoted any small humble country dwelling; it was not until the mid-18th century that it began to acquire modern connotations of tweeness.

▶ cot, cote

**cotton** [14] As with knowledge of the plant, its name *cotton* came to Europe from the Middle East. It originated in Arabic *qutn*, which passed via Spanish into the other languages of Europe. English acquired it via Old French *coton*. The verbal idiom *cotton (on) to* 'come to understand' developed in the 20th century from an earlier 'harmonize, agree.' This in turn has been traced back to a still earlier 'prosper,' which seems to have originated in the 16th century with the notion of the successful raising of the nap on cotton cloth.

**couch grass**   see QUICK

**cough**   [14]   Although it is largely disguised by the modern English pronunciation, *cough* is of onomatopoeic origin. It came from a prehistoric Germanic base *\*kokh-* (the *kh* pronounced not unlike the *ch* of *loch*), which imitated the sound of coughing. This has no recorded Old English descendant (although one probably existed, *\*cohhian*), and first appears in the language as Middle English *coughen*.

**could**   [16]   *Could* began life as *cūthe*, the past tense of Old English *cunnan* 'can.' By Middle English times this had become *couthe*, and in the 14th century it developed to *coude* under the influence of the standard past tense ending *-(e)de*. The *l* was introduced in the 16th century, to bring *coude* into line with *would* and *should*.

▶ kith, uncouth

**coulter**   see CUTLASS

**council**   [12]   Etymologically, a *council* is a body that has been 'called together' or 'summoned.' Latin *concilium* meant 'assembly, meeting'; it was formed from the prefix *com-* 'together' and *calāre* 'call, summon.' It passed into English via Anglo-Norman *cuncile*. It has no direct etymological connection with *counsel*, but the two are so similar that their meanings have tended to merge at various points down the centuries.

Latin *concilium* also formed the basis of the verb *conciliāre*, which originally meant 'bring together, unite.' Its metaphorical sense 'make more friendly, win over' is preserved in English *conciliate* [16].

▶ conciliate

**counsel**   see CONSULT

**count**   There are two distinct words *count* in English. *Count* 'enumerate' [14] comes ultimately from Latin *computāre* 'calculate' (source of English *compute*). It came into English from Old French *conter*, which had, via the notion of 'adding up and rendering an account,' developed the sense 'tell a story' (preserved in English in the derivatives *account* and *recount*). The derivative *counter* [14] began life as medieval Latin *computātōrium* 'place of accounts,' and entered English via Anglo-Norman *counteour*. Its modern sense 'surface for transactions in a shop' does not seem to have become firmly established until the early 19th century, although it was applied to similar objects in banks from the late 17th century.

The noble title *count* [16] comes via Old French *conte* from Latin *comes*, which originally meant 'companion, attendant' (it was a compound noun, formed from the

prefix *com-* 'with' and *īre* 'go,' and so its underlying etymological meaning is 'one who goes with another'). In the Roman empire it was used for the governor of a province, and in Anglo-Norman it was used to translate English *earl*. It has never been used as an English title, but the feminine form *countess* was adopted for the wife of an earl in the 12th century (and *viscount* was borrowed from Anglo-Norman *viscounte* in the 14th century). The Latin derivative *comitātus* was originally a collective noun denoting a 'group of companions,' but with the development of meaning in *comes* it came to mean first 'office of a governor' and latterly 'area controlled by a governor.' In England, this area was the 'shire,' and so *county* [14], acquired via Anglo-Norman *counte*, came to be a synonym for 'shire.' Another descendant of Latin *comes* is *concomitant* [17], from the present participle of late Latin *concomitārī*.

▶ account, compute, putative, recount / concomitant, county

**countenance**   [13]   A person's *countenance* has nothing to do with computation. Etymologically, it is how they 'contain' themselves, or conduct themselves, and the word itself is a parallel construction with *continence*. It was borrowed from Old French *contenance* (a derivative of the verb *contenir* 'contain'), which meant 'behaviour,' 'demeanour,' or 'calmness' as well as 'contents,' and originally had this somewhat abstract sense in English. It was not until the 14th century that the meaning began to develop through 'facial expression' to the now familiar 'face' (traces of the original sense survive in such expressions as 'put someone out of countenance,' meaning to make them lose their cool).

▶ contain, continence

**counter**   see COUNT

**counterpane**   see QUILT

**country**   [13]   Etymologically, the meaning of *country* is virtually 'surroundings.' It originated in medieval Latin *contrātus* 'lying on the opposite side,' an adjective formed from the preposition *contrā* 'against, opposite.' This was used in the phrase *terra contrāta* 'land opposite or before one, spread out around one,' and soon broke free to act as a noun in its own right. In Old French it became *cuntree*, the form in which it was borrowed into English. Its original notion of 'area of land' had quickly become narrowed down to 'district controlled or occupied by a particular people,' hence 'nation,' but its use for 'rural areas as opposed to cities' does not seem to have developed until the 16th century. The compound *countryside* originated in Scotland and northern England, probably in the 17th century.

**county**   see COUNT

**coupé**   [19]   *Coupé* is the past participle of the French verb *couper* 'cut,' and it was originally applied in the early 19th century to a type of four-wheeled covered carriage (in full a *carrosse coupé* 'cut-off carriage'). The notion behind the term is a truncated version of an earlier type of coach, known as a berlin, achieved by removing the rear seat. The first record of its application to closed two-door cars comes in 1908. The French verb *couper* is a derivative of the noun *coup* 'blow' (itself borrowed into English in the 18th century), which in turn came from medieval Latin *colpus* (ultimate source of English *coppice*, which etymologically denotes the 'cutting down' of trees). Earlier in time the word can be traced back via Latin *colaphus* to Greek *kólaphos* 'blow, punch.' A related word is *coupon*, borrowed from French in the 19th century.

▶ coppice, copse, coup

**couple** [13] The notion underlying *couple* is of 'joining.' The noun came into English via Old French from Latin *cōpula* 'tie, connection.' This was a compound noun formed from the prefix *com-*'together' and the verb *apere* 'fasten' (source of English *apt, adapt, adept*, and *inept*). Derived from it was the verb *cōpulāre*, source of English *copulate* [17].

▶ adapt, adept, apt, copulate, inept

**courage** [13] Modern English uses *heart* as a metaphor for 'innermost feelings or passions,' but this is nothing new. Vulgar Latin took the Latin word *cor* 'heart' and derived from it *\*corāticum*, a noun with just this sense. Borrowed into English via Old French *corage*, it was used from earliest times for a wide range of such passions, including 'anger' or 'lust,' and it was not until the early 17th century that it became narrowed down in application to 'bravery.'

▶ cordial

**courier**   see CURRENT

**course** [13] Etymologically, *course* denotes 'running.' It comes via Old French *cours* from Latin *cursus*, a derivative of the verb *currere* 'run' (from which English gets *current* and a wide range of other words, from *courier* to *occur*). Its earliest meaning in English was 'onward movement in a particular direction,' but over the centuries it has developed a network of additional senses. From the same Latin base *curs-* are *concourse* [14], *cursory* [17] (from Latin *cursōrius*), *discourse* [14] (and the related *discursive* [16]), *excursion* [16], *incursion* [15], *precursor* [16], and *recourse* [14]. The derived noun *courser* [13] is a doublet of *corsair*.

▶ corsair, courier, current, discourse, excursion, occur

**court** [12] Latin *cohors* designated an 'enclosed yard' (it was formed from the prefix *com-* 'with' and an element *hort-* which also appears in English *horticulture*). By extension it came to stand for those assembled in such a yard – a crowd of attendants or company of soldiers; hence the meaning of *cohort* familiar today. But both in its original sense and as 'retinue' the word took another and rather more disguised path into Eng-

lish. In late Latin the accusative form *cohortem* had already become *cortem*, and this passed into English via Old French *cort* and Anglo-Norman *curt*. It retains the underlying notion of 'area enclosed by walls or buildings' (now reinforced in the tautological compound *courtyard* [16]), but it seems that an early association of Old French *cort* with Latin *curia* 'sovereign's assembly' and 'legal tribunal' has contributed two of the word's commonest meanings in modern English.

The Italian version of the word is *corte*. From this was derived the verb *corteggiare* 'attend court, pay honour,' which produced the noun *corteggio*, borrowed into English via French as *cortège* [17]. Other derivatives include *courtesy* [13], from Old French *cortesie* (of which *curtsey* [16] is a specialized use) and *courtesan* [16], via French *courtisane* from Italian *cortigiana*.

▶ cohort, courtesy, curtsey, horticulture

**cousin** [13] The word *cousin* is etymologically related to *sister*. It comes via Old French *cosin* from Latin *consobrīnus*, which meant literally 'child of one's mother's sister' – that is, 'cousin on one's mother's side' (*consobrīnus* was a compound noun formed from the prefix *com-* 'together' and *sobrīnus* 'maternal cousin,' a derivative of *soror* 'sister' and relative of English *sister*). By the time it entered English, it had already broadened out in meaning to cover paternal as well as maternal cousins, and indeed in the Middle Ages it was applied more generally still to any relative other than one's parents or brother and sister (probably through association with Latin *consanguineus* 'blood relative').

▶ sister

**couvade**   see INCUBATE

**cove** [OE] Old English *cofa* meant 'small room,' as used for sleeping in or as a storeroom. It was descended from Germanic *\*kubon*, which was probably also the ultimate ancestor of *cubbyhole* [19] (the superficially similar *cubicle* is not related). In the late Old English period this seems to have developed in northern and Scottish dialects to 'small hollow place in coastal rocks, cave,' and hence (although not, apparently, until as late as the 16th century) to 'small bay.' (The other *cove* [16], a dated slang term for 'chap,' may come from Romany *kova* 'thing, person.')

▶ cubbyhole

**coven**   see CONVENT

**covenant** [13] The notion of 'agreement' in *covenant* comes originally from a literal 'coming together.' It was borrowed from Old French *covenant*, a noun use of the present participle of the verb *covenir* 'agree,' which was descended from Latin *convenire* 'come together' (source also of English *convene, convenient, convention, convent*, and *coven*). (Modern French has restored the *n*, giving *convenir*.)

▶ convenient, convent, convention, coven, venue

**cover** [13] *Cover* comes ultimately from Latin *cooperīre*, a compound verb formed from the intensive prefix *com-* 'completely' and *operīre* 'cover' (a relative of *aperīre* 'open,' from which English gets *aperient*). It passed into English via Old French *cuvrir* or *covrir*. Derivatives include *coverlet* [13] (in which the final element represents not the diminutive suffix but French *lit* 'bed,' the word being a borrowing from Anglo-Norman *covrelit*, literally 'bed-cover') and *kerchief* (literally 'head-cover'), as in *handkerchief*.

▸ aperient, discover

**covet** [13] *Covetousness* and *cupidity* are very closely related, etymologically as well as semantically. *Covet* comes via Old French *coveitier* from Vulgar Latin *cupiditāre*, a verb derived from the Latin noun *cupiditās* (from which English gets *cupidity*). Its ultimate source is the Latin verb *cupere* 'desire.'

▸ cupidity

**covey** see INCUBATE

**cow** English has two completely distinct words *cow*. The commoner, 'female of cattle' [OE], is a word of very ancient ancestry. It goes back via West and North Germanic *\*kōuz* to a hypothetical Indo-European *\*gwōus*, which was also the source of Latin *bōs* (from which English gets *bovine*, *beef*, and *bugle*, not to mention *Bovril*). In modern English its plural is *cows*, but Old English *cū* had an anomalous plural, *cȳ*, which in the remodelled form *kine* survived dialectally into the 20th century. The other *cow*, 'intimidate, daunt' [17], probably comes from Old Norse *kúga* 'oppress.'

▸ beef, bovine, bugle

**coward** [13] Etymologically, a *coward* seems to be 'someone who runs away with his tail between his legs.' It comes from Old French *cuard*, which was based on *\*cōda*, the Vulgar Latin descendant of Latin *cauda* 'tail.' (The apparently similar *cower* [13] is no relation, coming from Middle Low German *\*kūren* 'lie in wait.')

**cowslip** [OE] Old English *cūslyppe* literally meant 'cow dung' (a variant *cūsloppe*, which survived dialectally into the 20th century as *cowslop*, suggests that its second element is related to *slop* and *sloppy*). The name presumably came from the plant's growing in pastures where cows commonly graze, and perhaps even from some perceived symbiosis with cow-pats.

**coxswain** [15] A coxswain was originally a servant, or *swain*, whose job was to steer a ship's boat, or *cock* (*cock* comes from Old French *coque*, which was probably a descendant via late Latin *caudica* 'canoe' of Latin *caudex* 'treetrunk,' and *swain* is a borrowing from Old Norse *sveinn* 'boy, servant'). The abbreviation *cox* seems to have developed in the 19th century.

**coy** [14] Essentially, *coy* is the same word as *quiet*, and 'quiet' is what it meant when it first came into

English (it soon developed to 'shyly reserved,' and the sense 'quiet' died out in the 17th century). Its ultimate source was Latin *quiētus*, but whereas in the case of *quiet* this passed directly through Old French, *coy* came via the more circuitous route of Vulgar Latin *\*quētus*, which produced early Old French *quei*, and later *coi*, the source of the English word.

▸ quiet

**crab** *Crab* the crustacean [OE] and *crab* the apple [14] may be two distinct words. The word for the sea creature has several continental relatives (such as German *krebs* and Dutch *krabbe*) which show it to have been of Germanic origin, and some of them, such as Old Norse *krafla* 'scratch' and Old High German *krapho* 'hook,' suggest that the crab may have received its name on account of its claws. The origins of *crab* the fruit are not so clear. Some would claim that it is simply a metaphorical extension of the animal *crab*, from a perceived connection between the proverbial perversity or cantankerousness of the crustacean (compare *crabbed*) and the sourness of the apple, but others have proposed a connection with Swedish dialect *skrabba* 'wild apple,' noting that a form *scrab* was current in Scottish English from at least the 16th century.

▸ crayfish

**crabbed** [13] Because of their tendency to deploy their pincers at the slightest provocation, and also perhaps because of their sidelong method of locomotion, crabs seem always to have had a reputation for being short-tempered and perverse. Hence the creation of the adjective *crabbed*, which literally means 'like a crab.' Its meaning has subsequently been influenced by *crab* the apple, famous for its sourness. (The semantically similar *crabby* is a 16th-century formation.)

**crack** [OE] Old English had the verb *cracian* 'make a sudden sharp noise,' but English did not acquire the noun *crack* until the 14th century. Both are of Germanic origin (modern German has the related *krachen*, for instance, and Dutch has *kraken*), and the verb's hypothetical ancestor can be reconstructed as *\*krakojan*. The notion of 'sudden sharp noise' is semantically primary (presumably it was originally onomatopoeic), and the prevalent modern sense 'fissure' arises from the connection between the noise of something breaking and the resultant line of fracture.

▸ crock

**craft** [OE] The original notion contained in the word *craft* is that of 'strength' (that is the meaning of its relatives in other Germanic languages, such as German and Swedish *kraft*). Old English *cræft* had that sense too (it had largely died out by the 16th century), but it had also developed some other meanings, which are not shared by its Germanic cognates: 'skill,' for example (in a bad as well as a good sense, whence *crafty*) and 'trade' or 'profession.' Much later in origin, however

(17th-century in fact), is the sense 'ship.' It is not clear how this developed, but it may have been a shortening of some such expression as 'vessel of the sailor's craft' (that is, 'trade'). The word's Germanic stem was *krab- or *kraf-, which some have seen also as the source of crave [OE].

▶ crave

**cram**   [OE] Prehistoric Germanic had a base *kram-, *krem-which denoted 'compression' or 'bending.' Among its descendants were Old Norse kremja 'squeeze, pinch,' German krumm 'crooked' (source of English crumhorn [17], a curved Renaissance musical instrument), and Old English crammian (ancestor of cram), which meant 'press something into something else, stuff.' An extension of the base with p (*kramp-, *kremp-) produced Middle Low German and Middle Dutch krampe 'bent,' one or other of which was borrowed by Old French as crampe and passed on to English as cramp [14] (crampon [15] comes from a related source). Other products of the Germanic base were Old English crumb 'crooked,' a possible ancestor of crumpet, and perhaps crimp [17]. A non-nasalized version of the base produced Germanic *krappon 'hook,' source of grape and grapnel.

▶ crampon, crimp, crumhorn, crumpet, grape, grapnel

**crane**   [OE] Crane is a widespread Indo-European bird-name: related forms such as Latin grūs, Greek géranos (source of English geranium, also known as crane's-bill, from the long pointed 'beak' of its fruit), and Welsh garan point to a prehistoric Indo-European base *ger-, possibly imitative of the bird's raucous call. The resemblance of a crane lowering its long neck to feed or drink to the operation of a lifting apparatus with a long jib led to the application of crane to the latter in the 14th century (French grue and German kran show a similar semantic development). Cranberry [17] is a borrowing (originally American) of German cranbeere, literally 'craneberry,' so named from the stamens, which supposedly resemble a beak.

▶ cranberry, geranium, pedigree

**crank**   [OE] There appears to be a link between the words crank, cringe, and crinkle. They share the meaning element 'bending' or 'curling up' (which later developed metaphorically into 'becoming weak or sick,' as in the related German krank 'ill'), and probably all came from a prehistoric Germanic base *krank-. In Old English the word crank appeared only in the compound crancstæf, the name for a type of implement used by weavers; it is not recorded in isolation until the mid-15th century, when it appears in a Latin-English dictionary as a translation of Latin haustrum 'winch.' The adjective cranky [18] is no doubt related, but quite how closely is not clear. It may derive from an obsolete thieves' slang term crank meaning 'person feigning

sickness to gain money,' which may have connections with German krank. Modern English crank 'cranky person' is a back-formation from the adjective, coined in American English in the 19th century.

▶ cringe, crinkle

**cranny**   see CRENELLATE

**crash**   [14] Crash suddenly appeared from nowhere in Middle English (meaning 'break in pieces noisily'), with apparently no relatives in other Germanic languages. Its form suggests that it originated in imitation of the sound of noisy breaking, but it has been further suggested that it may be a blend of craze and dash. The financial or business sense of the noun, 'sudden collapse,' is first recorded in the early 19th century in the writings of Samuel Taylor Coleridge.

**crass**   see GREASE

**crate**   [17] Crate is usually connected with Latin crātis 'hurdle,' making it a relative of grate, griddle, and grill(e), and indeed an isolated example of crate in the early 16th century, which unequivocally means 'hurdle,' certainly must come from that source. However, the main body of evidence for crate begins in the late 17th century, and its meaning, 'large case or box,' is sufficiently far from 'hurdle' to raise doubts about its origins. Another possible source that has been suggested is Dutch krat 'basket.'

▶ grate, griddle, grill

**crater**   [17] Greek krateر meant 'bowl,' or more specifically 'mixing bowl': it was a derivative of the base *kerā-, which also produced the verb kerannýnai 'mix.' (Crater or krater is still used in English as a technical term for the bowl or jar used by the ancient Greeks for mixing wine and water in.) Borrowed into Latin as crātēr, it came to be used metaphorically for the bowl-shaped depression at the mouth of a volcano. Its acquisition by English is first recorded in Samuel Purchas's Pilgrimage 1619.

**cravat**   [17] The fashion for wearing scarves round the neck started in France in the 1650s. It was inspired by Croatian mercenaries employed there at that time, who regularly sported linen neckbands of that type. The Croats were called in French Cravates (the name comes via German Krabate from the original Serbo-Croat term Hrvat), and so their neckerchiefs came to be known as cravates too. English was quick to adopt the term.

**crave**   see CRAFT

**craven**   [13] Craven originally meant simply 'defeated,' and only gradually came to have the pejorative sense 'cowardly.' It probably came from Old French cravante 'defeated,' the past participle of the verb cravanter, which in turn came via Vulgar Latin *crepantāre from Latin crepāre; this meant 'creak, rattle, crack' (hence the English technical term *crepitation* [17]) but also secondarily 'burst' or 'break.'

▶ crepitation, crevice, decrepit

**crayfish** [14] The *crayfish* is related etymologically as well as biologically to the crab. The Old High German word for 'crab' was *krebiz* (source of modern German *krebs*). This was borrowed into Old French as *crevice* (modern French has preserved the variant form *écrevisse*), and transmitted to Middle English as *crevis*. Association of the final syllable with *fish* led by the 16th century to its transformation to *crayfish* (a variant Middle English form *cravis* became *crawfish*).

▶ crab, crawfish

**crazy** [16] *Crazy* originally meant literally 'cracked' (a sense preserved in the related *crazed*). This soon came to be extended metaphorically to 'frail, ill' (as in Shakespeare's 'some better place, fitter for sickness and crazy age,' *1 Henry VI*), and thence to 'mentally unbalanced.' It was derived from the verb *craze* [14], which was probably borrowed from an unrecorded Old Norse verb *\*krasa* 'shatter' (likely source, too, of French *écraser* 'crush, smash').

**cream** [14] *Cream* seems to have come from two distinct late Latin sources: *crānum* 'cream,' which may be of Gaulish origin, and *chrisma* 'ointment' (from which English gets *chrism* [OE]). These two were probably blended together to produce Old French *cresme* or *craime*, immediate source of the English word. (Modern French *crème* was borrowed into English in the 19th century.)

▶ chrism

**crease** [15] *Crease* and *crest* are ultimately the same word. The ridges produced by creasing cloth were regarded as similar to ridges or crests, and so the word *crease* (often *creast* in late Middle English) came to be applied to them. The loss of the final *-t* may have been due to the mistaken analysis of *creast* or *crest* as the past form of a verb.

▶ crest

**creature** [13] *Creature* and *creator*, both 13th-century borrowings from Old French, predate the introduction of the verb *create* into English by about a hundred years. This was a verbal use of an earlier adjective *create*, borrowed directly from Latin *creātus*, the past participle of *creāre* 'produce' (which in turn may have been a causative derivative of the verb *crēscere* 'grow,' source of English *crescent*). Another descendant of Latin *creāre* was Portuguese *criar* 'breed, nurse,' the probable ancestor of English *creole* [17].

▶ create, creole, crescent, croissant, increase

**creed** [OE] *Creed* was the first of a wide range of English words borrowed from Latin *crēdere* 'believe.' Others include *credible* [14] (from Latin *crēdibilis*), *credence* [14] (from Old French *credence*), *credential* [16] (from medieval Latin *crēdentiālis*), *credit* [16]

(from French *crédit*), and *credulous* [16] (from Latin *crēdulus*). Also ultimately from the same source are *grant* and *miscreant* [14] (from Old French *mescreant*, the present participle of *mescroire* 'disbelieve').

▶ credible, credit, grant, miscreant

**creek** [13] Now firmly associated with watercourses, the original connotations of *creek* seem to have been of 'narrow and secluded bendiness.' It appears to have been borrowed from Old Norse *kriki* 'nook,' which some have speculated may be related to Old Norse *krókr* 'hook' (source of English *crook*). *Creek* remains strictly a word for narrow waterways, a reminder of its beginnings.

▶ crook

**creep** [OE] *Creep* is an ancient verb, which has been traced back to Indo-European *\*greub-*. This was the source also of Dutch *kriupen* and Swedish *krypa* 'creep,' and of Lithuanian *grubineti* 'stumble,' and links have been suggested with English *cripple*. The related Indo-European *\*greug-* produced German *kriechen* 'creep.'

▶ cripple

**cremate** see HEARTH

**crenellate** [19] The 19th century seems a surprisingly late date for English to have acquired a term so closely associated with medieval battlements, but it is a little misleading. For essentially the same word entered the language in the 13th century as *kernel*. Both come ultimately from late Latin *crēna* 'notch' (probable source also of English *cranny* [15]). In Vulgar Latin this developed the diminutive form *\*crenellus*, metathesized in medieval Latin as *kernellus*.

▶ cranny

**creole** see CREATURE

**creosote** [19] The term *creosote* was coined as German *kreosot* in the early 1830s. Of creosote's various properties, the one perhaps most valued in the early days after its discovery was that of being antiseptic. Hence the name *kreosot*, which was intended to mean 'flesh-preserver.' The first element, *kreo-*, is a derivative of Greek *kréas* 'flesh'; this also produced English *pancreas*, and is a descendant of an Indo-European base which was also the source of English *crude, cruel*, and *raw*. The second comes from Greek *sōtér* 'saviour, preserver,' a derivative of Greek *sōs*.

▶ crude, cruel, pancreas, raw

**crepitation** see CREVICE

**crescent** [14] *Crescent* is one of a wide range of words (including *create, crescendo, concrete, crew, acretion, croissant, increase*, and *recruit*) bequeathed to English by the Latin verb *crēscere* 'grow.' In the case of *crescent*, it came in the form of the present participial stem *crēscent-*, which passed into English via Old French *creissant* and Anglo-Norman *cressaunt*. Its use in the Latin phrase *luna crescens* 'waxing moon' led later to its application to the shape of the new moon, hence the modern meaning of *crescent*. The modern French form *croissant* has given English the term for a crescent-shaped puff-pastry roll [19], so named allegedly from its original manufacture following the defeat of the Turkish beseigers of Budapest in 1686, whose Muslim symbol was the crescent.

▶ acretion, create, creature, croissant, increase, recruit

**cresset**   see GREASE

**crest**   [14]   The original etymological meaning of *crest* appears to have been 'tuft of hair.' It comes via Old French *creste* from Latin *crista* 'tuft, plume,' which may be related to Latin *crīnis* 'hair' (source of the English biological term *crinite* 'hairy' [16]). If so, *crest* belongs to the same word family as *crinoline*. The notion of *crest* as a 'surmounting ridge' is a secondary semantic development, which may have given rise to the word *crease*.

▶ crease

**cretin**   [18]   In the Swiss-French dialect of the high Alps the term *creitin* or *crestin* (their version of *christian*) was applied to people suffering from mental handicap and stunted growth – the notion being to emphasize that despite their abnormalities, such people were nevertheless as much human beings as any other 'Christian.' The word was adopted (via French *crétin*) as a clinical term for someone suffering from dwarfism and mental retardation as a result of a congenital thyroid deficiency, and was subsequently broadened out, towards the end of the 19th century, as a general disparaging term for a 'fool.'

▶ Christian

**crevice**   [14]   Rather like *crack*, the word *crevice* began with the notion of the sharp noise of breaking and gradually developed to denote the fissure caused by such a break. It comes ultimately from the Latin verb *crepāre* 'creak, rattle, crack' (source of English *crepitation* [17] and *decrepit*, and probably also of *craven*), which passed into Old French as *crever* 'burst, split.' From this was derived the noun *crevace*, borrowed into Middle English as *crevace* or *crevisse*. In modern French it developed into *crevasse*, which English reborrowed in the 19th century.

▶ craven, crepitation, crevasse, decrepit

**crib**   [OE]   *Crib* is a Germanic word, with relatives today in German (*krippe*) and Dutch (*kribbe*). In Old English it meant 'manger,' and not until the 17th century did it develop its familiar present-day sense 'child's bed.' An intermediate stage, now lost, was 'basket,' which appears to have given rise to its 18th-century use as a thieves' slang term for 'pilfer'; this in turn is probably the source of the modern colloquial sense 'plagiarize.' Vulgar Latin borrowed Old High German

*kripja* as *\*creppia*, from which modern French gets *crèche* (acquired by English in the 19th century).

▶ creche

**cricket**   English has two completely unrelated words *cricket*. The name of the small grasshopper-like insect [14] comes from Old French *criquet*, a derivative of the verb *criquer* 'click, creak,' which no doubt originated as an imitation of the sound itself. The origins of the name of the game *cricket* [16] have never been satisfactorily explained. One explanation often advanced is that it comes from Old French *criquet* 'stick,' or its possible source, Flemish *krick*, although it is not clear whether the original reference may have been to the stick at which the ball was aimed (the forerunner of the modern stumps) or to the stick, or bat, used to hit the ball. Another possible candidate is Flemish *krick-stoel*, a long low stool with a shape reminiscent of the early types of wicket.

**crime**   [14]   *Crime* is one of a wide range of English words (including *certain, crisis, critic, decree, discern, discrete, discriminate, excrement, riddle* 'seive,' *secret*, and *secretary*) which come ultimately from or are related to the Greek verb *krīnein* 'decide.' This was a relative of Latin *cernere* 'decide,' from whose root evolved the noun *crīmen* 'judgment, accusation, illegal act.' This passed via Old French *crimne* (later *crime*) into English, where traces of the original meaning 'accusation' survived until the 17th century.

▶ certain, critic, decree, discriminate, excrement, secret

**crimp**   see CRAM

**crimson**   [14]   The colour term *crimson* comes ultimately from the name of a small scale insect, the kermes, from whose dried bodies a red dyestuff is obtained. *Kermes* comes from Arabic *qirmaz*, which in turn was derived from Sanskrit *krmi-ja* '(dye) produced by a worm,' a compound formed from *krmi-* 'worm' and *ja-* 'produced, born.' From *qirmaz* was derived Arabic *qirmazī* 'red colour,' which passed into English via metathesized Old Spanish *cremesin*. The medieval Latin version *carmesīnum* is thought to have been the source of English *carmine* [18], through blending with *minium* 'red lead' (whence English *miniature*).

▶ carmine

**cringe**   [13]   Like *crank*, *cringe* appears to come ultimately from a prehistoric Germanic base *\*krank-* whose original meaning was 'bend' or 'curl up.' This produced an Old English verb *crincan* 'fall in battle, yield' (the association of 'curling up' and 'dying' is obvious), probable ancestor of modern English *crinkle* [14]. *Crincan* does not itself seem to be the source of *cringe*, which until the 16th century was usually spelled *crenge* or *crench*; to explain these *e-* forms it is necessary to postulate *\*crencean*, an unrecorded Old English causative derivative of *crincan*, meaning 'cause to curl up.'

▶ crank, crinkle

**crinite** see CREST

**crinoline** [19] The reason crinolines are called *crinolines* is that they were originally made from a stiff fabric woven from horsehair and linen thread. Italian *crino* 'horsehair' (from Latin *crīnus* 'hair,' a possible relative of English *crest*) and *lino* 'flax' (from Latin *līnum*, source of English *linen*) were combined to produce *crinolino*, which passed into English via French *crinoline*.

▶ crest, linen

**cripple** [OE] The etymological sense of *cripple* appears to be 'someone who creeps along,' for it probably goes back ultimately to the same Indo-European base, *greub-*, as *creep*. The word is widespread in the Germanic languages: German has *kruppel*, Dutch *kreupel*, and Norwegian *krypel*.

▶ creep

**crisp** [OE] Historically, *crisp* means 'curly.' It was borrowed into Old English from Latin *crispus* 'curled' (which was also the source of French *crêpe*, acquired by English as *crape* in the 17th century and then reborrowed in the original French form in the 19th century). The reason for the emergence of the word's modern sense 'brittle,' which happened in the early 16th century, is not clear; it may simply be that the sound of the word suggested brittleness.

▶ crape, crêpe

**crisscross** [16] *Crisscross* is an alteration of *Christscrosse*, a term used from the 16th to 18th centuries for the figure of a cross (not specifically, as the name would seem to suggest, the crucifix). Gradually the original signification of the first syllable came to be lost, and the term fell into the pattern of reduplicated words (such as *flipflop*, *singsong*) in which a syllable is repeated with variation of the vowel. This may have contributed to the broadening of the word's meaning to 'pattern of repeated crossings,' which happened in the 19th century.

**critic** [16] *Critic* and *crisis* both come ultimately from the Greek verb *krínein* 'decide' (a relative of Latin *cernere* 'decide,' which produced English *certain*, *crime*, *decree*, *discern*, *discrete*, *discriminate*, *excrement*, *riddle* 'seive,' *secret*, and *secretary*). The Greek derived noun *krísis* 'judgment' was used by the physicians Hippocrates and Galen for the 'turning point of a disease.' It passed as a medical term via Latin *crisis* into English in the 15th century, where it was not used in the .more general modern sense until the 17th century. The Greek derived noun *kritḗs* 'judge' produced in turn *kritikós* 'able to make judgments'; this came to be used as a noun, 'one who makes judgments,' which passed via Latin *criticus* into English. Another descendant of

*kritḗs* was Greek *kritḗrion* 'standard for making a judgment,' borrowed directly into English in the 17th century as *criterion*.

▶ certain, crime, crisis, criterion, discern, discriminate, excrement, secret

**crock** English has two words *crock*. The one meaning 'earthenware pot' [OE] is now almost never heard on its own, except perhaps in the phrase 'crock of gold,' but it is familiar from its derivative *crockery* [18]. Its immediate antecedents appear to be Germanic (Dutch, for instance, has the related *kruik*), but cognate forms appear in other Indo-European languages, including Welsh *crochan* and Greek *krōssós*. *Cruet* [13] comes from Anglo-Norman *cruet*, a diminutive frorm of Old French *crue* 'pot,' which was borrowed from Old Saxon *krūka*, a relative of English *crock*. *Crock* 'decrepit person, car, etc' [15] is earliest encountered (in Scottish English) in the sense 'old ewe.' The connotation of being 'broken-down,' and the existence of near synonyms such as Dutch *krak*, Flemish *krake*, and Swedish *krake*, all meaning 'worn-out old horse,' suggest some kind of link with the word *crack*.

▶ crockery, cruet

**crocodile** [13] The crocodile gets its name from its habit of basking in the sun on sandbanks or on the shores of rivers. The word means literally 'pebble-worm,' and it was coined in Greek from the nouns *krókē* 'pebbles' and *drilos* 'worm.' The resulting Greek compound *krokódrīlos* has never actually been found, for it lost its second *r*, giving *krokódīlos*, and this *r* reappeared and disappeared capriciously during the word's journey through Latin and Old French to English. Middle English had it – the 13th century form was *cokodrille* – but in the 16th century the modern *r*-less form took over, based on Latin *crocodīlus*.

**croissant** see CRESCENT

**crone** [14] *Crone* has a rather macabre history. Essentially it is the same word as *carrion*. It began life in Latin *carō* 'flesh,' which had a Vulgar Latin derivative *carōnia* 'carcass.' In Old Northern French this became *carogne*, which was applied metaphorically to a withered old woman (English *carrion* comes from the Anglo-Norman form *caroine*). Middle Dutch borrowed the word as *croonje*, applying it additionally to old ewes, and passed it on to English.

▶ carrion

**crony** [17] *Crony* originated as a piece of Cambridge university slang. Originally written *chrony*, it was based on Greek *khrónios* 'long-lasting,' a derivative of *khrónos* 'time' (source of English *chronicle*, *chronology*, *chronic*, etc), and seems to have been intended to mean 'friend of long-standing,' or perhaps 'contemporary.' The first recorded reference to it is in the diary of Samuel Pepys, a Cambridge man: 'Jack

Cole, my old school-fellow . . . who was a great chrony of mine,' 30 May 1665.

▶ chronic, chronicle, chronology

**crook** [12]   A *crook* 'criminal' is almost literally a 'bent' person. The underlying meaning of the word is 'bend, curve, hook,' as can be seen in other applications such as 'shepherd's staff with a crooked end,' and particularly in the derivative *crooked* [13]. *Crook* was borrowed into English from Old Norse *krókr* 'hook, corner.' Old French also acquired the Old Norse word, as *croc*, and passed it on to English in *crochet, croquet, crotchet,* and *encroach*; and the derived verbs *crocher* and *crochier* produced respectively a new noun *croche* 'hook,' source of English *crotch* [16], and the English verb *crouch* [14]. Moreover, Old French also had *croce*, resulting from an earlier borrowing of the word's ultimate West and North Germanic base *\*kruk-* introduced into Vulgar Latin as *\*croccus*, and this was eventually to form the basis of English *crosier* [14] and perhaps *lacrosse* [18].

▶ croquet, crosier, crotch, crotchet, crouch, encroach, lacrosse

**crop** [OE]   Old English *cropp* meant 'bird's craw' and 'rounded head of a plant,' and it was presumably the latter that gave rise to the word's most familiar modern sense, 'cultivated plant produce,' at some time in the 13th century. Its relatives in other Germanic languages, including German *kropf* and Dutch *krop*, are used for 'bird's craw' but also for various bodily swellings in the throat and elsewhere, indicating the word's underlying meaning is 'round mass, lump.' Its Germanic ancestor, *\*kruppō*, was borrowed into Vulgar Latin as *\*cruppa*, which made its way via Old French into English as *croup* 'horse's (round) rump' [13], and as the derivative *crupper* [13]. *Croupier* [18] is based on French *croupe*, having originally meant 'person who rides on the rump, behind the saddle.' The Germanic base *\*krup-* 'round mass, lump' is also the ancestor of English *group*.

▶ croup, croupier, crupper, group

**croquet** [19]   Old Norse *krókr* 'hook' (source of English *crook*) was borrowed into Old French as *croc*. This formed the basis of a diminutive, *crochet*, literally 'little hook,' which has passed into English in various guises over the centuries. First to arrive was *crotchet* [14], applied to musical notes from their hooked shape. *Crocket* 'curling ornamental device' followed in the 17th century, via the Old Northern French variant *croquet*. *Crochet* itself, in the 'knitting' sense, arrived in the 19th century. And in the mid 19th century *croquet*, apparently a dialectal variant of French *crochet*, was applied to the lawn game with balls and mallets newly introduced from Ireland to Britain. Old French *croc* was also the ancestor of *encroach*.

▶ crook, crotchet, encroach, lacrosse

**crosier**   see CROOK

**cross** [OE]   When the Anglo-Saxons embraced Christianity they acquired *cros*, in the first instance from Old Irish *cross*. The word's ultimate source was Latin *crux*, which may have been of Phoenician origin (although some have connected it with Latin *curvus* 'bent'). (*Crux* itself was borrowed into English in the 18th century.) The cross's shape formed the basis of the adjectival, adverbial, and verbal uses of the word, and also of *across*. (The notion of 'crossing' also lies behind *cruise* [17] a probable borrowing from the Dutch *kruisen* 'cross.') Derivatives of the Latin word include *crucial* [18], *crucible* [15], *crucifix* [13] (from late Latin *crucifixus*, literally 'fixed to a cross'), *crusade* [16], and *excruciate* [16].

▶ crucial, crucible, crucifix, crusade, excruciate

**crotch**   see CROOK
**crotchet**   see CROQUET
**crouch**   see CROOK
**croup**   see CROP
**croupier**   see CROP

**crow** [OE]   The verb *crow* began in prehistoric West Germanic as an imitation of the harsh call of the cockerel. Its relatives still survive in other Germanic languages, including German *krähen* and Dutch *kraaien*. Early examples of birds other than cockerels being described as 'crowing' are comparatively rare, but nevertheless there seems no doubt that the verb formed the basis of the name given to birds of the genus *Corvus* [OE]. The *crowbar* [19] was so named from the resemblance of its splayed end to a crow's foot.

**crowd** [OE]   The notion underlying *crowd* is of 'pushing' or 'pressing' (a semantic element shared by *throng* and of course by the now obsolete use of *press* for 'crowd,' and echoed in such current expressions as 'there's quite a crush in here'). The Old English verb *crūdan* meant simply 'press,' and of its relatives Middle Dutch *crūden* meant 'press, push' and Middle High German *kroten* meant 'oppress.' Old English also had a noun *croda* 'crowd,' but this does not seem to be the direct ancestor of the modern English noun, which does not appear until as late as the 16th century, as a derivative of the verb.

**crown** [12]   Crowns appear to have been named essentially from their circular shape. The word's ultimate source, Greek *korónē*, simply meant 'something curved' (it came from the adjective *korōnos* 'curved,' which was a relative of Latin *curvus* 'curved'). Latin borrowed it as *corōna* 'circular garland,' and passed it on via Old French *corone* and Anglo-Norman *corune* to English. Latin also derived a verb from it, *corōnāre*, which ultimately became the English verb *crown* and also, of course, formed the basis of English *coronation* [14]. Other English descendants of Latin *corōna* (which

itself became an English word in the 16th century) are
the two diminutives *coronet* [15] and *corolla* [17]
(source of *corollary*), *coroner* [14] (originally an 'officer of the crown'), and *coronary*. The use of *crown* for
certain coins (based of course on their being stamped
with the figure of a crown) dates in English from the
14th century; it is also reflected in such coin names as
Swedish *krona* and Danish and Norwegian *krone*.
► corollary, coronation, coroner, coronet, curve

**crucial**    see CROSS

**crucible**    see CROSS

**crucifix**    see CROSS

**cruel**    [13]    Aptly, *cruelty* and *crudeness* are
closely linked etymologically. *Cruel* comes via Old
French *cruel* from Latin *crūdēlis*, a relative of Latin
*crūdus* (which actually meant 'cruel' as well as 'raw'
and 'bloody'). Both come ultimately from an Indo-European base which also produced English *raw*, Greek
*kréas* 'flesh' (whence English *creosote* and *pancreas*),
and Old Slavic *kruvi* 'blood.' (*Crude* is a 14th-century
borrowing direct from Latin.)
► creosote, crude, pancreas, raw

**cruet**    see CROCK

**cruise**    see CROSS

**cruller**    see CURL

**crumb**    [OE]    Relatives of *crumb* are fairly widespread in the Germanic languages – German has
*krume*, for example, and Dutch *kruim* – and it is represented in some non-Germanic Indo-European languages, such as Greek *grūméa* and even Albanian
*grime*. As these forms indicate, the *b* is not original (the
Old English word was *cruma*); it first appeared in the
16th century, but *crum* remained an accepted spelling
well into the 19th century. The derivative *crumble* appeared in the 16th century.
► crumble

**crumhorn**    see CRAM

**crumpet**    [17]    An isolated late 14th-century instance of the phrase *crompid cake* suggests that etymologically a *crumpet* may be literally a 'curled-up' cake,
*crompid* perhaps being related to Old English *crumb*
'crooked.' This was one of a wide range of closely related words descended from the Germanic base *\*kram-* or
*\*krem-*, denoting 'pressure' (see CRAM). The colloquial
application of the word to 'women considered as sexually desirable' seems to date from the 1930s.
► cram

**crupper**    see CROP

**crusade**    see CROSS

**crush**    [14]    The emergence of *crush* is something
of a mystery. English borrowed it from Old French
*croissir*, but it is not clear where Old French got it from.
Some consider it to be of Romance origin, postulating a
hypothetical Vulgar Latin *\*cruscīre* to account for it,

but others suggest that Old French may have borrowed
it from Germanic, pointing to the similarity of Middle
Low German *krossen* 'crush.'

**crust**    [14]    Latin *crusta* meant 'hard outer covering, shell' (it is related to a number of words, including
ultimately *crystal*, denoting a hard surface caused by
freezing). Old French acquired it as *crouste* (the modern
French form *croûte* formed the basis of *croûton*, borrowed into English in the early 19th century), and
passed it on to Middle English as *cruste*. *Crusta* formed
the basis of the modern Latin adjective *crustāceus* 'having a shell,' applied in the early 19th century to the *crus-
tacea* or *crustaceans*. And a *custard* was originally a
kind of pie enclosed in a *crust*.
► croûton, crystal, custard

**cry**    [13]    *Cry* comes via Old French *crier* from Latin *quirītāre*, which, according to the Roman etymologist Marcus Terentius Varo, meant originally 'call for
the help of the Quirites.' This was a term for those who
held the rank of Roman citizen; it is of uncertain origin,
variously explained as coming from an Italic word for
'lance' and as denoting those who lived in the Sabine
town of Cures. The more banal truth, however, is that
the Latin verb was probably of imitative origin.

**crypt**    [18]    The Greek adjective *kruptós* meant
'hidden.' From it was derived *kruptikós*, which passed
into English via late Latin *crypticus* as *cryptic* [17]. The
feminine form of the original Greek adjective, *krúptē*,
was used as a noun meaning literally 'hidden place,'
thus 'underground chamber, vault'; English acquired it
via Latin *crypta*. From the same ultimate source comes
*apocrypha* [14], literally 'books of hidden - that is, unknown - authorship.'
► apocrypha

**crystal**    [OE]    The prehistoric Indo-Eurpean base
*\*kru-*produced several words denoting 'hard outer surface,' including English *crust*, Old High German *hrosa*
'crust,' and Old Norse *hrúthr* 'crust.' In some cases
they reflect a hardening caused by freezing: Old High
German *hrosa*, for example, also meant 'ice,' and
Greek *krúos* meant 'frost.' From this was derived *krus-
taímein* 'freeze,' which in turn formed the basis of *krús-
tallos* 'ice.' When Old English first acquired the word,
via Latin *crystallum* and Old French *cristal*, it still
meant 'ice,' a sense which survived until the 16th century, although losing ground all the time to the metaphorical extension 'clear mineral.'
► crust

**cubbyhole**    see COVE

**cube**    [16]    Greek *kúbos* meant literally 'six-sided
solid figure,' a sense handed down to English via Latin
*cubus*. Apart from more obvious metaphorical applications, such as 'dice,' the Greek word was used for the
internal cavity of the pelvis, a semantic feature which
links it with its possible relative, English *hip*. The fine-

art term *cubism* was introduced to English in 1911 from French, where it seems to have been coined in 1908 by an anonymous member of the Hanging Committee of the Salon des Indépendents. The story goes that when a painting by Georges Braque was being shown to the committee, he exclaimed 'Encore des Cubes! Assez de cubisme!'

**cubicle**   see CONCUBINE

**cuckold**   [13]   *Cuckold* is a derivative of *cuckoo*, the cuckoo's invasion of other birds' nests perhaps being viewed as analogous to the stealing of a wife's affections by another man. It is not an original English coinage, but was borrowed from an unrecorded Anglo-Norman *cucuald*, a variant of Old French *cucuault*, which in turn was formed from *cucu* 'cuckoo' and the pejorative suffix -*ault*.
▶cuckoo

**cuckoo**   [13]   So distinctive is the cuckoo's call that it is not always clear whether the names for the bird in various languages, based on the call, owe their similarity to borrowing or coincidence – Dutch, for instance, has *koekoek*, Russian *kukúshka*, Latin *cuculus*, and Greek *kókkūx*. In the case of English *cuckoo*, it seems to have been borrowed from Old French *cucu*, which was of imitative origin. Its first appearance is in the famous *Cuckoo song* of the late 13th century ('Sumer is icumen in, lhude sing, cuccu!'), where it replaced the native Middle English word *yeke* (from Old English *gēac*, also of imitative origin).

**cucumber**   [14]   English acquired this word as *cucumer*, by direct borrowing from Latin *cucumer*, which may originally have been a word of some pre-Italic Mediterranean language. The form spelled with a *b* did not appear until the 15th century. It seems to have been a blend of Middle English *cucumer* and Old French *coucombre*, which itself ultimately derived from Latin *cucumer*. Spellings based on the Old French form led to a pronunciation of the first syllable as 'cow,' which persisted until the early 19th century.

**cud**   [OE]   The etymological meaning of *cud* appears to be 'glutinous substance.' It is related to a wide range of Indo-European words in this general sense area, including Sanskrit *játu* 'gum,' German *kitt* 'putty,' and Swedish *kåda* 'resin,' and the first syllable of Latin *bitūmen* (source of English *bitumen* [15]) is generally referred to the same source. *Quid* 'piece of tobacco for chewing' is a variant of *cud*.
▶bitumen, quid

**cue**   *Cue* has several meanings in English, and it is not clear whether they can all be considered to be the same word. In the case of 'pigtail' and 'billiard stick,' both of which appeared in the 18th century, *cue* is clearly just a variant spelling of *queue*, but although *cue* 'actor's prompt' [16] has been referred by some to the same source (on the grounds that it represents the 'tail' –

from French *queue* 'tail' – of the previous actor's speech) there is no direct evidence for this. Another suggestion is that it represents *qu*, an abbreviation of Latin *quando* 'when' which was written in actor's scripts to remind them when to come in.
▶queue

**cuirass**   [15]   A *cuirass* 'breastplate' is literally, and was originally, a piece of body armour made of leather. The word comes, via French *cuirasse*, from Vulgar Latin *\*coriācia*, a nominal use of the Latin adjective *coriāceus* 'made of leather.' This was a derivative of *corium* 'leather,' which came ultimately from the Indo-Eurpean base *\*ker-* or *\*sker-* 'cut' (source also of English *shear*), the underlying notion being of removing the animal's hide with a knife. Other descendants of Latin *corium* include French *cuir* and Spanish *cuero*, both meaning 'leather.'
▶curtail, shear, shirt, short, skirt

**culinary**   see KILN

**cull**   [15]   Ultimately, *cull* is the same word as *collect*. It comes via Old French *cuillir* from Latin *colligere* 'gather together,' whose past participial stem *collēct-* formed the original basis of English *collect*. The Latin verb was a compound formed from the prefix *com-* 'together' and *legere* 'gather' (source also of English *elect, neglect, select*, etc).
▶collect, elect, lecture, legend, neglect, select

**culprit**   [17]   *Culprit* appears to be a fossilized survival of the mixture of English and French once used in English courts. The usually accepted account of its origin is that it is a lexicalization of an exchange in court between the accused and the prosecutor. If the prisoner pleaded 'not guilty' to the charge read out against him, the prosecutor would have countered, in Law French, with 'Culpable: prit d'averrer . . . ,' literally 'Guilty: ready to prove.' (English *culpable* [14] comes ultimately from Latin *culpa* 'guilt,' and *prit* is the Anglo-Norman form of what in modern French has become *prêt* 'ready,' from Latin *praestus* – source of English *presto*). The theory is that this would have been noted down by those recording the proceedings in abbreviated form as *cul. prit*, which eventually came to be apprehended as a term used for addressing the accused.
▶culpable, presto

**cult**   [17]   The Indo-European base *\*quel-,\*quol-* denoted primarily 'move around, turn' (it is the source of English *cycle* and *wheel*). By metaphorical extension it came to signify 'be busy,' which later branched out in two semantic directions: 'inhabiting a place' and 'making a wild place suitable for crops.' These are both channelled into Latin *colere*, which meant 'inhabit,' 'cultivate,' and also 'worship.' The notion of 'inhabiting' is reflected in its descendant *colony*, but its past participial stem *cult-* has bequeathed us other aspects of its meaning. 'Worship' is represented by *cult*, acquired via French *culte* or directly from Latin *cultus*. 'Developing the land' appears in *cultivate* [17], from the medieval Latin derivative *cultivāre*, and by metaphorical extension in *culture* [15], from French *culture*, which originally meant 'piece of tilled land.'

▶ colony, cultivate, culture, cycle, wheel

**cunning**   [13]   Cunning did not always have its present-day negative connotations. At first it was a term of approval, meaning 'learned.' It is connected in some way to the verb *can*, which originally meant 'know,' although it is not altogether clear whether it is a direct use of the present participle of the English verb, or whether it was borrowed from the related Old Norse *kunnandi*, present participle of *kunna* 'know.' Either way, it is a parallel formation to *canny* [16]. The sense 'skilfully deceitful' developed towards the end of the 16th century.

▶ canny

**cunt**   [13]   The first known reference to the word *cunt* is in an early medieval Oxford street-name: *Gropecuntlane* (it was afterwards renamed *Magpie lane*). This was around 1230, and from later in the same century there are records of a street of the same name (presumably the haunt of prostitutes) in London, probably around the area of modern Cheapside. York, too, had its *Grapcunt lane* in the 15th century. *Cunt* has a number of Germanic cognates, including Old Norse *kunta*, Middle Dutch *kunte*, and possibly Middle High German *kotze* 'prostitute,' which point to a prehistoric Germanic ancestor *kunton* 'female genitals,' but beyond that its origins are not known. A link has been suggested with Latin *cuneus* 'wedge.'

**cup**   [OE]   Cup is a member of a large Indo-European family of words denoting broadly 'round container' that go back ultimately to the bases *kaup- (source of English *head*) and *keup-. This produced Greek *kúpellon* 'drinking vessel,' English *hive*, and Latin *cūpa* 'barrel,' source of English *coop* [13] (via Middle Dutch *kūpe*) and *cooper* 'barrel-maker' [14] (from a derivative of Middle Dutch *kūpe*). A post-classical by-form of *cūpa* was *cuppa*, from which came German *kopf* 'head' and English *cup*.

▶ coop, cupola

**cupboard**   [14]   A *cupboard* was originally exactly that: a 'board,' or table, on which cups (and other pieces of crockery or plate) were placed for display. Essentially, it was what we would now call a *sideboard*. The modern sense, 'recess with doors and shelves,' did not develop until the 16th century. (An earlier, and now largely superseded, term for 'cupboard' was *press* [14]. *Cabinet* is roughly contemporary with *cupboard* in its modern sense, and *closet* developed this meaning in the 17th century.)

**cupidity**   [15]   The Latin verb *cupere* meant 'desire' (related forms such as Sanskrit *kup*- 'become agitated,' Church Slavonic *kypeti* 'boil,' and Latvian *kūpēt* 'boil, steam' suggest that its underlying notion is 'agitation'). One of its derivatives was the noun *cupīdō* 'desire,' which was used as the name of the Roman god of love – hence English *cupid* [14]. Another was the adjective *cupidus* 'desirous,' which produced the further noun *cupiditās*, source, perhaps via French, of English *cupidity*, and also ultimately of English *covet*. *Concupiscence* [14] also comes from Latin *cupere*.

▶ concupiscence, covet

**curate**   see CURE

**curb**   [15]   Ultimately, *curb* and *curve* are the same word. Latin *curvāre* 'bend' passed into Old French as *courber*, which Middle English borrowed as *courbe* 'bend.' This seems to have formed the basis of a noun *courbe* or *curb*, which was originally used for a strap to restrain a horse, the underlying meaning perhaps being that pulling on the strap 'bent' the horse's neck, thereby restraining it. The sense 'enclosing framework' began to emerge in the early 16th century, perhaps mainly through the influence of the French noun *courbe*, which meant 'curved piece of timber, iron, etc used in building.' Its chief modern descendant is 'pavement edge,' a 19th-century development, which has generally been spelled *kerb* in British English.

▶ circle, crown, curve

**curd**   [14]   Curd began life as *crud*, a word which has survived in its own right. In the 15th century it underwent a process known as metathesis, by which the sounds *r* and *u* became transposed, producing *curd*. A derivative of this, dating from the 16th century, is *curdle*. The word's ultimate ancestry is not known, although some consider that Gaelic *gruth* may be related.

**cure**   [13]   The Latin noun *cūra* 'care' has fathered a wide range of English words. On their introduction to English, via Old French, both the noun and the verb *cure* denoted 'looking after,' but it was not long before the specific sense 'medical care' led to 'successful medical care' – that is, 'healing' (the Latin verb *cūrāre* could mean 'cure' too, but this sense seems not to have survived into Old French). The notion of 'looking after' now scarcely survives in *cure* itself, but it is preserved in the derived nouns *curate* [14] (and its French version *curé* [17]), who looks after souls, and *curator* [14]. The Latin adjective *cūriōsus* originally meant 'careful,' a sense preserved through Old French *curios* into English *curious* [14] but defunct since the 18th century. The secondary sense 'inquisitive' developed in Latin, but it was not until the word reached Old French that the meaning 'interesting' emerged. *Curio* [19] is an abbreviation of *curiosity* [14], probably modelled on Italian nouns of the same form. *Curette* [18] and its derivative *curettage* [19] were both formed from the French verb *curer*, in the sense 'clean.'

Other English descendants of Latin *cūra* include *scour*, *secure*, and *sinecure*.

▶ curate, curious, scour, secure, sinecure

**curfew** [13] *Curfew* means literally 'cover-fire.' It was introduced into English via Anglo-Norman *coeverfu* from Old French *covrefeu*, which was formed from *covrir* 'cover' and *feu* 'fire' (*feu* was a descendant of Latin *focus* 'hearth,' which has given English *focus*, *foyer*, *fuel*, and *fusillade*). The notion underlying the word is that of a signal given at a particular time in the evening to extinguish all fires in a town, camp, etc; its original purpose seems to have been to prevent accidental fires breaking out at night.

▶ cover, focus, foyer, fuel

**curio**  see CURE

**curious**  see CURE

**curl** [14] *Curl* seems to have been borrowed from Middle Dutch *krul* 'curly,' and indeed the original English forms of the word were *crolle* and *crulle*. The present-day form arose in the 15th century by a process known as metathesis, whereby the sounds *r* and *u* were transposed. The Middle Dutch word came from a Germanic *\*krusl-*, source also of German *kraus* 'curly.' Modern Dutch *krul*, meanwhile, has given English *cruller* 'small cake of twisted shape' [19].

▶ cruller

**curlew** [14] The name of the curlew was no doubt originally inspired by its haunting flute-like call, but it has been speculated that other forces have been at work too. The word was borrowed from Old French *courlieu*, which bears more than a passing resemblance to Old French *courliu* 'messenger' (a compound formed from *courre* 'run' and *lieu* 'place,' from Latin *locus*), and it seems quite possible that the latter may have influenced the formation of the former.

**currant** [14] Etymologically, *currants* are grapes from 'Corinth.' In the Middle Ages Corinth, in Greece, exported small dried grapes of particularly high quality, which became known in Old French as *raisins de Corinthe* 'grapes of Corinth.' This phrase passed via Anglo-Norman *raisins de corauntz* into Middle English as *raisins of coraunce*. By the 16th century, *coraunce* had come to be regarded as a plural form, and a new singular was coined from it – at first *coren*, and then in the 17th century *currant*. In the late 16th century, too, the name was transferred to fruit such as the blackcurrant and redcurrant, under the mistaken impression that the 'dried-grape' currant was made from them.

**current** [13] *Current* literally means 'running.' It comes from Old French *corant*, the present participle of *courre* 'run,' which in turn was descended from Latin *currere* 'run.' This has been traced back to a prehistoric root denoting 'swift movement,' which probably also produced *car*, *career*, *carry*, and *charge*. The Latin verb itself has a wide range of descendants in English, from the obvious *courier* [16] to the more heavily disguised *corridor* [16] (originally literally 'a run'), *occur* and *succour*. For the English offspring of its past participle *cursus* see COURSE. The sense 'of the present time' (first recorded in the 17th century) comes from the notion of 'running in time' or 'being in progress.'

▶ car, carry, charge, corridor, courier, course, occur, succour

**curry** Of the two English words *curry*, the older, 'groom a horse' [13], is now almost forgotten except in the compound *currycomb* and the phrase *curry favour*. It comes, via Old French *correier*, from Vulgar Latin *\*conrēdāre* 'arrange, prepare, get ready,' which seems to have been an adaptation and partial translation of a prehistoric Germanic verb *\*garǣthjan*, a derivative of the base which produced English *ready*. The expression *curry favour* is a partial translation of Old French *estriller favel* or *torcher favel*, literally 'groom a chestnut horse,' which, for reasons that are not known, was used as a metaphor for hypocritical behaviour; the word *favel*, unfamiliar to English speakers, was replaced with the semantically appropriate *favour*.

*Curry* 'spiced dish' [16] was borrowed from Tamil *kari* 'sauce.'

▶ ready

**cursary**  see COURSE

**curse** [OE] *Curse* first appeared in late Old English (in the early 11th century) as *curs*. It has no known linguistic relatives, and it is not clear where it comes from. Perhaps the most plausible suggestion is that it was borrowed from Old French *curuz* 'anger' (which probably came from the verb *\*corruptiāre*, a Vulgar Latin derivative of Latin *corrumpere* 'destroy' – source of English *corrupt*), and that *curse* itself therefore originally meant 'anger, wrath.' The colloquial alteration *cuss* dates from the 18th century.

▶ corrupt, rupture

**curtail** [16] The now defunct English noun *curtal* meant 'horse with a docked tail.' It was borrowed in the 16th century from French *courtault*, a derivative of the adjective *court* 'short.' Like English *curt* [17] this came from Latin *curtus* 'cut off, shortened,' which in common with English *short* and *shear*, can be traced back to an Indo-European base *\*ker-* or *\*sker-*'cut.' In the late 16th century the noun was converted into a verb, originally meaning literally 'dock a horse,' and the close semantic link with 'tails' led to its alteration to *curtail*.

▶ cuirass, curt, shear, shirt, short, skirt

**curtain** [13] Latin *cortīna* meant 'round vessel, cauldron,' but in the 4th-century Vulgate we find it being used to translate Greek *aulaía* 'curtain.' The reason for this considerable semantic leap seems to have been a link perceived to exist between Greek *aulaía*, a derivative of *aulē* 'court,' and Latin *cohort-* 'court' (source of English *court*), although in fact there is no etymological connection between *cohort-* and *cortīna*. The word passed into Old French as *cortine*, and from there was acquired by English.

**curtsey**   see COURT

**curve**   [15]   *Curve* has a wide circle of relations in English. It comes from Latin *curvus* 'curved,' which had connections with Greek *kurtós* 'curved,' Greek *korōnos* 'curved' (source of English *crown*), and Greek *kírkos* 'ring, circle' (source of English *circle*). When English acquired it, it was still an adjective, and English did not convert it into a noun until the 17th century.

▶ circle, crown, curb

**cushion**   [14]   Ultimately, *cushion* and *quilt* are the same word. Both come from Latin *culcita* 'mattress, cushion,' which is related to Sanskrit *kūrcás* 'bundle,' and both reached English via rather circuitous routes. In Gallo-Roman (the descendant of Latin spoken in France from the 5th to the 9th centuries) *culcita* underwent a transformation which produced Old French *coissin* and *cussin*, which Middle English borrowed as *quisshon* and *cushin*. The complexity of forms spawned by these was quite staggering – the OED records nearly seventy spellings of the word – but by the 17th century things had settled down, with *cushion* emerging the winner.

*Cushy* [20], incidentally, is quite unrelated, being a borrowing from Hindi *khūsh* 'pleasant.'

▶ quilt

**cuspidor**   see SPIT

**custard**   [15]   A *custard* was originally a pie, which took its name from its 'crust' (Anglo-Norman *\*crustade*, the source of the word, was a derivative of Old French *crouste*, from which English got *crust*). The earliest English form was *crustade*, and intermediate spellings *crustarde* and *custade* occur. The reference in the name is to the pie's pastry shell, not to its lid, for it had none: it was an open pie, of meat or fruit, filled up with stock or milk. This liquid was often thickened with eggs, and by around 1600 the term had moved across to name a dish in its own right made of eggs beaten into milk and cooked.

▶ crust

**custom**   [12]   *Custom* comes ultimately from Latin *consuēscere*, a compound verb formed from the intensive prefix *com-* and *suēscere* 'become accustomed.' This in turn was derived from *suī*, the genitive singular of the reflexive pronoun *suus* 'oneself'; the notion underlying its formation was therefore 'that which is one's own,' a semantic element echoed in Greek *ethos* 'custom, usage, trait,' which was based ultimately on Indo-European *\*swe-* 'oneself.' From *consuēscere* was formed the Latin noun *consuētūdō* 'being accustomed' (source of the English legal noun *consuetude* 'custom' [14]). This passed into early Old French

as *\*costudne*, which developed via *\*costumne* to *custome*, the form borrowed into Middle English (English *costume* came from the same ultimate source, but via Italian *costume*). The word's original sense, 'habitual practice,' developed various secondary associations, including 'customary tax' (whence *customs duties*) and 'customary business patronage' (whence *customer*). The derivative *accustom* [15] was borrowed from Anglo-Norman *acustumer*.

▶ accustom, costume

**cut**   [13]   There is no direct evidence that Old English had the word *cut* – the Old English terms were *sceran* 'shear,' *ceorfan* 'carve,' and *hēawan* 'hew' – but many etymologists have speculated that a pre-Conquest *\*cyttan* did exist. Forms such as Norwegian *kutte* 'cut,' Swedish *kåta* 'whittle,' and Icelandic *kuta* 'cut with a knife' suggest an origin in a North Germanic base *\*kut-*.

**cutaneous**   see HIDE

**cuticle**   see HIDE

**cutlass**   [16]   Appropriate as the name sounds, *cutlass* has no etymological connection with *cut*. It comes from Old French *cutelas*, a derivative (denoting large size) of *coutel* 'knife.' This in turn goes back to Latin *cultellus*, a diminutive of *culter* 'knife, ploughshare' (source of English *coulter* [OE] and *cutler* [14], whence *cutlery* [14]).

▶ coulter, cutlery

**cutlet**   see COAST

**cuttlefish**   [11]   The *cuttlefish* probably gets its name from its resemblance to a bag when its internal shell is removed. Its earliest recorded designation is *cudele* (the compound *cuttlefish* does not appear until the 16th century), which is generally taken to be a derivative of the same base as produced *cod* 'pouch' (as in *codpiece* and *peascod*). In the 16th century the variant *scuttlefish* arose, perhaps partly with reference to the creature's swift movements.

▶ cod

**cybernetics**   [20]   *Cybernetics* was first coined in French, as *cybernétique*, in the 1830s. But then it was used literally for the 'art of governing' (it is a derivative of Greek *kubernḗtēs* 'steersman, governor,' from *kubernan* 'steer,' source of English *govern*). The English term, 'theory of control and communication processes,' is a new formation, introduced in the late 1940s by the founder of cybernetics, the US mathematician Norbert Wiener (1894–1964).

▶ govern

**cycle**   [14]   *Cycle* is one of a wide range of English words (including *pole, colony,* and *cult*) which go back ultimately to the Indo-European base *\*qwel-*, *\*qwol-*, which signified 'move around.' Its reduplicated form, *\*qweqwelo-*, produced English *wheel*, Sanskrit *cakra* 'wheel, circle' (ultimate source of the polo term *chuk-*

*ker* [19]), and Greek *kúklos* 'circle.' English acquired this via French *cycle* or late Latin *cyclus*. Its use as a cover term for bicycles, tricycles, etc (of which words in this context it is an abbreviation) dates from the late 19th century. Related forms in English include *cyclone* 'mass of rapidly circulating wind' [19] (probably a modification of Greek *kúklōma*), *cyclamen* [16] (so named from its bulbous roots), and *encyclopedia*.

▶ bicycle, chukker, colony, cult, encyclopedia, pole, wheel

**cygnet** [15]   A *cygnet* is literally a 'small swan.' The late Old French term for 'swan' was *cigne*, and this was modified with the diminutive suffix -*et*, probably in Anglo-Norman, to produce *\*cignet*, the source of the English word. *Cigne*, precursor of modern French *cygne*, strikes a familiar chord, but in fact its Latin source, *cygnus*, is a comparatively late development. The standard classical Latin word for 'swan' was *cycnus*, from Greek *kúknos*, which produced in early Old French *cisne*. A trace of it survives in Spanish *cisne* 'swan.'

**cymbal** [14]   The notion underlying *cymbal* is of a 'hollow vessel.' Greek *kúmbē* meant 'cup, bowl.' From it was derived *kúmbalon*, which passed via Latin *cymbalum* into Old French as *cimbal* 'metal plate struck to make a noise.' This did not survive much beyond the 10th century (although it may have given rise before its demise to *chime*), but the word was reborrowed via Old French *symbale* in the 14th century.

▶ chime

**cynic** [16]   Originally, the Cynics were a group of ascetic philosophers in ancient Greece. Their founder, around 400BC, was Antisthenes, a follower of Socrates. They advocated the view that virtue and self-control are the highest good and, particularly under their later leader Diogenes, came to exhibit a contempt for the frailties of their fellow human beings that is traditionally said to have earned them their name: Greek *kúon* meant 'dog' (it is related to English *hound*), and the philosophers were allegedly dubbed *kunikós* on account of their 'doglike' sneering. A more prosaic but more likely explanation of the term is that it comes from the *Kunósarge*, the gymnasium where Antisthenes taught (perhaps later influenced by *kúon*). English acquired the word via Latin *cynicus*.

# D

**dabchick**  see DEEP

**dachshund**  [19] *Dachshund* means literally 'badger-dog' in German. It was originally bred in Germany for badger-hunting, its long thin body enabling it to burrow into the animals' setts. The first known reference to it in English (in the anglicized form *dachshound*) is in a poem by Matthew Arnold of around 1881, *Poor Matthias*: 'Max, a dachshound without blot.'
▶ hound

**dado**  see DATE

**daffodil**  [16] Originally, this word was *affodil*, and referred to a plant of the lily family, the asphodel; it came from medieval Latin *affodillus*, and the reason for the change from *asph-*(or *asf-*, as it often was in medieval texts) to *aff-* is probably that the *s* in medieval manuscripts looked very like an *f*. The first evidence of its use to refer to a 'daffodil,' rather than an 'asphodel,' comes in the middle of the 16th century. It is not entirely clear where the initial *d* came from, but the likeliest explanation is that *daffodil* represents Dutch *de affodil* 'the daffodil' (the Dutch were then as now leading exponents of bulb cultivation).

**daft**  [13] *Daft* was not always a term of reproach. It originally meant 'mild, gentle,' and only in late Middle English slid to 'stupid' (in a semantic decline perhaps paralleling that of *silly*, which started off as 'happy, blessed'). Middle English *dafte* corresponds directly to an Old English *gedæfte*, whose underlying sense seems to have been 'fit, suitable' (the sense connection was apparently that mild unassuming people were considered as behaving suitably). There is no direct evidence of its use with this meaning, but Old English had a verb *gedæftan* 'make fit or ready, prepare' which, together with the Gothic verb *gedaban* 'be suitable,' points to its origin in a Germanic base *dab-* 'fit, suitable.' This ties in with the semantic development of *deft*, a variant of *daft*, which has moved from a prehistoric 'fit, suitable' to 'skilful.'
▶ deft

**dagger**  [14] *Dagger* has an uncertain history. There was a verb *dag* in Middle English, meaning 'stab,' which suggests that *dagger* may simply be 'something that stabs,' but similarity of form and sense indicates a connection too with Old French *dague* 'dagger.' This appears to have come via Old Provençal or Old Italian *daga* from a hypothetical Vulgar Latin *\*daca*, which meant literally 'Dacian knife' (from Latin *Dācus* 'Dacian'). *Dacia* was the ancient name for an area roughly corresponding to modern Rumania.

**dago**  [18] *Dago* originated in the USA as a contemptuous term for a Spanish-speaking person. It is an alteration of *Diego* (the Spanish version of *James*), a common Spanish forename, which itself was used in English in the 17th century for 'Spaniard': 'Next follows one whose lines aloft do raise Don Coriat, chief Diego of our days.' By the late 19th century the application of *dago* had broadened out to include anyone of Spanish, Portuguese, or Italian descent.
▶ James

**dahlia**  [19] The *dahlia* was named in 1791 in honour of Anders Dahl, an 18th-century Swedish botanist who discovered the plant in Mexico in 1788. The first record of the term in English is from 1804. During the 19th century it was used for a particular shade of red: 'One of the many ugly shades that are to be worn this season is dahlia,' *Pall Mall Gazette* 29 September 1892.

**dainty**  [13] In origin, *dainty* is the same word as *dignity*. The direct descendant of Latin *dignitās* in Old French was *daintie* or *deintie*, but Old French later reborrowed the word as *dignete*. It was the latter that became English *dignity*, but *daintie* took a route via Anglo-Norman *dainte* to give English *dainty*. At first it meant 'honour, esteem,' but before a century was up it had passed through 'pleasure, joy' to 'something choice, luxury.' The first record of its adjectival use comes in the 14th century, when it meant 'choice, excellent, delightful'; this soon developed to 'delicately pretty.'

▶ dignity

**dairy** [13] Etymologically, a *dairy* is a place where a female kneader of bread works. The term for such an operative in Old English was *dæge*, which came from the same Indo-European base (*\*dheigh-*) as produced *dough* and the second syllable of *lady*. In Middle English this became *deie* or *daye*, and gradually progressed in meaning through 'female servant' in general to 'female farm-servant' and 'dairy-maid,' concerned with the keeping of milk and making it into butter and cheese (the word survived into modern times in Scottish English). From it was derived *deierie* or *dayerie*, to denote the place where such a woman worked.

▶ dough, lady

**dais** [13] Ultimately, *dais* and *disc* are the same word. Both came from Latin *discus* 'quoit,' which by medieval times had come to mean 'table' (see DESK). Its Old French descendant was *deis*, which was borrowed into Middle English as *deis*. It died out in English around 1600, but it survived in Scottish English, and was revived in England by antiquarians, its spelling based on the modern French form *dais*. Historically it is a monosyllabic word, and the modern two-syllable pronunciation represents an attempt to render the unfamiliar French word.

▶ desk, disc, dish

**daisy** [OE] The Anglo-Saxons named this familiar flower *dæges ēage*, literally 'day's eye,' from the fact that some species open in daylight hours to reveal their yellow disc, and close again at dusk. (The medieval Latin name for the daisy was *solis oculus* 'sun's eye.')

▶ day, eye

**dale** [OE] Both *dale* and *dell* [OE] come ultimately from the Germanic base *\*dal-* (which also produced German *tal*, ultimate source of English *dollar*). *Dale* goes back to the Germanic derivative *\*dalam, \*dalaz*, *dell* to the derivative *\*daljō*. Cognate forms such as Old Norse *dalr* 'bow' and, outside Germanic, Greek *thólos* show that the underlying meaning of the word family is 'bend, curve.' Those members which mean 'valley' (including Gothic *dals*, which also signified 'ditch') were no doubt named from their rounded, hollowed-out shape.

▶ dell, dollar

**dam** [12] *Dam*, appropriately enough for a word related to the human control of water-courses, seems to have been borrowed from Middle Dutch *dam*. It appears to have been a fairly widespread West and East Germanic word, subsequently borrowed into North Germanic, but its ultimate source is not known.

**damage** [14] *Damage* comes from Latin *damnum* 'loss, damage' (source of English *damn*). It passed into Old French as *dam*, from which was formed the derivative *damage*. English borrowed and has preserved the Old French form, but in modern French it has become *dommage*. Besides *damn*, another English relative is *indemnity* [15], ultimately from Latin *indemnis* 'undamaged.'

▶ damn, indemnity

**damask** [14] Originally, *damask* was 'cloth from Damascus' (which was known as *Damaske* in Middle English). This Syrian city was a notable centre for export to the West in the Middle Ages, and has provided English with the *damson* [14] (originally the *damascene* plum, or plum from Damascus) and the *damask rose* [16]. In addition, the term for the method of inlaying steel known as *damascening* [19], or earlier *damaskining* [16], comes via French and Italian from the name of Damascus (where such steel was once produced).

▶ damson

**dame** [13] Latin *domina* was the feminine form of *dominus* 'lord' (see DOMINION). English acquired it via Old French *dame*, but it has also spread through the other Romance languages, including Spanish *dueña* (source of English *duenna* [17]) and Italian *donna* (whence English *prima donna*, literally 'first lady' [18]). The Vulgar Latin diminutive form of *domina* was *\*dominicella*, literally 'little lady.' This passed into Old French as *donsele*, was modified by association with *dame* to *damisele*, and acquired in the 13th century by English, in which it subsequently became *damsel* (the archaic variant *damosel* came from the 16th-century French form *damoiselle*).

▶ damsel, danger, dominate, dominion, duenna, prima donna

**damn** [13] *Damn* comes via Old French *damner* from Latin *damnāre*, a derivative of the noun *damnum*. This originally meant 'loss, harm' (it is the source of English *damage*), but the verb soon spread its application to 'pronounce judgment upon,' in both the legal and the theological sense. These meanings (reflected also in the derived *condemn*) followed the verb through Old French into English, which dropped the strict legal sense around the 16th century but has persisted with the theological one and its more profane offshoots.

▶ condemn, damage, indemnity

**damp** [14] The familiar adjectival use of *damp* as 'slightly wet' is a comparatively recent development, from the 18th century. When the word was first borrowed into English, from Middle Low German *damp*, it was a noun meaning 'vapour' (an application which survives in *fire-damp*). It comes ultimately from a Germanic base *\*thump-*. The first line of semantic development taken by the word in English was of a 'noxious exhalation' (including gas or even smoke, not just vapour), and this is reflected in its earliest adjectival use, in the late 16th century, meaning 'dazed,' as if affected by such harmful fumes: 'with looks downcast and damp,' John Milton, *Paradise Lost* 1667. Another contemporary sense was 'noxious.' But the 17th century saw the noun used more and more for specifically wet turbidity: 'mist,' or simply 'moisture.' And this formed the basis of the present-day adjectival sense.

**damson**   see DAMASK

**dance**   [13]   The history of the word *dance*, now widespread amongst European languages (French *dansir*, Spanish *danzar*, Italian *danzare*, German *tanzen*, Swedish *dansa*, Russian *tancovat'*), is disappointingly obscure. All these forms, including the English word, stem from an original Old French *danser*. This developed from an assumed Vulgar Latin *\*dansāre*, which may have been borrowed from a Frankish *\*dintjan* (Frisian *dintje* 'tremble' has been compared).

**dandelion**   [13]   *Dandelion* means literally 'lion's tooth.' It was borrowed from French *dent-de-lion*, which itself was a translation of medieval Latin *dēns leōnis*. It was presumably so called from the toothlike points of its leaves (although some have speculated that the name comes from the long taproot). The plant has a variety of local dialectal names, many of them (*clock*, *farmer's clocks*, *schoolboy's clock*, *tell-time*, *time flower*) reflecting the traditional practice of telling the time by blowing off all the plant's tufted seeds (the number of puffs needed indicates the hour). *Piss-a-bed*, like its French counterpart *pissenlit*, betrays the plant's diuretic properties.
▶ dentist, lion

**dandruff**   [16]   The word *dandruff* (or *dandriff*, as it commonly used to be) first appears, out of the blue, in the mid-16th century, with no known relatives. Its first element, *dand-*, remains utterly obscure, but the second part may have been borrowed from Old Norse *hrufa* or Middle Low German *rōve*, both meaning 'scab' (Middle English had a word *roufe* 'scab, scurf,' and modern Dutch has *roof*).

**dandy**   [18]   The first record of the word *dandy* comes in Scottish border ballads of the late 18th century, but by the early 19th century it had become a buzz term in fashionable London society. It is generally explained as being an abbreviation of *jack-a-dandy* 'affected man,' a word first recorded in the 17th century which apparently incorporates *Dandy*, a colloquial Scottish abbreviation of the name *Andrew*. The word's adjectival use started in the 19th century in close semantic relationship to the noun – 'affectedly trim or neat' – but American English has rehabilitated it to 'excellent' in the 20th century.
▶ Andrew

**danger**   [13]   Etymologically, *danger* is a parallel formation to *dominion*. It comes ultimately from Vulgar Latin *\*domniārium* 'power or sway of a lord, dominion, jurisdiction,' a derivative of Latin *dominus* 'lord, master.' English acquired the word via Old French *dangier* and Anglo-Norman *daunger*, retaining the word's original sense until the 17th century ('You stand within his [Shylock's] danger, do you not?' says Portia to Antonio in Shakespeare's *Merchant of Venice*). But things had been happening to its meaning in Old French, particularly in the phrase *estre en dangier* 'be in danger.' The notions of being *in someone's danger* (that is, 'in his power, at his mercy') and of being *in danger of something* (that is, 'liable to something unpleasant, such as loss or punishment' – a sense preserved in the 1611 translation of the Sermon on the Mount: 'Whosoever is angry with his brother without a cause shall be in danger of the judgment,' Matthew 5:22) led directly to the sense 'peril,' acquired by English in the 14th century.
▶ dame, dome, dominate, dominion, dungeon

**dapper**   [15]   Modern English *dapper* connotes neatness, alertness, and liveliness, but its etymological significance as revealed by distant relatives such as Old High German *tapfar* 'heavy,' Old Prussian *debīkan* 'large,' and Old Slavic *debelu* 'thick,' is 'heavy.' The notion of 'weightiness' spread to 'firmness, endurance in battle,' and hence 'courage' (German *tapfer* and Dutch *dapper* both mean 'brave'). English acquired the word, with an apparently ironical change of meaning, from Middle Dutch or Middle Low German *dapper* 'heavy, stout, bold.'

**dapple**   [14]   *Dapple* is a puzzling word. It is presumably derived from or linked in some way to its contemporary *dapple-grey* (although this has never been proved), which has formal and semantic links with several colour terms in other Germanic languages (such as Old Norse *apalgrár*, German *apfelgrau*, and Dutch *appelgrauw*) that are surely too strong to be coincidental. They all mean literally 'apple-grey.' Add to this such forms as French *gris-pommelé*, again literally 'apple-grey,' and Russian *yablokakh* 'dappled,' a derivative of *yábloko* 'apple,' and the inference becomes even more compelling – that *dappled* is related in some way as yet unexplained to *apple*. Many of the above terms were applied specifically to grey horses marked with round blotches, and so perhaps the word had its beginnings in a perceived resemblance in shape between such markings and apples.

**dare**   [OE]   *Dare* used to be a widespread Germanic verb, with relatives in Old High German (*giturran*) and Gothic (*gadaursan*), but today it survives only in English (the similar-looking Danish *turde* and Swedish *töras* are probably not related). It comes via Germanic *\*ders-* from an Indo-European *\*dhers-*, which also produced Greek *thrasús* 'bold' and Old Slavic *druzate* 'be bold.' In Old English it was a conjugationally complex verb, with anomalous present and past forms, but most of its oddities have now been ironed out: the past form *durst* is now on its last legs, and only the 3rd present singular form remains unusual, especially in negative contexts and questions: *she daren't* rather than *she dares not*.

**dark**    [OE]    *Dark* comes ultimately from a Germanic base *\*derk-*, *\*dark-*, which also produced Old High German *tarchanjan* 'hide' and Middle Low German *dork* 'place where dirt collects' (outside Germanic, Lithuanian *dargus* has been compared). In Old English the word usually denoted absence of light, particularly with reference to 'night'; the application to colours did not develop until the 16th century.

**darn**    English has two distinct words *darn*. The verb 'mend with stitches' [16] may come ultimately from an Old English verb *diernan* 'hide,' a derivative of the adjective *dierne* 'secret,' which in turn was descended from West Germanic *\*darnjaz*. *Darn* the mild curse [18], which arose in American English, is usually taken to be a euphemistic alteration of *damn*, although it has been suggested, not very plausibly, that it too came from *dern*, the modern English descendant of Old English *dierne*, in the sense 'dark, dreary.'

**dash**    [13]    *Dash* is probably of Scandinavian origin – Danish *daske* 'beat' has been compared – but whether it was a borrowing or a home-grown word, it was no doubt formed in imitation of rapid impulsive violent movement. Its original sense in English was 'hit, smash' (now rather eclipsed, put preserved in such phrases as 'dash someone's hopes'). 'Move quickly and violently' followed in the 14th century, and the noun sense 'stroke of a pen' in the 16th century (this probably gave rise to the use of the word as a euphemism for *damned*, from the replacement of that word in print with a dash).

**date**    *Date* 'time of an event' and *date* 'fruit' are distinct words in English, and perhaps unexpectedly the latter [13] entered the language a century before the former. It came via Old French *date* and Latin *dactylus* from Greek *dáktulos*, which originally meant literally 'finger' or 'toe.' The term was originally applied from the supposed resemblance of a date to a little brown finger or toe. *Date* 'time' [14] was acquired from Old French *date*, a descendant of medieval Latin *data*, which represented a nominal use of the feminine form of Latin *datus*, the past participle of the verb *dare* 'give.' It originated in such phrases as *data Romae* 'given at Rome,' the ancient Roman way of dating letters. (*Data* 'information' [17], on the other hand, is the plural of the neuter form of the past participle, *datum*.) Among the wide range of other English words descended from Latin *dare* (which can be traced back ultimately

to an Indo-European base *\*dō-*) are *antidote* [15] (etymologically 'what is given against something'), *condone* [19], *dado* [17] (a borrowing from Italian, 'cube'), *dative* [15], *donation* [15], *dice, dowry* and *endow* (both ultimately from Latin *dōs* 'dowry,' a relative of *dare*), *edit*, and *pardon* [13].

▶ pterodactyl / antidote, condone, data, dative, dice, donation, edit, endow, pardon

**daub**    [14]    The ultimate source of *daub*, Latin *dēalbāre*, meant literally 'whiten.' It was derived from the adjective *albus* 'white,' ancestor of English *albino* and *album*. It developed the specific meaning 'cover with some white substance, such as whitewash or plaster,' and by the time it reached English, via Old French *dauber*, it referred to the applying of a coating of mortar, plaster, etc to a wall. This was generally a messy process (particularly in the smearing of a mixture of mud and dung on to a framework of laths to produce wattle-and-daub walls), and led in due course to the broader sense 'apply crudely.'

▶ albino, album, auburn

**daughter**    [OE]    *Daughter* is an ancient word which goes back to Indo-European *\*dhughətēr*. Apart from Latin and the Romance languages (with *fīlia* and its descendants) and Celtic (Welsh has *merch*), all the Indo-European languages have inherited this form: Greek had *thugátēr*, Armenian *dustr*, Old Slavic *dusti* (whence Russian *doch'*), and Sanskrit *duhitar-*. The prehistoric Germanic word was *\*dohtēr*, which produced Gothic *dauhtar*, German *tochter*, Dutch *dochter*, Swedish *dotter*, Danish *datter*, and of course English *daughter*. It is not known where the Indo-European word ultimately came from, although correspondencies have been suggested with Sanskrit *duh-* 'milk' and Greek *teúkho* 'make.'

**daunt**    see TAME

**dauphin**    [15]    The eldest sons of the French king were from 1349–1830 designated by a title which is essentially the same word as English *dolphin*. It was originally applied to the lords of the Viennois, an area in the southeast of France, whose coat of arms incorporated three dolphins. After the Viennois province of Dauphiné was sold by Charles of Valois to the French crown in 1343, the king gave it to his eldest son, and from then on all eldest sons inherited it along with the title *dauphin*.

▶ dolphin

**dawn**    [15]    *Dawn* was originally formed from *day*. The Old English word *dæg* 'day' formed the basis of *dagung*, literally 'daying,' a word coined to designate the emergence of day from night. In Middle English this became *daiing* or *dawyng*, which in the 13th to 14th centuries evolved to *dai(e)ning* or *dawenyng*, on the model of some such Scandinavian form as Old

Swedish *daghning*. Then in the 15th century the *-ing* ending was dropped to produce *dawn*.

▶day

**day**  [OE]  *Day* and its Germanic relatives (German *tag*, Dutch, Danish, and Swedish *dag*, and Gothic *dags*) come from a prehistoric Germanic *\*dagaz*. It seems likely that the ultimate source of this was the Indo-European base *\*dhegh-*, which also produced Sanskrit *dah-* 'burn' and *nidāgha-* 'heat, summer,' and that the underlying etymological meaning of *day* is thus 'time when the sun is hot.'

▶dawn

**dead**  [OE]  *Dead* is part of a Germanic family of adjectives (including also German *tot*, Dutch *dood*, Swedish *död*, and Gothic *dauths*) which come from a prehistoric Germanic adjective *\*dauthaz*. This in turn came from an earlier *\*dhautós*, which was the past participle of the verb base that eventually produced English *die* (thus etymologically *dead* is in effect a precursor of *died*). The word's ultimate source was Indo-European *\*dheu-*, which some have linked with Greek *thánatos* 'dead.'

▶die

**deaf**  [OE]  Ultimately, *deaf* and *dumb* come from the same source, and moreover they are related to a Greek word for 'blind.' The common denominator 'sensory or mental impairment' goes back to an Indo-European base *\*dheubh-*, which denoted 'confusion, stupefaction, dizziness.' It produced Greek *tuphlós* 'blind'; English *dumb*; and a prehistoric Germanic adjective *\*daubaz* 'dull, stupefied, slow.' Many of the modern descendants of *\*daubaz* retain this general sense – Danish *doven* means 'lazy' – but English has specialized it to 'dull in hearing.' *Duffer* may ultimately be derived from Old Norse *daufr* 'deaf' in which the sense 'dull, stupid' is preserved.

▶duffer, dumb

**deal**  English has two words *deal*. The one which now means chiefly 'distribute' goes back to Old English *dǣl* 'part' and its verbal derivative *dǣlan* 'divide.' The noun (together with its relatives German *teil*, Dutch *deel*, and Gothic *dails*) goes back to a prehistoric Germanic *\*dailiz*, a derivative of the base *\*dail-*, which also produced English *dole* and *ordeal*. The ultimate source of this base is not known. *Deal* '(plank of) pine' [14] was borrowed from Middle Dutch or Middle Low German *dele*.

▶dole, ordeal

**dean**  [14]  Etymologically, a *dean* is someone in charge of a group of ten people. That was the meaning of its ancestor, Greek *dekānós*, a word formed from *déka* 'ten.' This eventually came to designate specifically someone in charge of ten monks, and this sense passed via late Latin *decānus*, Old French *deien*, and Anglo-Norman *deen* into English as the 'head of a ca-

thedral.' The modern French descendant of *deien*, *doyen*, was reborrowed into English in the 17th century.

▶doyen

**dear**  [OE]  *Dear* is one of the English language's more semantically stable words. By the 11th century it had already developed its two major present-day senses, 'much-loved' and 'expensive,' which are shared by its Germanic relative, German *teuer* (Dutch has differentiated *dier* 'much loved' from *duur* 'expensive'). All these words go back to a prehistoric West and North Germanic *\*deurjaz*, whose ultimate origin is not known. In the 13th century an abstract noun, *dearth*, was derived from the adjective. It seems likely that this originally meant 'expensiveness' (although instances of this sense, which has since disappeared, are not recorded before the late 15th century). This developed to 'period when food is expensive, because scarce,' and eventually to 'scarcity' generally.

▶dearth

**death**  [OE]  Like *dead*, *death* comes from a Germanic verb base *\*dau-*, which also produced English *die*. To it was added the abstract noun suffix *\*-tus*, later *\*-thuz*, meaning 'act, process, condition.' This produced prehistoric Germanic *\*dauthuz*, source of Gothic *dauthus*, Old Norse *dauthr*, and Old English *dēath*. Its modern English descendant, *death*, thus means literally 'act or process of dying,' in the same way as *birth* means 'act or process of bearing' and *strength* means 'condition of being strong.'

▶dead, die

**débâcle**  [19]  A *débâcle* is etymologically an 'act of unbarring,' the notion behind it being that once a restraining bar is removed, a rush of disasters follows. It was borrowed at the start of the 19th century (originally in the technical geological sense of a 'sudden violent surge of water in a river') from French, where it was a derivative of *débâcler*, a verb formed from *dé-* 'de-, un-' and *bâcler* 'bar.' This was acquired from Provençal *baclar* 'bar a door,' which came from medieval Latin *\*bacculāre*, a derivative of Latin *bacculus* 'stick' (responsible also for English *bacillus* and *bacterium*).

▶bacillus, bacterium

**debenture**  [15]  *Debenture* is simply an anglicization of Latin *dēbentur*, literally 'they are due,' the third person plural present passive of the verb *dēbēre* 'owe.' It supposedly arose from the practice of writing *debentur* on IOUs in the late Middle Ages. The English word originally signified such IOUs issued by the government or the Crown – certificates of indebtedness, to give them their formal designation – and it was not until the mid-19th century that the modern meaning, 'unsecured bond backed by the general credit of a company,' came into use.

▶debt, due, duty

**debility**  [15]  Despite the passing similarity, *debility* has no connection with *ability*. It comes via Old French *debilite* from Latin *dēilitās*, a derivative of the adjective *dēbilis* 'weak.' This was a compound formed from the prefix *de-* 'not' and a second element meaning 'strong,' represented also in Sanskrit *bálam* 'strength,' Greek *beltíon* 'better,' and Old Slavic *bolij* 'larger' (ultimate source of *bolshevik*).

**debt**  [13]  *Debt* originated as *dēbita*, the plural of Latin *dēbitum* 'that which is owed,' a noun formed from the past participle of the verb *dēbēre* 'owe.' In Vulgar Latin, *dēbita* was evidently viewed as a feminine singular noun, and it passed thus into Old French as *dette*, the form in which English originally acquired the word. From the 13th to the 16th centuries the French spelling was latinized as *debte*, a reform which English adopted in the 16th century. In the 15th century English independently borrowed Latin *dēbitum* as *debit*. (Latin *dēbēre* 'owe,' source also of English *debenture*, *due*, and *duty*, was originally a compound verb formed from the prefix *dē-* 'away' and *habēre* 'have,' literally 'have away,' that is, 'keep in one's possession what belongs to someone else.')

▶ debenture, due, duty, endeavour

**decade**  see DECIMAL

**decant**  [17]  The word *decant* depends on a metaphorical connection perceived in the ancient world between the 'corner of someone's eye' (Greek *kánthos*) and the 'lip of a jug.' On the basis of this, Latin acquired the word *canthus* 'lip of a jug.' From this was formed in medieval Latin the verb *dēcanthāre* 'pour out,' a word originally used by alchemists to denote the careful pouring off of a liquid from its sediment. English probably acquired the verb direct from Latin.

**decay**  [15]  The notion underlying *decay* and its close relative *decadence* is of a 'falling off' from a condition of health or perfection. *Decay* comes from Old Northern French *decair*, a descendant of Vulgar Latin *\*dēcadere*, which in turn came from Latin *dēcidere*, a compound verb formed from the prefix *dē-* 'down, off, away' and *cadere* 'fall' (source of English *case* and a wide range of related words). *Decadence* [16] was acquired via the medieval derivative *dēcadentia*.

To the same word-family belongs *deciduous* [17], from Latin *dēciduus*, literally denoting the 'falling off' of leaves from trees.

▶ accident, case, chance, decadence, deciduous

**decease**  see PREDECESSOR

**deceive**  [13]  Etymologically, to *deceive* someone is to 'catch' or 'ensnare' them. The word comes ultimately from Latin *dēcipere* 'ensnare, take in,' a compound verb formed from the pejorative prefix *dē-* and *capere* 'take, seize' (source of English *capture* and a wide range of related words). It passed into English via Old French *deceivre* and *decevoir*. English has two noun derivatives of *deceive*: *deceit* [13] comes ultimately from the past participle of Old French *decevoir*, while *deception* [14] comes from *dēcept-*, the past participial stem of Latin *dēcipere*.

▶ capable, capture, conceive, deceit, receive

**December**  [13]  *December* was originally so named by the ancient Romans (Latin *December*) because it was the tenth month of their calendar (which began with March). The term was derived from Latin *decem* 'ten.' It reached English via Old French *decembre*.

▶ decimal, ten

**decent**  [16]  *Decent* comes ultimately from Latin *decere* 'be fitting or suitable,' close relatives of which have produced *decorate*, *dignity*, and (from Greek) *orthodox*. Its present participial stem *decent-* was acquired by English, either directly or via French *décent*.

▶ dainty, decorate, dignity, orthodox

**decide**  [14]  Etymologically, *decide* denotes a resolving of alternatives or difficulties by cutting through them as if with a knife or a sword – dealing with them 'at a stroke.' The word comes, perhaps via French *décider*, from Latin *dēcidere*, a compound verb formed from the prefix *dē-* 'off' and *caedere* 'cut, strike.' It is not clear where this comes from, although Sanskrit *khid-* 'press, tear' has been compared. Its other descendants in English include *chisel*, *cement*, *concise*, and *scissors*. (Other verbs for 'decide' which contain the basic meaning element 'cut through' or 'separate' include Latin *dēcernere* and German *entscheiden*.)

▶ cement, chisel, concise, excise, incision, precise, scissors

**deciduous**  see DECAY

**decimal**  [17]  *Decimal* comes from *decimālis*, a medieval Latin coinage based on *decimus* 'tenth,' the ordinal derivative of Latin *decem* 'ten' (a relative of English *ten*). Other descendants of *decem* include *December*, *decimate*, *dime*, and the prefix *deci-*, while its Greek cousin *déka* has given us *decade* [15] and the prefix *deca-*.

▶ decade, December, decimate, dime, ten, tithe

**decimate**  [17]  *Decimate* is a cause célèbre amongst those who apparently believe that words should never change their meanings. The original general signification of its Latin source, the verb *decimāre*, was the removal or destruction of one tenth (it was derived from Latin *decem* 'ten'), and it may perhaps strike the 20th century as odd to have a particular word for such an apparently abstruse operation. It does, however, arise out of two very specific procedures in the ancient world: the exaction of a tax of one tenth (for which indeed English has the ultimately related word *tithe*), and the practice in the Roman army of punishing a body of soldiers guilty of some crime such as mutiny by choosing one in ten of them by lot to be put to death. Modern English does not perhaps have much use for a verb with such specialized senses, but the general notion of impassive and indiscriminate slaughter implied in the Roman military use led, apparently as early as the mid-17th century, to the modern sense 'kill or destroy most of.'

▶ decimal, ten

**deck** [15] Ultimately, *deck* (both the noun and the verb) is the same word as *thatch*. The meaning element they share is of a 'covering over the top.' The noun was borrowed from Middle Dutch *dec*, which meant 'covering' in general, and more specifically 'roof' and 'cloak' (its ultimate source was Germanic *\*thakjam*, source of English *thatch*). Its modern nautical sense did not develop in English until the early 16th century, and as its antecedents suggest, its original signification was of a covering, perhaps of canvas or tarpaulin, for a boat. Only gradually has the perception of it changed from a roof protecting what is beneath to a floor for those walking above. The word's application to a pack of cards, which dates from the 16th century, perhaps comes from the notion of the cards in a pile being on top of one another like the successive decks of a ship.

The verb *deck* [16] comes from Middle Dutch *dekken* 'cover.'

▶ detect, thatch, toga

**declare** [14] To *declare* something is to make it 'clear.' English acquired the word from Latin *dēclārāre* 'make clear,' a compound verb formed from the intensive prefix *dē-* and *clārāre* 'make clear,' a derivative of *clārus* 'clear.'

▶ claret, clear

**decline** [14] The notion underlying *decline* is of 'bending away.' It comes via Old French *decliner* from Latin *dēclīnāre* 'turn aside, go down,' a compound verb formed from the prefix *dē-* 'away, aside' and *clīnāre* 'bend,' which also produced English *incline* and *recline* and is related to *lean*. Its Latin nominal derivative *dēclīnātiō* has bifurcated in English, to produce *declination* [14] and, via Old French *declinaison*, *declension* [15]. The latter is used only in the specialized grammatical sense 'set of inflectional endings of a noun,' already present in Latin, which derives from the concept that every inflected form of a word represents a 'falling away' from its uninflected base form (the same underlying notion appears in the term *oblique case* 'any grammatical sense other than the nominative or vocative,' and indeed the word *case* itself, whose etymological meaning is 'fall'; and there are perhaps traces of it in *inflection*, literally 'bending').

▶ declension, incline, lean, recline

**decorate** [16] *Decorate* comes from Latin *decorātus*, the past participle of *decorāre* 'make beauti-

ful,' a verb derived from *decus* 'ornament.' Its root, *decor-*, also produced the adjective *decorus* 'beautiful, seemly,' from which English gets *decorous* [17] and, via its neuter singular form, *decorum* [16]. *Décor* is a 19th-century borrowing from French, where it was a derivative of the verb *décorer*. From the same ultimate source come *decent* and *dignity*.

▶ decent, dignity, decorous

**decoy** [16] Dutch *kooi* means 'cage' (it comes from Latin *cavea* 'cage,' source of English *cage*). The term came to be applied specifically to a pond which had been surrounded with nets into which wildfowl were lured for capture. English took it over, but brought with it the Dutch definite article *de*, so that Dutch *de kooi* 'the decoy' became English *decoy*.

▶ cage

**decrease** [14] Etymologically, *decrease* means 'ungrow.' It comes from *de(s)creiss-*, the present stem of Old French *de(s)creistre*, which was a descendant of Vulgar Latin *discrēscĕre*. This was an alteration of Latin *dēcrēscĕre*, a compound verb formed from the prefix *dē-*, denoting reversal of a previous condition, and *crēscĕre* 'grow' (source of English *crescent* and a wide range of other words).

▶ crescent, croissant, increase

**decree**   see DISCERN

**decrepit** [15] The underlying meaning of *decrepit* is 'cracked.' It comes from Latin *dēcrepitus*, an adjective formed (with the intensive prefix *dē-*) from the past participle of *crepāre* 'creak, rattle, crack' (ultimate source also of English *crepitation, crevice*, and probably *craven*).

**deed** [OE] Etymologically, a *deed* is 'that which is done.' An ancient word, it can be traced back as far as a hypothetical *\*dhētis*, a noun derived from *\*dhē-*, *\*dhō-* 'place, put,' the Indo-European base from which *do* comes. This passed into Germanic as *\*dædiz*, which produced German *tat*, Dutch *daad*, and Swedish *dåad* as well as English *deed*. The word's application to a legal document is a 14th-century development.

▶ do

**deed poll** [16] Contrary to what the term's modern pronunciation might seem to suggest, with the main stress on its first element rather than its second, a *deed poll* is a sort of *deed*, not a sort of *poll*. It originally referred to a legal document made and signed by one person only. Such documents were drawn up on parchment cut evenly, or 'polled,' rather than indented, as was the case with documents relating to two or more people.

**deep** [OE] *Deep* is a member of a quite extensive and heterogeneous family of English words. It comes from a prehistoric Germanic *\*deupaz* (source also of German *tief*, Dutch *diep*, and Swedish *djup*), which was a derivative of the base *d(e)u-* 'deep, hollow.' This may also have been the ancestor of the first syllable of *dabchick* 'little grebe' [16] (which would thus mean literally 'diving duck'), while a nasalized version of it may underlie *dimple*. It produced *dip*, and a variant has given us *dive*.

▶ dabchick, dimple, dip, dive

**deer** [OE] In Old English, *dēor* meant 'animal' in general, as opposed to 'human being' (as its modern Germanic relatives, German *tier*, Dutch *dier*, and Swedish *djur*, still do). Apparently connected forms in some other Indo-European languages, such as Lithuanian *dusti* 'gasp' and Church Slavonic *dychati* 'breathe,' suggest that it comes via a prehistoric Germanic *deuzom* from Indo-European *dheusóm*, which meant 'creature that breathes' (English *animal* and Sanskrit *prānin-* 'living creature' have similar semantic origins). Traces of specialization in meaning to 'deer' occur as early as the 9th century (although the main Old English word for 'deer' was *heorot*, source of modern English *hart*), and during the Middle English period it became firmly established, driving out 'animal' by the 15th century.

**defalcate** [15] *Defalcate* comes from medieval Latin *dēfalcāre* 'cut off,' a compound verb formed from the prefix *dē-* 'off' and *falx* 'sickle' (source of French *faux* 'scythe'). At first it meant simply 'deduct' in English; the modern legal sense 'embezzle' did not develop until the 19th century.

**defame** [14] The main source of *defame* (originally, in Middle English, *diffame*) is Old French *diffamer*, which came from Latin *diffāmāre* 'spread damaging rumours about,' a compound verb formed from the prefix *dis-*, denoting 'ruination,' and *fāma* 'report, fame' (source of English *fame*).

▶ fame

**defeat** [14] Etymologically, to *defeat* someone is literally to 'undo' them. The verb comes from Anglo-Norman *defeter*, a derivative of the noun *defet*. This in turn came from Old French *desfait*, the past participle of the verb *desfaire*. This was a descendant of medieval Latin *disfacere*, literally 'undo,' a compound verb formed from the prefix *dis-*, denoting reversal, and Latin *facere* 'do, make.' Its original metaphorical extension was to 'ruination' or 'destruction,' and the now central sense 'conquer' is not recorded in English before the 16th century.

A classical Latin combination of *facere* with the prefix *dē-* rather than *dis-* produced *defect*, *deficient*, and *deficit*.

▶ defect, deficient, deficit

**defect** see DEFICIENT

**defend** [13] *Defend* comes via Old French *defendre* from Latin *dēfendere* 'ward off,' a compound verb formed from the prefix *dē-* 'off, away' and an ele-

ment that survives elsewhere only in other compound forms (represented in English by *offend*). It has been suggested that this is related to Sanskrit *han-* 'strike' and Old English *gūth* 'battle,' and that it can be traced ultimately to a prehistoric Indo-European *gwendh-*. *Defend* had not long become established in English when it produced the offspring *fend*, dispensing with the first syllable. This in turn formed the basis of the derivatives *fender* [15] and *forfend* [14]. *Fence* likewise comes from *defence*.

▶ fence, fend

**defer** English has two distinct verbs *defer*. The one meaning 'delay' [14] is ultimately the same word as *differ*. It comes via Old French *differer* from Latin *differre* 'carry apart, delay,' a compound verb formed from the prefix *dis-* 'apart' and *ferre* 'carry' (related to English *bear*). The Latin verb's past participle, *dīlātus*, is the source of English *dilatory* [15]. *Defer* 'submit' [15] comes via Old French *deferer* from Latin *dēferre* 'carry away,' a compound verb formed from the prefix *dē-* 'away' and *ferre*. The notion of submission seems to have arisen from an earlier application to referring, or 'carrying,' a matter to someone else.

▶ bear, dilatory

**deficient** [16] *Deficient* was acquired from Latin *dēficient-*, the present participial stem of *dēficere* 'undo, fail, leave, be lacking,' a compound verb formed from the prefix *dē-* 'away' and *facere* 'do, make' (a parallel formation lies behind English *defeat*). The past participial stem of the Latin verb, *dēfect-*, produced English *defect* [15], while its third person present singular *dēficit* was borrowed by English as *deficit*.

▶ defeat, defect, deficit

**defile** *Defile* 'make dirty' [14] and *defile* 'narrow pass' [17] are distinct words in English. The former has a rather complex history. It was originally acquired in the 13th century as *defoul*, borrowed from Old French *defouler* 'trample down, injure'; this was a compound verb formed from the prefix *de-* 'down' and *fouler* 'tread,' which in turn goes back via Vulgar Latin *fullāre* to Latin *fullō* 'person who cleans and thickens cloth by stamping on it,' source of English *fuller* [OE]. In the 14th century *defoul* started to turn into *defile* under the influence of the synonymous (and now obsolete) *befile* [OE], a compound verb derived ultimately from the adjective *foul*. *Defile* 'narrow pass' was borrowed from French *défilé*, originally the past participle of *défiler*, a compound verb based on *filer* 'march in a column' (which is a close relative of English *file*).

▶ fuller / file

**define** see FINE

**defunct** [16] The *-funct* in *defunct* is the same ultimately as that in *function* and *perfunctory*. It comes from the past participle of Latin *fungī* 'perform, discharge.' In combination with the intensive prefix *dē-*

this produced *dēfunctus* 'discharged, finished,' hence 'dead,' which was borrowed directly into English.

▶ function, perfunctory

**defy** [14] The underlying notion of *defy* is of the renunciation of allegiance. It comes via Old French *defier* from a Vulgar Latin *\*disfīdāre* 'renounce one's faith,' a compound verb formed from the prefix *dis-*, denoting reversal, and Latin *fīdus* 'trusting.' This adjective came from a lengthened variant of the stem which produced *fidēs* 'faith,' source of English *faith*. The word's current main sense represents a slight shift from 'being disloyal' to actively 'challenging someone's power.' The verb's noun derivative *defiance* [14], borrowed from Old French, has a first cousin in *diffidence* [15], originally 'distrustfulness,' which came from the classical Latin compound verb *diffīdere* 'mistrust.'

▶ diffidence, faith

**degree** [13] Etymologically, *degree* means 'step down,' a sense revealed more clearly in its relative *degrade* [14]. It comes via Old French *degre* from Vulgar Latin *\*dēgradus*, a compound noun formed from the prefix *dē-* 'down' and *gradus* 'step' (source of English *gradual* and a wide range of other words). The word's modern meanings, such as 'academic rank' and 'unit of temperature,' come from an underlying abstract notion of a hierarchy of steps or ranks. *Degrade* represents a parallel but distinct formation, originally coined as ecclesiastical Latin *dēgradāre* and passed into English via Old French *degrader*.

▶ degrade, gradual, progress

**deign** see DISDAIN

**deity** [14] *Deity* comes via Old French *deite* from late Latin *deitās* 'godhood, divinity,' a derivative of Latin *deus* 'god.' This traces its ancestry back to Indo-European *\*deiwos*, which has links with other words meaning 'sky' and 'day' and probably comes ultimately from a base with the sense 'bright, shining.' Amongst its other descendants are English *divine*, the personifications Greek *Zeus*, Latin *Iuppiter* and *Iovis* (source of English *jovial*), and Old English *Tīw* (source of English *Tuesday*), and Sanskrit *dēvás* 'god' (source of English *deodar* 'variety of cedar' [19], literally 'divine wood'); the superficially similar Greek *theós* 'god,' however, is not related. English is also indebted to Latin *deus* for *deify* [14] and, via a somewhat circuitous route, the *joss* [18] of *joss-stick*, a Pidgin English word which comes from *deos*, the Portuguese descendant of *deus*.

▶ divine, joss, jovial, Tuesday

**delay** [13] English acquired *delay* from Old French *delaier*, a compound verb formed from the prefix *de-* 'off' and *laier* 'leave.' This verb, which also crops up in English *relay*, appears to have been a variant of *laissier* (source of English *lease*), which came from

Latin *laxāre* 'slacken, undo.' This in turn was derived from the adjective *laxus* 'loose.'

▶ lax, lease, relay

**delegate** see LEGAL

**deliberate** see DELIVER

**delicate** [14] *Delicate* comes either from Old French *delicat* or direct from its source, Latin *dēlicātus*, but its ultimate history is obscure. Its formal similarity to *delicious* and *delight*, and the fact that 'addicted to pleasure' was one of the meanings of Latin *dēlicātus*, suggest that the three words may have an ancestor in common. *Delicatessen* [19] was borrowed from German *delikatessen*, plural of *delikatesse* 'delicacy,' which in turn was acquired by German from French *délicatesse*.

▶ delicatessen

**delicious** [13] The underlying meaning of *delicious* is 'tempting, luring one aside from the straight and narrow.' It comes via Old French *delicious* from late Latin *dēliciōsus*, a derivative of Latin *dēlicia* 'delight.' This in turn was formed from *dēlicere* 'entice away,' a compound verb made from the prefix *dē-* 'away' and *lacere* 'lure, deceive' (source also of English *elicit* and related to *lace, lasso*, and possibly *latch*). Latin *dēlectāre*, a derivative of *dēlicere* denoting repeated action, produced Old French *delit*, source of English *delight* [13], and Italian *dilettante*, literally 'lover,' borrowed by English in the 18th century in the positive sense 'someone who takes delight in fine art.'

▶ delight, dilettante, elicit, lace, lasso

**delinquent** see RELIC

**delirious** see LAST

**deliver** [13] To *deliver* something is etymologically to 'set it free.' The word comes via Old French *delivrer* from late Latin *dēlīberāre*, a compound verb formed from the intensive prefix *dē-* and Latin *līberāre* 'set free,' a derivative of the adjective *līber* 'free.' Its meaning developed through 'set free' to 'give up, surrender' and finally 'hand over to someone else.' (Classical Latin *dēlīberāre*, source of English *deliberate* [15], is an entirely different verb, derived from Latin *lībra* 'scales.')

▶ liberate

**dell** see DALE

**delphinium** see DOLPHIN

**delta** [16] *Delta* was the fourth letter of the Greek alphabet, corresponding to English *d*. Its capital form was written in the shape of a tall triangle, and already in the ancient world the word was being applied metaphorically to the triangular deposit of sand, mud, etc which forms at the mouth of rivers (the Greek historian Herodotus, for instance, used it with reference to the mouth of the Nile). Greek acquired the word itself from some Semitic language; it is related to *dāleth*, the name of the fourth letter of the Hebrew alphabet.

**deluge** see LAVATORY

**delusion** see ILLUSION

**demagogue** [17] A *demagogue* is literally a 'leader of the people.' The word represents Greek *demagōgós*, a compound formed from *demos* 'common people' and *agōgós* 'leader.' (This was derived from *ágein* 'drive, lead,' a verb related to Latin *agere* 'do,' and hence to its host of English descendants, from *act* to *prodigal*.) In ancient Greece the term was applied particularly to a set of unofficial leaders drawn from the common people who controlled the government of Athens in the 4th century BC, and whose irresponsible rule (as their critics saw it) has given *demagogue* a bad name ever since.

▶ act, agent

**demand** [13] Latin *dēmandāre* meant 'entrust something to someone.' It was a compound verb formed from the intensive prefix *dē-* and *mandāre* 'entrust, commit' (source of English *mandate*). As it passed via Old French *demander* into English, its meaning developed to 'give someone the responsibility of doing something,' and finally 'order.'

▶ mandate

**demeanour** [15] A person's *demeanour* is how they 'conduct' themselves. The word goes back ultimately to the literal notion of driving animals along. It is a derivative of the now virtually obsolete reflexive verb *demean* 'behave,' borrowed in the 13th century from Old French *demener*. This was a compound formed from the intensive prefix *de-* and *mener* 'lead,' a descendant of Latin *mināre* 'drive a herd of animals' (whose original connotation of 'urging on with threats' is revealed by its close relationship with *minārī* 'threaten,' source of English *menace*).

This obsolete *demean* should not, incidentally, be confused with *demean* 'degrade' [17], which was formed from the adjective *mean*.

▶ menace

**demesne** [14] Ultimately, *demesne* is the same word as *domain*. It comes via Old French *demeine* from Latin *dominicus*, an adjective meaning 'of a lord' (see DOMINION), and hence etymologically means 'land belonging to a lord.' Under the feudal system it denoted land retained by the lord for his own use, rather than let out to tenants. The -*s*- was inserted into the word in Anglo-Norman, partly as a graphic device to indicate a long vowel and partly through association with Old French *mesnie* 'household,' which came ultimately from Latin *mansio* 'place to stay' (source of English *mansion*).

▶ dame, danger, domain, dominion

**demijohn** [18] *Demijohn* 'large globular bottle' has no connection with half of the common male forename. It arose through a process known as folk etymology, by which an unfamiliar or slightly outlandish foreign word is deconstructed and then reassembled using similar-sounding elements in the host language. In this case the source was French *dame-jeanne*, literally 'Lady Jane,' a term used in French for such a container since the 17th century.

**demise** see DISMISS

**democracy** [16] *Democracy* means literally 'government by the populace at large.' It comes via Old French *democratie* and medieval Latin *dēmocratia* from Greek *dēmokratíā*, a compound formed from *demos* 'people' and -*kratíā* 'rule,' a derivative of the noun *krátos* 'power, authority,' which has contributed a number of terms for types of government to English. The original meaning of Greek *demos* was 'district, land,' but eventually it came to denote the people living in such a district, particularly the ordinary people considered as a social class participating in government – hence *democracy*. The derivative *democrat* [18] was coined in French at the time of the Revolution.

▶ epidemic

**demolish** [16] To *demolish* something is etymologically to 'deconstruct' it. The word comes from *demoliss-*, the stem of Old French *demolir*, which in turn came from Latin *dēmōlīrī* 'throw down, demolish.' This was a compound verb formed from the prefix *dē-*, denoting reversal of a previous condition, and *mōlīrī*, which among other things meant 'build, construct.' This was a derivative of *mōles* 'mass, huge mass, massive structure' (source of English *mole* 'harbour wall' and *molecule*).

▶ mole, molecule

**demon** [14] English acquired this word from Latin in two forms, classical Latin *daemōn* and medieval Latin *dēmōn*, which were once used fairly interchangeably for 'evil spirit' but have now split apart. *Demon* retains the sense 'evil spirit,' but this was in fact a relatively late semantic development. Greek *daímōn* (source of Latin *daemōn*) meant 'divine power, fate, god' (it is probably related to Greek *daíomai* 'distribute, allot,' which comes from an Indo-European base whose descendants include English *tide* and *time*). It was used in Greek myths as a term for a minor deity, and it was also applied to a 'guiding spirit' (senses now usually denoted by *daemon* in English). It seems to be from this latter usage that the sense 'evil spirit' (found in the Greek Septuagint and New Testament and in the Latin Vulgate) arose.

▶ pandemonium, time, tide

**demonstrate**   see MONSTER

**demur**   [13]   Like its French cousin *demeurer*, *demur* originally meant 'stay, linger.' It was not until the 17th century that the current sense, 'raise objections,' developed, via earlier 'delay' and 'hesitate in uncertainty.' The word comes via Old French *demorer* and Vulgar Latin *dēmorāre* from Latin *dēmorārī*, a compound verb formed from the intensive prefix *dē*- and *morārī* 'delay' (source also of English *moratorium* [19]).

▶ demure, moratorium

**demure**   [14]   Etymologically, someone who is *demure* is quiet and settled, not agitated. The word comes from *demore*, the past participle of Old French *demorer* 'stay' (source of English *demur*), and so semantically is a parallel formation to *staid*. One of its earliest recorded uses in English was actually to describe the sea as 'calm,' and it was not until the late 17th century that its modern slightly pejorative connotations of coyness began to emerge.

▶ demur

**den**   [OE]   Related forms such as German *tenne* 'threshing floor' and possibly Greek *thenar* 'palm of the hand' suggest that the underlying meaning of *den* may be 'flat area.' Old English *denn* denoted 'wild animal's lair,' perhaps with reference to animals' flattening an area of vegetation to form a sleeping place. *Dean* [OE], a word for 'valley' now surviving only in place-names, comes from the same source.

**denigrate**   [16]   To *denigrate* people is literally to 'blacken' them. The word comes from Latin *dēnigrāre* 'blacken,' a compound verb formed from the intensive prefix *dē*- and *niger* 'black.' This adjective, which is of unknown origin, also produced French *noir* 'black' and Italian *nero* 'black,' and is the source (via Spanish *negro*) of English *negro* [16] and the now taboo *nigger* [18]. *Denigrate* originally meant 'physically turn something black' as well as the metaphorical 'defame, belittle': 'This lotion will denigrate the hairs of hoary heads,' Richard Tomlinson, *Renodaeus' Medicinal dispensatory* 1657.

▶ negro, nigger

**denim**   [17]   The name of the fabric from which jeans are made had its origins in a sort of serge produced in the southern French town of Nîmes. The French naturally enough called it *serge de Nîmes*, but the original meaning of this soon became lost when English borrowed it as *serge de Nim*, and the last two words came to be run together as *denim*.

**denizen**   [15]   Etymologically, *denizen* means 'someone who is inside,' and it is related to French *dans* 'in.' It comes from Anglo-Norman *deinzein*, a derivative of Old French *deinz* 'inside.' This had grown out of the Latin phrase *dē intus*, literally 'from inside.' Hence *denizen*'s original meaning of someone who lives 'in' a country, as opposed to a *foreigner*. In the 16th and 17th centuries the verb *denize* existed, coined by back-formation from *denizen*; it meant roughly the same as modern English *naturalize*.

**denouement**   [18]   A *denouement* is literally an 'untying of a knot.' It was borrowed from French (its first recorded use in English is by Lord Chesterfield in one of his famous letters to his son (1752)), where it was a derivative of *dénouer* 'undo.' This was a compound verb formed from the prefix *dé*- 'un-' and *nouer* 'tie,' which came ultimately from Latin *nōdus* 'knot' (source of English *newel, node, nodule*, and *noose*).

▶ newel, node, nodule, noose

**denounce**   see PRONOUNCE

**dent**   see DINT

**dentist**   [18]   *Dentist* was borrowed from French *dentiste*, and at first was ridiculed as a high-falutin foreign term: '*Dentist* figures it now in our newspapers, and may do well enough for a French puffer; but we fancy Rutter is content with being called a *tooth-drawer*,' *Edinburgh Chronicle* 15 September 1759. It was a derivative of French *dent* 'tooth,' which goes back via Latin *dēns* to an Indo-European base *dont-, *dent-*, source also of English *tooth*. Other English descendants of Latin *dēns* include *dental* [16] and *denture* [19].

▶ indent, tooth

**deny**   see RENEGADE

**deodar**   see DEITY

**depart**   [13]   *Depart* originally meant 'divide.' This was the sense of its ultimate Latin ancestor *dispertīre*, literally 'separate up into constituent parts,' a compound verb formed from the prefix *dis-*, denoting separation, and *partīre* 'divide, distribute,' a derivative of the noun *pars* 'part.' It passed into English via Vulgar Latin *dēpartīre* and Old French *departir*, by which time the notions of 'division' and 'separation' had already produced the intransitive sense 'go away.'

▶ part

**department**   [15]   English has borrowed *department* from French *département* on two completely separate occasions. Originally, in late Middle English, it was used for 'departure,' but this died out in the mid-17th century. Then in the 18th century it was re-acquired in the different sense 'distinct division'; Dr Johnson, in his *Dictionary* 1755, dismisses it as a French term.

**depend**   [15]   To *depend* on something is literally to 'hang down' from it. The word comes, via Old French *dependre*, from Latin *dēpendēre*, a compound verb formed from the prefix *dē*-'down' and *pendēre* 'hang' (source of English *pendant, pendulum, penthouse*, and a host of derivatives from *appendix* to *suspend*). Its original literal sense survives in English, just, as a conscious archaism, but essentially the metaphorical extensions 'be contingent' (echoed in the parallel use of *hang on*) and 'rely' have taken the verb over.

▶ appendix, pendent, pendulum, penthouse, suspend

**depict** see PICTURE

**depilatory** see PILE

**deplete** see FULL

**deploy** see DISPLAY

**deport** see PORT

**depot** [18] A *depot* is literally a 'place where something is deposited,' a 'depository.' The word comes, via French *dépôt*, from Latin *dēpositum* (source of English *deposit* [17]), the past participle of *dēpōnere* 'put down.' This was a compound verb formed from the prefix *dē-* 'down' and *pōnere* 'put, place' (source of English *position*), and also produced English *depose* [13] and *deponent* [15].

▶ deponent, depose, deposit, position

**deprecate** see PRAY

**depreciate** see PRICE

**depredation** see PREY

**depress** see PRESS

**deprive** see PRIVATE

**depth** [14] *Depth* is not as old as it looks. Similar nouns, such as *length* and *strength*, existed in Old English, but *depth*, like *breadth*, is a much later creation. In Old English the nouns denoting 'quality of being deep' were *dīepe* and *dēopnes* 'deepness.'

▶ deep

**deputy** [16] A *deputy* is literally 'someone who has been deputed to act on someone else's behalf.' It represents a reformulation of the Middle English noun *depute*. This was borrowed from the past participle of Old French *deputer* (source of the English verb *depute* [15] and hence of *deputation* [16]), which in turn came from late Latin *dēputāre* 'assign, allot.' In classical times this meant literally 'cut off' (it was a compound verb formed from the prefix *dē-* 'off' and *putāre*, which meant 'cut' – as in *amputate* – as well as 'esteem, consider, reckon, think' – as in *compute*, *dispute*, *impute*, and *repute*).

▶ amputate, compute, count, dispute, impute, putative, repute

**derive** [14] Like *rival*, *derive* comes ultimately from Latin *rīvus* 'stream.' This was used as the basis of a verb *dērīvāre*, formed with the prefix *dē-* 'away,' which originally designated literally the 'drawing off of water from a source.' This sense was subsequently generalized to 'divert,' and extended figuratively to 'derive' (a metaphor reminiscent of *spring from*). English acquired the word via Old French *deriver*.

▶ rival

**derrick** [16] Around the end of the 16th century there was a famous Tyburn hangman called *Derick*. His name came to be used as a personification of hangmen in general, and subsequently as a metaphor for the 'gallows.' Gradually, however, these macabre associations were lost, and by the 18th century *derrick* had progressed in meaning to 'hoisting apparatus.'

**derring-do** [16] *Derring-do* arose from a misunderstanding of the Middle English phrase *dorring do*, which literally meant 'daring to do' (*dorren* was the Middle English form of *dare*). In some 16th-century editions of medieval authors this was misprinted as *derring do*. The poet Edmund Spenser came across it and used it several times in his often deliberately archaic verse – but as a noun, meaning 'boldness,' rather than as the verbal phrase it actually was: 'a man of mickle name, renowned much in arms and derring do,' *Faerie Queene* 1596. Spenser's usage was picked up and popularized by Sir Walter Scott in the early 19th century.

▶ dare

**descant** [14] Etymologically, *descant* is a parallel formation to English *part song*. English acquired it via Old French *deschant* from medieval Latin *discantus* 'refrain,' a compound noun formed from the prefix *dis-* 'apart' and *cantus* 'song.' The notion originally underlying it is of a separate vocal line 'apart' from the main musical theme. The Middle English form of the word was *deschaunt*; *descant* represents a partial 16th-century reversion to Latin *discantus*.

▶ canto, chant

**descend** [13] Etymologically, *descend* means 'climb down.' Like its opposite, *ascend* [14], it comes ultimately from Latin *scandere* 'climb,' which also produced English *scan* and *scansion* and is related to *echelon*, *escalate*, *scale* 'set of graduated marks,' *scandal*, and *slander*. The Latin verb was a product of the Indo-European base *\*skand-* 'jump.'

▶ ascend, echelon, escalate, scale, scan, scandal, slander

**describe** [15] To *describe* something is literally to 'write it down.' The word comes from Latin *dēscrībere*, a compound verb formed from the prefix *dē-* 'down' and *scrībere* 'write' (source of English *scribe*, *script*, etc). English originally borrowed it via Old French *descrivre* in the 13th century as *descrive*, in which the metaphorical sense 'give an account of' had already developed, and this was grafted on to the Latin verb when it was reborrowed directly in the 15th century. The derivative *nondescript* was coined (originally as a term in biological classification) in the 17th century.

▶ ascribe, scribe, script

**desert** English has three distinct words *desert*, which come from two separate sources. *Desert* 'what one deserves' [13] (now usually used in the plural) is related, as its meaning suggests, to the verb *deserve*. It comes from Old French *desert* or *deserte*, which were formed from the past participle of *deservir* 'deserve.'

(*Dessert* 'sweet course' [17] is its first cousin, coming from French *desservir* 'clear the table' – literally 'unserve' – a compound verb formed, like *deserve*, from the verb *serve* but with the prefix *dis-* rather than *de-*.)

The noun *desert* 'barren region' [13] and the verb *desert* 'abandon' [15] both come ultimately from *dēsertus*, the past participle of Latin *dēserere* 'abandon.' This was a compound verb formed from the prefix *dē-* denoting reversal and *serere* 'join' (a derivative of which gave English '*serried* ranks').

▶ serve / serried

**deserve** [13] Latin *dēservīre* meant 'serve well or enthusiastically' (it was a compound verb formed from the intensive prefix *dē-* and *servīre* 'serve'). Hence in late Latin it came to mean 'become entitled to because of meritorious service,' a sense which passed via Old French *deservir* into English. The more general modern English 'be worthy of' developed in the 15th century.

▶ serve

**desiccate** see SACK

**design** [16] The semantic history of *design* is a little complicated. It comes ultimately from the past participle of Latin *dēsignāre* 'mark out' (source also of English *designate* [15]), a compound verb formed from the prefix *dē-* 'out' and *signāre* 'mark,' a derivative of *signum* 'sign.' But English acquired it largely via French, in which a three-way split of form and meaning had taken place. In both respects *désigner* 'point out, denote' remains closest to the original Latin, but this use of the word has now died out in English, having been taken over by *designate*. This has left the field open to the metaphorical use 'plan,' represented in French on the one hand by *dessein* 'purpose, intention' and on the other by *dessin* 'pattern, drawing' and its related verb *dessiner*. They represent the two main areas of meaning covered by the word in modern English, although English has stuck to the more latinate spelling.

▶ designate, sign

**desire** [13] The underlying etymological meaning of *desire* is something of a mystery. Like *consider*, it comes ultimately from a base related to Latin *sīdus* 'star,' but the links in the semantic chain that would lead us back from 'desire' to 'star' have not all been successfully reconstructed. It does at least seem, though, that before the word denoted 'wanting,' it signified 'lack.' English acquired it via Old French *desirer*, but has also gone back directly to the past participle of Latin *dēsīderāre* for *desideratum* 'something desirable' [17].

▶ consider, sidereal

**desist** see STATUE

**desk** [14] *Desk, disc, dish,* and *dais* – strange bedfellows semantically – form a little gang of words going back ultimately, via Latin *discus*, to Greek *dískos* 'quoit.' *Desk* seems perhaps the least likely descendant

of 'quoit,' but it came about like this: Latin *discus* was used metaphorically, on the basis of its circular shape, for a 'tray' or 'platter, dish'; and when such a tray was set on legs, it became a table. (German *tisch* 'table' comes directly from Vulgar Latin in this sense.) By the time English acquired it from medieval Latin it seems already to have developed the specialized meaning 'table for writing or reading on.'

▶ dais, disc, dish

**desolate** see SOLE

**despair** [14] Etymologically, *despair* is literally 'lack of hope.' The word comes via Old French *desperer* from Latin *dēspērāre*, a compound verb formed from the prefix *dē-*, denoting reversal, and *spērāre*, a derivative of the noun *spēs* 'hope.' Its past participle, *dēspērātus*, produced English *desperate* [15], from which *desperado* is a 17th-century mock-Spanish coinage.

▶ desperate

**despond** [17] Latin had a phrase *animam dēspondēre*, literally 'give up one's soul,' hence 'lose heart.' The verb *dēspondēre* came to be used on its own in this sense, and was borrowed thus by English. It was a compound verb, formed from the prefix *dē-* 'away' and *spondēre* 'promise' (source of English *sponsor, spontaneous, spouse, respond,* and *riposte*), and originally meant 'promise to give away,' hence 'give up.'

▶ respond, riposte, sponsor, spontaneous, spouse

**despot** [16] The ultimate source of *despot* is Greek *despótēs* 'lord.' It is related to Sanskrit *dampati* 'master of the house,' and both probably go back to an Indo-European compound formed from *\*domo-* 'house' (source of Latin *domus* 'house,' and hence of English *domestic*) and another element related to Latin *potis* 'able' and English *power*. (Latin *dominus* 'lord,' a derivative of *domus* 'house' and originally meaning 'master of the house,' is a semantically parallel formation.) Greek *despótēs* was used for 'lord, master' or 'ruler' in various contexts, with no particular pejorative connotation (in modern Greek it means 'bishop'). But most rulers in ancient times enjoyed absolute power, and so eventually the word (which entered English via medieval Latin *despota* and early modern French *despot*) came to mean 'tyrannical ruler'; this sense became firmly established at the time of the French Revolution.

▶ domestic, dominion

**dessert** see DESERT

**destiny** [14] Etymologically, one's *destiny* is that which has been firmly established or determined for one (as if by fate). The word comes from *destinee*, the Old French descendant of Latin *dēstinātus*. This was the past participle of *dēstināre* 'make firm, establish,' a compound verb formed from the intensive prefix *dē-* and *\*stanāre* 'fix' (source also of English *obstinate*). This in turn was a derivative of *stare* 'stand,' a relative of English *stand*. The Latin verb also gave English *destine* [14] and hence *destination* [15], whose current use comes from an earlier *place of destination* 'place for which one is bound.'

▶ destination, obstinate, stand

**destitute**    SEE STATUE

**destroy**    [13]    As in the case of *demolish*, to *destroy* something is almost literally to 'unbuild' it. The word comes via Old French *destruire* from *\*dēstrūgere*, a Vulgar Latin alteration of Latin *dēstrū-ere*. This was a compound verb formed from the prefix *dē-*, denoting reversal of a previous state, and *struere* 'pile up, build' (source of English *construct* and *structure*). Its past participle, *dēstructus*, has produced English *destruction* [14], *destructive* [15], and the verb *destruct* (recorded once in the 17th century but revived in the 1950s by back-formation from *destruction*).

▶ construct, destruction, structure

**desultory**    [16]    Latin *dēsultor* designated a circus trick-rider who jumped from the back of one horse to another while they were galloping along (it was a derivative of *dēsilīre*, a compound verb formed from *dē-* 'down' and *salīre* 'jump,' source of or related to English *assail*, *assault*, *insult*, *salacious*, *salient*, and *sally*). From it was derived an adjective *dēsultōrius* 'jumping from one thing to another like a *dēsultor*,' hence 'superficial,' and eventually 'unmethodical, irregular,' the sense which survives in English.

▶ assail, assault, insult, salacious, salient

**detail**    [17]    Etymologically, a *detail* is a 'little piece cut off.' It comes from French *détail*, a derivative of *détailler* 'cut up.' This was a compound verb formed from the intensive prefix *dé-* and *tailler* 'cut' (a relative of English *tailor* and *tally*). English acquired the word via the French phrase *en détail* 'piece by piece, item by item,' source of the central modern meaning 'individual item, particular.'

▶ tailor, tally

**detect**    SEE PROTECT

**détente**    [20]    English originally acquired this word from French in the 17th century as *detent*, which denotes a catch that regulates the movement of a clock. French *détente*, which originally signified a device for releasing a crossbow string, came from the past participle of Old French *destendre* 'release,' a compound verb formed from the prefix *des-* 'apart' and *tendre* 'stretch' (related to English *tension*). But English-speakers, mistakenly associating it with *detain* [15] (a verb of completely different origin, via Old French *detenir* from Latin *dētinēre* 'keep back') completely reversed its meaning, applying to a restraining catch rather than a releasing one.

French, the language of diplomacy, re-lent *détente* to

English in the first decade of the 20th century in the sense 'relaxation of international tension.'

▶ tension

**deter**    SEE TERROR

**detergent**    [17]    A *detergent* is literally something that 'wipes away.' The word comes from *dētergent-*, the present participial stem of Latin *dētergēre*, a compound verb formed from *dē-* 'away' and *tergēre* 'wipe' (its past participle produced English *terse*). English *detergent* originally meant simply 'cleansing agent' (used particularly in a medical or surgical context); the specific application to a cleanser made from synthetic chemical compounds (as opposed to *soap*, which is made from fats and lye) is a 20th-century development.

▶ terse

**deteriorate**    [16]    The meaning of *deteriorate* resides etymologically in its first syllable, which represents the Latin preposition *dē* 'down.' To this was added the adjectival suffix *-ter*, to produce *\*dēter* 'bad,' and this in turn was modified with the comparative suffix *-ior* to *dēterior* 'worse.' *Dēterior* formed the basis of the verb *dēteriorāre* 'get worse,' source of English *deteriorate*.

**determine**    [14]    The central meaning of *determine* is 'fix a limit to,' as in 'determine the scope of an enquiry.' It comes via Old French *determiner* from Latin *dētermināre*, a compound verb formed from the prefix *dē-* 'off' and *termināre* 'limit' (source of English *terminate*). Its connotations of 'firm resolve,' a 17th-century development, came via an intermediate sense 'come to a firm decision on.'

▶ terminate

**detest**    [16]    Latin *dētestārī*, source of *detest*, meant 'denounce.' It was a compound verb formed from the pejorative prefix *dē-* and *testārī* 'bear witness.' This in turn was a derivative of *testis* 'witness,' source of English *testify*, *testimony*, and *testicle*. It retained its original sense of 'cursing' or 'execration' when first borrowed into English, but by the 18th century this had weakened from open denunciation to internal 'loathing.'

▶ testicle, testify, testimony

**detonate**    [18]    *Detonate* is related to *thunder*. It comes from the past participle of Latin *dētonāre*, a compound verb formed from the prefix *dē-* 'down' and *tonāre* 'thunder, roar,' which goes back to the same Indo-European base (*\*ten-*, *\*ton-*) as *thunder*. Latin *dētonāre* never actually meant 'cause to explode,' though; that sense comes from its French descendant *détoner*.

▶ thunder

**detriment**    [15]    Etymologically, *detriment* denotes damage caused by 'wearing away.' The word comes via Old French from Latin *dētrīmentum*, a derivative of *dēterere* 'wear away' (whose past participle is the source of English *detritus* [18]). This was a compound verb formed from the prefix *dē-* 'away' and *terere* 'rub' (from which English gets *attrition* and *trite*). The generalized metaphorical sense 'harm' had already developed in classical Latin.

▶ attrition, detritus, trite

**deuce** [15] The underlying meaning of *deuce* emerges most clearly in its application to playing cards and dice: the number two. It comes from Old French *deus* 'two,' which goes back to *duōs*, the accusative case of Latin *duo* 'two' (English *two* comes ultimately from the same source). Its use in tennis comes from the French phrase *à deux*, literally 'at two,' which signifies that a player must score two successive points to win a game. It is generally thought that the mild oath *deuce* came from *duus*, the Low German descendant of Latin *duōs*, which gamblers supposedly cried out in disgust when they threw the lowest score, a two.

**devastate** [17] Etymologically as well as semantically, *devastate* is related to 'lay *waste*.' It comes from the past participle of Latin *dēvāstāre*, a compound verb formed from the intensive prefix *dē-* and *vāstāre* 'lay waste.' This was a derivative of *vāstus* 'waste,' source of English *waste*.

▶ vast, waste

**develop** [17] The history of *develop* and its close relative *envelop* is hazy. English acquired it from *développer*, the modern French descendant of Old French *desveloper*. This was a compound verb formed from the prefix *des-* 'un-' and *voloper* 'wrap.' But where did *voloper* come from? Some have proposed a hypothetical Celtic base *\*vol-* 'roll,' while others have pointed to similarities, formal and semantic, with Italian *viluppo* 'bundle' and *viluppare* 'wrap,' which come from an assumed late Latin *\*faluppa* 'husk.' Beyond that, however, the trail has gone cold.

▶ envelop

**deviate** see DEVIOUS

**device** [13] A *device* is something which has been devised – which, etymologically speaking, amounts to 'something which has been divided.' For ultimately *devise* and *divide* come from the same source. The noun *device* comes in the first instance from Old French *devis* 'division, contrivance' and latterly (in the 15th century) from Old French *devise* 'plan,' both of which were derivatives of the verb *deviser* 'divide, devise' (source of English *devise* [13]). This in turn came from Vulgar Latin *\*dīvisāre*, a verb based on the past participial stem of Latin *dīvidere*, source of English *divide*. The semantic development by which 'divide' passed to 'contrive,' presumably based on the notion that dividing something up and distributing it needs some planning, happened before the word reached Eng-

lish, and English *device* has never meant 'division.' The sense 'simple machine' essentially evolved in the 16th century.

▶ devise, divide, individual, widow

**devil** [OE] English acquired *devil* in the 8th century via late Latin *diabolus* from Greek *diábolos*, which originally meant 'slanderer.' It was a derivative of *diabállein* 'slander,' a compound verb literally meaning 'throw across,' formed from *diá* 'across' and *bállein* 'throw' (whence English *ballistics*). The Greek word has reached most European languages: for example French *diable*, Italian *diavolo*, German *teufel*, Dutch *duivel*, Swedish *djävul*, and Russian *djavol*. It has also given English *diabolical* [16], and indeed *diabolo* [20], a game played by spinning a top (named from a variant of Italian *diavolo*) on a string.

▶ ballistics, diabolical

**devious** [16] *Devious* and its close relative *deviate* [17] are both based on the notion of going 'out of the way.' They come respectively from Latin *dēvius* and *dēviāre*, compound adjective and verb formed from the prefix *dē-* 'from' and *via* 'way.'

▶ deviate, via

**devolution** see VOLUME

**devout** [13] Essentially, *devout* and *devote* [16] are the same word; they come from an identical source, but reached English along different routes. That source is *dēvōtus*, the past participle of Latin *dēvovēre*, which was a compound formed from the intensive prefix *dē-* and *vovēre* 'promise' (source of English *vote* and *vow*). This entered English originally via Old French *devot* as an adjective, and was then reborrowed directly from Latin in the 16th century as the basis for a verb.

▶ devote, vote, vow

**dew** [OE] *Dew* is an ancient word, which can be traced back to the Indo-European base *\*dheu-*; this also produced Greek *thein* 'run' and Sanskrit *dhāv* 'flow, wash' (whence, via Hindi, English *dhobi* 'Indian washerman' [19]) and *dhaūtís* 'brook.' Its Germanic descendant was *\*dauwaz*, which produced (besides English *dew*) German *tau*, Dutch *dauw*, and Swedish *dagg*.

▶ dhobi

**dextrous** [17] Just as the left hand has always been associated with awkwardness or maladroitness (*cack-handed*), so the right hand has traditionally been credited with skill: hence *dextrous*, a derivative of Latin *dexter*, which meant 'on the right side' and thus by extension 'skilful.' This came ultimately, like Greek *dexiós*, Gothic *taihswa*, Breton *dehou*, Russian *desnoj*, and many other related forms in the general semantic area 'right-hand side,' from an Indo-European base *\*dek-*. English acquired the Latin adjective itself as a heraldic term in the 16th century.

**dhobi**  see DEW

**diabetes**  [16]  *Diabetes* means literally 'passing through'; it was originally so named in Greek because one of the symptoms of the disease is excessive discharge of urine. Greek *diabétēs* was a derivative of *diabaínein* 'pass through,' a compound verb formed from the prefix *dia-* 'through' and *baínein* 'go' (a relative of English *basis* and *come*). English acquired it via medieval Latin *diabētēs*. Compare DIARRHOEA.

▶ basis, come

**diabolical**  see DEVIL

**diadem**  [13]  A *diadem* was originally something that was bound round someone's head. The word comes, via Old French *diademe* and Latin *diadēma*, from Greek *diádēma*; this was a derivative of *diadein*, a compound verb formed from the prefix *dia-* 'across' and *dein* 'bind.' In Greek it was often applied specifically to the regal headband worn by Alexander the Great and his successors.

**diaeresis**  see HERESY

**diagnosis**  [17]  The underlying meaning of Greek *diágnōsis* was 'knowing apart.' It was derived from *diagignṓskein* 'distinguish, discern,' a compound verb formed from the prefix *dia-* 'apart' and *gignṓskein* 'know, perceive' (a relative of English *know*). In postclassical times the general notion of 'distinguishing' or 'discerning' was applied specifically to medical examination in order to determine the nature of a disease.

▶ know

**diagonal**  [16]  *Diagonal* is commonly used simply as a synonym for *oblique*, but in strict mathematical terms it denotes a line joining two non-adjacent angles of a polygon. This reveals far more clearly its origins. It comes from *diagōnālis*, a Latin adjective derived from Greek *diagṓnios*. This was a compound formed from the prefix *dia-* 'across' and *gōníā* 'angle' (as in English *polygon*), meaning 'from angle to angle.' *Gōníā* is related ultimately to English *knee* and *genuine*.

▶ genuine, knee, polygon

**dial**  [15]  The original application of the word *dial* in English is 'sundial.' The evidence for its prehistory is patchy, but it is generally presumed to have come from medieval Latin *diālis* 'daily,' a derivative of Latin *diēs* 'day,' the underlying notion being that it records the passage of a 24-hour period.

**dialect**  [16]  The notion underlying *dialect* and its relatives *dialectic* [14] and *dialogue* [13] is of 'conversation.' They come ultimately from Greek *dialégesthai* 'converse,' a compound verb formed from the prefix *dia-* 'with each other' and *légein* 'speak' (source of English *lecture* and a wide range of related words). This formed the basis of two derived nouns. First *diálektos* 'conversation, discourse,' hence 'way of speaking' and eventually 'local speech,' which passed into English via Latin *dialectus* and Old French *dialecte* (from it was produced the adjective *dialektikós* 'of conversation, discussion, or debate,' which was eventually to become English *dialectic*). Secondly *diálogos* 'conversation,' which again reached English via Latin and Old French.

▶ lecture

**dialysis**  [16]  As in the case of its close relative *analysis*, the underlying etymological notion contained in *dialysis* is of undoing or loosening, so that the component parts are separated. The word comes ultimately from Greek *diálusis*, a derivative of *dialúein* 'tear apart'; this was a compound verb formed from the prefix *dia-* 'apart' and *lúein* 'loosen, free' (related to English *less, loose, lose,* and *loss*). In Greek it meant simply 'separation,' but it was borrowed into English, via Latin *dialysis*, as a rhetorical term denoting a set of propositions without a connecting conjunction. The chemical sense, 'separation of molecules or particles' (from which the modern application to 'renal dialysis' comes), was introduced in the 1860s by the chemist Thomas Graham (1805–69).

▶ analysis, less, loose, lose, loss

**diamond**  [13]  *Diamond* is an alteration of *adamant*, a rather archaic term which nowadays refers to hard substances in general, but formerly was also used specifically for 'diamond.' The alteration appears to have come about in Latin of post-classical times: *adamant-* (stem of Latin *adamas*) evidently became Vulgar Latin *\*adimant-* (source of French *aimant* 'magnet'), which appears to have opened the way to confusion, or at least association, with words beginning *dia-*. The result was medieval Latin *diamant-*, which passed into English via Old French *diamant*.

▶ adamant

**diapason**  [14]  *Diapason*, a musical term now used mainly for the main stops on an organ, and also metaphorically for 'range, scope' in general, originally meant literally 'through all.' It comes, via Latin *diapāsōn*, from the Greek phrase *hē dia pasōn khordon sumphonía* 'concord through all the notes': *dia* means 'through,' and *pasōn* is the feminine genitive plural of *pas* 'all' (as in the English prefix *pan-* 'all').

**diaper**  [14]  The notion underlying *diaper* is of extreme whiteness. It comes ultimately from Byzantine Greek *díaspros*, which was a compound formed from the intensive prefix *dia-* and *áspros* 'white.' (*Aspros* itself has an involved history: it started life as Latin *asper* 'rough' – source of English *asperity* – which was applied particularly to bas-relief on carvings and coins; it was borrowed into Byzantine Greek and used as a noun to designate silver coins, and their brightness and shininess led to its reconversion into an adjective, meaning 'white.') *Díaspros* appears originally to have been applied to ecclesiastical vestments, and subsequently to any shiny fabric. When the word first entered English, via medieval Latin *diasprum* and Old French *diapre*, it referred to a rather rich silk fabric embellished with gold thread, but by the 16th century it was being used for less glamorous textiles, of white linen, with a small diamond-shaped pattern. The specific application to a piece of such cloth used as a baby's nappy (still current in American English) seems to have developed in the 16th century.

▸ asperity

**diaphanous** [17] Semantically, *diaphanous* is the ancestor of modern English *see-through*. It comes, via medieval Latin *diaphanus*, from Greek *diaphanés*, a compound adjective formed from *dia-* 'through' and the verb *phaínein* 'show'. Originally in English it meant simply 'transparent,' without its present-day connotations of delicacy: 'Aristotle called light a quality inherent, or cleaving to a Diaphanous body,' Walter Raleigh, *History of the World* 1614.

**diaphragm** [17] The etymological notion underlying *diaphragm* is of a sort of 'fence' or 'partition' within the body. It comes via late Latin *diaphragma* from Greek *diáphragma*. This in turn was a derivative of *diaphrássein* 'divide off, barricade,' a compound verb formed from the intensive prefix *dia-* and *phrássein* 'fence in, enclose.' Originally in Greek *diáphragma* was applied to other bodily partitions than that between the thorax and the abdomen – to the septum which divides the two nostrils, for instance.

**diarrhoea** [16] *Diarrhoea* means literally 'through-flow' (and hence semantically is a parallel formation to *diabetes*). It comes via late Latin *diarrhoea* from Greek *diárrhoia*, a term coined by the physician Hippocrates for 'abnormally frequent defecation.' It was formed from the prefix *dia-* 'through' and *rhein* 'flow' (a relative of English *rheumatism* and *stream*). Of other *-rrhoea* formations (or *-rrhea*, as it is generally spelled in American English), *pyorrhoea* 'inflammation of the tooth sockets' was coined in the early 19th century, and *logorrhoea* at around the turn of the 20th, originally as a clinical term in psychology (although subsequently hijacked as a facetious synonym for 'talkativeness').

▸ rheumatism, stream

**diary** [16] Like its semantic cousin *journal*, a *diary* is literally a 'daily' record. It comes from Latin *diarium*, a derivative of *diēs* 'day.' Originally in classical Latin the word meant 'daily allowance of food or pay,' and only subsequently came to be applied to a 'record of daily events.' From the 17th to the 19th century English also had an adjective *diary*, from Latin *diarius*, meaning 'lasting for one day.'

**diaspora**     see SPORADIC

**diatribe** [16] *Diatribe*'s connotations of acrimoniousness and abusiveness are a relatively recent

(19th-century) development. Originally in English it meant simply 'learned discourse or disquisition.' It comes via Latin *diatriba* from Greek *diatribé* 'that which passes, or literally wears away, the time,' and hence, in scholarly circles, 'study' or 'discourse.' This was a derivative of *diatríbein* 'pass, waste, while away,' a compound verb formed from the intensive prefix *dia-* and *tríbein* 'rub.'

▸ attrition, detriment, trite

**dice** [14] *Dice* originated, as every schoolboy knows, as the plural of *die*, which it has now virtually replaced in British English as the term for a 'cube marked with numbers.' *Die* itself comes via Old French *de* from Latin *datum*, the past participle of the verb *dare* (and source also of English *date*). The main meaning of *dare* was 'give,' but it also had the secondary sense 'play,' as in 'play a chess piece.' The plural of the Old French word was *dez* (itself occasionally used as a singular), which gave rise to such Middle English forms as *des*, *dees*, and *deys* and, by around 1500, *dyse*.

The singular *die* survives for 'dice' in American English, and also in the later subsidiary sense 'block or other device for stamping or impressing' (which originated around 1700).

▸ date, donate

**dictionary** [16] The term *dictionary* was coined in medieval Latin, probably in the 13th century, on the basis of the Latin adjective *dictionārius* 'of words,' a derivative of Latin *dictiō* 'saying,' or, in medieval Latin, 'word.' English picked it up comparatively late; the first known reference to it is in *The pilgrimage of perfection* 1526: 'and so Peter Bercharius [Pierre Bercheur, a 15th-century French lexicographer] in his dictionary describeth it.'

Latin *dictiō* (source also of English *diction* [15]) was a derivative of the verb *dicere* 'say.' Its original meaning was 'point out' rather than 'utter,' as demonstrated by its derivative *indicāre* (source of English *indicate*) and words in other languages, such as Greek *deiknúnai* 'show,' Sanskrit *diç-*'show' (later 'say'), and German *zeihen* 'accuse,' which come from the same ultimate source. Its past participle gave English *dictum* [16], and the derived verb *dictāre* 'assert' produced English *dictate* [17] and *dictator* [14]. It has been the basis of a wide range of other English words, from the more obvious derivatives like *addict* and *predict* to more heavily disguised offspring such as *condition, index,* and *judge*.

▸ addict, condition, dictate, diction, ditto, index, indicate, judge, predict

**didactic**     see DOCTOR

**die** English has two distinct words *die*. The noun, 'cube marked with numbers,' is now more familiar in its plural form (see DICE). The verb, 'stop living' [12], was probably borrowed from Old Norse *deyja* 'die.' This, like English *dead* and *death*, goes back ultimately to an

Indo-European base *dheu-, which some have linked with Greek thánatos 'dead.' It may seem strange at first sight that English should have borrowed a verb for such a basic concept as 'dying' (although some have speculated that a native Old English verb *dīegan or *dēgan did exist), but in fact it is a not uncommon phenomenon for 'die' verbs to change their meaning euphemistically, and therefore to need replacing by new verbs. In the case of the Old English verbs for 'die,' steorfan survives as starve and sweltan in its derivative swelter, while cwelan is represented by the related cwellan 'kill,' which has come down to us as quell.

▶ dead, death

**diet** [13] Diet comes, via Old French diete and Latin diaeta, from Greek díaita 'mode of life.' This was used by medical writers, such as Hippocrates, in the specific sense 'prescribed mode of life,' and hence 'prescribed regimen of food.' It has been speculated that Latin diaeta, presumably in the yet further restricted sense 'day's allowance of food,' came to be associated with Latin diēs 'day.' This gave rise to medieval Latin diēta 'day's journey,' 'day's work,' etc, hence 'day appointed for a meeting,' and thus 'meeting (of legislators).' English acquired this word (coming orthographically full circle as diet) in the 15th century, but it is now mainly used for referring to various foreign legislatures.

**different** [14] English acquired different via Old French different from different-, the present participial stem of Latin differre, a compound verb formed from the prefix dis-'apart' and ferre 'carry' (related to English bear). Latin differre had two distinct strands of meaning that sprang from the original literal 'carry apart, scatter, disperse, separate': one was 'put off, delay,' from which English gets defer; the other 'become or be unlike,' whence English differ [14] and different. The derived indifferent [14] originally meant 'not differentiating or discriminating.'

▶ bear, dilatory

**difficult** [14] Difficult means literally 'not easy.' It is a back-formation from difficulty [14], which was borrowed from Latin difficultās. This was a derivative of the adjective difficilis (source of French difficile), which was a compound formed from the prefix dis- 'not' and facilis 'easy' (whence English facile [15]).

▶ facile

**diffidence** see DEFY

**dig** [13] The origins of dig are not altogether clear. It does not appear to have existed in Old English, although it has been speculated that there was an Old English verb *dīcigian, never recorded, derived from dīc 'ditch' (the standard Old English verbs for 'dig' were delfan and grafan, whence modern English delve and grave). Another theory is that it was borrowed from Old

French diguer 'make a dyke, hollow out the earth.' This was a derivative of the noun digue 'dyke,' which itself was borrowed from a Germanic source that also produced Old English dīc (and indeed modern English dyke).

▶ ditch, dyke

**digest** [15] English took the verb digest from dīgest-, the past participle of Latin dīgerere. This was a compound verb formed from the prefix dī- 'apart' and gerere 'carry,' and originally meant 'divide, distribute' – a sense which developed via 'dissolve' into the specifically physiological 'dissolve and obtain nutrients from food in the body.' A further semantic offshoot of 'distribute' was 'orderly arrangement,' and in fact the earliest use of the word in English was as the noun digest 'summary of information' [14], from Latin dīgesta, the neuter plural of the past participle, literally 'things arranged.'

▶ congest, gesture, ingest

**digit** [15] Digit was borrowed from Latin digitus. This meant 'finger or toe,' but its underlying etymological sense is probably 'pointer'; it appears to come from an Indo-European base *deik-, which also produced Latin dicere 'say' (originally 'point out'), Greek deiknúnai 'show,' Sanskrit diç- 'show,' and possibly English toe. The word was used in classical times for a measure of length, a 'finger's breadth,' but the mathematical sense 'any of the numbers from 0 to 9' (originally as counted on the fingers) is a later development.

Digitalis [17], the scientific name of the 'foxglove,' is a modern Latin use of the Latin adjective digitālis 'of the finger,' perhaps in allusion to the foxglove's German name fingerhut 'thimble,' literally 'finger-hat.'

▶ toe

**dignity** [13] Dignity comes via Old French dignete from Latin dignitās, a derivative of dignus 'worthy.' Also from the same source was Latin dignāre (source of English deign and its derivative disdain) and late Latin dignificāre (source of English dignify [15]). Dignus itself probably came from an earlier unrecorded *decnus 'suitable, fitting,' a derivative of the verb decere, which produced English decent. Other related words in English include condign [15] and indignant [16], while dignitās also produced, via a different line of descent, English dainty.

▶ condign, dainty, deign, disdain, indignant

**digress** see GRADUAL

**dilapidate** [16] It is a common misconception that dilapidate means literally 'fall apart stone by stone,' since the word comes ultimately from Latin lapis 'stone' (as in lapis lazuli [14], literally 'azure stone'). But in fact Latin dīlapidāre meant 'squander' (a sense once current in English, but now superseded). It was a compound verb formed from the prefix dis- 'apart' and lapidāre 'throw stones,' and thus originally must have meant literally 'scatter like stones,' but its only recorded sense is the metaphorical extension 'throw away or destroy wantonly, squander.' The application of the word to the destruction of buildings is a piece of later etymologizing.

▶lapis lazuli

**dilate** [14] Latin *lātus* meant 'wide' (it probably came from an earlier *\*stlātos*, represented in Church Slavonic *stilati* 'spread out,' and has given English *latitude*). It was used with the prefix *dis-* 'apart' to form the verb *dīlātāre* 'expand, extend,' which English acquired via Old French *dilater*. The word has two English nominal derivatives: *dilatation* [14], from late Latin *dīlātātiō*, now mainly restricted to medical contexts, and *dilation* [15], an English formation.

▶latitude

**dilatory** see DEFER

**dilemma** [16] *Dilemma* was originally a technical term in rhetoric, denoting a form of argument in which one's opponent is faced with a choice of two unfavourable alternatives. It comes via Latin *dilemma* from Greek *dilēmma*, a compound formed from *di-* 'two' and *lēmma* 'proposition, premise.' (*Lēmma* itself, which English acquired in the 16th century, came ultimately from *\*lab-*, the base of Greek *lambánein* 'talk.') The 'looser' general sense 'choice between unpleasant alternatives' developed in the late 16th century.

**diligent** [14] The underlying meaning of *diligent* is 'loving.' It comes via Old French *diligent* from the present participial stem of Latin *dīligere* 'esteem highly, love.' This was a compound verb formed from the prefix *dis-* 'apart' and *legere* 'choose' (source of English *elect*, *neglect*, and *select*), and so originally meant literally 'single out.' It gradually passed semantically via 'love' to 'attentiveness,' 'carefulness,' and finally 'steady effort.'

▶elect, neglect, select

**dilute** see LAVATORY

**dime** [14] *Dime* originally meant 'tenth part,' and often specifically a 'tax of one tenth, tithe': 'From all times it was ordained to pay dimes or tithes unto the Lord,' James Howell, *Lexicon tetraglotton* 1660. It came via Old French *disme* from Latin *decima* 'tenth part,' a derivative of *decem* 'ten' (to which English *ten* is related). The application of the word to a coin worth one tenth of a US dollar dates from the 1780s.

▶decimal, ten

**dimension** see MEASURE

**diminish** [15] *Diminish* is a hybrid verb, the result of a marriage between the now obsolete *diminue* [14] and the virtually obsolete *minish* [14], both of which meant 'make smaller.' *Diminue* came via Old French *diminuer* from Latin *dīminuere* 'break into

small pieces'; it was a compound verb formed from the prefix *dē-*'from' and *minuere* 'lessen' (source of English *minute*). *Minish* came via Old French *menuiser* from Vulgar Latin *\*minūtiāre*, a derivative of Latin *minūtus* 'small'; this, bringing the history of *diminish* full circle, was an adjectival use of the past participle of *minuere*.

▶minute

**dimity** see DRILL

**dimple** [13] *Dimple* originally meant 'pothole,' and was not applied to an 'indentation in the flesh' until the 14th century. There is no surviving record of the word in Old English, but it probably existed, as *\*dympel*; Old High German had the cognate *tumphilo*, ancestor of modern German *tümpel* 'pool, puddle.' Both go back to a Germanic *\*dump-*, which may be a nasalized version of *\*d(e)up-*, source of English *deep* and *dip*.

▶deep, dip

**din** [OE] *Din* is an ancient word, traceable back via Old English *dyne* and Germanic *\*dunjaz* to an Indo-European base *\*dhun-*, signifying 'loud noise.' This is also represented in Sanskrit *dhúnis* 'roaring' and Lithuanian *dundéti* 'sound.'

**dine** see DINNER

**dingy** [18] Nobody is quite sure where *dingy* comes from, but the very occasional occurrence of *ding* or *dinge* as Middle English forms of *dung* suggests that it may originally have signified 'dung-coloured' (although if it came from such a source it might have been expected to rhyme with *springy* rather than *stingy*). *Dung* [OE] itself appears to go back ultimately to an Indo-European base *\*dhengh-* denoting 'covering' (relatives include the Lithuanian verb *dengti* 'cover'), so its etymological significance is 'material spread over the earth (for fertilization)' rather than 'excrement.'

▶dung

**dinner** [13] The etymological meaning of *dinner* is 'breakfast.' The word comes ultimately from an unrecorded Vulgar Latin verb *\*disjūnāre*, a compound formed from the prefix *dis-* 'un-' and *jējūnus* 'fasting, hungry' (source of English *jejune* [17]): hence, 'break one's fast.' Old French adopted it in two phases: as *desiuner*, which became modern French *déjeuner* (originally 'breakfast' but later 'lunch'), borrowed by English in the 18th century; and as *disner*. In later Old French this developed into *diner* (source of English *dine* [13]), which came to be used as a noun – from which English acquired *dinner*.

In English it has always denoted the main meal of the day, although the timing of this has varied over the centuries, and continues to do so, according to region, social class, etc.

▶jejune

**dinosaur** [19] *Dinosaur* means literally 'terrible lizard' (something of a misnomer, since dinosaurs are not particularly closely related to modern lizards). The word was coined around 1840 from Greek *deinós* 'terrible' (which goes back to the same Indo-European base, *\*dwei-*, as produced English *dire* [16]) and *sauros* 'lizard' (which occurs in its Latin form *saurus* in the names of specific dinosaurs, such as *brontosaurus* and *tyrannosaurus*).

▶dire

**dint** [OE] *Dint* originally signified a 'blow' or 'hit,' particularly one inflicted by a sword or similar weapon. Its meaning broadened out in the 14th century to 'force of attack or impact,' and this is the source of the modern English phrase *by dint of*, which to begin with denoted 'by force of.' In the 13th century a variant form *dent* arose, which by the 16th century had moved on metaphorically to the sense 'depression made by a blow.'

**diocese** [14] Etymologically, *diocese* means 'administration,' and only gradually did the word become more concrete and specific, via 'area administered, province' to 'ecclesiastical province.' It comes ultimately from Greek *dioíkēsis*, a derivative of *dioikein* 'keep house,' hence 'administer'; this was a compound verb formed from the intensive prefix *dia-* and *oikein* 'inhabit,' which in turn was a derivative of *oikos* 'house' (a distant relative of the *-wich*, *-wick* ending in some British place-names). Its ecclesiastical meaning developed in Greek, and came to the fore as the word passed via Latin *dioecēsis* and late Latin *diocēsis* into Old French *diocise* (source of English *diocese*). In English that has always been the only living sense of the word, although it has been used in historical contexts to refer to provinces of the Roman empire.

**dip** [OE] Like *deep*, *dip* comes ultimately from a Germanic base *\*d(e)up-* 'deep, hollow.' The derived verb, *\*dupjan*, produced Old English *dyppan*, ancestor of modern English *dip*. It originally meant quite specifically 'immerse' in Old English, sometimes with reference to baptism; the sense 'incline downwards' is a 17th-century development.

▶deep, dimple

**diphtheria** [19] The disease *diphtheria* is characterized by the formation of a false membrane in the throat which obstructs breathing, and when the French physician Pierre Bretonneau described it in the 1820s, he coined a name for it based on Greek *diphthéra*, which means 'piece of leather.' Using the suffix *-itis*, denoting inflammation, he formed the modern Latin term *diphtheritis* (used in English until the 1850s) and its French equivalent *diphthérit*. He subsequently substituted *diphthérie*, and this was borrowed into and established in English in the late 1850s when an epidemic of the disease (then also termed *Boulogne sore*

throat*, from its first having been observed in Boulogne) struck Britain.

**diploma** [17] Etymologically, a *diploma* is a 'folded paper.' It comes via Latin *diplōma* from Greek *díplōma*; this was a derivative of the verb *diploun* 'fold,' which in turn came from *diplous* 'double' (a distant cousin of English *double*). Since official letters tended to be folded over, *díplōma* eventually came to mean 'document, especially one issued by the government' – the sense in which the word was acquired by English.

In the 17th and 18th centuries, the use of the derived Latin adjective *diplōmaticus* 'relating to official documents' with specific reference to the field of international relations led eventually to its French descendant, *diplomatique*, coming to mean 'relating to international relations.' English acquired the word as *diplomatic* in the 18th century.

▶double

**dire** SEE DINOSAUR

**direct** [14] English acquired *direct* from *dīrectus*, the past participle of Latin *dīrigere* 'arrange in distinct lines,' hence 'straighten, guide.' This was a compound verb formed from the prefix *dis-* 'apart' and *regere* 'guide, rule' (source of English *regent, region*, etc). The first recorded use of the verb in English was 'write something and send it to a particular person,' a sense now preserved more specifically in the related *address*. (Also ultimately from Latin *dīrigere* is *dirigible* 'steerable airship' [19], a borrowing from French *dirigeable*; this was a derivative of *diriger*, the French descendant of *dīrigere*.)

▶address, dirigible, dress, regent, region

**dirge** [16] *Dirge* is an anglicization of Latin *dīrige*, the imperative singular of *dīrigere* 'guide' (source of English *direct*). It is the first word in the Latin version of Psalm 5, verse 8: *Dirige, Domine, Deus meus, in conspectu tuo viam meam* 'Direct, O Lord, my God, my way in thy sight' (the Authorized Version expands this to 'Lead me, O Lord, in thy righteousness because of my enemies; make thy way straight before thy face'). This formed an antiphon in the Office of the Dead (the funeral service) and hence came to be associated with songs of mourning, and with gloomy singing in general.

▶direct

**dirham** SEE DRAM

**dirt** [13] *Dirt* was originally *drit*, and meant 'excrement' (it was borrowed from Old Norse *drit*, which goes back to a prehistoric Germanic base *\*drit-* that also produced Dutch *dreet* 'excrement'). The toned-down sense 'soiling substance' is of equal antiquity with 'excrement' in English, and the modern English form *dirt* first appeared in the 15th century, by a process known as metathesis in which two sounds are reversed.

**disappoint** [15] *Disappoint* (a borrowing from French *désappointer*) originally meant 'remove from a post or office, sack' – that is, literally, 'deprive of an appointment': 'A monarch . . . hath power . . . to appoint or to disappoint the greatest officers,' Thomas Bowes, *De La Primaudraye's French academie* 1586. This semantic line has now died out, but parallel with it was a sense 'fail to keep an appointment,' which appears to be the ancestor of modern English 'fail to satisfy, frustrate, thwart.'

**disaster** [16] The word *disaster* has astrological connotations. It comes, perhaps via French *désastre*, from Italian *disastro*; this was a back-formation from *disastrato*, literally 'ill-starred,' a compound adjective formed from the pejorative prefix *dis-* and *astro* 'star,' a descendant of Latin *astrum* 'star.' This in turn came from Greek *astron* 'star,' source of English *astronomy* and related to English *star*. So the underlying meaning of the word is 'malevolant astral influence.' Provençal has the parallel *malastre* 'misfortune.'

**disc** [17] *Disc* comes ultimately from Greek *dískos* 'quoit,' a derivative of the verb *dikein* 'throw.' This passed into Latin as *discus*, adopted by English in the 17th century in its original athletic sense. The most salient semantic feature of the *discus* was perhaps its shape, and it was this that English took over in the form *disc* (either adapted from Latin or borrowed from French *disque*). The spelling *disk* is preferred in American English, and it is the standard form used for 'disc-shaped computer storage device.' Other English words ultimately derived from Latin *discus* are *dais*, *desk*, and *dish*.

▶ dais, desk, dish

**discern** [14] *Discern, discreet, discrete,* and *discriminate* all come ultimately from the same source, Latin *discernere*, literally 'separate by sifting,' hence 'distinguish.' This was a compound verb formed from the prefix *dis-* 'apart' and *cernere* 'sift, separate' (source of English *crime* and *secret* and related to *crisis*). The derived noun *discrimen* formed the basis of a new Latin verb *discrimināre*, from which English gets *discriminate* [17]. (Closely related is *decree* [14], whose ultimate source is Latin *dēcernere* 'decide,' also a derivative of *cernere* but with the prefix *dē-*, denoting removal.)

▶ certain, crime, crisis, decree, discreet, discrete, discriminate, excrement, secret

**discipline** [13] The Latin word for 'learner' was *discipulus*, a derivative of the verb *discere* 'learn' (which was related to *docēre* 'teach,' source of English *doctor, doctrine,* and *document*). English acquired the word in Anglo-Saxon times, as *discipul*, and it was subsequently reformulated as *disciple* on the model of Old French *deciple*. Derived from *discipulus* was the noun *disciplīna* 'instruction, knowledge.' Its meaning devel-

oped gradually into 'maintenance of order (necessary for giving instruction),' the sense in which the word first entered English (via Old French *discipline*).

▶ disciple, doctor, doctrine, document

**discomfit** [14] The underlying etymological sense of *discomfit* is 'destroy.' It comes from *desconfit*, the past participle of Old French *desconfire* 'defeat'; this in turn was a descendant of Vulgar Latin *\*disconficere* 'destroy, undo,' a compound verb formed from the prefix *dis-* 'un-' and *conficere* 'put together, complete, accomplish' (source of English *comfit, confection,* and *confetti*). Its original English meaning 'defeat' has weakened over the centuries to 'disconcert,' probably due to the influence of *discomfort*, with which it is often confused.

▶ comfit, confection, confetti

**discord**    see CONCORD
**discourse**    see COURSE

**discreet** [14] *Discreet* and *discrete* [14] are ultimately the same word. Both come from Latin *discrētus*, the past participle of *discernere* 'distinguish' (source of English *discern*). *Discrete* was borrowed direct from Latin, and retains its original meaning more closely: 'distinct, separate.' The Latin abstract noun formed from the past participle, *discrētiō* (source of English *discretion* [14]), developed the sense 'power to make distinctions.' This fed back into the adjective, giving it the meaning 'showing good judgment,' the semantic guise in which English acquired it from Old French *discret*. This was usually spelled *discrete* too until the 16th century, when *discreet* (based on the *-ee-* spelling commonly used in words like *sweet* and *feet* which rhymed with *discrete*) became the established form for the more widely used sense 'judicious.'

▶ certain, discern, discrete, secret

**discriminate**    see DISCERN
**discursive**    see COURSE

**discuss** [14] The ultimate source of *discuss* meant 'smash to pieces.' It comes from *discuss-*, the past participial stem of Latin *discutere*, a compound verb formed from the prefix *dis-*'apart' and *quatere* 'shake' (from which English also gets *concussion* and *quash*). Its literal meaning was 'smash apart, break up,' and this gradually developed via 'scatter, disperse' to, in post-classical times, 'investigate, examine' and eventually 'debate.' The apparently wide semantic discrepancy between 'scatter, disperse' and 'examine' was probably bridged by some such intermediate notion as 'disperse or separate in the mind so as to distinguish and identify each component.'

▶ concussion, quash

**disdain** [14] *Disdain* comes via Old French *desdeigner* from *\*disdignāre*, a Vulgar Latin alteration of Latin *dēdignāri* 'scorn.' This was a compound verb formed from the prefix *dē-* 'un-, not' and *dignāre* 'consider worthy' (source of English *deign* [13]).

▶ dainty, deign, dignity

**disease** [14] *Disease* and *malaise* are parallel formations: both denote etymologically an 'impairment of ease or comfort.' *Disease* comes from Old French *desaise*, a compound formed from the prefix *dis-*'not, lacking' and *aise* 'ease,' and in fact at first meant literally 'discomfort' or 'uneasiness.' It was only towards the end of the 14th century that this sense began to narrow down in English to 'sickness.' (*Malaise* was borrowed from French *malaise*, an Old French formation from *mal* 'bad' and *aise*.)

▶ ease, malaise

**disguise** see GEEZER

**disgust** [16] Something that *disgusts* one is literally 'not to one's taste.' The word comes from Old French *desguster*, a compound verb formed from the prefix *des-* 'not' and *goust* 'taste.' This in turn came from Latin *gustus* (ultimate source of English *gusto*); its modern French descendant is *goût*. Originally, as its derivation implies, *disgust* meant simply 'cause to feel aversion, displease' (and also, with subject and object reversed, 'dislike, loathe': 'Had he not known that I disgusted it, it had never been spoke or done by him,' Robert South, *Sermons* 1716); but over the centuries it has hardened into 'sicken, repel.'

▶ gusto

**dish** [OE] Like *dais*, *desk*, and *disc*, *dish* comes ultimately from Greek *dískos* 'quoit.' As their diversity of form and meaning suggests, they were acquired at various times and by various routes. English got *dish* around 700AD from Latin *discus*, in which the original meaning 'quoit' had been extended metaphorically to 'tray, platter, dish' on the basis of the semantic features 'roundness' and 'flatness.'

▶ dais, desk, disc

**dishevelled** [15] Semantically, *dishevelled* 'with untidy hair' and *unkempt* 'with uncombed hair' are closely parallel formations. *Dishevelled* originated as an adaptation of *deschevele*, the past participle of Old French *descheveler* 'disarrange the hair.' This was a compound verb formed from the prefix *dis-* 'apart' and *chevel* 'hair,' a descendant of Latin *capillus* 'hair' (from which English got *capillary* [17]). In Middle English its meaning was extended to 'without a head-dress,' and even to 'undressed,' but its modern metaphorical application is the more general 'untidy.' (The verb *dishevel* was a late 16th-century back-formation from *dishevelled*.)

▶ capillary

**dismal** [13] Etymologically, *dismal* means 'bad day.' It comes, via Anglo-Norman *dis mal*, from Latin *diēs malī*, literally 'evil days,' a term used to denote the two days in each month which according to ancient superstition were supposed to be unlucky (these days, of set date, were said originally to have been computed by Egyptian astrologers, and were hence also called *Egyptian days*). The term *dismal* thus acquired connotations of 'gloom' and 'calamity.' Its earliest adjectival use, somewhat tautologically, was in the phrase *dismal day*, but in the late 16th century it broadened out considerably in application.

**dismay** [13] The underlying meaning of *dismay* is 'deprive of power' – its second syllable is ultimately the same word as the verb *may*. It comes via Old French *desmaier* from Vulgar Latin *\*dismagāre* 'deprive of power,' a compound verb formed from the prefix *dis-* 'un-' and the borrowed Germanic base *\*mag-*'power, ability' (source of English *may*).

▶ may

**dismiss** [15] Ultimately, *dismiss* and *demise* [16] are the same word: both come from Old French *desmis* or *demis* 'sent away.' These in turn came from *dismissus*, the medieval descendant of Latin *dīmissus*, which was the past participle of *dīmittere*, a compound verb formed from *dis-* 'away' and *mittere* 'send.' In the case of *dismiss*, English originally acquired the word, more logically, in the form *dismit*, based on the Latin infinitive, but in the late 15th century *dismiss*, in the past participial form *dismissed* modelled on the French past participle, began to replace it. *Demise* comes from Anglo-Norman *\*demise*, which represents a nominal use of the feminine form of Old French *demis*. It was originally a technical legal term signifying the transference of property or title, and only in the 18th century came to be used for the 'death' which often brought this about.

▶ commit, demise, mission, transmit

**disparage** see PAIR

**dispatch** [16] *Dispatch* appears to have been borrowed from Spanish *despachar* 'expedite,' but its ultimate origins are not clear. The likeliest source of the Spanish word is Old French *despeechier* 'set free' (source of modern French *dépêcher* 'hurry'), a compound verb formed from the prefix *des-* 'un-' and the verbal element *-peechier* 'impede, hinder,' which is also represented in English *impeach* and goes back ultimately to Latin *pedica* 'shackle.' The semantic history of *dispatch* thus appears to be 'unshackle,' 'set free,' 'send away, get rid of,' and hence (with the notion of 'freeing from restraint') 'send away quickly.' (The currency of the alternative spelling *despatch* is due to its occurrence in Dr Johnson's *Dictionary* 1755.)

▶ impeach

**dispel** see PULSE

**dispense** [14] *Dispense* comes ultimately from Latin *dispendere* 'weigh out' (partial source of English *spend*). This was a compound verb formed from the prefix *dis-* 'away' and *pendere* 'weigh,' a relative of *pendēre* 'hang,' from which English gets *pendulum, pendant*, and *penthouse*. It had a derivative, *dispensāre*, denoting repeated action: hence 'pay out, distribute,' senses which passed into English via Old French *dispenser*. In medieval Latin *dispensāre* also came to mean 'administer justice,' and hence 'exempt, condone'; this was the source of the English usage *dispense with* 'do without.'

▶ pendulum, pendant, penthouse, spend

**display** [14] *Display* originally meant 'unfold,' and it is related not to modern English *play* but to *ply*. It comes via Old French *despleier* (whose modern French descendant, *déployer*, is the source of English *deploy* [18]) from Latin *displicāre*. This was a compound verb formed from the prefix *dis-* 'un-' and *plicāre* 'fold' (source of or related to English *accomplish, complicated, ply*, and *simple*), and in classical Latin seems only to have had the metaphorical meaning 'scatter.' In medieval Latin, however, it returned to its underlying literal sense 'unfold,' which was originally retained in English, particularly with reference to sails or flags. The notion of 'spreading out' is retained in *splay*, which was formed by lopping off the first syllable of *display* in the 14th century.

▶ accomplish, complicate, deploy, ply, simple

**disport** see SPORT

**dispose** see POSITION

**dispute** [13] *Dispute* comes via Old French *disputer* from Latin *disputāre*, a compound verb formed from the prefix *dis-* 'separately' and *putāre* 'consider, reckon, think' (source of a wide range of English words, from *computer* to *reputation*). It was originally a commercial term, denoting the calculation of a sum by considering each of its items separately, but its meaning eventually broadened out to 'estimate, examine, weigh up' – either mentally or (the sense which prevailed) by discussion with others. The neutral sense 'discuss' held centre stage in classical Latin, but later (in the Vulgate, for instance) a note of acrimony appeared, signalling the beginnings of *dispute*'s current sense 'argue.'

▶ computer, count, putative, reputation

**disrupt** see ROUT

**dissect** see SECTION

**dissemble** see SIMILAR

**disseminate** see SEED

**dissent** see SENSE

**dissolve** see SOLVE

**dissonant** see SOUND

**dissuade** see PERSUADE

**distaff** [OE] The compound noun *distaff* 'rod for holding flax, wool, etc in spinning' was a late Old English formation from *\*dis* 'bunch of flax' (a word which survives in *bedizen* [17], a derivative of the obsolete *dizen*, which originally meant 'put flax on to a rod'

and hence 'dress up in finery') and *staff*. The now fairly archaic use of phrases such as *distaff side* to refer to 'women' comes from the traditional pigeon-holing of spinning as a woman's job.

▶ bedizen

**distance** [13] Etymologically, things that are *distant* stand far apart from each other. The word comes via Old French from Latin *distantia*, an abstract noun formed from *distāns*, the present participle of *distāre* 'be remote.' This was a compound verb formed from the prefix *dis-* 'apart' and *stāre* 'stand' (source of English *state, station, statue*, etc and related to English *stand*).

▶ stand, state, station, statue

**distemper** English has two distinct words *distemper*, although ultimately they come from the same source, Latin *temperāre* 'mingle' (source of English *temper, temperate*, and *temperature*). This formed the basis of two separate medieval Latin verbs, both compounded from the prefix *dis-* but using it in quite different ways. *Dis-*in the sense 'reversal of a current state' joined with *temperāre* in the specialized meaning 'mingle in proper proportion' to produce *distemperāre* 'upset the proper balance of bodily humours,' hence 'vex, make ill.' This passed directly into English as *distemper* [14], and survives today mainly as the term for an infectious disease of dogs. *Dis-*joined with *temperāre* in its intensive function produced medieval Latin *distemperāre* 'mix thoroughly, soak,' which entered English via Old French *destemprer* in the 14th century. The meaning 'soak, steep, infuse' survived until the 17th century: 'Give the Horse thereof every morning . . . the quantity of a Hasel-nut distempered in a quart of Wine,' Edward Topsell, *History of Four-footed Beasts* 1607. The word's modern application, to a water-based decorator's paint, comes from the fact that the pigment is mixed with or infused in water (the same notion lies behind English *tempera* [19], borrowed from Italian).

▶ temper, temperate, temperature

**distend** see TEND

**distil** see STILL

**distinct** [14] Etymologically, *distinct* is the past participle of *distinguish*. It comes from *distinctus*, past participle of Latin *distinguere* 'separate, discriminate' (source, via the present stem of Old French *distinguer*, of English *distinguish* [16]). This was a compound verb formed from the prefix *dis-* 'apart' and the verbal element *-stinguere* 'prick, stick,' and hence meant originally 'separate by pricking' (*-stinguere*, related to English *stick* and *instigate*, is not found as an independent verb in Latin in the sense 'prick,' but *stinguere* does occur in the remote metaphorical meaning 'quench' – a development mirrored in German *ersticken* 'stifle, suffocate' – which lies behind English *ex-*

*tinct* and *extinguish*). *Distingué* is an early 19th-century adoption of the past participle of French *distinguer*.

▶ distinguish, extinct, instigate, stick

**distraught**   see STRAIGHT

**distribute**   see TRIBE

**district**   [17]   *District* started life as the past participle of the verb which gave English *distrain* [13] and *strain*. It came via French *district* from medieval Latin *districtus*; this meant literally 'seized, compelled,' and hence was used as a noun in the sense 'seizure of offenders,' and hence 'exercise of justice,' and finally 'area in which justice is so exercised (in the feudal system).' This was the word's meaning when it was first borrowed into English, and it was not really until the early 18th century that its much more general modern application developed. *Districtus* was the past participle of Latin *distringere*, a compound verb formed from the prefix *dis-* 'apart' and *stringere* 'pull tight' (source of English *strain, strict, stringent, stress*, etc). In classical times it meant 'draw apart, detain, hinder,' but by the Middle Ages this had moved on to 'seize, compel,' which were the main senses in which it entered English as *distrain* (via Old French *destreindre*). Latin *districtus* was also the source of a Vulgar Latin noun *\*districtia* 'narrowness,' which passed via Old French *destresse* into English as *distress* [13].

▶ distrain, distress, strain, stress, strict, stringent

**disturb**   see TROUBLE

**ditch**   [OE]   Like its close relative *dyke* [13], *ditch* probably comes ultimately from a long-lost language once spoken on the shores of the Baltic. Its source-word seems to have represented an all-embracing notion of 'excavation,' including not just the hole dug but also the mound formed from the excavated earth (which perhaps supports the suggestion that *dig* belongs to the same word-family). This dichotemy of sense is preserved in *dyke*, whose original meaning, from Old Norse *dík*, was 'ditch,' but which came in the 15th century to denote 'embankment' (probably under the influence of Middle Dutch *dijc* 'dam').

▶ dig, dyke

**ditto**   [17]   *Ditto* is a precisely parallel formation to English *said* 'aforementioned' (as in 'the said John Smith'). It is the Tuscan dialect version of Italian *detto*, which comes from *dictus*, the past participle of Latin *dīcere* 'say' (source of English *dictionary* and a vast range of related words). It was originally used in Italian to avoid repeating the name of the month when giving a series of dates, much as *inst* and *ult* are used in commercial English.

▶ diction, dictionary

**diurnal**   see JOURNEY

**diva**   see DIVINE

**divan**   [16]   The word *divan* has a long and spectacularly variegated semantic history. It started out as Persian *dēvān*, which originally meant 'small book.' This came to be used specifically for 'account book,' and eventually for 'accountant's office.' From this its application broadened out to cover various official chambers and the bodies which occupied them, such as tax offices, customs collectors, courts, and councils of state. And finally it developed to 'long seat,' of the sort which lined the walls of such Oriental chambers. The word carried these meanings with it via Arabic *dīwān* and Turkish *dīvān* into the European languages, and English acquired most of them as a package deal from French *divan* or Italian *devano* (it did not, however, include the 'customs' sense which, via the Turkish variant *duwan*, survives in French *douane*, Italian *dogana*, Spanish *aduana*, etc). The 19th-century sense 'smoking lounge' seems to be an exclusively European development.

**dive**   [OE]   Old English *dȳfan* 'dive' came from a prehistoric Germanic *\*dūbjan*. This was a derivative of the base *\*d(e)ub-*, a variant of which, *\*d(e)up-*, was the source of English *deep* and *dip*. The colloquial use of the noun for a disreputable bar, nightclub, etc, which comes from 1880s America, is probably a reference to someone 'diving' out of sight into such an establishment, which was often in a basement.

▶ deep, dip

**diverge**   see VERGE

**diverse**   [13]   *Diverse* is one of a small family of English words, including also *divers, divert*, and *divorce*, which come ultimately from Latin *dīvertere*. This was a compound verb formed from the prefix *dis-* 'aside' and *vertere* 'turn' (source of English *verse, version, vertebra*, etc and related to *worth*), and hence meant literally 'turn aside, turn out of the way.' It developed in various metaphorical directions, however. One was 'turn one's husband or wife out of the way' which, via the variant *dīvortere*, gave English *divorce* [14]. The central sense of the verb passed more or less unchanged into English, via French *divertir*, as *divert* [15], but its past participle *diversus* illustrates a further metaphorical strand, in which 'turned aside' has become 'separate, different.' English acquired this via Old French in the 13th century in two distinct forms: masculine *divers* and feminine *diverse*. The present-day semantic distinction between the former ('various, several') and the latter ('different') had established itself by around 1700.

▶ divert, divorce, verse, version, worth

**divest**  see VEST

**divide**  [14]  Etymologically, *divide* shares its underlying notion of 'separation' with *widow* 'woman parted from or bereft of her husband,' which comes ultimately from the same source. English acquired it from Latin *dīvidere* 'split up, divide.' This was a compound verb formed from the prefix *dis-* 'apart' and *-videre*, a verbal element meaning 'separate' which is represented in Sanskrit *vindháte* 'is empty' as well as in *widow*, and goes back to an Indo-European base *weidh-* 'separate.'

English *device* and *devise* come ultimately from *dīvisāre*, a Vulgar Latin derivative of *dīvidere*, and *individual* belongs to the same word family.

▶ device, individual, widow

**divine**  [14]  Like *deity*, *divine* comes ultimately from Indo-European *deiwos*, an ancestor whose godly connotations seem to have developed from earlier associations with 'sky' and 'day,' and which probably originally meant 'shining.' Its Latin descendants included *deus* 'god' (source of English *deity*) and the adjective *dīvus* 'godlike' (the noun use of its feminine form, *dīva*, for 'goddess' entered English via Italian as *diva* 'prima donna' [19]). From *dīvus* was derived the further adjective *dīvīnus*, which became Old French *devin* and eventually English *divine*. *Dīvīnus* was used as a noun meaning, in classical times, 'soothsayer' (whence, via the Latin derivative *dīvīnāre*, the English verb *divine*) and in the Middle Ages 'theologian' (whence the nominal use of English *divine* in the same sense).

▶ deity

**divorce**  see DIVERSE

**divulge**  [15]  Etymologically, to *divulge* something is to make it known to the vulgar masses. The word comes from Latin *dīvulgāre*, a compound verb formed from the prefix *dis-* 'widely' and *vulgāre* 'make common, publish.' This in turn was derived from *vulgus* 'common people,' source of English *vulgar*. At first in English it was semantically neutral, meaning 'make widely known' ('fame of his ouvrages [works, achievements] hath been divulged,' William Caxton, *Book of Eneydos* 1490), but by the 17th century the word's modern connotations of 'disclosing what should be secret' had developed.

▶ vulgar

**dizzy**  [OE]  *Dizzy* originally signified 'foolish, stupid,' a meaning which from the 13th century retreated into dialectal use and has only comparatively recently returned to the mainstream language in the milder form 'scatterbrained.' The now central sense 'giddy' is recorded from the 14th century. The word comes from a West Germanic base *dus-*, which also produced Dutch *duizelen* 'be giddy.' Its formal and semantic similarity to *doze* and *tizzy* are obvious, but no actual etymological link between the three seems ever to have been established.

**do**  [OE]  Not surprisingly, *do* is a verb of great antiquity. It goes back to the Indo-European base *dhē-* (source also of English *deed* and *doom*), which signified 'place, put.' This sense remains uppermost in descendants such as Sanskrit *dhā-* and Greek *títhēmi* (related to English *theme*), but a progression to 'make, do' shows itself in Latin *facere* (source of English *fact* and a host of other words) and West Germanic *dōn*. 'Make' is now the central signification of English *do*, although traces of the earlier 'put, place' survive in such fossilized forms as *don* and *doff*, and 'do someone to death.' Other Germanic relatives include German *tun* and Dutch *doen*, but the Scandinavian languages have not adopted the verb, preferring instead for 'do' one which originally meant 'make ready' (Danish *gøre*, Swedish *gåra*) and which is related to English *gear*.

▶ deed, doom, fact, fashion, theme

**dock**  English has no fewer than four distinct words *dock*. The oldest is the plant-name, which comes from Old English *docce*. *Dock* for ships [14] was borrowed from Middle Low German or Middle Dutch *docke*, which may have come from Vulgar Latin *ductia* 'duct, conduit,' a hypothetical derivative of Latin *dūcere* 'lead' (source of English *duke, educate*, etc). *Dock* 'cut off' [14] was originally a verbal application of the noun *dock* 'horse's short tail,' which appears to go back to a Germanic *dukk-* 'bundle'; it may be the source of *docket* [15]. *Dock* for prisoners [16] was originally thieves' slang, borrowed from Flemish *dok* 'cage.'

▶ duke, educate, induce / docket

**doctor**  [14]  *Doctor, doctrine*, and *document* all go back ultimately to the Latin verb *docēre* 'teach.' This in turn was a descendant of an Indo-European base *dok-, *dek-* which also produced Greek *dokein* 'seem, think' (source of English *dogma* [17], *orthodox*, and *paradox*) and *didáskein* 'learn' (source of English *didactic* [17]) and Latin *decere* 'be fitting or suitable' (source of English *decent, decorate*, and *dignity*) and *dexter* (source of English *dextrous*). Latin *doctor* was derived from *doctus*, the past participle of *docēre*, and came into English via Old French *doctour*. It originally meant 'teacher,' and the main modern sense of 'medical practitioner,' although sporadically recorded in Middle English, did not become firmly established until the late 16th century. Latin *doctrīna* 'teaching, learning,' a derivative of Latin *doctor*, produced English *doctrine* [14]. Latin *documentum*, which came directly from *docēre*, originally meant 'lesson,' but in medieval Latin its signification had passed through 'written instruction' to 'official paper.' English acquired it as *document* [15]. The derivative *documentary* is 19th-century.

▶ dainty, decent, decorate, dextrous, didactic, dignity, doctrine, document, dogma, orthodox, paradox

**dodo**  [17]  When Portuguese explorers first encountered the unfortunate dodo on the island of Mauritius, it struck them as a clumsy and foolish bird, so they applied to it the Portuguese word *doudo* 'simpleton.' The name has stuck in English (although in the 17th century it had some competition from the French and Dutch term *dronte*). The first record of the simile 'dead as a dodo' comes from 1904, over 200 years after the extinction of the species, although the word had been used since the late 19th century as a metaphor for someone or something hopelessly out of date: 'He belongs to the Dodo race of real unmitigated toryism,' Lisle Carr, *Judith Gwynne* 1874.

**doff**  [14]  *Doff, don* [14], and the now obsolete *dout* [16] and *dup* [16], contractions respectively of 'do off, on, out, and up,' preserve the ancient meaning of *do*, 'put, place.' They were standard Middle English forms, but gradually fell out of the mainstream language into dialect (from which *dout* and *dup* never emerged). Sir Walter Scott, however, included *doff* and *don*, in their specific sense 'remove *or* put on clothing,' in his long list of medieval lexical revivals ('My experience has been in donning steel gauntlets on mailed knights,' *Fair Maid of Perth* 1828), and they have survived as archaisms ever since.

**dog**  [11]  *Dog* is one of the celebrated mystery words of English etymology. It appears once in late Old English, in the *Prudentius glosses*, where it translates Latin *canis*, but its use does not seem to have proliferated until the 13th century, and it did not replace the native *hound* as the main word for the animal until the 16th century. It has no known relatives of equal antiquity in other European languages, although several borrowed it in the 16th and 17th centuries for particular sorts of 'dog': German *dogge* 'large dog, such as a mastiff,' for instance, French *dogue* 'mastiff,' and Swedish *dogg* 'bulldog.'

**dogma**  see DOCTOR

**doily**  [17]  In the latter part of the 17th century a certain Mr Doily kept a celebrated draper's shop in the Strand, London, not too far from where the Aldwych now is ('The famous Doily is still fresh in every one's Memory, who raised a Fortune by finding out Materials for such Stuffs as might be at once cheap and genteel,' *Spectator* 1712). He gave his name first to a sort of light fabric used for summer wear ('Some Doily Petticoats and Manto's we have,' John Dryden, *Kind Keeper* 1678) and then, early in the 18th century, to a variety of ornamental table napkin ('After dinner we had coarse Doily-napkins, fringed at each end, upon the table to drink with,' Jonathan Swift, *Journal to Stella* 1711).

**dole**  [OE]  In Old English, the noun *dāl* meant simply 'part, portion' (it came from a Germanic base *dail-*, which also produced English *deal*). By the 14th century this had developed into the more specific 'portion (of food, money, etc) handed out as a charitable donation to those in need.' This is the source of the phrase *on the dole* 'receiving government benefit,' first recorded in the 1920s. The verb *dole* 'distribute' arose in the 15th century; its modern use, *dole out*, is an 18th-century development.

▸ deal

**doll**  [16]  *Doll* comes from the name *Dorothy*: the changing of *r* to *l* in personal names is a common English phenomenon of long standing, from Shakespeare's Prince *Hal* (for *Harry*) to the currently familiar *Del* and *Tel* (for *Derek* and *Terry*). The word was originally applied to a man's mistress (much like *moll*, which came from *Mary*), but in the 18th century it came to be applied to a 'toy baby.' The pet form *dolly* dates from the 17th century.

**dollar**  [16]  English originally acquired the word *dollar* in the form *doler*; this was the Low German form of German *taler*, a large silver coin in use in the German states from the 16th century. The word was short for *Joachimstaler*, literally 'of Joachim's valley,' and is a reference to the fact that silver from which the coins were made was mined near Joachimstal (modern Jachymov) in the Erzgebirge mountains, Czechoslovakia. By around 1700 the spelling *dollar* had become fairly standard, and in 1785 the term was formally adopted for the main unit of currency in the USA. It has since been taken up by over thirty countries around the world.

▸ dale

**dolmen**  [19]  English acquired the word *dolmen* for a 'prehistoric structure of two upright stones surmounted by a horizontal one' from French, but its ultimate source is Celtic. The element *men* means 'stone' (it occurs also in *menhir* [19], literally 'long stone') but there is disagreement about the first syllable. It is usually said to represent *tōl* 'table,' a Breton borrowing from Latin *tabula* 'board, plank,' but another view is that it is Cornish *tol* 'hole,' and that the compound as a whole means literally 'stone hole,' a reference to the aperture formed by the top stone lying on the two side stones.

▸ menhir

**dolphin**  [13]  The ultimate source of *dolphin* is Greek *delphís* 'dolphin,' which some have linked with Greek *delphýs* 'womb.' From it was derived *delphínion*, a name given to the plant larkspur on account of the dolphin-like shape of part of its flower, acquired by English via Latin as *delphinium* [17]. Latin took over Greek *delphís* as *delphīnus*, which passed into English along two channels. The classical form was borrowed as *delfyn* or *delphin*, which did not survive the 17th century. But the Vulgar Latin form *\*dalphīnus* progressed to Old French *daulphin* (ultimate source of English *dauphin*), which English acquired as *dalphyn*.

*Dolphin*, first recorded in the 14th century, appears to be an English alteration of the form *da(u)lphin*.

▶ dauphin, delphinium

**dolt**   see DULL

**domain**   [17] Etymologically, *domain* means 'land belonging to a lord,' but its resemblance to such words as *dominate* and *dominion* is somewhat adventitious. Until the 17th century it was essentially the same word as *demesne*: *demaine* or *demeine* 'lord's estate' was the Old French equivalent of (and indeed source of) English *demesne*. It came ultimately from Latin *dominicus* 'of a lord,' but its etymological connection with Latin *dominus* 'lord' had become somewhat obscured over the centuries. But then, around 1600, by association with Latin *dominium* (source of English *dominion*), French *demaine* became altered to *domaine*, which English borrowed as *domain*.

▶ dame, demesne, dominate, dominion

**dome**   [16] *Dome* originally meant 'house' in English – it was borrowed from Latin *domus* 'house' (source of English *domestic*). However, in other European languages the descendants of *domus* had come to signify more than a humble dwelling house, and its new meanings spread to English. The word increasingly encompassed stately mansions and important places of worship. Italian *duomo* and German *dom* mean 'cathedral,' for instance (a sense adopted by English in the late 17th and early 18th centuries), and since a leading characteristic of Italian cathedrals is their cupola, the word was soon applied to this.

▶ domestic

**domestic**   [16] *Domestic* comes, via French *domestique*, from Latin *domesticus*, a derivative of *domus* 'house.' This can be traced back to an Indo-European *\*domo-*, *\*domu-*, which was also the source of Greek *dómos* and Sanskrit *dama-* 'house,' and goes back in its turn to a base *\*dem-*, *\*dom-* 'build' which gave rise to English *daunt, tame, timber*, and probably *despot*. A further derivative of *domus* is *domicile* [15], from Latin *domicilium* 'dwelling-place,' and it is also the ultimate source of the wide range of English words (*dominate, dominion*, etc) based immediately on Latin *dominus* 'master.'

▶ dame, daunt, dome, dominion, tame, timber

**dominion**   [15] *Dominion*, in common with *demesne, domain, dominant, dominate, domineer, dominie, domino*, and *don*, and indeed *danger* and *dungeon*, comes ultimately from Latin *dominus* 'lord, master.' This was a derivative of Latin *domus* 'house' (source of English *dome*) and, like the parallel Greek formation *despótēs* (source of English *despot*), originally meant 'master of the house.' Its most direct descendant in modern English is *don* [17]. This is the Spanish reflex of Latin *dominus*, used as a title of respect for Spanish lords or gentlemen, and has been ap-

plied since the mid 17th century (originally as a piece of university slang) to university teachers. Of derivatives, *dominion* comes from Latin *dominium* 'property' (of which a post-classical descendant was *dominiō* or *domniō*, source of English *dungeon*); *dominate* [17] and *dominant* [15] come from the verb *dominārī* 'be lord and master'; *domineer* [16] is also from *dominārī*, via French *dominer* and early modern Dutch *domineren*; and *dominie* [17], a Scottish term for a 'schoolmaster,' probably comes from the Latin vocative case *dominē*.

▶ dame, danger, demesne, despot, dome, domestic, dominate

**domino**   [18] The word *domino* was borrowed from French, where it originally signified (in the 16th century) a sort of hooded cloak worn by priests. It presumably represents a form of Latin *dominus* 'lord, master,' but the reason for the application has never been satisfactorily explained (one suggestion is that it comes from the ritual formula *benedicamus Domino* 'let us bless the Lord'). By the time English acquired it, it had come to mean 'hooded cloak with a half-mask, worn at masquerades,' and by the 19th century it was being used for the mask itself. It is far from clear whether the application to the game played with small rectangular blocks, which dates in English from the 19th century, represents a new use of the same word or a return to the original Latin, but either way the reason behind the usage is not known. A possibility that has been advanced is that the winner of the game originally shouted *domino!* 'lord!'

**don**   see DOFF

**donation**   see DATE

**donkey**   [18] The usual English word for 'donkey' from Anglo-Saxon times was *ass*, and *donkey* is not recorded until Francis Grose entered it in his *Dictionary of the vulgar tonge* 1785: 'Donkey or Donkey Dick, a he or Jack-ass.' No one really knows where it came from. The usual explanation offered is that it was based on *dun* 'brownish grey' and the diminutive suffix *-ey*, with the intermediate *k* added in imitation of *monkey* (*donkey* originally rhymed with *monkey*).

▶ dun

**doom**   [OE] *Doom* derives ultimately from *\*dō-*, the Germanic base from which the verb *do* comes. This originally meant 'put, place,' and so Germanic *\*dōmaz* signified literally 'that which is put.' By the time it reached Old English as *dōm* a more concrete sense 'law, decree, judgment' had developed (this lies behind the compound *doomsday* 'day of judgment' [OE], whose early Middle English spelling has been preserved in *Domesday book*). The modern sense '(evil) fate' first appeared in the 14th century.

▶ deem, do

**door**   [OE] Old English had two closely related words for 'door': *duru* (mirrored by German *tür* 'door') and *dor* (which corresponds to German *tor* 'gate'). They gradually came together during the Middle English period. Both go back ultimately to the Indo-European base *\*dhwer-*, which also produced Greek *thúrā* 'door' (source of English *thyroid*), Latin *foris* 'door' (source of English *foreign* and *forest*) and *forum*, Sanskrit *dvar-*'door,' Russian *dver'* 'door,' Lithuanian *dùrys* 'gate,' etc.

▶ foreign, forest, thyroid

**dope** [19] *Dope* originated in the USA, where it was borrowed from Dutch *doop* 'sauce.' This was a derivative of the verb *doopen* 'dip,' which is related to English *dip*. It was at first used as a general colloquialism for any thick semi-liquid preparation, whether used as a food or, for example, as a lubricant, but during the 19th century some specific strands began to emerge: notably 'drug,' and in particular 'opium,' and 'varnish painted on the fabric of an aircraft.' The effects of the former led to its use in the sense 'fool,' and to the coinage of the adjective *dopey*, first recorded in the 1890s. The sense 'information' dates from around 1900.

▶ deep, dip

**doppelganger** [19] English borrowed *doppelganger* from German *doppelgänger*, which means literally 'double-goer.' It was originally used in the sense 'ghostly apparition of a living person, especially one that haunts its real counterpart' ('hell-hounds, doppel-gangers, boggleboes,' M A Denham, *Denham tracts* 1851), but in the course of the 20th century it has become increasingly restricted to a flesh-and-blood 'person identical to another, double.'

▶ double

**dormant** [14] Like *dormitory* and *dormer*, *dormant* comes ultimately from Latin *dormīre* 'sleep,' which is related to Sanskrit *drā-* 'sleep' and Russian *dremat'* 'doze.' *Dormant* was borrowed from French *dormant*, the present participle of *dormir* 'sleep,' while *dormitory* [15] comes from Latin *dormītōrium*, a derivative of the past participle of *dormīre*. *Dormer* [16], from Old French *dormeor*, a derivative of *dormir*, originally signified a 'dormitory window.' (It is not clear whether *dormouse* [15] is related, but if it is it would mean literally 'sleeping mouse,' or conceivably even 'sleeper,' from French *dormeuse*, the feminine of *dormeur* 'sleeper.')

▶ dormer, dormitory

**dorsal** see DOSS

**dose** [15] A *dose* is literally 'that which is given to one' – etymologically and semantically, it is a parallel formation to *donation*. It comes via French *dose* and late Latin *dosis* from Greek *dósis*, a derivative of the verb *didónai* 'give' (which is related to English *date*, *donate*, etc). It originally meant simply 'giving, gift,' but was used by Greek physicians such as Galen for

'portion of medicine administered,' and it is that application that has proved most durable. The modern slang sense 'venereal infection' dates from just before World War I.

▶ date, donate

**doss** [18] The use of *doss* in senses associated with 'lying down on a bed' comes from an earlier notion of 'lying on one's back.' In the 18th century the word was *dorse*, a borrowing from Latin *dorsum* 'back,' but by the 19th century it had become *doss*, perhaps owing to the influence of French *dos*. Other English words from the same source include *endorse*, the adjective *dorsal* [15], and *dossier* [19]. This was acquired from French *dossier*, a derivative of *dos*, which originally signified a 'bunch of papers with a label on the back.'

▶ dorsal, dossier, endorse

**dot** [OE] The underlying meaning of *dot* seems to be 'small lump or raised mark.' In Old English (in which there is only a single record of its use) it meant 'head of a boil,' and it could well be related to English *tit* 'nipple.' The word disappears from written texts between the 11th and the 16th centuries, and resurfaces in the sense 'small lump.' The modern meaning 'small roundish mark' does not appear until the 17th century. *Dottle* 'unburnt tobacco in the bottom of a pipe' [15] is a diminutive form of *dot*.

▶ dottle, tit

**dote** [13] English may have borrowed *dote* from Middle Dutch *doten* 'be silly,' but its ultimate origins are not known. To begin with it meant 'be silly' in English too (a sense now mainly preserved in its various derivatives), and 'show excessive fondness' did not develop until the 15th century. Related forms include *dotage* [14], where the notion of 'simple-mindedness due to senility' (implicit in the verb from earliest times) has passed to simply 'senility'; *dotterel* [15], the name of a sort of plover, supposedly so called because it was foolish enough to allow itself to get caught; and *dotty* [19], an alteration of Scottish English *dottle* 'fool,' which was a derivative of *dote*.

▶ dotage, dotterel, dotty

**dottle** see DOT

**double** [13] *Double* comes via Old French *doble* or *duble* from Latin *duplus* (direct source of English *duple* [16]). This was a compound adjective formed from *duo* 'two' and an Indo-European element *\*pl-* which denoted 'folding' (it is present also in English *fold* and *ply*). The same semantic elements went to make up English *twofold*, and indeed *duplex* (see DUPLICATE), and also Greek *diplous* (source of English *diploma* and *diplomat*). The underlying meaning of *doublet* 'close-fitting jacket' [14] (borrowed from French *doublet*, a derivative of *double*) is 'something folded,' while *doubloon* [17], borrowed via French *doublon* from

Spanish *doblón* (a derivative of *doble* 'double') was originally a gold coin worth 'double' a pistole.

▶diploma, diplomat, dub, duplicate, fold, ply

**doubt** [13] English acquired the verb *doubt* from Old French *doter* or *duter*, a descendant of Latin *dubitāre* 'waver, be uncertain' (the *b* was reintroduced from the Latin spelling in the 15th century). *Dubitāre* was closely related to Latin *dubius* 'uncertain' (ultimate source of English *dubious* [16]), which appears to have been based on *duo* 'two,' and thus to have meant originally 'wavering between two possibilities.' In Old French, the sense 'fear' developed, and this was an important meaning of the word in Middle English; it survives in the derivative *redoubtable* [14], literally 'fearable.'

▶dubious, redoubtable

**douche** see DUCT

**dough** [OE] *Dough* is an ancient word, with related forms scattered throughout the Indo-European languages. It goes back to an Indo-European base *dheigh-*, which meant 'mould, form, knead,' and produced Latin *fingere* 'mould' and *figūra* 'figure' (source between them of English *effigy, faint, feign, fiction, figment,* and *figure*), Sanskrit *dih-* 'smear,' Gothic *digan* 'mould, form,' Avestan (a dialect of Old Iranian) *diz* 'mould, form' (source of the last syllable of English *paradise*), and the Old English element *dig-* 'knead,' which forms the last syllable of *lady*. It also produced the prehistoric Germanic *daigaz* 'something kneaded,' hence 'dough,' whose modern Germanic descendants include German *teig*, Dutch *deg*, Swedish *deg*, Danish *dej*, and English *dough*.

In northern areas *dough* used to be pronounced /duf/, which has given modern English the 'plum *duff*' [19].

▶dairy, duff, effigy, faint, fiction, figure, lady, paradise

**doughty** [11] *Doughty* originally had the rather general sense 'worthy, virtuous' – 'brave' is a secondary specialization. It comes from late Old English *dohtig*, an unexplained variant of an earlier Old English *dyhtig*, which appears to have derived ultimately from a prehistoric Germanic *duhtiz* 'ability, capacity.' This in turn came from a verb *dugan* 'be able or strong,' which itself came into Old English and survived dialectally until the 19th century as *dow* 'be able to do something' or 'thrive.'

**down** Effectively, English now has three distinct words *down*, but two of them are intimately related: for *down* 'to or at a lower place' [11] originally meant 'from the hill' – and the Old English word for hill in this instance was *dūn*. This may have been borrowed from an unrecorded Celtic word which some have viewed as the ultimate source also of *dune* [18] (borrowed by English from Middle Dutch *dūne*) and even of *town*. Its usage is now largely restricted to the plural form, used as a geographical term for various ranges of hills (the applica-

tion to the North and South Downs in southern England dates from at least the 15th century).

The Old English phrase *of dūne* 'from the hill' had by the 10th century become merged into a single word, *adūne*, and broadened out semantically to 'to a lower place, down,' and in the 11th century it started to lose its first syllable – hence *down*. Its use as a preposition dates from the 16th century. (The history of *down* is closely paralleled in that of French *à val*, literally 'to the valley,' which also came to be used for 'down'; it is the source of French *avaler* 'descend, swallow,' which played a part in the development of *avalanche*.)

*Down* 'feathers' [14] was borrowed from Old Norse *dúnn*.

▶dune

**dowry** [14] English acquired *dowry* via Anglo-Norman *dowarie* from Old French *douaire* (source of the originally synonymous but now little-used *dower* [14]). This in turn came from medieval Latin *dōtārium*, a derivative of Latin *dōs* 'dowry,' which was related to *dāre* 'give' (source of English *date, donate*, etc). Its associated verb, *dōtāre* 'endow,' is the ancestor of English *endow*.

▶date, donate, endow

**dozen** [13] *Dozen* traces its ancestry back to the Latin word for 'twelve,' *duodecim*. This was a compound formed from *duo* 'two' and *decem* 'ten.' This gradually developed in the post-classical period via *dōdece* to *doze*, which, with the addition of the suffix *-ēna*, produced Old French *dozeine*, source of the English word.

▶duodenum

**drab** [16] *Drab* is a variant of the now obsolete form *drap*, which was borrowed from Old French *drap* 'cloth' (source also of English *drape, draper*, and *trappings*). It was originally a noun meaning 'cloth' in English too, but the beginnings of its transition to the modern English adjective meaning 'faded and dull' can be seen in the 17th century. The word came to be used particularly for natural undyed cloth, of a dull yellowish-brown colour, and hence for the colour itself (an application best preserved in the *olive-drab* colour of American service uniforms). The figurative development to 'dull and faded' is a comparatively recent one, first recorded a little over a hundred years ago.

▶drape, trappings

**drachma** see DRAM

**draconian** [18] *Draconian* 'excessively harsh' is a monument to the severe code of laws drawn up in 621BC by the Athenian statesman Draco. Its purpose was to banish inequities in the system which were leading at the time to rumblings and threats of rebellion among the common people, and to an extent it succeeded, but all it is now remembered for is its almost pathological harshness: the most trivial infraction was punished with death. When taxed with his laws' severity, Draco is said to have replied 'Small crimes deserve death, and for great crimes I know of no penalty severer.'

**drag** [14] *Drag* has two possible sources, each with equally plausible claims: Old English *dragan*, source of modern English *draw*, or the related Old Norse *draga*. Both go back to a common Germanic source. Of the modern colloquial applications of the word, 'women's clothes worn by men' seems to have originated in 19th-century theatrical slang, in reference to the 'dragging' of a woman's long skirts along the ground (an unusual sensation for someone used to wearing trousers).

▶ draw

**dragée** SEE DREDGE

**dragoman** [16] *Dragoman* 'Arabic guide or interpreter' comes via early modern French *dragoman*, Italian *dragomano*, medieval Greek *dragómanos*, early Arabic *targumān*, and Aramaic *tūrgemānā* from Akkadian *targumānu* 'interpreter,' a derivative of the verb *ragāmu* 'call.' It is one of the few English nouns ending in *-man* which forms its plural simply by adding *-s* (*desman* 'small molelike animal' is another).

**dragon** [13] English acquired *dragon* via Old French *dragon* and Latin *dracō* from Greek *drákōn*. Originally the word signified simply 'snake,' but over the centuries this 'snake' increased in size, and many terrifying mythical attributes (such as wings and the breathing of fire) came to be added to it, several of them latterly from Chinese sources. The Greek form is usually connected with words for 'look at, glance, flash, gleam,' such as Greek *drakein* and Sanskrit *darç*, as if its underlying meaning were 'creature that looks at you (with a deadly glance).'

*Dragon* is second time around for English as far as this word is concerned: it originally came by it in the Old English period, via Germanic, as *drake*.

*Dragoons* [17] (an adaptation of French *dragon*) were originally mounted infantry, so called because they carried muskets nicknamed by the French *dragon* 'fire-breather.'

▶ dragoon, drake, rankle

**drain** [OE] The underlying meaning of *drain* seems to be 'making dry.' It comes ultimately from *\*draug-*, the same prehistoric Germanic base as produced English *drought* and *dry*, and in Old English it meant 'strain through a cloth or similar porous medium.' There then follows a curious gap in the history of the word: there is no written record of its use between about 1000AD and the end of the 14th century, and when it re-emerged it began to give the first evidence of its main modern meaning 'draw off a liquid.'

▶ drought, dry

**drake** English has two words *drake*, but the older, 'dragon' [OE] (which comes via prehistoric West Germanic *\*drako* from Latin *dracō*, source of English *dragon*), has now more or less disappeared from general use (it is still employed for a sort of fishing fly). *Drake* 'male duck' [13] probably goes back to (another) prehistoric West Germanic *\*drako*, preserved also in the second element of German *enterich* 'male duck.'

▶ dragon

**dram** [15] *Dram* was borrowed from Old French *drame* or medieval Latin *drama*, which were variants respectively of *dragme* or *dragma*. Both came from *drachma*, the Latin version of Greek *drakhmē*. This was used in the Athens of classical times for both a measure of weight (hence the meaning of modern English *dram*) and a silver coin (hence modern Greek *drakhmē*, in English *drachma* [16]). It is thought to have originated in the notion of the 'amount of coins that can be held in one hand,' and to have been formed from *\*drakh-*, the base which also produced Greek *drássesthai* 'grasp.' (Latin *drachma* is also the source of *dirham* [18], the name of the monetary unit used in Morocco and the United Arab Emirates.)

▶ dirham, drachma

**drama** [17] Etymologically, *drama* is simply 'that which is done' (in that respect it closely resembles *act*, which has the neutral, general meaning 'do something,' as well as the more specific 'perform on stage'). It comes via late Latin *drāma* from Greek *drama*, originally 'deed, action,' and hence 'play.' This was a derivative of the verb *dran* 'do,' whose past participle was the ultimate source of English *drastic* [17].

▶ drastic

**drape** [15] The verb *drape* originally meant 'weave wool into cloth.' It was borrowed from Old French *draper*, which was a derivative of *drap* 'cloth' (source of English *drab*). This in turn came from late Latin *drappus*, which was ultimately of Celtic origin. Other offspring of *drap* which found their way into English are *draper* [14], *drapery* [14], and *trappings*. The use of *drapery* for 'loose voluminous cloth covering' eventually fed back into the verb *drape*, producing in the 19th century its current sense 'cover loosely with cloth.'

▶ drab, draper, trappings

**drastic** SEE DRAMA

**draught** [12] *Draught* and *draft* are essentially the same word, but *draft* (more accurately representing its modern English pronunciation) has become established since the 18th century as the spelling for 'preliminary drawing or plan,' 'money order,' and (in American English) 'conscription.' The word itself probably comes from an unrecorded Old Norse *\*drahtr*, an abstract noun meaning 'pulling' derived from a prehistoric Germanic verb *\*dragan* (source of English *drag* and draw). Most of its modern English meanings are fairly transparently descended from the idea of 'pulling': 'draught beer,' for example, is 'drawn' from a barrel. Of the less obvious ones, 'current of air' is air that is 'drawn' through an opening; the game *draughts* comes from an earlier, Middle English sense of *draught*, 'act of drawing a piece across the board in chess and similar games'; while *draft* 'provisional plan' was originally 'something drawn or sketched.'

▶ draft, drag, draw

**draw** [OE]   The Old English ancestor of modern English *draw* was *dragan*, which came from a prehistoric Germanic verb *\*dragan* (source also of English *drag*). This seems to have meant originally 'carry' (which is what its German and Dutch descendants *tragen* and *dragen* still mean). In English and the Scandinavian languages, however (Swedish *draga*, for instance), it has evolved to 'pull.' 'Sketch,' perhaps the word's most common modern English sense, developed in Middle English from the notion of 'drawing' or 'pulling' a pencil, brush, etc across a surface.

*Dray* 'wagon' [14] is related to, and perhaps originally came from, Old English *dragan*.

▶ drag, draught, dray

**drawer** [16]   A *drawer* is literally something that is 'drawn' or 'pulled' out. The coinage was perhaps based on French *tiroir* 'drawer,' which was similarly derived from the verb *tirer* 'pull.' The same basic notion underlies the formation of *drawers* [16], a superannuated term for 'knickers,' which were originally 'garment pulled on.'

**dray**   see DRAW

**dread** [12]   Old English had the verb *ondrædan* 'fear.' Its first syllable is generally taken to be the prefix *\*and-* 'against,' which is related to German *ent-* 'away, un-' and Greek *anti-* (source of English *anti-*) and appears also in English *answer*. The second part, however, remains a mystery. There are one or two related forms in other West Germanic languages, such as Old High German *intrātan*, but where they come from has never been established satisfactorily. By the end of the Old English period this obsolete prefix had shrunk to *a-* (*adread* survived until around 1400), and in the 12th century it started to disappear altogether.

**dream** [13]   Old English had a word *drēam*, which meant 'joy, merrymaking, music,' but it is not at all clear that this is the same word as modern English *dream* (the recorded Old English words for 'dream' were *swefn* and *mǣting*). Semantically, the two are quite a long way apart, and on balance it seems more likely that Old English had a homonym *\*drēam* 'dream,' which has not survived in the written records, and which was perhaps subsequently reinforced by Old Norse *draumr*. Both these and the related German *traum* and Dutch *droom* have been traced back to an In-

do-European base denoting 'deception,' represented also in Sanskrit *druh-*'seek to harm' and Avestan (a dialect of Old Iranian) *druz-* 'lie, deceive.'

**dreary** [OE]   In Old English, *dreary* (or *drēorig*, as it then was) meant 'dripping with blood, gory,' but its etymological connections are with 'dripping, falling' rather than with 'blood.' It goes back to a West Germanic base *\*dreuz-*, *\*drauz-* which also produced Old English *drēosna* 'drop, fall,' probably the ultimate source of *drizzle* [16] and *drowsy*. The literal sense 'bloody' disappeared before the end of the Old English period in the face of successive metaphorical extensions: 'dire, horrid'; 'sad' (echoed in the related German *traurig* 'sad'); and, in the 17th century, the main modern sense 'gloomy, dull.' *Drear* is a conscious archaism, created from *dreary* in the 17th century.

▶ drizzle, drowsy

**dredge**   English has two distinct words *dredge*, neither with a particularly well-documented past. *Dredge* 'clear mud, silt, etc from waterway' [16] may be related in some way to the 15th-century Scottish term *dreg-boat*, and similarities have been pointed out with Middle Dutch *dregghe* 'drag-net,' although if the two are connected, it is not clear who borrowed from whom. It has also been suggested that it is related ultimately to *drag*. *Dredge* 'sprinkle with sugar, flour, etc' [16] is a verbal use based on a now obsolete noun *dredge*, earlier *dradge*, which meant 'sweet.' This was borrowed from Old French *dragie* (its modern French descendant gave English *dragée* [19]), which may be connected in some way to Latin *tragēmata* and Greek *tragēmata* 'spices, condiments' (these Latin and Greek terms, incidentally, may play some part in the obscure history of English *tracklements* 'condiments to accompany meat' [20], which the English food writer Dorothy Hartley claimed to have 'invented' on the basis of an earlier – but unrecorded – dialect word meaning more generally 'appurtenances').

▶ dragée

**drench** [OE]   Originally, *drench* meant simply 'cause to drink.' It comes ultimately from the prehistoric Germanic verb *\*drangkjan*, which was a causative variant of *\*drengkan* (source of English *drink*) – that is to say, it denoted 'causing someone to do the action of the verb *drink*.' That particular sense now survives only as a technical usage in veterinary medicine, but already by the Middle English period it had moved on metaphorically to 'drown' (now obsolete, and succeeded by the related *drown*) and 'soak thoroughly.'

▶ drink, drown

**dress** [14]   *Dress* originally meant literally 'put right, put straight.' It comes via Old French *dresser* from Vulgar Latin *\*dīrectiāre*, a derivative of Latin *dīrectus* 'straight' (from which English gets *direct*). Traces of this underlying sense survive in the word's application to the correct aligning of columns of troops, but its main modern signification, 'clothe,' comes via a more generalized line of semantic development 'prepare' (as in 'dress a turkey for the oven'), and hence 'array, equip.' (English *address* developed in parallel with *dress*, and comes from the same ultimate source.) *Dresser* 'sideboard' [15] was borrowed from Old French *dresseur*, a derivative of *dresser* in the sense 'prepare.'

▶ address, direct

**drift** [13] *Drift* comes ultimately from the same Germanic base as produced *drive*, and etymologically means 'driving or being driven,' but as far as we can tell it did not exist in Old English, and the word as we now have it is a borrowing from other Germanic languages. Its first recorded use is in the sense 'snowdrift,' which points to Old Norse *drift* as the source, but later more general applications were probably reinforced by Dutch *drift*.

▶ drive

**drill** English has no fewer than four separate words *drill*, all of them comparatively recent acquisitions. *Drill* 'make a hole' [16] was borrowed from Middle Dutch *drillen*, but beyond that its history is obscure. The word's military application, to 'repetitive training,' dates from earliest times, and also existed in the Dutch verb in the 16th century; it seems to have originated as a metaphorical extension of the notion of 'turning round' – that is, of troops marching around in circles. *Drill* 'small furrow for sowing seeds' [18] may come from the now obsolete noun *drill* 'rivulet,' but the origins of this are purely conjectural: some have linked it with the obsolete verb *drill* 'trickle.' *Drill* 'strong fabric' [18] gets its name from originally being woven from three threads. An earlier form of the word was *drilling*, an adaptation of German *drillich*; this in turn was descended from Latin *trilix*, a compound formed from *tri-* 'three' and *līcium* 'thread' (*trellis* is a doublet, coming ultimately from the same Latin source). (Cloth woven from two threads, incidentally, is *twill* [14], or alternatively – from Greek *dímitos* – *dimity* [15].) *Drill* 'African baboon' [17] comes from a West African word. It occurs also in the compound *mandrill* [18], the name of a related baboon, which appears to have been formed with English *man*.

▶ trellis / mandrill

**drink** [OE] *Drink* comes ultimately from a prehistoric Germanic verb *\*drengkan*, which is widely represented in other modern Germanic languages: German *trinken*, for instance, Dutch *drinken*, Swedish *dricka*, and Danish *drikke*. Variants of it also produced English *drench* and *drown*. Its pre-Germanic history is not clear, however: some have suggested that the original underlying notion contained in it is of 'sucking liquid in or up,' and that it is thus related to English *draw*

(a parallel semantic connection has been perceived between Latin *dūcere* 'lead, draw' and the related *tsuk-* 'drink' in Tocharian A, an extinct Indo-European language of central Asia).

▶ drench, drown

**drip** see DROP

**drive** [OE] As far as is known, *drive* is an exclusively Germanic word. It and its relatives German *treiben*, Dutch *drijven*, Swedish *driva*, Danish *drive*, and Gothic *dreiban* point to a prehistoric Germanic ancestor *\*drīban*. Its base also produced English *drift* and *drove* [OE]. The central modern sense of *drive*, 'drive a car,' comes from the earlier notion of driving a horse, ox, etc by pushing it, whipping it, etc from behind, forcing it onwards, but in most other modern European languages the verb for 'driving a vehicle' denotes basically 'leading' or 'guiding' (French *conduire*, for example, or German *lenken*).

▶ drift, drove

**drizzle** see DREARY

**dromedary** [14] The dromedary, or one-humped camel, got its name from its swiftness of foot. The word comes via Old French *dromedaire* from late Latin *dromedārius*, an adjective formed from *dromas*, the Latin term for 'camel.' This in turn was derived from the Greek *dromás* 'runner,' a close relative of *drómos* 'running, course,' which is the source of the *-drome* in such English words as *hippodrome*, *aerodrome*, and *palindrome*.

▶ aerodrome, hippodrome, palindrome

**drop** [OE] *Drop*, *droop*, and *drip* are closely related. *Droop* [13] was borrowed from Old Norse *drúpa*, which came from a Germanic base *\*drūp-*. A variant of this, *\*drup-*, produced Middle Danish *drippe*, the probable source of English *drip* [15], and a further variant, *\*drop-*, lies behind Old English *dropa*, ancestor of modern English *drop*. All three go back ultimately to a prehistoric Indo-European *\*dhreub-*, source of Irish *drucht* 'dew.'

The English noun originally meant 'globule of liquid,' and its related verb 'fall in drops.' The main modern transitive sense, 'allow to fall,' developed in the 14th century, giving English a single word for the concept of 'letting fall' not shared by, for example, French and German, which have to use phrases to express it: respectively, *laisser tomber* and *fallen lassen*.

▶ drip, droop

**drought** [OE] Etymologically, *drought* means simply 'dryness.' The prehistoric Germanic base that produced English *dry* (and indeed *drain*) was *\*draug-*, *\*drūg-*. To this was added the suffix *-th*, used for creating abstract nouns from adjectives, as in *length*, *strength*, and *truth*; this gave Old English *drūgath*. The subsequent change of -*th* to -*t* (which began in the 13th century) is mirrored in such words as *height* and *theft*.

▶ drain, dry

**drove**   see DRIVE

**drown**   [13]   Drown is not found in texts until the end of the 13th century (when it began to replace the related *drench* in the sense 'suffocate in water') but an Old English verb *drūnian* could well have existed. The earliest occurrences of the word are from the North of England and Scotland, which suggests a possible borrowing from, or influence of, Old Norse *drukna* 'be drowned'; this came ultimately from Germanic *drungk-*, a variant of the base which produced English *drink*.

▶ drench, drink

**drowsy**   [15]   The etymological notion underlying *drowsy* seems to be of heaviness, with eyelids falling and the head nodding over the chest. The word probably comes from a Germanic base *drūs-*, which also produced *drūsian*, an Old English verb meaning 'be slow and sleepy' which did not survive into the Middle English period (modern English *drowse* [16] is a back-formation from *drowsy*). A variant of this base is the possible source of English *dreary* and *drizzle*.

▶ dream, drizzle

**drub**   [17]   Drub appears to have been introduced to the English language by Sir Thomas Herbert (1606–82), a traveller in the Orient, who used the word several times in his *Relation of some yeares travaile into Afrique and the greater Asia* 1634: '[The pasha] made the Petitioner be almost drub'd to death.' It came from Arabic *dáraraba*, which meant not just 'beat,' but also specifically 'bastinado' – 'beat on the soles of the feet as a punishment or torture.'

**drudge**   [15]   No one is quite sure where *drudge* comes from. It is first recorded, as a noun, towards the end of the 15th century, and the verb followed about fifty years later. One possible source may be the Middle English verb *drugge* 'pull laboriously,' a possible relative of English *drag*; another suggestion is the Old English verb *drēogan* 'work.'

**drug**   [14]   Drug is one of the mystery words of the language. It is clear that English acquired it from Old French *drogue*, but no one is certain where the French word came from. One suggestion is that it originated in Arabic *dūrawā* 'chaff'; another, rather more likely, is that its source was Dutch *droog* 'dry,' via either the phrase *droge waere* 'dry goods' or *droge vate* 'dry barrels,' a common expression for 'goods packed in barrels.' It has spread to many other European languages, including Italian and Spanish *droga*, German *droge*, and Swedish *drog*.

**druid**   [16]   Druid is, not surprisingly, of Celtic origin, although English probably acquired it via French *druide* or the Latin plural *druides*. The source of these forms was Gaulish *druides*, which came ultimately from Old Celtic *derwíjes*. There are two opposing theories on the derivation of this: one is that it comes from an Old Celtic adjective *derwos* 'true' (source of Welsh *derw* 'true'), in which case its etymological meaning would be 'someone who says the truth' (a parallel formation to English *soothsayer*); the other is that it was formed from the Old Celtic base *dru-* 'tree' (source of Welsh *derwen* and Irish *daur* 'oak-tree' and related to Greek *drus* 'oak' and English *tree*) in reference to the central role played by oak-trees in druidic ceremonies.

**drum**   [16]   Belying the total lack of similarity between the instruments, *drum, trumpet*, and *trombone* seem to be closely related. *Drum* appears to be a shortening of a slightly earlier English word *drumslade* 'drum, drummer,' which was borrowed from Low German *trommelslag* 'drumbeat.' This was a compound noun formed from *trommel* 'drum' and *slag* 'hit' (related to English *slay*). An alternative view is that English simply acquired the word from Middle Dutch *tromme*. Both these Germanic forms meant simply 'drum,' but the picture becomes more complex with Middle High German *tromme* 'drum,' for originally this had the sense 'trumpet,' and what is more it had a variant form *trumbe* (its ancestor, Old High German *trumpa*, ultimate source of English *trumpet* and *trombone*, only meant 'trumpet'). So the picture that emerges is of a word that originally referred in a fairly undifferentiated way to any musical instrument that made a loud noise.

▶ trombone, trumpet

**dry**   [OE]   Dry comes ultimately from prehistoric Germanic *draugiz*, a derivative of the base *draug-*, *drūg-*, which also produced English *drought* and *drain*. Its other Germanic relatives are Dutch *droog* and German *trocken*, and some have connected it with Old Norse *drjūgr* 'lasting, strong,' Old Prussian *drūktai* 'firmly,' and Lithuanian dialect *drūktas* 'thick, strong' – the theory being that strength and endurance are linked with 'drying out.'

▶ drain, drought

**dryad**   see TREE

**dual**   [17]   Dual was borrowed from Latin *duālis*, a derivative of *duo* 'two' (which is a distant relative of English *two*). In Latin it was used particularly by grammarians, to denote the category 'two people or things' (as opposed to the plural, referring to three or more), and this was the earliest sense of the word adopted by English. (Incidentally, despite its formal similarity, and a common meaning element – two people participate – *duel* [15] is not etymologically related to *dual*; it comes from medieval Latin *duellum*, which was originally an archaic form of Latin *bellum* 'war.'

▶ two

**dub**   English has two words *dub*. By far the older, 'create a knight, name' [11], was one of the first linguistic fruits of the Norman conquest, which was during the Middle English period to contribute such a vast number of French words to the English language. It came from Anglo-Norman *duber*, which was a reduced form of *aduber*, the Anglo-Norman version of Old French *adober*. This meant 'equip, repair, arrange,' but also specifically 'equip with armour,' which led metaphorically to 'confer the rank of knighthood on.' The sense 'arrange' has remained in use in various technical areas up to the present time, and its application to the dressing of leather with grease formed the basis of the noun *dubbin* 'mixture of oil and tallow for softening and waterproofing leather' [18].

Dub 'insert soundtrack' [20] is a shortened version of *double*.

▶ dubbin / double

**dubious**   see DOUBT

**ducat**   see DUKE

**duchess**   see DUKE

**duchy**   see DUKE

**duck**   [OE]   A *duck* is a bird that 'ducks' – as simple as that. It gets its name from its habit of diving down under the surface of the water. There is no actual record of an English verb *duck* until the 14th century, but it is generally assumed that an Old English verb *ducan* did exist, which would have formed the basis of the noun *duck*. It came from a prehistoric West Germanic verb *dukjan*, which also produced German *tauchen* 'dive.' English is the only language which uses this word for the bird, although Swedish has the term *dykand*, literally 'dive-duck,' which refers to the 'diver,' a sort of large waterbird. Nor is it the original English word: the Anglo-Saxons mainly called the duck *ened*, a term which survived until the 15th century. This represents the main Indo-European name for the duck, which comes from an original *anəti- and is found in Greek *nessa*, Latin *anas*, German *ente*, Dutch *eend*, Swedish *and*, and Russian *utka*.

**duct**   [17]   *Duct* comes from Latin *ductus*, a noun formed from the past participle of the verb *dūcere* 'lead.' This is among the most prolific Latin sources of English words. It appears in numerous prefixed forms, all containing to some extent the underlying meaning element 'lead,' such as *deduce, introduce, produce*, and *reduce*, as well as *educate* and, in less obvious form, *subdue*. Its past participle produced *aqueduct* and *ductile* [14], not to mention (via Vulgar Latin *ductiāre* and Italian *docciare*) *douche* [18]. And furthermore it comes ultimately from the same Indo-European source as produced English *team, teem, tie, tight, tow*, and *tug*.

▶ aqueduct, conduct, deduce, deduct, douche, duke, edu-

cate, introduce, produce, reduce, seduce, team, tie, tight, tow, tug

**due**   see DUTY

**duel**   see DUAL

**duenna**   see DAME

**duet**   [18]   The original term for 'two musicians' was Italian *duo*, a descendant of Latin *duo* 'two.' English acquired this in the 16th century. But Italian (the major source of Western musical vocabulary) also produced a diminutive form *duetto*, literally 'little duo,' which English borrowed either directly (the unanglicized form *duetto* was used in English for about a hundred years from the 1720s) or pehaps via German *duett*.

▶ two

**duff**   see DOUGH

**duffel**   [17]   Duffel is actually a sort of heavy woollen material, and like so many names of fabrics it comes from the place where it was originally made or exported from – in this case Duffel, a town in Belgium, near Antwerp. However, the term *duffel coat* (which dates back to the late 17th century) has in modern times become associated with a particular design of coat (with a hood and toggles) as much as with the material it is made from. *Duffel bag* [20], a term of American origin, was to begin with a bag for 'personal belongings and equipment,' or *duffel*, as it is called in American English (the application seems to have started with 'spare clothes made of duffel').

**duffer**   see DEAF

**duke**   [12]   *Duke* is one of a wide range of English words which come ultimately from the Latin verb *dūcere* 'lead' (see DUCT). In this case its source was the Latin derivative *dux* 'leader' (ancestor also of Italian *duce*, the title adopted by the 20th-century dictator Benito Mussolini), which passed into English via Old French *duc*. In Latin the word signified 'military commander of a province,' and in the so-called Dark Ages it was taken up in various European languages as the term for a 'prince ruling a small state.' Old English never adopted it though, preferring its own word *earl*, and it was not until the 14th century that it was formally introduced, by Edward III, as a rank of the English peerage. Before that the word had been used in English only in the titles of foreign dukes, or (echoing the word's etymological meaning) as a general term for 'leader' or 'military commmander.' The feminine form *duchess* [14] comes from Old French, while English has two terms for a duke's rank or territory: the native *dukedom* [15], and *duchy* [14], borrowed from Old French *duche* (this came partly from medieval Latin *ducātus*, ultimate source of English *ducat* [14], a former Italian coin).

▶ conduct, ducat, duchess, duchy, duct, produce

**dull** [13] *Dull* originally meant 'slow-witted.' It was borrowed from Middle Low German *dul*, a descendant of the prehistoric Germanic adjective *\*dulaz*, which also produced German *toll* and Old English *dol* 'stupid' (the Old English adjective does not seem to have survived beyond the 10th century). The modern meaning 'boring' developed in the 15th century. The now little-used *dullard* [15] is a derivative (reflecting the adjective's original sense), as also is probably *dolt* [16].

▶dolt

**dumb** [OE] The notion underlying *dumb* is of 'sensory or mental impairment.' It goes back to a nasalized version of prehistoric Indo-European *\*dheubh-*, denoting 'confusion, stupefaction, or dizziness,' which was also the ultimate source of English *deaf*. This developed two strands of meaning. The first, through association of 'sensory or mental impairment' and 'slow-wittedness,' led to forms such as German *dumm* and Dutch *dom*, which mean 'stupid' (the use of *dumb* to mean 'stupid' did not develop until the 19th century, in American English, presumably under the influence of the German and Dutch adjectives). The other was semantic specialization to a particular sort of mental impairment, the inability to speak, which produced Gothic *dumbs*, Old Norse *dumbr*, and English *dumb*. (The German word for 'dumb,' *stumm*, is related to English *stammer* and *stumble*, as are Dutch *stom* and Swedish *stum*.)

*Dummy* [16] is a derivative; it originally meant 'dumb person.'

▶deaf, dummy

**dump** [14] *Dump* is probably of Scandinavian origin.– Danish and Norwegian have the similar *dumpe* and *dumpa*, which mean 'fall suddenly' – although Dutch *dompen* 'immerse, topple' is another candidate that has been put forward. Either way, there does not seem to be any direct connection with the *dumps* [16], which was probably originally a metaphorical use of Dutch *domp* 'haze,' in the sense 'miasma of depression.' Nor has any relationship been established with the obsolete noun *dump* 'lump' [18], which appears to have close ties with *dumpling* [16] and *dumpy* [16], although whether as source or descendant (by back-formation) is a debatable point.

**dun** English has two words *dun*. The colour adjective, 'greyish brown' [OE] , comes ultimately from Indo-European *\*donnos*, *\*dusnos*, which is also the source of English *dusk*. The now rather dated noun, 'debt-collector' [17], is an abbreviation of *dunkirk*, a 17th-century term for a 'privateer,' a privately owned vessel officially allowed to attack enemy shipping during wartime. It was originally applied from such privateers that sailed from the port of Dunkirk, on the northern coast of France, to attack British ships, and its connotations of unwarranted piracy soon spread metaphorically to one who was constantly importuning for the repayment of his loan.

▶donkey, dusk, obfuscate

**dunce** [16] *Dunce* originated as a contemptuous term for those who continued in the 16th century to adhere to the theological views of the Scottish scholar John Duns Scotus (*c*1265–1308). Renaissance philosophers ridiculed them as narrow-minded hair-splitters, and so before long the application of the word spread metaphorically to any 'stuffy pedant' in general, and hence, through the implication of a lack of true intellect, to 'stupid person.' The conical *dunce's cap* seems to have originated in the 19th century.

**dune** see DOWN

**dung** see DINGY

**dungeon** [14] In common with a wide range of other English words, including *danger, demesne, dominion, domino*, and *don*, *dungeon* comes ultimately from Latin *dominus* 'lord, master.' Derived from this was *dominium* 'property' (source of English *dominion*), which in post-classical times became *dominiō* or *domniō*, meaning 'lord's tower.' In Old French this became *donjon*, the term for a 'castle keep,' and eventually, by extension, a 'secure (underground) cell.' English acquired the package in the 14th century, but in common usage has retained only the latter sense, in the adapted Middle English spelling (although the original Old French form remains in use as a technical term for a 'castle keep').

▶dame, danger, demesne, dominion, dominate

**duodenum** [14] The term *duodenum*, for the first part of the small intestine, originated as a measure of length. It comes from the medieval Latin phrase *intestinum duodēnum digitōrum* 'intestine of twelve digits' – that is, twelve finger-breadths long, or just over 20 centimetres. Latin *duodēnī* meant literally 'twelve each'; it was a derivative of *duodecim* 'twelve' (source also of English *dozen*).

▶dozen

**dupe** [17] English borrowed *dupe* from French, where it was probably originally a humorous application of a dialect word for a 'hoopoe,' an extravagantly crested bird whose flamboyant appearance seems to have made it the butt of jokes. It presumably represents ultimately an alteration of Old French *huppe* 'hoopoe,' sometimes explained as being a conflation of *de huppe* 'of the hoopoe.' (English *hoopoe* [17] is an alteration of an earlier *hoop*, which came from Old French *huppe*; its ultimate source was Latin *upupa*, which originated as an imitation of the bird's cry.)

▶hoopoe

**duple**   see DOUBLE

**duplicate**   [15]   Like its close relative *double*, *duplicate* comes ultimately from Latin *duplus* 'twofold,' a compound adjective based on Latin *duo* 'two' and an Indo-European element *\*pl-* which denoted 'folding' (it is present also in English *fold* and *ply*). English acquired this in the 16th century, and its synonym *duplex* (based on the extended stem *\*plic-*) in the 19th century. In Latin, *duplus* formed the basis of a verb *duplicāre* 'make twofold, double,' from whose past participle English gets *duplicate*, while *duplex* has given us *duplicity* [15].

▶ double, duplicity, fold, ply, two

**duress**   [14]   Etymologically, *duress* means literally 'hardness,' and that was what it was used for when English first acquired it. It comes via Old French *duresse* from Latin *dūritia*, a derivative of the adjective *dūrus* 'hard' (from which English gets *during*). The current sense 'constraint' developed during the 15th century.

▶ during, endure

**during**   [14]   *During*, like *durable* [14], *durance* [15], *duration* [14], *duress*, and *endure* [14], comes ultimately from the Latin adjective *dūrus* 'hard.' This goes back to an earlier *\*drūros*, which is related to Irish *dron* 'solid,' Lithuanian *drūtas* 'strong, solid,' and Sanskrit *dāruna-* 'strong, hard,' and links with Irish *daur* 'oak' (a possible relative of *druid*) and Greek *drus* 'oak' suggest that its original underlying meaning was 'oak wood,' from which 'hard' developed as a metaphorical extension. The Latin verb *dūrāre* meant originally literally 'harden,' but this widened (perhaps with memories of an underlying sense 'strong, resilient') to 'continue in existence, last.' It is these notions of 'continuance,' 'strength,' and 'perseverance' that emerge in different proportions in *durable, duration*, and *endure*, and indeed in *during*, which is a translation of Old French *durant*, the present participle of *durer* 'last': phrases such as 'during the day' mean etymologically 'as long as the day lasts.' *Durance*, an archaic term for 'imprisonment,' originally denoted 'length of sentence,' and so is virtually equivalent to the modern 'for the duration.'

▶ durable, duration, duress, endure

**dusk**   [OE]   In Anglo-Saxon times, *dusk* was an adjective meaning 'dark in colour' (a sense preserved today in the derived adjective *dusky* [16]). Its modern noun use 'twilight' is not recorded until as recently as the early 17th century. The Old English form of the word was *dox*, which was descended from the same ultimate Indo-European ancestor as Latin *fuscus* 'dark' (source of English *obfuscate* [16]).

▶ dun, obfuscate

**dust**   [OE]   The notion ultimately underlying *dust* seems to be that of 'smoke' or 'vapour.' It goes back to a prehistoric Indo-European base *\*dheu-*, which also produced Latin *fūmus* and Sanskrit *dhūma-* 'smoke.' A Germanic descendant of this, *\*dunstu-*, picks up the idea of a cloud of fine particles being blown about like smoke, and is the basis of Norwegian *dust* 'dust' and *duft* 'finely ground grain,' German *duft* 'fragrance' (from an earlier Middle High German *tuft* 'vapour, dew'), and English *dust*.

**duty**   [13]   *Duty* comes from Anglo-Norman *dueté*. This was a derivative of Old French *deu* 'owed' (source of English *due* [13]), which in turn came from Latin *dēbitus*, past participle of *dēbēre* 'owe' and source of English *debit* and *debt*. (Latin *dēbēre* was originally a compound verb formed from the prefix *dē-* 'away' and *habēre* 'have,' literally 'have away,' that is 'keep in one's possession what belongs to someone else.') So etymologically one's *duty* is what one 'owes' to others.

▶ debit, debt, due

**dwarf**   [OE]   *Dwarf* is descended via Germanic *\*dwergaz* from Indo-European *\*dhwergwhos*, which denoted 'something tiny.' In English, it originally meant simply 'person of abnormally small stature'; the modern connotation of 'small manlike creature that lives underground and works metal,' a product of Germanic mythology, is not recorded until the late 18th century. The word's German relative, *zwerg*, is the source of English *quartz*.

▶ quartz

**dwell**   [OE]   *Dwell* has changed its meaning remarkably over the centuries. In Old English it meant 'confuse, lead astray.' It goes back to a Germanic base *\*dwel-*, *\*dwal-*, *\*dwul-*, which also produced Old English *dwola* 'error,' Gothic *dwals* 'foolish,' and Old High German *gitwelan* 'be stunned,' and beyond that to Indo-European *\*dhwel-*, source of Greek *tholós* 'dirt' and Irish *dall* 'blind.' Already by the end of the Old English period, 'lead astray' had progressed to 'hinder, delay,' probably under the influence of the related Old Norse *dvelja* 'delay,' and this subsequently developed through 'linger' to (in the 13th century) 'make one's home in a place.'

**dye**   [OE]   *Dye* is something of a mystery word. Its original meaning seems to have been simply 'colour,' its modern connotations of 'artificially changing colour' a secondary development, but its source remains unknown. A connection has been suggested with Old English *dēagol* 'secret, hidden,' but what the implications of that would be for its semantic history are not clear. The convention of spelling the word *dye* did not become established until as recently as the 19th century; until then *die* was equally common, and orthographic confusion with *die* 'cease to live' was rife.

**dyke** see DITCH

**dynamic** [19] Greek *dúnamis* (a word of unknown origin) meant 'strength.' It was used by the Swedish chemist Alfred Nobel in 1867 to form the name of the new explosive he had invented, *dynamite*. From it was derived the adjective *dunamikós* 'powerful,' which French adopted in the 17th century as *dynamique*, and English acquired it in the early 19th century. Related to *dúnamis* was the verb *dúnasthai* 'be strong' or 'be able'; from this was derived the noun *dunasteíā* 'power, domination,' source, via French or late Latin, of English *dynasty* [15]. Part of the same word family is *dynamo* [19], short for *dynamo-electric machine*, a term coined in 1867 by the electrical engineer Werner Siemens.

▶ dynamite, dynasty

# E

**each** [OE] *Each* comes from Old English *ǣlc.* This, brief as it is, was in fact originally a compound adjective; it was descended from West Germanic *\*aiwō galīkaz,* literally 'ever alike' (*\*aiwō* is the source of English *aye* 'ever' [12], *\*galīkaz* the source of English *alike*). *Ǣlc* also formed the second element of an Old English expression, literally 'ever each,' which has become modern English *every.*

▶ alike, aye

**eager** [13] As its close etymological connection with *vinegar* and *acid* might suggest, the underlying sense of *eager* is 'sharp.' It comes ultimately from the Indo-European base *\*ak-* 'sharp, pointed,' amongst whose other English descendants are *acne, edge,* and *oxygen.* It was the source of Latin *ācer* 'keen, sharp,' which was used in relation both to sight, hearing, etc, and to temperamental qualities – hence 'ardent, zealous.' The Latin adjective (from which English also gets *acid* and *acrid*) became *\*acrum* in post-classical times, and from this came Old French *aigre* (source of the *-egar* of *vinegar*), which passed into English via Anglo-Norman *egre.* English retained the literal senses 'pungent, sour' and 'sharp-edged' until the early 19th century.

▶ acid, acne, acrid, acute, edge, oxygen

**eagle** [14] *Eagle* comes via Old French *aigle* from Latin *aquila* (source also of English *aquiline* [17]). This was presumably a derivative of the adjective *aquilus* 'dark-coloured,' suggesting that the eagle's name originally signified simply 'dark-coloured bird' (Greek had the term *melanáetos* 'black eagle'). Before the French word was introduced, the English term for 'eagle' was *erne,* which still survives dialectally.

▶ aquiline

**ear** *Ear* for hearing and *ear* of corn seem in some way to belong together, but in fact they are two quite distinct words etymologically. *Ear* for hearing [OE] is an ancient term that goes right back to the Indo-European roots of the language. Its ancestor is the base *\*aus-,* whose underlying signification was perhaps 'perception' (a variant, *\*au-,* produced Greek *aisthánomai* 'perceive'). This lies behind the term for 'ear' in the majority of European languages: French *oreille,* for example, Italian *orecchio,* Spanish *oreja,* Rumanian *ureche,* Irish *ó,* Russian and Polish *ucho,* and modern Greek *autí.* Its Germanic descendant, *\*auzon,* produced German *ohr,* Dutch *oor,* Gothic *ausō,* Swedish *öra,* and English *ear.*

The etymological sense of *ear* of corn [OE] is 'spike' of corn. The word comes from a prehistoric Germanic *\*akhuz,* which goes back ultimately to the Indo-European base *\*ak-* 'be pointed or sharp' (ultimate source of English *acid, acne, acute, eager, edge,* and *oxygen*).

▶ acid, acne, acute, eager, edge, oxygen

**early** [OE] Broken down into its equivalent parts in modern English, *early* means 'before-ly.' It was a compound formed from Old English *ǣr* (ancestor of modern English *ere* 'before') and the adverb ending *-ly,* modelled probably on the parallel Old Norse form *árligr.* *Ere* itself was actually originally a comparative form, which before it was used for 'before' meant 'earlier.' Old English *ǣr* came from prehistoric Germanic *\*airiz,* the comparative form of *\*air* 'early.' Related forms in other Indo-European languages, such as Greek *eri* 'in the morning' and Avestan (the sacred form of Old Iranian) *ayarə* 'day,' suggest that its underlying meaning is 'early in the morning.'

▶ ere

**earn** [OE] The underlying sense of *earn* is 'gain as a result of one's labour.' It comes from a prehistoric West Germanic verb *\*aznōjan,* which was based on the noun *\*aznu* 'work, labour.' This seems often to have been used specifically for 'work in the fields,' for several other related forms in the Germanic languages, such as German *ernte* and Gothic *asans,* denote 'harvest,' which in some cases has been metaphorically extended to apply to 'autumn.'

**earnest** [OE] *Earnest* was originally a much more red-blooded word than it is today. It comes ultimately from a Germanic base *\*ern-* which denoted 'vigour' or 'briskness.' To this was added the noun suffix -*ost* (*earnest* was originally a noun), giving Old English *eornost*, which appears at first to have meant 'intense passion,' and particularly 'zeal in battle.' However, by the end of the Old English period there is already evidence of a semantic toning down from 'intensity of feeling' to 'seriousness of feeling' (as opposed to 'frivolity'), a process which has culminated in modern English connotations of 'over-seriousness.'

**earth** [OE] *Earth* comes ultimately from an Indo-European base *\*er-*. This produced the prehistoric Germanic noun *\*erthō*, ancestor of German *erde*, Dutch *aarde* (whence, via early Afrikaans, English *aardvark* [19], literally 'earth-pig'), Swedish and Danish *jord*, and English *earth*. Related forms outside Germanic include Greek *éraze* 'on the ground' and Welsh *erw* 'field.' The word's basic range of modern senses, 'ground,' 'world,' and 'soil,' all date back to the Old English period.

▶ aardvark

**earwig** [OE] A colloquial Old English term for 'insect' was *wicga* (which would have been pronounced something like 'widger'). It probably came from the same prehistoric Germanic base (*\*wig-*) as produced English *wiggle* [13], and so is roughly equivalent in spirit to modern English *creepy-crawly*. There used to be a belief (perhaps still is) that earwigs creep into people's ears and penetrate inside their heads, and so the Anglo-Saxons called them *ēarwicga*, literally 'ear-insect.' The same notion lies behind French *perce-oreille*, literally 'pierce-ear,' and German *ohrwurm*, literally 'earworm,' both of which stand for 'earwig.'

▶ wiggle

**easel** [17] *Easel* was borrowed from Dutch *ezel*, which means literally 'donkey' (it is related to English *ass*). The notion of loading a painting on to a stand, much as a burden is loaded on to a donkey, is echoed in the use of *clotheshorse* for a stand for hanging clothes on to dry or air.

▶ ass

**east** [OE] Etymologically, *east* is the point of the compass at which the sun rises (and hence is a parallel formation to *orient*, which comes from a Latin word originally meaning 'rising'). It goes back to an Indo-European base *\*aus-*, source of a range of terms meaning not only 'east' but also 'dawn': Latin *aurora*, for instance, and Greek *aúōs*, had both senses. Its Germanic descendant, *\*austo-*, produced German *ost*, Dutch *oosten*, Swedish *öster*, and English *east* (which was subsequently borrowed by French as *est*). It was also the source of *\*Austron*, the name of a goddess of the prehistoric Germanic peoples, originally the dawn-goddess, whose festival occurred in spring. In Old English her name was *Ēastre*, which is generally taken to be the ulti-

mate source of English *Easter* (German *Ostern* 'Easter' has a parallel origin).

▶ Easter

**easy** [12] *Easy* comes via Anglo-Norman *aise* from Old French *aisie*, the past participle of *aisier* 'put at ease,' which in turn was a derivative of *aise*. This noun (source of English *ease* [13]) originally meant 'convenience' rather than 'comfort.' It came from *\*adjaces*, the Vulgar Latin descendant of Latin *adjacēns* 'nearby' (source of English *adjacent* and related to *adjective*), which was the present participle of the verb *adjacēre* 'lie near.' The progression of senses is thus 'nearby,' 'handy,' 'convenient,' and eventually 'comfortable.' The subsequent development to 'not difficult,' which took place in the 14th century, is purely English, although Breton took the parallel step of borrowing French *aise*, as *aes*, to mean 'not difficult.'

▶ adjacent, adjective

**eat** [OE] *Eat* is a very ancient and basic verb. It goes back to Indo-European *\*ed-* 'eat' (distant ancestor of English *tooth*), which produced the basic word for 'eat' in most European languages, apart from French, Italian, Rumanian, and the Celtic languages: Greek *édein*, for example, Latin *edere* (source of English *comestible* [15], from Latin *comedere* 'eat up,' and of *obese* [17]), and Russian *jest'*. Its Germanic descendant was *\*etan* (ultimate source of English *etch*), which produced German *essen*, Dutch *eten*, Swedish *öta*, and English *eat* (and also lies behind English *fret*).

▶ comestible, etch, fret, obese, tooth

**eaves** [OE] The etymological meaning of *eaves* appears to be 'going over the edge, projecting.' It comes from a prehistoric Germanic *\*obaswa*, which was probably formed on *\*ob-*, the base from which English *over* ultimately derives. The *eavesdrip* or *eavesdrop* is, or was, the area of ground on which rainwater thrown off by the eaves falls, so that somebody who stood within this area, with his or her ear to the door or window trying to listen in on private conversations, became known as an *eavesdropper* [15].

▶ over

**ebb** [OE] Water that is *ebbing* is literally going 'off' or 'away.' The word comes from West Germanic *\*abjon*, a noun formed from *\*ab*, ancestor of modern English *of, off*, which denoted removal or departure.

▶ of, off

**ebony** [15] *Ebony* is ultimately of Semitic origin. The Greeks took it from some Middle Eastern source, perhaps Egyptian *hbnj*, and turned it into *ébenos*. This made its way via Latin *ebenus*, later *ebanus*, and Old French *eban* into English. At first English simply used the French form (which as *ebon* survived into modern times as an archaism), but from the 16th century forms ending in -*y* began to supersede it.

**ecclesiastical** [15] In classical Greek, an *ekklēspcf4iíā* was an 'assembly' (the word was derived from *ekkalein*, a compound verb formed from the prefix *ek-* 'out' and *kallein* 'call'). With the introduction of Christianity, it was adopted as the term for 'church,' and an *ekklēsiastēs*, originally 'someone who addressed an assembly,' became a 'preacher' or 'priest.' The derived adjective, *ekklēsiastikos*, passed into English via either French or Latin.

**echelon** see SCALE

**echo** [14] *Echo* comes via Old French or Latin from Greek *ēkhó*, a word related to *ēkhḗ* 'sound.' It may have originated as a personification of the concept 'sound,' which developed eventually into the mythological mountain nymph *Echo*, who faded away for love of Narcissus until nothing but her voice was left. (The Greek verb derived from *ēkhḗ*, *ēkhein*, is the ultimate source of English *catechism*.)

▶ catechism

**éclat** see SLAT

**eclipse** [13] From the point of view of the observer, an object which has been *eclipsed* has 'gone away' – is no longer there. And that in fact is the etymological foundation of the word. It comes, via Old French and Latin, from Greek *ékleipsis*, a derivative of *ekleípein* 'no longer appear or be present.' This was a compound verb formed from the prefix *ek-* 'out, away' and *leípein* 'leave' (a distant relative of English *leave*). Its adjectival derivative, *ekleiptikós*, passed into English as *ecliptic* [14], which was applied to the apparent path of the Sun relative to the stars because that is the line along which eclipses caused by the moon occur.

▶ leave

**ecology** [19] Interpreted literally, *ecology* means 'study of houses.' The word was coined, as *ökologie*, by the German zoologist Ernst Haeckel in the 1870s, on the basis of Greek *oikos* (as in *economy*). This means literally 'house,' but Haeckel was using it in the wider sense 'dwelling, habitat.' English adopted the word soon after its coinage, originally in the quasi-Latin form *oecology*.

▶ economy

**economy** [16] The underlying notion contained in the word *economy* is of 'household management.' It comes, via French or Latin, from Greek *oikonomíā*, a derivative of *oikonómos*, a term for the 'steward of a household.' This was a compound noun formed from *oikos* 'house' (a word related to the *-wich* element in many English place-names) and *némein* 'manage' (ultimate source of English *antinomian* and *nomad*). The original sense 'household management' was carried through into English. It broadened out in the 17th century to the management of a nation's resources (a concept at first termed more fully *political economy*),

while the use of the derivative *economics* for the theoretical study of the creation and consumption of wealth dates from the early 19th century.

▶ antinomian, ecology, nomad

**ecstasy** [14] Etymologically, someone who is *ecstatic* is out of his or her mind. The word comes, via Old French *extasie* and late Latin *extasis*, from Greek *ékstasis*, a derivative of the verb *existánai* 'displace, drive out of one's mind.' This was a compound formed from the prefix *ek-* 'out' and *histánai* 'place' (a distant relative of English *stand*). The underlying notion of being 'beside oneself, in the grip of extreme passion' survives in modern English in relation to mystic experiences or trances, and also, albeit archaically, in such phrases as 'an ecstasy of rage,' and the specific sense 'delight' developed only comparatively recently, apparently in the 17th century.

▶ stand

**eczema** [18] A person suffering from *eczema* has a skin that is, in a rather gruesome metaphor, 'boiling over.' The word comes from Greek *ékzema* 'eruption,' a compound formed from the prefix *ek-* 'out' and the verb *zein* 'boil, ferment.' This in turn goes back to the Indo-European base *\*jes-*, source also of Sanskrit *yas-* 'boil, foam,' Welsh *ias* 'boiling,' and English *yeast*.

▶ yeast

**eddy** [15] The ultimate source of *eddy* appears to be a prehistoric Germanic particle meaning 'back, again,' represented in Old English by *ed-*, in Old High German by *et-*, and in Old Norse by *ith-* (it is related to Latin *et* 'and' and its various Romance descendants, such as French *et* and Italian *ed*). According to this theory, an *eddy* would thus be 'water that flows back.' What is not altogether clear, however, is precisely how that prehistoric particle became *eddy*. Perhaps the most likely candidate as the missing link is Old Norse *itha* 'whirlpool,' but it has also been suggested that Old English may have had a word *\*edwǣg*, whose second element, 'wave,' would be related to English *way* and *vogue*.

**edge** [OE] *Edge* is probably the main native English representative of the Indo-European base *\*ak-* 'be sharp or pointed,' which has contributed so many words to the language via Latin and Greek (such as *acid, acrid, acute, acne, alacrity,* and *oxygen*). Its Germanic descendant was *\*ag-*, on which was based the noun *\*agjā*, source of German *ecke* 'corner,' Swedish *egg* 'edge' (a probable relative of English *egg* 'urge'), and English *edge*. The word's application to a 'border' or 'boundary' dates from the late 14th century.

▶ acid, acne, acrid, acute, alacrity, egg, oxygen

**edict** [15] An *edict* is literally that which is 'spoken out' or 'proclaimed.' It was acquired directly from Latin *ēdictum*, which comes from the past participle of *ēdīcere* 'proclaim.' This was a compound verb formed from the prefix *ex-* 'out' and *dīcere* 'say' (source of English *diction, dictionary, dictate* amongst a host of others). The passing resemblance of *edict* to *edit* is quite fortuitous, for they are completely unrelated.

▶ dictate, diction, dictionary

**edify** [14] As its close relative *edifice* [14] suggests, *edify* has to do literally with 'building.' And in fact its underlying etymological sense is 'building a hearth.' That was the original sense of Latin *aedis*. Gradually, though, it was extended, in a familiar metaphorical transition, from 'hearth' to 'home' and 'dwelling.' Addition of a verbal element related to *facere* 'make' produced *aedificāre* 'build a house,' or simply 'build.' Its figurative application to 'instruction' or 'enlightenment' took place in Latin, and has no doubt been reinforced in English (which acquired the word from Old French *edifier*) by its accidental similarity to *educate*.

**edit** [18] Etymologically, someone who *edits* a newspaper 'gives it out,' or in effect 'publishes' it. And that in fact is how the word was first used in English: when William Enfield wrote in his 1791 translation of Brucker's *Historia critica philosophiae* that a certain author 'wrote many philosophical treatises which have never been edited,' he meant 'published.' This usage comes directly from *ēditus*, the past participle of Latin *ēdere* 'put out, exhibit, publish,' which was a compound verb formed from the prefix *ex-*'out' and *dare* 'put, give' (source of English *date, donate*, etc). In its modern application, 'prepare for publication,' it is mainly a back-formation from *editor* [17], which acquired this particular sense in the 18th century. (French *éditeur* still means 'publisher,' and the term *editor* is used in that sense in some British publishing houses.)

▶ date, donate

**educate** [15] To *educate* people is literally to 'lead them out.' The word comes from the past participle of Latin *ēducāre*, which meant 'bring up, rear' as well as more specifically 'educate.' It was related to *ēducere* 'lead out' (source of English *educe* [15]), a compound verb formed from the prefix *ex-* 'out' and *dūcere* 'lead' (source of English *duct, duke*, and a whole host of derivatives such as *deduce* and *seduce*).

▶ conduct, deduce, duct, duke, educe, produce, seduce

**eerie** [13] *Eerie* seems to come ultimately from Old English *earg* 'cowardly,' a descendant of prehistoric Germanic *\*arg-*, although the connection has not been established for certain. It emerged in Scotland and northern England in the 13th century in the sense 'cowardly, fearful,' and it was not until the 18th century that it began to veer round semantically from 'afraid' to 'causing fear.' Burns was one of the first to use it so in print: 'Be thou a bogle by the eerie side of an auld thorn.' In the course of the 19th century its use gradually spread further south to become general English.

**effect** [14] Etymologically, an *effect* is that which is 'accomplished' or 'done.' The word comes (probably via Old French *effect*) from *effectus*, the past participle of Latin *efficere* 'perform, accomplish, complete,' or literally 'work out.' This was a compound verb formed from the prefix *ex-* 'out' and *facere* 'make, do' (source of English *fact, factory*, etc). The English verbal use, 'bring about,' is a 16th-century development based on the noun. (The similar *affect* also comes ultimately from Latin *facere*, but with the prefix *ad-* 'to' rather than *ex-*.) Latin *efficere* is also the source of English *efficacious* [16] and *efficient* [14].

The *feck-* of *feckless* is an abbreviated version of *effect*.

▶ efficacious, efficient, fact, factory, fashion, feckless

**effendi** SEE AUTHENTIC

**effervescent** SEE FERVENT

**effete** [17] Latin *effētus* meant literally 'that has given birth.' It was a compound adjective, based on the prefix *ex-*'out' and *fētus* 'childbearing, offspring' (source of English *foetus*). Its use spread metaphorically first to 'worn out by giving birth' and finally to simply 'exhausted,' the senses in which English originally acquired it. The word's modern connotations of 'over-refinement' and 'decadence' did not develop until the 19th century.

**efficacious** SEE EFFECT

**efficient** SEE EFFECT

**effigy** [16] *Effigy* comes ultimately from the Latin verb *effingere* 'form, portray.' This was a compound formed from the prefix *ex-* 'out' and *fingere* 'make, shape' (source of English *faint, feign, fiction, figment*, and related to English *dairy* and *dough*). It formed the basis of the noun *effigiēs* 'representation, likeness, portrait,' which was borrowed into English in the 16th century as *effigies*: 'If that you were the good Sir Rowland's son, as you have whisper'd faithfully you were, and as mine eye doth his effigies witness most truly limn'd and living in your face, be truly welcome hither,' Shakespeare, *As you like it* 1600. By the 18th century, however, this had come to be regarded as a plural form, and so a new singular, *effigy*, was created.

▶ dairy, dough, faint, fiction, figment

**effluent** [19] *Effluent* is that which 'flows out.' The word comes from the present participle of Latin *effluere*, a compound verb formed from the prefix *ex-* 'out' and *fluere* 'flow' (source of English *fluctuate, fluent, fluid, flux*, and a host of derivatives). English originally acquired it as an adjective in the 18th century, but did not begin to use it in its present-day noun senses until the mid 19th century. From the same source come *effluvium* [17] and *efflux* [17].

▶ fluctuate, fluent, fluid, flux

**effort** [15] Etymologically, *effort* is the 'putting out' or 'showing' of 'force.' It comes ultimately from Vulgar Latin *\*exfortiāre*, a compound verb formed from the prefix *ex-* 'out' and the adjective *fortis* 'strong.' This passed into Old French as *esforcier* 'force, exert,' from which was derived the noun *esforz*. English borrowed it in its later form *effort*.

▶ force

**effrontery** [18] The notion of 'audacity' or 'impudence' is often expressed in terms of 'exposing or pushing forward the face': a 'barefaced lie' or 'putting on a bold front,' for instance. And *effrontery* is no exception. It comes ultimately from late Latin *effrōns* 'barefaced, shameless,' a compound adjective formed from the prefix *ex-* 'out of' and *frōns* 'forehead' (source of English *front*). This seems subsequently to have been reformulated along the lines of its original components, giving Vulgar Latin *\*exfrontātus*, source of Old French *esfronte*. This in turn developed to French *effronté*, whose derived noun *effronterie* was acquired by English as *effrontery*.

▶ front

**egalitarian**    see EQUAL

**egg**    English has two distinct words *egg*, but surprisingly the noun, in the form in which we now have it, has not been in the language as long as the verb. *Egg* 'reproductive body' [14] was borrowed from Old Norse *egg*. Old English had a related word, *ǣg*, which survived until the 16th century as *eye* (plural *eyren*). Although it does not begin to show up in the written records until the 14th century, the form *egg* was presumably introduced into English by Norse immigrants considerably earlier, but even so, as late as the end of the 15th century there was still considerable competition between the native *eye* and the imported *egg*: 'What sholde a man in thyse dayes now wryte, egges or eyren, certaynly it is harde to playse every man,' William Caxton, *Eneydos* 1490. Both the Old English and the Old Norse forms came from a prehistoric Germanic *\*ajjaz* (source also of German and Dutch *ei*). This in turn was a descendant of an Indo-European *\*ōwo-* (whence Greek *ōión*, Latin *ōvum*, French *oeuf*, Italian *uovo*, Spanish *huevo*, and Russian *jajco*), which was probably derived ultimately from a base signifying 'bird' (source of Sanskrit *vís* and Latin *avis* 'bird,' the ancestor of English *aviary*).

*Egg* 'incite' [10], as in 'egg on,' is a Scandinavian borrowing too. It comes from Old Norse *eggja*, which was a relative or derivative of *egg* 'edge' (a cousin of English *edge*).

▶ aviary / edge

**ego** [19]    *Ego* is Latin for 'I' (and comes in fact from the same Indo-European base as produced English *I*). English originally acquired it in the early 19th century as a philosophical term for the 'conscious self,' and the more familiar modern uses – 'self-esteem,' or more

derogatorily 'self-importance,' and the psychologist's term (taken up by Freud) for the 'conscious self' – date from the end of the century.

Derivatives include *egoism* [18], borrowed from French *égoïsme*, and *egotism* [18], perhaps deliberately coined with the *t* to distinguish it from *egoism*. And the acquisitions do not end there: *alter ego*, literally 'other I, second self,' was borrowed in the 16th century, and the Freudian term *superego*, 'beyond I,' entered the language in the 1920s.

▶ I

**egregious**    see SEGREGATE

**eight** [OE]    Virtually all the ancient basic Indo-European 'number'-words are very stable, remaining recognizably the same as they spread and developed over the millenia, and the ancestor of English *eight* is no exception. It was *\*oktō*, which produced Sanskrit *astáu*, Latin *octō* (source of French *huit*, Italian *otto*, and Spanish *ocho*), Greek *oktố*, and Irish *ocht*. Its prehistoric Germanic decendant was *\*akhtō*, source of German and Dutch *acht*, Swedish *åtta*, and English *eight*.

▶ October

**eisteddfod** [19]    An *eisteddfod* is literally a 'session' or 'sitting.' It comes from the Welsh verb *eistedd* 'sit,' a derivative of *sedd* 'seat,' which goes back to the same Indo-European base (*\*sed-*) as produced English *sit* and *session*. The final element, *-fod*, comes from the Welsh verb *bod* 'be.'

▶ session, sit

**either** [OE]    *Either* is the modern descendant of an ancient Germanic phrase which meant literally 'always each of two.' Its constituents were *\*aiwō*, source of English *aye* 'ever, always,' (which was also one of the building blocks of which *each* was made) and *\*gikhwatharaz*, ancestor of English *whether*. In Old English this became lexicalized as the compound *ǣgehwæther*, subsequently contracted to *ǣgther*, from which developed modern English *either*. Despite its similarity, *neither* is more than just *either* with a negative prefix tacked on: its history is parallel but slightly different.

▶ aye, whether

**ejaculate** [16]    Etymologically, *ejaculate* means 'dart out.' It comes from Latin *ejaculārī*, a compound verb formed ultimately from the prefix *ex-* 'out' and *jaculum* 'dart, javelin.' This in turn was a derivative of *jacere* 'throw' (which itself combined with *ex-* to form *ejicere*, source of English *eject* [15]). The word's original sense 'throw out suddenly' survived (or perhaps has revived) for a time in English, but essentially it has been for its metaphorical uses ('emit semen' and 'exclaim') that it has been preserved.

▶ eject, jesses, jet, object, reject, subject

**eke** [12]    No Old English evidence of this verb, which originally meant 'increase,' has been found, but related forms in other Germanic languages, such as Old Norse *auka* and Gothic *aukan*, suggest that it did exist. Both these and a range of non-Germanic verbs, such as Latin *augēre* (source of English *auction, augment*, and *author*) and Greek *aúkhein*, point to an ultimate Indo-European ancestor *\*aug-* (from which comes English *wax* 'grow'). The first syllable of *nickname* was originally *eke*.

Until comparatively recently English had another word *eke* [OE], which meant 'also' (German *auch* and Dutch *ook* 'also' are related to it). It is not clear whether it is ultimately the same word as the verb *eke*.

▶ auction, augment, author, nickname, wax

**elaborate** [16] Etymologically, something that is *elaborate* has been produced by hard work. The word comes from *ēlabōrātus*, the past participle of Latin *ēlabōrāre*; this was a compound verb formed from the prefix *ex-* 'out' and *labor* 'work' (source of English *labour*). The notion of 'painstaking work' had passed by the early 17th century into 'extreme detail.'

▶ labour

**eland** [18] Although the eland is an African animal, it has an ancient European name, given to it by Dutch settlers in South Africa. *Eland* is the Dutch word for an 'elk' (the European version of the North American moose); it comes via German from Lithuanian *élnis*, which goes back ultimately to a prehistoric Indo-European source (*\*oln-, \*eln-*) which also produced English *elk*.

▶ elk

**elastic** [17] Greek *elaúnein* meant 'drive.' From it was derived the late Greek adjective *elastikós*, which had the sense 'driving, propelling.' Its Latin version *elasticus* was used by the French scientist Jean Pecquet (1622–74) in describing the expansive properties of gases, and that is the sense in which it was originally adopted into English. Its transference to the wider meaning 'returning to a former state after contracting' took place towards the end of the 17th century.

**elate** [16] *Elate* means literally 'lift up,' and that is how it was originally used in English: 'Placus doth elate his shady forehead,' George Chapman, *Iliad* 1611. The word comes from *ēlātus*, the past participle of Latin *efferre*. This was a compound verb formed from the prefix *ex-* 'out' and *ferre* 'carry' (a relative of English *bear*). Its metaphorical extension to a 'lifting of the spirits, exultation' had already started in the Latin word, and had completely ousted the literal meaning in English before the end of the 18th century.

▶ relate

**elbow** [OE] Logically enough, *elbow* means etymologically 'arm bend.' It comes from a prehistoric West and North Germanic *\*alinobogan* (which also produced German *ellenbogen*, Dutch *elleboog*, and Danish *albue*). This was a compound formed from

*\*alinā* 'forearm' and *\*bogan* (source of English *bow*). However, there is a further twist. For *\*alinā* (source also of English *ell* [OE], a measure of length equal to that of the forearm) itself goes back ultimately to an Indo-European base *\*el-, \*ele-* which itself meant 'bend,' and produced not just words for 'forearm' (such as Latin *ulna*), but also words for 'elbow' (such as Welsh *elin*). So at this deepest level of all, *elbow* means tautologically 'bend bend.'

▶ bow, ell, ulna

**elder** *Elder* 'older' [OE] is not, of course, the same word as *elder* the tree-name [OE]. The former began life in prehistoric Germanic as *\*althizon*, the comparative form of *\*althaz* 'old.' Gradually, the vowel *i* had an effect on the preceding vowel *a*, and by Old English times the word had become *eldra* – hence modern English *elder*. The regularized form *older* appeared in the 16th century. The derivative *elderly* dates from the 17th century.

The tree-name comes from Old English *ellærn*, a word whose origin is not known for certain (although it may perhaps be related to English *alder*). The intrusive *d* began to appear in the 14th century.

▶ old

**eldorado** [16] *Eldorado* was the name given by the Spanish to a country or city which they believed to exist in the heart of the Amazonian jungle, rich in precious metals and gems. It means 'the gilded one': *el* is the Spanish definite article, and *dorado* is the past participle of the Spanish verb *dorar* 'gild,' a descendant of Latin *dēaurāre*. This was a compound verb formed from the intensive prefix *dē-* and *aurum* 'gold.' The first known use of the word in English is in the title of Sir Walter Raleigh's book *Discoverie of Guiana, with a relation of the Great and Golden City of Manoa (which the Spaniards call El Dorado)* 1596.

**elect** [15] To *elect* somebody is literally to 'choose them out' of a range of possibilities. The word comes from *ēlectus*, the past participle of Latin *ēligere* 'pick out, select.' This was a compound verb formed from the prefix *ex-* 'out' and *legere* 'gather, choose' (source also of English *collect, neglect*, and *select* and, from its secondary meaning 'read,' *legible* and *lecture*). The notion of 'choosing by ballot' is the oldest of the verb's senses in English.

A person who may be 'elected' or 'chosen' is *eligible* [15] (an acquisition via French from the late Latin derivative *ēligibilis*). And someone who has been 'picked out' from the crowd is a member of the *élite* [18] (a borrowing of the feminine form of the past participle of French *élire* 'elect'). Also closely related is *elegant*.

▶ collect, elegant, eligible, elite, lecture, legible, neglect, select

**electricity** [17] The earliest manifestation of electricity was that produced by rubbing amber, and hence the name, based on *ēlectrum*, Latin for 'amber' (which in turn derives from Greek *élektron*). The first evidence of this in a Latin text is in William Gilbert's *De magnete* 1600, but by the middle of the century we find the word being used in English treatises, notably Sir Thomas Browne's *Pseudodoxia epidemica* 1646. (At this early stage, of course, it referred only to the ability of rubbed amber, etc to attract light bodies, the only property of electricity then known about; it was not until later that the full range of other electrical phenomena came to be included under the term.)

**eleemosynary**   see ALMS

**elegant**   [15]   Someone who made careful, fastidious choices was termed in Latin *ēlegāns*. This was the present participle of a hypothetical verb *ēlegāre*, a derivative of *ēligere* 'pick out, select' (source of English *elect*). Originally it seems to have been a derogatory term – 'fussy, foppish' – but by classical times it signified more approvingly 'making refined choices,' and was also transferred to the things chosen – 'choice, tasteful.' English probably acquired the word via French.

▶ elect

**elegy**   [16]   Greek *élegos* originally signified simply 'song' (Aristophanes, for example, used it for the song of a nightingale in his play *Birds*). It is not clear where it came from, although it has been speculated that the Greeks may have borrowed it from the Phrygians, an Indo-European people of western and central Asia Minor, and that originally it denoted 'flute song' (the long-held derivation from Greek *e e légein* 'cry woe! woe!' is not tenable). Later on it came to mean specifically 'song of mourning,' and its adjective derivative *elegeíā* passed as a noun via Latin and French into English.

**elephant**   [13]   Elephants were named from their tusks. Greek *eléphās* (probably a borrowing from a non-Indo-European language) meant originally 'ivory' (hence *chryselephantine* 'of gold and ivory' [19]). Only later did it come to denote the animal itself, and it passed in this sense into Latin as *elephantus*. By post-classical times this had become *olifantus*, and it is a measure of the unfamiliarity of the beast in northern Europe in the first millenium AD that when Old English acquired the word, as *olfend*, it was used for the 'camel.' Old French also had *olifant* (referring to the 'elephant' this time) and passed it on to English as *olifaunt*. It was not until the 14th century that, under the influence of the classical Latin form, this began to change to *elephant*. In the 16th and 17th centuries there was a learned revival of the sense 'ivory': Alexander Pope, for instance, in his translation of the *Odyssey* 1725, refers to 'the handle . . . with steel and polish'd elephant adorn'd.'

The notion of the *white elephant* as 'something unwanted' arose apparently from the practice of the kings of Siam presenting courtiers who had incurred their displeasure with real white elephants, the cost of whose proper upkeep was ruinously high.

**eleven**   [OE]   Originally, *eleven* and *twelve* seem to have meant literally 'one over' and 'two over.' *Eleven* comes ultimately from a prehistoric Germanic *ainlif-* (source also of German *elf* and Swedish *elva*) in which the first element *ainaz* is 'one' and the second is probably related to English *leave*. The compound would thus have signified 'one left (over ten),' hence 'ten plus one.'

▶ leave, one

**elf**   [OE]   In Germanic legend, elves were potent supernatural beings, capable of exercising considerable magic powers to the benefit or harm of human beings. Their decline to their modern status as small mischievous sprites seems to have begun in the 16th century. The word comes from a prehistoric Germanic *albiz*, a variant of which produced Old Norse *álfr* (source of English *oaf* [17]) and German *alp* 'nightmare.'

▶ oaf

**eligible**   see ELECT

**eliminate**   [16]   To *eliminate* somebody is literally to 'kick them out of doors.' The word comes from the past participle of Latin *ēlīmināre*, a compound verb formed from the prefix *ex-* 'out' and *līmen* 'threshhold' (source also of English *subliminal* and probably *sublime*). At first it was used in English with its original Latin sense ('the secounde sorte thearfore, that eliminate Poets out of their citie gates,' Giles Fletcher, *Christ's Victorie* 1610), and it was not until the early 18th century that the more general modern notion of 'exclusion' began to develop.

▶ sublime, subliminal

**élite**   see ELECT

**elixir**   [14]   Although nowadays we think of an *elixir* as liquid, it probably originated in the Greek word for 'dry,' *xērós* (whence English *xerox*). From this was derived a term for a 'dry' powder for treating wounds, *xérion*, and it has been speculated that this was borrowed by Arabic as (with the definite article *al*) *aliksīr*. Medieval alchemists used this as a word for a substance which could change base metals into gold, and also for a substance (according to some the same substance) which could confer immortality (known more fully as the *elixir of life*).

▶ xerox

**elk**   [OE]   The Indo-European base *ol-, *el-* produced a number of names for deerlike animals – Greek *élaphos* 'stag,' for example, and Welsh *elain* 'hind,' not to mention English *eland*. In its Germanic descendants, two main lines of development are evident: its extensions *olk-* and *elk-* produced respectively Germanic *algiz* (whence Old Norse *elgr*) and Germanic *elkho(n)*- (whence Old English *eolh*). It is not actually entirely clear which of these two is represented by modern English *elk*, which is first unequivocally recorded in the late 15th century. It is formally possible that it could be a survival of the Old English word, with its final /kh/ sound changed to /k/, but the long gap in the written record between Old English *eolh* and Middle English *elk* suggests that it could be an Old Norse borrowing.

▶ eland

**ell**  see ELBOW

**ellipse**  [18]  Greek *élleipsis* meant literally 'defect, failure.' It was a derivative of *elleípein*, literally 'leave in,' hence 'leave behind, leave out, fall short, fail,' a compound verb formed from the prefix *en-* 'in' and *leípein* 'leave' (which is related to English *loan* and *relinquish*). It was borrowed into English in the 17th century as *ellipsis* in the grammatical sense 'omission of a word or words,' but its mathematical use for an 'oval' (enshrined in the form *ellipse*, borrowed via French *ellipse* and Latin *ellīpsis*) comes from the notion that a square drawn on lines passing vertically and laterally through the centre of an ellipse 'falls short' of the entire length of the lateral line.

▶ loan, relinquish

**elm**  [OE]  The tree-name *elm* is widely distributed throughout the Indo-European languages of Europe. Latin had *ulmus*, for instance (source of German *ulme* and Dutch *olm*) and Irish has *leamh*. Of the Germanic languages (those whose native forms have not been supplanted by Latin *ulmus*) Swedish and Norwegian have *alm* beside English *elm*.

**elope**  [17]  Etymologically, *elope* signifies 'leap away.' It was originally an Anglo-Norman legal term applied to a married woman running off with a lover, and only in the past couple of hundred years has it come to be applied to a couple leaving home to get married when parental permission is denied. It is thought that the Anglo-Norman term was an adaptation of Middle English *alopen*, past participle of an unrecorded verb *alepen* 'run away,' which would have been formed from the prefix *a-* 'away' and *lepen* 'run, leap' (source of modern English *leap* and related to *lope* and German *laufen* 'run').

▶ leap, lope

**eloquent**  see VENTRILOQUIST

**else**  [OE]  *Else* shares its sense of 'otherness' with related words in other parts of the Indo-European language family. It comes ultimately from the base *al-*, which also produced Latin *alter* 'other' (source of English *alter*) and *alius* 'other' (source of English *alibi* and *alien*) and Greek *állos* 'other' (source of the prefix *allo-* in such English words as *allopathy*, *allophone*, and *allotropy*). Its Germanic descendant was *aljo-* 'other,'

whose genitive neuter case *aljaz*, used adverbially, eventually became English *else*.

▶ alibi, alien, alter

**elude**  see ILLUSION

**emaciate**  see MEAGRE

**emancipate**  [17]  Despite modern associations with women's liberation, *emancipate* has no etymological connection with *man*. It comes from Latin *ēmancipāre*, which meant originally 'free from parental power.' This was a compound verb formed from the prefix *ex-* 'out of' and *mancipium* 'ownership,' and referred in Roman law to the freeing of a son from the legal authority of the male head of the family, thus making him responsible for himself in law. *Mancipium* (source of the archaic English noun *manciple* 'steward, purveyor' [13]) was ultimately a compound noun formed from *manus* 'hand' (as in English *manual*) and *capere* 'take' (as in English *captive* and *capture*). The association of the verb with the 'freeing of slaves,' the basis of the present English meanings, is a modern development.

▶ captive, capture, manciple, manual

**embargo**  [16]  Something that has been *embargoed* has been literally 'placed behind bars' (compare EMBARRASS). The word comes from Vulgar Latin *imbarricāre*, which was formed from the Latin prefix *in-* 'in' and Vulgar Latin *barra* (source of English *bar*). This passed into Spanish as *embargar* 'impede, restrain,' and its derived noun *embargo* was borrowed into English.

▶ bar, barrier

**embark**  [16]  To *embark* is literally to 'put or get on to a boat' – or more specifically a *barque* [15] (a word acquired ultimately from late Latin *barca*, which is probably related to English *barge*). Its immediate French ancestor, *barque*, formed the basis of a compound verb *embarquer*, borrowed by English as *embark*. The antonym *disembark* also dates from the 16th century.

▶ barge, barque

**embarrass**  [17]  As in the case of *embargo*, the etymological meaning of *embarrass* is 'put behind bars.' It comes ultimately from Italian *imbarrare* 'surround with bars,' hence 'impede,' a compound verb formed from the prefix *in-* 'in' and Vulgar Latin *barra* 'bar' (source of English *bar*). From this was derived *imbarazzare*, which passed into English via Spanish *embarazar* and French *embarrasser*. Its original meaning 'impede, hamper' remains in use, chiefly in the context 'financially embarrassed,' but has been overtaken in frequency by 'disconcert.'

▶ bar, barrier

**embassy**  [16]  Ultimately, *embassy* comes from the same source as *ambassador*, the Vulgar Latin verb *ambactiāre 'go on a mission' (a derivative, via a rather circuitous route, of Latin *ambactus* 'vassal,' which was of Celtic origin). From the verb was derived the Old French noun *ambassade*, which was borrowed into English in the 15th century but was gradually supplanted from the 16th century onwards by *embassy*, acquired from another Old French derivative *ambassee*.

▶ ambassador

**embellish** [14] To *embellish* something is literally to 'make it beautiful.' It comes from Old French *embellir*, a compound verb formed from the prefix *en-*, which denotes 'causing' or 'making,' and *bel* 'beautiful.' This Old French adjective (source of modern French *beau*) came from Latin *bellus* 'beautiful,' and its other English offspring include *beau, belle*, and *beauty*.

▶ beau, beauty, belle

**ember** [OE] *Ember* goes back to a prehistoric Germanic *aimuzjōn*, although it is possible that the modern English word represents a borrowing from the related Old Norse *eimyrja* rather than a direct line of descent from Old English *æmyrge*. The *ember* of *Ember days* [10], incidentally, 'days following certain Christian festivals,' is a completely different word. It comes from Old English *ymbryne* 'circuit,' literally 'running round,' a compound formed from *ymb* 'round' and *ryne* 'course, running,' a relative of modern English *run*. It was applied to these particular days of the Christian calendar because they 'come round' four times a year.

**embezzle** [15] Originally, *embezzle* meant simply 'steal': 'See that no victuals nor no other stuff of the same household be embezzled out,' *Household Ordinances* 1469. The modern legal sense 'convert fraudulently' did not develop until the late 16th century. The word itself comes from Anglo-Norman *enbesiler*, a compound formed from the intensive prefix *en-* and the Old French verb *besiller*, of unknown origin.

**emblem** [15] The Latin term *emblēma* referred to 'inlaid work' – designs formed by setting some material such as wood or ivory, or enamel, into a contrasting surface. This usage survived into English as a conscious archaism ('The ground more colour'd then with stone of costliest emblem,' John Milton, *Paradise Lost* 1667), but for the most part English has used the word metaphorically, for a 'design which symbolizes something.' The Latin word was borrowed from Greek *émblēma*, a derivative of *embállein* 'throw in, put in, insert.' This was a compound verb formed from the prefix *en-* 'in' and *bállein* 'throw' (source of the second syllable of English *problem*, and closely related to that of *symbol*).

▶ problem, symbol

**embrace** [14] To *embrace* someone is literally to 'put your arms round' them. It comes via Old French from Vulgar Latin *imbracchiāre*, a compound verb formed from the prefix *in-* 'in' and Latin *bracchium*

'arm' (ultimate source of English *brace, bracelet*, and *bra*, and of French *bras* 'arm'). The transferred sense 'include' developed in the 17th century (a course also taken by modern French *embrasser*, whose original 'clasp in the arms' has moved on to 'kiss' in response to the progression of *baiser* from 'kiss' to 'have sex with').

▶ bra, brace, bracelet

**embrocation** [15] The semantic notion underlying *embrocation* is of 'wetness,' for it comes ultimately from the Greek word for 'rain,' *brokhē*. This was the basis of a verb *embrékhein*, used for 'treat medically by the application of liquid,' from which in turn was derived the noun *embrokhē* 'lotion.' Latin took this over and in the Middle Ages formed a verb from it, *embrocāre* 'treat with healing liquid,' which was actually borrowed into English as *embrocate*: 'In wounds of gun-shot . . . embrocate often,' John Woodall, *Surgion's Mate* 1612. This had died out by the mid 19th century, but its noun, *embrocation* (used in the concrete sense 'lotion' since the 17th century), survives.

**embroidery** [14] *Embroidery* comes from Anglo-Norman *enbrouderie*, a derivative of the verb *enbrouder*. This was a compound verb formed from the prefix *en-* 'in' and *broisder* 'embroider' (a borrowing from Frankish *brusdan*). English originally borrowed the verb as *embroud*, but soon extended it to *embrouder* (the early substitution of *-broid-* for *-broud-* may have been due to the influence of *broiden*, the Middle English past participle of *braid*).

**embryo** [16] The idea underlying *embryo* is of 'growing within.' The word comes from Greek *émbruon*, a compound verb formed from the prefix *en-* 'in' and the verb *brúein* 'swell, grow,' which meant literally 'something that grows inside the body.' English acquired it via late Latin *embryo*.

**emend** see MEND

**emerald** [13] *Emerald* traces its history back to an ancient Semitic verb 'shine' – *bāraq*. From this there seems to have been formed a noun *bāraqt* meaning 'gem.' This was taken over into the ancient vernacular languages of India (main source of gems in early times) as *maragada-*. Greek acquired the word as *máragdos* 'green gem,' which was soon superseded as the main form by a variant *smáragdos*. Latin adopted this as *smaragdus* (which passed into English, probably via Old French, as *smaragd*, a term used for the 'emerald' from the 13th to the 18th century, and revived as an archaism in the 19th century). In post-classical times Latin *smaragdus* became *smaralda*, and as this became disseminated through the Romance languages it acquired in many cases an additional syllable: Spanish *esmeralda*, for instance (source of the English forename) and Old French *esmeraude*, borrowed into Middle English as *emeraud*.

**emerge**　see MERGE
**emery**　see SMEAR
**emetic**　see VOMIT
**émeute**　see EMOTION
**eminent**　[15]　Someone who is *eminent* literally 'stands out.' The word comes from the present participle of Latin *ēminēre* 'stand out,' a compound verb formed from the prefix *ex-* 'out' and a verbal element *-minēre* 'stand, project' which occurs also in *imminent* and *prominent* and may be related ultimately to Latin *mōns* 'mountain,' source of English *mount* and *mountain*.
▶ imminent, mount, mountain, prominent

**emir**　see ADMIRAL

**emolument**　[15]　Just as a *salary* was originally a 'payment for salt,' so *emolument* appears to have been a particular kind of payment – in this case for flour – which later became generalized in meaning. Latin *ēmolere* meant 'grind out' (it was a compound verb formed from the prefix *ex-* 'out' and *molere* 'grind,' a relative of English *mill* and *meal* 'ground grain'), and hence the derivative *ēmolumentum* was used originally for 'fee paid to a miller for grinding grain.' The metaphorical sense 'gain' was already present in classical Latin.
▶ meal, mill

**emotion**　[16]　The semantic notion underlying *emotion* – of applying 'physical movement' metaphorically to 'strong feeling' – is an ancient one: Latin used the phrase *mōtus animā*, literally 'movement of the spirit,' in this sense. *Emotion* itself is a post-classical Latin formation; it comes ultimately from Vulgar Latin *\*exmovēre*, literally 'move out,' hence 'excite,' a compound verb formed from the prefix *ex-* 'out' and *movēre* 'move' (source of English *move*). In French this became *émouvoir*, and English borrowed its derived noun *émotion*, but at first used it only in the literal sense 'moving, agitation' ('The waters continuing in the caverns . . . caused the emotion or earthquake,' *Philosophical transactions of the Royal Society* 1758) and the metaphorically extended 'political agitation or disturbance' (a sense now preserved only in *émeute* [19], another derivative of French *émouvoir*). It was not until the late 17th century that the sense 'strong feeling' really came to the fore. The back-formation *emote* is a 20th-century phenomenon, of US origin.
▶ émeute, move

**emperor**　see EMPIRE

**emphasis**　[16]　In Greek, *émphasis* originally meant simply 'appearance.' It was a derivative of *emphaínein* 'exhibit, indicate,' a compound verb formed from the prefix *en-* 'in' and *phaínein* 'show' (source of English *phase*). It came to be used as a grammatical term denoting 'implication' (as opposed to 'directly ex-

pressed meaning') and passed in this sense via Latin *emphasis* into English. Its main modern use, 'special importance placed on something,' derives from the stressing of a particular word or phrase in speech to show that it is intended to imply something other than its literal meaning might seem to suggest.
▶ phase

**empire**　[13]　*Empire* and its close relatives *emperor* [13], *imperial* [14], *imperious* [16], and *imperative* [16] all come ultimately from the Latin verb *imperāre* 'command.' This was a compound verb formed from the prefix *in-* 'in relation to' and *parāre* 'make ready' (source of English *prepare*), and hence originally meant 'make preparations for' before shifting metaphorically to 'issue commands for.' Of its derivatives, *imperātor* (source of English *emperor*) was used originally for 'commander of an army,' and only secondarily for the ruler of the Roman empire, while the primary sense of *imperium* (source of English *empire*) was 'a command,' and hence 'authority.'
▶ imperative, imperial, prepare

**empirical**　[16]　Despite their formal resemblance, *empirical* and *empire* are completely unrelated. *Empirical* comes ultimately from the Greek adjective *émpeiros* 'skilled or experienced in,' a compound formed from the prefix *en-* 'in' and *peira* 'attempt, trial' (a relative of English *expert, peril, pirate*, and *repertory*). From this were derived successively the noun *empeiría* 'experience' and *empeirikós*, which English acquired via Latin *empiricus*.
▶ expert, peril, pirate, repertory

**employ**　[15]　Essentially, *employ* is the same word as *imply* [14] and *implicate* [16]. All three come ultimately from Latin *implicāre* 'enfold, involve,' a compound verb formed from the prefix *in-* 'in' and *plicāre* 'fold' (source of English *ply* and related to English *fold*). This passed into Old French as *emplier*, which in turn was transmitted into English as *imply*; this originally retained the literal sense 'enfold,' and it was only gradually that the metaphorical 'involve as a necessary condition' developed. However, Old French *emplier* had a variant *empleier*, later *emploier*, which took a slightly different semantic route – from simply 'involve' to 'involve in or apply to a particular purpose.' This was the sense in which English acquired it as *employ*.
▶ fold, implicate, imply, ply

**empty**　[OE]　The original meaning of Old English *ǣmtig* appears to have been 'unoccupied, at leisure,' and it was only secondarily that it developed the physical connotations of 'not full' which have come down to us in *empty*. (It also meant 'unmarried.') It was a derivative of the noun *ǣmetta* 'rest, leisure.' This is a word of uncertain history, but it has been plausibly analysed as the negative prefix *ǣ-* plus a derivative of the root which produced modern English *mete* (as in 'mete out'), meaning something like 'not assigned.'

▶ mete

## emulate  see IMITATE

## emulsion  [17] An emulsion is an undissolved suspension of tiny drops of one liquid dispersed throughout another. The classic example of this is milk – whence its name. It comes from modern Latin *ēmulsiō*, a derivative of *ēmulgēre* 'drain out, milk out.' This was a compound verb formed from the prefix *ex-* 'out' and *mulgēre* 'milk,' a distant relative of English *milk*. The word's familiar modern application to paint dates from the 1930s.

▶ milk

## enamel  [14] The underlying meaning element in *enamel* is 'melting.' It comes ultimately from a pre-historic Germanic base *\*smalt-* (source of English *schmaltz* 'sentimentality' [20], borrowed via Yiddish from German *schmalz* 'fat, dripping'), and related Germanic forms produced English *smelt, melt,* and *malt*. Old French acquired the Germanic word and turned it into *esmauz*; this in turn was re-formed to *esmail,* and Anglo-Norman adopted it as *amail*. This formed the basis, with the prefix *en-* 'in,' of a verb *enamailler* 'decorate with enamel.' English borrowed it, and by the mid-15th century it was being used as a noun for the substance itself (the noun *amel,* a direct borrowing from Anglo-Norman, had in fact been used in this sense since the 14th century, and it did not finally die out until the 18th century). Its application to the substance covering teeth dates from the early 18th century.

▶ malt, melt, schmaltz, smelt

## encaustic  see INK

## enclose  see INCLUDE

## encroach  [14] Something that *encroaches* on something else literally seizes it with its 'hooks.' The word was borrowed from Old French *encrochier* 'catch in a hook,' hence 'seize.' This was a compound formed from the prefix *en-* and *croc* 'hook' (source of English *crochet, crocket,* and *croquet*), a noun borrowed from Old Norse *krókr* 'hook' (source of English *crook*). The verb's original use in English was transitive, in the sense 'seize wrongfully'; the modern sense 'intrude, trespass' did not develop until the 16th century.

▶ crochet, crook, croquet

## encyclopedia  [16] Etymologically, *encyclopedia* means 'general education.' It is a medieval formation, based on the Greek phrase *egkúklios paideíā* (*egkúklios,* a compound adjective formed from the prefix *en-* 'in' and *kúklos* 'circle' – source of English *cycle* – meant originally 'circular,' and hence 'general,' and is the ultimate source of English *encyclical* [17]; *paideíā* 'education' was a derivative of *país* 'boy, child,' which has given English *paederast* [18],

*paedophilia* [20], *pedagogue* [14], *pedant* [16], and *pediatrician* [20]). This referred to the general course of education which it was customary to give a child in classical Greece, and after it was merged into a single word *egkuklopaideíā* and transmitted via medieval Latin *encyclopedia* into English, it retained that meaning at first. However, in the 17th century the term began to be applied to compendious reference works (the first, or at least the one which did most to establish the name, was perhaps that of J H Alsted in 1632). The *Encyclopedia Britannica* was first published in 1768.

▶ cycle, encyclical, paederast, pedagogue, pedant, pediatrician

## end  [OE] *End* is an ancient word, that has been traced back to an Indo-European *\*antjó*. This also produced Sanskrit *ántas* 'end,' as well as Latin *ante* 'before' and Greek *antí* 'opposite.' Its Germanic descendant was *\*andja,* from which came Gothic *andeis,* German *ende,* Dutch *einde,* Swedish *ända,* and English *end*.

## endeavour  [14] Despite its plausible appearance, *endeavour* is not a borrowing from French or Latin but a purely English creation. It was coined from the Middle English phrase *put in dever,* which was a partial translation of Old French *mettre en deveir,* literally 'put in duty,' hence 'make it one's duty to do something' (*deveir,* ancestor of modern French *devoir* 'duty,' came ultimately from Latin *dēbēre* 'owe,' source of English *debit* and *debt*). In the 14th century the last two words were joined together to form the verb *endeavour* 'make an effort.'

▶ debit, debt

## endorse  [16] To *endorse* something is literally to write 'on the back' of it. The word comes from medieval Latin *indorsāre,* a compound verb formed from the prefix *in-* 'in' and *dorsum* 'back' (source of English *dorsal, doss,* and *dossier*). (An earlier English version of the word was *endoss* [14], acquired via Old French *endosser,* which died out in the 17th century.)

▶ dorsal, doss, dossier

## endow  see DOWRY

## endure  see DURING

## enemy  [13] An *enemy* is literally someone who is 'not a friend.' The word comes, via Old French *enemi,* from Latin *inimīcus,* a compound formed from the prefix *in-* 'not' and *amīcus* 'friend' (source of English *amicable* and related to English *amiable*). The late Latin derivative *inimīcālis* produced English *inimical* [17].

▶ amicable, inimical

## energy  [16] *Energy* comes ultimately from Greek *érgon* 'deed, work.' This was a descendant of Indo-European *\*wergon,* which also produced English *work, liturgy, organ,* and *orgy*. Addition of the prefix

*en-* 'at' produced the adjective *energés* or *energós* 'at work,' hence 'active,' which Aristotle used in his *Rhetoric* as the basis of a noun *enérgeio*, signifying a metaphor which conjured up an image of something moving or being active. This later came to mean 'forceful expression,' or more broadly still 'activity, operation.' English acquired the word via late Latin *energīa*.

▶ liturgy, organ, orgy, work

**engage** [15] Vulgar Latin had a noun *\*wadium* 'pledge' (it came from Germanic *\*wathjam*, source also of English *wed* and *wage*). From it was derived a verb *\*wadiāre* 'pledge,' which formed the basis of a compound *\*inwadiāre*. Germanic *w* became *g* in French (hence French *Guillaume* for *William*), so the Old French descendant of *\*inwadiāre* was *engager*, acquired by English as *engage*. (The superficially similar *gauge* [15] is probably not related, although it is not known for certain what its ultimate source is.)

▶ wage, wed

**engine** [13] The underlying etymological meaning of *engine* is 'natural talent.' It comes ultimately from Latin *ingenium* (source also of English *ingenious*) which was formed from the base *\*gen-* (as in *genetic*) denoting 'reproduction' and meant literally 'skill or aptitude one was born with.' Abstract meanings related to this (such as 'ingenuity' and 'genius') have now died out in English (which acquired the word via Old French *engin*), but what remains is a more specific strand of meaning in the Latin word – 'clever device, contrivance.' Originally this was an abstract concept (often used in a bad sense 'trick, cunning ruse'), but as early as about 1300 there is evidence of a more concrete application in English to a 'mechanical device.' The word's modern use for 'machine producing motion' originates in its early 19th-century application to the steam engine.

*Engineer* [14] comes via Old French *engigneor* from medieval Latin *ingeniātōr*, a derivative of the verb *ingeniāre* 'contrive,' which in turn came from *ingenium*.

▶ gin, ingenious

**English** [OE] The people and language of England take their name from the Angles, a West Germanic people who settled in Britain in the 5th and 6th centuries AD. They came originally from the Angul district of Schleswig, an area of the Jutland peninsula to the south of modern Denmark. This had a shape vaguely reminiscent of a fishhook, and so its inhabitants used their word for 'fishhook' (a relative of modern English *angler* and *angling*) to name it. From earliest times the adjective *English* seems to have been used for all the Germanic peoples who came to Britain, including the Saxons and Jutes, as well as the Angles (at the beginning of the 8th century Bede referred to them collectively as *gens anglorum* 'race of Angles'). The earliest record of its use

with reference to the English language is by Alfred the Great.

▶ angler, angling

**engrave** see GRAVE

**engross** see GROSS

**enhance** [14] To *enhance* something is literally to 'make it higher.' The word comes via Anglo-Norman *enhauncer* from Old French *enhaucer*, a descendant of Vulgar Latin *\*inaltiāre* 'raise.' This was a verb formed from the Latin intensive prefix *in-* and the adjective *altus* 'high' (source of English *altitude*). This original literal sense persisted into English ('It was a stone, the which was enhanced upright,' William Caxton, *Charles the Great* 1485), but had largely died out by the end of the 16th century, leaving the field clear for the metaphorical 'augment.'

▶ altitude

**enigma** [16] *Enigma* comes, via Latin, from Greek *aínigma* 'riddle, obscure statement.' This was a derivative of the verb *ainíssesthai* 'talk in riddles,' which in turn came from the noun *ainos* 'tale, story.' Its modern English use for 'something puzzling' dates from the early 17th century.

**enjoy** [14] Originally, *enjoy* was used intransitively in English, rather as in the modern American Yiddish-influenced injunction 'Enjoy!': 'Yet he never enjoyed after, but in conclusion pitifully wasted his painful life,' Robert Laneham 1549. However, by the end of the 16th century the transitive sense 'take pleasure in' had virtually taken over the field. The word probably comes from Old French *enjoïr*, a compound formed from the prefix *en-* 'in' and *joïr* 'rejoice,' which in turn came from Latin *gaudēre* (ultimate source of English *joy*). Old French did have another, similar verb, however, *enjoier* (formed from the noun *joie*), which probably also played a part in the English acquisition.

▶ joy

**ennui** see ANNOY

**enormous** [16] Etymologically, *enormous* is a parallel formation to *abnormal* and *extraordinary*. It comes from Latin *ēnormis*, a compound adjective formed from the prefix *ex-* 'out of' and *norma* 'pattern, rule' – hence literally 'out of the usual pattern.' It originally had a range of meanings in English, including 'abnormal, unusual' ('entered the choir in a military habit, and other enormous disguises,' Thomas Warton, *History of English Poetry* 1774) and 'outrageous.' By the beginning of the 19th century these had mostly died out, leaving the field clear for modern English 'huge,' although the notion of 'outrageousness' remains in the noun derivative *enormity* [15].

▶ abnormal, normal

**enough** [OE] *Enough* is a widespread word in the Germanic languages. German has *genug*, Dutch *ge-*

*noeg*, and Swedish and Danish the reduced forms *nog* and *nok*. All go back to a prehistoric Germanic *\*ganō-gaz*, a compound formed from the collective prefix *\*ga-* and an Indo-European element *\*nak-* whose underlying meaning is probably 'reach, attain' (it occurs in Sanskrit *na* and Latin *naniscī*, both of which have that sense).

**enquire** [13] The *-quire* element in *enquire* (or *inquire*, as it is alternatively spelled) is etymologically related to English *query* and *question*. The word comes via Old French *enquerre* from *\*inquaerere*, the Vulgar Latin descendant of Latin *inquīrere*. This was a compound verb formed from the intensive prefix *in-*and *quaerere* 'seek, ask.' The modern English spelling with *i* in the second syllable comes from a 15th-century reintroduction of the vowel of Latin *inquīrere*. *Inquest* [13] comes from the Latin verb's past participle.

▶ inquest, query, question

**ensconce**    see SCONCE

**ensemble**    see SIMILAR

**ensign**    see SIGN

**ensue**    see SUE

**ensure**    see INSURE

**entablature**    see TABLE

**entail** [14] *Entail* means literally 'put a tail on' – but not the sort that grows. This is a *tail* in the sense of a 'legal limitation.' It came from Old French *taille*, meaning literally 'cut,' which is also related to English *detail, retail, tailor*, and *tally*. The coining of *entail* itself probably took place in Anglo-Norman. Its current main meaning 'have as a necessary or logical consequence' did not develop until as late as the 19th century.

▶ detail, retail, tailor, tally

**enter** [13] *Enter* comes ultimately from a Latin preposition and adverb, *intrā*, which meant 'inside' (and was formed from *in* 'in' and the suffix *-trā*, as in *extra*). This was taken as the basis of a Latin verb, *intrāre* 'enter,' which passed into English via Old French *entrer*. Of its derivatives, *entry* [13] has the longer history, going back to a Vulgar Latin *\*intrāta*; *entrance* [16] is an Old French formation.

**enterprise** [15] *Enterprise* is the Romance-language equivalent of the native English formation *undertaking*. It comes from the past participle of Old French *entreprendre*, a compound verb formed from *entre* 'between' and *prendre* 'take' (a word with many relatives in English, from *comprehend* to *surprise*). The original Old French version of the word was *emprise* (from Vulgar Latin *\*imprendere* 'undertake,' in which the prefix was *in-* rather than *inter-*), and English actually borrowed this in the 13th century; it survived as an archaism into the 19th century. The underlying meaning of both versions is probably 'taking something in *or* between one's hands' so as to do something about it.

▶ apprehend, comprehend, comprise, surprise

**enthusiasm** [17] *Enthusiasm* has had a chequered semantic history. Like *giddyness*, it meant originally 'state of being inspired by a god.' It comes ultimately from Greek *énthous* or *éntheos* 'possessed, inspired,' a compound formed from the prefix *en-* 'in' and *theós* 'god' (as in English *theology*). From this in turn was derived the verb *enthousiázein* 'be inspired' and the noun *enthousiasmós*, which passed into English via Latin or French, still with the sense 'divine inspiration' ('Doth he think they knew it by enthusiasm or revelation from heaven?' Richard Baxter, *Infants' church membership and baptism* 1651). In the stern climate of Puritanism, however, divine inspiration was not something to be encouraged, and as the 17th century progressed *enthusiasm* took on derogatory connotations of 'excessive religious emotion.' The modern approbatory meaning, 'eagerness,' had its beginnings at the start of the 18th century, and by the early 19th century had ousted the deprecatory sense from leading place.

▶ theology

**entice** [13] *Entice* is an inflammatory sort of word. It comes ultimately from Latin *tītiō* 'firebrand,' which was used, with the prefix *in-* 'in,' to form the Vulgar Latin verb *\*intītiāre* 'set on fire.' This passed into English via Old French *enticier*, and originally retained much of the heat and vigour of its origins: 'Your master is enticed and provoked by the Duke of Burgundy,' Richard Grafton, *Chronicles of the Affairs of England* 1568; but by the 17th century the process of softening from 'incitement' to 'allurement' was all but complete.

**entire** [14] *Entire* and *integrity* [15] have the same source – Latin *integer*. This meant 'whole, complete,' and was formed from the prefix *in-* 'in' and *\*tag-*, the base which produced Latin *tangere* 'touch,' source of English *tactile* and *tangible* (and indeed of *intact* [15], a parallel formation to *entire* and *integrity*). English borrowed *integer* [16] itself as a mathematical term denoting a 'whole' number, and several of its Latin derivatives – not just *integrity* but also *integral* [16], from late Latin *integrālis*, and *integrate* [17], from Latin *integrāre* 'make whole.' As its difference in form suggests, however, *entire* came via a different route. The Latin accusative form *integrum* produced Vulgar Latin *\*integro*, which passed into Old French as *entier* – hence English *entire*.

▶ intact, integrity, tactile, tangible

**entitle**    see TITLE

**entomology**    see INSECT

**entrails** [13] *Entrails* means literally just 'insides' – and indeed there is an unbroken semantic undercurrent to the word from earliest times to the present day signifying exactly that (as in 'entrails of the earth'). It comes ultimately from the Latin adjective *interāneus* 'internal,' a derivative of the adverb and preposition *in-*

*ter* 'inside, among.' Its neuter plural form *interānea* came to be used as a noun, and at some point underwent a metamorphosis to medieval Latin *intrālia* 'inner parts, intestines.' English acquired the word via Old French *entrailles*.

**entrance**   see ENTER

**entrechat**   [18]   An *entrechat* has no connection with cats, despite the passing resemblance to French *chat*. It comes from French, indeed, but there the original form was not *entrechat* but *entrechas*, a derivative of the verb *entrechasser* 'chase in and out,' the notion being that the dancer's feet cross, or 'chase,' each other several times while she or he is in the air. The verb is a compound formed from *entre* 'between' and *chasser* 'pursue,' a relative of English *chase*.

▶chase

**entropy**   [19]   The term *entropy* was coined (as *entropie*) in 1865 by the German physicist Rudolph Clausius (1822–88), formulator of the second law of thermodynamics. It was he who developed the concept of entropy (a measure of the disorder of a system at atomic or molecular level), and he created the name for it (on the model of *energy*) from Greek *en-* 'in' and *tropé* 'turning, transformation' (source of English *trophy* and *tropical*). The first record of the English version of the word is from 1868.

▶trophy, tropical

**entry**   see ENTER

**enumerate**   see NUMBER

**envelope**   [18]   English borrowed *envelope* from French *enveloppe* in the sense 'wrapper,' and more specifically 'cover for a letter,' at the start of the 18th century. It was a derivative of the verb *envelopper* 'wrap,' whose ancestor, *envoloper*, gave English *envelop* in the 14th century. As in the case of its first cousin *develop*, the origin of the verb remains a mystery. It is a compound formed from the prefix *en-* 'in' and *voloper* 'wrap,' but the source of *voloper* has never been satisfactorily explained. It may come from a hypothetical Celtic base **vol-* 'roll,' but an equally good candidate is late Latin **faluppa* 'husk,' from which come Italian *viluppo* 'bundle' and *viluppare* 'wrap.'

▶develop

**envoy**   [14]   English has acquired *envoy* – literally 'sent on one's way' – twice. The first time, it meant 'final part of a poem' (this is now usually spelled *envoi*); the second time (in the 17th century) it meant 'diplomatic representative.' Both came from the past participle of the French verb *envoyer* 'send,' which in turn was a descendant of late Latin *inviāre* 'put on the way,' a compound based on the noun *via* 'way.' Its plural formed the basis of *invoice* [16].

▶invoice

**envy**   [13]   The underlying meaning of *envy* is simply 'look at someone' – the implication being, 'with malice or resentment.' The word comes via Old French *envie* from Latin *invidia* 'malice' (source of English *invidious* [17]), which was a derivative of *invidēre* 'look at with malice.' This in turn was a compound verb formed from the prefix *in-* 'in, on' and *vidēre* 'see' (whence English *vision*).

▶invidious, view, vision

**épée**   see SPADE

**ephemeral**   [16]   *Ephemeral*, now used fairly loosely for 'transitory,' originally meant specifically 'lasting only one day.' It comes from Greek *ephémeros*, a compound formed from the prefix *epí-* 'on' and *hēmérā* 'day.' The Greeks named the mayfly *ephémeron*, since its adult form lives only one day, and English adopted *ephemeron* [16] as the scientific name for the insect.

**epicure**   [16]   The Greek philosopher Epicurus (Greek *Epíkouros*) (341–270BC) evolved a code of life and behaviour which stressed the avoidance of pain, but since his time it has been stood on its head to signify the active seeking of pleasure – and particularly the pleasures of the table. Indeed, when the word *epicure* (which arrived via Latin *epicūrus*) was introduced into English it was even used for a 'glutton' – since toned down somewhat to 'connoisseur of fine food and wine.'

**epidemic**   [17]   An *epidemic* is literally something that has an effect 'among the people.' The word comes from French *épidémique*, a derivative of the noun *épidémie*, which goes back via late Latin *epidēmia* to Greek *epidēmíā* 'disease prevalent among the people.' This was a noun use of *epidēmios*, a compound adjective formed from the prefix *epí-* 'among' and *demos* 'people' (source of English *democracy*).

▶democracy

**epiglottis**   see GLOSS

**epilepsy**   [16]   Etymologically, *epilepsy* is the Greek equivalent of English *seizure* or *attack*. The word comes, via French or Latin, from Greek *epilēpsíā*, a derivative of *epilambánein* 'seize upon.' This was a compound verb formed from the prefix *epí-* 'on' and *lambánein* 'take hold of.'

**episode**   [17]   In modern English, an *episode* is a component in a series of connected events, but originally it was something incidental, coming in adventitiously from the side. The word comes from Greek *epeisódion* 'addition,' a noun use of the adjective *epeisódios* 'coming in besides.' This was a compound formed from the prefix *epí-* 'besides' and the noun *eísodos* 'coming in, entrance' – which in turn was a compound formed from the preposition *eis* 'into' and *hodós* 'way' (a relative of Russian *chodit'* 'go').

▶exodus

**epistle** [14] *Epistle* has never really caught on in English as a general term for a 'letter' – too high-falutin – but in fact from a semantic point of view its origins are quite simple. It comes ultimately from Greek *epistolē*, which meant 'something sent to someone.' This was a derivative of *epistéllein*, a compound verb formed from the prefix *epi-* 'to' and *stellein* 'send' (as in *apostle*, literally 'someone sent out'). English actually acquired the word for the first time during the Anglo-Saxon period, directly from Latin *epistola*, and it survived into the 16th century in the reduced form *pistle*. In the 14th century, however, it was reborrowed, via Old French, as *epistle*.

► apostle

**epitaph** [14] Greek *táphos* meant 'tomb,' and so an oration that was *epitáphios* (an adjective formed with the prefix *epi-*'over') was given 'over the tomb.' Eventually the adjective was made into a noun, *epitáphion*, and this reached English via Latin *epitaphium* and Old French *epitaphe*.

**epithet** [16] Etymologically, an *epithet* is a word that is 'put on' to or 'added' to another. The term comes from Greek *epítheton*, which meant literally 'addition,' but was used by Greek grammarians for 'adjective.' It was a derivative of *epitithénai* 'put on, add,' a compound verb formed from the prefix *epi-* 'on' and *tithénai* 'place, put' (a relative of English *do* and *theme*). By the time the word reached English (via French or Latin) it had moved over from the vocabulary of the grammarian to that of the layman, in the sense 'descriptive appellation.'

► do, theme

**epoch** [17] Historically, *epoch* means 'point in time,' but its particular application to 'point marking the beginning of a new period of time' has led increasingly to its use in modern English for simply 'historical period.' The word comes via modern Latin *epocha* from Greek *epokhē*, literally 'pause, stoppage,' and hence 'fixed point in time.' This was a derivative of *epékhein* 'pause, hold back,' a compound verb formed from the prefix *epi-* 'back' and *ékhein* 'hold' (source of English *hectic* and related to *scheme* and *sketch*).

► hectic, scheme, sketch

**equal** [14] Latin *aequus* (a word of unknown ancestry) meant 'level' or 'even.' From it was derived the adjective *aequālis* 'equal,' which has provided the term for 'equal' in all the modern Romance languages, including French *égal* (source of English *egalitarian* [19]), Italian *uguale*, and Spanish *igual*. English, however, is the only Germanic language in which it constitutes a major borrowing.

English also possesses, of course, a host of related words, including *adequate* [17], *equanimity* [17], *equate* [15], *equation* [14], *equator* [14] (etymologically the line of latitude that 'equalizes' day and night), and *iniquity* [14] (etymologically the equivalent of *inequality*), not to mention all those beginning with the prefix *equi-*, such as *equidistant* [16], *equilibrium* [17] (literally 'equal balance,' from Latin *lībra* 'balance'), *equinox* [14], *equity* [14], and *equivalent* [15].

► adequate, egalitarian, equator, equity, iniquity

**equerry** [16] Nowadays in Britain simply royal attendants, equerries' long and traditional association with the royal stables has led to association of the word *equerry* with Latin *equus* 'horse,' but in fact the two are quite unrelated. *Equerry* originally meant 'stable,' and was borrowed from the obsolete French *escuirie* (now *écurie*). It is not clear where this came from: some etymologists have linked it with Old High German *scūr* 'barn, shed,' while others have derived it from Old French *escuier* 'groom' (source of English *esquire* and *squire*), according to which view it would mean 'place where a groom stayed or worked.' (*Escuier* itself came ultimately from Latin *scūtārius* 'shield-bearer.') Forms such as *escurie* remained current in English up until the 18th century, but already by the 17th century *equus*-influenced spellings had begun to appear.

The person in charge of such a stable was formerly termed in French *escuier d'escuirie* 'squire of the stable,' and in English *groom of the equerry*, and there are records from quite early in the 16th century indicating that *equerry* was being used on its own as the term for such a groom.

► esquire, squire

**equestrian** [17] *Equestrian* was adapted from Latin *equester*, an adjective derived from *eques* 'horseman.' *Eques* in turn was based on *equus* 'horse' (source of English *equine* [18]). This was the Latin descendant of *\*ekwos*, the prehistoric Indo-European term for 'horse,' which was once found in all the daughter languages of Indo-European except for the Slavic branch: Old English had *eoh*, for example, Old Irish *ech*, Sanskrit *aśva*, and ancient Greek *híppos* (source of English *hippodrome* and *hippopotamus*). It is a remarkable circumstance, however, that over the past thousand years *equus* and its relatives have (other than in derivatives such as *equine*) died out, to be replaced by secondary terms such as French *cheval* (from Latin *caballus*, probably a non-Indo-European borrowing), German *pferd* (from late Latin *paraverēdus* 'extra post-horse,' source also of English *palfrey*), and English *horse*.

► equine, hippopotamus

**equip** [16] Etymologically, *equip* means 'fit out or provide crew for a ship.' Its immediate source was French *équiper*, but this appears to have been a borrowing from Old Norse *skipa* 'fit out a ship,' a verb derived from *skip* 'ship' (first cousin of English *ship*). The earliest examples of its use in English are in the much broader sense 'supply with necessary materials,' and its specific links with the sea were soon severed.

▶ ship

**era** [17] In ancient Rome, small discs or tokens made of 'brass' (Latin *aes*, a descendant, like English *ore* [OE], of Indo-European *\*ajes*) used for counting were known as *aera*. In due course this developed the metaphorical meaning 'number as a basis for calculation,' and from around the 5th century AD it came to be used in Spain, North Africa, and southern Gaul as a prefix for dates, somewhat analogous to modern English AD. By extension it was then applied to a 'system of chronological notation, as dated from a particular event or point in time,' the sense in which English acquired the word. The more general 'historical period' is an 18th-century semantic development.

▶ ore

**eradicate** [16] Semantically, *eradicate* is an analogous formation to *uproot*. It comes from the past participle of Latin *ērādicāre* 'pull out by the roots,' a compound verb formed from the prefix *ex-* 'out' and *rādix* 'root' (source of English *radical* and *radish* and related to English *root*). In the 16th and 17th centuries it was often used literally ('oaks eradicated by a prodigious whirlwind,' Thomas Nabbes, *Hannibal and Scipio* 1637), but since then the metaphorical 'remove totally' has taken over.

▶ radish, root

**erase** [17] Like *abrade, rascal, rase,* and *razor, erase* comes ultimately from Latin *rādere* 'scrape.' This formed the basis of a compound verb *ērādere* 'scrape out, scrape off' (its first element is the Latin prefix *ex-* 'out'). *Eraser* 'rubber' seems to be a 19th-century coinage.

▶ abrade, rascal, rase, razor

**erect** [14] *Erect* was borrowed from Latin *ērectus*, the past participle of *ērigere* 'raise up, set up.' This was a compound verb formed from the prefix *ex-* 'out, up' and *regere* 'keep straight, set, direct' (source of English *regent, region*, etc). The use of the derivative *erection* [15] for the enlargement of the penis dates from the 16th century.

▶ correct, direct, regent, region

**ermine** [12] The term *ermine* was introduced to English from Old French as a name for the 'stoat,' but as in the case of other words of French origin like *mutton* and *pork* which soon came to be used for the dead animals' product rather than the live animals themselves, it was not long (about a hundred years in fact) before *ermine* was being applied to the stoat's fur, and specifically to its white winter fur. The source of the French word is not entirely clear. One school of thought derives it from medieval Latin *mūs Armenius* 'Armenian mouse,' on the assumption that this denoted a 'stoat' or 'weasel,' but an alternative possibility is Germanic origin.

**erode** SEE ROSTRUM

**erotic** [17] *Érōs* was the Greek word for 'sexual love' (as opposed to *agápē* 'brotherly love' and *philía* 'friendship'). The concept was personified in Greek mythology as *Érōs*, the boy-god of love. Its adjectival derivative *erōtikós* arrived in English via French *érotique*.

**err** [14] *Err, erratic* [14], *erroneous* [14], and *error* [13] all go back to a prehistoric base *\*er-*, which meant 'wandering about' (the semantic progression from 'wandering' to 'making mistakes' is reproduced in several other quite unrelated word groups in the Indo-European language family). This produced Gothic *airzei* 'error,' Old High German *irri* 'astray' (source of modern German *irre* 'angry'), Old English *ierre* 'astray,' and Latin *errāre* 'wander, make mistakes' – from which, via Old French *errer*, English got *err*.

▶ erratic, error

**errand** [OE] Despite the passing similarity, *errand* has no etymological connection with *err* and *error*. It comes from a prehistoric Germanic *\*ærundjam*, which meant 'message' – a sense which in fact survived in English until as recently as the 18th century (Miles Coverdale, for example, in his 1535 translation of 1 Samuel 11:5 wrote 'So they told him the errand of the men of Jabesh' – where the Authorized Version has 'tidings'). The main modern meaning, 'task one goes to perform,' developed in the 13th century (in American English it has latterly gained specific connotations of 'shopping'). The source of the Germanic word is not known, but it is no doubt related to Swedish *ärende* and Danish *ærinde* 'errand, message, business.'

**error** SEE ERR

**eructate** SEE REEK

**erudite** [15] To be *erudite* is literally to be the opposite of 'rude.' Latin *rudis* (source of English *rude*) meant 'rough, unpolished,' and so *ērudīre*, a compound verb formed with the prefix *ex-* 'out of, from,' signified 'take the roughness out of,' hence 'polish, teach.' Its past participle formed the basis of an adjective, *ērudītus* '(well) taught,' which as borrowed into English has acquired the greater gravitas of 'learned.'

▶ rude

**erupt** [17] Etymologically, *erupt* means simply 'break out.' It comes from the past participle of Latin *ērumpere*, a compound verb formed from the prefix *ex-* 'out, from' and *rumpere* 'break' (source of English *rout, route, routine,* and *rupture*, and related to *bereave, rob,* and *robe*). English actually acquired the derived noun *eruption* [15] before the verb.

▶ bereave, corrupt, disrupt, rob, rout, route, routine, rupture

**erythrocyte**   see RED

**escalate**   [20] *Escalate* is a back-formation from *escalator* [20], which was originally a trade-name for a moving staircase first made in the USA around 1900 by the Otis Elevator Company. This in turn seems to have been coined (probably on the model of *elevator*) from *escalade* [16], a term in medieval warfare signifying the scaling of a fortified wall, which came via French and Spanish from medieval Latin *scalāre*, source of English *scale* 'climb.' *Escalate* originally meant simply 'ascend on an escalator'; the metaphorical sense 'increase' developed at the end of the 1950s.

**escape**   [14] Originally, *escape* meant literally 'take off one's cloak,' and signified metaphorically 'throw off restraint' – much as we might say *unbutton*. The word appears to come ultimately from Vulgar Latin *\*excappāre*, a hypothetical compound verb formed from the prefix *ex-* 'out, off' and *cappa* 'cloak' (source of English *cape*). This passed into Old Northern French as *escaper* (immediate source of the English word), by which time the metaphor had progressed from 'throwing off restraint' to 'gaining one's liberty.'
▶ cape

**eschew**   [14] *Eschew* is ultimately of Germanic origin, although it reached English via French. Its remote ancestor is prehistoric Germanic *\*skeukhwaz*, source also of English *shy*. A verb based on this, *\*skeukhwan*, was borrowed into Vulgar Latin as *\*skīvāre*, which in Old French became *eschiver* or *eschuer* – whence English *eschew*. An Old Northern French variant of the Old French form, *eskiuer*, gave English *skew* [14] (which originally meant 'escape'), while modern French *esquiver* 'dodge' (actually a reborrowing from Italian *schivare* rather than a direct descendant of Old French *eschiver*) could be the source of English *skive* [20], a probable borrowing by British servicemen in France during World War I.
▶ skew, skive

**escort**   [16] The notion underlying *escort* is of 'guidance,' of 'showing the right path.' The word comes via French from Italian *scorta* 'guide,' a noun use of the past participle of *scorgere* 'show, guide.' This in turn came from Vulgar Latin *\*excorrigere*, a compound verb formed from the prefix *ex-* 'out' and Latin *corrigere* 'put right' (source of English *correct*).
▶ correct

**escrow**   see SCROLL

**escutcheon**   see SQUIRE

**especial**   see SPECIAL

**espionage**   see SPY

**esplanade**   [17] Essentially, *esplanade* is the same word as *explain*, but whereas *explain* has lost its underlying literal meaning, *esplanade* has retained at least a memory of it. It comes ultimately from Latin *ex-*

*plānāre*, which meant 'flatten out,' and so *esplanade* (acquired via French from the Spanish past participle *esplanada*) was originally simply a 'large level area.' Its application to the 'promenade' at seaside towns is a comparatively recent development.
▶ explain

**espouse**   [15] Etymologically, to *espouse* something is the same as to *sponsor* it. Both words go back ultimately to Latin *spondēre* 'promise solemnly.' From it developed late Latin *spōnsāre*, which produced Old French *espouser*, source of the English verb. It originally meant 'promise to marry,' but this particular semantic strand has survived only in the related noun *spouse*, and by the 17th century the now familiar metaphorical sense 'adopt and support a cause' had developed.
▶ sponsor, spouse

**espy**   see SPY

**esquire**   see SQUIRE

**essay**   [15] *Essay* and *assay* [14] are fundamentally the same word, and only began to diverge in the 15th century. Both come via Old French *assaier* from Vulgar Latin *\*exagiāre* 'weigh out,' a verb derived from late Latin *exagium* 'weighing'; this in turn was formed from the Latin verb *exigere* 'weigh' (source of English *exact* and *examine*). Accordingly, both originally had underlying connotations of 'testing by weighing.' But while these have become more concrete in *assay* 'analyse precious metals,' *essay* has, under the influence of French *essayer*, gone down the more metaphorical route from 'test' to 'try.' The verb now survives only in fairly formal use, but the noun is much more frequent, owing to its application to a 'short nonfictional literary composition.' It was first used thus in English by Francis Bacon in 1597 as the title of a collection of such pieces, and it is generally assumed that he borrowed the idea from the *Essais* of Montaigne, published in 1580.
▶ assay, exact, examine

**essence**   [14] *Essence* and its derivative *essential* [14] are the English descendants of the Latin verb 'to be,' *esse* (which came ultimately from the Indo-European base *\*es-* 'be,' source also of English *is*). From it was formed the abstract noun *essentia* 'being, existence,' acquired by English through Old French *essence*. In the adjective *essential*, the sense 'absolutely necessary' developed via 'inherent' and 'indispensable' in the 16th century.
▶ is

**establish**   [14] Etymologically, to *establish* something is to 'make it firm.' The word comes via Old French *establir* from Latin *stabilīre*, a derivative of *stabilis* 'firm, secure' (source of English *stable* and related to English *stand*). English originally acquired it at the end of the 13th century as *stablish*, but by the end of the 14th century the more 'French' spelling had been introduced, and gradually took over.

▶ stable, stand

**estate** [13] Essentially, *estate* and *state* are the same word, and originally their meanings were very close (the now archaic 'reach man's estate,' for instance, signifies 'reach the state of manhood'). From the 15th century, however, they began to diverge, *estate* taking a semantic path via 'interest in property' to 'such property itself,' and finally, in the 18th century, to the 'land owned by someone.' Both come via Old French *estat* from Latin *status* 'way of standing, condition' (source of English *status*), a derivative of the verb *stāre* 'stand' (a relative of English *stand*).

▶ stand, state, statue, status

**esteem** [15] *Esteem* and *estimate* [16] are fairly open about their relationship, but there is another, more heavily disguised member of the family: *aim*. All three come ultimately from Latin *aestimāre*. *Estimate* was a straightforward borrowing from the Latin past participle *aestimātus*, but *esteem* came via Old French *estimer*, and *aim* from the reduced Old French form *esmer*. Originally, *esteem* meant much the same as *estimate* does: 'evaluate, assess.' But as early as the 16th century it had passed into 'think highly of' (a semantic development interestingly paralleled in the 20th century by *rate*).

▶ aim, estimate

**estrange**    see STRANGE

**etch** [17] A line that has been *etched* has been literally 'eaten' away by acid or other corrosives. The word was borrowed from Dutch *etsen*, which in turn came from German *ätzen* 'corrode, etch.' This can be traced back to a prehistoric Germanic *\*atjan* 'cause to eat, feed,' a relation of *\*etan* 'eat' (from which English gets *eat*).

▶ eat

**eternal** [14] Something that is *eternal* lasts literally for 'aeons.' The word comes via Old French *eternal* from *aeternālis*, a late Latin development of the Latin adjective *aeternus* 'eternal.' This in turn was a derivative of *aevum* 'age' (which crops up in English *medieval, primeval*, etc), a relative of Greek *aiōn* 'age' (from which English gets *aeon*) and archaic English *aye* 'ever.'

▶ aeon, aye, ever

**ether** [17] Greek *aithḗr* denoted the 'upper atmosphere,' and by extension the 'substance that permeated the cosmos,' from which the stars and planets were made. It was a derivative of the verb *aíthein* 'ignite, blaze, shine,' a relative of Latin *aestās* 'summer,' from which English gets *aestivate* [17]. It passed into English via Latin *aethēr*, and to begin with was used in its original Greek senses. Its application to the liquid with anaesthetic properties dates from the mid 18th century, the

use of its first syllable in the names of organic compounds in the bicarbon series (such as *ethyl* and *ethane*) from the mid 19th century.

▶ aestivate, ethyl

**ethical** [17] The underlying meaning of Greek *ēthos* was 'personal disposition.' It came ultimately from prehistoric Indo-European *\*swedh-*, a compound formed from the reflexive pronoun *\*swe-* 'oneself' and *dhē-* 'put' (from which English gets *do*). Gradually the meaning broadened out to 'trait, character' and then 'custom,' or in the plural 'manners' or 'morals.' English acquired it, in the sense 'distinctive characteristic' (based on the usage of Aristotle), in the 19th century. The Greek derived adjective *ēthikós* entered English, via Latin *ēthicus*, as *ethic* in the 16th century. This had largely been replaced by *ethical* by the end of the 17th century, but it has survived as a noun (as in 'the work ethic'), which actually predates the adjective in English by about two hundred years. The plural usage *ethics* 'science of morals' dates from the beginning of the 17th century.

▶ do

**ethnic** [14] Greek *éthnos* meant 'nation, people.' However, its use in the Septuagint (the early Greek translation of the Old Testament) to render the Hebrew word for 'gentile' led to its derived adjective *ethnikós*, and hence Latin *ethnicus*, meaning virtually 'heathen.' It was in this sense that English first acquired the word ('an ethnic and a pagan king,' Nicholas Udall, *Paraphrase of Erasmus* 1545); indeed, early etymologists thought that English *heathen* came from *éthnos*. The word's modern anthropological sense is a mid-19th-century return to its roots.

**etiquette** [18] *Etiquette* is, almost literally, 'just the ticket.' The primary meanings of French *étiquette* are 'ticket' and 'label' – and indeed it is the source of English *ticket*. A particular application of it in former times was to a small card which had written or printed on it directions as to how to behave properly at court – hence it came to mean 'prescribed code of social behaviour.'

▶ ticket

**etymology** [14] The underlying meaning of *etymology* is 'finding the underlying or 'true' meaning of words.' Its ultimate source is Greek *étumos* 'real, true.' From this was derived *étumon* 'true or literal sense of a word' (acquired by English in the 16th century as *etymon*). Post-classical grammarians came to use this in the sense 'root from which a particular word was derived,' as a result of which modern etymology, the study of etymons, deals with their history rather than their meaning.

**eucalyptus** [19] Europeans first encountered eucalyptus trees in Australia at the end of the 18th century. The French botanist Charles Louis l'Héritier based its Latin name, which he coined in 1788, on the fact that its flower buds have a characteristic conical cover (the Greek prefix *eu-* means 'well' and Greek *kaluptós* means 'covered').

**eucharist** [14] The Greek-based *eucharist* corresponds to native English *thanksgiving*. It comes via Old French *eucariste* and late Latin *eucharistia* from Greek *eukharistíā* 'gratitude.' This was a derivative of *eukháristos* 'grateful,' a compound adjective formed from the prefix *eu-* 'well' and *kharízesthai* 'show favour.' The verb in turn was formed from the noun *kháris* 'favour, grace' (source of English *charisma* [19] and probably a distant relative of *yearn* [OE]).

▶ yearn

**eunuch** [15] *Eunuch* has no etymological connection with 'castration.' It is simply the fact that in former times male harem attendants in Oriental courts had their testicles removed, to ensure that they were not distracted from their work, that has led ultimately to the equation of *eunuch* with 'castrated man.' Literally, the word means 'bed-guard': it comes via Latin from Greek *eunoukhos*, a compound formed from *eunḗ* 'bed' and *ékhein* 'have charge of, keep.'

**euphemism** [17] Etymologically, *euphemism* means 'speaking with good words.' Greek *euphēmismós*, a compound formed ultimately from the prefix *eu-* 'good, well' and *phḗmē* 'speech, saying' (a relative of English *fable, fame,* and *fate*), originally denoted the avoidance of words of ill omen at religious ceremonies, but it was subsequently taken up by grammarians to signify the substitution of a less for a more offensive word. Its opposite, *dysphemism* 'use of a more offensive word,' is a modern coinage, formed in the late 19th century using the Greek prefix *dus-* 'bad, difficult.'

▶ fable, fame, fate

**eureka** [16] The Greek mathematician Archimedes (*c*287–212 BC) was commissioned by King Hiero II of Syracuse to find out whether the goldsmith who had made a new crown for him had fraudulently mixed some silver in with the gold. In order to do so, Archimedes needed to ascertain the metal's specific gravity. But how to do this? According to Plutarch, he decided to take a bath to ponder the problem. He filled the bath too full, and some of the water overflowed – and it suddenly occurred to Archimedes that a pure-gold crown would displace more water if immersed than one made from an alloy. Elated at this piece of lateral thinking, Archimedes is said to have leapt out of the bath shouting *heúrēka*! 'I have found!', the perfect indicative of Greek *heurískein* 'find' (source of English *heuristic* [19]). The earliest occurrence of the word in an English text as an exclamation of delight at discovery is in John Dee's *Preface*, but there it appears in Greek characters; the first English author to fully naturalize it

was probably Henry Fielding in *Joseph Andrews* 1742: 'Adams returned overjoyed cring out 'Eureka!'' (The goldsmith, incidentally, had adulterated the gold.)

▶ heuristic

**euthanasia** [17] Etymologically, *euthanasia* means 'good death,' and that was more or less its signification when it was introduced into English: 'Give me but gentle Death: Euthanasia, Euthanasia, that is all I implore,' *Tatler* 1709. The modern use of the word, 'mercy killing,' seems to have originated in the 1860s; the first recorded use of it was by William Lecky in his *History of European morals* 1869. The term is borrowed from Greek *euthanasíā*, a compound based on the prefix *eu-* 'good' and *thánatos* 'death.'

**evanescent**   see VANISH

**evangelist** [12] The original sense of *evangelist* was 'writer of a gospel.' English used to have the word *evangel* 'gospel.' This came via Old French *evangile* and ecclesiastical Latin *evangelium* from Greek *euaggélion*, which in classical times meant 're-ward for bringing good news' (it was a compound based ultimately on the prefix *eu-* 'good, well' and the noun *ággelos* 'messenger' – source of English *angel*). Later on it came to mean simply 'good news,' and in early Christian texts written in Greek it denoted specifically any of the four books of the New Testament written by Matthew, Mark, Luke, and John. (English *gospel* was originally a literal translation of it.) *Evangelist* itself comes from the Greek derivative *euaggelistḗs*.

▶ angel

**even** [OE] *Even* can be traced back to a prehistoric Germanic \**ebnaz*, although it is not clear whether it meant originally 'flat, level' or 'equal, alike' (both strands of meaning are still present in the word, the latter in such expressions as 'get even with' and 'even number,' and also in its various adverbial uses, the former in 'even keel,' 'even light,' etc).

**evening** [OE] *Evening* is a derivative of *even* [OE], a word for 'evening' now restricted to bad poetry. This came ultimately from an Indo-European base, whose general meaning of 'lateness' is pointed up by other descendants such as Sanskrit *apara-* 'later, western,' Greek *opsé* 'late,' and Gothic *iftuma* 'following, later.' The specific application to 'latter part of the day' seems only to have occurred in the Germanic languages, where it is represented in German *abend* and Dutch *avond*, and also possibly in Swedish *afton* and Danish *aften* (although these could be from another source). The Old English word was *ǣfen*, which formed the basis of a verb *ǣfnian* 'become evening'; the verbal noun derived from this has become English *evening*. *Eve* [13], as in 'Christmas eve,' is a Middle English reduction of *even*.

**ever** [OE] For such a common and long-established word, the origins of *ever* are surprisingly obscure. It has no relatives in other Germanic languages, so it must be a purely English creation. Its first element probably comes from Germanic *aiwō (which is also represented in English aye 'ever' [12] and either, and is related to Latin aevum 'age,' source of English eternal). The second element is a puzzle, though. Candidates that have been put forward include Old English feorh 'life' (thus, 'ever in life') and Old English byre 'occasion' (giving the underlying sense 'on any occasion'). Never was formed in the Old English period with the negative particle ne-.

▶ aye, either, eternal

**every** [OE] Stripped down into its component parts, every means literally 'ever each.' It was originally an Old English compound made up of ǣfre 'ever' and ǣlc 'each,' in which basically the 'ever' was performing an emphasizing function; in modern English terms it signified something like 'every single,' or, in colloquial American, 'every which.' By late Old English times the two elements had fused to form a single word.

▶ each, ever

**evict** [15] Ultimately, evict and evince [17] are the same word, although they have diverged considerably over the centuries. Both come from Latin ēvincere, a compound verb formed from the prefix ex- 'out' and vincere (source of English victory). This originally meant 'defeat, conquer,' but a whole range of secondary legal senses developed: 'recover something by defeating an opponent in a legal action'; 'eject by judicial process'; and 'prove by legal argument.' Both evict (acquired from the Latin past participle ēvictus) and evince have in the past been used for 'conquer' and 'prove,' and it was not until the 18th century that they settled into their present meanings.

▶ evince, victory

**evident** [14] Something that is evident is literally something that can be 'seen.' The word comes via Old French from Latin ēvidēns 'clear, obvious,' a compound formed from the intensive prefix ex- and the present participle of videre 'see' (source of English vision). The Latin derivative ēvidentia (from which English gets evidence [13]) meant originally 'distinction' and later 'proof,' basis of the main current sense of evidence, 'testimony which establishes the facts.'

▶ view, vision

**evil** [OE] Evil has got distinctly worse over the millenia. Originally it seems to have signified nothing more sinister than 'uppity,' and in the Old and Middle English period it meant simply 'bad'; it is only in modern English that its connotations of 'extreme moral wickedness' came to the fore. It probably comes ultimately from *upelo-, a derivative of the Indo-European base *upo- 'under' (source of Greek hupó 'under,' Sanskrit upa 'at, to,' and English up and over), and so its underlying connotation is of 'exceeding due limits, ex-

tremism.' Its Germanic descendant was *ubilaz, source of German übel 'evil' as well as English evil.

▶ over, up

**evince**    see EVICT

**evoke**    see VOCATION

**evolution** [17] Evolution originally meant simply 'unfolding,' or metaphorically 'development'; it was not used in its main current sense, 'gradual change in form of a species over the centuries,' until the early 19th century. The Scottish geologist Charles Lyell appears to have been the first to do so, in his Principles of Geology 1832, and it was subsequently taken up by Charles Darwin. The word comes from Latin ēvolūtiō, which denoted specifically the unrolling of a papyrus or parchment roll. It was a derivative of ēvolvere, a compound formed from the prefix ex- 'out' and volvere 'roll' (source also of English convolution, involve, and revolve and related to vault, voluble, volume, vulva, and wallow).

▶ convolution, involve, revolve, volume, wallow

**exact** [15] The adjective exact 'precise' and the verb exact 'demand with severity' have undergone considerable semantic divergance over the centuries, but they both go back to the same source, the Latin verb exigere (from which English also got essay, examine, exigent [15], and exiguous [17]). This, a compound of the prefix ex- 'out' and agere 'lead, drive' (source of English act and agent), meant originally 'drive out,' but in due course it developed the metaphorical senses 'demand' (preserved in the English verb), 'weigh accurately,' and 'bring to completion or perfection.' These last two were taken up adjectivally in the Latin past participle exactus, from which English gets exact.

▶ act, agent, essay, examine

**exaggerate** [16] Something that is exaggerated is literally 'piled up' out of all due proportion; indeed that is what it originally meant in English: 'With their flipping and flapping up and down in the dirt they exaggerate a mountain of mire,' Philip Stubbes, Anatomy of Abuses 1583. It was not really until the 17th century that the current sense 'overemphasize' came to the fore, although it was already present in the word's Latin original. This was exaggerāre, a compound formed from the intensive prefix ex- and aggerāre 'pile up' (a derivative of agger 'heap').

**examine** [14] Like essay and exact, examine comes ultimately from Latin exigere, a compound verb formed from the prefix ex-'out' and agere 'lead, drive' (source of English act and agent). This originally meant literally 'drive out,' but a metaphorical sense 'weigh accurately' developed which was carried over into a derived noun exāmen 'weighing.' This in turn formed the basis of another derivative, the verb exāmināre 'weigh,' hence 'weigh up, ponder, consider, test, examine.' The abbreviation *exam* for *examination* dates from the late 19th century.

▶ act, agent, essay, exact

**example** [14] Etymologically, an *example* is something that has been 'taken out,' so that it can be considered separately. The word comes via Old French *example* from Latin *exemplum* 'example,' a derivative of *eximere* 'take out.' This was a compound verb formed from the prefix *ex-* 'out' and *emere* 'take, buy' (source of English *peremptory, pre-empt, premium*, and *prompt*), and also yielded English *exempt* [14]. (An earlier Old French version of the word, *essample*, was borrowed into English in the 13th century as *asample*, which was the ancestor of modern English *sample*.)

▶ exempt, peremptory, premium, prompt, sample

**excellent** [14] The underlying notion of *excellent* is of physically 'rising above' others. It comes via Old French from the present participle of Latin *excellere*. This was a compound verb formed from the prefix *ex-* 'out' and a hypothetical verbal element *\*cellere*, which evidently meant something like 'rise, be high': it derived ultimately from an Indo-European base *\*kol-, \*kel-* which also produced English *column, culminate*, and *hill*. There is little evidence of its literal use in Latin; the metaphorical 'be outstanding' evidently elbowed it aside at an early stage. (English acquired *excel* itself in the 15th century, incidentally.)

▶ column, culminate, hill

**except** [14] If you *except* something, you literally 'take it out.' The verb comes from *exceptus*, the past participle of Latin *excipere*, a compound formed from the prefix *ex-* 'out' and *capere* 'take' (source of English *capture*). The use of the word as a preposition, and subsequently as a conjunction, arose from the adjectival use of the Latin past participle *exceptus* for 'excepted, excluded' (as in modern English 'present company excepted').

▶ captive, capture, chase, heave

**excerpt** SEE SCARCE

**exchange** [14] Like *change, exchange* comes ultimately from Latin *cambīre* 'barter.' In post-classical times this had the prefix *ex-* added to it, here functioning as an indicator of 'change,' producing late Latin *\*excambiāre*. In Old French this became *eschangier* (whence modern French *échanger*), which English acquired via Anglo-Norman *eschaunge*. A 15th-century reversion to the original Latin spelling of the prefix produced modern English *exchange*.

▶ change

**exchequer** [13] Etymologically, an *exchequer* is something that has 'checks' or squares on it, and indeed the earliest use of the word in English was for 'chessboard.' It came via Anglo-Norman *escheker* from medieval Latin *scaccārium* 'chessboard,' a derivative of Vulgar Latin *scaccus* 'check' (source of English

*check* 'verify'). In the early Middle Ages the office of state, in both England and Normandy, which dealt with the collection and management of the royal revenue, used a table with a chequered cloth on it as a sort of rudimentary adding machine, counters being placed on various squares as an aid to calculation. And by the 14th century it had become the custom to refer to this department, from its chessboard-like table cloth, as the *exchequer* (Robert Mannyng, for instance, in his *Chronicle* 1331, records that 'to Berwick came the king's exchequer, Sir Hugh of Cressyngham he was chancellor, Walter of Admundesham he was treasurer'). *Exchequer* was the source of *chequer* [13], which by further reduction produced *check* 'pattern of squares.'

▶ check, chess

**excise** English has two words *excise*. The one meaning 'tax' [15] is essentially a Dutch usage. English borrowed it in the late 15th century from Middle Dutch *excijs*, which came via Old French *acceis* from Vulgar Latin *\*accēnsum*, a compound noun formed from the Latin prefix *ad-* 'against, to' and *cēnsus* 'tax' (source of English *census* [17]). At first it was used broadly for any 'tax,' but in 1643 (following the example of Holland) it was officially adopted as the term for a tax imposed on certain forms of goods (originally domestically produced or imported, but since the 19th century only domestically produced – the tax on imports being termed *customs duty*). Dr Johnson in his *Dictionary* 1755 defined *excise* as 'a hateful tax levied upon commodities, and ajudged not by the common judges of property, but by wretches hired by those to whome excise is paid.'

*Excise* 'cut out' [16] comes from the past participle of Latin *excīdere*, a compound verb formed from the prefix *ex-* 'out' and *caedere* 'cut' (source also of English *concise, decide*, and *incision*).

▶ census, concise, decide, incision

**excite** [14] The use of the word *excite* to convey 'agitated elation' is a comparatively recent development, first recorded from the mid 19th century. Before that it was a fairly neutral verb, meaning 'produce a response, provoke' (as in the rather formal 'excite much comment'). It comes, perhaps via Old French *exciter*, from Latin *excitāre* 'call forth, arouse, produce.' This was a variant of *exciēre*, a compound verb formed from the prefix *ex-* 'out' and *ciēre* 'move, call' (source also of English *cite, incite, recite*, and *solicit*).

▶ cite, incite, recite, solicit

**exclude** SEE SLUICE

**excrement** [16] Latin *excrēmentum* meant originally 'that which is sifted out' (it was a derivative of the verb *excernere*, a compound formed from the prefix *ex-* 'out' and *cernere* 'sift, decide,' from which English gets *certain*). Hence it was applied metaphorically to any substance that is excreted from or secreted by the body, including sweat, nasal mucus, and milk, as well as faeces. (English acquired *excrete* [17], incidentally, from the past participle of *excernere, excrētus*.) This very general sense survived in English into the mid 18th century, when it was finally ousted by the more specific 'faeces.' (*Increment*, by the way, is a completely unrelated word, coming ultimately from Latin *crēscere* 'grow.')

▶ certain, crime, critic, discern, discriminate, secret

**excursion**    see COURSE

**excuse**    [13] Etymologically, *excuse* means 'free of accusation.' It comes via Old French from Latin *excūsāre*, a compound verb formed from the prefix *ex-*, denoting removal, and *causa* 'cause' – but 'cause' in the sense not of something that produces a result, but of 'legal action, accusation' (a meaning preserved in English 'cause list,' for example). Originally, the *s* of both the noun and the verb was pronounced /z/; the /s/ of the modern English noun arose by analogy with such nouns as *use* and *abuse*.

▶ accuse, cause

**execute**    [14] The original meaning of *execute* in English was 'carry out,' but the sense 'kill judicially' had already developed by the end of the 15th century (it comes from the notion of 'carrying out' a sentence). The word came via Old French *executer* from medieval Latin *executāre*, a derivative of Latin *exsequī*. This, a compound formed from the intensive prefix *ex-* and *sequī* 'follow' (source of English *consecutive, consequent, obsequious, sequence, subsequent*, etc), meant originally 'follow to the end, pursue,' and hence 'follow through, carry out, fulfil.' Its derivative *exsequiās* 'funeral procession' produced English *exequies* [14].

▶ consecutive, consequent, obsequious, sequence, subsequent

**exempt**    see EXAMPLE

**exercise**    [14] The notion underlying *exercise* is of 'removal of restraint.' It comes ultimately from Latin *exercēre*, a compound verb formed from the prefix *ex-* 'out of, from' and *arcēre* 'restrain, enclose' (source of English *arcane* and related to English *ark*). It has been speculated that this originally denoted the driving of draught animals out into the fields to plough, but however that may be, it soon developed the general senses 'set to work, keep at work' and 'drill, practise' which form the semantic basis of English *exercise*.

▶ arcane, ark

**exigent**    see EXACT

**exile**    [13] Latin *exul* meant 'banished person.' This was formed from the prefix *ex-* 'out' and a prehistoric Indo-European base *\*ul-* 'go' (represented also in Latin *ambulāre* 'walk,' source of English *amble* and *ambulance*). From it was created the noun *exilium* 'ban-

ishment,' which in Old French became *essil*. This was subsequently remodelled to *exil*, on the basis of its Latin source, and passed on to English.

▶ amble, ambulance

**exist**    [17] The 'existential' use of *exist* is a secondary development; to begin with it had the more concrete meaning 'stand out, so as to be perceptible.' It comes from Latin *existere*, a compound verb formed from the prefix *ex-* 'out' and *sistere* 'be placed, stand firm or still' (a distant relative of English *stand*). Its original sense 'stand out, stand forth' developed through 'emerge' and 'be visible' to 'exist.' The available evidence suggests that it entered English at a surprisingly late date, some centuries after the derivative *existence* [14] (of which the English verb may be a back-formation).

▶ stand, statue

**exit**    [16] Ultimately, *exit* is the same word as English *issue*. Both come from Latin *exīre*, a compound verb formed from the prefix *ex-* 'out' and *īre* 'go.' This Latin verb, which can be traced back to an Indo-European base *\*ei-*, also produced English *coitus* [18], *obituary*, and *transient* (as well as the French future tense *irai* 'will go'). The earliest use of *exit* in English was as a stage direction (it means literally 'he or she goes out' in Latin). The sense 'way out' is a late 17th-century development, the more concrete 'door by which one leaves' as recent as the late 19th century.

▶ coitus, obituary, transient

**exodus**    see PERIOD

**expand**    see SPAWN

**expect**    [16] Someone who *expects* something literally 'looks out' for it. The word comes from Latin *expectāre*, a compound verb formed from the prefix *ex-* 'out' and *spectāre* 'look' (source of English *spectacle, spectre, spectrum*, and *speculate*). Already in Latin the literal 'look out' had shifted metaphorically to 'look forward to, anticipate' and 'await,' meanings adopted wholesale by English ('await' has since been dropped).

▶ espionage, spectacle, speculate, spy

**expedition**    [15] The Latin verb *expedīre* originally had the rather mundane meaning 'free one's feet' – from a snare, for example. It was formed from the prefix *ex-* 'out' and *pēs* 'foot' (source of English *pedal, pedestrian*, etc and related to English *foot*). Its literal meaning was soon lost sight of, progressing via 'extricate, liberate' to 'bring out, make ready' and 'put in order, arrange, set right.' The notion of 'freeing' something, enabling it to go forward without hindrance, is reflected in the verb's English descendant *expedite* [17]. It also survives in the derived noun *expedition*, as 'promptness, dispatch'; in the main, however, this has taken a different semantic route, via 'sending out a military force' to 'long organized journey for a particular purpose.'

▶ expedite, foot, pedal, pedestrian

**expel**   see PULSE

**expend**   see SPEND

**experience**   [14]   *Experience, experiment* [14], and *expert* [14] all come from the same source, Latin *experīrī*. This was a compound verb formed from the prefix *ex-* 'out' and a prehistoric base *\*per-* denoting 'attempt, trial' (found also in English *empirical, peril, pirate*, and *repertory*), and meant 'try, test.' The original meaning is best preserved in *experiment*, but in fact *experience* too meant at first 'putting to the test' in English. From this developed the notion of 'actually observing phenomena in order to gain knowledge of them,' which in turn led to the more subjective 'condition of having undergone or been affected by a particular event.' The sense 'knowledge or skill gained from such observation or from undergoing such events' did not, however, emerge until the late 15th century. *Expert* was originally only an adjective, meaning 'having experience of something,' or 'trained by such experience'; its use as a noun only developed in the 19th century.

▶ empirical, experiment, expert, peril, pirate, repertory

**expiate**   see PIOUS

**expire**   see SPIRIT

**explain**   [15]   To *explain* a matter is literally to 'make it plain.' The word comes from Latin *explānāre*, a compound verb formed from the intensive prefix *ex-* and the adjective *plānus* 'flat' (source of English *plain*). This originally meant 'flatten out, make smooth,' but the metaphorical sense 'make clear' soon took over, and accompanied the verb into English (although in the 16th and 17th centuries a few scholars attempted to revive the literal sense: 'He must calm and explain his forehead,' Sir Thomas Chalenor, translation of Desiderus Erasmus' *Praise of Folly* 1549).

▶ esplanade, plain

**expletive**   [17]   Originally, an *expletive* word was simply one used to 'fill up' a line of verse, to complete its metrical pattern (*expletive* comes from Latin *explētus*, the past participle of *explēre* 'fill out,' a compound formed from the prefix *ex-* 'out' and *plēre* 'fill,' source of English *complete* and related to English *fill*). Hence the term came to be used for a redundant word, not contributing anything to the meaning of the sentence: "The Key my loose, powerless fingers forsook," a lame and expletive way of saying "I dropt the key," Robert Southey 1804. The first recorded example of its euphemistic application as a noun to 'profanities' is by Sir Walter Scott in *Guy Mannering* 1815: 'retaining only such of their expletives as are least offensive.'

▶ complete, full

**explicit**   [17]   Something that is *explicit* has literally been 'unfolded.' Like the earlier borrowing *explicate* [16], the word comes from the past participle of Latin *explicāre*, a compound verb formed from the prefix *ex-* 'un-' and *plicāre* 'fold' (source of English *ply* and related to English *fold*). At first, in the 16th and 17th centuries, English retained the literal sense of the original, but gradually it dropped out in favour of the metaphorical 'make clear, distinct, and open' (already present in Latin).

▶ exploit, fold, ply

**explode**   [16]   The use of *explode* to mean 'burst with destructive force' is a comparatively recent, late 19th-century development. The Latin verb *explōdere*, from which it comes, signified something quite different – 'drive off the stage with hisses and boos' (it was a compound formed from the prefix *ex-* 'out' and *plaudere* 'clap,' source of English *applaud* and *plaudits*). From this developed the figurative sense 'reject, disapprove,' which was how the word was used when it was first taken over into English: 'Not that I wholly explode Astrology; I believe there is something in it,' Thomas Tryon, *Miscellanea* 1696 (the modern notion of 'exploding a theory' is descended from this usage). In the 17th century, however, the Latin verb's original sense was reintroduced, and it survived into the 19th century: 'In the playhouse when he doth wrong, no critic is so apt to hiss and explode him,' Henry Fielding, *Tom Jones* 1749. Towards the end of the 17th century we find the first traces of a metaphorical use that combines the notion of 'driving out, expelling' with 'loud noise' ('the effects of Lightning, exploded from the Clouds,' Robert Plot, *Natural History of Staffordshire* 1679), but it was not to be for more than a century that the meaning element 'drive out' was replaced by the 'burst, shatter' of present-day English *explode* (Dr Johnson makes no mention of it in his *Dictionary* 1755, for example). Today the notion of 'bursting violently' is primary, that of 'loud noise' probably secondary, although still present.

▶ applause, plaudits

**exploit**   [14]   Latin *explicāre* (source of English *explicate* and *explicit*) meant 'unfold.' A Vulgar Latin descendant of its past participle was *\*explictum* 'something unfolded,' which passed into Old French as *exploit* or *esplait*. In the process, the original sense of 'unfolding' had developed through 'bringing out, development' and 'advantage, success' to 'achievement.' In the case of the English noun, it is the latter meaning which has survived, and in fact originally the verb too denoted 'achieve, accomplish.' This seems to have died out in the 18th century, however, and when the verb reappears in the 19th century it is closer to the earlier 'develop' in meaning, particularly as applied to 'getting the most out of' natural resources. The modern derogatory sense 'use for one's own selfish ends' emerged from this.

▶ explicit, fold, ply

**export**   see PORT

**expose**   see POSITION

**express**   [14]   Something that is *expressed* is literally 'pressed out.' The word comes via Old French from Vulgar Latin *\*expressāre*, a compound verb formed from the prefix *ex-* 'out' and *pressāre* 'press.' Its meaning developed metaphorically from 'press out' to 'form by pressure' (presumably applied originally to modelling in clay or some similar substance, and subsequently to sculpture and then painting), and finally to 'make known in words.'

The Vulgar Latin verb was in fact moving in on territory already occupied by its classical Latin forerunner *exprimere* (source of French *exprimer* 'express' and perhaps of English *sprain* [17]). The past participle of this was *expressus*, used adjectivally for 'prominent, distinct, explicit.' Old French took it over as *expres* and passed it on to English in the 14th century. By now its meaning was moving towards 'intended for a particular purpose,' and in the 19th century it was applied to 'special' trains (as in 'football specials'). It did not take long, however, for this to slip via 'train for people wanting to go to a particular place, and therefore not stopping anywhere else' to 'fast train.' Hence the modern sense of *express*, 'fast,' was born.

▶ press, sprain

**expunge**   see PUNCTUATION

**expurgate**   see PURGE

**exquisite**   [15]   Etymologically,   *exquisite* means 'sought out.' It comes from the past participle of Latin *exquīrere*, a compound formed from the prefix *ex-* 'out' and *quaerere* 'search' (source of English *query, quest,* and *question*). Already in Latin it had acquired the metaphorical sense 'sought after, choice, excellent,' which it brought with it into English. From the 15th to the 18th centuries, however, the adjective underwent something of an explosion (being used in such widely varied senses as 'ingenious, far-fetched,' 'abstruse,' 'affected,' 'careful,' 'elaborate,' and even – in relation to diseases – 'true, typical': 'an exquisite diabetes caused by attraction of urine,' translation of Théophile Bonet's *Mercurius Compitalitius* 1684) before settling back into the now familiar 'excellent in beauty.'

▶ query, quest, question

**extempore**   [16]   An *extempore* speech is one that is given literally 'out of time' – that is, 'on the spur of the moment.' That was the meaning of the Latin phrase *ex tempore* (*ex* 'out of' and *tempore*, the ablative case of *tempus* 'time'), which was the source of the Latin adjectives *extemporālis* and *extemporāneus*. Both of these were acquired by English, as *extemporal* [16] and

*extemporaneous* [17], but only the latter has survived. *Ex tempore* itself was first lexicalized in English as an adverb, and was not used as an adjective until the 17th century.

**extend**   [14]   Etymologically, to *extend* something is to 'stretch it out.' The word comes from Latin *extendere*, a compound verb formed from the prefix *ex-* 'out' and *tendere* 'stretch' (source of English *tend* and *tension* and a wide range of derivatives, including *contend, intend,* and *pretend*). English *standard* derives from its Old French descendant *estendre*.

▶ contend, intend, pretend, standard, tend, tension

**exterior**   see EXTRA

**extinct**   [15]   Latin *stinguere* appears originally to have meant 'prick, stick' (a sense revealed in the derivative from which English gets *distinct*), but in historical times the only record of it we have is in the later, and rather remote metaphorical meaning 'quench.' With the addition of the prefix *ex-* 'out' it became *extinguere* 'put out,' whence English *extinguish* [16]. *Extinct* comes from its past participle, *extinctus,* and originally meant 'put out, no longer alight': 'That fire was extinct,' Ranulph Higden, *Polychronicon* 1432–50. Its modern use, 'having died out,' dates – in relation to species, families, etc – from the late 17th century.

▶ distinct, extinguish

**extol**   see TOLERATE

**extort**   see TORMENT

**extra**   [18]   In its modern English use, 'beyond what is normal' or 'additional,' *extra* is probably an abbreviation of *extraordinary* [15], in which the prefix represents Latin *extrā* 'outside, beyond.' This in turn was short for *exterā*, the ablative feminine case of the adjective *exterus* 'outer' (from which English gets *exterior* [16]). And *exterus* itself began life as a compound form based on Latin *ex* 'out.'

▶ exterior, extreme

**extradite**   [19]   *Extradite* is a back-formation from *extradition* [19]. This was borrowed from French *extradition*, which was a coinage (apparently of Voltaire's) based on Latin *ex* 'out' and *trāditiō* 'handing over, deliverance' (source of English *tradition*).

▶ tradition, treason

**extraneous**   see STRANGE

**extraordinary**   see EXTRA

**extravagant**   [14]   An *extravagant* person is literally one who 'wanders out of' the proper course. The word comes from the present participle of medieval Latin *extrāvagārī*, a compound formed from the prefix *extrā-* 'outside' and *vagārī* 'wander' (source of English *vagabond, vagary,* and *vagrant*), which seems originally to have been used adjectivally with reference to certain uncodified or 'stray' papal decrees. This was the word's original application in English, and the present-day meanings 'wildly excessive' and 'spending too lavishly' did not really establish themselves before the early 18th century.

▶ vagabond, vagary, vagrant

**extreme**  [15]  Etymologically, *extreme* is the latinate equivalent of the native English *utmost*. It comes via Old French *extreme* from Latin *extrēmus* 'farthest, last, excessive,' which began life as a superlative form based on Latin *ex* 'out' – hence originally 'most out, utmost.' The underlying notion of 'furthest outlying' still survives in, for example, the use of *extremities* for the 'hands' or 'feet.'

**extricate**  see TRICK
**extrinsic**  see INTRINSIC
**extrude**  see ABSTRUSE

**exuberant**  [15]  *Exuberant* comes via French from the present participle of Latin *exūberāre* 'be abundant.' This was a compound verb formed from the intensive prefix *ex-* and *ūberāre* 'be productive,' a derivative of *ūber* 'fertile.' This in turn was an adjectival use of the noun *ūber* 'udder,' which came from the same ultimate source (Indo-European *\*ūdhr-*) as English *udder*.

▶ udder

**exude**  see SWEAT

**eye**  [OE]  In Old English times *eye* was *ēage*, which is related to a whole range of words for 'eye' in other European languages. Its immediate derivation is from prehistoric Germanic *\*augon*, which was also the source of German *auge*, Dutch *oog*, Swedish *öga*, and many others. And *\*augon* in its turn goes back to an Indo-European *oqw-*, which supplied the word for 'eye' to all the other Indo-European languages except the Celtic ones, including Russian *óko* (now obsolete), Greek *ophthalmós*, and Latin *oculus* (with all its subsequent derivatives such as French *oeuil*, Italian *occhio*, and Spanish *ojo*). Amongst its more surprising English relatives are *atrocious, ferocious, inoculate, ullage*, and *window*.

▶ atrocious, ferocious, inoculate, ocular, ullage, window

**eyot**  see ISLAND

**eyrie**  [16]  Latin *ager* (source of English *agriculture* and related to English *acre*) meant 'field,' or more broadly 'piece of land.' In post-classical times this extended via 'native land' to 'lair of a wild animal, particularly a bird of prey,' the meaning of its Old French descendant *aire*. The Old French form was taken back into medieval Latin as *aeria*, the immediate source of the English word.

▶ acre, agriculture

# F

**fable** [13] The Indo-European base *bha- 'speak' has produced a wide range of English words, including (via Germanic) ban and (via Latin fārī 'speak') affable, confess, fairy, fame, fate, ineffable, infant, nefarious, and profess. Fable is a member of this latter group; it comes via Old French fable from Latin fābula 'narrative, story' (source also of English fabulous [15]), which was a derivative of fārī. Fib [17] is probably short for an earlier fible-fable 'nonsense,' a fanciful reduplication of fable.

▶ affable, ban, confess, fabulous, fairy, fame, fate, fib, ineffable, infant, nefarious, profess, prophet

**fabric** [15] Latin faber was a term for an artisan who worked with hard materials – a carpenter, for example, or a smith (it probably came from a prehistoric Indo-European base meaning 'fit things together'). From it was derived fabrica, which denoted the trade such a man followed, the place where he worked, or in general terms the product of his work – in the case of a carpenter, a 'building.' And 'building' was the original sense of the word in English when it acquired it via French fabrique: 'He had neuer studye in newe fabrykes ne buyldynges,' William Caxton, Golden Legend 1483. Remnants of the usage survive in the current sense 'walls, roof, and floor of a building.' It was not until the mid 18th century that the underlying notion of 'manufactured material' gave rise to the word's main present-day meaning 'textile.' Derivatives include fabricate [18], from Latin fabricāre, and forge.

▶ forge

**face** [13] The notion that a person's face 'is' their appearance, what they look like to the rest of the world, lies behind the word face. It probably comes from a prehistoric base *fac-, signifying 'appear.' This gave rise to Latin faciēs, which originally meant 'appearance, aspect, form,' and only secondarily, by figurative extension, 'face.' In due course it passed via Vulgar Latin *facia into Old French as face, from which English acquired it (French, incidentally, dropped the sense 'face' in the 17th century, although the word face is retained for 'front, aspect,' etc). Related forms in English include facade [17], facet [17] (originally a diminutive), superficial and surface.

▶ facade, facet, superficial, surface

**facile** see FACULTY

**fact** [16] A fact is literally 'something that is done.' It comes from Latin factum 'deed,' a noun based on the past participle of facere 'do.' This verb, a distant relative of English do, has contributed richly to English vocabulary, from obvious derivatives like factitious [17] and factitive [19] to more heavily disguised forms such as difficult, effect, fashion, feasible, feature, and fetish, not to mention the -fic suffix of words like horrific and pacific, and the related verbal suffix -fy. To begin with, English adopted the word in its original Latin sense 'deed,' but this now survives only in legal contexts, such as 'accessory after the fact.' There is sporadic evidence in classical Latin, however, of its use for 'something that happens, event,' and this developed in post-classical times to produce 'what actually is,' the word's main modern sense in French fait and Italian fatto as well as in their English relative fact.

Feat is essentially the same word as fact, filtered through Old French.

▶ difficult, do, effect, fashion, feasible, feature, fetish

**faction** see FASHION

**factory** [16] Latin factor, a derivative of facere 'make,' meant 'maker, doer' (it was introduced into English in the 15th century as 'agent,' but was not adopted as a mathematical term until the mid 17th century). Among its post-classical derivatives were late Latin factōrium 'oil-press' and medieval Latin factōria 'establishment for factors or agents.' It appears that the latter must have been the original source of the word factory in English, which at first meant 'factorship, agency.' However, this does not fit in at all with its main modern sense 'place where things are made,' first recorded in the early 17th century, which presumably must go back in some way to Latin factōrium.

▶ fact

**factotum** [16] A *factotum* is literally someone who 'does everything.' It was coined from *fac*, the imperative form of the Latin verb *facere* 'do,' and *tōtum* 'all' (source of English *total*). Originally it was used virtually as a name, in phrases such as 'Master Factotum,' and it does not seem to have been until the late 18th century that it settled into its current role as an ordinary noun.

▶ fact, total

**faculty** [14] If one has a *faculty* for doing something, one finds it 'easy' to do. The word comes, via Old French *faculte*, from Latin *facultās*. This was a parallel form to *facilitās* (source of English *facility* [15]). Both were derived from Latin *facilis* 'easy' (whence English *facile* [15]), an adjective formed from the verb *facere* 'do.' Since *facilitās* more closely resembled *facilis*, it retained its connotations of 'easiness,' whereas by the classical period *facultās* had more or less lost them, coming to mean 'capability, power.'

▶ facile, facility

**fade** [14] *Fade* comes from Old French *fader*, a derivative of the adjective *fade* 'faded, vapid.' This in turn came from Vulgar Latin *\*fatidus*, which probably represents an alteration of Latin *fatuus* 'stupid, insipid' (source of English *fatuous* [17]) under the influence of Latin *vapidus* 'flat, lifeless' (source of English *vapid*).

▶ fatuous, vapid

**fag** English has three distinct words *fag*, none of whose origins is altogether clear. The oldest is the one which denotes 'drudgery.' It is first recorded as a verb in the 16th century, meaning 'droop, decline'; its more common noun uses, 'hard boring work' and 'boy who does tasks for an older boy in a British public school,' appear to have developed in the late 18th century. It is generally taken to have been originally an alteration of *flag* 'lose vigour, droop,' although there is no conclusive proof of this. *Fag* 'cigarette' [19] is an abbreviation of *fag-end* [17], which originally meant generally 'extreme end.' It was a compound formed from an earlier *fag* [15], whose underlying meaning seems to have been something like 'piece hanging down loosely, flap' (and which conceivably could be related to *fag* 'drudgery'). *Fag* 'homosexual' [20] is short for *faggot* [13], a derogatory term applied to male homosexuals in American English since the early 20th century; the usage is probably based on the slightly earlier uncomplimentary use of the word for 'woman.' *Faggot* means literally 'bundle of sticks,' and comes via Old French *fagot* from Italian *faggotto* (which is used also for 'bassoon'). This in turn is a diminutive form of Vulgar Latin *\*facus*, which was based ultimately on Greek *phákelos* 'bundle.' The notion of applying a term for 'bundle' abusively to 'women' is perhaps echoed in *baggage*.

**fail** [13] *Fail, fallacy* [15], *fallible, false,* and *fault* all come ultimately from the same source – the

Latin verb *fallere*. This originally meant 'deceive,' but it developed semantically to 'deceive someone's hopes, disappoint someone,' and in its Vulgar Latin descendant *\*fallīre* this meaning had progressed to 'be defective, fail.' English acquired the word via Old French *faillir*. Its Anglo-Norman form, *failer*, came to be used as a noun, and is the source of English *failure* [17].

▶ fallacy, fallible, false, fault

**faint** [13] *Faint* comes from Old French *faint*, which was originally the past participle of the verb *faindre, feindre* 'pretend, shirk' (whence English *feign*). This meant 'pretended, simulated,' 'lazy, shirking,' and 'cowardly,' and all these senses were originally taken over by English. None now survives except the last, in the phrase *faint heart*, but in their place the underlying notion of 'feebleness' has produced 'not bright, dim' and 'weak and dizzy.' The verb, based on the second of these, developed in the late 14th century. The variant spelling *feint*, used of printed lines, was introduced in the mid 19th century.

▶ feign

**fair** English has two distinct words *fair*, one Germanic and the other Romance. The older, meaning 'beautiful' [OE], comes from a prehistoric Germanic *\*fagraz*, which survives also in Swedish *fager* 'beautiful.' It derived from a base *\*fag-*, which seems originally to have meant 'fitting, suitable' (a variant of it was the ultimate source of *fake* and possibly also of the now archaic noun *fig* 'clothes, array,' as in 'in full fig'). Of its main present-day meanings, 'just, equitable' developed in the 14th century and 'not dark' in the mid 16th century.

*Fair* 'festive event' [13] comes from Old French *feire*. This was a descendant of late Latin *fēria*, a singular use of a noun which in classical times had been used in the plural, *fēriae*, for 'holiday.' A close relative of *fēriae* was the adjective *festus* 'joyous,' source of English *feast, festival, festoon,* and *fête*.

▶ fake, feast, festival, festoon, fête, fig

**fairy** [14] *Fairy* is an Old French coinage. It comes from Old French *faerie*, which meant 'enchantment, magic' and was derived from *fae* 'fairy' (source of English *fay* [14]). This in turn came from the Latin plural *fāta*, used in personifying the Fates, three goddesses who in ancient mythology governed human destiny. The original notion of the French noun survives in the mock-medieval term *faerie* (introduced by Edmund Spenser in his *Faerie Queene* 1590), but in *fairy* itself it has been gradually replaced by the meaning of the word from which it was originally derived – *fay*.

▶ fable, fame, fate

**faith** [12] *Faith* comes ultimately from the prehistoric Indo-European *\*bhidh-, \*bhoidh-* (source also of English *federal*). It produced Latin *fidēs* 'faith,' which lies behind a wide range of English words, including *confide*, *defy*, *diffident* (which originally meant 'distrustful'), *fealty* [14], *fidelity* [15], *fiduciary* [17], and *perfidy* [16]. Its descendants in the Romance languages include Italian *fede*, Portuguese *fé* (as in *auto-da-fé*, literally 'act of faith,' acquired by English in the 18th century), and Old French *feid*. This was pronounced much as modern English *faith* is pronounced, and Middle English took it over as *feth* or *feith*. (A later Old French form *fei*, foreshadowing modern French *foi*, produced the now defunct English *fay* [13].)

▶ confide, defy, diffident, federal, fidelity, fiduciary, perfidy

**fake** [19] The use of *fake* for 'produce a fraudulent copy of' is a comparatively recent development. It used to mean 'do up something spurious to make it seem genuine,' and in this sense seems to be a descendant of the long-obsolete verb *feague* [16]. Essentially it is a piece of underworld slang, and as such has a rather slippery semantic history. In the 19th century it was used, like its ancestor *feague*, for any number of nefarious operations, including beating up and killing ('to *fake* a man *out and out*, is to kill him,' J H Vaux, *Vocabulary of the Flash Language* 1812), but its current sense leads back in a straight line to its probable ultimate source, German *fegen* 'polish, refurbish.' This (like English *fig* 'clothes, array') was a derivative of the prehistoric Germanic base *feg-*, a variant of *fag-*, from which English gets *fair* 'beautiful.'

▶ fair, feast, fig

**falcon** [13] English acquired *falcon* via Old French *faucon*, but it is probably ultimately of Germanic origin. Related forms such as German *falke* and Dutch *valk* suggest a prehistoric Germanic *falkon*, adopted into late Latin as *falcō*, and passing from there into Old French.

**fall** [OE] The verb *fall* comes from prehistoric Germanic *fallan*, which also produced German *fallen*, Dutch *vallen*, and Swedish *falla*. The noun is partly a survival of Old English *feall*, partly a borrowing from the related Old Norse *fall*, but probably mostly a new formation based on the verb. The sense 'autumn,' now restricted to American English, originated in the 16th century from an earlier phrase *fall of the leaf*. (*Fell* 'cut down' is related; etymologically it means 'cause to fall.')

▶ fell

**fallacy** see FAIL

**fallow** English has two words *fallow*, both of considerable antiquity. *Fallow* 'uncultivated' [OE] originally meant 'ploughed land.' Its present-day adjectival mear.ing 'ploughed but not sown' or, more broadly, just 'uncultivated,' developed in the 15th century. *Fallow* 'pale yellowish-brown' [OE] (now used only in *fallow deer*) comes via Germanic *falwaz* from Indo-European *polwos*, a derivative of the base *pol-*, *pel-*, which al-

so produced English *appal* [14] (originally 'grow pale'), *pale*, and *pallid*. Its Germanic relatives include German *fahl* 'pale, fawn' and *falb* 'pale yellow.' (Germanic *falwaz*, incidentally, was the ancestor of French *fauve* 'wild animal,' source of the term *fauvism* [20] applied to an early 20th-century European art movement that favoured simplified forms and bold colours.)

▶ appal, pale, pallid

**false** [OE] *False* appears originally to have been borrowed directly from Latin *falsus* at the end of the 10th century, but without making much of an impression. It was only in the 12th century that it began being used with any frequency, probably as the result of an extra impetus given by reborrowing it via Old French *fals*. The word's ultimate source was the Latin verb *fallere* 'deceive,' from which English also gets *fail*, *fallacy*, *fallible*, and *fault*.

▶ fail, fallacy, fallible, fault

**fame** [13] Etymologically, *fame* is 'being talked about.' The word comes via Old French *fame* from Latin *fāma* 'talk, reputation.' This in turn goes back ultimately to the Indo-European base *bha-* 'speak,' which also produced English *confess*, *fable*, *fate*, *ineffable*, etc. The derivatives *famous* and *infamous* are both 14th-century acquisitions.

▶ confess, fable, fairy, fate, ineffable, profess

**familiar** [14] *Familiar* originally meant simply 'of the family' (it came, partly via Old French *familier*, from Latin *familiāris*). Its usual use in this sense was in phrases such as *familiar enemy* and *familiar foe*, denoting a treacherous enemy from within one's own family or household. It gradually broadened out semantically via 'intimately associated' (preserved in *familiar spirit*, and in the noun use 'intimate friend') to 'well-known from constant association.'

▶ family

**family** [15] Latin *famulus*, a word of unknown origin, meant 'servant.' From it was derived *familia*, a collective term for all the domestic servants of a household. Only rarely was it used for the entire household, including the servants' employers too, and when it first entered English it was with the original Latin sense (which indeed survived until the late 18th century). Gradually, however, the English word broadened out to 'whole household,' and then in the mid-17th century narrowed down again to the current main sense 'group of related people.'

▶ familiar

**famine** [14] Both *famine* and *famish* [14] come ultimately from Latin *famēs* 'hunger.' Its Vulgar Latin derivative *faminis* produced Old French *famine*, source of English *famine*. *Famish* has come via a more circuitous route: another Vulgar Latin derivative of *famēs* was *affamāre*, a compound verb formed with the prefix *ad-* 'towards'; in Old French this became *afamer*, which was borrowed into Middle English, with loss of its first syllable, as *fame* 'starve'; and before long this had the suffix *-ish* added to it, on the model of other verbs such as *abolish* and *diminish*.

▶ famish

**fan**   English has two words *fan*. By far the older [OE] came from Latin *vannus*; it originally meant 'device for winnowing grain,' and its now familiar sense 'handheld device for creating a cooling draught' did not develop until the 16th century. Its characteristic semicircular shape gave rise to the term *fanlight* [19] (since applied to a rectangular window above a door). *Fan* 'supporter' is short for *fanatic*. There is a one-off example of its use in the 17th century, in *New news from Bedlam* 1682, but the origins of the modern word were in late 19th-century America, where it was used for sports supporters.

**fancy**   [15]   Ultimately, *fancy* is the same word as *fantasy* [15], from which it emerged by a process of contraction and gradually became differentiated in meaning. Both go back originally to the Greek verb *phaínein* 'show' (source also of English *diaphanous* and *phenomenon*). From it was derived *phantázein* 'make visible,' which produced the noun *phantasíā* 'appearance, perception, imagination' and its associated adjective *phantastikós* 'able to make visible' (and also incidentally *phántasma*, from which English gets *phantasm* and *phantom*). The noun passed into English via Latin *phantasia* and Old French *fantasie*, bringing with it the original Greek senses and also some others which it had picked up on the way, including 'caprice.' The semantic split between *fantasy*, which has basically taken the road of 'imagination,' and *fancy*, which has tended more to 'capricious preference,' was more or less complete by about 1600. The quasi-Greek spelling *phantasy* was introduced in the 16th century, and has persisted for the noun, although the contemporary *phantastic* for the adjective has now died out. The Italian form *fantasia* was borrowed in the 18th century for a fanciful musical composition. (*Fancy* and *fantasy* have no etymological connection with the superficially similar *fanatic*, incidentally, which comes ultimately from Latin *fānum* 'temple.')

▶ diaphanous, fantasy, pant, phantom

**fane**   SEE PROFANE

**fang**   [11]   *Fang* originally meant 'prey, spoils' – a sense which survived well into the 18th century ('Snap went the sheers, then in a wink, The fang was stow'd behind a bink [bench],' Morrison, *Poems* 1790). It was related to a verb *fang* 'take, capture' which was very common in the Old and Middle English period, and which, like its surviving cousins German *fangen*, Dutch *vangen*, and Swedish *fånga*, goes back to a prehistoric Germanic *fangg-*(English *newfangled* [15] is a memory of it). The application of the word to an animal's tooth does not emerge until as late as the 16th century, and although the broad semantic connection between

'seizing' and 'sharp canine tooth' is clear, the precise mechanism behind the development is not known.

▶ newfangled

**fantasy**   SEE FANCY

**far**   [OE]   *Far* is a word of ancient ancestry. It goes back to Indo-European *per-, which also produced Greek *pérā* 'beyond, further' and Sanskrit *paras* 'beyond.' The Germanic descendant of the Indo-European form was *fer-, whose comparative form *ferrō 'further' passed into Old English as *feorr*, having lost its comparative connotations and come to mean simply 'far.' The Old English comparative was *fierr*, but in early Middle English this too lost its comparative force and a new form was created with the *-er* ending, *ferrer*, later *farrer*. This in turn was gradually replaced by *further* (a completely different – although probably distantly related – word, based on *forth*), of which *farther* is a 13th-century variant modelled on *far*.

**farce**   [14]   *Farce* originally meant 'stuff' (widening gastronomic knowledge in the late 20th century has made us more familiar with its French cousin *farcir* 'stuff,' and the *force-* of *forcemeat* [17] is the same word). It came via Old French *farsir* from Latin *farcīre* 'stuff.' The Latin verb was used in the Middle Ages for the notion of inserting additional passages into the text of the Mass, and hence to padding out any text. A particular application was the insertion of impromptu, usually comical interludes into religious plays, which had led by the 16th century to something approaching the modern meaning of *farce*.

▶ forcemeat

**fare**   [OE]   Both the verb *fare* (now only an archaism) and the noun go back ultimately to the Indo-European base *por-* 'going, passage,' which has produced a wide range of other English words, including *emporium, ferry, fiord, ford, importune, opportunity, pore,* and *port*. Its Germanic descendant was *fer-* 'go,' which produced in Old English the nouns *fær* and *faru* 'journey' and the verb *faran* 'go on a journey' (its German cousin *fahren* is still a standard verb for 'travel'). Of the noun's current senses, 'food' (which seems to have originated in the notion of 'how well one was faring,' 'how one was provided for') dates back to the 13th century, and 'money paid for travelling' to the 15th century. The derivative *welfare* dates from the 14th century.

▶ emporium, ferry, fiord, ford, importune, opportunity, pore, port

**farinaceous**   SEE FARRAGO

**farm**   [13]   The specifically agricultural connotations of *farm* are surprisingly recent. The word comes ultimately from Latin *firmāre* 'make firm, fix,' which produced a medieval Latin derived noun *firma*, denoting 'fixed payment.' English acquired the word via Old

French *ferme*, and originally used it in just this sense ('I will each of them all have 4d to drink when they pay their farm,' *Bury Wills* 1463); something of this early sense is preserved in the verbal usage *farm out*, which to begin with signified 'rent out.' By the 16th century the noun was shifting semantically from 'fixed (rental) payment' to 'land leased for such payment, for the purpose of cultivation,' but only very gradually did the notion of a farm being specifically a leased piece of land die out.

▶ firm

**farrago** [17] The notion of a *farrago* being a 'heterogeneous mixture' comes originally from the mixture of various grains for animal feed. Latin *farrāgo* was a derivative of *far* 'corn' (source of English *farinaceous* [17] and related to *barley* and *barn*), and was extended metaphorically to 'medley, hotch-potch' in classical times.

▶ barley, barn, farinaceous

**farrier** [16] Etymologically, a *farrier* is a 'worker in iron.' The word comes via Old French *ferrier* from Latin *ferrārius*, a derivative of *ferum*. This meant literally 'iron' (it is the source of English *ferrous* [19], and may well have been borrowed from a Semitic source), and already in classical times was being applied metaphorically to implements made from iron, particularly 'swords.' Its use for 'horseshoe,' on which the meaning of *farrier* is based, is a medieval Latin development.

▶ ferrous

**farrow** [OE] *Farrow*, nowadays used mainly as a verb for 'give birth to a litter of pigs,' originally meant 'young pig.' Its ultimate source was Indo-European *\*porkos* (from which English also gets *pork*). The Germanic descendant of this was *\*farkhaz*, which produced German *ferkel* 'young pig' and Dutch *varken* 'pig' (as in *aardvark*, literally 'earth-pig,' originally from Afrikaans) as well as *farrow*.

▶ aardvark, pork

**fart** [OE] *Fart* is a widespread and ancient word in the Indo-European languages, and goes back to a prehistoric Indo-European *\*perd-*, which may originally have been an imitation of the sound of a fart. Its other offspring besides *fart* include German *farzen* and *furzen*, Swedish *fjärta*, Danish *fjerte*, Russian *perdet'*, Polish *pierdziec*, Greek *pordízō*, and Welsh *rhechain*.

**farthing** [OE] *Farthing* has a long history as an English coin-name, going back to the 10th century, when it was used in translations of the Bible to render Latin *quadrans*, a quarter of a denarius. It was introduced into English currency (as a silver coin equal to a quarter of a penny) in the reign of Edward I; in Charles II's time copper was used for it, and from 1860 until its abolition in 1971 it was a bronze coin. Appropriately, the term means literally 'quarter'; it was originally a de-

rivative of Old English *fēortha* 'fourth,' formed with the suffix *-ing* denoting 'fractional part' (found also in *riding* [11], former name of the administrative areas of Yorkshire, which etymologically means 'third part').

▶ four

**fascinate** [16] To *fascinate* somebody is literally to 'bewitch' them. The word comes from the past participle of the Latin verb *fascināre*, which was a derivative of *fascinum* 'witchcraft.' The Roman phallic deity, incidentally, was named *Fascinus*, because an amulet in the shape of a penis was hung around children's necks in ancient times to ward off evil spells.

**fascist** [20] The early 20th-century Italian *fascisti*, under Benito Mussolini, took their name from Italian *fascio*, literally 'bundle' but figuratively 'group, association.' Its source was Latin *fascis* 'bundle,' from whose diminutive form *fasciculus* English gets *fascicle* [15]. Closely related was Latin *fascia* 'band, bandage, strip,' borrowed by English in the 16th century.

▶ fascia, fascicle

**fashion** [13] The underlying notion of *fashion* is of 'making,' 'forming,' or 'shaping.' The main modern sense of the word developed via 'particular shape or style,' 'way, manner,' and 'prevailing or current manner.' English acquired it via Anglo-Norman *fasun* from Latin *factiō*, a derivative of *facere* 'make, do' (which has contributed an enormous range of vocabulary to English, from *fact* to *difficult*, and is distantly related to English *do* itself). Latin *factiō* was only rarely used in the literal sense 'making.' In classical times it was generally applied to a 'group of people acting together' (hence English *faction* [16]), and the metaphorical extension to 'way, manner' and 'custom' taken up by English *fashion* is a post-classical development.

▶ difficult, fact, faction, factory

**fast** [OE] Widely dissimilar as they now seem, *fast* 'quick' and *fast* 'abstain from food' in fact come from the same ultimate source. This was Germanic *\*fastuz*, which denoted 'firm.' That underlying sense persists in various contexts, such as 'hold fast' and 'fast friend.' The verbal application to 'eating no food' originated in the notion of 'holding fast to a particular observance' – specifically, abstinence from food. The use of *fast* for 'quick' is a much later development, dating from the 13th century. It probably comes from a perception of *fast* 'firm' containing an underlying connotation of 'extremity' or 'severity.'

**fasten** [OE] Etymologically, *fasten* means 'make fast'; it goes back ultimately to Germanic *\*fastuz*, source of English *fast*. From this was derived a verb *\*fastinōjan*, which passed into Old English as *fæstnian*. To begin with this seems only to have been used in the metaphorical sense 'settle, establish.' The more concrete 'attach' is not recorded until the 12th century, and the earliest reference to its use for locking or bolting a door comes from as late as the mid-18th century.

▶ fast

**fat**  [OE]  *Fat* is one of a large Indo-European family of words denoting the substance 'fat' or its consequences in terms of obesity – the probably related Greek *pímelē* and Latin *pinguis*, for instance, signified respectively 'lard' and 'fat.' The Germanic members of the family, which include German *fett*, Dutch *vet*, and Swedish *fet* as well as English *fat*, go back to a prehistoric Germanic *\*faitaz*.

**fate**  [14]  Etymologically, *fate* is 'that which is spoken' – that is, by the gods. Like so many other English words, from *fable* to *profess*, it goes back ultimately to the Indo-European base *\*bha-* 'speak.' Its immediate source was Italian *fato*, a descendant of Latin *fātum*, which was formed from the past participle of the verb *fārī* 'speak.' That which the gods say determines the destiny of human beings, and so Latin *fātum* came to signify 'what is preordained, destiny.' It was used in the plural *fāta* to personify the Fates, the three goddesses who preside over human destiny – their direct etymological descendants in English have been diminished to *fairies*. The derivative *fatal* [14] comes from Latin *fatālis*, perhaps via Old French *fatal*.

▶ confess, fable, fairy, profess

**father**  [OE]  *Father* is the English representative of a general Indo-European family of words for 'male parent.' Its ancestor is Indo-European *pətér*, which probably originated (like the words for 'mother,' and indeed like English *daddy* and *papa* and Welsh *tad* 'father') in prearticulate syllables interpreted by proud parents as words. Its multifarious descendants include Greek *patér*, Latin *pater* (whence French *père*, Italian and Spanish *padre* – borrowed into English in the 16th century – and English *pater, paternal, patriarch, patrician, patriot*, and *patron*), Irish *athair*, Armenian *hayr*, German *vater*, Dutch *vader*, Swedish and Danish *fader*, and English *father*. A less obvious relation is *perpetrate* [16]; this comes ultimately from Latin *perpetrāre*, a derivative of the verb *patrāre*, which originally meant literally 'perform or accomplish in the capacity of a father.'

▶ paternal, patriot, patron, perpetrate

**fathom**  [OE]  The underlying etymological meaning of *fathom* appears to be 'stretching out, spreading.' It probably comes ultimately from the Indo-European base *\*pot-, \*pet-*, which also produced Latin *patēre* 'be open' (source of English *patent*) and Greek *pétalos* 'outspread' (source of English *petal*). Its Germanic descendant was *\*fath-*, which produced the noun *\*fathmaz*, direct ancestor of Old English *fæthm*. Here, the notion of 'stretching out' seems to have spread via 'stretching out the arms' to, on the one hand 'embrace' (and one meaning of Old English *fæthm* was 'embrace,

bosom'), and on the other 'length spanned by outstretched arms' – about six feet.

▶ patent, petal

**fatigue**  [17]  In English a relatively formal term, *fatigue* goes back ultimately to a Latin expression roughly equivalent to the English notion of having 'had it up to here.' It was borrowed from French *fatiguer*, a descendant of Latin *fatigāre* 'tire.' This appears to have been related to the adverb *affatim* 'sufficiently,' suggesting that underlying *fatigāre* was the idea of having 'had enough.' The derivative *indefatigable* 'tireless' [16] comes from Latin *indēfatigābilis*.

**fatuous**  see FADE

**faucal**  see SUFFOCATE

**fault**  [13]  Like *fail, fallacy, fallible*, and *false*, *fault* comes ultimately from Latin *fallere* 'deceive, fail.' Its past participle formed the basis of a Vulgar Latin noun *\*fallita* 'failing, falling short,' which passed into English via Old French *faute* in the sense 'lack, deficiency.' The notion of 'moral culpability' does not seem to have become incorporated into the word until the late 14th century.

▶ fail, fallacy, fallible, false

**fauna**  [18]  Fauna was a Roman goddess of the countryside, sister of Faunus (the Roman equivalent of Greek Pan) who was a nature and fertility god worshipped by shepherds, farmers, etc. The Swedish naturalist Carolus Linnaeus applied her name in 1746 to his catalogue of the animals of Sweden, *Fauna suecica* 'Swedish Fauna,' and it has been used since then as a collective term for the animal life of a region (one of the earliest records of its use in English is by the naturalist Gilbert White in 1771). (*Faunus*, source of English *faun* [14], may be related ultimately to Latin *favēre* 'regard favourably,' source of English *favour*.)

▶ faun

**fauvism**  see FALLOW

**favour**  [14]  Latin *favēre* meant 'regard favourably, side with, protect.' It came ultimately from Indo-European *\*dhegh-, \*dhogh-* 'burn,' which also produced Latin *fovēre* 'heat, cherish' (source of English *foment* [15]) and English *day*. From it was derived the Latin noun *favor*, which passed into English via Old French *favour*. *Favourite* [16] came via early modern French *favorit* from Italian *favorito*, the past participle of the verb *favorire* 'favour.'

▶ day, foment

**fawn**  *Fawn* 'young deer' [14] and *fawn* 'grovel' [13] are two distinct words. The latter did not always have the negative associations of 'servility' which it usually carries today. Originally it simply referred to dogs showing they were happy – by wagging their tails, for instance. It was a derivative of Old English *fægen* 'happy,' an adjective of Germanic origin which survives in the archaic *fain* 'willingly' (as in 'I would fain go'). *Fawn* 'young deer' comes via Old French *faon* 'young of an animal' and Vulgar Latin *\*fētō* from Latin *fētus* 'giving birth, offspring' (whence English *foetus*). The general sense 'young of an animal' survived into the early 17th century in English (James I's translation of the *Psalms*, for instance, in 1603, has 'the fawn of unicorns' in Psalm 29, where the Authorized Version simply refers to 'a young unicorn'), but on the whole 'young of the deer' seems to have been the main sense of the word from the 15th century onwards. Its use as a colour term, after the pale yellowish brown of a young deer's coat, dates from the 19th century.

▶ fain, foetus

**fay**    see FAIRY

**faze**    [19]   *Faze* 'disconcert' is now mainly restricted to American English, but in fact it has an extensive prehistory stretching back to Anglo-Saxon times. It is a variant of *feeze*, a verb meaning 'drive away' or 'alarm' as well as 'disconcert' which survives in American English and in some British dialects, and which comes from Old English *fēsian* 'drive away.'

**fealty**    see FAITH

**fear**    [OE]   'Being frightened' seems to be a comparatively recent development in the semantic history of the word *fear*. In Old English times the verb meant 'be afraid,' but the noun meant 'sudden terrible event, danger,' and it did not develop its modern sense – possibly under the influence of the verb – until the 13th century (the Old English nouns for 'fear' were *ege* and *fyrhto*, source of modern English *fright*). Related words, such as German *gefahr* and Dutch *gevaar*, both meaning 'danger,' confirm that this is the earlier sense (as would Latin *perīculum* 'danger' – source of English *peril* – if, as has been suggested, it too is connected). Taking the search wider, possible links with Latin *perītus* 'experienced,' Greek *peráo* 'go through,' and English *fare* 'go' point to an underlying meaning 'what one undergoes, experience.'

▶ peril

**feasible**    [15]   Something that is *feasible* is literally something 'that can be done.' The word was borrowed from French *faisable*, a derivative of the stem of the verb *faire* 'do, make.' This is the French descendant of Latin *facere*, which has contributed so voluminously to English vocabulary, from *fact* to *difficult*.

▶ difficult, fact, factory, fashion, feat, feature

**feast**    [13]   The notion of 'eating' is a secondary semantic development for *feast*, whose underlying meaning (as may be guessed from the related *festival* [14] and *festivity* [14]) has more to do with joyousness than with the appeasement of hunger. Its ultimate source is the Latin adjective *festus*, which meant 'joyful, merry.' This was used as a plural noun, *festa*, meaning 'celebratory ceremonies, particularly of a reli-

gious nature,' which came down to Old French as *feste*. This was the source of English *feast*, and its modern French descendant gave English *fête* [18]. Incidentally, the sense 'sumptuous meal,' present in *feast* but not in *fête*, goes back to the Latin singular noun *festum*.

Also related is *festoon* [17], acquired via French from Italian *festone*, which originally meant 'ornament for a festive occasion'; and *fair* (as in *fairground*) comes ultimately from Latin *fēria*, first cousin to *festus*.

▶ fair, festival, festoon, fête

**feat**    [14]   Etymologically, a *feat* is 'something that is done.' The word comes via Old French *fet* from Latin *factum* 'deed,' a noun based on the past participle of *facere* 'make, do,' and is hence a doublet of English *fact* – that is to say, both words go back to an identical source, but have become differentiated (in this case because *fact* came directly from Latin, whereas *feat* was filtered through Old French).

▶ fact, factory, fashion, feasible, feature

**feather**    [OE]   The concept of 'feathers' is closely bound up with those of 'wings' and 'flying,' and not surprisingly *feather* belongs to a word family in which all three of these meanings are represented. Its ultimate source is the prehistoric Indo-European base *\*pet-*, which also produced Greek *ptéron* 'wing' (as in English *pterodactyl*), Latin *penna* 'feather, wing' (source of English *pen*), and Sanskrit *pátati* 'fly.' Its Germanic descendant was *\*fethrō*, from which came German *feder*, Dutch *veer*, Swedish *fjäder* and English *feather* (itself used in the plural for 'wings' in Anglo-Saxon times).

▶ pen, pterodactyl

**feature**    [14]   *Feature* comes ultimately from Latin *factūra*, a derivative of the verb *facere* 'do, make' which meant literally 'making, formation.' Elements of this original sense remained when the word reached English via Old French *faiture* – when John Dymmok wrote in 1600 of 'horses of a fine feature,' for example, he was referring to their shape or general conformation – but already a semantic narrowing down to the 'way in which the face is shaped' had taken place. This meaning was then distributed, as it were, to the individual components of the face, and hence (in the 17th century) to any distinctive or characteristic part.

▶ difficult, fact, factory, fashion, feasible, feat

**February**    [13]   Etymologically, *February* is the 'month of purification.' The word comes via Old French *feverier* and late Latin *febrārius* from Latin *februārius* (English reintroduced the Latin *-ruar-* spelling in the 14th century). This was a derivative of *februa*, a word borrowed into Latin from the language of the ancient Sabine people of Italy which was used to designate a festival of purification held on 15 February.

**feckless**    [16]   From an etymological point of view, *feckless* is simply another way of saying *ineffective*. It originated in Scotland, where from the 15th century the local population economized on the pronunciation of *effect*, reducing it to *feck* (this survived into modern times in the sense 'efficacy'). From it was formed *feckless*, literally 'having no effect,' and also *feckful* 'efficient, vigorous,' which never made it further south than northern England.

▶ effect

**fecund**  see FOETUS

**federal**  [17] The modern political use of *federal* and its various derivatives is a comparatively recent development, ushered in by the formation of the USA in the late 18th century. Its original meaning was 'of a league or treaty' (it was formed from Latin *foedus* 'league, treaty,' which came from the same ultimate Indo-European base – *bhidh-*, *bhoidh-* – as *faith*), and its application to a 'joining together of states into a single unit' seems to have arisen from such phrases as *federal union*, which would originally have meant 'union by treaty.'

▶ confide, defy, faith, perfidy

**fee**  [14] *Fee* is a word bequeathed to modern English by the feudal system (and indeed it is closely related etymologically to *feudal*). It came via Anglo-Norman *fee* from medieval Latin *feodum* or *feudum* (source also of *feudal* [17]). This denoted 'land or other property whose use was granted as a reward for service,' a meaning which persists in its essentials in modern English 'payment for work done.' The secondary signification of *fee*, 'feudal estate,' is no longer a live sense, but it is represented in the related *fief* [17], a descendant of *feodum*, which English acquired through French rather than Anglo-Norman. The ultimate derivation of the medieval Latin term itself is not altogether clear, although it is usually assigned to an unrecorded Frankish *fehu-ōd*, literally 'cattle-property' (*fehu* has related forms in Old English *fēoh* 'cattle, property' and Old Norse *fé* 'cattle, money' – joint sources of the first syllable of English *fellow* – and in modern German *viehe* 'cattle'; they all go back ultimately to Indo-European *peku-*, ancestor of a wide range of words meaning 'cattle' which, since in former times cattle were symbolic of wealth, in many cases came to signify 'property' too).

▶ fellow, feudal, fief

**feeble**  [12] Semantically, *feeble* was originally a close relative of *deplorable* and *lamentable*, but over the centuries it has diverged markedly from them. Its ultimate source was Latin *flēbilis*, a derivative of the verb *flēre* 'weep.' In classical times this meant literally 'worthy of being cried over, lamentable,' but later it came to signify 'weak.' It passed in this sense into Old French as *fleible*, which subsequently became *feible* or *feble* (source of English *feeble*), and later still *foible* (whence English *foible* [17]) and *faible* (the modern French form).

▶ foible

**feed**  [OE] *Feed* was formed from the noun *food* in prehistoric Germanic times. It comes via Old English *fēdan* from Germanic *fōthjan*, a derivative of *fōthon*, the noun from which modern English *food* is descended. Its use as a noun, for 'food, fodder,' dates from the 16th century.

▶ food

**feel**  [OE] Like its West Germanic cousins, German *fühlen* and Dutch *voelen*, *feel* is part of a wider Indo-European word-family covering notions like 'touching' and 'handling,' including Greek *palámē* and Latin *palma* 'palm of the hand' and Latin *palpāre*, originally 'stroke, touch lightly,' later 'feel' (source of English *palpable* and *palpitation*). Its ultimate ancestor was the Indo-European base *pōl-*, *pal-*.

▶ palm, palpable, palpitation

**feign**  [13] *Feign* is first cousin to *faint*. It comes from the present stem of Old French *faindre* or *feindre* 'pretend, shirk,' whose past participle gave English *faint*. This in turn came from Latin *fingere* 'make, shape,' which also gave English *effigy*, *fiction*, *figure*, and *figment* and is related to English *dairy* and *dough*. The semantic progression from 'make, shape' to 'reform or change fraudulently,' and hence 'pretend,' had already begun in classical Latin times.

▶ dairy, dough, effigy, faint, fiction, figure

**feint**  The noun *feint* [17] and the adjective *feint* [19] are essentially different words, but they have a common ultimate origin. *Feint* 'misleading mock attack' was borrowed from French *feinte*, a noun use of the feminine form of the past participle of *feindre* 'pretend' (from which English got *feign*). *Feint* 'printed with pale lines' is an artificial variant of *faint* introduced in the printing trade in the mid 19th century (and *faint* itself originally came from the past participle of *feindre*).

▶ faint, feign

**feisty**  [19] *Feisty*, nowadays a colloquial Americanism for 'quarrelsome' or 'spirited,' originated in Middle English as a term for a 'farting dog.' It goes back to the now obsolete English verb *fist* 'fart,' which came ultimately from Indo-European *pezd-* (source also of Latin *pēdere* 'break wind,' whence English *petard* 'small bomb' [16], as in 'hoist with one's own petard'); like *perd-*, the Indo-European ancestor of English *fart*, this was probably of imitative origin. In the 16th and 17th centuries the expression *fisting dog*, literally 'farting dog,' was applied contemptuously to a 'mongrel' or 'cur.' This eventually became shortened to *feist*, and (mongrels being notoriously combative) *feisty* was born.

▶ fizzle, petard

**felicity**  [14] *Felicity* and its relatives *felicitous* [18] and *felicitate* [17] all come ultimately from Latin *fēlīx*. This originally meant 'fruitful' (it is probably related to English *fecund* and *foetus*) but by classical times had progressed semantically via 'favourable, fortunate' to 'happy.'

▶ fecund, foetus

**fell**   English has no fewer than four separate words *fell*, not counting the past tense of *fall*. *Fell* 'cut down' [OE] originated as the 'causative' version of *fall* – that is to say, it means literally 'cause to fall.' It comes ultimately from prehistoric Germanic *\*falljan*, causative of *\*fallan* 'fall.' *Fell* 'animal's skin' [OE] goes back via Germanic *\*fellam* (source also of English *film*) to Indo-European *\*pello-* (whence Latin *pellis* 'skin,' from which English gets *pellagra* [19], *pellicle* [16], and *pelt* 'skin' [15]). *Fell* 'hill' [13] was borrowed from Old Norse *fjall* 'hill'; this seems to be related to German *fels* 'rock,' whose ultimate ancestor was Indo-European *\*pels-*. And the adjective *fell* 'fierce, lethal' [13] was borrowed from Old French *fel*, ancestor of English *felon*.

▶ fall / film, pelt / felon

**fellow**   [11] Etymologically, a *fellow* is somebody who 'lays money.' The word originated as an Old Norse compound *félagi*, formed from *fé* 'money' and *\*lag-*, a verbal base denoting 'lay.' Someone who puts down money with someone else in a joint venture is his or her associate: hence a *fellow* is a 'companion' or 'partner.' When English adopted the Old Norse word in the 11th century, it translated its first element into Old English *fēoh* 'property,' giving late Old English *fēolaga* and eventually modern English *fellow*. (Both Old English *fēoh* and Old Norse *fé* originally meant 'cattle,' and are probably related to modern English *fee*.)

▶ fee, lay

**felon**   [13] Medieval Latin *fellō* (a word of uncertain origin, sometimes referred to Latin *fel* 'gall, poison') meant 'evil-doer.' Its nominative form gave English the adjective *fell* 'fierce, lethal,' via Old French *fel*, while its stem form, *fellōn-*, passed into English through Old French *felon*. The derivative *felony* [13] comes from Old French *felonie*.

▶ fell

**felt**   [OE] Etymologically, *felt* is a fabric that is formed by 'beating' (as indeed is the case, for it is made from compressed fibres). The word comes via West Germanic *\*feltaz* or *\*filtiz* (source also of German *filz* and Dutch *vilt* 'felt,' and of English *filter*) from prehistoric Indo-European *\*peldos*, a derivative of the same base as produced Latin *pellere* 'strike, beat' and the second syllable of English *anvil*.

▶ anvil, filter

**female**   [14] The symmetry between *female* and *male* is a comparatively recent development. *Female* started as Latin *fēmella*, a diminutive form of *fēmina* 'woman' (whence English *feminine* [14]). This in turn was a derivative of Latin *fēlāre* 'suck,' and so etymo-

logically signified 'person from whom milk is sucked' (it came ultimately from the Indo-European base *\*dhēi-*, which also produced Latin *fīlia* 'daughter' and *fīlia* 'son,' source of English *filial* [15]). *Fēmella* passed into English via Old French *femelle* as *femele*, but as early as the end of the 14th century began to change, by association with *male*, to *female*.

▶ feminine, filial

**fence**   [14] *Fence* is short for *defence*, and indeed until the 16th century meant 'defence' ('Yet, for [that is, despite] the fence that he could make, she struck it from his hand,' *Felon Sowe Rokeby* 1500). Of its present-day meanings, 'enclosing structure' (originally a 'defence' against intruders) and 'sword-fighting' (originally the use of a sword for 'self-defence,' now used only as a verb) developed in the 16th century. The sense 'dealer in stolen property' came along in the 17th century; it arose from the notion that such transactions are carried out under the cover, or 'defence,' of secrecy.

Similarly, *fend* [13] and *fender* [15] came by loss of the initial syllable from *defend*.

▶ defence, fend, fender

**feral**   SEE FIERCE

**ferment**   SEE FERVENT

**fern**   [OE] *Fern* is a fairly widespread Indo-European word, represented among the other West Germanic languages by German *farn* and Dutch *varen*. It comes ultimately from Indo-European *\*porno-*. This also produced Sanskrit *parnám*, which meant 'feather' as well as 'leaf,' suggesting that the fern may have been named originally from the feathery leaves of some species.

**ferocious**   [17] Etymologically, *ferocious* means 'wild-eyed.' It comes from Latin *ferox*, which was originally a compound formed from *ferus* 'fierce, wild' (source of English *feral* [17]) and an element *-oc-*, *-ox* meaning 'looking, appearing.' This also appears in *atrocious* and *ocular*, and goes back to an Indo-European source which also produced Greek *ōps* 'eye' and English *eye*.

▶ atrocious, eye, feral, ocular

**ferret**   [14] A *ferret* is, from an etymological point of view, a 'thieving animal.' The word comes via Old French *fuiret* or *furet* from Vulgar Latin *\*fūrittus*, literally 'little thief.' This was a derivative of Latin *fūr* 'thief,' which is related to English *furtive*. The verbal senses 'search about' and 'search out' developed in the 16th century.

▶ furtive

**ferrous**   SEE FARRIER

**ferrule**   [17] Despite appearances, *ferrule* 'metal cap on the end of a stick' has no etymological connection with Latin *ferrum* 'iron,' although its present form has been heavily influenced by it. It is an alteration of an earlier *virolle*, which was borrowed in the 15th century from Old French. The Old French word in turn came from Latin *viriola* 'little bracelet,' a diminutive form of *viriae* 'bracelet.'

**ferry** [12] A *ferry* is etymologically a boat on which you 'travel' from one place to another. The word comes ultimately from the Indo-European base *\*por-* 'going, passage,' which has produced a wide range of other English words, including *emporium*, *ford*, and *port*. Its Germanic descendant was *\*fer-* 'go,' source of English *fare* as well as *ferry*. *Ferry* itself was probably borrowed from the Old Norse element *ferju-*, denoting 'passage across water,' and that was what it at first meant in English. The word's main modern use, which is essentially an abbreviation of *ferry-boat*, is not recorded before the 16th century, and does not seem to have really become established until the 20th century.

▶ emporium, fare, ford, port

**fertile** [15] Etymologically, something that is *fertile* can 'bear' offspring. The word comes via French from Latin *fertilis*. This was a derivative of *\*fertus*, the original past participle of *ferre* 'bear' (a distant relative of English *bear*).

▶ bear

**fervent** [14] *Fervent* comes from the present participle of Latin *fervēre* 'boil.' This verb also produced English *effervescent* [17] and *comfrey* [15], a plant-name which means literally 'boil together,' and moreover its derivative *fermentum* led to English *ferment* [14]. It goes back ultimately to the Indo-European base *\*bhreu-* or *\*bhru-*, from which English also gets *brew*, *broth*, and *fry*, and possibly *bread* and *burn*.

▶ brew, broth, comfrey, effervescent, ferment, fry

**festival** see FEAST

**festoon** see FEAST

**fetch** [OE] *Fetch* comes from the Old English verb *fetian* 'go and get,' which survived dialectally as *fet* well into the 19th century. In the late Old English period a variant *feccan* developed, from which we get the modern English verb's /ch/ ending. Its ultimate origin has been disputed. Perhaps the likeliest explanation is that it comes from a prehistoric Germanic *\*fat-* 'hold' (source also of Old English *fetel* 'girdle, strap,' from which modern English gets *fettle*).

**fête** see FEAST

**fetish** [17] *Fetish* is a doublet of *factitious*: that is to say, the two words have a common origin, but have subsequently diverged widely. Both come ultimately from Latin *factītius* 'made by art,' an adjective derived from the past participle of *facere* 'do, make' (whence English *effect*, *fact*, *fashion*, among a host of other related words). Its Portuguese descendant, *feitiço*, was used as a noun meaning 'charm, sorcery.' French took this over as *fétiche* and passed it on to English, where it was used in the concrete sense 'charm, amulet,' particu-

larly as worshipped by various West African peoples. 'Object irrationally or obsessively venerated' is a 19th-century semantic development.

▶ effect, fact, factory, fashion

**fetter** [OE] Etymologically, *fetters* are shackles for restraining the 'feet.' The word comes from prehistoric Germanic *\*feterō*, which derived ultimately from the same Indo-European base, *\*ped-*, as produced English *foot*. The parallel Latin formation, incidentally, was *pedica* 'fetter,' from which English gets *impeach*.

▶ foot, impeach, pedal

**fettle** see FETCH

**feud** [13] *Feud* signifies etymologically the 'condition of being a foe.' It was borrowed from Old French *fede* or *feide*, and originally meant simply 'hostility'; the modern sense 'vendetta' did not develop until the 15th century. The Old French word in turn was a borrowing from Old High German *fēhida*. This was a descendant of a prehistoric Germanic *\*faikhithō*, a compound based on *\*faikh-* 'hostility' (whence English *foe*). Old English had a parallel descendant, *fǣhthu* 'enmity,' which appears to have died out before the Middle English period. It is not clear how the original Middle English form *fede* turned into modern English *feud* (the first signs of which began to appear in the late 16th century).

▶ foe

**feudal** see FEE

**fever** [OE] The underlying meaning of *fever*, 'high temperature,' suggests that it goes back ultimately to Indo-European *\*dhegh-*, *\*dhogh-* 'burn' (which also produced English *day*, *favour*, and *foment*). Descended from it was Latin *febris* 'fever,' which English acquired during Anglo-Saxon times as *fēfor*. The modern form of the word is partly due to the influence of the related Old French *fievre*.

▶ day, favour, foment

**few** [OE] *Few* traces its history back to the Indo-European base *\*pau-*, denoting smallness of quantity or number, amongst whose other descendants are Latin *paucus* 'little' (source of English *paucity* [15], French *peu* 'few,' and Italian and Spanish *poco* 'a little'), Latin (and hence English) *pauper* 'poor,' and English *poor* and *poverty*. In Germanic it produced *\*faw-*, whose modern representatives are Swedish *få*, Danish *faa*, and English *few*.

▶ pauper, poor, poverty

**fiasco** [19] In Italian, a *fiasco* is literally a 'bottle' (the word comes from medieval Latin *flasco*, source of English *flagon* and *flask*). Its figurative use apparently stems from the phrase *far fiasco*, literally 'make a bottle,' used traditionally in Italian theatrical slang for 'suffer a complete breakdown in performance.' The usual range of fanciful theories has been advanced for the origin of the usage, but none is particularly convincing.

▶ flagon, flask

**fib**    see FABLE

**fichu**    see FIX

**fiction**    [14]    Fiction is literally 'something made or invented' – and indeed that was the original meaning of the word in English. It seems always to have been used in the sense 'story or set of "facts" invented' rather than of some concrete invention, however, and by the end of the 16th century it was being applied specifically to a literary genre of 'invented narrative.' The word comes via Old French from Latin fictiō, a derivative of the verb fingere 'make, shape,' from which English also gets effigy, faint, feign, figure, and figment.

▶ effigy, faint, feign, figure, figment

**fiddle**    [OE]    Like its distant cousin violin, fiddle comes ultimately from the name of a Roman goddess of joy and victory. This was Vītula, who probably originated among the pre-Roman Sabine people of the Italian peninsula. A Latin verb was coined from her name, vītulārī, meaning 'hold joyful celebrations,' which in post-classical times produced the noun vītula 'stringed instrument, originally as played at such festivals.' In the Romance languages this went on to give viola, violin, etc, but prehistoric West and North Germanic borrowed it as *fithulōn, whence German fiedel, Dutch vedel, and English fiddle. In English, the word has remained in use for the instrument which has developed into the modern violin, but since the 16th century it has gradually been replaced as the main term by violin, and it is now only a colloquial or dialectal alternative. The sense 'swindle' originated in the USA in the mid-to-late 19th century.

▶ violin

**fidelity**    see FAITH

**fiduciary**    see FAITH

**fief**    see FEE

**field**    [OE]    Like plain, field seems originally to have meant 'area of flat, open land.' It comes ultimately from the Indo-European base *plth-, which also produced Greek platús 'broad,' English place and plaice, and possibly also English flan and flat. A noun derived from it, *peltus, entered prehistoric West Germanic as *felthuz, which subsequently disseminated as German feld, Dutch veld (English acquired veld or veldt [19] via its Afrikaans offshoot), and English field.

▶ flan, flat, place, plaice, veld

**fiend**    [OE]    Fiend seems originally to have meant 'hated person.' It was formed in prehistoric times from the past participle of a Germanic verb meaning 'hate' (represented in historic times by, for example, Old English fēon, Old High German fiēn, and Gothic fijan). In Old English its meaning had progressed to 'enemy'

(which is what its German relative feind still means). Then towards the end of the first millenium AD we see evidence of its being applied to the 'enemy' of mankind, the Devil. From there it was a short step to an 'evil spirit' in general, and hence to any 'diabolically wicked person.'

**fierce**    [13]    Fierce has not always had exclusively negative connotations of 'aggression,' although admittedly they do go back a long way. Its source, Latin ferus (which also gave English feral) meant originally 'wild, untamed,' but it subsequently developed the metaphorical sense 'uncultivated, savage, cruel.' However, when English acquired the word, via Anglo-Norman fers and Old French fiers, it was used for 'brave' and 'proud' as well as 'wildly hostile or menacing.' 'Brave' died out in the 16th century, although across the Channel 'proud' has survived to become the only sense of modern French fiers.

▶ feral

**fig**    English has two words fig. Fig the fruit [13] comes via Old French figue, Provençal figua, and Vulgar Latin *fica from Latin ficus. This, together with its Greek relative súkon (source of English sycamore and sycophant), came from a pre-Indo-European language of the Mediterranean area, possibly Semitic. Greek súkon was, and modern Italian fica (a relative of fico 'fig') still is, used for 'cunt,' apparently in reference to the appearance of a ripe fig when opened. English adopted the term in the 16th and 17th centuries as fig, fico, or figo, signifying an 'indecent gesture made by putting the thumb between two fingers or into the mouth' ('The figo for thee then!' says Pistol to the disguised king in Shakespeare's Henry V 1599).

The now little used fig 'dress, array' [19], as in 'in full fig,' probably comes from an earlier, now obsolete feague, which in turn was very likely borrowed from German fegen 'polish.' This was a derivative of the same prehistoric Germanic base, *feg-, as produced English fake.

▶ sycamore, sycophant / fake

**fight**    [OE]    The deadly earnestness of fighting seems to have had its etymological origins in the rather petty act of pulling someone's hair. Fight, together with German fechten and Dutch vechten, goes back to a prehistoric Germanic *fekhtan, which appears to come from the same ultimate source as Latin pectere 'comb' and Greek péko 'comb.' The missing links in the apparently far-fetched semantic chain between 'fighting' and 'combing' are provided by such words as Spanish pelear 'fight, quarrel,' a derivative of pelo 'hair,' which originally meant 'pull hair'; German raufen 'pull out, pluck,' which when used reflexively means 'fight'; and English tussle, which originally meant 'pull roughly,' and may be related to tousle.

**figure** [13] *Figure* comes via Old French from Latin *figūra* 'form, shape, figure,' a derivative of the same base (*\*fig-*) as produced *fingere* 'make, shape' (whence English *effigy, faint, feign,* and *fiction*). Many of the technical Latin uses of the word, including 'geometric figure,' are direct translations of Greek *skhéma*, which also meant literally 'form, shape,' but the sense 'numerical symbol' is a later development.

Also from the base *\*fig-* was derived Latin *figmentum* 'something created or invented,' from which English gets *figment* [15].

▶ effigy, faint, feign, fiction, figment

**filbert** [14] Hazelnuts begin to ripen around the end of August, and so in medieval times they were named after Saint Philibert, a 7th-century Frankish abbot whose feast day falls on the 22nd of that month. Thus in Anglo-Norman they were *\*noix de Philibert* or *noix de filbert* – whence English *filbert*.

**file** The *file* for smoothing and rubbing [OE] and the *file* for storing things in [16] are quite different words. The former comes from a prehistoric Germanic *\*fīkhalā* (source also of German *feile* and Dutch *vijl*), which goes back ultimately to Indo-European *\*pik-, \*peik-*, denoting 'cut.' The latter, on the other hand, comes from Old French *fil*, a descendant of Latin *filum* 'thread,' which was applied to a piece of string or wire suspended from two points and used for hanging documents and records on for easy reference. As methods of document storage and retrieval became more sophisticated, the word *file* followed them. The later *file* '(military) column', first recorded at the end of the 16th century, probably represents a reborrowing from French, but it is ultimately the same word.

*Fillet* [14] originated as a diminutive form of Latin *filum*.

▶ filigree, fillet

**filial** see FEMALE

**filibuster** [16] *Filibuster* and *freebooter* [16] are doublets: that is to say, they come from the same ultimate source, but have subsequently diverged. *Freebooter* 'pirate' was borrowed from Dutch *vrijbuiter*, a compound formed from *vrij* 'free' and *buiter* 'plunderer' (this was a derivative of *buit* 'loot,' to which English *booty* is related). But English was not the only language to adopt it; French wanted it too, but mangled it somewhat in the borrowing, to *flibustier*. It was then handed on to Spanish, as *filibustero*. It is not clear where the 16th-century English use of the word with an *l* spelling rather than an *r* spelling (which is recorded in only one text) comes from. The French form *flibustier* was borrowed towards the end of the 18th century, and present-day *filibuster* came from the Spanish form in the mid-19th century. The use of the term for 'obstructing a legislature with an overlong speech' (which has now virtu-

ally obliterated its former semantic equivalence to *freebooter*) originated in the USA in the 1880s.

▶ booty, free, freebooter

**filigree** [17] Etymologically, *filigree* describes very accurately how filigree was originally made: it was delicate ornamental work constructed from threads (Latin *filum*) and beads (Latin *grānum* 'grain, seed'). The Italian descendants of these two Latin words were combined to form *filigrana*, which passed into English via French as *filigrane*. This gradually metamorphosed through *filigreen* to *filigree*.

▶ file, grain

**fill** [OE] *Fill* originated in prehistoric Germanic times as a derivative of the adjective *\*fullaz* 'full,' source of modern English *full*. This was *\*fulljan*, which produced German *füllen*, Dutch *vullen*, Swedish *fylla*, Danish *fylde*, and English *fill*.

▶ full

**fillet** see FILE

**filly** see FOAL

**film** [OE] The notion underlying *film* is of a thin 'skin.' The word comes ultimately from a prehistoric Germanic *\*fellam*, which was related to Latin *pellis* 'skin' (source of English *pelt* 'skin'). From this was derived *\*filminjam*, which produced Old English *filmen*, a word used for various sorts of anatomical membrane or thin skin, including the peritoneum and the foreskin of the penis. It was generalized from the late 16th century to any thin membrane, and was applied by early 19th-century photographers to a thin layer of gel spread on photographic plates ('The film of isinglass . . . peels off and will be found to bear a minute copy of the original,' William Thornthwaite, *Guide to Photography* 1845). As photographic technique moved on to cellulose coated with photosensitive emulsion, it took the term *film* with it.

▶ pelt

**filter** [14] Ultimately, *filter* is the same word as *felt* – and indeed that is what it first meant in English ('They dwell all in tents made of black filter,' John Mandeville, *Travels* 1400). It comes via Old French *filtre* from medieval Latin *filtrum*, which was borrowed from prehistoric West Germanic *\*filtiz*, source of English *felt*. The modern sense of *filter* did not develop until the 17th century; it came from the use of felt for removing impurities from liquid. The derivative *infiltrate* dates from the 18th century. (The homophonic *philtre* [16] is not related; it comes ultimately from Greek *phílos* 'beloved.')

▶ felt, infiltrate

**filth** see FOUL

**fin** [OE] *Fin* is a word common to the Germanic languages of northeast Europe (German has *finne*, Dutch *vin*), but its ultimate source is not clear. The likeliest candidate is Latin *pinna* 'feather, wing' (source of English *pin, pinion,* and *pinnacle*), although another suggestion is Latin *spīna* 'thorn, spike.'

▶ pin, pinion, pinnacle

**final** [14] Of all the English descendants of Latin *fīnis* 'final moment, end' or 'limit' (see FINANCE, FINE, and FINISH), *final,* which comes via Old French *final* from Latin *fīnālis* 'last,' preserves most closely the meaning of its source. But although by classical times *fīnis* denoted a temporal conclusion, its original use was for a physical boundary, and it appears to be related to *fīgere* 'fix' (source of English *fix*) – as if its underlying meaning were 'fixed mark.'

▶ finance, fine, finish

**finance** [14] *Finance* comes ultimately from Latin *fīnis* 'end,' and its present-day monetary connotations derive from the notion of 'finally settling a debt by payment.' Its immediate source is Old French *finance,* a derivative of the verb *finer* 'end, settle,' which when it was originally acquired by English still meant literally 'end': 'God, that all things did make of nought . . . puttest each creature to his finance,' *Coventry Mystery Plays* 1400. The debt-settling sense had already developed by that time, but this did not broaden out into the current 'management of monetary resources' until the 18th century.

▶ final, fine, finish

**find** [OE] *Find* is a widespread Germanic verb, with relations in German (*finden*), Dutch (*vinden*), Swedish (*finna*), and Danish (*finde*). Further back in time, however, its ancestry is disputed. Some have connected it with various words for 'path, way' in Indo-European languages, such as Sanskrit *panthās* and Russian *put',* and with related forms denoting 'go, journey,' like Old Saxon *fāthi* 'going' and Old High German *fendeo* 'walker'; others have suggested a link with Latin *petere* 'seek.'

**fine** [12] Both the adjective and the noun *fine* have come a very long way since their beginnings in Latin *fīnis* 'end.' The etymological sense of the adjective is 'finished' – hence, 'of high quality.' It comes via Old French *fin* from Vulgar Latin *\*fīnus,* an adjective formed from the Latin verb *fīnīre* 'limit, complete' (source of English *finish*). (A derivative of *\*fīnus* was the noun *\*fīnitia,* from which ultimately English gets *finesse* [15].) The noun *fine* also comes from an Old French *fin,* this time a noun descended directly from Latin *fīnis.* In medieval times this was used for 'money to be paid at the completion of legal proceedings' – hence the present-day sense 'payment imposed as a punishment.' From the same ultimate source, but reflecting different aspects of it, come *confine* [16] and *define* [14] ('limitation') and *refine* [16] ('high quality').

▶ confine, define, final, finance, finesse, finish, refine

**finger** [OE] Widespread among the Germanic languages (German, Swedish, and Danish all have *finger,* and Dutch *vinger*), *finger* is not found in any other branch of Indo-European. It is usually referred to a prehistoric Indo-European ancestor *\*pengkrós* 'number of five,' a derivative (like *fist*) of *\*pengke* 'five.'

▶ fist, five

**finish** [14] The Latin verb *\*fīnīre,* a derivative of *fīnis* 'end, limit,' signified 'limit' as well as 'complete,' but it is the latter which has come down to English via *feniss-,* the stem of Old French *fenir.* The Latin past participle, *fīnītus,* gave English *finite* [15].

▶ final, finance, fine, finite

**fiord** see FORD

**fir** [14] As with many Indo-European tree-names, *fir* is a widespread term, but it does not mean the same thing wherever it occurs. Its prehistoric Indo-European ancestor was *\*perkos,* which in Latin became *quercus,* the name for the 'oak.' Nor was the application confined to southern Europe, for Swiss German has a related *ferch* 'oak wood.' But by and large, the Germanic languages took the term over and applied it to the 'pine': German *föhre,* Swedish *fura,* and Danish *fyr* all mean 'pine.' So also did Old English *furh* (known only in the compound *furhwudu* 'pine-wood'), but this appears to have died out. It was replaced semantically by *pine,* but formally by Middle English *firre,* a borrowing from the Old Norse form *fyri-* (also known only in compounds). This was used as a name not for the 'pine,' but for the 'fir' (which in Old English times had been called *sæppe* or *gyr*).

**fire** [OE] Appropriately enough for one of the mainsprings of human civilization, the word *fire* is widespread amongst Indo-European languages (although it is only one of two competing 'fire' strands, the other being represented in English by *ignite*). Among its relatives are Greek *pur* (whence English *pyre, pyrotechnic,* and, by a very circuitous route, *bureau*), Czech *pýr* 'embers,' Armenian *hūr,* and Hittite *pahhur,* pointing back to a prehistoric Indo-European *\*pūr.* Its Germanic descendant was *\*fūir,* from which came German *feuer,* Dutch *vuur,* and English *fire.*

▶ bureau, pyre, pyrotechnic

**firm** [14] *Firm* comes ultimately from Latin *firmus* 'stable, strong, immovable.' In its adjectival use, the English word's semantic line of descent from its Latin original is perfectly clear, but the noun presents a very different story. From *firmus* was derived the verb *firmāre* 'make firm, fix,' which in post-classical times came to mean 'confirm.' It passed into Italian as *firmare,* which was used in the sense 'confirm by one's signature,' hence simply 'sign.' It formed the basis of a noun *firma* 'signature,' and by extension the 'name under which a business is carried on,' and finally the 'business' itself. English took the noun over with the latter two meanings in the 18th century.

Other English words that trace their ancestry back to Latin *firmus* are *firmament* [13], from Latin *firmāmentum* (this originally meant simply 'strengthening, support,' and acquired the sense 'sky' in post-classical times as a literal Biblical translation of Greek *steréōma* 'heavenly vault,' a derivative of *stereós* 'firm,' which in turn was a literal translation of Hebrew *rāqī' a* 'heavenly vault,' also derived from a word meaning 'firm'); *furl* [16], originally a blend formed in Old French from *ferm* 'firm' and *lier* 'tie' (a relative of English *liable*); and *farm*, whose semantic history is quite similar to that of the noun *firm*.

▶ farm, firmament, furl

**first** [OE] As its -*st* ending suggests, *first* was originally a superlative form. Its distant ancestor was Indo-European *\*pro*, denoting 'before, in front' (amongst whose other descendants to have reached English are *prime* and the prefix *proto-*). Its Germanic offspring was *\*fur*, *\*for* (source also of English *for* and *fore*), from which the superlative *\*furistaz*, literally 'most in front,' was formed. Besides English *first* and the related Swedish *först* and Danish *forst* (which etymologically are the equivalent of *foremost*), this has produced German *fürst* and Dutch *vorst* 'prince.'

▶ for, fore, prime

**firth** see FORD

**fiscal** [16] Latin *fiscus* originally denoted a 'small rush basket,' used for example for keeping olives in. Evidently, though, the main purpose to which it was put was as a purse, for it soon acquired the figurative sense 'public purse, public revenue.' Hence the adjective *fiscālis* 'of the imperial treasury,' which passed into English via French *fiscal*.

**fish** [OE] *Fish* goes back to an ancient Indo-European word *\*piskos*, which produced on the one hand Latin *piscis* (source of French *poisson*, Italian *pesce*, Spanish *pez*, Breton *pesk*, and Welsh *pysgodyn*) and on the other Germanic *\*fiskaz* (source of Gothic *fisks*, German *fisch*, Dutch *visch*, Swedish and Danish *fisk*, and English *fish*). (English, incidentally, gets *piscatorial* [19], *piscina* [16], and the zodiacal sign *Pisces* [14] from Latin *piscis*.) But not all Indo-European languages share the word, by any means: Greek had *ikhthús* for 'fish' (whence English *ichthyology* 'study of fish' [17]), and Russian, Polish, and Czech have *ryba*.

▶ piscatorial, Pisces

**fissure** see VENT

**fist** [OE] Like *finger*, *fist* seems etymologically to be a reference to the number of fingers on the hand. It comes from a prehistoric West Germanic *\*fūstiz* (source also of German *faust* and Dutch *vuist*). This may represent an earlier *\*fungkhstiz*, which has been referred to an Indo-European ancestor *\*pngkstis*, a derivative of *\*pengke* 'five.' (Dutch *vuist* 'fist,' incidentally, is probably the source of English *foist* [16], which originally denoted the dishonest concealing of a dice in one's hand.)

▶ finger, five, foist

**fit** English has three distinct words *fit*, but the history of them all is very problematical. The verb *fit* 'make suitable, be the right size, etc' [16], and the presumably related adjective 'proper, appropriate' [14] may come from a Middle English verb *fitten* 'marshal troops,' but that only pushes the difficulty one stage further back, for no one knows where *fitten* came from. (The derivative *outfit* dates from the 18th century.) *Fit* 'seizure, sudden outburst' [14] may be the same word as Old English *fitt* 'conflict,' whose antecedents again are obscure (*fitful* was formed from it in around 1600, but was not widely used before the 19th century). *Fit* 'section of a poem' [OE] also comes from an Old English *fitt*, which might conceivably be identical with Old English *fitt* 'conflict'; but an alternative possibility is some connection with Old High German *fizza* 'skein' and Old Norse *fit* 'hem.'

**five** [OE] *Five* is one of a general Indo-European family of words signifying 'five.' It goes back ultimately to Indo-European *\*pengke*, which also produced Greek *pénte* (source of English *pentagon* [16], *pentecost* [OE] – literally 'fiftieth day' – *pentagram* [19], etc), Sanskrit *pañca* (source of English *punch* 'spiced drink'), and Latin *quīnque*. In due course this underwent a phonetc transformation to *\*pempe*, which was the direct ancestor of prehistoric Germanic *\*fimfi*. This led on in its turn to German *fünf*, Dutch *vijf*, Swedish and Danish *fem*, and English *five*.

▶ finger, fist, pentagon, punch

**fix** [15] *Fix* comes ultimately from Latin *fīgere* 'fasten.' Its past participle *fīxus* made its way into English along two distinct routes, partly via the Old French adjective *fix* 'fixed,' and partly via the medieval Latin verb *fīxāre*. Derived forms in English include *affix* [15], *prefix* [17], *suffix* [18], and *transfix* [16], and also *fichu* 'scarf' [19]: this came from the past participle of French *ficher* 'attach,' which is descended from Vulgar Latin *\*fīgicāre*, another derivative of *fīgere*.

▶ affix, prefix, suffix, transfix

**fizzle** [16] Originally, *fizzle* meant 'fart silently or unobtrusively': 'And then in court they poisoned one another with their fizzles,' Benjamin Walsh's translation of Aristophanes' *Knights* 1837. Then in the mid-19th century it started to be used for a 'weak spluttering hissing sound,' and hence figuratively 'end feebly.' In the earlier sense, *fizzle* was probably a derivative of the now obsolete English verb *fist* 'fart' (source of *feisty*), which came ultimately from Indo-European *\*pezd-* (no doubt imitative of the sound of breaking wind). The later sense is close enough semantically to suggest that it is probably a metaphorical extension of the earlier, but it could also be a new formation, based on *fizz* [17] (which was also of onomatopoeic origin).

▶ feisty

**fjord**    see FORD

**flag**    English has at least three separate words *flag*, none of whose origins are known for certain. Both the noun 'cloth used as an emblem' [16] and the verb 'droop, decline' [16] may have developed from an obsolete 16th-century adjective *flag* 'drooping, hanging down,' but no one knows where that came from. *Flag* the plant [14] is probably related to Danish *flæg* 'yellow iris,' but beyond that the trail goes cold. *Flag* as in *flagstone* [15] originally meant 'piece of turf.' It probably came from Old Norse *flaga* 'stone slab.' This also gave English *flaw* (which originally meant 'flake'), which is related to English *floe*, and goes back to a Germanic base, a variant of which produced English *flake*.

▶ flake, flaw, floe

**flagellation**    see FLAIL

**flageolet**    see FLUTE

**flagon**    see FLASK

**flagrant**    [15]    Etymologically, *flagrant* means 'burning, blazing.' It comes, via French, from the present participle of Latin *flagrāre* 'burn' (source of English *conflagration* [16]). This in turn went back to Indo-European *\*bhleg-*, which also produced English *flame*. The use of *flagrant* for 'shameless, shocking,' an 18th-century development, comes from the Latin phrase *in flagrante delicto* 'red-handed,' literally 'with the crime still blazing.'

▶ conflagration, flame

**flail**    [OE]    *Flail* is a distant relative of *flagellation* [15]. Both go back ultimately to Latin *flagrum* 'whip.' This had a diminutive form *flagellum*, which in prehistoric times was borrowed into West Germanic as *\*flagil-*. It is assumed that Old English inherited it as *\*flegil* (although this is not actually recorded), which, reinforced in Middle English times by the related Old French *flaiel*, produced modern English *flail*. *Flagellation* comes from the derived Latin verb *flagellāre* 'whip.'

▶ flagellation

**flake**    [14]    *Flake* appears to go back to a prehistoric Germanic source which denoted the splitting of rocks into strata. This was *\*flak-*, a variant of which produced English *flaw* [14] (which originally meant 'flake'), the second syllable of *whitlow* [14] (which probably means etymologically 'white fissure'), *floe* [19], and probably *flag* 'stone slab.'

▶ flag, flaw, floe, whitlow

**flame**    [14]    *Flame* traces its history back to an Indo-European *\*bhleg-*, *\*phleg-*, which also produced Greek *phlóx* 'flame' (source of English *phlox*, and relat-

ed to *phlegm* and *phlegmatic*), Latin *flāgrāre* 'burn, blaze' (source of English *flagrant*), Latin *fulmen* (source of English *fulminate*), and Latin *fulgēre* 'shine' (source of English *refulgent* [16]). The relevant descendant in this case was Latin *flamma* 'flame,' acquired by English via Old French *flame*. It had a diminutive form *flammula*, which produced Old French *flambe* 'small flame,' ultimate source of English *flambé* [19] and *flamboyant* [19] (originally an architectural term applied to a 15th- and 16th-century French Gothic style characterized by wavy flamelike forms).

▶ flagrant, flamboyant, flamingo, phlegm, refulgent

**flamingo**    [16]    *Flamingos* get their name from their reddish-pink plumage, which earned them the epithet 'fire-bird.' This was expressed in Provençal (the language of southern French coastal areas, where flamingos abound) as *flamenc*, a compound formed from *flama* 'flame' (a descendant of Latin *flamma*) and the Germanic suffix *-ing* 'belonging to.' English acquired the word via Portuguese *flamengo*. (It has, incidentally, no etymological connection with *flamenco* 'Spanish dance' [19], which comes from the Spanish word for 'Flemish': the people of Flanders seem to have had a reputation in the Middle Ages for bright, flamboyant dress, and hence 'Flemish' in Spanish became synonymous with 'gipsy-like.')

▶ flame

**flan**    [19]    The word *flan* itself is a relatively recent addition to English, adopted on our behalf from French by the chef Alexis Soyer (a Frenchman working in England), but in that form it is in fact simply a reborrowing of a word which originally crossed the Channel in the 13th century as *flawn*, denoting some sort of custard tart or cheesecake. Its Old French source was *flaon*, which came from medieval Latin *fladō*, but this was originally borrowed from Germanic *\*fladu-* (source of German *fladen* 'flat cake, cowpat' and Dutch *vlade* 'pancake'), which is probably related ultimately to Sanskrit *prthūs* 'broad,' Greek *platūs* 'broad,' and English *flat*.

▶ flat

**flank**    see LINK

**flannel**    [14]    *Flannel* is probably one of the few Welsh contributions to the English language. It appears to be an alteration of Middle English *flanen* 'sackcloth,' which was borrowed from Welsh *gwlanen* 'woollen cloth,' a derivative of *gwlân* 'wool.' This in turn is related to Latin *lāna* 'wool' and English *wool*. It is not clear where the British colloquial sense 'insincere talk' (which seems to date from the 1920s) comes from, although it may well have been inspired by Shakespeare's unflattering application of the word to a Welshman in the *Merry Wives of Windsor* 1598: 'I am not able to answer the Welsh flannel,' says Falstaff of Hugh Evans, a Welsh parson.

▶ wool

**flash** [14] The earliest recorded use of *flash* is as a verb, referring to the swift turbulent splashing movement of water (a memory of which is probably preserved in modern English *flash flood*). The glints of light on the splashing surface of such water seems to have given rise in the 16th century, or perhaps before, to the main present-day sense of the word 'burst out with sudden light.' It was presumably originally imitative of the sound of splashing water.

**flask** [14] English acquired *flask* via French *flasque* from medieval Latin *flasca*, a word of uncertain origin. It occurs widely in the Germanic languages (German has *flasche*, for instance, and Dutch *vlesch*, and the related word *flasce* existed in Old English, although it did not survive into Middle English), but it is not clear whether the medieval Latin word was borrowed from Germanic, or whether the Germanic languages originally got it from a Latin word (Latin *vāsculum* 'small vessel,' a diminutive form of *vās* – whence English *vascular*, *vase*, and *vessel* – has been suggested as a source). The sense 'gunpowder container,' first recorded in the 16th century, may have been inspired by Italian *fiasco* (source of English *fiasco*), which came from a variant medieval Latin form *flascō*. This also produced English *flagon* [15].
▶ fiasco, flagon

**flat** [14] The Old English word for 'flat' was *efen* 'even,' and *flat* was not acquired until Middle English times, from Old Norse *flatr*. This came from a prehistoric Germanic *\*flataz*, source also of German *platt* 'flat.' And *\*flataz* probably goes back to an Indo-European *\*pelə-*, *\*plā-*, denoting 'spread out flat,' from which came Sanskrit *prthūs* 'broad,' Greek *platús* 'broad' (source of English *place*, *plaice*, *plane* [the tree], and *platypus*), Latin *plānus* 'flat' (whence English *plane* and *plain* 'unadorned'), and also English *place*, *plaice*, *plant*, and *flan*. *Flat* 'single-storey dwelling' [19] is ultimately the same word, but it has a more circuitous history. It is an alteration (inspired no doubt by the adjective *flat*) of a now obsolete Scottish word *flet* 'interior of a house,' which came from a prehistoric Germanic *\*flatjam* 'flat surface, floor,' a derivative of the same source (*\*flataz*) as produced the adjective.
▶ flan, flatter, floor, place, plaice, plane, platypus

**flatter** [13] Etymologically, *flatter* means 'smooth down or caress with the flat of the hand.' It comes from Old French *flatter*, in which the original literal notion of 'caressing' had already passed into the figurative 'buttering up.' The Old French verb in turn was based on Frankish *\*flat*, the 'flat or palm of someone's hand,' a word which shared a common source with English *flat*.
▶ flat

**flavour** [14] The form of the word *flavour*, and probably to some extent its meaning, owe a lot to *sa-*

*vour*. It was borrowed from Old French *flaor*, and originally meant 'smell' (the current association with 'taste' did not develop until the 17th century). The *savour*-influenced change from *flaor* to *flavour* seems to have happened somewhere in the crack between Old French and Middle English: there is no evidence of a *v*-spelling in Old French. The Old French word itself came from Vulgar Latin *\*flātor* 'smell,' a derivative of Latin *flātus* 'blowing, breeze, breath' (possibly influenced by Latin *foetor* 'foul smell'). *Flātus* in turn came from the past participle of *flāre* 'blow.'

**flaw** see FLAKE

**flea** see PUCE

**fledge** [16] The notion underlying *fledge* is the 'ability to fly.' Historically, the idea of 'having feathers' is simply a secondary development of that underlying notion. The verb comes from an obsolete adjective *fledge* 'feathered,' which goes back ultimately to a prehistoric West Germanic *\*fluggja* (source also of German *flügge* 'fledged'). This was derived from a variant of the base which produced English *fly*. There is no immediate connection with *fletcher* 'arrow-maker' [14], despite the formal resemblance and the semantic connection with 'putting feathered flights on arrows,' but further back in time there may be a link. *Fletcher* came from Old French *flechier*, a derivative of *fleche* 'arrow.' A possible source for this was an unrecorded Frankish *\*fliugika*, which, like *fledge*, could be traceable back to the same Germanic ancestor as that of English *fly*.
▶ fly

**flee** [OE] *Flee*, like its close relatives German *fliehe*, Dutch *vlieden*, and Swedish and Danish *fly*, comes from a prehistoric Germanic *\*thleukhan*, a word of unknown origin. In Old English, *flee* and *fly* had the same past tense and past participle (and indeed the same derivatives, represented in modern English by *flight*), and this, together with a certain similarity in meaning, has led to the two verbs being associated and often confused, but there is no reliable evidence that they are etymologically connected.

**fleece** [OE] *Fleece* comes from a prehistoric Germanic *\*flūsaz*. This probably goes back to an Indo-European *\*plus-*, which also produced Latin *plūma* 'down,' later 'feathers,' and Lithuanian *plunksna* 'feather.' The metaphorical sense of the verb, 'swindle,' developed in the 16th century from the literal 'remove the fleece from.'
▶ plume

**fleet** [OE] *Fleet* is one of a vast tangled web of words which traces its history back ultimately to Indo-European *\*pleu-*, denoting 'flow, float' (amongst its other English descendants are *fly*, *flood*, *flow*, *fledge*, *fowl*, *plover*, and *pluvial*). *Fleet* itself comes from the extended Indo-European base *\*pleud-*, via the Germanic verb *\*fleutan* and Old English *flēotan* 'float, swim' (modern English *float* comes from the related Old English *flotian*). The verb has now virtually died out, but it survives in the form of the present participial adjective *fleeting*, which developed the sense 'transient' in the 16th century, and in the derived noun *fleet*: Old English seems to have had two distinct nouns *flēot* based on the verb *flēotan*, one of which meant 'ships,' and the other of which signified 'creek, inlet' (it survives in the name of London's Fleet Street, which runs down to the now covered-up Thames tributary, the river Fleet). The adjective *fleet* 'quick' (as in 'fleet of foot') was probably borrowed from Old Norse *fljótr*, likewise a descendant of Germanic *fleut-.

► fledge, float, flood, flow, fowl, plover, pluvial

**flesh** [OE] The etymological notion underlying *flesh*, and its near relative *flitch* 'side of bacon' [OE], is of 'slitting open and cutting up an animal's carcase for food.' It, together with its continental cousins, German *fleisch* and Dutch *vleesch* 'flesh' and Swedish *fläsk* 'bacon,' comes ultimately from Indo-European *pel-* 'split.' Consequently, the earliest recorded sense of the Old English word *flæsc* is 'meat'; the broader 'soft animal tissue,' not necessarily considered as food, seems to have developed in the late Old English period.

► flitch

**fletcher** see FLEDGE

**fleur-de-lys** see LILY

**flight** [OE] English has two distinct, etymologically unrelated words *flight*. One, 'flying,' comes from a prehistoric West Germanic *flukhtiz*, a derivative of the same base as produced *fly* (the sense 'series of stairs,' which developed in the 18th century, was perhaps modelled on French *volée d'escalier*, literally 'flight of stairs'). The other, 'escape,' comes from a hypothetical Old English *flyht*, never actually recorded, which goes back ultimately to the same Germanic base as produced *flee*.

► flee, fly

**flinch** see LINK

**flit** see FLOAT

**flitch** see FLESH

**float** [OE] Germanic *fleut-*, which produced English *fleet*, had the so-called 'weak grades' (that is, variant forms which because they were weakly stressed had different vowels) *flot-* and *flut-*. The former was the source of Germanic *flotōjan*, which passed into late Old English as *flotian* and eventually ousted *flēotan* (modern English *fleet*) from its original meaning 'float.' It also seems to have been borrowed into the Romance languages, producing French *flotter*, Italian *fiottare*, and Spanish *flotar* (a diminutive of the Spanish noun derivative *flota* gave English *flotilla* [18]). The latter formed the basis of Old Norse *flytja*, acquired by

English as *flit* [12], and of Old English *floterian*, which became modern English *flutter*.

► fleet, flit, flotilla, flutter

**floe** see FLAKE

**flood** [OE] *Flood* goes back to a prehistoric Germanic *flōthuz*, which also produced German *flut*, Dutch *vloed*, and Swedish *flod* 'flood.' It was derived ultimately from Indo-European *plō-*, a variant of *pleu-* 'flow, float' which also produced English *fleet*, *float*, *fly*, *fledge*, and *fowl*.

► fleet, float, fly, fowl

**floor** [OE] *Floor* and its first cousins, German *flur* 'paved floor' and Dutch *vloer* 'floor,' go back to a prehistoric Germanic *flōruz*. They are related to various Celtic words for 'floor,' including Old Irish *lār*, Welsh *llawr*, and Breton *leur*, and it has been speculated that both the Germanic and the Celtic words come ultimately from the same source as Latin *plānus* 'flat' and English *flat*, and denote etymologically 'flat surface.'

► flat

**flora** [16] Latin *flōs* meant 'flower' (it was the source of English *flower*). From it was derived *Flora*, the name given to the Roman goddess of flowers. English took over the term in this mythological sense, and in the 17th century it began to be used in the titles of botanical works (for example John Ray's *Flora, seu de florum cultura* 'Flora, or concerning the cultivation of flowers'). In particular, it was used for books describing all the plants in a particular area or country, and in the 18th century it came, like its animal counterpart *fauna*, to be applied as a collective term to such plants. The adjective *floral* [17] comes from Latin *flōs*.

► flower

**florid** see FLOWER

**florin** [14] *Florin* came via Old French *florin* from Italian *fiorino*, a diminutive of *fiore* 'flower.' This was used as the name of a gold coin first issued in Florence, Italy in 1252, which had the figure of a lily on its obverse side. In the 15th century it was adopted as the term for an English gold coin worth variously 6 shillings and 6 shillings and 8 pence, issued in the reign of Edward III, and it was revived in 1849 when a new 2 shilling silver coin was issued.

► flower

**florist** see FLOWER

**flotilla** see FLOAT

**flour** [13] Etymologically, *flour* is the same word as *flower*. It originally meant the 'flower,' or 'finest part,' of ground grain, and hence eventually just 'ground (and more or less sifted) grain.' The distinction in spelling between *flour* and *flower* did not emerge until the late 18th century, and the spelling *flower* for 'flour' persisted into the early 19th century.

► flower

**flourish** [13] To *flourish* is etymologically to 'flower' – and indeed 'come into flower, bloom' is originally what the verb literally meant in English: 'to smell the sweet savour of the vine when it flourisheth,' Geoffrey Chaucer, *Parson's Tale* 1386. The metaphorical 'thrive' developed in the 14th century. The word comes from Old French *floriss-*, the stem of *florir* 'bloom,' which goes back via Vulgar Latin *\*florīre* to classical Latin *florēre*, a derivative of *flōs* 'flower.'

▶ flower

**flow** [OE] The prehistoric Indo-European *\*pleu-*, ancestor of a heterogeneous range of English vocabulary, from *fleet* to *plover*, denoted 'flow, float.' It had a variant form *\*plō-*, which passed into Germanic as *\*flō-*. This formed the basis of the Old English verb *flōwan* (whence modern English *flow*) and also of the noun *flood*.

▶ fleet, flood, fowl, plover, pluvial

**flower** [13] The Old English word for 'flower' was *blōstm*, which is ultimately related to *flower*. Both come from Indo-European *\*bhlō-*, which probably originally meant 'swell,' and also gave English *bloom*, *blade*, and the now archaic *blow* 'come into flower.' Its Latin descendant was *flōs*, whose stem form *flōr-* passed via Old French *flour* and Anglo-Norman *flur* into English, where it gradually replaced *blossom* as the main word for 'flower.'

Close English relatives include *floral*, *florid* [17] (from Latin *flōridus*), *florin*, *florist* [17] (an English coinage), *flour*, and *flourish*.

▶ blade, bloom, blow, floral, florid, flour, flourish

**flu** [19] *Flu* is short for *influenza* [18]. The first record of its use is in a letter of 1839 by the poet Robert Southey (who spelled it, as was commonly the practice in the 19th century, *flue*): 'I have had a pretty fair share of the Flue.' *Influenza* means literally 'influence' in Italian, and was used metaphorically for the 'outbreak of a particular disease' (hence an *influenza di febbre scarlattina* was an 'outbeak of scarlet fever,' a 'scarlet fever epidemic'). The severe epidemic of the disease we now know as *flu*, which struck Italy in 1743 and spread from there throughout Europe, was called an *influenza di catarro* 'catarrh epidemic,' or simply an *influenza* – and hence *influenza* became the English word for the disease.

▶ influence, influenza

**fluctuate** see FLUX

**fluent** see FLUX

**fluid** see FLUX

**flush** see FLUX

**flute** [14] Provençal *flaut* was probably the original source of *flute*, and it reached English via Old French *floute* or *floite*. Where *flaut* came from, however, is another matter, and a much disputed one. Some

etymologists claim that it is ultimately simply an imitation of a high-pitched sound, its initial consonant cluster perhaps provided by Provençal *flajol* 'small flute or whistle' (source of English *flageolet* [17], but itself of unknown origin) and Latin *flāre* 'blow'; others suggest a specific blend of *flajol* with Provençal *laut*, source of English *lute*. The sense 'groove' developed in English in the 17th century, from a comparison with the long thin shape of the instrument.

Related forms in English include *flautist* [19], whose immediate source, Italian *flautisto*, preserves the *au* diphthong of the Provençal source word *flaut* (American English prefers the older, native English formation *flutist* [17]); and perhaps *flout* [16], which may come from Dutch *fluiten* 'play the flute,' hence 'whistle at, mock.'

▶ flout

**flux** [14] *Flux* denotes generally 'flowing,' and comes from Latin *fluxus*, a derivative of the past participle of *fluere* 'flow.' This verb, similar in form and meaning to English *flow* but in fact unrelated to it, is responsible for a very wide range of English words: its past participle has given us *fluctuate* [17], its present participle *fluent* [16] and a spectrum of derived forms, such as *affluent*, *effluent* [18], and *influence*, and other descendants include *fluid* [15] (literally 'flowing,' from Latin *fluidus*), *mellifluous* (literally 'flowing with honey'), *superfluous* [15], and *fluvial* [14] (from Latin *fluvius* 'river,' a derivative of *fluere*). Latin *fluxus* also produced the card-playing term *flush* [16].

▶ affluent, effluent, fluctuate, fluent, fluid, influence, mellifluous, superfluous

**fly** [OE] Historically, 'move through the air' is something of a secondary semantic development for *fly*. Its distant Indo-European ancestor, *\*pleu-*, denoted rapid motion in general, and in particular 'flowing' or 'floating,' and it produced such offspring as Greek *pléo* 'sail, float' and Sanskrit *plu-* 'sail, swim,' as well as English *fleet*, *flood*, *flow*, *fowl*, *plover*, and *pluvial*. An extension to that base, *\*pleuk-*, gave rise to Lithuanian *plaukti* 'float, sail, swim,' and to prehistoric West and North Germanic *\*fleugan*, source of German *fliegen*, Dutch *vliegen*, Swedish *flyga*, and English *fly*, all meaning 'move with wings.' The insect-name *fly* is also of considerable antiquity, going back to a prehistoric Germanic derivative *\*fleugōn* or *\*fleugjōn*, but the origins of the adjective *fly* 'crafty, sharp' [19] are not known.

▶ fleet, flood, flow, fowl, plover, pluvial

**foal** [OE] *Foal* goes back to a prehistoric source meaning 'young, offspring,' which also produced Latin *puer* 'child' and English *pony, poultry, pullet, pullulate*, and even *pool* 'common fund.' Its main Germanic descendant was *\*folon*, which gave German *fohlen* and *füllen*, Dutch *veulen*, Swedish *föl*, and English *foal*, but another derivative of the same Germanic base produced English *filly* [15], probably borrowed from Old Norse *fylja*.

▶ filly, pony, pool, poultry, pullet, pullulate

**foam** [OE] *Foam* is an ancient word, with several relatives widespread among the Indo-European languages, all denoting generally 'substance made up of bubbles': Latin *pūmex*, for instance, from which English gets *pumice*, and probably Latin *spūma*, from which we get *spume* [14]. These and other forms, such as Sanskrit *phénas* and Russian *pena* 'foam,' point to a common Indo-European source *poimo-*, which produced prehistoric West Germanic *faimaz* – whence English *foam*.

▶ pumice, spume

**focus** [17] Latin *focus* meant 'fireplace,' and in post-classical times it came to be used for 'fire' itself – hence French *feu*, Italian *fuoco*, Spanish *fuego*, all meaning 'fire,' and hence too the English derivatives *fuel* and *fusillade*. The first writer known to have used it in its modern sense 'point of convergence' was the German astronomer Johannes Kepler, in 1604, but the reason for his choice of word is not clear. It may have been some metaphorical notion of the 'hearth' symbolizing the 'centre of the home,' but it has also been suggested that it may have been preceded and inspired by the use of *focus* for the 'burning point' of a mirror (not actually recorded until somewhat later). The philosopher Thomas Hobbes appears to have introduced the term into English, in 1656.

A medieval Latin derivative of *focus* was *focārius*, from which French got *foyer* 'hearth, home,' borrowed by English in the 19th century for a public entrance hall or lobby.

▶ foyer, fuel, fusillade

**fodder**   see FOOD

**foe** [OE] *Foe* is the modern descendant of the Old English noun *gefā* 'enemy,' a derivative of Germanic *faikh-*. This also produced the Old English adjective *fāh* 'hostile,' and was the ultimate source of modern English *feud*.

▶ feud

**foetus** [14] *Foetus* comes from Latin *fētus* 'giving birth, offspring,' which also gave English *fawn* 'young deer.' It was a noun use of the adjective *fētus* 'pregnant, productive,' from whose derivative *effētus* English got *effete*. Probably it was related to Latin *fēcundas* (source of English *fecund* [14]) and *fēlix* 'happy' (whence English *felicity*), and there could even be etymological links with *fēmina* 'woman,' from which English gets *feminine* and *female*.

▶ effete, fecund, felicity

**fog** [16] The word *fog* is something of a mystery. It first appears in the 14th century meaning 'long grass,' a use which persists in *Yorkshire fog*, the name of a spe-

cies of grass. This may be of Scandinavian origin. The relationship, if any, between *fog* 'grass' and *fog* 'mist' is not immediately clear, but it has been speculated that the adjective *foggy*, which to begin with referred to places overgrown with long grass, and then passed via 'of grassy wetlands' to 'boggy, marshy' may have given rise via this last sense to a noun *fog* denoting the misty exhalations from such marshy ground. A rather far-fetched semantic chain, perhaps, lacking documentary evidence at crucial points, and perhaps Danish *fog* 'spray, shower' may be closer to the real source.

**foible**   see FEEBLE

**foil** English has three separate words *foil*. The oldest, 'thwart' [13], originally meant 'trample.' It probably comes via Anglo-Norman *fuler* from Vulgar Latin *fullāre*, a derivative of Latin *fullō* 'person who cleans and bulks out cloth, originally by treading' (whence English *fuller* [OE]). *Foil* 'metallic paper' [14] comes via Old French from Latin *folium* 'leaf' (source also of English *foliage* [15] and *folio* [16]). It originally meant 'leaf' in English too, but that usage died out in the 15th century. The modern notion of 'one that enhances another by contrast' comes from the practice of backing a gem with metal foil to increase its brilliancy. (Latin *folium*, incidentally, goes back to an Indo-European *bhel-*, an extended form of which, *bhlō-*, produced English *blade, bloom, blossom*, and *flower*.) The source of *foil* 'sword ' [16] is not known, although the semantic development of *blade* from 'leaf' to 'cutting part' suggests the possibility that a similar process took place in the case of *foil* 'leaf.'

▶ fuller / blade, bloom, blossom, flower, foliage

**foist**   see FIST

**fold** [OE] The verb *fold* comes ultimately from the Indo-European base *pel-*, which also produced Latin *plicāre* 'fold' (source of or related to English *accomplice, complicated, explicit, perplex, plait, pleat, pliant, pliers, plight, ply, reply*, and *supple*) and the final element *-ple* or *-ble* in such words as *simple, double*, or *triple* (which are hence related to the parallel Germanic formations *twofold, threefold*, etc). Its Germanic descendant was *falthan*, from which were descended German *falten*, Dutch *vouwen*, Danish *folde*, and English *fold*. The noun *fold* 'enclosure for animals' is of Germanic origin (Dutch has the related *vaalt*), but its distant antecedents are unknown.

▶ accomplice, complicated, explicit, perplex, plait, pleat, pliers, plight, ply, reply, supple

**foliage**   see FOIL

**folio**   see FOIL

**folk** [OE] *Folk* comes from a prehistoric Germanic *folkam*, which also produced German and Dutch *volk* and Swedish and Danish *folk*. It is not clear where this came from, although it has been linked with the Indo-European base *pel-, *plē- 'fill,' which might also have produced Latin *populus* 'people.' On the other hand Russian *polk*, thought to have been borrowed from the Germanic form, means 'division of an army,' and it is conceivable that this may preserve an earlier semantic stratum, represented also in Old Norse *folk*, which signified both 'people' and 'army.'

**follow** [OE] *Follow* is a widespread Germanic verb (German has *folgen*, for instance, Dutch *volgen*, Swedish *följa*, and Danish *følge*, pointing to a prehistoric West and North Germanic *fulg-), but its ultimate origins are not known.

**folly** see FOOL

**foment** see FAVOUR

**fond** [14] *Fond* originally meant 'foolish,' and the likeliest explanation of its rather problematic origin is that it was a derivative of the Middle English noun *fon* 'fool' (its Middle English spelling *fonned* suggests that it was formed with the suffix *-ed*, just as *wretched* was formed from *wretch*). However, where *fon* (probably a relative of modern English *fun*) comes from is another matter. Links with Swedish *fåne* 'fool' have been suggested but never established for certain. The adjective's modern meaning 'having a great liking,' incidentally, developed in the 16th century via an intermediate 'foolishly doting.'

*Fondle* [17] is a back-formation from the now obsolete *fondling* 'foolish person,' a derivative of *fond*.
▸ fondle, fun

**font** English has two words *font*. The older, 'basin for baptismal water' [OE], comes from *font-*, the stem of Latin *fons* 'spring, fountain' (from which English also gets *fountain*). It may well have been introduced into the language via Old Irish *fant* or *font* (it was often spelled *fant* in Old English). *Font* 'set of type' [16] (or *fount*, as it is often also spelled) was borrowed from French *fonte*, a derivative of *fondre* 'melt' (whence also English *fondant, fondu*, and *foundry*).
▸ fountain / fondant, foundry

**food** [OE] *Food* and its Germanic relatives, German *futter* 'fodder,' Dutch *voedsel* 'food,' and Swedish *föda* 'food,' all go back ultimately to a prehistoric Indo-European base *pā-, *pī-, which also produced Latin *pābulum* 'fodder,' Russian *pisca* 'food,' and Czech *pice* 'fodder.' The immediate source of all the Germanic forms was *fōth-*, which had two important derivatives: *fōthram*, which gave English *fodder* [OE] and (via Old French) *forage* [14] and *foray* [14] (etymologically probably a 'search for food'); and *fōstrom*, source of English *foster*.
▸ feed, fodder, forage, foray, foster

**fool** [13] *Fool* comes via Old French *fol* from Latin *follis*, which originally meant 'bellows' (and may come ultimately from Indo-European *bhel-, which

produced English *bellows*). In post-classical times it developed semantically via 'windbag' and 'fatuous person' to 'idiot.' *Fool* 'dessert of puréed fruit and cream' [16] appears to be the same word, applied (like *trifle*) to a light insubstantial dessert. *Folly* [13] comes from the Old French derivative *folie*.
▸ folly

**foot** [OE] *Foot* traces its ancestry back to Indo-European *pōd-, *ped-, which provided the word for 'foot' in most modern Indo-European languages (the exceptions are the Slavic languages, whose 'foot'-words, such as Russian *noga* and Czech *noha*, come from a source that meant 'claw,' and the Celtic languages – such as Welsh *troed* and Irish *troigh*). Descendants include Greek *poús* 'foot' (whence English *antipodes, pew, podium* [18], and *tripod*, literally 'three-footed,' a formation mirrored exactly by Latin *trivet* [15] and Hindi *teapoy* [19]), Persian *pāē* or *pay* (whence English *pyjama*), Sanskrit *pādas* 'foot' (source of *pie* 'unit of Indian currency'), and Lithuanian *pedà* 'footstep,' but the most fruitful of all from the point of view of the English lexicon has been Latin *pēs*, source of *impede, pawn* 'chess piece,' *pedal, pedestal, pedestrian, pedicure, pedigree, pedometer, peon, pioneer, quadruped, vamp*, and *velocipede* (it also, of course, gave French *pied*, Italian *piede*, and Spanish *pie*). Its Germanic descendant was *fōt-*, which produced German *fuss*, Dutch *voet*, Swedish *fot*, Danish *fod*, and English *foot*. Other related forms in English include *pilot* and *trapeze*.
▸ antipodes, impede, pawn, pedal, pedestal, pedestrian, pedigree, pilot, pioneer, podium, pyjamas, quadruped, trapeze, tripod, vamp

**footle** [19] *Footling* appears to have originated as a euphemistic equivalent to *fucking*. It probably comes from a dialectal *footer* 'mess about, fuck around,' which may well have been acquired from French *foutre* 'copulate with,' a descendant of Latin *futuere* 'copulate with' (whose origin is not known).

**footpad** see PAD

**for** [OE] *For* comes from a prehistoric Germanic *fora*, which denoted 'before' – both 'before' in time and 'in front' in place. *For* itself meant 'before' in the Old English period, and the same notion is preserved in related forms such as *first, fore, foremost, former, from*, and of course *before*. Germanic *fora* itself goes back to Indo-European *pr*, source also of Latin *prae* 'before,' *pro* 'for,' and *primus* 'first' (whence English *premier, primary*, etc), Greek *pará* 'by, past,' *pró* 'before,' and *protos* 'first' (whence English *protocol, prototype*, etc), and English *forth* and *further*.
▸ before, first, fore, former, forth, from, further, premier, primary

**forage**    see FOOD

**foray**    see FOOD

**forbid**    [OE] *Forbid* is a compound verb that appears to have been coined in prehistoric Germanic times from the prefix *\*fer-*, denoting negation or exclusion (as in *forget*) and *\*bithjan*, source of English *bid* – hence, 'command not to do something.' It produced German *verbieten* and Dutch *verbieden* 'forbid' as well as English *forbid*.

▶ bid

**force**    [13] The ultimate source of *force* is Latin *fortis* 'strong,' which also gave English *comfort, effort, fort*, etc. In post-classical times a noun was formed from it, *\*fortia* 'strength,' which passed into English via Old French *force*. (The *force* of *forcemeat* [17], incidentally, is a variant of *farce*, in its original sense 'stuff,' and is not etymologically related to *force* 'strength.')

▶ comfort, effort, fort

**ford**    [OE] *Ford* is an ancient word, whose origins can be traced back as far as prehistoric Indo-European *\*prtús*, a derivative of *\*por-* 'going, passage,' which also produced English *fare* and *ferry*. Descendants of *\*prtús* include Latin *portus* 'harbour' (source of English *port*), Welsh *rhyd* 'ford,' West Germanic *\*furduz* (whence German *furt* 'ford' and English *ford*) and North Germanic *\*ferthuz* (source of English *fiord* or *fjord* [17] and *firth* [15]).

▶ fare, ferry, fiord, firth, fjord, ford, port

**foreign**    [13] Etymologically, *foreign* means 'out of doors.' It comes via Old French *forein* from Vulgar Latin *\*forānus*, a derivative of Latin *forās* 'out of doors, abroad.' This originated as the accusative plural of *\*fora*, an unrecorded variant form of *forēs* 'door' (to which English *door* is related). The literal sense 'outdoor' survived into Middle English (the *chambre forene* mentioned by Robert of Gloucester in his *Chronicle* 1297, for instance, was an 'outside loo'), but by the early 15th century the metaphorical 'of other countries, abroad' had more or less elbowed it aside.

▶ door, forest, forfeit

**foremost**    see FORMER

**forensic**    see FORUM

**forest**    [13] The underlying sense of *forest* appears to be 'outside wooded area.' It comes from the late Latin phrase *forestis silva* (Latin *silva* means 'wood'), which was applied to the royal forests of Charlemagne. The adjective *forestis* (which became the Old French noun *forest*) was probably a derivative of Latin *forīs* 'outdoor, outside,' which, like *forās* (source of English *foreign*), was related to Latin *forēs* 'door.' In this context, 'outside' presumably meant 'beyond the main or central fenced area of woodland.'

▶ door, foreign, forfeit

**forfeit**    [13] A *forfeit* was originally a 'transgression' or 'misdemeanour.' The word comes from Old French *forfet*, a derivative of the verb *forfaire* or *forsfaire* 'commit a crime.' This was a compound formed from *fors-* 'beyond (what is permitted or legal),' which is descended from Latin *forīs* 'outdoor, outside' (source of English *forest* and related to *foreign*), and *faire* 'do, act,' which came from Latin *facere* (whence English *fact, fashion, feature*, etc). The etymological meaning 'misdeed' was originally taken over from Old French into Middle English ('Peter was in hand nummen [taken] for forfait he had done,' *Cursor mundi* 1300), but by the 15th century it was being edged out by 'penalty imposed for committing such a misdeed.'

▶ door, fact, factory, fashion, forest, foreign

**forfend**    see DEFEND

**forge**    *Forge* 'make' [13] and *forge ahead* [17] are two quite distinct and unrelated words in English. The former's now common connotation of 'faking' is in fact a purely English development (dating from the late 14th century) in a word whose relatives in other languages (such as French *forger*) mean simply 'make – especially by working heated metal.' It comes via Old French *forger* from Latin *fabricāre* 'make' (source also of English *fabricate*, which has similarly dubious connotations). The related noun *forge* goes back to Latin *fabrica* (whence also English *fabric*), amongst whose specialized senses was 'blacksmith's workshop.'

*Forge* 'move powerfully,' as in *forge ahead*, may be an alteration of *force*.

▶ fabric

**forget**    [OE] From a formal point of view, *forget* is exactly what it seems – a combination of *for* and *get*. However, this is not the modern English preposition *for*, but a prefix that in former times was a live building block of the language, denoting negation or exclusion. So here, *forget*'s Germanic ancestor *\*fergetan* meant literally 'not get,' hence 'lose one's hold on' and metaphorically 'lose one's memory of.'

▶ get

**forgive**    [OE] *Forgive* is what is known technically as a 'calque' or loan translation – that is, it was created by taking the component parts of a foreign word, translating them literally, and then putting them back together to form a new word. In this case the foreign word was Latin *perdōnāre* 'forgive' (source of English *pardon*), which was a compound verb formed from *per-* 'thoroughly' and *dōnāre* 'give' (its underlying sense was 'give wholeheartedly'). These two elements were translated in prehistoric Germanic times and assembled to give *\*fergeban*, from which have come German *vergeben*, Dutch *vergeven*, and English *forgive*.

▶ give

**fork** [OE] *Fork* comes from Latin *furca*, a word of unknown origin which denoted 'two-pronged fork or stake.' It provided most of the Romance and Celtic languages with their terms for 'fork,' as well as English (French *fourche*, for instance, Italian *forca*, Spanish *horca*, Welsh *fforch*, and Breton *forc'h*). The term was not widely used for 'table forks' until they came into general use, from Italy, in the 15th and 16th centuries; several languages have used diminutive forms in this context, such as French *fourchette* and Rumanian *furculita*. *Bifurcate* [17] is a derivative, descended from Latin *bifurcus* 'two-pronged.'

▶ bifurcate, carfax

**forlorn** [12] *Forlorn* began life as the past participle of Old English *forlēosan* 'lose completely, forfeit, abandon,' a compound verb formed in prehistoric Germanic times from the intensive prefix *\*fer-* and *\*leusan* (a relative of modern English *lose*). It retains some of its early connotations of being 'abandoned,' but the main modern sense 'miserable, downcast' developed in the 14th century. The *forlorn* of *forlorn hope* [16], incidentally, is a translation of the related Dutch *verloren* 'lost,' but *hope* has no etymological connection with English *hope*. It is simply an anglicization of Dutch *hoop* 'troop, band' (to which English *heap* is related). The word was originally used for a squad of soldiers sent out on a very dangerous mission, with little hope that they would return. The modern sense 'hopeless undertaking' developed in the 17th century, 'misguided hope' probably even more recently.

▶ lose

**form** [13] *Form* comes via Old French *forme* from Latin *forma* 'shape, contour,' a word whose origins have never been satisfactorily explained. Its semantic similarity to Greek *morphḗ* 'form, shape' (source of English *morphology* [19]) is striking, and has led some etymologists to suggest that the Latin word may be an alteration of the Greek one, presumably by metathesis (the reversal of sounds, in this case /m/ and /f/). Another possibility, however, is that it comes from *ferīre* 'strike,' from the notion of an impression, image, or shape being created by beating. Of the word's wide diversity of modern senses, 'school class,' a 16th-century introduction, was inspired by the late Latin usage *forma prima, forma secunda*, etc for different orders of clergy, while 'bench' may go back to the Old French expression *s'asseoir en forme* 'sit in a row.' Amongst *forma*'s derivatives that have found their way into English are *formal* [14], *format* [19], *formula* [17] (from a Latin diminutive form), and *uniform*.

▶ formal, format, formula, inform, uniform

**formaldehyde**    see ANT

**former** [12] *Former* is a comparative form based on Middle English *forme* 'first (in time or order),' on the analogy of the superlative *foremost* [16] (which

was originally *formost* [12]; the modern spelling came about through association with *fore* and *most*). *Forme* itself goes back to Old English *forma*, which was a descendant of a prehistoric Germanic superlative form derived from *\*fora* 'before' (whence also English *first, for,* and *fore*). So untangling the suffixal accretions of centuries, *former* means etymologically 'more most before.'

▶ first, for, fore, primary

**formic acid**    see ANT

**formidable** [15] Latin *formīdō* meant 'fear' (it may have links with Greek *mormṓ* 'bugbear, goblin,' which came from an Indo-European *\*mormo*). From it was derived the verb *formīdāre*, which in turn produced the adjective *formīdābilis*, which English originally acquired in the literal sense 'inspiring fear.' The weaker 'impressive in size, difficulty, etc' is a 17th-century development.

**formula**    see FORM

**fornication** [13] Latin *fornix* denoted an 'arch' or 'vault,' and hence came to be used in the late republican period for the sort of vaulted underground dwellings where the dregs of Roman society – tramps, prostitutes, petty criminals, etc – lived. Early Christian writers homed in on the prostitutes, and employed the term with the specific meaning 'brothel,' whence the verb *fornicārī* 'have illicit sexual intercourse' and its derivative *fornicātiō*, source of English *fornication*.

**forsake**    see SAKE

**fort** [15] Etymologically, a *fort* is a 'strong place.' The word comes either from Old French *fort* or from Italian *forte*, both noun uses of an adjective descended from Latin *fortis* 'strong.' A similar semantic result, but achieved by derivation rather than conversion, can be seen in *fortress* [13], a borrowing from Old French *forteresse*, which goes back to Vulgar Latin *\*fortaritia*, a derivative of Latin *fortis*. (The nearest native English equivalent of both words is *stronghold*.) Other words inherited by English from *fortis* include *fortify* [15], *fortitude* [15], the noun *forte* 'strong point' [17] (it was borrowed, despite its modern Italianate pronunciation, from French *fort*, and was subsequently remodelled on the French feminine form *forte*), and the musical direction *forte* 'loud' [18] (from Italian), which appears also in *pianoforte*.

▶ force, fortify, fortress

**forth** [OE] *Forth* can be traced back to the same Indo-European source, *\*pr*, as produced English *first, for, fore, foremost, former, from,* and *before*. It formed the basis of a word *\*prto* 'forwards,' whose Germanic descendant *\*furtha* gave German *fort*, Dutch *voort*, and English *forth*. Modern English *forward(s)* [OE], which has largely replaced *forth* in general use, was originally a compound formed from *forth* and *-ward*. Other related forms include *afford*, which originally meant 'accomplish, fulfil,' *forthwith* [14], at first literally 'along with,' hence 'at the same time as' and 'immediately,' and *further*.

▶ afford, before, first, for, fore, former, from, further

**fortnight** [13] The ancient Germanic peoples recorded the passing of time in units of 'nights' rather than, as we do, in units of 'days': hence a period of two weeks was in Old English *fēowertīene niht*, or 'fourteen nights.' By early Middle English times this was starting to be contracted to the single word *fortnight*. (The parallel *sennight* 'week' [15] – literally 'seven nights' – survived dialectally into the 20th century.)

▶ fourteen

**fortress** see FORT

**fortune** [13] Latin *fors* meant 'chance' (it came ultimately from Indo-European *\*bhrtis*, a derivative of the same base as produced English *bear* 'carry,' and hence signified etymologically 'that which fate brings along'). Formed from *fors* was *fortuna*, which was used both for the personification of 'chance' as a goddess, and for 'luck' in general – and in particular for 'good luck.' The notion of 'good luck' persists in most of the word's modern descendants, including English *fortune* (acquired via Old French *fortune*) and *fortunate* [14], although Italian *fortunale* has opted for the downside of 'luck' – it means 'storm at sea.'

Another derivative of Latin *fors* was the adjective *fortuitus* 'happening by chance,' from which English gets *fortuitous* [17].

▶ bear, fortuitous

**forum** [15] Originally Latin *forum* denoted an 'out-of-doors place' – it was related to *forīs* 'out-of-doors, outside' and to *forēs* 'door,' a distant cousin of English *door*. It came to be used for any outdoor open space or public place, and in particular for a market place (the most famous of which was the one in Rome, where public assemblies, tribunals, etc were held). Other English words from the same source are *foreign*, *forest*, and *forensic* 'of legal proceedings' [17] (from Latin *forēnsis* 'of a forum as a place of public discussion').

▶ door, foreign, forensic, forest

**forward** see FORTH

**fossil** [17] Etymologically, a *fossil* is something 'dug' out of the ground. It comes via French *fossile* from Latin *fossilis* 'dug up,' a derivative of the verb *fodere* 'dig.' The English adjective originally meant virtually the same as Latin *fossilis* ('Seven unmixt fossil Metals are forecited,' Robert Vilvain, *Epitome of Essais* 1654), and this sense survives in the present-day expression *fossil fuel*, but the word's main modern connotation 'excavated relic of a former life-form' had begun to emerge by the mid 17th century.

**foster** [OE] The etymological notion underlying *foster* is of 'giving food.' Indeed, the Old English verb *fōstrian* meant 'feed, nourish,' and it was not until the 13th century that secondary metaphorical senses, such as 'rear a child' and 'encourage, cultivate,' began to emerge. It was a derivative of the Old English noun *fōstor* 'food,' which in turn was formed from the same Germanic source, *\*fōth-*, as produced English *food*.

▶ food

**foul** [OE] The underlying meaning of *foul* is probably 'rotten, putrid,' with overtones of 'evil-smelling.' It goes back to an Indo-European *\*pu-*, which may originally have been inspired by the same reaction as produced the English exclamation of disgust at a bad smell, *pooh*. Amongst its other offspring were Latin *pūs*, source of English *pus*, *purulent*, and *supurate*, and Latin *putridus*, source of English *putrid*. Its Germanic descendant was *\*fu-*, on which the adjective *\*fūlaz* was based. This produced German *faul* 'rotten, lazy,' Dutch *vuil* 'dirty,' and English *foul*, and also the derived noun *filth* [OE]. *Defile* 'make dirty' is not directly related, but its form was influenced by the now obsolete verb *befile*, which was connected with *foul*.

▶ filth, pus, putrid, suppurate

**found** Aside from the past form of *find*, there are two distinct words *found* in English. *Found* 'establish' [13] comes via Old French *fonder* from Latin *fundāre*, a derivative of *fundus* 'bottom' (which, like English *bottom*, goes back ultimately to Indo-European *\*bhud-* or *\*bhund-*). The Latin words also gave English *founder*, *fund* and *fundamental*. *Found* 'melt' [14], which is now mainly represented by the derived *foundry* [17], comes via Old French *fondre* from Latin *fundere* 'pour, melt.' This goes back to Indo-European *\*ghud-*, *\*gheud-*, from which English also gets *ingot*. Amongst related forms in English are (from French *fondre*) *font*, *fondant*, and *fondu*, (from Latin *fundere*) *funnel*, (from the Latin past participle *fūsus*) *fuse* and *fusion*, and (from *\*fud-*, the immediate root of Latin *fundere*) *futile* [16], which etymologically means 'that pours away,' hence 'useless.'

▶ bottom, founder, fund, fundamental / fondant, funnel, fuse, fusion, futile, ingot

**founder** [13] Etymologically, *founder* means 'sink to the bottom.' Its history can be traced back to Latin *fundus* 'bottom' (source also of English *found* 'establish,' *fund*, and *fundamental*), which formed the basis of a Vulgar Latin verb *\*fundorāre*. This passed into Old French *fondrer*, which meant 'submerge,' but also, by extension, 'fall in ruins, collapse' – both of which groups of senses English took over in *founder*.

▶ found, fund, fundamental

**fountain** [15] Latin *fons* meant 'spring of water' (it was related to Sanskrit *dhan-* 'run, flow'). The feminine form of its adjectival derivative, *fontāna* 'of a spring,' came to be used in late Latin as a noun, also meaning 'spring,' and this passed via Old French *fontaine* into English, still carrying its original sense 'spring' with it. This survives in the reduced form *fount* [16], which is usually used metaphorically for a 'source,' but *fountain* itself has from the 16th century been mainly applied to an 'artificial jet of water.' Other descendants of Latin *fontāna*, incidentally, include Italian *fontana*, Rumanian *fîntîna*, and Welsh *ffynon*.

*Fontanelle* 'space between infant's skull bones' [16] comes ultimately from Old French *fontenelle*, a diminutive form of *fontaine*. The underlying notion appears to be of an anatomical 'hollow,' as if from which a spring of water would come.

▸ fontanelle, fount

**four** [OE] The distant Indo-European ancestor of English *four* was *qwetwōr-*, which also produced Latin *quattuor* (whence French *quatre*, Italian *quattro*, Spanish *cuatro*, etc), Greek *téssares*, Sanskrit *catvāras*, Russian *chetvero*, and Welsh *pedwar*. Its Germanic descendant was *petwor-*, from which come German and Dutch *vier*, Swedish *fyra*, and English *four*. Amongst the word's perhaps more surprising relatives in English are *carfax* 'crossroads' (ultimately from a post-classical Latin compound which meant literally 'four forks'), *quarantine* (denoting etymologically a 'period of 40 days'), *quire* 'set of four sheets of paper,' and *trapeze* (literally 'four-footed').

▸ carfax, quarantine, quire, trapeze

**fowl** [OE] *Fowl* was the main term for 'bird' in the Old English period, but in Middle English it was gradually replaced by *bird*. (It remains in use in compounds, such as *wildfowl* and *waterfowl*, and is sometimes still applied to 'chickens.') It goes back to a prehistoric Germanic *foglaz* or *fuglaz*, which also produced the still very much current German and Dutch *vogel*, Swedish *fåagel*, and Danish *fugl*, all signifying 'bird,' and which may have been a derivative of the same source (*fleug-*) as gave English *fly* – in which case *fowl* would mean literally 'flying creature.'

▸ fly

**fox** [OE] *Fox* probably means literally 'tailed animal' – the fox's brush being perhaps its most distinctive feature. It has been traced back to a prehistoric Indo-European *puk-*, which also produced Sanskrit *púcchas* 'tail.' In West Germanic this gave *fukhs*, from which come German *fuchs*, Dutch *vos*, and English *fox*. The fox is also named after its tail in Spanish (*raposa* 'fox' is a derivative of *rabo* 'tail') and in Welsh (*llwynog* 'fox' comes from *llwyn* 'bush' – that is, 'bushy tail').

**fraction** [14] Like *fracture* [15], which preserves its etymological meaning more closely, *fraction* comes ultimately from *fractus*, the past participle of Latin *frangere* 'break.' This verb goes back to prehis-

toric Indo-European *bhr(e)g-*, which also produced English *break*. The Latin derived noun *fractiō* simply meant 'breaking,' particularly with reference to the breaking of Communion bread, but all trace of this literal sense has now virtually died out in English, leaving only the mathematical sense 'number produced by division' and its metaphorical offshoots. Amongst the English meanings that have disappeared is 'discord, quarreling,' but before it went it produced *fractious* [18].

▸ fracture, fragile, frail

**fragile** [17] *Fragile* and *frail* [13] are doublets: that is to say, they have the same ultimate source but have evolved in different ways. In this case the source was Latin *fragilis* 'breakable,' a derivative of the same base (*frag-*) as produced *frangere* 'break' (whence English *fractious*). *Fragile* was acquired either directly from the Latin adjective or via French *fragile*, but *frail* passed through Old French *frale* or *frele* on its way to English. Other English words to come from *frag-* include *fragment* [15] (from Latin *fragmentum*) and *saxifrage*, literally 'rock-breaker.'

▸ fraction, fracture, fragment, frail, saxifrage

**frame** [OE] *Frame* comes from the preposition *from*, whose underlying notion is of 'forward progress.' This was incorporated into a verb *framian* in Old English times, which meant 'make progress.' Its modern meaning started to develop in the early Middle English period, from 'prepare, make ready,' via the more specific 'prepare timber for building,' to 'construct, shape' (the Middle English transitive uses may have been introduced by the related Old Norse *fremja*). The noun *frame* was derived from the verb in the 14th century. Incidentally, if the connection between *from* and *frame* should seem at first sight far-fetched, it is paralleled very closely by *furnish*, which came from the same prehistoric Germanic source as *from*.

▸ from

**franc** SEE FRANK

**franchise** [13] Originally, *franchise* meant 'freedom' (as it still does in French today): 'We will for our franchise fight and for our land,' Robert of Gloucester's *Chronicle* 1297. Gradually, though, it became more specialized in sense, narrowing down via 'particular legal privilege' to (in the 18th century) 'right to vote.' It comes from Old French *franchise*, a derivative of *franc* 'free' (whence English *frank*).

▸ frank

**frank** [13] To call someone *frank* is to link them with the Germanic people who conquered Gaul around 500AD, the Franks, who gave their name to modern France and the French. After the conquest, full political freedom was granted only to ethnic Franks or to those of the subjugated Celts who were specifically brought under their protection. Hence, *franc* came to be used as

an adjective meaning 'free' – a sense it retained when English acquired it from Old French: 'He was frank and free born in a free city,' John Tiptoft, *Julius Caesar's commentaries* 1470. In both French and English, however, it gradually progressed semantically via 'liberal, generous' and 'open' to 'candid.' Of related words in English, *frankincense* [14] comes from Old French *franc encens*, literally 'superior incense' ('superior' being a now obsolete sense of French *franc*), and *franc* [14], the French unit of currency, comes from the Latin phrase *Francorum rex* 'king of the Franks,' which appeared on the coins minted during the reign of Jean le Bon (1350–64). The Franks, incidentally, supposedly got their name from their preferred weapon, the throwing spear, in Old English *franca*.
▶ French

**frantic** [14] *Frantic* comes via Old French *frenetique* and Latin *phreneticus* from late Greek *phrenētikús*, a derivative of *phrenîtis* 'delirium.' This in turn was based on Greek *phrén* 'mind' (source also of English *phrenology* 'study of cranial bumps to determine intelligence, character, etc' [19]). The Old French form split into two virtually distinct words once English got hold of it: in one, the French three-syllable form was preserved, and even partially remodelled on its Latin ancestor, to give what has become modern English *phrenetic*, while in the other it was reduced to *frentik* which, for reasons that have never been satisfactorily explained, subsequently became *frantic*. The related noun *frenzy* [14] retains the original vowel.
▶ frenzy, phrenology

**fraternal** [15] Etymologically as well as semantically, *fraternal* is 'brotherly.' It comes from *frāternālis*, a medieval Latin derivative of Latin *frāter* 'brother.' This goes back to the same prehistoric Indo-European source, *\*bhrāter*, as produced English *brother*. The Latin accusative form, *frātrem*, produced French *frère* 'brother,' from which English gets *friar* [13].
▶ brother, friar, pal

**fraud**   see FRUSTRATE

**fraught** [14] *Fraught* and *freight* [15] are related, and share the underlying meaning 'load.' But whereas *freight* has stayed close to its semantic roots, *fraught*, which started out as 'laden,' has moved on via 'supplied or filled with something' to specifically 'filled with anxiety or tension.' It was originally the past participle of a now obsolete verb *fraught* 'load a ship,' which was borrowed from Middle Dutch *vrachten*. This in turn was a derivative of the noun *vracht* 'load, cargo,' a variant of *vrecht* (from which English gets *freight*). Both *vracht* and *vrecht* probably go back to a prehistoric Germanic noun *\*fraaikhtiz*, whose second element *\*-aikhtiz* is related to English *owe* and *own*.
▶ freight

**free** [OE] The prehistoric ancestor of *free* was a term of affection uniting the members of a family in a common bond, and implicitly excluding their servants or slaves – those who were not 'free.' It comes ultimately from Indo-European *\*prijos*, whose signification 'dear, beloved' is revealed in such collateral descendants as Sanskrit *priyás* 'dear,' Russian *prijatel'* 'friend,' and indeed English *friend*. Its Germanic offspring, *\*frijaz*, displays the shift from 'affection' to 'liberty,' as shown in German *frei*, Dutch *vrij*, Swedish and Danish *fri*, and English *free*. Welsh *rhydd* 'free' comes from the same Indo-European source.
▶ Friday, friend

**freebooter**   see FILIBUSTER

**freeze** [OE] *Freeze* is an ancient word, which traces its history back to Indo-European *\*preus-* (source also of Latin *pruīna* 'hoarfrost'). Its Germanic descendant was *\*freusan*, from which come German *frieren*, Dutch *vriezen*, Swedish *frysa*, and English *freeze*. The noun *frost* [OE] was formed in the prehistoric Germanic period from a weakly stressed variant of the base of *\*freusan* plus the suffix *-t*.
▶ frost

**freight**   see FRAUGHT

**frenzy**   see FRANTIC

**frequent** [16] *Frequent* comes from Latin *frequēns*, which meant 'crowded' as well as 'regularly repeated' (it is not known what the origins of *frequēns* were, although it may be related to Latin *farcīre* 'stuff,' source of English *farce*). The sense 'crowded' was carried over into English along with 'regularly repeated,' but it had virtually died out by the end of the 18th century. The verb *frequent* [15] goes back to Latin *frequentāre* 'visit frequently or regularly.'

**fresh** [12] *Fresh* is of Germanic origin, but in its present form reached English via French. Its ultimate source was the prehistoric Germanic adjective *\*friskaz*, which also produced German *frisch*, Dutch *vers*, Swedish *färsk*, and possibly English *frisk* [16]. It was borrowed into the common source of the Romance languages as *\*friscus*, from which came French *frais* and Italian and Spanish *fresco* (the Italian form gave English *fresco* [16], painting done on 'fresh' – that is, still wet – plaster, and *alfresco* [18], literally 'in the fresh air'). English acquired *fresh* from the Old French predecessor of *frais, freis*. The colloquial sense 'making presumptuous sexual advances,' first recorded in the USA in the mid 19th century, probably owes much to German *frech* 'cheeky.'
▶ alfresco, fresco, frisk

**fret** English has three separate words *fret*. *Fret* 'irritate, distress' [OE] goes back to a prehistoric Germanic compound verb formed from the intensive prefix *\*fra-* and the verb *\*etan* (ancestor of English *eat*), which meant 'eat up, devour.' Its modern Germanic descendants include German *fressen* 'eat' (used of animals). In Old English, it gave *fretan*, which also meant 'devour,' but this literal meaning had died out by the early 15th century, leaving the figurative 'gnaw at, worry, distress.' *Fret* 'decorate with interlaced or pierced design' [14] (now usually encountered only in *fretted, fretwork*, and *fretsaw*) comes from Old French *freter*, a derivative of *frete* 'trellis, embossed or interlaced work,' whose origins are obscure. Also lost in the mists of time are the antecedents of *fret* 'ridge across the fingerboard of a guitar' [16].

▶ eat

**friar**   see FRATERNAL

**Friday**   [OE]   *Friday* was named for Frigg, in Scandinavian mythology the wife of Odin and goddess of married love and of the hearth (*Frigg*, or in Old English *Frīg*, is thought to have come from prehistoric Germanic *\*frijaz* 'noble,' source of English *free*). 'Frigg's day' was a direct adaptation of Latin *Veneris dies* 'Venus's day' (whence French *vendredi* 'Friday'), which in turn was based on Greek *Aphrodítēs hēméra* 'Aphrodite's day.'

▶ free

**friend**   [OE]   Etymologically, *friend* means 'loving.' It and its Germanic relatives (German *freund*, Dutch *vriend*, Swedish *frände*, etc) go back to the present participle of the prehistoric Germanic verb *\*frijōjan* 'love' (historically, the German present participle ends in *-nd*, as in modern German *-end*; English *-ng* is an alteration of this). *\*Frijōjan* itself was a derivative of the adjective *\*frijaz*, from which modern English gets *free*, but which originally meant 'dear, beloved.'

▶ free

**frieze**   [16]   Phrygia, in western and central Asia Minor, was noted in ancient times for its embroidery. Hence classical Latin *Phrygium* 'of Phrygia' was pressed into service in medieval Latin (as *frigium*, or later *frisium*) for 'embroidered cloth.' English acquired the word via Old French *frise*, by which time it had progressed semantically via 'fringe' to 'decorative band along the top of a wall.'

**fright**   [OE]   Prehistoric Germanic *\*furkhtaz*, an adjective of unknown origin (not related to English *fear*), meant 'afraid.' From it was derived a noun *\*furkhtīn*, which was the basis of one of the main words for 'fear' among the ancient Germanic languages (not superseded as the chief English term by *fear* until the 13th century). Its modern descendants include German *furcht* and English *fright* (in which the original sequence 'vowel plus *r*' was reversed by the process known as metathesis – something which also happened to Middle Low German *vruchte*, from which Swedish *fruktan* and Danish *frygt* 'fear' were borrowed).

**fringe**   [14]   Late Latin *fimbria* meant 'fibre, thread' (it is used in modern English as an anatomical term for a threadlike structure, such as the filaments at the opening of the Fallopian tube). In the plural it was applied to a 'fringe,' and eventually this meaning fed back into the singular. In Vulgar Latin *fimbria*, by the sound-reversal process known as metathesis, became *\*frimbia*, which passed into Old French as *fringe* or *frenge* – source of the English word.

**fritter**   see FRY

**frizz**   see FRY

**fro**   see FROM

**frock**   [14]   *Frock* is a Germanic word, although English acquired it via Old French *froc*. It originally meant 'long coat or tunic' – a sense reflected in the related Old High German *hroc* 'mantle, coat,' and preserved in English *frock coat* and *unfrock* 'dismiss from the office of clergyman' (*frock* once having denoted a 'priest's cassock,' and hence symbolized the priestly office). Its application to a 'woman's dress' dates from the 16th century.

**frog**   [OE]   *Frog* comes from Old English *frogga*, which probably started life as a playful alternative to the more serious *frosc* or *forsc*. This derived from the prehistoric Germanic *\*fruskaz*, which also produced German *frosch* and Dutch *vorsch*. Its use as a derogatory synonym for 'French person' goes back to the late 18th century, and was presumably inspired by the proverbial French appetite for the animals' legs (although in fact *frog* as a general term of abuse can be traced back to the 14th century, and in the 17th century it was used for 'Dutch person'). It is not clear whether *frog* 'horny wedge-shaped pad in a horse's hoof' [17] and *frog* 'ornamental braiding' [18] are the same word; the former may have been influenced by French *fourchette* and Italian *forchetta*, both literally 'little fork.'

**frolic**   [16]   Like its source, Dutch *vrolijk*, and the related German *fröhlich, frolic* was originally an adjective meaning 'happy.' This usage had died out by the end of the 18th century, but in the meantime the adjective had been converted into a verb, and thence into a noun, both of which are still with us. (Dutch *vrolijk* was formed from the adjective *vro* 'happy,' which probably goes back ultimately to a prehistoric Indo-European source which meant primarily 'spring upwards, move swiftly.')

**from**   [OE]   *From* goes back ultimately to Indo-European *\*pr*, which also produced English *first, for, fore, foremost, former*, and *before*. The addition of a suffix *-m* gave a word denoting 'forward movement, advancement' (as in Greek *prómos* 'foremost'). By the time it reached Old English as *from* or *fram* the notion of 'moving forward or onward' had passed into 'moving away.' The related *fro* [12], now little used except in *to and fro*, comes from Old Norse *frá*.

▶ before, first, for, fore, former, forth, fro, primary

**front**   [13]   As its close French relative *front* still does, *front* used to mean 'forehead.' Both come from Latin *frōns*, a word of dubious origins whose primary meaning was 'forehead,' but which already in the classical period was extending figuratively to the 'most forwardly prominent part' of anything. In present-day English, only distant memories remain of the original sense, in such contexts as 'put up a brave front' (a now virtually dead metaphor in which the forehead, and hence the countenance in general, once stood for the 'demeanour'). The related *frontier* [14], borrowed from Old French *frontiere*, originally meant 'front part'; its modern sense is a secondary development.

▶ frontier

**frontispiece**   [16]   The final syllable of *frontispiece* has no etymological connection with *piece*. It comes from *\*spic-*, a root denoting 'see' which is also represented in *conspicuous* and *spectator*. Here, as in the related *auspices*, its particular application is 'divination by observation.' Added to Latin *frōns* 'forehead' it produced late Latin *frontispicium*, which originally meant 'judgment of character through interpretation of facial features.' Gradually it weakened semantically through 'face' to simply 'front part,' and when English first acquired it, it was used for the 'principal façade of a building' ('an indiscreet builder, who preferreth the care of his frontispiece before the maine foundation,' Richard Brathwait, *English Gentleman* 1630). By the 17th century, however, the word's modern meaning 'illustration facing the title page' was becoming established. (Spellings based on an erroneous association with *piece*, incidentally, occur as early as the 16th century.)

▶ auspices, conspicuous, front, inspect, spectator, spy

**frost**   see FREEZE

**frown**   [14]   Probably the underlying notion of *frowning* is 'snorting' rather than 'wrinkling the brows.' It comes from Old French *froignier*, which meant 'snort' as well as 'frown.' It is assumed to have been adopted into French from a Celtic language of Gaul, and would therefore have been related to Welsh *ffroen* 'nostril.'

**fructify**   see FRUIT

**fructose**   see FRUIT

**frugal**   [16]   Paradoxically, *frugal* comes from a source that meant 'fruitful.' English borrowed it from Latin *frūgālis*, which was derived from the adjective *frūgī* 'useful.' This in turn was the dative case of the noun *frūx* 'fruit, value,' which came from the same base as *frūctus*, the source of English *fruit*. The links in the semantic chain seem to have been that something that

was 'useful, valuable, or productive' was also 'profitable,' and that in order to be 'profitable' it must be 'economical' – hence *frugal*'s connotations of 'careful expenditure.'

▶ fruit

**fruit**   [12]   English acquired *fruit* via Old French *fruit* from Latin *frūctus*, a source more clearly on display in *fructify* [14], *fructose* [19], etc. The underlying meaning of the Latin noun seems to have been 'enjoyment of that which is produced,' for it came, like *frūx* (source of English *frugal*), from a base which also produced the verb *fruī* 'enjoy.' By classical times, however, it had passed from 'enjoyment' to the 'product' itself – the 'rewards' of an enterprise, the 'return' on an investment, or the 'produce' obtained from the soil or from farm animals. When it reached English this latter meaning had narrowed down somewhat, but it was still capable of being used far more broadly, for any 'edible vegetable,' than we would do today, except in certain archaic expressions such as 'fruits of the earth.' The modern restriction to the edible reproductive body of a tree, bush, etc dates from the 13th century. English retains, of course, the more general sense 'product, result,' although this is now usually expressed by the plural *fruits*.

▶ fructify, frugal

**frustrate**   [15]   *Frustrate* comes from Latin *frūstrātus* 'disappointed, frustrated,' the past participle of a verb formed from the adverb *frūstrā* 'in error, in vain, uselessly.' This was a relative of Latin *fraus*, which originally meant 'injury, harm,' hence 'deceit' and then 'error' (its English descendant, *fraud* [14], preserves 'deceit'). Both go back to an original Indo-European *\*dhreu*-which denoted 'injure.'

▶ fraud

**fry**   *Fry* 'cook in fat' [13] and *fry* 'young fish' [14] are quite distinct words. The former comes via Old French *frire* from Latin *frīgere*, a cooking term which covered what we would now distinguish as 'roasting' and 'frying.' It goes back ultimately to Indo-European *\*bhreu*-, which also produced Latin *fervēre* 'boil' (source of English *fervent*). Its past participle *frictus* formed the basis of Vulgar Latin *\*frīctūra*, from which, via Old French, English gets *fritter* [14]; and the past participial stem of the French verb, *fris-*, may lie behind English *frizz* [17]. *Fry* 'small fish' may come from Anglo-Norman *frie*, a derivative of Old French *freier* 'rub, spawn,' which in turn goes back to Latin *frīgere* 'rub.'

▶ fervent, fritter, frizz

**fuck**   [16]   The most celebrated of the so-called 'Anglo-Saxon' four-letter words goes back in written form no further than the early 16th century – a far cry from the Old English period. A personal name *John le Fucker*, however, recorded from 1278, shows that it was around before 1500 (perhaps not committed to paper because even then it was under a taboo). There is little doubt that it is of Germanic origin, but its precise source has never been satisfactorily identified. All the earliest known examples of the word come from Scotland, which may suggest a Scandinavian source, related to Norwegian dialect *fukka* 'copulate,' and Swedish dialect *focka* 'copulate, hit' and *fock* 'penis.'

**fudge** [17] *Fudge* the verb, 'evade,' probably comes from an earlier *fadge*, which meant 'fake, deceive,' and hence 'adjust, fit,' and this in turn probably goes back to a Middle English noun *fage* 'deceit' – but where *fage* came from is not clear. *Fudge* as the name of a type of toffee, which is first recorded in the late 19th century, may be a different use of the same word – perhaps originally 'toffee 'cooked up' or 'bodged up' in an impromptu manner.'

**fuel** [14] The notions of 'fuel' and 'fire' are closely connected etymologically. *Fuel* comes via Anglo-Norman *fuaille* from medieval Latin *focālia*, which was used in legal documents as a term for the 'right to demand material for making a fire.' It was a derivative of Latin *focus* 'fireplace, fire,' which also gave English *focus*, *foyer*, and *fusillade*.

▶ focus, foyer, fusillade

**fugitive** see REFUGE

**fugue** see REFUGE

**full** [OE] *Full* and its verbal derivative *fill* go back ultimately to the Indo-European base *\*plē-*, which also produced Latin *plēnus* 'full' (source of English *plenary*, *plenty*, and *replenish*, and of French *plein* and Italian *pieno* 'full') and English *complete*, *deplete* [19] (literally 'unfill, empty'), *implement*, *plebeian*, *plethora*, *plural*, *plus*, *replete* [14], *supply*, and *surplus* [14]. The Indo-European derivative *\*plnós* passed into prehistoric Germanic as *\*fulnaz*, which eventually became *\*fullaz*, source of German *voll*, Dutch *vol*, and Swedish and English *full*. *Fulfil* dates from the late Old English period; it originally meant literally 'fill full, fill up.'

▶ complete, deplete, fill, implement, plenty, plethora, plural, plus, replete, supply, surplus

**fuller** see FOIL

**fulminate** [15] Etymologically, *fulminate* means 'strike with lightning.' It comes from Latin *fulmināre*, a derivative of *fulmen* 'lightning.' In medieval Latin its literal meaning gave way to the metaphorical 'pronounce an ecclesiastical censure on,' and this provided the semantic basis for its English derivative *fulminate*, although in the 17th and 18th centuries there were sporadic learned reintroductions of its original meteorological sense: 'Shall our Mountains be fulminated and thunder-struck,' William Sancroft, *Lex ignea* 1666.

**fume** [14] *Fume* comes via Old French *fum* from Latin *fūmus* 'smoke, steam.' This in turn went back to a prehistoric Indo-European *\*dhūmo-*, which also produced Sanskrit *dhūmás* 'smoke' and Russian and Polish *dym* 'smoke.' The word's verbal use, 'be very angry,' comes, like *seethe*, from the notion of being 'hot or steaming with fury.' Derived words in English include *fumigate* [16] and *perfume*.

▶ fumigate, perfume

**fun** [17] A *fun* was originally a 'trick, hoax, practical joke': 'A Hackney Coachman he did hug her, and was not this a very good Fun?' Thomas D'Urfey, *Pills to Purge Melancholy* 1719. It came from the contemporary verb *fun* 'cheat, hoax,' which was presumably a variant of the Middle English verb *fon* 'make a fool of.' This in turn was a verbal use of the noun *fon* 'fool,' probable origin of modern English *fond*. The current sense of *fun*, 'amusement, merriment,' did not develop until the 18th century. The derived adjective *funny*, in the sense 'amusing,' was roughly contemporary with it; 'strange, odd' is an early 19th-century semantic development.

▶ fond

**funambulist** see FUNICULAR

**function** [16] The ultimate source of *function* is the Latin verb *fungī* 'perform, discharge,' which may be related to Sanskrit *bhunkte* 'he enjoys.' From its past participle, *functus*, was formed the abstract noun *functiō* 'performance, activity,' which passed into English via Old French *fonction*. Other English derivatives of *fungī* include *defunct* and *perfunctory* [16], etymologically 'done only to discharge an obligation.'

▶ defunct, perfunctory

**fund** [17] Latin *fundus* meant 'bottom.' English originally acquired it via French as *fond*, and in the course of the 17th century re-latinized it to *fund*. The literal meaning 'bottom' was retained until the mid 18th century ('a Glass-Bubble fix'd to the Fund of a Vessel,' *British Apollo* 1709), but gradually it gave way to the metaphorical 'basic supply, particularly of money.' From *fundus* was derived the Latin verb *fundāre* 'lay the bottom for, establish' (source of English *found*), and the next step on from this was the noun *fundāmentum* 'bottom part, foundation,' which gave English *fundament* [13] and *fundamental* [15].

▶ found, fundament

**funeral** [14] Latin *fūnus*, a word of uncertain origin, meant 'funeral' and, probably secondarily, 'corpse.' From it was derived the adjective *fūnerālis*, which English acquired via Old French in the 14th century. The noun *funeral* followed in the 16th century; it came from the same ultimate source, of course, but by a slightly different route – from medieval Latin *fūnerālia* via Old French *funeraille*.

**fungus** [16] *Fungus* was introduced into English in the early 16th century as a learned and more all-embracing alternative to *mushroom*. It was borrowed from Latin *fungus*, which probably came from Greek *sphóngos* 'sponge,' source of English *sponge*.

▶ sponge

**funicular** [19] A *funicular* railway is literally one that runs on a 'rope.' The word was coined from Latin *fūniculus*, a diminutive form of *fūnis* 'rope' (a word of uncertain origin from which comes Italian *fune* 'cable, rope'). *Fūnus* also gave English *funambulist* 'tightrope walker' [18].

▶ funambulist

**funnel** [15] Etymologically, a *funnel* is something used for 'pouring in.' The word comes via Provençal *fonilh* from Latin *infundibulum* 'funnel.' This was a derivative of *infundere* 'pour in,' a compound verb formed from *in-* 'in' and *fundere* 'pour' (source of English *found* 'melt,' *foundry*, and *fuse*).

▶ found, foundry, fuse

**fur** [14] Old English did not have a distinct word for 'animal's hair' – the nearest approach to it was *fell* 'animal's hide.' Then in the 13th century English acquired the verb *fur* 'line with fur' from Anglo-Norman *furrer* or Old French *forrer* 'encase, line.' These were derivatives of the Old French noun *forre* 'sheath, case,' a loanword from prehistoric Germanic *fōthram* 'sheath,' which in turn goes back to the Indo-European base *pō-* 'protect.' In the 14th century the new English verb was taken as the basis for a noun, which originally meant 'trimming for a garment, made from fur,' or more loosely 'garment made from fur'; it was not until the 15th century that it was used for 'animal's hair.'

**furl** see FIRM

**furlong** [OE] *Furlong* 'eighth of a mile,' which has now virtually died out except in horse-racing terminology, is part of a vocabulary of length-measuring bequeathed to us by the agricultural practices of our ancestors. It originated as an Old English compound formed from *furh* 'furrow' and *lang* 'long' – that is, the length of a furrow ploughed across a standard-sized square field of ten acres. Since the term *acre* varied somewhat in its application at different times and places, the length of a furlong could not be computed with great precision from it, but in practice from about the 9th century the *furlong* was pegged to the *stadium*, a measure equal to one eighth of a Roman mile.

▶ furrow, long

**furnace** [13] Etymologically, *furnace* means roughly 'warm place.' It comes via Old French *fornais* from Latin *fornāx* 'furnace.' This was a derivative of *fornus* 'oven,' a word related to *formus* 'warm,' which goes back to the same Indo-European source, *ghworm-*, *ghwerm-*, as probably produced English *warm*.

▶ fornication

**furnish** [15] Far apart as they may now seem, *furnish* is closely parallel in its development with *frame*. Both originated as verbs based on *from*, in its earliest signification 'forward movement, advancement, progress.' *Frame* was a purely English formation, but *furnish* goes back beyond that to prehistoric Germanic, where it was formed as *frumjan*. This was borrowed into Vulgar Latin as *fromīre*, which in due course diversified to *formīre* and *fornīre*, the form adopted into Old French as *furnir*. Its lengthened stem *furniss-* provided English with *furnish*. To begin with this retained the ancestral sense 'advance to completion, accomplish, fulfil' ('Behight [promise] no thing but that ye may furnish and hold it,' *Melusine* 1500). However, this died out in the mid 16th century, leaving the field clear for the semantic extension 'provide.' The derivative *furniture* [16] comes from French *fourniture*, but its main meaning, 'chairs, tables, etc.,' recorded from as early as the 1570s, is a purely English development (the majority of European languages get their word for 'furniture' from Latin *mōbīle* 'movable': French *meubles*, Italian *mobili*, Spanish *muebles*, German *möbel*, Swedish *möbler*, Dutch *meubelen*, Russian *mebel'* – indeed, even Middle English had *mobles*, though it retained the broader meaning 'movable property'). By another route, Old French *furnir* has also given English *veneer*.

▶ from, furniture, veneer

**furrow** [OE] *Furrow* is an ancient agricultural term, going back to the prehistoric Indo-European base *prk-*, which also produced Welsh *rhych* 'furrow,' Armenian *herk* 'newly ploughed land,' Latin *porca* 'ridge between furrows,' and possibly also Sanskrit *parçāna-* 'chasm' and Latin *porcus* 'grave.' Its Germanic descendant was *furkh-*, which produced German *furche*, Dutch *voor*, Swedish *fåra*, and English *furrow*.

▶ furlong

**further** [OE] Etymologically, *further* is simply a comparative form of *forth*, and originally meant nothing more than simply 'more forward.' Its more metaphorical senses, 'in addition' and 'to a greater extent,' are secondary developments. It was formed in the prehistoric Germanic period, and so has relatives in other Germanic languages, such as German *vorder*. Its verbal use is apparently equally ancient.

▶ forth

**furtive** [15] Etymologically, someone who is *furtive* 'carries things away like a thief.' The word comes via Old French *furtif* from Latin *furtīvus* 'stealthy, hidden,' a derivative of *furtum* 'theft,' which in turn was based on *fūr* 'thief.' This was either borrowed from or related to Greek *phór* 'thief,' which came ultimately from Indo-European *bher-* 'carry' (source of English *bear*) and thus meant literally 'someone who carries things off.' A *ferret* is etymologically a 'furtive' animal.

▶ bear, ferret

**furze**   see GORSE

**fuse**   English has two distinct words *fuse*. The noun, 'igniting device' [17], comes via Italian *fuso* from Latin *fūsus* 'spindle,' a word of unknown origin. Its modern application comes from the fact that the long thin shape of the original gunpowder-filled tubes used for setting off bombs reminded people of spindles. The Vulgar Latin diminutive form of *fūsus*, *\*fūsellus*, gave French *fuseau* 'spindle,' which is the ultimate source of English *fuselage* [20] (etymologically, 'something shaped like a spindle'). The verb *fuse* 'melt' [17] probably comes from *fūsus*, the past participle of Latin *fundere* 'pour, melt' (source of English *found*, *foundry*, and *fusion* [16]).

▶ fuselage / found, foundry, fusion

**fuss**   [18]   The early use of *fuss* by Irish-born writers such as Jonathan Swift and George Farquhar has led to the supposition that it is of Anglo-Irish origin, but no substantiation for this has ever been found on the other side of the Irish Sea. Among suggestions as to how it came into being have been that it was an alteration of *force*, as in the now obsolete phrase *make no force of* 'not bother about,' and that it was simply onomatopoeic, imitating the sound of someone puffing and blowing and making a fuss.

**fusty**   see BEAT

**futile**   see FOUND

**future**   [14]   *Future* comes via Old French *future* from Latin *futūrus* 'going to be, about to be,' which was used as the future participle of *esse* 'be.' It was a descendant of the Indo-European base *\*bheu-* or *\*bhu-*, which originally denoted 'grow,' and also produced English *be*, the German present first and second person singular forms *bin* and *bist*, and the Latin perfect tense of *esse* (*fuī* 'I was,' etc).

▶ be

# G

---

**gabardine**  [16]  The use of *gabardine* for a sort of worsted material is an early 20th-century development, but the word itself has been around much longer than that. Its central meaning (for which the usual spelling is *gaberdine*) is 'long coarse outer garment.' English acquired it from Old French *gauvardine*, which was a development of an earlier *gallevardine*. This was probably derived from Middle High German *wallevart* 'pilgrimage' (a compound formed from *wallen* 'roam' and *vart* 'journey, way'), and hence etymologically meant 'pilgrim's garment.'

**gable**  [14]  The notion underlying *gable* is probably of 'topping' or 'surmounting,' for it has been traced back by some to prehistoric Indo-European *\*ghebhalā*, which also produced Greek *kephalḗ* 'head.' Its immediate source was Old Norse *gafl*, which gave English the form *gavel*, subsequently remodelled on the basis of Old French *gable* (itself probably borrowed originally from the Old Norse word).

► cephalic

**gadfly**  see YARD

**gadget**  [19]  *Gadget* is an elusive sort of word, as vague in its history as it is unspecific in its meaning. It seems to have originated as a piece of sailors' slang, and is said to have been current as long ago as the 1850s, but the earliest record of it in print is from 1886, in R Brown's *Spun Yarn and Spindrift*: 'Then the names of all the other things on board a ship! I don't know half of them yet; even the sailors forget at times, and if the exact name of anything they want happens to slip from their memory, they call it a chicken-fixing, or a gadjet, or a gill-guy, or a timmey-noggy, or a wim-wom – just *pro tem.*, you know.' As for its source, suggestions have included French *gâchette* 'catch of a mechanism' and French dialect *gagée* 'tool.'

**gag**  [15]  Middle English *gaggen* meant 'strangle, suffocate,' so the word started out with strong connotations that seem to have become submerged in local dialects as it came to be used more commonly in the milder sense 'obstruct someone's mouth.' In the 20th century,

however, they have re-emerged in the intransitive sense 'choke.' It is not clear how the 19th-century noun sense 'joke' is connected, if at all. As for the word's source, it is generally said to have originated as an imitation of someone retching or choking.

**gain**  [15]  *Gain* is Germanic in origin, although English acquired it via Old French. Its distant ancestor is the Germanic noun *\*waithā*. The etymological meaning of this was 'hunting ground' (it came ultimately from a prehistoric Indo-European base *\*wei-*, which also produced Lithuanian *vyti* 'pursue, hunt' and Sanskrit *veti, vayati* 'seeks, follows'), but gradually this extended via 'place where food or fodder is sought' to 'grazing place' (its modern German and Dutch descendant *weide* means 'pasture'). From it was formed a verb *\*waithanjan* 'hunt' and 'graze, pasture,' which Vulgar Latin took over as *\*gwadanjāre*. This preserved the semantic dichotomy that had grown up in Germanic: the agricultural sense developed to 'cultivate land,' and it appears that the 'hunting' sense gave rise metaphorically to 'win, earn.' Both passed into Old French *gaaignier*, but evidently by the time English acquired the word, the former meaning had all but died out (although it is interesting to note that it was introduced into English as a pseudo-archaism in the 17th and 18th centuries: 'Of old to gain land was as much as to till and manure it,' *Termes de la ley* 1708).

**gaiter**  [18]  Etymologically as well as semantically, *gaiter* is an 'ankle covering.' It comes from French *guêtre* 'gaiter,' which may well have been formed from Germanic *\*wirst-*. This denoted 'twist, turn,' and it has several modern derivatives which mean essentially 'twisting joint': German *rist*, for example, which has now migrated anatomically to the 'instep' and the 'back of the hand,' originally signified 'ankle, wrist,' and although English *wrist* now refers only to the hand/arm joint, it was formerly used dialectally for the 'ankle.'

► wrist

**gala** [17] *Gala* comes ultimately from Arabic *khil'a*, which denoted an 'especially fine garment given as a presentation.' This original meaning persisted through Spanish *gala* and into Italian and French *gala*, from one or other of which English got it ('Whereupon this King and the whole Court put on Galas [special festive attire],' *Cabala sive scrinia sacra* 1654) and survived into the 19th century ('Apparelled on Sunday morning in gala, as if for the drawing-room, he constantly marched out all his household to the parish church,' George Bancroft, *History of the United States* 1876). Nowadays, however, all that remains is the extended sense 'festive occasion,' first recorded in the late 18th century.

**galaxy** [14] The Greeks had a word for the 'Milky Way' – and indeed it was very much the same as ours. They called it *galaxías*, which was originally an adjective, 'milky,' derived from the noun *gála* 'milk.' English acquired it via late Latin *galaxiās* and Old French *galaxie*. (The term *Milky Way*, incidentally, which originated as a translation of Latin *via lactea*, is of roughly equal antiquity in English with *galaxy*. Their common inspiration is the white appearance of the myriad stars packed densely together.)

**gale** [16] *Gale* is a puzzling word. An isolated early example of what appears to be the word, in the phrase *gale wind* ('Our life like smoke or chaff is carried away as with a gale wind,' Zachary Boyd, *The Last Battle* 1619), suggests that it may originally have been an adjective. If this is so, a possible candidate as a source may be Norwegian *galen* 'bad' – making *gale* etymologically a 'bad wind.' The Norwegian adjective in turn may go back to Old Norse *galinn* 'bewitched, enchanted,' a derivative of *gala* 'sing, bewitch, enchant' (source of English *yell* and related to the final syllable of *nightingale*).

▶ nightingale, yell

**gall** *Gall* 'bile' [12], and by metaphorical extension 'bitterness' and 'effrontery,' was borrowed from Old Norse *gall*. It gets its name ultimately from its colour, for its prehistoric Germanic ancestor *\*gallam* or *\*gallon* (which also produced German *galle* and Dutch *gal*) goes back to Indo-European *\*ghol-, \*ghel-*, which also gave English *gold, jaundice, yellow*, and *yolk*. The relationship of the two other English words *gall* ('skin sore' [14], whence the verbal use 'exasperate,' and 'plant swelling' [14]) to *gall* 'bile' and to each other is not clear. The immediate source of 'skin sore' was Middle Low German *galle* 'sore,' but 'bile' could easily have led via 'astringent substance' to 'sore place,' and it may be that ultimately the Middle Low German word is connected with *gall* 'bile.' *Gall* 'plant swelling' has been traced back via Old French *galle* to Latin *galla* 'plant gall,' but some later descendants of this were used for

'swelling on an animal's leg,' further adding to the confusion.

▶ gold, jaundice, yellow, yolk

**gallant** [14] *Gallant* originated as the present participle of Old French *galer* 'make merry, rejoice.' This probably came from Gallo-Romance *\*walāre*, a derivative of Frankish *\*wala* 'well' (of which English *well* is a relative). Following its French model, the English adjective originally meant 'showy, splendid, gorgeous' as well as 'spirited, brave' and 'courteous, polished' (the last of which led in the 17th century to 'courteously attentive to women' and 'amorous'). *Regale* [17] too goes back to Old French *galer*.

▶ regale, well

**gallery** [15] The original meaning of *gallery* in English was 'long roofed walkway along the wall of a building'; the present sense 'room or building for the exhibition of paintings, sculpture, etc' did not develop until the end of the 16th century. English borrowed the word from Old French *galerie* 'portico,' which came via Italian *galleria* from medieval Latin *galeria*. This may have been an alteration of *galilea* (source of English *galilee* [16], as in *galilee chapel*), thought to have been applied to a porch or chapel at the far or western end of a church in allusion to the position of Galilee as the province of Palestine most distant from Jerusalem.

**Gallic**    see GALLOSHES

**gallilee**    see GALLERY

**gallon** [13] English acquired *gallon* from Old Northern French *galon*. This was a descendant of medieval Latin *gallēta*, a word for a 'jug' which was also used as a unit of measurement for wine. It may have been of Celtic origin. An early modern English dialect form of *gallon* was *gawn*, which added to *tree* produced *gantry* [16], originally a 'wooden stand for barrels.'

▶ gantry

**gallows** [13] *Gallows* was probably borrowed from Old Norse *gálgi* (the related Old English *galga* does not seem to have survived into the Middle English period). Both go back to a prehistoric Germanic *\*galgon* 'pole,' whose descendants, which also include Old High German *galgo* and Gothic *galga*, were often used for the 'cross on which Christ was crucified.' The plurality of modern English *gallows* presumably comes from the fact that technically a gallows consists of two upright poles with a cross-piece in between (as opposed to a gibbet, which has a single upright).

**galoshes** [14] In modern terms, *galoshes* might be etymologically rendered as 'little French shoes.' The word comes from Old French *galoche*, which was an alteration of late Latin *gallicula*. This in turn was a diminutive form of Latin *gallica*, short for *gallica solea* 'Gallic sandal, sandal from Gaul' (the name *Gaul*, incidentally, and the Latin-based *Gallic*

[17], come ultimately from prehistoric Germanic *walkhoz 'foreigners,' which is related also to *Walloon, walnut,* and *Welsh*). The term *galosh* was originally used in English for a sort of clog; the modern sense 'overshoe' did not develop until the early 19th century.

▶ Gallic, Walloon, walnut, Welsh

**galvanize** [19] The verb *galvanize* commemorates the work of Italian physicist Luigi Galvani (1737–98), who in 1762 discovered voltaic electricity by attaching the legs of dead frogs to pairs of different metals. It was first used literally, for the production of muscular spasms by electrical means (Sydney Smith in 1825: 'Galvanize a frog, don't galvanize a tiger'), but by the mid-19th century it was being employed figuratively, for 'stimulate, spur.' The sense 'coat electrolytically with metal, dates from the 1830s.

**gambit** [17] Like *gambol* [16], *gambit* originated in an Italian noun meaning literally 'tripping up.' The Italian for 'leg' is *gamba* (a relative of English *gammon* 'bacon'). From it were derived *gambetto* and *gambata*, both of which signified 'trip-up.' The former was borrowed into Spanish as *gambito*, where its underlying notion of 'underhanded procedure' was first applied specifically to a chess manoeuvre in the mid-16th century. It passed into English mainly via French *gambit*. More frivolous, light-hearted aspects of 'tripping' are preserved in *gambata*, which English originally took over via French as *gambade* and gradually transformed into *gambol*.

▶ gambol, gammon

**gamble** [18] Although its ancestry has never been established beyond all doubt, it seems overwhelmingly likely that *gamble* is essentially the same word as *game* (in which the sense 'gamble' is preserved in such contexts as *gaming tables* and *betting and gaming*). The Middle English form of *game* was *gamen*, and it is thought that this may have produced a variant form *gamel* (recorded in the 16th century) which in due course became *gamble*.

▶ game

**game** There are two *games* in English. The noun *game* 'pastime, sport' [OE] used to be a fairly widespread word in the Germanic languages (Swedish and Danish still preserve it as *gamman* and *gammen* respectively) and may well go back to a prehistoric Germanic compound formed from the collective prefix *ga-* and *mann-*'person' (source of English *man*), and denoting literally 'people together, participating.' Its Old English descendant was *gamen* which, before it became reduced to *game* (a process which began in the 13th century but was not complete until the 16th century), bequeathed *gammon* (as in *backgammon*) and probably also *gamble* to modern English. *Game* 'plucky' [18] is probably an adjectival use of the same word. *Game* 'lame' [18], however, and its derivative *gammy* [19],

are not related; they may come from archaic French *gambi* 'crooked.'

▶ gamble, man / gammy

**gammon** *Gammon* 'bacon' [15] is not related to the *gammon* [18] of *backgammon*. It comes from Old Northern French *gambon* (source also of modern French *jambon* 'ham'), which was a derivative of *gambe* 'leg' – hence etymologically 'leg meat.' This seems to go back ultimately to Greek *kampḗ* 'bend,' which was used particularly as an anatomical term for joints of the body. Latin took it over as a veterinary expression, *gamba*, denoting a 'horse's hoof,' and it passed into due course into Italian as *gamba* (whence English *gambit, gambol, jamb* [14], and the *gamba* of *viola da gamba* [18], played between the legs) and into French as *jambe*, both meaning 'leg.' The *gammon* of *backgammon* comes from Middle English *gamen*, the ancestor of modern English *game* (see also BACKGAMMON).

▶ gambit, gambol, jamb

**gamut** [15] *Gamut* began life as a medieval musical term. The 11th-century French-born musical theorist Guido d'Arezzo devised the 'hexachord,' a six-note scale used for sight-reading music (and forerunner of the modern tonic sol-fa). The notes were mnemonically named *ut, re, mi, fa, sol, la* (after, according to legend, syllables in a Latin hymn to St John: '*Ut* queant laxis *re*sonāre fibris *Mi*ra gestorum *fa*muli tuorum, *Sol*ve polluti *la*bii reatum' – 'Absolve the crime of the polluted lip in order that the slaves may be able with relaxed chords to praise with sound your marvellous deeds'). The note below the lowest note (*ut*) became known as *gamma-ut* (*gamma*, the name of the Greek equivalent of *g*, having been used in medieval notation for the note bottom G). And in due course *gamma-ut*, or by contraction in English *gamut*, came to be applied to the whole scale, and hence figuratively to any 'complete range' (an early 17th-century development).

**gander** see GANNET

**gang** [12] *Gang* originally meant 'going, journey.' It was borrowed from Old Norse *gangr*, which goes back ultimately to the same Germanic source (the verb *\*ganggan* 'go') as produced the German past participle *gegangen* 'gone' and Old English *gangan* 'go' – still preserved in Scottish *gang* 'go' and in *gangway* [17], originally literally a 'way for going.' The word's modern meaning seems to have developed via 'quantity carried on a journey' (a common usage in Scottish English well into the 19th century) and 'set of articles carried together' to (in the 17th century) 'group of workmen' and 'group of people acting together for a (bad) purpose.'

**gannet** [OE] The gannet used to be known dialectally as the *solan goose* (*solan* was a compound formed in the 15th century from Old Norse *súla* 'gannet' and *önd* 'duck'), and in fact the name *gannet* too reveals a perceived similarity between the gannet and the goose. For it comes ultimately from a prehistoric Germanic *ganitaz* or *ganoton*, a word formed from the same base as produced English *gander* [10].

▶ gander

**gantry**   see GALLON

**gaol**   see JAIL

**gape**   [13]   Gape and the related *gap* [14] are of Scandinavian origin. English borrowed the verb from Old Norse *gapa* 'open the mouth,' which survives in modern Scandinavian languages as Swedish *gapa* and Danish *gabe*. Old Norse *gap* 'chasm' (source of Swedish *gap* 'mouth' and Danish *gab* 'opening, open mouth') was originally taken over by English in the specific sense 'hole in a wall or hedge'; the broader modern range of meanings began to emerge in the 16th century.

▶ gap, yawn

**garage**   [20]   As the motor-car age got under way at the start of the 20th century, a gap opened up in the lexicon for a word for 'car-storage place.' English filled it in 1902 by borrowing French *garage*. The first references to it show that the term (*station* was an early alternative) was originally applied to large commercially run shelters housing many vehicles – the equivalent more of modern multi-storey car parks than of garages (the *Daily Mail*, for example, on 11 January 1902, reports the 'new 'garage' founded by Mr Harrington Moore, hon. secretary of the Automobile Club . . . The 'garage,' which is situated at the City end of Queen Victoria-street, has accommodation for 80 cars,' and Alfred Harmsworth, in *Motors* 1902, wrote of 'stations or 'garages' where a number of cars can be kept'). It was not long, however, before individual houses got more personalized garages, and the application to an establishment where vehicle repairs are carried out and fuel sold soon followed. The French word *garage* itself is a derivative of the verb *garer*, which originally meant 'dock ships.' It comes from Old French *garer* 'protect, defend,' a loanword from Old High German *warōn* (to which English *ward, warn*, and the *-ware* of *beware* are related).

▶ beware, ward, warn

**garb**   see GEAR

**garble**   [15]   Garble used not to have its present-day negative connotations. It originally meant simply 'cleanse, sift, cull': '[At Alexandria] all sorts of spices be garbled after the bargain is made,' Richard Hakluyt, *Voyages* 1599. Gradually, though, 'taking out the worst' and 'selecting the best' passed into 'making an unfair selection,' 'distorting by leaving things out' and eventually simply 'distorting meaning.' The word itself has a convoluted pre-English history: English got it from Italian *garbellare*, which in turn came from Arabic *gharbala* 'sift, select,' a term probably wide-

spread in the commercial linguae francae of the Mediterranean seaboard in medieval and Renaissance times. This verb was a derivative of the Arabic noun *ghirbāl* 'sieve,' which seems to have been based on the Latin verb *crībellāre* 'seive' – itself derived from *crībellum*, a diminutive form of *crībum* 'seive,' which was related to Latin *cernere* 'sift' (source of English *discern* and *discrete*).

▶ certain, discern, discrete

**garden**   [14]   Ultimately, *garden* and *yard* are the same word. Both come from prehistoric Germanic *gardon*, but whereas *yard* reached English via a direct Germanic route, *garden* diverted via the Romance languages. Vulgar Latin borrowed *gardon* as *gardo* 'enclosure,' and formed from it the adjective *gardīnus* 'enclosed.' The phrase *hortus gardīnus* 'enclosed garden' came to be abbreviated to *gardīnus*, which gave Old Northern French *gardin*, the source of the English word (more southerly dialects of Old French had *jardin*, borrowed by Italian as *giardino*).

▶ yard

**gargoyle**   [15]   The ancient root *garg-, *gurg-* originated as an imitation of throat sounds. From it were derived such guttural words as Greek *gargarízein* 'gargle' (whence Latin *gargarizāre* 'gargle') and Latin *gurguliō* 'gullet' (Latin *gurges*, source of English *gorge* and *regurgitate*, had moved further figuratively to 'whirlpool'). Among the offspring of *gurguliō* are Vulgar Latin *gurguliāre*, source of English *gurgle* [16], and Old French *gargouille* 'throat.' Roof spouts carved in the shape of grotesque creatures had the term *gargouille* applied to them from the notion that the rainwater was coming out of their throats – hence English *gargoyle*. *Gargouille* also formed the basis of the verb *gargouiller* 'gargle, gurgle,' from which English gets *gargle* [16].

▶ gargle, gurgle

**garlic**   see GOAD

**garner**   see GRAIN

**garnet**   [13]   Garnet, as a term for a semiprecious stone, was borrowed from Middle Dutch *garnate*. This in turn came from Old French *grenat* 'dark red,' the colour of the garnet, whose original inspiration was probably the pomegranate (in Old French *pome grenate*), with its vivid scarlet pulp.

▶ grain, pomegranate

**garnish**   [14]   Garnish was originally a fairly utilitarian verb, meaning simply 'fit out, equip, supply' or 'adorn.' Its modern culinary application did not develop until the late 17th century. It came from *garniss-*, the lengthened stem of the Old French verb *garnir* 'equip, adorn.' This was borrowed from prehistoric Germanic *warnjan*, which presumably came from the same base as produced *warnōjan* 'be cautious, guard, provide for' (source of English *warn*). The notion of 'warning' is preserved in the legal term *garnishee* [17], applied to someone who is served with a judicial warning not to pay their debt to anyone other than the person who is seeking repayment.

▶ warn

**garotte** [17] *Garotte* is widely used simply for 'strangle,' but its strict application is to a former Spanish method of capital punishment by strangulation or breaking the neck, in which a metal collar was screwed increasingly tight. It got its name from Spanish *garrote*, which originally meant 'cudgel': in earlier, less sophisticated or more impromptu versions of the execution, a cudgel or stick was inserted into a band around the neck and twisted round and round so as to tighten the band. The immediate source of *garrote* was no doubt Old French *garrot*, from an earlier *guaroc* 'club, stick, rod for turning,' whose form suggests a Celtic origin.

**garrison** [13] The notion underlying *garrison* is of 'protection.' Its ultimate source was Germanic *\*war-*, denoting 'caution,' which also produced English *ward, warn, wary*, and the *-ware* of *beware*. This produced the verb *\*warjan* 'protect, defend,' which Old French borrowed as *garir* (the related *garer* gave English *garage*). From it was derived the Old French noun *garison* 'defence, protection,' from which English borrowed *garrison*. The concrete senses 'fortress,' and hence 'detachment of troops in such a fortress,' developed in the 15th century.

▶ beware, garage, ward, warn, wary

**garter** [14] The ultimate source of *garter* was probably an unrecorded Gaulish word meaning 'leg' (related to Welsh *gar* 'leg'). It was borrowed into Old French at some point and used as the basis of the noun *garet*, which (in relation to people) meant 'place where the leg bends, knee.' From this in turn was derived Old French *gartier* 'band just above or below the knee,' source of English *garter*. The British Order of the Garter dates, according to the medieval French chronicler Jean Froissart, from around 1344. The story of its origin, not recorded until over 250 years later and never authenticated, is that while the Countess of Salisbury was dancing with King Edward III, her garter fell off; the king picked it up and put it on his own leg, remarking somewhat cryptically in Anglo-French 'Honi soit qui mal y pense' – 'Shamed be he who thinks evil of it,' and named the order of knighthood which he founded after this very garter.

**garth**  see YARD

**gas** [17] We get *gas* from a Flemish pronunciation of Greek *kháos* 'chasm, void' (a derivative of Indo-European *\*ghǝw-*'hollow,' and source of English *chaos* [15]). The Flemish chemist J B van Helmont (1577–1644) used the Greek word to denote an occult principal, supposedly an ultra-refined form of water, which he postulated as existing in all matter. The sound of

Greek *kh* is roughly equivalent of that represented by Dutch and Flemish *g*, and so the word came to be spelled *gas*. Its modern application to any indefinitely expanding substance dates from the late 18th century.

The derivative *gasolene*, source of American English *gas* 'petrol,' dates from the late 19th century.

▶ chaos

**gash** [16] Greek *kharássein* meant 'sharpen, engrave, cut' (it gave English *character*). It was borrowed into Latin as *charaxāre*, which appears to have found its way into Old Northern French as *garser* 'cut, slash.' English took this over as *garse*, which survived, mainly as a surgical term meaning 'make incisions,' into the 17th century. An intermediate form *garsh*, recorded in the 16th century, suggests that this was the source of modern English *gash*.

▶ character

**gasket** [17] Although it has never been·established for certain, it seems likely that *gasket* may have originated as a word meaning 'little girl' – namely French *garcette*. This is a diminutive of *garce* 'girl,' the feminine form of *gars* 'boy' (whence *garçon*). It is used figuratively for a 'small rope,' and was originally borrowed into English in the 17th century as *gassit*, used as a nautical term for a 'small rope for attaching a furled sail to a mast.' Modern English *gasket*, first recorded in the early 17th century, seems to be an alteration of this. The main present-day sense 'joint seal' (originally made from tow or plaited hemp) developed in the early 19th century.

**gastric** [17] Grek *gastér* meant 'stomach' (it was related to Greek *gráō* 'gnaw, eat' and Sanskrit *gras-* 'devour'). It was used as the basis of the modern Latin adjective *gastricus* 'of the stomach,' which English acquired via French *gastrique*. Derivatives include *gastronomy* 'culinary connoisseurship' [19], originally a French coinage, and *gastropod* 'mollusc' [19], literally 'stomach-foot' (from the ventral disc used by molluscs as a 'foot').

**gate** Of the two English words *gate*, only one survives in general use. *Gate* 'doorlike structure' [OE] comes from a prehistoric Germanic *\*gatam*, whose other descendants, including Dutch *gat* 'hole, opening,' suggest that it originally denoted an 'opening in a wall' rather than the 'structure used to close such an opening.' Irish has borrowed it as *geata*. The other *gate* 'way, path' [13] now survives only in street-names, particularly in the North of England (for instance, York's *Micklegate* and *Coppergate*); its other main meaning, 'way of walking,' has been partitioned off since the 18th century in the spelling *gait*. It was borrowed from Old Norse *gata* 'path, passage,' which comes ultimately from prehistoric Germanic *\*gatwōn*.

**gather** [OE] *Gather* goes back ultimately to Germanic *\*gath-*'bring together, unite' (which also produced English *good*). From it was derived *\*gadurī* (source of English *together*), which in turn formed the basis of a verb *\*gadurōjan*. Its offspring include Middle High German *gaten* 'come together,' Old Frisian *gadia* 'unite,' and Old English *gaderian*, whence modern English *gather*. It also produced German *gatte* 'husband, spouse,' originally 'companion.'

▶ good, together

**gaudy** [16] Middle English had a colour term *gaudy-green* 'yellowish-green,' which originally denoted 'green produced by dye obtained from the plant dyer's rocket, *Reseda luteola*,' a plant formerly known as *weld* [14]. The word *weld* came from a Germanic source which, borrowed into Old French, produced *gaude* – whence English *gaudy-green*. It has been claimed that this *gaudy* soon lost its literal meaning 'produced from weld-dye,' and came to be interpreted as 'bright.' Other etymologists, however, favour the explanation that *gaudy* comes from *gaud* 'joke, plaything' [14], which was adapted from Old French *gaudir* 'rejoice,' a descendant of Latin *gaudēre* 'delight in' (from which English gets *joy*).

**gauge**    see ENGAGE

**gauntlet** The *gauntlet* of 'run the gauntlet' has no etymological connection with *gauntlet* 'glove' [15]. The latter was borrowed from Old French *gantelet*, a diminutive form of *gant* 'glove.' This was orginally a Germanic loanword, with surviving relatives in Swedish and Danish *vante* 'glove.' As for 'running the gauntlet,' it was to begin with 'running the gantlope,' in which *gantlope* signified 'two lines of people armed with sticks, who attacked someone forced to run between them.' This was borrowed in the 17th century from Swedish *gatlopp*, a descendant of Old Swedish *gatulop* 'passageway'; this was a compound noun formed from *gata* 'way' (related to English *gate, gait*) and *lop* 'course' (related to English *leap* and *lope*). Under the influence of *gauntlet* 'glove,' English changed *gatlopp* to *gantlope*, and thence to *gantlet* (now restricted in use to an 'overlapping section of railway track') and *gauntlet* (as in 'run the gauntlet').

▶ gait, gate, leap, lope

**gauze** [16] Many terms for various types of fabric come from the name of a place they were originally associated with, from obvious derivatives such as *damask* from Damascus to more obscure associations like *denim* from Nîmes in France, and *gauze* appears to be no exception. It was borrowed from French *gaze*, which is generally assumed to have been named after Gaza, a city in medieval Palestine which was closely associated with the production of gauze.

**gay** [13] English borrowed *gay* from Old French *gai*, an adjective of uncertain origin connected by some with Old High German *gāhi* 'sudden, impulsive.' 'Happy' is its ancestral meaning, stretching back to Old

French *gai*. The 20th-century sense 'homosexual,' which first came into general usage in the 1950s, seems to have arisen from an earlier American slang term *gay cat*, which originally denoted a young male tramp who was the companion of an older tramp. The implications of a homosexual relationship which this carried had led by the 1930s to the use of *gay cat* for any young male homosexual, and the application of *gay* to 'homosexual' was probably generalized from this.

**gaze** [14] *Gaze* is probably of Scandinavian origin, although its precise antecedents have never been pinned down. Swedish has a dialect verb *gasa* 'gape, stare,' which may be related, and it could be connected in some way with Old Norse *gá* 'heed,' source of a Middle English verb *gaw* 'gape, stare,' which may lie behind modern English *gawk* [18]. These suggestions fit semantically, for the earliest use of *gaze* in English was in the sense 'gawp, stare'; only gradually was this overtaken by the politer 'look intently.' *Gazebo* [18] probably originated as a 'humorous' quasi-Latin coinage based on *gaze*, using the Latin first person singular future suffix *-ēbō*, as if *gazebo* meant 'I shall gaze.'

▶ gazebo

**gazette** [17] If the *Sun* or the *Mirror* were called the *22p*, they would be echoing the origins of the word *gazette*. In Renaissance Venice, a 'newspaper' was termed casually *gazeta de la novita* (*gazeta* for short), literally a 'pennyworth of news' – for a *gazeta* was the name of a small Venetian copper coin (probably a diminutive form of *gazza* 'magpie'). Italian took the word over as *gazzetta*, and passed it on to English via French. The verbal use of *gazette*, 'announce a military promotion officially,' arises from the practice of printing such announcements in the British government newspaper, the *London Gazette* (first published in the 17th century).

The derived *gazeteer* [17], ultimately from Italian *gazzettiere*, originally meant 'journalist.' Its current sense 'index of places' was inspired by Laurence Echard's *The Gazetteer's; or a Newsman's Interpreter: Being a Geographical Index* 1693.

**gear** [13] The etymological meaning of *gear* is roughly 'that which puts one in a state of readiness' – hence 'equipment, apparatus.' Its ultimate source is prehistoric Indo-European *\*garw-*, which also produced the now obsolete English adjective *yare* 'ready' and (via Germanic, Italian, and French) *garb* [16]. A derivative *\*garwīn-* passed into Old Norse as *gervi*, which English borrowed as *gear*. The mechanical sense of the word developed in the 16th century.

▶ garb

**geezer** [19] Originally, a *geezer* seems to have been 'someone who went around in disguise.' The word probably represents a dialectal pronunciation of the now obsolete *guiser* 'someone wearing a masquerade as part of a performance, mummer.' This was a derivative of *guise* [13], which, together with *disguise* [14], goes back ultimately to prehistoric Germanic *wīsōn, ancestor of archaic English *wise* 'manner.'

▶ disguise, guise, wise

**gel** see JELLY

**gelatine** see JELLY

**gem** [14] *Gem* comes via Old French *gemme* from Latin *gemma*. This originally meant 'bud,' and the sense 'precious stone' was only a secondary metaphorical extension. The underlying semantic stratum still appears in such botanical terms as *gemmation* 'formation of buds' [18].

**general** [13] *General* is one of a vast range of English words which go back ultimately to the prehistoric Indo-European base *gen-, *gon-, *gn-, denoting 'produce.' Its Germanic offshoots include *kin, kind,* and probably *king,* but for sheer numbers it is the Latin descendants *genus* 'race, type,' *gēns* 'race, people,' *gignere* 'beget,' and *nāscī* 'be born' (source of *nation, nature,* etc) that have been the providers. From *genus* come *gender* [14] and its French-derived counterpart *genre* [19], *generate* [16], *generation* [13], *generic* [17], *generous,* and *genus* [16] itself. *Gēns* produced *genteel, gentile, gentle,* and *gentry,* while *gignere* was the source of *genital* [14], *genitive* [14], *gingerly* [16] (originally 'daintily,' as if befitting someone of 'noble birth'), *indigenous,* and *ingenuous.* A separate Latin strand is represented by *genius* and *genie,* and its derivative *genial,* while Greek descendants of Indo-European *gen-, *gon-* are responsible for *gene* [20], *genealogy* [13], *genesis* [OE], *genetic* [19], *genocide* [20] (apparently coined by the Polish-born American jurist Raphael Lemkin in 1944), and *gonorrhoea* [16] (literally 'flow of semen').

As for *general* itself, it comes via Old French *general* from Latin *generālis* 'of the genus or type (as a whole),' particularly as contrasted with *speciālis* 'of the species' (source of English *special*). The application of the noun *general* to 'senior military officer' originated in the 16th century as an abbreviation of the phrase *captain general* (where the *general* was an adjective), a translation of French *capitaine générale*.

▶ gender, gene, genealogy, generate, generous, genesis, genetic, genie, genital, genius, genocide, gingerly, gonorrhoea, indigenous, ingenuous, jaunty, kin, kind

**generous** [16] *Generous* comes via Old French *genereux* from Latin *generōsus,* which originally meant 'of noble birth' (a sense which survived in English into the late 17th century – Richard Knolles, for instance, in his *General history of the Turks* 1603, wrote of 'many knights of generous extraction'). It was a derivative of *genus* in the sense 'birth, stock, race,' and harks back semantically to its ultimate source in the Indo-European base *gen- 'produce' (see GENERAL). Its

semantic progression from 'nobly born' through 'noble-minded, magnanimous' to 'liberal in giving' took place largely in Latin.

▶ general

**genetic** see GENERAL

**genital** see GENERAL

**genitive** see GENERAL

**genius** [16] Latin *genius* originally meant 'deity of generation and birth.' It came ultimately from the Indo-European base *gen- 'produce' (source of English *gene, generate, genitive,* etc), probably via a derivative *gnjos. It broadened out considerably in meaning, initially to 'attendant spirit,' the sense in which English originally acquired it (French took it over as *génie,* a word which, because of its phonetic and semantic similarity to Arabic *jinn,* 18th-century translators of the *Arabian nights* eagerly adopted into English as *genie*). The main modern English sense, 'person of outstanding intellectual ability,' which dates from the 17th century, goes back to a comparatively rare Latin 'intellectual capacity.' *Genial* [16] comes from Latin *geniālis,* a derivative of *genius,* which again originally meant 'of generation and birth' (a sense which survived into English: 'And thou, glad Genius! in whose gentle hand the bridal bower and genial bed remain,' Edmund Spenser, *Epithalamion* 1595). It later developed in Latin to 'pleasant, festive.'

▶ general

**genocide** see GENERAL

**genre** see GENERAL

**gentle** [13] Expressions like 'of gentle birth,' and related forms such as *gentility* [14] and *gentleman* [13] point up the original link between *gentle* and 'family, stock, birth.' The word comes via Old French *gentil* from Latin *gentīlis,* a derivative of *gēns* 'family, stock,' which in turn goes back to the Indo-European base *gen- 'produce' (source of English *gene, generate, genitive,* etc). To begin with it meant 'of the same family,' but by post-classical times it had shifted to 'of good family,' the sense in which English originally acquired it. Like the closely related *generous,* it then moved on semantically from 'well-born' to 'having a noble character, generous, courteous,' but interestingly this sense has virtually died out in English (except in such fixed phrases as *gentle knight* and *gentle reader*), having been replaced since the 16th century by 'mild, tender.'

French *gentil* was reborrowed into English in the 16th century as *genteel,* in which again connotations of good breeding figure highly. Attempts at a French accent resulted ultimately in *jaunty* [17], which originally meant 'well-bred' or 'elegant.'

The other English descendant of Latin *gentīlis* is the directly borrowed *gentile* [14], whose application to 'non-Jewish people' comes from its use in the Vulgate, the Latin version of the Bible.

▶ general

**genuine** [16] Latin *genu* meant 'knee' (it comes from the same Indo-European ancestor as English *knee*, and gave English *genuflection* [16]). In Rome and elsewhere in the ancient world, it was the convention for a father to acknowledge a newly-born child as his own by placing it on his knee – hence the child was *genuinus*.

▶ genuflection, knee

**genus**   see GENERAL

**geography** [16] All the English '*geo-*' words (*geography, geology* [18], *geometry* [14], etc) come ultimately from Greek *gē* 'earth,' a word probably of pre-Indo-European origin, whose Homeric form *gaia* was used as the name of the Greek goddess of the earth. *Geography* denotes literally the 'describing of the earth'; *geometry* the 'measuring of the earth' (from its early application to the measuring of land and surveying).

▶ geology, geometry

**geranium** [16] The native English name for the 'geranium,' *cranesbill*, shows that the same thought occurred independently to the speakers of two independent languages many miles and centuries apart. For the plant's seed case is long and pointed, very much like the beak of a crane; and *geranium* comes via Latin from Greek *geránion*, literally 'little crane,' a diminutive form of *géranos* 'crane' (which is related to English *crane*).

▶ crane

**germ** [17] As its close relatives *germane* and *germinate* [17] suggest, *germ* has more to do etymologically with 'sprouting' and 'coming to life' than with 'disease.' It comes via Old French *germe* from Latin *germen* 'sprout, offshoot,' which may go back ultimately to the Indo-European base *\*gen-* 'produce' (source of English *gene, generate, genitive*, etc). The meaning 'sprout, from which new life develops' persisted into English (and still occurs in such contexts as *wheatgerm* – and indeed in metaphorical expressions like 'the germ of an idea'). Then at the beginning of the 19th century it began to be used to put into words the idea of a 'seed' from which a disease grew: 'The vaccine virus must act in one or other of these two ways: either it must destroy the germe of the small-pox . . . or it must neutralize this germe,' *Medical Journal* 1803. By the end of the century it was an accepted colloquialism for 'harmful microorganism.'

▶ germane, germinate

**germane** [19] *Germane* is an alteration of *german* 'closely related' [14], which now survives only in the rather archaic expression *cousin-german*. This came via Old French *germain* from Latin *germānus*, which meant 'of the same race' (it was a derivative of *germen* 'sprout, offspring,' from which English gets *germ*). The use of *germane* for 'relevant' as opposed to simply 'related' seems to have been inspired by Hamlet's comment that a remark of Osric's would have been 'more german to the matter, if we could carry cannon by our sides.' (The nationality term *German* [16], incidentally, is probably of Celtic origin, and has no etymological connection with *germane*.)

▶ germ

**germinate**   see GERM

**gerrymander** [19] The story goes that in 1812 the governor of Massachusetts, Elbridge Gerry, instituted some electoral boundary changes favourable to his party, the Democrats. When a painter named Stuart saw these outlined on a map in the office of a newspaper editor, he remarked that the resulting area resembled a salamander in shape. 'A gerrymander, you mean!' replied the editor – and the term caught on for 'unfair manipulation of constituency boundaries.'

**gestation** [16] Etymologically, *gestation* is the period during which unborn young is 'carried' inside the womb. Indeed, to begin with the word meant simply 'carrying' in English ('*Gestacion*, that is to be carried of another thing, without any travail of the body itself,' William Bullein, *Bulwark of Defence Against All Sickness* 1562). It comes from Latin *gestātiō*, a derivative of the verb *gerere* 'carry, conduct oneself, act.' This has given a wide variety of words to English, including *congest, digest, gerund, gesture, jester, register*, and *suggest* (*gerund* [16] comes from Latin *gerundum*, a variant of *gerendum* 'carrying on,' the gerund of *gerere*).

▶ congest, digest, gesture, jester, register, suggest

**gesture** [15] Originally, a person's *gesture* was their 'bearing,' the way they 'carried' themselves: 'He was a knight of yours full true, and comely of gesture,' *Sir Cleges* 1410. But by the 16th century it was well on its way via 'bodily movement' to 'bodily movement conveying a particular message.' The word came from medieval Latin *gestūra*, a derivative of Latin *gerere* 'carry, conduct oneself, act.' A parallel derivative was *gestus* 'action' (ultimate source of English *jest* and *jester*), whose diminutive *gesticulus* produced English *gesticulate* [17].

▶ gestation, gesticulate, jest, jester

**get** [13] *Get*, now one of the most pervasive of English words, has only been in the language for the (comparatively) short period of 800 years. It was borrowed from Old Norse *geta* (although a related, hundred-per-cent English *-get*, which occurs in *beget* and *forget*, dates back to Old English times). Both come via a prehistoric Germanic *\*getan* from Indo-European *\*ghed-*, which signified 'seize' (*guess* is ultimately from the same source). *Gotten* is often quoted as an American survival of a primeval past participle since abandoned by British English, but in fact the original past participle of *got* was *getten*, which lasted into the 16th century; *gotten* was a Middle English innovation, based on such models as *spoken* and *stolen*. *Got* originated as an abbreviated form of *gotten*, which in due course came to be used, on both sides of the Atlantic, as the past tense of the verb (replacing the original *gat*).

▶ beget, forget, guess

**geyser** see GUST

**ghastly** [14] Despite its similarity in form and sense, *ghastly* is not related to *ghost*. It was formed from the Middle English verb *gasten* 'terrify,' which may have been a descendant of the Old English verb *gǣstan* 'torment' (source of *aghast*). The spelling with *gh-*, based on *ghost*, was first used by the 16th-century poet Edmund Spenser, and in due course caught on generally.

▶ aghast

**gherkin** [17] Etymologically, a *gherkin* may be a 'little unripe one.' The word was borrowed from an assumed early Dutch *\*gurkkijn*, a diminutive form of *gurk*, which probably came from Lithuanian *agurkas*. This in turn goes back via Polish *ogurek* to medieval Greek *angoúrion*, which has been linked with classical Greek *ágouros* 'youth.'

**ghetto** [17] English acquired *ghetto* from Italian, but its precise history is uncertain. Among the suggestions are that it represents Italian *getto* 'foundry,' from a Jewish enclave in Venice established on the site of a medieval foundry in 1516; that it is short for Italian *borghetto*, a diminutive form of *borgo* 'settlement outside city walls' (to which English *borough* is related); and that it was an alteration of Latin *Aegyptus* 'Egypt,' presumably an allusion to the captivity of the Jews in Egypt.

**ghost** [OE] In Old English times, *ghost* was simply a synonym for 'spirit' or 'soul' (a sense preserved in *Holy Ghost*); it did not acquire its modern connotations of the 'disembodied spirit of a dead person appearing among the living' until the 14th century. However, since it has been traced back to Indo-European *\*ghois-* or *\*gheis-*, which also produced Old Norse *geisa* 'rage,' Sanskrit *hédas* 'anger,' and Gothic *usgaisjan* 'terrify,' it could well be that its distant ancestor denoted as frightening concept as the modern English word does. The Old English form of the word was *gāst*, which in Middle English became *gost*; the *gh-* spelling, probably inspired by Flemish *gheest*, first appeared at the end of the 15th century, and gradually established itself over the next hundred years.

**giblets** [14] French *gibier* means 'game' – in the sense 'hunted animals' (it comes from Frankish *\*gabaiti* 'hunting with falcons'). In the Old French period this seems to have produced a diminutive form

*\*giberet*, literally 'small game,' which, though never recorded, is assumed to have been the basis of Old French *gibelet* (*l* and *r* are very close phonetically, and each is easily substituted for the other). *Gibelet* is only known in the sense 'game stew,' but it seems quite plausible that it could have originally meant 'entrails of hunted animals' (Walloon, the French dialect of southern Belgium, has *giblè d'awe* 'goose giblets').

**giddy** [OE] Like *enthusiastic*, the etymological meaning of *giddy* is 'possessed by a god.' Its distant ancestor was a prehistoric Germanic adjective *\*guthigaz*, which was derived from *\*gutham* 'god.' This produced Old English *gidig*, which meant 'insane' or 'stupid.' It was not until the 16th century that it acquired its main present-day meaning, 'dizzy.'

▶ god

**gift** [13] Prehistoric Germanic *\*geb-*, the source from which English gets the verb *give*, produced the derivative *\*geftiz*. This passed into Old English as *gift*, which, as far as is known, meant only 'bride price,' and seems to have died out by the Middle English period. Modern English *gift* represents a borrowing of the related Old Norse *gipt* or *gift*. (Modern German, Swedish, and Danish *gift* and Dutch *gif* are used euphemistically for 'poison.')

▶ give

**gild** see GOLD

**gill** English has three separate words *gill*. The oldest, *gill* 'ravine' [11], was borrowed from Old Norse *gil*, a word of unknown ancestry. *Gill* 'fishes' breathing organ' [14] probably also comes from an Old Norse *\*gil*, never actually recorded, but deduced from modern Swedish *gäl* and Danish *gjælle* 'gill.' It may well go back to a prehistoric Indo-European source which also produced Greek *kheilos* 'lip.' *Gill* 'quarter of a pint' [14] comes via Old French *gille* from medieval Latin *gillo* 'water-pot.'

**gillyflower** see CLOVE

**gilt** see GOLD

**gimmick** [20] *Gimmick* originally meant 'dishonest contrivance' – indeed, in the first known printed reference to it, in George Maine's and Bruce Grant's *Wise-crack dictionary* 1926 (an American publication), it is defined specifically as a 'device for making a fair game crooked.' The modern sense 'stratagem for gaining attention' seems to have come to the fore in the 1940s. The origins of the word are a mystery, although it has been suggested that it began as *gimac*, an anagram of *magic* used by conjurers.

**gin** *Gin* 'alcoholic drink' [18] and *gin* 'trap' [13] are different words, but both originated as abbreviations. The latter comes from Old French *engin* (source of English *engine*), while the former is short for *geneva*. This now obsolete term for the spirit was borrowed via Dutch *genever* from Old French *genevre*, a derivative of Latin *jūniperus* 'juniper' (juniper being the chief flavouring agent of gin). English *geneva* was remodelled on the basis of the name of the Swiss city.

▸ engine / juniper

**ginger** [OE] Few foodstuffs can have been as exhaustively etymologized as *ginger* – Professor Alan Ross, for instance, begetter of the U/non-U distinction, wrote an entire 74-page monograph on the history of the word in 1952. And deservedly so, for its ancestry is extraordinarily complex. Its ultimate source was Sanskrit *śṛṅgavēram*, a compound formed from *śṛṅgam* 'horn' and *vēra-* 'body'; the term was applied to 'ginger' because of the shape of its edible root. This passed via Prakrit *singabēra* and Greek *ziggíberis* into Latin as *zinziberi*. In post-classical times the Latin form developed to *gingiber* or *gingiver*, which Old English borrowed as *gingifer*. English reborrowed the word in the 13th century from Old French *gingivre*, which combined with the descendant of the Old English form to produce Middle English *gingivere* – whence modern English *ginger*.

Its verbal use, as in 'ginger up,' appears to come from the practice of putting a piece of ginger into a lazy horse's anus to make it buck its ideas up.

**gingerbread** [13] The idea that *gingerbread* does not much resemble bread is entirely justified by the word's history. For originally it was *gingebras* (a borrowing from Old French), and it meant 'preserved ginger.' By the mid-14th century, by the process known as folk etymology (the substitution of a more for a less familiar form), *-bread* had begun to replace *-bras*, and it was only a matter of time (the early 15th century, apparently) before sense followed form.

The expression 'take the gilt off the gingerbread' (not recorded before the late 19th century) comes from the fact that formerly gingerbread was often decorated with gold leaf.

**gingerly** see GENERAL

**gipsy** [16] In the 16th century, it was widely thought that the Romany people originated in Egypt. They were therefore called *gipcyans* or *gipsens*, which was simply an alteration of *Egyptian*. The modern form of the word developed in the 17th century (perhaps influenced by Latin *Aegyptius*). In American English the spelling *gypsy* is generally preferred. (Spanish *gitano* 'gipsy,' incidentally, has a similar origin.)

▸ Egyptian

**giraffe** [17] The 16th-century name for the 'giraffe' was *camelopard*, a compound of *camel* and *leopard* appropriate enough in view of the animal's long neck and leopard-like spots, but in the 17th century a rival term came on the scene – *giraffe*. This was borrowed from either French *girafe* or Italian *giraffa*, both

of which go back to Arabic *zirāfah*, a word probably of African origin.

**girdle** English has two words *girdle*. The more familiar, 'belt' [OE], goes back, together with its relatives *garth*, *gird* [OE], and *girth* [14], to a prehistoric Germanic *\*gurd-*, *\*gard-*, *\*gerd-* which denoted 'surrounding .' From *\*gurd-* came the verb *\*gurthjan*, which produced both *gird* and *girdle* (as well as relatives in other Germanic languages, such as German *gürtel*, Dutch *gordel*, and Swedish *gördel*, all meaning 'belt'), while *\*gerd-* formed the basis of *\*gerdō*, acquired by English via Old Norse *gjorth* as *girth*.

*Girdle* 'metal baking plate' [15] (as in *girdle cake*) is a Scottish alteration of *griddle* (see GRID).

▸ garth, gird, girth

**girl** [13] Where *girl* comes from is one of the unsolved puzzles of English etymology. What is at least clear is that originally it meant 'child' in general rather than specifically 'female child' (a mid 15th-century text refers to *knave-gerlys* 'male children'), but where it came from is not known. Among suggestions for words that may be connected are Low German *göre* 'child, kid' and Norwegian dialect *gurre* 'lamb.'

**gist** [18] *Cest action gist*, literally 'this action lies,' was an Old French expression denoting that a case was sustainable in law and could be proceeded with. English took over *gist*, which was the third person singular of the verb *gésir* 'lie,' as a legal term meaning 'grounds for action in a suit.' The more general modern meaning, 'central point,' developed in the 19th century.

**give** [OE] *Give* is part of a widespread Germanic family of verbs, including also German *geben*, Dutch *geven*, Swedish *giva*, and Danish *give*, not to mention Gothic *giban*. They all come from a prehistoric Germanic *\*geban*, a verb of uncertain ancestry (it has been suggested that it was related to Latin *habēre* 'have,' their opposite meaning being accounted for by a shared notion of 'reaching out the hands' – either to 'take and have' or to 'give').

**gizzard** [14] Latin *gigeria* denoted the 'cooked entrails of poultry,' something of a delicacy in ancient Rome (the word may have been borrowed from Persian *jigar*). This produced a Vulgar Latin *\*gicerium*, which passed into Old French as *giser*. English acquired it, but did not change it from *giser* to *gizzard* until the 16th century (the addition of a so-called 'parasitic' *d* or *t* to the end of a word also accounts for *pilchard*, *varmint*, and the now obsolete *scholard* for *scholar*, among others).

**glacier** [18] Latin *glaciēs* meant 'ice' (it probably came from Indo-European *\*gel-* 'cold,' which also produced English *cold* and Latin *gelidus* 'cold'). Its Vulgar Latin descendant was *\*glacia*, which passed into French as *glace* (whence English *glacé* 'iced, crystallized' [19]). A derivative *glacière* was used in French-speaking areas of the Alps for a 'moving mass of ice.' It later became *glacier*, the form in which English borrowed it.

*Glacial* [17] comes from the Latin derivative *glaciālis*.

▶ cold, glance, jelly

**glad** [OE] The original meaning of Old English *glæd* was 'bright, shining.' It went back to a prehistoric Germanic *\*glathaz*, which was related to Latin *glaber* 'smooth, bald' (source of English *glabrous* [17] and Old Slavic *gladuku* 'smooth'). 'Happy' is a secondary semantic development, which evidently took place before the various Germanic dialects went their own way, for it is shared by Swedish and Danish *glad* (the sense 'smooth,' also an extension of 'bright, shining,' is preserved in German *glatt*).

▶ glabrous

**gladiator** [16] The main Latin word for 'sword' was *gladius*. It was probably borrowed from a Celtic word, in which case its relatives would include Irish *claideb*, Welsh *cleddyf*, and Scots Gaelic *claidheamh* (which with the addition of *mór* 'great' produced English *claymore* [18]). Among its derivatives were *gladiātor*, literally 'swordsman,' and *gladiolus*, literally 'little sword,' acquired by English in the 16th century.

▶ claymore, gladiolus

**glamour** [18] Unlikely as it may seem, *glamour* is ultimately the same word as *grammar*. This seems to have been used in the Middle Ages for 'learning' in general, and hence, by superstitious association, for 'magic' (there is no actual record of this, but the related *gramarye* was employed in that sense). Scottish English had the form *glamour* for *grammar* (*l* is phonetically close to *r*, and the two are liable to change places), used for 'enchantment,' or a 'spell,' for whose introduction to general English Sir Walter Scott was largely responsible. The literal sense 'enchanted' has now slipped into disuse, gradually replaced since the early 19th century by 'delusive charm,' and latterly 'fashionable attractiveness.'

▶ grammar

**glance** [15] 'Touch or deflect lightly,' as in 'glance off something' and a 'glancing blow,' is the primary meaning of *glance*; 'look briefly' did not develop until the 16th century. The word may have originated as an alteration of the Middle English verb *glacen* 'glide, slide' (probably under the influence of Middle English *glenten*, the ancestor of modern English *glint*). *Glacen* was borrowed from Old French *glacier* 'slide,' a derivative of *glace* 'ice' (from which English also gets *glacier*).

▶ glacier

**glare** see GLASS

**glasnost** [20] Russian *glasnost* means literally 'publicity'; it is a derivative of *glas* 'voice.' It was originally applied to the concept of 'freedom of information within a society' by Lenin, but the man responsible for introducing the word to the English language in 1985 was Soviet President Mikhail Gorbachev (see also PERESTROIKA).

**glass** [OE] The making of glass goes back to ancient Egyptian times, and so most of the words for it in the various Indo-European languages are of considerable antiquity. In those days, it was far easier to make coloured glass than the familiar clear glass of today. In particular, Roman glass was standardly bluish-green, and many words for 'glass' originated in colour terms signifying 'blue' or 'green.' In the case of *glass*, its distant ancestor was Indo-European *\*gel-*or *\*ghel-*, which produced a host of colour adjectives ranging in application from 'grey' through 'blue' and 'green' to 'yellow.' Among its descendants was West Germanic *\*glasam*, which gave German, Dutch, Swedish, and Danish *glas* and English *glass*. A secondary semantic development of the word's base, glass being a shiny substance, was 'shine, gleam'; this probably lies behind English *glare* [13], whose primary sense is 'shine dazzlingly' (the change of *s* to *r* is a well-known phonetic phenomenon, termed 'rhoticization'). Irish *gloine* 'glass' also comes from Indo-European *\*g(h)el-*, and French *verre* and Italian *vetro* 'glass' go back to Latin *vitrum* 'glass' (source of English *vitreous*), which also meant 'woad,' a plant which gives a blue dye.

The use of the plural *glasses* for 'spectacles' dates from the mid-17th century. The verb *glaze* [14] is an English derivative of *glass*.

▶ glaze

**gleam** [OE] *Gleam* is one of a very wide range of English words beginning with *gl* that denote 'shining' (others include *glare*, *glint*, *glister*, *glitter*, and *glow*). Originally it was a noun, which came from Germanic *\*glaim-*, *\*glim-* (source also of *glimmer* [15]); the verb is a 13th-century development.

▶ glimmer, glimpse

**glebe** see GLOBE

**glee** [OE] *Glee* has had a strange history. It was common in Old English times, both for 'entertainment, having fun' (source of the modern sense 'joy, delight'), and in the more specific sense 'musical entertainment' (from which we get the 'unaccompanied part-song' of glee clubs). It survived healthily into the 15th century but then went into long-term decline. By the 17th century it seems virtually to have become extinct. However, in 1755 Dr Johnson in his *Dictionary* said that it was 'not now used except in ludicrous writing, or with some mixture of irony and contempt,' signalling the start of a revival which got fully under way towards the end of the 18th century. How and why it came back from the dead in this way is not known. Its source was Germanic *gliujam.

**glimmer**    see GLEAM

**glimpse**   [14]   Glimpse originally meant 'shine faintly.' It comes from the same Germanic source (*glaim-, *glim-) as produced English gleam and glimmer. The modern sense 'see briefly' developed in the 18th century from the noun glimpse, originally a 'momentary or dim flash,' hence 'faint brief appearance,' and finally 'sight of something afforded by such an appearance.'

▶ gleam, glimmer

**glitter**   [14]   Glitter goes back to a Germanic *glit-, denoting 'shining, bright,' which also produced German glitzern 'sparkle' (source of English glitz) and gleissen 'glisten' and Swedish glittra 'glitter.' English probably acquired it via Old Norse glitra.

▶ glitz

**glitz**   [20]   Glitz, a sort of 'shallow but exciting and fashionable sparkle and showiness,' is a back-formation from glitzy, an American slang term fashionable in the early 1980s. This in turn was derived from Yiddish glitz 'glitter,' which came from German glitzern 'sparkle' (a relative of English glitter). Its fortuitous resemblance to a blend of glamour and Ritz contributes to its expressiveness.

▶ glitter

**globe**   [16]   Globe comes from Latin globus, probably via Old French globe. Globus was related to glēba 'lump of earth' (source of English glebe [14]), and may denote etymologically 'something rolled up into a ball.'

▶ glebe

**glory**   [13]   Latin glōria had two separate descendants in Old French: glore, which produced modern French gloire, and glorie, which English took over via Anglo-Norman. The source of the Latin word, which is also the ancestor of Italian and Spanish gloria and Irish Gaelic glóir, is not known. The now obsolete English sense 'pride,' inherited from Latin, is preserved in vainglorious [15].

**gloss**   English has two words gloss. The one meaning 'shining surface' [16] is of unknown origin, although no doubt it belongs ultimately to the general nexus of words beginning gl- which mean broadly 'bright, shining.' Forms such as Icelandic glossi 'spark' and Swedish dialect glossa 'glow' suggest a Scandinavian origin. Gloss 'explanation, definition' [16] goes back to Greek glossa 'tongue,' source also of English epiglottis [17]. This developed the secondary sense 'language' (as English tongue itself has done), and was borrowed by Latin as glōssa meaning 'foreign word needing an explanation,' and eventually the 'explana-

tion' itself. It passed into English via medieval Latin glōsa and Old French glose as gloze in the 14th century, and was reformulated as gloss on the basis of classical Latin glōssa in the 16th century. Glossary [14] comes from the Latin derivative glossārium.

▶ epiglottis, glossary

**glove**   [OE]   Not surprisingly, most words for 'glove' in European languages are related in some way to words for 'hand': German handschuh and Dutch handschoen, for example, mean literally 'handshoe'; Greek kheirís was derived from kheíris 'hand'; and Rumanian manusa was based on Latin manus 'hand.' And glove appears to be no exception; it probably goes back to a prehistoric Germanic *galōfō, in which *ga- was a collective prefix and lōfō meant 'hand' (Swedish dialect loof 'palm of the hand' comes from it).

**glow**   [OE]   Glow comes ultimately from Indo-European *ghlō-, in which the ghl- seems originally to have had some sort of symbolic function, as if directly representing the notion of 'brightness, shining' in speech. Its Germanic descendant *glō- produced German glühen, Dutch gloeien, and Swedish glöda (all meaning 'glow') as well as English glow and probably also glower [16].

▶ glower

**glucose**    see GLYCERINE

**glue**   [14]   Glue is an ancient word, whose ancestry can be traced back all the way to Indo-European *gloi-, *glei-, *gli- 'stick.' Its Latin descendant was glūten, from which English gets gluten [16], glutinous [16], and agglutinate [16]. In post-classical times this spawned a new form, glūs, which English acquired via Old French glu as glue.

▶ agglutinate, gluten, glutinous

**glutton**   [13]   Indo-European *gel- produced a wide range of descendants in the general semantic area 'swallow,' among them Latin gula 'throat' and its offspring French gueule 'mouth' and English gullet; German kehle 'throat'; and Latin gluttīre 'swallow,' which was probably the ultimate source of English glut [14]. Another was Latin gluttō 'overeater,' which English acquired via Old French gluton.

▶ glut, gullet

**glycerine**   [19]   Greek glukús meant 'sweet' (its derivative gleukos 'sweet thing' is the ancestor of English glucose [19]). It had a variant glukerós, which the French chemist Michel-Eugène Chevreul took as the basis of a name of a recently discovered syrupy liquid obtained from fats or oils – glycerin (adopted by English as glycerine or glycerin).

▶ glucose

**gnarled**   [17]   Gnarled is essentially a 19th-century word. It is recorded once before then, in Shakespeare's Measure for measure 1603 ('Thy sharp and sulphurous bolt splits the unwedgable and gnarled oak'), but its modern currency is due to its adoption by early 19th-century romantic writers. It is probably a variant of *knurled* [17], itself a derivative of *knur* or *knor* 'rough misshapen lump, as on a tree trunk' [14], which is related to German *knorren* 'knot, gnarled branch or trunk.'

▶ knurled

**gnome** [18] *Gnome* comes via French from Latin *gnomus*, a word coined by the 16th-century Swiss physician Paracelsus for a type of being that lives in the earth, in the same way that fish live in water. It seems to have been a pure invention on his part, and is not based on or related to Greek *gnómē* 'opinion, judgment' (source of English *gnomic* [19] and connected with *agnostic*, *diagnosis*, and *know*).

The term *gnomes of Zürich* for 'Swiss financiers' is first recorded in the early 1960s.

**go** [OE] *Go* is an ancient verb, traceable back to a prehistoric Indo-European base *ghēi-* or *ghē-*. This seems to have been relatively unproductive outside the Germanic languages (Sanskrit *hā-*, *hī-* 'leave' and Greek *kikhánō* 'reach' may be descendants of it), but it has provided the basic word for 'move along, proceed' in all the Germanic languages, including German *gehen*, Dutch *gaan*, Swedish *gå*, Danish *gaa*, and English *go*. In Old and Middle English its past tense was *ēode*, later *yode*, a word of uncertain origin, but from about 1500 this was replaced by *went*, originally the past tense of *wend*.

**goad** [OE] *Goad* comes via prehistoric Germanic *gaidō* from an Indo-European base *ghai-*. This also produced an Old English word for 'spear,' *gār*, which survives today in *garlic* [OE], etymologically 'spear leek.'

▶ garlic

**goal** [16] The earliest examples of what can confidently be identified as the word *goal* come from the first half of the 16th century, when it was used for both the 'finishing line of a race' and the 'posts through which the ball is sent in football.' Before that we are in the realm of speculation. A 14th-century text from Kent has the word *gol* 'boundary,' which could quite plausibly be the ancestor of the 16th-century *goal*, and *gol* suggest an Old English *gāl*. No such word has come down to us, but the Old English verb *gǣlan* 'hinder,' which looks as though it could have been related to a noun *gāl*, indicates that if it existed it might have meant 'obstacle, barrier' (which would lead on quite logically through 'boundary' and 'finishing line' to 'something to be aimed at').

**goat** [OE] Old English had no all-purpose word for 'goat'; the male goat was a *bucca* ('buck') and the female goat was a *gāt*. In early Middle English, *goat* began to encroach on the semantic territory of *buck*, and

by the 14th century it had come to be the dominant form for both sexes, as is shown by the emergence around that time of the distinguishing terms *she-goat* and *he-goat* (*nanny-goat* and *billy-goat* are much later – 18th-century and 19th-century respectively). *Goat* itself comes via prehistoric Germanic *gaitaz* (source of German *geiss*, Dutch *geit*, Swedish *get*, and Danish *ged*) from Indo-European *ghaidos*. This may be related to Lithuanian *zaidziu* 'play,' and if so, the *goat* could be etymologically the 'animal that jumps about' (semantic development in the opposite direction has given English *caper* from Latin *caper* 'goat').

**goblin** [14] *Goblin* probably came via Anglo-Norman from medieval Latin *gobelīnus*, which was reported by the 12th-century English chronicler Ordericus Vitalis as haunting the area around Évreux in northwestern France. It is thought that this could have been based on German *kobold* 'goblin,' source of English *cobalt*.

▶ cobalt

**god** [OE] Similar in form though it may be, and appropriate as the semantic connection would be, *god* is not etymologically related to *good*. It probably comes from an Indo-European *ghut-*. This may be related to Sanskrit *havate* and Old Church Slavonic *zovetu*, both meaning 'call,' and if so the underlying etymological meaning of *god* would be 'that which is invoked.' The English word's immediate ancestor was prehistoric Germanic *guth-*, which also produced German *gott*, Dutch *god*, and Swedish and Danish *gud*.

**goffer** see WAFER

**gold** [OE] *Gold* gets its name from its colour. The perception of what this is has varied. In the ancient Germanic languages, *red* was often used as a poetic epithet for 'gold,' and in English this survives into the present day as an archaism. And Latin *aurum* 'gold,' source of French *or* and Italian and Spanish *oro*, is probably related to words for 'dawn' (such as Latin *aurora*), the inspiration in both cases being 'redness.' The word *gold*, however, depends on the metal's yellowness. It goes back to Indo-European *ghel-*, source of English *yellow*. From this was formed *ghltom* 'gold,' which was the ancestor of Russian *zoloto* 'gold,' Polish *złoto* (whence *złoty* 'golden,' used as the name of a Polish coin), Sanskrit *hiranya-* 'gold,' and the various Germanic words for 'gold': English and German *gold*, Dutch *goud*, and Swedish and Danish *guld*.

*Golden* [13] is a Middle English derivative of *gold*, replacing the earlier *gilden*, which came from Old English *gylden*. Of related forms in other Germanic languages, Dutch *gulden* is the source of the coin-name *guilder* [15]. The verb *gild*, from Old English *gyldan*, retains its original vowel; *gilt* [14] began life as its past participle.

▶ gall, gild, gilt, guilder, yellow

**golliwog** [19] It was Florence Upton (1873–1922), an American-born illustrator and writer of children's books, who dreamed up the black-faced male doll we now know as the *golliwog*. It first appeared in the story *The Adventures of Two Dutch Dolls* – and *a 'Golliwog'* 1895, with verses by Florence's mother Bertha. The inspiration for the word may have been *golly* [19], a euphemism for *God*, and *polliwog*, an American term for a 'tadpole' (which came from Middle English *polwygle*, a compound of *pol* 'head' and the verb *wiglen* 'wiggle'). The offensive *wog* [20] for 'black person' is probably short for *golliwog*.

**gondola** [16] The *gondola*, the narrow boat used on Venetian canals, gets its name from the way it rocks gently in the water. Italian *gondola* is an adaptation of *gondolà*, a word meaning 'roll, rock' in the Rhaeto-Romanic dialect of Friuli, in northeastern Italy (Rhaeto-Romanic is a cover term for a group of Romance-language dialects spoken in southern Switzerland, northern Italy, and the Tyrol). *Gondola* was first applied to the cabin suspended from an airship or balloon in the 1890s (probably as a translation of German *gondel*).

**gonorrhoea**   see GENERAL

**good** [OE] *Good* is such a general, all-embracing word for anything regarded in a positive light that it perhaps comes as something of a surprise that it is not an ancient primary term distributed throughout the Indo-European languages. It is a strictly Germanic word (German has *gut*, Dutch *goed*, and Swedish and Danish *god*), and it goes back to prehistoric Germanic *\*gath-* 'bring together' (source of English *gather* and *together*); the progression of senses appears to be 'brought together, united,' 'fitting, suitable,' 'pleasing.' and 'good.' See also BEST.

▶ gather, together

**good-bye** [16] The *good* of *good-bye* was originally *God*. The expression is a contraction of *God be with you*, a form of farewell first recorded in the late 16th century. Its gradual reduction can be traced through a series of metamorphoses (Shakespeare, for instance, had *God be wy you* and *God buy' ye*), and it did not reach modern *good-bye* until the 18th century. The substitution of *good* for *God* seems to have been mainly due to the influence of such phrases as *good day* and *good night*.

▶ god

**googol** [20] There are comparatively few 'new' words in the English language – that is, words which have not been made up from combinations of old words, or borrowed from other languages, but have sprung up as entirely new growths – but this is one of them. When in the 1930s the American mathematician Dr Edward Kasmer was trying to think of a name for an unimaginably large number, ten to the power of a hundred, he asked his nine-year-old nephew for a suggestion, and *googol* was what he got. It has never really caught on in technical use, although it has spawned a compound of its own – the *googolplex*, ten to the power of a googol.

**goose** [OE] *Goose* has relatives throughout the Indo-European languages: Latin *ānser*, Greek *khḗn*, Sanskrit *hansás*, Russian *gus'*, Czech *husa*, German and Dutch *gans*, and Swedish *gåas* (not to mention Irish Gaelic *gēis* 'swan') all go back to a prehistoric Indo-European *\*ghans-*, which probably originated as an imitation of the honking of geese. (The only major exceptions to this cosy family are French *oie* and Italian and Spanish *oca*, which come from Latin *avicula* 'little bird.') A Germanic extension of the base was *\*ganit-* or *\*ganot-*, which produced not only English *gander* 'male goose' but also *gannet*. *Gosling* [15] was borrowed from the Old Norse diminutive *gáeslingr*, literally 'little goose'; and *goshawk* [OE] is a compound of *goose* and *hawk*.

The verb *goose* 'jab between the buttocks,' first recorded in the 1870s, may come from a supposed resemblance between the upturned thumb with which such jabbing may be done and the neck of a goose.

▶ gooseberry, goshawk

**gooseberry** [16] Probably, when all is said and done, *gooseberry* is simply a compound of *goose* and *berry*. But no one has ever been able to explain satisfactorily why the *gooseberry* should have been named after the *goose*, and there has been no lack of alternative etymological suggestions for the word – notably that *goose* is an alteration of an old dialect word for the 'gooseberry', such as *groser* or *gozell*, borrowed ultimately from French *groseille* 'gooseberry.' The quaint alteration *goosegog* dates from at least the early 19th century.

*Play gooseberry* 'be an uncomfortably superfluous third person with two lovers' also goes back to the early 19th century, and may have originated in the notion of a chaperone (ostensibly) occupying herself with picking gooseberries while the couple being chaperoned did what they were doing (*gooseberry-picker* was an early 19th-century term for a 'chaperone').

**gore** English has three separate words *gore*, two of them perhaps ultimately related. *Gore* 'blood' [OE] originally meant 'dung, shit,' or more generally 'filth, dirt, slime,' and related words in other languages, such as Dutch *goor* 'mud, filth,' Old Norse *gor* 'slime,' and Welsh *gôr* 'pus,' round out a semantic picture of 'unpleasant semi-liquid material,' with frequent specific application to 'bodily excretions.' It was from this background that the sense 'blood,' and particularly 'coagulated blood,' emerged in the mid-16th century. *Gore* 'triangular piece of cloth, as let into a skirt' [OE] comes from Old English *gāra* 'triangular piece of land' (a sense preserved in the London street-name *Kensing-*

ton *Gore*). This was related to Old English *gār* 'spear' (as in *garlic*; see GOAD), the semantic connection being that a spearhead is roughly triangular. *Gore* 'wound with horns' [14] originally meant simply 'stab, pierce'; it too may come ultimately from *gār* 'spear,' although there is some doubt about this.

▶ garlic

**gorge** [14] *Gorge* originally meant 'throat'; the metaphorical extension to 'rocky ravine' did not really take place until the mid 18th century (the semantic connection was presumably 'narrow opening between which things pass'). The word was borrowed from Old French *gorge* 'throat,' which goes back via Vulgar Latin *\*gurga* to Latin *gurges* 'whirlpool' from which English gets *regurgitate* [17].

The superficially similar *gorgeous* [15], incidentally, is not related. It was adapted from Old French *gorgias* 'fine, elegant,' but no one knows where that came from.

▶ regurgitate

**gorilla** [19] The first we hear of *gorilla* is as a word used in a Greek translation of the 5th-century BC Carthaginian explorer Hanno's account of a voyage to West Africa. He reported encountering there a tribe of wild hairy people, whose females were, according to a local interpreter, called *goríllas*. In 1847 the American missionary and scientist Thomas Savage adopted the word as the species name of the great ape *Troglodytes gorilla*, and by the 1850s it had passed into general use.

**gorse** [OE] *Gorse* appears to mean etymologically 'prickly bush.' It has been traced back to an Indo-European source *\*ghrzd-* denoting 'roughness' or 'prickliness,' which also produced German *gerste* 'barley.' Of the plant's other names, *furze* [OE] is of unknown origin, while *whin* [11] was probably borrowed from a Scandinavian language.

**goshawk**     see GOOSE
**gosling**     see GOOSE
**gospel** [OE] Etymologically, *gospel* is 'good news.' It was coined in Old English as *gōdspel*, a compound of *gōd* 'good' and *spel* 'discourse, tidings, news' (the same word as the modern English magic *spell*), which was a direct translation of Latin *bona annuntiatio*. This in turn was a literal interpretation or gloss of ecclesiastical Latin *evangelium* (whence English *evangelist*) and its source, Greek *euaggélion*, which originally meant 'reward for bringing good news,' but in its later sense 'good news' *tout court* was applied to any of the four accounts of Christ's life written by Matthew, Mark, Luke, and John.

▶ good

**gossamer** [14] It would be pleasant to think that *gossamer*, originally 'fine cobwebs,' is a descendant of an earlier *goose-summer*, but unfortunately

there is not enough evidence to make this more than a conjecture. The theory goes as follows: mid-autumn is a time when geese for the table are plentiful (November was once known as *gänsemonat* 'geese-month' in German), and so a warm period around then might have been termed *goose-summer* (we now call it an *Indian summer*); the silken filaments of *gossamer* are most commonly observed floating in the air on such warm autumnal days; and so the spiders' webs were christened with the name of the season.

**gossip** [OE] The Anglo-Saxons' term for a 'godparent' was *godsibb*, a compound formed from *god* 'god' (just as in modern English *godmother, godfather*, etc) and *sib* 'relative' (a word of unknown origin from which modern English gets *sibling*). It denotes one's 'relative in God,' one's 'spiritual relative.' By Middle English times, however, it had come down in the world somewhat, to mean simply 'close friend,' and by the 16th century it was being used for 'one who indulges in idle talk.' The modern sense 'idle talk' developed from the verb in the 19th century.

▶ god, sibling

**gouge** [15] *Gouge* may be of Celtic origin – a resemblance to forms such as Welsh *gylf* 'beak' and Cornish *gilb* 'borer' has been noted. But its earliest positively identifiable ancestor is late Latin *gubia*, whose Old French descendant *gouge* was borrowed by English.

**gout** [13] Latin *gutta* meant literally 'drop' (the spelling of *gutta* in English *gutta percha* [19] shows its influence, although in fact the term originated in Malay *getah percha* 'gum tree'). It was applied metaphorically to various diseases ascribed to the precipitation of fluids from one part of the body to another, among them pain in the joints which was supposed to be caused by poisonous material deposited from the blood (not far wide of the mark, for the condition now known as *gout* is due to the accumulation of uric-acid products in the joints). English acquired the word via Old French *goute*.

▶ gutter

**govern** [13] Politicians' clichés about 'steering the ship of state' are no new thing; for the distant ancestor of English *govern* is the Greek verb *kubernán* 'steer a ship' (source also of English *cybernetics*). It developed the metaphorical sense 'guide, rule,' and it was this that passed with it via Latin *gubernāre* and Old French *governer* into English. The Latin form is preserved in *gubernatorial* 'of a governer' [18].

▶ cybernetics, gubernatorial

**grab** [16] *Grab* is a Germanic word. It was probably borrowed from Middle Dutch or Middle Low German *grabben*. These were descendants of a prehistoric Germanic *\*grab-*, which could well have been related to the *graip-*, *grip-* which produced *grip*, *gripe*, and *grope*.

▶ grip, gripe, grope

**grace** [12] Latin *grātus* meant 'pleasing.' Its most obvious English descendants are *grateful*, *gratify*, *gratuity*, etc, but it is also responsible for *grace* (not to mention the even better disguised *agree*). Its derived noun *grātia* 'pleasure, favour, thanks' passed into English via Old French *grace*. *Gracious* [13] comes ultimately from Latin *grātiōsus*; *grateful* [15] is an English formation. (The apparently similar *gracile* 'slender' [17], incidentally, is not etymologically related; it comes from Latin *gracilis* 'slender.')

▶ agree, grateful

**gradual** [16] Latin *grādus* 'step' has been a remarkably prolific source of English words. Beside *grade* [16] itself, it has contributed the derivatives *gradation* [16], *gradient* [19], *gradual* (from medieval Latin *graduālis*, literally 'proceeding by steps'), *graduate* [15], and *retrograde* [14]. The derived verb *gradī* 'walk, go' has produced *ingredient*, and its past participial stem *gress-* has given, among others, *aggression*, *congress*, *digress* [16], *progress* [15], and *transgress* [16]. And *degrade* and *degree* are of the same parentage, the latter filtered through Old French. The origins of Latin *grādus* itself are not known.

▶ aggression, congress, degrade, degree, digress, grade, gradient, ingredient, progress, transgress

**graffiti** [19] Although it denotes 'writing,' *graffiti* has no etymological connection with Greek *gráphein*, source of English *graphic*. It comes from the plural of Italian *graffito*, a diminutive form of the noun *graffio* 'scratching.' This was derived from the verb *graffiare* 'scratch,' itself originally formed from *graffio* 'hook.'

**graft** [15] *Graft*, in its original sense 'plant part inserted into a living plant' (the application to skin and other animal tissue is a late 19th-century development), came from its resemblance in shape to a pencil. Greek *graphíon* meant 'writing implement, stylus' (it was a derivative of the verb *gráphein* 'write,' source of English *graphic*). It passed via Latin *graphium* into Old French as *grafe*, gradually changing in its precise application with the advance of writing technology. By the time it reached Old French it denoted a 'pencil,' and it was then that the resemblance to two artificially united plant stems was noted and the metaphor born. English took the word over as *graff* in the late 14th century (it actually survived in that form into the 19th century), and within a hundred years had added a *-t* to the end to give modern English *graft*. *Graft* 'corruption,' first recorded in mid 19th-century America, may be the same word, perhaps derived from the notion of a *graft* as an 'insertion,' hence 'something extra, on the side.' *Graft* 'hard work' [19], on the other hand, is probably a differ-

ent word, perhaps based on the English dialect verb *graft* 'dig,' an alteration of *grave* 'dig.'

▶ graphic

**grain** [13] *Grain* comes via Old French from Latin *grānum* 'seed.' Its prehistoric Indo-European ancestor was *\*grnóm*, literally 'worn-down particle,' which also produced English *corn*, and it has given English a remarkably wide range of related forms: not just obvious derivatives like *granary* [16], *granule* [17], and *ingrained* [16], but also *garner* [12] (originally a noun derived from Latin *grānārium* 'granary'), *gram* 'chick-pea' [18] (from the Portuguese descendant of *grānum*, now mainly encountered in 'gram flour'), *grange*, *granite*, *gravy*, *grenade*, and the second halves of *filigree* and *pomegranate*.

▶ filigree, garner, granary, granite, gravy, grenade, ingrained, pomegranate

**gram** [18] *Gram*, or *gramme* as it is sometimes spelled, was borrowed at the end of the 18th century from French *gramme*, the term adopted in 1799 as the basic unit of weight in the metric system. The word itself goes back via late Latin *gramma* 'small unit' to Greek *grámma* (source of English *grammar*), which originally meant 'letter of the alphabet' but later came to be used for 'small weight.'

▶ grammar

**grammar** [14] Etymologically, *grammar* is the 'art of letters.' The word comes via Anglo-Norman *gramere*, Old French *gramaire*, and Latin *grammatica* from Greek *grammatikē*, a noun use of the adjective *grammatikós* 'of letters' (whence English *grammatical* [16]). This was a derivative of the noun *grámma* 'something written,' hence 'letter of the alphabet,' which was related to the verb *gráphein* 'write' (source of English *graphic*) and also gave English *gram* and the suffix *-gram* that appears in a wide range of English words, from *anagram* and *diagram* to *telegram* and *kissagram*.

▶ glamour, gram, graphic

**gramophone** [19] The term *gramophone* was registered as a trademark in 1887 by the German-born American inventor Emil Berliner for a sound recording and reproducing device he had developed using a disc (as opposed to the cylinder of Edison's phonograph). He coined it simply by reversing the elements of *phonogram*, a term adopted for a 'sound recording' in the early 1880s and composed of descendants of Greek *phōnē* 'voice, sound' and *grámma* 'something written.' It seems to have begun to give way to *record player* in the mid 1950s.

**granary**        see GRAIN

**grand** [16] The original Latin word for 'big' was *magnus* (as in *magnify*, *magnitude*, etc). However, it also had *grandis*. This not only denoted great physical size; it also had connotations of moral greatness or sublimity, and in addition often carried the specialized meaning 'full-grown.' This last, together with a possibly etymologically connected Greek *brénthos* 'pride' and Old Church Slavonic *gradi* 'breast' suggest that its underlying meaning may be 'swelling.' French (*grand*) and Italian and Spanish (*grande*) have taken it over as their main adjective for 'big,' but in English it remains a more specialized word, for things or people that are 'great' or 'imposing.' Its use for denoting family relationships separated by two generations, as in *grandmother*, was adopted from Old French, and goes back, in the case of *grandame* and *grandsire*, to the 13th century, well before the independent adjective *grand* itself was borrowed. But the underlying notion is as old as the Greeks and Romans, who used *mégas* and *magnus* in the same way.

**grand prix**   see PRIZE

**grange**   [13]   Originally, a *grange* was 'somewhere for storing grain,' a 'barn.' The word comes via Old French *grange* from medieval Latin *grānica*, a noun use of an unrecorded adjective *\*grānicus* 'of grain,' which was derived from *grānum* 'grain, seed' (source of English *grain*). Of its present-day meanings, 'farm-house' developed in the 14th century, 'country house' in the 16th century.

▶ grain

**granite**   [17]   Etymologically, *granite* is 'grainy or granular rock.' The word was borrowed from Italian *granito*, a derivative of *grano* 'grain' (which is related to English *grain*). (English acquired the Italian feminine form *granita* in the 19th century as a term for a granular form of water ice.)

▶ grain

**grant**   [13]   To *grant* something etymologically implies an element of 'belief' or 'trust,' although there is virtually no semantic trace of these left in the word today. Its ultimate source was *crēdens*, the present participle of Latin *crēdere* 'believe' (source of English *credence, credible*, etc). This was used as the basis of a new Vulgar Latin verb *\*crēdentāre*, which passed into Old French as *creanter* 'insure, guarantee.' Its later variant *greanter* or *granter* gave English *grant*.

▶ credence, credible, credit

**grape**   [13]   Not surprisingly, given the northerliness of the British Isles, English does not have its own native word for 'grape.' In Old English it was called *wīnberige*, literally 'wineberry,' and the Old French word *grape* which Middle English borrowed as *grape* meant 'bunch of grapes,' not 'grape.' It was probably a derivative of the verb *graper* 'gather grapes,' which itself was based on the noun *grape* 'hook' (a relative of English *cramp, crampon*, and *grapnel* [14]). The underlying notion is of a bunch of grapes being gathered with a sort of pruning hook. (The use of a word that originally meant 'bunch' for 'grape' is in fact fairly common: Czech *hrozen*, Rumanian

*stugure*, German *traube*, and Lithuanian *keke* all follow the same pattern, as does French *raisin*, source of English *raisin*.)

▶ cramp, crampon, grapnel

**graphic**   [17]   The profoundest influence that Greek *gráphein* 'write' has had on English has no doubt been through its combining form *-graphos*, which has provided us with a whole host of words, both original Greek formations and new English ones, from *autograph* to *telegraph*. But descendants in their own right include *graphic* (which came via Latin *graphicus* from the Greek derivative *graphikós*), *graphite* [18] (originally coined in German as *graphit*, from its being used in writing implements), and *graph* [19] (short for *graphic formular*, a term used in chemistry for a diagram representing in lines the relationship between elements). Greek *gráphein* itself originally meant 'scratch' (it is etymologically related to English *carve*); it was applied to early methods of writing, by scratching on clay tablets with a stylus, and kept its job when writing technology moved on.

▶ carve, graft, graph, graphite

**grapnel**   see GRAPE

**grass**   [OE]   Reflecting its status as the commonest and most obvious of plants (and, for agricultural communities, the most important), *grass* etymologically simply means 'that which grows.' It comes from *\*grō-, \*gra-*, the prehistoric Germanic base which also produced *grow* (and *green*). This gave the noun *\*grasam*, from which German and Dutch get *gras*, Swedish *gräs*, and English *grass*.

▶ graze, green, grow

**grate**   *Grate* 'framework for holding burning fuel' [14] and *grate* 'rub' [15] are different words. The former comes via Old French *grate* 'grille' and Vulgar Latin *\*grāta* from Latin *crātis* 'wickerwork, hurdle.' *Grate* 'rub' is ultimately Germanic (its ultimate ancestor was the Germanic verb *\*krattōn*, source of modern German *kratzen* 'scratch'), but it reached English via Old French *grater* 'scrape.' *Gratin* [19] comes from the derived French noun *gratin*.

▶ gratin

**grateful**   [16]   *Grateful* is a curious sort of adjective. The *grate* that a *grateful* person is full of is a now obsolete adjective, meaning 'pleasing' and 'thankful,' which was derived from Latin *grātus*. It is unusual for adjectives ending in *-ful* themselves to be formed from adjectives, rather than from nouns, and it has been suggested in this case that the related Italian *gradevole* 'pleasing' may have had some influence. Latin *grātus* itself meant 'pleasing' as well as 'thankful,' and has also given English *congratulate* [16], *gratify* [16]. *gratitude* [16], and *gratuity* [16], and, via the derived noun *grātia, grace* and *gratis* [15].

▶ congratulate, grace, gratis, gratitude

**gratin** see GRATE

**grave** Modern English has essentially two words
grave. *Grave* 'burial place' goes back ultimately to prehistoric Indo-European *\*ghrebh-*'dig,' which also produced Latvian *grebt* 'hollow out' and Old Church
Slavonic *pogreti* 'bury.' Its Germanic descendant had
variants *\*grōb-* (source of *groove*), *\*grub-* (whence
*grub*), and *\*grab-*. This last formed the basis of
*\*graban*, from which have come the verbs for 'dig' in
most Germanic languages, including German *graben*,
Dutch *graven*, Swedish *gräva*, and Danish *grave*. The
English member of the family, *grave*, is now virtually
obsolete as a verb (although its derivative *engrave* [16]
survives); but its nominal relative *grave*, also formed
from *\*grab-*, is still very much with us. *Grave* 'serious'
[16] comes via Old French *grave* from Latin *gravis*
'heavy, important,' source also of English *gravity* and
*grief*. Its application to a backward-leaning accent (as in
è) comes from the original use of such an accent-mark to
indicate low or deep intonation.

▶ engrave, groove, grub / gravity, grief

**gravel** [13] *Gravel* is of Celtic origin. It has been
traced to a prehistoric Celtic *\*gravo-* 'gravel,' never actually recorded but deduced from Breton *grouan* and
Cornish *grow* 'soft granite.' French borrowed it as
*grave* 'gravel, pebbles' (perhaps the source of the English verb *grave* 'clean a ship's bottom' [15], now encountered virtually only in *graving dock*, from the
notion of ships being hauled up on to the pebbles of the
seashore for cleaning). The Old French diminutive of
*grave* was *gravelle* – whence English *gravel*.

**gravity** [16] *Gravity* comes from Latin
*gravitās*, a derivative of the adjective *gravis* 'heavy,
important.' This in turn goes back to a prehistoric Indo-
European *\*gru-*, which also produced Greek *bárus*
'heavy' (source of English *baritone* [19] and *barium*
[19]), Sanskrit *gurús* 'heavy, dignified' (whence English *guru* [17]), Latin *brūtus* 'heavy,' hence 'cumber-
some, stupid' (from which English gets *brute*), Gothic
*kaurus* 'heavy,' and Latvian *grūts* 'heavy, pregnant.'
English descendants of *gravis*, apart from *gravity*, include *grave* 'serious,' *gravid* 'pregnant' [16], *gravitate*
[17], *grief*, and *grudge*.

▶ baritone, barium, brute, grave, grief, grudge, guru

**gravy** [14] To begin with, the word *gravy* signified a sort of spiced stock-based sauce served with white
meat; it was not until the 16th century that its modern
sense 'meat juices' or 'sauce made from them'
emerged. Its origins are problematical. It is generally
agreed that its *v* represents a misreading of an *n* in the
Old French word, *grané*, from which it was borrowed
(modern *v* was written *u* in medieval manuscripts, and
was often very hard to distinguish from *n*); but what the
source of *grané* was is not clear. The favourite candidate is perhaps *grain* (source of English *grain*), as if

'sauce flavoured with grains of spice,' but *graine*
'meat' has also been suggested.

▶ grain

**graze** [OE] There is no difficulty about the etymology of *graze* 'feed on grass': it was formed in Old
English times as a derivative of the noun *græs* (modern
English *grass*). But what about *graze* in the sense
'scrape lightly,' first recorded in the 17th century? In
the absence of any convincing alternative candidates, it
is usually taken to be simply a special use of *graze* 'feed
on grass,' in the sense 'remove grass close to the
ground,' as some animals do in grazing – like a 'close
shave,' in fact.

▶ grass

**grease** [13] Latin *crassus* meant 'solid, thick,
fat,' and hence 'gross, stupid' (English borrowed it in
this latter metaphorical sense as *crass* [16], and it is also
the source of French *gras* 'fat'). On it was based the
Vulgar Latin derived noun *\*crassia* '(melted) animal
fat,' which passed into English via Old French *craisse*,
later *graisse*, and Anglo-Norman *gresse* or *grece*. Old
French *craisse* was the source of *craisset* 'oil lamp,'
from which English got *cresset* [14].

▶ crass, cresset

**great** [OE] The main adjective for 'large' in the
Anglo-Saxon period was the now virtually obsolete
*mickle*. *Great* at that time was for the most part restricted in meaning to 'stout, thick.' In the Middle English
period *great* broadened out in meaning, gradually taking over from *mickle*, but in modern English has itself
been superseded by *big* and *large*, and is now used only
in reference to non-material things. Its origins are a
problem. It comes from a prehistoric West Germanic
*\*grautaz*, which also produced German *gross* and
Dutch *groot* (source of English *groat* 'small coin' [14],
etymologically a 'big' or 'thick' coin), but it is not clear
where *\*grautaz* came from. A resemblance to *grit* and
*groats* has suggested a common origin in Indo-
European *\*ghrēu-* 'rub, pound.'

▶ grit, groat

**green** [OE] *Green* is preeminently the colour of
growing plants, and so appropriately it was formed
from the same prehistoric Germanic base, *\*grō-*, as produced the verb *grow*. Its West and North Germanic derivative *\*gronjaz* gave German *grün*, Dutch *groen*,
Swedish *grön*, and Danish *grøn* as well as English
*green*.

▶ grass, grow

**gregarious** see SEGREGATE

**grenade** [16] The original *grenades* were
small spherical explosive-filled cases with a wick on
top. In shape, they bore more than a passing resemblance to pomegranates. The Old French term for
'pomegranate' was *pome grenate*, or just *grenate* for
short, and it was this abbreviated form, altered to *gre-*

*nade* under the influence of the related Spanish *granada*, that was applied to the explosive device. *Grenadier* [17] came from the French derivative *grenadier* 'grenade-thrower.'

▶ grain, grenadier, pomegranate

**grey** [OE] *Grey* is an ancient colour term, traceable back all the way to a prehistoric Indo-European *\*ghrēghwos*. From this was descended West and North Germanic *\*grǣwaz*, which produced German *grau*, Dutch *grauw*, Swedish *grå*, and Danish *graa* as well as English *grey*. The distinction in spelling between British *grey* and American *gray* is a comparatively recent one. Dr Johnson in his *Dictionary* 1755 gave *gray* as the main form, and even into the early 20th century it was still quite common in Britain (*The Times* used it, for instance). Nor is *grey* by any means unknown in America.

**greyhound** [OE] Most greyhounds are not grey – and there is no etymological reason why they should be. For the element *grey-*in their name has no connection with the colour-term *grey*. It comes from an unrecorded Old English *\*grīeg* 'bitch,' a relative of Old Norse *grøy* 'bitch.'

**grid** [19] *Grid* is simply an abbreviated version of *gridiron* [13]. This in turn seems to have been an alteration (through association with *iron*) of *griddle* [13], which is traceable back via Old French *gridil* to a hypothetical Vulgar Latin *\*crāticulum*, a diminutive form of Latin *crātis* 'wickerwork, hurdle' (from which English gets *grate*). A parallel feminine Vulgar Latin derivative, *crāticula*, produced English *grill* [17] and *grille* [17].

▶ grate, griddle, grill

**grief** [13] 'Oppressiveness' is the link between modern English *grief* and Latin *gravis* (source of English *gravity*). The Latin adjective meant 'heavy, weighty,' and it formed the basis of a verb *gravāre* 'weigh upon, oppress.' This passed into Old French as *grever* 'cause to suffer, harrass' (source of English *grieve* [13]), from which was derived the noun *grief* or *gref* 'suffering, hardship.' Its modern sense, 'feeling caused by such trouble or hardship, sorrow,' developed in the 14th century.

▶ grave, gravity, grieve

**grill** see GRID

**grim** [OE] Indo-European *\*ghrem-*, *\*ghrom-* probably originated in imitation of the sound of rumbling (amongst its descendants was *grumins* 'thunder' in the extinct Baltic language Old Prussian). In Germanic it became *\*grem-*, *\*gram-*, *\*grum-*, which not only produced the adjective *\*grimmaz* (source of German *grimm*, Swedish *grym*, and English, Dutch, and Danish *grim*) and the English verb *grumble* [16], but was adopted into Spanish as *grima* 'fright,' which eventually arrived in English as *grimace* [17].

▶ grimace, grumble

**grin** [OE] Modern English *grin* and *groan* are scarcely semantic neighbours, but a possible common ancestor may provide the link: prehistoric Indo-European *\*ghrei-*, which seems to have meant something like 'be open.' It has been suggested as the source of a range of verbs which started off denoting simply 'open the mouth,' but have since differentiated along the lines 'make noise' and 'grimace.' *Grin* has taken the latter course, but close relatives, such as Old High German *grennan* 'mutter' and Old Norse *grenja* 'howl,' show that the parting of the semantic ways was not so distant in time. Old English *grennian* actually meant 'draw back the lips and bare the teeth in pain or anger.' Traces of this survive in such distinctly unfunny expressions as 'grinning skull,' but the modern sense 'draw back the lips in amusement' did not begin to emerge until the 15th century. *Groan* [OE], on the other hand, is firmly in the 'make noise' camp.

▶ groan

**grind** [OE] *Grind* is part of the ancient Indo-European word-stock. Relatives such as Latin *frendere* 'crush' and Lithuanian *grendu* 'rub' point back to an Indo-European *\*ghrendh-*. This perhaps denoted 'crushing' rather than what we would today call 'grinding'; for in earliest times grain was crushed rather than ground to produce meal. The connotations of the word seem to have changed in step with advances in grain-pulverizing technology. (The same is true, incidentally, in the case of Indo-European *\*mel-*, which produced the majority of modern European words for 'grind,' from German *mahlen* and Spanish *moler* to Russian *molot'*, and also gave English *meal, mill, molar*, etc.)

*Grist* [OE] was formed from the same base as produced *grind*, and until the 15th century meant simply 'grinding.'

▶ grist

**grip** [OE] *Grip* comes from a prehistoric Germanic verb *\*gripjan*, derived from a base *\*grip-*. Variants of this base produced *gripe* [OE] (which originally meant simply 'grasp'), *grope* [OE], and possibly also *grab*. French borrowed it as *gripper* 'seize,' from which English gets the now obsolete *grippe* 'flu' [18].

▶ grab, gripe, grope

**grisly** [OE] Middle English had a verb *grise* 'be terrified,' which points back via an unrecorded Old English *\*grīsan* to a West Germanic *\*grī-* denoting 'fear, terror,' from which *grisly* would have been formed. Dutch has the parallel formation *grijzelijk*. In 1900, the *Oxford English Dictionary* described *grisly* as 'now only *arch* and *lit*,' but since then its fortunes have recovered strongly, and it is now firmly part of the general language.

**grist** see GRIND

**grit** [OE] Etymologically, *grit* is 'something produced by pounding.' Prehistoric Indo-European *ghrēu-* denoted 'rub, pound, crush,' and from it came Germanic *greutam* 'tiny particles of crushed or pounded rock,' hence 'sand, gravel.' Its modern descendants include English *grit* and German *griess* 'gravel, grit, coarse sand,' and it was also used in the formation of the Old English word for 'pearl,' *meregrot*, literally 'sea-pebble,' an alteration of Latin *margarīta* 'pearl.' *Groats* 'husked grain' [OE] comes from the same source.

The sense 'determination, resolve' originated in the USA in the early 19th century, presumably as a metaphorical extension of *grit* meaning 'hard sandstone' (as in *millstone grit*).

▶ groats

**grizzle** [18] *Grizzle* 'whine, complain' is a bit of a puzzle. It has no obvious ancestor, and it is tempting to conclude that it originated as an ironic allusion to 'patient Griselda' (popularly *Grizel* from the 14th to the 19th centuries), the proverbial meek, uncomplaining wife. Against this it has to be said that in the earliest recorded examples of the verb it means 'grin,' and that the sense 'whine, complain' did not emerge until the 19th century; however, *grizzle* 'grin' may be a different word. The adjective *grizzle* 'grey' [15] is now obsolete, but it lives on in its derivatives *grizzled* 'grey-haired' [15] and *grizzly* [16] (as in *grizzly bear*). It was borrowed from Old French *grisel*, a derivative of *gris* 'grey,' which goes back ultimately to prehistoric Germanic *grīsiaz*.

**groan** see GRIN

**groats** see GRIT

**grocer** [15] Etymologically, a *grocer* is simply somebody who sells 'in gross' – that is, wholesale. The word's ancestor is medieval Latin *grossārius* 'wholesale dealer,' a derivative of late Latin *grossus* 'large, bulky' (from which English gets *gross*). It passed into English via Old French *grossier* and Anglo-Norman *grosser*. In practice, the term seems largely restricted in Britain from earliest times to merchants who dealt in spices and similar imported edible goods, and as early as the mid 15th century it was being used for retailers who sold such goods in small quantities to the public. *Greengrocer* is an 18th-century formation.

▶ gross

**grog** [18] *Grog* comes from the nickname of Edward Vernon (1684–1757), the British admiral who in 1740 introduced the practice of serving rum and water (*grog*) to sailors in the Royal Navy rather than the hitherto customary neat rum (it was discontinued in 1970). His nickname was 'Old Grogram,' said to be an allusion to the grogram cloak he always wore (*grogram* 'coarse fabric' [16] comes from French *gros grain*, literally 'coarse grain'). *Groggy* [18], originally 'drunk,' is a derivative.

**groin** [15] Unravelling the history of *groin* required a good deal of detective work, and the answer that the 19th-century etymologist Walter Skeat came up with was the rather surprising one that it is related to *ground*. The root on which this was formed was prehistoric Germanic *grundu-*, which also produced the derivative *grundja-*. This passed into Old English as *grynde*, which seems originally to have meant 'depression in the ground' (although the more extreme 'abyss' is its only recorded sense). It appears to correspond to Middle English *grynde* 'groin' ('If the pricking be in the foot, anoint the grynde with hot common oil,' *Lanfranc's Science of Surgery* 1400 – evidently an example of reflexology), and the theory is that the original sense 'depression in the ground' became transferred figuratively to the 'depression between the abdomen and the thighs.' By the late 15th century *grynde* had become *gryne*, and (by the not uncommon phonetic change of /ee/ to /oi/) this metamorphosed to *groin* in the late 16th century. (*Groyne* 'wall projecting into the sea' [16] is a different word. It is a transferred use of the now obsolete *groin* 'pig's snout' [14], which came via Old French *groin* from Latin *grunnīre* 'grunt.')

**groom** [13] No one has ever been able satisfactorily to explain where the word *groom* came from. It suddenly appears in early Middle English, meaning 'boy, male servant' (the sense 'one who takes care of horses' is a 17th-century development), and none of the words with a superficial similarity to it, such as Old French *grommet* 'servant' and Old Norse *grómr* 'man,' can be shown to be related. *Bridegroom* is a 14th-century alteration of Old English *brȳdguma* (the element *guma* 'man' is related to Latin *homō* 'man') under the influence of *groom*.

**groove** see GRUB

**grope** see GRIP

**gross** [14] *Gross* comes via Old French *gros* from late Latin *grossus* 'large, bulky,' a word of unknown origin (not related to German *gross* 'large'). Its association with literal physical size has now largely died out in English, in the face of a growing figurative role in such senses as 'coarse, vulgar' and (of amounts) 'total, entire.' Its use as a noun meaning '144,' which dates from the 15th century, comes from the French phrase *grosse douzaine* 'large dozen.' *Grocer* is a derivative, as is *engross* [14]; this originally meant 'buy up wholesale,' hence 'gain exclusive possession of' and, by metaphorical extension, 'occupy all the attention of.'

▶ engross, grocer

**grotesque** [16] Etymologically, *grotesque* means 'grotto-like.' Its Italian source, *grottesco*, was used in the phrase *pittura grottesca*, literally 'grotto-like pictures,' denoting wall paintings of the sort discovered in the excavated basements of old buildings.

Many of them were evidently bizarre or highly imaginative, and so *grottesca* came to mean 'fanciful, fantastic.' English acquired the word via Old French *crotesque* (*crotescque* was the earliest English spelling, later re-formed as *grotesque* on the basis of French *grotesque* and Italian *grottesca*), and in general use from the mid-18th century onward it slid towards the pejorativeness of 'ludicrous, absurd.' The colloquial abbreviation *grotty* is first recorded in print in 1964.
▶ grotto

**grotto**   [17]   *Grotto* and *crypt* are ultimately the same word. The source of both was Greek *krúptē*, originally 'hidden place,' hence 'vault.' English acquired *crypt* directly from *krúptē*'s Latin descendant, *crypta*, but *grotto* came via a more circuitous route. *Crypta* became *\*crupta* or *\*grupta* in Vulgar Latin, and this produced Italian *grotta*, later *grotto*. French borrowed it as *grotte*, and the earliest English form, the now obsolete *grot* [16], came from French, but in the 17th century the Italian version of the word established itself.
▶ crypt, grotesque

**ground**   [OE]   *Ground* is part of a widespread family of Germanic words, which include also German, Swedish, and Danish *grund* and Dutch *grond*. A common meaning element of all these is 'bottom,' particularly of the sea (preserved in English 'run *aground*'), and it seems that their prehistoric Germanic ancestor *\*grunduz* may originally have denoted something like 'deep place.'

**groundsel**   [OE]   The *-sel* of *groundsel* represents Old English *swelgan* 'swallow' (ancestor of modern English *swallow*), and if *ground-* genuinely represents *ground*, then *groundsel* would mean etymologically 'ground-swallower' – presumably a reference to its rapid and invasive growth. However, in early texts the form *gundæswelgiæ* appears, the first element of which suggests Old English *gund* 'pus.' If this is the word's true origin, it would mean literally 'pus-swallower,' an allusion to its use in poultices to absorb pus, and *groundsel* would be a variant introduced through association with *ground*.
▶ swallow

**group**   [17]   *Group* was originally a term in art criticism. It referred to the disposition of a set of figures or objects in a painting, drawing, etc. Not until the 18th century was it used in its current general sense. It comes via French *groupe* from Italian *gruppo*, which was borrowed originally from prehistoric Germanic *\*kruppaz* 'round mass, lump' (formed from the same base as produced English *crop*).
▶ crop

**grouse**   English has two words *grouse*, neither of whose ancestries are adequately documented. It has been speculated that *grouse* the game-bird [16] originated as the plural of a now lost *\*grue*, which may

have come from the medieval Latin bird-name *grūta*, or from Welsh *grugiar*, a compound of *grug* 'heath' and *iar* 'hen.' *Grouse* 'complain' [19] is first recorded in the poetry of Rudyard Kipling. It seems originally to have been pronounced to rhyme with *moose*, but in the 20th century has come into line phonetically with *grouse* the bird. It is not known where it came from.

**grovel**   [16]   Old and Middle English had a suffix *-ling*, used for making adverbs denoting direction or condition. Few survive, and of those that do, most have had their *-ling* changed to the more logical-sounding *-long* (*headlong* and *sidelong*, for instance, used to be *headling* and *sideling*; *darkling* still hangs on – just – unchanged). Among them was *grovelling*, an adverb meaning 'face downwards' based on the phrase *on grufe* 'on the face or stomach,' which in turn was a partial translation of Old Norse *á grúfu*, literally 'on proneness' (*grúfu* may be related to English *creep*). It was not long before *grovelling* came to be regarded as a present participle, and the new verb *grovel* was coined from it.
▶ creep

**grow**   [OE]   *Grow* comes from a prehistoric Germanic base *\*grō-*, which also produced Dutch *groeien* 'grow' and English *grass* and *green*. Latin *grāmen* 'grass' may indicate connections outside Germanic, but this is not certain.
▶ grass, green

**grub**   [13]   *Grub* 'dig' comes ultimately from prehistoric Germanic *\*grub-*, perhaps via Old English *\*grybban*, although no record of such a verb has actually come down to us (the related Germanic *\*grab-* gave English *grave*, while a further variant *\*grōb-* produced *groove* [15]). The relationship of *grub* 'dig' to the various noun uses of the word is far from clear. *Grub* 'larva,' first recorded in the 15th century, may have been inspired by the notion of larvae digging their way through wood or earth, but equally it could be connected (via the idea of 'smallness') with the contemporary but now obsolete *grub* 'short, dwarfish fellow' – an entirely mysterious word. *Grub* 'food,' which dates from the 17th century, is usually said to have been suggested by birds' partiality for grubs or larvae as part of their diet. And in the 19th century a *grub* was also a 'dirty child' – perhaps originally one who got dirty by digging or grubbing around in the earth – which may have been the source of *grubby* 'dirty' [19].
▶ grave, groove

**gruesome**   [16]   The novels of Sir Walter Scott had an enormous influence in introducing Scotticisms into the general English language, and *gruesome* is a case in point. It was apparently coined in the 16th century from an earlier verb *grue* 'be terrified,' which was probably of Scandinavian origin. For over 200 years it remained restricted in distribution to Scotland and northern England, but Scott started using it ('He's as grave and grewsome an auld Dutchman as e'er I saw,' *Old Mortality* 1816), immediately ensuring it an entrée into homes all over Britain thanks to Scott's huge readership. It has never looked back.

**grumble**  see GRIM

**grundyism**  [19] The term *grundyism* 'prudishness' was based on Mrs Grundy, a character in Thomas Moreton's play *Speed the Plough* 1798 who became proverbial for her extreme rigidity in matters of sexual morality. Dame Ashfield, another character in the play, when contemplating some ticklish moral dilemma would invariably ask herself 'What would Mrs Grundy say?'

**guarantee**  [17] *Guarantee* is essentially the same word as *warrant*, which is of Germanic origin (Germanic initial *w*-became *g(u)*- in the Romance languages). It was probably borrowed into English from the Spanish form *garante* (this is suggested by early spellings *garanté* and *garante* in English), and later changed to *guarantee* through confusion with *guaranty* [16] (itself originally a variant of *warranty*).
▶ warrant

**guard**  [15] Prehistoric West Germanic *\*warthōn* produced English *ward*. It was borrowed into Vulgar Latin as *\*wardāre*, and following the general phonetic trend by which Germanic initial *w* became *g(u)* in the Romance languages, it produced Italian *guardare*, Spanish *guardar*, and French *garder*. The noun derived from the latter, *garde*, gave English *guard*. *Guardian* [15], borrowed from Old French *gardien*, has a doublet in *warden*.
▶ ward

**gubernatorial**  see GOVERN

**guerilla**  [19] Etymologically, a *guerilla* is a 'little war.' English acquired the word during the Peninsular War (1808–14) from Spanish *guerrilla*, which is a diminutive form of *guerra* 'war' (a word ultimately of Germanic origin, related to English *war*). In Spanish it still means 'skirmish,' and until well into the 19th century it was used in English for a 'war characterized by irregular skirmishing' (the famous *Times* war correspondent William Russell, for instance, reported on 18 March 1862 that 'Arkansas is now the theatre of a large guerilla'). The first recorded use of the word in its present-day sense is by the Duke of Wellington, the British military commander in Spain, in a despatch of 1809: 'I have recommended to the Junta to set the Guerillas to work towards Madrid.'
▶ war

**guess**  [13] In the earliest records we have of the verb *guess*, it is used for 'take aim.' The modern sense 'estimate' did not emerge until the mid-14th century. It seems to be of Scandinavian origin, and probably comes ultimately from the same base as produced *get*

(Old Norse *geta* meant 'guess' as well as 'get,' and the semantic progression hinted at by the intermediate 'take aim' is probably via 'lock on to something in one's sights' to 'fix on a particular figure' – by implication, without exact calculation).

*Guesstimate*, a blend of *guess* and *estimate*, is a US coinage of the 1930s.
▶ get

**guest**  [13] *Guest* comes ultimately from the same source as produced *host*. Their family tree diverged in prehistoric times, but their close relationship is pointed up by the fact that the related French *hôte* means both 'guest' and 'host.' The common ancestor was Indo-European *\*ghostis* 'stranger,' whose Germanic descendant *\*gastiz* produced German and Dutch *gast*, Swedish *gäst*, Danish *gæst*, and English *guest*. The Old English version of the word was *giest*, which would have produced modern English *\*yest*, but it was elbowed out in Middle English times by Old Norse *gestr*. The spelling *gu-*, indicating a hard /g/ sound, developed in the 16th century.
▶ host, xenophobia

**guide**  [14] The ancestor of *guide* was Germanic *\*wit-*'know,' source of English *wise*, *wit*, and *witness*. From it was derived a verb *\*wītan*, and the Franks, a West Germanic people who conquered Gaul in the 3rd and 4th centuries AD, brought it with them. It eventually became Old French *guider*, and was borrowed by English. The semantic progression from 'knowing' to 'showing' is also displayed in the related German *weisen* 'show, direct, indicate.'
▶ wise, wit, witness

**guild**  [14] *Guilds* probably got their name from the subscriptions paid by their members. It goes back to a Germanic *\*gelth-* 'pay,' which also produced German and Dutch *geld* 'money.' An association to which people contributed in order to further a common effort was a *\*gelthjōn*, which probably passed into English via Middle Low German or Middle Dutch *gilde*. English *yield* is a relative; it originally meant 'pay.'
▶ yield

**guilder**  see GOLD

**guillotine**  [18] Joseph Ignace Guillotin (1738–1814), a French doctor, did not invent the device named after him – such contraptions had been around for some time – but it was he who saw the advantages, in terms of speed and efficiency, of an easily resettable blade for beheading in a time of peak demand, and he recommended it to the Revolutionary authorities. The term used for it, first recorded in English in 1793, is a fitting memorial to him. Its application to the limitation of discussion in a legislature dates from the 1890s.

**guilt**  [OE] *Guilt* is a strictly English word; no other Germanic, or indeed Indo-European language has it, and it is not clear where it came from. One theory is that, like *guild* and *yield*, it comes ultimately from Germanic *gelth-* 'pay,' and originally meant 'debt.' This is not generally accepted, but it is notable that the German word *schuld* means 'debt' as well as 'guilt,' with 'debt' being the original sense.

**guinea** [17]   *Guinea* first emerged as the name of a section of the West African continent in the late 16th century (its origins are not known, but presumably it was based on an African word). In 1663 the Royal Mint began to produce a gold coin valued at 20 shillings 'for the use of the Company of Royal Adventurers of England trading with Africa.' It had the figure of an elephant on it. Straightaway it became known as a *guinea*, both because its use was connected with the Guinea coast and because it was made from gold obtained there. And what is more, the coins soon came to be much in demand for domestic use: on 29 October 1666 Samuel Pepys recorded 'And so to my goldsmith to bid him look out for some gold for me; and he tells me that Ginnys, which I bought 2000 of not long ago, and cost me but 18½d. change, will now cost me 22d., and but very few to be had at any price. However, some more I will have, for they are very convenient - and of easy disposal.' Its value fluctuated, and was not fixed at 21 shillings until 1717. The last one was minted in 1813, but *guinea* as a term for the amount 21 shillings stayed in use until the early 1970s, when the decimalization of British currency dealt it the deathblow.

The *guineapig* [17], incidentally, comes from South America, and its name probably arose from a confusion between Guinea and Guiana, on the northern coast of South America.

**guise**   see GEEZER

**guitar** [17]   The Greek *kithárā* was a stringed musical instrument of the lyre family, which has bequeathed its name to a variety of successors. Via Latin *cithara* came English *citole* [14], a medieval stringed instrument, and German *zither* (borrowed by English in the 19th century), while Arabic took it over as *qītār* and passed it on to Spanish as *guitarra*. French adopted it in the form *guitare* (which eventually superseded the earlier *guiterne*), and it eventually reached English. (The history of *guiterne*, incidentally, is not entirely clear, although it is obviously a member of the *kithárā* family. English acquired it as *gittern* [14], applied to an early form of guitar, and it seems to have been blended with Latin *cithara* to produce English *cithern* or *cittern* [16], the name of a plucked stringed instrument of Renaissance times.)

▶ zither

**gules**   see GULLET

**gulf** [14]   *Gulf* comes from Greek *kólphos*, which meant originally 'bosom.' It was later extended metaphorically to denote 'bag,' and also 'trough between

waves,' and these senses (the latter modified to 'abyss') followed it through Vulgar Latin *\*colphus*, Italian *golfo*, and French *golphe* into English. The derivative *engulf*, based on the sense 'abyss,' dates from the mid-16th century.

**gull** [15]   *Gull* is a Celtic contribution to English. It was probably borrowed from Welsh *gwylan*, which together with Cornish *guilan*, Breton *gwelan*, and Old Irish *foilenn*, goes back to a prehistoric Old Celtic *\*voilenno-*. (The Old English word for 'gull' was *mǽw*, as in modern English *sea mew*.)

**gullet** [14]   Latin *gula* meant 'throat.' It was a descendant of Indo-European *\*gel-* 'swallow,' which also produced German *kehle* 'throat' and English *glut* and *glutton*. *Gula* passed into Old French as *gole* or *goule* (whence modern French *gueule* 'mouth'), where it formed the basis of a diminutive form *goulet*, acquired by English as *gullet* (and later, in the 16th century, as *gully*, which originally meant 'gullet'). The English heraldic term *gules* 'red' [14] also comes from Old French *gole, goule*, in the specialized sense 'red fur neckpiece.'

▶ glut, glutton, gules, gully

**gullible** [19]   *Gullible* is a derivative of the now archaic *gull* 'dupe,' itself a verbal use of the noun *gull* 'gullible person, simpleton.' This appears to have been a figurative extension of an earlier *gull* 'newly hatched bird' [14], which survived dialectally into the late 19th century, and was itself perhaps a noun use of the obsolete adjective *gull* 'yellow' (borrowed from Old Norse *gulr* and still extant in Swedish and Danish *gul* 'yellow'). Some etymologists, however, derive the noun *gull* 'simpleton' from an obsolete verb *gull* 'swallow' [16], which goes back ultimately to Old French *gole, goule* 'throat' (source of English *gullet*).

**gum**   English has three words *gum*. The oldest, 'tissue surrounding the teeth' [OE], originally meant 'mucous lining of the mouth and throat'; its present-day meaning did not emerge until the 14th century. It is not clear where it came from, although it is related to German *gaumen* 'roof of the mouth,' and perhaps to Lithuanian *gomurys* 'gum' and even Latin *fauces* 'throat' (source of English *suffocate*). *Gum* 'sticky material' [14] comes ultimately from Egyptian *kemai*, which passed into English via Greek *kómmi*, Latin *cummi* or *gummi*, Vulgar Latin *\*gumma*, and Old French *gomme*. And *gum* in the exclamation *by gum* [19] is a euphemistic alteration of *god*.

**gun** [14]   *Gun* probably comes, unlikely as it may seem, from the Scandinavian female forename *Gunnhildr* (originally a compound of *gunnr* 'war' and *hildr* 'war'). It is by no means unusual for large fearsome weapons to be named after women (for reasons perhaps best left to psychologists): the huge German artillery weapon of World War I, *Big Bertha*, and the old British army musket, *Brown Bess*, are cases in point. And it seems that in the Middle Ages *Gunnhildr* or *Gunhild* was applied to various large rock-hurling seige weapons, such as the ballista, and later to cannon. The earliest recorded sense of *gun* (on this theory representing *Gunne*, a pet form of *Gunhild*) is 'cannon,' but it was applied to hand-held firearms as they developed in the 15th century.

**gurgle**   see GARGOYLE

**guru**   see GRAVITY

**gust**   [16]   The underlying meaning of *gust* is 'sudden rush or gush,' and related words refer to water or steam rather than wind. It was borrowed from Old Norse *gustr* 'gust,' and the closely connected *geysa* 'gush' produced English *geyser* [18].

▶ geyser

**gusto**   [17]   *Gusto* originally meant 'taste.' It was borrowed from Italian *gusto*, which, like French *goût*, comes from Latin *gustus* 'taste.' Its semantic progress from 'taste' via 'liking for a particular food' and 'liking in general' to 'zest, enthusiasm' is paralleled in *relish*. (Latin *gustus* itself came from an Indo-European *geus-*, which also produced English *choose*.)

▶ choose

**gut**   [OE]   *Gut* probably comes ultimately from prehistoric Indo-European *gh(e)u-* 'pour' (source also of English *foundry, funnel, fusion*, etc), and presumably has the underlying meaning 'tube through which digested food flows.' From the same source came Greek *khūmós* 'animal or plant juice,' from which English got the technical term *chyme* 'mass of semidigested food in the stomach' [17].

The use of the plural *guts* for 'vigour' or 'courage' dates from the late 19th century.

▶ foundry, funnel, fusion

**gutta percha**   see GOUT

**gutter**   [13]   Etymologically, a *gutter* is something along which 'drops' of water run. Its distant ancestor is Latin *gutta* 'drop' (source also of English *gout*). From it was formed the Vulgar Latin derivative *guttāria*, which passed into English via Anglo-Norman *gotere*. The use of the word as a verb, meaning (of a flame) 'flicker on the point of going out,' comes from the channel, or 'gutter,' formed down one side of a candle by the melted wax flowing away.

▶ gout

**guy**   English has two separate words *guy*. The *guy* of *guy rope* [14] was probably borrowed from a Low German word (of which Dutch *gei* 'rope used for hauling a sail in' may well be a descendant), but its ultimate ancestry is not clear. *Guy* 'fellow, man' [19] originated as an American English generalization of *guy* 'effigy of Guy Fawkes burned on 5 November' – a sense first recorded in 1806.

**gymkhana**   [19]   The British brought the word *gymkhana* back with them from India, where they found it as Hindi *gendkhāna*, literally 'ball-house,' the name given to a racket court. The first syllable *gym-* is generally assumed to be an alteration of *gend-* on the analogy of *gymnasium*. The term was originally used for a 'sports ground'; the current sense 'horse-riding contest' seems to have developed after World War I.

**gymnasium**   [16]   Greek *gumnós* meant 'naked.' It was customary in ancient times for athletes to train naked, and so the verb *gumnázein* came to mean 'train, practise' -- particularly by doing exercises (whence English *gymnast* [16]). From the verb was derived the noun *gumnásion*, which Latin borrowed as *gymnasium* 'school.' This academic sense has never caught on to any extent in English (although it is the word's only application in German); we have preferred to go back to the original athletic connotations.

**gynaecology**   [19]   The Greek word for 'woman' was *guné*. It has relatives in several modern Indo-European languages, including Swedish *kvinna*, Danish *kvinde*, Irish Gaelic *bean*, Welsh *benyw*, Czech *zhena*, Russian *zhenshchina*, Persian *zan* (whence ultimately English *zenana* 'harem' [18]), and the now obsolete English *quean* [OE], and goes back to Indo-European *gwen-*. The resumption of the study of Greek in the 16th century led to increasing adoption of compounds involving *guné* into English. The earliest recorded ones are *gyneconome* 'member of a board of Athenian magistrates whose job was to ensure that women behaved properly' [16] and *gynocracy* 'rule by women' [17]. *Gynaecology* is a comparative latecomer, not appearing before the 1840s.

▶ queen, zenana

**gypsum**   [17]   The word *gypsum* originated among the Semitic languages, with a relative or ancestor of Arabic *jibs* and Hebrew *gephes* 'plaster.' Greek adopted this unknown form as *gúpsos*, which passed into Latin as *gypsum*. (An Italian descendant of *gypsum* is *gesso* 'plaster,' borrowed by English in the 16th century for 'plaster as a surface for painting on.')

▶ gesso

# H

--------- ---------

**habeas corpus** [15] *Habeas corpus* means literally 'you should have the body.' They are the first words of a Latin writ, apparently in use in England since the 13th century, requiring a person to be brought before a court of law. It begins *Habeas corpus ad subjiciendum* 'You should have the body to undergo,' that is, 'You must produce the person in court so that he or she may undergo what the court decides.' It applies in particular to the bringing of a detained person before a court so that a judge may decide whether he or she is being legally held – a safeguard against unlawful detention enshrined in England in the Habeas Corpus Act 1679.

**haberdasher** [14] No one is too sure what Anglo-Norman *hapertas* meant – perhaps 'piece of cloth,' perhaps 'small goods' – but it is the nearest we can come to the origin of that curious word *haberdasher*. The theory is that it had an Anglo-Norman derivative, *\*habertasser* or *\*haberdasser*, never actually recorded, which passed into Middle English as *haberdassher*. The term seems originally to have denoted a 'seller of small fancy goods' – and indeed in the 16th and 17th centuries it was often used synonymously with *milliner*, which had a similar broad meaning in those days – but gradually it passed into two more specific applications, 'seller of hats' (now obsolete in British English, but surviving in the American sense 'seller of men's hats, gloves, etc') and 'seller of dressmaking accessories.'

**habit** [13] Etymologically, a *habit* is 'what one has.' The word comes via Old French *abit* from Latin *habitus*, originally the past participle of the verb *habēre* 'have.' This was used reflexively for 'be,' and so the past participle came to be used as a noun for 'how one is' – one's 'state' or 'condition.' Subsequently this developed along the lines of both 'outward condition or appearance,' hence 'clothing,' and 'inner condition, quality, nature, character,' later 'usual way of behaving.' This proliferation of meaning took place in Latin, and was taken over lock, stock, and barrel by English,

although the 'clothing' sense now survives only in relation to monks, nuns, and horseriders. (Incidentally, the notion of adapting the verb *have* to express 'how one is, how one comports oneself' recurs in *behave*.)

Derived from Latin *habitus* was the verb *habitāre*, originally literally 'have something frequently or habitually,' hence 'live in a place.' This has given English *habitation* [14], *inhabit* [14], and also *habitat* [18], literally 'it dwells,' the third person present singular of *habitāre*, which was used in medieval and Renaissance books on natural history to describe the sort of place in which a particular species lived.

*Malady* [13] comes via Old French from an unrecorded Vulgar Latin *\*male habitus* 'in bad condition.'
▶habitat, inhabit, malady

**hack** English has two distinct words *hack*. By far the older, 'cut savagely or randomly' [OE], goes back via Old English *haccian* to a prehistoric West Germanic *\*khak-*, also reproduced in German *hacken* and Dutch *hakken*. It perhaps originated in imitation of the sound of chopping. *Hack* 'worn-out horse' [17] is short for *hackney* (as in *hackney carriage*), a word in use since the 14th century in connection with hired horses. It is thought that this may be an adaptation of the name of *Hackney*, now an inner-London borough but once a village on the northeastern outskirts of the capital where horses were raised before being taken into the city for sale or hire. Most rented horses being past their best from long and probably ill usage, *hackney* came to mean 'broken-down horse' and hence in general 'drudge.' This quickly became respecified to 'someone who writes for hire, and hence unimaginatively,' which influenced the development of *hackneyed* 'trite' [18]. The modern sense of *hacker*, 'someone who gains unauthorized access to computer records,' comes from a slightly earlier 'one who works like a hack – that is, very hard – at writing and experimenting with software.'

**haemorrhage** [17] *Haemorrhage* means literally a 'bursting forth of blood.' It comes ultimately from Greek *haimorrhagía*, a compound formed from Greek *haima* 'blood' and an element derived from the same source as the verb *rhēgnúnai* 'break, burst.' *Haima*, a word of unknown origin, has been a generous contributor to English vocabulary. Besides *haemorrhage*, it has given *haematite* [17], literally 'blood-like stone,' a type of iron ore, *haemoglobin* [19], a shortening of an earlier *haemoglobulin*, *haemorrhoid* [14] (in the 16th and 17th centuries spelled *emerod*), literally 'flowing with blood,' and many more.

**haggard** [16] *Haggard* was originally a falconer's term for a hawk as yet untamed. It has been suggested that its ultimate source was Germanic *\*khag-*, which also produced English *hedge*, the implication being that a haggard was a hawk that sat in a hedge rather than on the falconer's arm. The modern meaning 'gaunt' developed in the 17th century, probably by association with *hag* 'ugly old woman' [13] (perhaps a shortening of Old English *hægtesse* 'witch,' a word of unknown origin related to German *hexe* 'witch').

▶ hedge

**haggis** [15] Improbable as it may seem, the leading candidate for the source of the word *haggis* is Old French *agace* 'magpie.' Corroborative evidence for this, circumstantial but powerful, is the word *pie*, which also originally meant 'magpie' (modern English *magpie* comes from it) but was apparently applied to a 'baked pastry case with a filling' from the notion that the collection of edible odds and ends a pie contained was similar to the collection of trinkets assembled by the acquisitive magpie. On this view, the miscellaneous assortment of sheep's entrails and other ingredients in a haggis represents the magpie's hoard. An alternative possibility, however, is that the word comes from the northern Middle English verb *haggen* 'chop,' a borrowing from Old Norse related ultimately to English *hew*.

**hail** Not surprisingly, *hail* 'frozen rain' [OE] and *hail* 'call out' [12] are quite unrelated. The former, together with its German and Dutch relative *hagel*, comes from a prehistoric West Germanic *\*hagalaz*, which is related ultimately to Greek *kákhlēx* 'pebble.' The verb *hail* is closely related to *hale* and *whole*. It comes from the noun *hail*, which in turn was a nominal use of the now obsolete adjective *hail* 'healthy' (preserved in *wassail*, literally 'be healthy'). This was borrowed from *heill*, the Old Norse counterpart of English *whole*.

▶ hale, wassail, whole

**hair** [OE] No general Indo-European term for 'hair' has come down to us. All the 'hair'-words in modern European languages are descended from terms for particular types of hair – hair on the head, hair on other parts of the body, animal hair – or for single hairs or hair collectively, and indeed many retain these specialized meanings: French *cheveu*, for instance, means 'hair of the head,' whereas *poil* denotes 'body hair' or

'animal hair.' In the case of English *hair*, unfortunately, it is not clear which of these categories originally applied, although some have suggested a connection with Lithuanian *serys* 'brush,' which might indicate that the prehistoric ancestor of *hair* was a 'bristly' word. The furthest back in time we can trace it is to West and North Germanic *\*khǣram*, source also of German, Dutch, and Danish *haar* and Swedish *hår*.

The slang use of *hairy* for 'difficult' is first recorded in the mid 19th century, in an erudite context that suggests that it may have been inspired by Latin *horridus* (source of English *horrid*), which originally meant (of hair) 'standing on end.' Its current use, in which 'difficult' passes into 'dangerous,' seems to have emerged in the 1960s, and was presumably based on *hair-raising*, which dates from around 1900. It is fascinatingly foreshadowed by *harsh*, which is a derivative of *hair* and originally meant 'hairy.'

**hake** see HOOK

**halcyon** [14] *Halcyon* days, originally 'days of calm weather,' but now used figuratively for a 'past period of happiness and success,' are literally 'days of the kingfisher.' The expression comes from Greek *alkuonídes emérai* 'kingfisher's days,' a term used in the ancient world for a period of 14 days fine or calm weather around the winter solstice which was attributed to the magical influence of the kingfisher. The origin of Greek *alkúon* is not known, although it was from earliest times associated with Greek *háls* 'sea' and *kúōn* 'conceiving' (whence the spelling *halcyon*).

**hale** see WHOLE

**half** [OE] *Half* comes from prehistoric Germanic *\*khalbaz*, which also produced German *halb*, Dutch *half*, and Swedish and Danish *halv*. If, as some have suggested, it is connected with Latin *scalpere* 'cut' (source of English *scalpel* and *sculpture*) and Greek *skóloph* 'spike,' its underlying meaning would be 'cut, divided.'

**halibut** see TURBOT

**hall** [OE] Etymologically, a *hall* is a 'roofed or covered place.' Its ultimate ancestor was prehistoric West and North Germanic *\*khallō*, a derivative of *\*khal-*, *\*khel-* 'cover, hide' (a slightly different derivative produced English *hell*, and *cell*, *clandestine*, *conceal*, *hull* 'pod,' and possibly *colour* and *holster* are all relatives, close or distant). It retained much of its original meaning in Old English *heall*, which denoted simply a 'large place covered by a roof.' This gradually became specialized to, on the one hand, 'large residence,' and on the other, 'large public room.' The main current sense, 'entrance corridor,' dates from the 17th century (it derives from the fact that in former times the principal room of a house usually opened directly off the front door).

▶ cell, clandestine, conceal, hell, hull

**hallow** [OE] *Hallow* is essentially the same word as *holy*. The noun, as in *Halloween*, the eve of All Hallows, or All Saints, comes from a noun use of Old English *hālig*, which as an adjective developed into modern English *holy*; and the verb was formed in pre-historic Germanic times from the root *\*khailag-*, source also of *holy*.

► holy

**halt** English has two words *halt*. By far the older, meaning 'lame' [OE], has virtually died out as a living part of English vocabulary except in the verbal deriva-tive *halting* 'stopping and starting uncertainly.' It came from a prehistoric Germanic *\*khaltaz*, which also pro-duced Swedish and Danish *halt* 'lame.' *Halt* 'stop' [17], originally a noun, comes from German *halt*, which began life as the imperative form of the verb *halten* 'hold, stop' (a relative of English *hold*).

► hold

**ham** [OE] The etymological meaning of *ham* is 'bend' – it comes from Germanic *\*kham-* 'be crooked' – and up until the 16th century it denoted exclusively the 'part of the leg at the back of the knee' (a portion of the anatomy now without a word of its own in English). *Hamstring* [16] reflects this original meaning. From the mid-16th century, it gradually extended semantically to 'back of the thigh' and hence 'thigh' generally, and by the 17th century it was being used for the 'thigh of a slaughtered animal, especially a pig, preserved and used for food.'

*Ham* in the sense 'performer who overacts,' first rec-orded in the late 19th century, apparently comes from an earlier *hamfatter* 'bad actor,' which may have been inspired by the Negro minstrel song 'The Ham-fat Man.'

**hamlet** [14] *Hamlet* is a double diminutive: ety-mologically it means 'little little village.' It comes from Old French *hamelet*, a diminutive form of *hamel*, which was itself a diminutive of *ham* 'village.' This was bor-rowed from a Germanic word related to English *home*, and to the *-ham* in many English place-names.

► home

**hammer** [OE] *Hammer* is part of a widespread Germanic word-family, including also German and Danish *hammer*, Dutch *hamer*, and Swedish *hammar*. The ancestor of the Scandinavian forms, Old Norse *hamarr*, meant 'stone crag' as well as 'hammer.' This and possible connections with the standard words for 'stone, rock' in the Indo-Iranian and Balto-Slavonic language groups (such as Sanskrit *açman* and Russian *kamen'*) suggest that *hammer* originally denoted some sort of tool with a stone head.

**hammock** [16] *Hammock* is a product of early European explorations in the New World. When Span-ish crews first sailed into the Caribbean, they encoun-tered a word in the Taino language of the Arawakan people for a hanging bed suspended between two trees. They adopted it into Spanish as *hamaca*, which English borrowed as *hamaca* or 'Englished' as *hammaker* (*hammock* is a 17th-century alteration).

**hamster** [17] The hamster is a native of west-ern Asia and southeastern Europe, and its English name is of Slavic origin. In Old Slavic it was called *chomes-toru*, and it appears that at some point in the past an an-cestor of this was borrowed into Germanic. Old High German had *hamustro*, which became modern German *hamster*, source of the English word. In the 18th cen-tury the animal was also called the *German rat*.

**hand** [OE] *Hand* is a widespread Germanic word (German, Dutch, and Swedish also have it), but it has no relatives outside Germanic, and no one is too sure where it comes from. Perhaps the likeliest explanation is that it is related to Gothic *frahinthan* 'seize, pursue,' Swedish *hinna* 'reach,' and English *hunt*, and that its underlying meaning is 'body part used for seizing.'

The derived adjective *handsome* [15] originally meant simply 'easy to handle.' The modern sense 'at-tractive' did not develop until the late 16th century.

► handsome, hunt

**handicap** [17] The word *handicap* originally denoted a sort of game of chance in which one person put up one of his or her personal possessions against an article belonging to someone else (for example one might match a gold watch against the other's horse) and an umpire was appointed to adjudicate on the respective values of the articles. All three parties put their hands into a hat, together with a wager, and on hearing the um-pire's verdict the two opponents had to withdraw them in such a way as to indicate whether they wished to pro-ceed with the game. If they agreed, either in favour of proceeding or against, the umpire took the money; but if they disagreed, the one who wanted to proceed took it. It was the concealing of the hands in the hat that gave the game its name *hand in cap, hand i' cap*, source of mod-ern English *handicap*.

In the 18th century the same term was applied to a sort of horse race between two horses, in which an umpire decided on a weight disadvantage to be imposed on a su-perior horse and again the owners of the horses sig-nalled their assent to or dissent from his adjudication by the way in which they withdrew their hands from a hat. Such a race became known as a *handicap race*, and in the 19th century the term *handicap* first broadened out to any contest in which inequalities are artificially evened out, and was eventually transferred to the 'dis-advantage' imposed on superior contestants – whence the main modern meaning, 'disadvantage, disability.'

**handkerchief** [16] *Handkerchief* is a com-pound formed from *hand* and the now obsolete *kerchief* 'cloth for covering the head' [13] (what in modern Eng-lish would be called a *head-scarf*). This was acquired via Anglo-Norman *courchef* from Old French *couvrechef*, a compound of *couvrir* 'cover' and *chief* 'head.' The colloquial abbreviation *hanky* is first recorded in the 1890s.

▶ chef, chief, cover, hand, kerchief

**handle** [OE] Etymologically, a *handle* is nothing more or less than 'something to be held in the hand.' Likewise the verb *handle*, together with Germanic relatives like German *handeln* and Swedish *handla*, began life as 'hold, touch, feel with the hands' (the German and Swedish verbs have since lost this original literal meaning, and now have only the metaphorical senses 'deal with,' 'trade,' etc).

▶ hand

**handsome** see HAND

**hang** [OE] *Hang* is a general Germanic verb, represented also in German and Dutch *hangen* and Swedish *hänga*. These point back to a prehistoric Germanic *\*khang-*, which some have linked with the Latin verb *cunctārī* 'deal.' *Hanker* [17] (which originally meant 'loiter, hang about') probably comes ultimately from the same source, as does *hinge*; but *hangar* 'structure housing aircraft' [19] does not – it goes back via French *hangar* to medieval Latin *angarium* 'shed in which horses are shod.'

▶ hanker, hinge

**hank** see HOOK

**hansom** [19] The hansom cab, the taxi of the second half of the 19th century, was the brainchild of James Aloysius Hansom (1803–82), an architect, whose other main claim to fame is that he designed Birmingham town hall. In 1834 he took out a patent for a Safety Cab, which included many features incorporated into the hansom cab when it came into general use in the late 1840s. In the 1890s the word was used as a verb: 'To think that I . . . a raging Democrat, should be hansoming it to and fro between my Ladies and Honourables,' Sabine Baring-Gould *Armine* 1890.

**happen** [14] Surprisingly for such a common verb, *happen* is a comparatively recent addition to the English language. Old English had a number of verbs denoting 'occurrence,' all long since defunct, including *gelimpan* and *gescēon*, and in the 13th century *befall* began to be used for 'happen,' but the first signs we see of the coming of *happen* are when English acquired the noun *hap* 'chance, luck' in the 13th century. It was borrowed from Old Norse *happ*, a word of uncertain ancestry but probably related to Old Slavic *kobu* 'fate' and Old Irish *cob* 'victory,' and represented in Old English by *gehæp* 'fit.' In the 14th century it began to be used as a verb meaning 'happen by chance,' and hence simply 'happen,' and before the century was very old it had been extended with the verbal suffix *-en* to *happen*.

▶ happy, perhaps

**happy** [14] The Old and Middle English word for 'happy' was what in modern English has become *silly*. This began to change its meaning around the 15th century, and obviously an opportunity began to open up for an adjective expressing 'contentment' (as opposed to positive 'joy,' denoted then by *glad, fain*, and *joyful*). The gap was partly filled by a weakening in the meaning of *glad*, but waiting in the wings was *happy*, a derivative of the noun *hap* 'chance, luck' (source of *happen*), which when it was coined in the 14th century meant 'lucky, fortunate, prosperous.' The main modern sense 'highly pleased or contented' developed in the early 16th century.

▶ happen

**hara-kiri** [19] Hara-kiri is a Japanese form of ritual suicide, now little practised, involving disembowelment. The term, which means literally 'belly-cutting,' is a relatively colloquial one in Japanese; the more dignified expression is *seppuku*, literally 'cut open the stomach.'

**harangue** [15] The original notion underlying *harangue* may have been of a large group of people crowded round, with the idea of 'addressing' them only developing later. The word comes via Old French *harangue* from medieval Latin *harenga*, and it has been speculated that this was perhaps acquired from a prehistoric Germanic *\*kharikhring-* 'assembly,' a compound of *\*kharjaz* 'crowd' (source of English *harbinger, harbour, harry*, and *herald* and related to *harness*) and *\*khringaz* 'ring.'

▶ harbinger, harbour, harness, harry, herald

**harbinger** [12] Originally, a *harbinger* was simply someone who provided 'harbour' – that is, 'shelter, lodging.' The word began life as a derivative of Old French *herberge* 'lodging,' a borrowing from *heriberga*, the Old Saxon equivalent of Old English *herebeorg* (whence modern English *harbour*). English acquired it as *herbergere*, and the *n* did not put in an appearance until the 15th century (it was quite a common phenomenon, seen also in *messenger* and *passenger*). As for its meaning, it developed in the 14th century to 'someone sent on ahead to arrange for lodging for an army, an official royal party, etc,' and from this came the present-day figurative sense 'forerunner.'

▶ harbour

**harbour** [OE] Etymologically, a *harbour* is a 'shelter for a crowd of people.' English acquired it in the late Anglo-Saxon period as *herebeorg*, perhaps borrowed from Old Norse *herbergi*, but it began life as a compound of prehistoric Germanic *\*kharjaz*, originally 'crowd,' later specifically 'army' (source also of English *harry* and related to *harness*) and *\*berg-* 'protect' (which occurs in a range of English words, including *barrow* 'mound,' *borough, borrow*, and *bury*). The original sense 'shelter for a crowd or army' had broadened out by historic times to the more general 'shelter, lodging.' That is what Old English *herebeorg* meant, and gradually it underwent further semantic development, via 'place in which shelter can be obtained,' to (as recently as the 16th century) 'place of shelter for ships, port.'

▶ barrow, borough, borrow, bury, harbinger, harness, harry, herald

**hard** [OE] *Hard* comes ultimately from a prehistoric Indo-European *\*krátus*, which denoted 'power, strength.' This original meaning was carried over into Greek *krátos* 'strength, power, authority' (source of the ending -*cracy* in such English words as *democracy* and *plutocracy*), but the Germanic languages took it over mainly in the sense 'resistant to physical pressure.' The prehistoric Germanic form *\*kharthuz* produced, besides English *hard*, German *hart*, Dutch *hard*, Swedish *hård*, and Danish *haard*. The sense 'difficult,' incidentally, developed in the 14th and 15th century from the notion 'resistant to one's efforts.'

A Germanic derived verb *\*kharthjan* 'harden' was borrowed into Old French as *hardir* 'embolden,' and its past participle *hardi* 'bold' reached English as *hardy* [13]. Its main modern sense, 'robust, tough,' presumably a harking back to its distant English relative *hard*, developed in the 16th century.

▶ hardy

**hare** [OE] The *hare* seems originally to have been named from its colour. The word comes from prehistoric West and North Germanic *\*khason*, which also produced German *hase*, Dutch *haas*, and Swedish and Danish *hare*, and if as has been suggested it is related to Old English *hasu* 'grey' and Latin *cascus* 'old,' its underlying meaning would appear to be 'grey animal' (just as the bear and the beaver are etymologically the 'brown animal,' and the herring may be the 'grey fish'). *Harrier* 'dog for hunting hares' [16] was derived from *hare* on the model of Old French *levrier* (French *lièvre* means 'hare,' and is related to English *leveret* 'young hare' [15]); it was originally *harer*, and the present-day form arose from confusion with *harrier* 'falcon' [16], a derivative of the verb *harry*.

▶ harrier, herring, hoar

**harem** [17] Etymologically, Arabic *harīm* is a 'forbidden place.' It is a derivative of the verb *harama* 'prohibit' (whence also *harmatan*, literally 'the forbidden one,' the name of a dry dusty Saharan wind). Hence it came to be applied to a part of a Muslim house reserved for women, and by extension to the women who lived there – the wives and concubines of the master of the household. Synonymous terms in English include *seraglio*, which comes via Italian and Turkish from Persian *serāi* 'residence, palace,' and forms the second element of *caravanserai*, and *zenana*, which is derived

ultimately from Persian *zan* 'woman,' a relative of Greek *gunē* 'woman' (as in English *gynaecology*).

**harlequin** [16] Harlequin, a brightly-clad character in the Italian commedia dell'arte, has a murky history. He seems to have originated in a mythical figure known in Old French as *Herlequin* or *Hellequin*, who was the leader of a ghostly troop of horsemen who rode across the sky at night. And *Herlequin* could well be a later incarnation of King Herla (in Old English *Herla cyning*), a legendary personage who has been identified with the chief Anglo-Saxon god Woden. It seems likely that another piece of the jigsaw could be the *erlking*, the supernatural abductor of children described in a Goethe poem memorably set to music by Schubert; its name is generally traced back to Danish *ellerkonge*, a variant of *elverkonge*, literally 'king of the elves,' which bears a resemblance to *Herlequin* that is surely too strong to be coincidental. In early modern French *Herlequin* became *Harlequin*, the form borrowed by English (present-day French *arlequin* shows the influence of Italian *arlecchino*).

▶ king

**harlot** [13] The use of *harlot* for 'prostitute' is a comparatively recent development in the word's history. It originally meant 'tramp, beggar,' and did not come to mean 'prostitute' until the 15th century. It was borrowed from Old French *harlot* or *herlot* 'vagabond,' a word of unknown ancestry with relatives in Italian (*arlotto*) and Provençal (*arlot*).

**harm** [OE] The ideas of 'physical damage' and 'grief' are intimately associated in the word *harm*: indeed, until the early 17th century it had both meanings, and its relatives, German and Swedish *harm*, mean exclusively 'grief.' It appears to be related to Russian *sram* 'shame, scandal,' but its ultimate ancestry is not known.

**harmony** [14] The etymological idea behind *harmony* is 'fitting things together' – that is, of combining notes in an aesthetically pleasing manner. It comes via Old French *harmonie* and Latin *harmonia* from Greek *harmonía* 'means of joining,' hence 'agreement, concord,' a derivative of *harmós* 'joint.' As a musical term in Greek it appears to have denoted 'scale,' or more simply just 'music,' and its original use in English was for what we would now call 'melody.' It was not applied to the combination of notes to form chords (a practice which originated in the 9th century) until the 16th century.

The term *harmonica* was coined in 1762 by the American physicist and statesman Benjamin Franklin for a musical instrument consisting of a set of water-filled glasses tuned to different notes and played with the fingers. It was first applied to the mouth-organ in the 19th century.

**harness** [13] Etymologically, *harness* is 'equipment for an army.' It comes via Old French *herneis* 'military equipment' from an unrecorded Old Norse *\*hernest*, a compound formed from *herr* 'army' (a descendant of prehistoric Germanic *\*kharjaz* 'crowd' and related to English *harangue, harbinger, harbour*, and *harry*) and *nest* 'provisions.' English took it over in the general sense 'equipment,' and did not apply it specifically to the straps, buckles, etc of a horse until the 14th century (it was originally used for any equestrian equipment, including reins, saddles, etc, but now it denotes exclusively the gear of a draught horse).

▶ harangue, harbinger, harbour, harry, herald

**harpsichord** [17] *Harpsichord* means literally 'harp-string.' *Harp* [OE] is a Germanic word. It comes from a prehistoric West and North Germanic *\*kharpōn*, which also produced German *harfe*, Dutch *harp*, and Swedish *harpa*, and was borrowed into the Romance languages via late Latin *harpa* (its Italian descendant, *arpa*, gave English *arpeggio* [18]). When the harpsichord was developed in the late 16th century, it was named in Italian *arpicordo*, a compound formed with *corda* 'string.' English acquired the term via the now obsolete French *harpechorde*, for some unknown reason inserting an *s* in the process.

▶ arpeggio, harp

**harrier** see HARE

**harry** [OE] Etymologically, to *harry* is to 'go on a raid as an army does.' The word comes ultimately from prehistoric Germanic *\*kharjaz*, which meant 'crowd of people' and also 'army' (it also produced English *harangue, harbinger, harbour*, and *harness*). From it was formed the verb *\*kharōjan*, which passed into Old English as *hergian*. This developed into modern English *harry*, and it also produced the verb *harrow* 'rob, plunder,' now obsolete except in the expression *harrowing of hell* (which denotes the rescuing by Christ, after his crucifixion, of the souls of the righteous held in captivity in hell).

▶ harangue, harbinger, harbour, harness, harrow

**harsh** [16] *Harsh* originally meant 'hairy.' Its ancestor, Middle Low German *harsch*, was a derivative of the noun *haer* 'hair,' and its exact English equivalent would have been *hairish*. By the time English acquired it, it had broadened out in meaning to 'rough,' both literally and figuratively.

**harvest** [OE] The idea underlying the word *harvest* is of 'plucking, gathering, cropping' – it comes ultimately from Indo-European *\*karp-*, which also produced Greek *karpós* 'fruit, crop, harvest' (whence English *carpel* [19]) and Latin *carpere* 'pluck' (source of English *carpet, excerpt*, and *scarce*) – but its original meaning in English was 'time of gathering crops' rather than 'act of gathering crops.' Indeed, until as recently as the 18th century it was used as the name for the season

now known as *autumn* (as its German relative *herbst* still is), and it was not until the 16th century that the present-day senses 'act of gathering crops' and 'crops gathered' began to develop.

▶ carpet, excerpt, scarce

**haste** [13] *Haste* is a Germanic word, but English acquired it through Old French. The furthest back it can be traced is to a prehistoric West Germanic *\*khaistiz*, which produced such now defunct offspring as Old English *hǣst* 'violence' and Old High German *heisti* 'powerful.' Its survival is due to its acquisition by Old French as *haste*, which not only gave English the noun *haste*, but also contributed a related verb to German (*hasten*), Dutch (*haasten*), Swedish (*hasta*), and English (*haste*, largely superseded since the 16th century by *hasten*). The modern French noun is *hâte*.

**hat** [OE] *Hat* and *hood* are ultimately the same word, and denote literally 'head-covering.' Both go back to Indo-European *\*kadh-* 'cover, protect,' which in the case of *hat* produced a Germanic derivative *\*khadnús*, later *\*khattus*. This was the source of English *hat*, and also of Swedish *hatt* and Danish *hat* (German *hutt* and Dutch *hoed* 'hat' are more closely related to English *hood*).

▶ hood

**hatchment** see ACHIEVE

**hate** [OE] There are indications that the ancestral meaning of *hate* may have been a neutral 'strong feeling' rather than the positive 'dislike.' It has been traced to a prehistoric Indo-European *\*kədes-*, amongst whose other descendants were Greek *kedos*, which meant 'care, anxiety, grief,' and Old Irish *caiss*, which meant 'love' as well as 'hate.' It is clear, though, that the notion of strong dislike became established fairly early, and that it was certainly the sense transmitted via Germanic *\*khatis-*, source of German *hass*, Dutch *haat*, Swedish *hat*, Danish *had*, and English *hate*. The derivative *hatred* was formed from the verb in the 13th century with the suffix *-red* 'condition,' as in *kindred*.

Old French borrowed the Germanic verb *\*khatjan* 'hate' as *haïr*, and derived from it the adjective *haïneus*, acquired by English as *heinous* [14].

▶ heinous

**haughty** [16] To be *haughty* is to be 'above oneself,' or, to put it another way, to be 'on one's high horse.' For etymologically, *haughty* means simply 'high.' It is an alteration of an earlier, now dead English adjective *haught*, which was borrowed from Old French *haut* 'high,' a descendant of Latin *altus* (whence English *altitude*).

▶ altitude

**haunt** [13] Etymologically, a ghost that *haunts* a building is only using the place as its 'home.' The word's distant ancestor is the prehistoric Germanic verb *\*khaimatjan*, a derivative of the noun *\*khaimaz* (source of English *home*). This was borrowed by Old French as *hanter* 'frequent a place,' and passed on to English as *haunt*. Its main modern supernatural meaning did not develop until the 16th century (the first records of this sense come in Shakespeare's plays).

▶ home

**have** [OE] *Have* and its Germanic cousins, German *haben*, Dutch *hebben*, Swedish *ha*, and Danish *have*, come from a prehistoric Germanic ancestor *\*khabēn*. This was probably a product of Indo-European *\*kap-*, which was also the source of English *heave* and Latin *capere* 'seize' (whence English *capable, capture*, etc). In all the Germanic languages it shares the function of denoting 'possession' with that of forming the perfect tense. (It appears, incidentally, to have no etymological connection with the superficially similar Latin *habēre* 'have.')

▶ capable, captive, capture

**haven** [11] Etymologically, a *haven* is probably a 'container' for ships. The word appears to go back ultimately to Indo-European *\*kap-*, source also of Latin *capere* 'seize' (whence English *capable, capture*, etc). This produced Old Norse *höfn* or *hafn*, which lies behind the modern Scandinavian words for 'harbour' (such as Swedish *hamn* and Danish *havn*), and was borrowed into late Old English as *hæfen*, whence modern English *haven*. Closely related is Dutch *haven*, from which German borrowed *hafen* 'harbour.'

▶ capable, captive, capture

**haversack** [18] Etymologically, a *haversack* is a 'bag for oats.' The word comes via French *havresac* from German *habersack*, a compound formed from the now dialectal *haber* 'oats' and *sack* 'bag.' This denoted originally a bag used in the army for feeding oats to horses, but by the time it reached English it had broadened out to a 'bag for soldiers' provisions,' carried over the shoulders (northern dialects of English, incidentally, had the term *haver* for 'oats,' probably borrowed from Old Norse *hafri*, and related forms are still widespread among the Germanic languages, including German *hafer*, Dutch *haver*, and Swedish and Danish *havre*. It has been speculated that the word is related to Latin *caper* and Old Norse *hafr* 'goat,' in which case it would mean etymologically 'goat's food').

**havoc** [15] The ancestry of *havoc* is a mystery, but it seems originally to have been an exclamation, probably Germanic, used as a signal to begin plundering. This was adopted into Old French as *havot*, which was used in the phrase *crier havot* 'shout 'havot','' hence 'let loose destruction and plunder.' *Havot* became altered in Anglo-Norman to *havok*, the form in which English adopted it; and in due course *cry havoc* gave rise to the independent use of *havoc* as 'destruction, devastation.'

**hawk** English has three current words *hawk*. The oldest, denoting the bird of prey [OE] , comes from a prehistoric West and North Germanic *\*khabukaz*, which also produced German *habicht*, Dutch *havik*, Swedish *hök*, and Danish *høg*. *Hawk* 'peddle' [16] is a back-formation from *hawker*. This was probably borrowed from Low German *höker*, a derivative ultimately of Middle Low German *höken* 'peddle,' which may well have been formed from the same base as produced English *huckster*. *Hawk* 'clear the throat' [16] probably originated as an imitation of the noise it denotes.

▶ huckster

**hawthorn** [OE] The *hawthorn* appears to be etymologically the 'hedgethorn.' Its first element, *haw*, which in Old English was *haga*, goes back to a prehistoric Germanic *\*khag-*, which also produced English *hedge* and possibly *haggard* (German *hagedorn*, Dutch *haagdoorn*, and Swedish *hagtorn* share the same ancestry). The name of the tree's fruit, *haw* [OE], is presumably either a back-formation from *hawthorn*, or an abbreviation of some lost term such as *\*hawberry* 'hedgeberry.' *Hawfinch* dates from the 17th century.

▶ haggard, hedge

**hay** [OE] Etymologically, *hay* is 'that which is cut down.' It comes ultimately from the prehistoric Germanic verb *\*khauwan*, source also of English *hew*, which was formed from the Indo-European base *\*kou-*, *\*kow-*. From it was derived the noun *\*khaujam*, which has become German *hau*, Dutch *hooi*, Swedish and Danish *hä*, and English *hay* – 'grass cut down and dried.' Other English descendants of Germanic *\*khauwan* 'cut down' are *haggle* [16], which originally meant 'hack, mutilate' and was derived from an earlier *hag* 'cut,' a borrowing from Old Norse *höggva* 'cut'; and *hoe* [14], which comes via Old French *houe* from Frankish *\*hauwa* 'cut.'

▶ haggle, hew, hoe

**hazard** [13] The word *hazard* was introduced to English as the name for a game played with dice. It was borrowed from Old French *hasard*, which came via Spanish *azar* from Arabic *azzahr*, earlier *al-zahr* 'luck, chance.' Its associations were thus from the first with 'uncertainty,' and its central modern sense 'danger' did not develop until the 16th century.

**hazel** [OE] *Hazel* is a very ancient tree-name. It can be traced right back to Indo-European *\*kosolos* or *\*koselos*, which also produced French *coudrier* and Welsh *collen*. Its Germanic descendant was *\*khasalaz*, from which come German *hasel*, Dutch *hazel-*, and Swedish and Danish *hassel* as well as English *hazel*. The earliest known use of the word to describe the colour of eyes comes in Shakespeare's *Romeo and Juliet* 1592: 'Thou wilt quarrel with a man for cracking nuts, having no other reason, but thou hast hazel eyes.'

**he** [OE] *He* comes ultimately from a prehistoric Indo-European base *\*ki-*, *\*ko-*, which denoted in general terms 'this, here' (as opposed to 'that, there') and occurs in a number of modern English demonstrative pronouns and adverbs, such as *here* and *hence*. The most direct use of the demonstrative is for the 'person or thing referred to,' and so *\*ki-* has come down directly via Germanic *\*khi-* as the third person singular pronoun *he* (of which *him, his, she, her*, and *it* are all derivatives).
► him, his, it, she

**head** [OE] The word *head* can be traced back ultimately to Indo-European *\*kauput-*, *\*kaupet-*, which probably had connotations of 'bowl' (as in 'skull') as well as 'head,' although which came first is not clear. From it was descended prehistoric Germanic *\*khaubutham*, *\*khaubitham*, which produced German *haupt*, Dutch *hoofd*, Swedish *huvud*, and English *head*. A variant of the Indo-European ancestor, *\*kaput-*, seems to have been responsible for the Latin word for 'head,' *caput* (source of a wide range of English words, including *capillary, capital, captain*, and *chief*), and also for Sanskrit *kapucchala-* 'hair at the back of the head' and Danish *hoved* 'head.' And a further related form, *\*keup-*, produced English *hive*, Latin *cūpa* 'barrel,' and medieval Latin *cuppa* (source of English *cup* and German *kopf* 'head').
► capital, captain, chief, cup

**health** [OE] Etymologically, *health* is the 'state of being whole.' The word was formed in prehistoric Germanic times from the adjective *\*khailaz*, ancestor of modern English *whole*. To this was added the abstract noun suffix *\*-itha*, producing *\*khailitha*, whence English *health*. The verb *heal* [OE] comes from the same source.
► heal, whole

**heap** [OE] *Heap* is an ancient word, with still the odd non-Germanic relative surviving. Its immediate West Germanic ancestor was *\*khaupaz*, which also produced Dutch *hoop* (the *hope* of English *forlorn hope*), and forms such as German *haufen* 'heap' and Lithuanian *kaupas* 'heap,' while not in exactly the same line of descent, point to a common Indo-European source.

**hear** [OE] The prehistoric Germanic verb for 'hear' was *\*khauzjan*, which produced German *hören*, Dutch *hooren*, Swedish *höra*, Danish *høre*, and English *hear*. Some etymologists have suggested links with Greek *akoúein* 'hear' (source of English *acoustic*), and also with Latin *cavēre* 'beware' and Russian *chuvstvovat'* 'feel, perceive,' but these have not been conclusively demonstrated.

**hearse** [14] The ancestor of *hearse* seems to have been a word in an ancient Italic language meaning 'wolf' – Oscan *hirpus*. The salient feature of wolves being their teeth, the Romans took the word over as *hirpex* and used it for a 'large rake, of the sort used for breaking up fields.' It passed via Vulgar Latin *\*herpica* into Old French as *herse*, and by now had moved another semantic step further away from its original sense 'wolf,' for, since agricultural harrows in those times were typically toothed triangular frames, the word *herse* was applied to a triangular frame for holding candles, as used in a church, and particularly as placed over a coffin at funeral services. This was its meaning when English acquired it, and it only gradually developed via 'canopy placed over a coffin' and 'coffin, bier' to the modern sense 'funeral carriage' (first recorded in the mid-17th century).
► rehearse

**heart** [OE] *Heart* is part of a widespread Indo-European family of words for the 'cardiac muscle,' which all go back to the common ancestor *\*kerd-*. From it come Greek *kardíā* (source of English *cardiac* [17]), Latin *cor* (whence French *coeur*, Italian *cuor*, Spanish *corazón*, not to mention a wide range of English descendants, including *concord, cordial, courage, quarry* 'hunted animal,' and *record*), modern Irish *croidhe*, Russian *serdce*, and Latvian *sirds*. Its Germanic offspring was *\*khertōn*, which produced German *herz*, Dutch *hart*, Swedish *hjärta*, Danish *hjerte*, and English *heart*. The only major Indo-European languages to have taken a different path are Rumanian, whose *inima* 'heart' comes from Latin *anima* 'soul,' and Welsh, which keeps *craidd* for the metaphorical sense 'centre,' but for the bodily organ has *calon*, a descendant of Latin *caldus* 'warm.'
► cardiac, concord, cordial, courage, quarry, record

**hearth** [OE] Etymologically, *hearth* seems to mean 'burning place.' It has been suggested that its West Germanic ancestor *\*kherthaz*, which also produced German *herd* and Dutch *haard*, may be connected with Latin *cremāre* 'burn' (source of English *cremate* [19]) and Lithuanian *kurti* 'heat.'
► cremate

**heat** [OE] From an etymological point of view, *heat* is simply 'hotness' – that is, the adjective *hot* with an abstract noun suffix added to it. But the addition took place a long time ago, in the prehistoric ancestor of Old English. The suffix *\*-īn* 'state, condition' was tacked on to the adjective *\*khaitaz* 'hot' to produce *\*khaitīn*, which eventually became modern English *heat*. The verb *heat* is equally ancient, and was independently formed from *\*khiataz* (*het*, as in 'het up,' comes from a dialectal form of its past participle).
► het, hot

**heath** [OE] *Heath* goes back to Indo-European *\*kait-*, denoting 'open, unploughed country.' Its Germanic descendant *\*khaithiz* produced German and Dutch *heide* and English *heath*. One of the commonest plants of such habitats is the heather, and this was accordingly named in prehistoric Germanic *khaithjō, a derivative of the same base as produced *khaithiz, which in modern English has become *heath* 'plant of the heather family.' (The word *heather* [14] itself, incidentally, does not appear to be related. It comes from a Scottish or Northern Middle English *hadder* or *hathir*, and its modern English form is due to association with *heath*.)

**heathen** [OE] Etymologically, a *heathen* is 'someone who lives on the heath' – that is, someone who lives in a wild upcountry area, and is uncivilized and savage (the word was derived in prehistoric Germanic times from *khaithiz* 'heath,' and is also represented in German *heide*, Dutch *heiden*, and Swedish and Danish *heden*). Its specific use for 'person who is not a Christian' seems to have been directly inspired by Latin *pāgānus* (source of English *pagan*), which likewise originally meant 'country-dweller.' (Etymologically, *savages* too were to begin with dwellers in 'wild woodland' areas, while *civilized* or *urbane* people lived in cities or towns.) The now archaic *hoyden* 'high-spirited girl' [16] was borrowed from Dutch *heiden* 'heathen.'

▶ heath, hoyden

**heather** see HEATH

**heave** [OE] *Heave* is part of a major family of English words that can trace their ancestry back to Indo-European *kap-'seize.' One of its Latin descendants was the verb *capere* 'take,' which has given English *capable, capacious, capstan, caption, captious, capture, case* (for carrying things), *cater, chase, prince*, and many others. To Germanic it gave *khabjan*, from which come German *heben* 'lift' and English *heave* (which also originally meant 'lift'; 'throw' and 'haul' are 16th-century developments). *Haft* [OE] (literally 'something by which one seizes or holds on to something') and *heavy* are derived from the same base as *heave*, and *have* may be related.

*Hefty* [19] comes from *heft* 'weight, heaviness' [16], which was formed from *heave* on the analogy of such pairs as *weave* and *weft*.

▶ capable, capacious, capstan, caption, captive, capture, case, cater, chase, haft, heavy, hefty, prince

**heaven** [OE] The precise origins of the word *heaven* have never been satisfactorily explained. Could it perhaps be related in some way to Greek *kamára* 'vault, covering,' and thus originally have denoted 'sky thought of as arching over or covering the earth' ('sky' is at least as ancient a meaning of *heaven* as 'abode of god(s),' although it now has an archaic air)? Are the tantalizingly similar German, Swedish, and Danish *himmel* and Dutch *hemel* related to it (going back perhaps to a common Germanic source *hibn-in which the /b/ sound, which became /v/ in English, was lost – as in

*e'en* for *even* – and a suffix *-ila-* was adopted rather than the *-ina-* that produced English *heaven*), or are they completely different words? The etymological jury is still out.

**heavy** [OE] From the prehistoric Germanic verb *khabjan* 'lift' was derived the noun *khabiz* 'weight.' This in turn was the source of the adjective *khabiga-* 'weighty,' from which have come Dutch *hevig* and English *heavy* (the other Germanic languages once had related forms, but have long since abandoned them in favour of other ways of expressing 'heaviness').

▶ heave

**hectic** [14] The use of *hectic* for referring to 'great haste or confusion' is a surprisingly recent development, not recorded before the first decade of the 20th century. It originally meant in English 'suffering from fever, particularly of the sort that characterizes tuberculosis or septicaemia' (the metaphorical progression to 'feverishly active' is an obvious one). English acquired the word via Old French *etique* and late Latin *hecticus* from Greek *hektikós*, which meant literally 'habitual,' and hence 'suffering from a habitual or recurrent fever, consumptive.' It was a derivative of *héxis* 'condition, habit,' which in turn was formed from the verb *ékhein* 'hold, be in a particular condition,' which has also given English *epoch*. (The original English form of the word was *etik*; *hectic* represents a 16th-century return to the Latin form.)

**hedge** [OE] *Hedge* traces its ancestry back to a prehistoric Germanic *khag-*, which also produced the *haw* of *hawthorn* and possibly *haggard* and *quay* too. From it was derived the West Germanic noun *khagjō*, which has since become differentiated into German *hecke*, Dutch *heg*, and English *hedge*. The compound *hedgehog*, an allusion to the animal's piglike nose, dates from the 15th century (*porcupine*, literally 'pig spine,' conveys much the same idea).

▶ haggard, hawthorn, quay

**heel** English has two separate words *heel*. The one that names the rear part of the foot [OE] comes ultimately from Germanic *khangkh-*, which also produced English *hock* 'quadruped's joint corresponding to the human ankle.' From it was derived *khākhil-*, source of Dutch *hiel*, Swedish *häl*, Danish *hæl*, and English *heel*. *Heel* 'tilt, list' [16] is probably descended from the Old English verb *hieldan* 'incline' (which survived dialectally into the 19th century), its *-d* mistaken as a past tense or past participial ending and removed to form a new infinitive. *Hieldan* itself came ultimately from the prehistoric Germanic adjective *khalthaz* 'inclined.'

▶ hock

**hefty** see HEAVE

**hegemony** [16] *Hegemony* 'dominating influence of one nation over another' etymologically denotes 'leadership.' It was borrowed from Greek *hēgemoníā* 'authority, rule,' a derivative of the verb *hegeisthai* 'lead' (to which English *seek* is distantly related).

▶seek

**height** [OE] Etymologically as well as semantically, *height* is the 'condition of being high.' It was formed in prehistoric Germanic from *\*khaukh-* (source of *high*) and *\*-ithā*, an abstract noun suffix: combined, they came down to Old English as *hēhthu*. The change of final *-th* to *-t* seems to have begun in the 13th century. The spelling *ei* reflects the word's pronunciation in Middle English times, when it rhymed approximately with modern English *hate*.

▶high

**heinous**    see HATE

**heist**    see HOIST

**helicopter** [19] The term *helicopter* was coined in the mid-19th century from Greek *hélix* 'spiral' (source of English *helix* [16] and *helical* [17]) and Greek *ptéron* 'wing' (source of English *pterodactyl* and related to *feather*). The French were first in the field with *hélicoptère*, and the earliest record of the word in English, in 1861, was the barely anglicized *helicoptere*, but by the late 1880s the modern form *helicopter* was being used. (These 19th-century helicopters were of course a far cry from the present-day rotor-blade-driven craft, which were introduced in the late 1930s; as their name suggests, they were lifted – or more usually not lifted – by rotating spiral-shaped aerofoils.)

▶feather, helical, helix, pterodactyl

**heliotrope** [17] The *heliotrope*, a plant of the forget-me-not family, gets its name because its flowers always turn to face the sun (the word comes via Latin *hēliotropium* from Greek *hēliotrópion*, a compound formed from *hélios* 'sun' and *-tropos* 'turning' – as in English *trophy* and *tropical* – which designated such plants, and was also used for 'sundial'). In early times the word was applied to the 'sunflower,' which has similar heliotactic habits and in Italian is called *girasole* (literally 'turn-sun'), source of the *Jerusalem* in English *Jerusalem artichoke*. Another application of Greek *hēliotrópion* carried over into English was to a sort of green quartz which was believed to turn the sun's rays blood-red if thrown into water.

▶trophy, tropical

**hell** [OE] Etymologically, *hell* is a 'hidden place.' It goes back ultimately to Indo-European *\*kel-* 'cover, hide,' which has contributed an extraordinary number of words to English, including *apocalypse, cell, cellar, conceal, helmet, hull* 'pod,' *occult,* and possibly *colour* and *holster*. Its Germanic descendant was *\*khel-, \*khal-,* whose derivatives included *\*khallō* and *\*khaljō*. The first became modern English *hall*, the second modern English *hell* – so both *hall* and *hell* were originally 'concealed or covered places,' although in

very different ways: the *hall* with a roof, *hell* with at least six feet of earth. Related Germanic forms include German *hölle*, Dutch *hel*, and Swedish *helvete* (in which *vete* means 'punishment').

▶apocalypse, cell, conceal, hall, helmet, hull, occult

**helmet** [15] A *helmet* is literally a 'little protective hat.' The word was borrowed from Old French *helmet*, a diminutive form of *helme* 'helmet.' This in turn was acquired by Old French from Germanic *\*khelmaz* (source of English *helm* [OE]), which goes back ultimately to Indo-European *\*kel-* 'hide, cover' (source of a wide range of English words, including *apocalypse, cell, cellar, conceal, hall, hell,* and *occult*).

▶hell, helm

**help** [OE] Today, *help* is essentially a Germanic word. Related forms such as German *helfen*, Dutch *helpen*, Swedish *hjälpa*, and Danish *hjælpe* point to a Germanic ancestor *\*khelp-*. But there is one clue – Lithuanian *shélpti* 'help, support' – that suggests that formerly it may have been much more widespread throughout the Indo-European languages, and came from an Indo-European source *\*kelp-*.

**hem** [OE] If, as seems likely, *hem* is related to Old Frisian *hemme* 'enclosed piece of land,' its underlying meaning would be 'edge, border.' However, a link has also been suggested with Armenian *kamel* 'press.'

**hemp** [OE] *Hemp* is ultimately the same word as *cannabis* (as, bizarrely, is *canvas*, which was originally made from hemp). Both go back to a common ancestor which produced Persian *kanab*, Russian *konóplya*, Greek *kánnabis* (source of English *cannabis*), and a prehistoric Germanic *\*khanipiz* or *\*khanapiz*. From the latter are descended German *hanf*, Dutch *hennep*, Swedish *hampa*, Danish *hamp*, and English *hemp*.

▶cannabis

**hen** [OE] Etymologically, a *hen* is a 'singing bird.' The word goes back ultimately to a prehistoric Germanic *\*khanon* 'male fowl, cock,' which was related to the Latin verb *canere* 'sing' (source of English *chant*). In the West Germanic dialects a feminine form developed, *\*khannjō*, which has become German *henne*, Dutch *hen*, Swedish *höna*, Danish *høne*, and English *hen*. (The original masculine form survives in German *hahn*, Dutch *haan*, and Swedish and Danish *hane*, but English has given it up – the Old English word was *hana*, and if it had survived to the present day it would probably be *\*hane*.) The metaphorical extension of the term to any female bird took place in the 14th century.

▶chant

**henchman** [14] Early spellings such as *hengestman* and *henxstman* suggest that this word is a compound of Old English *hengest* 'stallion' and *man* 'man.' There are chronological difficulties, for *hengest* seems to have gone out of general use in the 13th century, and *henchman* is not recorded until the mid-14th century, but it seems highly likely nevertheless that the compound must originally have meant 'horse servant, groom.' The word *hengest* would no doubt have remained alive in popular consciousness as the name of the Jutish chieftain Hengist who conquered Kent in the 5th century with his brother Horsa; it is related to modern German *hengst* 'stallion,' and goes back ultimately to a prehistoric Indo-European *kǝnku-*, which denoted 'jump.' *Henchman* remained in use for 'squire' or 'page' until the 17th century, but then seems to have drifted out of use, and it was Sir Walter Scott who revived it in the early 19th century, in the sense 'trusty right-hand man.'

**her** [OE] *Her* is the modern English descendant of Old English *hire*, a derivative of the same Germanic base, *khi-*, as produced *he*. It was the genitive and dative case of the feminine personal pronoun: the former, which we would now express as *of her*, has become the possessive adjective, as in 'her job,' and the latter is now the object form, as in 'follow her.' The possessive pronoun *hers* dates from the 14th century.

▶ he

**herald** [14] Etymologically, a *herald* is a 'leader of an army.' The word comes via Old French *herault* from a prehistoric Germanic *khariwald-*, a compound formed from *kharjaz* 'army' (which occurs also in English *harangue*, *harbinger*, *harbour*, *harness*, and *harry*) and *wald-* 'rule' (source of English *wield*). It is identical in origin with the personal name *Harold*.

▶ harangue, harbinger, harbour, harness, harry, wield

**herd** [OE] *Herd* is part of a widespread Indo-European family of words denoting 'group' (others include Sanskrit *çárdhas* 'troop, multitude' and Welsh *cordd* 'tribe, family'). It goes back to an Indo-European *kherdhā-*, whose Germanic descendant *kherthō* produced German *herde*, Swedish and Danish *hjord*, and English *herd*. *Herd* 'herdsman,' now found only in compounds such as *shepherd* and *goatherd*, is a different word, albeit derived from the same Germanic source. Its Germanic relatives are German *hirte*, Swedish *herde*, and Danish *hyrde*.

**here** [OE] Like *he*, *here* can be traced back ultimately to a prehistoric Indo-European base *ki-*, *ko-*, which denoted 'thisness' or 'hereness' (as opposed to 'thatness' or 'thereness'). The adverbial suffix *-r* (as in *there* and *where*) links it to the concept of 'place.'

▶ there, where

**hereditary** [16] Latin *hērēs* 'heir' (a relative of Greek *khéra* 'widow' and Sanskrit *hā-* 'leave, lose') has been quite a prolific source of English words. For one thing there is *heir* [13] itself, acquired via Old French *heir*. And then there are all the derivatives of the Latin stem form *hērēd-*, including *hereditament* [15],

*hereditary*, *heredity* [16], and, via the late Latin verb *hērēditāre*, *heritage* [13] and *inherit* [14].

▶ heredity, heritage, inherit

**heresy** [13] Etymologically, a *heresy* is a 'choice' one makes. The word comes ultimately from Greek *haíresis* 'choice,' a derivative of *hairein* 'take, choose.' This was applied metaphorically to a 'course of action or thought which one chooses to take,' hence to a particular 'school of thought,' and ultimately to a 'faction' or 'sect.' The word passed into Latin as *haeresis*, which early Christian writers used for 'unorthodox sect or doctrine,' and thence via Vulgar Latin *heresia* and Old French *heresie* into English. (Another derivative of *hairein*, incidentally, was *diairein* 'divide,' from which English gets *diaeresis* [17].)

▶ diaeresis

**heritage**    see HEREDITARY

**hermaphrodite** [15] Biologically a combination of male and female, *hermaphrodite* is etymologically a blend of the names of Hermes, the messenger of the Greek gods, and Aphrodite, the Greek goddess of love. According to Ovid *Hermaphróditos*, the son of Hermes and Aphrodite, was beloved of the nymph Salmacis with an ardour so strong that she prayed for complete union with him – with the result that their two bodies became fused into one, with dual sexual characteristics. English acquired the term via Latin *hermaphrodītus*.

**hermetic** [17] *Hermetic* means literally 'of Hermes.' Not Hermes the messenger of the Greek gods, though, but an Egyptian priest of the time of Moses, who in the Middle Ages was regarded as identical with the versatile Hermes in his capacity of patron of science and invention, and who was thus named *Hermes Trismegistus* 'Hermes the thrice greatest.' This shadowy figure was the supposed author of various works on alchemy and magic, and so the term *hermetic* came to be roughly synonymous with *alchemical*. One of the inventions credited to Hermes Trismegistus was a magic seal to make containers airtight, and by the 1660s we find *hermetic* being used for 'airtight.'

**hermit** [13] Etymologically, a *hermit* is someone who lives alone in the desert. The word comes ultimately from Greek *érēmos* 'solitary,' from which was derived *erēmíā* 'desert, solitude.' Many of the early Christian hermits, notably Saint Anthony, lived not only alone but in the desert, so it was appropriate that the term *erēmítēs* was applied to them. It came into English via medieval Latin *herēmīta* and Old French *hermite*.

**hero** [14] *Hero* is a Greek word – *hérōs* – applied in ancient times to men of superhuman ability or courage, and in due course by extension to demigods. At first it was used in English simply to render this Greek notion, and it was not until the late 16th century that the extended and more general sense 'brave or otherwise admirable man' began to emerge. 'Chief character in a story' is a late 17th-century development. English acquired the word via Latin *hērōs* as *heros*, but it was not long before this became interpreted as a plural, and a new singular *hero* was formed. *Heroin* [19] comes from German *heroin*, said to have been coined from the delusions of heroism which afflict those who take the drug.

▶ heroin

**heron** [OE] *Heron* may well have originated in imitation of the bird's cry, for its source was probably Indo-European *\*qriq-* (whence also Russian *krichat'* 'call out, shout'). From this was descended prehistoric Germanic *\*khaigaron* (source of Swedish *häger* 'heron'), which was borrowed into Old French as *hairon*. English took it over as *heron* or *hern* (the latter now a memory surviving in personal names and place-names, such as *Earnshaw*).

**herpes** see SERPENT
**herpetology** see SERPENT
**herring** [OE] Just as the hare is probably the 'grey animal,' so the herring could well be the 'grey fish.' Old English *hēring* goes back to a prehistoric West Germanic *\*khēringgaz*, in which the first syllable could represent the ancestor of English *hoar* 'silvery-grey' – the colour of the herring. French *hareng* comes from a variant of the West Germanic word.

▶ hare, hoar

**hesitate** [17] Etymologically, to *hesitate* is to become 'stuck.' The word comes from Latin *haesitāre*, a derivative of *haerēre* 'hold fast, stick' (which gave English *adhere*). The underlying idea is of being 'held back,' or in speech of 'stammering,' and hence of being unable to act or speak promptly or decisively.

▶ adhere

**hessian** [19] In common with many other sorts of textile, such as denim, jersey, and worsted, hessian's name reveals its place of origin. In this case it was Hesse, formerly a grand duchy, nowadays a state of West Germany, in the western central part of the country.

**heuristic** see EUREKA
**heyday** [16] Etymologically, the *-day* of *heyday* has no connection with the English noun *day*, although it has come to resemble it over the centuries. Nor is *hey-* related to *hay*. Originally the word was *heyda*, an exclamation roughly equivalent to modern English *hurrah*. Probably it was just an extension of *hey*, modelled partly on Low German *heida* 'hurrah.' Its earliest noun use (first recorded in the 1590s) was in the sense 'state of exultation'; the influence of the *day*-like second syllable did not make itself felt until the mid-18th century, when the modern sense 'period of greatest success' began to emerge.

**hiatus** see YAWN
**hibernate** [19] The Latin word for 'winter' was *hiems* (it is the source of French *hiver*, Italian *inverno*, and Spanish *invierno*, and is related to a number of other 'winter' or 'snow' words, such as Greek *kheima*, modern Irish *geimhreadh*, Russian *zima*, and Sanskrit *hima-* – the *Himalayas* are etymologically the 'snowy' mountains – which point back to a common Indo-European ancestor *\*gheim-*, *\*ghyem-*). From it was derived the adjective *hībernus*, whose neuter plural form *hīberna* was used as a noun meaning 'winter quarters.' This in turn formed the basis of a verb *hībernāre* 'pass the winter,' whose English descendant *hibernate* was apparently first used by the British naturalist Erasmus Darwin (grandfather of Charles) around 1800. (*Hibernia*, incidentally, the Romans' name for 'Ireland,' comes ultimately from Old Celtic *\*Iveriu*, source also of *Erin* and the *Ire-* of *Ireland*, but its Latin form was influenced by *hībernus*, as if it meant 'wintry land.')

▶ Himalayas

**hide** English has two words *hide* in current usage, probably from an identical Indo-European source. The verb, 'conceal' [OE], which has no living relatives among the Germanic languages, comes from a prehistoric West Germanic *\*khūdjan*. This was derived from a base which probably also produced English *hoard*, *huddle*, and *hut*, and goes back to Indo-European *\*keudh-*, source also of Greek *keúthein* 'cover, hide,' Welsh *cuddio* 'hide,' and Breton *kuzat* 'hide.' *Hide* 'skin' [OE] and its Germanic relatives, German *haut*, Dutch *huid*, and Swedish and Danish *hud*, come ultimately from Indo-European *\*keut-*, which also produced Latin *cutis* 'skin' (source of English *cuticle* [17] and *cutaneous* [16]) and Welsh *cwd* 'scrotum.' The semantic link between the two *hides* is 'covering.'

▶ hoard, huddle, hut / cutaneous, cuticle

**hierarchy** [14] Greek *hierós* meant 'sacred, holy.' Combined with *-arkhēs* 'ruling' (as in English *archbishop*) it produced *hierárkhēs* 'chief priest.' A derivative of this, *hierarkhíā*, passed via medieval Latin *hierarchia* and Old French *ierarchie* into Middle English as *ierarchie* (the modern spelling was introduced on the basis of the Latin form in the 16th century). At first the word was used in English for the medieval categorization of angels (into cherubs and seraphs, powers and dominions, etc), and it was not until the early 17th century that it was applied to the clergy and their grades and ranks. The metaphorical use for any graded system soon followed.

**hieroglyphic** [16] Etymologically, *hieroglyphic* means 'of sacred carving.' It came via French *hiéroglyphique* from Greek *hierogluphikós*, a compound of *hierós* 'sacred' and *gluphḗ* 'carving' (which derived from the same source as English *cleave* 'split'). It was applied to the picture writing of the ancient Egyptians because this was used in sacred texts.

▶ cleave

**high** [OE] *High* is an ancient word. It goes right back to Indo-European *\*koukos*, which is related to a number of terms denoting roughly 'rounded protuberance': Sanskrit *kucas* 'breast,' for instance, Russian *húcha* 'heap,' and Lithuanian *kaukas* 'swelling, boil.' Evidently the notion of 'tallness,' central to modern English *high*, is historically a secondary development from the notion of being 'heaped up' or 'arched up.' The Germanic descendant of *\*koukos* was *\*khaukhaz*, which produced German *hoch*, Dutch *hoog*, Swedish *hög*, Danish *høj*, and English *high*. *Height* is a derivative of *\*khaukh-*.

▶ height

**hill** [OE] The ultimate source of *hill* was Indo-European *\*kel-*, *\*kol-*, which denoted 'height' and also produced English *column, culminate*, and *excellent*. A derivative *\*kulnís* produced Germanic *\*khulniz*, which now has no surviving descendants apart from English *hill*, but related words for 'hill' or 'mountain' in other Indo-European language groups include French *colline*, Italian *colle*, and Spanish and Rumanian *colina* (all from Latin *collis* 'hill'), Lithuanian *kálnas*, and Latvian *kalns*.

▶ column, culminate, excellent

**him** [OE] *Him* was originally the dative case of Old English *hē* 'he,' which in the late Old English period gradually started to take over from the original accusative *hine* as the general object form (the *'un* or *'n* still occasionally found in southern English dialects for 'him' may represent the last vestiges of this). The dative ending *-m* is also found in, for example, German *ihm* (dative of *er* 'he') and Dutch *hem*.

▶ he

**hind** English has two words *hind*. The adjective meaning 'rear' [13] probably came mainly from *behind*, a compound formed in Old English times from *bi-* 'by' and *hindan* 'from behind,' whose ultimate origins are unknown. Related are German *hinter* 'behind,' the first element of *hinterland*, which English borrowed in the 19th century, and the verb *hinder* [OE], etymologically 'put behind or back.' *Hind* 'female deer' [OE] comes ultimately from Indo-European *\*kemti-*, a derivative of *\*kem-* 'hornless.'

▶ behind, hinder, hinterland

**hinge** [13] *Hinge* is generally agreed to be related to the verb *hang*, and to mean etymologically 'something on which a door hangs,' but the circumstances of its formation are obscure (as indeed are the reasons for

its rhyming with *singe*, a 16th-century development; before that it rhymed with *sing*).

▶ hang

**hip** English has two *hips*. The anatomical *hip* [OE] comes from a prehistoric Germanic *\*khupiz*, whose formal and semantic similarity to Greek *kúbos* 'six-sided figure,' hence 'pelvic cavity' (source of English *cube*) suggests that the two may be related. The rose-*hip* [OE] goes back to a West Germanic *\*kheup-*, which survives also in Dutch *joop* 'rose-hip.'

▶ cube

**hippopotamus** [16] Etymologically, a *hippopotamus* is a 'river horse.' The word comes, via Latin, from late Greek *hippopótamos*, a lexicalization of an earlier phrase *híppos ho potámios*, literally 'horse of the river.' Other English descendants of *híppos* (a relative of Latin *equus* 'horse') include *hippodrome* [16], from a Greek compound that meant originally 'horse-race' (*-drome* occurs also in *aerodrome* and *dromedary*), and the name *Philip*, literally 'lover of horses.' The abbreviation *hippo*, incidentally, dates from the mid-19th century.

▶ equine, hippodrome

**hire** [OE] *Hire* probably originated in North Germany, in the area where the set of dialects known as Low German was spoken. It comes from a prehistoric *\*khūr-*, which also produced Dutch *huren* (Swedish *hyra* and Danish *hyre* were borrowed from Low German).

**his** [OE] *His* originated as the standard genitive form of the masculine personal pronoun *he*, with the genitive ending *-s* – what in modern English would be expressed as *of him*. But comparatively early in the Old English period it began to replace the ancestral third person possessive adjective *sīn* (a relative of modern German *sein* 'his'), and by the year 1000 it was also being used as a possessive pronoun, as in 'It's his.'

▶ he

**history** [15] Etymologically, *history* denotes simply 'knowledge'; its much more specific modern meaning is decidedly a secondary development. Its story begins with Greek *hístōr* 'learned man,' a descendant of Indo-European *\*wid-* 'know, see,' which also produced English *wit* and Latin *vidēre* 'see.' From *hístōr* was derived *historía* 'knowledge obtained by enquiry,' hence 'written account of one's enquiries, narrative, history.' English acquired it via Latin *historia*, and at first used it for 'fictional narrative' as well as 'account of actual events in the past' (a sense now restricted to *story*, essentially the same word but acquired via Anglo-Norman).

▶ story, vision, wit

**hit** [11] *Hit* is one of those words, now so common that we assume it has always been around, that is in fact a comparative latecomer to the English language, and one, what is more, whose ancestry is not at all clear. The standard Old English verb for 'strike' was *slēan* (modern English *slay*), but at the end of the Old English period *hit* suddenly appeared. It was borrowed from Old Norse *hitta*, a verb of unknown origin which meant not 'strike' but 'come upon, find' (as Swedish *hitta* still does). This sense was carried over into English (and still survives in *hit upon*), and it was not until the 13th century that the meaning 'strike' began to appear.

**hive** [OE] *Hive* comes ultimately from Indo-European *\*keup-*, which denoted 'round container, bowl' and also produced Greek *kúpellon* 'drinking vessel,' Latin *cūpa* 'barrel' (source of English *coop, cooper,* and *cupola*), and its post-classical offshoot *cuppa* (whence English *cup*). (A variant of the Indo-European base was the source of English *head*.) The Germanic descendant of *\*keup-* was *\*khūf-*, from which came Old Norse *húfr* 'ship's hull' and English *hive*.

▶ coop, cooper, cupola, cup, head

**hoar** [OE] *Hoar* now survives mainly in *hoary*, a disparaging term for 'old,' and *hoarfrost*, literally 'white frost.' Between them, they encapsulate the meaning of *hoar* – 'greyish-white haired with age.' But it is the colour that is historically primary, not the age. The word goes back to an Indo-European *\*koi-*, whose other descendants include German *heiter* 'bright' and Russian *ser'iy* 'grey.' Another Germanic offshoot was *\*khairaz* – but here the association between 'grey hair' and 'age, venerability' began to cloud the issue. For while English took the word purely as a colour term, German and Dutch have turned it into a title of respect, originally for an elderly man, now for any man: *herr* and *mijnheer* respectively.

▶ hare, herring

**hoard** [OE] Etymologically, a *hoard* is 'that which one hides.' The word comes from a prehistoric Germanic *\*khuzdam*, which was derived from the same base as the verb *hide*. (*Hoarding* [19], incidentally, is not etymologically connected; it comes from an earlier *hoard* 'fence,' which probably goes back via Old French *hourd* or *hord* to a prehistoric German form that also produced English *hurdle* [OE]. Nor is the identically pronounced *horde* [16] related: it goes back via Polish *horda* to Turkish *ordū* 'camp,' source also of *Urdu* [18], etymologically the 'language of the camp.')

▶ hide

**hoax**  see HOCUS POCUS

**hob**  see HUB

**hobby** *Hobby* in the sense 'pastime' is short for *hobbyhorse*. This originated in the 16th century as a term for the figure of a horse used in morris dances: the element *hobby*, used since the 14th century for a 'small horse,' was derived from *Hob*, a pet form of the man's name *Robert* or *Robin* which survives also in *hobgoblin*

[16] . From the morris-dance hobbyhorse was descended the toy hobbyhorse, a stick with a horse's head on top; and the notion of 'riding a hobbyhorse,' which could not actually take you anywhere, passed metaphorically into 'doing something only for amusement' – hence the meaning 'pastime,' first recorded for *hobbyhorse* in the 17th century and for the shortened *hobby* in the early 19th century.

*Hobby* 'bird of prey' [15] comes from Old French *hobet*, a diminutive form of *hobe* 'small bird of prey,' whose origins are not known.

▶ hobbyhorse, hobgoblin

**hobnob** [18] In Shakespeare's *Twelfth Night*, Sir Toby Belch says 'Hob, nob, is his word: give't or take't'; from which it has been deduced that the *hob* of *hobnob* represents *have* and that the *nob* represents the now obsolete *nave* 'not have' (formed in the Old English period by adding the negative particle *ne* to *have*). In Middle English these would have been *habbe* and *nabbe*. When *hobnob* first appears as a verb, in the mid 18th century, it means 'drink together' – perhaps from the notion of buying alternate rounds of drinks, or drinking toasts to each other in turn. The modern sense 'associate familiarly, socialize' is not recorded before the early 19th century.

▶ have

**hock** English has three words *hock*. The oldest, 'joint of a quadruped corresponding to the human ankle' [16] , is short for an earlier *hockshin*, which comes from Old English *hōhsinu*. This meant literally 'heel-sinew,' and the *hōh* came from the same prehistoric Germanic source as produced modern English *heel*. In its original sense it can also be spelled *hough*, but for 'joint of bacon,' first recorded in the 18th century, *hock* is the only spelling. *Hock* 'Rhinewine' [17] is short for an earlier *hockamore*, an anglicization of *Hochheimer* (Hochheim, on the river Main, is a centre of German wine production). *Hock* 'pawn, debt' [19] comes from Dutch *hok* 'prison,' hence 'debt'; it was introduced to English by Dutch immigrants in the USA. The -*hock* of *hollyhock*, incidentally, comes from Old English *hoc* 'mallow' (and the *holly*- is an alteration of *holy*, and has no connection with *holly*).

▶ heel

**hockey** [19] The first known unequivocal reference to the game of hockey comes in William Holloway's *General Dictionary of Provincialisms* 1838, where he calls it *hawkey*, and describes it as 'a game played by several boys on each side with sticks, called hawkey-bats, and a ball' (the term came from West Sussex). It is not known for certain where the word originated, but it is generally assumed to be related in some way to *hook*, with reference to the hockey stick's curved end. The *Galway Statutes* of 1527 refer to the 'hurling of the little ball with hockie sticks or staves,' which may mean 'curved sticks.'

▶hook

**hocus pocus** [17]  Hocus pocus came from a phoney Latin phrase – in full hax pax max Deus adimax – used by travelling conjurers to impress their audiences. It was originally used for such a 'conjurer,' or for a 'trickster' in general ('a Persian hocus pocus performed rare tricks with hands and feet,' Sir Thomas Herbert, Travels into Africa and the Greater Asia 1634), but this had largely died out by the end of the 17th century, leaving 'trickery, deception' in full possession. Hoax [18] probably originated as a shortened version of hocus.

▶hoax

**hoe**     see HAY

**hog**  [OE]  Hog generally means 'pig,' of course, and has done so since the late Old English period, but it is also a technical term used by farmers and stockmen for a 'young sheep before its first sheering,' a usage which seems to go back at least to the 14th century, so it could well be that originally the term hog denoted not a type of animal, but its age. Its ultimate source may have been Celtic.

**hogmanay**  [17]  Hogmanay is the Scottish term for 'New Year's Eve,' and so might reasonably be supposed to be of Gaelic origin, but in fact it is not. It appears to come from hoguinané, the Norman dialect version of Old French aguillanneuf, a greeting given when exchanging New Year's gifts (and possibly a contraction of accueillis l' an neuf 'welcome the new year').

**hoi polloi**     see POLYP

**hoist**  [16]  The history of hoist cannot be traced back very far. It is an alteration of a now defunct hoise (probably due to the mistaking of the past form hoised for a present form), which itself was an alteration of an earlier heise. This probably came from, or at least was related to, Dutch hijsen or Low German hissen 'raise.' Heist 'robbery, hold-up' [20], which originated in the USA, is a variant of hoist, and perhaps represents a survival of heise.

▶heist

**hold**  Hold 'grasp, clasp' [OE] and hold 'cargo store' [16] are not the same word. The verb goes back to a prehistoric Germanic source which meant 'watch, guard.' This ancestral sense is preserved in the derivative behold [OE], but the simple verb hold, together with its relatives German halten (source of English halt), Dutch houden, Swedish hålla, and Danish holde, has moved on via 'keep' to 'have in the hands.' The cargo hold, on the other hand, is simply an alteration (influenced by the verb hold) of an earlier hole or holl –

which was either the English word hole or a borrowing of its Dutch relative hol.

▶behold, halt / hole

**hole**  [OE]  Etymologically, a hole is a 'hollow' place. It originated as a noun use of the Old English adjective hol 'hollow' which, together with German hohl, Dutch hol, and Danish hul, all meaning 'hollow,' goes back to a prehistoric German *khulaz. The source of this is disputed, but it may be related to Indo-European *kel- 'cover, hide' (source of English apocalypse, cell, cellar, conceal, hall, hell, helmet, hull 'pod,' and occult). The semantic connection is presumably that a place that is 'deep' or 'hollowed out' is also 'hidden.'

▶apocalypse, cell, conceal, hall, hell, helmet, occult

**holiday**  [OE]  A holiday was originally a 'holy day,' a day set aside as a religious festival. The first signs of the word being used for a 'day on which no work is done' (originally because of its religious significance) appear in the 14th century.

▶holy

**holism**     see HOLOCAUST

**hollow**  [12]  Modern English hole comes from an Old English adjective meaning 'hollow,' and by a coincidental swap hollow originated in an Old English word for 'hole' (the two are probably ultimately related). Old English holh meant 'hollow place,' 'hole,' or 'cave,' and presumably came from the same source as produced Old English hol 'hollow.' In the early Middle English period it began to be used as an adjective, its inflected form holge having become holwe, later holew or hollow.

▶cauliflower

**hollyhock**     see HOLY

**holocaust**  [13]  Etymologically, a holocaust is a 'complete burning,' and the word was originally used in English for a 'burnt offering,' a 'sacrifice completely consumed by fire' (Mark 12, 33, 'more than all whole burnt offerings and sacrifices' in the Authorized Version, was translated by William Tindale in 1526 as 'a greater thing than all holocausts and sacrifices'). It comes via Old French and Latin from Greek holókauston, a compound formed from hólos 'whole' (as in English holograph [17] and holism [20], a coinage of the South African statesman Jan Smuts) and kaustós, a relative of Greek kaúein 'burn' (from which English gets caustic [14] and cauterize [14]). John Milton was the first English writer to use the word in the wider sense 'complete destruction by fire,' in the late 17th century, and in the succeeding centuries several precedents were set for its modern application to 'nuclear destruction' and 'mass murder' – Bishop Ken, for instance, wrote in 1711 'Should general Flame this World consume . . . An Holocaust for Fontal Sin,' and Leitch Ritchie in Wanderings by the Loire 1833 refers to Louis VII making 'a holocaust of thirteen hundred persons in a church.'

▶ caustic, cauterize, holism

**holster** [17] *Holster* was probably borrowed from Dutch *holster*, and may well be related to Old English *heolster* 'cover,' which did not survive into the Middle English period. It seems likely that its ultimate source was Indo-European *\*kel-* 'cover, hide,' a prolific progenitor of English words including *apocalypse, cell, cellar, conceal, hall, hell, helmet, hole, hollow, hull* 'pod,' and *occult*.

▶ apocalypse, cell, conceal, hall, hell, helmet, occult

**holy** [OE] *Holy* originated as a derivative of the prehistoric Germanic adjective which produced modern English *whole*, and so its etymological meaning is perhaps 'unimpaired, inviolate.' This ancestral form was *\*khailagaz*, which diversified into German and Dutch *heilig*, Swedish *helig*, and Danish *hellig* as well as English *holy*. *Hallow* is essentially the same word, and compounds with *holy* as a now hidden component include *hollyhock* [13] as well as *holiday*.

▶ hallow, holiday

**home** [OE] Old English *hām* meant 'place where one lives, house, village.' The last of these survives only in place-names (such as *Birmingham, Fulham*), and it is the 'house, abode' sense that has come through into modern English *home*. Its ancestor was prehistoric Germanic *\*khaim-*, which also produced German *heim*, Dutch *heem*, Swedish *hem*, and Danish *hjem*. It is not clear where this came from, although some have connected it with Latin *cīvis* 'citizen.'

**homeopathy** [19] Greek *hómoios* meant 'like, similar.' It was derived from *homós* 'same,' a word ultimately related to English *same* which has contributed *homogeneous* [17], *homonym* [17], *homophone* [17], and *homosexual* [19] to the English language. Combined with *-pátheia*, a derivative of Greek *páthos* 'passion, suffering,' it produced German *homöopathie*, which was borrowed by English around 1830. Etymologically, the word means 'cure by similarity' – that is, by administering minute quantities of the same substance as caused the disease – and contrasts with *allopathy* [19], based on Greek *állos* 'other.'

▶ same

**homily** [14] Etymologically, a *homily* is a discourse addressed to a 'crowd of people.' The word comes via Old French *omelie* and late Latin *homīlia* from Greek *homīlíā* 'discourse.' This was a derivative of *hōmílos* 'crowd,' originally a compound noun formed from *homou* 'together' and *ilē* 'crowd.' Its moral connotations emerged in the original Greek.

**hominy** [17] Hominy, a gruel or porridge made from coarsely ground maize kernels, is a North American dish, and appropriately enough its linguistic origins are probably American too. A likely source is Algon-

quian *appuminnéonash* 'parched corn,' a compound noun formed from *appwóon* 'he bakes' and *minneash* 'grains, corn.' The first reference to it in an English text is by Captain John Smith, an early English colonist in America, in 1629: 'Their servants commonly feed upon Milk Homini, which is bruised Indian corn pounded, and boiled thick, and milk for the sauce.'

**homonym**   see HOMEOPATHY

**homosexual**   see HOMEOPATHY

**honest** [13] *Honest* comes via Old French *honeste* from Latin *honestus*, a derivative of *honōs*, from which English gets *honour*. The new Latin noun formed from *honestus* was *\*honestitās*, literally 'honestness,' recorded only in the later contracted form *honestās*. From it English acquired *honesty* [14], whose application to plants of the genus *Lunaria* was inspired by their nearly transparent seed-pods.

▶ honour

**honey** [OE] Our Indo-European ancestors were very fond of honey, and their word for it, based on *\*melit-*, has come down to many modern European languages, such as French and Spanish *miel*, Italian *miele*, and Welsh *mel* (it also contributed to English *mellifluous, mildew*, and *molasses*). The Germanic languages, however, have not persisted with it. Their words for 'honey' (which also include German *honig*, Dutch *honing*, Swedish *honung*, and Danish *honning*) come from a prehistoric West and North Germanic *\*khunagom* or *\*khunanggom*. This may originally have described the colour of honey; it has been linked with Greek *knēkós* 'pale yellow' and Sanskrit *kāñcana-* 'golden.'

**honeymoon** [16] The word *honeymoon* first appeared in print in the middle of the 16th century. Richard Huloet in his *Abecedarium Anglico Latinum* 1552 defined it as 'a term proverbially applied to such as be new married, which will not fall out at the first, but the one loueth the other at the beginning exceedingly, the likelihood of their exceeding love appearing to assuage, the which time the vulgar people call the honey moon.' His description suggests not only that the term had already been around for some time by the 1550s, but also that it was probably inspired by the notion that although married love was at first as sweet as honey, it soon waned like the moon.

**honour** [12] English acquired *honour* via Old French *honour* from *honōr-*, the stem form of Latin *honōs* (later *honor*). It is not known where the Latin word came from. Derivatives to reach English include *honest, honesty, honorary* [17], and *honorarium* [17] (which in Latin denoted virtually a bribe paid in order to get appointed to an honorary post).

▶ honest, honesty

**hood** [OE] Ultimately *hood* and *hat* are the same word, and both mean etymologically 'head-covering.'

They go back to an Indo-European *kadh-* 'cover, protect,' which in the case of *hood* produced a West Germanic derivative *khōdaz*. From it are descended German *hut* 'hat,' Dutch *hoed* 'hat,' and English *hood*. *Hoodwink* [16] originally meant literally 'cover someone's eyes with a hood or blindfold so that they could not see'; the modern figurative sense 'deceive' is first recorded in the 17th century.

▶ hat

**hook**   [OE]   *Hook* and its Germanic relatives, German *haken*, Dutch *haak*, Swedish *hake*, and Danish *hage*, go back to a prehistoric *keg-* or *keng-* 'bent object,' from which English also gets *hank* [14] (via Old Norse *hanku*). Old Norse *haki* 'hook' was the source of a now obsolete English *hake* 'hook,' which may have been the inspiration for the fish-name *hake* [15] (the hake having a hook-shaped lower jaw). *Hookah* 'waterpipe' [18], incidentally, has no etymological connection with *hook*; it comes via Urdu from Arabic *huqqah* 'small box.'

▶ hake, hank

**hoopoe**   see DUPE

**hope**   [OE]   The origins of the word *hope* are obscure. It appears to have started life among the Low German dialects of northern Germany (whence English *hope* and Dutch *hoop*), and later spread to Scandinavia (giving Swedish *hopp* and Danish *haab*) and High German (modern German has the verb *hoffen* and the derived noun *hoffnung* 'hope'). Where did the original Low German forms come from, though? A suggestion that has found some favour is that the word is related to *hop*, and that it started from the notion of 'jumping to safety.' The theory goes that the 'place of refuge' thus reached gives one 'hope,' but it has an air of desperation.

**horde**   see HOARD

**horizon**   [14]   Etymologically, the *horizon* is simply a 'line forming a boundary.' The word comes via Old French *orizon* and late Latin *horīzōn* from Greek *horízōn*, a derivative of the verb *horízein* 'divide, separate' (source also of English *aphorism* [16], originally a 'definition'). This in turn came from the noun *hóros* 'boundary, limit.' *Horizontal* [16], which came either from French or directly from late Latin, originally meant simply 'of the horizon'; it was not until the 17th century that it began to be used in its modern sense 'flat, level.'

▶ aphorism

**horn**   [OE]   *Horn* belongs to a very large Indo-European word-family that has made an enormous number of contributions to English. Its ultimate source is Indo-European *ker-*, whose offspring predominantly denote 'animal's horn,' but also include words for 'top' and 'head.' Its Germanic descendant, *khornaz*, has not been that prolific (it has produced English, German,

Swedish, and Danish *horn* and Dutch *hoorn*, and *hornet* is probably a derivative), but other branches of the family have been more fruitful sources. From Latin *cornū* 'horn,' for example, come English *corn* 'hard skin,' *cornea*, *corner*, *cornet*, *cornucopia*, *unicorn*, and possibly *scerzo* and *scorn*; Greek *kéras* 'horn' has given English *keratin*, *rhinoceros*, and *triceratops*; while Sanskrit *śṛṅgam* 'horn' lies behind English *ginger*. And besides these, English *hart* 'male deer' [OE] goes back to a derivative of *ker-*.

▶ corn, corner, cornet, ginger, hart, hornet, keratin, rhinoceros, triceratops

**horoscope**   see HOUR

**horrible**   [14]   The Latin verb *horrēre* was used for hair standing on end or bristling. A common cause of this phenomenon is of course fear, and so in due course *horrēre* came to mean 'tremble, shake, be filled with fear and revulsion.' The latter sense has been carried through into English in the derivatives *horrible*, *horrid* [16], and *horror* [14]. (*Horrid*, incidentally, from Latin *horridus*, was originally used in English in the etymological sense 'shaggy, hairy, bristling' – 'a rugged attire, hirsute head, horrid beard,' Robert Burton, *Anatomy of Melancholy* 1621 – but this did not survive beyond the early 19th century.) The Old French descendant of *horridus* was *ord* 'filthy,' from a derivative of which English gets *ordure* [14].

▶ horrid, horror, ordure

**hors d'oeuvre**   [18]   In French, *hors d'oeuvre* means literally 'outside the work' – that is, 'not part of the ordinary set of courses in a meal.' The earliest record of its use in English is in the general sense 'out of the ordinary' ('The Frenzy of one who is given up for a Lunatick, is a Frenzy *hors d'oeuvre* . . . something which is singular in its kind,' Joseph Addison, *Spectator* 1714), but this did not survive beyond the 18th century. Alexander Pope, in his *Dunciad* 1742, was the first to use the word in its modern culinary sense. (French *oeuvre* 'work,' incidentally, comes from Latin *opera* 'work,' source of or related to English *copious*, *manoeuvre*, *opera*, *operate*, and *opulent*.)

▶ d'oeuvre copious, manoeuvre, manure, opera, operate, opulent

**horse**   [OE]   The Germanic languages have gone their own way as far as the horse is concerned. The prehistoric Indo-European term for the animal was *ekwos*, which produced Latin *equus* (source of English *equestrian* and *equine*), Greek *híppos* (whence English *hippodrome* and *hippopotamus*), Sanskrit *açvás*, and Old English *eoh*. Remarkably, though, this has virtually died out as the day-to-day word for 'horse' in the modern European branches of the Indo-European languages. In the case of English, it has been replaced by a descendant of prehistoric Germanic *khorsam* or *khorsaz*: *horse* (German *ross*, now mainly a literary term equivalent to English *steed*, is related). Its source is not known, although some have linked it with Latin *currere* 'run.'

**hose** [OE] The original meaning of *hose* was 'leg-covering, stocking.' It comes from a prehistoric Germanic *\*khuson*, which also produced German *hose* and Dutch *hoos*. It appears that the metaphorical transference from a 'long tubular stocking' to a 'long tube for conveying liquid' was first made in Dutch; it was introduced into English in the 15th century.

**hospital** [13] Like *hospices, hostels*, and *hotels, hospitals* were originally simply places at which guests were received. The word comes via Old French *hospital* from medieval Latin *hospitāle*, a noun use of the adjective *hospitālis* 'of a guest.' This in turn was derived from *hospit-*, the stem of Latin *hospes* 'guest, host.' In English, *hospital* began its semantic shift in the 15th century, being used for a 'home for the elderly or infirm, or for down-and-outs'; and the modern sense 'place where the sick are treated' first appeared in the 16th century. The original notion of 'receiving guests' survives, of course, in *hospitality* [14] and *hospitable* [16].

*Hospice* [19] comes via French from Latin *hospitium* 'hospitality,' another derivative of *hospes*.
▶ hospice, hospitable, host, hostel, hotel

**host** Indo-European *\*ghostis* denoted 'stranger.' From it were descended Germanic *\*gastiz* (source of English *guest*), Greek *xénos* 'guest, stranger' (source of English *xenon* and *xenophobia*), and Latin *hostis* 'stranger, enemy.' This original meaning is retained in the derived adjective *hostile* [16], but the noun itself in post-classical times came to mean 'army,' and that is where (via Old French) English got *host* 'army' [13] from. Its main modern sense, 'large number,' is a 17th-century development. But Latin had another noun, *hospes* 'host,' which was probably derived from *hostis*. Its stem form, *hospit-*, passed into Old French as *hoste* (whose modern French descendant *hôte* means both 'host' and 'guest'). English borrowed this in the 13th century, giving it a second noun *host*, quite distinct in meaning, but ultimately of the same origin. (Other English words that owe their existence to Latin *hospes* include *hospice, hospital, hostel, hotel*, and *ostler*.)

But that is not the end of the *host* story. English has yet another noun *host*, meaning 'bread of the Eucharist' [14]. This comes via Old French *hoiste* from Latin *hostia* 'sacrifice, victim.'
▶ guest, hospital, hostile, hotel, ostler, xenon, xenophobia

**hostage** [13] Despite its similarity, *hostage* is not related to any of the English words *host*. It comes via Old French *hostage* from *\*obsidāticum*, a Vulgar Latin derivative of late Latin *obsidātus* 'condition of being held as a security for the fulfilment of an undertaking.'

This in turn was based on Latin *obses* 'hostage,' a compound noun formed from the prefix *ob-* 'before' and the base of *sedēre* 'sit' (English *obsess* [16] is made up of virtually the same elements). The use of *hostage* for the 'person held' was established before English took it over.
▶ obsess

**hostel** see HOTEL

**hot** [OE] *Hot* is the English member of a family of adjectives widespread in Germanic, but with very few outside relatives. Its first cousins are German *heiss*, Dutch *heet*, Swedish *het*, and Danish *hed*, which point back to a prehistoric Germanic ancestor *\*khaitaz* (the English noun and verb *heat* come from the same source). Lithuanian *kaisti* and Latvian *kaist* 'become hot' are allied forms.
▶ heat

**hotchpotch** [15] *Hotchpotch* is an alteration (for the sake of the rhyme) of an earlier *hotchpot*. This was borrowed from an Old French compound made up of *hocher* 'shake' (perhaps from Frankish *hottisōn*) and *pot* 'pot.' So originally the word meant literally 'shake the pot' – presumably to blend an assortment of ingredients, although it is not certain that the allusion was in the first instance culinary. (Old French *hocher*, incidentally, may well have been the source of the Scottish verb *hotch* 'shake, fidget' [14].)

**hotel** [17] Ultimately, *hotel* and *hospital* are the same word, but they have diverged widely over the centuries. Both go back to medieval Latin *hospitāle* 'place where guests are received, hospice,' but this developed in two different ways in Old French. One branch led with little change to English *hospital*, but a reduced form *hostel* also emerged (borrowed by English as *hostel* [13]). Its modern French descendant is *hôtel*, from which English gets *hotel* (originally used in the sense 'large residence,' as in the French *hôtel de ville* 'town hall,' but since the 18th century increasingly restricted to its present-day sense). Other contributions made to English by Old French *hostel* are the derivatives *hostelry* [14] and *ostler* [13], originally (as *hosteler*) 'someone who receives guests' but since the 14th century used for someone who looks after horses at an inn.
▶ hospital, host, hostel, hostelry, ostler

**hound** [OE] Until superseded around the 16th century by *dog, hound* was the main English word for 'dog' (and indeed its relatives in the other Germanic languages remain so – German, Swedish, and Danish *hund*, for instance, and Dutch *hond*). It goes back ultimately to Indo-European *\*kuntos*, a derivative of the base which also produced Greek *kúōn* 'dog' (source of English *cynic* and, according to some etymologists, *quinsy*), Latin *canis* 'dog' (whence French *chien* and Italian *cane*, not to mention English *canine, canary, chenille*, and *kennel*), Welsh *ci* 'dog' (as in *corgi* [20], literally 'dwarf dog'), and Russian *sobaka* 'dog.' Since the 16th century, English *hound* has been used largely for 'hunting dog.'

▶ canary, canine, chenille, cynic, kennel, quinsy

**hour** [13] Greek *hṓrā* (a distant relative of English *year*) was originally a rather vague term, denoting 'period of time, season.' In due course it came to be applied more specifically to 'one twelfth of a day (from sunrise to sunset),' but as this varied in length according to the time of the year, *hṓrā* was still far from being a precise unit of time. Not until the Middle Ages (when *hṓrā* had passed via Latin *hora* and Old French *hore* into English as *hour*) did the term become fixed to a period of sixty minutes. (The same sort of vague relationship between 'time' in general or 'period of time' and 'fixed period' is shown in Swedish *timme*, which is related to English *time* but means 'hour'; in German *stunde*, which originally meant 'period of time,' but now means 'hour'; and indeed in English *tide*, which in Old English times meant 'hour' but now, insofar as it survives as a temporal term, denotes 'season' – as in *Whitsuntide*.) English *horoscope* [16] comes ultimately from Greek *hōroskópos*, a compound which meant literally 'observer of time' – that is, of the 'time of birth.'

▶ horoscope, year

**house** [OE] The ultimate origins of *house* are uncertain. The furthest it can be positively traced into the past is to a prehistoric Germanic *\*khūsam*, which also produced German *haus*, Dutch *huus* (probably a close relative of English *husk*), and Swedish *hus* (descendant of Old Norse *hús*, which provided the *hus*-of English *husband*). Beyond that, all is speculation: some have argued, for instance, that *\*khūsam* came from an Indo-European *\*keudh-* 'cover, hide,' source also of English *hide, hoard*, and *hut*.

▶ husband, husk, husting

**how** [OE] *How* belongs to the large family of question-words which in Indo-European began with *qw-* (as in English *quantity, query*, etc). The phonetic descendant of this in prehistoric Germanic was *khw-*, which in modern English is represented by *wh-*. *How* itself comes from a West Germanic adverb *\*khwō* formed from the base that also produced English *what* and *who*; like *who* it has lost its /w/ sound, but since *who* did not lose it until considerably later the spelling *wh* remains as a reminder of it.

The *how!* with which North American Indians supposedly greet each other is not the same word, incidentally. It is an imitation of a Sioux word, such as Dakota *háo* or Omaha *hau*.

▶ what, who

**howitzer** [17] Czech *houfnice* denotes a 'large catapult' for hurling stones at the enemy. It was borrowed into German as *houfenitz*, and this made its way into English as *howitz* at the end of the 17th century.

This had died out within a hundred years, but at around the same time English acquired *howitzer*, probably via Dutch *houwitser*, which has stood the test of time.

**hoyden** SEE HEATHEN

**hub** [17] *Hub* is one of those words that emerge unheralded from the undergrowth of language, its forbears uncertain. It seems originally to have meant 'lump,' and is probably ultimately the same word as *hob* [16]. This was at first spelled *hub* and may have denoted a lump of clay used as a bakestone, or a brick or clay projection at the back of a fire on which things were placed to keep warm. And *hobnail* [16] is etymologically a nail with a large 'lumpy' head.

▶ hob

**hubbub** [16] *Hubbub* is an Irish contribution to English. It comes from Irish Gaelic *hooboobbes*, which appears to be related to the Old Irish battle-cry *abú*. This was a derivative of *buide* 'victory' (a relative of which across the Irish Sea formed the basis of the name *Boudicca* or *Boadicea*, the Ancient Britons' version of *Victoria*). English acquired the word (and the now disused longer form *hubbuboo*) in the mid 16th century, and originally used it for the 'war-cry of a savage tribe'; the modern sense 'noisy turmoil' developed in the 17th century.

**huckster** [12] The Low German dialects of northern Germany appear to have had in prehistoric times a root *\*huk-* which denoted 'sell.' It has been suggested that this was the source of English *hawker* 'peddlar,' and with the alternative agent suffix *-ster* (which originally signified 'female doer,' but in Low German was used for males) it produced *huckster* – perhaps borrowed from Middle Dutch *hokester*.

▶ hawk

**huddle** [16] *Huddle* originally meant 'hide' ('to chop off the head of the sentence, and slyly huddle the rest,' James Bell's translation of *Walter Haddon against Orosius* 1581), suggesting that it could well be a derivative of the same base as produced English *hide* (its form indicates that it would have come via a Low German dialect). But virtually from the first *huddling* was more than just 'hiding' – it was 'hiding in a heap or among a crowd'; and from this has developed the word's modern meaning 'crowd or draw together.'

**hug** [16] Etymologically, *hug* seems to convey the notion of 'consolation, solicitude'; the expression of such feelings by clasping someone in one's arms is apparently a secondary semantic development. The word is of Scandinavian origin, and is probably related to, if not borrowed from Old Norse *hugga* 'comfort, console.' This was descended from a prehistoric Germanic *\*hugjan*, which also produced Old English *hogian* 'think, consider, be solicitous.'

**hull** [OE] The notion underlying the word *hull* is of 'covering' or 'concealing.' It originally meant 'peapod' – etymologically, the 'covering' of peas – and comes ultimately from the same Indo-European source as produced English *cell, clandestine, conceal, hall, hell,* and possibly *colour* and *holster.* It is generally assumed that *hull* 'main body of a ship,' which first appeared in the 15th century, is the same word (a ship's hull resembling an open peapod), although some etymologists have suggested that it may be connected with *hollow.*

▶ cell, clandestine, conceal, hall, hell, occult

**human** [14] *Human* comes via Old French *humain* from Latin *hūmānus.* Like *homō* 'person,' this was related to Latin *humus* 'earth,' and was used originally for 'people' in the sense 'earthly beings' (in contrast with the immortal gods). *Humane* is essentially the same word, and became established in the 18th century as a distinct spelling (and pronunciation) for two or three specific senses of *human.* Other English derivatives include *humanism* [19], *humanity* [14], and *humanitarian* [19].

▶ humane, humble, humus

**humble** [13] Etymologically, *humble* means 'close to the ground.' It comes via Old French *umble* from Latin *humilis* 'low, lowly.' This was a derivative of *humus* 'earth,' which is related to English *chameleon* and *human* and was itself acquired by English in the 18th century. In post-classical times the verb *humiliāre* was formed from *humilis,* and English gets *humiliate* [16] from it.

▶ chameleon, human, humiliate, humus

**humble pie** [17] Until the 19th century, *humble pie* was simply a pie made from the internal organs of a deer or other animal ('Mrs Turner did bring us an umble pie hot out of her oven,' Samuel Pepys, *Diary* 8 July 1663). *Humble* has no etymological connection with the adjective *humble* 'meek'; it is an alteration of the now extinct *numbles* 'offal' [14] (which came ultimately from Latin *lumulus,* a diminutive of *lumbus* 'loin,' from which English gets *loin* and *lumbar*). *Numbles* became *umbles* (perhaps from misanalysis of *a numble* as *an umble* in contexts such as *numble pie*), and from there it was a short step to *humble*; but the expression *eat humble pie* is not recorded in the sense 'be humiliated' until the 1830s. It combines the notion of 'food fit only for those of lowly status' with a fortuitous resemblance to the adjective *humble.*

▶ loin, lumbar

**humiliate** see HUMBLE

**humour** [14] Latin *hūmēre* meant 'be moist' (from it was derived *hūmidus,* source of English *humid* [16]). And related to it was the noun *hūmor,* which signified originally simply 'liquid.' In due course it came to be applied specifically to any of the four bodily fluids

(blood, phlegm, choler, and black bile) whose combinations according to medieval theories of physiology determined a person's general health and temperament. This was the sense in which English acquired the word, via Anglo-Norman *humour,* and it gradually developed in meaning via 'mental disposition at a particular time, mood' and 'inclination, whim' to, in the late 17th century, the main modern sense 'funniness.'

▶ humid

**hump** [18] *Hump* seems to have originated among the Low German dialects of North Germany and the Low Countries – Dutch, for instance, has the probably related *homp* 'lump.' It first appeared in English towards the end of the 17th century in the compound *hump-backed,* but by the first decade of the 18th century it was being used on its own. (Another theory is that it arose from a blend of the now obsolete *crumpbacked* with *hunchbacked* [16], whose *hunch-* is of unknown origin.)

**humus** see HUMBLE

**hundred** [OE] The main Old English word for 'hundred' was *hund,* whose history can be traced back via a prehistoric Germanic \**khundam* to Indo-European \**kmtóm*; this was also the source of Latin *centum,* Greek *hekatón,* and Sanskrit *çatám,* all meaning 'hundred.' The form *hundred* did not appear until the 10th century. Its *-red* ending (represented also in German *hundert,* Dutch *honderd,* and Swedish *hundrade*) comes from a prehistoric Germanic \**rath* 'number.'

▶ cent, rate, thousand

**hunger** [OE] *Hunger* is a widespread word in the Germanic languages, shared by German, Swedish, and Danish as well as English (Dutch spells it *honger*), but it is not represented in any of the other Indo-European languages. Indeed, no related forms have been identified for certain, although Greek *kégkein* 'be hungry' and Sanskrit *kákat* 'be thirsty' are possibilities.

**hunt** [OE] *Hunt* is an ancient word, probably traceable back to an Indo-European \**kend-,* which also produced Swedish *hinna* 'reach.' Its original Old English descendant was *hentan* 'seize,' of which *huntian* (source of modern English *hunt*) was a derivative. Etymologically, therefore, *hunt* means 'try to seize.'

▶ hand

**hurdle** see HOARD

**hurricane** [16] European voyagers first encountered the swirling winds of the hurricane in the Gulf of Mexico and the Caribbean, and they borrowed a local word to name it – Carib *huracan.* This found its way into English via Spanish. (An early alternative form was *furacano,* which came from a Carib variant *furacan.*)

**hurry** [16] The earliest known occurrences of the verb *hurry* are in the plays of Shakespeare, who uses it quite frequently. This suggests that it may have been a word well known to him in his native West Midland dialect, but it is not clear whether it is identical with the *horye* that occurs in a 14th-century Middle English poem from the same general area. A possible relative is Middle High German *hurren* 'move quickly.'

**hurt** [12] English borrowed *hurt* from Old French *hurter*, which meant 'knock' (as its modern French descendant *heurter* still does). This sense died out in English in the 17th century, leaving only the metaphorically extended 'wound, harm.' It is not clear where the Old French word came from, although it may ultimately be of Germanic origin. *Hurtle* [13], a derivative of *hurt*, also originally meant 'knock,' and did not develop its present connotations of precipitate speed until the 16th century.

► hurtle

**husband** [OE] The Anglo-Saxons used *wer* 'man' (as in *werewolf*) for 'husband,' and not until the late 13th century was the word *husband* drafted in for 'male spouse.' This had originally meant 'master of a household,' and was borrowed from Old Norse *húsbóndi*, a compound formed from *hús* 'house' and *bóndi*. *Bóndi* in turn was a contraction of an earlier *bóandi*, *búandi* 'dweller,' a noun use of the present participle of *bóa*, *búa* 'dwell.' This was derived from the Germanic base *\*bū-* 'dwell,' which also produced English *be*, *boor*, *booth*, *bound* 'intending to go,' *bower*, *build*, *burly*, *byelaw*, *byre*, and the *-bour* of *neighbour*. The ancient link between 'dwelling in a place' and 'farming the land' comes out in *husbandman* [14] and *husbandry* [14], reflecting a now obsolete sense of *husband*, 'farmer.' The abbreviated form *hubby* dates from the 17th century.

► be, boor, booth, bower, build, byre, house

**husk** [14] Etymologically, a *husk* is probably a 'little house.' It seems to have been adapted from Middle Dutch *húskijn*, a diminutive form of *hús* 'house' – the notion being, of course, that it 'houses' seeds or fruits. The derivative *husky* was coined in the 16th century; its use for 'hoarse' comes from the idea of having dry husks in the throat (the *husky* dog [19] is an entirely different word, probably an alteration of *Eskimo*).

► house

**hussar** [15] Ultimately, *hussar* is the same word as *corsair*. Its remote ancestor is Italian *corsaro*, which was borrowed via Old Serbian *husar* into Hungarian as *huszár*. This originally retained the meaning of *corsair*, 'plunderer,' but gradually developed into 'horseman,' and it was as 'Hungarian horseman' that English borrowed it.

► corsair

**husting** [11] In the late Old English period, a *husting* was a sort of deliberative assembly or council

summoned by the king. The word was borrowed from Old Norse *hústhing*, literally 'house assembly,' which denoted a council consisting of members of the king's immediate household, rather than a general assembly (*thing*, which is the same word as modern English *thing*, is represented in modern Scandinavian languages by *ting* or *thing* 'parliament, court'). In the 12th century the word came to be used for a court of law held in London's Guildhall, which for many centuries was the City of London's senior court, and in the 17th century it is recorded as meaning the 'platform at the upper end of the Guildhall,' on which the Lord Mayor and Aldermen sat during sessions of the court. In the early 18th century this was transferred metaphorically to the 'platform on which candidates stood to address electors,' and subsequently it was widened to include the whole 'election proceedings.'

► house, thing

**hut** [17] Etymologically, a *hut* is probably a 'covering structure.' The word has plausibly been traced back to Germanic *\*khūd-*, which also produced English *hide* and probably *hoard*, *house*, and *huddle*. This would have been the source of Middle High German *hütte*, which eventually found its way into French as *hutte* – whence English *hut*.

► hide, hoard, house, huddle

**hyacinth** [16] Greek *huákinthos* denoted a plant with deep red flowers which according to legend sprang from the blood of Hyacinthus, a beautiful youth whom Apollo loved but accidentally killed. It probably came from some pre-Hellenic Mediterranean language, and was remodelled in Greek on the basis of Hyacinthus's name. It is not clear what sort of plant the original hyacinth was, but by the time the word reached English (via Latin *hyacinthus* and French *hyacinthe*) it had been adopted for the bluebell and its immediate relatives. Greek *huákinthos* was also used for a variety of precious stone, probably originally the sapphire. This meaning too followed the word into English, but is now little used, having been taken over by *jacinth* [13] – itself a descendant of Latin *hyacinthus*.

► jacinth

**hydrogen** [18] Greek *húdōr* 'water' (a distant relative of English *water*) has been a prolific source of English vocabulary. Amongst its contributions are *hydrangea* [18] (literally 'water-vessel,' so named from the cuplike shape of its seedpods), *hydrant* [19], *hydrate* [18], *hydraulic* [17] (literally 'of a water-pipe'), *hydrofoil* [20], and *hydroponics* [20] (literally 'water-culture'). *Hydrogen* itself means literally 'generating water,' and was coined in French as *hydrogène* in the late 1780s for hydrogen's property of forming water when oxidized. It is first recorded in English in 1791.

► water

**hyena**   see SOW

**hygiene**   [19]   Greek *hugiḗs* meant 'healthy.' From it were formed the noun *hugíeia* 'health' (personified as *Hygieia*, the Greek goddess of health) and the adjective *hugieinós* 'healthful.' This came to be used as a noun, *hugieinḗ*, 'science of healthy living,' which passed via modern Latin *hygieina* and French *hygiène* into English.

**hymen**   see SEW

**hymn**   [13]   For the ancient Greeks, a *húmnos* was a 'song of praise' – but not necessarily a religious one. It could be used to celebrate the deeds of heroes as well as to compliment the gods. However, the Greek Septuagint uses it to render various Hebrew words meaning 'song praising God,' and it was this meaning that was carried via Latin *hymnus* and Old French *ymne* into English as *imne* (the spelling *hymn* is a 16th-century latinization).

**hypnosis**   [19]   *Húpnos* was Greek for 'sleep.' From it was derived the adjective *hūpnotikós* 'sleepy, narcotic,' which English acquired via Latin and French as *hypnotic* [17]. At first this was used only with reference to sleep-inducing drugs, but then in the late 18th and early 19th centuries the techniques of inducing deep sleep or trance by suggestion were developed. Early terms for the procedure included *animal magnetism* and *mesmerism* (SEE MESMERIZE), and then in 1842 Dr James Braid coined *neuro-hypnotism* for what he called the 'condition of nervous sleep.' By the end of the 1840s this had become simply *hypnotism*. *Hypnosis* was coined in the 1870s as an alternative, on the model of a hypothetical Greek \**hupnosis*.

**hypochondria**   [16]   Originally, *hypochondria* was an anatomical term, denoting the 'area of the abdomen beneath the ribs.' It comes via Latin from Greek *hupokhóndrion*, a compound noun formed from the prefix *hupo-* 'under' and *khóndros* 'cartilage.' This particular part of the body was formerly supposed to be the seat of melancholy, and so in the 17th century the word came to be used for 'low spirits, depression.' The modern sense 'belief of being ill' originally belonged to the derived *hypochondriasis* [18], but was transferred in the 19th century to *hypochondria*.

**hypocrite**   [13]   Etymologically, a *hypocrite* is someone who is 'playing a part,' merely pretending. The word comes via Old French *ypocrite* and late Latin *hypocrita* from Greek *hupokritḗs* 'actor, hypocrite.' This was a derivative of *hupokrínein*, a compound verb formed from the prefix *hupo-* 'under' and *krínein* 'separate,' which originally meant literally 'separate gradually,' and eventually passed via 'answer' and 'answer one's fellow actor on stage' to 'play a part,' and hence 'pretend.'

**hypotenuse**   [16]   The *hypotenuse* is etymologically a line that is 'stretched under' the right angle of a triangle. The word comes via Latin *hypotēnūsa* from Greek *hupoteínousa*, a derivative of *hupoteínein*. This was a compound verb formed from the prefix *hupo-* 'under' and *teínein* 'stretch' (a relative of English *tend, tense*, etc).

▶ tend, tense

**hysteria**   [19]   Greek *hustérā* meant 'womb' (it is related to Latin *uterus* 'womb'). The adjective derived from it was *husterikós* 'suffering in the womb.' This passed into Latin as *hystericus*, which formed the basis of the modern Latin noun *hysteria*, a term coined in the 19th century for a neurotic condition supposedly peculiar to women (in popular parlance it was called 'the vapours'). *Hysterectomy* 'surgical removal of the womb' dates from the late 19th century.

▶ uterus

# I

**I** [OE] Essentially all the Indo-European languages share the same first person singular pronoun, although naturally it has diverged in form over the millennia. French has *je*, for example, Italian *io*, Russian *ja*, and Greek *egṓ*. The prehistoric Germanic pronoun was *\*eka*, and this has produced German *ich*, Dutch *ik*, Swedish *jag*, Danish *jeg*, and English *I*. The affirmative answer *aye* 'yes' [16] is probably ultimately the same word as *I*.

▶ aye, ego

**ibex** see IVY

**ice** [OE] *Ice* is a widespread word among the Germanic languages – German has *eis*, for instance, Dutch *ijs*, and Swedish and Danish *is* – but beyond that its connections are somewhat dubious. Some of the more easterly Indo-European languages have or had similar-looking forms, including Old Iranian *isu-* 'frosty, icy,' modern Iranian *yak* 'ice,' and Afghan *asaī* 'frost,' which suggest the possibility of a common source.

*Iceberg* [18] was perhaps an adaptation of Danish and Norwegian *isberg*, literally 'ice mountain.'

**ichneumon** [16] *Ichneumon* comes from a Greek word which meant literally 'tracker.' This was *ikhneúmōn*, a derivative of *íkhnos* 'track, footstep.' Aristotle used it as the name for a species of wasp that hunted spiders, and it was adopted into English in this sense for the *ichneumon fly*, a wasplike insect with parasitic larvae, in the 17th century. Its original English application, however, was to a variety of African mongoose which 'tracks down' or hunts out crocodile eggs.

**ichthyology** see FISH

**icicle** [14] Historically, *icicle* is a tautology, meaning literally 'ice icicle.' It originated in Middle English as a compound of *ice* and *ickel* 'icicle.' This word, which survived dialectally into the 20th century as *ickle*, goes back to Old English *gicel*, which in turn was descended from a prehistoric Germanic *\*jakulaz* (source also of modern Icelandic *jökull* 'glacier').

**icon** [16] The etymological idea underlying *icon* is of 'similarity.' It comes via Latin *īcōn* from Greek *eikṓn*, which was derived from a prehistoric base meaning 'be like.' From 'likeness, similarity,' *eikṓn* progressed semantically via 'image' to 'portrait, picture.' That was the general sense in which English acquired the word ('The Icon, or forme of the same birde, I have caused thus to bee figured,' John Bossewell, *Workes of Armorie* 1572), and it was not until the early 19th century that the particular application to a 'sacred portrait in the Eastern Orthodox church' entered the language.

**iconoclast** [17] The original iconoclasts were members of the Eastern Orthodox church in the 8th and 9th centuries AD who were opposed to the use or worship of religious images. In more extreme cases their opposition took the form of smashing icons (the word *iconoclast* comes via medieval Latin from medieval Greek *eikonoklástēs*, a compound formed from *eikṓn* 'icon' and the verb *klan* 'break'). The term subsequently came to be applied to extreme Protestants in England in the 16th and 17th centuries who expressed their disapproval of graven images (and popish practices in general) in similar ways. Its general use for an 'attacker of orthodoxy' dates from the early 19th century.

**idea** [16] Etymologically, an *idea* is the 'look' of something – it comes ultimately from the same source as produced the Greek verb *ídein* 'see.' Greek *idéā* itself was used by Plato in the specialized sense 'archetypal form of something,' which survives in the derived adjective *ideal* [17], but as far as the modern English noun is concerned, its sense 'notion, mental conception' developed (in Greek) via 'look, appearance,' 'image,' and 'mental image.' *Ideology* [18] is a derivative, coined originally in French at the end of the 18th century.

▶ ideology, idol

**identity** [16] The historical meaning of *identity* is best preserved in its derivative *identical* [17] – 'the same.' For its ultimate source was Latin *idem* 'same,' a pronoun (formed from *id* 'it, that one' with the suffix *-dem*) used in English since the 17th century for referring to a previously cited author or text. This formed the basis of late Latin *identitās*, which meant literally 'sameness'; the main meaning of its English descendant *identity*, 'individuality, set of definitive characteristics,' arose from the notion of something always being the same or always being itself (rather than something else).

**ideology**   see IDEA

**idiosyncracy**   [17]   Greek *ídios* meant 'of a particular person, personal, private, own.' Among the words it has contributed to English are *idiom* [16] (etymologically 'one's own particular way of speaking'), *idiot*, and *idiosyncracy*. This was a compound formed in Greek with *súgkrāsis*, itself a compound noun made up of *sún* 'together' and *krāsis* 'mixture' (a relative of English *crater*). *Súgkrāsis* originally meant literally 'mixture,' but it was later used metaphorically for 'mixture of personal characteristics, temperament,' and so *idiosúgkrāsis* was 'one's own particular mix of traits.'

▶ idiom, idiot

**idiot**   [13]   The etymological idea underlying *idiot* is of a 'private individual.' That is what Greek *idiṓtēs* (a derivative of *ídios* 'personal, private') originally meant. It was extended to the ordinary 'common man,' particularly a lay person without any specialized knowledge, and so came to be used rather patronizingly for an 'ignorant person.' It is this derogatory sense that has come down to English via Latin *idiōta* and Old French *idiot*.

▶ idiosyncracy

**idle**   [OE]   'Lazy' is only a secondary meaning of *idle*. It originally meant 'useless, worthless' (as in 'idle threats'), and the sense 'lazy' did not develop until the 13th century (the Old English words for 'lazy' were *slow* and *slack*). *Idle* is shared by other West Germanic languages, and its relatives (German *eitel* 'vain, futile' and Dutch *ijdel* 'vain, useless, conceited') point up its original English meaning, but it is not known what its ultimate origins are.

**idol**   [13]   Greek *eidos* meant 'form, shape' (it came from the same root as *idéā*, source of English *idea*). From it was derived *eídōlon*, which originally meant 'appearance,' and in particular 'apparition, phantom.' It developed from there to 'image,' either a 'mental image' or a 'physical image,' such as a 'statue'; and in the early Christian era it and its Latin descendant *īdōlum* were used for an 'image of a false god.' English acquired the word via Old French *idole* or *idele*.

Another English offspring of Greek *eidos*, in the sense 'picture,' is *idyll* [17], which was borrowed from the diminutive form *eidúllion* 'little picture,' hence 'small descriptive poem.'

▶ idea, idyll

**if**   [OE]   The Old English version of *if* was *gif*, but its initial *g* was closer to modern Englsh *y* in pronunciation than to *g*, and the conjunction gradually evolved through Middle English *yif* to *if*. It is not known where it ultimately came from; it is evidently connected with Old High German *iba* 'condition' and Old Norse *ef* 'doubt,' but whether it started life as a noun like these or was from the beginning a conjunction is not clear. Its surviving Germanic relatives are German *ob* 'whether' and Dutch *of* 'if.'

**ignite**   [17]   The Latin word for 'fire' was *ignis* (it has been traced back to a prehistoric Indo-European *\*egni-* or *\*ogni-*, which also produced Sanskrit *agni-* and Lithuanian *ugnìs* 'fire'). From it were derived the verb *ignīre* 'set light to,' source of English *ignite*, and the adjective *igneus*, from which English got *igneous* [17]. Another contribution the Latin noun has made to English is *ignis fatuus* 'will-o'-the-wisp' [16], literally 'foolish fire,' so called perhaps from its erratic flickering, as if scatter-brained.

**ignoble**   see NOBLE

**ignore**   [17]   The Latin verb for 'not know,' and hence 'disregard,' was *īgnōrāre*, which was formed with a negative prefix from the stem *gnō-* 'know' (ultimate source also of English *narrate*). From it English got *ignore*, and from its derivative *īgnōrantia* the noun *ignorance* [13]. Its first person present plural was *īgnōrāmus* 'we do not know.' This was originally used in English in the 16th century as a legal term, in the sense 'we ignore,' used by a Grand Jury in rejecting an indictment for lack of evidence. Not until the early 17th century was it applied to an 'ignorant person.'

▶ narrate

**iliac**   see JADE

**ilk**   [OE]   Historically *ilk* means simply 'same.' Its Old English form was *ilca*, which was ultimately a compound made up of the demonstrative particle *\*i-* 'that (same)' and *\*līk-* 'form' (as in the English verb *like*). It had virtually died out by the mid-16th century as a straight synonym for *same*, but one context in which it survived, particularly in Scottish English, was in the increasingly fossilized phrase *of that ilk* 'of the same,' which was used originally to express the notion that someone's name was the same as that of the place they came from: thus *Nairn of that ilk* would have signified 'someone called Nairn from a place called Nairn.' In due course it came to be applied specifically to landed Scottish families, and so strong did the connection with 'family' become that by the 19th century we see the first signs of *ilk* being treated as if it were a noun, meaning 'family.' That led on in time to an even more general sense 'type, sort,' capable of use in such expressions as 'of a different ilk.'

**ill** [12] 'Sick' is not the original meaning of *ill*. To start with it meant 'bad' (a sense which survives, of course, in contexts such as 'ill-will,' 'ill-mannered,' etc), and 'sick' did not come on the scene until the 15th century. The word was borrowed from Old Norse *illr*, which is something of a mystery: it has other modern descendants in Swedish *illa* and Danish *ilde* 'badly,' but its other relations are highly dubious (Irish *olc* has been compared) and no one knows where it originally came from. The sense 'sick' was probably inspired by an impersonal usage in Old Norse which meant literally 'it is bad to me.'
▶ like

**illicit** see LEISURE

**illuminate** [16] Etymologically, *illuminate* is a parallel construction to *enlighten*. It was formed in the late Latin period from the prefix *in*- and *lūmen* 'light' (source of English *luminous*). The past participle of the resulting *illumināre* gave English *illuminate*. The medieval-sounding sense 'illustrate manuscripts' is actually quite recent, replacing in the 18th century the parallel formation *enlumine*, acquired by English in the 14th century via Old French *enluminer* from medieval Latin *inlūmināre*. *Illumine* [14] came via Old French *illuminer*. *Illustrate* is closely related.
▶ illustrate, luminous

**illusion** [14] The notion of 'play' is at the etymological heart of *illusion* (as indeed of its close relatives *allusion* [16], *delusion* [15], and *elude* [16]). It came via Old French from Latin *illūsiō*, a derivative of *illūdere* 'make fun of.' This was a compound verb formed from the prefix *in*- and *lūdere* 'play' (source of English *ludicrous* [17]). In classical Latin *illūsiō* meant 'mockery,' and no semantic shift seems to have taken place until post-classical times, when it moved to 'deceit' (a sense originally taken over by English).
▶ allusion, delusion, elude, ludicrous

**illustrate** [16] *Illustrate* is closely related etymologically to *illuminate*. It goes back to Latin *illustrāre*, a compound verb formed from the prefix *in*- and *lustrāre* 'make bright,' which came from the same base as produced Latin *lūmen* (source of *illuminate*) and *lūx* 'light,' and indeed English *light*. Originally it meant literally 'throw light on,' but this eventually passed via 'elucidate' to, in the 17th century, 'exemplify' and 'add pictures to.' More of the original sense of 'brightness' survives, albeit metaphorically, in *illustrious* [16], which comes from Latin *illustris* 'shining, clear,' a back-formation from *illustrāre*.
▶ illuminate, illustrious, light, luminous, lustre

**image** [13] Latin *imāgō* meant a 'likeness of something' (it probably came from the same source as *imitate*). It subsequently developed a range of secondary senses, such as 'echo' and 'ghost,' which have not survived the journey via Old French into English, but the central 'likeness' remains in place. Derived from the noun in Latin was the verb *imāginārī* 'form an image of in one's mind, picture to oneself,' which became English *imagine* [14]. (Latin *imāgō*, incidentally, was used in the 1760s by the Swedish naturalist Linnaeus for an 'adult insect' – based on the Latin sense 'natural shape,' the idea being that the insect had achieved its final perfect form after various pupal forms – and English took the term over at the end of the 18th century.)
▶ imitate

**imbecile** [16] Etymologically *imbecile* means 'without support,' hence 'weak.' It came via French from Latin *imbēcillus*, a compound adjective formed from the prefix *in*- 'not' and an unrecorded *\*bēcillum*, a diminutive variant of *baculum* 'stick' (from which English gets *bacillus* and *bacterium*). Anyone or anything without a stick or staff for support is by extension weak, and so the Latin adjective came to mean 'weak, feeble.' This broadened out to 'weak in mind,' and was even used as a noun for 'weak-minded person,' but English did not adopt these metaphorical uses until the late 18th century.
▶ bacillus, bacterium

**imitate** [16] Latin *imitārī* meant 'make a copy of.' It was formed from the base *\*im*-, which also lies behind the Latin ancestors of English *emulate* [16] and *image*; all three words share the basic meaning element 'likeness.' English acquired the word via the Latin past participle *imitātus*.
▶ emulate, image

**immaculate** [15] A *macula* in Latin was a 'spot' or 'stain' (as well as a 'hole in a net,' which gave English the *mail* of *chainmail*). Hence anything that was *immaculātus* (an adjective formed with the negative prefix *in*-) was 'spotless' – 'perfect.'
▶ chainmail

**immediate** see MEDIUM

**immense** see MEASURE

**immerse** see MERGE

**imminent** see PROMINENT

**immolate** see MILL

**immune** [15] The *-mune* of *immune* is the same as that of *remunerate* and of *commune* (and hence of *common*). It represents Latin *mūnis* 'ready to give service.' The addition of the negative prefix *in*- gave *immūnis*, which in classical Latin denoted literally 'exempt from a service, charge, etc,' and hence by metaphorical extension 'free from something, devoid of something.' This general sense still survives, of course, in English (as in 'grant immunity from prosecution'); and the more specific 'not liable to infection' did not emerge until as recently as the 1870s, probably under the influence of French or German.
▶ common, commune, remunerate

**immure**   see MURAL

**imp**   [OE]   Old English *impe* meant 'new shoot, sapling.' Its ultimate source was medieval Latin *impotus* 'graft,' a borrowing from Greek *émphutos*, which itself was an adjective derived from the verb *emphúein* 'implant.' In the early Middle English period it began to be transferred from plants to people, carrying its connotations of 'newness' or 'youth' with it, so that by the 14th century it had come to mean 'child.' And in the 16th century, in a development similar to that which produced the now obsolete sense of *limb* 'naughty child,' it was applied to 'mischievous children, children of the Devil,' and hence to 'mischievous or evil spirits.'

**impair**   [14]   If to *repair* something is to 'put it right,' it seems logical that to *impair* something should be to 'make it wrong.' In fact, though, logic has nothing to do with it, for the two words are quite unrelated. *Repair* comes ultimately from Latin *parāre* 'make ready,' whereas *impair* goes back via Old French *empeirier* to Vulgar Latin *\*impējōrāre* 'make worse.'

**impeach**   [14]   *Impeach* has nothing to do with peaches. In fact it is closely related to *impede*, and indeed originally meant 'impede' in English. Both verbs comes ultimately from Latin *pēs* 'foot.' *Impede* [17] goes back to Latin *impedīre*, a compound verb based on *pēs* which originally meant literally 'tie the feet together.' *Impeach*, on the other hand, comes via Old French *empecher* (ancestor of modern French *empêcher*) from late Latin *impedicāre* 'fetter, entangle, ensnare,' a compound verb based on the noun *pedica* 'fetter,' which itself came from the same base as *pēs*. Its original meaning 'impede, prevent' survived in English until the late 17th century ('a Ditch of sufficient breadth, and depth, to impeach the Assaults of an Enemy,' William Leybourn, *Cursus Mathematicus* 1690). Its use for 'charge, accuse' arose in the 14th century from an erroneous association with Latin *impetere* 'attack, accuse' (source of English *impetuous*).

▶ foot, impede, pedal

**impede**   see PEDAL
**impend**   see PENDULUM
**imperative**   see EMPIRE
**imperial**   see EMPIRE
**impersonate**   see PERSON

**impetuous**   [14]   Etymologically, *impetuous* means 'having impetus.' It comes from Latin *impetuōsus*, a derivative of the noun *impetus* 'attack' (source of English *impetus* [17]), which in turn was based on *impetere* 'attack.' This was a compound verb formed from the prefix *in-* 'against' and *petere* 'go towards, seek, attack' (source of English *appetite*, *compete*, *perpetuate*, *petition*, *petulant*, and *repeat*). The etymological idea underlying both words is thus of 'rushing towards something with great violence or aggression.' Another member of the same family is *impetigo* [16], the name of a sort of skin disease. This was borrowed from Latin *impetīgō*, whose medical meaning was a specialization of an earlier and much more general 'attack' (as in 'an attack of eczema').

▶ appetite, compete, impetus, perpetuate, petulant, repeat

**implacable**   see PLEASE

**implement**   [15]   The idea underlying *implement* is of 'filling up.' It comes ultimately from Latin *implēre*, a compound verb formed from the intensive prefix *in-* and *plēre* 'fill' (as in English *complete*). This originally meant 'fill up,' and hence 'fulfil,' but in postclassical times, under the influence of *implicāre* (source of English *employ*) it came to mean 'use, employ,' and so the derived plural noun *implēmenta* denoted 'things used, equipment.' It was originally used in the plural in English too, and it was not until the 16th century that the singular 'tool' emerged. The original Latin sense 'fulfil' is preserved much more closely in the verb *implement*, which was an independent and considerably later introduction, first recorded in Scottish English in the 19th century. (From the same source come English *complement* and *supplement*.)

▶ complement, complete, supplement

**implicate**   see EMPLOY
**imply**   see EMPLOY

**important**   [16]   *Important* and *import* (the opposite of *export*) come from the same source – Latin *importāre*, a compound verb formed from the prefix *in-* and *portāre* 'carry' (as in English *portable*). Its original literal sense (as represented in the English verb *import* [16]) was 'bring in,' but in the Middle Ages this developed metaphorically to 'imply, mean' (which is what French *importer* and Italian *importare* signify), and its present participle *importāns* gave English *important*.

▶ import, port, portable

**impostor**   [16]   An *impostor* is etymologically someone who 'imposes' on others. The word comes via French *imposteur* from late Latin *impostor*, a contraction of classical Latin *impositor*. This was a derivative of *imponere* 'put on,' hence 'inflict, deceive' (a compound verb based on *ponere* 'put, place'), which also gave English *impose* [15], *impost* 'tax' [16], and *imposture* [16]. It is the 'deceive' sense of *imponere*, of course, that has come through into *impostor*.

▶ compose, depose, impose, position

**imprecation**   see PRAY
**impregnable**   see PREY

**impresario**   [18]   *Impresario* has no etymological connection with 'impressing' people (often though it is mistakenly spelled *impressario*). It was borrowed from Italian, where it was a derivative of *impresa* 'undertaking.' This in turn came from the verb *im-*

*prendere* 'undertake,' which goes back to a hypothetical Vulgar Latin *\*imprendere* (source of the archaic English *emprise* 'enterprise' [13]), a compound based on Latin *prendere* 'take.' Hence an *impresario* is literally someone who 'undertakes' something.

**impress**     see PRESS

**improve**     [16]   The *-prove* of *improve* has no direct connection with the verb *prove*, although the two have come to resemble each other over the centuries. It comes ultimately from late Latin *prōde* 'advantageous' (source of English *proud*). This gave Old French *prou* 'profit,' which was combined in Anglo-Norman with the causative prefix *em-* to produce the verb *emprouer*. This originally meant 'turn to a profit, turn to one's advantage,' a sense which survives in English in one or two fossilized contexts such as 'improve the shining hour.' Modern English 'make or get better' developed in the 17th century.
▶ proud

**improvise**     [19]   Etymologically, if you *improvise* something, it is because it has not been 'provided' for in advance. The word comes via French *improviser* from the Italian adjective *improvviso* 'extempore,' a descendant of Latin *imprōvīsus* 'unforeseen.' This in turn was formed from the negative prefix *in-* and the past participle of *prōvidēre* 'foresee' (source of English *provide*). The earliest recorded use of the verb in English is by Benjamin Disraeli in *Vivian Grey* 1826: 'He possessed also the singular faculty of being able to improvise quotations.' (The closely related *improvident* 'not providing for the future' [16] preserves even more closely the sense of its Latin original.)
▶ provide

**impugn**     see PUGNACIOUS

**in**     [OE]   *In* is a widespread preposition amongst the Indo-European languages. Greek had *en*, Latin *in* (whence French and Italian *en* and Spanish *in*), and amongst modern languages German and Dutch have *in*, Swedish *i*, Welsh *yn*, and Russian *v*, all of which point back to an original Indo-European *\*en* or *\*n*. The adverb *in* was not originally the same word; it comes from a conflation of two Old English adverbs, *inn* and *inne*, both ultimately related to the preposition *in*. (An *inn* is etymologically a place 'in' which people live or stay.)
▶ inn

**inaugurate**     see AUGUR

**incense**     English has two distinct words *incense*, but both come ultimately from the same source. The noun, 'aromatic burnt substance' [13], comes via Old French *encens* from late Latin *incensum*, a noun use of the verb *incendere* 'set fire to' (source of English *incendiary* [17]). This in turn was formed from a derivative of *candēre* 'glow' (source of English *candle*). (From *encens* was derived Old French *censier*, which passed into

English via Anglo-Norman as *censer* [13].) Besides the literal 'set fire to,' *incendere* was used figuratively for 'enrage,' which English acquired as the verb *incense* [15] via Old French.
▶ censer, incendiary

**incest**     [13]   Etymologically, *incest* is virtually the same word as *unchaste*. It was borrowed from Latin *incestus*, a noun use of an adjective formed from the negative prefix *in-* and *castus* 'pure' (source of English *chaste*). The Latin word denoted 'unchastity' in general, but in practice was often applied specifically to 'sexual contact between close relatives.'
▶ chaste

**inch**     [OE]   *Inch* and *ounce* both mean etymologically 'one twelfth,' but while this ancestral sense has largely been lost sight of in the case of *ounce*, for *inch* it remains in force. The words' common ancestor is Latin *uncia*, a term for a 'twelfth part' derived from *unus* 'one.' This was borrowed into prehistoric Germanic as *\*ungkja*, but it has not survived in any other Germanic language but English.
▶ one, ounce

**incident**     [15]   An *incident* is literally that which 'befalls.' In common with *accident* and *occident*, and a wide range of other English words, from *cadaver* to *occasion*, it comes ultimately from Latin *cadere* 'fall.' This was combined with the prefix *in-* 'on' to produce *incidere* 'fall on,' hence 'befall, happen to.' Its present participial stem *incident-* passed into English either directly or via French. The use of a word that literally means 'fall' to denote the concept of 'happening' is quite a common phenomenon. It occurs also in *befall* and *chance*, and operates in other languages than English: Welsh *digwydd* 'happen,' for instance, is derived from *cwyddo* 'fall.'
▶ accident, cadence, case, occasion

**incline**     [13]   Latin *-clīnāre* (a relative of English *lean*, but itself only ever recorded in compounds) meant 'bend, lean.' Add to this the prefix *in-* and you had *inclīnāre* 'lean towards.' This was originally borrowed into English via Old French *encliner* as *encline* – a form which survived until the 17th century, when the latinized *incline* began to take over. The metaphorical use of the word to indicate a person's disposition or preference dates back to Roman times.
▶ lean

**include**     [15]   The idea of 'shutting in' or 'enclosure' is etymologically central to *include* – indeed, it is virtually the same word as *enclose*. It was borrowed from Latin *inclūdere*, a compound verb formed from the prefix *in-* and *claudere* 'shut' (source of English *close*). (A probable Vulgar Latin descendant of *inclūdere* was *\*inclaudere*, which passed into Old French as *enclore*. English took over its past participle *enclose* as the verb *enclose* [14].) The metaphorical sense 'comprise' was already developing in classical Latin.

▶ close, enclose

**increase** [14] The *-crease* element in *increase* (which occurs also, of course, in its antonym *decrease*) means 'grow.' It comes from Latin *crēscere* 'grow' (source of English *crescent*), which combined with the prefix *in-* to produce *incrēscere* 'grow in, grow on.' This passed into Old French as *encreistre*, which English originally took over as *encres*. The Latin-style spelling, with *in-* instead of *en-*, was reintroduced in the 15th century. Derived from Latin *incrēscere* was *incrēmentum* 'growth, increase,' which gave English *increment* [15].

▶ crescent, croissant, decrease, increment

**incubate** [18] Latin *incubāre*, the source of English *incubate*, meant literally 'lie down on.' It was based on the verb *cubāre* 'lie,' which also produced English *concubine* and *cubicle*. The notion of 'lying on eggs to hatch them' seems later to have fed back into the simple verb *cubāre*, which in this sense gave English *couvade* 'male mimicking of child-bearing' [19] (an anthropological term borrowed from French) and *covey* [14]. Another English descendant of *incubāre* is *incubus* 'male demon that has sex with a sleeping woman' [14], literally 'one who lies down on another' (its counterpart is the *succubus* 'female demon that has sex with a sleeping man' [16], literally 'one who lies down under another').

The nasalized version of the stem of Latin *cubāre* gave English *incumbent* [16] (which etymologically means 'resting upon as a duty') and *recumbent* [17].

▶ cubicle, concubine, covey, incubus, incumbent, recumbent, succubus, succumb

**incunabulum** [19] An *incunabulum* is a book printed before 1501. But etymologically the word has nothing to do with books. It comes from the Latin plural noun *incūnābula*, which had a range of meanings, including 'swaddling clothes,' 'cradle,' and 'infancy,' which point back to its original source, Latin *cūnae* 'cradle.' Nineteenth-century antiquarians and bibliographers applied the term to early printed books since they represented the 'infancy' of book production.

**incursion** see COURSE

**indefatigable** see FATIGUE

**indemnity** see DAMAGE

**indent** Etymologically, English has two separate words *indent*, although they have converged to a considerable extent over the centuries (particularly in the virtually shared derivative *indentation*). The one meaning '(make) a hole or depression' [14] is simply a derivative of *dent*, which itself probably originated as a variant of *dint*. *Indent* 'make notches in' [14], however,

owes its origin to Latin *dēns* 'tooth.' This formed the basis of an Anglo-Latin verb *indentāre*, which denoted the drawing up of a contract between two parties on two identical documents, which were cut along a matching line of notches or 'teeth' which could subsequently be rejoined to prove their authenticity. A particular use of such contracts was between master craftsmen and their trainees, who hence became known as *indentured apprentices*.

▶ dent, dint / dentist

**index** [16] Latin *index* originally meant 'indicator,' and hence more specifically 'forefinger' – the finger used for pointing things out. It was based on the same stem, *\*dik-* 'point out,' as produced Latin *dīcere* 'say' (source of English *diction, dictionary*, etc). The metaphorically extended sense 'list of contents' had already developed in Latin before English took it over. *Indicate* is a parallel but apparently independent formation.

▶ diction, dictionary, indicate

**indicate** [17] Like *index*, *indicate* has its origins in the Latin stem *\*dik-* 'point out.' In this case the base form was the verbal derivative *dicāre* 'proclaim,' which with the addition of the prefix *in-* produced *indicāre* 'show' – which English adopted as *indicate*. First cousin of Latin *dicāre* was *dīcere* 'say' (source of English *diction, dictionary*, etc). Addition of the prefix *in-* to this produced *indicere* 'proclaim,' which formed the basis of Vulgar Latin *\*indictāre* 'declare, dictate.' This has given English two separate verbs: via Old French *enditier* the now archaic *indite* [14]; and via Anglo-Norman *enditer*, with subsequent latinization of the spelling, *indict* [14].

**indifferent** see DIFFERENT

**indigenous** [17] The *-gen-* of *indigenous* comes from the same ultimate source – Indo-European *\*gen-* – as produced English *gender, generate, genital*, etc. It denoted 'produce.' The addition of the Latin prefix *indi-* 'in, within,' earlier *indu-* (a strengthened form of *in-* originally formed with *de* 'down,' which also appears in *indigent* 'poor' [14] and *industry*) produced *indigena* 'born or produced in a particular place, native,' which English adopted and adapted as *indigenous*.

▶ gender, general, generate, genital, kind

**indignant** see DIGNITY

**indigo** [16] Etymologically *indigo*, a blue dye, is the 'Indian dye' – so named because supplies of it were obtained from India. The term is an ancient one. It originated in Greek *indikón*, literally the 'Indian substance,' a derivative of the adjective *Indikós* 'Indian,' and passed via Latin *indicum* and Spanish *indico* into English as *indico*. This was replaced in the 17th century by the Portuguese form *indigo*, and it was Portuguese influence, stemming from their commercial activities in India, that really established the term among the Euro-

pean languages (hitherto the commoner term for the dye had been *anil*, a word of Sanskrit origins). (The name *India*, incidentally, to which *indigo* is related, comes ultimately from Old Persian *hiñd'u*, which originally meant 'river,' was subsequently applied specifically to the river Indus, and finally became the name for the country through which the Indus flowed.)
▶ India

**individual**    [15]    To begin with, *individual* retained in English its ancestral meaning 'not able to be divided': 'in the name of the holy and individual Trinity,' Richard Whitbourne, *Discourse and Discovery of Newfoundland* 1623. It was borrowed from medieval Latin *indīviduālis*, a derivative of Latin *indīviduus* 'not divisible,' which in turn was based on *dīviduus*, a derivative of the verb *dīvidere* 'divide.' The semantic move from 'not divisible' to 'single, separate' took place in the 17th century. (English acquired the formally parallel *indivisible*, incidentally, in the 14th century.)
▶ divide

**indomitable**    see TAME

**indulge**    [17]    The *-dulg-* of *indulge* may be related to such words as Greek *dolikhós* and Russian *dólgij*, meaning 'long.' In that case Latin *indulgēre*, the immediate source of the English word, may to begin with have signified 'allow long enough for.' Its only recorded senses, however, are the same as those of modern English *indulge*.

**industry**    [15]    *Industry* comes, partly via Old French *industrie*, from Latin *industria*, which meant 'quality of being hard-working, diligence.' This was a derivative of the adjective *industrius* 'diligent,' which went back to an Old Latin *indostruus*, formed from the prefix *indu-* 'in' (see INDIGENOUS) and the element *-struus* (a relative of the verb *struere* 'build,' from which English gets *construct, destroy*, etc).
▶ construct, destroy, structure

**inebriate**    [15]    Latin *ēbrius* (a relative of *sōbrius*, from which English gets *sober*) meant 'drunk.' From it was formed the verb *ēbriāre* 'intoxicate,' which with the addition of the intensive prefix *in-* produced *inēbriāre* 'make very drunk' – whence English *inebriate*.
▶ sober

**ineffable**    [15]    *Ineffable* literally means 'that cannot be spoken.' Its ultimate source was the Latin verb *fārī* 'speak,' which has also given English *fable, fame, fate*, etc. Addition of the prefix *ex-* 'out' produced *effārī* 'speak out,' from which the adjective *ineffābilis* was derived. In 19th-century English the word was used as a plural noun, like *unmentionables*, as a humorous euphemism for 'trousers' or 'nether garments': 'shoes off, ineffables tucked up,' William Cory, *Letters and Journals* 1867.
▶ fable, fame, fate

**inert**    [17]    The *-ert* of *inert* is the same word as *art*. The word comes from Latin *iners*, which originally meant 'unskilled,' but soon developed semantically to 'inactive.' It was formed with the negative prefix *in-* from *ars* 'skill,' source of English *art*. The derivative *inertia* [18] is a Latin formation. In classical times it meant simply 'lack of skill, idleness'; it was Johannes Kepler who first used it as a technical term in physics in the 17th century.
▶ art, inertia

**inevitable**    [15]    Latin *ēvītāre* meant 'avoid.' It was a compound verb formed from the prefix *ex-* 'away, from' and *vītāre* 'shun,' and actually produced an English verb *evite* 'avoid,' a scholarly 16th-century introduction which survived as an archaism into the 19th century. Its derived adjective was *ēvītābilis* 'avoidable,' which with the negative prefix became *inēvītābilis*.

**inexorable**    [16]    Etymologically, *inexorable* means 'that cannot be removed by praying.' It is an adjective of many layers, of which the original is Latin *ōrāre* 'pray' (source of English *oracle, orator*, etc). Addition of the prefix *ex-* 'out' produced *exōrāre* 'remove by pleading or entreating,' and further prefixation and suffixation gave *inexōrābilis*, which entered English partly via French *inexorable*.
▶ oracle, orator

**infamous**    [14]    The negative connotations of *infamous* go back a long way – to the word's source, in fact, Latin *infāmis*. This did not mean simply 'not well known'; the prefix *in-* denoted positively 'bad,' and so *infāmis* signified 'of ill repute.' In post-classical times *infāmis* became *infamōsus*, which passed into English as *infamous*.
▶ famous

**infant**    [14]    Etymologically, an *infant* is 'someone who cannot yet speak.' The word comes via Old French *enfant* from Latin *infāns* 'young child,' a noun use of the adjective *infāns*, originally 'unable to speak,' which was formed from the negative prefix *in-* and the present participle of *fārī* 'speak' (source of English *fable, fame, fate*, etc). The somewhat improbable derivative *infantry* [16] comes via French from Italian *infanteria*; this was based on *infante*, whose original meaning 'young person' had shifted to 'foot soldier' (a development distantly reminiscent of the use of British English *lads* for 'male members of a group, team, etc').
▶ fable, fame, fate

**infect**    [14]    Latin *inficere* originally meant 'put in' – it was a compound verb formed from the prefix *in-* and *facere* 'put, do' (source of English *fact, fashion*, etc). Its earliest specialized extension was 'dip in,' which was applied specifically to the dipping of cloth into dye. From this it moved on to 'stain,' and then it was a short step to 'taint, spoil.' 'Affect with disease' was a post-Latin development. English acquired the word via the Latin past participial stem *infect-*.

▶ fact, factory, fashion, perfect

**inferior** see UNDER

**inflate** [16] *Inflate* comes from *inflātus*, the past participle of Latin *inflāre* 'blow into.' This was a compound verb formed from the prefix *in-* and *flāre* 'blow' (a distant relative of English *blow*). The use of *inflate* and *inflation* as technical terms in economics to denote uncontrolled growth in money supply, credit, etc originated in 1830s America.

▶ blow

**inflict** see PROFLIGATE

**influence** [14] *Influence* began life as an astrological term. It was coined in medieval Latin as *influentia* from the present participle of Latin *influere* 'flow in,' a compound verb based on *fluere* 'flow,' and to begin with denoted a sort of fluid that was supposed to be given off by the stars and to influence human life. English originally acquired the word with this meaning, and it was not until the end of the 16th century that the main current sense 'power to produce effects' started to establish itself. The more concrete notion of an 'emanation' that affected people also lay behind the use of Italian *influenza* for 'epidemic,' from which English got *influenza* (see FLU).

Another English acquisition from Latin *influere* is *influx* [17], which comes from its past participle.

▶ flu, fluent, influx

**influenza** see FLU

**inform** [14] When English first acquired *inform* (via Old French *enfourmer*) it was used simply for 'give form or shape to.' However, its Latin original, *informāre* (a compound verb based on *forma* 'form'), had in classical times moved on from the primary notion of 'shaping' via 'forming an idea of something' and 'describing it' to 'telling or instructing people about something.' English took this sense over too, and has persevered with it, but 'give shape to' was dropped in the 17th century.

▶ form

**ingenious** [15] *Ingenious* used to be a more elevated term than it is today. To begin with it meant 'highly intelligent,' but already by the 16th century it was starting to come down in the world somewhat to 'cleverly inventive.' It comes, partly via French *ingénieux*, from Latin *ingeniōsus*, a derivative of *ingenium* 'natural talent, skill' (a word which, like English *gene, generate, genital*, etc, goes back ultimately to Indo-European *\*gen-* 'produce,' and was also the source of English *engine*). Its formal similarity to the distantly related *ingenuous* has led in the past to its being used for 'honest, open, frank,' and indeed its semantic deriva-

tive *ingenuity* 'quality of being ingenious' [16] belongs etymologically to *ingenuous*.

▶ gene, general, generate, genital

**ingenuous** [16] Etymologically, *ingenuous* means 'inborn.' English acquired it from Latin *ingenuus*, which was composed of the prefix *in-* and the element *\*gen-*, denoting 'production, birth.' This was originally used for 'born in a particular place, native, not foreign,' but it soon began to take on connotations of 'freeborn, not a slave,' and hence 'of noble birth.' Metaphorical transference to qualities thought characteristic of the nobility – uprightness, candour, straightforwardness, etc – soon followed, and that was the word's semantic slant when English acquired it. By the 17th century, however, it had started to slide towards 'artlessness, innocence' (a sense reflected in *ingénue*, borrowed from French in the 19th century).

▶ gene, general, generate, genital, ingénue

**ingot** [14] The etymological meaning of *ingot* is 'poured in.' It was formed in Middle English from *in* and an apparent survival of *goten*, the past participle of Old English *geotan* 'pour.' It originally meant 'mould for casting metal' (the idea being that the molten metal was 'poured into' the mould), but towards the end of the 16th century it started being used for the lump of metal formed in this way. (When French borrowed the word in the 15th century it grafted its definite article on to it, giving modern French *lingot* 'ingot.')

**ingrain** [17] *Ingrain* means literally 'work into the grain' (of fabric, originally) – whence the main metaphorical sense of *ingrained*, 'deep-seated.' But there is much more to the story of *ingrain* than that. Its ultimate source was *engrainer* 'dye,' an Old French verb based on *graine* 'cochineal dye.' English borrowed this in the 14th century as *engrain* 'dye crimson with cochineal,' which remained a live sense of the word into the 17th century. Gradually awareness of the word's original specific connections with the colour crimson died out, and the verb was virtually formed anew in the mid 17th century using the concept of the *grain* or 'texture' of cloth, but the spelling *engrain* remained, and remains as a secondary variant to this day, to remind us of the word's origins.

▶ grain

**ingredient** [15] The *-gredi-* of *ingredient* represents the Latin verb *gradī* 'step, go' (whose past participial stem *gress-* has given English *aggression, congress, digress*, etc). From it was formed *ingredī* 'go in, enter,' whose present participle *ingrediēns* became English *ingredient*. The word's etymological meaning is thus 'that which 'enters into' a mixture.' It was originally used mainly with reference to medicines, and its current application to food recipes seems to be a comparatively recent development.

▶ aggression, congress, grade, gradual

**inhabit** see HABIT
**inherit** see HEREDITARY
**inimical** see ENEMY
**iniquity** see EQUAL

**injury** [14] Etymologically, an *injury* is something 'unjust.' It comes via Anglo-Norman *injurie* from Latin *injūria*, a noun use of *injūrius* 'unjust,' which was a compound adjective based on *jūs* 'right' (source of English *just*). Its original meaning in English was 'wrongful action,' and it was only gradually that the notion of 'harm' (which had actually been present in the word from classical Latin times) began to come to the fore.
▶ just

**ink** [13] The Greeks had a method of painting which involved applying coloured wax to a surface and then fixing it with heat. The verb describing this process was *egkaíein* 'burn in,' a compound of *en-* 'in' and *kaíein* 'burn,' whose derivative *egkaustikós* is the ancestor of the term used for the technique in English – *encaustic* [17]. Another derivative, *égkauston*, was applied to the purple ink used by emperors in ancient times for signing documents. As it passed via late Latin *encaustum* or *encautum* into Old French *enque* it gradually lost its imperial associations, and by the time it reached English as *enke* it was being used for any dark writing fluid.
▶ caustic

**inn** [OE] An *inn* was originally literally a place one lived or stayed 'in.' It comes from a prehistoric Germanic *\*innam*, which was a derivative of the ancestor of the modern English adverb *in*, and in Old English it meant simply 'house where one lives, abode, home.' This sense survived into the 17th century ('Queen Mary gave this House to Nicholas Heth, Archbishop of York, and his successors for ever, to be their Inne or Lodging for their Repair to London,' James Howell, *Londinopolis* 1657), and a memory of it remains in London's Inns of Court, which originated as lodgings for lawyers. The later sense 'public house, tavern' developed towards the end of the 14th century.
▶ in

**innate** see NATIVE

**innocent** [14] Someone who is *innocent* is literally 'harmless.' The word comes, partly via Old French, from Latin *innocēns*, an adjective formed with the negative prefix *in-* from the present participle of *nocēre* 'harm' (source of English *nuisance*) – hence, 'not harming.' The slight semantic shift from 'not harming' to 'blameless, guiltless' took place in Latin.
▶ nuisance

**innuendo** [17] An *innuendo* was originally a hint given with a 'nod' or a wink. The word is a derivative of Latin *innuere* 'signal to by means of a nod,' a compound verb formed from *in-* 'towards' and *nuere* 'nod.' The ablative case of its gerund, *innuendō* 'by nodding,' was used in medieval legal documents as the equivalent of 'that is to say, i.e.' In particular, it introduced the derogatory meaning claimed by the plaintiff in a libel case to be contained in or implied by a statement, and this formed the basis for its metaphorical transference to any 'oblique derogatory implication.'

**inoculate** [15] Far-fetched as the connection may seem, *inoculate* actually comes ultimately from Latin *oculus* 'eye' (source of English *ocular* [16] and *oculist* [17]). By metaphorical extension *oculus* was applied to the 'bud' of a plant (much like the *eye* of a potato in English), and the verb *inoculāre* was coined to denote the grafting on of a bud or other plant part. That was how it was used when originally adopted into English ('Peaches have their Season at May Kalends them to inoculate,' *Palladius on Husbandry* 1440), and the modern sense 'introduce antigens into the body' did not emerge before the early 18th century, based on the notion of 'engrafting' or 'implanting' an immunising virus into a person. It was originally used with reference to smallpox.
▶ eye, ferocious, ocular

**inquest** see ENQUIRE

**insect** [17] The Greek word for 'insect' was *éntomon* (source of English *entomology* [18]). It was derived from *entémnein* 'cut up,' a compound verb formed from *en-* 'in' and *témnein* 'cut' (a close relative of English *tome*), and denoted literally 'creature divided up into segments.' The term was translated literally into Latin as *insectum* (originally the past participle of *insecāre*, a compound verb formed from *in-* and *secāre* 'cut'), and seems to have been introduced into English in Philemon Holland's translation of Pliny's *Natural History* 1601.
▶ section

**insert** see SERIES

**inside** [16] *Inside* (a compound, of course, of *in* and *side*) was originally a noun, meaning 'inner surface' ('Solomon builded the walls on the inside with Cedar timber,' Miles Coverdale's translation of I Kings 6:15 1535), and it was not used as an adjective until the early 17th century – by Shakespeare, in fact. Adverbial and prepositional use are more recent still, from around the end of the 18th century.
▶ side

**insidious** see SESSION
**insignia** see SIGN
**insist** see STATUE
**insouciant** see SOLICIT
**inspire** see SPIRIT
**instal** [16] To *instal* someone was originally literally to put them 'into a stall.' The word comes from

medieval Latin *installāre*, a compound verb based on the noun *stallum* 'stall,' and referred originally to the formal induction of someone into an office by ceremonially placing them in a seat or 'stall,' such as the choir-stall of a cathedral. The *instal-* of *instalment* [18], incidentally, is a different word, although the two are ultimately related. It is an alteration of an earlier *estallment* 'arrangement for payment,' which came from Anglo-Norman *estaler* 'fix payments.' This was a derivative of *estal* 'fixed position,' which was borrowed from Old High German *stal* 'place' (source also of medieval Latin *stallum*).

▶ instalment, stall

## instant [15]
Latin *instāre* meant 'be present' (it was a compound verb formed from the prefix *in-* 'upon' and *stāre* 'stand'). Its present participle *instāns* was used adjectivally for 'present,' and hence by extension for 'urgent.' The latter was actually the meaning originally taken up by English, but it has now virtually died out. 'Present' was introduced in the mid-16th century (it now survives in the abbreviation *inst*, used in giving dates to signify 'the present month'), and by the end of the century this had evolved into the main current sense 'immediate.' The noun *instant* 'moment' comes from medieval Latin *tempus instāns* 'present time.' Derived from *instāns* was the Latin noun *instantia* 'presence, urgency.' Again it was the latter that originally came into English with *instance* [14]. The main modern sense 'example,' first recorded in the 16th century, appears to come ultimately from a semantic progression in medieval Latin from 'urgency' to 'eager solicitation' and hence to 'legal pleading.' Further metaphoricization took it on to 'new argument or example adduced to counter a previous one,' and hence in due course to simply 'example.'

▶ instance, stand, station, statue

## instead [13]
*Instead* is the English end of a chain of loan translations that goes back to Latin *in locō* (in loan translations, the individual components of a foreign word or expression are translated into their equivalents in the borrowing language, and then reassembled). The Latin phrase meant literally 'in place (of),' and this was translated into Old French as *en lieu de*. Middle English rendered the French expression in turn as *in stead of* or *in the stead of* (*stead* 'place,' now obsolete except in certain fixed compounds and expressions, comes ultimately from the same Indo-European source as *stand, station*, etc). It began to be written as one word towards the end of the 16th century.

▶ stand, station, statue, stead

## instigate see STICK

## instil see STILL

## instinct [15]
The etymological notion underlying *instinct* (and also the closely related *instigate*) is of 'goading onwards with a pointed stick.' Its ultimate source is Latin *instinguere* 'urge onwards, incite,' a compound verb formed from the prefix *in-* 'on' and *stinguere* 'prick, goad.' Source also of English *distinct* and *extinct*, this goes back to the same root, *\*stig-*, as produced English *stick* and Latin *stīgāre* 'prick, goad,' the ancestor of English *instigate* [16]. The noun derived from it, *instinctus*, originally meant 'incitement, instigation,' but it eventually moved on to 'impulse,' the sense it had when English acquired it. The more specialized 'innate impulse' developed in the mid 16th century.

▶ distinct, extinct, instigate, stick

## institute [15]
An *institute* is etymologically something 'established' or 'set up.' Its ancestor is Latin *instituere* 'establish,' a compound verb formed from the prefix *in-* and *statuere* 'set up' (itself a derivative of *stāre* 'stand' and source of English *prostitute, statute*, etc). The noun derived from this was *institūtum*, which meant 'purpose, plan, practice.' Word and senses were taken over as a package by English, but these meanings are now dead or dying, having been taken over since the 19th century by 'organization that promotes a particular cause or pursuit' (this originated in French at the end of the 18th century). The verb *institute*, however, remains far closer to the original Latin meaning.

▶ prostitute, stand, station, statute

## instruct [15]
The *-struct* of *instruct* occurs also in *construction, destruction, structure*, etc. It comes from the past participle of Latin *struere* 'build.' In the case of *instruct*, combination with the prefix *in-* produced *instruere* 'build, prepare, equip, teach,' whose past participle stem *instruct-*formed the basis of the English verb.

▶ construct, destroy, instrument, structure

## instrument [13]
*Instrument* comes from the same source as *instruct*: the Latin verb *instruere* 'build, prepare, equip, teach.' From it was derived the noun *instrūmentum*, which meant 'tool, equipment.' When introduced into English via Old French at the end of the 13th century it was used for a 'musical instrument,' but the more general 'implement' and the metaphorical 'means' soon followed in the 14th century.

▶ construct, destroy, instruct, structure

## insular see ISLAND

## insulin [20]
Insulin, a hormone which promotes the utilization of blood sugar, was first isolated in 1921 by F G Banting and C H Best. Its name, which was inspired by the fact that insulin is secreted by groups of cells known as the *islets of Langerhans* (*insula* is Latin for 'island'), was actually coined in French around 1909, and was independently proposed in English on a couple of further occasions before the substance itself was anything more than a hypothesis.

▶ isle, peninsula

**insult** [16] The *-sult* of *insult* comes from a word that meant 'jump.' Its source was Latin *insultāre* 'jump on,' a compound verb based on *saltāre* 'jump.' This was a derivative of *salīre* 'jump,' source in one way or another of English *assail, assault, desultory, salacious*, and *salient*. Old French took *insultāre* over as *insulter* and used it for 'triumph over in an arrogant way.' This was how the word was originally used in English, but at the beginning of the 17th century the now familiar sense 'abuse' (which had actually developed first in the Latin verb) was introduced.

▶ assail, assault, desultory, salacious, salient

**insuperable** see SUPER

**insure** [15] *Insure* and *ensure* [14] are ultimately the same word. And their common ancestor started out, in fact, as a variant of *assure* [14]. This came via Old French *asseurer* from Vulgar Latin *\*assēcūrāre*, a compound verb formed from the Latin prefix *ad-* 'to' and the adjective *sēcūrus* 'safe' (source of English *secure* and *sure*). Anglo-Norman had a variant form, *enseurer*, which produced English *ensure*. From fairly early on this had been alternatively spelled *insure* (using the Latinate prefix *in-*), but it was not until the 17th century that this version became established in the sense 'provide cover against loss, damage, etc' (for which previously the more usual term had actually been *assure*).

▶ assure, ensure, secure, sure

**intact** see ENTIRE

**integral** see ENTIRE

**integrity** see ENTIRE

**integument** see PROTECT

**intellect** [14] *Intellect* and *intelligent* come from the same ultimate source: Latin *intelligere* 'perceive, choose between.' This was a compound verb formed from the prefix *inter-*'between' and *legere* 'gather, choose, read' (source of English *lecture, legible*, etc). Its past participle *intellectus* came to be used as a noun meaning 'perception, comprehension,' which English acquired as *intellect* via Old French; while its present participle *intelligēns* gave English *intelligent* [16]. The derivative *intelligentsia* [20] was borrowed from Russian *intelligyentsia*, which in turn came via Polish *inteligiencja* from Latin *intelligentia* 'intelligence.'

▶ intelligent, lecture, legible

**intend** [14] The Latin verb *intendere* (a compound formed from the prefix *in-* 'towards' and *tendere* 'stretch') had a variety of metaphorical meanings, some of which have come through into English. Principal among them was 'form a plan or purpose,' an extension of an earlier 'direct or 'stretch' one's thoughts towards something,' which has given English *intend* and the derived *intention* [14]. The noun *intent* [13] belongs with this group too, but the adjective *intent* [17] looks back to the earlier 'direct one's mind towards a particular thing,' and *intense* [14] comes from the even more literal 'stretched tight.' A medieval Latin addition to the meanings of *intendere* was 'understand,' which English adopted in the 14th century. It had largely died out in English by the end of the 17th century, but it has persisted in the Romance languages, and has even developed further to 'hear' (which is what French *entendre* means).

▶ intense, intention, tense

**interest** [15] The Latin verb *interesse* meant literally 'be between' (it was a compound of *inter* 'between' and *esse* 'be'). It was used metaphorically for 'be of concern, be important, matter,' and appears to have been borrowed into Anglo-Norman as a noun, meaning 'what one has a legal concern in or share of.' English took this over in the 14th century as *interesse*, but it gradually changed over the next hundred years or so into *interest*, mainly due to the influence of Old French *interest* 'damage,' which came from the third person present singular form of the Latin verb. The main modern sense 'curiosity' developed towards the end of the 18th century.

**interloper** [16] An *interloper* is literally someone who 'runs between.' The word was coined in English, but based on Dutch *loper*, a derivative of *lopen* 'run' (to which English *leap* is related). It originally denoted someone who engaged in trade without authorization, and only in the 17th century took on its present-day meaning 'interfering outsider.'

▶ leap

**intermediate** see MEDIUM

**intermezzo** see MEDIUM

**internecine** [17] Etymologically, *internecine* denotes 'attended by great slaughter.' Its modern connotations of 'conflict within a group,' which can be traced back to the 18th century (Dr Johnson in his *Dictionary* 1755 defines it as 'endeavouring mutual destruction'), presumably arise from the standard interpretation of *inter-* as 'among, between.' But in fact in the case of *internecine* it was originally used simply as an intensive prefix. The word was borrowed from Latin *internecīnus*, a derivative of *internecāre* 'slaughter, exterminate.' This was a compound verb formed with the intensive *inter-*from *necāre* 'kill' (a relative of English *necromancy* and *pernicious*).

▶ necromancy, pernicious

**interpolate** [17] The Latin ancestor of *interpolate* meant literally 'polish up.' It was *interpolāre*, based on a verbal element *-polāre* that was related to *polīre* 'polish' (source of English *polish*). Its meaning gradually progressed metaphorically via 'refurbish' and 'alter the appearance of' to 'falsify, particularly by the insertion of new material' (this last presumably arising from a reassertion of the central meaning of *inter-*, 'between'). English originally took it over in the sense 'alter, tamper with,' but before the middle of the 17th century the notion of 'insertion, interjection' had begun to emerge in its own right, and has gradually taken over from 'alter.'

▶polish

**interpose**   see POSITION

**interregnum**   see REIGN

**interrogate**   see PREROGATIVE

**interrupt**   [15] Etymologically, *interrupt* means 'break between.' It comes from the past participle of Latin *interrumpere* 'break in,' a compound verb formed from the prefix *inter-* 'between' and *rumpere* 'break' (source of English *rout* and *rupture*).

▶corrupt, rout, rupture

**intersect**   see SECTION

**interval**   [13] The *val-* of *interval* represents Latin *vallum* 'rampart' (source of English *wall*) – so etymologically the word means 'space between ramparts.' That was the original sense of its Latin ancestor, *intervallum*, but already in the classical period the metaphorical 'gap in time, pause' was developing.

▶wall

**intestate**   see TESTAMENT

**intransigent**   [19] In the 18th century there was an extreme leftist political party in Spain which, because of its unwillingness ever to compromise, was known as *los intransigentes*. The name was formed with the negative prefix *in-* from *transigentes*, the present participle of Spanish *transigir* 'compromise.' This was a descendant of Latin *transigere*, literally 'drive through,' hence 'come to an understanding, accomplish' (source of English *transact*), a compound verb formed from *trans-* 'through' and *agere* 'drive' (from which English gets *action, agent*, etc). French took the Spanish word over as a general adjective meaning 'uncompromising,' and English acquired it in the early 1880s.

▶act, action, agent, transact

**intrepid**   [17] The *-trepid* of *intrepid* represents Latin *trepidus* 'alarmed' (source also of English *trepidation* [17]), which goes back to an Indo-European source in which the notion of 'fear' seems to be linked with or derived from that of 'scurrying away.' Addition of the negative prefix *in-* produced *intrepidus* 'undaunted,' which reached English partly via French *intrépide*.

▶trepidation

**intricate**   see TRICK

**intrinsic**   [15] The Latin adverb *intrinsecus* meant 'on the inside.' It was formed from *\*intrim* 'inward,' an unrecorded derivative of the adverb *intrā* 'within,' and *secus* 'alongside' (a relative of English *second, sect, sequal*, etc). In the post-classical period it

came to be used as an adjective, meaning 'inward,' and it passed into Old French as *intrinseque* 'inner, internal.' This general concrete sense accompanied the word into English, but it now survives only as an anatomical term, meaning 'situated within a body part.' The abstract sense 'inherent,' now the adjective's main meaning, developed in the 17th century.

The derivation of the antonym *extrinsic* [16] is precisely parallel, with Latin *extrā* 'outside' taking the place of *intrā*.

▶extrinsic, second, sect, sequal

**introduce**   [[16] *Introduce* means etymologically 'lead inside.' It was borrowed from Latin *intrōdūcere* 'lead in,' a compound verb formed from the prefix *intrō-* 'in, inside' and *dūcere* 'lead' (source of English *duct, duke, educate, produce*, etc). Of its main secondary meanings, 'use for the first time, originate' emerged in Latin but 'make known personally to others' seems to have been a later development.

▶duct, duke, educate, produce

**intrude**   see ABSTRUSE

**inundate**   see UNDULATE

**invalid**   see VALID

**inveigh**   [15] *Inveigh* originally meant 'carry in, introduce' ('In them are two colours quarterly put: the one into the other, and so one colour is inveighed into another,' *Book of Saint Albans* 1486). Its second syllable comes from Latin *vehere* 'carry' (source of English *vector, vehicle*, and *vex*). *Invehere* meant simply 'carry in,' but its passive infinitive form *invehī* denoted 'be carried into,' 'go into,' and hence 'attack (physically or verbally).' This latter sense was imported into English *inveigh* in the early 16th century, and into the derivative *invective* [15].

▶invective, vehicle, vex

**inveigle**   [15] The French verb *aveugler* means 'blind' (it is a derivative of the adjective *aveugle* 'blind,' whose probable source was the medieval Latin phrase *ab oculīs* 'without eyes'). It passed into Anglo-Norman, with alteration of the prefix, as *envegler*, and English acquired this originally in the metaphorical sense 'deceive' – which in the 16th century developed to 'entice, seduce, persuade.'

**invent**   [15] *Invent* originally meant 'find' ('Since that Eve was procreated out of Adam's side, could not such newels [novelties] in this land be invented,' wrote the anonymous author of a 15th-century song). It was based on *invent-*, the past participial stem of Latin *invenīre* 'come upon, find,' a compound verb formed from the prefix *in-* 'on' and *venīre* 'come.' The sense 'devise,' which developed via 'discover,' actually existed in the Latin verb, but English did not take it on board until the 16th century.

The derivative *inventory* [16] was borrowed from

medieval Latin *inventōrium* 'list,' an alteration of late Latin *inventārium*, which originally meant a 'finding out,' hence an 'enumeration.'

▶ adventure, inventory

**invert** see VERSE

**invest** [16] The etymological notion underlying *invest* is of 'putting on clothes.' It comes via Old French *investir* from Latin *investīre*, a compound verb formed from the prefix *in-* and *vestis* 'clothes' (source of English *vest, vestment, travesty*, etc). It retained that original literal sense 'clothe' in English for several centuries, but now it survives only in its metaphorical descendant 'instal in an office' (as originally performed by clothing in special garments). Its financial sense, first recorded in English in the early 17th century, is thought to have originated in Italian *investire* from the idea of dressing one's capital up in different clothes by putting it into a particular business, stock, etc.

▶ travesty, vest, vestment

**investigate** [16] To *investigate* something is etymologically to look for traces, or 'vestiges,' of it. The word comes from Latin *investīgāre* 'search into,' a compound verb based on *vestīgāre* 'track, trace.' This in turn was a derivative of *vestīgium* 'footprint,' hence 'track, trace' (source of English *vestige*).

▶ vestige

**invidious** see ENVY

**invigorate** see VIGOUR

**invincible** see VANQUISH

**invite** [16] *Invite* comes from Latin *invītāre*, probably by way of French *inviter*, but there our certain knowledge of its ancestry ends; for the Latin verb is something of a mystery word. No one is too sure where the element *-vītāre* comes from. One suggestion is that it is related to Greek *hiesthai* 'be desirous of.'

▶ vie

**invoice** see ENVOY

**invoke** see VOCATION

**involve** see VOLUME

**iodine** [19] *Íon* was the Greek word for 'violet' (indeed it is related to English *violet*). From it was derived the adjective *iōdēs* 'violet-coloured,' which was taken by the chemist Joseph Louis Gay-Lussac as the basis of *iode*, the French term for 'iodine' (iodine gives off a purple vapour when heated). The British chemist Sir Humphry Davy adopted it into English, adding the suffix *-ine* to produce *iodine*.

▶ violet

**ire** see OESTRUS

**irk** [13] *Irk* originally meant 'grow tired,' and although it is not known for certain, its underlying sense could be 'work until one is weary': for a possible source may be Old Norse *yrkja* 'work.' The present-day sense 'annoy' is first recorded in the 15th century.

**iron** [OE] *Iron* is probably a Celtic contribution to English, but the borrowing took place in the prehistoric period, before the Germanic dialects separated, and so English shares the word with German (*eisen*), Dutch (*ijzen*), Swedish (*järn*), etc. The prehistoric Celtic form from which these all ultimately came was *\*īsarnon*, which some have linked with Latin *aes* 'bronze' and Sanskrit *isira-* 'strong.' The ancient Indo-European peoples had already split up into groups speaking mutually unintelligible tongues by the time iron came into general use, so there was never any common Indo-European term for it.

**irony** [16] *Irony* has no etymological connection with *iron*. It comes via Latin *īrōnia* from Greek *eirōneía*, which signified 'deliberately pretending ignorance, particularly as a rhetorical device to get the better of one's opponent in argument.' This was a derivative of *eírōn* 'dissembler,' which in turn came from the verb *eírein* 'say.' This original sense of 'dissimulation' survives in the expression *Socratic irony*, a reference to Socrates' use of such feigned ignorance as a pedagogical method, but it has been overtaken as the main sense of the word by 'saying the opposite of what one means.'

**isinglass** [16] Early modern Dutch *huysen* meant 'sturgeon' and *blas* denoted 'bladder.' Put them together and you had *huysenblas*, which English took over as a term not for the sturgeon's air bladder itself, but for the gelatinous substance obtained from it – isinglass. In the process of adoption the more familiar *glass* was substituted for *-blas*.

**island** [OE] Despite their similarity, *island* has no etymological connection with *isle* (their resemblance is due to a 16th-century change in the spelling of *island* under the influence of its semantic neighbour *isle*). *Island* comes ultimately from a prehistoric Germanic *\*aujō*, which denoted 'land associated with water,' and was distantly related to Latin *aqua* 'water.' This passed into Old English as *īeg* 'island,' which was subsequently compounded with *land* to form *īegland* 'island.' By the late Middle English period this had developed to *iland*, the form which was turned into *island*. (A diminutive form of Old English *īeg*, incidentally, has given us *eyot* 'small island in a river' [OE].)

*Isle* [13] itself comes via Old French *ile* from Latin *insula* (the *s* is a 15th-century reintroduction from Latin). Other contributions made by *insula* to English include *insular* [17], *insulate* [16], *insulin, isolate* (via Italian) [18], and *peninsula* [16].

▶ eyot

**isotope** [20] The term *isotope* for a version of an element with a particular atomic weight was coined in 1913 by the British chemist Frederick Soddy. It means literally 'equal place' and was formed from two Greek components, the prefix *iso-* 'equal' and the noun *tópos* 'place' (source of English *topic*). The reason for the coinage was that although isotopes of the same element have different atomic weights, they occupy the 'same place' in the periodic table of elements.

▶ topic

**issue**    [13]    The words *issue* and *exit* are closely related etymologically. Both go back ultimately to the Latin verb *exīre* 'go out.' Its past participle *exitus* became in Vulgar Latin *exūtus*, whose feminine form *exūta* was used as a noun meaning 'going out, exit.' This passed into Old French as *eissue*, later *issue*, and thence into English. The original literal sense of the word still survives in English, particularly in relation to the outflow of liquid, but has been overtaken in frequency by various metaphorical extensions denoting a 'giving out' – such as the 'issue' of a book or magazine. The sense 'point of discussion or consideration' probably comes from a medieval legal expression *join issue*, which originally meant 'jointly submit a disputed matter to the decision of the court,' and hence 'argue about something.'

▶ exit

**it**    [OE]    *It* (or *hit*, as it was in Old English) comes ultimately from the same prehistoric Germanic demonstrative stem form, *\*khi-*, as produced *he*. The possessive form *its* is a comparatively recent development, dating from the end of the 16th century; until then, *his* was used for 'its.'

▶ he

**itinerary**    see OBITUARY

**ivory**    [13]    As is hardly surprising, *ivory* goes back ultimately to an African word which meant both 'ivory' and 'elephant.' A likely candidate as this source is Egyptian *āb*, which may well lie behind Latin *ebur* 'ivory.' This passed into English via Old French *ivurie*.

The expression *ivory tower* 'place where reality is evaded' is a translation of French *tour d'ivoire*. This was originally used in 1837 by the French critic Sainte-Beuve with reference to the poet Alfred de Vigny, whom he accused of excessive aloofness from the practicalities of the world. The English version is first recorded in 1911.

**ivy**    [OE]    *Ivy* has been traced back to a prehistoric Germanic *\*ibakhs*, which also lies behind modern German *efeu* and Dutch *eilof*. This has been linked by some etymologists with Latin *ibex* 'mountain goat' (itself acquired by English in the 17th century), the semantic connection being 'climber.'

The expression *Ivy League*, denoting the eight old-established and prestigious universities of the north-eastern USA (Brown, Columbia, Cornell, Dartmouth, Harvard, Pennsylvania, Princeton, and Yale), was inspired by the idea of ancient ivy-covered walls. It dates from the 1930s.

# J

**jacinth**   see HYACINTH

**jade**   English has two words *jade*, of which by far the commoner nowadays is the name of the green stone [18]. Despite the mineral's close association with China and Japan, the term has no Oriental connections. It is of Latin origin, and started life in fact as a description of the stone's medical applications. Latin *īlia* denoted the 'sides of the lower torso,' the 'flanks,' the part of the body where the kidneys are situated (English gets *iliac* [16] from it). In Vulgar Latin this became *\*iliata*, which passed into Spanish as *ijada*. Now it was thought in former times that jade could cure pain in the renal area, so the Spanish called it *piedra de ijada*, literally 'stone of the flanks.' In due course this was reduced to simply *ijada*, which passed into English via French. (Jade's alternative name, *nephrite* [18], is based on the same idea; it comes from Greek *nephrós* 'kidney.')

English's other word *jade* [14] now survives really only in its derivative adjective *jaded* 'tired, sated' [16]. It originally meant 'worn-out horse,' and was later transferred metaphorically to 'disreputable woman.' Its origins are not known.

▶ iliac / jaded

**jail**   [13]   Etymologically, a *jail* is a 'little cage.' The word comes ultimately from Vulgar Latin *\*gaviola*, which was an alteration of an earlier *\*caveola*, a diminutive form of Latin *cavea* 'cage' (source of English *cage*). It passed into English in two distinct versions: *jail* came via Old French *jaiole*; but the Old Northern French form of the word was *gaiole*, and this produced English *gaol*. Until the 17th century *gaol* was pronounced with a hard /g/ sound, but then it gradually fell into line phonetically with *jail*. There has been a tendency for British English to use the spelling *gaol*, while American prefers *jail*, but there are now signs that *jail* is on the increase in Britain.

▶ cage

**jam**   [18]   The verb *jam*, meaning 'press tightly together,' first appears in the early 18th century (the earliest-known unequivocal example of its transitive use is in Daniel Defoe's *Robinson Crusoe* 1719: 'The ship stuck fast, jaum'd in between two rocks'). It is not known where it came from, but it is generally assumed to be imitative or symbolic in some way of the effort of pushing. Equally mysterious are the origins of *jam* the sweet substance spread on bread, which appeared around the same time. Contemporary etymologists were nonplussed (Nathan Bailey had a stab in the 1730s: 'prob. of *J' aime*, i.e. I love it; as Children used to say in French formerly, when they liked any Thing'; but Dr Johnson in 1755 confessed 'I know not whence derived'); and even today the best guess that can be made is that the word refers to the 'jamming' or crushing of fruit into jars.

**jamb**   see GAMMON

**January**   [14]   The ancient Romans had a god named Janus whose head had two faces, looking in opposite directions. He was the tutelary deity of doorways, and his festival month was at the beginning of the year, when he could look both backwards at the old year and forwards to the new one. This month was therefore called *Jānuārius mensis* 'month of Janus' – whence English *January*.

**japan**   [17]   The hard laquer varnish called *japan* received its name, of course, because it came from Japan. But where did the name *Japan* come from? For the Japanese call their country *Nippon*. The answer is Chinese, where *jih pun* means literally 'sunrise' (*jih* is 'sun,' and the equivalent term in Japanese is *ni*, so Japanese *Nippon* too is the 'land of the rising sun'). The Chinese word came into English via Malay *Japang*. Another English derivative is the name of the shrub *japonica* [19], which originated in Japan.

**jaundice**   [14]   *Jaundice* is literally 'yellowness.' The word came from Old French *jaunice*, which was a derivative of the adjective *jaune* 'yellow' (the *d* in the middle appeared towards the end of the 14th century). The derived adjective *jaundiced* [17] originally meant simply 'suffering from jaundice,' but the association of the yellowish colour with bitterness and envy soon produced the figurative meaning familiar today.

▶ yellow

**jaunty**   see GENTLE

**jaw**   [14]   Given that it is a fairly important part of the body, our knowledge of the origins of the word for 'jaw' is surprisingly sketchy. The Old English terms for 'jaw' were *cēace* (modern English *cheek*) and *ceafl* (ancestor of modern English *jowl*), and when *jaw* first turns up towards the end of the 14th century it is in the form *iowe*. This strongly suggests a derivation frpm Old French *joe* 'cheek,' but the connection has never been established for certain, and many etymologists consider it more likely that it is related to *chew*.

**jay**   [13]   Like the robin, the jay may have been christened originally with a human name: Latin *Gaius*. At all events, the term for it in post-classical Latin was *gaius*, which passed into English via Old French *jay*. The term *jaywalker* for 'one who crosses the road illegally' originated in the USA around the time of World War I; it was based on an American use of *jay* for a 'fool' or 'simpleton.'

**jazz**   [20]   Words of unknown origin always attract speculation, and it is hardly surprising that such an unusual and high-profile one as *jazz* (first recorded in 1909) should have had more than its fair share. Since the term arose out of the Black English of the southern states of America, most attention has focussed on trying to pinpoint an ancestor from Africa. And perhaps the likeliest explanation is that *jazz* originated in a West African language, was for a long time a Black slang term in America for 'strenuous activity,' particularly 'sexual intercourse,' and surfaced in the mainstream English language when it was applied to syncopated Black American music.

**jealous**   [13]   Etymologically, *jealousy* and *zeal* are two sides of the same coin. Both come ultimately from Greek *zelos*. This passed into post-classical Latin as *zēlus*, which later produced the adjective *zēlōsus*. Old French took this over as *gelos* or *jelous* and passed it on to English. The Greek word denoted 'jealousy' as well as 'fervour, enthusiasm,' and it is this strand of meaning that has come down to us in *jealous*. *Jalousie*, incidentally, the French equivalent of *jealousy*, was borrowed into English in the 19th century in the sense 'blind, shutter' – the underlying notion apparently being that one can look through the slats without oneself being seen.

▶ zeal

**jeans**   [19]   Jeans of the sort we would recognize today – close-fitting working trousers made of hardwearing, typically blue cloth – emerged in America in the mid-19th century. But their antecedents have to be sought in a far distant place. The first known reference to trousers called *jeans* actually comes from mid-19th-

century England: 'Septimus arrived flourishin' his cambric, with his white jeans strapped under his chammy leather opera boots,' R S Surtees, *Handley Cross* 1843. Why the name *jeans*? Because they were made of *jean*, a sort of tough twilled cotton cloth. This was short for *jean fustian*, a term first introduced into English in the mid-16th century, in which the *jean* represented a modification of *Janne*, the Old French name of the Italian city of Genoa. So *jean fustian* was 'cotton fabric from Genoa,' so named because that was where it was first made.

**jejune**   see DINNER

**jelly**   [14]   The central idea of 'coagulation' takes us back to the ultimate source of *jelly*, the Latin verb *gelāre* 'freeze' (which also gave English *congeal* [14]). Its feminine past participle *gelāta* was used in Vulgar Latin for a substance solidified out of a liquid, and this passed into Old French as *gelee*, meaning both 'frost' and 'jelly' – whence the English word. (Culinarily, *jelly* at first denoted a savoury substance, made from gelatinous parts of animals; it was not really until the early 19th century that the ancestors of modern fruit jellies began to catch on in a big way.)

The Italian descendant of *gelāta* was *gelata*. From it was formed a diminutive, *gelatina*, which English acquired via French as *gelatine* [19]. *Gel* [19] is an abbreviation of it.

▶ cold, congeal, gel, gelatine

**jeopardy**   [14]   The semantic focus of *jeopardy* has changed subtly over the centuries. Originally it meant 'even chance,' but gambling being the risky business it is, and human nature having a strong streak of pessimism, attention was soon focussed on the 'chanciness' rather than the 'evenness,' and by the late 14th century *jeopardy* was being used in its modern sense 'risk of loss or harm, danger.' The word originated in the Old French expression *jeu parti*, literally 'divided play,' hence 'even chance.' It was to begin with a term in chess and similar board games.

**jet**   English has two distinct words *jet*. The older, which denotes a type of black stone used in jewellery [14], comes via Old French *jaiet* and Latin *gagātēs* from Greek *gagátēs*, which denoted 'stone from Gagai,' a town in Lycia, in Asia Minor, where it was found.

The *jet* of 'jet engines' [16] goes back ultimately to a word that meant 'throw' – Latin *jacere* (from which English also gets *inject, project, reject*, etc). A derivative of this was *jactāre*, which also meant 'throw.' It passed via Vulgar Latin *\*jectāre* into Old French as *jeter*, and when English took it over it was originally used for 'protrude, stick out': 'the houses jetting over aloft like the poops of ships, to shadow the streets,' George Sandys, *Travels* 1615. This sense is perhaps best preserved in *jetty* 'projecting pier,' and in the variant form *jut* [16], while the underlying meaning 'throw' is still present in *jettison* 'throw things overboard' and its contracted form *jetsam*. But back with the verb *jet*, in the 17th century it began to be used for 'spurt out in a forceful stream.' The notion of using such a stream to create forward motion was first encapsulated in the term *jet propulsion* in the mid 19th century, but it did not take concrete form for nearly a hundred years (the term *jet engine* is not recorded until 1943).

▶ inject, jetsam, jettison, jetty, jut, project, reject, subject

**jettison** [15] Etymologically, to *jettison* something is to 'throw' it overboard. Like *jet*, as in 'jet engine,' the word comes from Latin *jactāre* 'throw.' The abstract noun derived from this was *jactātiō*, which entered English via Anglo-Norman *getteson*. It was used for the 'action of throwing cargo overboard, especially in order to lighten a ship,' but it was not converted to its familiar modern role, as a verb, until as recently as the 19th century. The contracted form *jetson*, later *jetsam*, emerged in the 16th century, and later came to be used for such jettisoned material washed ashore.

▶ jet, jetsam

**jetty** [15] A *jetty* is a structure that literally projects or is 'thrown' out beyond what surrounds it. The word was borrowed from Old French *jetee*, where it originated as the past participle of the verb *jeter* 'throw' (source also of English *jet*, as in 'jet engine'). It was used originally both for a structure jutting out into a body of water, and for a projecting upper storey of a house, of which the latter now survives only as a technical term in architectural history.

▶ jet

**jewel** [13] Originally, *jewel* meant 'costly adornment made from precious stones or metals' – a sense now largely restricted to the collective form *jewellery* [14]. The main modern sense 'gem' emerged towards the end of the 16th century. The word comes from Anglo-Norman *juel*, but exactly where that came from is not known for certain. It is generally assumed to be a derivative of *jeu* 'game,' which came from Latin *jocus* (source of English *jocular*, *joke*, etc).

▶ jeopardy, jocular, joke

**jingo** [17] The exclamation *by jingo!* has been around since at least the late 17th century, and the element *jingo* probably originated as a euphemistic alteration of *Jesus*. But it took on a new lease of life in 1878 when G W Hunt incorporated it into a music-hall song he was writing in support of Disraeli's hawkish foreign policy towards the Russians. Its refrain went 'We don't want to fight, yet by Jingo! if we do, We've got the ships, we've got the men, and got the money too.' *By jingo!* was taken up as a nationalistic rallying call: those who supported Disraeli's plan to send in the fleet were called *jingoes*, and their attitude was dubbed *jingoism*. But these were terms used by their opponents, not by the

jingoes themselves, and they were essentially derogatory, and when *jingoism* later broadened out in meaning, it denoted a mindless gung-ho patriotism.

**job** [16] The origins of *job* are uncertain. Its likeliest source is an earlier and now obsolete noun *job* which meant 'piece.' It is quite plausible that *job of work*, literally 'piece of work,' could have become shortened to *job*. But where this earlier *job* came from is not known, so the mystery remains open.

**jocular** see JOKE

**join** [13] *Join* goes back ultimately to a prehistoric Indo-European *\*jug-* (which also produced English *adjust, conjugal, jostle, joust, jugular, juxtapose, subjugate, yoga,* and *yoke*). Its Latin descendant was *jungere* 'join,' which passed into English via *joign-*, the present stem of Old French *joindre*. The Latin past participial stem *junct-* gave English *junction* [18] and *juncture* [14], and also, via Spanish, *junta* [17] (etymologically a body of people 'joined' together for a particular purpose, hence a 'governing committee').

▶ adjust, conjugal, joust, jugular, junction, junta, juxtapose, subjugate, yoga, yoke

**joist** [14] Etymologically, a *joist* is a wooden beam on which boards 'lie' down. The word's ultimate ancestor is the Latin verb *jacēre* 'lie down' (from which English also gets *adjacent*). Its neuter past participle *jacitum* was taken into Old French as a noun, *giste*, which denoted a 'beam supporting a bridge' (its modern French descendant, *gîte* 'home' – that is, 'place where one lies down' – is currently infiltrating English). Middle English took over the Old French word, which from the 15th century gradually began to change to *joist*.

▶ adjacent

**joke** [17] Latin *jocus* meant 'jest, joke' (a possible link with Old High German *gehan* 'say' and Sanskrit *yācati* 'he implores' suggests that its underlying meaning was 'word-play'). It passed into Old French as *jeu*, which lies behind English *jeopardy* and probably also *jewel*. But English also went direct to Latin for a set of words connected with 'fun' and 'humour,' among them *jocose* [17] and *jocular* [17], both from Latin derivatives of *jocus* (the superficially similar *jocund*, incidentally, is etymologically unrelated), and *joke* itself, which was originally introduced in the form *joque* or *joc* ('coming off with so many dry joques and biting repartees,' Bishop Kennett's translation of Erasmus's *Encomium Moriae* 1683). *Juggler* belongs to the same word family.

▶ jeopardy, jewel, jocular, juggler

**jolly** [14] Old French *jolif* meant 'pleasant, merry, festive' (it has been speculated that it may have been derived from *jól*, the Old Norse term for the midwinter festival, to which English *yule* is closely related). English took the adjective over, and whereas in French (the modern form is *joli*) it has come to mean 'pretty,' in English it kept closer to the original sense 'merry.'

▶ yule

**joss** see DEITY

**jostle** see JOUST

**journey** [13] Etymologically, a *journey* is a 'day's' travel. The word comes via Old French *jornee* from Vulgar Latin *\*diurnāta*. This in turn was derived from Latin *diurnum* 'daily allowance or ration,' a noun use of the adjective *diurnus* 'daily,' which was based on *diēs* 'day.' The specific notion of a 'day's' travel had died out by the mid-16th century, leaving only the more general 'travel.' But before going altogether, 'day' left its mark on another manifestation of the word *journey*: the word *journeyman* 'qualified worker' [15]. This has no connection with 'travelling'; it originally denoted one who was qualified to do a 'day's' work.

Another Latin derivative of *diurnus* was the adjective *diurnālis*, which has given English *diurnal* [15], *journal* [14] (first cousin to *diary*), and *journalism* [19]. So-*journ* belongs to the same language family.

▶ diary, diurnal, journal, sojourn

**joust** [13] The underlying meaning of *joust* is simply an 'encounter.' The word came from Old French *juster*, which originally meant 'bring together,' and hence by extension 'join battle' and 'fight on horse-back.' The Old French verb goes back to Vulgar Latin *\*juxtāre* 'come together,' a derivative of Latin *juxtā* 'close' (source of English *juxtaposition* [17]). And *juxtā* itself comes from the same ultimate source as English *join* and *yoke*.

*Jostle* [14] originated as a derivative of *joust*.

▶ join, jostle, juxtapose

**jovial** [16] Etymologically, *jovial* simply means 'born under the influence of the planet Jupiter.' It comes via French from Italian *gioviale*, a derivative of *Giove* 'Jupiter,' which itself goes back to the Latin stem *Jov-* (from which English also gets *Jove* [14], as in *by Jove!*). Jupiter was thought of as endowing those born under its sign with happiness, and so by extension *jovial* came to mean 'jolly, good-humoured.'

The word *Jupiter* [13] itself represents a Latin compound of *Jov-* and *pater* 'father.'

**jowl** English has two words *jowl*, which are quite close together in meaning but are etymologically unrelated. The older, which means 'jaw,' goes back ultimately to Old English *ceafl*. It is now encountered virtually only in the expression 'cheek by jowl.' *Jowl* 'flesh around the throat' (now usually used in the plural) first appears in the 16th century. It may well be a development of Middle English *cholle*, which in turn probably goes back to Old English *ceole* 'throat' (a relative of German *kehle* 'throat').

**joy** [13] Latin *gaudēre* meant 'rejoice' (it came from a prehistoric base *\*gāu-*, which also produced Greek *gēthein* 'rejoice'). From it was derived the noun *gaudium* 'joy,' which passed into English via Old French *joye*. From the same source come English *enjoy* and *rejoice*.

The use of *joystick* for the 'control stick of an aircraft' (perhaps inspired by an earlier slang sense 'penis') dates from around 1910.

▶ enjoy, rejoice

**jubilee** [14] Despite their similarity, *jubilee* has no etymological connection with *jubilation* [14] and *jubilant* [17]; but they have exerted a considerable influence on it over the centuries. It was originally a Hebrew word: Hebrew *yōbhēl* meant 'leading animal, ram,' and by extension 'ram's horn,' and since a ram's horn was blown to announce the start of a special year (set aside once every fifty years according to ancient Hebrew law) in which slaves were freed, land left untilled, etc, the term *yōbēl* came to be used for the year itself. Greek took it over as *iōbēlos* and formed an adjective from it, *iōbēlaios*. This was passed on to Latin, and it was here that *jubilation* took a hand. Latin *jūbilāre* (source of English *jubilation*) originally meant simply 'call out,' but early Christian writers used it for 'shout for joy.' Under its influence Greek *iōbēlaios* became Latin *jūbilaeus*, which was used in the expression *annus jūbilaeus* to denote this special Jewish year. It soon came to be used as a noun in its own right, and in this role passed via Old French *jubile* into English. By this time the ideas of 'fifty years' and 'joy, celebration' had mingled to such an extent that the word was being used for a 'fiftieth anniversary' or its celebration, a sense which remained current until the early 20th century (in present-day English it means simply 'anniversary,' usually of a monarch's accession, and the period involved has to be defined by *golden, silver*, etc).

**judge** [13] Etymologically, a *judge* is someone who 'speaks the law.' The word comes via Old French *juge* from Latin *jūdex*, which was originally a compound noun made up of *jūs* 'law' and the element *-dicus* 'speaking' (related to English *diction, dictionary*, etc). Parallel formations to have reached English are *juridical* [16] and *jurisdiction* [13], while derivatives of *jūdex* itself include *judicature* [16], *judicial* [14], *judiciary* [16], and *judicious* [16].

▶ diction, dictionary, judicious, jury, just

**juggernaut** [17] Hindi *Jagganath* is a title of Krishna, one of the avatars, or incarnations, of the god Vishnu, the Preserver. It comes from Sanskrit *Jagganātha*, a compound of *jagat-* 'world' and *nāthás* 'lord.' It is applied also to a large wagon on which an image of the god is carried in procession (notably in an annual festival in Puri, a town in the northeastern Indian state of Orissa). It used to be said, apocryphally, that worshippers of Krishna threw themselves under the wheels of the wagon in an access of religious ecstacsy, and so *juggernaut* came to be used metaphorically in English for an 'irresistible crushing force': 'A neighbouring people were crushed beneath the worse than Jaggernaut car of wild and fierce democracy,' J W Warter, *Last of the Old Squires* 1854). The current application to large heavy lorries is prefIgured as long ago as 1841 in William Thackeray's *Second Funeral of Napoleon* ('Fancy, then, the body landed at day-break and transferred to the car; and fancy the car, a huge Juggernaut of a machine'); but it did not become firmly established until the late 1960s.

**juggler** [12] A *juggler* was originally a 'jester,' and the word is related to English *joke*. Its ultimate source was Latin *joculātor*, a derivative of *jocus* 'jest' (from which English gets *joke*). This passed into Old French as *jogleor*, and was borrowed into English at the beginning of the 12th century. It denoted a general entertainer or buffoon, but it was also used for a magician or conjurer, and it was presumably an underlying notion of dexterity or sleight of hand that led by the 17th century to its being used for someone who keeps several objects in the air at the same time. Old French *jogleor* became modern French *jougleur*, and this spawned the variant form *jongleur*, which was borrowed into English in the 18th century.

▶ jocular, joke

**jugular** see YOKE

**juice** [13] *Juice* appears to come ultimately from a prehistoric root which meant 'mix.' This had early descendants denoting 'soup' – Latin *jūs*, for instance, Sanskrit *yūa*, and Old Slavic *jucha* – and the Latin form passed into Old French as *jus*, whence English *juice*.

**July** [13] July was the month in which Julius Caesar was born. Originally in ancient Rome it was called *Quintilis*, literally 'fifth month' (the Roman year began in March), but after the death and deification of Caesar its name was changed in his honour. Latin *Jūlius* passed into English via Anglo-Norman *julie*, and until the 18th century the word was usually pronounced to rhyme with *truly* (as the related woman's name *Julie* still is).

**jump** [16] Until the early modern English period, the words for 'jump' were *leap* and *spring*. Then, apparently out of nowhere, the verb *jump* appeared. Its provenance has never been satisfactorily explained, and etymologists fall back on the notion that it may originally have been intended to suggest the sound of jumping feet hitting the ground (the similar-sounding *bump* and *thump* are used to support this theory). And certainly one of the earliest known instances of the word's use

connotes as much 'making heavy contact' as 'rising': 'The said anchor held us from jumping and beating upon the said rock,' Sir Richard Guylforde, *Pilgrimage to the Holy Land* 1511.

*Jumper* 'sweater' [19], incidentally, appears to have no etymological connection with *jump*. It was probably derived from an earlier dialectal *jump* or *jup*, which denoted a short coat for men or a sort of woman's underbodice. This in turn was borrowed from French *juppe*, a variant of *jupe* 'skirt,' whose ultimate source was Arabic *jubbah*, the name of a sort of loose outer garment.

**junction** see JOIN
**juncture** see JOIN

**June** [13] *June* is the month of Juno, the Roman goddess of women and marriage, and wife and sister of Jupiter. Its Latin name was *Jūnius mēnsis*, 'Juno's month,' and *Jūnius* passed into English via Old French *juin*.

**jungle** [18] Not surprisingly, *jungle* is a tropical word, but its ancestor denoted quite the opposite of the lush vegetation it now refers to. It comes from Sanskrit *jangala*, which originally meant 'dry,' and hence 'desert.' Its Hindi descendant *jangal* was used for an 'area of wasteland,' and hence 'such an area overgrown with scrub,' and when it was taken over into Anglo-Indian it was gradually extended to an 'area of thick tangled trees.'

**junta** see JOIN
**Jupiter** see JOVIAL
**jurisdiction** see JUDGE

**just** [14] Latin *jūs* originated in the terminology of religious cults, perhaps to begin with signifying something like 'sacred formula.' By classical times, however, it denoted 'right,' and particularly 'legal right, law,' and it has provided English with a number of words connected with 'rightness' in general and with the process of law. The derived adjective *jūstus* has produced *just* and, by further derivation, *justice* [12] and *justify* [14]. The stem form *jūr-* has given *injury*, *jury* [14], *objurgate* [17], and *perjury* [14]. And combination with the element *-dic-* 'say' has produced *judge*, *judicial*, *juridical*, and *jurisdiction*. Not part of the same word family, however, is *adjust* [17], which comes ultimately from Vulgar Latin *\*adjuxtāre* 'put close to,' a compound verb based on Latin *juxtā* 'close' (whence English *juxtaposition*).

▶ injury, judge, jury, objurgate, perjury

**jut** see JET
**juxtaposition** see JOUST

# K

**kale**  see CAULIFLOWER

**kaleidoscope**  [19]  Greek *kalós* meant 'beautiful' (it was related to Sanskrit *kalyāna* 'beautiful'). It has given English a number of compound words: *calligraphy* [17], for instance, etymologically 'beautiful writing,' *callipygian* [18], 'having beautiful buttocks,' and *callisthenics* [19], literally 'beauty and strength.' The Scottish physicist Sir David Brewster used it, along with Greek *eidos* 'shape' and the element *-scope* denoting 'observation instrument,' to name a device he invented in 1817 for looking at rotating patterns of coloured glass – a 'beautiful-shape viewer.'
► calligraphy, callisthenics

**kangaroo**  [18]  The first English speakers to refer in writing to the *kangaroo* were Captain Cook and the botanist Joseph Banks, who both mentioned it in 1770 in the journals they kept of their visit to Australia (Banks, for instance, noted 'the largest [quadruped] was called by the natives *kangooroo*'). They reported that it was the name used for the animal by the aborigines along the banks of the Endeavour River, Queensland. Doubt has subsequently been cast on this, but no definitive alternative source has been discovered. The element *-roo* was used in the 19th century to produce *jackeroo*, which denoted a 'new immigrant in Australia,' and is first recorded as an independent abbreviation for *kangaroo* in the first decade of the 20th century.

The term *kangaroo court* 'unofficial court,' which dates from the 1850s, is an allusion to the court's irregular proceedings, which supposedly resemble the jumps of a kangaroo.

**kaolin**  [18]  The word *kaolin* comes ultimately from *gaō ling*, the name of a hill in Jiangxi province, northern China, from which fine white china clay was first obtained (it means literally 'high hill'). It reached English via French.

**keen**  [OE]  The ancestral meaning of *keen* is 'brave.' That is what its German and Dutch relatives, *kühn* and *koen*, mean, and that is what *keen* itself meant in the Old English period. But this sense had died out by the 17th century, having been replaced by the meanings familiar today, such as 'eager' and 'sharp.'

**keep**  [OE]  For all that it is one of the commonest verbs in the language, remarkably little is known about the history of *keep*. It first appears in texts around the year 1000. It is assumed to have existed before then, but not to have belonged to a sufficiently 'literary' level of the language to have been written down. Nor has a link been established for certain with any words in other Germanic languages, although suggestions that have been put forward include Old High German *kuofa* 'barrel' (a relative of English *coop*), from the notion of its being something for 'keeping' things in, and also (since in the late Old English period *keep* was used for 'watch') Old Norse *kópa* 'stare.'

**keepsake**  see SAKE

**ken**  [OE]  Once a widespread verb throughout English, *ken* is now restricted largely to Scotland, having taken over the semantic territory elsewhere monopolized by *know*. In Old English it actually meant not 'know' but 'make known'; it was the causative version of *cunnan* 'know' (ancestor of modern English *can*). Its relatives in other Germanic languages made the change from 'make known' to 'know' early – hence German *kennen* 'know,' for example. In the case of English *ken*, the impetus is thought to have come from Old Norse *kenna* 'know.' The derived noun *ken*, as in 'beyond one's ken,' dates from the 16th century.
► can

**kennel**  [14]  Appropriately enough for a word for 'dog-house,' *kennel* comes ultimately from Latin *canis* 'dog' (a relative of English *hound*). *Canis* was the basis of a Vulgar Latin derivative *\*canīle*, which passed into English via Anglo-Norman *\*kenil*. Other English derivatives of Latin *canis* include *canary, canine* [17], and *chenille* 'fabric made from soft yarn' [18], a borrowing from French *chenille*, literally 'hairy caterpillar,' which came from a diminutive form of *canis*.
► canary, canine, chenille, hound

**kerchief**    see HANDKERCHIEF

**kernel**    [OE] Etymologically, a *kernel* is a 'little seed.' Old English *corn*, ancestor of modern English *corn*, meant 'seed, grain,' and its diminutive form *cyrnel* was applied to 'pips' (now obsolete), to 'seeds' (a sense which now survives only in the context of cereals), and to the 'inner part of nuts, fruit stones, etc.'

▶ corn

**ketchup**    [17] *Ketchup* is a Chinese word in origin. In the Amoy dialect of southeastern China, *kôechiap* means 'brine of fish.' It was acquired by English, probably via Malay *kichap*, towards the end of the 17th century, when it was usually spelled *catchup* (the *New Dictionary of the Canting Crew* 1690 defines it as 'a high East-India Sauce'). Shortly afterwards the spelling *catsup* came into vogue (Jonathan Swift is the first on record as using it, in 1730), and it remains the main form in American English. But in Britain *ketchup* has gradually established itself since the early 18th century.

**kettle**    [13] Latin *catīnus* denoted a 'deep pan or dish in which food was cooked or served.' Its diminutive form *catillus* was borrowed into prehistoric Germanic as *katilaz*, which passed into Old English in the form *cetel*. This produced Middle English *chetel*, which died out in the 15th century, having been ousted by the related Old Norse form *ketill*. Originally the term denoted any metal vessel for boiling liquid, and it is only really in the past century that its meaning has narrowed down to an 'enclosed pot with a spout.' The original sense lingers on in the term *fish kettle*, and is still very much alive in related Germanic forms such as German *kessel* and Swedish *kittel*.

**key**    [OE] The Old English ancestor of *key* was *cǣg*. This produced a modern English word which to begin with was pronounced to rhyme with *bay*, and its present-day pronunciation, rhyming with *bee*, did not come to the fore until the 18th century. No one knows where the word originally came from; it has no living relatives in other Germanic languages.

**khaki**    [19] *Khaki* is part of the large linguistic legacy of British rule in India. In Urdu *khākī* means 'dusty,' and is a derivative of the noun *khāk* 'dust' (a word of Persian origin). It seems first to have been used with reference to the colour of military uniforms in the Guide Corps of the Indian army in the late 1840s. The term followed the colour when it was more widely adopted by the British army for camouflage purposes during the South African wars at the end of the 19th century.

**kick**    [14] *Kick* is one of the mystery words of English. It first appears towards the end of the 14th century, but no one knows where it came from, and it has no relatives in the other Indo-European languages. It may have been a Scandinavian borrowing.

**kidney**    [14] The origins of *kidney* are a matter of guesswork rather than certain knowledge. Probably the most widely accepted theory is that the *-ey* element represents *ey*, the Middle English word for 'egg,' in allusion to the shape of the kidneys. The first syllable is more problematical, but one possible source is Old English *cwith* 'womb' or the related Old Norse *kvithr* 'belly, womb,' in which case *kidney* would mean etymologically 'belly-egg.'

▶ egg

**kill**    [13] The Old English verbs for 'kill' were *slēan*, source of modern English *slay*, and *cwellan*, which has become modern English *quell*. The latter came from a prehistoric Germanic *kwaljan*, which it has been suggested may have had a variant *kuljan* that could have become Old English *cyllan*. If such a verb did exist, it would be a plausible ancestor for modern English *kill*. When this first appeared in early Middle English it was used for 'hit,' but the meanings 'hit' and 'kill' often coexist in the same word (*slay* once meant 'hit' as well as 'kill,' as is shown by the related *sledgehammer*); the sense 'deprive of life' emerged in the 14th century.

**kiln**    [OE] Etymologically a *kiln* is for 'cooking,' not for burning or drying. Its distant ancestor was Latin *coquīna* 'kitchen,' a derivative of the verb *coquere* 'cook.' This produced an unexplained variant *culīna* (source of English *culinary* [17]), which was used not only for 'kitchen,' but also for 'cooking-stove.' Old English adopted it as *cylene*, which has become modern English *kiln*.

▶ cook, culinary, kitchen

**kilo**    [19] *Khílioi* was Greek for a 'thousand.' It was adopted in French in the 1790s as the prefix for 'thousand' in expressions of quantity under the new metric system, and various compound forms (*kilogram, kilolitre, kilometre*, etc) began to find their way into English from the first decade of the 19th century onwards. The first recorded instance of *kilo* being used in English for *kilogram* dates from 1870.

**kin**    [OE] *Kin* is the central English member of the Germanic branch of a vast family of words that trace their ancestry back to the prehistoric Indo-European base *gen-, *gon-, *gn-*, denoting 'produce' (the Latin branch has given English *gender, general, generate, genital, nature*, etc, the Greek branch *gene, genetic, gonorrhoea*, etc). Amongst the Germanic descendants of this base was *kun-*, from which was derived the noun *kunjam*, source of Swedish *kön* 'sex' and English *kin* 'family.' *Kindred* [12] was formed from *kin* in early Middle English by adding the suffix *-red* 'condition' (as in *hatred*). Also closely related are *kind* and *king*.

▶ gender, gene, general, generate, genital, kind, kindred, king, nature

**kind**    [OE] *Kind* the noun and *kind* the adjective are ultimately the same word, but they split apart in prehistoric times. Their common source was Germanic *kunjam*, the ancestor of English *kin*. From it, using the collective prefix *ga- and the abstract suffix *-diz, was derived the noun *gakundiz, which passed into Old English as *gecynde* 'birth, origin, nature, race.' The prefix *ge-* disappeared in the early Middle English period.

Germanic *gakundiz formed the basis of an adjective, *gakundjaz, which in Old English converged with its source to produce *gecynde*. It meant 'natural, innate,' but gradually progressed via 'of noble birth' and 'well-disposed by nature' to (in the 14th century) 'benign, compassionate' (a semantic development remarkably similar to that of the distantly related *gentle*).

▶ kin

## kindred   see KIN

## king   [OE]   The prehistoric Germanic ancestor of *king* (as of German *könig*, Dutch *koning*, Swedish *konung*, and Danish *konge*) was *kuninggaz. This seems to have been a derivative of *kunjam 'race, people' (source of English *kin*). If it was, *king* means etymologically 'descendant of the race, offspring of the people.'

▶ kin

## kipper   [OE]   There is a single Old English instance, in a text of around the year 1000, of a fish called *cypera*. The context suggests that this was a 'salmon,' which would tie in with the later use of the word *kipper*, from the 16th to the 20th centuries, for 'male salmon during the spawning season.' What is not clear, however, despite the obvious semantic link 'fish,' is whether this is the same word as *kipper* 'cured herring or other fish,' first recorded in the 14th century. Nor is it altogether clear where the term originally came from, although it is usually held to be a derivative of Old English *copor* 'copper,' in allusion to the colour of the fish.

## kiss   [OE]   *Kiss* is a widespread Germanic word, represented also in German *küssen*, Dutch *kussen*, Swedish *kyssa*, and Danish *kysse*. It probably goes back to some prehistoric syllable imitative of the sound or action of kissing, such as *ku or *kus, which would also lie behind Greek *kunein* 'kiss,' Sanskrit *cumb-* 'kiss,' and Hittite *kuwass-* 'kiss.' There is not sufficient linguistic evidence, however, to show whether the Indo-Europeans expressed affection by kissing each other.

## kitchen   [OE]   The Latin word for 'kitchen' was *coquīna*, a derivative of the verb *coquere* 'cook' (ultimate source of English *cook, culinary, kiln, precocious*, etc). It had a colloquial variant, *cocīna, which spread far and wide throughout the Roman empire. In French it became *cuisine* (borrowed by English in the 18th century), while prehistoric West Germanic took it over as *kocina. This has subsequently become German *küche*, Dutch *keuken*, and English *kitchen* – etymologically, a room where one 'cooks.'

▶ apricot, cook, culinary, kiln, precocious

## knapsack   [17]   The *-sack* of *knapsack* is no doubt essentially the same word as English *sack*, but the *knap-* presents slightly more of a problem. The term was borrowed from Low German *knappsack*, and so probably *knapp-* represents Low German *knappen* 'eat' – the bag having originally been named because it carried a traveller's supply of food.

## knee   [OE]   The majority of modern European words for 'knee' go back to a common Indo-European ancestor which probably originally signified 'bend.' This was *g(e)neu or *goneu, which lies behind Latin *genu* 'knee' (source of French *genou* and Italian *ginocchio*, and also of English *genuine*) and may well be connected with Greek *gōníā* 'angle,' from which English gets *diagonal*. It passed into Germanic as *knewam, which over the centuries has diversified into German and Dutch *knie*, Swedish *knä*, Danish *knœ*, and English *knee*. The derivative *kneel* [OE] was formed before the Anglo-Saxons reached Britain, and is shared by Dutch (*knielen*). *Knuckle* [14], a borrowing from Low German, may well be related.

▶ genuine, kneel, knuckle

## knickers   [19]   The use of the word *knickers* for 'women's underpants' dates back to the 1880s: a writer in the magazine *Queen* in 1882 recommended 'flannel knickers in preference to flannel petticoat,' and *Home Chat* in 1895 was advertising 'serge knickers for girls from twelve to sixteen.' Over the decades, of course, the precise application of the term has changed with the nature of the garment, and today's legless briefs are a far cry from the kneelength 'knickers' of the 1880s. They got their name because of their similarity to the original knickers, which were kneelength trousers for men (*The Times* in 1900 reported the 'Imperial Yeomanry . . . in their well-made, loosely-fitting khaki tunics and riding knickers'). And *knickers* itself was short for *knickerbockers*, a term used for such trousers since the 1850s. This came from Diedrich Knickerbocker, a fictitious Dutch-sounding name invented by the American writer Washington Irving for the 'author' of his *History of New York* 1809. The reason for the application seems to have been that the original knickerbockers resembled the sort of knee-breeches supposedly worn by Dutchmen.

## knife   [11]   *Knife* is not a native English word, but a borrowing. It came from Old Norse *knífr*, which survives also in modern Swedish *knif* and Danish *knif*. It can be traced back to a prehistoric Germanic *knībaz, which also produced German *kneif* 'cobbler's knife,' and was borrowed by French as *canif* 'knife,' but its previous ancestry is not known.

**knight** [OE] The word *knight* has come up in the world over the centuries. In the Old English period it simply meant 'boy' or 'young man.' By the 10th century it had broadened out to 'male servant,' and within a hundred years of that we find it being used for 'military servant, soldier.' This is the general level or 'rank' at which the word's continental relatives, German and Dutch *knecht*, have remained. But in England, in the course of the early Middle Ages, *knight* came to denote, in the feudal system, 'one who bore arms in return for land,' and later 'one raised to noble rank in return for military service.' The modern notion of knighthood as a rung in the nobility, without any necessary connotations of military prowess, dates from the 16th century.

**knit** see KNOT

**knob** see KNOT

**knock** [OE] *Knock* is a classic onomatopoeic word: that is to say, it originated in a direct imitation of the sound it denotes. The similar Swedish *knacka* 'knock' may be related. The figurative use of the word for 'criticize' originated in late 19th-century America.

**knot** [OE] The word *knot* goes back ultimately to a prehistoric Germanic *knūdn-*, whose underlying meaning was 'round lump.' This only emerged in the English word (in such senses as 'point from which a branch has grown') in the Middle English period, but it can be seen in *knoll* [OE], which is a derivative of the same base (the related German *knolle* means 'lump'). *Knob* [14] may be related too, although this has never been conclusively demonstrated. The Germanic form diversified into English and Dutch *knot*, German *knoten*, Swedish *knut*, and Danish *knode* (whose Old Norse ancestor *knútr* was borrowed into Russian as *knut* 'whip,' acquired by English as *knout* [18]). *Knit* [OE], which originally meant 'tie in knots,' was derived in prehistoric West Germanic from *knot*.

▶ knit

**know** [11] The words for 'know' in the various Indo-European languages mostly belong to one large many-branched family which goes back ultimately to the base *\*gn-*, which also produced English *can* and *ken*. Its Latin offspring was *nōscere*, from which English gets *cognition, incognito, note, quaint*, etc. From its Greek branch come English *agnostic* and *diagnosis*. And in other Indo-European languages it is represented by, among others, Sanskrit *jānáti* 'know,' Old Irish *gnáth* 'known,' and Russian *znat'*. In the other Germanic languages it is the immediate relatives of English *can* (German and Dutch *kennen*, Swedish *känna*, Danish *kende*) that are used for 'know'; *know* itself, which was originally a reduplicated form, survives only in English.

The *-ledge* of *knowledge* [13] was probably originally the suffix *-lock* 'action, process,' which otherwise survives only in *wedlock*. *Acknowledge* [15] is derived from *knowledge*.

▶ agnostic, can, cognition, diagnosis, incognito, ken, knowledge, note, quaint, recognize

**knuckle** see KNEE

**knurled** see GNARLED

**kohlrabi** see CAULIFLOWER, RAPE

**kowtow** [19] The approved Chinese method of signifying respect for the emperor or other august personages was to prostrate oneself so that one's forehead touched the ground. This was expressed in Mandarin Chinese by the term *ke tóu* (*ke* means 'knock, bump' and *tóu* 'head'). English took the word over in the early 19th century and spelled it in various experimental ways (*koo-too, ka-tou, kotow*, etc) before settling on *kowtow* in the early 20th century. The first writer on record as using the word in the metaphorical sense 'defer servilely' was Benjamin Disraeli in his *Vivian Grey* 1826: 'The Marqess kotooed like a first-rate Mandarin, and vowed 'that her will was his conduct'.'

**kraal** see CORRAL

# L

laager  see LAIR
label  see LAP
labial  see LIP
labour  [13] *Labour* comes via Old French *labour* from Latin *labor*. This has been linked with the verb *labāre* 'slip,' and if the two were related it would mean that the underlying etymological meaning of *labour* was something like 'stumble under a burden.' Most of the modern European descendants of Latin *labor* have progressed from the broad sense 'work, exertion' to more specialized meanings – French *labourer* denotes 'plough,' for instance, and Spanish *labrar* 'plough, carve, embroider,' etc. English has retained it as a formal alternative to *work*, although the additional obstetric sense developed in the 16th century.

lace  [13] *Lace* originally meant 'noose' or 'snare,' and its underlying semantic connections are not with 'string' or 'thread' but with 'entrapment' or 'enticement.' Its ultimate source was Latin *laqueus* 'noose,' which was related to the verb *lacere* 'lure, deceive' (source of English *delicious* and *elicit*). This passed into Vulgar Latin as *\*lacium*, which in due course diversified into Italian *laccio*, Spanish *lazo* (source of English *lasso* [19]), and French *lacs*. It was the latter's Old French predecessor, *laz* or *las*, that gave English *lace*. The sense 'noose' had died out by the early 17th century, but by then it had already developed via 'string, cord' to 'cord used for fastening clothes.' 'Open fabric made of threads' emerged in the mid-16th century. *Latch* [14] is thought to be distantly related.
▶ delicious, elicit, lasso, latch

lachrymal  see TEAR
lachrymose  see TEAR
lack  [12] The word *lack* is not known to have existed in Old English, although it is by no means impossible that it did. If it was a borrowing, a possible source would have been Middle Dutch *lak* 'deficiency, fault.' This has been traced back to a prehistoric Germanic *\*lak-*, a variant of which produced English *leak*.
▶ leak

lackey  [16] By a circuitous series of steps, *lackey* is of Arabic origin. English borrowed it from French *laquais*, which originally denoted a sort of foot-soldier, and hence a 'footman' or 'servant.' French in turn got it from Catalan *alacay*, whose source was Arabic *al-qādī* 'the judge' (the Spanish version *alcalde* 'magistrate' was acquired by English in the 17th century).

laconic  [16] The Greek term for an inhabitant of the ancient region of Laconia, in the southern Peloponnese, and of its capital Sparta, was *Lákōn*. The Spartans were renowned for not using two words where one would do (there is a story that when Philip of Macedon threatened invasion with 'If I enter Laconia, I will raze Sparta to the ground,' the Spartans' only reply was 'If'), and so English used the adjective *laconic* (from Greek *Lakōnikós*) for 'sparing of speech.'

lacquer  see LAKE
lacrosse  [18] French *la crosse* means 'the hooked stick' (*crosse* was originally borrowed from a prehistoric Germanic *\*kruk-*, from which English got *crook* and *crutch*). French speakers in Canada used the term *jeu de la crosse* 'game of the hooked stick' to name a game played by the native Americans with netted sticks, and in due course this became reduced and lexicalized to *lacrosse*.
▶ crook, crutch

lactation  see LETTUCE
lacuna  see LAKE
lad  [13] *Lad* originally meant 'male of low status or social rank,' and hence 'male servant,' but by the 14th century its progression to the present-day 'young male' was well under way. It is not known where it came from, but there seems to be a strong likelihood of a Scandinavian origin (Norwegian has -*ladd* in compounds referring to '(male) persons').

ladder  [OE] Etymologically, a *ladder* is something that is 'leant' up against a wall. Like Greek *klîmax* 'ladder' (source of English *climax*), it goes back ultimately to the Indo-European base *\*khli-*, source of English *lean*. Its West Germanic relatives are German *leiter* and Dutch *leer*.

▶ climax, lean

**lade**     see LOAD

**ladle**     see LOAD

**lady** [OE] Originally, the term *lady* denoted a 'kneader of bread.' It comes from Old English *hlǽfdige*, a compound formed from *hlǽf* 'bread' (ancestor of modern English *loaf*) and an element *\*dig-* 'knead' (related to English *dough*). It is a measure of the symbolic (and actual) importance of bread in medieval households that (like *lord*, also a derivative of *loaf*) *lady* came, as a provider of bread, to be applied to someone in a position of authority within a house.

▶ dairy, dough, loaf, lord

**lag** English has three distinct words *lag*. The verb 'fall behind' [16] is perhaps of Scandinavian origin (Norwegian has *lagga* 'go slowly'), although a link has been suggested with the *lag* of *fog, seg, lag*, a dialect expression used in children's games which represents an alteration of *first, second, last*. *Lag* 'insulate' [19] comes from an earlier noun *lag* 'barrel stave,' which was also probably borrowed from a Scandinavian language (Swedish has *lagg* 'stave'); the original material used for 'lagging' was wooden laths. And finally the noun *lag* 'prisoner' [19] seems to have come from an earlier verb *lag*, which originally meant 'steal,' and then 'catch, imprison'; but no one knows where this came from.

**lager** [19] *Lager* is etymologically beer that has been matured by being kept in a 'store.' English borrowed the term from German *lagerbier*, a compound based on the noun *lager* 'storeroom' (to which English *laager* and *lair* are closely related).

▶ laager, lair

**lagoon**     see LAKE

**lair** [OE] Etymologically a *lair* is a place where you 'lie' down. For it comes ultimately from the same Germanic base, *\*leg-*, as produced English *lie*. In Old English it had a range of meanings, from 'bed' to 'grave,' which are now defunct, and the modern sense 'place where an animal lives' did not emerge until the 15th century. Related Germanic forms show different patterns of semantic development: Dutch *leger*, for instance, means 'bed' and 'camp' (it has given English *beleaguer* [16] and, via Afrikaans, *laager* [19]) and German *lager* (source of English *lager*) means 'bed,' 'camp,' and 'storeroom.'

*Layer* in the sense 'stratum' [17] (which to begin with was a culinary term) may have originated as a variant of *lair*.

▶ beleaguer, laager, lager, lay, layer, lie

**lake** English has two words *lake*. The one meaning 'body of water' [13] comes via Old French *lac* from Lat-

in *lacus*. This goes back to the same prehistoric source as produced Gaelic *loch* (acquired by English in the 14th century) and Latin *lacūna* 'hole, pit, pool' (from which English got *lacuna* [17] and, via Italian or Spanish, *lagoon* [17]); this seems to have denoted 'hole, basin,' the notion of 'water-filled hole' being a secondary development.

*Lake* the colour [17], now usually encountered only in *crimson lake*, is a variant of *lac*, a term for a reddish resin or dye that comes via Dutch or French from Hindi *lākh*, and forms the second syllable of English *shellac*. Its ultimate source is Sanskrit *lākshā*. *Lacquer* [16] comes via early modern French *lacre* 'sealing-wax' from *laca*, the Portuguese version of *lac*.

▶ lacuna, lagoon / lacquer, shellac

**lamb** [OE] *Lamb* is a widespread word throughout the Germanic languages (German and Swedish have *lamm* and Dutch and Danish have *lam*), but no connections have ever been established with any animal-names in non-Germanic languages. In Gothic, *lamb* was used for 'adult sheep' as well as 'lamb.'

**lambent**     see LAP

**lame** [OE] Prehistoric Germanic had an adjective *\*lamon* which meant 'weak-limbed,' and seems to have originated in a base which meant something like 'break by hitting' (English *lam* 'hit' [16], as in 'lam into someone,' and its derivative *lambaste* [17] probably come from the same source). In the modern Germanic languages it has diversified into two strands of meaning: Dutch, Swedish, and Danish *lam* denote mainly 'paralysed,' a sense also present in German *lahm*, while English *lame* has taken the path of 'limping, crippled.'

▶ lam, lambaste

**laminate**     see OMELETTE

**Lammas**     see LOAF

**lamp** [12] A *lamp* is literally something that 'shines.' The word comes via Old French *lampe* and Latin *lampas* from Greek *lampás*, which was derived from the verb *lámpein* 'give light, shine' (source also of English *lantern*). The Greek word originally denoted a 'bunch of burning sticks, torch,' but in post-classical times it was applied to an 'oil lamp.' The Old English word for 'lamp' was *lēohtfæt*, literally 'light-vessel.'

▶ lantern

**lamprey** [12] The words *lamprey* and *limpet* [OE] come from the same source: medieval Latin *lampreda*. This was an alteration of an earlier, 5th-century *lampetra*, which has been plausibly explained as literally 'stone-licker' (from Latin *lambēre* 'lick,' source of English *lambent*, and *petra* 'stone'). The reason for applying such a name to the limpet is fairly obvious – it clings fast to rocks – but in fact the lamprey too holds on to rocks, with its jawless sucking mouth.

▶ lambent, limpet, petrol

**lance** [13] *Lance* is now a fairly widespread word throughout the European languages: German has *lanze*, for instance, Swedish *lans*, Italian *lancia*, and Spanish *lanza*. English acquired the word from Old French *lance*, which in turn came from Latin *lancea*, but its ultimate origin may have been Celtic. Derived words in English include *élan* and *launch*.

*Lance corporals* [18] were not named because they carried lances. The term was based on the now obsolete *lancepesade* 'officer of lowest rank,' which came via Old French from Old Italian *lancia spezzata*, literally 'broken lance,' hence 'old soldier.'

▶ élan, launch

**land** [OE] *Land* goes back to a prehistoric Germanic *\*landam*. This seems originally to have meant 'particular (enclosed) area' (ancestor of the modern sense 'nation'), but in due course it branched out to 'solid surface of the earth in general.' The term is now common to all the Germanic languages, and it has distant relatives in Welsh *llan* 'enclosure, church' and Breton *lann* 'heath' (source of French *lande* 'heath, moor,' from which English gets *lawn*).

▶ lawn

**language** [13] Like English *tongue*, Latin *lingua* 'tongue' was used figuratively for 'language'; from it English gets *linguist* [16] and *linguistic* [19]. In the Vulgar Latin spoken by the inhabitants of Gaul, the derivative *\*linguāticum* emerged, and this became in due course Old French *langage*, source of English *language*. (The *u* in the English word, which goes back to the end of the 13th century, is due to association with French *langue* 'tongue.')

▶ linguistic

**languish** see RELISH

**lank** see LINK

**lanolin** see WOOL

**lantern** [13] Like *lamp, lantern* comes ultimately from the Greek verb *lámbein* 'give light, shine.' Derived from this was the noun *lamptér*, which originally denoted 'bunch of burning sticks, torch,' but was later extended to 'lamp.' Latin borrowed it, and tacked on the ending of *lucerna* 'lamp' to produce *lanterna*, which English acquired via Old French *lanterne*. The translucent cover of lanterns was in former times usually made of horn, and so popular etymology from the 16th to the 19th centuries produced the spelling *lanthorn*.

▶ lamp

**lap** English now has three distinct words *lap*, but probably two of them are ultimately related. *Lap* 'upper legs of a seated person' [OE] originally meant 'flap of a garment,' and it goes back to a prehistoric Germanic source which also produced German *lappen* 'rag, cloth, flap, lobe,' and which may lie behind *label* [14]. It

seems likely that *lap* in the sense 'folds of a garment' was the basis of the Middle English verb *lap*, which meant 'wrap,' and hence 'extend beyond.' From this come both the verb *overlap* [18] and the noun *lap* [18], whose modern meaning 'one circuit of a course' emerged in the 19th century.

*Lap* 'lick up' [OE] comes from a prehistoric Germanic base *\*lap-*, which was related to Latin *lambēre* 'lick' (source of English *lambent* [17], and possibly responsible also for *lamprey* and *limpet*).

▶ label / lambent

**lapis lazuli** see DELAPIDATE

**lapwing** [OE] The present-day form of the word *lapwing* is due to the notion that it describes the way the bird's wings overlap in flight, but in fact although it did originally refer to the way the bird flies, it has no etymological connection with *lap* or *wing*. Its Old English form was *hlēapwince*, whose first element came from the ancestor of modern English *leap*, and whose second element went back to a base meaning 'move from side to side' that also produced English *wink*. So etymologically the *lapwing* is the 'leapwink,' the bird that tumbles and jinks in flight – as indeed it does.

Its alternative name *peewit* [13] describes its call.

**larceny** [15] The Latin word for 'robber' was *latrō*. Its original meaning was 'mercenary soldier,' and it came from Greek *látron* 'pay' (a relative of *latreíā* 'service, worship,' which provided the suffix in such English words as *idolatry* and *bardolatry*). From *latrō* was derived *latrōcinium* 'robbery,' which passed into English via Old French *larcin* and its Anglo-Norman derivative *\*larcenie*.

▶ idolatry

**large** [12] Latin *largus*, a word of unknown origin, meant 'abundant' and also 'generous.' It retained the latter meaning when it came into English via Old French *large* ('the poor King Reignier, whose large style agrees not with the leanness of his purse,' Shakespeare, *2 Henry VI* 1593), but this now survives only in the derivative *largesse* [13]. 'Abundant,' on the other hand, has provided the basis of the main modern English meaning 'of great size,' which emerged in the 15th century.

**lascivious** see LUST

**lass** [13] Like its male counterpart *lad, lass* has an obscure past. The form *lasce*, recorded in the 13th and 14th centuries, suggests the possibility that it may originally have come from a Scandinavian adjective related to Old Swedish *løsk* 'unmarried.'

**lassitude** see LATE

**lasso** see LACE

**last** [OE] Modern English has three separate words *last*, two of which are related. The adjective, meaning 'after all others,' originated in prehistoric Germanic as the superlative form of *late*; its modern Germanic relatives include German *letzt* and Dutch *laatst*. The verb *last* 'continue' goes back to a prehistoric Germanic *laistjan* 'follow a track,' which also produced modern German *leisten* 'perform, afford.' This was derived from *laisti-*, as was ultimately the noun *last*, which in Old English meant 'footprint' ('shoemaker's model foot' is a secondary development). The general semantic thread 'following a track' can be traced back further via Germanic *lais-* (a variant of which gave English *learn*) to Indo-European *leis-* (source of Latin *dēlīrāre*, literally 'deviate from a straight track,' from which English gets *delirious* [18]).

► delirious, late, learn

**latch**    see LACE

**late**    [OE]    English and Dutch (with *laat*) are the only modern European languages to use this word to express the idea of 'behind time.' It comes from an Indo-European base *lad-* 'slow, weary,' which also produced Latin *lassus* 'tired' (source of English *alas* [13] and *lassitude* [16]). In prehistoric Germanic this gave *lataz* 'slow, sluggish.' Its English descendant *late* originally meant 'slow' (and the related German *lass* still means 'lazy'), but although this survived dialectally into the 19th century, in the mainstream language 'delayed' had virtually replaced it by the 15th century. From the same ultimate Indo-European source come English *lease, let,* and *liege*.

► alas, lassitude, last, lease, let, liege

**lather**    [OE]    Indo-European *lou-* denoted 'wash' (from it English gets *laundry, lavatory, lotion*, etc). Addition of the suffix *-tro-* produced *loutrom*, which passed via Germanic *lauthram* into English as *lather*. In Old English this is only recorded as meaning 'washing soda,' and the modern sense 'soap bubbles' does not emerge until the late 16th century.

► ablution, laundry, lavatory, lotion

**latitude**    [14]    Latin *lātus* meant 'broad.' From it were derived *dīlātāre* 'spread out' (source of English *dilate*) and *lātitūdō*, which English took over as *latitude*. Its use as a cartographical term stems from the oblong maps of the ancient world, in which distance from north to south represented 'breadth' (hence *latitude*), and distance from east to west represented 'length' (hence *longitude* [16], from Latin *longitūdō*, a derivative of *longus* 'long').

► dilate

**latrine**    see LAVATORY

**laudanum**    [16]    *Laudanum*, the name of a tincture of opium, a forerunner of modern heroin and crack, was coined by the 16th-century Swiss physician Paracelsus. He used it for a medicine of his own devising which according to the prescription he gave out contained all sorts of expensive ingredients such as gold

leaf and pearls. It was generally believed, however, that the reason for the medicine's effectiveness was a generous measure of opium in the mixture, and so in due course *laudanum* came to have its current use. It is not known where Paracelsus got the name from, but he could well have based it on Latin *lādanum* 'resin,' which came from Greek *ládanon*, a derivative of *ledon* 'mastic.'

**laugh**    [OE]    The word *laugh* is ultimately onomatopoeic, imitative of the sound of laughter. It goes back to Indo-European *klak-*, *klōk-*, which also produced Greek *klóssein*, a verb denoting the clucking of hens, and Latin *clangere* 'sound' (source of English *clangor* [16]). Its Germanic descendants were *khlakh-*, *khlōkh-*, from which come German and Dutch *lachen*, Swedish and Danish *le*, and English *laugh*.

► clangor

**launch**    English has two separate words *launch*. The verb, 'propel' [14], is related to *lance*. Lances are propelled by throwing, and so the derived Old French verb *lancier* was used for 'throw.' English acquired it via the Anglo-Norman form *launcher*. The sense 'put a boat into the water' emerged at the end of the 14th century. From the same source came modern French *élancer* 'throw out,' whose derivative *élan* was acquired by English in the 19th century.

Launch 'boat' [17] comes via Portuguese *lancha* from a Malay word related to *lancharan* 'boat.'

► élan, lance

**laundry**    [16]    Although it is better disguised than most of its relatives, *laundry* is one of a large family of English words derived from Latin *lavāre* 'wash' (see LAVATORY). It is a contraction of an earlier *lavendry*, which came via Old French *lavanderie* from Latin *lavandārium* 'things to be washed.' By the time it reached English it had also acquired the meaning 'place where things are washed.'

► lavatory

**lavatory**    [14]    The notion of 'washing' was represented in prehistoric Indo-European by *lou-*, which produced Greek *loúein* 'wash,' English *lather*, and Latin *lavāre* 'wash.' This last has been a fruitful source of English words, not all of them as obvious as *lavatory*, which originally meant simply 'place or vessel for washing' (its use for a 'room containing a water closet' appears to date from the 19th century). Among its relatives are *deluge* [14], *latrine* [17] (from a contraction of Latin *lavātrīna*), *laundry, lava* [18] (from Italian *lava*, which originally denoted a 'stream caused by sudden rain'), *lavish* [15] (from the metaphorical notion of an 'outpouring'), and *lotion* [14]. And from Latin *luere*, the form taken on by *lavāre* after prefixes, we get *ablution* [14] and *dilute* [16]. *Lavender* [15] looks as though it should belong to the same family, but no actual connection has ever been demonstrated.

▶ ablution, deluge, dilute, lather, latrine, laundry, lava, lavish, lotion

**law** [10] Etymologically, a *law* is that which has been 'laid' down. English borrowed the word from Old Norse *lagu* (replacing the native Old English *ǣ* 'law'), which was the plural of *lag* 'laying, good order.' This came ultimately from the prehistoric Germanic base *lag-* 'put,' from which English gets *lay*. It has no etymological connection with the semantically similar *legal*.

▶ lay

**lawn** English has two words *lawn*. 'Grassy area' [16] is ultimately the same word as *land*. It is an alteration of an earlier *laund* 'glade,' which came from Old French *launde* 'heath,' a borrowing from the same prehistoric Germanic source as produced English *land*. *Lawn* was originally used for 'glade' too, and it was not until the 18th century that its present-day meaning emerged. *Lawn* 'fine linen or cotton' [15] probably comes from *Laon*, the name of a town in northern France where linen was formerly manufactured.

▶ land

**lax** see LEASE, RELISH

**lay** English has three words *lay*. The common verb, 'cause to lie' [OE], goes back to the prehistoric Germanic base *lag-* 'put,' a variant of which produced *lie*. From it was derived *lagjan*, whose modern descendants are German *legen*, Dutch *leggen*, Swedish *lägga*, Danish *lægge*, and English *lay*. *Law* comes from the same source, and it is possible that *ledge* [14] may be an offshoot of *lay* (which in Middle English was *legge*). *Ledger* could well be related too.

*Lay* 'secular' [14] comes via Old French *lai* and Latin *lāicus* from Greek *lāikós*, a derivative of *lāós* 'the people.' And *lay* 'ballad' [13] comes from Old French *lai*, a word of unknown origin.

▶ law, lie, ledger / liturgy

**layer** see LAIR

**lazy** [16] *Lazy* is one of the problem words of English. It suddenly appears in the middle of the 16th century, and gradually replaces the native terms *slack, slothful*, and *idle* as the main word for expressing the concept 'averse to work,' but no one knows for sure where it came from. Early spellings such as *laysy* led 19th-century etymologists to speculate that it may have been derived from *lay*, but the more generally accepted theory nowadays is that it was borrowed from Low German. Middle Low German had the similar *lasich* 'lazy, loose,' which may go back to an Indo-European form denoting 'slack.'

**lead** [OE] English has two words *lead*, spelled the same but of course pronounced differently and with a very different history. The verb goes back to a prehistoric West and North Germanic *laithjan*. This was derived from *laithō* 'way, journey' (from which English gets *load*); so etymologically *lead* means 'cause to go along one's way.' Its Germanic relatives include German *leiten*, Dutch *leiden*, Swedish *leda*, and Danish *lede*.

*Lead* the metal is probably of Celtic origin. The prehistoric Celtic word for 'lead' was *loudiā*, which may have come ultimately from an Indo-European source meaning 'flow' (a reference to the metal's low melting point). Its modern descendants include Irish *luaidhe* and Gaelic *luaidh*. It could well have been borrowed into prehistoric West Germanic as *lauda*, which would have produced modern German *lot* 'solder,' Dutch *lood* 'lead,' and English *lead*.

▶ load

**leaf** [OE] *Leaf* goes back to a prehistoric Germanic *laubaz*, which also produced words for 'foliage' in other modern Germanic languages (German *laub*, Dutch *loof*, Swedish *löf*, and Danish *løv*). It is not known for certain where the Germanic word came from, although a connection has been suggested with Russian *lupit* 'bark.' It may also lie behind the modern English words *lobby* and *lodge*.

▶ lobby, lodge

**leak** [15] The ultimate source of *leak* is probably a prehistoric Germanic *lek-*, which denoted 'deficiency' (a variant *lak-* gave English *lack*). It is not clear how this reached English; it could have been via Old Norse *leka*, or through Middle Dutch *lēken*.

▶ lack

**lean** [OE] *Lean* 'thin' and *lean* 'incline' are of course of completely different origin. The adjective goes back to a prehistoric Germanic *khlainjaz*. The verb can be traced to an Indo-European base *kli-* 'lean, slope,' which has given English a wealth of vocabulary. Via Greek intermediaries have come *climate, climax*, and *clinic*, while its Latin descendant *clīnāre* has produced *decline, incline*, and *recline*. The prehistoric Germanic verb formed from it was *khlinōjan*, which has diversified into modern German *lehnen*, Dutch *leunen*, and English *lean*. From the same Germanic base come *ladder*, and also perhaps *links* 'golf course' [OE], which originally meant 'sloping or rising ground.'

▶ climate, climax, clinic, decline, incline, ladder, links, recline

**leap** [OE] Prehistoric Germanic *khlaupan* was the source of English *leap*, and of its relatives German *laufen* and Dutch *loopen* (these both denote 'run,' a meaning which *leap* used to have – and which is preserved in its first cousins *lope* [15], a borrowing from Old Norse, and *elope*). It is not known where it ultimately came from, although a connection has been suggested with Indo-European *kloub-, source of Lithuanian šlubuoti 'limp.' The verb loaf may be related.

▶ loaf, lope

**leap year** [14] The inspiration for the term leap year is probably simply that in such a year the day on which any given date falls 'jumps' one day ahead of where it would have been in an ordinary year. The metaphorical application of the notion of 'jumping' to this phenomenon predates the first record of the term leap year: medieval Latin, for instance, used the term saltus lunae 'moon's jump' for the nineteen-yearly omission of a day from the lunar calendar, and this was translated into Old English as mōnan hlȳp 'moon's leap.'

**learn** [OE] Learn comes from a prehistoric West Germanic *liznōjan, which also produced German lernen. This goes back ultimately to an Indo-European *leis- 'track,' and so seems to carry the underlying notion of 'gaining experience by following a track.' Very closely related are terms in various Germanic languages for 'teach' (German lehren, for instance, and Dutch leeren, Swedish löra, and Danish lære – the last three also mean 'learn'). English used to have such a verb for 'teach' too: lere. It had largely died out by the 19th century, but the related lore 'knowledge' [OE] survives.

▶ last, lore

**lease** [15] The etymological idea underlying lease is of 'letting go' – a notion more readily apparent in its close relative release. Its ultimate ancestor is the Latin adjective laxus 'loose,' source of English lax [14]. From this was derived the verb laxāre 'loosen, let go,' which passed into Old French as laissier (its modern descendant is laisser 'leave, let'). Anglo-Norman took it over as lesser, and used it for 'letting something go' to someone else for a certain period under the terms of a legal contract. Hence English lease. The derivatives lessee [15] and lessor [15] also come from Anglo-Norman.

▶ lax, release

**least** [OE] In origin, least is simply the superlative form of less. The prehistoric Germanic ancestor of less was *laisiz (itself a comparative form). Addition of the superlative suffix produced *laisistaz, which passed into Old English as lǣsest. Unchanged, this would have become in modern English *lessest, but it was contracted in the Old English period to lǣst, and so modern English has least.

▶ less

**leather** [OE] The Indo-European ancestor of leather was *letrom. It has descendants in two branches of the Indo-European language family: in Celtic, Welsh lledr, Irish leathar, and Breton ler; and in Germanic, German leder, Dutch leer, Swedish läder, Danish læder, and English leather.

**leave** [OE] English has two distinct words leave. The noun, meaning 'permission,' comes from a prehistoric West Germanic *laubā, which was derived from a root meaning 'pleasure, approval' (other English words from the same source include believe and love). It passed semantically through 'be well disposed to' to 'trust' (a sense preserved in the related believe, and also in the cognate German glauben 'believe'), and from there to 'permit.'

The verb leave 'go away' comes from a prehistoric Germanic *laibjan 'remain.' It has been speculated that this is related ultimately to various Indo-European words for 'sticky substances' or 'stickiness' (Sanskrit lipta- 'sticky,' for instance, and Greek lípos 'grease,' source of English lipid [20]), and that its underlying meaning is 'remaining stuck,' hence 'staying in a place.' The sense 'remain' survived into English, but it died out in the 16th century, leaving as its legacy the secondary causative sense 'cause to remain.' The apparently opposite sense 'go away,' which emerged in the 13th century, arose from viewing the action of the verb from the point of view of the person doing the leaving rather than of the thing being left. The related German bleiben, which incorporates the prefix bi-, still retains the sense 'remain.' Other related English words, distant and close respectively, are eclipse and eleven.

▶ believe, love / eclipse, eleven, lipid, twelve

**lecher** [12] Etymologically, a lecher is a 'licker.' English borrowed the word from Old French lecheor, a derivative of the verb lechier 'lick,' which was used figuratively for 'live a life of debauchery.' This in turn came from Frankish *likkōn, a descendant of the same prehistoric Germanic source as English lick [OE]. The inspiration of the metaphor, which originally encompassed the pleasures of the table as well as of the bed, was presumably the tongue as an organ of sensual gratification.

▶ lick

**lecture** [14] The Latin verb legere has been a prodigious contributor to English vocabulary. It originally meant 'gather, choose,' and in that guise has given us collect, elect, elegant, intelligent, legion [13] (etymologically a 'chosen' body), neglect, and select. It subsequently developed semantically to 'read,' and from that mode English has taken lecture, lectern [14] (from the medieval Latin derivative lectrīnum), legend [14] (etymologically 'things to be read'), and lesson.

▶ collect, elect, elegant, intelligent, legend, legible, legion, lesson, neglect, select

**ledger** [15] Etymologically, a ledger is a book that 'lies' in one place. The term was used in 15th- and 16th-century English with various specific applications, including a 'large copy of the Breviary' (the Roman catholic service book), and a 'large register or record-book' – both big volumes that would not have been moved around much – but it finally settled on the 'main book in the set of books used for keeping accounts.' It probably comes from Dutch *legger* or *ligger*, agent nouns derived respectively from *leggen* 'lay' and *liggen* 'lie' (relatives of English *lay* and *lie*).

▶ lay, lie

**left** [13] The Old English word for 'left' was *winestra*. Etymologically this meant 'friendlier' (it is related to Swedish *vän* 'friend'), and its euphemistic application to 'left' is a reminder that historically the left-hand side of the body has been superstitiously regarded as of ill omen. To call it 'friendly' (a usage which survives in Swedish *vänster* and Danish *venstre* 'left') was an attempt to placate the evil forces of the left. (Latin *sinister* 'left' is similarly fraught with negative connotations. It too had euphemistic origins – it came from a source meaning 'more useful' – and it developed the figurative senses 'unfavourable,' 'injurious,' etc, taken over and extended by English in *sinister* [15].)

An ancestor of *left* existed in Old English – *left* or *\*lyft*. But it meant 'weak' or 'foolish,' and it was not until the 13th century that it came to be used as the partner of *right*. Its ultimate origins are not known.

**leg** [13] *Shank* was the word used in Old English for 'leg.' Not until the late 13th was *leg* acquired, from Old Norse *leggr*. It goes back to a prehistoric Germanic *\*lagjaz*, which may ultimately come from a source that meant 'bend.' No other Germanic language any longer uses it for 'leg,' but Swedish and Danish retain *lägg* and *læg* respectively for 'calf.'

**legal** [16] The Latin term for a 'law' was *lex*. From its stem form *leg-* come English *legal, legislator* [17] (which goes back to a Latin compound meaning literally 'one who proposes a law'), and *legitimate* [15]. *Loyal* is a doublet of *legal*, acquired via Old French rather than directly from Latin. Another derivative of *leg-* was the Latin verb *lēgāre* 'depute, commission, bequeath,' which has given English *colleague, college, delegate* [14], *legacy* [14], and *legation* [15].

▶ colleague, college, delegate, legacy, loyal

**legend** see LECTURE
**legion** see LECTURE
**legume** see LOBE

**leisure** [14] The etymological idea underlying *leisure* is that of 'having permission,' and hence of 'having the freedom to do as one likes.' The word came via Anglo-Norman *leisour* from Old French *leisir*. This was a noun use of a verb that meant 'be permitted,' and came from Latin *licēre* 'be permitted' (source of English *illicit* [17] and *licence* [14]).

▶ illicit, licence

**lemon** see LIME

**lend** [15] *Lend* and *loan* are closely related – come in fact from the same ultimate source (which also

produced English *delinquent, ellipse*, and *relinquish*). Why then does the verb have a *d* while the noun does not? Originally there was no *d*. The Old English verb 'lend' was *lǣnan*, which in Middle English became *lene*. But gradually during the Middle English period the past form *lende* came to be reinterpreted as a present form, and by the 15th century it was established as the new infinitive.

▶ delinquent, ellipse, loan, relinquish

**length** [OE] *Length* was coined in the prehistoric Germanic period from the adjective *\*langgaz* (source of English *long*) and the abstract noun suffix *\*-ithō*. The resultant *\*langgithō* has subsequently diversified to Dutch *lengte*, Swedish *längd*, Danish *længde*, and English *length*. (German has plumped for the different noun derivative *länge* 'length,' whose English relative *lenge* 'length' survived until the 17th century.)

▶ long

**lens** [17] The Latin word for a 'lentil' was *lēns*; and when 17th-century scientists wanted a term for a round biconvex (lentil-shaped) piece of glass, they needed to look no further than *lens*. English *lentil* [13] itself comes via Old French from Latin *lenticula*, a diminutive form of *lēns*

▶ lentil

**Lent** [OE] The etymological meaning of *Lent* is 'long days.' It comes from *\*langgitīnaz*, a prehistoric West Germanic compound formed from *\*lanngaz* 'long' and an element *\*tīna-* denoting 'day.' This signified originally 'spring,' an allusion to the lengthening days at that time of year. It passed into Old English as *lencten*, which became Middle English *lenten*, but in the 13th century the *-en* was dropped from the noun, leaving *Lenten* to function as an adjective. By this time too the secular sense 'spring' was fast dying out, having been usurped by the application of *Lent* to the period between Ash Wednesday and Easter.

▶ long

**lentil** see LENS

**leper** [13] Etymologically, a person suffering from leprosy has 'scaly' skin. The Greek word for 'scale' was *lépos* or *lepís*. From them was derived the adjective *leprós* 'scaly,' whose feminine form *léprā* was used as a noun meaning 'leprosy.' This passed via Latin *lepra* and Old French *lepre* into English as *leper*, where it still denoted 'leprosy.' In the 14th century it came to be used for a 'person suffering from leprosy.'

**leprechaun** [17] *Leprechaun* means literally 'little body.' It comes from an Irish compound noun made up of the adjective *lu* 'little' and *corp* 'body' (a borrowing from Latin *corpus*). Its original Old Irish form was *luchorpán*, and in modern Irish this became *leipracán*. The first record of its use in English is in Thomas Middleton's *Honest whore* 1604: 'as for your

Irish lubrican, that spirit whom by preposterous charms thy lust hath rais'd in a wrong circle.'

▶corpse

**less** [OE] In origin, *less* is a comparative form. It goes back ultimately to Indo-European *\*loiso-* 'small,' which in prehistoric Germanic had the comparative suffix added to it to produce *\*laisiz* – whence English *less*. It is not found in any of the other modern Germanic languages.

▶least

**lessee** SEE LEASE

**lesson** [13] Etymologically, a *lesson* is 'something read' – as indeed the lesson read in church still is. The word comes via Old French *lecon* from Latin *lectiō* 'reading,' a derivative of the verb *legere* 'read' (from which English gets *lectern, lecture*, etc). The word's educational sense arose from the notion of a passage of text that a child had to read and learn.

▶lectern, lecture, legible

**let** [OE] English has two distinct verbs *let*, of diametrically opposite meaning, but they are probably ultimately related. The one meaning 'allow' goes back to a prehistoric Germanic *\*lǣt-* (source also of German *lassen* and Dutch *laten*) which, like the related *late*, is connected with a range of words denoting 'slowness' or 'weariness.' It therefore appears that the underlying etymological meaning of *let* is 'let go of something because one is too tired to hold on to it.' By the time the verb reached Old English this had developed to 'leave behind' and 'omit to do,' senses now defunct, as well as to 'allow.'

A close relative of the base *\*lǣt-* was *\*lat-*, direct ancestor of English *late*. From this was formed the Germanic verb *\*latjan*, which gave English its other verb *let*, meaning 'prevent,' now largely obsolete except as a noun, in the phrase *without let or hindrance* or as a tennis term.

▶late

**lethargy** [14] Greek *léthé* meant 'oblivion' (the Romans used it for the name of a river in Hades whose water induced forgetfulness, and its influence has also been traced in changing Latin *lētum* 'death' to *lēthum*, source of English *lethal* [17]). From it was formed the adjective *lēthargos*, which in turn produced the noun *lēthargíā*, source (via Latin and Old French) of English *lethargy*.

▶lethal

**letter** [13] The distant ancestry of the word *letter* has never been satisfactorily explained. One possible candidate as a source that has been put forward is Greek *diphthérai* 'writing tablets.' But the earliest precursor that can be positively identified is Latin *littera*. This meant 'alphabetic symbol,' or in the plural 'document' and 'epistle.' English acquired it via Old French *lettre*.

Also from Latin *littera* are English *literature* and *obliterate* [16], which means etymologically 'remove letters.'

▶literature, obliterate

**lettuce** [13] The lettuce was named for the milky white sap that exudes from its stalk when cut. The Latin for milk is *lac* (source of English *lactation* [17] and *lactose* [19]), and so the lettuce was christened *lactūca*. This passed into English via *laituës*, the plural of Old French *laituë*.

▶lactation, lactose

**leukaemia** SEE LIGHT

**level** [14] The Latin word for a 'balance' or 'scales' was *libra* (it has given English *Libra* the zodiacal sign [14] and also lies behind many terms for units of measurement, including *litre* and the abbreviation *lb* for 'pound'). Its diminutive form was *lībella*, which denoted an 'instrument for checking horizontality,' and hence a 'horizontal line.' It passed into Old French as *livel* (which in modern French has become *niveau* 'level'), and English took it over as *level*.

▶litre

**liable** [15] Today's main meaning of *liable*, 'likely to,' is a comparatively recent development. Its primary sense is 'legally bound or obliged' (as in 'liable for someone else's debts'), which goes right back to the word's ultimate source, Latin *ligāre* 'tie.' Its Old French descendant *lier* is assumed to have give rise to an Anglo-Norman derivative *\*liable*, literally 'bindable,' which English took over. Other English words that come ultimately from *ligāre* include *ally, liaison* [17], *lien* [16] (etymologically a 'bond'), *ligament* [14], *ligature* [14], *oblige, religion*, and *rely*.

▶ally, liaison, lien, ligament, ligature, oblige, religion, rely

**libel** SEE LIBRARY

**liberal** [14] The Latin word for 'free' was *līber*. It came from the same prehistoric source as Greek *eleútheros* 'free,' which may have denoted 'people, nation' (in which case the underlying etymological meaning of the word would be 'being a member of the (free) people,' as opposed to 'being a slave'). From *līber* was derived *līberālis* 'of freedom,' which passed into English via Old French *liberal*. Its earliest English meanings were 'generous' and 'appropriate to the cultural pursuits of a 'free' man' (as in 'the liberal arts'). The connotations of 'tolerance' and 'lack of prejudice' did not emerge until the 18th century, and the word's use as a designation of a particular political party in Britain dates from the early 19th century.

Also from Latin *līber* come English *libertine* [14] and *liberty* [14].

▶libertine, liberty

**libidinous**   see LOVE

**library**   [14]   The Latin word for 'book' was *liber*. It is related to Russian *lub* 'bark' and Lithuanian *luba* 'board,' and originally denoted 'bark,' as used for writing on before the introduction of papyrus. From it was derived *librāria* 'bookseller's shop,' which Old French took over as *librairie* and passed on to English. The English word has only ever been used for a 'place where books are kept,' or for a 'collection of books,' but French *librairie* now exclusively means 'bookseller's shop.' Other English derivatives of Latin *liber* include *libel* [13] (from the diminutive form *libellus* 'little book'; it originally denoted in English simply a 'formal written claim by a plaintiff,' and did not take on its current connotations of 'defamation' until the 17th century) and *libretto* [18] (also literally a 'little book,' from an Italian diminutive form).

▶ libel, libretto

**licence**   see LEISURE

**lick**   see LECHER

**lid**   [OE]   The prehistoric Germanic ancestor of *lid* was *khlitham*, which also produced Dutch *lid* and the *-lid* of German *augenlid* 'eyelid.' It comes ultimately from the Indo-European base *kli-* 'cover, shut.'

**lie**   [OE]   English has two words *lie*. The verb 'recline' goes back, together with its Germanic relatives (German *liegen*, Dutch *liggen*, Swedish *ligga*, Danish *ligge*), to a prehistoric base *leg-*, a variant of the base *lag-* which produced *lay*. Both come ultimately from Indo-European *legh-*, *logh-*, whose other English descendants include *litter* and *low*.

The verb 'tell untruths' and its related noun come from a Germanic base *leug-*, *loug-*, represented also in German *lügen*, Dutch *liegen*, Swedish *ljuga*, and Danish *lyve*. The second syllable of English *warlock* comes from the same source.

▶ lay, lig, litter, low / warlock

**lien**   see LIABLE

**lieutenant**   [14]   Etymologically, a *lieutenant* is someone who 'holds the place' of another (more senior) officer – that is, deputizes for him. The word comes from French *lieutenant*, a compound formed from *lieu* 'place' and *tenant* (source of English *tenant*). *Lieu* (borrowed independently by English as *lieu* [13] in the phrase 'in lieu of') comes in turn from Latin *locus* 'place,' source of English *local*. *Locum tenens* [17] (or *locum* for short) 'temporary replacement,' literally 'holding the place,' is thus a parallel formation with *lieutenant*. Spellings of *lieutenant* with *-f-*, indicating the still current British pronunciation /lef-/, first appear as early as the 14th century.

▶ lieu, local, tenant

**life**   [OE]   Prehistoric Germanic *līb-* denoted 'remain, be left.' From this was formed the noun *lībam*, which in due course produced English *life* (the semantic connection between 'remaining' and *life* – and the closely related *live* – is thought to lie in the notion of being 'left alive after a battle'). Of the noun's Germanic relatives, Swedish and Danish *liv* still mean 'life,' but German *leib* and Dutch *lijf* have moved on semantically to 'body.'

English *alive* is a derivative of *life*, not of the verb *live*.

▶ live

**lift**   see LOFT

**lig**   [20]   The verb *lig*, meaning 'freeload, sponge,' and its derivative *ligger*, achieved a particular prominence in late 20th-century British English. But in fact its roots go back far into the past. In origin it is simply a variant version of the verb *lie* 'recline.' In Old English times this was *licgan*, and although in the mainstream language *licgan* became *lie*, *liggen* survived dialectally. The sense 'lie about' passed naturally into 'lounge about lazily,' and apparently merged with another dialectal sense 'steal' to produce the word's current meaning.

▶ lie

**ligament**   see LIABLE

**ligature**   see LIABLE

**light**   [OE]   English has two distinct words *light*. The one meaning 'illumination' comes ultimately from Indo-European *leuk-*, *louk-*, *luk-*, which also produced Greek *leukós* 'white' (source of English *leukaemia* [20]) and Latin *lūx* 'light' (from which English gets *lucifer* [OE], literally 'light-bearer'), *lūmen* 'light' (whence English *luminous* [15]), *lūcēre* 'shine' (source of English *lucid* [16]), *lūstrāre* 'light up' (whence English *illustrate* and *lustre* [16]), and *lūna* 'moon' (source of English *lunar*). Its main prehistoric West Germanic derivative was *leukhtam*, from which come German and Dutch *licht* and English *light*. The word *lynx* may be related.

*Light* 'not heavy' comes from a prehistoric Germanic *lingkhtaz*, a close relative of which produced English *lung* (the word *lung* thus etymologically denotes 'something full of air and not heavy,' and indeed lungs were, and animal lungs still are called *lights* in English).

▶ illustrate, leukaemia, lucid, luminous, lunar, lustre, lynx / lung

**lightning**   [14]   Etymologically, *lightning* is simply something that illuminates, or 'lightens,' the sky. The word is a contraction of an earlier *lightening*, a derivative of *lighten* 'make light.' The Old English word for 'lightning' was *lēget*, which is related to *light*. In Middle English it became *leit*, and later *leiting*, but in the 14th century *lightning* took over as the main form.

▶ light

**like**    English has a diverse group of words spelled *like*, but they all come ultimately from the same source. This was prehistoric Germanic *\*līkam* 'appearance, form, body' (source also of the *lych-* of English *lychgate* [15], which originally signified the gate through which a coffin was carried into a churchyard). From it was derived the verb *\*līkōjan*, which passed into English as *like*. It originally meant 'please,' but by the 12th century had done a semantic somersault to 'find pleasing.' The same Germanic *\*līkam* produced English *alike*, literally 'similar in appearance,' whose Old Norse relative *līkr* was borrowed into English as the adjective *like* [12]. Its adverbial and prepositional uses developed in the later Middle Ages. Also from Old Norse came the derived adjective *likely* [13].

English *each* and *such* were formed from the ancestor of *like*.
▶ each, such

**lilac**    [17]    Like the river Nile, the *lilac* gets its name from its colour. The Sanskrit word for 'dark blue' was *nīla*. This passed into Persian as *nīl*, from which was derived *nīlak* 'bluish.' This developed a variant *līlak*, which English acquired via Arabic *līlak*, Spanish *lilac*, and early modern French *lilac*. Along the way it was applied to a shrub of the genus *Syringa*, on account of its mauve flowers.

**lily**    [OE]    *Lily* probably originated in a pre-Indo-European language of the Mediterranean seaboard. Latin acquired it (either independently or via Greek *leírion*) as *līlium*, and passed it on to English in the 10th century. It is now common to virtually all western European languages, including German (*lilie*), Dutch (*lelie*), Swedish (*lilja*), Spanish (*lirio*), Italian (the more radically altered *giglio*), and French (*lis*, acquired by English in *fleur-de-lis*, literally 'lily flower' [19]).

**limb**    [OE]    The Old English word for 'limb' was *lim*. Like *thumb*, it later (in the 16th century) acquired an intrusive *b*, which has long since ceased to be pronounced. It has cognates in Swedish and Danish *lem*, and Dutch *lid* 'limb' is probably related too.

**lime**    English has three distinct words *lime*, of which by far the oldest is *lime* the 'chalky substance' [OE]. It goes back to a prehistoric Germanic *\*līm-* (shared also by German *leim*, Dutch *lijm*, and Swedish *limma*), a variant of which also produced English *loam* [OE]. *Lime* the 'citrus fruit' [17] comes via French *lime* and Provençal *limo* from Arabic *līmah* 'citrus fruit,' which was also the source of English *lemon* [14]. And *lime* the 'tree' [17] is an alteration of an earlier *line*, a variant of *lind* 'lime tree' (the closely related *linden* was acquired in the 16th century, from German *lindenbaum* or early modern Dutch *lindenboom* 'lime tree').
▶ loam / lemon / linden

**limerick**    [19]    The best-known writer of limericks is of course Edward Lear, but ironically the term *limerick* was not born until after Lear was dead. It is first recorded in 1896, and is said to have come from a Victorian custom of singing nonsense songs at parties, in the limerick rhyme-scheme (*aabba*), which always ended with the line 'Will you come up to Limerick?' (Limerick of course being a county and town in Ireland).

**limit**    [14]    Latin *līmes* originally denoted a 'path between fields,' but it became extended metaphorically to any 'boundary' or 'limit,' and that was the sense in which English acquired it (in its stem form *līmit-*).
▶ lintel

**limousine**    [20]    Limousin is a former province of central France. Its inhabitants commonly wore a distinctive style of cloak, and when at the beginning of the 20th century a new and luxurious type of car was designed with a closed passenger compartment and an open but roofed seat for the driver, it evidently struck someone that the roof resembled a Limousin cloak, and so the car was named a *limousine*. The American abbreviation *limo* is first recorded from the 1960s.

**limp**    English has two words *limp*, which perhaps share a common ancestry. Neither is particularly old. The verb first crops up in the 16th century (until then the word for 'walk lamely' had been *halt*, which now survives, barely, as an adjective). It was probably adapted from the now obsolete adjective *limphalt* 'lame', a descendant of Old English *lemphealt* (which goes back ultimately to Indo-European *\*lomb-*). The adjective *limp* is first recorded in the 18th century, and in view of the common meaning element 'lack of firmness, infirmity' it seems likely that it is related to the verb.

**limpet**    see LAMPREY
**limpid**    see LYMPH
**linden**    see LIME

**line**    [OE]    The closest modern English *line* comes to its ancestor is probably in the fisherman's 'rod and line' – a 'string' or 'chord.' For it goes back to Latin *līnea* 'string.' This was a derivative of *līnum* 'flax' (source of English *linen*), and hence meant etymologically 'flaxen thread.' English acquired it in two separate phases. First of all it was borrowed directly from Latin in the Old English period, and then it made a return appearance via Old French *ligne* in the 14th century; the two have coalesced to form modern English *line*. Derived forms include *lineage* [14], *lineal* [15], *lineament* [15], and *liner* [19]. The last is based on the sense 'shipping line,' which goes back to the notion of a 'line' or succession of ships plying between ports.
▶ align, lineal, linen, liner

**linen**    [OE]    The word for 'flax' is an ancient one, shared by numerous Indo-European languages: Greek *línon*, Latin *līnum* (source of English *line*), and prehistoric West Germanic *\*līnam* among them. The latter passed into Old English as *līn*, but now survives only in the compound *linseed* (literally 'flax-seed'). Its adjectival derivative, however, *\*linīn*, lives on in the form *linen*, nowadays used as a noun meaning 'cloth made from flax.' The Latin word, or its French descendants *lin* or *linge*, have contributed several other derivatives to English, including *crinoline, lingerie* [19] (literally 'linen garments'), *linnet* [16] (etymologically a 'flax-eating bird'), *linoleum* [19], and *lint* [14].

▶ crinoline, line, lingerie, linnet, linoleum, lint

**liner**   see LINE

**linger**   [13] Etymologically, to *linger* is to remain 'longer' than one should. Like its relatives, German *längen* and Dutch *lengen*, it goes back to a prehistoric Germanic *\*langgjan* 'lengthen.' In Old Norse this became *lengja*, which was borrowed into English in the 10th century as *leng*. By now, 'lengthen' had progressed metaphorically via 'prolong' to 'delay,' which is what it meant when *linger* was derived from it in the 13th century.

▶ long

**lingerie**   see LINEN
**linguist**   see LANGUAGE

**link**   [14] *Link* goes back ultimately to prehistoric Germanic *\*khlangkjaz*, whose underlying meaning element was 'bending' (it also has close relatives in English *flank* [12], *flinch* [16], and *lank* [OE]). 'Bending' implies 'joints' and 'links,' and this is the meaning which is the word is presumed to have had when it passed into Old Norse as *\*hlenkr* – from which English acquired *link*.

There is, incidentally, no etymological connection with the now obsolete *link* 'torch' [16], which may have come via medieval Latin *linchinus* from Greek *lúkhnos* 'lamp,' nor with the *links* on which golf is played, which goes back to Old English *hlincas*, the plural of *hlinc* 'rising ground, ridge.'

▶ flank, flinch, lank

**links**   see LEAN
**linnet**   see LINEN
**linoleum**   see LINEN
**lint**   see LINEN

**lintel**   [14] *Lintel* is the result of the blending of two Latin words: *līmes* 'boundary' (source of English *limit*) and *līmen* 'threshold' (source of English *subliminal* and possibly also of *sublime*). *Līmen* had a derived adjective, *līmināris* 'of a threshold.' In the post-classical period, under the influence of *līmes*, this became altered to *\*līmitāris*, which was used in Vulgar Latin as a noun meaning 'threshold.' This passed into English via Old French *lintier*, later *lintel*.

▶ limit, subliminal

**lion**   [13] The word for 'lion' in virtually all modern European languages goes back to Greek *léōn*, which was presumably borrowed from some non-Indo-Euro-

pean source. From it came Latin *lēo*, which Old English took over as *lēo*. The modern English form *lion* was introduced in the 13th century via Anglo-French *liun*. Related forms include French *lion*, Italian *leone*, Spanish *león*, Rumanian *leu*, German *löwe*, Dutch *leeuw*, Swedish *lejon*, Danish *løve*, Russian *lev*, and Welsh *llew*.

The *-leon* of *chameleon* represents Greek *léōn*.

▶ chameleon

**lip**   [OE] *Lip* has been traced back to Indo-European *\*leb-*, which also produced Latin *labrum* 'lip,' source of French *lèvre* 'lip' and English *labial* [16]. Its Germanic descendant was *\*lepaz-*, from which come German *lippe*, Dutch *lip*, Swedish *läppe*, Danish *læbe*, and English *lip*.

▶ labial

**lipid**   see LEAVE

**liquid**   [14] Latin *liquēre* meant 'be fluid.' From it was derived the adjective *liquidus*, which reached English via Old French (it was not used as a noun in the sense 'liquid substance' until the early 18th century). Also derived from *liquēre* was the noun *liquor*, which passed into Old French as *licur* or *licour*. English has borrowed this twice: first in the 13th century as *licour*, which was subsequently 're-latinized' as *liquor*, and then in the 18th century in the form of its modern French descendant *liqueur*. From the same ultimate source come *liquefy* [16], *liquidate* [16] (which goes back to a metaphorical sense of Latin *liquēre*, 'be clear' – thus 'clear a debt'; the modern meaning 'destroy' was directly inspired by Russian *likvidirovat'*), and the final syllable of *prolix* [15].

▶ liquor, prolix

**liquorice**   [13] *Liquorice*, or *licorice* as it is usually spelled in American English, has no direct etymological connection with *liquor* (although *liquor* has played a significant role in its development). It goes back to Greek *glukúrrhiza*, which meant literally 'sweet root' (it was a compound of *glukús* 'sweet,' source of English *glycerine*, and *rhíza* 'root,' source of English *rhizome* [19]). Under the influence of *liquor*, this was borrowed into post-classical Latin as *liquiritia*, which passed into English via Old French *licoresse* and Anglo-Norman *lycorys*.

▶ glycerine, rhizome

**list**   Over the centuries, English has had no fewer than five different words *list*, only two of which are now in everyday common usage. *List* 'catalogue' [17] was borrowed from French *liste* 'band, border, strip of paper, catalogue.' This goes back to a prehistoric Germanic *\*līstōn*, source also of English *list* 'border, strip' [OE], which now survives only in the plural *lists* 'tournament arena.' *List* 'tilt' [17] is of unknown origin. *List* 'listen' [OE], which goes back to Indo-European *\*klu-*, has been replaced by the related *listen*. And the archaic *list* 'desire' [OE] (source of *listless* [15]) goes back to the same source as *lust*.

▸listless, lust

**listen** [OE] The Indo-European base *\*klu-* denoted 'hearing' (it is the ultimate source of English *loud*). From its extended form *\*klus-* were derived in prehistoric Germanic the noun *\*khlustiz* 'hearing,' which eventually produced the now archaic English verb *list* 'listen,' and the verb *\*khlusnōjan* 'hear,' which became English *listen*.

▸loud

**listless** see LIST

**literature** [14] Latin *littera* meant 'letter,' and was the source of English *letter*. From it was derived *literātus* 'having knowledge of letters,' hence 'educated, learned' (source of English *literate* [15]); and this formed the basis of the further derivative *litterātūra*, which denoted 'writing formed with letters,' and by extension 'learning, grammar.' English took it over partly direct, partly via French *littérature*. From the same source comes English *literal* [14].

▸letter, literal, obliterate

**lithograph** [19] Greek *líthos* meant 'stone.' It has contributed a small cluster of words to English, including *lithium* [19] (a metal so named from its mineral origin), *lithops* [20] (the name of a small pebble-like plant, coined in the 1920s, which means literally 'stone-face' in Greek), *lithosphere* [19] (the solid outer layer of the Earth), *lithotomy* [18] (the surgical removal of stones from the bladder), *megalith* [19], *monolith* [19], and the various terms for subdivisions of the Stone Age, such as *Neolithic* [19] and *Paleolithic* [19]. *Lithography* itself, which denotes a method of printing from a flat surface, means etymologically 'stone-writing,' reflecting the fact that the original printing surfaces in this process were of stone (they are now usually metal).

**litmus** see MOSS

**litre** [19] *Litre* goes back to Greek *lítrā*, a term which denoted a Sicilian monetary unit. This found its way via medieval Latin *litrā* into French as *litron*, where it was used for a unit of capacity. By the 18th century it had rather fallen out of use, but in 1793 it was revived, in the form *litre*, as the name for the basic unit of capacity in the new metric system. It is first recorded in English in 1810.

The Greek word was descended from an earlier, unrecorded *\*līthrā*, which was borrowed into Latin as *lībra* 'pound.' This is the source of various modern terms for units of weight, and hence of currency, including Italian *lira* and the now disused French *livre*, and it also lies behind the English symbol £ for 'pound.'

▸level, lira

**litter** [13] The word *litter* has come a long way semantically since it was born, from 'bed' to 'rubbish

scattered untidily.' It goes back ultimately to Latin *lectus* 'bed,' a distant relative of English *lie* and source of French *lit* 'bed' (which forms the final syllable of English *coverlet* [13], etymologically 'bed-cover'). From *lectus* was derived medieval Latin *lectāria*, which passed into English via Old French *litiere* and Anglo-Norman *litere* 'bed.' This original sense was soon extended in English to a 'portable conveyance or stretcher,' which still survives, just, as an archaism, but the word's main modern sense, which first emerged fully in the 18th century, derives from the notion of scattering straw over the floor for bedding.

▸coverlet

**little** [OE] *Little* goes back to the prehistoric West Germanic base *\*lut-*, which also produced Dutch *luttel* and may have been the source of the Old English verb *lūtan* 'bow down.' Some have detected a link with Old English *lot* 'deceit,' Old Norse *lýta* 'dishonour, blame,' Russian *ludit'* 'deceive,' and Serbo-Croat *lud* 'foolish.'

**liturgy** [16] Etymologically, *liturgy* means 'public performance.' It comes via late Latin *līturgia* from Greek *leitourgíā* 'public service or worship.' This was a derivative of *leitourgós* 'public servant,' hence 'priest,' a compound formed from *leit-*, the stem of *léós* 'people, multitude' (from which English gets *layman*), and *érgon* 'work, action' (source of English *energy*).

▸laity, lay, enery

**live** [OE] Modern English *live* represents a conflation of two Old English verbs, *libban* and *lifian*, both of which go back ultimately to the same prehistoric Germanic source, *\*lib-* 'remain, continue.' Variants of this produced *leave* 'depart' and *life*. The adjective *live* [16] is a reduced form of *alive*, which derived from *life*.

▸life

**livid** see SLOE

**lizard** [14] *Lizard* goes back to Latin *lacertus* or *lacerta*, words of unknown origin. It reached English via Old French *lesard*. The Latin word was used for 'muscle' as well as 'lizard,' perhaps because the ripple of a muscle beneath the skin reminded people of a lizard's movement (an exactly parallel development links *mouse* and *muscle*). And in heavily disguised form, owing to a detour via Arabic, *alligator* is the same word.

▸alligator

**load** [OE] *Load* originally meant 'way, course' and 'conveyance, carriage.' It goes back to prehistoric Germanic *\*laithō*, which also lies behind English *lead* 'conduct.' Not until the 13th century did it begin to move over to its current sense 'burden,' under the direct influence of *lade* [OE] (a verb of Germanic origin which now survives mainly in its past participial adjective *laden* and the derived noun *ladle* [OE]).

The word's original sense 'way' is preserved in *lodestar* [14], etymologically a 'guiding star,' and *lode-*

*stone* [16], likewise a 'guiding stone,' named from its use as a compass.

▶laden, lead

**loaf**   English has two words *loaf*. By far the older is 'portion of bread' [OE], which goes back to a prehistoric Germanic *\*khlaibaz*. This also produced German *laib* and Danish *lev* 'loaf,' and was borrowed, originally into Gothic, from an Old Slavic *chleb* (source of modern Russian and Polish *chleb* 'bread, loaf'). Heavily disguised, *loaf* forms part of both *lady* and *lord* (which etymologically mean respectively 'loaf-kneader' and 'loaf-guardian'), and it also contributed the first syllable to *Lammas* [OE], literally 'loaf-mass.'

The verb *loaf* 'dawdle, mooch' [19] seems to have been a back-formation from *loafer*, which was probably adapted in 19th-century American English from German *landläufer* 'vagabond,' a compound of *land* 'land' and *läufer* 'runner' (to which English *leap* is related).

▶lady, lord / leap

**loam**   see LIME

**loan**   [13]   Old English had a noun *lǣn*, a close relative of the verb *lǣnan* (precursor of modern English *lend*). It meant 'gift,' but it died out before the Middle English period, and was replaced by the related Old Norse *lán*, which has become modern English *loan*. Both go back ultimately to prehistoric Indo-European *\*loiq-*, *\*leiq-*, *\*liq-*, which also produced Greek *leípein* 'leave' (source of English *ellipse*) and Latin *linquere* 'leave' (source of English *delinquent*, *relic*, and *relinquish*).

▶delinquent, lend, relic, relinquish

**loathe**   [OE]   *Loathe* originated as a derivative of the adjective *loath* or *loth* [OE]. This originally meant 'hostile' or 'loathsome,' and goes back to a prehistoric Germanic *\*laithaz*, which also produced Swedish *led* 'fed up' and German *leid* 'sorrow,' and was borrowed into the Romance languages, giving French *laid* and Italian *laido* 'ugly.'

**lobby**   see LODGE

**lobe**   [16]   Greek *lobós* denoted 'something round,' such as the circular part of the ear or the liver, or a round seed pod. It came from a prehistoric *\*logwós*, a close relative of which produced Latin *legūmen* 'seed pod' (source of English *legume* [17]). *Lobós* was borrowed into late Latin as *lobus*, and from there made its way into English.

▶legume

**lobster**   [OE]   The Latin word *locusta* denoted both the voracious grasshopper, the 'locust,' and the 'lobster' or similar crustaceans, such as the crayfish (if, as has been suggested, the word is related to Greek *lēkan* 'jump,' then presumably the 'grasshopper' sense was primary, and the 'lobster' application arose from some supposed resemblance between the two crea-

tures). English has borrowed the Latin word twice. Most recently it came in the easily recognizable guise *locust* [13], but *lobster* too goes back to the same source. The radical change of form may be due to the influence of the Old English word *loppe* 'spider' – the Old English precursor of *lobster* was *loppestre* or *lopystre*.

▶locust

**local**   [15]   Latin *locus* meant 'place' (it became in due course French *lieu*, acquired by English in the 13th century, and was itself adopted into English as a mathematical term in the 18th century). From it was derived the verb *locāre* 'place,' source of English *locate* [18] and *location* [16], and the post-classical adjective *locālis*, from which English gets *local*. The noun *locale* is a mock frenchification of an earlier *local* [18], an adoption of the French use of the adjective *local* as a noun.

▶lieu, locomotive, locus

**lock**   [OE]   English has two words *lock*. The one meaning 'fastening mechanism' goes back ultimately to a prehistoric Germanic *\*luk-* or *\*lūk-*, denoting 'close,' which also produced German *loch* 'hole' and Swedish *lock* 'lid.' Closely related are *locker* [15], etymologically a 'box with a lock,' and *locket* [14], which was acquired from Old French *locquet*, a diminutive form of *loc* (which itself was a borrowing from Germanic *\*luk-*).

*Lock* 'piece of hair' goes back to a prehistoric Indo-European *\*lug-*, which denoted 'bending.' Its Germanic relatives include German *locke*, Dutch and Danish *lok*, and Swedish *lock*.

**locomotive**   [17]   *Locomotive* denotes etymologically 'moving by change of place.' It is an anglicization of modern Latin *locōmōtīvus*, a compound formed from *locus* 'place' and *mōtīvus* 'causing to move' (source of English *motive*). Originally it was used strictly as an adjective, and it was not until the early 19th century that the present-day noun use (which began life as an abbreviation of *locomotive engine*) emerged.

**locust**   see LOBSTER

**lodestone**   see LOAD

**lodge**   [13]   The distant ancestor of *lodge* was Germanic *\*laubja* 'shelter,' which may well have been a derivative of *\*laubam* 'leaf' (source of English *leaf*) – the underlying idea being of a sheltered place formed by or constructed from leafy branches. German *laube* 'summer-house, covered way' comes from the same source. Medieval Latin took over the Germanic form as *laubia* or *lobia* (from which English gets *lobby* [16]), and passed it on via Old French *loge* to English in the form *lodge*.

▶leaf, lobby

**loft** [OE] The notion underlying *loft* is of being 'high up in the air' – and indeed originally *loft*, like its close German relative *luft*, meant 'air.' Not until the 13th century do we find it being used in English for 'upper room' (although in fact its source, Old Norse *lopt*, had both meanings). All these words go back to a common ancestor, prehistoric Germanic *\*luftuz* 'air, sky.' From this was derived a verb *\*luftjan*, which, again via Old Norse, has given English *lift* [13] (the use of the derived noun for an 'elevator,' incidentally, dates from the mid 19th century).

▶ lift

**log** [14] *Log* is a mystery word. It first turns up (in the sense 'felled timber') towards the end of the 14th century, but it has no ascertainable relatives in any other language. Nor is it altogether clear how the sense 'ship's record' came about. It was inspired by the use of *log* for a thin piece of wood floated in the water from a line to determine the speed of a ship, but some etymologists have speculated that this is not the same word as *log* 'piece of timber,' but was adapted from Arabic *lauh* 'tablet.'

**logarithm** [17] Greek *lógos* had a remarkably wide spread of meanings, ranging from 'speech, saying' to 'reason, reckoning, calculation,' and 'ratio.' The more 'verbal' end of its spectrum has given English the suffixes *-logue* and *-logy* (as in *dialogue, tautology*, etc), while the 'reasoning' component has contributed *logic* [14] (from the Greek derivative *logikḗ*), *logistic* [17] (from the Greek derivative *logistikós* 'of calculation'), and *logarithm*, coined in the early 17th century by the English mathematician John Napier from Greek *logós* 'ratio' and *arithmós* 'number' (source of English *arithmetic* [13]).

▶ arithmetic, logic, logistic

**loin** [14] *Loin* has had a circuitous history. Its distant ancestor was probably Germanic, but it was borrowed early on into Latin as *lumbus* 'loin' (source of English *lumbar* [17], *lumbago* [17], and the *numbles* or *umbles* which became the *humble* of *humble pie*). *Lumbus* passed via Vulgar Latin *\*lumbia* into Old French as *longe*. This had an eastern dialectal form *loigne*, which English acquired as *loin*.

▶ humble pie, lumbago, lumbar

**lonely** [16] *Lonely* is a derivative of *lone* [14], itself a truncated form of *alone*. Another coinage based on *lone* is *lonesome* [17].

**long** [OE] *Long* goes back to a prehistoric Germanic *\*langgaz*, which also produced German, Dutch, and Danish *lang* and Swedish *lång*. It is presumably related to Latin *longus* 'long' (source of French *long*, Italian *lungo*, and Rumanian *lung*) but quite how has not been established. The derived verb *long* is of equal antiquity, and originally meant simply 'grow long'; the current sense 'yearn' developed via 'seem long.' De-

rived forms, more or less heavily disguised, include *belong, Lent, linger, lunge*, and *purloin* [15], etymologically 'take a long way away,' hence 'remove.'

▶ belong, length, Lent, linger, lunge, purloin

**longitude** see LATITUDE

**loo** [20] *Loo* presents one of the more celebrated puzzles of English etymology. Not the least of its problematical points is that there is no reliable evidence of its existance before the 1920s, whereas most of its suggested sources have a more dated air than that. Amongst them, the most widely touted is of course *gardy loo!*, a shout of warning (based on French *gardez l'eau* 'beware of the water') supposedly used when emptying chamber pots from upper-storey windows in the days before modern plumbing; but there is no real evidence for this. Other possibilities are that it is short for *Waterloo* ('O yes, *mon loup*. How much cost? Waterloo. Watercloset,' James Joyce, *Ulysses* 1922), and that it comes from *louvre*, from the use of slatted screens for a makeshift lavatory. But perhaps the likeliest explanation is that it derives from French *lieux d'aisances*, literally 'places of ease,' hence 'lavatory' (perhaps picked up by British servicemen in France during World War I).

**look** [OE] For such a common word, *look* is surprisingly isolated. It goes back to prehistoric West Germanic *\*lōkōjan*, which has no other descendants in the modern Germanic languages, and its only distant relative is the German verb *lugen* 'show, be visible.'

**loose** [13] *Loose* is one of a large family of words that go back ultimately to Indo-European *\*lau-, \*leu-, \*lu-*, which denoted 'undoing.' It includes (via Greek) *analyse* and *paralyse*, (via Latin) *dissolve* and *solution*, and (via Germanic) *lose* and the suffix *-less*. *Loose* itself was borrowed from Old Norse *laus*, which was descended from a prehistoric Germanic *\*lausaz*.

▶ analyse, dissolve, lose, paralyse, solution

**lope** see LEAP

**loquacious** see VENTRILOQUIST

**lord** [OE] It is a measure of the centrality of bread to human society that the word *lord* denotes etymologically 'guardian of the loaf.' It goes back to a primitive Old English *\*khlaibward*, a compound formed from *\*khlaib* 'loaf' and *\*ward* 'guardian, keeper' (ancestor of modern English *ward*). This gradually developed in Old English via *hlāfweard* to *hlāford*, and in the 14th century it lost its middle /v/ to become the single-syllable word we know today.

*Lady* was likewise originally based on the word *loaf*.

▶ guard, loaf, ward

**lore** see LEARN

**lorry** [19] The first record we have of the word *lorry* is from the northwest of England in the early

1830s, when it denoted a 'low wagon' (it was often used for railway wagons). The modern application to a motor vehicle emerged at the beginning of the 20th century. It is not clear where it came from, although it has been speculated that it was based on the personal name *Laurie* (perhaps someone called Laurie invented the vehicle). Another possibility is some connection with the Northern dialect verb *lurry* 'pull.'

**lose** [OE]  The verb *lose* originated as a derivative of the Old English noun *los* 'loss,' which went back ultimately to the same Indo-European source (*lau-, *leu-, lu-) as produced English *loose* and the suffix *-less*. In Old English it was *losian*, which eventually ousted the original *lēosan* to become the only verb for 'lose.' The noun *los* died out before the Middle English period, and was replaced by *loss* [14], probably a derivative of the past participle *lost*. The past participle of *lēosan* 'lose' was *loren*, which survives in *forlorn* and *love-lorn*.
▶ loose

**lot** [OE]  *Lot* goes back to a prehistoric Germanic *khlut-*, which appears to have denoted the use of objects to make decisions by chance (Old English *hlot* was used for such an object). The first inklings of the modern range of senses did not emerge until the 18th century, when *lot* began to be used for a 'set of things.' 'Large number, many' followed in the 19th century. The Germanic word was borrowed into the Romance languages, and of its descendants English has acquired *allot* [16] (from Old French) and *lotto* [18] (from Italian). *Lottery* [16] comes from the Dutch derivative *loterij*.
▶ allot, lottery, lotto

**loth**    see LOATHE

**loud** [OE]  The underlying meaning of *loud* is 'heard, audible' – for it goes back ultimately to an Indo-European *klu-* 'hear' (source also of English *listen*). The past participial form based on this, *klūtós*, passed into prehistoric West Germanic as *khluthaz*, which has since differentiated into German *laut*, Dutch *luid*, and English *loud*.
▶ listen

**lounge** [16]  It is the verb *lounge* (originally 'move indolently') which came first; its application as a noun to a 'room where one can sit and take one's ease' came later, in the 18th century. It is not at all clear where the word came from, but some have linked it with the long obsolete noun *lungis*, which denoted both a 'gangling foolish fellow' and 'someone who is slow or dilatory at doing things.' This was borrowed in the 16th century from French *longis*, which was apparently a generic application of *Longīnus*, the name of the Roman centurion who pierced Christ's side with a spear as he was hanging on the cross.

**love** [OE]  The word *love* goes back to an Indo-European *leubh-*, which has spawned a huge lexical progeny: not just words for 'love' (*love*'s Germanic relatives, such as German *liebe* and Dutch *liefde*, as well as the archaic English *lief* 'dear' [OE] and Latin *libīdō* 'strong desire,' source of English *libidinous* [15]) but also words for 'praise' (German *lob* and Dutch *lof*) and 'belief' (German *glauben*, Dutch *gelooven*, English *believe*). The sense 'find pleasing' is primary; it subsequently developed to 'praise' and, probably via 'be satisfied with,' to 'trust, believe.'

The derivative *lovely* [OE] originally meant 'affectionate' and 'lovable'; the modern sense 'beautiful' did not develop until the late 13th century.
▶ believe, leave, lief

**low**  English has two words *low*, of which surprisingly the 'noise made by cattle' [OE] is the older. It goes back ultimately to the onomatopoeic Indo-European base *klā-*. This also produced Latin *clārus* (which originally meant 'loud,' and gave English *clear* and *declare*), *clāmāre* 'cry out' (source of English *acclaim, claim, exclaim*, etc), and *calāre* 'proclaim, summon' (source of English *council*). It produced a prehistoric Germanic *khlō-*, whose only survivor other than English *low* is Dutch *loeien*.

*Low* 'not high' [12] was borrowed from Old Norse *lágr* (source also of Swedish *låg* 'low'). This goes back to a prehistoric Germanic *lǣgjaz*, which was derived from the same base as produced the English verb *lie* 'recline.'
▶ acclaim, claim, clear, council, exclaim / lie

**loyal** [16]  *Loyal*, ultimately the same word as *legal*, has a double history in English. It was originally acquired in the 13th century as *leal*. This came from Anglo-Norman *leal*, a descendant of Latin *lēgālis* 'legal.' Then in the 16th century it was reborrowed from the modern French form *loyal*. The semantic link is 'faithfully carrying out (legal) obligations.'
▶ legal

**lubricate**    see SLIP

**lucid**    see LIGHT

**lucifer**    see LIGHT

**luck** [15]  The antecedents of *luck* are not at all clear. Its likeliest source is Low German *luk*. This is clearly a close relative of modern Dutch *geluk*, whose prefix *ge-* is found also in Middle High German *gelücke* (source of modern German *glück* 'good fortune, happiness'). But where the element *lu(c)k* came from is not known.

**ludicrous**    see ILLUSION

**luff**    see ALOOF

**lug**  English has three words *lug*, two of them possibly connected. The verb , 'pull' [14], may be related to Swedish *lugga* 'pull someone's hair,' suggesting a Scandinavian origin. And it has been pointed out that the various meanings of the noun *lug* [15], such as 'ear' and 'projecting handle,' share a common semantic element 'capable of being held (and pulled),' so the noun may have been derived from the verb. The *lug-* of *lugworm* [17] may be of Celtic origin.

**lukewarm**   [14]   *Lukewarm* is a compound adjective based on the now obsolete Middle English *luke* 'tepid.' It is not altogether clear where this came from, but it is generally assumed to be a derivative of the also now obsolete *lew* '(fairly) warm,' with perhaps a diminutive suffix. *Lew* goes back to an Old English *hlēow* 'warm,' a variant of which became modern English *lee* 'shelter.' It is related to Latin *calor* 'heat' (source of English *calorie*), *calidus* 'hot' (source of English *caudle, cauldron,* and *chowder*), and *calēre* 'be hot' (source of English *nonchalant*).

▶ calorie, cauldron, chowder, lee, nonchalant

**lull**   [14]   There are several words similar to *lull* in various Germanic languages, including Swedish *lulla* 'lull' and Dutch *lullen* 'prattle,' but it is not clear to what extent they are interconnected. But either individually or collectively they all no doubt go back ultimately to a repitition of the syllable *lu* or *la*, used in singing a baby to sleep. *Lullaby* was coined from *lull* in the 16th century, perhaps using the final syllable of *goodbye.*

**lumbago**   see LOIN
**lumbar**   see LOIN
**lumber**   [14]   Swedish has a dialectal verb *loma* 'move heavily,' which is the only clue we have to the antecedents of the otherwise mysterious English verb *lumber*. The noun, too, which first appears in the 16th century, is difficult to account for. In the absence of any other convincing candidates, it is presumed to have been derived from the verb (its earliest recorded sense is 'useless or inconvenient articles,' plausibly close to the verb; 'cut timber' did not emerge until the 17th century, in North America).

**luminous**   see LIGHT

**lump**   [13]   The origins of *lump* are obscure. It presumably emerged from an imperfectly recorded medieval Germanic substratum of words for 'coarse or shapeless things' (also represented perhaps by Low German *lump* 'coarse, heavy' and Dutch *lomp* 'rag'), but where this began is not known. The *lump* of *like it or lump it* [19] is a different word, of even more mysterious ancestry.

**lunar**   [17]   Latin *lūna* 'moon' came from an Indo-European base which also produced English *light* (not to mention a range of Latin 'light'-words, such as *lūx* and *lūmen*, which have given English *illustrate, lucid, luminous, lustre*, etc). It had two adjectival derivatives: *lūnāris*, which simply meant 'of the moon,' and was borrowed by English as *lunar*; and *lūnāticus*. This was originally used for 'living on the moon,' but subsequently came to employed in the sense 'crazy,' from the

notion that certain sorts of periodic madness were caused by the phases of the moon. English acquired it via Old French *lunatique* as *lunatic* [13].

▶ illustrate, light, luminous, lunatic, lustre

**lunch**   [16]   When *lunch* first appeared on the scene, at the end of the 16th century, it was used for a 'slice or hunk of food' ('He shall take bread and cut it into little lunches into a pan with cheese,' Richard Surfleet, *Country Farm* 1600). It appears to have been borrowed from Spanish *lonja* 'slice.' The roughly contemporaneous *luncheon*, probably just an arbitrary lengthening of *lunch*, came to be used in the early 17th century for a 'snack' (the link with 'hunk or piece of food' is obvious), and eventually for a 'light meal.' *Lunch* returned to the language in this sense at the beginning of the 19th century, as an abbreviation of *luncheon*.

**lung**   [OE]   Lungs, insubstantial air-filled sacs, got their name because they weigh so little. It comes ultimately from Indo-European *lnggh-*, a variant of which produced English *light* 'not heavy.' In prehistoric Germanic this became *lungg-*, which over the centuries has differentiated to German *lunge*, Dutch *long*, Swedish *lunga*, and English *lung*. The similarly motivated use of the word *lights* for 'lungs' dates from the 12th century; it is now restricted to 'animals' lungs used as food,' but it was formerly a general term.

▶ light

**lunge**   [18]   'Length' is the etymological notion underlying the word *lunge*. It comes ultimately from French *allonger* 'lengthen,' a verb based on the adjective *long* 'long.' Its fencing application derived, in French, from the idea of 'extending one's sword to strike a blow.' It was originally borrowed into English in the 17th century as *allonge*, but this was soon shortened to *lunge*.

**lupin**   see WOLF

**lurch**   English has two words *lurch*, both with rather obscure histories. The verb, 'stagger' [19], appears to come from an earlier *lee-lurch*, which in turn may have been an alteration of an 18th-century nautical term *lee-latch*, denoting 'drifting to leeward.' The *latch* element may have come from French *lâcher* 'let go.'

The *lurch* of *leave someone in the lurch* [16] originated as a term in backgammon, denoting a 'defeat,' 'low score,' or 'position of disadvantage.' It was borrowed from French *lourche*, which probably goes back to Middle High German *lurz* 'left,' hence 'wrong,' 'defeat.'

**lust**   [OE]   *Lust* is a Germanic word; it goes back to a prehistoric Germanic *lust-*, which as well as English *lust* had produced German *lust* (now used for 'pleasure' rather than 'desire'). Swedish *lust* 'inclination, pleasure, desire' was borrowed from Low German. From the same Germanic ancestor came the now archaic verb *list* 'desire,' source of *listless*. And it is possible that *lasciv-*

*ious* [15], acquired from late Latin *lascīviōsus*, may ultimately be related.

▶ lascivious, listless

**lustre**  see LIGHT

**luxury**  [14]  *Luxury* was originally a pejorative word, denoting 'sinful self-indulgence.' Not until the 17th century did it begin to acquire its positive modern connotations of costliness, comfort, and desirability. It came via Old French from Latin *luxuria* 'excess,' a derivative of *luxus* 'excess, abundance, extravagance.' The Latin derived verb *luxuriāre* 'grow profusely' has given English *luxuriant* [16] and *luxuriate* [17].

**lycanthropy**  see WOLF

**lychgate**  see LIKE

**lymph**  [17]  Despite its Greek appearance, *lymph* comes, perhaps via French, from Latin. Its distant ancestor was Latin *limpa* or *lumpa*, which meant 'water.' And that was the original sense of English *lymph*; not until the 18th century was it used for 'clear bodily fluid.' The alteration of the Latin word to *lympha* appears to have been due to association with Greek *numphḗ* 'nymph.'

English *limpid* [17] comes from Latin *limpidus* 'clear,' which may have been related to *limpa*.

**lynch**  [19]  This verb for 'punishing someone without an official trial' owes its existence to one William Lynch, a planter and justice of the peace of Pittsylvania, Virginia, USA, who at the beginning of the 19th century took it upon himself to set up unofficial tribunals to try suspects. His rough and ready method of administering justice was termed *Lynch's law*, later *lynch law*, and the verb followed in the 1830s.

**lynx**  [14]  The lynx, a member of the cat family, probably gets its name from its clear sight. It comes via Latin *lynx* from Greek *lúgx*, which probably derived from the same Indo-European root (*leuk*-) as produced English *light* and (via Latin) *illuminate, illustrate, lucid, luminous, lunar*, and *lustre*. A precedent for its application to 'seeing' is provided by Greek *leússein* 'see.'

▶ illustrate, light, ounce

# M

**macabre** [15] *Macabre* is now used generally for 'ghastly,' but that is a late 19th-century development. It originated in the very specific phrase *dance macabre*, which denoted a dance in which a figure representing death enticed people to dance with him until they dropped down dead. This was borrowed from French *danse macabre*, which was probably an alteration of an earlier *danse Macabé*. This in turn was a translation of medieval Latin *chorea Machabaeorum* 'dance of the Maccabees,' which is thought originally to have referred to a stylized representation of the slaughter of the Maccabees (a Jewish dynasty of biblical times) in a medieval miracle play.

**macaroni** [16] *Macaroni* was the earliest of the Italian pasta terms to be borrowed into English, and so it now differs more than any other from its original. When English acquired it, the Italian word was *maccaroni* (it came ultimately from late Greek *makaría* 'food made from barley'), but now it has become *maccheroni*.

The colloquial 18th-century application of *macaroni* to a 'dandy' is thought to have been an allusion to such people's supposed liking for foreign food. And the derivative *macaronic* [17], used for a sort of verse in which Latin words are mixed in with vernacular ones for comic effect, was originally coined in Italian, comparing the verse's crude mixture of languages with the homely hotchpotch of a macaroni dish.

*Macaroon* [17] comes from *macaron*, the French descendant of Italian *maccaroni*.

► macaroon

**machine** [16] The ultimate source of both *machine* and *mechanic* [14] was *makhos*, a Greek word meaning 'contrivance, means,' and related distantly to English *may* 'be able' and *might*. From it was derived *mēkhané*, whose Doric dialect form *mākhaná* passed into Latin as *māchina* 'engine, contrivance.' English acquired the word via Old French *machine*. Meanwhile *mēkhané* had spawned an adjectival derivative

*mēkhanikós*, which was in due course to find its way into English through Latin *mēchanicus*.

► mechanic

**macho** see MALE

**mackintosh** [19] The rubberized material from which this waterproof coat was originally made was invented in the early 1820s by the British chemist Charles Macintosh (1766–1843). His name (misspelled with a *k*) is first recorded as being applied to the coat in 1836. The abbreviated form *mac* (or occasionally *mack*) dates from around the turn of the 20th century.

**mad** [13] The underlying etymological meaning of *mad* is 'changed.' It goes back ultimately to Indo-European *\*moitó-*, a past participial form based on *\*moi-*, *\*mei-* 'change' (source also of Latin *mūtāre* 'change,' from which English gets *mutate*). Prehistoric Germanic inherited it, adding the collective prefix *\*ga-*to form *\*gamaithaz*, which passed into Old English as *gemād* 'insane.' From this was derived the verb *gemǣdan* 'madden,' whose past participle *gemǣded* eventually became a new adjective *gemǣdd*. By the Middle English period this had become *amadd*, and the reduced prefix *a-* eventually disappeared, leaving *mad*.

► mutate

**madrigal** [16] Etymologically, *madrigal* denotes a 'simple song, such as might just have sprung from the mother's womb.' It comes ultimately from medieval Latin *mātricālis* 'simple, primitive,' a derivative of Latin *mātrix* 'womb.' (And *mātrix* itself, source of English *matrix* [16] and *matriculate* [16] – etymologically 'put on a list,' from a later metaphorical use of the Latin noun for 'list' – was a derivative of *māter* 'mother.') *Mātricālis* passed into Italian as *madrigale*, where it was used as a noun for a 'simple unaccompanied song.'

► matriculate, matrix

**maenad** see MANIA

**magazine** [16] The original meaning of *magazine*, now disused, was 'storehouse.' The word comes, via French *magasin* and Italian *magazzino*, from Arabic *makhāzin*, the plural of *makhzan* 'store-house' (a derivative of the verb *khazana* 'store'). It was soon applied specifically to a 'store for arms,' and the modern sense 'journal,' first recorded in the early 18th century, goes back to a 17th-century metaphorical application to a 'storehouse of information.'

**maggot**   see MAWKISH

**magic**   [14]   Greek *mágos*, a word of Persian origin, meant 'sorcerer' (Latin borrowed it as *magus*, whose plural *magi* is used in English for the three 'Wise Men' who visited the infant Christ). From *mágos* was derived the adjective *magikós*. Its use in the phrase *magikḗ tékhnē* 'sorcerer's art' led eventually to *magikḗ* itself being regarded as a noun, and it passed into English via late Latin *magica* and Old French *magique*.

▶ magi

**magistrate**   [14]   By far the most widely used contributions of Latin *magister* 'master' to English are the heavily disguised *master* and *mister*, but more obvious derivatives have made the trip too. The late Latin adjective *magisterius* 'of a master,' modified through medieval Latin *magisteriālis*, has given us *magisterial* [17]; and *magistrātus*, source of English *magistrate*, denoted a 'state official' in ancient Rome.

▶ master, mister

**magma**   see MAKE

**magnanimous**   see MAGNITUDE

**magnate**   see MAGNITUDE

**magnet**   [15]   Greek *Mágnēs líthos* meant 'stone from Magnesia' – Magnesia being a region of Thessaly, Greece where much metal was obtained. It had two specific applications: to ore with magnetic properties, and to stone with a metallic sheen. And it was the first of these that has come down to English via Latin *magnēta* as *magnet*. English *magnesia* [14] comes from the same source, but it is not clear how it came to be applied (in the 18th century) to 'magnesium oxide,' for it originally denoted, in the rather vague terminology of the alchemists, a 'constituent of the philosopher's stone.' In the 17th century it was used for 'manganese' (and *manganese* [17] itself comes via French from Italian *manganese*, an alteration of medieval Latin *magnēsia*). And when the term *magnesium* [19] was introduced (at the suggestion of the chemist Sir Humphry Davy), it too at first denoted 'manganese.'

▶ magnesium, manganese

**magnitude**   [14]   *Magnitude* is one of a large family of words for which English is indebted to Latin *magnus* 'large.' This goes back to an Indo-European *meg-* or *megh-*, source also of Greek *mégas* 'large' (from which English gets the prefix *mega-*) and prehistoric Germanic *mikil-*, ancestor of English *much*. Apart from *magnitude*, English descendants of *magnus* include *magnanimous* [16] (etymologically 'large-

minded'), *magnate* [15] (a 'large' or 'important' person), *magnificat* [12] (from the first words of Luke 1:46, *Magnificat anima mea dominum* 'My soul doth magnify the lord,' where *magnificat* is the 3rd person present singular of Latin *magnificāre*, a derivative of *magnus* and source of English *magnify* [14]), *magnificent* [16] (etymologically 'doing great deeds'), and *magnum* [18] (the application to a double-sized wine bottle is a modern one). In addition *maxim* and *maximum* come from the superlative of *magnus* and *major* and *mayor* from its comparative, and *master* and the month-name *May* could also be related.

▶ magnum, major, maxim, mayor, much

**magpie**   [17]   The original name of the magpie was simply *pie*, which came via Old French from Latin *pīca*. This is thought to go back ultimately to Indo-European *spi-* or *pi-*, denoting 'pointedness,' in reference to its beak (the Latin masculine form, *pīcus*, was applied to a 'woodpecker'). *Pie* arrived in English as long ago as the 13th century, but not until the 16th century do we begin to find pet-forms of the name *Margaret* applied to it (one of the earliest was *maggot-pie*). By the 17th century *magpie* had become the institutionalized form.

Some etymologists consider that the term for the edible *pie* comes from the bird's name, based on a comparison of the miscellaneous contents of pies with the hoard of assorted stolen treasures supposedly accumulated by the magpie.

▶ pie

**maharajah**   see RAJ

**maiden**   [OE]   *Maiden* goes back to a prehistoric Germanic *magadiz* 'young (sexually inexperienced) woman,' which is also the source of German *mädchen* 'girl.' Its diminutive form, *magadīnam*, passed into Old English as *mægden*, the antecedent of modern English *maiden*. *Maid* is a 12th-century abbreviation.

**mail**   English has two extant words *mail*. The one meaning 'post' [13] goes back via Old French to Old High German *malha*, which meant 'bag, pouch.' That indeed was what the word originally denoted in English (and modern French *malle* is still used for a 'bag'). It was not until the 17th century that a specific application to a 'bag for carrying letters' emerged, and this was followed in the next century by the 'letters, etc so carried.'

*Mail* 'chain-armour' [14] comes via Old French *maille* 'mesh' from Latin *macula*, which originally meant 'spot, stain' (hence English *immaculate* [15], etymologically 'spotless'), but was tranferred to the 'holes in a net,' from their appearance of being spots or marks. The word *maquis*, made familiar in English during World War II as a term for the French resistance forces, means literally 'scrub, undergrowth' in French. It was borrowed from Italian *macchia*, a descendant of

Latin *macula*, whose literal sense 'spot' was applied metaphorically to 'bushes dotted over a hillside.'

English once had a third word *mail*, meaning 'payment, tax' [12]. It was borrowed from Old Norse *mál* 'speech, agreement.' It now survives only in *blackmail* [16].

► immaculate, maquis

**maim** [13] *Maim* and *mayhem* [15] are ultimately the same word. Both go back to a Vulgar Latin verb *\*mahagnāre* 'wound,' whose origins are unknown. This passed into Old French as *mahaignier* (whose probable Anglo-Norman derivative *\*mahangler* was the source of English *mangle* 'mutilate' [14]). *Mahaignier* became *mayner*, and passed into Middle English as *mayn*. But it also had a noun derivative, *mahaing* or *main*, which in due course became *mayhem*. This seems to have been borrowed into English twice. First, in the 14th century, as *maheym* or *maim* 'severe injury'; this has now died out, but has left its mark on the verb, which it has changed from *mayn* to *maim*. And second, in the 15th century, via Anglo-Norman, as *mayhem*.

► mayhem

**main** [OE] *Main* goes back to prehistoric Germanic *\*mag-* 'be able, have power' (source also of English *may* and *might*, and distantly related to *machine*). From it was descended Old English *mægen* 'strength.' This now survives as a noun only in the expression *with might and main*, but it was also used attributively in Old English to mean 'of large size, great,' and by the 13th century (helped along partly by the related Old Norse *megenn* or *megn* 'strong') it was being used as an adjective in its own right. At first it still meant just 'large,' but by the 15th century its modern sense 'chief' had evolved.

► may, might

**maintain** [13] Etymologically, *maintain* means 'hold in the hand.' It comes via Old French *maintenir* from Vulgar Latin *\*manūtenēre* 'support,' a compound verb formed from *manū*, the ablative case of *manus* 'hand,' and *tenēre* 'hold.' The derivative *maintenance* [14] comes from Old French.

► maintenance, manual, tenant

**maisonette** SEE MANOR

**major** [16] Latin *mājor* 'larger' was the comparative form of *magnus* 'large,' from which English gets *magnitude, magnum* etc (in early Latin it was *\*māgjōs*). English originally acquired it as an adjective. Its noun use, for an army officer, followed in the 17th century. This represented a borrowing from French *major*, which was short for *sergent-major* (in those days, 'sergeant major' was a more elevated rank than it is today). The derivative *majority* [16] comes via French *majorité* from medieval Latin *mājōritās*.

*Mayor* comes from Latin *mājor*, routed via Old French.

► magnitude, magnum, mayor

**make** [OE] *Make* probably goes back ultimately to an Indo-European base *\*mag-* denoting 'kneading' (also the source of Greek *mágma* 'salve made by kneading,' from which English gets *magma* [15]). A prehistoric Germanic descendant was *\*mako-* (source of English *match* 'go together'). From this was derived the West Germanic verb *\*makōjan*, which over the centuries differentiated into German *machen*, Dutch *maken*, and English *make*. *Make* was not a particularly common verb in Old English (*gewyrcan*, ancestor of modern English *work*, was the most usual way of expressing the notion 'make'), but in the Middle English period its use proliferated.

► magma, match

**makeshift** SEE SHIFT

**malachite** SEE MAUVE

**malady** SEE MALIGN

**malaise** SEE MALIGN

**malapropism** [19] English owes the word *malapropism* to Mrs Malaprop, a character in Richard Sheridan's play *The Rivals* 1775 whose grandiloquent impulses led her to use slightly (but ludicrously) the wrong word: amongst the most familiar of her errors are 'contagious countries' (for *contiguous*), 'a supercilious knowledge in accounts' (for *superficial*), and 'as headstrong as an allegory on the banks of the Nile.' Sheridan based the name on *malapropos* 'inappropriate' [17], an anglicization of French *mal à propos*, literally 'badly to the purpose' (on *mal*, see MALIGN).

► malign, propose

**malaria** [18] The original English term for an 'attack of malarial fever' was *ague*. The word *malaria* did not come on the scene until the mid-18th century. It was borrowed from Italian *mal' aria*, a conflation of *mala aria*, literally 'bad air.' This was an allusion to the former belief that malaria was caused by foul air, and particularly by vapours given off by swamps.

► air, malign

**male** [14] The Latin word for 'male' was *masculus* (from which of course English gets *masculine* [14]). It passed into Old French as *masle*, which later became *male* – hence English *male*. The Spanish descendant of *masculus* is *macho*, which means 'virile' as well as simply 'male,' and has given English *macho* [20] and the derivative *machismo* [20]. Another close relative is probably *mallard*, which seems to mean etymologically 'male bird.'

*Female*, incidentally, despite its similarity, is not etymologically related to *male*, although the two have converged formally owing to their semantic closeness.

► macho, mallard, masculine

**malic**   see POMEGRANATE

**malign**   [14]  *Malign* comes, probably via Old French, from Latin *malignus* 'wicked.' This was derived from *malus* 'bad,' a word of unknown origin (some have tried to link it with English *small*). *Malus* is of course the starting point for a wide range of other English words, including *malady* [13] (ultimately from Vulgar Latin *\*male habitus* 'in bad condition'); *malaise* [18] (which originated in Old French as a conflation of *mal aise* 'bad ease'); *malapropism*; *malaria*; *malediction* [15] (etymologically 'evil saying'); *malevolent* [16] (literally 'wishing evil'); *malice* [13] (from Latin *malitia*, a derivative of *malus*); and *malingerer* [18] (from French *malingre*, which may have been a compound of *mal-* and *haingre* 'weak'). *Malignant* [16] comes from the present participle of Latin *malignāre* 'act with malice,' a verb derived from *malignus*.

▶ malady, malaise, malaria, malignant, malingerer

**mall**   see MALLET

**mallard**   [14]  Etymologically, a *mallard* seems to be a 'male bird.' It comes from Old French *mallart*, which was probably a development of an earlier *\*maslart*, a derivative of *masle* 'male' (source of English *male*). It was originally used for the 'male of the wild duck,' but now it denotes either sex of the species (*Anas platyrhynchos*).

▶ male

**mallet**   [15]  Latin *malleus* meant 'hammer' (it may be related to Latin *molere* 'grind,' and to Russian *mólot* and Polish *młot* 'hammer'). It passed into Old French as *mail*, of which the derivative *maillet* eventually reached English as *mallet*. *Mail* itself was borrowed into English as *maul* 'hammer' [13], but it now survives only as a verb (which originally meant 'hit with a hammer').

The Latin verb derived from *malleus* was *malleāre* 'hit with a hammer,' from which ultimately English gets *malleable* [14]. And the Italian descendant of *malleus*, *maglio*, was combined with a word for 'ball,' *palla*, to form the name of a croquet-like game, *pallamaglio*; via French this passed into English as *pall-mall* [17], remembered in the London street-names *Pall Mall* and *The Mall* (whence the use of *mall* [18] for a 'walkway' or 'promenade,' and latterly for a 'shopping precinct').

▶ mall, malleable, maul, pall-mall

**malt**   [OE]  *Malt* goes back to prehistoric Germanic *\*malt-*, a variant of which produced English *melt*. Hence it seems to denote etymologically the 'softening' of the barley or other grain by steeping it in water preparatory to germinating it for use in brewing (German *malz* means 'soft' as well as 'malt').

▶ melt

**mammal**   [19]  Etymologically, *mammal* denotes an 'animal that suckles its young.' The word is a derivative of *mammalia* [18], the term for that whole class of animals, coined by the Swedish naturalist Linnaeus from Latin *mammālis* 'of the breast.' This in turn was based on *mamma* 'mother, breast,' which has been traced back to a prehistoric Indo-European *\*mammā*. There are obvious links with 'mother'-terms in other languages, such as Greek *mámmē*, French *maman*, Italian *mamma*, Russian *mama*, Welsh *mam*, and English *mamma* and *mummy*, but whether a sustained chain of descent and borrowing is involved, or simply parallel formation based on the syllable *ma*, imitative of the sound of a suckling baby, is not clear.

*Mammary* [17] is an English derivative of Latin *mamma*, in the sense 'breast.'

▶ mamma, mammary, mummy

**mammoth**   [18]  *Mammoth* is a Russian contribution to English. The word was borrowed from early modern Russian *mammot'*, an adaptation of Tatar *mamont* 'earth' (the reason for the animal being so named is that the first remains of mammoths to be found were dug out of the frozen soil of Siberia). The adjectival use of the word for 'huge' dates from the early 19th century ('The dancing very bad; the performers all had mammoth legs,' private diary of Sir Robert Wilson, 1814).

**man**   [OE]  *Man* is a widespread Germanic word (with relatives in German *mann* 'man' and *mensch* 'person,' Dutch and Swedish *man* 'man,' Danish *mand* 'man,' and Swedish *menniska* 'person'), and connections have even been found outside Germanic (Sanskrit, for instance, had *mánu-* 'man'). But no decisive evidence has been found for an ultimate Indo-European source. Among the suggestions put forward have been links with a base *\*men-* 'think' or 'breathe,' or with Latin *manus* 'hand.'

The etymologically primary sense of the word is 'human being, person,' and that is what it generally meant in Old English: the sexes were generally distinguished by *wer* 'man' (which survives probably in *werewolf* and is related to *world*) and *wīf* (source of modern English *wife*) or *cwene* 'woman.' But during the Middle English and early modern English periods 'male person' gradually came to the fore, and today 'person' is decidedly on the decline (helped on its way by those who feel that the usage discriminates against women). *Woman* originated in Old English as a compound of *wīf* 'woman, female' and *man* 'person.'

*Manikin* [17] was borrowed from Dutch *manneken*, a diminutive form of *man* 'man'; and *mannequin* [18] is the same word acquired via French.

▶ manikin, mannequin

**manacle**   see MANUAL

**manage**   [16] Etymologically, *manage* means 'handle.' It comes via Italian *maneggiare* 'control a horse' from Vulgar Latin *manidiare*, a derivative of Latin *manus* 'hand.' To begin with it was used in the context of 'horse-training' in English, but eventually the French form *manège* took over in this sense. The more general sense 'handle, control' is of virtually equal antiquity in English, though.
▶ manual

**manciple**   see EMANCIPATE

**mandarin**   [16] Although it refers to a Chinese official, *mandarin* is not a Chinese word. Sanskrit *mantrin* meant 'counsellor' (it was a derivative of *mantra* 'counsel,' which itself was based on *man* 'think,' a distant relative of English *mind*). Its Hindi descendant *mantrī* passed into English via Malay *mēteri* and Portuguese *mandarin*. The word's application to a variety of small loose-skinned orange, which dates in English from the 19th century, was inspired by the yellow robes worn by mandarins.
▶ mind

**mandate**   [16] Etymologically, *mandate* means 'give one's hand.' It comes from *mandātum* (source also of English *maundy*), a noun use of the past participle of Latin *mandāre* 'commit, command.' This verb was formed by blending *manus* 'hand' and *dāre* 'give.' English verbs derived from *mandāre* are *command*, *commend*, *demand*, and *remand*.
▶ command, commend, date, demand, donation, manual, maundy, remand

**mandolin**   see BANJO

**mandrake**   [14] The mandrake is a Mediterranean plant of the potato family with medicinal uses. Its name is an alteration of *mandragora*, which goes back via Latin to Greek *mandragóras*, a word probably of non-Indo-European origin. The change arose owing to an association with *man* (the mandrake has a large forked root which supposedly resembles a human being) and *drake* 'dragon' (an allusion to the root's supposedly magical properties).

**mandrill**   see DRILL

**mane**   [OE] *Mane* goes back to a prehistoric Germanic *manō*, which also produced German *mähne* and Dutch *mane*. Related forms such as Swedish *manke* 'neck,' Irish *muin* 'nape of the neck,' archaic Welsh *mwn* 'neck,' Latin *monīle* 'necklace,' and Sanskrit *manyā-* 'nape of the neck' suggest that historically 'neck' is the primary, 'neck-hair' a secondary meaning of this word-family. It has been speculated that it goes back ultimately to Indo-European *men-* 'project' (source of English *eminent*, *prominent*, etc).

**manganese**   see MAGNET

**manger**   [14] Etymologically, a *manger* is an 'eater,' or 'feeding place.' It comes from Old French *mangeoire*, a descendant of Vulgar Latin *mandūcātōria*. This was derived from Latin *mandūcāre* 'chew,' which in modern French has become *manger* 'eat'; the use of this as a noun, meaning 'edible substance,' forms the ultimate basis of English *blancmange*, literally 'white food.' From a parallel source comes the name of the skin disease *mange* [14], an allusion to its 'eating' or irritating the skin; *mangy* is a 16th-century derivative.
▶ blancmange, mange

**mangle**   see MAIM

**mania**   [14] Greek *maníā* meant 'madness.' It goes back ultimately to Indo-European *mn-*, *men-* 'think,' the same source as produced English *mind*. It reached English via late Latin *mania*. Of its derivatives, *maniac* [17] comes from late Greek *maniakós*, but *manic* [20] is an English formation. Closely related to *maníā* was the Greek verb *maínesthai* 'be mad'; from it was derived *mainás*, the name for a fanatical female follower of Dionysus, which English has adopted via Latin as *maenad* [16].
▶ maenad, manic, mind

**manicure**   see MANUAL

**manifest**   [14] That which is *manifest* is etymologically 'grasped by the hand' – that is, 'palpable, obvious.' The word comes via Old French from Latin *manifestus*. This was a later form of *manufestus*, a compound formed from *manus* 'hand' and *festus* 'gripped.' *Manifesto* [17] is a borrowing from Italian; it originally meant 'evidence, proof,' and only gradually developed to the present-day 'political statement.'
▶ manifesto, manual

**manifold**   see MANY

**manikin**   see MAN

**manipulate**   see MANUAL

**manna**   [OE] *Manna* was introduced into Old English by Latin, which got it from Aramaic *mannā*. This was a derivative of Hebrew *mān*, one of a family of Semitic words denoting an edible substance exuded by a sort of tamarisk tree that grows in the Sinai desert.

**mannequin**   see MAN

**manner**   [12] Etymologically, a *manner* is a method of 'handling' something. It comes via Anglo-Norman *manere* from Vulgar Latin *manuāria* 'way of handling.' This was a noun use of the Latin adjective *manuārius* 'of the hand,' a derivative of *manus* 'hand.' The adoption of *manner* as a conventional translation of Latin *modus* 'method' helped to establish the far broader range of meanings it has today.
▶ manual

**manoeuvre** [18] Essentially *manoeuvre* and *manure* [14] are the same word. Both go back ultimately to a Latin expression denoting 'manual labour.' This was *manū operārī*, literally 'work with the hand.' It was lexicalized in medieval Latin as the verb *manuoperāre*, and this passed into Old French as *manovrer*. Middle English took it over via Anglo-Norman *mainoverer* as *maynoyre* or *manour*, which at first was used for 'administer land,' and more specifically 'cultivate land.' Not until the mid 16th century did the noun *manure*, denoting 'dung spread in cultivating the land,' emerge. Meanwhile Old French *manovrer* developed into modern French *manoeuvrer*, which English borrowed in the 18th century.

▶ manual, manure, operate

**manor** [13] Etymologically, a *manor* is a place where one 'stays' or 'dwells.' It goes back ultimately to the Latin verb *manēre* 'remain, stay,' which in postclassical times was used for 'dwell, live.' Its Old French descendant *maneir* came to be used as a noun, meaning 'dwelling place.' This passed into English via Anglo-Norman *maner*, and was originally used for 'country house.' In the 14th century it came to be incorporated into the terminology of the feudal system, from which its present-day meanings come.

The past participial stem of *manēre* was *māns-*, from which was derived the Latin noun *mānsiō* 'place to stay.' Old French took this over in two forms: *maison* (whence the modern French word for 'house,' source of English *maisonette* [19]) and *mansion*. English borrowed this as *mansion* [14], and originally used it for 'place of abode, house.' The present-day connotations of a 'large stately house' did not emerge until as recently as the 19th century.

*Manse* [15] comes from the same ultimate source, as do *menagerie* [18] (whose immediate French source originally denoted the 'management of domestic animals'), *permanent*, and *remain*.

▶ maisonette, manse, mansion, menagerie, permanent, remain

**mantis** SEE NECROMANCY

**mantle** [13] *Mantle* comes via Old French *mantel* from Latin *mantellum* 'cloak,' a word of uncertain (possibly Celtic) origin. Related forms to find their way into English from other languages include *mantilla* [18] (a Spanish diminutive of *manta* 'cape,' which came from Latin *mantus*, a shortened form of *mantellum*) and *mantua*, a term used in the 17th and 18th centuries for a woman's loose gown, which arose from the association of modern French *manteau* with the name of the Italian city of Mantua, once famous for its silks. And the *mantel* [15] of *mantelpiece* is a variant spelling of *mantle*.

▶ mantel

**manual** [15] The Latin word for 'hand' was *manus* (it came from an Indo-European base *\*mən-*, and

its modern descendants include French *main*, Italian and Spanish *mano*, and Rumanian *mîna*). It has contributed generously to English vocabulary, and *manual* (from the Latin adjective *manuālis*) is among its least heavily disguised derivatives. Others include *amanuensis* [17] (from the Latin phrase *servus ā manū* 'servant at hand(writing),' hence 'secretary'); *emancipate*; *manacle* [14] (from Latin *manicula* 'little hand'); *manage*; *mandate* (and its relatives *command*, *demand*, etc); *manicure* [19]; *manifest*; *manipulate* [19] (from Latin *manipulus* 'handful'); *manner*; *manoeuvre*; *manufacture* [16] (ultimately from Latin *manū factum* 'made by hand'); *manure*; *manuscript* [16] (in Latin literally 'written by hand'); *mastiff*; and possibly *masturbate* [17], which comes from Latin *masturbārī*, perhaps a lexicalization of the phrase *manū stuprāre* 'defile with the hand.'

▶ amanuensis, command, demand, emancipate, manacle, manage, mandate, manifest, manipulate, manner, manoeuvre, manure, mastiff, masturbate, maundy, remand

**manure** SEE MANOEUVRE

**many** [OE] *Many* goes back ultimately to Indo-European *\*monogho-*, *\*menogho-*, which also produced Russian *mnogij* 'many' and Welsh *mynych* 'often.' From it was descended prehistoric Germanic *\*managaz*, *\*manigaz*, which have differentiated into German *manch*, Dutch *menig*, Swedish *många*, Danish *mange*, and English *many*. The pronunciation /meni/ dates from the 13th century; it perhaps arose from association with the unrelated *any*. The derived *manifold* [OE] preserves the original pronunciation.

▶ manifold

**map** [16] *Map* is closely related to *apron* and *napkin*. It comes from Latin *mappa*, which denoted a 'cloth,' 'towel,' 'sheet,' 'table-cloth,' etc. This was used in the expression *mappa mundī*, literally 'sheet of the world,' which referred to a graphical representation of the earth's surface – a 'map,' in other words.

▶ apron, napkin

**maquis** [20] The French word *maquis* literally means 'undergrowth, scrub,' and its use for the resistance fighters who opposed German occupation during World War II is an allusion to their hide-outs in scrubby country. It is a borrowing, via Corsica, of Italian *macchia*. This originally meant 'spot' (it came from Latin *macula* 'spot, stain,' source of English *immaculate* and *mail* 'armour'), but was transferred metaphorically to a 'bush or thicket seen from the distance as a spot on a hillside.'

▶ immaculate, mail

**marathon** [19] When the Greek army defeated the Persians at Marathon, on the northeast coast of Attica, in 490BC, the runner Pheidippides was dispatched to bring the good news to Athens. With the instigation of the modern Olympic games in Athens in 1896, a long-distance race was introduced to commemorate his feat, run over a course supposedly equal in distance to the journey from Marathon to Athens – 26 miles 385 yards.

**marble**   [12]   Greek *mármaros*, a word of unknown origin, denoted to begin with 'any hard stone,' but association with the verb *marmaírein* 'shine' led to a particular application to 'marble.' Latin took it over as *marmor*, and it passed into Old French as *marbre*. Here, by a process known as dissimilation, in which one of two similar sounds is replaced by a different one, *marbre* became *marble* – whence English *marble*. The use of the word for the little ball with which the game of 'marbles' is played dates from the late 17th century.

**march**   English has three words *march*. The commonest is also the most recent: *march* 'walk as a soldier' [16]. Etymologically, this means virtually 'trample down.' It comes via French *marcher* from Gallo-Roman *\*marcāre*, a verb derived from late Latin *marcus* 'hammer.' The month-name *March* [12] goes back via Old French to Latin *Martius*, literally the 'month of Mars, the god of war' (Mars also gave English *martial*). *March* 'boundary' [13] has now almost died out, apart from its use in the plural ('the Marches') as a geographical name. It comes via Old French *marche* from medieval Latin *marca* (source also of *marquis* and *marchioness*); and *marca* in turn goes back through Frankish *\*marka* to prehistoric Germanic *\*markō*, source of English *mark*.

▶ martial / mark, marquis

**mare**   see MARSHAL

**margarine**   [19]   Margarine was invented in 1869 by the French food technologist Hippolyte Mège-Mouriès. Its name was based on *margaric acid*, a term coined by the French biochemist Michel-Eugène Chevreuil for a fatty acid which he believed to be one of the constituents of animal fats (the earliest margarine was made from clarified beef fat). He derived it from Greek *margarítēs* 'pearl' (source also of English *marguerite* [19], and of the names *Margaret* and *Margot*), an allusion to the pearly lustre of the acid crystals. The abbreviation *marge* dates from the 1920s.

▶ marguerite

**margin**   [14]   *Margin* comes from *margin-*, the stem form of Latin *margō* 'margin.' This appears to go back to the same ultimate source as English *mark* (which originally meant 'boundary'). The now archaic synonym *marge* [15] was borrowed from the Latin word's French descendant.

▶ march, mark

**marigold**   [14]   The Old English term for this yellow-to-orange-flowered plant was *golde*, which was presumably derived from *gold*, in allusion to the colour. In the Middle Ages the name *Mary* (no doubt a refer-

ence to the Virgin Mary) was added to it. Another English word based ultimately on *Mary* is *marionette* [17], which was borrowed from a French word derived from the diminutive form *Marion*.

**marinade**   [17]   Etymologically, to put food in a *marinade* is virtually to dunk it in the 'sea'; for the word comes via French from Spanish *marinada*, a derivative of *marina* 'of the sea.' It originally signified strictly a 'brine pickle' (hence the reference to the sea), and only gradually broadened out to include vinegar and other preservatives. The related verb *marinate* [17] comes from French *mariner* or Italian *marinare*.

▶ marine

**marine**   [15]   The Latin word for 'sea' was *mare* (borrowed into English in the 19th century as a term for any of the sea-like dark areas on the moon). It goes back to Indo-European *\*mori-*, *\*mari-*, which also produced Russian *more* 'sea,' Welsh *mor* 'sea,' and English *mere* 'lake' (the *mer-* of *mermaid*). The Romance-language terms for 'sea' (French *mer*, Italian and Rumanian *mare*, and Spanish *mar*) are descended from it. And its derived adjective, *marīnus*, has given English *marine* (and *mariner* [13]). *Maritime* [16] is another derivative. *Marina* [19] was borrowed from Italian.

▶ marinade, maritime, mere

**mark**   English has two words *mark*, although they may be ultimately related. *Mark* 'sign, trace' [OE] goes back to a prehistoric Germanic *\*markō*. This seems originally to have denoted 'boundary' (that is what Old English *mearc* meant, and related forms such as *march* 'border' and *margin* still bear witness to it), but the notion of a 'sign denoting a boundary' seems to have led early on to the development of the word's main present-day sense. *Remark* is closely related, as are *marquis* and *marchioness*, and *marquetry* [16], borrowed from French *marqueterie*, a derivative of *marque* 'mark,' denotes etymologically work that is 'marked' with patterns.

   *Mark* 'coin' [OE] comes from medieval Latin *marcus* or *marca*, which may well derive ultimately from the ancestor of *mark* 'sign, trace' (its etymological meaning being 'mark on a piece of metal, constituting a coin').

▶ march, margin, marquetry, marquis, remark

**market**   [12]   The Latin word for 'goods to be sold' was *merx* (source of English *commerce*, *merchant*, and *mercury*). From it was derived the verb *mercārī* 'buy,' and its past participle produced the noun *mercātus* 'trade, market.' In Vulgar Latin this became *\*marcātus*, which was adopted into early Middle English as *market*. The now seldom used synonym *mart* [15] comes from early modern Dutch *mart*, a variant of *markt* 'market.'

▶ commerce, mart, merchant, mercury

**marmalade** [16] The word *marmalade* originally denoted 'quince jam.' It comes via French from Portuguese *marmelada*, a derivative of *marmelo* 'quince.' And *marmelo* goes back via Latin *melimēlum* to Greek *melímēlon*, a term meaning literally 'honey-apple' which was applied to the fruit of an apple tree grafted on to a quince (the second element, *melon* 'apple,' is the source of English *melon*). Not until the 17th century was *marmalade* used for a preserve made from citrus fruits.

▶ melon

**marmot** see MOUSE

**maroon** English has two distinct and completely unrelated words *maroon*. The one denoting 'brownish red' and 'firework' [16] has had a chequered semantic history, as its present-day diversity of meanings suggests. It comes ultimately from medieval Greek *máraon* 'sweet chestnut,' and reached English via Italian *marrone* and French *marron* (as in *marrons glacés*). It was originally used for 'chestnut' in English too, but that sense died out in the early 18th century, leaving behind the colour term (an allusion to the reddish brown of the chestnut's inner shell) and 'firework, exploding projectile' (perhaps a reference to the shape of such devices).

*Maroon* 'abandon' [17] comes from the noun *maroon*. This originally meant 'runaway slave,' and comes via French from American Spanish *cimarron*. The most widely accepted derivation of this is that it was based on Spanish *cima* 'summit,' a descendant of Latin *cȳma* 'sprout,' and that it thus denotes etymologically 'one who lives on the mountain tops.'

**marquetry** see MARK

**marquis** [14] Etymologically, a *marquis* is a lord of the 'marches' or borderlands. The word comes from Old French *marquis*, an alteration of an earlier *marchis*. This was a derivative of medieval Latin *marca* 'border, frontier,' source of archaic English *march* 'border.' The feminine form *marchioness* [16] comes from medieval Latin *marchionissa*, a derivative of *marchiō* 'lord of the marches,' which likewise was based on *marca*.

The French feminine form of *marquis* is *marquise*. This was borrowed into English in the 17th century and used for a 'large tent.' It soon came to be misanalysed as a plural form, and so a new 'singular,' *marquee*, was born.

▶ march, mark, marquee

**marry** [13] Latin *marītus* meant 'husband' (it may go back to an Indo-European *mer-, *mor-, which meant something like 'young person' – Lithuanian has the related *marti* 'bride' – and in that case would denote etymologically 'man who has been provided with a young woman as a bride'). From it was derived the verb *marītāre* 'marry,' which passed into English via Old

French *marier*. *Marriage* [13] likewise comes from Old French.

**marsh** [OE] The immediate origin of *marsh* is Germanic: it comes from a prehistoric West Germanic *marisk-, which also produced German *marsch* and Dutch *marsk*. This was probably a derivative of Germanic *mari 'sea' (source of English *mere* 'lake'), whose relatives included Latin *mare* 'sea' (source of English *marine*).

▶ marine, mere

**marshal** [13] Etymologically, a *marshal* is a 'horse-servant.' The word goes back to a prehistoric Germanic *markhaskalkaz 'groom,' a compound based on *markhaz 'horse' (source of English *mare* [OE]) and *skalkaz 'servant.' This was borrowed into late Latin as *mariscalcus*, and passed from there via Old French *mareschal* into English. In the course of its journey its status gradually rose, and by the time it reached English it denoted a 'high officer of state.'

▶ mare

**mart** see MARKET

**martial** [14] Latin *mārtiālis* denoted 'of Mars, the god of war' (his name goes back to an early Latin *Māvors*). In its journey via Old French to English it acquired the meaning 'of war.' The application of the name *Mars* to the red planet dates back to Roman times, as does the adjective *Martian* [14] (from Latin *Mārtiānus*), which in modern English refers exclusively to the astronomical Mars. The god also gave his name to the first month of the Roman calendar – whence English *March*.

▶ Mars

**martinet** [17] The word *martinet* comes from the name of Jean Martinet, a 17th-century French army officer who invented a system of drill. Indeed, it was as the term for this new drill that *martinet* was first used in English ('What, d'ye find fault with Martinet? . . . 'tis the best exercise in the World,' William Wycherley, *The Plain-Dealer* 1676); not until the 18th century did the figurative sense 'rigid disciplinarian' emerge.

**martyr** [OE] Etymologically, a *martyr* is a 'witness' – that was the original meaning of Greek *mártur*, which came ultimately from Indo-European *mer 're-member' (source of English *memory, mourn, remember*, etc). In Christian usage, the notion of someone dying as a 'witness' to their faith led to the application of *mártur* to 'martyr,' and it was in this sense that it passed via Latin *martyr* into Old English.

▶ memory, mourn, remember

**marvel** see MIRROR

**marzipan** [19] If the early 20th-century etymologist Kluyver is to be believed, the word *marzipan* has an incredibly convoluted history. According to him, it started life as Arabic *mawthabān*, which meant literally 'king who sits still.' This was applied by the Saracens to a medieval Venetian coin which had a figure of the seated Christ on it. In the Italian dialect of Venice the word became *matapan*, and eventually, in general Italian *marzapane*; and its signification supposedly progressed from the 'coin' via 'measure of weight or capacity,' 'box of such capacity,' and 'such a box containing confectionery' to 'contents of such a box.' Whether or not this tale is true, what is generally agreed is that *marzapane* and its relatives in other languages (such as early modern French *marcepain*) entered English in the 16th century, and from the confusion of forms the consensus spelling *marchpane* emerged. This remained the standard English word for 'marzipan' until the 19th century, when *marzipan* was borrowed from German; this was an alteration of Italian *marzapane*, based on the misconception that it came from Latin *marci pānis* 'Mark's bread.'

## masculine   see MALE

## mask   [16]   *Mask* may be of Arabic origin. The word *maskharah* 'buffoon' has been postulated as the source of Italian *maschera*, from which, via French *masque*, English got *mask*. In modern English, the word is largely restricted to 'face covering,' but a range of other senses developed during the 16th and 17th centuries, including 'masked ball' and 'allegorical dramatic entertainment,' which are now lumped together under the French spelling *masque*. The derivative *masquerade* [16] was borrowed from French *mascarade*, with the spelling of *masque* later grafted on to it.

▶ masque, masquerade

## masochism   [19]   The term *masochism* was based on the name of Leopold von Sacher-Masoch (1836–95), an Austrian novelist who used the theme of gaining sexual gratification from the infliction of pain on oneself in his writings.

## mason   [13]   English originally acquired *mason* in the form *machun*, from Anglo-Norman. In the 14th century it was remodelled as *masoun* or *mason* on the basis of Old French *masson*. The derivation of this is disputed. Some etymologists claim that it comes via a Vulgar Latin *matiō* from prehistoric Germanic *mattjon* (source of German *steinmetz* 'stonemason'), but an alternative theory traces it back to a Frankish *makjo*, a derivative of *makōn* 'make.'

## masquerade   see MASK

## mass   English has two distinct words *mass*. The one meaning 'Eucharist' [OE] comes from late Latin *missa*, a noun use of the feminine past participle of *mittere* 'send' (source of English *admit, commit, dismiss, mission*, etc) possibly arising from *Ite, missa est* 'Go, it is the dismissal,' the last words of the Latin Eucharist service.

*Mass* 'amount of matter' [14] comes via Old French *masse* and Latin *massa* from Greek *maza* 'barley cake,'

hence 'lump, mass.' The derivative *massive* [15] goes back ultimately to Vulgar Latin *massīceus*. A possible relative is *massage* [19], a borrowing from French. It was a derivative of *masser* 'massage,' which may have been acquired from Portuguese *amassar* 'knead,' a verb based on *massa* 'mass, dough.'

▶ admit, commit, dismiss, mission, transmit / massage, massive

## master   [OE]   The Latin word for 'master, chief' was *magister* (which is generally assumed to have been based on the root of Latin *magis* 'more' and *magnus* 'big,' source of English *magnify, magnitude*, etc). Its more obvious English descendants include *magistrate* and *magisterial*, and indeed English originally acquired *magister* itself in the 10th century in the form *mægister*, but over the years (partly under the influence of Old French *maistre*) this developed to *master*.

The feminine counterpart *mistress* [14] was borrowed from Old French *maistresse*, a form maintained in English for some time. The alteration of *mais-* to *mis-* began in the 15th century, due probably to the weakly-stressed use of the word as a title (a phenomenon also responsible for the emergence of *mister* [16] from *master*). The abbreviated *miss* followed in the 17th century.

▶ magistrate, magnitude, magnum, miss, mister, mistress

## mastiff   [14]   Despite its rather fierce reputation, a *mastiff* may etymologically be a 'tamed' dog, a dog 'accustomed to the hand.' The word seems to have come into the language as an alteration of Old French *mastin*, which was a descendant of the Vulgar Latin *mānsuētīnus* 'tame.' This in turn went back to Latin *mānsuētus*, a compound adjective based on *manus* 'hand' and *suēscere* 'accustom.'

▶ manual

## masturbate   see MANUAL

## mat   English has two distinct words *mat*. The one meaning 'small carpet' [OE] is ultimately of Latin origin (*matta*), but it found its way into the West Germanic group of languages in prehistoric times, and has produced German *matte* and Dutch *mat* as well as English *mat*. *Mat* (or *matt*) meaning 'dull' [17] comes from French *mat* 'dead,' which is also the source of the chess term *mate*.

▶ mate

## matador   see MATE

## match   There are two unrelated words *match* in English, of which the older is 'counterpart' [OE]. This goes back to an Old English *gemæcca* 'mate,' whose ancestry can be traced to a prehistoric *gamakjon*, a word based on the collective prefix *ga-* and *mak-* 'fit' (source of English *make*). Its etymological meaning is thus 'fitting well together.' The use of the word as a verb emerged in the 14th century. *Match* 'ignitable stick'

[14] originally meant 'wick.' It comes via Old French *meiche* from Latin *myxa* 'lamp nozzle.' The first record of its modern use for 'ignitable stick' comes from 1831 (the synonymous *lucifer* is exactly contemporary, but had virtually died out by the end of the 19th century).

▶ make

**mate** [14] *Mate* 'friend' and *mate* the chess term are two distinct words. The former was borrowed from Middle Low German *mate* or *gemate* 'companion' (source also of Dutch *maat*), which goes back to a prehistoric West Germanic *\*gamaton*. This was formed from the collective prefix *\*ga-* and *\*mat-* 'measure,' which was also the source of English *meat*; so etymologically *mate* (like *companion*) is 'someone you eat with or share your food with.'

The chess term *mate* comes from Old French *mat* 'dead.' This was short for *eschec mat* (source of English *checkmate*), which comes from Persian *shāh māt* 'the king is dead.' Persian *māt* 'dead' also contributed the verb *matar* 'kill' to Spanish, from which was derived *matador* [17], literally 'killer.'

▶ meat / mat, matador, matte

**material** [14] Etymologically, *material* is simply a derivative of *matter*. It comes via Old French *materiel* from late Latin *māteriālis*, a derivative of Latin *māteria* 'matter' (source of English *matter*). The modern French form of the word was reborrowed as *materiel* 'military equipment' [19].

▶ materiel, matter

**maternal** [15] *Maternal* and *maternity* [17] are the central English representatives of the Romance-language branch of the great Indo-European 'mother' word-family. Both go back to Latin *māter* 'mother' (source of French *mère* and Italian and Spanish *madre*), whose derived adjective *māternus* reached English via Old French *maternel*. Other English words that come ultimately from *māter* include *material* and *matter*, *matrix* [16] (from which also come *madrigal* and *matriculate* [16], etymologically 'enter on a matrix or list'), and *matrimony* [14].

▶ mother

**mathematics** [16] Etymologically, *mathematics* means 'something learned.' Its ultimate source was the Greek verb *manthánein* 'learn,' which came from the same Indo-European base (*\*men-*, *\*mon-*, *\*mn-* 'think') as produced English *memory* and *mind*. Its stem form *math-* served as a basis of a noun *máthēma* 'science,' whose derived adjective *mathēmatikós* passed via Latin *mathēmaticus* and Old French *mathematique* into English as *mathematic*, now superseded by the contemporary *mathematical* [16]. *Mathematics* probably comes from French *les mathématiques*, a rendering of the Latin plural noun *mathēmatica*. From earliest times the notion of 'science' was bound up with that of 'numerical reasoning,'

and when *mathematics* reached English it was still being used for various scientific disciplines that involved geometrical calculation, such as astronomy and physics, but gradually over the centuries it has been narrowed down to a cover term for the abstract numerical sciences such as arithmetic, algebra, and geometry.

The abbreviated form *maths* dates from the early 20th century, the preferred American form *math* from the late 19th century.

The original meaning of the word's Greek ancestor is preserved in English *polymath* 'person of wide learning' [17].

▶ memory, mind, polymath

**matins** see MATURE

**matriculate** see MADRIGAL

**matrix** see MADRIGAL

**matter** [14] *Matter* comes via Anglo-Norman *matere* from Latin *māteria* 'matter.' This was originally applied to the 'hard inner wood of a tree,' and etymologically denoted the 'matrix' or 'mother' from which the tree's new growth came (it was a derivative of Latin *māter* 'mother'). The verbal use of *matter* dates from the late 16th century.

*Material* originated as a derivative of Latin *māteria*.

▶ material, mother

**mattress** [13] Etymologically, a *mattress* is something 'thrown' down on the floor to lie on. The word comes via Old French *materas* and Italian *materasso* from Arabic *matrah* 'mat, cushion,' a derivative of the verb *taraha* 'throw.'

**mature** [15] 'Earliness' is the etymological notion underlying the word *mature*. It goes back ultimately to a pre-Latin base *\*mātu-*, which produced the Latin adjective *mātūrus* 'timely, early,' direct source of the English word (in Old French *mātūrus* became *mur* 'ripe,' which played a part in the emergence of English *demure*). Another Latin derivative of *\*mātu-* was *Mātūta*, the name of the Roman goddess of the dawn. From this in turn was derived the adjective *mātūtīnus* 'of the morning,' source of English *matins* [13] and *matutinal* 'of the morning' [17].

▶ demure, matins

**maudlin** [16] *Maudlin* represents a gradual erosion of the pronunciation of *Magdalen* (exhibited also in the case of the Oxford and Cambridge colleges that have taken that name). The word originated as the name given to a woman called Mary who came from Magdala on the Sea of Galilee, and who according to the Bible was present at Christ's crucifixion and was the first to meet him after he had risen from the dead. In the Middle Ages she was generally represented in paintings as crying, and so *maudlin* came to be used for 'oversentimental.'

**maul** see MALLET

**maulstick** see MOLE

**maundy** [13] Maundy Thursday commemorates Christ's washing of the apostles' feet at the Last Supper. The first antiphon sung at the Catholic Maundy service begins *Mandātum novum dō vōbis* 'I give you a new commandment,' and so in medieval Latin *mandātum* (source of English *mandate*) came to be used as the name for the commemorative ceremony. The word passed into Old French as *mandé*, whence English *maundy*.

▶ mandate, manual

**mausoleum** [16] The original mausoleum was a vast marble tomb (one of the seven wonders of the ancient world) erected in 353 BC for Mausolus, king of Caria in Asia Minor by his widow Artemisia. Its architect was Pythius, and its site was at Halicarnassus (now Bodrum in Turkey). Its Greek name was *mausōleion*, and it passed into English as a generic term for a 'large tomb' via Latin *mausōlēum*.

**mauve** [19] Etymologically, *mauve* is the colour of the 'mallow' flower. The word was borrowed from French *mauve*, whose original meaning was 'mallow,' and which was descended from Latin *malva* 'mallow.' English took over *malva* in the Old English period as *mealuwe*, which has become modern English *mallow*. And Greek *molókhē* 'mallow,' a probable relative of *malva*, is the ultimate source of English *malachite* [16].

▶ malachite, mallow

**mawkish** [17] The underlying meaning of *mawkish* is 'maggotish.' It was derived from a now obsolete word *mawk*, which meant literally 'maggot' but was used figuratively (like *maggot* itself) for a 'whim' or 'fastidious fancy.' Hence *mawkish* originally meant 'nauseated, as if repelled by something one is too fastidious to eat.' In the 18th century the notion of 'sickness' or 'sickliness' produced the present-day sense 'oversentimental.' *Mawk* itself went back to a Middle English *mathek* 'maggot' (possible source of *maggot* [14]), which was borrowed from Old Norse *mathkr*.

▶ maggot

**maximum** [18] *Maximum* was adopted, via French, from *maximum*, the neuter form of Latin *maximus* 'largest.' This was the superlative of *magnus* 'large' (source of English *magnitude, magnum*, etc). From the same ultimate source comes *maxim* [15], which goes back via French *maxime* to Latin *maxima*. This was short for *maxima prōpositio* 'largest proposition,' a term used in medieval philosophy for a 'fundamental axiom.'

▶ magnitude, magnum, maxim

**may** English has basically two words *may*, although one of them has now virtually split into two. The auxiliary verb *may* [OE] goes back ultimately to the Indo-European base *mogh-, *megh-*, denoting 'power, ability,' which also produced English *machine, main*, and *might*. Its Germanic descendant *magan* lies behind German and Dutch *mag*, Swedish *må*, and Danish *maa* as well as English *may*. The compound *maybe* dates from the 15th century, and *dismay* is also related.

*May* the month-name [13] comes via Old French *mai* from Latin *Maius*. This was originally an adjective meaning 'of Maia,' Maia being a Roman goddess and wife of Vulcan (her name may go back to the same source as Latin *magnus* 'large,' and hence denote 'growth' or 'increase'). In the month of May the hawthorn comes into flower, and so in the 16th century the tree received the name *may*.

▶ dismay, machine, main, might

**mayhem** see MAIM

**mayonnaise** [19] There are several conflicting theories about the origin of the term *mayonnaise*, among them that it is an alteration of *bayonnaise*, as if the sauce originated in Bayonne, in southwestern France; that it was derived from the French verb *manier* 'stir'; and that it goes back to Old French *moyeu* 'egg yolk.' But the early variant spelling *mahonnaise* strongly suggests that it originally meant literally 'of Mahon,' and that the sauce was so named to commemorate the taking of Port Mahon, the capital of the island of Minorca, by the duc de Richelieu in 1756.

**mayor** [13] *Mayor* and *major* are ultimately the same word. The ancestor of *mayor* is Latin *mājor* 'larger,' which reached English via medieval Latin *mājor* (used nominally as the title of various officials) and Old French *maire*. In Middle English the word was *mair* or *mer*, and *mayor* represents a partial return to the Latin form.

▶ major

**maze** [13] *Maze* was originally a verb (now obsolete) meaning 'daze,' which arose by shortening of *amaze*. When it was first used as a noun it meant 'delusion, delirium,' and it was not until the late 14th century that it began to be used for a 'structure of bewildering complexity.'

▶ amaze

**me** [OE] *Me* is an ancient and widespread word. It goes back to Indo-European *me*, which is the source of the pronoun corresponding to *me* in all modern Indo-European languages (for instance German *mich*, Dutch *mij*, Swedish *mig*, French, Italian, and Spanish *me*, Greek *me, emé*, and Welsh and Irish *mi*). The derivative *mine* is equally ancient, but *my* is a later shortening of *mine*.

▶ mine

**mead** [OE] *Mead* goes back ultimately to Indo-European *medhu-*, which meant 'sweet drink' (it was also the source of Greek *méthu* 'wine,' from which English gets *methyl* [19] and hence *methylated spirits* [19]). Its prehistoric Germanic descendant was *\*meduz*, from which come German *met*, Dutch *mede*, Swedish *mjöd*, and Danish *mjød* as well as English *mead*.

▶ methyl

**meadow** [OE] Etymologically, *meadow* means 'mowed land.' It goes back ultimately to an Indo-European *\*mētwá*, a derivative of the base *\*mē-* 'mow' (source of English *mow* [OE]). In prehistoric Germanic this became *\*mædwō* (whence German *matte* 'meadow'), which passed into Old English as *mæd*. The modern English descendant of this, *mead*, now survives only as an archaism, but its inflected form, *mædwe*, has become modern English *meadow*.

▶ mow

**meagre** [14] *Meagre* originally meant literally 'thin' (it goes back via Anglo-Norman *megre* and Old French *maigre* to Latin *macer* 'thin,' source also of English *emaciate* [17]). Not until the 16th century did the modern figurative sense 'scanty' begin to emerge. (Its distant Indo-European ancestor, incidentally, *\*makró-*, also produced a parallel Germanic form *mager* 'thin,' shared by German, Dutch, Swedish, and Danish.)

▶ emaciate

**meal** [OE] *Meal* 'repast' and *meal* 'flour' are two distinct words. The former originally meant 'measure': it goes back via prehistoric Germanic *\*mǣlaz* (source of German *mal* 'time, occasion' and *mahl* 'meal,' Dutch *maal* 'time, meal,' and Swedish *mål* 'meal') to the Indo-European base *\*me-* 'measure,' which is also the ancestor of English *measure*. The semantic progression from 'measure' (which died out for *meal* in the Middle English period, but survives in the compound *piecemeal* [13], etymologically 'measured piece by piece') to 'repast' was via 'measured or fixed time' (hence the meaning 'time, occasion' in many of the related Germanic forms) and 'time fixed for eating.'

*Meal* 'flour' (as in *oatmeal*) goes back ultimately to Indo-European *\*mel-*, *\*mol-*, *\*ml-* 'grind,' source of a wide range of other English words from *mild* and *mill* to *molar* and *mould*. From it was descended West and North Germanic *\*melwam*, which has differentiated to German *mehl*, Dutch *meel*, Swedish *mjöl*, Danish *mel*, and English *meal*. It has been speculated that *mellow* [15] may have originated in the use of Old English *melu* 'meal' as an adjective, in the sense 'soft and rich like flour.'

▶ measure, piecemeal / mellow, mild, mill, molar, mould

**mean** English has three distinct words *mean*. The oldest, 'intend' [OE], goes back via a prehistoric West Germanic *\*mainjan* to the Indo-European base *\*men-* 'think' (source also of English *memory, mention, mind*, etc).

The adjective 'petty, stingy' [12] originally meant 'common, shared by all.' It comes from a prehistoric Germanic *\*gamainiz* (source also of German *gemein* 'common, shared'), which was formed from the collective prefix *\*ga-* and *\*mainiz*. This went back to an Indo-European base *\*moi-*, *\*mei-* 'change, exchange,' which also lies behind English *mad, moult, mutate, mutual*, and the second syllable of *common*. *Mean*'s semantic history can be traced from 'common to all' via 'inferior' and 'low, ignoble' to 'petty.'

The adjective 'intermediate, average' [14] came via Anglo-Norman *meen* and Old French *meien* from Latin *mediānus* (source of English *median*), a derivative of *medius* 'middle' (source of English *medium*). It forms the basis of the plural noun *means* 'method' [14], and of the compound adverb *meanwhile* [15].

▶ memory, mention, mind / common, mad, moult, mutate, mutual / median, medium

**meander** [16] The word *meander* comes from the name of an actual river, the Maeander (now known as the Büyük Menderes), which flows through Turkey into the Aegean sea. It was famous in ancient times for its winding course, and so Greek *maíandros* came to be used as a generic term for 'winding course.' The word passed into English via Latin *maeander*, and was turned into a verb in the 17th century.

**measles** [14] *Measles* means literally 'spots, blemishes.' The word was originally borrowed from Middle Dutch *māsel* 'blemish,' which went back to a prehistoric Germanic base *\*mas-* 'spot, blemish, excrescence.' The earliest English form of the word was thus *maseles*, and the change to *measles* (which began in the 14th century) may have been due to association with the now obsolete *mesel* 'leper,' a descendant of Latin *miser* 'wretched, unfortunate' (source of English *misery*).

**measure** [13] The distant ancestor of English *measure* was the Indo-European base *\*ma-*, *\*me-* 'measure.' This has generated a wide range of often unexpected English progeny, including *meal* 'repast,' *month*, and *moon*. *Measure* itself comes from an extension of the base, *\*mat-*, *\*met-*, from which was derived the Latin verb *mētīrī* 'measure.' Its past participial stem *mēns-*formed the basis of the noun *mēnsūra* 'measure,' which passed into English via Old French *mesure* as *measure*. From the same Latin stem come *commensurate* [17], *dimension* [14], and *immense* [15] (literally 'unmeasurable'); and other related forms that go back to the base *\*mat-*, *\*met-* (or *\*med-*) include *mate* 'friend,' *meat, meditate, meet* 'suitable,' *mete, mode, moderate, modest*, and *modify*.

▶ commensurate, dimension, immense, mate, meal, meat, meditate, meet, mete, metre, mode, moderate, modest, month, moon

**meat** [OE] Etymologically, *meat* is a 'portion of food measured out.' The word's ultimate source is Indo-European *mat-, *met-'measure,' which also lies behind English *measure*. This produced a prehistoric Germanic *matiz, which by the time it passed into Old English as *mete* had broadened out in meaning from 'portion of food' to simply 'food.' That is still the meaning of its Germanic relatives, Swedish *mat* and Danish *mad*, and it survives for English *meat* in certain fixed contexts, such as *meat and drink* and *What's one man's meat is another man's poison*, but for the most part the more specific 'flesh used as food,' which began to emerge in the 14th century, now dominates.

▶ measure

**medal**   see METAL

**meddle**   see MIX

**medial**   see MEDIUM

**median**   see MEDIUM

**mediate**   see MEDIUM

**medicine**   [13] Latin *medērī* 'heal' underlies all the English 'medical'-words (it was formed from the base *med-, which also produced English *remedy*). From it was derived *medicus* 'doctor,' which has given English *medical* [17]; and on *medicus* in turn were based Latin *medicīna* 'practice of medicine' (source of English *medicine*) and *medicārī* 'give medicine to' (source of English *medicament* [14] and *medicate* [17]). The informal *medico* [17] comes via Italian.

▶ remedy

**medieval**   see MEDIUM

**mediocre**   [16] Etymologically, *mediocre* means 'halfway up a mountain.' It comes from Latin *mediocris* 'of middle height, in a middle state,' which was formed from *medius* 'middle' (source of English *medium*) and *ocris* 'rough stony mountain.'

▶ medium

**medium**   [16] Latin *medius* meant 'middle' (it came from an Indo-European source that also produced English *mid* and *middle*). Its neuter form, used as a noun, has given English *medium*, but it has made several other contributions to the language, including *mean* 'average,' *medial* [16], *median* [16], *mediate* [16] (and its derivatives *immediate* [16] – etymologically 'acting directly, without any mediation' – and *intermediate* [17]), *medieval* [19] (literally 'of the Middle Ages'), *mediocre*, *meridian*, *mitten*, and *moiety*. Its Italian descendant is *mezzo* 'half,' which has given English *intermezzo* [19], *mezzanine* [18], *mezzosoprano* [18], and *mezzotint* [18].

▶ immediate, intermezzo, mean, median, mediate, middle, mitten

**medley**   see MIX

**meek**   see MUCK

**meerschaum**   see SCUM

**meet**   [OE] English has two words *meet*, although one of them has almost died out. The verb comes

from a prehistoric Germanic *gamōtjan, a derivative of the noun *mōtam 'meeting' (from which English gets *moot*). Its Germanic relatives include Dutch *moeten*, Swedish *möta*, and Danish *møde*. The adjective, 'suitable,' originally meant literally 'fitting,' and goes back via Old English *gemǣte* to the prehistoric Germanic base *mǣt-, *met- 'measure' (source also of the verb *mete* 'measure' [OE], as in *mete out*, and related ultimately to English *measure*).

▶ moot / measure, mete

**megalith**   see LITHOGRAPH

**melancholy**   [14] Etymologically, *melancholy* means 'black gall.' The word comes via Old French *melancolie* and late Latin *melancholia* from Greek *melagkholía*, a compound formed from *mélās* 'black' (source also of English *melanin* [19] and *melanoma* [19]) and *kholế* 'bile' (a relative of English *gall*). This 'black bile' was one of the four bodily substances or 'humours' whose relative preponderance, according to medieval medical theory, determined a person's physical and mental state. Excess of black bile was thought to cause depression – hence the modern meaning of *melancholy*.

▶ gall, melanoma

**mêlée**   see MIX

**mellifluous**   see FLUX, MOLASSES

**mellow**   see MEAL

**melody**   [13] Greek *mélos* originally meant 'limb' (it is related to Cornish *mal* 'joint'), but it was transferred metaphorically to a 'limb or 'part' of a piece of music,' a 'musical phrase,' and from there to 'song.' It was combined with the element *ōid- 'singing' (source of English *ode*) to form *melōidíā* 'choral song,' which passed into English via late Latin *melōdia* and Old French *melodie*. The compound *melodrama* [19] is of French origin.

▶ melodrama, ode

**melon**   [14] Greek *mēlon* actually meant 'apple.' But combination with *pépōn* 'ripe' (a relative of English *peptic* [17]) produced *mēlopépōn*, which was used for 'melon.' This passed into Latin as *mēlopepō*, but the -*pepō* part was subsequently dropped, giving *mēlō* – source, via Old French, of English *melon*.

▶ marmalade

**melt**   [OE] *Melt* goes back ultimately to an Indo-European *meld-, *mold-, *mld-, denoting 'softness,' which also produced English *mild* and Latin *mollis* 'soft' (source of English *mollify* and *mollusc*). Its prehistoric Germanic descendant *melt-, *malt- produced the verb *maltjan 'dissolve,' which has become English *melt*. *Malt* comes from the same Germanic source, and *smelt* [15], a borrowing from Middle Low German, goes back to *smelt-, a variant of the base *melt-.

▶ malt, mild, mollify, mollusc, smelt

**member** [13] Latin *membrum* originally meant 'part of the body, limb, organ' (it has been connected tentatively with various words in other Indo-European languages meaning 'flesh, meat,' including Sanskrit *māmsám* and Gothic *mimz*). But it was early broadened out metaphorically to 'part of anything, one that belongs,' and brought that meaning with it via Old French *membre* into English. The original sense still survives, though, particularly with reference to the 'penis' (an application that originated in Latin – *membrōsus* denoted 'having a large penis').

Derived from Latin *membrum* was the adjective *membrānus*. Its feminine form *membrāna* was used as a noun meaning 'skin covering an organ or limb' – whence English *membrane* [16].

▸ membrane

**memory** [14] The Indo-European base *\*men-*, *\*mon-*'think' has contributed an enormously wide range of words to the English lexicon, from *comment* to *mind*. One particular semantic family denotes 'memory,' and goes back to *memor* 'mindful,' a Latin descendant of *\*men-*. From it was derived the noun *memoria* 'memory,' which has given English *memory, memorize* [16], *memorial* [14], and, via modern French, *memoir* [16]; and the verb *memorāre* 'remember,' from which English gets *commemorate* [16], *memorable* [15], and *memorandum* [16] (not forgetting its abbreviation *memo* [19]). Also from *memor* comes *remember*; and three other Latin descendants of *\*men-*, *meminisse* 'remember,' *reminiscī* 'remember,' and *mentiō* 'remembrance,' gave English *memento* [15], *reminiscence* [16], and *mention* respectively. The distantly related *remind* carries the same idea.

▸ commemorate, comment, mention, mind, remind, reminisce

**menace** [13] Latin *mināx* meant 'threatening' (it was formed from a base *\*min-* 'jut' which also produced English *eminent* and *prominent*, and hence etymologically denoted 'overhanging'). From it was derived the noun *minācia* 'threatening things,' which passed into English via Old French *manace*.

The closely related *demeanour* comes ultimately from a word denoting 'drive animals with threats.'

▸ eminent, prominent

**menagerie**   SEE MANOR

**mend** [12] *Mend* originated as a shortened form of *amend* [13] – or rather, of the Old French source of *amend*, which did not arrive in English until after *mend*. The Old French verb was *amender*, a descendant of Vulgar Latin *\*admendāre* 'remove faults, correct.' This in turn was an alteration of classical Latin *ēmendāre* (source of English *emend* [15]), a compound verb formed from the prefix *ex-* denoting 'removal' and *menda, mendum* 'fault, defect.' (Other Latin derivatives of *mendum* were *mendīcus* 'injured,' which was

used as a noun meaning 'beggar' – hence English *mendicant* [15]; and perhaps *mendāx* 'speaking faultily,' hence 'lying,' from which English gets *mendacious* [17].)

▸ amend, emend, mendicant

**menhir**   SEE DOLMEN

**menstrual** [14] Etymologically, *menstrual* means 'monthly.' It comes from Latin *mēnstruālis*, an adjective derived from *mēnsis* 'month' (a close relative of English *month*). From the same source comes *menses* [16], originally the plural of Latin *mēnsis*, and *menopause* [19] is based on the related Greek word for 'month,' *mén*. Their gynaecological application comes, of course, from the 'monthly' flow of blood from the uterus.

▸ menopause, month

**mental**   SEE MIND

**menthol**   SEE MINT

**mention** [14] The etymological notion underlying *mention* is of 'reminding.' For it comes via Old French from Latin *mentiō*, which originally meant 'remembrance' (it was a derivative of the Indo-European base *\*men-*, which also produced English *memory, remember*, etc). It developed via 'cause to remember something by speaking or writing of it' (a sense still present in Middle English) to simply 'refer to something.'

▸ memory, mind, remember

**menu**   SEE MINUTE

**merchant** [13] Latin *merx* denoted 'goods for sale.' From it was derived the verb *mercārī* 'trade' (whose past participle was the source of English *market*). *Mercārī* was adapted in Vulgar Latin to *mercātāre*, whose present participle *mercātāns* produced the Old French noun *marcheant* 'trader,' source of English *merchant*. *Merchandise* [13] comes from a derivative of *marcheant*; and other English descendants of Latin *merx* are *commerce* and *mercury*.

▸ commerce, market, mercury

**mercury** [14] The Roman god Mercury got his name from his original role as patron of trade and tradesmen: Latin *Mercurius* was a derivative of *merx* 'goods for sale' (source of English *commerce* and *merchant*). The inspiration for the medieval application of the term to the fluid metal was its use as a planet-name, which dates from the classical Latin period.

▸ commerce, merchant

**mercy** [12] Latin *mercēs* meant 'payment, reward.' In the Christian era the notion of a 'reward' was taken up and reapplied metaphorically to the 'compassion given freely by God to humankind,' and the word passed into Old French (in the form *merci*) with the broader sense 'compassion,' and hence 'forbearance from punishment.' English took it over and has continued to use it in much the same way, but its main role in modern French is as the word for 'thankyou.'

**mere** see MERMAID

**merge** [17] *Merge* comes from Latin *mergere*, which meant 'dive, plunge' (it was also the source of English *emerge* [16], which etymologically means 'rise out of a liquid,' *immerse* [17], and *submerge* [17]). *Merge* was originally used for 'immerse' in English too, and the modern meaning 'combine into one' did not emerge fully until as recently as the 20th century. It arose from the notion of one thing 'sinking' into another and losing its identity; in the 1920s this was applied to two business companies amalgamating, and the general sense 'combine' followed from it.

▶ emerge, immerse, submerge

**meridian** [14] Etymologically, *meridian* denotes the 'middle of the day.' It comes via Old French from Latin *merīdiānus*, a derivative of *merīdiēs* 'midday.' This was an alteration of an earlier *medidiēs*, a compound noun formed from *medius* 'middle' (source of English *medium*) and *diēs* 'day.' The application of the word to a circle passing round the Earth or the celestial sphere, which is an ancient one, comes from the notion of the sun crossing it at noon.

▶ medium

**mermaid** [14] A *mermaid* is literally a 'sea-maiden.' The word was coined on the basis of English *mere* [OE], which is now a little-used term for 'lake,' but originally denoted 'sea' (it came ultimately from Indo-European *\*mori-*, *\*mari-* 'sea,' which also produced German *meer* 'sea' and Latin *mare* 'sea,' source of French *mer* and English *marine*). *Mermaid* served in due course as a model for *merman* [17].

▶ marine, mere

**merry** [OE] *Merry* goes back to a prehistoric Germanic *\*murgjaz*, which appears to have been derived from a base meaning 'short.' By the time it reached Old English, as *myrige*, it meant 'pleasant' – a semantic leap perhaps inspired by the notion of 'shortening' time by passing it pleasantly. The modern meaning 'jolly' did not emerge until the 14th century. A derivative of *\*murgjaz* was the noun *\*murgithō*, source of English *mirth* [OE]; Dutch has the related *merchte* 'mirth.'

▶ mirth

**mesmerize** [19] Franz Anton Mesmer (1734–1815) was an Austrian doctor whose experiments with what he called 'animal magnetism,' by which he induced a trance-like state in his subjects, are considered to be the forerunner of modern hypnotism (formerly called *mesmerism* [19]). The broader sense of *mesmerize*, 'enthral,' dates from the early 20th century.

**mess** [13] *Mess* comes via Old French *mes* from late Latin *missus*, a derivative of the verb *mittere* 'send' (source of English *admit, mission, transmit*, etc). This meant 'sending, placement,' and its original metaphori-

cal application was to a 'round or heat of a contest,' but it was also used for a 'course of a meal,' and this was the sense in which it originally entered English. Traces of the food connection survive in the *mess of pottage* (literally a 'dish of porridge or gruel' made from lentils) for which Esau sold his birthright to Jacob, and in the sense 'communal eating place' (as in 'sergeants' mess'), which developed in the 16th century. But the main present-day meaning, 'disorderly thing or condition,' did not emerge until as recently as the 19th century, apparently based on the notion of a *mess* as a 'dish of assorted foodstuffs dumped unceremoniously and without thought on to a plate.'

▶ admit, commit, mission, permit, transmit

**message** [13] Etymologically, a *message* is something that is 'sent.' The word comes via Old French *message* from Vulgar Latin *\*missāticum*, a derivative of the Latin verb *mittere* (from which English also gets *admit, mission, transmit*, etc). *Messenger* [13] comes from the Old French derivative *messager*, and was originally *messager* in English; the *n* is a 14th-century intruder, found also in such words as *harbinger* and *passenger*.

▶ admit, commit, mess, mission, permit

**messieurs** see SIR

**messrs** see SIR

**metal** [13] Greek *métallon*, a word of unknown origin, had a range of meanings, including 'mine' (the original sense) and 'mineral' as well as 'metal.' These were carried over into Latin *metallum*, but by the time the word reached English, via Old French *metal*, 'metal' was all that was left. *Mettle* [16] is a variant spelling of *metal*, used to distinguish its metaphorical senses.

Closely related is *medal* [16], which etymologically means 'something made of metal.' It comes via French *médaille* and Italian *medaglia* from a general Romance form *\*medallia*. This was an alteration of Vulgar Latin *\*metallea*, a derivative of Latin *metallum*. *Medallion* [17] goes back via French to Italian *medaglione* 'large medal.'

▶ medal, medallion

**mete** see MEET

**meteor** [15] Greek *meteóron* meant literally 'something high up,' and was used to denote 'phenomena in the sky or heavens.' It was a compound noun formed from the intensive prefix *metá-* and *\*eōr-*, a variant form of the base of the verb *aeírein* 'raise.' When English first took it over, via medieval Latin *meteōrum*, it was still in the sense 'phenomenon of the atmosphere or weather' ('hoar frosts . . . and such like cold meteors,' Abraham Fleming, *Panoplie of Epistles* 1576), an application which survives, of course, in the derivative *meteorology* [17]. The earliest evidence of the specific use of *meteor* for a 'shooting star' comes from the end of the 16th century. The derivative *meteor-*

*ite*, for a meteor that hits the ground, was coined in the early 19th century.

▶ meteorology

**meter** see METRE

**method** [16] *Method* comes via French *méthode* and Latin *methodus* from Greek *méthodos*, which meant 'pursuit.' It was a compound noun formed from the prefix *metá-* 'after' and *hodós* 'way, journey' (found also in English *episode, exodus*, and *period*). 'Pursuit' of a particular objective gradually developed into a 'procedure for attaining it,' the meaning which the word had when it reached English.

The derivative *methodist* [16], originally simply 'someone who followed a particular method,' was first applied to the followers of John Wesley in the 18th century.

▶ episode, exodus, period

**methyl** see MEAD
**métier** see MINISTER
**metre** [14] Greek *métron* meant 'measure': it came ultimately from the Indo-European base *\*me-* 'measure,' which also produced English *measure, immense*, etc. English originally acquired it, via Latin *metrum* and Old French *metre*, in the sense 'measured rhythmic pattern of verse.' Then at the end of the 18th century French *mètre* was designated as the standard measure of length in the new metric system, and English reborrowed it as *metre*.

*Meter* 'measuring device' [19] is probably a nominalization of the element *-meter*, occurring in such compounds as *galvanometer* [19], *gasometer* [18], and *pedometer* [18], which itself went back via French *-mètre* or modern Latin *-metrum* to Greek *métron*.

▶ commensurate, immense, measure, mete

**metropolis** [16] A *metropolis* is etymologically a 'mother city.' The word comes via late Latin *mētropolis* from Greek *mētrópolis*, a compound formed from *mētēr* 'mother' (a distant relative of English *mother*) and *pólis* 'city' (source of English *police, policy, politics*, etc).

▶ mother, police, policy, politics

**mews** [14] In former times, a *mew* was a place where trained falcons were kept (etymologically the word means 'moulting-place'; it came from Old French *mue*, a derivative of *muer* 'moult,' which was descended from Latin *mūtāre* 'change'). In the latter part of the 14th century the Royal Mews were built in London on the site of what is now Trafalgar Square, to house the royal hawks. By Henry VII's time they were being used as stables, and from at least the early 17th century the term *mews* was used for 'stabling around an open yard.' The modern application to a 'street of former stables converted to human dwellings' dates from the early 19th century.

▶ moult, mutate

**mezzanine** see MEDIUM

**mica** [18] Latin *mīca* meant 'grain,' and its original use in English (perhaps influenced by the similar but unrelated Latin verb *micāre* 'shine') was to 'small shiny particles or platelets' in certain sorts of rock. The modern application to a group of related silicates, which contain such shiny plates, dates from the 1790s.

**micro** [19] The conversion of the prefix *micro-* into a noun (standing, for instance, for a *microskirt* or *microcomputer*) is not as recent as one might have supposed: as long ago as the 1860s it was being used for a sort of tiny moth (short for *microlepidoptera*). The prefix itself comes from Greek *mīkrós* 'small,' a variant of *smīkrós*, which may be distantly related to English *small*. The earliest English word containing it appears to have been *microcosm* [15], etymologically 'little world.' From the 17th century come *micrometer, microphone*, and *microscope*. *Microbe* [19] means etymologically 'little life' (from Greek *bíos* 'life'), hence 'little creature.'

**micturate** see ANT
**midden** see MUCK
**middle** [OE] *Middle* traces its ancestry back to Indo-European *\*medhjo-*, which also produced Latin *medius* 'middle' (source of English *mediate, medium*, etc) and Greek *mésos* 'middle' (source of the English prefix *meso-*). Its prehistoric Germanic descendant was *\*mithja-*, which has given English the adjective *mid* [OE] and the derived noun *midst* [14]. From *\*mithja-* was formed in West Germanic the adjective *\*middila*, which has given modern German *mittel*, Dutch *middel*, and English *middle*.

▶ mediate, medium

**midge** see MOSQUITO
**midget** see MOSQUITO
**midwife** [14] A *midwife* is etymologically a 'with-woman.' The *mid-* element represents the long extinct preposition *mid* 'with' (its Germanic relatives are still alive and well: German *mit*, Dutch *met*, and Swedish and Danish *med*). *Wife* preserves the original meaning of Old English *wīf*, 'woman.' The idea underlying the word is that a midwife is 'with' a woman giving birth.

**might** [OE] *Might* goes back ultimately to Indo-European *\*mag-* 'be able, have power,' the same base as produced the auxiliary verb *may*. The noun *might* was formed with the Germanic suffix *\*-tiz*, which also gave German and Dutch *macht* 'power'; and the verb *might*, the past form of *may*, contains the past inflectional suffix (in modern English *-(e)d*).

▶ may

**migraine** [14] The earliest English forms of this word were *mygrame* and *mygrane*, but eventually it became institutionalized as *megrim*. Not until the 18th century did what is now the standard form, *migraine*, begin to appear on the scene, probably as a reborrowing of the word's original source, French *migraine*. This came via late Latin *hēmicrānia* from Greek *hēmikrāníā*, literally 'half-skull' (*krāníon* is the source of English *cranium* [16], and is distantly related to English *horn*). The etymological idea underlying the word is of 'pain in one side of the head.'

▶ cranium, horn

**migrate** SEE MUTATE

**milch** SEE MILK

**mild** [OE] *Mild* goes back ultimately to Indo-European *meld-, *mold-, *mld-, which denoted 'softness' and also produced English *melt* and Latin *mollis* 'soft,' source of English *mollify* and *mollusc*. From it was derived the Germanic adjective *milthjaz*, whose modern descendant has shown remarkable formal stability: German, Dutch, Swedish, Danish, and English all share the word *mild*.

▶ melt, mollify, mollusc, smelt

**mildew** [OE] *Mildew* originally meant 'honey-dew' (which is a sort of sticky substance exuded by aphids and similar insects on to leaves). It is a compound noun formed in the prehistoric Germanic period from *melith* 'honey' (a relative of Latin *mel* 'honey,' source of English *mellifluous* and *molasses*) and *dawwaz*, ancestor of English *dew*. The metaphorical transference from 'honey-dew' to a less pleasant, fungal growth on plants, etc took place in the 14th century.

▶ dew, mellifluous, molasses

**mile** [OE] Latin *mīlle* denoted 'thousand' (it is the source of English *millennium* [17], etymologically a 'thousand years,' and, via Italian and French, of *million* [14]). Its plural *mīllia* was used in ancient Rome for a measure of length equal to a thousand paces. This was borrowed into prehistoric West Germanic as *mīlja*, which has subsequently differentiated into German *meile*, Dutch *mijl*, and English *mile*. (The English mile is over 100 yards longer than the Roman one was.)

▶ millennium, million

**military** [16] *Military* traces its history back to Latin *mīles* 'soldier,' a word possibly of Etruscan origin. Its derived adjective *mīlitāris* entered English via French *militaire*. Also based on *mīles* was the verb *mīlitāre* 'serve as a soldier,' which has given English *militant* [15] and *militate* [17], a verb whose meaning has changed sharply over the centuries: at first it was used in the same way as its Latin ancestor, but then it developed via 'conflict with' to 'be evidence against,' and finally, in the 20th century, to 'make unlikely.' *Mi-*

*litia* [16] comes from Latin *mīlitia* 'warfare,' another derivative of *mīles*.

**milk** [OE] Far back into prehistory, *milk* traces its ancestry to an Indo-European base *melg-, which denoted 'wiping' or 'stroking.' The way of obtaining milk from animals is to pull one's hand down their teats, and so *melg- came in due course to be used for 'milk.' It passed into Germanic as *melk-, which formed the basis of the noun *meluks, and this over the centuries has become German *milch*, Dutch and Danish *melk*, Swedish *mjölk*, and English *milk*. The now virtually obsolete adjective *milch* 'giving milk' [OE] (as in *milch cow*) goes back to a Germanic derivative of *meluks*.

Another derivative of Indo-European *melg- was the Latin verb *mulgēre* 'milk,' which has given English *emulsion* and *promulgate*.

▶ emulsion, promulgate

**mill** [OE] *Mill* is one of a large family of English words that go back ultimately to the Indo-European base *mel-, *mol-, *ml-, denoting 'grind.' It includes *meal* 'flour,' *mollify, mollusc, mould* and (via the extended form *meld-, *mold-) *melt* and *mild*. One particular subset of the family comes from closely related Latin sources: the verb *molere* 'grind' has produced *emolument* and *ormolu* [18] (etymologically 'ground gold'); the noun *mola* 'grindstone' has given *molar* [16] and (via a later sense 'flour mixed with salt, sprinkled on sacrificial victims') *immolate* [16]; and late Latin *molīnus* 'grindstone,' which replaced classical Latin *mola*, was borrowed into Old English as *mylen*, from which we get modern English *mill*.

▶ emolument, meal, melt, mild, molar, mollify, mollusc, mould, ormolu

**millennium** SEE MILE

**milliner** [16] The Italian city of Milan was famous in medieval and Renaissance times for the fabrics, laces, etc that it manufactured; and a merchant who imported such 'Milan ware' became known as a *Milaner*. In due course the term became associated with 'makers of female garments,' which would have incorporated such Italian haberdashery, and by the 19th century it had narrowed down specifically to 'maker of women's hats.'

**million** SEE MILE

**mime** [17] Greek *mimos* meant 'imitator,' and hence 'actor.' English took it over via Latin *mīmus*, and lost no time in turning it into a verb. The derived Greek adjective *mīmikós* has given English *mimic* [16], and other related forms include *mimeograph* [19], so called because it copies things, and *mimosa* [18], named from its tendency to curl up when touched, as if in 'imitation' of animal behaviour. The compound *pantomime* means etymologically 'complete mime.'

▶ mimeograph, mimosa, pantomime

**mince** [14] Etymologically, to *mince* something is to make it extremely 'small.' The word comes via Old French *mincier* from Vulgar Latin *\*minūtiāre*, a derivative of Latin *minūtia* 'small thing.' This in turn was based on *minūtus* 'small,' source of English *minute*.

▶ minute

**mind** [12] *Mind* is a member of a large and diverse family of English words (including *mandarin, mathematics, memory,* and *reminisce*) that go back ultimately to the Indo-European base *\*men-* 'think.' Amongst its other descendants were Latin *mēns* 'mind,' source of English *mental* [15], and prehistoric Germanic *\*gamunthiz* (formed with the collective prefix *\*ga-*). This passed into Old English as *gemynd*, but its prefix was dropped in the early Middle English period, giving modern English *mind*. Historically, 'memory' has been as important an element in the word's meaning as 'mental faculty,' but it now survives mainly in the derived verb *remind*.

▶ mandarin, mathematics, memory, mental, reminisce

**mine** English has two quite distinct words *mine*. The first person possessive pronoun [OE] goes back to a prehistoric Germanic *\*mīnaz* (source also of German *mein*, Dutch *mijn*, and Swedish and Danish *min*), which was derived from the same Indo-European source as produced English *me*. Originally it was an adjective, but in the 13th century the *-n* was dropped before consonants, and eventually the resulting *my* took over the adjective slot altogether, leaving *mine* as a pronoun only.

*Mine* 'excavation' [14] is of uncertain origin. It comes via Old French from an assumed Vulgar Latin *\*mina*, which may go back ultimately to a Celtic *\*meini-* 'ore' (Gaelic has *mein* 'ore, mine' and Welsh *mwyn* 'ore'). The use of the word for an 'explosive device,' which dates from the 17th century, arose from the practice of digging tunnels or 'mines' beneath enemy positions and then blowing them up.

▶ me, my

**mineral** [15] A *mineral* is etymologically something obtained by 'mining.' The word comes from medieval Latin *minerāle*, a derivative of the adjective *minerālis*. This in turn was derived from *minera* 'ore,' a latinization of Old French *miniere*. And *miniere* itself came from Vulgar Latin *\*mināria*, a derivative of *\*mina* – source of English *mine*.

▶ mine

**mingle** see AMONG

**miniature** [16] 'Smallness' is a purely secondary semantic development as far as *miniature* is concerned, inspired by its accidental similarity to the *min-* element of words like *minimum* and *minute*. It in fact comes ultimately from Latin *minium* 'red lead.' Red lead was used in ancient and medieval times for making a sort of red ink with which manuscripts were decorat-

ed, and so the derived medieval Latin verb *miniāre* was coined for 'illuminate a manuscript.'

Italian took this over as *miniare*, and derived *miniatura* 'painting, illustrating' from it. It referred particularly to the small paintings in manuscripts, and when English borrowed it as *miniature* it was soon broadened out to any 'small image.' Association with *minute*, etc led by the early 18th century to its adjectival use for 'small.'

**minimum** see MINUTE

**minister** [13] Etymologically, a *minister* is a person of 'lower' status, a 'servant.' The word goes back via Old French *ministre* to Latin *minister* 'servant, attendant,' which was derived from *minus* 'less.' It retained this meaning when it arrived in English, and indeed it still survives in the verb *minister*. But already by the Middle Ages a specialized application to a 'church functionary' had developed, and in the 16th century this hardened into the present-day 'clergyman.' The political sense of the word developed in the 17th century, from the notion of a 'servant' of the crown.

Derivatives from other languages to have established themselves in English include *métier* [18], which came via French from Vulgar Latin *\*misterium*, an alteration of Latin *ministerium* 'service' (source of English *ministry* [14]), and *minstrel*. And etymologically, *minister* is the antonym of *master*, whose Latin ancestor was based on *magis* 'more.'

▶ métier, minstrel, minus

**minor** [13] Latin *minor* 'less' was a comparative form based on the element *min-* 'small' (source of English *minute* and a whole range of other 'small'-words). The noun derived from it, *minus* 'less,' was taken over by English in the 15th century.

▶ minute

**minster** see MONK

**minstrel** [13] Originally *minstrel*, like its close relative *minister*, denoted a 'servant.' Its musical associations are a comparatively recent development. It goes back ultimately to late Latin *ministeriālis* 'official,' a derivative of Latin *ministerium* (source of English *ministry*). Old French took it over as *menestral*, and it was here that a gradual specialization in meaning took place, from 'servant' via 'entertainer' to 'singer.'

▶ minister

**mint** [OE] English has two completely unconnected words *mint*. The 'money factory' comes ultimately from Latin *monēta* 'mint, money' (source also of English *money*). It was borrowed into prehistoric West Germanic as *\*munita*, which in due course produced Old English *mynet*. This denoted 'coin' (as its modern German relative *münze* still does), and it was not until the 15th century that the modern sense 'place where money is made' emerged.

*Mint* the plant originated in Greek *mínthē*, and

reached English via Latin *mentha* (source of *menthol* [19], a German coinage) and prehistoric West Germanic *\*minta*.

▶ money / menthol

**minute** [14] Latin *minūtus* 'small' was a derivative of the verb *minuere* 'lessen' (source of English *diminish*), which itself was based on the element *min-* 'small.' In medieval Latin the term *pars minuta prima* 'first small part' was applied to a 'sixtieth part of a whole' – originally of a circle, later of an hour (likewise a *second* was originally a *secunda minuta*, a sixtieth of a sixtieth). Hence *minūta* itself came to be used for the unit of time, and that was the original meaning of *minute* when English acquired it via Old French. Its use for 'note, record' may derive from the Latin expression *minuta scriptura*, which denoted the writing of a rough draft in 'small' writing. The adjective *minute* 'small' was an independent 15th-century borrowing direct from Latin. A French descendant of *minūtus* is the adjective *menu* 'small'; its extended sense 'detailed' has led to its noun use for 'list,' and the expression *menu de repas* 'meal list' has given English *menu* [19].

Other members of the extended family of English words that come ultimately from Latin *min-* include *métier, mince, minim* [15], *minimum* [17], *minister, minor, minstrel, minuet* [17], *minus, minuscule* [18], and *minutia* [15].

▶ menu, métier, mince, minister, minor, minstrel, minus, minuscule

**mirror** [13] *Mirror* belongs to a small family of English words which illustrate how a Latin term originally signifying 'wonder at' weakened (presumably via 'stare in wonder at') to 'look at.' Etymologically, a *mirror* is something you 'look at' yourself in. The word comes via Old French *mirour* from Vulgar Latin *\*mīrātōrium*, a derivative of *\*mirāre* 'look at.' This was closely related to classical Latin *mīrārī* 'wonder at' (a derivative of *mīrus* 'wonderful'), which passed into Old French as *mirer* 'look at,' source of English *mirage* [19]. Based on *mīrārī* were Latin *mīrābilis* 'wonderful' (source of English *marvel* [13]) and *mīrāculum* 'something to be wondered at' (source of English *miracle* [12]).

▶ marvel, miracle, mirage

**mirth** see MERRY

**miscegenation** see MIX

**miscellaneous** see MIX

**mischief** [13] Etymologically, *mischief* is something that 'happens amiss.' The word comes from Old French *meschef*, a derivative of the verb *meschever* 'meet with misfortune.' This was a compound verb formed from the prefix *mis-* 'wrongly, amiss' and *chever* 'happen' (which came ultimately from Latin *caput* 'head,' and etymologically meant 'come to a head'). It still meant 'misfortune' when English ac-

quired it; in the 14th century the sense 'harm, damage' emerged, but the more trivial modern sense 'naughtiness' did not develop until the 18th century.

**miscreant** see CREED

**misery** [14] Latin *miser* meant 'miserable, wretched.' From it were derived *miseria* 'wretchedness,' source of English *misery*, and *miserābilis* 'pitiable,' source of English *miserable* [16]. Fitting in with the general semantic pattern, English *miser* [16] (a direct nominalization of the Latin adjective) originally meant 'wretched person.' But people who hoarded money were evidently viewed as being basically unhappy, and so right from the beginning *miser* was used for an 'avaricious person.'

▶ miser

**miss** English has two words *miss*. The one used as a title for an unmarried woman [17], which originated as a shortened form of *mistress* (see MASTER), is a comparatively recent introduction, but the verb *miss* [OE] has a much longer history. It comes from a prehistoric Germanic *\*missjan* (source of German and Dutch *missen*, Swedish *mista*, and Danish *miste*), which was derived from the base *\*missa-* 'wrongly, amiss' (ancestor of the English prefix *mis-*).

▶ master

**mission** [16] *Mission*, etymologically a 'sending,' is the hub of a large family of English words that come from the Latin verb *mittere* 'let go, send' or its stem *miss-*. Most are prefixed forms – *admit, commit, permit, promise, transmit,* etc – but the unadorned verb is represented in *mass* 'eucharist,' *mess, missile* [17] (literally 'something capable of being sent'), *mission* itself and its derivative *missionary* [17], and *missive* [15] ('something sent'). The source of *mittere* is not known, but what does seem clear is that it originally meant 'let go, throw.' This subsequently developed to 'send' and, in the post-classical period, to 'put' (hence French *mettre* 'put').

▶ admit, commit, mess, message, missile, missive, permit, promise, submit, transmit

**mist** [OE] *Mist* is a member of quite a widespread Indo-European family of 'mist'-words. Dutch and Swedish share *mist*, and among the non-Germanic languages Greek has *omíkhlē*, Lithuanian and Latvia *migla*, Serbo-Croat *màgla*, Polish *mgła*, and Russian *mgla*, all meaning 'mist,' besides Sanskrit *mēghas* 'cloud,' which all point back to an Indo-European ancestor *\*migh-, \*meigh-*.

**mistake** [13] *Mistake* originally meant literally 'take in error, take the wrong thing.' It was borrowed from Old Norse *mistaka*, a compound verb formed from the prefix *mis-* 'wrongly' and *taka* 'take.' This sense survived in English for some time ('to be ever busy, and mistake away the bottles and cans . . . before they be but half drunk of,' Ben Jonson, *Bartholomew Fair*

1614), but gradually through the late Middle English period the notion of 'error' came to the fore (it was already present in the Old Norse verb, which was used reflexively for 'go wrong,' and was probably reinforced by Old French *mesprendre*, literally 'take wrongly,' which was also used for 'err'). The noun use, 'error,' emerged in the 17th century.

▶ take

**mister**   see MASTER

**mistletoe**   [OE]   *Mistletoe* is a mystery word. It means literally 'mistletoe twig,' and comes from an Old English compound *misteltān* formed from *mistel* 'mistletoe' and *tān* 'twig.' The origins of *mistel*, however (which has relatives in German *mistil* and Dutch and Swedish *mistel*), are unknown. The *mistle thrush* [18], or *missel thrush*, got its name from its predilection for mistletoe berries.

**mistress**   see MASTER

**mite**   English has two words *mite*, although they probably share a common origin. The older, 'tiny insect-like creature' [OE], goes back to a prehistoric Germanic *\*mītōn*, which was probably derived from a base meaning 'cut' (hence 'something cut up small'). Dutch has the related *mijt*. The original meaning of *mite* 'small thing' [14] was 'small coin' (as in the 'widow's mite'). It was used in Flanders for such a coin, worth a third of a penny, and Middle Dutch *mīte* was borrowed into English. It too goes back to a Germanic *mītōn*, which is probably the same word as produced the animated *mite*.

**mitten**   [14]   Etymologically, a *mitten* is 'half a glove.' The word comes via Old French *mitaine* from Vulgar Latin *\*medietāna* 'cut off in the middle' (originally an adjective, and applied to gloves, but subsequently used independently as a noun meaning 'cut-off glove'). This in turn came from Latin *medietās* 'half' (source of English *moiety* [15]), a derivative of *medius* 'middle' (source of English *medium*).

The abbreviated *mitt* dates from the 18th century.

▶ medium, moiety

**mix**   [15]   English originally acquired this word in the form *mixt* or *mixed*, a past participial adjective, and did not coin the new verb *mix* from it until the 16th century. *Mixt* came via Old French from Latin *mixtus*, the past participle of the verb *miscēre* 'mix.' Derivatives of *miscēre* to have reached English include *miscellaneous* [17] and *promiscuous* [17], and its Vulgar Latin descendant *\*misculāre* 'mix up' has given English *meddle* [14], *medley* [14], and *mêlée* [17]. *Miscegenation* [19] was coined in the USA around 1863 from *miscēre* and Latin *genus* 'race.'

▶ meddle, medley, miscellaneous, mustang, promiscuous

**moat**   [14]   The word *moat* originally meant a 'mound' or 'embankment' (this has since been hived off

into the specialized form *motte*). The word was borrowed from Old French *mote* or *motte* 'hill, mound,' whose ultimate source was probably a Gaulish *mutt* or *mutta*. The use of the word for the mound on which a castle keep was built led in Old French or Anglo-Norman to its reapplication to the ditch surrounding such a mound.

**mob**   [17]   *Mob* is famous as one of the then new 'slang' abbreviations against which Joseph Addison and Jonathan Swift inveighed at the beginning of the 18th century (others included *pozz* for *positively* and *rep* for *reputation*). *Mob* was short for *mobile*, which itself was a truncated form of *mobile vulgus*, a Latin phrase meaning 'fickle crowd.' Latin *mōbilis* 'movable,' hence metaphorically 'fickle' (source of English *mobile* [15]), came from the base of the verb *movēre* 'move' (source of English *move*).

▶ mobile, move

**model**   [16]   Latin *modus* meant originally 'measure' (it came from the same Indo-European base, *\*met-*, *\*med-*, as produced English *measure* and *metre*). It subsequently spread out semantically to 'size,' 'limit,' 'way, method,' and 'rhythm, harmony.' From it was derived the diminutive form *modulus*, source of English *modulate* [16], *module* [16], and *mould* 'form.' It was altered in Vulgar Latin to *\*modellus*, and passed into English via Italian *modello* and early modern French *modelle*. Its original application in English was to an 'architect's plans,' but the familiar modern sense 'three-dimensional representation' is recorded as early as the start of the 17th century. The notion of an 'artist's model' emerged in the late 17th century, but a 'model who shows off clothes' is an early 20th-century development.

Other English descendants of *modus* include *modern*, *modicum* [15], *modify* [14], and of course *mode* [16] itself (of which *mood* 'set of verb forms' is an alteration).

▶ measure, mete, metre, mode, modern, modulate, mood, mould

**moderate**   [14]   Latin *moderārī* or *moderāre* meant 'reduce, control.' They were derived from an unrecorded *\*modes-* (source also of *modest*), which was related to *modus* 'measure' (source of English *mode* and *model*), and hence denoted etymologically 'keep within due measure.' Their past participle *moderātus* was taken over by English as an adjective, and converted into a verb in the 15th century.

▶ mode, model, modern, modest

**modern**   [16]   Latin *modus* (source of English *mode* and *model*) meant 'measure.' Its ablative form *modō* hence originally denoted 'to the measure,' but it subsequently came to be used as an adverb meaning 'just now.' And in post-classical times an adjective *modernus* was derived from it, signifying 'of the pres-

ent time' – source, via French, of English *modern*. At first it was used strictly for 'of the present moment,' but before the end of the 16th century the now familiar sense 'of the present age' had begun to emerge.
▶ mode, model

**modest** [16] Etymologically, *modest* means 'kept within due measure.' It comes via French from Latin *modestus*, a derivative of the same source as produced English *moderate*. This was *\*modes-*, a close relative of Latin *modus* 'measure' (from which English gets *mode* and *model*).
▶ mode, model

**modicum** see MODEL
**modify** see MODEL
**module** see MODEL
**moiety** see MITTEN

**moist** [14] Latin *mūcidus* meant 'mouldy' and 'snivelling' (it was a derivative of *mūcus*, source of English *mucus*). In Vulgar Latin it became altered to *\*muscidus*, which is thought to have branched out in meaning to 'wet,' and passed in this sense into Old French as *moiste* – whence English *moist*.

From the 15th to the 17th centuries the derived adjective *moisty* 'damp' existed (it was revived in the 19th century). *Musty* [16] is thought to have originated as an alteration of it, perhaps under the influence of *must* 'grape juice.'
▶ mucus, musty

**molar** see MILL

**molasses** [16] The etymological connections of *molasses* are with 'honey' rather than 'sugar.' It comes via Portuguese *melaço* from late Latin *mellāceum* 'fermenting grape juice, new wine.' This was a derivative of *mel* 'honey,' source of English *mellifluous* [15] and related to *mildew*.
▶ mellifluous, mildew

**mole** English has four distinct words *mole*. The oldest is 'brown spot' [OE]. It is the descendant of Old English *māl*, which meant broadly 'discoloured mark.' This developed in Middle English to 'spot on the skin,' but the specific sense 'brown mark' did not emerge until fairly recently. The word goes back to a prehistoric Germanic *\*mailam*, a derivative of a base meaning 'spot, mark' which also produced German *malen* 'paint' and Dutch *maalen* 'paint' (source of English *maulstick* 'stick used as a rest by painters' [17]).

*Mole* the animal [14] was borrowed from Middle Dutch *mol*. No one knows for sure where this came from, but its similarity to the now obsolete *mouldwarp* 'mole' [14] (a compound noun whose etymological meaning is 'earth-thrower') suggests that it could represent a truncated version of *mouldwarp*'s prehistoric Germanic ancestor. The metaphorical application of the word to a 'traitor working secretly' has been traced back

as far as the 17th century, but its modern currency is due to its use by the British espionage writer John le Carré.

*Mole* 'harbour wall' [16] comes via French *môle* and medieval Greek *mólos* from Latin *mōlēs* 'mass, massive structure.' The diminutive form of this, coined in modern times, is *mōlēcula*, from which, via French *molécule*, English gets *molecule* [18]. Other relatives are *demolish* and, possibly, *molest* [14], which comes ultimately from Latin *molestus* 'troublesome,' connected by some scholars with *mōlēs*. And German *mol*, a convenient shortening of *molekulargewicht* 'molecular weight,' has given English its fourth *mole* [20], used as the basic unit of measurement for the amount of a substance.
▶ maulstick / molecule, molest

**mollusc** [18] Etymologically, a *mollusc* is a 'soft' creature. The word comes ultimately from Latin *molluscus* 'soft,' a derivative of *mollis* 'soft.' In classical times it was used as a noun for various 'soft' things, such as a sort of thin-shelled nut and a species of fungus that grew from maple trees, but its application to a range of invertebrate animals seems to have been introduced by the Swedish naturalist Linnaeus in the mid-18th century. Latin *mollis* (source also of English *mollify* [15]) goes back ultimately to Indo-European *\*mel-*, *\*mol-*, *\*ml-* 'grind,' which also produced English *meal* 'flour,' *mill*, and *molar*.
▶ meal, melt, mild, mill, molar, mollify

**moment** [14] As the closely related *momentum* [17] suggests, 'movement' is the etymological notion underlying *moment*. It comes via Old French *moment* from Latin *mōmentum*. This was a contraction of an assumed earlier *\*movimentum*, a derivative of *movēre* 'move' (source of English *move*), and it had a wide range of meanings: from the literal 'movement' (preserved in English in the directly borrowed *momentum*) developed the metaphorical 'instant of time' (which arose from the notion of a particle so small as only just to 'move' the pointer of a scale) and 'importance' – both preserved in English *moment*. The former has been allotted the derived adjective *momentary* [16], the latter *momentous* [17].
▶ momentous, momentum, move

**monastery** see MONK

**Monday** [OE] Etymologically, *Monday* is the 'moon's day.' It comes from a prehistoric German translation of Latin *lūnae diēs* 'day of the moon,' which also produced German *montag*, Dutch *maandag*, Swedish *måandag*, and Danish *mandag*. In the Romance languages, the Latin term has become French *lundi*, Italian *lunedì*, Spanish *lunes*, and Rumanian *luni*. (The various words for 'Monday' in the Slavic languages, incidentally, such as Russian *ponedel'nik*, mean basically 'after Sunday.')
▶ moon

**money** [13] An epithet used in ancient Rome for the goddess Juno was *Monēta* (derived by some etymologists in the past from the Latin verb *monēre* 'advise, warn,' although this is now regarded as rather dubious). The name was also applied to her temple in Rome, which contained a mint. And so in due course *monēta* came to mean 'mint' (a sense retained in English *mint*, which goes back via a circuitous route to *monēta*), then 'stamp for coining,' and finally 'coin' – the meaning transmitted via Old French *moneie* to English *money*.

▶ mint

**mongrel** [15] The etymological notion underlying *mongrel* is of a 'mixture.' For the word goes back ultimately to the prehistoric Germanic base *\*mong-* 'mix,' which also produced English *among* and *mingle* [14].

▶ among, mingle

**monitor** see MONSTER

**monk** [OE] Etymologically, a *monk* is someone who lives 'alone.' The word comes ultimately from late Greek *mónachos* 'solitary person, hermit,' which was derived from Greek *mónos* 'alone' (source of the English prefix *mono-*). It passed into late Latin as *monachus* (by which time it had come to denote 'monk'), and eventually found its way to Old English as *munuc* – whence modern English *monk*.

Another derivative of Greek *mónos* was *monázein* 'live alone.' On this was based late Greek *monastérion*, whose late Latin form *monastērium* has been acquired by English in two distinct phases: first in the Anglo-Saxon period as *mynster*, which has given modern English *minster* [OE], and then in the 15th century as *monastery*.

▶ minster, monastery

**monkey** [16] No one is too sure where *monkey* came from. Spanish has *mono* 'monkey,' and Old Italian had *monno* 'monkey,' both probably borrowed from Arabic *maimūn* 'monkey,' and it could be that an ancestor of these was borrowed into Low German and given the diminutive suffix *-ke*. This would account for *monkey*. No related Germanic form has been found to substantiate this, although the name *Moneke* does occur in Middle Low German.

**monolith** see LITHOGRAPH

**monsieur** see SIR

**monster** [13] *Monster* originated as a word for a 'divine omen or warning.' It goes back via Old French *monstre* to Latin *mōnstrum*, a derivative of the verb *monēre* 'warn.' From its original sense 'warning of misfortune, evil omen,' *mōnstrum* was transferred to the sort of thing that could function as such an omen – a 'prodigy,' or a 'misshapen or horrifying creature' – whence the meaning of English *monster*. The word's connotations of 'largeness' seem to be rather more recent, first emerging in English in the 16th century.

Other English derivatives of *mōnstrum*, some of them reflecting a later sense of *monēre*, 'show, inform,' rather than the original 'warn,' include *demonstrate* [16], *monstrance* [16], *muster* [13] (which originally meant 'display'), and *remonstrate* [16]. And from *monēre* itself come *admonish*, *monitor* [16], *monument* [13], *premonition* [16], and *summon* [13].

▶ admonish, demonstrate, monitor, monument, muster, premonition, remonstrate, summon

**month** [OE] In ancient times the passing of time was recorded by noting the revolutions of the moon. Consequently prehistoric Indo-European had a single word, *\*mēnes-*, which denoted both 'moon' and 'month.' The Romance languages retain it only for 'month': Latin *mēnsis* (source of English *menstrual*) has given French *mois*, Italian *mese*, and Spanish *mes*. The Germanic languages, however, have kept both, distinguishing them by different forms. In the case of 'month,' the Germanic word was *\*mǣnōth*, which has differentiated into German *monat*, Dutch *maand*, Swedish *månad*, Danish *maaned*, and English *month*.

▶ menstrual, moon

**monument** see MONSTER

**mood** English has two words *mood*. The original one, 'emotional state' [OE], goes back to a prehistoric Germanic *\*mōthaz* or *\*mōtham*, whose descendants have denoted a wide range of such states: 'anger,' for instance (Old Norse *móthr*), and 'courage' (German *mut*). Old English *mōd* meant 'mind, thought,' 'pride,' 'courage,' and 'anger' as well as 'frame of mind,' but it is only the last that has survived.

*Mood* 'set of verb forms indicating attitude (such as the subjunctive)' [16] is an alteration of *mode*, influenced by *mood* 'frame of mind.'

▶ mode

**moon** [OE] Indo-European *\*mēnes-* meant both 'moon' and 'month.' It was probably a derivative of the base *\*me-* (source of English *measure*), reflecting the fact that in ancient times the passage of time was measured by the revolutions of the moon. Both strands of meaning have been preserved in the Germanic languages, represented by different forms: the 'moon' strand has differentiated into German *mond*, Dutch *maan*, Swedish *måane*, Danish *maane*, and English *moon*. Etymologically, *Monday* is 'moon day.'

▶ measure, metre, Monday, month

**moor** Counting the capitalized form, English has three separate words *moor*. The oldest, 'open land' [OE], comes from a prehistoric Germanic *\*mōraz* or *\*mōram*, whose other modern descendants, such as German *moor*, mean 'swamp,' suggest the possibility of some connection with English *mere* 'lake' (see MARINE).

*Moor* 'tie up a boat' [15] was probably borrowed from a Middle Low German *mōren*, a relative of Dutch *meren* 'moor.' And *Moor* 'inhabitant of North Africa' [14] comes ultimately from Greek *Mauros*, a word no doubt of North African origin from which the name of the modern state Mauretania is derived. English relatives include *morello* [17], the name of a dark-skinned cherry which comes via Italian from Latin *morellus* or *maurellus*, a derivative of *Maurus* 'Moor'; and *morris dance*.

▶ marine, mere / morello, morris dance

**moose** [17] The moose's name is a native American word. It comes from Natick *moos*, which has been linked by some with Narragansett *moosu* 'he strips,' an allusion to the moose's habit of stripping the bark from trees.

**moot** [OE] Etymologically, a 'moot point' is one talked about at a 'meeting.' For 'meeting' is the original sense of the noun *moot* – particularly as applied in early medieval England to a meeting functioning as a court of law. The word goes back to a prehistoric Germanic *mōtam* 'meeting,' source also of English *meet*. Its modern adjectival usage seems to have emerged in the 16th century. The derived verb *moot* goes back to Old English times (*mōtian* 'converse, plead in court'), but again its present-day use, for 'suggest, propose,' is a more recent development, dating from the 17th century.

▶ meet

**mop** [15] *Mop* first appeared in the guise *mappe*, a late 15th-century sailors' term for an improvised brush used for caulking ships' seams with tar. The modern form *mop*, presumably the same word, did not emerge until the mid-17th-century. It may be a truncation of an earlier *mapple* 'mop' [15], which came from late Latin *mappula* 'towel, cloth,' a diminutive form of Latin *mappa* 'cloth' (source of English *map*).

▶ map

**moral** [14] Latin *mōs* 'custom' is the starting point of the English family of 'morality'-words (and its plural *mōres* was acquired by English as *mores* in the 20th century). Its derived adjective *mōrālis* was coined, according to some by Cicero, as a direct translation of Greek *ēthikós* 'ethical,' to denote the 'typical or proper behaviour of human beings in society,' and was borrowed directly into English in the 14th century. *Morale* [18] was borrowed from French, where it is the feminine form of the adjective *moral*. At first it was used in English for 'morality, moral principles'; its modern sense 'condition with regard to optimism, cheerfulness, etc' is not recorded until the early 19th century.

▶ morale, mores

**moratorium** see DEMUR
**mordant** see MORSEL
**more** [OE] The Indo-European term for 'more' was *meis* (it was formed from the same base as produced Latin *magis* 'more,' source of Spanish *mas* 'more' and English *master*, and Latin *magnus* 'large,' source of English *magnitude*). Its Germanic descendant was *maiz*, which evolved into modern German *mehr* 'more,' and also into Old English *mā* 'more,' which survived dialectally until fairly recently as *mo*. From the adverb *maiz* was derived the adjective *maizon*, and it was this that has given English *more*. *Most* is, of course, closely related.

▶ magnitude, master, most

**morello** see MOOR
**morganatic** [18] A morganatic marriage is one between people of different social status, in which the rank and entitlements of the higher-status partner are not shared by the lower or their offspring. The word *morganatic* is a survival of an ancient Germanic marriage custom. On the morning after the wedding night, after the marriage had been consummated, the husband gave the wife a symbolic gift, which removed any further legal claim the wife or their children might have on his possessions. The term for this useful gift was *morgangeba*, a compound formed from *morgan* (ancestor of English *morning*) and *geba* (a noun formed from the same base as produced English *give*). The word was adopted into medieval Latin as *morganaticus*, from which (via either French or German) English got *morganatic*.

▶ morning, give

**morgue** [19] The original Morgue was a Parisian mortuary where unidentified corpses were displayed for visitors to try and put names to faces (a process described in gruesome detail by Émile Zola in *Thérèse Raquin* 1867). Its name is presumed to be a re-application of an earlier French *morgue* 'room in a prison where new prisoners were examined,' which may ultimately be the same word as *morgue* 'haughty superiority' (used in English from the 16th to the 19th centuries). *Morgue* was first adopted as a generic English term for 'mortuary' in the USA in the 1880s.

**morning** [13] The Old English word for 'morning' was *morgen*. It came from a prehistoric Germanic *murganaz* (source also of German, Dutch, and Danish *morgen* 'morning'), and links have been suggested with forms such as Old Church Slavonic *mruknati* 'darken' and Lithuanian *mirgeti* 'twinkle,' which may point to an underlying etymological notion of the 'glimmer of morning twilight.' By the Middle English period the word *morgen* had evolved to what we now know as *morn*, and *morning* was derived from it on the analogy of *evening*. A parallel development of *mor-*

*gen* was to Middle English *morwe*, from which we get modern English *morrow* (and hence *tomorrow*).

▶ morn, tomorrow

## morphology    see FORM

## morris    [15] Etymologically, the *morris dance* is a 'Moorish dance.' The name, probably borrowed into English from Flemish *mooriske dans*, implies a perceived connection with a dance performed by the Moors, presumably in Spain, but the dance to which it is applied has far more ancient cultural roots than this would suggest. (The *morris* of *nine men's morris*, incidentally, a sort of old board game, is a different word, perhaps going back ultimately to Old French *merel* 'token, counter.')

▶ Moor, morello

## morse    [19] People had for some years been experimenting with the magnetic telegraph, but it was the American inventor Samuel Morse (1791–1872) who in 1836 produced the first workable system. And with his assistant Alexander Bain he devised a set of dots and dashes representing letters and numbers which could be used for transmitting messages, and which came to be known as the *Morse code*. In the first half of the 20th century *morse* was also used as a verb: 'It can be used for Morsing instructions about breakfast to the cook,' *Punch* 31 March 1920.

## morsel    [13] Etymologically, a *morsel* is a piece 'bitten' off. The word comes from Old French *morsel*, a diminutive of *mors* 'bite.' This in turn goes back to Latin *morsus*, a derivative of the same base as the verb *mordēre* 'bite.' Other English words from the same source include *mordant* [15] and *remorse*.

▶ mordant, remorse

## mortal    [14] *Mortal* goes back ultimately to the Indo-European base *\*mor-*, *\*mr-* 'die' (source also of English *murder*). From it were descended the Latin words *mortuus* 'dead' (source of English *mortuary* [14] and the 19th-century American coinage *mortician*) and *mors* 'death.' The adjectival derivative of *mors* was *mortālis*, which reached English via Old French *mortal, mortel*. Also based on *mors* was the late Latin verb *mortificāre* 'kill,' hence metaphorically 'subdue desires,' from which English gets *mortify* [14].

▶ mortgage, mortify, mortuary, murder

## mortar    [13] Latin *mortārium*, a word of unknown origin, denoted both a 'bowl for grinding' and, by extension, the 'substance made in such a bowl.' These twin meanings survived through Anglo-Norman *morter* into modern English *mortar* as the 'bowl used with a pestle' and a 'building mixture of cement, sand, and water.' The shape of the former led in the 17th century to the word's application to a 'short cannon.' The use of *mortarboard* for a 'square flat academic cap' dates from the mid-19th century.

## mortgage    [14] *Mortgage* means literally 'dead pledge.' It comes from Old French *mortgage*, a compound formed from *mort* 'dead' and *gage* 'pledge' (source of English *gage* and closely related to English *wage*). The notion behind the word is supposedly that if the mortgagor fails to repay the loan, the property pledged as security is lost, or becomes 'dead,' to him or her.

▶ mortal, wage

## mortuary    see MORTAL

## mosaic    [16] *Mosaic* work is etymologically work 'of the muses.' The word comes ultimately from Greek *mouseion*, which originally meant literally 'place of the muses,' and has also given English *museum*. Somehow in medieval Latin it became altered to *mūsaicus* or *mōsaicus*, and passed via early modern Italian *mosaico* and French *mosaïque* into English as *mosaic*. It has no etymological connection, incidentally, with *Mosaic* 'of Moses' [17].

▶ muse, museum

## mosque    [17] *Mosque* means etymologically a place where you 'bow down' in prayer and is, not surprisingly, of Arabic origin. It comes from Arabic *masjid* 'place of worship,' a derivative of the verb *sajada* 'bow down.' English acquired the word via Italian *moschea* and French *mosquée* as *mosquee*, but soon dropped the final *-e*. (The Arabic form *masjid* or *musjid* has been intermittently used in English in the 19th and 20th centuries.)

## mosquito    [16] *Mosquito* comes ultimately from the Latin word for 'fly,' *musca* (this went back to an Indo-European base *\*mu-*, probably imitative of the sound of humming, which also produced English *midge* [OE], and hence its derivative *midget* [19] – originally a 'tiny sand-fly'). *Musca* became Spanish *mosca*, whose diminutive form reached English as *mosquito* – etymologically a 'small fly.' (The Italian descendant of *musca*, incidentally, is also *mosca*, and *its* diminutive, *moschetto*, was applied with black humour to the 'bolt of a crossbow.' From it English gets *musket* [16].)

▶ midge, midget, musket

## moss    [OE] The prehistoric Germanic ancestor of *moss* was *\*musam*. This had two distinct meanings: 'swamp' and 'moss.' It is not altogether clear which was primary, but it seems more probable than not that 'moss' (a plant which frequents damp places) was derived from 'swamp.' The only meaning recorded for its Old English descendant *mos* was 'swamp' (which survives in place-names), but no doubt 'moss' (not evidenced before the 14th century) was current too. Words from the same ultimate source to have found their way into English include *mire* [14] (borrowed from Old Norse *mýrr* 'swamp'), *mousse* [19] (borrowed from French, which got it from Middle Low German *mos* 'moss'), and *litmus* [16] (whose Old Norse source

*litmosi* meant literally 'dye-moss' – litmus is a dye extracted from lichens).

▶ litmus, mire, mousse

**most** [OE] Like *more, most* comes ultimately from prehistoric Germanic *maiz*. Addition of the superlative suffix produced *maistaz*, which passed into Old English as *mæst*. This subsequently evolved to *most* in Middle English under the influence of *more*.

▶ magnitude, master, more

**mother** [OE] The ancestral Indo-European word for 'mother' was *māter-*, which has descendants in virtually all the modern European languages. It was probably based on the syllable *ma*, suggested by the burbling of a suckling baby, which also lies behind English *mama, mamma* (and indeed *mammal*). Amongst its immediate descendants were Latin *māter* (source of English *madrigal, material, maternal, matrimony, matrix, matron*, and *matter*) and Greek *métēr* (from which English gets *metropolis*). In prehistoric Germanic it evolved to *mōthar-*, which has differentiated to German *mutter*, Dutch *moeder*, Swedish and Danish *moder*, and English *mother*.

▶ madrigal, mamma, mammal, material, maternal, matrimony, matrix, matron, matter, metropolis

**motor** [16] The most direct English descendant of Latin *movēre* 'move' is of course *move*, but several more have found their way into the language via derivatives. From *mōtiō* 'movement' comes *motion* [15] (and its collateral forms *commotion* [15], *emotion*, and *promotion* [15]); from *mōtīvus* 'causing to move' come *motivate* [19], *motive* [14], and (via modern French) *motif* [19]; and *mōtor* 'mover' has given *motor*. Originally this was used for the rather generalized notion of a 'moving force'; the modern application to an 'engine' did not emerge until the mid-19th century. Also from *movēre* come English *moment* and *mutiny*.

▶ commotion, emotion, moment, motif, motion, motive, move, mutiny, promotion

**mould** English has three words *mould*. By some way the oldest is 'earth, soil' [OE], which comes ultimately from the Indo-European base *mel-*, *mol-*, *ml-* 'grind' (source also of English *meal* 'flour,' *mill*, etc). *Moulder* [16] may be derived from it. *Mould* 'form' [13] is assumed to come from Old French *modle* 'form, shape, pattern.' This was descended from Latin *modulus* 'small measure' (source of English *module*), a diminutive form of *modus* 'measure' (source of English *mode, model*, etc). *Mould* 'fungus' [15] appears to have originated as an adjective, meaning 'mouldy.' This in turn was an adjectival use of the past participle of a now obsolete verb *moul* 'go mouldy,' which was borrowed from an assumed Old Norse *mugla*.

▶ meal, mill, molar, moulder / mode, model, mood

**moult** [14] The etymological meaning of *moult* is simply 'change.' It comes (via an assumed but never

recorded Old English *mūtian*) from a prehistoric Germanic verb borrowed from Latin *mūtāre* 'change' (source of English *mutate*). The extreme semantic narrowing down from 'change' to 'change a coat of feathers' is shown too in the related *mews*, which originally denoted 'cages for moulting hawks.' The spelling with *l*, which started to appear in the 16th century, is due to association with words such as *fault*, whose *l* at that time was generally not pronounced. When it began to be, *moult* followed suit.

▶ mews, mutate

**mountain** [13] Latin *mōns* 'mountain' could well go back ultimately to a variant of the base *min-* 'jut' which produced English *eminent, imminent, menace*, and *prominent*. English acquired it originally direct from Latin as a noun, *mount* [OE], which is now used only in the names of mountains. The verb *mount* followed in the 14th century, via Old French *munter*. Latin *mōns* had a derived adjective *montānus* 'mountainous,' which was adapted in Vulgar Latin to the noun *montānea* 'mountainous area.' This made its way into Old French as *montaigne*, by which time it meant simply 'mountain' – whence English *mountain*.

*Amount* [13] comes ultimately from the Latin phrase *ad montem* 'to the mountain,' hence 'upwards'; and *paramount* [16] in turn derives from an Old French phrase *par amont* 'by above,' hence 'superior.'

▶ amount, eminent, imminent, menace, mount, paramount, prominent, tantamount

**mouse** [OE] *Mouse* is an ancient word, with relatives today in all the Germanic and Slavic languages. Its Indo-European ancestor was *mūs-*, which produced Greek *mūs*, Latin *mūs* (something of a dead end: the modern Romance languages have abandoned it), Sanskrit *mūs* (source, via a very circuitous route, of English *musk*), and prehistoric Germanic *mūs-*. This has evolved into German *maus*, Dutch *muis*, Swedish and Danish *mus*, and English *mouse*. And the Slavic branch of the 'mouse'-family includes Russian *mysh'*, Polish *mysz*, and Serbo-Croat *mish*. English relatives of *mouse* include *muscle* and *mussel* (ultimately the same word) and *marmot* [17], which goes back to a Vulgar Latin accusative form *mūrem montis* 'mouse of the mountain.'

▶ marmot, muscle, musk, mussel

**mousse** see MOSS

**moustache** [16] *Moustache* comes via French from Italian *mostaccio*, which goes back ultimately to Greek *mústax* 'upper lip, moustache.' The synonymous *mustachio* [16] appears to have originated as a blend of *mostaccio* with the related Spanish *mostacho*.

**mouth** [OE] *Mouth* is part of a general Germanic family of 'mouth'-words that go back to a prehistoric *munthaz*: its modern relatives include German and Danish *mund*, Dutch *mond*, and Swedish *mun*. The loss of the nasal consonant is part of a general phenomenon that happened in primitive Old English (and also in Old Frisian and Old Saxon) whose effects can be seen also in *goose* (beside German *gans*) and *tooth* (beside German *zahn*). It is thought that *\*munthaz* itself comes from the same Indo-European source as produced Latin *mentum* 'chin.'

**move** [13] *Move* comes via Anglo-Norman *mover* from Latin *movēre* 'move,' which was related to Sanskrit *mīv-* 'push, press.' Derivatives of the Latin verb have been a rich source of English vocabulary, including *emotion, moment, motion, motor*, and *mutiny*.

▶ emotion, moment, motion, motor, mutiny

**much** [13] The Old English word for 'much' was *mycel* (a relative of Old Norse *mikill*, from which English got the now archaic *mickle* [13]). It goes back ultimately to the same Indo-European base as produced Latin *magis* 'more' (source of English *master*) and *magnus* 'large' (source of English *magnitude*) and Greek *mégas* 'large' (source of the English prefix *mega-*). *Mycel* became early Middle English *muchel*, which began to lose its second syllable in the 13th century.

▶ magnitude, master, more

**mucilage** see MUCUS

**muck** [13] The original meaning of *muck* is 'excrement'; the more general 'dirt' is a 14th-century development. It goes back to a prehistoric Germanic *\*muk-, \*meuk-* 'soft.' This was also the source of Danish *møg* 'dung' (which provides the first syllable of *midden* [14], a borrowing from the ancestor of Danish *mødding*, literally 'dung-heap'). The same Germanic base lies behind English *meek* [12], whose immediate Old Norse antecedent *mjúkr* meant 'soft, pliant' – leading on in due course to English 'submissive.'

▶ meek, midden

**mucus** [17] *Mucus* was borrowed from Latin *mūcus* 'nasal mucus,' which was related to two ancient verbs for 'blow the nose': Greek *mússesthai* and Latin *ēmungere*. The homophonic adjectival derivative *mucous* [17] (as in *mucous membrane*) comes from Latin *mūcōsus*. Related forms to have reached English are *mucilage* [14], from the late Latin derivative *mūcilāgō*, and *moist*.

▶ moist, mucilage

**mud** [14] The Old English word for 'mud' was *fen*, which now survives only in the sense 'swamp.' It was replaced in the Middle English period by *mud*, probably a borrowing from Middle Low German *mudde*. This goes back ultimately to a prehistoric base *\*meu-, \*mu-* that has produced a range of words in the Indo-European languages denoting 'dirt' or 'wet': Greek *múdos* 'damp,' for instance, and Polish *muł* 'slime.' *Muddle* [17] may come from Middle Dutch *moddelen* 'make muddy,' a derivative of *modde* 'mud.'

**muesli** [20] Etymologically, *muesli* means 'little pap.' It is a Swiss-German diminutive form of German *mus* 'pulp, purée.' Old English had the cognate *mōs*, which survived into the 16th century in the compound *apple-mose* 'dish made from a purée of stewed apples.'

**mule** English has two words *mule*. The 'donkey-like animal' [13] comes via Old French *mul* from Latin *mūlus*, which was borrowed from a pre-Latin language of the Mediterranean area; Albanian *mušk* 'mule' is related. *Mule* the 'slipper' [16] is probably an adaptation of Latin *mulleus*, which denoted a sort of red or purple shoe worn by high-ranking magistrates in Rome. This was short for *mulleus calceus* 'red shoe,' and *mulleus* itself appears to have been derived from *mullus* 'red mullet' (ultimate source of English *mullet* [15]), which in turn came from Greek *múllos*, a relative of *mélās* 'black.'

▶ mullet

**multiply** [13] *Multiply* is one of a large family of English words based on Latin *multus* 'much,' a word of uncertain origin which may be related to Greek *mála* 'very' and Latin *melior* 'better.' *Multiply* itself comes from the Latin derivative *multiplicāre*, formed with the element *plic-* 'fold' found also in *complicated, explicit*, etc, and therefore very closely parallel to the native English compound *manifold*. Other members of the family include *multiple* [17], from late Latin *multiplus* (the *-plus* is a relative of the *-plic-* in *multiplicāre*); *multitude* [14], from Latin *multitūdō* 'crowd,' formed with the abstract noun suffix *-tūdō*; and of course the host of words formed since the 16th century with the prefix *multi-*, including *multifarious* [17] (based on Latin *-fārius* 'doing'), *multilateral* [17], *multinational* [20], *multiracial* [20], and *multistorey* [20].

▶ fold

**mum** see MUMMY, MUMPS

**mumble** see MUMPS

**mummer** see MUMPS

**mummy** English has two words *mummy*. The one meaning 'mother' [19], although not recorded in print until comparatively recently, is one of a range of colloquial 'mother'-words, such as *mama* and *mammy*, that go back ultimately to the syllable *ma*, imitative of a suckling baby (see MAMMAL and MOTHER), and was probably common in dialect speech much earlier. The 19th century saw its adoption into the general language. The abbreviation *mum* [19] has a parallel history.

The Egyptian *mummy* [14] comes ultimately from Arabic *mūmiyā* 'embalmed body,' a derivative of *mūm* 'embalming wax,' but when it first arrived in English (via medieval Latin *mumia* and Old French *mumie*) it was used for a 'medicinal ointment prepared from mummified bodies' ('Take myrrh, sarcocol [a gum-resin], and mummy . . . and lay it on the nucha [spinal cord],' *Lanfranc's Science of Cirurgie, c* 1400). The word's original sense 'embalmed body' did not emerge in English until the early 17th century.

▶ mama, mammy

**mumps** [16] The dialect noun *mump* meant 'grimace'; and the use of its plural *mumps* for the disease is thought to have been originally an allusion to the distorted expression caused by the swollen neckglands. *Mump* itself is presumably related to the verb *mump* 'sulk' [16], and belongs to a family of words (including also *mumble* [14]) based on the syllable *mum*, representing an 'indistinct sound made through closed lips' (*mum* 'silent' [14] itself, as in 'keep mum,' comes from this source, as does *mummer* [15], originally 'mime actor').

▶ mum, mumble, mummer

**municipal** [16] Latin *mūnus* meant 'office, duty, gift.' Combined with *-ceps* 'taker' (a derivative of the verb *capere* 'take,' source of English *capture*) it formed *mūniceps*, which denoted a 'citizen of a Roman city (known as a *mūnicipium*) whose inhabitants had Roman citizenship but could not be magistrates.' From *mūnicipium* was derived the adjective *mūnicipālis*, source of English *municipal*; this was originally used for 'of the internal affairs of a state, domestic,' and the modern application to the sphere of local government did not emerge strongly until the 19th century. The stem of Latin *mūnus* also crops up in *commūnis* (source of English *common*), and so *community* and *municipality* are etymologically related.

*Mūnus* in the later sense 'gift' formed the basis of the Latin adjective *mūnificus* 'giving gifts,' hence 'generous,' from which ultimately English gets *munificent* [16].

▶ capture, common

**mural** [16] The Latin for 'wall' was *mūrus*, derivatives of which have given English *immure* [16] and *mural*. It came from an earlier form *moerus*, to which was related *moenia* 'walls,' source of the verb *mūnīre* 'fortify, defend.' This has given English *muniment* 'documentary proof of ownership, which 'defends' one's right to something' [15] and *munition* [16] (whence *ammunition*).

▶ ammunition, immure, muniment, munition

**murder** [OE] The ultimate source of *murder* is the Indo-European base *\*mor-, \*mr-* 'die' (source also of English *mortal*). Its extension *\*mrt-* produced a prehistoric Germanic *\*mortam* (source of German, Swedish, and Danish *mord* and Dutch *moord* 'murder') and *\*murthram*, from which comes English *murder*.

▶ mortal

**muscat** see MUSK

**muscle** [16] Ultimately, *muscle* and *mussel* [OE] are the same word, and both owe their origin to a

supposed resemblance to a mouse. They go back to Latin *mūsculus*, literally 'little mouse,' a diminutive form of *mūs* 'mouse,' which was applied to the shellfish because of a similarity in shape and colour, and to 'muscle' because the shape and movement of certain muscles beneath the skin, such as the biceps, reminded people of a mouse. Latin *mūsculus* 'mussel' was borrowed into Old English as *muscle* or *muxle*; the *-ss-* spelling began to emerge in the 15th century, inspired by Middle Low German *mussel* (which came from *\*muscula*, a Vulgar Latin feminization of Latin *mūsculus* and source of French *moule* 'mussel') and reinforced in the 16th century by the introduction via Old French of *muscle* for 'muscle.'

The notion of resemblance to a mouse also lies behind English *musk*.

▶ mouse, mussel

**museum** [17] Etymologically, a *museum* is a place devoted to the 'muses.' It comes via Latin *mūsēum* 'library, study' from Greek *mouseion* 'place of the muses,' a noun based on the adjective *mouseios* 'of the muses.' This in turn was derived from *mousa* 'muse,' source of English *muse* [14]. Other English words from the same source are *mosaic* and *music*. But *muse* 'ponder' is not related; it comes, like its first cousin *amuse*, from Old French *muse* 'animal's mouth.'

▶ mosaic, muse, music

**music** [13] Etymologically, *music* comes from the 'muses,' Greek goddesses who inspired poets, painters, musicians, etc. The word traces its history back via Old French *musique* and Latin *mūsica* to Greek *mousikḗ*, a noun use of *mousikós* 'of the muses,' an adjective derived from *mousa* 'muse.' The specialization of the word's meaning began in Greek – first to 'poetry sung to music,' and subsequently to 'music' alone.

▶ muse, museum

**musk** [14] Like the substance musk itself, the name *musk* came to Europe from the East. Its ultimate ancestor appears to have been Sanskrit *muska* 'scrotum, testicle.' This meant literally 'little mouse' (it was a diminutive form of Sanskrit *mūs* 'mouse'), and its metaphorical reapplication was due to a supposed similarity in shape between mice and testicles (a parallel inspiration gave rise to English *muscle* and *mussel*). The gland from which the male musk deer secretes musk was held to resemble a scrotum, and so Persian took the Sanskrit word for 'scrotum' over, as *mushk*, and used it for 'musk.' It reached English via late Latin *muscus*.

The *-meg* of English *nutmeg* comes ultimately from Latin *muscus*, and other English relatives include *muscat* [16], the name of a grape that supposedly smells of musk, and its derivative *muscatel* [14].

▶ mouse, muscatel, muscle, mussel, nutmeg

**musket** see MOSQUITO

**muslin** [17] Etymologically, *muslin* is 'cloth from Mosul,' a city in Iraq where fine cotton fabric was once made. The Arabic form *mūslin* was adopted into Italian as *mussolino*, and made its way into English via French *mousseline*.

**mussel** see MUSCLE

**must** English has three words *must*. By far the commonest is of course the verb, 'have to' [OE], which originated in Old English as the past tense of the now obsolete *mūt* 'may, must.' It has relatives in German *muss* and Dutch *moet*, but its ultimate origins are not known for certain (there may be some distant link with Germanic 'measure'-words, such as English *mete*, suggesting a semantic progression from an original 'time measured out for doing something' through 'have time to do something,' 'be able to do something,' and 'be allowed to do something' to 'have to do something').

*Must* 'unfermented grape juice for making into wine' [OE] comes from Latin *mustum* 'new wine,' a noun use of the adjective *mustus* 'new.' *Mustard* is a derivative. And the esoteric *must* 'sexual frenzy in elephants, camels, etc' [19] comes via Urdu from Persian *mast* 'drunk.'

▶ mustard

**mustachio** see MOUSTACHE

**mustang** [19] Etymologically, a *mustang* is a 'mixed' animal. The word comes from Mexican Spanish *mestengo*, which originally in Spanish meant 'stray.' This was derived from *mesta* 'annual roundup of cattle, participated in by all the herdsmen, in which stray cattle were disposed of,' which in turn goes back to medieval Latin *mixta*. And *mixta* (literally 'mixed') was used for the wild or stray animals that got 'mixed' in with the graziers' herds (it was a noun use of the feminine past participle of *miscēre* 'mix,' source of English *miscellaneous* and *mix*). The word passed early on from 'stray cattle' to 'stray horses.'

▶ miscellaneous, mix

**mustard** [13] Mustard was originally made by mixing the crushed seeds of various plants of the cabbage family with the freshly pressed juice of grapes – the 'must.' Hence its name, which comes from Old French *moustarde*, a word derived from a descendant of Latin *mustum* 'new wine' (source of English *must* 'grape juice').

▶ must

**muster** see MONSTER

**musty** see MOIST

**mutate** [19] Semantically, *mutate* is probably the most direct English descendant of the Indo-European base *moi-, *mei- 'change, exchange,' which has also given English *mad, mean* 'unworthy, ignoble,' *municipal, mutual* [15] (from Latin *mūtuus* 'exchanged, reciprocal'), the final syllable of *common*, and probably *migrate* [17]. *Mutate* itself comes from Latin *mūtāre* 'change' (source also of English *mews* and *moult*), and was preceded into English by some centuries by the derivatives *mutable* [14] and *mutation* [14].

▶ mews, moult, mutual

**mutiny** [16] Etymologically, a *mutiny* is simply a 'movement.' The word was adapted from the now obsolete *mutine*, a borrowing from French *mutin* 'rebellion.' This in turn was a derivative of an earlier *muete*, literally 'movement,' hence 'rebellion' (remembered in English in the related *émeute* 'uprising'), which came from Vulgar Latin *movita*, a descendant of Latin *movēre* 'move' (source of English *move*).

▶ émeute, motion, move

**muzzle** see AMUSE

**my** [12] *My* is simply a reduced form of *mine*, which used to be an adjective, but is now restricted almost entirely to pronoun use. At first it was used only before consonants (except *h*), but gradually from the 14th century it came to be used before all nouns, whatever their initial sound. The first record of its use as an exclamation (short, of course, for *my goodness!, my word!*, etc) comes from the early 18th century.

▶ me, mine

**myrmedon** see ANT

**mystery** [14] Greek *mūein* meant 'close one's eyes or mouth,' and hence was used figuratively for 'keep secret.' Its association with secret initiation ceremonies inspired the formation from it of *muein* 'initiate,' whose derivative *mústēs* meant 'initiated person.' This in turn formed the basis of *mustérion* 'secret ceremony, secret thing,' which passed into English via Latin *mystērium*. Also derived from *mústēs* was *mustikós*, from which ultimately English gets *mystic* [14] and *mystical* [15].

▶ mystic

# N

**nail** [OE] The Indo-European ancestor of *nail* was *\*nogh-* or *\*onogh-*. The latter was the source of Latin *unguis* (which evolved into French *ongle* and Italian *unghia* and has given English *ungulate* [19]) and Greek *ónux* (source of English *onyx*). Both these strands refer only to the sort of nails that grow on fingers and toes, but the Germanic branch of the family (which has come from *\*nogh-* through a prehistoric Germanic *\*naglaz*) has differentiated into a 'fastening pin' – originally of wood, latterly of metal. Hence English *nail* and German *nagel* cover both meanings (although Dutch and Swedish *nagel* and Danish *negl* are used only for the anatomical 'nail').

▶ onyx, ungulate

**naive** see NATIVE

**naked** [OE] *Naked* goes back ultimately to Indo-European *\*nogw-* 'unclothed,' which also produced Latin *nūdus* (source of English *nude* [16]) and Russian *nagój* 'naked.' The past participial form derived from this, *\*nogwedhos*, passed into prehistoric Germanic as *\*naquethaz*, which has subsequently differentiated into German *nackt*, Dutch *naakt*, Swedish *naken*, Danish *nøgen*, and English *naked*.

▶ nude

**namby-pamby** [18] *Namby-pamby* originated in the early 18th century as a derisive nickname for the English poet Ambrose Philips (1674–1749), who wrote feebly sentimental pastorals ('Dimply damsel, sweetly smiling' gives something of their flavour). They appear to have got on the nerves particularly of his contemporary, the author Henry Carey (?1687–1741), who is credited with coining the nickname (based, of course, on the first syllable of Philips's forename). The first record of its use as a general term comes from 1745.

**name** [OE] *Name* is an ancient word, which traces its history back to Indo-European *\*-nomen-*. This has produced Latin *nōmen* (source of English *nominate*, *noun*, etc), Greek *ónoma* (source of English *anonymous* [17] – etymologically 'nameless' – and *synonym* [16]), Welsh *enw*, and Russian *imja*, among many others. Its prehistoric Germanic descendant was *\*namōn*, which has evolved to German and English *name*, Dutch *naam*, Swedish *namn*, and Danish *navn*.

▶ anonymous, nominate, noun, synonym

**namesake** see SAKE

**napkin** [15] Latin *mappa* meant 'cloth' (it is the source of English *map*). As it passed into Old French its *m* became transformed into an *n*, producing *nappe*. This was borrowed into English as the long-defunct *nape* 'cloth,' which, with the addition of the diminutive suffix *-kin*, has bequeathed *napkin* to modern English. The abbreviation *nappy* dates from the early 20th century. From derivatives of Old French *nappe* English also gets *apron* and *napery* [14].

▶ apron, map

**narcotic** [14] Greek *nárkē* meant 'numbness.' From it was derived the verb *narkoun* 'make numb,' which in turn formed the basis of the adjective *narkōtikós* 'numbing,' which passed into English via medieval Latin *narcōticus* and Old French *narcotique*.

**narrate** [17] To *narrate* something is etymologically to 'make it known.' The word comes from Latin *narrāre* 'give an account of,' which was derived from *gnārus* 'knowing' and is hence related to English *ignore, recognize*, and, distantly, *know*. English acquired the derived noun *narration* [15] considerably earlier than the verb (which was widely condemned in the 18th century for its inelegance), and it could be that *narrate* represents a back-formation from *narration* rather than a new introduction directly from the Latin verb.

▶ ignore, know, recognize

**narrow** [OE] *Narrow* comes from a prehistoric Germanic *\*narwaz*, whose only other modern representative is Dutch *naar* 'unpleasant, sad' (although it also occurs in *Norva-sund*, the Old Norse term for the 'Straits of Gibraltar'). It is not known for certain where it comes from, but a connection has been suggested with Latin *nervus* 'sinew, bowstring' (source of English *nerve*) and Old High German *snuor* 'string,' which might point back to an ancestral sense 'tying together tightly.'

**nascent**  see NATIVE

**nasturtium**  [17]  The nasturtium plant has a peppery taste (its immature flower buds are often used as an alternative to capers), and tradition has it that the Romans named it *nasturtium* because its pungency made them pucker up their noses. According to this theory, the word is an alteration of an earlier *\*nāsitortium*, which would have been a compound formed from *nāsus* 'nose' and *tort-*, the past participial stem of *torquēre* 'twist' (source of English *torture*).

**nasty**  [14]  *Nasty*, now such a widespread term of disapproval, is not that ancient a word in English, and it is not too certain where it came from. In the 14th and 15th centuries it was often spelled *naxty*, and this, together with one early 17th-century example of *nasky*, has suggested some connection with Swedish dialect *naskug* 'dirty, nasty.' And a link has also been proposed with Dutch *nestig* 'dirty,' which may denote etymologically 'made dirty like a bird's nest.' 'Dirty' was the original sense of the English adjective; the more general 'unpleasant' did not begin to emerge until the end of the 17th century.

**natal**  see NATIVE

**nation**  [13]  Etymologically a *nation* is a 'breed' or 'stock.' It is one of a wide range of English words that go back ultimately to Latin *nāscī* 'be born,' and its immediate source is the derived noun *nātiō*. This literally meant 'that which has been born,' a 'breed,' but was soon used by extension for a 'species' or 'race,' and then by further narrowing down for a 'race of people, nation.' The notion of 'common ancestry' underlying the term survived into English, but over the centuries has gradually been overtaken by the political concept of an organized territorial unit. The derivative *nationality* dates from the 17th century.

▶ native

**native**  [14]  *Native* is one of a large family of English words that go back ultimately to the Latin verb *nāscī*. This meant 'be born,' and was a descendant of the Indo-European base *\*gen-*, *\*gn-* 'produce,' which also gave English *gene, general, generate*, etc. From its past participial stem *nāt-* was formed the adjective *nātīvus* 'from birth, born,' which has produced English *native* (and also, via Old French, *naive* [17], which is etymologically the equivalent of 'born yesterday'), and also its derivative *nativity* [12] (applied from earliest times specifically to the birth of Christ). Other English words from the same source include *cognate* [17], *innate* [15], *nascent* [17], *natal* [14], *nation, nature, noel* (earlier *nowel* [14], from an Old French descendant of

Latin *nātālis* 'of birth'), *pregnant, puny*, and *renaissance* [19] (literally 'rebirth').

▶ cognate, gene, general, generate, innate, naive, nascent, nation, nature, noel, pregnant, puny, renaissance

**natty**  see NEAT

**nature**  [13]  Etymologically, someone's *nature* is the qualities they were 'born' with. The word comes via Old French *nature* from Latin *nātūra*, a derivative of the verb *nāscī* 'be born' (source of English *nation, native*, etc). This originally meant simply 'birth,' but by classical times it had developed to the 'innate properties or qualities of something or someone,' and hence to the 'inherent course of things,' the 'way things are in the world.' The common English sense 'physical world' (as in *nature study*) first began to emerge in the 16th century.

▶ native

**navy**  [14]  Latin *nāvis* 'ship' is the ultimate source of *navy*. In post-classical times it spawned an offspring *nāvia* 'fleet,' which passed into English via Old French *navie*. Other Latin derivatives of *nāvis* were *nāvālis*, source of English *naval* [16], and the verb *nāvigāre* 'manage a ship,' from which English gets *navigate* [16] (*navvy* [19] originated as a colloquial abbreviation for *navigator*, a term applied to someone who dug 'navigation canals'). In medieval Latin *nāvis* was applied to the central part of a church, from the passing resemblance in shape to a ship, and the word was anglicized as *nave* [17].

*Nāvis* was related to Greek *naus* 'ship,' whose contributions to English include *nautical* [16], *nautilus* [17], *nausea* [16] (etymologically 'seasickness'), and, somewhat surprisingly, *noise*.

▶ nausea, nautical, navigate, noise

**nay**  see NO

**near**  [12]  Historically, *near* is a comparative form, and its ancestor originally meant 'nearer.' It was borrowed from Old Norse *náer*, the comparative of *ná-* 'near,' which came from the same prehistoric Germanic source as produced English *nigh* [OE] and *next* (not to mention German *nah* 'near'). By the time it reached English it had lost its comparative force, and simply meant 'close' (which is also the sense of its modern Scandinavian descendants, Swedish *nära* and Danish *nær*).

▶ neighbour, next, nigh

**neat**  English has two words *neat*. The older is now virtually obsolete, while the commoner is a comparatively recent introduction. *Neat* 'tidy' [16] was borrowed from French *net* 'neat, clean.' This goes back to Latin *nitidus* 'elegant, shiny,' a derivative of the verb *nitēre* 'shine.' English originally acquired the word in the 14th century as *net* 'clean, tidy' (from which the modern *net* 'with deductions' developed). This had a

16th-century derivative *netty*, which may be the source of modern English *natty* [18].

*Neat* 'cow, ox' [OE] is now encountered only in gastronomic contexts, such as 'neat's foot jelly,' and even then is an archaism. It goes back to prehistoric Germanic *nautam*, a derivative of a base meaning 'use,' and hence reflects (like *cattle* itself) the original notion of cattle as 'useful property.'

▶ natty, net

**nebula**   [17]   As its form suggests, *nebula* was originally a Latin word, but it goes back to a prehistoric Indo-European base (*nebh- 'cloud') which produced a wide range of other descendants, including German *nebel* 'cloud,' Greek *néphos* 'cloud,' and Latvian *debess* 'sky.' It also got into Old English, as *nifol* 'dark.' The Latin word was originally used in English for a sort of 'cataract' over the eye, and the present-day astronomical application to a 'cloud' of stars did not emerge until the early 18th century. The derivative *nebulous* [16] is an earlier borrowing.

**necessary**   [14]   The original Latin adjective meaning 'necessary' was *necesse* (it was formed with the negative particle *ne*-from the stem of *cēdere* 'yield,' source of English *cede*, and hence meant etymologically 'unyielding'). This was subsequently extended to *necessārius*, and English acquired it via Anglo-Norman *necessarie*.

▶ cede, concede, proceed

**neck**   [OE]   *Neck* originally meant only the 'back or nape of the neck' (that is what its modern German relative *nacken* denotes, and in Old English times the usual word for 'neck' in general was *heals*). It seems to go back to a prehistoric Indo-European base *knok- signifying 'high point, ridge,' which also produced Irish *cnoc* 'hill.' The use of the verb *neck* for 'kiss and cuddle' dates back at least to the early 19th century.

**necromancy**   [13]   Greek *nekrós* meant 'corpse' (it has given English *necrophilia* [19], *necropolis* 'cemetery' [19], and *necrosis* 'death of tissue' [17] as well as *necromancy*, and goes back to a base *nek- 'kill' which also produced Latin *nex* 'killing,' source of English *internecine* and *pernicious*, and possibly Greek *néktar*, source of English *nectar*). Addition of *manteíā* 'divination,' a derivative of *mántis* 'prophet, diviner' (from which English gets the insect-name *mantis* [17], an allusion to its raised front legs, which give it an appearance of praying), produced *nekromanteíā* 'foretelling the future by talking to the dead,' which passed into late Latin as *necromantīa*. By the Middle Ages the application of the term had broadened out to 'black magic' in general, and this led to an association of the first element of the word with Latin *niger* 'black.' Hence when it first arrived in English it was in the form *nigromancy*,

and the restoration of the original *necro-* did not happen until the 16th century.

▶ internecine, mantis, pernicious

**nectar**   [16]   Nectar was originally the drink of the Greek gods, but soon after the word's arrival in English it was being used metaphorically for any 'delicious drink.' It comes via Latin *nectar* from Greek *néktar*, and it has been speculated that this may have been derived from the base *nek- 'kill' (source also of English *necromancy*), as some sort of allusion to the 'immortality' of the gods. *Nectarine* [17], the name of a sort of peach based on the now disused adjective *nectarine* 'like nectar,' was probably inspired by German *nektarpfirsich* 'nectar-peach.'

**need**   [OE]   *Need* is a widespread Germanic noun, with relatives also in German *not*, Dutch *nood*, Swedish *nöd*, and Danish *nød*. It comes from a prehistoric Germanic *nauthiz*, whose non-Germanic relatives, such as Old Prussian *nautin* 'necessity, distress' and Czech *nyti* 'languish,' reveal its darker past, in which the accent was on 'distress' and 'straitened circumstances' rather than just the desirability of having something (these connotations survive in German *not*, which means 'misery, danger, emergency' as well as 'need').

**needle**   [OE]   Etymologically, a *needle* is a 'sewing' implement. The word comes from a prehistoric Germanic *nēthlō* (source also of German *nadel*, Dutch *naald*, Swedish *nål*, and Danish *naal*), which was derived from an Indo-European base *nē- 'sew' (represented also in English *nerve* and *neural*).

▶ nerve, neural

**nefarious**   [16]   Latin *nefās* 'sin' denoted etymologically something that was contrary to the divine law. It was a compound noun formed from the negative particle *ne-* and *fās* 'divine law, dictates of religion.' From it was derived the adjective *nefārius*, source of English *nefarious*.

**negative**   SEE RENEGADE

**negotiate**   [16]   The etymological notion underlying *negotiate* is of 'not being at leisure,' and hence of 'being busy.' The word comes ultimately from Latin *negōtium* 'business,' which was a compound formed from the negative particle *neg* and *ōtium* 'leisure' (source of English *otiose* [18]). From it was derived the verb *negōtiārī* 'do business,' which passed into English as *negotiate*. There is some early evidence in the derivatives *negotiation* and *negotiator* that the original Latin sense of the word survived into English, but in the verb itself it had already developed via 'transact business' and 'hold business discussions' to 'hold discussions' generally.

▶ otiose

**negro**    see DENIGRATE

**neighbour**    [OE] Etymologically, your *neighbour* is simply someone who 'lives near' you. It is a compound formed in the Old English period from *nēah* (ancestor of modern English *nigh*) and *gebūr* 'dweller' (a descendant of the prolific Germanic base *bū- 'dwell,' which also produced English *be, booth, bower, build,* etc). Parallel formations in other Germanic languages include German *nachbar* and Swedish and Danish *nabo*. The derivative *neighbourhood* dates from the 15th century, but was not used in its main modern sense 'district' until the late 17th century.

▶ be, booth, bower, build, burly, byre, husband, near

**neither**    [13] Despite the two words' similarity, *neither* is not just *either* with a negative prefix tacked on. It comes ultimately from Old English *nāhwæther* 'neither,' a compound formed from *nā* 'not' (which survives as *no* in modern English 'whether or no') and *hwæther* 'which of two' (ancestor of modern English *whether*). In the late Old English period it was contracted to *nawther*, and in Middle English, under the influence of *either*, this became transformed into *neither*.

▶ whether

**nemesis**    see NOMAD

**Neolithic**    see LITHOGRAPH

**neophyte**    [16] *Neophyte* is one of an ever-growing family of English words containing the prefix *neo-*, which comes from Greek *néos* 'new' (a relative of English *new*). Most of them are English formations (*neoclassical* [19], *Neolithic* [19], *neologism* [18], *neonatal* [20], *neoplatonism* [19], etc), but *neophyte* goes back to a Greek compound, *neóphutos*, which meant literally 'newly planted.' Also derived from Greek *néos* is the name of the gas *neon* [19], so called in 1898 because it was 'newly' discovered.

▶ neon, new

**nephew**    [13] *Nephew* goes back ultimately to Indo-European *nepōt-*, which denoted a range of indirect male descendants, including 'grandson' and 'nephew.' Among its offspring were Greek *anepsiós* 'nephew,' Sanskrit *nápāt* 'grandson,' Germanic *nebon* (source of German *neffe* and Dutch *neef* 'nephew'), and Latin *nepōs* 'nephew, grandson' (source of English *nepotism* [17], etymologically 'favouring one's nephews'). This passed into Old French as *neveu*, from which English got *nephew* (replacing the related native English term *neve*). The corresponding Indo-European feminine form was *neptī-*, which is the ultimate source of English *niece*.

▶ nepotism, niece

**nephrite**    see JADE

**nerve**    [16] Latin *nervus* meant 'sinew, bowstring.' It and its Greek relative *neuron* (source of English *neural*) may belong to a wider family of words that includes Latin *nēre* 'spin' (a relative of English *needle*) and possibly also English *narrow*, perhaps with a common meaning element. The application to 'bundle of fibres carrying sensory or other impulses' seems to have begun in Greek, but was soon adopted into the Latin word, and was brought with it into English. Metaphorically, the Romans used *nervus* for 'strength, force,' an application perhaps lying behind the English sense 'courage,' first recorded in the early 19th century. The use of the plural *nerves* for 'agitation, apprehension' (and of the adjective *nervous* [14] for 'apprehensive') is an English development, which probably started in the mid-18th century.

▶ needle, neural

**ness**    see NOSE

**nest**    [OE] Etymologically, a *nest* is a place for 'sitting down.' It is a very ancient word, and traces its history all the way back to Indo-European *nizdo-*, a compound formed from *ni* 'down' (source of English *beneath* and *nether*) and *sed-* (ancestor of English *sit*). From it came English *nest* (a word shared by German and Dutch), and also Latin *nīdus* 'nest,' source of Old French *niche* 'nest' – whence English *niche* [17]. *Nestle* [OE] was derived from *nest*.

▶ beneath, nestle, nether, sit

**net**    English has two distinct words *net*. The commoner and more ancient, 'mesh' [OE], is a widespread Germanic word: German has the related *netz*, Dutch and Danish *net*, and Swedish *nät*. Its ultimate origins are not known, although a link with Latin *nassa* 'wicker basket for catching fish' has been suggested. *Net* 'without deductions' [14] comes from French *net*, which was borrowed into English again two centuries later as *neat*. It was originally used, like its French source, for 'trim, clean,' but this developed via 'unadulterated, unmixed' to, by the early 16th century, 'free from any (further) deduction.' The alternative spelling *nett* dates from the 16th century.

▶ neat

**nether**    see BENEATH

**neural**    [19] *Neural* is one of a wide range of words for which English is indebted to Greek *neuron* 'nerve' (a relative of Latin *nervus*, from which English gets *nerve*). Others include *neuralgia* [19] (etymologically 'nerve-pain'), *neurology* [17], *neurosis* [18], and *neurotic* [17].

▶ nerve

**neuter**    [14] From a formal point of view, Latin *neuter* is virtually identical to English *neither*. Both originated as compounds formed from a negative particle and an element meaning 'which of two.' In the case of *neuter* these were *ne* and *uter*, which in combination denoted etymologically 'neither one thing nor the other.' The specialized application to grammatical gender soon emerged, and it was in this sense that *neuter* was first adopted into English. The derivative *neutral* [16] goes back to Latin *neutrālis*.

**new** [OE] *New* goes back a long way – to Indo-European *\*newos*, in fact. This also produced Greek *néos* 'new' (source of English *neophyte* and a range of other *neo-* compounds), Latin *novus* 'new' (ancestor of French *nouveau*, Italian *nuovo*, and Spanish *nuevo*, and source of English *novel, novice*, etc), Welsh *newydd* 'new,' Lithuanian *naujas* 'new,' and Russian *novyj*. Its prehistoric Germanic descendant was *\*neujaz*, which has fanned out into German *neu*, Dutch *nieuw*, Swedish and Danish *ny*, and English *new*. The use of the plural noun *news* for 'information' dates from the 15th century.

▶ neon, novel, novice

**newel** see NOOSE
**newfangled** see FANG
**newt** see NICKNAME

**next** [OE] Etymologically, something that is *next* is 'nearest.' The word comes, like its Germanic relatives, German *nächste*, Dutch *naaste*, Swedish *näst*, and Danish *næst*, from a prehistoric ancestor formed from *\*nēkh-* 'near' (from which English *nigh* is descended) and the superlative suffix *\*-istaz*. A parallel comparative formation has given English *near*.

▶ near, nigh

**nexus** see CONNECT

**nice** [13] *Nice* is one of the more celebrated examples in English of a word changing its meaning out of all recognition over the centuries – in this case, from 'stupid' to 'pleasant.' Its ultimate source was Latin *nescius* 'ignorant,' a compound adjective formed from the negative particle *ne-* and the base of the verb *scīre* 'know' (source of English *science*). This passed into English via Old French *nice* with minimal change of meaning, but from then on a slow but sure semantic transformation took place, from 'foolish' via 'shy,' 'fastidious,' and 'refined' to on the one hand 'minutely accurate or discriminating' (as in a 'nice distinction') and on the other 'pleasant, agreeable' (first recorded in the second half of the 18th century).

▶ science

**niche** see NEST

**nickel** [18] The element nickel was named in 1754 by the Swedish mineralogist Axel von Cronstedt. The word he chose was a truncated form of *kupfernickel*, a term formerly used by German miners for niccolite, a nickle-bearing ore. This meant literally 'copper-demon,' an allusion probably to the fact that niccolite looks as though it contains copper, but does not. The *-nickel* part of the term represents a pet form of the name *Nikolaus*, perhaps chosen for its resemblance to German *nix* 'water-sprite.' *Nickel* was first used for a US

five-cent coin (made of a copper and nickel alloy) in the 1880s.

**nickname** [14] A *nickname* is etymologically an 'additional name.' The word was originally *ekename*, whose *eke* 'addition' was a derivative of the verb *eke* (as in 'eke out'). But by the 15th century *an ekename* was becoming misinterpreted as *a nekename* – hence *nickname* (the same process produced *newt* [15] from *ewt*, ancestor of modern English *eft* 'newt,' and the reverse happened to *adder, apron*, and *umpire*).

▶ eke

**nicotine** [19] *Nicotene* gets its name ultimately from Jean Nicot, 16th-century French ambassador in Lisbon, who in 1560 got hold of some samples of the new 'tobacco' and sent them to the French queen Catherine de Medici. The tobacco-plant was named *herba nicotiana* 'herb of Nicot' in his honour (whence the modern English term *nicotiana* for all plants of this genus), and *nicotine* was derived from *nicotiana*, originally in French, for the addictive alkaloid obtained from it.

**niece** [13] *Niece* comes ultimately from *\*neptī-*, the feminine form of Indo-European *\*nepōt-* (source of English *nephew*). This passed into Latin as *neptis* 'granddaughter, niece,' which in post-classical times became *\*neptia*. Old French took it over as *niece* – whence English *niece*. *\*Neptī-* also had a Germanic descendant, *\*niptiz*, which now survives only in German *nichte* and Dutch *nicht* 'niece.'

▶ nephew

**nigger** see DENIGRATE
**nigh** see NEAR

**night** [OE] *Night* is the English member of an ancient Indo-European family of 'night'-words, represented in virtually all the modern European languages. The ancestral form was *\*nokt-*, and from this have come Greek *núx*, Latin *nox* (source of English *nocturnal* [15] and *nocturne* [19], and forerunner of French *nuit*, Italian *notte*, and Spanish *noche*), Welsh *nos*, Latvian *nakts*, and Russian *noch'*. The Germanic descendant of *\*nokt-* was *\*nakht-*, source of modern German and Dutch *nacht*, Swedish *natt*, Danish *nat*, and English *night*. The only exception to the general European picture is modern Irish *oidhche* 'night,' a word of unknown origin.

▶ nocturnal

**nightingale** [OE] The nightingale's name, appropriately enough, means literally 'night-singer.' It represents a 13th-century alteration of an earlier *niht-gale*, which goes back to a prehistoric Germanic compound formed from *\*nakht* 'night' and *\*galan* 'sing' (a relative of English *yell* [OE] and possibly of *gale*). Related Germanic forms include German *nachtigall*,

Dutch *nachtegaal*, Swedish *näktergal*, and Danish *nattergal*.

**nightmare** [13] The *mare* of *nightmare* is not the same word as *mare* 'female horse.' It comes from Old English *mære*, which denoted a sort of evil spirit or goblin which sat on sleepers' chests and gave them bad dreams. That is what the compound *nightmare* meant too when it emerged in the early Middle English period, and the metaphorical application to the bad dream supposedly caused by this incubus is not recorded until the mid-16th century.

▶ yell

**nil** [19] Latin *nil* was a contracted form of *nihil* 'nothing' (source of English *nihilism* [19]). This in turn was a shortening of an earlier *nihilum*, a compound formed from the negative particle *nī* and *hīlum* 'small or trivial thing,' and thus denoted etymologically 'not a jot.'

▶ nihilism

**nine** [OE] *Nine* is part of a general Indo-European family of '9'-words, which trace their ancestry back to a prehistoric *\*newn* or *\*enewn*. Among the descendants of these are Greek *ennéa*, Latin *novem* (source of English *November*), Irish *nóin*, Lithuanian *devynì*, and Russian *devyat'*. Its Germanic forms *\*niwun* or *\*nigun* have differentiated into German *neun*, Dutch *negen*, Swedish *nio*, Danish *ni*, and English *nine*. *Noon* is so called from being originally the 'ninth' hour.

▶ noon

**no** English has three words *no*, which come from quite distinct sources (although they all, of course, contain the ancient negative particle *ne*). *No* the negative reply [OE] means etymologically 'not ever, never.' It originated as a compound of *ne* and *ā* 'ever' (a relative of archaic modern English *aye* 'ever,' whose own negative form is *nay* [12]) and the resulting *nā* became in the 13th century *no*. The history of *no* 'not' [OE] (which is now used virtually only in the expression 'whether or no') is almost exactly parallel: it was formed from Old English *ō* 'ever,' a variant of *ā*. The adjective *no* 'not any' [13] is a reduced form of *none*, its final *n* originally dispensed with before consonants.

▶ aye, nay / none

**noble** [13] Etymologically, to be *noble* is simply to be 'well known.' The word reached English via Old French *noble* from Latin *nōbilis*. But this was only a later form of an original *gnōbilis* (preserved in the negative form *ignoble* [16]), which was derived from the base *\*gnō-* 'know,' source also of English *notorious*. It thus originally meant 'knowable,' hence 'known,' and only subsequently broadened out via 'well known' to 'noble' (which in ancient Rome denoted 'belonging to a family

of which many members had held high office in the state').

▶ cognition, ignoble, know, notorious, recognize

**nocturnal** SEE NIGHT

**nodule** SEE NOOSE

**noel** SEE NATIVE

**noise** [13] Unlikely as it may seem, the ancestor of English *noise* meant 'sickness.' It comes from Latin *nausea*, source also, of course, of English *nausea*. This was used colloquially for the sort of 'hubbub' or 'confusion' which is often coincident with someone being sick (and particularly seasick, which was what *nausea* originally implied), and Old French took it over, as *noise*, with roughly these senses. They later developed to 'noisy dispute,' and modern French *noise* has retained the 'dispute' element of this, while English *noise* has gone for the 'intrusive sound.'

▶ nausea, nautical, navy

**noisome** [14] *Noisome* has no etymological connection with *noise*. Its closest English relative is *annoy*. This had a shortened form *noy* 'trouble, annoy, harm,' current from the 13th to the 17th centuries, which was combined with the suffix *-some* to form *noysome*, later *noisome*, 'harmful.'

▶ annoy

**nomad** [16] The Greek verb *némein* had a very wide range of senses. It originally meant 'deal out, dispense,' a signification mirrored in the derived *nemesis* [16] (etymologically the 'dealing out' of what is due) and the possibly related *number*. It developed subsequently to 'inhabit' and to 'control, manage' (which is represented in English *economy*). But a further strand was 'put out to pasture'; and from the same stem as produced *némein* was formed the adjective *nomás* 'wandering about to find pasture for herds or flocks.' Its plural *nomádes* was used to denote pastoral people who lived in this way, and the word was passed on via Latin *nomades* and French (singular) *nomade* into English.

▶ economy, nemesis

**nominate** [16] *Nominate* is one of a small band of English words descended from *nōmen*, the Latin representative of the Indo-European 'name' word family that also includes English *name*. It was based on the derived verb *nōmināre* 'name,' which has also given English, via French, *nominee* [17]. Other English words from the same source include *nominal* [15], *nomenclature* [17] (from Latin *nōmenclātūra*, whose second element was based on the verb *calāre* 'call'), *noun*, and *renown*.

▶ name, noun, renown

**nonchalant** [18] To be *nonchalant* is etymologically 'not to get hot under the collar.' The word comes from French *nonchalant*, an adjective formed with the prefix *non-* 'not' from the present participle of the verb *chaloir* 'be concerned.' This goes back ultimately to Latin *calēre* 'be hot' (a relative of English *calorie* and *cauldron*).

▶ calorie, cauldron, lukewarm

**none** [OE] Etymologically, *none* is simply 'not one.' It was formed in the Old English period from the negative particle *ne* and *ān*, ancestor of modern English *one*. It was originally both a pronoun and an adjective, but in the latter role it has been replaced by its reduced form *no*.

▶ one

**nonpareil**  see PAIR

**nonplus**  see PLURAL

**noon** [OE] *Noon* denotes etymologically the 'ninth' hour. It was adopted in the Old English period from Latin *nōna*, short for *nōna hōra*, the 'ninth hour.' Reckoning the day from sunrise, on average six o'clock, this meant that 'noon' was three o'clock in the afternoon (which was originally when the office of *nones* [18] – a related word – was said in the Roman catholic church). By the 12th century, however, we find *noon* being used for a 'midday meal,' and in the early 13th century it had moved on to simply 'midday,' so it appears that some forward shifting of a meal that had originally taken place in mid afternoon was responsible for altering the meaning of *noon* (modern English terms for mealtimes, such as *tea* and *dinner*, are equally slippery).

▶ nine

**noose** [15] The notion underlying the word *noose* is of a 'knot,' rather than of a 'loop of rope made with a knot.' The word comes from *nos* or *nous*, the Old French descendant of Latin *nodus* 'knot.' This was the source of English *node* [16], of course, and of the diminutive form *nodule* [16], but it has also made a couple of less obvious contributions to English: *dénouement* [18], which comes via a French word denoting literally the 'untying of a knot,' and *newel* [14] 'staircase post,' which was borrowed from Old French *nouel* 'knob,' a descendant of the medieval Latin diminutive *nōdellus*.

▶ dénouement, newel, node, nodule

**nor** [14] *Nor* began life in the Old English period as *nother*. This was a compound formed from the negative particle and an unrecorded \**ōther*, a word related to *either* which expressed the notion of 'alternative.' In the Middle English period this was contracted to *nor*.

▶ either

**normal** [17] Latin *norma* originally denoted a sort of set square used by carpenters, masons, etc for measuring right angles. It was extended metaphorically to a 'rule, pattern, precept,' but English originally took over its derivative *normālis* as a mathematical term, in the fairly literal sense 'perpendicular.' The more familiar modern sense 'standard, usual' did not emerge until

the 19th century, at about the same time as *normality*, *normalcy*, and *norm* itself began to appear on the scene.

**north** [OE] *North* is a general West and North Germanic word for 'north,' represented also in German, Swedish, and Danish *nord* and Dutch *noorden*. It was also borrowed into French (from Old English) as *nord*, from where it spread into Italian and Rumanian as *nord* and into Spanish as *norte*. It is not known for certain where it came from, but a link has been suggested with *nertro-*, a word for 'left' in the extinct Oscan-Umbrian languages of Italy, which might mean that the underlying meaning of *north* is 'to the left as one faces the rising sun' (modern Irish *tuaisceart* 'north' was based on a word meaning 'left').

**nose** [OE] *Nose* is the English member of a widespread family of 'nose'-words that trace their ancestry back to Indo-European \**nas-*. This has produced Latin *nāsus* (source of English *nasal* [17]), Sanskrit *nás*, Lithuanian *nósis*, and Russian, Polish, Czech, and Serbo-Croat *nos*. Its Germanic descendant has differentiated into German *nase*, Dutch *neus*, Swedish *näsa*, Danish *næse*, and English *nose*. *Nozzle* [17] and *nuzzle* [15] are probably derived from *nose*, and *ness* 'promontory, headland' [OE] (now encountered only in place-names) is related to it.

▶ nasal, ness, nostril, nozzle, nuzzle

**nostril** [OE] Etymologically, a *nostril* is a 'nose-hole.' Its Old English ancestor was *nosthyrl*, a compound formed from *nosu* 'nose' and *thӯrl* 'hole.' This was a derivative of *thurh* 'through,' and still survives as *thirl*, a dialectal word for 'hole.'

▶ nose, thrill, through

**not** [14] In Old English and early Middle English the simple particle *ne* was used for making negative sentences. But it was evidently often felt to be in need of some reinforcement, for purposes of emphasis, and to do this job *noht* was brought in. Ancestor of modern English *nought* [OE], it was a compound formed from *ne* and *ōwiht* 'anything' (precursor of archaic modern English *ought*). By the end of the 13th century this was being widely used as the sole negator in sentences, the *ne* having been dispensed with, and we soon find spellings reflecting the sort of reduction in pronunciation from *nought* to *not* that one would expect from its often weakly-stressed position.

▶ nought, ought

**notable**  see NOTE

**notary**  see NOTE

**notch** [16] Not much is known for certain about the word *notch*, apart from the fact that its immediate source, Anglo-Norman *noche*, existed at least a couple of centuries before English acquired it. There may well be some connection with Old French *oche* 'groove, notch' (probable source of the English darts term *oche* 'line where the dart-thrower stands'); the initial *n* could well have arisen by misdivision of a preceding indefinite article (as happened with *nickname*).

► oche

**note** [13] Latin *nota* had a remarkably wide range of meanings. Its original sense was 'sign, mark,' but already in classical times it had broadened out semantically to include 'alphabetical character,' 'shorthand sign,' 'brief letter,' 'musical note,' and 'characteristic quality.' Many of these followed it via Old French *note* into English, where they were supplemented by 'distinction, reputation,' perhaps inspired by the derived adjective *notable* [14]. From the same source came *notary* [14], etymologically a 'shorthand-writer.'

**notice** [15] One of the main Latin verbs for 'know' was *nōscere* (earlier *gnōscere*), a distant relative of English *know* and, via the derived *cognōscere*, source of a wide range of English words, from *cognizance* to *reconnaissance*. From its past participle *nōtus* was formed the noun *nōtitia*, which denoted 'knowledge, acquaintance.' English took this over via Old French *notice*, and at first used it only for 'advance knowledge, warning' (as in 'give someone notice of something'). The main modern sense, 'heed, attention' (as in 'take notice of'), did not emerge until the end of the 16th century (and the use of the verb *notice* for 'observe, perceive' is later still, dating from the mid-18th century). Also from the Latin past participial stem *nōt*- come *notify* [14], *notion* [16], and *notorious*.

► cognition, know, noble, notion, notorious, reconnaissance

**notorious** [16] *Notorious* originally meant simply 'well known.' It was borrowed from medieval Latin *nōtōrius*, which was a derivative of *nōtus* 'known,' the past participle of Latin *nōscere* 'know' (source also of English *notice, notion,* etc). The English word very soon came to be used in association with derogatory nouns (as in 'a notorious liar'), and by the early 17th century the adjective itself had taken on negative connotations. (*Noble*, which comes from the same ultimate source and likewise etymologically means 'known,' has gone up in the world as far as *notorious* has gone down.)

► notice

**nougat** see NUT
**nought** see NOT
**noun** [14] Etymologically, a *noun* is simply a 'name.' Latin *nomen* 'name' (a relative of English *name*) was used by classical grammarians for a 'noun' – that is, a word that 'names' something – and English acquired it via Old French *non* and Anglo-Norman *noun*.

**nourish** see NURSE
**novel** English has acquired the word *novel* in several distinct instalments. First to arrive was the adjective, 'new' [15], which came via Old French from Latin *novellus*, a derivative of *novus* 'new' (to which English *new* is distantly related). (The Old French derived noun *novelte* had already reached English as *novelty* [14].) Next on the scene was a now obsolete noun *novel* 'new thing, novelty' [15], which went back to Latin *novella*, a noun use of the neuter plural of *novellus*. In Italian, *novellus* became *novello*, and this was used in *storia novella*, literally 'new story,' a term which denoted 'short story.' English adopted this as a third *novel* [16], at first referring specifically to Italian short stories of the type written by Boccaccio, but by the mid-17th century being extended to a longer 'prose narrative' (the original Italian *novella* was reborrowed in the early 20th century for a 'short novel'). English is also indebted to Latin *novus* for *nova* [19] (etymologically a 'new star') and *novice* [14].

**November** [13] The ancient Romans calculated the beginning of their year from March. Hence they named their ninth month *novembris* or *november mēnsis*. *November* and *novembris* were derivatives of Latin *novem* 'nine.'

**novice** see NOVEL
**now** [OE] *Now* is the English member of a widespread family of words denoting 'present time' that are traceable back to Indo-European *nu- or *nū- (a relative of the ancestor of *new*). Others include Greek *nun*, Latin *nunc*, Sanskrit *nū*, Czech *nyní*, and, among the Germanic languages, German *nun* and Dutch, Swedish, and Danish *nu*. (French *maintenant* 'now,' incidentally, originally meant literally 'holding in the hand,' and developed its present sense via 'at hand' and 'soon.')

**noxious** [17] *Noxious* was adapted from Latin *noxius* 'harmful,' a derivative of *noxa* 'damage, injury.' (An earlier borrowing was *obnoxious* [16], from Latin *obnoxius*, which contains the prefix *ob-* 'to.') Related to *noxa* were Latin *nex* 'destruction, death, slaughter' (source of English *internecine* and *pernicious*) and *nocēre* 'injure' (source of English *innocent, innocuous,* and *nuisance*).

► innocent, innocuous, internecine, nuisance, obnoxious, pernicious

**nozzle** see NOSE
**nubile** [17] In modern English, *nubile* is generally used as a facetious synonym for 'sexy, attractive,' but etymologically it means 'suitable for marriage.' It comes from Latin *nūbilis*, a derivative of *nūbere* 'take a husband.' This has also given English *nuptial* [15] and *connubial* [17], and is related to *nymph*.

► connubial, nuptial, nymph

**nuclear** see NUT

**nucleus** see NUT

**nude** see NAKED

**nuisance** [15] *Nuisance* has become much less serious over the centuries. When English originally acquired it, it meant 'harm, injury' ('Helpe me to weye ageyn the feend . . . keepe vs from his nusance,' Thomas Hoccleve, *Mother of God* 1410), reflecting its origins in Latin *nocēre* 'injure' (source also of English *innocent* and *innocuous*). But gradually it softened to 'troublesomeness,' and by the early 19th century it had acquired its present-day connotations of 'petty annoyance.'

**number** [13] The etymological notion underlying the word *number* is probably 'distribution.' Its ultimate source, Latin *numerus*, may have been related to Greek *némein* 'deal out, distribute' (source of English *nemesis* and related to *nomad*). *Numerus* passed into Old French as *nombre* (subsequently borrowed by German as *nummer*), and English acquired it via Anglo-Norman *numbre*. Derivatives of Latin *numerus* to have reached English include *enumerate* [17], *numeral* [16], *numerate* [20], *numerical* [17], and *numerous* [16].

▶ enumerate, numerous

**nun** [OE] In medieval Latin, *nunnus* and *nunna* were titles of respect accorded respectively to old men and old women in general. In due course they came to be applied specifically to 'monks' and 'nuns.' The masculine form has since disappeared, but the feminine *nonna* was borrowed into Old English as *nunne*. This was subsequently reinforced in the 13th century by Old French *nonne*.

**nuptial** see NUBILE

**nurse** [13] The ultimate source of *nurse* was Latin *nūtrīre* (which also gave English *nourish* [13], *nutriment* [16], and *nutrition* [16]). This originally meant 'suckle' (it is related to Sanskrit *snauti* 'drips, trickles'), but was later generalized to 'feed, nourish' and 'look after.' Both 'suckle' and 'look after' are preserved in *nurse*, which comes via Old French *nourice* from the late Latin derivative *nūtrīcia*, although originally the 'looking after' was restricted to children: the notion of a *nurse* as a 'carer for sick people' did not emerge in English until the end of the 16th century. The derivative *nursery* [16] retains its associations with children, and by extension with young plants. Late Latin *nūtrītūra* 'feeding,' based on *nūtrīre*, gave English *nurture* [14].

▶ nourish, nurture, nutriment, nutrition

**nut** [OE] *Nut* is a member of a restricted family of Indo-European 'nut'-words, present only in the Ger-

manic, Romance, and Celtic languages, that were derived ultimately from the Indo-European base *\*knu-*, denoting 'lump.' Latin *nux* (source of French *noix*, Italian *noce*, and Spanish *nuez*) came from an extended base *\*knuk-*. Its derivative *nucleus* 'nut, kernel' has given English *nucleus* [18] and *nuclear* [19], and Vulgar Latin *\*nucātum* is the source of English *nougat* [19]. The Germanic branch of the family, on the other hand, comes from an extended base *\*knut-*, which has produced German *nuss*, Dutch *noot*, Swedish *nöt*, Danish *nød*, and English *nut*.

The adjectival use of the plural, *nuts*, for 'crazy' dates back to the mid-19th century. It came from the metaphorical application of *nut* to 'head' – hence *off one's nut* 'deranged,' and in due course *nuts*.

▶ nougat, nuclear, nucleus

**nutmeg** [13] Etymologically, the *nutmeg* is the 'musk-flavoured nut.' The word originated as a partial anglicization of Anglo-Norman *\*nois mugue*, which came via Old French *nois muguede* from Vulgar Latin *\*nuce muscāta*, literally 'musky nut.' This 'musky' connection, now effectively concealed in English, is still apparent in, for example, German *muskatnuss*, Swedish *muskotnöt*, and French *noix muscade*.

▶ musk, nut

**nutriment** see NURSE

**nutrition** see NURSE

**nuzzle** see NOSE

**nylon** [20] English has a long history of naming fabrics after their places of origin: *denim* from Nîmes, for instance, *muslin* from Mosul, and *calico* from Calicut in India. It is not surprising, therefore, that the popular myth has grown up that *nylon* took its name from New York (*ny-*) and London (*-lon*). The truth, however, is more prosaic. Du Pont, nylon's inventors, took the element *-on* (as in *cotton* and *rayon*) and simply added the arbitrary syllable *nyl-*. The word was coined in 1938, and its plural was in use for 'nylon stockings' as early as 1940.

**nymph** [14] Greek *númphē* originally meant 'bride' (it was related to Latin *nūbere* 'take a husband,' source of English *connubial* and *nubile*). It subsequently became extended, however, to 'beautiful young woman' and 'female nature spirit, particularly one frequenting water,' and it was in the latter sense that the word first entered English, via Latin *nympha* and Old French *nimphe*. The original sense 'bride' lies behind *nymphomania*, coined in the second half of the 18th century.

▶ connubial, nubile

# O

oaf    see ELF

**oak**    [OE]    *Oak* is an ancient Germanic tree-name, shared by German (*eiche*), Dutch (*eik*), Swedish (*ek*), and Danish (*eg*). These point back to a common Germanic ancestor *\*aiks*. There is no conclusive evidence of any related forms outside Germanic, however, although similarities have been noted with Greek *aigílops*, a term for a sort of oak tree, and Latin *aesculus* 'oak sacred to Jupiter.' Despite its passing similarity, *acorn* is not etymologically related.

The oak was one of the commonest trees in the ancient European forests, and many terms that started out as names for it became generalized to simply 'tree': English *tree*, for instance, comes from an Indo-European ancestor that probably originally meant 'oak.'

**oar**    [OE]    *Oar* is a general northern Germanic term, traceable back to an ancestral *\*airō*, source also of Swedish *år*, Danish *aare*, and, by borrowing, Finnish *airo*. It is not clear where it comes from, although it may ultimately be related to Latin *rēmus* 'oar' (as in *trirēmis*, source of English *trireme* [17]).
▶ trireme

**oasis**    [17]    The ultimate origins of the word *oasis* no doubt lie in North Africa, and although no positive link has been established, it is likely to be related in some way to Coptic *ouahe*. This means literally 'dwelling area' (it is derived from the verb *ouih* 'dwell'), but since isolated fertile spots in the desert are natural centres of habitation, it is used also for 'oasis.' The farthest back we can actually trace English *oasis* is, via Latin, to Greek *óasis*.

**oasthouse**    [18]    Although the compound *oasthouse* is not recorded until the mid 18th century, *oast* itself, which means 'kiln,' goes right back to Old English, and beyond, to Indo-European *\*aidh-* 'burn.' This was also the source of Latin *aestās* 'summer,' etymologically the 'hot season,' from which are descended French *été* 'summer' and English *aestivate* [17]. Originally *oast* was simply a general term for 'kiln,' and the

specific application to a 'hop-drying kiln' did not begin to emerge until the 16th century.
▶ aestivate

**obese**    see EAT

**obey**    [13]    'To hear is to obey' carries more than a germ of etymological truth. For *obey* comes via Old French *obeir* from Latin *ōbēdīre*, which meant literally 'listen to.' It was a compound verb formed from the prefix *ob-* 'to' and *audīre* 'hear' (source of English *audible*). By classical times the metaphorical sense 'obey' had virtually taken over from the original 'listen to,' and it is this sense that informs the related *obedient* [13] and *obeisance* [14].
▶ audible, obedient

**obfuscate**    see DUSK

**obituary**    [18]    *Obituary* goes back ultimately to a Latin euphemism for 'die,' meaning literally 'go down, make an exit.' This was *obīre*, a compound verb formed from the prefix *ob-* 'down' and *īre* 'go.' From it was derived *obitus* 'death,' which formed the basis of the medieval Latin adjective *obituārius* 'of death,' source of English *obituary*. A parallel Latin formation was the adverb *obiter* 'on the way, in passing along,' based on the noun *iter* 'journey' (a relative of *īre* and source of English *itinerant* [16] and *itinerary* [15]). English preserves it in *obiter dictum* [19], literally a 'statement in passing.'
▶ itinerant

**object**    *Object* the noun [14] and *object* the verb [15] have diverged considerably over the centuries, but they come from the same ultimate source: Latin *obicere*. This was a compound verb formed from the prefix *ob-* 'towards' and *jacere* 'throw' (source of English *ejaculate, inject, subject*, etc), and hence originally meant literally 'throw towards,' but by classical times it had been extended metaphorically to 'place a hindrance in the way of, oppose.' This was the strand of the word's meaning taken up by English in the verb *object*, and also originally in the noun ('how Christ answered to objects [that is, objections] of false Jews,' John Wycliffe

1380). The standard present-day meaning of the noun, however, comes from a post-classical meaning of Latin *objectum* (the noun formed from the past participle of *obicere*): 'something put in someone's way so that it can be seen,' hence a 'visible object.'

▶ ejaculate, inject, jet, subject

**objurgate**   see JUST

**oblation**   see OFFER

**oblige**   [13]   To *oblige* someone is etymologically to 'bind them to' something with a promise. The word comes via Old French *obliger* from Latin *obligāre*, a compound verb formed from the prefix *ob-* 'to' and *ligāre* 'tie' (source of English *liable, ligament*, etc). By classical times its original literal sense had been extended figuratively to 'make liable, put under an obligation.' The synonymous *obligate* [16] comes from its past participial stem, as does *obligatory* [15].

▶ liable, ligament, obligatory

**obliterate**   see LETTER

**obnoxious**   see NOXIOUS

**oboe**   [18]   The oboe gets its name from its high pitch. Its ultimate ancestor was French *hautbois*, a compound of *haut* 'high' and *bois* 'wood' (the oboe is a woodwind instrument). English acquired this in the 16th century as *hautboy*, but from the 18th century it was gradually ousted by the Italian version of the word, *oboe* (itself originally an acquisition from French).

▶ bush

**obscure**   see SKY

**obsequious**   see SEQUENCE

**observe**   [14]   Latin *observāre* meant 'watch, pay attention to, look to, comply with.' It was a compound verb, formed with the prefix *ob-* 'to' from *servāre* 'keep safe,' hence 'guard, watch, heed' (no relation to *servīre*, source of English *serve* and *servant*). The two semantic strands 'seeing, noting' and 'complying' have remained together in the English verb, but have diverged in its derived nouns, the former going to *observation* [14], the latter to *observance* [13].

▶ conserve, reserve

**obstetric**   [18]   An *obstetric* nurse is etymologically one who 'stands before' a woman giving birth to render assistance. The word is an adaptation of Latin *obstetrīcius*, a derivative of *obstetrīx* 'midwife.' This in turn was formed from *obstāre* 'stand in the way' (source also of English *obstacle* [14] and *oust* [16]), a compound verb formed from the prefix *ob-* 'before' and *stāre* 'stand.'

▶ obstacle, oust, stand, station, statue

**obstruct**   see STRUCTURE

**obtain**   [15]   *Obtain* is one of the large family of English words (*attain, contain, continue, tenor*, etc) that come ultimately from Latin *tenēre* 'hold.' In this case its source, by way of Old French *obtenir*, was Latin

*obtinēre*, a compound formed with the intensive prefix *ob-*, which denoted both 'get possession of' and 'prevail, be established.'

▶ attain, contain, continue, tenor

**obtuse**   [16]   The etymological meaning of *obtuse* is 'beaten down, blunted.' It comes from Latin *obtūsus*, the past participle of *obtundere*, a compound verb formed from the prefix *ob-* 'against' and *tundere* 'beat' (source of English *contusion* and related to *toil*). The notion of being 'dulled' or 'blunted' led to its being used for 'having dulled wits, stupid,' and the idea of bluntness also lies behind its geometrical use for an angle of more than 90 degrees (as contrasted with the 'sharp' acute angle).

▶ contusion, toil

**ocarina**   [19]   The ocarina, a primitive sort of musical instrument played by blowing, gets its name from a supposed resemblance to a goose (it is shaped like an elongated egg, with a neck-like mouthpiece). Italian *ocarina* means literally 'little goose.' It is a diminutive form of *oca* 'goose,' which in turn goes back to Latin *auca*, a derivative of *avis* 'bird.'

▶ aviary

**occasion**   [14]   Like English *befall, occasion* depends on a metaphorical connection between 'falling' and 'happening.' Its ultimate source is the Latin verb *occidere* 'go down,' a compound formed from the prefix *ob-* 'down' and *cadere* 'fall' (source of English *cadence, case* 'circumstance,' *decadent*, etc). The figurative notion of a 'falling together of favourable circumstances' led to the coining of a derived noun *occasiō*, meaning 'appropriate time, opportunity,' and hence 'reason' and 'cause.' English acquired it via Old French *occasion*.

Also from Latin *occidere* comes English *occident* [14], a reference to the 'west' as the quarter in which the sun 'goes down' or sets.

▶ cadaver, cadence, case, decadent, occident

**occult**   [16]   Something that is *occult* is etymologically 'hidden.' The word comes from the past participle of Latin *occulere* 'hide,' a compound verb formed from the prefix *ob-* and an unrecorded *\*celere*, a relative of *cēlāre* 'hide' (which forms the second syllable of English *conceal*). When English acquired it, it still meant broadly 'secret, hidden' ('Metals are nothing else but the earth's hid and occult plants,' John Maplet, *Green Forest* 1567), a sense preserved in the derived astronomical term *occultation* 'obscuring of one celestial body by another' [16]. The modern associations with supernatural mysteries did not begin to emerge until the 17th century.

▶ cell, conceal, hall, hell

**occupy**   [14]   *Occupy* comes via Anglo-Norman *\*occupier* from Latin *occupāre* 'seize,' a compound verb formed from the intensive prefix *ob-* and *capere*

'take' (source of English *capture, chase*, etc). In the 16th and 17th centuries it was used in English for 'have sex (with)' ('as king Edwin occupied Alfgifa his concubine,' John Bale, *English Votaries* 1546), and fell temporarily out of 'polite' usage: as Doll Tearsheet complained in Shakespeare's *2 Henry IV* 1597, 'A captain! God's light, these villains will make the word 'captain' as odious as the word 'occupy,' which was an excellent good word before it was ill sorted.'
▶ captive, capture, chase

**occur** [16] Etymologically, *occur* means 'run towards.' It was borrowed from Latin *occurrere*, a compound verb formed from the prefix *ob-* 'towards' and *currere* 'run' (source of English *course, current*, etc). This had the sense 'run to meet,' hence simply 'meet,' which survived into English: 'The whole multitude might freely move . . . with very little occurring or interfering,' Richard Bentley, *Boyle Lectures* 1692. But 'meeting' also passed into 'presenting itself,' 'appearing,' and hence 'happening' – from which the main present-day meaning of English *occur* comes.
▶ course, current

**ocean** [13] In Greek mythology, *Ōkeanós* was a great river or sea that completely encircled the world. This was personified as *Ōkeanós*, a Titan who was god of this outer sea. The name passed into English via Latin *ōceanus* and Old French *occean*, and to begin with was used only for this mythical sea, or for the whole body of water surrounding the Eurasian landmass, with which it was identified. Not until the end of the 14th century did it begin to be applied to large individual sections of the Earth's seas.

**oche** see NOTCH

**October** [OE] The Romans calculated the beginning of their year from March, and so the eighth month was called *octōber* or *octōbris mēnsis*, literally 'eighth month' (terms derived from Latin *octō* 'eight'). Other English words derived from Latin *octō* or its close Greek relative *oktṓ* include *octagon* [17], *octane* [19], *octave* [14], *octet* [19], and *octopus* [18] (from Greek *oktṓpous*, literally 'eightfoot').
▶ octane, octave, octopus

**ocular** see INOCULATE

**odd** [14] The etymological idea underlying *odd* is of 'pointing upwards.' Its ultimate ancestor is a prehistoric Indo-European *\*uzdho-*, a compound formed from *\*uz-* 'up' and *\*dho-* 'put, place' (source of English *do*). From the notion of a 'pointed vertical object' developed 'triangle,' which in turn introduced the idea of 'three' and 'one left over from two,' hence 'indivisible by two.' This is the meaning *odd* had when English borrowed it from Old Norse *oddi*, and the modern sense 'peculiar' (as if the 'odd one out') did not emerge until the late 16th century.
▶ do

**ode** see PROSODY

**odontology** see TOOTH

**odour** [13] The Latin noun for 'smell' was *odor*. It was descended from the Indo-European base *\*od-*, source also of the Greek verb *ózein* 'smell' (from which English gets *ozone* [19]), the Latin verb *olēre* 'smell' (ancestor of English *redolent*), and the Latin verb *olfacere* 'smell' (source of English *olfactory*). It passed into English via Anglo-Norman *odour*. (It has, incidentally, no etymological connection with *odious* [14], which comes from Latin *odium* 'hatred.')
▶ olfactory, redolent

**oenology** see WINE

**oestrus** [17] Greek *oistros* had an extraordinarily wide range of meanings, from 'madness, frenzy' through 'sting' to 'gadfly,' and including also 'breeze.' If, as has been suggested, it is related to Latin *īra* 'anger' (source of English *ire* [13]), Lithuanian *aistra* 'passion,' etc, 'frenzy' is presumably the primary sense, but in fact English originally adopted it (via Latin *oestrus*) as the genus name for a variety of horse-fly or bot-fly. 'Sting' was taken up, in the sense 'impetus, goad,' as a learned borrowing in the mid-19th century ('They too were pricked by the oestrus of intellectual responsibility,' John Morley, *On Compromise* 1874), but *oestrus* was not used for 'period of sexual receptiveness in female animals' (based of course on the notion of sexual 'frenzy') until the end of the 19th century. The derived *oestrogen* dates from the 1920s.
▶ ire

**of** [OE] *Of* has an ancient ancestry, going back to the prehistoric Indo-European preposition of 'removal' or 'origin,' *\*ap*. Its Germanic descendant was *\*ab*, source of modern German *ab* (now only an adverb, meaning 'away'), Dutch *af*, Swedish *av*, and English *of*. Latin *ab* 'from' (as in English *abduct, abject*, etc) also came from Indo-European *\*ap*.
▶ off

**off** [OE] *Off* originated simply as the adverbial use of *of*. The spelling *off*, denoting the extra emphasis given to the adverb, began to appear in the 15th century, but the orthographic distinction between *off* for the adverb, and for prepositional uses associated with it ('removal, disengagement'), and *of* for the ordinary preposition did not become firmly established until after 1600.
▶ of

**offal** [14] Etymologically, *offal* is simply material that has 'fallen off.' English borrowed the word from Middle Dutch *afval*, a compound formed from *af* 'off' and *vallen* 'fall' which denoted both the 'extremities of animals cut off by the butcher, such as feet, tail, etc' and 'shavings, peelings, or general refuse.' English originally took it over in the latter sense, but by the 15th century *offal* was being used for 'animals' entrails.'

▶ fall, off

**offend** [14] Latin *offendere* meant 'strike against.' It was a compound verb formed from the prefix *ob-* 'against' and *-fendere* 'hit' (source also of English *defend*). Its literal sense survived into English ('The navy is a great defence and surety of this realm in time of war, as well to offend as defend' proclaimed an act of parliament of Henry VIII's time), and continues to do so in the derivatives *offence* [14] and *offensive* [16], but as far as the verb is concerned only the metaphorical 'hurt the feelings' and 'violate' remain.

▶ defend, fend

**offer** [OE] Latin *offerre* was a compound verb formed from the prefix *ob-* 'to' and *ferre* 'bring, carry' (a distant relative of English *bear*), and it meant 'present, offer.' It was borrowed into Old English from Christian Latin texts as *offrian*, in the specific sense 'offer up a sacrifice'; the more general spread of modern meanings was introduced via Old French *offrir* in the 14th century. The past participle of *offerre* was *oblātus*, from which English gets *oblation* [15].

▶ bear, oblation

**office** [13] *Office* comes from a Latin source that originally meant 'do work.' This was *officium*, a reduced form of an earlier *\*opificium*, which was compounded from *opus* 'work' (source of English *opera*, *operate*, etc) and *-ficium*, a derivative of *facere* 'do' (source of English *fact, faction*, etc). That original literal sense has now disappeared from English (which got the word via Old French *office*), but it has left its mark in 'position, post, job' and 'place where work is done,' both of which existed in Latin. English has a small cluster of derivatives, including *officer* [14], *official* [14], *officiate* [17], and *officious* [16].

▶ fact, factory, fashion, opera, operate

**often** [14] *Oft* was the Old English word for 'often.' It came from a prehistoric Germanic adverb of unknown origin, which also produced German *oft*, Swedish *ofta*, and Danish *ofte*. In early Middle English it was extended to *ofte*. This developed a form *often* before vowels and *h*, which by the 16th century had begun to oust *oft(e)*.

**oil** [12] Around the Mediterranean in ancient times the only sort of oil encountered was that produced by pressing olives, and so 'oil' was named after the olive. The Greek word for 'olive' was *elaía*, and from it was derived *elaíon* 'olive oil.' This passed into Latin as *oleum*, and reached English via Old French *oile*. By now it had begun to be applied to similar substances pressed from nuts, seeds, etc, but its specific modern use for the mineral oil 'petroleum' is a much more recent, essentially 19th-century development.

▶ olive

**OK** [19] Few English expressions have had so many weird and wonderful explanations offered for their origin as *OK*. There is still some doubt about it, but the theory now most widely accepted is that the letters stand for *orl korrect*, a facetious early 19th-century American phonetic spelling of *all correct*; and that this was reinforced by the fact that they were also coincidentally the initial letters of *Old Kinderhook*, the nickname of US president Martin Van Buren (who was born in Kinderhook, in New York State), which were used as a slogan in the presidential election of 1840 (a year after the first record of *OK* in print).

**old** [OE] Etymologically, *old* means 'grown-up.' It comes from a prehistoric West Germanic *\*altha* (source also of German *alt* and Dutch *oud*) which was a past-participial adjective formed from the base of a verb meaning 'grow, nourish.' (A precisely similar formation from the related Latin verb *adolēscere* 'grow' has given English *adult*, and Latin *altus* 'high' – source of English *altitude* [14] – was originally a past-participial adjective too, derived from *alēre* 'nourish,' although it has metaphoricized 'growing' to 'height' rather than 'age.') *Elderly* and the comparative and superlative *elder, eldest* come ultimately from the same source.

*World* began life as a compound noun of which the noun *\*ald-* 'age,' a relative of *old*, formed the second element.

▶ adult, altitude, elder, world

**olfactory** [17] *Olfactory* means etymologically 'making smell.' It was borrowed from Latin *\*olfactōrius*, a derivative of the verb *olfacere* 'smell.' This in turn was a blend of *olēre* 'smell' (source of English *redolent* and related to *odour*) and *facere* 'make' (source of English *fact, faction*, etc).

▶ odour, redolent

**olive** [13] The word *olive* probably originated in a pre-Indo-European language of the Mediterranean area. Greek took it over as *elaía*, and passed it on to English via Latin *olīva* and Old French *olive*. The olive's chief economic role is as a source of oil (indeed the very word *oil* comes from a Greek derivative of *elaía*), and before the word *olive* arrived in English, it was called *eleberge*, literally 'oil-berry.'

▶ oil

**ombudsman** [20] The word *ombudsman*, denoting an 'investigator of public complaints,' was introduced into English from Swedish, and was first used as a quasi-official term in the 1960s: New Zealand was the first English-speaking country to introduce such a post, in 1962, and Britain followed four years later. The Swedish word is a descendant of Old Norse *umboth-smathr*, literally 'administration-man'; and *umboth* was originally a compound of *um* 'about' and *both* 'command' (a relative of English *bid*).

▶ bid

**omelette** [17] The *omelette* seems to have been named for its thinness, like a sheet of metal. The word was borrowed from French *omelette*, the modern descendant of Old French *amelette*. This meant literally 'thin sheet of metal,' and was an alteration, by metathesis (the reversal of sounds) of *alumette*. This in turn was a variant of *alumelle*, which arose through the mistaking of *la lemelle* 'the blade' as *l'alemelle*. And *lemelle* goes back to Latin *lāmella* 'thin sheet of metal,' a diminutive form of *lāmina* 'plate, layer' (from which English gets *laminate* [17]).

▶ laminate

**omen** [16] *Omen* was a direct borrowing from Latin *ōmen*, whose derivative *ōminōsus* also gave English *ominous* [16]. From the same source comes *abominable*.

▶ abominable, ominous

**on** [OE] *On* is an ancient Germanic preposition, with relatives in German (*an*), Dutch (*aan*), and Swedish (*å*), and also connections outside Germanic (such as Greek *aná* 'on' and Russian *na* 'on').

**onager** see ASS

**once** [12] *Once* originated as the genitive form of *one* (the genitive case was widely used in Old and Middle English for making adverbs out of nouns – other examples include *always*, *needs*, *nowadays*, and *towards*). To begin with, this was clearly indicated by its spelling – *ones* – but from about the start of the 16th century *-es* was gradually replaced by *-ce* (reflecting the fact that *once* retained a voiceless /s/ at its end, whereas in *ones* it had been voiced to /z/).

▶ one

**one** [OE] *One* is the English member of an ancient and widespread family of 'one'-words that goes back ultimately to Indo-European *\*oinos*. This also produced Latin *ūnus* (ancestor of French *un* and Italian and Spanish *uno* and source of English *ounce*, *union*, *unit*, etc), Welsh *un*, Lithuanian *víenas*, Czech and Polish *jeden*, and Russian *odin*, all meaning 'one.' Its Germanic descendant was *\*ainaz*, which has fanned out into German *ein*, Dutch *een*, Swedish and Danish *en*, and English *one*. In many languages the word is used as the indefinite article, but in English the numeral *one* has become differentiated from the article *a*, *an*. *One* lies behind *alone*, *atone*, and *only* (all of which preserve its earlier diphthongal pronunciation) as well as *once*, and its negative form is *none*. The use of the word as an indefinite pronoun, denoting 'people in general,' dates from the late 15th century.

▶ alone, atone, eleven, inch, lonely, none, once, only, ounce, union, unit

**onion** [14] The usual Old English word for 'onion' was *cīpe* (a borrowing from Latin *cēpa*, source also of English *chives* and *chipolata*), but it also had *ynne*.

This came from Latin *ūniō*, a word of uncertain origin but possibly identical with *ūniō* (a derivative of *ūnus* 'one') which denoted a 'single large pearl' (according to Julius Moderatus Columella, *ūniō* was a farmer's term, and one can well imagine a proud onion-grower comparing his products with pearls). An alternative explanation, also based on a derivation from *ūnus*, is that the word is an allusion to the 'unity' formed by the layers of the onion. *Ynne* had died out by the Middle English period, and *onion* represents a reacquisition of the word via Anglo-Norman *union*.

▶ one

**only** [OE] *Only* is a compound formed in the Old English period from *ān*, ancestor of modern English *one*, and *-līc* '-ly.' It originally meant 'solitary' as well as 'unique,' but this sense has been taken over by the related *lonely*. *Only* preserves the early diphthongal pronunciation which its source *one* has lost.

▶ lonely, one

**onyx** [13] Greek *ónux* meant 'claw, fingernail' (it is distantly related to English *nail*). Certain sorts of onyx are pink with white streaks, and a resemblance to pink fingernails with their paler crescent-shaped mark at the base led the Greeks to name the stone *ónux*. The word travelled to English via Latin *onyx* and Old French *onix*.

▶ nail

**open** [OE] Etymologically, *open* means 'turned up' or 'put up.' It comes ultimately from a prehistoric Germanic *\*upanaz*, an adjective based on the ancestor of *up*, and therefore presumably denoted originally the raising of a lid or cover. The German verb *aufmachen* 'open,' literally 'make up,' contains the adverb *auf*, the German equivalent to English *up*. The English verb *open* [OE] is a derivative of the adjective.

▶ up

**operate** [17] *Operate* belongs to a small family of English words that trace their history back to Latin *opus* 'work,' which may be related to Sanskrit *ápas* 'work,' Old English *afol* 'power,' and Latin *ops* 'wealth' (source of English *copious*, *copy*, and *opulent* [17]). Its most direct English descendant is of course *opus* [18] itself, which was originally adopted in the phrase *magnum opus* 'great work.' *Opera* [17] goes back to the Latin plural, which came to be regarded as a feminine singular noun meaning 'that which is produced by work.' Italian gave it its musical sense, and passed it on to English. *Operate* itself came from the past-participial stem of the derived Latin verb *operārī* 'work.' It was originally used in English for 'produce an effect,' and the transitive sense, as in 'operate a machine,' did not emerge until as recently as the mid-19th century, in American English. The surgical sense is first recorded in the derivative *operation* [16] at the end of the 16th century. Other English descendants of *opus* include *cooperate* [17] and *manoeuvre*.

▶ copious, copy, manoeuvre, opera, opulent

**opinion** [13] *Opinion* comes via Old French from Latin *opīniō*, a derivative of *opīnārī* 'think.' It is not certain where this came from, although some have linked it with Latin *optāre* 'choose,' source of English *adopt* [16], *co-opt* [17], *opt* [19], and *option* [17].

▶ adopt, opt, option

**opium** [14] Etymologically, *opium* means 'little juice.' It comes via Latin from Greek *ópion* 'poppy juice,' which originated as a diminutive form of *opós* 'juice.' This in turn may be related to Persian *āb* 'water.' The derivative *opiate* [16] comes via medieval Latin *opiātus*.

**opportunity** [14] *Opportunity* has its origins in a Latin nautical term denoting 'favourable winds.' This was *opportūnus*, a compound adjective formed from the prefix *ob-* 'to' and *portus* 'harbour' (source of English *port*). It was used originally for winds, 'blowing towards the harbour,' and since it is good when such advantageous winds arrive, it developed metaphorically to 'coming at a convenient time.' From it English got *opportune* [15] and the derived *opportunity*. *Opportunism* [19] is a much more recent introduction, which originated in the world of Italian politics.

▶ port

**oppose** [14] *Oppose* is in origin an Old French re-formation of Latin *oppōnere*, based on *poser* (source of English *pose*). *Oppōnere* was a compound verb formed from the prefix *ob-* 'against' and *pōnere* 'put' (source also of English *position, posture*, etc). It originally meant literally 'set against,' but developed various figurative senses, including 'oppose in argument,' which is how it was originally used when it arrived in English. The notions of 'contention' and 'prevention' have remained uppermost in the English verb, as they have in *opponent* [16], which comes from the present participle of the Latin verb. But *opposite* [14] (from the Latin past participle) retains another metaphorical strand that began in Latin, of 'comparison' or 'contrast.'

▶ pose, position, posture

**oppress** see PRESS

**opt** see OPINION

**optical** [16] Greek *optós* meant 'visible' (it was presumably related to *ophthalmós* 'eye,' source of English *ophthalmic* [17], and belonged to the general Indo-European family of 'eye'/'see'-words – including English *eye* itself – that goes back to the base *oqw-*). From it was derived *optikós*, which has given English *optic* [16] and *optical*. *Optician* [17] originated as a French coinage.

▶ ophthalmic

**optimism** [18] Etymologically as well as semantically, *optimism* means hoping for 'the best.' It was coined in French (as *optimisme*) in 1737 as a term for the doctrine of the German philosopher Leibnitz (1646–1716) that the world is as good as it could possibly be. It was based on Latin *optimum* (source also of English *optimum* [19]), the neuter case of *optimus* 'best.' This may have been formed from the preposition *ob* 'in front of' and a superlative suffix.

**option** see OPINION
**opulent** see OPERATE
**opus** see OPERATE

**or** [12] The Old English word for 'or' was *oththe*. This appears to have been altered in the early Middle English period to *other*, probably due to the influence of similar words denoting 'choice between alternatives' and ending in *-er* (notably *either* and *whether*). *Other* was soon contracted to *or*, but it did not finally die out until the 15th century.

**oracle** see ORATOR

**oral** [17] *Oral* comes from Latin *ōs* 'mouth.' This went back to a prehistoric Indo-European *ōs-* or *ōus-*, which also produced Sanskrit *ās-* 'mouth' and Old Norse *óss* 'mouth of a river.' Its other contributions to English include *orifice* [16] (etymologically 'forming a mouth'), *oscillate, osculate* 'kiss' [17], and *usher*.

▶ orifice, oscillate, osculate, usher

**orange** [14] The name of the orange originated in northern India, as Sanskrit *nāranga*. This passed westwards via Persian *nārang* and Arabic *nāranj* to Spain. The Spanish form *naranj* filtered up to France, and became altered (perhaps under the influence of *Orange*, the name of a town in southeastern France which used to be a centre of the orange trade) to *orenge*, later *orange* – whence the English word.

**orang-utan** [17] Malay *ōrang ūtan* means literally 'wild man.' It probably originated as a term used by those who lived in open, more densely populated areas for the 'uncivilized' tribes who lived in the forest, but was taken by early European travellers to refer to the large red-haired ape that inhabits the same forests. The word may well have reached English via Dutch.

**orator** [14] *Orator* is one of a small family of English words that go back to the Latin verb *ōrāre* 'speak.' Others include *oracle* [14], *oration* [14] (whence, by back-formation, *orate* [16]), and *oratory* 'public speaking' [16]. And besides these, there is a special subset of words that depend on a later, extended sense of *ōrāre*, 'pray': *adore* [15] (etymologically 'pray to'), *inexorable, oratory* 'small chapel' [14] (whose Italian form has given English *oratorio* [18]), and the now archaic *orison* 'prayer' [12] (etymologically the same word as *oration*).

▶ adore, inexorable, oracle, orison

**orbit** [16] *Orbit* comes from Latin *orbita*. This was a derivative of the noun *orbis*, which originally meant 'circle, disc.' It was applied metaphorically to a number of circular things, including the 'circular path of a satellite' (from which the main meaning of *orbit* comes) and also the 'eye socket,' and eventually came to be applied to 'spheres' as well as 'circles' – whence English *orb* [16].

▶ orb

**orchard** [OE] Etymologically, an *orchard* is probably simply a 'plant-yard.' It appears to have been coined in the prehistoric Germanic period from *\*worti-*, the ancestor of the now archaic English noun *wort* 'plant, vegetable, herb' (which is distantly related to *root*), and *\*gardaz*, *\*gardon*, forerunner of English *yard* and *garden*. Originally, as its derivation suggests, it was quite a broad term, covering vegetable gardens as well as enclosures for fruit trees, but by the 15th century it had more or less become restricted to the latter.

▶ garden, yard

**orchestra** [17] In ancient Greece, the term *orkhḗstrā* denoted a 'semicircular space at the front of a theatre stage, in which the chorus danced' (it was a derivative of the verb *orkheisthai* 'dance'). English originally took it over (via Latin *orchēstra*) in this historical sense, but in the early 18th century *orchestra* began to be used for the 'part of a theatre where the musicians played,' and hence by extension for the 'group of musicians' itself. The derivative *orchestrate* [19] was adapted from French *orchestrer*.

**orchid** [19] Greek *órkhis* meant 'testicle' (a sense preserved in English *orchitis* 'inflammation of the testicles' [18]). The tuberous roots of the orchid supposedly resemble testicles (hence the old dialect name *ballock's-grass* for various sorts of wild orchid), and so the plant was named *órkhis*. The Latin form *orchis* was taken by botanists of the 16th and 17th centuries as the basis for the plant's scientific name (they smuggled an inauthentic *d* into it, under the mistaken impression that its stem form was *orchid-*), and it passed from there into English.

**ordain** see ORDER

**ordeal** [OE] The 'meting out of judgement' is the etymological notion immediately underlying *ordeal*, but at a more primitive level still than that it denotes simply 'distribution, giving out shares.' It comes ultimately from prehistoric Germanic *\*uzdailjan* 'share out,' a compound verb formed from *\*uz-* 'out' and *\*dailjan*, ancestor of English *deal*. The noun derived from this was *\*uzdailjam*, and it came to be used over the centuries for the 'handing out of judgements' (modern German *urteil*, for instance, means among other things 'judicial verdict or sentence'). Its Old English descendant, *ordāl*, denoted specifically a 'trial in which a person's guilt or innocence were determined by a haz-

ardous physical test, such as holding on to red-hot iron,' but the metaphorical extension to any 'trying experience' did not take place until as recently as the mid-17th century.

▶ deal

**order** [13] *Order* comes via Old French *ordre* from Latin *ōrdō*. This originally denoted a 'row, line, series, or other regular arrangement,' but it spawned a lot of other metaphorical meanings that have also come through into English, including 'regularity' and (from the general notion of a 'rank' or 'class') 'ecclesiastical rank or office' (preserved in English in 'holy orders' and in the derivatives *ordain* [13] and *ordination* [15]). The sense 'command, directive,' first recorded in English in the mid-16th century, presumably comes from the notion of 'keeping in order.' Other derivatives of *ōrdō* are represented by *ordinance* [14] and *ordinary*.

▶ ordain, ordinary, ordination

**ordinary** [14] Latin *ōrdinārius* meant 'following the usual course'; it was a derivative of *ōrdō*, source of English *order*. It was originally used in English as a noun, meaning 'someone with jurisdiction in ecclesiastical cases,' and right up until the 19th century the noun *ordinary* was common, with an amazingly wide range of meanings (including 'post, mail,' 'fixed allowance,' 'priest who visited people in the condemned cell,' and 'tavern'). Nowadays, however, the only (quasi-)nominal use at all frequently encountered is in the phrase *out of the ordinary*. English first took the word up as an adjective in the 15th century.

▶ order

**ordination** see ORDER

**ore** see ERA

**organ** [13] Greek *óganon* meant 'tool, implement, instrument.' It was a descendant of the Indo-European base *\*worg-* (source also of English *work*). Latin took the word over as *organum*, and in the post-classical period applied it to 'musical instruments.' At first it was a very general term, but gradually it narrowed down to 'wind instrument,' and in ecclesiastical Latin it came to be used for a musical instrument made from a number of pipes. When English acquired it, via Old French *organe*, it was in the intermediate sense 'wind instrument' (in the 1611 translation of Psalm 150, 'Praise him with stringed instruments and organs,' *organ* still means 'pipe'), but by the end of the 17th century this had died out. The sense 'functional part of the body' goes right back to the word's Greek source.

The derivative *organize* [15] comes via Old French from medieval Latin *organizāre*. This originally denoted literally 'furnish with organs so as to form into a living being,' and hence 'provide with a co-ordinated structure.'

▶ organize, orgy, work

**orgy** [16] *Orgy* comes ultimately from Greek *órgia* (like English *organ*, a descendant of the Indo-European base *\*worg-* 'work'), which denoted 'religious revels involving dancing, singing, getting drunk, and having sex.' It was a plural noun, and passed into English via Latin *orgia* and French *orgies* as *orgies*. This was very much a historical term, denoting the goings-on in ancient Greece, but in the 18th century it was singularized to *orgy*, and used for any 'copulatory revelry.'

▶ organ, work

**orient** English has two separate words *orient*, but they come ultimately from the same source: Latin *orīrī* 'rise' (from which English also gets *abort* and *origin*). Its present participle, *oriēns* 'rising,' was used for the direction of the 'rising sun,' and hence for the 'east,' and passed into English via Old French as the adjective and noun *orient* [14]. The verb *orient* [18] was borrowed from French *orienter*, a derivative of the adjective *orient*. It originally meant 'turn to face the east,' and was not used for 'ascertain or fix the direction of' until the 19th century. *Orientate* emerged in the mid-19th century, probably as a back-formation from *orientation* [19], itself a derivative of *orient*.

▶ abort, origin

**orifice** SEE ORAL

**origin** [14] Etymologically, *origin* denotes literally an 'arising.' The word was borrowed from Latin *orīgō* 'source,' a derivative of the verb *orīrī* 'rise.' This also produced English *abort* [16] (etymologically 'be born badly') and *orient*.

▶ abort, orient

**orison** SEE ORATOR

**ormolu** SEE MILL

**ornament** [14] *Ornament* comes from Latin *ōrnāmentum*, a derivative of the verb *ōrnāre* 'equip, get ready,' hence 'decorate.' This also forms the basis of English *adorn* [14] and *suborn* [16] (etymologically 'equip secretly').

▶ adorn, suborn

**orthodox** [16] Greek *orthós* meant 'straight, correct' (it enters into numerous English compounds, including *orthography* 'correct spelling' [15] and *orthopaedic* [19]). Greek *dóxa* meant 'opinion'; it was derived from the verb *dokein* 'think.' Put them together and you got *orthódoxos* 'having the right opinion,' which passed into English via ecclesiastical Latin *orthodoxus*.

**oscillate** [18] Latin *ōs* originally meant 'mouth' (it was the source of English *oral*), but it was also used for 'face.' Its diminutive form *ōscillum* 'little face' was applied to a mask depicting the god Bacchus that was hung up as a charm in vineyards, to be swung to and fro by the breeze. In due course its meaning broadened out to 'swing' generally, and a verb *ōscillāre*

'swing' was derived from it – whence English *oscillate*.

▶ oral

**osculate** SEE ORAL

**osprey** [15] Etymologically, the *osprey* is simply a 'bird of prey.' Its name comes from *ospreit*, the Old French descendant of Vulgar Latin *\*avispreda*, which in turn was a conflation of Latin *avis praedae* 'bird of prey' (*avis* is the source of English *augur*, *auspice*, *aviary*, and *aviation*, and *praeda* is the ancestor of English *prey*). The specific association with the 'osprey' came about in Old French through confusion with the coincidentally similar *osfraie* 'osprey.' This meant etymologically 'bone-breaker.' It came from Latin *ossifraga*, a compound formed from *os* 'bone' (source of English *ossify* [18]) and *frangere* 'break' (source of English *fracture, fragment*, etc). It was originally applied to the lammergeier, a large vulture, in allusion to its habit of dropping its prey from a great height on to rocks beneath in order to break its bones, but was subsequently also used for the osprey.

▶ aviary, prey

**ostensible** [18] *Ostensible* means literally 'that can be shown.' It comes via French from medieval Latin *ostensibilis*, a derivative of the Latin verb *ostendere* 'show' (itself a compound formed from the prefix *ob-* 'in front of' and *tendere* 'stretch,' source of English *extend, tend, tense* etc). Its original meaning 'showable' survived into English ('You should send me two letters – one confidential, another ostensible,' Jeremy Bentham, 1828), but seems to have died out by the mid-19th century. Two metaphorical strands came with it, though. One, 'vainly conspicuous,' goes right back to *ostendere*, and is still preserved in English *ostentation* [15], although it has disappeared as far as *ostensible* is concerned. The other, 'presented as real but not so,' is today the central meaning of the adjective.

▶ extend, ostentation, tend, tense

**ostler** SEE HOTEL

**ostracism** [16] In ancient Greece, when it was proposed that a particular person should be sent into exile for a period, because he was becoming a danger to the state, a democratic vote was taken on the matter. The method of registering one's vote was to inscribe the name of the prospective banishee on a piece of broken pottery. The pieces were counted, and if enough votes were cast against him away he would go for ten years. The fragment of pottery was called an *óstrakon*, a word related to Greek *ostéon* 'bone' (source of the English prefix *osteo-*) and *óstreon* 'oyster' (source of English *oyster*). To cast such a vote was therefore *ostrakízein* (whence English *ostracize* [17]), and the abstract now derived from this was *ostrakismós*, source of English *ostracism*.

**ostrich** [13] Greek *strouthós* seems originally to have meant 'sparrow.' *Mégas strouthós* 'great sparrow' – the understatement of the ancient world – was used for 'ostrich,' and the 'ostrich' was also called *strouthokámelos*, because of its long camel-like neck. Eventually *strouthós* came to be used on its own for 'ostrich.' From it was derived *strouthíon* 'ostrich,' which passed into late Latin as *strūthiō* (source of English *struthious* 'ostrich-like' [18]). Combined with Latin *avis* 'bird' (source of English *augur, aviary*, etc) this produced Vulgar Latin *\*avistrūthius*, which passed into English via Old French *ostrusce* as *ostrich*.

▶ struthious

**other** [OE] *Other* is one of a widespread family of Germanic words expressing 'alternative,' represented today also by German and Dutch *ander*. The prehistoric ancestor of all three was *\*antheraz*, which came ultimately from an Indo-European *\*ánteros*. This, a comparative formation based on *\*an-*, may have been related to Latin *alter* 'other' (source of English *alter, alternative*, etc).

**otiose** SEE NEGOTIATE

**otter** [OE] The *otter* is etymologically the 'water-animal.' Its name goes back ultimately to an Indo-European *\*udros*, source also of Greek *húdrā* 'water-snake' (the best-known example of which in English is the many-headed *Hydra* killed by Hercules). This was a derivative of the same base as produced English *water*. Its Germanic descendant was *\*otraz*, which has become *otter* in German, Dutch, and English.

▶ water

**ought** [OE] *Ought* began life as the past tense of *owe*, but the two have diverged widely over the centuries. The Old English ancestor of *owe* was *āgan*, and its past form was *āhte*. This originally shared all the meanings of its parent verb, of course, and continued to do so well into the 17th century ('He said this other day, you ought him a thousand pound,' Shakespeare, 1 *Henry IV* 1596). Indeed, it survived dialectally until comparatively recently. But steadily since the 1600s its role as a quasi-modal auxiliary verb, denoting 'obligation,' has come to the fore.

▶ owe

**ounce** English has two separate words *ounce*. The 'measure of weight' [14] is etymologically the same word as *inch*. It comes from the same ultimate source, Latin *uncia* 'twelfth part,' but whereas *inch* reached English via prehistoric Germanic, *ounce*'s route was through Old French *unce*. Its original use was in the Troy system of weights, where it still denotes 'one twelfth of a pound,' but in the avoirdupois system it came to be applied to 'one sixteenth of a pound.' Its abbreviation, *oz* [16], comes from Italian *onza*.

*Ounce* [13] 'big cat' comes from the same source as *lynx* (and indeed it originally meant 'lynx'; 'snow leopard' is an 18th-century reapplication of the name). It represents an alteration of Old French *lonce*, based on the misapprehension that the initial *l* represented the definite article. This in turn came via Vulgar Latin *\*luncia* from Latin *lynx*, source of English *lynx*.

▶ inch, one / light, lynx

**our** [OE] *Our* is the English member of the common Germanic family of first person plural possessive forms, which also includes German *unser* and Dutch *onze*. They all come from the same prehistoric base, *\*ons*, as produced English *us*.

▶ us

**oust** SEE OBSTETRIC

**out** [OE] *Out* is a widespread Germanic adverb (German *aus*, Dutch *uit*, Swedish *ut*, and Danish *ud* are its first cousins) which also has a relative on the far side of the Indo-European language area, Sanskrit *ud-* 'out.' Its former comparative form still survives in *utter* 'complete,' and *utmost* and the verb *utter* are also closely related.

▶ utmost, utter

**outfit** SEE FIT

**outrage** [13] *Outrage* has no etymological connection with either *out* or *rage*. It comes via Old French *outrage* from Vulgar Latin *\*ultrāticum* 'excess,' a noun derived from the Latin preposition *ultrā* 'beyond.' This of course has given English the prefix *ultra-*, and it is also the source of French *outré* 'eccentric,' borrowed by English in the 18th century.

▶ outré, ultra-

**outstrip** SEE STRIP

**ovary** [17] Latin *ōvum* 'egg' came from the same Indo-European base (*\*ōwo-*) as produced English *egg*. From it were derived the medieval Latin adjective *ōvālis* 'egg-shaped' (source of English *oval* [16]) and the modern Latin noun *ōvārium* (whence English *ovary*). Also from *ōvum* come English *ovate* [18] and *ovulate* [19], and the Latin noun itself was adopted as a technical term in biology in the early 18th century.

▶ egg

**over** [OE] Etymologically, *over* denotes 'more up, upper.' It originated as an Indo-European comparative form derived from the base *\*upó* 'under,' which gave rise to English *up*. This became prehistoric Germanic *\*uberi*, which has diversified into German *über*, Swedish *öfver*, and Dutch, Danish, and English *over*. A derivative of the same base forms the second syllable of English *above*, while amongst *over*'s more surprising relatives are *eaves* and *evil*.

▶ above, eaves, evil, up

**overlap**　see LAP
**overweening**　see WISH
**ovulate**　see OVARY

**owe**　[OE]　*Owe* goes back to a prehistoric Indo-European base *\*oik-*, *\*ik-* denoting 'possession.' Its Germanic descendant *\*aig-* produced a range of 'possession'-verbs, none of which now survives except Swedish *äga*, Danish *eie*, and English *owe*. In the Old English period this meant 'possess,' but that sense was gradually taken over by the related *own*, and *owe* developed in the 12th century to 'have to repay.' A more general notion of 'obligation' also emerged, which is now restricted to *ought*, originally the past tense of *owe*.
▶ought, own

**owl**　[OE]　*Owl* has several relatives in the other modern Germanic languages (German *eule*, Dutch *uil*, Swedish *uggla*), which point back to a prehistoric source *\*uwwalōn*, *\*uwwilōn*. Like most owl-names, such as Latin *ulula* and the possibly related German *uhu*, this no doubt originated as an imitation of the owl's call.

**own**　[OE]　The adjective *own* originated as the past participle of *\*aigan*, the prehistoric Germanic ancestor of English *owe*. Its original form was *\*aiganaz*, which has produced German and Dutch *eigen* and Swedish and Danish *egen* as well as English *own*. The verb *own* is a derivative of the adjective.
▶owe

**ox**　[OE]　*Ox* is an ancient word, traceable back to a prehistoric Indo-European *\*uksín-*. This also produced Welsh *ych* 'bull,' Irish *oss* 'stag,' and Sanskrit *ukshán* 'bull,' and it has been speculated that there may be some connection with Sanskrit *uks-* 'emit semen' and Greek

*hugrós* 'moist,' as if *\*uksín-* denoted etymologically 'male animal.' If this was so, the 'seed-bearing' function had clearly been lost sight of by the time it had evolved to Germanic *\*okhson*, which was reserved for a 'castrated bull.' *Ox*'s modern Germanic relatives are German *ochse* (taken over by English in the compound *aurochs* 'extinct wild ox' [18], which etymologically means 'original or primeval ox'), Dutch *os*, Swedish *oxe*, and Danish *okse*.
▶aurochs

**oxygen**　[18]　Etymologically, *oxygen* means 'acid-former.' The word was coined in French in the late 1780s as *oxygène*, based on Greek *oxús* 'sharp, acid' (a descendant of the same Indo-European base, *\*ak-* 'be pointed,' as produced English *acid, acute*, etc) and the Greek suffix *-genes*, denoting 'formation, creation' (a descendant of the Indo-European base *\*gen-* 'produce,' which has given English a vast range of words, from *gene* to *genocide*).
▶acid, acute, eager, gene, general, generate

**oyster**　[14]　The Greek word for 'oyster' was *óstreon* – etymologically an allusion to its shell. It came from a prehistoric Indo-European base *\*ost-* denoting 'bone,' which also produced Greek *ostéon* 'bone' (source of the English prefix *osteo-*), *ostakós* 'crustacean,' and *óstrakon* 'shell, piece of broken pottery' (source of English *ostracism*). *Óstreon* passed into Latin as *ostrea*, and from there came by way of Old French *oistre* into English as *oyster*.
▶osteo-

**oz**　see OUNCE
**ozone**　see ODOUR

# P

**pace** [13] Latin *passus* 'step,' the source of English *pace* (and also ultimately of English *pass*), denoted etymologically a 'stretch of the leg.' It was based on *passus*, the past participle of the verb *pandere* 'stretch' (source also of English *expand* and *spawn*). English acquired it via Old French *pas*, and at first used it not just for 'step' and 'rate of movement,' but also for a 'mountain defile.' In this last sense, though, it has since the early modern English period been converted to *pass*, partly through reassociation with French *pas*, partly through the influence of the verb *pass*.

▶ expand, pass, spawn

**pacific**   see PEACE

**pacify**   see PEACE

**pack** [13] The ultimate origins of *pack* are unknown. English borrowed it from one of the Germanic languages of northeastern Europe (both Middle Dutch and Middle Low German had *pak*), but where they got it from is not clear. Its derivatives *package* [16] and *packet* [16] are both English formations.

**pact**   see COMPACT

**pad** [16] English has two words *pad*, both of them borrowed from Low German or Dutch. The ancestral meaning of *pad* 'cushion' seems to be 'sole of the foot,' although that sense did not emerge in English until the 18th century. Flemish *pad* and Low German *pad* both denote 'sole,' as does the presumably related Lithuanian *pãdas*. *Pad* 'tread, walk' comes from Low German *padden*, a descendant of the same Germanic source as produced English *path*. It was originally a slang term used by 16th- and 17th-century highwaymen, muggers, and the like, and its corresponding noun *pad* survives in *footpad* [17]. *Paddle* 'walk in shallow water' [16] comes from a Low German or Dutch derivative (the other *paddle*, 'oar, bat' [15], is of unknown origin).

▶ paddle, path

**paddock** [17] *Paddock* is ultimately the same word as *park*. Their common ancestor was a prehistoric Germanic word which took a route through Latin and French to reach English as *park*. Its direct Old English descendant, however, was *pearruc*. This in due course became *parrock*, which survived dialectally into the 20th century. But in the early modern English period a variant form *paddock* appeared. It is not clear how this arose, but it may be a hyper-correct form reflecting the change in the opposite direction, from /d/ to /r/, in words such as *porridge* for *pottage* and *geraway* for *get away*.

▶ park

**pagan** [14] The history of *pagan* is a bizarre series of semantic twists and turns that takes it back ultimately to Latin *pāgus* (source also of English *peasant*). This originally meant 'something stuck in the ground as a landmark' (it came from a base *\*pāg-* 'fix' which also produced English *page, pale* 'stake,' and *pole* 'stick' and is closely related to *pact* and *peace*). It was extended metaphorically to 'country area, village,' and the noun *pāgānus* was derived from it, denoting 'country-dweller.' But then this in its turn began to shift semantically, first to 'civilian' and then (based on the early Christian notion that all members of the church were 'soldiers' of Christ) to 'heathen' – whence English *pagan*.

▶ pact, page, pale, peace, peasant, pole

**page**   English has two nouns *page*. The one that now denotes 'boy servant' originally meant simply 'boy' [13]. It was borrowed from Old French *page*, itself an adaptation of Italian *paggio*. This is generally assumed to have come from Greek *paidíon*, a diminutive form of *pais* 'boy, child' (source of English *encyclopedia*, *paediatric* [19], *paedophilia* [20], *pedagogue* [14], *pederast* [18], etc). *Page* of a book [15] depends ultimately on the notion of 'fastening.' It comes via Old French *page* from Latin *pāgina*, a derivative of the base *\*pāg-* 'fix' (source also of English *pagan, pale* 'stake,' etc). This was used for 'vine-stakes fastened together into a trellis,' which perhaps inspired its metaphorical application to a 'column of writing' in a scroll. When books replaced scrolls, *pāgina* was transferred to 'page.'

▶ encyclopedia, paediatric, pedagogue / pagan, pale, pole

**pagoda** [17] The immediate source of *pagoda* was Portuguese *pagode*, but this is generally assumed to have been an adaptation of Persian *butkada*, a compound put together from *but* 'idol' and *kada* 'dwelling, temple.' Its form was no doubt influenced by *bhagodī*, a word for 'holy' in the vernacular languages of India.

**pain** [13] 'Punishment' (now encountered only in such phrases as *on pain of death*) is the ancestral meaning of *pain*; 'suffering' is a secondary development. The word comes via Old French *peine* and Latin *poena* from Greek *poinḗ* 'punishment, penalty.' Its original connotations are preserved in the related *penal* [15], *penalty* [16], *penance* [13], *penitence* [12], and *punish*, its later associations in the related verb *pine*.

▶ penal, penalty, penance, pine, punish

**paint** [13] *Paint* comes ultimately from an Indo-European base *pik-, *pig-*. This originally meant 'cut' (English *file* comes from it), but it broadened out via 'decorate with cut marks' and simply 'decorate' to 'decorate with colour' (whence English *pigment*). A nasalized version of the base produced Latin *pingere* 'paint,' which reached English via Old French *peindre* and its past participle *peint* (the Latin past participle *pictus* is the source of English *Pict* and *picture*, and also lies behind *depict*).

▶ depict, picture, pigment

**pair** [13] Like English *par* [17], *parity* [16], and *peer* 'noble' [13], *pair* comes ultimately from Latin *pār* 'equal,' a word of unknown origin. Its derivative *paria* 'equal things, similar things' passed into English via Old French *paire*. Other English descendants of Latin *pār* include *compare*, *disparage* [14], *nonpareil* [15], and *umpire*.

▶ compare, disparage, nonpareil, par, parity, peer, umpire

**pal** [17] *Pal* is a Travellers' contribution to English. It was borrowed from British Romany *pal* 'brother, friend,' an alteration of continental Romany *pral*. This was descended ultimately from Sanskrit *bhrātar-* 'brother,' a member of the same Indo-European word-family as English *brother*.

▶ brother

**palace** [13] The *Palātium*, or *Mons Palātīnus* (in English the 'Palatine hill'), was one of the seven hills of ancient Rome. On it the emperor Augustus built a house, which in due course grew into a grand imperial palace, also called the *Palātium*. This came to be used as a generic term for such residences, and passed into English via Old French *paleis*. The derived Latin adjec-

tive *palātīnus* has given English *paladin* [16] and *palatine* [15].

▶ paladin, palatine

**Palaeolithic** see LITHOGRAPH

**palaver** [18] *Palaver* originated as a piece of naval slang picked up by English sailors in Africa. There they came across Portuguese traders negotiating with the local inhabitants, a process known in Portuguese as *palavra* 'speech' (a descendant of Latin *parabola*, source of English *parable*). They took the Portugese word over as *palaver*, applying it first to 'negotiations,' and then by extension to 'idle chatter.'

▶ parable

**pale** English has two words *pale*. The adjective [13] comes via Old French from Latin *pallidus* (source also of English *appal* – originally 'turn pale' – *pall* 'become wearisome' [14] – originally a shortening of *appal* – and *pallid* [17]). This was a derivative of the verb *pallēre* 'be pale,' which was descended from *pol-, *pel-*, the same Indo-European base as produced English *fallow*.

The noun *pale* [14] comes via Old French *pal* from Latin *pālus* 'stake.' This was a descendant of the base *pāg-* 'fix,' which also produced English *pagan, page*, and *pole* 'stick.' English *palisade* [17] comes ultimately from *pālicea*, a Vulgar Latin derivative of *pālus*, and the closely related Latin *pāla* 'spade' produced English *palette* [17] and *pallet* [16].

▶ appal, fallow, pall, pallid / pagan, page, palette, palisade, pallet, pole, travel

**palfrey** [12] Etymologically, a *palfrey* is an 'extra horse.' The word comes via Old French *palefrei* from medieval Latin *palefrēdus*, an alteration of an earlier *paraverēdus* (source of German *pferd* 'horse'). This was a compound formed from Greek *pará* 'extra' (source of the English prefix *para-*) and late Latin *verēdus* 'light fast horse used by couriers,' a word of Gaulish origin.

**palisade** see PALE

**pallet** see PALE

**pallid** see PALE

**palm** *Palm* the tree [OE] and the *palm* of the hand [14] are effectively distinct words in English, but they have the same ultimate source: Latin *palma*. This originally meant 'palm of the hand' (it is related to Irish *lám* 'hand' and Welsh *llaw* 'hand'), and the application to the tree is a secondary one, alluding to the shape of the cluster of palm leaves, like the fingers of a hand. The Latin word was borrowed into the Germanic dialects in prehistoric times in the tree sense, and is now widespread (German *palme* and Dutch and Swedish *palm* as well as English *palm*). English acquired it in the 'hand' sense via Old French *paume*, with subsequent reversion to the Latin spelling.

The French diminutive *palmette* denotes a stylized palm leaf used as a decorative device, particularly on cornices. It was borrowed into English in the mid-19th century, and is thought to have formed the basis of English *pelmet* [20].

▶ pelmet

**palpable** [14] Latin *palpāre* meant 'touch, stroke' (it may be related to English *feel*). From it in post-classical times was derived the adjective *palpābilis* 'touchable' – whence English *palpable*. Other derivatives were the verb *palpitāre* 'tremble, throb' (from which English gets *palpitate* [17]) and the noun *palpus* 'touching' (source of English *palp* [19]).

▶ palpitate

**pamphlet** [14] The original 'pamphlet' was *Pamphilus*, a short anonymous Latin love poem of the 12th century. It was very popular and widely reproduced, and its name was adapted in the vernacular to *Pamflet*; and by the end of the 14th century this was being used generically for any text shorter than a book. The word's more restricted modern connotations ('unbound' and 'dealing with controversial subjects') developed gradually over the centuries.

**pan** [OE] *Pan* is a general West Germanic word, with relatives in German (*pfanne*) and Dutch (*pan*), and also, by borrowing, in Swedish (*panna*) and Danish (*pande*). It may have been borrowed into Germanic from Latin *patina* 'dish' (source of English *paten* [13] and *patina* [18]), which itself went back to Greek *patánē* 'plate, dish.'

The verbal use *pan out* 'turn out, succeed' is an allusion to the getting of a result when 'panning' for gold – washing gold-bearing gravel, silt, etc in a shallow pan to separate out the metal. (*Pan* 'move a camera' [20], incidentally, is a different word altogether. It is an abbreviation of *panorama*.)

▶ paten, patina / panorama

**panache** see PIN

**pancreas** [16] Etymologically, *pancreas* means 'all-flesh.' It is a modern Latin adaptation of Greek *págkreas*, a compound formed from the prefix *pan-* 'all' and *kréas* 'flesh.' This was presumably an allusion to the homogeneous substance of the organ. The term *sweetbread*, denoting the 'pancreas used as food,' also dates from the 16th century. The -*bread* element may represent Old English *brǣd* 'flesh' rather than modern English *bread*.

▶ raw

**pandemonium** [17] *Pandemonium* was coined by John Milton as the name for the capital of Hell in his poem *Paradise lost* 1667: 'Meanwhile the winged heralds . . . throughout the host proclaim a solemn council forthwith to be held at Pandaemonium, the high capital of Satan and his peers.' He formed it from the prefix *pan-* 'all' and Greek *daímōn* 'demon' – hence

'place of all the demons.' The modern colloquial use of the word for 'uproar' developed in the mid-19th century.

▶ demon

**pander** [16] *Pandaro* was a character in Boccaccio's *Filostrato*. He was the cousin of Cressida, and acted as go-between in her affair with Troilus. Chaucer took him over in his *Troilus and Criseyde* as *Pandarus*, changing him from cousin to uncle but retaining his role. His name came to be used as a generic term for an 'arranger of sexual liaisons' ('If ever you prove false to one another, since I have taken such pains to bring you together, let all pitiful goers-between be call'd to the world's end after my name: call them all Panders,' says Pandarus in Shakespeare's *Troilus and Cressida* 1606), and by the mid-16th century was already well on the downward slope to 'pimp, procurer.' Its modern use as a verb, meaning 'indulge,' dates from the 19th century.

**panel** [13] Etymologically, a *panel* is nothing more than a 'small pane.' It comes via Old French from Vulgar Latin *\*pannellus*, a diminutive form of Latin *pannus* 'rag' (source of English *pane* [13]). Both *panel* and *pane* entered English with their original 'cloth' connotations intact, but they have now virtually died out, surviving only in the compound *counterpane* (which is actually an alteration of an earlier *counterpoint*), and 'shape' has taken over from 'substance' as the word's key semantic feature.

▶ pane

**panic** [17] *Panic* is etymologically 'terror caused by the god Pan.' The ancient Greeks believed that he lurked in lonely spots, and would frighten people by suddenly appearing, or making noises. He was evidently invoked to account for alarming but harmless natural phenomena, and so the element of 'irrationality' in the English word was present from the beginning. English acquired it (originally as an adjective) via French *panique* and modern Latin *pānicus* from Greek *pānikós* 'of Pan.'

▶ Pan

**panjandrum** [18] *Panjandrum* is an invented word, coined in 1755 by the English actor and playwright Samuel Foote (1720–77) to test the memory of the actor Charles Macklin, who claimed to be able to memorize and repeat anything said to him (it was one of several inventions in the same vein that Foote put to him: 'And there were present the Picninnies, and the Joblillies, and the Garyulies, and the Grand Panjandrum himself, with the little round button at top'). It does not seem to have been taken up as a general comical term for a 'pompous high-ranking person' until the 19th century.

**pannier** [13] Etymologically, a *pannier* is something for carrying 'bread' in. It comes via Old French *pannier* from Latin *pānārium* 'breadbasket,' a derivative of *pānis* 'bread.' This originally meant simply 'food' (it came from the same ultimate source as Latin *pābulum* 'food,' borrowed into English in the 17th century, and English *food*); 'bread' was a secondary development. It is the ancestor of the modern Romance words for 'bread' (French *pain*, Italian *pane*, Spanish *pan*, etc), and also gave English *pantry*.

▶ pantry

**panoply** [17] *Panoply* originally meant a 'full suit of armour'; the modern sense 'impressive array' is a metaphorical extension that did not emerge until the 19th century. The word comes via French from Greek *panoplía*, a compound formed from the prefix *pan-* 'all' and *hópla* 'arms, weapons.'

**panorama** [18] The word *panorama* was coined in the late 1780s by an Irish artist called Robert Barker for a method he had invented for painting a scene on the inside of a cylinder in such a way that its perspective would seem correct to someone viewing it from inside the cylinder. He put his invention into practice in 1793 when he opened his 'Panorama,' a large building in Leicester Square, London where the public could come and gaze at such all-encompassing scenes. By the early years of the 19th century the word (formed from the prefix *pan-* 'all' and Greek *hórāma* 'view,' a derivative of *horān* 'see') had acquired all its modern extended meanings.

**pansy** [15] French *pensée* means literally 'thought,' and it was presumably the pensive look of these flowers of the viola family that earned them the name. English originally took it over as *pensee*, but later anglicized it to *pansy*. The use of the word for an effeminate male homosexual dates from the 1920s.

French *pensée* itself is the feminine past participle of *penser* 'think' (source also of English *pensive* [14]). This was descended from Latin *pēnsāre* 'weigh,' which in post-classical times was used for 'think.'

▶ pensive

**pant** [15] It is the shock that makes you 'gasp' that lies behind the word *pant*. It is closely related to English *fancy*, *fantasy*, and *phantom*. It comes from Anglo-Norman \**panter*, a condensed version of Old French *pantaisier* 'gasp.' This in turn went back to Vulgar Latin *phantasiāre* 'gasp in horror, as if at a nightmare or ghost,' a derivative of Latin *phantasia* 'apparition' (source of English *fancy* and *fantasy* and first cousin to *phantom*).

▶ fancy, fantasy, phantom

**pantechnicon** [19] The original *Pantechnicon* was a huge complex of warehouses, wine vaults, and other storage facilities in Motcomb Street, in London's Belgravia. Built in 1830 and supposed to be fireproof, it was almost totally destroyed by fire in 1874. It seems originally to have been intended to be a bazaar, and its name was coined from the prefix *pan-*

'all' and Greek *tekhnikón*, the neuter form of *tekhnikós* 'artistic,' denoting that all sorts of manufactured wares were to be bought there. But it was its role as a furniture repository that brought it into the general language. Removal vans taking furniture there came to be known as *pantechnicon vans*, and by the 1890s *pantechnicon* was a generic term for 'removal vans.'

▶ architect, technical

**pantomime** [17] In ancient Rome, a *pantomīmus* was a 'mime artist,' a sort of Marcel Marceau performer who acted scenes, incidents, etc without words. The term was adopted from Greek *pantómōmos* 'complete imitator,' a compound formed from *panto-* 'all' and *mōmos* 'imitator, actor' (source of English *mime*). English originally took the word over in this historical sense, and it was not until the early 18th century that it began to be used first for a sort of mime ballet and then for a play without words, relating a popular tale, which gradually developed into the Christmas fairy-tale pantomimes of the 19th and 20th centuries. The abbreviation *panto* dates from the mid-19th century.

▶ mime

**pantry** [13] A *pantry* is etymologically a 'bread' room. The word comes from Old French *paneterie* 'cupboard for keeping bread,' a derivative of *panetier* 'servant in charge of bread.' This was adopted from medieval Latin *pānetārius*, an alteration of late Latin *pānārius* 'bread-seller,' which in turn was a derivative of Latin *pānis* 'bread' (source also of English *pannier*). The notion of 'bread storage' survived into English, but was gradually lost in the face of the extended 'food store.'

▶ pannier

**pants** [19] *Pants* is short for *pantaloons*, a term used since the 17th century for men's nether garments. The word originated in the name of a character in the old Italian commedia dell'arte, *Pantalone*, a silly old man with thin legs who encased them in tight trousers. English took the word over via French *pantalon*, and began to use it for 'tight breeches or trousers.' In American English it broadened out to 'trousers' generally, whence the current American use of *pants* for 'trousers.' British English, however, tends to use the abbreviation for undergarments, perhaps influenced by *pantalets*, a 19th-century diminutive denoting 'women's long frilly drawers.'

**papa**    see POPE
**papacy**    see POPE
**papal**    see POPE

**paper** [14] Paper gets its name from the papyrus, a sort of rush from which in ancient times paper was made. The Greek word for this (presumably borrowed from some Oriental language) was *pápūros*, and its Latin descendant *papȳrus* passed into English via Old French *papier* and Anglo-Norman *papir*. (English *papyrus* [14] itself was an independent borrowing direct from Latin.)

▶ papyrus, taper

**par** see PAIR

**parable** [14] The etymological idea underlying *parable* is of 'drawing analogies.' It comes via Old French *parabole* and Latin *parabola* from Greek *parabolḗ*, a derivative of *parabállein*. This was a compound verb formed from *pará* 'beside' and *bállein* 'throw' (source of English *ballistic* [18]). It meant 'put beside,' hence 'compare.' Its derived noun *parabolḗ* was used for a 'comparison' or 'analogy,' and hence in the Christian tradition for an 'allegorical or moral narrative.' The geometrical sense of the term, acquired by English directly from Latin as *parabola* [16], comes from the notion of 'comparability' or 'parallelism' between the section of a cone that forms the parabola and an element in the cone's surface. Etymologically the same word is *parole* [17], which reached English via Vulgar Latin *\*paraula* and Old French *parole* 'word.' Its use for 'conditional release' is based on the notion of the prisoner giving his 'word of honour' to be of good behaviour.

▶ ballistic, palaver, parabola, parliament, parole

**paradigm** see TEACH

**paradise** [12] *Paradise* comes from an ancient Persian word meaning 'enclosed place.' In Avestan, the Indo-European language in which the Zoroastrian religious texts were written, *pairidaēza* was a compound formed from *pairi* 'around' (a relative of Greek *péri*, from which English gets the prefix *peri-*) and *diz* 'make, form' (which comes from the same Indo-European source as produced English *dairy, dough*, and the second syllable of *lady*). Greek took the word over as *parádeisos*, and specialized 'enclosed place' to an 'enclosed park'; and in the Greek version of the Bible it was applied to the 'garden of Eden.' English acquired the word via Latin *paradīsus* and Old French *paradis*.

▶ dairy, dough, lady

**paraffin** [19] The term *paraffin* was coined in German around 1830 by the chemist Reichenbach. It was formed from Latin *parum* 'little' and *affinis* 'related' (source of English *affinity*), an allusion to the fact that paraffin is not closely related chemically to any other substance. The word is first recorded in English in 1838.

▶ affinity, fine

**paragon** [16] When we say someone is a 'paragon of virtue' – a perfect example of virtue, able to stand comparison with any other – we are unconsciously using the long-dead metaphor of 'sharpening' them against others. The word comes via archaic French *paragon* and Italian *paragone* from medieval Greek

*parakónē* 'sharpening stone, whetstone.' This was a derivative of *parakonan*, a compound verb formed from *pará* 'alongside' and *akonan* 'sharpen' (a descendant of the same base, *\*ak-* 'be pointed,' as produced English *acid, acute*, etc), which as well as meaning literally 'sharpen against' was also used figuratively for 'compare.'

▶ acid, acute, eager, oxygen

**parakeet** [16] *Parakeet* is an anglicization of Old French *paroquet*. Like the roughly contemporary *parrot*, this seems to have begun life as a diminutive form of the name *Pierre* 'Peter' (several species of bird, such as the *magpie* and *robin*, have been given human names).

**parallel** [16] Etymologically, *parallel* simply means 'beside each other.' It comes via French *parallèle* and Latin *parallēlus* from Greek *parállēlos*. This was a compound formed from *pará* 'beside' and *allḗlōn* 'each other,' a derivative of *állos* 'other' (to which English *else* is distantly related).

▶ else

**paramount** see MOUNTAIN

**paraphernalia** [17] In former times, when a woman married her property was divided into two categories: her dowry, which became the property of her husband, and the rest. The legal term for the latter was *paraphernalia*, which came via medieval Latin from late Latin *parapherna*, a borrowing from Greek *parápherna*. And the Greek word in turn was a compound formed from *pará* 'beside' and *phernḗ* 'dowry.' It is a measure of the light in which these remaining odds and ends were viewed that by the early 18th century the term *paraphernalia* had come to be used dismissively for 'equipment' or 'impedimenta.'

**parcel** [14] Etymologically, *parcel* is the same word as *particle*. Both go back to Latin *particula*, a diminutive form of *pars* (source of English *part*). *Particle* [14] was acquired direct from Latin, whereas *parcel* was routed via an unrecorded Vulgar Latin variant *\*particella* and Old French *parcelle*. It originally meant 'part' in English (a sense which survives in fossilized form in the phrase *part and parcel*); the modern meaning 'package' emerged in the 17th century via the notions of a 'number of parts forming a whole' and a 'collection of items.'

▶ part, particle

**parchment** [13] Under several layers of disguise lurks the geographical origin of *parchment*: the ancient town of Pergamum in western Turkey, whose inhabitants used the skin of sheep for writing on rather than papyrus. In Latin, such skin was known as *charta Pergamīna* 'paper from Pergamum,' or simply *pergamīna*. This was later blended with *Parthica pellis* 'Parthian leather' to produce a Vulgar Latin *\*particamīnum*, which passed into English via Old French *parchemin* (the ending was changed to -*ment* on the model of other English words, in the 15th century). The formal distinction between *parchment* (made from sheepskin) and *vellum* (made from calfskin) has never been particularly watertight in English.

**pardon**   see DATE, FORGIVE

**parent** [15] Latin *parere* meant 'bring forth, give birth.' Its present participle was used to form a noun, *parēns*, which denoted literally 'one who gives life to another,' hence a 'mother' or 'father.' Its stem form *parent*- passed into English via Old French *parent*. Other English descendants of Latin *parere* (which is related to *prepare*) include *parturition* 'giving birth, labour' [17], *puerperal* (a compound containing Latin *puer* 'child'), and *viviparous* 'giving birth to live young' [17].

▶ parturition, prepare, puerperal, viper, viviparous

**parish** [13] The etymological notion underlying *parish* is of 'living nearby.' It comes via Old French *paroisse* and late Latin *parochia* (source of English *parochial* [14]) from late Greek *paroikíā*. This was a derivative of *pároikos* 'living near,' a compound formed from *pará* 'beside' and *oikos* 'house' (source of English *economy*). Scholars have not been able to agree on precisely how the idea of 'living nearby' became transmuted into that of the 'parish': some consider the central concept to be of a 'community of neighbours,' while others view the 'near-dweller' here not as a permanent neighbour but as a temporary 'sojourner' or 'stranger,' an epithet applied to early Christians.

▶ economy, parochial

**parity**   see PAIR

**park** [13] The origins of *park* are Germanic. It goes back to a prehistoric Germanic base, meaning 'enclosed place,' which has also given English *paddock*. This reached English by direct descent, but *park* took a route via medieval Latin. Here it was *parricus*, which passed into English via Old French *parc*. The verbal use of *park*, for 'place a vehicle,' began to emerge in the early 19th century, and was based on the notion of putting military vehicles, artillery, etc in an 'enclosure.' *Parquet* [19] comes from a diminutive of French *parc*, in the sense 'small enclosed place.'

▶ paddock, parquet

**parliament** [13] The French verb *parler* 'talk' has made a small but significant contribution to English. Amongst its legacies are *parlance* [16], *parley* [16], *parlour* [13] (etymologically a 'room set aside for conversation'), and *parliament* itself. This came from the Old French derivative *parlement*, which originally meant 'talk, consultation, conference,' but soon passed to 'formal consultative body,' and hence to 'legislative body.' French *parler* was a descendant of medieval Latin *parabolāre* 'talk,' which was derived from the Latin

noun *parabola* (source of English *parable*, *parabola*, and *parole*).

▶ ballistic, parable, parlour

**parlous**   see PERIL
**parochial**   see PARISH
**parody**   see PROSODY
**parquet**   see PARK

**parrot** [16] The original English name for the 'parrot' was *popinjay* [13] (whose ultimate source, Arabic *babaghā*, probably arose as an imitation of the parrot's call). But in the early 16th century this began to be replaced by *parrot*, which seems to have originated (like its close relative *parakeet*) in French as a diminutive form of the name *Pierre* 'Peter.'

**parse**   see PART

**parsley** [14] The ultimate source of *parsley* is Greek *petrŏselínon*, a compound formed from *pétrā* 'rock' (source of English *petrify*, *petrol*, etc) and *sélīnon* 'parsley' (source of English *celery*). From it was descended Latin *petroselīnum*, which in post-classical times became *petrosilium*. This passed into English in two distinct phases: first, direct from Latin in the Old English period as *petersilie*, and secondly, in the 13th century via Old French *peresil* as *percil*. By the 14th century these had started to merge together into *percely*, later *parsely*.

▶ celery, petrol

**parsnip** [14] The Romans called the 'parsnip' (and the 'carrot') *pastināca*. This was a derivative of *pastinum*, a term for a sort of small two-pronged fork, inspired no doubt by the forked appearance of some examples of the vegetable. In Old French the word had become *pasnaie*, but when English took it over, it altered the final syllable to -*nep*, under the influence of Middle English *nep* 'turnip' (source of the second syllable of *turnip*).

**parson** [13] *Parson* and *person* started off as the same word (both come from Latin *persōna*) but split into two. It is not altogether clear why *parson* came to be used for a 'priest.' It may simply have been a specialized application of an extended post-classical sense of Latin *persōna*, 'person of rank, important person, personage' – hence 'person of high position within the church.' But it has also been speculated that it originated in the notion of the priest as the 'person' who legally embodied the parish (who could for example sue or be sued on behalf of the parish).

▶ person

**part** [13] Latin *pars*, a possible relative of *parāre* 'make ready' (source of English *prepare*), had a wide range of meanings – 'piece,' 'side,' 'share,' etc – many of them shared by its English descendant *part*. The word was originally acquired in the late Old English period, but does not seem to have survived, and as we now have it was reborrowed via Old French *part* in the 13th century. Other English descendants of *pars* include *parcel*, *parse* [16] (based on the notion of 'parts' of speech), *partake* [16] (a back-formation from *partaker* [14], itself created from *part* and *taker*), *partial* [15], *participate*, *participle*, *particle*, *particular*, *partisan*, *partition*, *partner*, and *party*.

▶ parcel, parse, partial, particle, partisan, partner, party

## participle
[14] The etymological notion underlying *participle* is of a word that shares or 'partakes' of the dual nature of an adjective and a noun. It comes via Old French *participle* from Latin *participium*, a derivative of *particeps* 'partaker' (the usage was a direct translation of Greek *metokhḗ* 'sharer, partaker,' which was likewise used as a grammatical term for 'participle'). *Particeps* (based on a variant of Latin *capere* 'take,' source of English *capture*) also spawned the verb *participāre* 'take part,' from which English gets *participate* [16].

▶ part, participate

## particle
see PARCEL

## particular
[14] Latin *particula* (source of English *parcel* and *particle*) was a diminutive form of *pars* 'part,' and denoted 'small part.' From it was derived the adjective *particulāris*, which denoted 'concerned with small parts, or details' (as opposed to 'concerned with wider aspects of a matter'). English acquired it via Old French *particuler*.

▶ part, particle

## partisan
[16] Etymologically, a *partisan* is someone who takes a 'part' – in the sense 'side' or 'cause.' The word comes via French *partisan* from *partisano*, a dialect form of mainstream Italian *partigiano*, which was based on *parte* 'part.'

▶ part

## partner
[14] *Partner* is related to *part* – but not quite so directly as might appear. When it first entered the language it was in the form *parcener* [13], which remains in existence as a legal term meaning 'joint heir.' This came via Anglo-Norman *parcener* 'partner' from Vulgar Latin *\*partiōnārius*, a derivative of Latin *partītiō* 'partition' (source of English *partition* [15]). This in turn was based on the verb *partīrī* 'divide up,' a derivative of *pars* 'part.' The change from *parcener* to *partner* began in the 14th century, prompted by the similarity to *part*.

▶ part, partition

## parturition
see PARENT

## party
[13] The Latin verb *partīrī* 'divide up' was derived from *pars* 'part' (source of English *part*). The feminine form of its past participle, *partīta*, was used in Vulgar Latin as a noun meaning 'part, side,' and passed into English via Old French *partie*. This was later reinforced by Old French *parti*, which came from the Vul-

gar Latin neuter form *\*partītum* and contributed the English word's more salient current senses 'political group' and (in the 18th century) 'social gathering.' Other contributions made to English by the Latin past participle are the element *-partite* of words like *bipartite*, *tripartite*, etc and (via Italian) the musical term *partita* [19].

▶ part

## pass
[13] Strictly speaking, English has two distinct words *pass*, although they come from the same ultimate source, and have now virtually merged together again. That source was Latin *passus* 'step,' which gave English *pace*. From it was derived the Vulgar Latin verb *\*passāre*, which came to English via Old French *passer*. The past participle of the English verb has become *past*; and other related English words include *passage* and *passenger*. The noun *pass* 'mountain defile' originated as a sense of *pace*, but since the early modern English period has been spelled (and pronounced) *pass*, partly through reassociation with French *pas*, partly under the influence of the verb *pass*.

▶ pace, passage, passenger

## passage
[13] *Passage* goes back to the Latin ancestor of modern French. Here, the noun *\*passāticum* was derived from *passāre* (source of English *pass*). This found its way into English via Old French *passage*. At first it simply meant 'passing' or 'way along which one passes'; the sense 'segment of music, text, etc' did not emerge in English until the 16th century.

▶ pass

## passenger
[14] Originally a *passenger* was a *passager* – someone who goes on a 'passage,' makes a journey. The word was borrowed from Old French *passager*, at first an adjective meaning 'passing,' which was derived from *passage*. The *n* began to appear in the mid-15th century, a product of the same phonetic process as produced the *n* of *harbinger* and *messenger*.

▶ pass

## passion
[12] Latin *patī* meant 'suffer' (it is the source of English *patient*). From its past participial stem *pass-* was coined in post-classical times the noun *passiō*, denoting specifically the 'suffering of Christ on the cross.' English acquired the word via Old French *passion*, but its familiar modern senses, in which 'strength of feeling' has been transferred from 'pain' to 'sexual attraction' and 'anger,' did not emerge until the 16th century. Also from the Latin stem *pass-* comes *passive* [14], etymologically 'capable of suffering.'

▶ passive, patient

## past
[13] *Past* originated simply as a variant spelling of *passed*, the past participle of *pass*. The earliest unequivocal examples of it are as a preposition, but its adjectival use followed in the 14th century, and by

the 16th century it was being employed as a noun too (*the past*).

▶ pass

**paste** [14] Greek *pástē* denoted a sort of 'porridge made from barley' (it was a derivative of the verb *pássein* 'sprinkle'). Late Latin borrowed it as *pasta*, by which time it had come to mean 'dough.' From this were descended Italian *pasta* (acquired by English in the late 19th century) and Old French *paste*, source of English *paste*. This at first meant 'pastry, dough,' a sense now largely taken over by the related *pastry*. The meaning 'glue' did not emerge until the 16th century, 'soft mixture' until as recently as the 17th century. Other related forms in English include *pastel* [17], which comes via French from the Italian diminutive *pastello*; *pastiche* [19], which comes, again via French, from Italian *pasticcio* 'pie,' hence 'hotchpotch'; and *pasty* [13], *paté* [18], and *patty* [18], all of which go back to medieval Latin *pastāta*.

▶ pasta, pastel, pastiche, pasty, paté, patty

**pastor** [14] Latin *pāstor* meant 'shepherd.' It came from the same base as produced *pāscere* 'feed,' source of English *pasture* and *repast*, and hence denoted etymologically 'one who grazes sheep.' The 'animal husbandry' sense is still fairly alive and well in the derivative *pastoral* [15], but in *pastor* itself it has largely been ousted by 'Christian minister,' inspired by the frequent metaphorical use of *shepherd* for 'minister, priest' in the Bible.

▶ pasture, repast

**pastry** [16] The original word in English for 'pastry' in English was *paste*. This is still in use as a technical term, but in everyday usage it has gradually been replaced by *pastry*. This was derived from *paste*, modelled apparently on Old French *pastaierie* 'pastry,' a derivative of *pastaier* 'pastrycook.' It originally meant 'article made from pastry' (as in *Danish pastries*), and not until as recently as the mid-19th century did it start being used for simply 'pastry.'

▶ paste

**pasty**  see PASTE
**patch**  see PIECE
**paté**  see PASTE
**paten**  see PAN

**patent** [14] Etymologically, *patent* means simply 'open.' Its ultimate source is *patēns*, the present participle of the Latin verb *patēre* 'be open' (a relative of English *fathom* and *petal*). It was used particularly in the term *letters patent*, which denoted an 'open letter,' particularly an official one which gave some particular authorization, injunction, etc. It soon came to be used as a noun in its own right, signifying such a letter, and by the end of the 16th century it had acquired the meaning 'exclusive licence granted by such a letter.' This gradually passed into the modern sense 'official protection granted to an invention.'

▶ fathom, petal

**paternal**  see PATRON
**paternity**  see PATRON
**paternoster**  see PATRON

**path** [OE] *Path* is a West Germanic word of uncertain ultimate origin. Its cousins German *pfad* and Dutch *pad* point back to a prehistoric West Germanic ancestor *patha*, but no one is too sure where this came from (one possibility is that it was borrowed somehow from Greek *pátos* 'path'). The verb *pad* 'tread, walk' and the *-pad* of *footpad* come from the same source.

▶ pad

**pathos**  see SYMPATHY

**patient** [14] Etymologically, a *patient* is someone who is 'suffering.' The word comes via Old French from the present participle of the Latin verb *patī* 'suffer' (source also of English *passion* and *passive*). As an adjective it had already in Latin taken on its present-day sense of 'bearing affliction with calmness,' but the medical connotations of the noun are a post-Latin development.

▶ passion, passive

**patina**  see PAN
**patriarch**  see PATRON
**patrician**  see PATRON
**patrimony**  see PATRON
**patriot**  see PATRON

**patrol** [17] What is now a reasonably dignified term began life as a colloquialism meaning 'paddle about in mud.' English acquired the word via German from French *patrouiller*, which originally denoted 'tramp around through the mud of a military camp - when doing guard duty, for instance.' This was an alteration of Old French *patouiller* 'walk or trample in mud,' a verb based on the noun *patte* 'paw.' Other English words which trace their history back to *patte* are *patois* [17] (which developed via the Old French verb *patoier* 'trample on,' hence 'treat roughly,' and originally meant 'rough speech') and *patten* 'wooden shoe' [14].

▶ patois, patten

**patron** [14] *Patron* is one of a large group of English words descended from *pater*, the Latin member of the Indo-European family of 'father'-words (which also includes English *father*). Among the others are *paternal* [17], *paternity* [15], *paternoster* [OE] (literally 'our father'), *patrician* [15], and *patrimony* [14]. *Patron* itself comes from Latin *patrōnus*, a derivative of *pater* which was used for 'one who protects the interests of another, as a father does.' By post-classical times it had acquired its current meanings, including that of a 'guardian saint.' *Pattern* is ultimately the same word as *patron*.

The Greek branch of the 'father'-family is represented by *patér*, from which English gets *patriarch* [12], *patriot* [16] (based ultimately on the notion of a 'fatherland'), and *patronymic* [17].

▶ father, paternal, pattern, patrician, patriot

**patten**   see PATROL

**pattern**   [14]   Etymologically, *pattern* and *patron* are the same word. When it arrived in Old French as *patron* (from Latin *patrōnus*), it had roughly the range of senses of modern English *patron*, including that of 'one who commissions work.' But it had also acquired one other. Someone who pays for work to be done often gives an example of what he wants for the workman to copy: and so *patrōnus* had developed the meaning 'example, exemplar.' This passed into English from Old French along with the other meanings of *patron*, and not until the 17th century did it begin to be differentiated by the spelling *pattern*. The sense 'decorative design' emerged in the 16th century.

▶ patron

**patty**   see PASTE

**paucity**   see FEW

**pauper**   see POOR

**pause**   [15]   Greek *paúein* meant 'stop.' Its noun derivative *pausis* passed into English via Latin *pausa* and Old French *pause*. The Greek word also lies behind English *pose* and *repose*. Its ultimate origins are not clear, although some etymologists have suggested links with Old Prussian *pausto* 'wild' and Old Church Slavonic *pustiti* 'let go.'

▶ pose, repose

**pavilion**   [13]   *Pavilion* got its name because some anonymous ancient Roman was reminded by a tent, with its two 'wings' spread out from a central crosspiece, of a 'butterfly.' Latin for 'butterfly' was *pāpiliō* (a word of unknown origin), which hence came to be used for 'tent.' English acquired it via Old French *pavillon*.

**pawn**   English has two words *pawn*. The older, 'chess piece' [14], means etymologically 'footsoldier.' It comes via Anglo-Norman *poun* from medieval Latin *pedō* 'infantryman,' a derivative of Latin *pēs* 'foot' (to which English *foot* is related). The footsoldier being the lowest of the low in the army, the term came to be applied to the 'chess piece of lowest rank.' (English gets *pioneer* from a derivative of *paon*, the Old French version of *poun*.)

*Pawn* 'pledge as security for a loan' [15] comes via Old French *pan* 'security, pledge' from a prehistoric West Germanic *\*panda* (source of modern German *pfand* 'pledge, security, pawn'). *Penny* may go back to the same source.

▶ foot, pedal, pioneer / penny

**pay**   [12]   Etymologically, to *pay* someone is to 'quieten them down by giving them the money they are owed.' For the word is closely related to English *peace*. It comes via Old French *payer* from Latin *pācāre* 'pacify,' a derivative of *pāx* 'peace.' The notion of the irate creditor needing to be appeased by payment led to the verb being used in medieval Latin for 'pay.' The original sense 'pacify, please' actually survived into English ('Well he weened with this tiding for to pay David the king,' *Cursor Mundi* 1300), but by the beginning of the 16th century it had virtually died out, leaving 'give money' in sole possession.

▶ pact, peace

**pea**   [17]   *Pea* is the mirror-image of *dice*. *Dice* started off as the plural of *die*, but has become a singular form; the singular form of *pea* was originally *pease*, but it came to be regarded as plural, and so a new singular *pea* was created. The word was originally acquired in the Old English period from Latin *pisa*, which in turn got it from Greek *píson*. The old singular form survives in *pease pudding*. Relatives of the word include French *pois*, Italian *pisello*, and Welsh *pysen*.

**peace**   [12]   The etymological notion underlying *peace* is of 'fastening,' so as to achieve a 'stable' condition. The word comes via Anglo-Norman *pes* from Latin *pāx* 'peace,' which was derived from the same base, *\*pāk-* 'fasten,' as lies behind English *pact*, and is closely related to *pagan*, *page*, *pale* 'stake,' and *pole* 'stick.' Derivatives of Latin *pāx* or its Old French descendant to reach English include *appease* [16], *pacific* [16], *pacify* [15], and *pay*.

▶ appease, pacific, pact, pagan, pale, pay, pole

**peach**   [14]   Etymologically, the *peach* is the 'Persian' fruit. The word comes via Old French *peche* from medieval Latin *persica*, an alteration of an earlier *persicum* 'peach.' This was short for *mālum Persicum*, literally 'Persian apple,' reflecting the fact that the peach, a native of China, first became widely known in Europe when it had reached Persia on its westward journey.

**peacock**   [14]   The original English name of the 'peacock' in the Anglo-Saxon period was *pēa*. This was borrowed from Latin *pāvō*, a word which appears to have been related to Greek *taós* 'peacock,' and which also gave French *paon*, Italian *pavone*, and Spanish *pavo* 'peacock.' The Old English word is presumed to have survived into Middle English, as *\*pe*, although no record of it survives, and in the 14th century it was formed into the compounds *peacock* and *peahen* to distinguish the sexes. The non-sex-specific *peafowl* is a 19th-century coinage.

**peak**   [16]   *Peak* seems to come ultimately from the noun *pick* 'pointed implement' (as in *toothpick*). From this in the 15th century was formed an adjective *picked* 'pointed,' which survived dialectally into the

19th century (S H A Hervey noted in the *Wedmore Chronicle* 1887 'Children still use 'picked' of a pencil with a good point to it'). It had a variant form *peaked*, from which *peak* appears to have been derived as a back-formation. The adjective *peaky* 'sickly' [19], incidentally, is not etymologically related. It comes from a now little used verb *peak* 'become sickly or pale' [16], whose origins are unknown.

▶ pick

**peal** see APPEAL

**pearl** [14] Latin *perna* originally signified 'leg,' and hence 'ham.' It came to be applied metaphorically to a variety of sea-mussel whose stalk-like foot resembled a ham in shape. Such mussels could contain pearls, and so a diminutive form *\*pernula* seems to have been coined in Vulgar Latin to designate 'pearl.' This was later contracted to *\*perla*, which passed into English via Old French *perle*.

**peat** see PIECE

**peculiar** [15] The etymological notion underlying *peculiar* is of 'not being shared with others,' of being 'one's own alone.' It was borrowed from Latin *pecūliāris* 'of private property,' a derivative of *pecūlium* 'private property,' which in turn was based on *pecus* 'cattle,' hence 'wealth' (source also of English *pecuniary* [16]). (A parallel semantic progression from 'cattle' to 'property' is shown in English *fee*.) The development of the adjective's meaning from 'belonging to oneself alone' through 'individual' to 'extraordinary, strange' took place in Latin. *Peculate* 'pilfer, embezzle' [18] also comes ultimately from Latin *pecūlium*.

▶ pecuniary

**pedagogue** see PAGE

**pedal** [17] *Pedal* is one of a group of English words which go back to Latin *pēs* 'foot' or its Romance descendants (to which English *foot* is related). Others include *impede* [17], *pedestal* [16] (which comes via French from Old Italian *piedestallo*, a conflation of *pie di stallo* 'foot of a stall'), *pedestrian* [18], *pedicure* [19], *pedigree*, and *pedometer* [18].

▶ foot, impede, pawn, pedestal, pedestrian, pedigree

**pederast** see PAGE

**pedigree** [15] Etymologically, *pedigree* means 'crane's-foot.' It comes from Anglo-Norman *\*pe de gru*, *pe* meaning 'foot' (from Latin *pēs*) and *gru* 'crane' (from Latin *grūs*). The notion behind the metaphor is that a bird's foot, with its three splayed-out toes, resembles the branching lines drawn to illustrate a family tree.

▶ crane, geranium

**pediment** see PYRAMID
**pedometer** see PEDAL
**pee** see PISS
**peel** see PILLAGE
**peer** see PAIR, PORE
**peewit** see LAPWING
**pelican** [OE] *Pelican* comes via Latin *pelicānus* from Greek *pelekán*. This is generally thought to have been derived from *pélekus* 'axe,' in allusion to the shape of the pelican's beak.

**pellagra** see FELL
**pellet** [14] Etymologically, a *pellet* is a 'little ball.' It comes via Old French *pelote* (a relative of Spanish *pelota* 'ball,' from which the name of the Basque ball-game *pelota* [19] comes) from Vulgar Latin *\*pilotta*, a diminutive form of Latin *pila* 'ball' (source of English *pill* [15] and *piles* 'haemorrhoids' [15]). *Pelt* 'throw things at' [15] may have originated as a contraction of *pellet* (although a possible alternative source is Latin *pultāre* 'hit'); and *platoon* comes from a diminutive form of French *pelote*.

▶ pelota, pelt, piles, platoon

**pellicle** see FELL
**pelmet** see PALM
**pelt** see FELL, PELLET
**pen** English has three words *pen*. The oldest, 'enclosure' [OE], is something of a mystery term. It has no known relatives in the other European languages, and even in English it is not unequivocally found in its current sense until the 14th century. *Pent* [16], as in 'pent up,' originated in the past participle of the verb *pen*.

The earliest writing implements known as 'pens' were of course made from feathers, and so it is not surprising that the word *pen* [13] comes from a word that meant 'feather.' This was Latin *penna*, source also of English *pennon* [14] and a distant relative of English *feather*. It entered English via Old French *penne*.

*Pen* 'female swan' [16] is of unknown origin.

▶ pent / feather, pennon

**penal** see PAIN
**penalty** see PAIN
**penance** see PAIN
**penchant** see PENDULUM
**pencil** [14] Etymologically, a *pencil* is a 'little penis.' It originally denoted a 'paintbrush' – the current sense 'writing implement filled with a graphite rod' did not emerge until the 17th century – and came via Old French *pincel* from Vulgar Latin *\*pēnicellum*, an alteration of Latin *pēnicillum* 'paintbrush.' This was a diminutive form of *pēniculus* 'brush,' which was in turn a diminutive of *pēnis*. *Pēnis* originally meant 'tail' (whence the metaphor of the 'brush'), and only by extension was it used for 'male sex organ' (in which sense

English adopted it as *penis* [17]). The term *penicillin* [20] was based on Latin *pēnicillum*, in allusion to the tuft-like shape of its spore-bearing structures.

▶ penicillin, penis

**pendulum** [17] A *pendulum* is etymologically simply something that 'hangs.' It is a noun use of the neuter form of the Latin adjective *pendulus* 'hanging' (source of English *pendulous* [18]). This was a derivative of the verb *pendēre* 'hang,' which has contributed a wide range of words to English, among them *penchant* [17], *pendant* [14], *pendent* [15], *pending* [17], and *penthouse*, and derived forms such as *append* [15], *appendix* [16], *depend, impend* [16], *perpendicular* [14], and *suspend*.

▶ append, appendix, depend, impend, penchant, pendant, pendent, penthouse, perpendicular, suspend

**penguin** [16] *Penguin* is one of the celebrated mystery words of English etymology. It first appears towards the end of the 16th century (referring to the 'great auk' as well as to the 'penguin') in accounts of voyages to the southern oceans, but no one has ever ascertained where it came from. A narrative of 1582 noted 'The countrymen call them *Penguins* (which seemeth to be a Welsh name),' and in 1613 John Selden speculated that the name came from Welsh *pen gwyn* 'white head.' Etymologists since have not been able to come up with a better guess than this, but if it is true it means that the word must originally have referred to the now extinct auk, and only later been applied to the similar-looking penguin, which has a black head.

**penicillin** see PENCIL

**peninsula** see ISLAND

**penis** see PENCIL

**penitence** see PAIN

**pennon** see PEN

**penny** [OE] *Penny* comes from a prehistoric Germanic *\*panninggaz*, which also produced German *pfennig* and Dutch and Swedish *penning*. It has been speculated that this was derived from *\*pand-* 'pledge, security,' which also produced English *pawn* – in which case it would denote etymologically a 'coin used in transactions involving the pledging of a sum as security.'

▶ pawn

**pension** see PONDER

**pensive** see PANSY

**pent** see PEN

**pentagon** see FIVE

**pentagram** see FIVE

**pentecost** see FIVE

**penthouse** [14] *Penthouse* has no etymological connection with *house*. It comes from Anglo-Norman *\*pentis*, an abbreviated version of Old French *apentis*. This in turn went back to Latin *appendicium*

'additional attached part,' a derivative of *appendēre* 'attach' (source of English *append* [15] and *appendix* [16]), which was a compound verb formed from the prefix *ad-* 'to' and *pendēre* 'hang' (source of English *pending, pendulum*, etc). It arrived in English as *pentis*, and was used for a sort of 'lean-to with a sloping roof.' A perceived semantic connection with houses led by the late 14th century to its reformulation as *penthouse*, but its application to a '(luxurious) flat on top of a tall block' did not emerge until the 20th century.

▶ append, pendulum

**penumbra** see UMBRAGE

**people** [13] *People* is one of a large family of English words (including also *popular* and *public*) descended from Latin *populus* 'people.' Its spelling and pronunciation are due to its route of entry into English, via Anglo-Norman *poeple, people* and Old French *pueple, pople* rather than direct from Latin.

▶ popular, population, public

**pepper** [OE] The pepper vine is a native of the East Indies, and its name is oriental in origin too. It comes ultimately from Sanskrit *pippalī*, which meant 'berry,' and hence 'peppercorn.' It came west via Greek *péperi* and Latin *piper*, and was borrowed in prehistoric times into the West Germanic languages, giving German *pfeffer*, Dutch *peper*, and English *pepper*. Its application to fruits of the capsicum family, or their pungent dried products (no relation to the original pepper), dates from the 16th century. *Pimpernel* is a derivative of Latin *piper*.

▶ pimpernel

**peptic** see MELON

**perchance** see PERHAPS

**percussion** see CONCUSSION

**peregrine** see PILGRIM

**peremptory** [16] *Peremptory* comes via Anglo-Norman *peremptorie* from Latin *peremptōrius*. This meant 'destructive,' and was derived from *perimere* 'take away completely,' a compound verb formed from the prefix *per-* 'completely' and *emere* 'obtain' (source of English *example, exempt, prompt*, etc). By extension it was used for 'taking away all possibility of debate,' and hence 'decisive.'

▶ example, exempt, prompt

**perestroika** [20] Along with *glasnost, perestroika* was catapulted into English from Russian in the mid-1980s by Mikhail Gorbachev's reforms in the Soviet Union. It means literally 'rebuilding, reconstruction, reform,' and is a compound formed from *pere-* 're-' and *stroika* 'building, construction.' In the context of Gorbachev's sweeping changes, it denotes a 'sweeping restructuring of Soviet society, industry, etc.'

**perfect** [13] Something that is *perfect* is etymologically 'completely made.' The word comes via Old

French *parfit* from Latin *perfectus*, the past participle of *perficere* 'finish.' This was a compound verb formed from the prefix *per-* 'completely' and *facere* 'do, make' (source of English *fact, fashion*, etc). The modern English form *perfect*, a reversion to the Latin spelling, emerged in the 15th century.

▶ fact, factory, fashion

**perfidy**   see FAITH

**perform**   [14]   If the word *perform* had carried on as it started out, it would now be *perfurnish* (as indeed it was in northern and Scottish English from the 14th to the 16th centuries). For it comes ultimately from Old French *parfournir*, a compound verb formed from the intensive prefix *par-* and *fournir* 'accomplish' (source of English *furnish*). By association with *forme* 'form,' this was altered in Anglo-Norman to *parformer* – whence English *perform*.

▶ furnish

**perfume**   [16]   The *-fume* of *perfume* is the same word as English *fumes*, but whereas *fumes* has gone downhill semantically, *perfume* has remained in the realms of pleasant odours. It comes from French *parfum*, a derivative of the verb *parfumer*. This was borrowed from early Italian *parfumare*, a compound formed from the prefix *par-* 'through' and *fumare* 'smoke,' which denoted a 'pervading by smoke.' When it first arrived in English, the semantic element 'burning' was still present, and *perfume* denoted the 'fumes produced by burning a substance, such as incense,' but this gradually dropped out in favour of the more general 'pleasant smell.'

▶ fume

**perfunctory**   see FUNCTION

**perhaps**   [16]   The phrase *by hap* or *by haps* 'by chance' originated in the 14th century (*hap* 'chance,' a borrowing from Old Norse, now survives in the derived *happen*). In the 16th century it was transformed into *perhaps* on the model of *perchance* [14] and the now obsolete *percase* [14], both borrowings from Anglo-Norman containing *per* 'by.'

▶ happen, happy

**perigee**   see APOGEE

**peril**   [13]   Etymologically, *peril* means a 'trying out of something,' an 'experiment.' The word comes via Old French *peril* from Latin *periculum* 'experiment, danger,' a noun formed from the base *\*per-* 'attempt' (which also lies behind English *empiric, experience, expert, pirate,* and *repertory*). Its derivative *periculōsus* originally reached English via Old French as *perilous* [13], but subsequently became contracted to *parlous* [14].

▶ empiric, experience, expert, parlous, pirate, repertory

**period**   [14]   *Period* means etymologically 'going round.' It comes via Old French *periode* and Latin

*periodus* from Greek *períodos*, a compound noun formed from the prefix *perí-* 'round' and *hódos* 'way' (source also of English *episode, exodus* [17], and *method*). The main sense of the word in modern English, 'interval of time' (which first emerged in post-classical Latin), comes from the notion of a 'repeated cycle of events' (now more obvious in the derivative *periodical* [17]).

▶ episode, exodus, method

**peripatetic**   [16]   *Peripatetic* means literally 'walking round.' It comes via Old French *peripatetique* and Latin *peripatēticus* from Greek *peripatētikós*. This was a derivative of *peripatein*, a compound verb formed from the prefix *perí-* 'round' and *patein* 'walk.' But the Greeks used it not simply for 'walk around,' but specifically for 'teach while walking around' – an allusion to the teaching methods of Aristotle, who discussed and argued with his pupils and followers while walking about in the Lyceum, a garden near the temple of Apollo in Athens. Hence adherents of Aristotle's school of philosophy are known as *Peripatetics*. The more general use of the adjective for 'itinerant' represents a relatively modern (17th-century) return to its etymological meaning.

**periphrasis**   see PHRASE
**periwig**   see WIG
**perjury**   see JUST
**permanent**   see REMAIN
**permit**   [15]   *Permit* is one of a large family of English words (including also *admit, commit*, etc) which go back to Latin *mittere* 'let go, send.' Combination with the prefix *per-* 'through' produced *permittere* 'let go, give up,' hence 'allow.' Amongst derivatives to have reached English are *permissible* [15], *permission* [15], and *permissive* [17].

▶ admit, commit, mission, permission, submit, transmit

**perpendicular**   see PENDULUM
**perpetrate**   see FATHER
**perpetual**   see REPEAT
**perplex**   see PLY
**persecute**   see SEQUENCE
**persist**   see STATUE
**person**   [13]   Latin *persōna* originally denoted a 'mask, particularly one worn by an actor' (it may have been borrowed from Etruscan *phersu* 'mask'). It gradually evolved through 'character played by an actor' (a meaning preserved in English *persona* [20], a term introduced by Jungian psychology) to 'individual human being.' It entered English via Old French *persone*, and by the normal processes of phonetic development has become *parson*. But this in the Middle English period was hived off (for reasons that have never been satisfactorily explained) to 'priest,' and the original Latinate spelling *person* was restored for 'human being.' Other

derivatives to have reached English include *imperson-ate* [17], *personage* [15], *personal* [14], *personality* [14], and, via French, *personnel* [19].

▶ impersonate, parson, personnel

**perspire**  see SPIRIT

**persuade**  [16] The *-suade* element of *per-suade* goes back to Latin *suādēre* 'advise, urge,' a de-scendant of the same Indo-European base (**swād-*) as produced English *assuage* [14], *suave* [16], and *sweet*. Addition of the intensive prefix *per-* produced *per-suādēre*, source of English *persuade*; while negation of *suādēre* with *dis-* has given English *dissuade* [15].

▶ assuage, suave, sweet

**peruke**  see WIG

**peruse**  see USE

**pervert**  see VERSE

**peseta**  see PONDER

**pessimism**  [18] The first English writer on record as using *pessimism* was the poet Coleridge, in the 1790s. But he employed it for the 'worst possible state.' The modern sense 'expecting the worst' did not emerge until the early 19th century. The word was probably coined first in French, and was based on Latin *pessimus* 'worst.'

**pestle**  see PISTON

**petard**  see FEISTY

**petition**  see REPEAT

**petrel**  [17] The petrel, a gull-like seabird, is al-leged to have been named after the apostle Peter, sup-posedly inspired by the resemblance between the petrel's habit of flying close to the surface of the sea and touching it with its feet, and Peter's reported feat of walking on the water, as reported in Matthew 14:29 – 'And when Peter was come down out of the ship, he walked on the water, to go to Jesus.'

**petrol**  [16] *Petrol* originally meant 'mineral oil, extracted from the ground' (what we would now call *pe-troleum* or, more loosely, simply *oil*); not until the end of the 19th century was it applied to the 'fuel refined from this.' The word was borrowed from French *pé-trole*, which in turn came from Latin *petroleum* (itself taken over directly into English in the 16th century). This means etymologically 'rock-oil.' It was formed from *petra* 'rock' and *oleum* 'oil.' Other English words that go back to Latin *petra* or its Greek source *pétrā* in-clude *parsley*, *petrify* [16], *saltpetre* [16] (so called be-cause it forms a crust like salt on rocks), and the name *Peter* (a reference to Jesus calling the apostle Simon the 'rock on which he would build his church' – hence 'Si-mon Peter').

▶ parsley, petrify, saltpetre

**petulant**  see REPEAT

**petunia**  see TOBACCO

**pew**  [14] Historically, *pew* and *podium* are the same word. Both go back ultimately to Greek *pódion* 'small foot, base,' a diminutive form of *poús* 'foot' (a distant relative of English *foot*). This passed into Latin as *podium* 'raised place, balcony,' acquired directly by English as *podium* [18]. Its plural *podia* passed into English via Old French *puie* 'raised seat, balcony' as *pew*. This was originally used for a sort of raised enclo-sure in a church, court, etc, rather like a pulpit or dock; then for an enclosure in a church set aside for particular people to sit in (now known as a *box pew*); and finally (in the 17th century) for a church bench.

▶ foot, pedal, podium

**phantom**  [13] Like *fancy* and *fantasy*, *phan-tom* goes back ultimately to the Greek verb *phantázein* 'make visible,' a derivative of *phaínein* 'show' (source also of English *diaphanous* and *phenomenon* [17]). From *phantázein* was derived the noun *phántasma* 'ap-parition, spectre,' which passed into Latin as *phantas-ma*. This reached English in two separate forms: as *phantom*, via Old French *fantosme*; and as *phantasm* [13], via Old French *fantasme*. The latter formed the ba-sis of the fanciful coinage (originally French) *phantas-magoria* [19]. Other related English words are *emphasis* and *pant*.

▶ diaphanous, emphasis, pant, phase, phenomenon

**phase**  [19] Greek *phásis* (a derivative of the verb *phaínein* 'show,' source of English *phantom*) meant 'appearance,' and also 'cyclical apparent form of a planet, moon, etc.' This was adopted into modern Lat-in as *phasis*, and it originally passed into English (in the 17th century) in the Latin plural form *phases*. *Phase* represents a new singular formed from this. The more familiar modern sense 'stage in a sequence' is a meta-phorical extension of the astronomical meaning.

▶ phantom

**pheasant**  [13] Etymologically, the *pheasant* is a bird from the 'Phasis.' This was a river in the Caucusus, where the pheasant is supposed according to legend to have originated. The Greeks therefore called it *phāsiānós*, the 'Phasian bird,' and the word passed in-to English via Latin *phāsiānus* and Anglo-Norman *fesaunt*.

**phenomenon**  see PHANTOM

**philander**  see PHILOSOPHY

**philanthropy**  see PHILOSOPHY

**philately**  [19] When a Monsieur Herpin, a French stamp-collector, was looking for an impressive and learned-sounding term for his hobby, he was ham-pered by the fact that the Greeks and Romans did not have postage stamps, and therefore there was no classi-cal term for them. So he decided to go back a stage beyond stamps, to the days of franking with a post-mark. In France, such letters were stamped *franc de port* 'carriage-free,' and the nearest he could get to this in Greek was *atelés* 'free of charge,' a compound formed from *a-* 'not' and *télos* 'payment.' Using the Greek prefix *phil-* 'loving, love of' (as in *philosophy* and a wide range of other English words) he created *philatélie*, which made its first appearance in English in 1865.

**philippic**  [16] The original philippics (in Greek *philippikós*) were a series of speeches in which the Athenian orator Demosthenes denounced the political ambitions of Philip of Macedon in the 4th century BC (the word was a derivative of the Greek name *Phílippos* 'Philip,' which etymologically means 'horse-lover'). The term was subsequently applied (as Latin *philippicus*) to the speeches of Cicero attacking Mark Anthony, and in due course became a general word for a 'fierce denunciation.'

**philistine**  [16] The original Philistines were inhabitants of Philistia, an area in the southwestern corner of ancient Palestine. They were famed for their aggression and harrying tactics, and so the word *Philistine* was often used metaphorically for an 'enemy into whose hands one might fall,' but the notion of a Philistine as a 'boorish person' is a comparatively recent development, not recorded in English until the 19th century. It appears to have originated in German universities (the German term is *Philister*), and the story goes that it comes from the use of the biblical quotation 'the Philistines be upon thee, Samson' as the text of a sermon delivered at the funeral service for a student killed in a town-and-gown riot in Jena.

**philosophy**  [14] Greek *phílos* (a word of uncertain origin) meant 'loving.' It has entered into an enormous range of English compounds, including *philander* [17] (adopted from a Greek word meaning 'loving men'), *philanthropy* [17], *philately*, and *philology* [17], not to mention all the terms suffixed with *-phil* or *-phile*, such as *Anglophile* [19] and *paedophile* [20]. *Philosophy* itself means etymologically 'loving wisdom.' It comes via Old French *filosofie* and Latin *philosophia* from Greek *philosophía*, whose second element was a derivative of *sophós* 'wise' (source of English *sophisticate*).

▶ sophisticate

**philtre**  see FILTER

**phlegm**  [14] Greek *phlégma* denoted 'bodily fluid produced by inflammation' (it was a derivative of *phlégein* 'burn,' which went back to the same Indo-European base as produced English *flagrant, flame, fulminate*, and *phlox* [18] – in Greek literally 'flame'). As Latin *phlegma* it came to be used for 'body fluid' in general, and was incorporated into the medieval system of bodily humours as a term for the 'cold moist humour,' which induced sluggishness (whence the meaning of

the derivative *phlegmatic* [16]). This came to be associated in the late Middle Ages with 'mucus, particularly as produced in the respiratory passage.' English acquired the word via Old French *fleume* as *fleume*, and did not revert to the latinate form until the 16th century.

▶ flagrant, flame, fulminate, phlox

**phoenix**  [OE] The phoenix, a fabuluous bird which every 500 years consumed itself by fire and then rose again from its own ashes, may get its name from the red flames in which it perished. The word comes via Latin *phoenix* from Greek *phoinix*, which as well as 'phoenix' denoted 'Phoenician' and 'purple,' and it has been speculated that it may be related to *phoinós* 'blood-red.'

**phone**  [20]  *Phone* is of course short for *telephone* [19], a compound word formed from Greek *tēle-* 'far off' and *phōnē* 'voice, sound' (a descendant of the Indo-European base *\*bha-* 'speak,' and related to English *fable, fame, fate*, etc). Other English words derived from or based on *phōnē* include *gramophone, megaphone* [19], *microphone, phonetic* [19], *phonology* [18], *saxophone*, and *xylophone*.

▶ fable, fame, fate

**phosphorus**  [17] Etymologically, *phosphorus* means 'bringing light.' The word comes via Latin *phōsphorus* from Greek *phōsphóros*, a compound adjective formed from *phōs* 'light' and the suffix *-phóros* 'carrying' (a relative of English *bear*), which was used as an epithet for the planet Venus as it appears at dawn. It was also applied to any substance that that glowed, and in the mid 17th century it was taken up as the term for the newly isolated element phosphorus, which catches fire when exposed to the air. *Phosphate* [18] was borrowed from French *phosphat*, a derivative of *phosphore* 'phosphorus.'

▶ bear, photo

**photo**  [19]  Greek *phōs* meant 'light' (it was related to Sanskrit *bhā-* 'shine'). Its stem form *phōto-* was used by the astronomer Sir John Herschel in 1839 to coin the term *photograph*, based on the Greek element *-graphos* 'writing,' and perhaps inspired by a parallel German formation *photographie* which had appeared a little earlier the same year. The word's living connection with the concept 'light' has now been virtually severed, but it still flourishes in, for example, *photoelectric* [19], *photometer* [18], *photon* [20], and *photosynthesis* [19].

▶ phosphorus, photon

**phrase**  [16]  Greek *phrásis* 'speech, way of speaking' was a derivative of the verb *phrázein* 'show, explain.' English adopted it via Latin *phrasis* as *phrasis*, whose plural *phrases* eventually gave rise to a new singular *phrase*. From the same source comes *periphrasis* [16].

▶ periphrasis

**phrenology**   see FRANTIC

**physics**   [16]   *Physics* comes ultimately from Greek *phúsis* 'nature,' a derivative of *phúein* 'bring forth, cause to grow.' The science of studying the natural world was hence *phusikḗ epistḗmē* 'knowledge of nature,' and *phusikḗ*, turned into a noun, passed into English via Latin *physica* and Old French *fisique* as *fisike*. By now its meaning had shifted from 'natural science' to 'medicine,' a sense preserved in the now archaic *physic* [13] and in the derivative *physician* [13], and the modern plural form, which restores the original meaning, was a direct translation of Greek *tà phusiká* 'the physics,' the title of Aristotle's writings on natural science. *Physique* [19] was borrowed from French.

▶ physique

**piano**   [19]   *Piano* is short for *pianoforte* [18], a term borrowed from Italian which means literally 'soft-loud.' It was a lexicalization of an epithet (*piano e forte* 'soft and loud') applied in the early 18th century to a new sort of harpsichord whose volume could be varied by the use of dampers. Italian *piano* itself is descended from Latin *plānus* 'flat, even,' later 'smooth,' source of English *plain*. It was introduced into English as a musical direction in the late 17th century.

▶ plain, plane

**piazza**   see PLACE

**pick**   English has two distinct words *pick*. The verb [15], which originally meant 'pierce' (a sense which survives in 'pick holes in'), appears to come via Old French *piquer* from a Vulgar Latin *\*piccāre* 'prick, pierce.' *Picket* [17], which originally meant 'pointed stake,' is probably derived from the same source (its modern sense 'guard,' which emerged in the 18th century, comes from the practice of soldiers tying their horses to stakes). *Pique* [16] is a slightly later borrowing from French.

   *Pick* 'sharp implement' [14] (as in *toothpick*) is probably related to Old English *pīc* 'pointed object,' source of English *pike* 'spear.' It also lies behind English *peak*. In view of their close semantic similarity, it seems likely that the two *picks* share a common ancestor, which was no doubt responsible also for Old French *picois* 'pickaxe,' altered in English, under the influence of *axe*, to *pickaxe* [15].

▶ picket, pique / peak, pike

**picnic**   [18]   *Picnic* was borrowed from French *piquenique*, a word which seems to have originated around the end of the 17th century. It is not clear where it came from, but one theory is that it was based on the verb *piquer* 'pick, peck' (source of English *pick*), with the rhyming *nique* perhaps added in half reminiscence of the obsolete *nique* 'trifle.' Originally the word denoted a sort of party to which everyone brought along some food; the notion of an 'outdoor meal' did not emerge until the 19th century.

**picture**   [15]   *Picture* and *paint* are very closely related. The Latin verb *pingere* 'paint' was the source of English *paint*, and its past participial stem *pict-* produced a noun, *pictūra* 'painting,' which was eventually to become English *picture*. The same source produced English *depict* [17] and *Pict* [OE] (etymologically the 'painted' or 'tattooed' people), while its ultimate ancestor, the Indo-European base *\*pik-*, *\*pig-* 'cut,' also evolved Latin *pigmentum* 'colouring substance,' from which English got *pigment* [14] and, via Spanish, *pimento* [17].

▶ depict, paint, pigment, pimento

**pidgin**   [19]   A pidgin is a reduced form of language used for communication between speech communities which do not share the same native language. A characteristic of such languages is that words in the base language from which the pidgin evolved become altered. And this is how the word *pidgin* itself arose. It comes from *pidgin English*, an alteration of *business English* in the commercial pidgin used in Far Eastern ports in the mid-19th century.

▶ business

**pie**   [14]   The characteristic feature of *pies* in the Middle Ages was that their filling consisted of a heterogeneous mixture of ingredients (as opposed to *pasties*, which had just one main ingredient). This has led etymologists to suggest that pies were named after *magpies* (or *pies*, as they were originally called), from a supposed resemblance between the miscellaneous contents of pies and the assortment of objects collected by thieving magpies.

   Although *pie* has now been superseded by *magpie* as the bird-name, it survives in *pied* [14] (etymologically 'coloured black and white like a magpie') and *piebald* [16] (etymologically 'streaked with black and white').

▶ magpie, pied, piebald

**piece**   [13]   *Piece* is probably ultimately of Celtic origin. It comes via Anglo-Norman *pece* from medieval Latin *pecia* or *petia*, which appears to have been borrowed from *\*pettia*, an unrecorded word in the Celtic language of ancient Gaul. This would have been descended from an Old Celtic base *\*pett-* that may also be the source of English *peat* [14]. Anglo-Norman *\*peche*, a variant form of *pece*, of dialectal origin, gave English *patch* [14].

▶ patch, peat

**piecemeal**   see MEAL

**pied**   see PIE

**piety**   see PITY

**pig**   [13]   The word *pig* is not recorded until the Middle English period, although it is assumed to have existed in Old English as *\*picga* or *\*pigga*. It originally meant 'young pig,' and did not become the general term for 'pig' until the 16th century (the usual word in Old and Middle English was *swine*). *Piglet* is a late 19th-century coinage. It is not known where the word *pig* came from, although some have suggested a connection with Old English *pīc* 'pointed object' (source of modern English *pike*), perhaps in allusion to the pig's pointed muzzle (if that is the truth of the matter, *pig* may be parallel as an animal-name with *pike*).

**pigeon**   [14]   *Pigeon* comes ultimately from late Latin *pīpiō*. This meant originally simply 'young bird,' and was formed from the onomatopoeic base *\*pīp-* (source also of English *pipe*), which imitated the chirps of young birds. It gradually specialized in use to 'young pigeon, squab,' and both the general and the specific senses passed via Vulgar Latin *\*pībiō* into Old French as *pijon*. By the time it arrived in English, however, only the 'young pigeon' sense survived, and this was soon overtaken by 'pigeon' in general.

▶ pipe

**pigment**   SEE PICTURE

**pike**   English has two *pikes* now in common usage, which are probably ultimately the same word. *Pike* 'spear' [OE] goes back to an Old English *pīc* 'pointed object,' which is closely related to English *peak* and *pick* 'sharp implement.' It had various specific applications in Old and Middle English, now long defunct, including 'pickaxe,' 'spike,' 'thorn,' 'point of a shoe,' and 'pitchfork' (and *pitchfork* [13] itself was originally *pickfork*, a fork with 'sharp points'; its current form, which emerged in the 16th century, is due to the association with 'pitching' or tossing hay on to a cart). But the sense 'weapon consisting of a long pole with a spike on top' did not appear until the 16th century, partly inspired by the related Old French *pique* 'pike.'

*Pike* the fish [14] was probably also named with the descendant of Old English *pīc*, in allusion to its long pointed jaws (a similar inspiration can be seen in French *brochet* 'pike,' a derivative of *broche* 'spit').

▶ peak, pick, pitchfork

**pilaster**   SEE PILLAR

**pile**   English has three words *pile*. The commonest, 'heap' [15], originally meant 'pillar.' It comes ultimately from Latin *pīla* 'pillar,' source also of English *pilaster, pillar*, etc. This evolved in meaning to 'pier or harbour wall made of stones,' and inspired a derived verb *pīlāre* 'heap up' (source of English *compile* [14]). The sense 'heap' came to the fore in Old French *pile*, and passed into English.

*Pile* 'post driven into the ground' [OE] was borrowed into Old English from Latin *pīlum* 'javelin.' It was originally used for a 'throwing spear,' 'arrow,' or 'spike,' and its present-day use did not emerge (via 'pointed stake or post') until the Middle English period.

*Pile* 'nap on cloth, carpets, etc' [15] probably comes via Anglo-Norman *pyle* from Latin *pilus* 'hair' (which

may be distantly related to English *pillage* and *pluck*, and lies behind English *depilatory* [17]).

▶ compile, pilaster, pillar / depilatory

**piles**   SEE PELLET

**pilfer**   [14]   Originally *pilfering* was quite a serious matter, roughly what would now be termed *plundering*, but gradually over the centuries is has become trivialized to 'stealing small things.' It was to begin with only a noun in English (the verb did not arrive until the 16th century), but its ultimate source was the Anglo-Norman verb *pelfrer* 'rob, plunder.' No one is too sure where that came from, although it may be related in some way to the now archaic *pelf* 'money' [14], which originally meant 'spoils, booty.'

**pilgrim**   [12]   Etymologically, a *pilgrim* is someone who goes on a journey. The word comes via Provençal *pelegrin* from Latin *peregrīnus* 'foreign.' This was a derivative of *pereger* 'on a journey, abroad,' a compound formed from *per* 'through' and *ager* 'country' (source of English *agriculture*). When it arrived in English it was still being used for 'traveller' (a sense which survives in the related *peregrinations* [16]), but the specific 'one who journeys for religious purposes' was well established by the 13th century.

The *peregrine falcon* [14] got its name because falconers took its young for hunting while they were 'journeying' from their breeding places, rather than from their nests.

▶ peregrine

**pill**   SEE PELLET

**pillage**   [14]   The origins of *pillage* are disputed. It comes from Old French *pillage*, a derivative of *piller* 'plunder,' but there the consensus breaks down. Some say that *piller* (which also meant 'tear up') was based on *pille* 'rag, cloth,' which may have been descended from Latin *pilleus* 'felt cap'; others that it came from a Vulgar Latin verb *\*pīliāre*, a derivative of Latin *pīlum* 'javelin' (source of English *pile* 'supporting stake'); and others again that it came from Latin *pilāre* 'remove hair' (source of English *peel* [13], which originally meant 'plunder'), a derivative of *pilus* 'hair' (source of English *pile* 'nap'), in which case it would be roughly parallel in inspiration to colloquial English *fleece* 'rob.'

**pillar**   [13]   *Pillar* comes ultimately from Latin *pīla* 'pillar' (source also of English *compile, pilaster* [16], and *pile* 'heap'). In Vulgar Latin this was extended to *\*pīlāre*, which passed into Anglo-Norman *piler*. This was the form in which English originally acquired it, and the *-ar* ending was not grafted on to it until the 14th century.

▶ compile, pilaster, pile

**pillion**   [16]   The word *pillion* long predates the invention of the motorcycle. It originally denoted a 'small light saddle on a horse,' particularly one placed behind a main saddle. It is ultimately of Latin origin, but it reached English via a Celtic route. English borrowed it from Scottish Gaelic *pillean*, a diminutive form of *peall* 'covering, cushion.' This in turn came from Latin *pellis* 'skin' (source of English *pelt* 'skin' and related to English *film*).

▶ film, pelt

**pillow** [OE] *Pillow* in a recognizable form emerged in the 14th century. It was based on an inflected form of Old English *pyle* 'pillow.' This came via a prehistoric West Germanic *pulwīn (source also of German *pfühl* and Dutch *peluw* 'pillow') from Latin *pulvīnus* 'pillow', a word of unknown origin.

**pilot** [16] *Pilot* comes ultimately from a Greek word for 'oar,' *pēdón*, which went back to the same Indo-European base as produced English *foot*. It plural, *pēdá*, was used for 'rudder,' and from this was derived medieval Greek *pēdótēs 'rudder, helmsman.' This in turn was borrowed into medieval Latin as *pedota*, which was later altered to *pilotus* – whence, via French, English *pilot*. For most of its career in English, of course, the word has been used in connection with the steering of ships, but in the middle of the 19th century it began to be applied to the steering of balloons, and the first record of its modern use for 'flier of an aeroplane' comes from 1907.

▶ foot

**pimento** see PICTURE

**pimpernel** [15] The burnet, a plant of the rose family, has fruit that look like peppercorns. It was therefore termed in Vulgar Latin *piperīnella, a derivative of *piperīnus 'pepper-like,' which in turn was based on Latin *piper* 'pepper' (source of English *pepper*). This passed into Old French as *piprenelle*, which was later altered to *pimpernelle* – hence English *pimpernel*. This too denoted the 'burnet,' and it is not clear how it came to be applied (as early as the 15th century) to the small red-flowered plant of the primrose family, its current usage.

▶ pepper

**pin** [OE] Latin *pinna* (a probable relative of English *fin*) meant 'wing, feather, pointed peak.' Amongst its derivatives were the diminutive *pinnāculum*, which has given English *pinnacle* [14] and, via French, *panache* [16] (which originally meant 'plume of feathers'), *pinnātus* 'feathered, winged,' source of English *pinnate* [18], and Vulgar Latin *pinniō, from which English gets *pinion* 'wing' [15]. *Pinna* itself was borrowed into Old English as *pinn*, and it was used for 'peg' (a sense which survives in various technical contexts); the application to a 'small thin metal fastener' did not emerge until the 14th century.

A *pinafore* [18] is etymologically a garment that is 'pinned afore,' that is, 'pinned to the front of a dress to protect it.'

▶ fin, panache, pinafore, pinion, pinnacle

**pine** [OE] English has two words *pine*. The tree-name was borrowed from Latin *pīnus*, which some have traced to the Indo-European base *pīt- 'resin' (source of English *pituitary* [17]). Pine-cones were originally called *pineapples* [14], but in the mid 17th century the name was transferred to the tropical plant whose juicy yellow-fleshed fruit was held to resemble a pine-cone. The Latin term for 'pine-cone' was *pīnea*, whose Vulgar Latin derivative *pīneolus has given English *pinion* 'cog-wheel' [17], and it seems likely that English *pinnace* [16] comes via French and Spanish from Vulgar Latin *pīnācea nāvis 'ship made of pine-wood.' And the *pinot noir* [20] grape is etymologically the grape with 'pine-cone'-shaped bunches.

*Pine* 'languish' is a derivative of an unrecorded Old English noun *pīne 'torture,' originally borrowed into Germanic from *pēna*, the post-classical descendant of Latin *poena* 'penalty' (source of English *pain*).

▶ pinion, pinnace, pituitary / pain

**pinion** see PIN, PINE

**pink** English has three distinct words *pink*. The colour term [18] appears to have come, by a bizarre series of twists, from an early Dutch word meaning 'small.' This was *pinck* (source also of the colloquial English *pinkie* 'little finger' [19]). It was used in the phrase *pinck oogen*, literally 'small eyes,' hence 'half-closed eyes,' which was borrowed into English and partially translated as *pink eyes*. It has been speculated that this was a name given to a plant of the species *Dianthus*, which first emerged in the abbreviated form *pink* in the 16th century. Many of these plants have pale red flowers, and so by the 18th century *pink* was being used for 'pale red.'

*Pink* 'pierce' [14], now preserved mainly in *pinking shears*, is probably of Low German origin (Low German has *pinken* 'peck'). And *pink* (of an engine) 'make knocking sounds' [20] is presumably imitative in origin.

**pinnace** see PINE

**pinnacle** see PIN

**pinnate** see PIN

**pinyin** [20] *Pinyin* is a system of writing Chinese in Roman characters which began to be introduced in China in the late 1950s. The term in Chinese means literally 'spell-sound.'

**pioneer** [16] *Pioneer* was borrowed from French *pionnier*, a descendant of Old French *paonier*. This originally denoted a 'foot soldier sent on ahead to clear the way,' and was a derivative of *paon* 'foot soldier' (whose Anglo-Norman version *poun* gave English *pawn*).

▶ foot, pawn, pedal

**pious** [17] *Pious* is one of a nexus of English words descended from Latin *pius*, an adjective of unknown origin. Its derivative *pietās* has given English *piety* and *pity*, and the derived verb *piāre* 'appease, atone' lies behind English *expiate* [16]. *Pious* itself was probably borrowed direct from Latin.

▶ expiate, piety, pity

**pipe** [OE] The etymological notion underlying *pipe* is of a 'piping' sound. The word goes back to a Common Romance *\*pīpa*, a derivative of the Latin verb *pīpāre* 'chirp.' This was formed from the base *\*pīp-*, imitative of the sounds made by young birds, which also lies behind English *pigeon*. Prehistoric Germanic took over *\*pīpa*, and it has since evolved to German *pfeife*, Dutch *pijp*, Swedish *pipa*, and English *pipe*. By the time it reached English it had broadened out semantically from its original 'tubular wind instrument which makes a piping sound' to 'tube' in general.

▶ pigeon

**pique** see PICK

**pirate** [15] A *pirate* is etymologically someone who makes an 'attempt' or 'attack' on someone. The word comes via Latin *pīrāta* (where the notion of a 'sea-robber' first emerged) from Greek *peirātés* 'attacker, marauder,' a derivative of the verb *peiran* 'attempt, attack.' This came from the same base, *\*per-* 'try,' as produced English *experience, expert, peril, repertory*, etc.

▶ experience, expert, peril, repertory

**piscatorial** see FISH

**Pisces** see FISH

**piscina** see FISH

**piss** [13] *Piss* probably originated in imitation of the sound of urinating. It has been traced back to a hypothetical Vulgar Latin *\*pisāre*, which passed into English via Old French *pisser*. It has become widely distributed throughout the other European languages (Italian *pisciare*, for instance, German and Dutch *pissen*, and Welsh *piso*). *Pee* [18] started life as a euphemism for *piss*.

▶ pee

**pistil** see PISTON

**pistol** [16] *Pistol* is one of a very small and select group of words contributed to English by Czech (others are *howitzer* and *robot*). It comes via German *pistole* from Czech *pišt'al*, which literally means 'pipe' (it is related to Russian *pischal* 'shepherd's pipe').

**piston** [18] The Latin verb *pinsere* meant 'beat, pound.' Its past participial stem *pist-* formed the basis for the noun *pistillum* 'grinding stick, pestle' (from which English gets *pistil* 'female flower part' [18], an

allusion to its shape). This passed into Italian as *pestello*, from which English gets *pestle* [14]. From the Italian stem *pest-* was formed *pestone* 'rammer,' whose variant *pistone* gave French *piston* – whence English *piston*.

▶ pestle, pistil

**pit** English has two words *pit*. The older, 'hole' [OE], comes ultimately from Latin *puteus* 'pit, well' (source also of French *puits* 'well, shaft'), but reached English via a Germanic route. It was borrowed in prehistoric times into West Germanic as *\*putti*, which has evolved into German *pfütze* 'pool,' Dutch *put* 'pit,' and English *pit*.

*Pit* 'fruit-stone' [19] may have been borrowed from Dutch *pit*, which goes back to a prehistoric West Germanic *\*pithan*, source of English *pith* [OE].

▶ pith

**pitcher** see BEAKER

**pitchfork** see PIKE

**pittance** see PITY

**pituitary** see PINE

**pity** [13] Latin *pius* 'pious,' an adjective of unknown origin which gave English *expiate* and *pious*, had a noun derivative *pietās*. This has come into English in three distinct forms. First to arrive, more or less contemporaneously, were *pity* and *piety* [13], which were borrowed from respectively Old French *pite* and *piete*. These both developed from Latin *pietās*, and were originally synonymous, but they became differentiated in meaning before they arrived in English. The Italian descendant of the Latin noun was *pietà*, which English took over in the 17th century as a term for a 'statue of Mary holding the body of the crucified Christ.'

Vulgar Latin *\*pietantia*, a derivative of *pietās*, meant 'charitable donation.' It has given English *pittance* [13].

▶ expiate, piety, pious, pittance

**placate** see PLEASE

**place** [13] A *place* is etymologically a 'broad' area. The word comes ultimately from the Greek expression *plateia hodós* 'broad way' (the adjective *platús* 'broad' is probably related to English *flat*). *Plateia* came to be used on its own as a noun, and passed into Latin as *platea* 'broad street, open area.' This became changed in post-classical times to *\*plattja*, which passed into English via Old French *place*. Probably the closest the English word comes to its ancestral meaning is as a street name (as in *Portland Place*), introduced under French influence in the late 16th century, which originally denoted more an 'open square' than a 'street.' But closer still are *piazza* [16] and *plaza* [17], borrowed respectively from the Italian and Spanish versions of the word.

The homophonous *plaice* the fish-name is a distant relative.

▶ flat, piazza, plaice, plate, platypus, plaza

**placebo** [13] *Placebo* started life as the first person future singular of the Latin verb *placēre* 'please' (source of English *please*), and hence meant originally 'I will please.' It was the first word of the antiphon to the first psalm in the Roman Catholic service for the dead, *Placēbo Dominō in rēgiōne vivōrum* 'I will please the Lord in the land of the living.' The word's medical use emerged at the end of the 18th, and arose from the notion of a medicine 'pleasing' the patient rather than having any direct physiological effect.

▶ please

**placenta** [17] Latin *placenta* originally meant 'flat cake.' It was borrowed from Greek *plakóenta*, the accusative form of *plakóeis* 'flat cake,' which was derived from *pláx* 'flat surface' (possible relative of English *plank*). Its application to the afterbirth (originally in the phrase *placenta uterīna* 'uterine cake') is a postclassical development, inspired by the flat round shape of the afterbirth.

**placid** see PLEASE

**plagiarize** [17] Latin *plagium* meant 'kidnapping' – it was a derivative of *plaga* 'net.' From it was formed *plagārius* 'kidnapper,' which was used metaphorically by the epigrammatist Martial for 'literary thief' – the sense in which the word reached English.

**plague** [14] Etymologically, *plague* means a 'blow' or 'stroke.' It goes back to the same prehistoric base, *\*plag-* 'hit,' as produced Latin *plangere* 'beat' (source of English *complain, plaintiff* [14], *plaintive* [14], and *plangent* [19] – which originally denoted the sound of waves 'beating' against the shore) and English *plankton*. From this was derived Greek *plāgā́* 'blow,' which was borrowed into Latin as *plāga* 'blow,' hence 'wound.' In the Vulgate it was used for an 'infectious disease,' and was borrowed in this sense (as well as the now defunct 'blow') via Old French into English. (*\*Plak-*, a parallel form to *\*plag-*, lies behind English *apoplexy* and *plectrum* [17].)

▶ apoplexy, complain, plaintive, plangent, plankton, plectrum

**plaice** [13] The *plaice* is etymologically the 'broad' fish. Its name goes back ultimately to Greek *platús* 'broad' (which makes it distantly related to *place*). From this was descended, via some missing links, late Latin *platessa* 'flatfish,' which became Old French *plaïs* – whence English *plaice*.

▶ place, plate, platypus

**plain** [13] *Plain* is etymologically the same word as *plane* in all its uses except the tree-name, and even that comes from the same ultimate source. This was Indo-European *\*plā-* 'flat,' which produced Greek *platús*

'broad' (source of English *place, plaice,* and *platypus*), Latin *plānus* 'flat, clear,' and possibly English *flat*. The Latin word passed into English via Old French *plain*, but its original 'flat' senses have been hived off into the separately acquired *plane*, leaving only the metaphorically derived 'clear' senses. The Italian descendant of *plānus* has given English *piano*.

▶ plane

**plaintiff** see PLAGUE

**plaintive** see PLAGUE

**plait** see PLEAT

**plan** [18] A *plan* is etymologically a design that has been 'planted' on the ground. Indeed in French, from which English acquired the word, it was originally *plant*, and was not altered to *plan* until the 16th century, under the influence of *plan* 'flat' (source of English *plane* 'flat'). It was a derivative of the verb *planter* 'plant,' and originally referred to the laying-out of the ground plan of a building. The metaphor seems first to have arisen in Italian *pianta* 'ground plan,' a relative of *plant*, which prompted its development in French.

▶ plant

**planchette** see PLANK

**plane** English has five distinct *planes*, four of which are essentially the same word as *plain*. These come ultimately from Latin *plānus*, but preserve its 'flat' meanings rather than (like *plain*) its 'clear' meanings. *Plane* 'flat surface' [17] comes from Latin *plānum*, a noun use of the neuter form of the adjective; it is the *plane* from which *aeroplane*, and hence its abbreviation *plane*, were formed. *Plane* 'carpenter's smoothing tool' [14] comes via Old French *plane* from late Latin *plāna*, a derivative of the verb *plānāre* 'make level,' itself a derivative of *plānus*. *Plane* 'flat' [17] is an alteration of *plain*, on the model of French *plan* 'flat.' And *plane* 'glide, soar' [17] comes from French *planer*, a derivative of *plan* 'level surface' (the underlying notion being of a bird soaring with level wings). The odd man out is *plane* the tree-name [14], which comes via Old French *plane* and Latin *platanus* from Greek *plátanos*, a derivative of *platús* 'broad' (source of English *place, plaice,* and *platypus*) – the reference being to its broad leaves. *Platanus* probably also underlies English *plantain*, as applied to the banana-like vegetable.

▶ piano, plain / place, plaice, plantain, plate, platypus

**planet** [12] A *planet* is etymologically a 'wanderer.' The word comes via Old French *planete* and late Latin *planēta* from Greek *planḗtos*, a derivative of the verb *planasthai* 'wander.' This was applied to any heavenly body that appeared to move or 'wander' across the skies among the fixed stars, which in ancient astronomy included the sun and moon as well as Mars, Venus, etc. The modern application to a 'body that orbits the sun (or similar star)' dates from the mid 17th century.

**plangent**  see PLAGUE

**plank**  [13]  The etymological idea underlying *plank* may be 'flatness.' It comes via *planke*, a northern dialect version of Old French *planche* (source of English *planchette* [19]), from late Latin *planca* 'slab,' a derivative of the adjective *plancus* 'flat.' This may have come from the same source as Greek *pláx* 'flat surface,' ancestor of English *placenta*.

▶ planchette

**plankton**  [19]  The ultimate source of *plankton* is Greek *plázein* 'hit,' a descendant of the same base as produced English *apoplexy*, *plague*, and *plectrum*. The link between these two unlikely-sounding relatives is that something that is hit moves or wanders, and plankton is minute organisms that wander or drift in the ocean. The Greek derivative *plagtón* meant 'wanderer,' and the application to 'plankton' was first made in German in the 1880s.

▶ plague

**plant**  [OE]  Etymologically, a *plant* is probably something you press into the ground with the 'sole' of your foot. The word was borrowed from Latin *planta* 'shoot, sprout, cutting,' a derivative of the verb *plantāre* 'plant, transplant,' and it has been speculated that this was based on Latin *planta* 'sole of the foot' (source of English *plantain* and *plantigrade* 'walking on the soles of the feet' [19]).

▶ plan, plantain

**plantain**  Two entirely unrelated plants have the name *plantain*. Both get it from their broad leaves. One, an insignificant-looking weed [14], comes via Old French *plantain* from Latin *plantāgō*, a derivative of *planta* 'sole of the foot' (source of English *plantigrade* and possibly *plant*). The other, a tropical plant of the banana family [16], was originally named by the Spaniards *plántano* 'plane tree,' a descendant of the same Latin source as produced English *plane* (which etymologically means 'broad-leaved'). This was adopted by English and quickly altered to the more familiar *plantain*.

▶ plan, plant / plane

**plasma**  see PLASTIC

**plaster**  [OE]  Like *plastic*, *plaster* comes ultimately from the Greek verb *plássein* 'mould.' Combination with the prefix *en-* 'in' produced *emplássein* 'daub on, plaster.' From its past participle *emplastós* was derived *émplastron* 'medicinal application to the skin,' which reached Latin as *emplastrum*. Medieval Latin shortened it to *plastrum*, which Old English adopted as *plaster*. Its use for a 'soft substance spread on walls, etc' was introduced via Old French *plastre* in the 14th century.

▶ plastic

**plastic**  [16]  *Plastic* is etymologically a 'mouldable' substance. The word comes via French *plastique* and Latin *plasticus* from Greek *plastikós* 'fit for moulding,' a derivative of the verb *plássein* 'mould' (source also of English *plasma* [18] and *plaster*). Up until the 20th century its main use in English was as an adjective, meaning 'pliable.' The first record of its use for a 'synthetic material made from organic compounds' comes from 1909. The trade-name *Plasticine* was coined from it in the 1890s.

▶ plasma, plaster

**plate**  [13]  Etymologically, a *plate* is something 'flat.' It comes from Vulgar Latin *\*plattus* 'flat,' which may go back to Greek *platús* 'broad' (source of English *place*, *plane* the tree, and *platypus*). It reached English via two separate Old French words, which have since coalesced: first *plate*, which gives the sense 'flat sheet,' as in *silver plate* and *plate glass*; and then, in the 15th century, *plat*, 'dish for food.' Related forms in English include *plateau* [18], *platform* [16] (etymologically a 'flat form'), *platinum* [19], *platitude* [19] (a 'flat' or dull remark), and *platter* [14].

▶ flat, place, plane, plateau, platform, platinum, platitude, platter, platypus

**platoon**  [17]  *Platoon* means etymologically 'little ball.' It comes from French *peloton*, a diminutive form of *pelote* 'ball' (source of English *pellet*). The notion of a 'small ball' was extended in French to a 'little cluster of people or group of soldiers' – hence the meaning of English *platoon*.

▶ pellet, pelota

**platter**  see PLATE

**platypus**  [18]  The platypus's name means literally 'flat-footed.' It was given to it at the end of the 18th century, and is first recorded in George Shaw's *Naturalists' Miscellany* 1799. It was adapted from Greek *platúpous*, a compound formed from *platús* 'flat' (source of English *place*, *plaice*, and *plane* the tree) and *poús* 'foot' (a relative of English *foot*).

▶ foot, place, plane, plate

**play**  [OE]  The origins of *play* are obscure. It had a relative in Middle Dutch *pleien* 'dance about, jump for joy,' but this has now died out, leaving it in splendid but puzzling isolation, its ancestry unaccounted for. Its underlying meaning appears to be 'make rapid movements for purposes of recreation,' but already in Old English times it was being used for 'perform on a musical instrument.' The earliest record of the use of the noun for a 'dramatic work' is from the 14th century.

**plead**  [13]  Essentially *plead* and *plea* are the same word. Both go back ultimately to Latin *placitum* 'something pleasant,' hence 'something that pleases both sides,' 'something agreed upon,' and finally 'opinion, decision.' This was a noun formed from the past participle of *placēre* 'please' (source of English *please*). It passed into Old French as *plaid* 'agreement, discussion, lawsuit,' and formed the basis of a verb *plaidier*, from which (via Anglo-Norman *pleder*) English got *plead*. In later Old French *plaid* became *plait*, and Anglo-Norman took it over as *plai* or *ple* – whence English *plea* [13].

▶ plea, please

**please**     [14]     *Please* is at the centre of a small family of English words that go back to Latin *placēre* 'please' (a derivative of the same base as produced *plācāre* 'calm, appease,' source of English *implacable* [16] and *placate* [17]). Related English words that started life in Latin include *complacent*, *placebo*, and *placid* [17]. It reached English via Old French *plaisir*, and other derivatives picked up via Old French or Anglo-Norman are *plea*, *plead*, *pleasant* [14], and *pleasure* [14] (originally a noun use of the verb *plaisir*).

▶ complacent, implacable, placate, placebo, placid, plea, plead, pleasant, pleasure

**pleat**     [14]     *Pleat, plait*, and *plight* 'predicament' are essentially the same word, but have become differentiated over the centuries. All three go back to Vulgar Latin *plicitum* or *plictum* 'fold,' a noun use of the past participle of Latin *plicāre* 'fold' (source of English *ply*). This became Old French *pleit*, which was originally borrowed into English as *plete* 'fold.' *Plete* was to become modern English *pleat*, but at first it was used only as a verb. For the noun, English borrowed *pleit* as *plait* [15] 'fold,' which did not begin to acquire its modern English meaning 'braid' until the 16th century. The Anglo-Norman version of *pleit* was *plit*, which gave English *plight* [14]. This too originally meant 'fold,' and the sense 'predicament' was presumably due to the influence of the other (completely unrelated) English word *plight* (see PLEDGE), which as a noun in Old and Middle English meant 'danger,' but is now mainly encountered in the expression 'plight one's troth.'

▶ fold, plait, plight, ply

**plebeian**     [16]     The *plēbs* were the 'common people' of ancient Rome (the word may connected with Greek *plēthos* 'multitude,' a relative of English *plethora*). English gets *plebeian* from its derived adjective *plēbēius*. The connotations of 'lower-classness' have been transferred from ancient Rome to the present day, and inspired the derogatory *pleb* [19]. A *plebiscite* [16] is etymologically a 'decree approved by the common people.'

**plectrum**     see PLAGUE

**pledge**     [14]     *Pledge* comes via Old French *plege* from late Latin *plebium*, a derivative of the verb *plebīre* 'pledge.' This was probably borrowed from Frankish

*plegan* 'guarantee,' a derivative of the same Germanic base as produced English *plight* 'pledge' [OE] (as in 'plight one's troth') and German *pflicht* 'duty.'

▶ plight

**plenty**     [13]     *Plenty* is one of a family of English words that trace their history back to Latin *plēnus* 'full' (a descendant of the same Indo-European base, *plē-*, as produced English *full* and *plethora*). Others include *plenary* [16], *plenipotentiary* [17], *plenitude* [15], *plenteous* [13], and *replenish*. *Plenty* itself comes via Old French *plentet* from the Latin derivative *plenitās*. Other close relatives contributed by Latin include *plural*, *plus*, and *surplus* and the range of words based on the verbal element *-plēre* 'fill' – *complete, deplete, implement, replete, supply*, etc.

▶ complete, deplete, full, implement, plethora, replete, supply

**plethora**     [16]     Greek *plēthōrē* meant 'fullness' (it was derived from the verb *pléthein* 'fill,' a descendant of the Indo-European base *plē-*, from which English gets *full, plenty*, etc). It was taken over into late Latin as *plēthōra*, and at first was widely used as a medical term, denoting an 'excess of blood or other fluids in the body.' That was what it originally denoted in English, but by the end of the 16th century the more general 'surplus' was coming into use.

▶ full

**pleurisy**     [14]     Greek *pleurá*, a word of unknown origin, denoted 'side' or 'rib.' It came to be used as an anatomical term for the 'inner lining of the chest, containing the lungs,' and the derivative *pleurîtis* 'inflammation of the chest lining' was coined (apparently by the physician Hippocrates). This passed into Latin as *pleurîtis*, which in post-classical times evolved to *pleurisis*. Old French took this over as *pleurisie*, whence English *pleurisy*.

**pliable**     see PLY
**pliant**     see PLY
**pliers**     see PLY
**plight**     see PLEAT
**plimsoll**     [20]     The British politician and social reformer Samuel Plimsoll (1824–98) was one of the leading instigators of the Merchant Shipping Act 1876. Amongst its provisions was that a line should be painted round the hulls of ships to indicate a safe limit for loading. This was Plimsoll's idea, and it became known as the *Plimsoll line*. It is thought that the word *plimsoll* was applied to 'gym shoes' in allusion to the line running round the shoes formed by the rubber welt or trimming.

**plot**     [11]     Two separate and unrelated words have come together to form modern English *plot*. The earlier was late Old English *plot*, a term of unknown origin which denoted 'area of ground' (as in a 'plot of land'). This subsequently developed to 'ground plan' and 'diagram,' which formed the basis of 'set of events in a story' (first recorded in the 17th century). The other ancestor was Old French *complot* 'secret scheme' (also of unknown origin), which was originally borrowed into English in the 16th century as *complot*, but soon lost its prefix *com-*, no doubt under the influence of the already existing noun *plot*.

**plough** [OE] *Plough* was not the original English word for an 'implement for turning over the soil.' That was Old English *sulh*, a relative of Latin *sulcus* 'furrow.' *Plough* was borrowed in the 10th century from Old Norse *plógr*, a descendant of prehistoric Germanic *plōgaz*. And this in turn was derived from a base *plōg-* acquired from one of the ancient Indo-European languages of northern Italy (source also of Latin *plaustrum* 'wagon'). The earliest record we have of the word being used for the characteristically shaped group of seven stars in Ursa major is from early 16th-century Scotland.

**plover** [14] Etymologically, the *plover* is the 'rain-bird.' Its name comes via Anglo-Norman *plover* from Vulgar Latin *\*ploviārius*, a derivative of Latin *pluvia* 'rain' (source of French *pluie*, Italian *pioggia*, and Spanish *lluvia* 'rain' and related to English *flow*). Various theories have been put forward as to how it came to be so called, among them that migrating plovers arrive in autumn, at the start of the rainy season; that plovers get restless at the approach of rain; and that some species have plumage spotted with pale marks, like raindrops.

▶ flow, pluvial

**pluck** [OE] *Pluck* is a widespread Germanic word (Flemish has *plokken*, Swedish *plocka*, and Danish *plukke*, and German and Dutch the closely related *pflücken* and *plukken*), but it is ultimately of Latin origin. Prehistoric Germanic *\*plukkōn* was acquired from a Vulgar Latin *\*piluccāre* (source also of Old French *peluchier* 'pluck' – from which English gets *plush* [16] – and Italian *piluccare* 'pluck'), a derivative of Latin *pilus* 'hair' (source of English *depilatory, pile* 'nap,' etc). The use of the noun *pluck* for 'courage' originated in the 18th century from an earlier literal application to the 'heart (and other internal organs) of a slaughtered animal,' which in turn was based on the notion of their being 'plucked' or removed from the carcase.

▶ depilatory, pile, plush

**plum** [OE] *Plum* and *prune* 'dried plum' are ultimately the same word. Their common ancestor was Greek *proumnon*, a word which originated somewhere in Asia Minor. This was later contracted to *prounon*, and borrowed into Latin as *prōnum*. Its plural *prōna* came to be regarded in post-classical times as a singular, and this is where English gets *prune* from, but *prōna* was also borrowed into prehistoric Germanic,

and many of its descendants here have had their *r* changed to *l* (the two are close together phonetically) – hence German *pflaume*, Swedish *plommon*, and English *plum*.

▶ prune

**plumb** [13] *Plumb* comes via Old French *\*plombe* from Latin *plumbum* 'lead,' a word of uncertain origin. Of its modern English uses, the verbal 'sound the depths' comes from the use of a line weighted with lead (a *plumb line*) to measure the depth of water and the adverbial 'exactly' from the use of a similar line to determine verticality. Related words in English include *aplomb; plumber* [14] (originally simply a 'worker in lead,' but eventually, since water pipes were once made of lead, a 'pipe-layer'); *plummet* [14] (a diminutive form coined in Old French); and *plunge* [14] (from the Vulgar Latin derivative *\*plumbicāre* 'sound with a plumb').

▶ aplomb, plumber, plummet, plunge

**plume** [14] Latin *plūma* originally denoted 'down, feathers' (it is probably related to English *fleece*). Eventually, though, it came to signify a 'single feather,' and evolved in this sense to Italian *piuma*, Spanish *pluma*, and French *plume* – source of English *plume*. The derivative *plumage* [15] originated in Old French.

▶ fleece, plumage

**plummet** see PLUMB

**plunder** [17] *Plunder* is of Dutch origin, and etymologically denotes something like 'rob of household odds and ends.' It was borrowed from Middle Dutch *plunderen*, which was presumably derived from the noun *plunde* or *plunne* 'household goods, clothes, etc,' whose origins are unknown.

**plunge** see PLUMB

**plural** [14] *Plural* is one of a range of English words that go back ultimately to Latin *plūs* 'more,' a descendant (like English *full* and Greek *pólus* 'much,' source of the English prefix *poly-*) of the Indo-European base *\*plē-* 'full.' This was borrowed into English directly as *plus* [17], in the sense 'with the addition of.' *Plural* comes via Old French *plurel* from the Latin derivative *plūrālis* 'more than one.' Other related words in English include *nonplus* [16] (etymologically 'put in a position where 'no more' - Latin *nōn plūs* - can be done'); *pluperfect* [16] (a lexicalization of the Latin phrase *plūs quam perfectum* 'more than perfect'); and *surplus*.

▶ nonplus, pluperfect, plus, surplus

**plus fours** [20] The term *plus fours* was introduced around 1920. It is an allusion the the fact that such trousers were made four inches longer in the leg than the standard knickerbockers or shorts of the time, which came to just above the knee.

**plush**   see PLUCK

**ply**   English has two distinct words *ply*, although ultimately they are related. The one meaning 'fold, twist, layer' [14], now mainly found in *plywood* [20] and in combinations such as *two-ply* and *three-ply*, comes from Old French *pli*, a derivative of the verb *plier* 'bend, fold' (source of English *apply* [14], *pliable* [15], *pliant* [14], *pliers* [16], and *reply*). This went back to Latin *plicāre* 'fold,' a relative of English *fold* and source of *accomplice, complicate* [17], *employ, explicit, imply, pleat, plight* 'predicament,' and *supplicate*. It was formed from a base that also produced English *perplex* [16] and the final syllables of *simple* and *supple*. The *apple pie* of *apple-pie bed* [18] is thought to be an alteration of French *nappe pliée* 'folded sheet.'

*Ply* 'travel a route regularly' or 'solicit' (as in 'ply for hire') [14] is short for *apply*, a relative of *ply* 'fold,' and originally meant 'apply, employ' (as in 'ply one's needle').

▶ accomplice, apply, complicate, comply, double, employ, explicit, fold, imply, perplex, pleat, pliable, pliers, plight, reply, simple, supple, supplicate

**pneumatic**   [17]   *Pneumatic* denotes etymologically 'of the wind or breath.' It comes via Latin *pneumaticus* from Greek *pneumatikós*, a derivative of *pneuma* 'wind, breath' (which is distantly related to English *sneeze*). Despite its similarity, *pneumonia* [17] does not come ultimately from the same source. It goes back to Greek *pleúmōn* 'lung,' a relative of Latin *pulmō* (source of English *pulmonary*), which was altered to *pneumōn* under the influence of *pneuma*. From this was derived *pneumonía*, acquired by English via Latin *pneumonia*.

▶ pneumonia, pulmonary

**poach**   English has two words *poach*, both of which go back ultimately to Old French *pocher* 'put in a bag,' a derivative of *poche* 'bag' (source of English *pocket* and *pouch*). The cookery term [15] is an allusion to the forming of little 'bags' or 'pockets' around the yolk of eggs by the coagulating white. *Poach* 'steal' [17] seems to mean etymologically 'put in one's pocket.'

▶ pocket, pouch

**pock**   see POX

**pocket**   [15]   A *pocket* is etymologically a 'small bag.' It comes from Anglo-Norman *poket*, a diminutive form of *poke* 'bag' (source of English *poke* 'bag' [13], now used only in the expression 'buy a pig in a poke'). Its Old French equivalent was *poche*, source of English *pouch* [14] (and of *poach*). This was acquired from Frankish *\*pokka* 'bag,' a derivative of the same Germanic base (*\*puk-*) as produced English *pock* (whose plural has become *pox*) and *pucker*.

▶ poach, pock, poke, pouch, pucker

**podium**   see PEW

**poem**   [16]   A *poem* is etymologically 'something created.' The word comes via Old French *poeme* and Latin *poēma* from Greek *póēma*, a derivative of *poeín* 'make, create.' The original sense 'something created' developed metaphorically via 'literary work' to 'poem.' From the same Greek verb was derived *poētés* 'maker,' hence 'poet,' which produced Latin *poēta* and in due course English *poet* [13] (the Old English word for 'poet' had been *scop*, a relative of modern English *scoff*). *Poetry* [14] originated as a medieval Latin derivative of *poēta*. *Poesy* 'poetry, poems' [14], like *poem* originally a derivative Greek *poeín*, now has an archaic air, but it has a living descendant in *posy* [16], which started life as a contraction of *poesy*.

▶ poesy, poet, poetry, posy

**poignant**   see PUNCTUATION

**point**   [13]   'Sharp end' is the etymological notion underlying *point*. For it comes ultimately from Latin *pungere* 'prick, pierce' (source also of English *expunge, poignant* and *pungent*). The neuter form of its past participle, *punctum*, was used as a noun, meaning 'small hole made by pricking, dot, particle, etc' (it is the source of English *punctual, punctuation*, etc), which passed into Old French as *point*. Then in the postclassical period a further noun was created, from the feminine past participle *puncta*, meaning 'sharp tip,' and this gave Old French *pointe*. The two have remained separate in French, but in English they have coalesced in *point*. The Spanish descendant of Latin *punctum, punta*, has given English *punt* 'bet.'

▶ compunction, expunge, poignant, punctual, punctuation, punt

**poise**   see PONDER

**poison**   [13]   Etymologically, *poison* is simply something you 'drink.' The word comes via Old French *poison* from Latin *pōtiō* 'drink' (source also of English *potion*), a derivative of the verb *pōtāre* 'drink' (from which English gets *potable*). The specialization in meaning from 'drink' to 'poisonous drink' took place in classical Latin, but the further progression to 'any poisonous substance' is a later development. Another probable relative is *pot*.

▶ potable, potion, symposium

**poke**   see POCKET

**poker**   English has two words *poker*. The earlier, *poker* for a fire [16], is simply the agent noun formed from *poke* [14], a verb borrowed from Middle Dutch or Middle Low German *poken* 'thrust, hit.' The card-game name [19] originated in the USA, but it is not clear where it came from: one suggestion is that it is connected with German *pochen* 'brag.'

**pole**   There are two separate words *pole* in English. *Pole* 'long thin piece of wood' [OE] comes from a prehistoric Germanic *pāl-(source also of German *pfahl*, Dutch *paal*, and Swedish *påla*). This was borrowed from Latin *pālus* 'stake,' from which English gets *pale* 'stake.' *Pole* 'extremity' [14] was acquired from Latin *polus*, which in turn went back to Greek *pólos* 'axis of a sphere.' This was a descendant of Indo-European *\*qwolo-* 'turn round' (source of English *wheel*), and has also given English *pulley*. The derivative *polar* [16] is an anglicization of the modern Latin coinage *polāris*.

▶ pale / polar, pulley, wheel

**police**  [16]  Etymologically, the *police* are in charge of the administration of a 'city.' In fact, *police* is essentially the same word as *policy* 'plan of action.' Both go back to Latin *polītīa* 'civil administration,' a descendant of Greek *pólis* 'city.' In medieval Latin a variant *polītia* emerged, which became French *police*. English took it over, and at first continued to use it for 'civil administration' (Edmund Burke as late as 1791 described the Turks as 'a barbarous nation, with a barbarous neglect of police, fatal to the human race'). Its specific application to the administration of public order emerged in France in the early 18th century, and the first body of public-order officers to be named *police* in England was the Marine Police, a force set up around 1798 to protect merchandise in the Port of London.

▶ politics

**policy**  English has two distinct and completely unrelated words *policy*. The one meaning 'plan of action' [14] comes via Old French *policie* from Latin *polītīa* 'civil administration,' source also of English *police* and the now archaic *polity* [16]. This in turn came from Greek *polīteíā*, a derivative of *pólis* 'city' (source of English *politics*). But the insurance *policy* [16] comes via French *police* 'document' and Provençal *polissa* from medieval Latin *apodissa*, an alteration of Latin *apodīxis* 'proof, demonstration,' which in turn was acquired from Greek *apódeixis*, a compound noun derived ultimately from the verb *deiknúnai* 'show.'

▶ politics / diction

**polio**  [20]  *Polio* is an abbreviation of *poliomyelitis* [19], a term coined in modern Latin from Greek *poliós* 'grey' and *muelós* 'marrow' (a derivative of *mūs* 'muscle') – hence 'inflammation of the 'grey matter' of the spinal chord.'

**polish**  [13]  Latin *polīre* 'make smooth and shiny' is the ultimate source of English *polish*. It passed into Old French as *polir*, whose stem form was *poliss-* – whence *polish*. The element *-pol-* of English *interpolate* is related to *polīre*.

▶ interpolate, polite

**polite**  [15]  Someone who is *polite* is etymologically 'polished' – indeed that is what the word originally meant in English ('The arch within and without was hiled [covered] with gold polite,' *Mirror of man's salvation* 1450). This had passed metaphorically into 're-

fined' by the 16th century, but not until the 17th century did the modern sense 'having refined manners' emerge. It was borrowed from *polītus*, the past participle of Latin *polīre* 'polish' (source of English *polish*).

▶ polish

**politics**  [16]  *Politics* is etymologically the art of 'civil administration.' It is an English rendering of Greek *tà polītiká* 'affairs of state.' Greek *polītikós* 'of the city or state, civil, political' was a derivative of *polítēs* 'citizen,' which in turn came from *pólis* 'city, state' (source also of English *police* and *policy* and related to Sanskrit *pūr* 'stronghold, fortified place'). It passed into English via Latin *polīticus* and Old French *politique* as *politic* [15], which originally meant 'political' as well as 'judicious' (*political* was coined in the 16th century).

▶ cosmopolitan, metropolis, police, policy

**polity**  see POLICY

**poll**  [13]  'Head' is the original and central meaning of *poll*, from which all its modern uses have derived. The 'voting' sort of *poll*, for instance, which emerged in the 17th century, is etymologically a counting of 'heads,' and the *poll tax* is a 'per capita' tax. The verb *poll* originally meant 'cut someone's hair,' a clear extension of the notion of 'top' or 'head' (the derived *pollard* [16] denotes an 'animal with its horns removed' or a 'tree with its top branches cut off'); this later developed to 'cut evenly across,' which is what the *poll* of *deed poll* means (originally it was a legal agreement cut evenly across, signifying that only one person was party to it – agreements made between two or more people were cut with a wavy line).

▶ pollard

**pollen**  [16]  *Pollen* originally meant 'flour' in English. Not until the 18th century was it taken up as a botanical term. It was borrowed from Latin *pollen* 'powder, dust, flour,' a relative of *pulvis* 'dust' (source of English *powder* and *pulverize*) and *polenta* 'pearl barley' (source of English *polenta* [16]).

▶ polenta, powder, pulverize

**polymath**  see MATHEMATICS

**polyp**  [16]  A *polyp* is etymologically a 'many-footed' creature. The word originally signified 'octopus,' but in the 18th century was broadened out into a general term for marine invertebrates with tentacles, such as hydras and sea anemones. It comes via French *polype* and Latin *polypus* from Greek *polúpous* 'cuttlefish,' a compound formed from *pólus* 'much, many' and *poús* 'foot' (source of English *pew* and *podium* and related to English *foot*). The metaphorical application of the word to a tumour growing from mucous membrane (an allusion to its tentacle-like outgrowths) originated in Greek.

Greek *pólus* (a distant relative of English *full* and *plural*) is of course the starting point of many English *poly-*

words, all with the underlying notion of 'several' – among them *polyglot* [17] (etymologically 'many tongues'), *polygon* [16], *polysyllable* [16], and *polytechnic* [19]. And its plural, *polloí* 'many,' is the origin of English *hoi polloi* [19], literally 'the many.'

▶ foot, full, hoi polloi, pedal, plural, plus, polygon

**pomegranate** [14] The *pomegranate* is etymologically the 'many-seeded apple.' The word's ultimate ancestor was Latin *mālum grānātum* (*mālum* gave English *malic* 'of apples' [18], and *grānātus* was derived from *grānum* 'seed,' source of English *grain*). In Vulgar Latin this became reduced to simply *\*grānāta*, which passed into Old French as *grenate* (source of English *grenade*, so named because early grenades looked like pomegranates). Before long *pome* 'apple' was added to the term, giving *pome grenate* – whence English *pomegranate*. *Pome* came from Latin *pōmum* 'apple, fruit,' which also gave English *pomade* [16] (an ointment so called because the original version was apple-scented), *pomander* [15] (etymologically an 'apple of amber'), *pommel* [14] (etymologically a 'little fruit'), and *pomology* [19].

▶ garnet, grain, grenade, pomade, pomander, pommel

**pomp** [14] Greek *pompḗ* meant literally 'sending' (it was derived from the verb *pémpein* 'send'). But it came to be used metaphorically for a 'solemn procession or parade' (as being something that was 'sent out' on its way), and hence for the concomitant 'display' or 'ostentation,' and passed with these senses into Latin as *pompa*. They survived into English, but 'procession' has gradually died out.

**pond** [13] *Pond* is historically the same word as *pound* 'enclosure.' The differentiation between the two was established early on, although *pound* continued to be used for 'pond' in Scotland and in some English dialects until quite recently. The common denominator is that *ponds* were originally specifically used for keeping fish in. The reason for the phonetic change from *pound* to *pond* is not known.

▶ pound

**ponder** [14] To *ponder* something is etymologically to 'weigh' it up. The word comes via Old French *ponderer* from Latin *ponderāre* 'weigh,' hence 'consider' (source also of English *preponderate* [17]). This was derived from *pondus* 'weight' (source of English *ponderous* [14]), a relative of *pendere* 'weigh' (source of English *compendium* [16], *compensate* [17], *dispense, expense, pansy, pension* [14], *pensive* [14], *peseta* [19], *poise* [15], and *spend*) and *pendēre* 'hang' (from which English gets *pendant, pendulum*, etc). Also closely related is English *pound*, the unit of weight.

▶ compendium, compensate, dispense, expense, pansy, pendant, pendulum, pension, pensive, peseta, poise, pound, preponderate, spend

**pontiff** [17] In ancient Rome, members of the highest college of priests were known by the epithet *pontifex*. This looks as though it should mean 'bridge-maker' (as if it were formed from Latin *pōns* 'bridge' – source of English *pontoon* – with the suffix *-fex*, from *facere* 'make'), but no one has ever been able to make any sense of this, and it is generally assumed that it originated as a loan-word, perhaps from Etruscan, and was subsequently adapted by folk etymology to *pontifex*. It was adopted into Christian usage in the sense 'bishop.' The pope was the 'sovereign pontifex,' and in due course *pontifex* came to designate the 'pope' himself. The word passed into French as *pontife*, from which English gets *pontiff*.

▶ punt

**pontoon** English has two words *pontoon*. The earlier, 'floating structure' [17], comes via French *ponton* from Latin *pontō* 'bridge made of boats,' a derivative of *pōns* 'bridge.' (*Pontō*, presumably the same word, was also used for a sort of Gaulish boat, and in that sense is the source of English *punt*.) *Pontoon* the card game [20] is an alteration of French *vingt-et-un* 'twenty-one' (the perfect score in pontoon being twenty-one) based on the other *pontoon*.

**pony** [18] Latin *pullus* denoted a 'young animal,' particularly a 'young horse' or 'young chicken' (it is related to English *foal*, and has given English *pool* 'collective amount,' *poultry*, and *pullet*). From it was derived in post-classical times *pullāmen*, which passed into Old French as *poulain* 'foal.' This had a diminutive form *poulenet*, and it is thought that this was the source of the early 18th-century Scottish term *powny*, which in due course spread southwards as *pony*.

▶ foal, pool, poultry, pullet

**pool** *Pool* of water [OE] and *pool* 'collective amount' [17] are distinct words in English. The former comes from a prehistoric West Germanic *\*pōl-*, source also of German *pfuhl* and Dutch *poel*. The latter was borrowed from French *poule* 'hen,' a descendant of Latin *pullus* 'young chicken' (source also of English *pony, poultry*, and *pullet*). There was a French game called *jeu de la poule*, the 'hen game,' involving throwing things at a hen – which you won as a prize if you hit it. Hence *poule* came to be used figuratively for 'target,' and also for 'that which is at stake in a game' – source of the original meaning of English *pool*, 'stake.' This evolved via 'stake made up of players' contributions' to 'collective amount' and 'collective resource.' *Pool* the snooker-like game is the same word; the game was originally played for a collective stake.

▶ foal, pony, poultry, pullet

**poor** [13] *Poor* came via Old French *povre* from Latin *pauper* 'poor.' This is thought originally to have been a compound meaning literally 'getting little,' formed from *paucus* 'little' (a distant relative of English *few*) and *parāre* 'get, prepare' (source of English *prepare*). Its derivative *paupertās* has given English *poverty* [12], and *pauper* itself was acquired by English in the 16th century as a noun meaning 'poor person.'

▶ few, pauper, poverty

**pope** [OE] Etymologically, the *pope* is the 'daddy' of the Roman Catholic church. Greek *páppas* was a nursery word for 'father,' based no doubt on the first syllable of *patér* 'father' (a relative of English *father*). In the form *pápas* it came to be used by early Christians for 'bishop,' and its Latin descendant *pāpa* was applied from the 5th century onwards to the bishop of Rome, the pope. English acquired the word in the Anglo-Saxon period, and so it has undergone the normal medieval phonetic changes to become *pope*, but the derivatives *papacy* [14] and *papal* [14] arrived later, and retain their *a*. Latin *pāpa* also gave English *papa* [17], via French *papa*.

▶ papa, papacy, poplin

**popinjay** see PARROT

**poplar** [14] The ancestor of *poplar* was Latin *pōpulus* 'poplar' (not to be confused with *populus* 'people'). This passed into Old French as *pople*, which with the addition of the tree-name suffix *-ier* became *poplier*. Its Anglo-Norman version was *popler*, from which English got *poplar*.

**poplin** [18] *Poplin* is etymologically the 'pope's cloth.' The word comes via obsolete French *papeline* from Italian *papalina*, a noun use of the feminine form of the adjective *papalino* 'papal,' and was applied to the cloth on the grounds that it was originally made in Avignon, in southern France, seat of the popes from 1309 to 1377.

▶ pope

**poppet** see PUPPET

**poppy** [OE] The Latin word for 'poppy' was *papāver*. A post-classical descendant, *\*papāvum*, was borrowed into prehistoric West Germanic as *\*papau*. This was later altered to *\*papāg*, which became Old English *popæg*, ancestor of modern English *poppy*. Italian *papavero* 'poppy' is a reminder of the Latin word.

**popular** [15] *Popular* is one of a range of English words that go back to Latin *populus* 'people.' Besides *people* (which came via Old French) and *popular* itself, these include *populace* [16], *population* [16], and *public*. It is not clear where *populus* itself came from, although some have linked it with the Indo-European base *\*plē-* 'fill,' source of English *full* and Greek *pléthos* 'multitude, common people' (a relative of English *plethora*).

▶ people, population, public

**porcelain** [16] The bizarre history of the word *porcelain* leads us back to a pig's vagina. It was origi-

nally applied to fine china in Italian, as *porcellana*. This meant literally 'cowrie shell,' and was used for the china in allusion to its shell-like sheen. *Porcellana* was a derivative of *porcella* 'little sow,' a diminutive form of *porca* 'sow' (to which English *pork* is related), and was applied to cowrie shells because they supposedly resembled the external genitalia of female pigs. English acquired the word via French *porcelaine*.

▶ pork

**porch** [13] *Porch* and *portico* [17] are ultimately the same word. Both go back to Italian *portico*, a descendant of Latin *porticus* 'covered gallery or entry,' but whereas *portico* was borrowed directly, *porch* came via Old French *porche*. *Porticus* was derived from Latin *porta* 'gate,' source of the *port* of English *porthole*.

▶ port, portico

**porcupine** [[14] The *porcupine* is etymologically a 'spiny pig.' Its name was coined in Vulgar Latin as *\*porcospīnus* from Latin *porcus* 'pig' (source of English *pork*) and *spīnus* 'spine.' It came to English via Old French *porc espin*. It underwent all sorts of traumas (*portpen, porpoynt, porpentine* – the form used by Shakespeare: the ghost of Hamlet's father speaks of the 'quills upon the fretful porpentine' – *porkenpick, porpin*, etc) before finally settling down in the 17th century to *porcupine*, and around 1700 the fanciful variant *porcupig* was coined.

▶ pork, spine

**pore** English has two words *pore*. The older, 'look attentively' [13], may go back to a hypothetical Old English *\*pūrian*, which might make it a relative of the nearly synonymous *peer* [16]. The *pore* in the skin [14] comes via Old French *pore* and Latin *porus* from Greek *póros* 'passage,' a descendant of the Indo-European base *\*por-* 'going, passage,' which also produced English *fare, ferry, opportunity*, and *port*. The development of the word's anatomical sense began in Greek. *Porous* [14] is derived from it.

▶ peer / fare, ferry, opportunity, porous, port

**pork** [13] Latin *porcus* 'pig' went back to a prehistoric Indo-European *\*porko-*, which also produced Russian *porosenok* 'pig,' Irish *orc* 'pig,' and English *farrow*. It passed into Old French as *porc*, which English adopted as a term for the 'flesh of pigs used as food.' Derivatives that have made it to English include *porcelain, porcupine*, and *porpoise*.

▶ farrow, porcelain, porcupine, porpoise

**pornography** [19] *Pornography* denotes etymologically the 'depiction of prostitutes'; and indeed *Webster's dictionary* 1864 defined the word as 'licentious painting employed to decorate the walls of rooms sacred to bacchanalian orgies, examples of which occur in Pompeii.' Originally in English it was mainly reserved to classical Greek and Roman examples of the genre, and the application to contemporary books, magazines, etc did not emerge strongly until the 1880s. The term originated in Greek, based on *pórnē* 'prostitute,' and reached English via French.

**porpoise** [14] The *porpoise* is etymologically the 'pig-fish.' The word comes via Old French *porpois* from Vulgar Latin *\*porcopiscis*, a compound formed from *porcus* 'pig' (source of English *pork*) and *piscis* 'fish' (a relative of English *fish*) and based on the model of Latin *porcus marīnus* 'sea-pig.' The name may have been suggested by the porpoise's snout.

▶ fish, pork

**porridge** [16] *Porridge* is a 16th-century alteration of *pottage* [13]. This originally denoted a stew of vegetables and sometimes meat, boiled to submission, but it gradually came to be applied to a gruel, of varying consistency, made of cereals, pulses, etc, and it was the sort made from oatmeal that eventually took over the word *porridge*. Its transformation from *pottage* took place via an intermediate *poddage* (the *t* pronounced /d/ as in American English), and the change to *r* is mirrored in such forms as *geraway* and *geroff* for *getaway* and *get off*. The same thing happened in the case of *porringer* 'dish' [16], which came from an earlier *pottinger*. *Pottage* itself was acquired from Old French *potage*, which etymologically meant simply 'something from a pot' (it was a derivative of *pot* 'pot'). English reborrowed it in the 16th century as *potage* 'soup.'

▶ pot, potage, pottage

**port** English has no fewer than five distinct words *port*, all of them going back to the Latin stem *port-*, a descendant of the Indo-European base *\*por-* 'going, passage' (from which English also gets *fare*, *ford*, etc). Based on this stem was *portus* 'harbour' (etymologically a 'place by which one enters'), which was borrowed into English as *port* 'harbour' [OE]. It is thought that the nautical *port* 'left' [17] originally denoted the side of the vessel facing harbour. And *port* the drink [17] gets its name from *Oporto* (literally 'the port'), the town at the mouth of the river Douro in Portugal through which port is shipped. From Latin *portus* was derived the verb *portāre*, which presumably originally meant 'bring into port,' but by classical times had broadened out to simply 'carry.' This gave English the military verb *port* 'carry' [16], and also underlies *deport* [15], *export* [15], *import*, *important*, *portable* [14], *portfolio* [18] (etymologically a 'carrier of leaves' or papers), *portly* [16], *portmanteau*, *report*, and *transport*. Also from *portus* comes English *opportunity*.

From the same stem came Latin *porta* 'gate, door,' which reached English via Old French *porte* as *port* 'gate' [13]. It came to be applied in the 14th century to an 'opening in the side of a ship,' and it is now most commonly encountered in the compound *porthole* [16]. *Portal* [14] and *portcullis* are among its descendants.

▶ fare, ferry, fiord, ford / deport, export, import, impor-

tant, opportunity, portable, portly, report, transport / porch, portal, portcullis, porthole, portico

**portcullis** [14] A *portcullis* is etymologically a 'sliding door.' The word comes from Old French *porte coleïce*, a term made up of *porte* 'door' (source of English *port*, as in *porthole*) and *coleïce* 'sliding.' This was a derivative of the verb *couler* 'slide,' which came ultimately from Latin *cōlum* 'seive' (source of English *colander* [14]).

▶ colander, porch, port, portico

**portend** see TEND

**porter** English has two distinct words *porter*, one for a 'person who carries things' [14] and the other for a 'door attendant' [13]. The former comes via Old French *portour* from medieval Latin *portātor*, a derivative of Latin *portāre* 'carry' (source of English *import*, *portable*, etc). It is generally assumed that *porter* the beer, first heard of in the 18th century, was so called from its being a favourite drink of porters. *Porter* 'door attendant' comes via Anglo-Norman *porter* from late Latin *portārius*, a derivative of Latin *porta* 'gate' (source of English *port*, as in *porthole*).

**portfolio** see PORT
**porthole** see PORT
**portico** see PORCH
**portly** see PORT

**portmanteau** [16] A *portmanteau* is etymologically something for 'carrying one's mantle' in. The word was borrowed from French *portemanteau*, a compound formed from *porter* 'carry' and *manteau* 'cloak' (source of English *mantle*). This originally denoted a 'court official whose duty was to carry the king's cloak,' but it was also applied to the bag in which he carried it, and hence eventually to any bag for carrying clothes and other items needed on a journey.

▶ mantle, port

**portrait** [16] *Portrait* was borrowed from French *portrait*, which originated as the past participle of the verb *portraire* 'depict' (source of English *portray* [14]). This was descended from Latin *prōtrahere*, a compound verb formed from the prefix *prō-* 'forth' and *trahere* 'draw' (source of English *tractor*). This originally meant 'draw out, reveal,' and also 'lengthen' (it has given English *protract* [16]), but in medieval Latin it came to be used for 'depict.'

▶ portray, protract, tractor

**pose** [16] *Pose* and *pause* come ultimately from the same source. This was late Latin *pausāre* 'stop, pause.' In Vulgar Latin it came to be associated with *pōnere* 'put,' and particularly, owing to the similarity of form, with its past participle *positum* (source of English *position*), and gradually started to take over its meaning. Hence Old French *poser*, source of the English word, meant 'put, place.' The noun *pose* is a modern acquisition from French, dating from the early 19th century.

▶ pause

**posh** [20] Although it only appeared as recently as the early 20th century, *posh* is one of the oldest chestnuts of English etymology. The story got around that it was an acronym for *port out, starboard home*, an allusion to the fact that wealthy passengers could afford the more expensive cabins on the port side of the ships going out to India, and on the starboard side returning to Britain, which kept them out of the heat of the sun. Pleasant as this story is, though, it has never been substantiated. Another possibility is that *posh* may be the same word as the now obsolete *posh* 'dandy, swell,' a slang term current around the end of the 19th century. This too is of unknown origin, but it has been tentatively linked with the still earlier 19th-century slang term *posh* 'halfpenny,' hence broadly 'money,' which may have come ultimately from Romany *posh* 'half.'

**position** [15] *Position* comes via Old French from Latin *positiō*, a noun formed from *posit-*, the past participial stem of Latin *pōnere* 'put, place.' This was also the source of English *posit* [17], *positive* [13] (which etymologically means 'placed down, laid down,' hence 'emphatically asserted'), *post* (in the senses 'mail' and 'job'), and *posture* [17]. And in addition it lies behind a wealth of English verbs (*compose, depose, dispose* [14], *expose* [15], *impose, interpose* [16], *oppose, repose, suppose, transpose* [14], etc) whose form underwent alteration by association with late Latin *pausāre* 'stop' (see POSE); *postpone* exceptionally has retained its link with *pōnere*.

▶ compose, depose, dispose, expose, impose, oppose, positive, post, postpone, repose, suppose, transpose

**posse** [17] *Posse* was the Latin verb for 'be able.' It was a conflation of an earlier expression *potis esse* 'be able'; and *potis* 'able' was descended from an Indo-European base *pot-* that also produced Sanskrit *pati-* 'master, husband' and Lithuanian *patis* 'husband.' In medieval Latin *posse* came to be used as a noun meaning 'power, force.' It formed the basis of the expression *posse comitātus*, literally 'force of the county,' denoting a body of men whom the sheriff of a county was empowered to raise for such purposes as suppressing a riot. The abbreviated form *posse* emerged at the end of the 17th century, but really came into its own in 18th-and 19th-century America.

▶ possible, potent

**possess** [15] Latin *potis* 'able, having power' (source of English *posse* and *potent*) was combined with the verb *sīdere* 'sit down' (a relative of English *sit*) to form a new verb *possīdere*. This meant literally 'sit down as the person in control,' hence by extension 'take

possession of' and ultimately 'have, own.' It passed into English via Old French *possesser*.

▶ possible, potent, sit

**possible** [14] Latin *posse* 'be able' (source of English *posse*) produced the derived adjective *possibilis* 'that can be done,' which came into English via Old French *possible*. (Its antonym *impossible* reached English at roughly the same time.)

▶ posse, potent

**post** Including the prefix *post-*, English has four different words *post*. The oldest, 'long upright piece of wood, metal, etc' [OE], was borrowed from Latin *postis*. From it was derived the verb *post* 'fix to a post,' which in turn produced *poster* [19], denoting a placard that can be 'posted' up. *Post* 'mail' [16] comes via French *poste* and Italian *posta* from Vulgar Latin *\*posta*, a contracted version of *posita*, the feminine form of the past participle of Latin *pōnere* 'put, place' (source of English *position*). The notion underlying the sense 'mail' is of riders 'placed' or stationed at intervals along a road so as to carry letters at speed by a relay system. *Post* 'job' [16] reached English via a very similar route, this time from the neuter form of the Latin past participle, *positum*. This became *\*postum* in Vulgar Latin, which produced Italian *posto*, French *poste*, and English *post*. Here again the word's original meaning, 'position where a soldier is placed,' reflects that of its Latin source *pōnere*. The prefix *post-* comes from the Latin preposition *post* 'after.' It occurs in a number of English words that go back to Latin ancestors (including *posterior* [16], *posthumous, postpone* [16], *postscript* [16], and the more heavily disguised *preposterous*), as well as being widely used to create new coinages (such as *postgraduate* [19] and *postwar* [20]).

▶ position

**posthumous** [17] Latin *postumus* functioned as a superlative form of *post* 'after,' and meant 'last of all.' It was often applied to a child 'born after the death of its father,' as being the final offspring that man could possibly have, and so began to pick up associations with the 'period after death.' This led in turn to the perception of a link with *humus* 'ground' (source of English *humble* and *humus*) and *humāre* 'bury,' and so *postumus* became *posthumus*. English adapted it direct from Latin.

**postpone**    see POST
**postscript**    see POST
**postulate** [16] The noun *postulate* originally meant 'demand, request.' It was an anglicization of *postulātum*, a noun use of the past participle of *postulāre* 'demand, request.' It was used in the mid-17th century by mathematicians and logicians for a proposition that (because it was a simple or uncontentious one) 'demanded' to be taken for granted for the sake of further reasoning, and from this it spread to more general us-

age. The notion of 'requesting' is better preserved in *postulant* [18], from the present participle of the Latin verb.

**posture**   see POSITION

**posy**   see POEM

**pot**   [OE]   *Pot* was borrowed in the late Old English period from medieval Latin *\*pottus*, which also produced French *pot* 'pot.' This may have been an alteration of *pōtus* 'drinking-cup,' which in classical Latin meant simply 'drink' (it was derived from the same stem as produced *pōtiō* 'drink,' source of English *poison* and *potion*). Related or derived forms in English include *porridge, potash, poteen* [19] (etymologically spirits distilled in a 'little pot' – Irish *poitín* is a diminutive of *pota* 'pot'), *pot-pourri* [18] (literally in French 'rotten pot'), *pottery* [15], and *putty*.

▶ porridge, potage, potash, poteen, pottage, putty

**potable**   see POTION

**potage**   see PORRIDGE

**potash**   [17]   Potassium carbonate was originally obtained by burning wood or other vegetable matter, soaking the ashes in water, and evaporating the resulting liquid in iron pots. The resulting substance was hence called in early modern Dutch *potasschen*, literally 'pot ashes,' and the word was adopted into English as *potash*. From it, or its French relative *potasse*, the chemist Sir Humphry Davy coined in 1807 the term *potassium* for the metallic element which occurs in potash.

▶ ash, pot, potassium

**potato**   [16]   *Potato* was originally the English name for the 'sweet potato' (when Falstaff in Shakespeare's *Merry Wives of Windsor* 1598 cried 'Let the sky rain potatoes!' it was to the sweet potato, and its supposed aphrodisiac properties, that he was referring). It did not begin to be used for the vegetable we now know as the *potato* until the very end of the 16th century. The word comes via Spanish *patata* from *batata*, the name for the 'sweet potato' in the Taino language of Haiti and other Caribbean islands.

**poteen**   see POT

**potent**   [15]   Latin *posse* (source of English *posse* and *possible*) meant 'be able or powerful.' It was a conflation of an earlier verbal phrase *potis esse* 'be able.' The precursor of *posse* was Old Latin *\*potēre*, whose present participle *potēns* survived to become the present participle of *posse*. And its stem form *potent-* has given English *potent, potentate* [14], and *potential* [14]. *Power* also comes from *\*potēre*.

▶ posse, possible, potentate, potential, power

**potion**   [13]   The Indo-European base *\*pō-, \*pī-* 'drink' has provided the verb for 'drink' in most modern European languages, apart from the Germanic ones: French *boire*, for instance, Russian *pit'*, and Welsh *yfed* all come from it. Amongst it Latin descendants were the

nouns *pōtiō* 'drink,' source of English *potion* (and also *poison*) and *pōtus* 'drink,' the probable ancestor of English *pot*, and the verb *pōtāre* 'drink,' from which English gets *potable* [16].

▶ poison, potable

**pot-pourri**   see POT

**potshot**   [19]   A *potshot* was originally a shot taken at an animal or bird simply in order to kill it for food – in order to get it into the 'pot,' in other words – rather than in accordance with the strict code and precise techniques of shooting as a 'sport.' Indeed to begin with it was distinctly a contemptuous term among the hunting and shooting fraternity. But gradually it broadened out in meaning to any 'casually aimed shot.'

**pottage**   see PORRIDGE

**potter**   see PUT

**pottery**   see POT

**pouch**   see POCKET

**poultry**   [14]   *Poultry* comes ultimately from a Latin word for a 'young animal,' which also gave English *pony*. It was borrowed from Old French *pouleterie*, a derivative of *pouletier* 'poultry dealer.' This in turn was based on *poulet* (source of English *pullet* [14]), a diminutive form of *poule* 'hen,' which went back via Vulgar Latin *\*pulla* to Latin *pullus* 'young animal, young horse, young chicken' (source of English *pony* and related to *foal*). *Punch*, as in 'Punch and Judy,' may come from *pullus* too.

▶ foal, pony, pullet

**pounce**   [15]   *Pounce* was originally a noun, denoting the 'claw of a bird of prey.' It is thought it may have come from *puncheon* 'stamping or perforating tool,' which was also abbreviated to *punch* 'stamping or perforating tool' and is probably related to *punch* 'hit.' The verb *pounce* emerged in the 17th century. It at first meant 'seize with talons,' and was not generalized to 'attack swoopingly' until the 18th century.

▶ punch

**pound**   English has three distinct words *pound*. The measure of weight and unit of currency [OE] goes back ultimately to Latin *pondō* '12-ounce weight,' a relative of *pondus* 'weight' (source of English *ponder*) and *pendere* 'weigh' (source of English *pension* and *poise*). It was borrowed into prehistoric Germanic as *\*pundo*, which has evolved into German *pfund*, Dutch *pond*, Swedish *pund*, and English *pound*. Its monetary use comes from the notion of a 'pound' weight of silver.

*Pound* 'enclosure' [14] is of unknown origin. It existed in Old English times in the compound *pundfald*, which has become modern English *pinfold*, and *pond* is a variant form of it.

*Pound* 'crush' [OE] is almost equally mysterious. In Old English it was *pūnian* (it did not acquire its final *d* until the 16th century, in fact), and it has been traced back to a Germanic *pūn-, which also produced Dutch puin 'rubbish.'

▶ pendant, pension, poise, ponder / pinfold, pond

**poverty**   see POOR

**powder**   [13]   The ultimate ancestor of powder is Latin pulvis 'dust' (source also of English pulverize [16]). This was related to Latin pollen 'fine flour' (source of English pollen), Latin puls 'gruel' (source of English poultice and pulse 'legume'), and Greek póltos 'gruel.'

▶ pollen, poultice, pulse, pulverize

**power**   [13]   Old Latin *potēre was the precursor of Latin posse 'be able or powerful' (source of English posse and possible). Its present participial stem potent- has given English potent. It seems to have remained current in colloquial speech, and by the 8th century AD was reasserting itself as the main form of the verb. It passed into Old French as poeir, later povoir (whence modern French pouvoir), and this came to be used as a noun, meaning 'ability to do things.' Its Anglo-Norman version poer passed into English, where it became power.

▶ posse, possible, potent

**pox**   [16]   Pox originated as an alteration of pocks, the plural of pock [OE]. This originally denoted a 'pustule,' and later the 'scar left by such a pustule, pockmark.' Pox used to be a common term for 'syphilis,' but today it is mainly found in compounds such as chicken-pox [18] (possibly a reference to the comparative mildness of the disease) and smallpox [16] (so called to distinguish it from the great pox, syphilis).

▶ pock, pocket

**practice**   [15]   The ultimate source of practice is Greek prássein 'do, practise.' From its base *prak- were derived the noun praxis 'doing, action' (source of English praxis [16]) and the adjective praktós 'to be done.' On this was based praktikós 'concerned with action, practical.' This passed into English via late Latin practicus as practic [14], which was later superseded by practical [17]. From practicus was derived the medieval Latin verb practicāre, later practizāre. This passed into English via Old French practiser as practise [15]. The derived noun practise was altered to practice in the 16th century, on the analogy of pairs like advice/advise.

▶ practical, practise, pragmatic, praxis

**pragmatic**   [16]   The base *prak-, which produced Greek praktós (source of English practice), also lies behind Greek prágma 'deed, affair.' From this was derived pragmatikós 'skilled in affairs,' which passed into English via late Latin pragmaticus.

▶ practice

**prairie**   [18]   Prairie comes ultimately from Latin prātum 'meadow' (source also of French pré 'meadow'). From it was derived Vulgar Latin *prātāria, which passed into English via French prairie. The word was from the start almost exclusively used with reference to the plains of North America.

**praise**   [13]   Despite a certain similarity in form and meaning, praise has no connection with pray. It comes ultimately from Latin pretium 'price,' which has also given English precious, price, prize, etc. From it was derived the late Latin verb pretiāre 'value highly, praise,' which English acquired via Old French preisier.

▶ precious, price, prize

**praxis**   see PRACTICE

**pray**   [13]   Latin precārī meant 'ask for, entreat, pray' (it has given English deprecate [17] and imprecation [16]). In Vulgar Latin it became *precāre, which passed into English via Old French preier. The noun prayer [13] goes back ultimately to the Latin adjective precārius 'obtained by asking or praying' (source also of English precarious), which was derived from precārī.

▶ deprecate, imprecation, precarious

**preach**   [13]   Preach goes back ultimately to Latin praedicāre 'proclaim' (source also of English predicament and predicate). Its Old French descendant was prechier, whence English preach (English had actually acquired the word before, directly from Latin in the Anglo-Saxon period, as predician 'preach,' but this had died out before the Old French word arrived). The semantic shift in the Latin verb from 'proclaiming' to 'preaching' took place in the early Christian period.

▶ predicament, predicate

**prebend**   [15]   A prebend is a salary paid to a clergyman from the revenue of his cathedral. The word comes via Old French prebende from late Latin praebenda 'salary, pension.' This was a noun use of the gerundive of praebēre 'give, grant, supply,' and hence meant literally 'things to be given.' Praebēre was a compound verb formed from the prefix prae- 'forth' and habēre 'have.' In Vulgar Latin, praebenda was altered to *prōbenda, from which English gets provender [14].

▶ provender

**precarious**   [17]   Precarious comes from Latin precārius (source also of English prayer), which meant 'obtained by asking or praying.' It was originally used in English as a legal term, in which 'obtained by asking' had undergone a slight change in focus to 'held through the favour of another.' This introduced the notion that the favour might be withdrawn, and that the possession was therefore uncertain, and so the adjective soon came to be used for 'depending on chance or caprice' and, in the 18th century, 'risky.' Latin precārius was derived from prex 'prayer,' a close relative of precārī 'ask, entreat, pray,' from which English gets pray.

▶ pray

**precede** [14] *Precede* is one of a large family of English words (including *concede, proceed, succeed,* and of course *cede*) which go back ultimately to Latin *cēdere* 'go away, withdraw, yield.' In this case the ancestor was Latin *praecēdere* 'go before,' a compound verb formed with the prefix *prae-* 'before,' which English acquired via Old French *preceder*. *Precedent* [15] goes back to the Latin verb's present participle, *precession* [16] to the late Latin derivative *praecessiō*.

▶ cede, concede, predecessor, proceed, succeed

**precinct** [15] The notion underlying *precinct* is of 'encirclement' or 'enclosure.' It comes from the past participle of Latin *praecingere* 'gird about, surround.' This was a compound verb formed from the prefix *prae-* 'before, around' and *cingere* 'encircle with a belt' (source of English *cincture* [16]). From the underlying notion come the twin modern meanings of an 'area enclosed by walls' and a 'delimited district within a city' (mainly used in American English).

▶ cincture

**precious** [13] Latin *pretiōsus* 'expensive, valuable, precious' was derived from *pretium* 'price' (source of English *praise, price,* and *prize*). English acquired it via Old French *precios*. The sense 'affected' was introduced from French in the early 18th century.

▶ praise, price, prize

**precipice** [16] The etymological notion underlying *precipice* is of falling 'headlong.' It comes via French *précipice* from Latin *praecipitium* 'headlong fall, steep place.' This was derived from *praecipitāre* 'throw headlong' (source of English *precipitate* [16] and *precipitous* [17]), a verb based on the adjective *praeceps* 'headlong, steep.' This in turn was a compound formed from the prefix *prae-* 'in front' and *caput* 'head' (source of English *capital, captain,* etc).

▶ capital, captain, chief

**precise** [16] Something that is *precise* is etymologically 'cut off in front.' The word was acquired via French *précis* (subsequently borrowed as the noun *précis* 'summary' in the 18th century) from Latin *praecīsus,* an adjectival use of the past participal of *praecīdere* 'shorten.' This was a compound verb formed from the prefix *prae-* 'in front' and *caedere* 'cut' (source also of English *concise, decide, excise,* etc). The notion of being 'shortened' gradually slipped via 'expressed shortly, leaving out extraneous matter' to 'exact.'

▶ concise, decide, excise, précis

**precocious** [17] *Precocious* means etymologically 'pre-cooked.' It was borrowed from Latin *praecox,* a derivative of the verb *praecoquere* 'cook in advance,' which was a compound formed from the prefix *prae-* 'before' and *coquere* 'cook' (a relative of English *cook* and *kitchen*). But *coquere* was also used

metaphorically for 'ripen,' and so *praecox* also meant 'early-ripening' – whence English *precocious* 'developing before its time.' The *apricot* is etymologically the 'precocious' fruit.

▶ apricot, cook, kiln, kitchen

**precursor** SEE COURSE
**predatory** SEE PREY
**predecessor** [14] Etymologically, *predecessor* is first cousin to *decease,* but it has never taken on *decease*'s connotations of 'dying.' Both go back to Latin *dēcēdere* 'go away' (a compound verb based on *cēdere* 'go away,' source of English *cede, concede, precede,* etc), whose derived noun *dēcessus* 'departure' came to be used euphemistically for 'death' – whence English *decease* [14]. Combination with the prefix *prae-* 'before' with the derived *dēcessor* 'leaver' produced *praedēcessor* 'one who leaves before.' Traces of this original meaning linger in English *predecessor* (acquired via Old French *predecesseur*) in the notion of 'one who left office before the present incumbent took over.'

▶ cede, concede, decease, precede, proceed, succeed

**predicament** [14] *Predicament* was originally a technical term in logic, denoting a 'category of attributes which may be asserted of a thing.' It broadened out in the 16th century to 'situation,' but it does not seem to have been until the 18th century that the specific modern sense 'awkward situation' became established. The word comes from late Latin *praedicāmentum,* a derivative of *praedicāre* 'proclaim' (source of English *preach* and *predicate* [16]). This was a compound verb formed from the prefix *prae-* 'in front of,' hence 'in public' and *dicāre* 'make known.'

▶ preach, predicate

**preen** [14] *Preen* is generally taken to be an alteration of *prune* 'cut branches,' under the influence of another now obsolete verb *preen* 'pierce,' a descendant of the Old English noun *prēon* 'pin' (the notion presumably being of a bird 'piercing' its feathers with its beak when cleaning them).

▶ prune

**preface** [14] *Preface* is a misleading sort of word. It has no connection with *face*. It comes ultimately from Latin *praefātiō,* a derivative of *praefārī* 'say beforehand.' This was a compound verb formed from the prefix *prae-* 'before' and *fārī* 'speak' (source of English *fable, fate,* etc). So etymologically, *preface* is virtually the equivalent of the native formation *foreword*.

▶ fable, fame, fate

**prefer** [14] To *prefer* one thing is etymologically to 'carry it before' others. The word comes via Old French *preferer* from Latin *praeferre* 'set before,' a compound verb formed from the prefix *prae-* 'before' and *ferre* 'carry' (source of English *fertile* and related to *bear*).

▶ bear

**prefix**     see FIX

**pregnant**     [16] Latin *praegnās* 'pregnant' probably originated as a compound formed from *prae* 'before' and *gnascī* or *nascī* 'be born' (source of English *nation, native*, etc). It was altered to *praegnāns*, bringing it in line with present participial adjectives ending in -*āns*, and was borrowed into English in its stem form as *pregnant*. From it was derived the verb *impregnāre*, from which English gets *impregnate* [16], but English *impregnable* is quite unrelated, despite its similarity – it comes from Latin *prehendere* 'seize' (source also of English *apprehend, comprehend*, etc).

▶ impregnate, nation, native, nature

**prehensile**     see PREY

**premier**     see PRIME

**premise**     [14] *Premise* comes via Old French *premisse* from medieval Latin *praemissa*, a noun use of the past participle of Latin *praemittere* 'send ahead.' This was a compound verb formed from the prefix *prae*-'before' and *mittere* 'send' (source of English *admit, commit, mission, transmit*, etc). It first entered English as a technical term in logic, in which its underlying meaning is of a proposition 'set before' someone. But it was also used in the plural as a legal term, meaning 'matters stated previously.' In a conveyance or will, such 'matters' were often houses or other buildings referred to specifically at the beginning of the document, and so the term *premises* came to denote such buildings.

▶ admit, commit, mission, permit, submit, transmit

**premonition**     see MONSTER

**prepare**     [15] Latin *parāre* 'make ready' lies behind a wide range of English words, from *apparatus* and *apparel* to *emperor* and *separate*. It combined with the prefix *prae*-'before' to produce *praeparāre* 'make ready in advance,' adopted into English via Old French *preparer*.

▶ apparatus, apparel, emperor, separate

**preponderate**     see PONDER

**preposterous**     [16] *Preposterous* originated as a Latin oxymoron, *praeposterus*. This was coined from *prae* 'before' and *posterus* 'coming after, next,' a derivative of *post* 'after.' It denoted 'the wrong way round, out of order' (and indeed that was how English *preposterous* was once used: 'The preposterous is a pardonable fault . . . We call it by a common saying to *set the cart before the horse*,' George Puttenham, *Art of English Poesie* 1589). But already in Latin the notion had developed via 'irrational' to 'absurd,' a sense quickly taken up by English.

**prerogative**     [14] Latin *praerogāre* meant 'ask before others' (it was a compound verb formed

from the prefix *prae*- 'before' and *rogāre* 'ask,' source also of English *interrogate* [15]). The term *praerogātīva* (based on its past participle) was applied to those electoral groups who were 'invited before others' to vote, or in other words had the privilege of voting first, in elections for state officials. Hence the word (acquired by English via Old French *prerogative*) came to mean in general 'right to precedence, privilege.'

▶ arrogant, interrogate

**presage**     see SEEK

**presbyterian**     see PRIEST

**present**     [13] The Latin adjective *praesēns* 'at hand, now here' originated as the present participle of *praeesse* 'be before one,' a compound verb formed from the prefix *prae*- 'in front' and *esse* 'be.' English acquired it via Old French *present*, the same route as was taken by its derivative *praesentia* on its way to English *presence* [14]. The use of the related noun *present* for 'gift' originated in Old French in the concept of 'bringing something into someone's presence,' and hence of giving it to them. The verb *present* [13] comes from the Latin derivative *praesentāre*.

**preserve**     [14] The -*serve* of *preserve* comes from Latin *servāre* 'keep safe' (no relation to *servīre* 'serve,' but source also of English *conserve, observe*, and *reserve*). Combination with *prae*- 'before' produced medieval Latin *praeservāre* 'guard beforehand, take steps to ward off possible harm,' which reached English via Old French *preserver*.

▶ conserve, observe, reserve

**president**     [14] A *president* is etymologically simply someone who 'presides.' The word comes via Old French *president* from Latin *praesidēns*, the present participle of *praesidēre* 'superintend' (it literally meant 'sit in front of' – it was formed from the prefix *prae*- 'before' and *sedēre* 'sit' – and it has given English *preside* [17]). Another Latin derivative was the noun *praesidium* 'garrison, fortification,' which English has acquired via Russian *prezídium* as *presidium* [20].

▶ preside, presidium, sit

**press**     English has two words *press*. The commoner, and older, 'exert force, push' [14], comes via Old French *presser* from Latin *pressāre*, a verb derived from the past participle of *premere* 'press' (source of English *print*). The corresponding noun *press* (which actually arrived in English a century earlier in the now archaic sense 'crowd') originated as a derivative of the Old French verb. Derived verbs in English include *compress* [14], *depress* [14], *express, impress* [14], *oppress* [14], *repress* [14], and *suppress* [14].

The other *press*, 'force' [16], is now found virtually only in the expression 'press into service' and in the compound *pressgang* [17]. It originally denoted 'compel to join the navy, army, etc,' and was an alteration, under the influence of *press* 'exert force,' of *prest* 'pay recruits.' This was a verbal use of Middle English *prest* 'money given to recruits,' which was borrowed from Old French *prest* 'loan.' This in turn was a derivative of the verb *prester* 'lend,' which went back to Latin *praestāre* 'provide,' a compound formed from the prefix *prae-* 'before' and *stāre* 'stand.' Related to *praestāre* was Latin *praestō* 'at hand,' from which have evolved French *prêt* 'ready' and Italian and Spanish *presto* 'quick' (English borrowed the Italian version as *presto* [16]).

▶ compress, depress, express, impress, oppress, print, repress, suppress / presto, station

**prestige** [17] As opponents of semantic change are fond of pointing out, *prestige* once meant 'trick, illusion,' and its use until the 19th century was usually derogatory. It comes via French *prestige* from Latin *praestigiae* 'illusions produced by a conjurer or juggler,' an alteration of an unrecorded *\*praestrigiae*. This would have been a derivative of *praestringere* 'blindfold,' hence 'confuse the sight, dazzle,' a compound verb formed from the prefix *prae-* 'before' and *stringere* 'bind' (source of English *strict*). The modern approbatory meaning appears to have been reintroduced from French.

▶ strict

**presto**   see PRESS

**pretend** [14] To *pretend* something is etymologically to 'hold it out' – as an excuse, or as something it is not. The word comes from Latin *praetendere*, a compound verb formed from the prefix *prae-* 'before' and *tendere* 'stretch' (source of English *tend, tense,* etc).

▶ extend, tend, tense

**pretext**   see TEXT

**pretty** [OE] In Old English *pretty* (or *prættig,* as it was then) meant 'clever' in a bad sense – 'crafty, cunning.' Not until the 15th century had it passed via 'clever,' 'skilfully made,' and 'fine' to 'beautiful.' It was a derivative of *prætt* 'trick, wile,' which came from a prehistoric West Germanic *\*pratt-* (source also of Dutch *part* 'trick').

**prevaricate** [16] Etymologically, *prevaricate* means 'walk crookedly,' and it goes back ultimately to a Latin adjective meaning 'knock-kneed,' *varus.* From this was derived the verb *vāricāre* 'straddle,' which was combined with the prefix *prae-* 'before, beyond' to produce *praevāricārī* 'walk crookedly,' hence 'deviate.' This developed in English to 'deviate from straightforward behaviour,' hence 'be evasive, equivocate.'

**prevent** [15] If you *prevent* someone, you 'come before' them (and indeed that literal meaning of the verb survived for some time: Thomas Cromwell wrote in 1538 'I have sent it unto him after the departure of the said Muriell, to the intent he might prevent the ambassadors post and you have leisure to consult and advise upon the same'; and as late as 1766 we find in Frances Sheridan's *Sidney Biddulph* 'I am an early riser, yet my lord V-- prevented me the next morning, for I found him in the parlour when I came downstairs'). The word comes from Latin *praevenīre,* a compound verb formed from the prefix *prae-* 'before' and *venīre* 'come.' Already in Latin, though, it had progressed semantically from 'come before' via 'act in advance of, anticipate' to 'hinder,' and this meaning emerged in English in the 16th century.

▶ adventure, venue

**prey** [13] *Prey* comes via Old French *preie* from Latin *praeda* 'booty' (from which was derived the verb *praedārī* 'plunder,' source of English *depredation* [15] and *predatory* [16]). This was a contraction of an earlier *praeheda,* a noun formed with the prefix *prae-* 'before' from the same base (*\*hed-* 'seize,' source also of English *get*) as produced the verb *praehendere* 'seize.' This has been a rich source of English vocabulary, contributing through different channels such a varied assortment as *prehensile* [18], *prison,* and *prize* 'something seized in war,' not to mention prefixed forms like *apprehend, comprehend* [14], *comprise* [15], *impregnable* [15], *reprehensible, reprieve,* and *surprise.* It is also the ancestor of French *prendre* 'take.'

▶ apprehend, comprehend, comprise, depredation, impregnable, predatory, prehensile, prison, reprehensible, reprieve, surprise

**price** [13] The Latin word for 'price' was *pretium* (it was probably derived ultimately from the Indo-European preposition *\*preti* 'back,' and so etymologically denoted 'recompense'). Its descendants have spread through most modern western European languages, including French *prix,* Italian *prezzo,* Spanish *precio,* German *preis,* and Dutch *prijs.* The last two were borrowed from Old French *pris,* the ancestor of modern *prix,* as was English *price.* The word differentiated in the 16th century into *price* and *prize*; and derivatives of the Latin original have given English *appreciate, depreciate* [15], *praise,* and *precious.*

▶ appraise, appreciate, depreciate, grand prix, praise, precious

**prick** [OE] *Prick* is a word of the Low German area, which English shares with Dutch (*prik*). Its ultimate origins, though, are not known. The earliest record of its use for 'penis' is from the late 16th century, and in the 16th and 17th centuries women employed it as a term of endearment – a usage which did not go down well in all quarters: 'One word alone hath troubled some, because the immodest maid soothing the young man, calls him her Prick. He who cannot away with this, instead of 'my Prick,' let him write 'my

Sweetheart',' H M, *Colloquies of Erasmus* 1671. *Prickle* [OE] is a diminutive derivative.

▶prickle

**pride** [OE] The original Old English noun for 'pride' was *prȳte*, a derivative of the adjective *prūd* 'proud' (ancestor of modern English *proud*). This changed in the 11th century to *prȳde*, probably under the influence of the adjective, and subsequently developed to *pride*. There is an isolated example of the use of the word for a 'group of lions' from the late 15th century, but the modern usage seems to be a 20th-century revival.

▶proud

**priest** [OE] *Priest* goes back ultimately to the Greek noun *presbúteros*, which meant literally 'elder' (it was formed from the comparative of the adjective *présbus* 'old'). It was used in the Greek translation of the New Testament for 'elder of the church, priest.' It was borrowed into Latin as *presbyter* (source of English *presbyterian* [17]). This subsequently became reduced to *\*prēster* (as in *Prester John*), which was taken over by Old English as *prēost*, ancestor of modern English *priest*.

▶presbyterian

**prim** [18] *Prim* etymologically means 'first.' It comes from Old French *prime*, the feminine form of *prin* 'fine, excellent,' which went back to Latin *prīmus* 'first' (source of English *prime*). The English meaning developed through a derogatory 'overrefined.'

▶first, prime

**prima donna** see DAME

**prime** [OE] Latin *prīmus* 'first' came from an earlier *\*prīsmo-* , which went back ultimately to Indo-European *\*pro* 'before, in front' (ancestor also of English *first*). English first acquired it direct from Latin in the Anglo-Saxon period as an ecclesiastical term for the earliest of the canonical hours, and this is the source of the modern English noun uses of the word (as in 'in one's prime'). The adjective *prime* was borrowed in the 14th century from Old French *prime*. English has a wide range of words that go back to derivatives of Latin *prīmus*, including *premier* [15], *prim*, *primal* [17], *primary* [15], *primate* [13], *primitive* [14], *prince, principal*, and *principle*. The trade-name *Primus* was first used for a sort of paraffin lamp in the early years of the 20th century.

▶first, premier, prim, primitive, prince, principle

**prince** [13] A *prince* is etymologically someone who 'takes first place,' hence a 'leader.' The word comes via Old French *prince* from Latin *princeps*, a compound formed from *prīmus* 'first' (source of English *prime*) and *capere* 'take' (source of English *captive, capture*, etc). (German *fürst* 'prince' was derived from Old High German *furist* 'first,' apparently in imi-

tation of the Latin word.) The derivative *princess* [14] was also acquired from Old French.

▶first, prime

**principle** [14] Frequently confused, *principal* [13] and *principle* come from distinct sources – but both sources were derived ultimately from Latin *princeps* 'chief' (from which English gets *prince*). *Principal* goes back via Old French *principal* to Latin *principālis* 'first, original,' while *principle* comes from *\*principle*, an assumed Anglo-Norman variant of Old French *principe*, which went back to Latin *principium* 'beginning, foundation.'

▶first, prime, prince

**print** [13] Latin *premere* meant 'press' (its past participial stem *press-* underlies English *press*). It passed into Old French as *preindre*, whose past participle formed the basis of a noun *preinte* 'impression, impressed mark' – source of English *print*. The verb first used for the activity of 'printing books' was the derived *imprint* [14] ('Because this said book is full of wholesome wisdom . . . I have purposed to imprint it,' William Caxton, *Game and Play of the Chess* 1474), but *print* soon followed at the beginning of the 16th century.

▶press

**prior** *Prior* the ecclesiastical rank [11] and *prior* 'previous' [18] are ultimately the same word. Both go back to Latin *prior* 'former, superior,' a comparative formation based on the Old Latin preposition *pri* 'before.' This came in post-classical times to be used as a noun meaning 'superior officer, administrator,' and it was taken over as such into the terminology of the monastic foundations.

**prism** [16] The etymological idea underlying the word *prism* is of its shape, that of a 'sawn-off' piece. It comes via medieval Latin *prisma* from Greek *prísma*, a derivative of the verb *prízein* 'saw.' Its optical application emerged in English at the beginning of the 17th century.

**prison** [12] Like *comprehend, prehensile*, etc, *prison* goes back ultimately to Latin *praehendere* 'seize.' From this was derived the noun *praehensiō* 'seizure,' later contracted to *prēnsiō*, which passed into Old French as *prisun*. By now it had come to be used specifically for 'imprisonment,' and from this it moved on in due course to the concrete 'place of imprisonment' – both senses which entered English from Old French in the 12th century.

▶apprehend, comprehensive, prehensile, prize, reprehensible

**private** [14] Latin *prīvus* meant 'single, individual.' From it was derived the verb *prīvāre*, source of English *deprive* [14] and *privation* [14]. This originally meant 'make solitary, isolate,' and although it later moved on metaphorically to 'bereave, deprive,' its earliest sense was preserved in the adjective formed from its past participle *prīvātus*. This denoted 'belonging to the individual alone,' hence 'not belonging or related to the state.' English has acquired the word twice: first, via Old French, as the now almost archaic *privy* [13], and later, directly from Latin, as *private*. *Privilege* [12] comes via Old French *privilege* from Latin *prīvilēgium*, a compound formed from *prīvus* and *lēx* 'law' (source of English *legal*) which etymologically meant 'law affecting an individual.'

▶ deprive, privilege, privy

**prize** English has four words *prize*. The one meaning 'reward' [16] is essentially the same word as *price*. This was originally *pris*, mirroring its immediate Old French ancestor *pris*. It became *prise*, to indicate the length of its vowel *i*, and in the 16th century this differentiated into *price* for 'amount to pay' and *prize* for 'reward.' (Modern French *prix* has given English *grand prix* [19], literally 'great prize,' first used for a 'car race' in 1908.) *Prize* 'esteem' [14] was based on *pris-*, the stem of Old French *preisier* 'praise' (source of English *praise*). *Prize* 'something captured in war' [14] comes via Old French *prise* 'capture, seizure, booty' from Vulgar Latin *\*prēsa* or *\*prēnsa* 'something seized.' This was a noun use of the past participle of *\*prēndere* 'seize,' a contraction of classical Latin *praehendere* (from which English gets *prehensile*, *prison*, etc). Another sense of Old French *prise* was 'grasp.' English borrowed this in the 14th century as *prize* 'lever,' which in due course was turned into modern English's fourth *prize*, the verb *prize*, or *prise*, 'lever' [17]. *Pry* 'lever' [19] is an alteration of *prize*, based on the misapprehension that it is a third-person singular present form (*\*pries*).

▶ grand prix, price / praise / comprehensive, prison, reprehensible / pry

**probable** [14] Latin *probāre* meant 'test, approve, prove' (it is the source of English *probate* [15], *probation* [15], *probe* [16], and *prove*). From it was derived the adjective *probābilis* 'provable,' hence 'likely.' It passed into English via Old French *probable*.

▶ probate, probation, probe, prove, reprobate

**probity** SEE PROVE

**problem** [14] A *problem* is etymologically something 'thrown forward.' The word comes via Old French *probleme* and Latin *problēma* from Greek *próblēma*, a derivative of *probállein* 'throw forward.' This was a compound verb formed from the prefix *pro-* 'forward' and *bállein* 'throw' (source of English *ballistic, emblem, parable*, etc). Things that are 'thrown out' project and can get in the way and hinder one, and so *próblēma* came to be used for an 'obstacle' or 'problem' – senses carried through into English *problem*.

▶ ballistic, emblem, parable, symbol

**proboscis** [17] The elephant's trunk was originally called *proboscis* because it is used for getting food – by pulling down leafy branches, for instance. The word comes via Latin from Greek *proboskís*, a compound formed from *pró* 'in front' and *bóskein* 'feed.'

**process** [14] Latin *prōcēdere* meant 'go forward': it was a compound verb formed from the prefix *prō-* 'forward' and *cēdere* 'go' (source of English *cede, concede*, etc), and has given English *proceed* [14] and *procedure* [17]. Its past participle *prōcessus* was used as a noun meaning 'advance, progress, lapse of time.' This passed via Old French *proces* into English, where the notion of something 'advancing during a period of time' led in the 17th century to the word's main modern sense 'set of operations for doing something.' *Procession* [12] comes from the Latin derivative *prōcessiō*.

▶ accede, cede, concede, exceed, precede, proceed, procession

**procrastinate** [16] *Crās* was Latin for 'tomorrow' (its antecedents are uncertain). The adjective derived from it was *crāstinus* 'of tomorrow,' which in turn formed the basis of a verb *prōcrāstināre* 'put forward to tomorrow' (*prō-* denotes 'forward'). By the time it reached English it had broadened out to simply 'delay.'

**procure** [13] The *-cure* of *procure* goes back to Latin *cūrāre* 'look after,' source of English *cure*. Combination with *prō-* 'for' produced *prōcūrāre* 'look after on behalf of someone else, manage,' which English acquired via Old French *procurer* as *procure*. The main modern sense 'obtain' developed via 'take care, take pains' and 'bring about by taking pains.' The agent noun derived from the Latin verb was *prōcūrātor* 'manager, agent'; English adopted this as *procurator* [13], and subsequently contracted it to *proctor* [14]. A similar process of contraction lies behind *proxy*, which goes back to Latin *prōcūrātiō*.

▶ cure, proctor, proxy

**produce** [15] To *produce* something is etymologically to 'lead it forward,' a meaning still discernable beneath the veil of metaphor that clothes the modern English word's range of meanings. It comes from Latin *prōdūcere*, a compound verb formed from the prefix *prō-* 'forward' and *dūcere* 'lead' (source of English *duct, duke, educate, introduce*, etc).

▶ duct, duke, educate, induce, introduce

**profane** [15] Anything that is *profane* is etymologically 'outside the temple' – hence, 'secular' or 'irreligious.' The word comes via Old French *prophane* from Latin *profānus*, a compound adjective formed from the prefix *prō-* 'before' (used here in the sense 'outside') and *fānum* 'temple' (source of archaic English *fane* [14]).

▶ fane

**profess** [14] *Profess* comes from *prōfessus*, the past participle of Latin *prōfitērī* 'declare publicly.' This was a compound verb formed from the prefix *prō-* 'forth, in public' and *fatērī* 'acknowledge, confess' (a relative of English *fable, fame,* and *fate* and source also of *confess*). A *professor* [14] is etymologically someone who 'makes a public claim' to knowledge in a particular field; and someone's *profession* [13] is the area of activity in which they 'profess' a skill or competence.

▶ confess, fable, fame, fate

**proficient** SEE PROFIT

**profile** [17] The *-file* of *profile* is etymologically a 'thread.' The word comes from early modern Italian *profilo,* a derivative of *profilare* 'draw in outline.' This was a compound verb formed from the prefix *pro-* 'forward' and *filare,* which used to mean 'draw a line'; and this in turn went back to Latin *fīlāre* 'spin,' a derivative of *fīlum* 'thread' (from which English gets *file* for storing things in).

▶ file

**profit** [14] Like *proficient, profit* goes back to Latin *prōficere* 'advance, be advantageous.' This was a compound verb formed from the prefix *prō-* 'forward' and *facere* 'do, make' (source of English *fact, fashion, feat,* etc). Its past participle *prōfectus* was used as a noun meaning 'progress, success, profit,' and this passed into English via Old French *profit.* The Latin present participle *prōficiēns* 'making progress' is the source of English *proficient* [16], which took its meaning on via 'making progress in learning' to 'adept.'

▶ fact, fashion, feat, proficient

**profligate** [16] Something that is *profligate* has etymologically been 'beaten down' to a state of ruination or degradation. The word was adapted from Latin *prōflīgātus* 'destroyed, dissolute,' an adjective based on the past participle of *prōflīgāre* 'beat down, destroy.' This was a compound verb formed from the prefix *prō-*'forward' (used here in the sense 'down') and *flīgere* 'hit' (source also of English *afflict, conflict* [15], and *inflict* [16]).

▶ afflict, conflict, inflict

**progress** [15] *Progress* is one of a large family of English words (including also *grade, gradual, transgress,* etc) that go back to Latin *gradus* 'step.' From it was derived the verb *gradī* 'go, step,' which in combination with the prefix *prō-* 'forward' produced *prōgredī* 'go forward.' English gets *progress* from its past participle *prōgressus.*

▶ grade, gradual, ingredient, regress, transgress

**proletarian** [17] A Roman citizen of the lowest class was termed a *prōlētārius.* The only service he was capable of performing for the state was that of producing children, to maintain its population level, and it was this function that gave the *prōlētārius* his name. For it was derived from *prōlēs* 'offspring,' a word based on the same source (*\*ol-* 'nourish') as produced English *adolescent, alimony,* etc. The abbreviation *prole* dates back to the late 19th century (George Bernard Shaw is the first writer on record as using it), but it was George Orwell in the 1930s who firmly established the term. The immediate source of *proletariat* [19] is French *prolétariat* (in the 19th century it was often anglicized to *proletariate*).

English is also indebted to Latin *prōlēs* for *prolific* [17], which comes from the medieval Latin derivative *prōlificus* 'producing offspring.'

▶ adolescent, alimentary, alimony, prolific

**prolix** SEE LIQUID

**promenade** [16] *Promenade* was borrowed from French. It was a derivative of *se promener* 'go for a walk,' which came from late Latin *prōmināre* 'drive forward.' This was a compound verb formed from the prefix *prō-* 'forward' and *mināre* 'drive.' It was originally used in English for a 'leisurely walk'; 'place for walking' followed in the mid-17th century, but it does not seem to have been applied specifically to a 'walkway by the sea' until the end of the 18th century. The abbreviation *prom* dates from the early 20th century. The term *promenade concert* originated in the 1830s.

**prominent** [16] *Prominent* comes from the present participle of Latin *prōminēre* 'jut out.' This was formed with the prefix *prō-* 'forwards, out' and *-minēre* 'project,' a verbal element which also lies behind English *eminent* and *imminent* [16]. It was derived from *\*min-* 'project,' a base which also gave English *menace* and may be related ultimately to Latin *mōns* 'mountain' (source of English *mount* and *mountain*). Combination of *prō-* and *mōns* itself produced Latin *prōmunturium* 'headland,' ancestor of English *promontory* [16].

▶ eminent, imminent, menace

**promiscuous** SEE MIX

**promise** [14] Latin *prōmittere* originally meant simply 'send forth' (it was a compound verb formed from the prefix *prō-* 'forward' and *mittere* 'send,' source of English *mission, missile, transmit,* etc). But it soon evolved metaphorically via 'say in advance, foretell' to 'cause to expect' and hence 'promise' – the sense adopted into English via its past participle *prōmissum.*

▶ admit, commit, missile, mission, submit, transmit

**promontory** SEE PROMINENT

**promotion** SEE MOTOR

**prompt** [14] Latin *prōmere* meant 'bring out, show' (it was a compound verb formed from the prefix *prō-* 'forward, forth' and *emere* 'take,' source also of English *assume* [15], *example, exempt, peremptory* [16], *redeem,* and *sample*). Its past participle was *promptus,* and this was used as an adjective in which the notion of 'shown, manifest' evolved via 'ready at hand, available' to 'quick, punctual' – whence English *prompt*. In Spanish, Latin *promptus* became *pronto*, which was borrowed into English in the mid-19th century.

▶ assume, example, exempt, peremptory, redeem, sample

**promulgate** [16] *Promulgate* owes its existence to an analogy drawn by the Romans between 'milking' and 'bringing out into the light of day.' The Latin verb for 'milk' was *mulgēre* (source of English *emulsion*). It was used metaphorically for 'cause to emerge,' and combination with the prefix *prō-* 'forth, out' produced *prōmulgāre* 'make known publicly, publish' – whence English *promulgate*.

▶ emulsion

**pronounce** [14] Latin *nuntius* meant 'messenger.' From it was derived the verb *nuntiāre* 'announce,' which has formed the basis of English *announce* [15], *annunciation* [14], *denounce* [13], *pronounce*, and *renounce* [14]. *Pronounce* itself goes back to Latin *prōnuntiāre* 'proclaim,' formed with the prefix *prō-* 'forth, out, in public.' Its specific application to the 'way in which a person speaks' emerged in English in the early 17th century.

▶ announce, denounce, nuncio, renounce

**pronto** see PROMPT

**proof** [13] *Proof* and *prove* are of course closely related. Both go back ultimately to Latin *probāre* 'test, prove.' From this in post-classical times was derived the noun *proba* 'proof,' which passed into English via Old French *preve* as *pref*. In the 14th and 15th centuries this gradually changed in the mainstream language to *proof*, due to the influence of the verb *prove*.

▶ probe, prove

**propaganda** [18] English gets the word *propaganda* from the term *Propaganda Fide*, the name of a Roman Catholic organization charged with the spreading of the gospel. This meant literally 'propagating the faith,' *prōpāgānda* being the feminine gerundive of Latin *prōpāgāre*, source of English *propagate* [16]. Originally *prōpāgāre* was a botanical verb, as its English descendant remains, only secondarily broadening out metaphorically to 'extend, spread.' It was derived from the noun *prōpāgo* 'cutting, scion,' which in turn was formed from the prefix *prō-* 'forth' and the base *\*pāg-* 'fix' (source of English *pagan, page, pale* 'stake,' etc).

▶ pagan, page, pale, propagate

**propel** see PULSE

**proper** [13] *Proper* originally meant 'belonging to itself, particular to itself' (a sense now defunct in English except in certain fossilized contexts, such as the astronomical term *proper motion*). It comes via Old

French *propre* from Latin *prōprius* 'one's own,' which may have been a lexicalization of the phrase *prō prīvō*, literally 'for the individual' (*prīvus* is the source of English *private*). The word developed widely in meaning in Latin, but its main modern English senses, 'correct' and 'morally right,' are of later evolution. *Appropriate* [15] goes back to a late Latin derivative.

▶ appropriate, property

**property** [13] *Property* and *propriety* [15] are doublets – that is to say, they have the same ancestor, but have diverged over the centuries. In this case the ancestor was Latin *prōprietās* 'ownership,' a derivative of *prōprius* (from which English gets *proper*). It passed into Old French as *propriete*, which originally reached English via Anglo-Norman *proprete* as *property*, and was subsequently reborrowed direct from Old French as *propriety* (this to begin with denoted 'property,' and did not begin to develop its present-day meaning until the 17th century). *Proprietary* [15] came from the late Latin derivative *prōprietārius*; and *proprietor* [17] was formed from *proprietary* by substituting the suffix *-or* for *-ary*.

▶ proper, proprietary, propriety

**prophet** [12] A *prophet* is etymologically someone who 'speaks for' another. The word comes via Old French *prophete* and Latin *prophēta* from Greek *prophḗtēs*, a compound noun formed from the prefix *pro-* 'for' and *-phḗtēs* 'speaker' (a derivative of *phánai* 'speak,' which goes back to the same Indo-European base, *\*bha-* 'speak,' as produced English *fable, fate*, etc). It meant literally 'spokesman,' and was frequently used specifically for 'one who interprets the will of the gods to humans.' The Greek translators of the Bible adopted it into Christian usage. *Prophecy* [13] comes ultimately from the Greek derivative *prophētíā*.

▶ fable, fame, fate

**prophylactic** [16] *Prophylactic* comes from Greek *prophulaktikós*, a derivative of the verb *prophulássein*. This meant literally 'keep guard in front of a place,' and hence 'take precautions against.' It was formed from the prefix *pro-* 'before' and *phulássein* 'guard.'

**propinquity** see PROXIMITY

**proponent** see PURPOSE

**propose** see PURPOSE

**propound** see PURPOSE

**propriety** see PROPER

**prose** [14] *Prose* is etymologically 'straightforward discourse' (as opposed to the more sophisticated discourse of poetry). The term comes via Old French *prose* from Latin *prōsa*, which was short for *prōsa ōrātiō* 'straightforward discourse.' *Prōsus* 'straightforward, direct' was a contraction of an earlier *prōversus*, the past participle of *prōvertere* 'turn forward.' This was a compound verb formed from the prefix *prō-* 'forward' and *vertere* 'turn' (source of English *verse, version*, etc).

▶ verse, version

**prosecute** [15] If you *prosecute* someone, etymologically you 'pursue' them. The word comes from *prōsecūt-*, the past participial stem of *prōsequī* 'pursue,' a compound verb formed from the prefix *prō-* 'forward' and *sequī* 'follow' (source of English *sequal, sequence*, etc). The word's legal application emerged in the late 16th century.

▶ pursue, sequal, sequence, suit

**proselyte** [14] A *proselyte* is etymologically someone who 'comes to' a new religion. The word comes via Latin *prosēlytus* from Greek *proséluthos* 'person who comes to a place,' a derivative of the verb *prosérkhesthai* 'come to, approach.'

**prosody** [15] Despite the passing similarity, *prosody* has no etymological connection with *prose*. In fact, its closest English relative is *ode*. It comes via Latin *prosōdia* from Greek *prosōidíā*, which originally meant 'song with an instrumental accompaniment.' This was a compound formed from *prós* 'in addition to' and *ōidé* 'song' (source of English *ode* [16] and also of *parody* [16], *rhapsody*, and probably *tragedy*).

▶ melody, ode, parody, rhapsody

**prostitute** [16] To *prostitute* something is etymologically to 'set it up in front of everyone.' The word comes from the past participle of Latin *prōstituere*, a compound formed from the prefix *prō-* 'before, in public' and *statuere* 'set, place' (source of English *statute*). The Latin verb evolved semantically via 'expose publicly' and 'offer for sale' to 'make available for sex in return for money,' and the feminine form of its past participle, *prōstitūta*, foreshadows its English noun descendant *prostitute*.

▶ statue, status, statute

**prostrate**  see STRATA

**protect** [16] The *-tect* element of *protect* goes back to the past participle of Latin *tegere* 'cover' (source of English *integument* [17] and *toga* [16] and related to *thatch*). Combination with the prefix *prō-* 'in front' produced *prōtegere* 'cover in front, protect.' Another English product of the past participle *tectus* is *detect* [15].

▶ detect, integument, thatch, toga

**protein** [19] The word *protein* was coined (as French *protéine*) by the Dutch chemist Mulder in the late 1830s. He based it on late Greek *prōteios* 'primary,' a derivative of Greek *prōtos* 'first' (see PROTO-ZOA), the notion being that proteins were substances of 'primary' importance to the proper functioning of the body.

**protest** [14] The noun *protest* comes from early modern French *protest*, a derivative of the verb *protester*, which goes back to Latin *prōtestārī* 'make a public declaration.' This was a compound verb formed from the prefix *prō-* 'out, in public' and *testārī* 'declare, bear witness' (source of or related to English *attest, contest, detest, testament, testify*, etc). The notion of 'making an objection' is a comparatively late development in the word's semantic history. *Protestant* [16], which comes from the Latin present participle, originated in 1529 as a term for those Germans who dissented from the decree of the Diet of Spires, an assembly of the estates of the Holy Roman Empire, which called for obedience to Rome. It was first used in English in 1539, and within a few years had broadened out in application to denote anyone dissenting from Roman Catholicism.

▶ attest, contest, detest, testament, testicle, testify

**protocol** [16] *Protocol* originally denoted an 'official record of a transaction.' Not until the end of the 19th century, as a reborrowing from French, did it come to be used for 'rules of etiquette' (the semantic link is an intermediate sense 'draft of a treaty or other diplomatic document,' which led to its use in French for the 'department in charge of diplomatic etiquette'). It goes back via Old French *prothocole* and medieval Latin *prōtocollum* to Greek *prōtókollon*, a compound formed from *prôtos* 'first' and *kólla* 'glue' which meant 'flyleaf glued to the front of a book giving a list of its contents.'

▶ colloid

**protozoa** [19] Greek *prôtos* meant 'first' (like English *first* and Latin *prīmus* 'first' it goes back ultimately to Indo-European *\*pro* 'before, in front'). It forms the basis of a wide range of English words, both original Greek compounds and post-classical formations, among them *protagonist* [17] (etymologically the 'first or leading actor'), *protein, protocol, proton* [20], *protoplasm* [19], and *prototype* [17]. *Protozoa* itself was coined in modern Latin by the zoologist Goldfuss in 1818 from *proto-* and Greek *zóia* 'animals' (source of English *zoo*), the notion being that the protozoa are the simplest or most primitive forms of life.

▶ zoo

**proud** [OE] *Proud* was borrowed in the 10th century from Old French *prud*. This came from a Vulgar Latin *\*prōdis*, a derivative of Latin *prōdesse* 'be beneficial,' which was a compound formed from *prōd-*, a variant of *prō-* 'for,' and *esse* 'be.' The Old French adjective meant 'good, brave,' and it is thought that the sense 'having a high opinion of oneself,' which does not occur in Old French but is the earliest recorded in English, may reflect what the Anglo-Saxons thought of Norman nobles who referred to themselves as *prud barun* or *prud chevalier*. A later form of Old French *prud* or *prod* was *prou*, whose derivative *proesce* 'bravery' passed into English as *prowess* [13]; and English is also indebted to *prud* for *prude*.

▶ pride, prowess, prude

**prove** [12] The ultimate source of *prove* was Latin *probus* 'good.' This went back (like the related Sanskrit *prabhu-* 'eminent, mighty') to a prehistoric Indo-European compound *pro-bhwo-* 'being in front,' hence 'excelling' (*pro-* meant 'in front,' and *bhwo-* was the ancestor of English *be*). From it was derived the verb *probāre* 'test, approve, prove,' which has given English *approve, probable, probe, proof, reprobate, reprove*, and of course *prove*, acquired via Old French *prover*. Another Latin derivative of *probus* was *probitās* 'honesty,' from which English gets *probity* [16].

▶ approve, probable, probe, proof, reprobate

**provender**    SEE PREBEND

**proverb** [14] Latin *prōverbium* meant literally 'set of words put forth' – that is, 'commonly uttered.' It was a compound formed from the prefix *prō-* 'forth' and *verbum* 'word' (source of English *verb, verbal*, etc). English acquired it via Old French *proverbe*.

▶ adverb, verb, verbal, word

**provide** [15] The *-vide* of *provide* goes back to Latin *vidēre* 'see' (source of English *vision*), which is a long way from the English verb's main present-day meaning, 'supply.' Its Latin ancestor *prōvidēre*, formed with the prefix *prō-* 'before,' meant 'foresee' – a sense which survived into English: 'evident and sufficient signs, whereby may be provided and foreseen the aborcement [abortion] before it comes,' Thomas Raynalde, *Birth of Mankind* 1545. But already in Latin it had moved on to 'exercise foresight by making preparations,' and this formed the basis of the later 'supply.' Other English descendants of *prōvidēre* include *improvise, provident* [15] (a close relative of *prudent*), *provision* [14], *proviso* [15], and *purvey* [13].

▶ improvise, provision, proviso, prudent, purvey, vision

**provoke**    SEE VOCATION

**provost** [OE] A *provost* is etymologically an official 'placed before' others – that is, put in charge of them. The word's ancestor is Latin *praepositus* 'superintendent,' a noun use of the past participle of *praepōnere*, a compound verb formed from the prefix *prae-* 'in front' and *pōnere* 'put' (source of English *position, post*, etc). In medieval Latin a variant form *prōpositus* emerged, which was borrowed into Old English as *profost*. This was supplemented in Middle English by the Anglo-Norman form *provost*.

▶ position

**prow** [16] 'Being in front' is the etymological notion that underlies *prow*. It comes ultimately from Greek *prŏira* 'front of a ship,' which was probably a de-

rivative of Indo-European *pro* 'before, in front.' It reached English via Latin *prōra* and Old French *proue*.

**prowess**    SEE PROUD

**proximity** [15] Latin *proximus* meant 'nearest, next' (it was the superlative form of an unrecorded *proqe* 'near,' a variant of *prope*, from which English gets *approach* and *propinquity* [14]). From it were formed the verb *proximāre* 'come near,' ultimate source of English *approximate* [15], and the noun *proximitās* 'nearness,' from which English gets *proximity*.

▶ approximate

**proxy** [15] *Proxy* has no etymological connection with 'closeness.' It is a much contracted form of *prōcūrātia*, the medieval version of Latin *prōcūrātiō* 'caring for, taking care of.' This was a noun derived from *prōcūrāre*, source of English *procure*. It originally entered English in the 13th century as *procuracy*, and gradually shrank via *procracy* and *prokecye* to *proxy*. The semantic notion underlying it is of 'taking care of another's interests.'

▶ procure

**prude** [18] Old French *prudefemme* 'virtuous woman' meant literally 'fine thing of a woman.' It was a lexicalization of the phrase *preu de femme*, in which *preu* meant 'fine, brave, virtuous' (its variant *prud* gave English *proud*). In the 17th century it was shortened to *prude* (Molière is the first writer on record as using it), with distinctly negative connotations of 'over-virtuousness.' It was borrowed into English at the beginning of the 18th century, and for a couple of hundred years continued to be used almost exclusively with reference to women.

▶ proud

**prudent** [14] *Prudent* and *provident* are as it were two separate goes at the same word. Both were formed from the Latin prefix *prō-* 'before, in advance' and *vidēns*, the present participle of *vidēre* 'see' (and hence etymologically mean 'foreseeing'). The pre-classical coinage was contracted to *prūdēns* 'farsighted, wise,' which reached English via Old French *prudent*. *Provident* comes from the uncontracted *prōvidēns*, part of the paradigm of *prōvidēre* (source of English *provide*).

▶ provide

**prune** English has two distinct words *prune*. The older, 'dried plum' [14], is ultimately the same word as *plum*, and indeed in the 16th and 17th century was often used for 'plum.' It comes via Old French *prune* from Vulgar Latin *prūna*, which also gave English (through Germanic) *plum*. *Prune* 'cut off unneeded parts' [15] denotes etymologically 'cut in a rounded shape in front.' It comes via Old French *proignier* from Vulgar Latin *prōrotundiāre*, a compound verb formed from the Latin prefix *prō-* 'in front' and *rotundus* 'round' (source of English *rotund* and *round*).

▶ plum / rotund, round

**pry** see PRIZE

**psalm** [OE] The Greek verb *psállein* originally meant 'pluck,' but it was extended figuratively to 'pluck harpstrings,' and hence 'sing to the accompaniment of the harp.' From it was derived the noun *psalmós* 'harp-song,' which was used in the Greek Septuagint to render Hebrew *mizmōr* 'song (of the sort sung to the harp by David).' It passed into Old English via late Latin *psalmus*. Another derivative of Greek *psállein* was *psaltérion* 'stringed instrument played by plucking,' which has given English *psalter* [OE] and *psaltery* [13].

**psephology** [20] The term *psephology* 'study of voting patterns' was coined in the early 1950s by R B McCallum from Greek *pséphos* 'pebble.' Pebbles were used in ancient Greece for casting votes, and so *pséphos* came to mean metaphorically 'vote' – hence *psephology*.

**pseudonym** [19] *Pseudonym* comes via French *pseudonyme* from Greek *pseudónumon*, a compound formed from *pseudés* 'false' and *ónoma* 'name.' *Pseudés*, a derivative of the verb *pseúdein* 'lie,' has given English the prolific prefix *pseudo-*, which in the mid 20th century yielded the noun and adjective *pseud*.

▶ name

**psyche** [17] Like Latin *animus* (source of English *animal*), Greek *psūkhé* started out meaning 'breath' and developed semantically to 'soul, spirit.' English adopted it via Latin *psȳchē* in the mid-17th century, but it did not really begin to come into its own until the middle of the 19th century, when the development of the sciences of the mind saw it pressed into service in such compound forms as *psychology* (first recorded in 1693, but not widely used until the 1830s) and *psychiatry* (first recorded in 1846), which etymologically means 'healing of the mind.'

▶ psychiatry, psychology

**ptarmigan** [16] *Ptarmigan* was borrowed from Scottish Gaelic *tarmachan*, a diminutive form of *tarmach* 'ptarmigan.' There is no etymological justification for the spelling *pt-*. It was foisted on the word in the late 17th century in the erroneous belief that it had some connection with Greek *pterón* 'wing' (source of English *pterodactyl*).

**pterodactyl** [19] *Pterodactyl* means literally 'wing-finger.' It was coined in the early 19th century, as Latin *pterodactylus*, from Greek *pterón* 'wing' (source of English *helicopter*, and descendant of the Indo-European base *\*pet-* 'fly,' which also produced English *feather*) and *dáktulos* 'finger' (source of English *date* the fruit).

▶ date, feather

**ptomaine** [19] *Ptomaine* denotes etymologically 'matter from a corpse.' It comes via French *ptomaïne* from Italian *ptomaina*, which was based on Greek *ptôma* 'corpse.' This in turn was derived from the verb *píptein* 'fall,' and originally meant literally 'fallen body.' The term was coined to name substances produced by decomposing flesh.

**puberty** [14] Latin *pūber* denoted 'adult,' and hence, by implication, 'covered in hair.' Both strands of meaning have followed the word into English: 'adulthood' by way of the derivative *pūbertās*, source of English *puberty*, and 'hairiness' in *pubescent* [17], which means 'downy' as well as 'having reached puberty.' And the two are combined in *pubic* 'relating to the region of the groin where hair begins to grow at puberty' [19].

**public** [15] *Public* means etymologically 'of the people.' It comes via Old French *public* from Latin *pūblicus*, an alteration (apparently inspired by *pūber* 'adult,' source of English *puberty*) of *poplicus* 'of the people,' which was derived from *populus* 'people' (source of English *people, popular*, etc). *Publicity* [19] was borrowed from the French derivative *publicité*.

▶ people, popular, pub, publish

**publican** [12] The modern use of *publican* for 'innkeeper' dates from the early 18th century, and presumably arose from an association with *public house*. Its original meaning was 'tax collector.' It comes via Old French *publicain* from Latin *pūblicānus* 'person who paid for the privilege of collecting the public revenues, in return for a percentage.' This in turn was derived from *pūblicum* 'public revenue,' a noun use of *pūblicus* 'public' (source of English *public*).

**publish** [14] To *publish* something is etymologically to make it 'public.' The word comes from *publiss-*, the stem of Old French *publier*, which was descended from Latin *pūblicāre* 'make public,' a derivative of *pūblicus* 'public.' The earliest record of its use in English for 'bring out a book' comes from the early 16th century.

▶ public

**puce** [18] *Puce* is etymologically 'flea-coloured.' It was borrowed from French *puce* 'flea,' a descendant of Latin *pūlex* 'flea,' which goes back to the same Indo-European source as English *flea* [OE].

▶ flea

**pucker** [16] The etymological notion underlying *pucker* seems to be of forming into 'pockets' or small baglike wrinkles (the same idea led to the use of the verb *purse* for 'wrinkle, pucker' – now dated in general usage, but fossilized in the expression *purse the lips*). The word was based on the stem *pock-* of *pocket*.

**puckish** [19] In English folklore from the late Middle Ages onward, *Puck* was a mischievous but essentially harmless sprite, up to all sorts of tricks (hence the coining of *puckish* for 'mischievous'). But his Anglo-Saxon ancestor *Pūca* was a far less pleasant proposition – for this was the Devil himself. He gradually dwindled over the centuries, but a hint of his former power remained in his placatory alternative name *Robin Goodfellow*. It is not known whether *pūca* is of Germanic or Celtic origin.

**pudding** [13] The original *puddings* were sausages – whose present-day survivor is the *black pudding*. They were encased in the intestines or stomachs of animals, and it was this casing that provided the springboard for the word's subsequent development in meaning. It came to be applied to any food cooked in a bag (hence the cannon-ball shape of the traditional Christmas pudding). Such dishes could be savoury (like today's steak-and-kidney pudding) or sweet, but it was not until the 20th century that *pudding* came to be used specifically for the 'sweet course of a meal.' The word comes via Old French *boudin* from Vulgar Latin *\*botellīnus*, a diminutive form of Latin *botellus* 'sausage' (source of English *botulism*).

▶ botulism

**puddle** [14] Old English *pudd*, a word of unknown origin, denoted 'ditch, furrow,' and *puddle* was a diminutive formed from it. In Middle English, it was often used for quite large bodies of water, what we would now call a *pond* or *pool*, but by the 17th century it had largely narrowed down to its present-day meaning.

**puerile** [17] Latin *puer* denoted 'child,' or more specifically 'boy' (like Greek *pais* 'child,' source of English *paediatric, pedagogue*, etc, it came ultimately from a base which signified 'smallness,' and also gave English *pusillanimous*). The derived adjective *puerīlis* 'childlike' began to acquire its negative connotations in Latin, and brought them with it into English. The related *puerperal* 'of childbirth' [18] comes from a Latin compound formed from *puer* and *parere* 'give birth' (source of English *parent*).

▶ pusillanimous

**puffin** [14] *Puffin* probably goes back to one of the ancestral Celtic languages of the British Isles – perhaps Cornish. Its English guise is no doubt due to its plump appearance, which suggested associations with *puff* [13] (a word which originated as an imitation of the sound of puffing).

**pugnacious** [17] Latin *pugnus* meant 'fist' (it may have been related to Greek *pugmé* 'fist,' source of English *pygmy*). From it was derived the verb *pugnāre* 'hit with the fist,' hence 'fight,' which has given English *impugn* [14], *repugnant* [14], and, via the further derivative *pugnāx* 'fond of fighting,' *pugnacious*.

▶ impugn, repugnant

**puke** [16] The first record of *puke* in English is in Jaques's famous 'Seven Ages of Man' speech in Shakespeare's *As You Like It* 1600: 'At first the infant, mewling and puking in the nurse's arms.' Its origins are not known for certain, but it presumably goes back ultimately to some Germanic base imitative of the sound of regurgitation (perhaps the same as produced German *spucken* 'spew, spit').

**pull** [OE] The main Old and Middle English word for 'pull' was *draw*, and *pull* did not really begin to come into its own until the late 16th century. It is not known for certain where it came from. Its original meaning was 'pluck' ('draw, drag' is a secondary development), and so it may well be related to Low German *pūlen* 'remove the shell or husk from, pluck' and Dutch *peul* 'shell, husk.'

**pullet** SEE POULTRY

**pulley** [14] Although *pulleys* are used for 'pulling,' there is no etymological connection between the two words. *Pulley* comes via Old French *polie* from Vulgar Latin *\*polidia*, which was probably borrowed from the plural of a medieval Greek *\*polidion*, a diminutive form of Greek *pólos* 'pole, pivot' (source of English *pole* 'extremity').

▶ pole

**pullulate** [17] The etymological notion underlying *pullulate* is of rapid 'new growth.' It goes back ultimately to Latin *pullus* 'young animal,' which also produced English *pony* and *poultry* and is distantly related to *foal*. From this was derived the verb *pullulāre* 'grow, sprout,' whose past participle provided English with *pullulate*. This too originally meant 'sprout,' a sense largely displaced since the 19th century by its metaphorical descendant 'swarm, teem.'

▶ foal, pony, poultry, pullet

**pulmonary** [18] Latin *pulmō* meant 'lung' (it was related to Greek *pleúmōn* 'lung,' ultimate source of English *pneumonia*). From it was formed the adjective *pulmōnārius*, which English adopted at the beginning of the 18th century as *pulmonary*.

**pulpit** [14] Classical Latin *pulpitum*, a word of unknown origin, denoted 'platform, stage.' This sense was originally carried over into English (Miles Coverdale, in his 1535 translation of II Chronicles 6:13, wrote 'Salomon had made a brasen pulpit . . . upon the same stood he,' where the 1611 Authorized Version was later to have 'Solomon had made a brasen scaffold . . . and upon it he stood'). But it was eventually swamped by a subsidiary sense which emerged in medieval Latin: *pulpitum* had been applied particularly to platforms on which people stood to speak in public, and in ecclesiastical usage it came to denote a 'raised structure on which preachers stand.'

**pulse** English has two separate words *pulse*. The older, 'seeds of beans, lentils, etc' [13], comes via Old French *pols* from Latin *puls* 'thick gruel (often made from beans and the like).' This was a relative of Latin *pollen* 'flour' (source of English *pollen*) and Latin *pulvis* 'powder' (source of English *powder* and *pulverize*). Its plural *pultes* has given English *poultice* [16].

*Pulse* 'beat of the blood' [14] comes via Old French *pouls* from Latin *pulsus* 'beating,' a noun use of the past participle of *pellere* 'drive, beat' (source of English *appeal*, *compel* [14], *dispel* [17], *expel* [14], *propel* [15], and *repel* [15]). The derivative *pulsāre* gave English *pulsate* [18], and also *push*.

▶ pollen, poultice, powder, pulverize / appeal, compel, dispel, expel, propel, pulsate, push, repel

**pulverize** SEE POWDER

**pumice** [15] *Pumice* comes via Old French *pomis* from Latin *pūmex* 'pumice.' This went back to a prehistoric Indo-European *poimo-*, source also of English *foam* and of Latin *spūma* 'foam, froth' (from which English gets *spume*).

▶ foam, spume

**pump** [15] The precise origins of *pump* have never been established. It is now widespread throughout the European languages, by dint of assiduous borrowing (French *pompe*, for instance), but its epicentre appears to have been northwestern Europe, with Middle Low German *pumpe* or Middle Dutch *pompe*. It started out, no doubt, as a vocal imitation of the sound of pumping.

**pumpkin** [17] Much as they look as though they had been blown up with a pump, *pumpkins* have no etymological connection with *pumps*. Greek *pépōn* denoted a variety of melon that was not eaten until it was fully ripe (the word was a noun use of the adjective *pépōn* 'ripe'). Latin took it over as *pepō*, and passed it on to Old French as *\*pepon*. Through a series of vicissitudes this evolved via *popon* to early modern French *pompon*. This was borrowed into English in the 16th century, and soon altered to *pompion*; and in the 17th century the native diminutive suffix *-kin* was grafted on to it to produce *pumpkin*.

**pun** [17] Snappy monosyllables produced by breaking off a piece of a longer word were all the rage in late 17th- and early 18th-century England (*mob* is a well-known example), and it is thought that *pun* may be one of them. It seems to be short for *pundigrion*, a short-lived fanciful 17th- and 18th-century term for a 'pun' or 'quibble' which may have been adapted from Italian *puntiglio* 'nice point, quibble' (source of English *punctilious*).

**punch** English has three distinct words *punch*, not counting the capitalized character in the Punch and Judy show, but two of them are probably ultimately related.

*Punch* 'hit' [14] originated as a variant of Middle English *pounce* 'pierce, prod.' This came from Old French *poinsonner* 'prick, stamp,' a derivative of the noun *poinson* 'pointed tool' (source of the now obsolete English *puncheon* 'pointed tool' [14]). And *poinson* in turn came from Vulgar Latin *\*punctiō*, a derivative of *\*punctiāre* 'pierce, prick,' which went back to the past participle of Latin *pungere* 'prick' (source of English *point*, *punctuation*, etc). *Punch* 'tool for making holes' [15] (as in 'ticket punch') probably originated as an abbreviated version of *puncheon*.

*Punch* 'drink' [17] is said to come from Hindi *pānch*, a descendant of Sanskrit *pañchan* 'five,' an allusion to the fact that the drink is traditionally made from five ingredients: spirits, water, lemon juice, sugar, and spice. This has never been definitely established, however, and an alternative possibility is that it is an abbreviation of *puncheon* 'barrel' [15], a word of uncertain origin.

The name of Mr *Punch* [17] is short for *Punchinello*, which comes from a Neapolitan dialect word *polecenella*. This may have been a diminutive of Italian *polecena* 'young turkey,' which goes back ultimately to Latin *pullus* 'young animal, young chicken' (source of English *poultry*). It is presumably an allusion to Punch's beaklike nose.

▶ point, punctuation

**punctuation** [16] *Punctuation* is one of a small family of English words that go back to *punctus*, the past participle of Latin *pungere* 'prick' (source of English *expunge* [17], *poignant* [14], and *pungent* [16]). They include *point*, which arrived via Old French; *punctilious* [17] (which comes via Italian and may be related to *pun*) and *punctual* [14], both of them containing the etymological notion of 'adherence to a precise point'; *puncture* [14]; *punt* 'bet'; and *punctuation* itself, whose present-day meaning comes from the insertion of 'points' or dots into written texts to indicate pauses (also termed *pointing* from the 15th to the 19th centuries).

▶ expunge, poignant, point, pungent, punt

**punish** [14] Latin *pūnīre* 'punish' was derived from the noun *poena* 'penalty, punishment' (source of English *pain*). It passed into Old French as *punir*, whose stem *puniss-* gave English *punish*. A derivative of *pūnīre* was *pūnitīvus* 'inflicting punishment,' which has given English *punitive* [17].

▶ pain

**punt** English has three separate words *punt*. The oldest is *punt* 'flat-bottomed boat' [15], which comes via Middle Low German *punte* or *punto* from Latin *pontō*, a term for a sort of Gaulish boat which also produced English *pontoon*. *Punt* 'bet' [18] (better known in the form of the agent noun *punter* 'better,' hence 'customer') comes from French *ponter*, a derivative of *ponte* 'bet against the banker in certain card games.'

This was adapted from Spanish *punto* 'point,' a descendant of Latin *punctum* (source of English *point*). *Punt* 'kick' [19] may be a variant of *bunt* 'push' [19] (now used as a baseball term, meaning 'hit the ball softly'); this could in turn be an alteration of *butt*, but it might also come from a Celtic source, related to Breton *bounta* 'butt.'

▶ pontoon / point, punctuation

**puny** [16] Etymologically, *puny* means 'born later.' It was borrowed from Old French *puisne*, a compound adjective formed from *puis* 'afterwards' and *ne* 'born' (a relative of English *native, nature*, etc). This signified 'junior,' in which sense it was originally acquired by English as *puisne*. This spelling survives (albeit pronounced the same as *puny*) as a term denoting a judge of junior rank, and the anglicized orthography has since the 18th century been reserved to 'feeble, small.'

▶ nation, native, nature

**pupil** [14] Latin *pūpus* and *pūpa* meant respectively 'boy' and 'girl' (*pūpa* was applied by the Swedish naturalist Linnaeus to 'chrysalises,' the underlying link being 'undeveloped creature,' and English adopted it as *pupa* [19]). The diminutive derivatives *pūpillus* and *pūpilla* denoted 'orphan,' a sense which remained with *pūpill-* as it passed via Old French *pupille* into English as *pupil*. 'Person being taught' did not emerge until the 16th century. The application of the word to the 'black aperture in the eye,' which reached English in the mid-16th century, goes back to Latin *pūpilla*, which was also used for 'doll' – the notion being that if you stand close to someone and look into their eyes, you can see yourself reflected in the pupils like a little 'doll.'

▶ pupa, puppet, puppy

**puppet** [16] *Puppet*, like its variant *poppet* [14], originally meant 'doll.' It comes from Old French *poupette*, a diminutive form of *\*poupe* 'doll.' This in turn came from Vulgar Latin *\*puppa*, a descendant of Latin *pūpa* 'girl, doll' (source of English *pupa* and *pupil*). The application to a 'moving doll controlled by strings' developed in the 16th century; in the case of *poppet* it has since died out, but it has taken over *puppet* completely.

▶ pupil

**puppy** [15] A *puppy* is etymologically a 'toy' dog. The word was borrowed from Old French *popee* 'doll,' hence 'toy,' which went back via Vulgar Latin *\*puppa* (source of English *puppet*) to Latin *pūpa* 'girl, doll' (source of English *pupa* and *pupil*). The shift from 'toy dog, lapdog' to 'young dog' happened towards the end of the 16th century. (The Old and Middle English word for 'puppy,' incidentally, was *whelp*.)

▶ pupil

**purchase** [13] To *purchase* something is etymologically to 'hunt it down.' It comes from Old French *pourchacier* 'pursue,' hence 'try to obtain,' a

compound verb formed from the intensive prefix *pour-* and *chacier* 'pursue' (source of English *chase*). It arrived in English meaning 'obtain.' This sense had virtually died out by the end of the 17th century, but not before it had evolved in the 14th century to 'buy.'

▶ chase

**pure** [13] *Pure* goes back ultimately to Latin *pūrus* 'clean,' a word of ancient ancestry which was related to Sanskrit *pūtás* 'purified.' It reached English via Old French *pur*. Amongst its Latin derivatives were the verbs *pūrificāre* 'make pure,' source of English *purify* [14]; *pūrāre* 'make pure,' which became French *purer* 'purify, strain,' source of English *purée* [19]; and *pūrigāre*, later *pūrgāre* 'purify,' source of English *expurgate* [17] and *purge* [14].

▶ expurgate, purge

**purlieu** [15] *Purlieu* has no etymological connection with French *lieu* 'place,' which seems to have been grafted on to it in the 16th century in ignorance of its origins. It comes from Anglo-Norman *puralee* 'act of walking round,' hence 'area of land beyond a perimeter fixed by walking round.' This was a noun use of the past participle of Old French *pouraler* 'go through, traverse,' a compound verb formed from the prefix *pour-* 'round' and *aler* 'go.'

**purloin** see LONG

**purple** [OE] Greek *porphúrā*, a word of Semitic origin, denoted a sort of shellfish from which a reddish dye was obtained (known as *Tyrian purple*, because it was produced around Tyre, in what is now Lebanon, it was highly prized in ancient times, and used for dyeing royal garments). It hence came to be used for the dye itself, and for cloth coloured with it, and it passed in this latter sense (with the particular connotation of 'royal cloth') via Latin *purpura* into Old English as *purpura*. Its derived adjective *purpuran* became *purple* by a process known as dissimilation, by which one of two similar speech sounds (here /r/) is altered.

**purpose** [13] *Purpose, propose* [14], and *propound* [16] are ultimately the same word. All go back to Latin *prōpōnere* 'put forward, declare,' a compound verb formed from the prefix *prō-* 'forward' and *pōnere* 'place' (source of English *pose, position*, etc). Its past participle *prōpositus* was the source of two distinct Old French verbs: the minimally altered *proposer*, source of English *propose*; and *purposer*, which contains the Old French descendant of the Latin prefix *prō-*, source of English *purpose*. *Propound* is an alteration of an earlier *propone* (source of *proponent* [16]), which was based directly on *prōpōnere*.

▶ pose, position, propose, proponent, propound

**purse** [OE] *Purse* was borrowed into Old English from late Latin *bursa* (source of English *bursar* [13] and *reimburse* [17]), which went back to Greek *búrsa*. This originally meant 'skin, leather,' and hence came to be used for 'wineskin, bag.' The Latin word was also borrowed into the Celtic languages, where it produced Gaelic *sporan*, source of English *sporran*.

▶ bursar, reimburse, sporran

**pursue** [13]   *Pursue* is first cousin to *prosecute*. Both go back ultimately to Latin *prōsequī* 'follow up, pursue.' This led fairly directly to English *prosecute*, but it also seems to have had a Vulgar Latin descendant *\*prōsequere*, which passed into English via Old French *porsivre* and Anglo-Norman *pursuer* as *pursue*.

▶ prosecute, sue, suit

**purvey**   SEE PROVIDE

**pus** [16]   English borrowed *pus* from Latin *pūs*, which was descended from the prehistoric Indo-European base *\*pū-*(source also of English *foul* and Latin *puter* 'rotten,' from which English gets *putrid* [16]). Its stem form *pūr-* has given English *purulent* [16] and *suppurate* [16]. The Greek relative of Latin *pūs* was *púon* 'pus,' from which English gets *pyorrhoea* [18].

▶ foul, purulent, putrid, pyorrhoea, suppurate

**push** [13]   *Push* comes ultimately from the same source as English *pulsate* and *pulse* – *pulsus*, the past participle of Latin *pellere* 'drive, push, beat.' From it was formed the verb *pulsāre* 'push, beat,' which in Old French became *poulser*, later *pousser*. Anglo-Norman took this over as *\*pusser*, and passed it on to English as *push*.

▶ pulsate, pulse

**pusillanimous** [16]   *Pusillanimous* means etymologically 'tiny-spirited.' It comes from late Latin *pūsillanimis*, a compound adjective formed from *pūsillus* 'very small or weak' (a descendant of the same base as produced Latin *puer* 'child, boy,' source of English *puerile*) and *animus* 'mind, spirit' (source of English *animate*).

▶ animal, animate, puerile

**puss**   English has two distinct words *puss*. The origins of the one meaning 'cat' [16] are rather mysterious. It appears to have been borrowed from Middle Low German *pūs*, but there the trail goes cold. Since it is basically used for calling cats, it may have originated simply in an exclamation (like *pss*) used for gaining their attention. *Puss* the slang term for 'mouth' or 'face' [19] comes from Irish *bus* 'lip, mouth.' *Pussy* 'cat' [18] is derived from *puss*, of course, but *pussy* the slang term for 'cunt' [19] may be of Low German or Scandinavian origin (Low German had *pūse* 'vulva' and Old Norse *púss* 'pocket, pouch').

**pustule** [14]   Despite the fact that pustules contain pus, there is no etymological connection between the two words. *Pustule* comes via Old French *pustule* from Latin *pustula* 'blister.' This was a derivative of a prehistoric Indo-European base *\*pu-* signifying 'blow,' so etymologically it means 'inflated area.'

**put** [12]   *Put* is one of the commonest of English verbs, but its origins are uncertain. It goes back to an Old English *\*putian*, never actually recorded but inferred from the verbal noun *putung* 'instigation,' but where that came from is not known. It was presumably related to Old English *potian* 'push, thrust,' whose Middle English descendant *pote* formed the basis of modern English *potter* [16]. The golfing term *putt* [18] is essentially the same word as *put*, differentiated in spelling and pronunciation.

▶ potter, putt

**putrid**   SEE PUS

**putty** [17]   Etymologically, *putty* is something that comes from a *pot*. It was borrowed from French *potée* 'contents of a pot,' a derivative of *pot* 'pot.' By the time English acquired it, it had come to be applied to a powder made from heated tin, used by jewellers for polishing, and for a cement made from lime and water, used as a top coating on plaster – both substances made in pots. The latter led on in English in the 18th century to the now familiar application to the window-pane sealant.

▶ pot

**puzzle** [16]   The origin of *puzzle* is, appropriately, a puzzle. One suggestion is that it may be derived from the now obsolete verb *pose* 'interrogate, perplex' (which survives in *poser* 'difficult question or problem'), a shortened form of *appose* 'interrogate or question severely.' This came from Old French *aposer*, a variant of *oposer*, from which English gets *oppose*. Another possibility is some connection with the Old English verb *puslian* 'pick out the best bits,' which is reminiscent of *puzzle out* 'find or solve by laborious reasoning' (although that sense of *puzzle* is not recorded until the end of the 18th century).

**pygmy** [14]   Greek *pugmḗ* meant 'fist' (it may have been related to Latin *pugnus* 'fist,' source of English *pugnacious*). By extension, it was used for a 'measure of length equal to the distance from the elbows to the knuckles.' From it was derived *pugmaîos* 'dwarfish,' which passed into English via Latin *pygmaeus*. In ancient and medieval times it was used as a noun to designate various apocryphal or mythical races of short stature, but it was not until the late 19th century that it was applied to the people of equatorial Africa who now bear the name.

▶ pugnacious

**pyjama** [18]   *Pyjamas* are etymologically 'leg-garments' – that is, 'trousers.' The word comes from Hindi *pāejāma*, a compound formed from Persian *pāī* 'foot,' hence 'leg' (which goes back to the same Indo-European ancestor as English *foot*) and *jāmah* 'clothing.' It denoted the loose trousers worn in India and the Middle East. Europeans living in that part of the world took to wearing them, especially for sleeping in. They brought them back to Europe, where, for reasons of temperature or propriety, a jacket was added to the trousers, in due course being subsumed under the term *pyjama*.

▶ foot, pedal

**pyorrhoea**    see PUS

**pyramid**    [16]   Egypt seems a likely ultimate source for *pyramid*, but its earliest known ancestor is Greek *puramís*, which passed into English via Latin *pyramis*. *Pediment* 'triangular gable' [17] probably originated as a garbling of *pyramid*, later influenced by *ped-*, the stem of Latin *pēs* 'foot.'

▶ pediment

**pyrotechnic**    [18]   The Greek word for 'fire' was *pūr* (it came from the same prehistoric Indo-European source as English *fire*). It underlies a range of English words, including *pyracantha* [17] (etymologically 'fire-thorn'), *pyre* [17], *pyrethrum* [16], and *pyrites* [16]. *Pyrotechnic* itself was derived from an earlier *pyrotechny*, which was originally used for the 'manufacture of gunpowder, firearms, bombs, etc.' The application to 'fireworks' did not emerge until the 17th century.

▶ fire, pyre, pyrites

**pyx**    see BOX

# Q

**quack**  English has two words *quack*. The one denoting the call of a duck [17] originated of course as an imitation of the sound itself. *Quack* 'person claiming to be a doctor' [17] is short for an earlier *quacksalver*, which etymologically denoted 'someone who prattles on or boasts about the efficacy of his remedies.' It was borrowed from early modern Dutch *quacksalver*, a compound formed from the now obsolete *quacken* 'chatter, prattle' and *salf*, the Dutch relative of English *salve*.

**quad**  see QUARTER

**quagmire**  [16]  The now virtually defunct word *quag* denoted a 'marsh,' particularly one with a top layer of turf that moved when you trod on it. Combination with *mire* (which also originally meant 'marsh,' and is related to English *moss*) produced *quagmire*. It is not known where *quag* came from, but its underlying meaning is generally taken to be 'shake, tremble,' and it may ultimately be of imitative origin.

**quail**  *Quail* the bird [14] and *quail* 'cower' [15] are not related. The former comes via Old French *quaille* from medieval Latin *coacula*, which probably originated in imitation of the bird's grating cry. It is not known for certain where the verb (which originally meant 'decline, wither, give way') came from, although some have linked it with another verb *quail*, now obsolete, which meant 'curdle.' This came via Old French *quailler* from Latin *coāgulāre*, source of English *coagulate*.
► coagulate

**quaint**  [13]  *Quaint* was once a more wholehearted term of approval than it is now. In Middle English it meant 'clever' or 'finely or skilfully made.' Its current sense 'pleasantly curious' did not emerge until the 18th century. It comes via Old French *coint* from Latin *cognitus* 'known,' the past participle of *cognōscere* 'know' (source of English *recognize*). The word's meaning evolved in Old French via the notion of someone who 'knows' about something, and hence is an expert at it or is skilful in doing it.
► cognition, recognize

**quality**  [13]  The ultimate source of *quality* is Latin *quālis* 'of what sort?,' a compound pronoun formed from *quī* 'who' and the adjectival suffix *-ālis*. From it were derived the noun *quālitās*, source of English *quality*, and *quālificāre*, from which English gets *qualify* [16].
► qualify

**quandary**  [16]  *Quandary* may have originated as a quasi-latinism. One of its early forms was *quandare*, which suggests that it may have been a pseudo-Latin infinitive verb, coined on the fanciful notion that Latin *quandō* 'when' was a first person present singular form.

**quantity**  [14]  Latin *quantus* meant 'how much' (it was a compound adjective formed from *quī* 'who'). From it was derived the noun *quantitās* 'extent, amount,' which passed into English via Old French *quantite*. *Quantum* [17], a noun use of the neuter form of the Latin adjective, originally denoted simply 'amount'; its specific application to a 'minimum amount of matter' was introduced by Max Planck in 1900, and reinforced by Einstein in 1905.
► quantum

**quarantine**  [17]  *Quarantine* denotes etymologically a period of 'forty' days. It goes back ultimately to Latin *quadrāgintā* 'forty,' whose Italian descendant *quaranta* formed the basis of the noun *quarantina* 'period of forty days.' English used it originally for a 'period of forty days' isolation,' but gradually the stipulation of the number of days faded out.
► quarter

**quark**  [20]  The term *quark* was applied to a type of fundamental particle by its discoverer, the American physicist Murray Gell-Mann. He seems first to have used *quork*, but then he remembered *quark*, a nonsense word used by James Joyce in *Finnegan's Wake* 1939, and he decided to plump for that. It first appeared in print in 1964.

**quarrel**  English has two words *quarrel*, one of them now little more than a historical memory. *Quarrel* 'argument' [14] goes back via Old French *querele* to Latin *querēla*, a derivative of *querī* 'complain.' Also based on *querī* was *querulus* 'complaining,' from which English gets *querulous* [15]. *Quarrel* 'crossbow arrow' [13] comes via Old French *quarel* from Vulgar Latin *\*quadrellus*, a diminutive form of late Latin *quadrus* 'square' (the quarrel had a 'square' head). And *quadrus* was based on the stem *quadr-* 'four,' source of English *quadrangle, quadrant, quadruped*, etc.

▶ querulous / quarter

**quarry** *Quarry* from which stone is extracted [15] and *quarry* which one hunts [14] are quite different words. The former was borrowed from Old French *quarriere*, a derivative of *\*quarre* 'square stone.' This went back to Latin *quadrum* 'square,' which was based on the stem *quadr-* 'four,' source of English *quadrangle, quadrant, quadruped*, etc. The sort of *quarry* that is pursued came from Anglo-Norman *\*quire* or *\*quere*, which denoted 'entrails of a killed deer given to the hounds to eat.' This went back to Old French *cuiree*, which was an alteration of an earlier *couree* or *coree*. And this in turn was descended from Vulgar Latin *\*corāta* 'entrails,' a derivative of Latin *cor* 'heart.' The present-day sense of the English word emerged in the 15th century.

▶ quarter / cordial, courage, record

**quarter** [13] *Quarter* is one of a large family of English words that go back ultimately to Latin *quattuor* 'four' and its relatives. Direct descendants of *quattuor* itself are actually fairly few – among them *quatrain* [16] and *quatrefoil* [15] (both via Old French). But its ordinal form *quārtus* 'fourth' has been most prolific: English is indebted to it for *quart* [14], *quarter* (via the Latin derivative *quartārius* 'fourth part'), *quartet* [18], and *quarto* [16]. In compounds *quattuor* assumed the form *quadr-*, which has given English *quadrangle* [15] (and its abbreviation *quad* [19]), *quadrant* [14], *quadratic* [17], *quadrille* [18], *quadruped* [17], *quadruplet* [18] (also abbreviated to *quad* [19]), *quarantine, quarrel* 'arrow,' not to mention the more heavily disguised *cadre* [19], *carfax* [14] (which means etymologically 'four-forked'), *squad*, and *square*. And the derivative *quater* 'four times' has contributed *carillon* [18] (etymologically a peal of 'four' bells), *quaternary* [15], and *quire* of paper [15] (etymologically a set of 'four' sheets of paper).

▶ cadre, carfax, carillon, quad, quarrel, quarry, quire, squad, square

**quash** [14] *Quash* goes back ultimately to Latin *quatere* 'shake' (source also of English *rescue* [14], which etymologically means 'shake off, drive away,' and of *concussion* and *percussion*). From it evolved *quassāre* 'shake to pieces, break,' which passed into Old French as *quasser* (its modern descendant is *casser*, from which English gets *cashier* 'dismiss from the

army'). English took *quasser* over as *quash*. *Squash* [16] comes ultimately from the Vulgar Latin derivative *\*exquassāre*.

▶ concussion, percussion, rescue, squash

**quaver** [15] *Quaver* was derived from an earlier and now obsolete Middle English *quave* 'tremble.' This was of Germanic origin (Low German has the related *quabbeln* 'tremble'), and probably started life as a vocal realization of the action of tembling. The use of the noun *quaver* for a short musical note (first recorded in the 16th century) comes from the original singing of such notes with a trill.

**quay** [14] *Quay* is of Celtic origin. Its immediate source was Old French *kai*, but this was borrowed from Gaulish *caio*, which went back to an Old Celtic *\*kagio-*. The spelling *quay* was introduced from modern French in the 17th century. The homophonic *cay* 'small coral island' [18] comes from *cayo*, a Spanish borrowing from French *quai*.

▶ cay

**quean** see GYNAECOLOGY

**queen** [OE] *Queen* goes back ultimately to prehistoric Indo-European *\*gwen-* 'woman,' source also of Greek *gunḗ* 'woman' (from which English gets *gynaecology*), Persian *zan* 'woman' (from which English gets *zenana* 'harem'), Swedish *kvinna* 'woman,' and the now obsolete English *quean* 'woman.' In its very earliest use in Old English *queen* (or *cwēn*, as it then was) was used for a 'wife,' but not just any wife: it denoted the wife of a man of particular distinction, and usually a king. It was not long before it became institutionalized as 'king's wife,' and hence 'woman ruling in her own right.'

▶ gynaecology, quean, zenana

**queer** [16] *Queer* was probably borrowed from German *quer* 'across, oblique,' hence 'perverse.' This went back to a prehistoric Indo-European *\*twerk-*, which also produced English *thwart* and Latin *torquēre* 'twist' (source of English *torch, torture*, etc).

▶ thwart, torch, torment, tort, torture

**quell** [OE] *Quell* and *kill* are probably closely related – indeed, in Old and Middle English *quell* was used for 'kill' ('birds and small beasts with his bow he quells,' *William of Palerne* 1350). *Quell* goes back to a prehistoric Germanic *\*kwaljan* (source also of German *quälen* 'torture'), which may have had a variant *\*kuljan*, that could have produced English *kill*. The milder modern sense of *quell* developed in the 14th century.

**querulous** see QUARREL

**question** [13] *Question* is one of a large family of English words that go back to the Latin verb *quaerere* 'seek, ask.' Its past participle *quaestus* formed the basis of a noun, *quaestiō*, which has become English *ques-*

*tion*. An earlier form of the past participle was *quaesītus*, and its feminine version *quaesīta* eventually passed into English via Old French as *quest* [14]. Other English words from the same source include *acquire*, *conquer*, *enquire*, *exquisite*, *inquest*, *request*, and *require*; and *query* [17] is an anglicization of *quaere*, the imperative form of *quaerere*.

▸ acquire, conquer, enquire, exquisite, inquest, query, quest, request, require

**queue** [16] Etymologically a *queue* is simply a 'tail.' That was the meaning of its Latin ancestor *cauda*, a word of unknown origin which has also given English *caudal* 'of a tail' [17] and, via Italian, *coda* [18] (literally a 'tail'-piece). To begin with in English *queue* (acquired via French) was used only as a technical term in heraldry for a 'tail.' It was not until the 18th century that metaphorical applications started to appear: to a 'billiard stick' (now spelled *cue*) and a 'pigtail.' 'Line of people waiting' (which has never caught on in American English) emerged in the early 19th century.

▸ coda

**quibble** [17] *Quibble* probably originated as a rather ponderous learned joke-word. It is derived from an earlier and now obsolete *quib* 'pun,' which appears to have been based on *quibus*, the dative and ablative plural of Latin *quī* 'who, what.' The notion is that since *quibus* made frequent appearances in legal documents written in Latin, it became associated with pettifogging points of law.

**quick** [OE] Originally *quick* meant 'alive' (as in the now fossilized phrase *the quick and the dead*); it was not until the 13th century that the sense 'rapid' began to emerge. It goes back to a prehistoric Germanic *\*kwikwaz* (which also produced Swedish *kvick* 'rapid'); and this was descended from an Indo-European base *\*gwej-*, which branched out into Latin *vīvus* 'alive' (source of English *vivid*), Greek *bíos* 'life' (source of English *biology*), Welsh *byw* 'alive,' Russian *zhivoj* 'alive,' etc.

The *couch* of *couch grass* [16] is a variant of the now seldom encountered *quitch*, whose Old English ancestor *cwice* may be related to *quick* (the allusion presumably being to its vigorous growth).

▸ biology, vivid

**quid** English has two words *quid*. The colloquial term for a 'pound' appears to be the same word as Latin *quid* 'something,' and may have been inspired by the expression *quid pro quo* [16], literally 'something for something.' *Quid* 'piece of chewing tobacco' [18] is a variant of *cud*.

▸ cud

**quiet** [14] The Latin noun *quiēs* meant 'quiet' (it came from a prehistoric Indo-European base *\*qwi-* 'rest,' which also produced English *while* and the final syllable of *tranquil*). From it was derived the verb

*quiēscere* 'be still' (source of English *quiescent* [17]). Its past participle *quiētus* has given English *quiet* (and its Siamese twin *coy*), *quit*, and *quite*, not to mention the derived forms *acquit* and *require*.

▸ acquit, coy, quit, quite, requite, tranquil, while

**quilt** [13] The ultimate source of *quilt* is Latin *culcita* 'mattress,' which passed into English via Old French *cuilte*. Its function gradually evolved from that of a mattress for lying on to that of a coverlet for lying under. A longstanding characteristic of such quilts is that their stuffing is held in place by cross-stitching. This does not emerge as a distinct meaning of the verb *quilt* ('sew padded cloth in a crisscross pattern') until the mid-16th century, but it is reflected in the medieval Latin term *culcita puncta* 'pricked mattress' – that is, a mattress that has been stitched. This passed into English via Old French as *counterpoint*, which was subsequently altered, by association with *pane* 'panel,' to *counterpane* [17].

▸ counterpane

**quince** [14] Etymologically, the *quince* is the 'fruit from Khaniá,' a port on the northwest coast of Crete from which quinces were exported. In ancient times Khaniá was known as Cydonia (in Greek *Kudốnia*), so the Greeks called the fruit *mēlon Kudốnion* 'Cydonian apple.' Latin took the term over as *cydōneum*, later *cotōneum*, which passed into English via Old French *cooin*. The original English form of the word was *quoyn*, later *quyn*, but already by the early 14th century its plural *quyns* was coming to be regarded as a singular – whence modern English *quince*.

**quinsy** [14] *Quinsy*, a now virtually obsolete term for 'sore throat,' has one of those etymologies that strain credulity to the limit. For it comes ultimately from a Greek term that meant literally 'dog-strangling.' This was *kunágkhē*, a compound formed from *kúon* 'dog' (a distant relative of English *hound*) and *ágkhein* 'strangle,' which originally denoted a sort of throat infection of dogs, which impaired their breathing, and was subsequently extended to a similar complaint in humans. English acquired the word via medieval Latin *quinancia* and Old French *quinencie*.

▸ hound

**quintessence** [15] Just as modern particle physicists search for the ultimate constituent of matter, the common denominator of all known forces, so medieval alchemists tried to find a fifth primary essence, which together with earth, air, fire, and water formed the substance of all heaven and earth. This fifth essence, higher and more etherial than the other four, was postulated by Aristotle, who called it *aithḗr* 'ether.' Another Greek term for it was *pemptē ousía* 'fifth essence,' which was translated into medieval Latin as *quinta essentia* – whence, via French, English *quintessence*. The metaphorical sense 'most perfect or characteristic embodiment' began to emerge in the second half of the 16th century.

Other English words based on *quintus* 'fifth,' the ordinal form of Latin *quinque* 'five,' include *quintet* [19] and *quintuple* [16].

**quire**    see QUARTER

**quisling**    [20]    Vidkun Quisling was a Norwegian politician who from 1933 led the National Union Party, the Norwegian fascist party (Quisling was not his real name – he was born Abraham Lauritz Jonsson). When the Germans invaded Norway in 1940 he gave them active support, urging his fellow Norwegians not to resist them, and in 1942 he was installed by Hitler as a puppet premier. In 1945 he was shot for treason. The earliest recorded use of his name in English as a generic term for a 'traitor' comes from April 1940.

**quit**    [13]    *Quit* comes from the same ultimate source as *quiet* – Latin *quiētus*. This originally meant simply 'quiet, calm,' but in medieval Latin it developed a wider range of senses, including 'unharmed' and 'free.' From it was derived the verb *quiētāre* 'set free, discharge,' which reached English via Old French *quiter*. The derived forms *acquit* and *requite* [16] come from the same source, and *quite* is essentially the same word as *quit*.
▶ quiet

**quite**    [14]    *Quite* is essentially the same word as the adjective *quit* 'free, absolved, discharged, cleared' (which in Middle English commonly took the alternative form *quite*). It came to be used as an adverb meaning 'thoroughly, clearly.' The weaker modern sense 'fairly' did not develop until as recently as the mid-19th century.
▶ quit

**quixotic**    [18]    *Quixotic* commemorates Don Quixote, the hero of Cervantes's novel of the same name (published in two parts in 1605 and 1615). He was a slightly dotty Spanish gentleman whose head became turned by tales of chivalric derring-do, which he sought to emulate in real life. His most famous exploit was to charge with his lance at windmills, under the mistaken impression that they were giants.

**quiz**    [19]    No one has ever been able satisfactorily to explain the origins of *quiz*. A word of that form first appeared at the end of the 18th century, meaning 'odd person' or, as a verb, 'make fun of' (in the early 19th century it was claimed to have been coined by a Dublin theatre proprietor by the name of Daly, but no proof has ever been found for this). The verb later came to be used for 'look at mockingly or questioningly through a monocle,' and it may be that this led on (perhaps helped by associations with *inquisitive* or Latin *quis?* 'who?, what?') to the sense 'interrogate.'

**quorum**    [15]    *Quorum* began life as the genitive plural of the Latin pronoun *quī* 'who.' This appeared in former times in the Latin text of commissions issued to persons who because of some special expertise were required to act as justices of the peace in a particular case (if two JPs were required, for instance, the wording would be *quorum vos . . . duos esse volumnus* 'of whom we wish that you . . . be two'). In due course the word came to be used as a noun, denoting the 'number of justices who must be present in order to try the case,' and in the 17th century this was generalized to 'minimum number of members necessary for a valid meeting.'

**quote**    [14]    Latin *quot* meant 'how many.' From it was derived the adjective *quotus* 'of what number,' whose feminine form *quota* was used in post-classical times as a noun, denoting literally 'how great a part' – whence English *quota* [17]. *Quotus* also formed the basis of the medieval Latin verb *quotāre* 'number,' which was used specifically for the practice of marking sections of text in manuscripts with numbers, as reference points. English took the verb over as *quote*, and by the 16th century was using it for 'cite' or 'refer to.' The derived *unquote* is first recorded in a letter by e e cummings, dated 1935.

Also based on *quot* was Latin *quotiēns* 'how many times,' which has given English *quotient* [15]; and *quotidian* 'daily' [14] goes back ultimately to a Latin compound formed from *quotus* and *diēs* 'day.' But the archaic *quoth* [OE], despite a certain similarity in form and sense, is not related; it comes from *cwæth*, the past tense of Old English *cwethan* 'say.'
▶ quota, quotient

**quoth**    see BEQUEATH

# R

**rabbi** [14] Hebrew *rabbī* meant 'my master.' It was a compound formed from *rabh* 'great one' and the pronoun suffix *-ī* 'my.' English originally acquired the word, via Latin, at the end of the Old English period, but only in biblical contexts, as a term of address equivalent to English *master* (as in 'Jesus . . . saith unto them, What seek ye? They said unto him, Rabbi (which is to say, being interpreted, Master), where dwellest thou?' John 1:38). Not until the 14th century did it begin to be used as an ordinary noun, meaning 'Jewish spiritual leader.'

**rabbit** [14] *Rabbit* was probably introduced into English from Old French. No immediate source is known to have existed, but we do have corroborative evidence in French dialect *rabotte* 'young rabbit' and Walloon *robète*. The latter was a diminutive derivative of Flemish *robbe* (Walloon is the form of French spoken in Flanders and Belgium), and it seems likely that the word's ultimate origins are Low German. At first it was used only for 'young rabbit' in English, and it did not really begin to take over from *cony* as the general term for the animal until the 18th century.

**rabies** [17] Latin *rabiēs* meant 'fury, madness' (it is the source of English *rage*). Hence it came to be used for 'madness in dogs,' and was subsequently adopted as the name of the disease causing this, when it came to be identified. The word was derived from the verb *rabere* 'be mad,' as also was *rabidus*, source of English *rabid* [17].
▶ rabid, rage

**race** For such a common word – or rather two words, for 'people, population' [16] and 'speed competition' [13] are unrelated – surprisingly little is known about the origins of *race*. The former comes via French from Italian *razza*, but the antecedents of *razza* are obscure. The 'running' *race* originally meant 'rush,' and was borrowed from Old Norse *rás* 'rush, running, race' – again, of unknown origin.

**raceme**   SEE RAISIN
▶ wrack, wreak, wreck

**rack**   English has no fewer than four distinct words *rack*. The oldest, 'framework' [14], was borrowed from Dutch *rak*, which was probably a derivative of the Middle Dutch verb *recken* 'stretch.' *Rack* 'destruction' [16], now used only in the phrase *rack and ruin*, is a variant of *wrack*, which is closely related to *wreak* and *wreck*. *Rack*, or *wrack*, 'mass of wind-driven cloud' [14] was probably acquired from Old Norse (Swedish has the probably related *rak*). And *rack* 'drain wine off its lees' [15] was borrowed from Provençal *arracar*, a derivative of *raca* 'dregs.'

**racket**   *Racket* for playing tennis [16] and *racket* 'noise' [16] are unrelated words. The former was borrowed from French *raquette*, which originally meant 'palm of the hand.' This goes back via Italian *racchetta* to Arabic *rāhat*, a variant of *rāha* 'palm of the hand.' The origins of *racket* 'noise' are not known, although the probability is that it started life as a verbal imitation of an uproar.

**radar**   see RADIO

**radical** [14] Etymologically, *radical* means 'of roots.' Its modern political meaning, based on the metaphor of fundamental change, going to the 'roots' of things, did not begin to emerge until the 18th century. The word was borrowed from late Latin *rādīcālis*, a derivative of Latin *rādīx* 'root' (source of English *radish* [OE] and probably related to *root*).
▶ radish, ramify, root

**radio** [20] *Radio* began life, in the first decade of the 20th century, as an abbreviation of *radiotelegraphy*, a compound based on Latin *radius*. This originally meant 'staff, stake,' but it is its secondary meanings that have contributed significantly to English: 'spoke of a wheel,' for instance, lies behind English *radius* [16], and the notion of a 'ray' has produced *radiant* [15], *radiate* [17], *radium* [19] (etymologically a metal emitting 'rays'), and indeed *ray*. *Radiotelegraphy* itself denoted the sending of messages by electromagnetic 'rays.' *Radar* [20], coined in the USA in 1941, is an acronym formed from *ra*dio *d*etection *a*nd *r*anging.

▶ radar, radiate, radius, radium, ray

**radish**    see RADICAL

**raffish**    see RAFT

**raffle**    [14]    *Raffle* was originally the name of a game played with three dice; the modern application to a 'prize draw' did not emerge until the 18th century. The word was borrowed from Old French *raffle* 'act of snatching,' but where this came from is not known.

**raft**    [15]    The ancestor of *raft* meant 'beam, rafter.' This was Old Norse *raptr*. Not until it got into English, apparently, was it used for a 'craft made by tying logs together.' (It should not, incidentally, be confused with the mainly American *raft* 'large collection, lot' [19], which is an alteration of Scottish English *raff* 'rubbish' – probable source of English *raffish* [19]. This too may well be of Scandinavian origin – Swedish has *rafs* 'rubbish.') *Rafter* [OE] comes from a Germanic source that was probably also responsible for *raft*.

▶ raffish, rafter

**rag**    English has four separate words *rag*, none of them with very well-documented histories. The origins of the oldest, 'rough building stone' [13], are completely unknown. *Rag* 'piece of cloth' [14] is probably a back-formation from *ragged* [13], which was adapted from Old Norse *roggvathr* 'tufted.' This in turn was derived from *rogg* 'tuft of fur,' but no one knows where that came from. *Rag* 'taunt, piece of fun' [18] is completely mysterious, although some connection with Danish dialect *rag* 'grudge' has been suggested. And finally *rag* 'syncopated jazz' [19] is short for *ragtime*, which is probably an alteration of *ragged time*.

**rage**    [13]    *Rage* is a close relative of *rabies*. It comes via Old French *rage* from Vulgar Latin *\*rabia*, an alteration of Latin *rabiēs* 'madness, frenzy, fury' (from which English gets *rabies*). (French *rage* still means 'rabies' as well as 'anger.')

▶ rabies

**raid**    [15]    *Raid* and *road* are doublets – that is to say, they have a common ancestor, but have diverged over the centuries. In this case the ancestor was Old English *rād* 'riding,' hence 'hostile incursion on horseback,' a relative of *ride*. South of the border this developed to *road*, and lost its predatory connotations (although they are preserved in *inroads*), but in Scottish English it became *raid*. This had more or less died out by the end of the 16th century, but Sir Walter Scott revived it at the beginning of the 19th century, and it has gone from strength to strength ever since.

▶ ride, road

**rail**    English has three words *rail*. The oldest, 'rod, bar' [13], comes via Old French *reille* 'iron bar' from Latin *rēgula* 'straight stick, rod,' source of English *reg-*

*ular* and *rule*. The bird-name *rail* [15] goes back via Old Northern French *raille* to Vulgar Latin *\*rascula*, which probably originated in imitation of the bird's hoarse cry. And *rail* 'complain, be abusive' [15] comes via Old French *railler* 'mock' and Provençal *ralhar* 'scoff' from Vulgar Latin *\*ragulāre* 'bray,' an alteration of *ragere* 'neigh, roar.' This in turn was a blend of Latin *rugīre* 'bellow' and Vulgar Latin *\*bragere* 'bray' (source of English *bray* [13]). *Raillery* [17] and *rally* 'tease' [17] come from the same source.

▶ regular, rule / bray, rally

**rain**    [OE]    *Rain* is an exclusively Germanic word, not shared by any other language group in the Indo-European family. Its prehistoric ancestor *\*reg-* has evolved into German and Dutch *regen*, Swedish and Danish *regn*, and English *rain*. There may be some connection with Old Norse *rakr* 'wet.'

**raise**    [12]    *Raise* is first cousin to *rear*. It was borrowed from Old Norse *reisa*, which was descended from the same prehistoric Germanic verb as produced English *rear* 'lift, rise.' This was *\*raizjan*, a derivative of the same source as gave English *rise*.

▶ rear, rise

**raisin**    [13]    *Raisin* comes ultimately from a Latin word that meant 'bunch of grapes.' This was *racēmus* (source also of English *raceme* [18]). It passed via Vulgar Latin *\*racīmus* into Old French as *raisin*, by which time it had come to mean just 'grape' rather 'bunch of grapes.' And it was already developing further to 'dried grape' by the time English acquired it.

▶ raceme

**raj**    [18]    English acquired the word *raj*, of course, from the period of British rule in India. It was borrowed from Hindi *rāj* 'reign,' which goes back to Sanskrit *rā-jā*, a derivative of *rājati* 'he rules.' Closely related is *rajah* [16], which came (probably via Portuguese) from Hindi *rājā*, a descendant of Sanskrit *rājan* 'king' (the Sanskrit feminine form *rājnī* produced *ranee* [17]). The whole family of words goes back to an Indo-European base *\*rēg-*, which also produced Latin *rēx* 'king,' source of English *regal* and *royal*. *Maharajah* [17] means literally 'great ruler' (Hindi *mahā* 'great' comes from the same source as Latin *magnus* 'great,' ancestor of English *magnify, magnitude*, etc).

▶ regal, royal

**rake**    English has three distinct words *rake*. The oldest, 'toothed implement' [OE], goes back to a prehistoric Germanic *\*rak-* or *\*rek-* 'gather, heap up,' which also produced German *rechen* 'rake.' It may be descended ultimately from Indo-European *\*rog-*, *\*reg-* 'stretch' (source of Latin *regere* 'rule' and English *right*), the notion of 'stretching' developing via 'stretch out the hand' to 'collect, gather.' *Rake* 'slant, inclination' [17] is of uncertain origin, although it seems likely that it is related to German *ragen* 'project.' It formed the basis of the adjective *rakish* [19] (inspired originally by the backward-inclined masts on certain fast sailing ships), but this has since become associated with the third *rake*, 'dissolute man' [17]. This was short for the now defunct *rakehell* [16], which comes from the notion that one would have to search through hell with a rake to find such a bad man.

▶ right / rakish

**ram**　　[OE]　　*Ram* is a general West Germanic word for 'male sheep,' now shared only by Dutch (although German has the derivative *ramme* 'rammer'). It may be related to Old Norse *ramr* 'strong,' the allusion being to the ram's strength in butting. This is reflected in the word's metaphorical applications: it was being used in Old English for a 'battering-ram,' and by the 14th century the verb *ram* had emerged. Another relative is the verb *ramble* [17], which etymologically denotes 'wander around like a randy ram, looking for ewes to copulate with.' It was borrowed from Middle Dutch *rammelen*, a derivative of *rammen* 'copulate with,' which is connected with *ram*.

▶ ramble

**ramify**　　[16]　　*Ramify* has no connection with rams. It comes ultimately from Latin *rāmus* 'branch,' which probably goes back to the same source as produced Latin *rādīx* 'root' (ancestor of English *radical* and *radish*) and English *root*. From it was derived the medieval Latin verb *rāmificāre*, which passed into English via Old French *ramifier*.

▶ radical, radish

**ramp**　　[18]　　A *ramp* is etymologically something you 'climb' up. The word was borrowed from French *rampe*, a derivative of the verb *ramper* 'climb,' hence 'slope.' This goes back to a Frankish *\*rampōn*, and was borrowed into English in the 13th century as *ramp*. It now survives mainly in the form of its present participle, *rampant* [14], which preserves the sense 'rearing up.' *Rampage* [18] may be a derivative.

**rampart**　　[16]　　*Rampart*, which means etymologically 'fortified place,' has a very convoluted history. Its ultimate ancestor is Latin *parāre* 'prepare' (source of English *prepare*). To this was added the prefix *ante-* 'before' to produce the Vulgar Latin verb *\*anteparāre* 'prepare for defence.' This passed via Provençal *amparar* into Old French as *emparer* 'defend, fortify,' which had the intensive *re-* prefixed to it, giving *remparer* 'fortify.' From this was derived the noun *remper* or *ramper*, which was altered (apparently under the influence of *boulevart*, source of English *boulevard*) to *rempart* or *rampart* – whence English *rampart*.

▶ prepare

**ramshackle**　　see RANSACK

**rancour**　　[14]　　To account for *rancour* and its close relative *rancid* we have to postulate a Latin verb

*\*rancēre* 'stink,' never actually recorded but inferrable from its present participle *rancēns* 'stinking, putrid.' From it were derived the adjective *rancidus*, source of English *rancid* [17], and in post-classical times the noun *rancor*, source of English *rancour*.

▶ rancid

**random**　　[14]　　The antecedents of *random* are somewhat murky. It originally meant 'impetuosity, sudden speed, violence,' and only in the mid 17th century emerged as an adjective meaning 'haphazard.' It was borrowed from Old French *randon*, which was probably a derivative of the verb *randir* 'run impetuously.' This in turn was based on Frankish *\*rant* 'running,' which was apparently descended from prehistoric Germanic *\*randa*. This originally meant 'edge' (it is the source of English *rand* [OE], now obsolete as a term for 'edge,' but reintroduced in the 20th century via Afrikaans as the name of the basic South African currency unit), but it was also widely used for 'shield,' and it is thought that the link with 'running impetuously' may be the notion of soldiers running along with their shields.

▶ rand

**ranee**　　see RAJ

**range**　　[13]　　*Range* and *rank* come ultimately from the same source: Old French *ranc*. This was borrowed directly into English as *rank*, but it subsequently developed to *rang*, from which was derived the verb *rangier* 'set in a row' (ancestor of English *arrange*). This in turn produced the noun *range* 'rank, row.'

▶ rank

**rank**　　English has two words *rank*. The one meaning 'row, line' [16], and hence 'position of seniority,' was borrowed from Old French *ranc* (source also of English *range*), which goes back via Frankish *\*hring* to a prehistoric Germanic *\*khrengaz* 'circle, ring' (ancestor of English *ring*). *Rank* 'absolute, downright' [OE], as in 'rank bad manners,' has had an eventful semantic history. It originally meant 'haughty' and 'full-grown,' and came from a prehistoric Germanic *\*rangkaz*, which also produced Old Norse *rakkr* 'erect.' 'Full-grown' evolved via 'growing vigorously, luxuriant' (which still survives) into 'gross, disgusting,' on which the present-day intensive usage is based.

▶ range, ring

**rankle**　　[14]　　Etymologically, if something *rankles*, it festers from the effects of a 'dragon's' bite. Nowadays the word is only used metaphorically, but it originally meant literally 'be sore, fester.' It was borrowed from Old French *rancler*, a variant of *draoncler*. This was derived from *draoncle* 'ulcer,' which in turn came from *dranculus*, the medieval Latin descendant of *dracunculus*, a diminutive form of Latin *dracō* 'snake' (source of English *dragon*). The notion underlying the word is of an ulcer caused by the bite of a snake.

▶ dragon

**ransack** [13]   *Ransack* means etymologically 'search a house.' It was borrowed from Old Norse *rann-saka*, a compound verb formed from *rann* 'house' (a relative of Old English *ærn* 'house,' which underlies English *barn*) and *-saka* 'search' (a relative of English *seek*). A now defunct derivative was *ransackle* or *ran-shackle*, from which we get modern English *ramshack-le* [19].

▶ barn, ramshackle, seek

**ransom** [13]   Heavily disguised, *ransom* is the same word ultimately as *redemption*. It was borrowed from Old French *ransoun*, which, much weathered over the centuries, was descended from Latin *redemptiō*, source of English *redemption*. The etymological notion underlying the word is thus of money paid to 'redeem' or rescue a hostage.

▶ redemption

**rapacious**   see RAPTURE

**rape**   English has three distinct words *rape*, only two of them now in general usage. The commonest, 'violate sexually' [14], comes via Anglo-Norman *raper* from Latin *rapere* 'seize by force,' a generous contributor to English vocabulary which has also given us *rapid, rapt, rapture*, etc. *Rape* the plant-name [14] was borrowed from Latin *rāpa* or *rāpum*. Like its Latin ancestor, it originally denoted 'turnip,' but since the 16th century it has come to be used exclusively for another plant of the brassica family, grown for its oil-rich seeds. (The *-rabi* of *kohlrabi* also comes ultimately from Latin *rāpa*; and Italian dialect *raviolo*, a diminutive of *rava* 'turnip,' has given English *ravioli* [19].) The oldest *rape* [11] is now only of historical interest. It denoted any of the six administrative areas into which Sussex was once divided. It is the same word ultimately as *rope*, and etymologically denotes the partitioning off of land with rope.

▶ rapid, rapt, rapture / kohlrabi, ravioli / rope

**rapid** [17]   Like *rape* and *rapture*, *rapid* comes ultimately from Latin *rapere* 'seize by force.' From this was derived the adjective *rapidus*, which originally denoted 'carrying off by force.' The notion of 'swiftness' soon became incorporated into the meaning, however, and although the Latin adjective retained its original connotations of violence (it suggested 'impetuous speed' or 'haste'), by the time it reached English it had simply become synonymous with 'quick.'

▶ rapture

**rapscallion**   see RASCAL

**rapture** [17]   *Rapture* is one of a large family of English words that go back ultimately to Latin *rapere* 'seize by force.' Its past participle was *raptus* (source of English *rapt* [14]), which formed the basis of the medieval Latin noun *raptūra* 'seizure,' hence 'ecstasy' – whence English *rapture*. From the same source come

*rapacious* [17], *rape* 'violate sexually,' *rapid, rapine* [15], *ravage, ravenous, ravine, ravish, surreptitious*, and *usurp*.

▶ rapacious, rape, rapid, ravage, ravenous, ravine, ravish, surreptitious, usurp

**rare**   *Rare* 'uncommon' [15] and *rare* 'underdone' [17] are not the same word. The former was borrowed from Latin *rārus*, which originally signified 'having a loose texture, widely separated' – hence 'scarce.' It is not known what its ultimate source is. The latter is an alteration of the now obsolete *rear* 'underdone' (originally used mainly of eggs: 'They had at their dinner rear eggs,' *Book of the knight of the tower* 1450), which goes back to Old English *hrēr* – again of unknown origin.

**rascal** [14]   *Rascal* has been traced back ultimately to Latin *rādere* 'scratch.' Its past participial stem *rās*-(source of English *erase* and *razor*) formed the basis of a Vulgar Latin verb *\*rāsicāre*. From this was derived the noun *\*rāsica* 'scurf, scab, dregs, filth,' which passed into Old Northern French as *\*rasque* (its central Old French counterpart, *rasche*, may be the source of English *rash*). And it could well be that this *\*rasque* lies behind Old French *rascaille* 'mob, rabble,' which gave English *rascal* (the English word originally meant 'rabble' too, but the application to an individual person emerged in the 15th and 16th centuries). *Rap-scallion* [17] is an alteration of a now defunct *rascal-lion*, which may have derived from *rascal*.

▶ erase, rapscallion, rash, razor

**rash**   English has two words *rash*. The older, 'impetuous' [14], probably comes from an unrecorded Old English *\*ræsc*, which together with its relatives German *rasch* 'quick' and Swedish *rask* 'active, vigorous' goes back to a prehistoric Germanic *\*raskuz*. This was probably derived from the same base as produced English *rather*, which originally meant 'more quickly.' *Rash* 'skin condition' [18] may have been borrowed from the now obsolete French *rache*, a descendant of Old French *rasche*, whose Old Northern French counterpart *\*rasque* is the possible source of English *rascal*.

▶ rather / rascal

**raspberry** [17]   The origins of the word *raspberry* are a mystery. At first, the fruit was known simply as *raspes* or *raspis* (recorded in an Anglo-Latin text as early as the 13th century), and the *-berry* was not tacked on until the early 17th century – but no one knows where *raspes* came from. Its use for a 'rude noise made by blowing,' first recorded in the 1890s, comes from rhyming slang *raspberry tart* 'fart.'

**rat** [OE]   *Rat* is a general western European term, with relatives in French *rat*, Italian *ratto*, Spanish *rata*, German *ratte*, Dutch *rat*, Swedish *råatta*, and Danish *rotte*. These all come from Vulgar Latin *\*rattus*, whose origin is unknown.

**ratafia**  see TOFFEE

**ratchet**  [17]  *Ratchet* was originally acquired, in the form *rochet*, from French *rochet*. This was a diminutive form descended ultimately from Frankish *\*rokko* 'spool,' which is related to English *rocket*. The notion of having teeth, which is central to the idea of a *ratchet*, therefore appears to be historically secondary; it presumably arose from the addition of 'teeth' to a rotating 'spool' or 'spindle' in a machine. The change from *rochet* to *ratchet*, which began in the 18th century, may have been influenced by German *ratsch* 'ratchet.'
▶ rocket

**rate**  English has two words *rate*. The commoner, 'relative quantity' [15], comes via Old French *rate* from medieval Latin *rata* 'calculated, fixed,' as used in the expression *pro rata parte* 'according to a fixed part, proportionally.' This was the feminine form of *ratus*, the past participle of *rērī* 'think, calculate,' from which English also gets *ratio, ration, reason*, etc. The other *rate*, 'scold' [14], is now seldom encountered except in its derivative *berate* [16]. It is not certain where it comes from, although a possible source is Old French *reter* 'accuse, blame,' which comes from Latin *reputāre* (ancestor of English *reputation*).
▶ ratio, ration, reason / berate

**rather**  [OE]  *Rather* originated as the comparative form of the now obsolete adjective *rathe* 'quick,' and so to begin with meant 'more quickly,' hence 'earlier, sooner.' Its most frequent modern meaning, 'more willingly,' emerged as recently as the 16th century. *Rathe* itself went back to a prehistoric Germanic *\*khrathaz*, which may have been derived from the same base as produced English *rash* 'impetuous.'
▶ rash

**ration**  [18]  *Ration*, like *reason*, comes from Latin *ratiō*, a derivative of the verb *rērī* 'think, calculate.' This meant, among other things, 'calculation, computation,' in which sense it has yielded English *ratio* [17]. In the Middle Ages it was used for an 'amount of provisions calculated for a soldier,' and that meaning has channelled via Spanish *ración* and French *ration* into English as *ration*. The 'thinking' sense of *ratiō* has reached English as *reason*, but its derivative *rational* [14] is less heavily disguised. Other English descendants of Latin *rērī* include *rate* and *ratify* [14], and the *-red* of *hundred* comes from a prehistoric Germanic *\*rath* 'number,' which came ultimately from Latin *ratiō*.
▶ hundred, rate, ratio, reason

**rattle**  [14]  *Rattle* probably existed in Old English, but in the absence of any direct evidence, it is usually suggested that the word was borrowed from Middle Low German *rattelen*, a relative of German *rasseln* 'rattle.' Whatever its ultimate source, it no doubt originally imitated the sound of rattling.

**raven**  English has two separate words *raven*. The bird-name [OE] is a general Germanic term, related to German *rabe*, Dutch *raaf*, and Danish *ravn*. It goes back to a prehistoric Germanic *\*khrabnaz* or *\*khraben*, which originated in an imitation of the raven's harsh croaking. The verb *raven* 'prey, plunder' [15], nowadays encountered virtually only in its present participle *ravening* and the derived *ravenous*, goes back ultimakely to Latin *rapere* 'seize by force.'
▶ rape, rapture, ravenous

**ravenous**  [15]  *Ravenous* was borrowed from Old French *ravineux*, a derivative of the verb *raviner* 'seize by force' (source of English *raven*, which nowadays appears mainly in its present participial form *ravening*). This came from Latin *rapere* 'seize by force,' ancestor also of English *rape*. The central modern meaning of *ravenous*, 'very hungry,' developed from the notion of predatory animals that 'seize' and eat their prey. Other English descendants of Latin *rapere* include *rapacious, rapid, rapture, ravage, ravine, ravish* [13], *surreptitious*, and *usurp*.
▶ rape, rapture, raven

**ravine**  [15]  *Ravine* and the now seldom encountered *rapine* 'plunder' [15] are essentially the same word. Both come ultimately from Latin *rapīna* 'plunder,' a derivative of *rapere* 'seize by force' (from which English gets *rape, rapid, rapture, ravenous*, etc). This passed directly into English via Old French as *rapine*, but a variant Old French form also developed, *ravine*, whose meaning appears to have been influenced by Latin *rapidus* 'rapid.' It denoted 'violent rush, impetus' – which is how it was used in its brief and very spasmodic career in Middle English. It did not become firmly established as an English word until the 19th century, when it was reborrowed from French in the sense 'gorge' – originally as carved out by a 'violent rush' or torrent of water.
▶ rape, rapine, rapture

**ravioli**  see RAPE

**ravish**  see RAVENOUS

**raw**  [OE]  *Raw* has relatives in German (*roh*), Dutch (*rauw*), Swedish (*rå*), and Danish (*ra*). These all go back to a prehistoric Germanic ancestor *\*khrawaz*, whose ultimate source was Indo-European *\*krowos* (other descendants of the same base include Greek *kréas* 'flesh,' from which English gets *creosote* and *pancreas*, and Latin *crūdus* 'raw,' source of English *crude* and *cruel*).
▶ creosote, crude, cruel, pancreas

**ray**  *Ray* the 'beam of light or energy' [14] and *ray* the fish-name [14] are two different words. The former comes from *rai*, the Old French descendant of Latin *radius* 'spoke of a wheel, ray' (source also of English *radiant, radio, radius*, etc). The textile term *rayon* was coined from it in the early 1920s. *Ray* the fish-name comes via Old French *raie* from Latin *raia*, a word of unknown origin.

▶ radio, radius

**razor** [13] A *razor* is etymologically a 'scraper.' The word was borrowed from Old French *rasor*, a derivative of *raser* 'scrape, shave' (from which English gets *raze* [16]). This in turn went back via Vulgar Latin *\*rasāre* to Latin *rādere* 'scrape,' source also of English *abrade* [17], *erase*, and possibly *rascal*.

▶ abrade, erase, rascal

**reach** [OE] *Reach* goes back ultimately to a prehistoric West Germanic *\*raikjan*, a word of uncertain origin which also produced German *reichen* and Dutch *reiken*. It originally meant 'stretch out the hand,' and 'attain' and 'arrive at' are secondary semantic developments.

**read** [OE] In most western European languages, the word for 'read' goes back ultimately to a source which meant literally 'gather, pick up': French *lire*, for instance, which comes from Latin *legere* (source of English *legible* and *collect*), and German *lesen*. English *read*, however, is an exception. Its underlying meaning is 'advise, consider' (it is related to German *raten* 'advise,' and a memory of this original sense lives on in the archaic *rede* 'advise,' which is essentially the same word as *read*, and also in *unready* 'ill-advised,' the epithet applied to the Anglo-Saxon king Ethelred II), and the sense 'read' developed via 'interpret' (preserved in the related *riddle*).

▶ riddle

**ready** [12] *Ready* is a derivative of Old English *rǣde* 'ready,' which went back to a prehistoric Germanic *\*raithjō* 'arranged,' hence 'prepared.' This also produced German *bereit* 'ready,' Dutch *gereed* 'ready,' and Swedish *reda* 'ready,' and it lies behind the second syllable of *curry* 'groom a horse.'

**real** [15] *Real* and its various derivatives (such as *realism* [19], *reality* [16], and *realize* [17]) go back ultimately to Latin *rēs* 'thing,' a word of uncertain origin related to Sanskrit *rās* 'riches.' It had a post-classical derivative *reālis*, which English originally acquired via Anglo-Norman *real* and used strictly in the legal sense 'of fixed property' (as in *real estate*). The broader modern range of meanings was probably instigated by the reintroduction of the word direct from Latin in the mid-16th century.

▶ realize

**realm** [13] *Realm. régime*, and *regimen* are ultimately the same word. All three come from Latin *regimen* 'system of government,' a derivative of the verb *regere* 'rule' (from which English gets *rector*, *regent*, *register*, etc). This passed into Old French, where *reiel* 'royal' was grafted into it, producing *realme* – whence English *realm*.

▶ rector, regal, régime, regimen, register, royal

**ream** English has two distinct words *ream*. The one denoting an amount of paper [14] comes via Old French *remme* from Arabic *risma* 'bundle,' a derivative of the verb *rasama* 'collect into a bundle.' *Ream* 'make or enlarge a hole' [19] may be the same word as Middle English *reme* 'open up, make room,' which goes back to Old English *rȳman* 'widen,' a derivative of the same base as English *room*.

▶ room

**reap** SEE RIPE

**rear** There are two separate words *rear* in English. The older, 'raise' [OE], is a descendant of prehistoric Germanic *\*raizjan*, which also produced Old Norse *reisa*, source of English *raise*. The Germanic verb denoted literally 'cause to rise,' and was derived from *\*reisan*, which evolved into English *rise*. *Rear* 'hind' [16] is descended ultimately from Latin *retrō-* 'behind,' but it is not clear whether it came into the language as an abbreviation of *arrear* [18], which goes back via Old French *arere* to medieval Latin *adretrō* 'to the rear' (the Anglo-Norman noun *areres* existed in the 14th century, so the chronological disparity may not be crucial), or was extracted from *rearguard* [15], a borrowing from Old French *rereguarde*.

▶ raise, rise / arrear, retro-

**reason** [13] *Reason*, together with *rational*, represent in English the 'thinking' aspects of the Latin verb *rērī* (it also meant 'calculate,' and in that guise has given English *rate*, *ration*, etc). From it was derived the noun *ratiō* 'thinking, calculation' (source of English *ratio* and the rest). This spawned a Vulgar Latin variant *\*ratiōne*, which passed into Old French as *reisun* – whence English *reason*.

▶ rate, ratio, ration

**rebate** [15] A *rebate* is etymologically an amount that has been 're-abated.' The word, originally a verb, comes from Old French *rabattre* 'beat down again,' hence 'reduce,' a compound formed from the prefix *re-* 'again' and *abattre* 'beat down' (source of English *abate* [13], and also of *abattoir* [19], euphemistically a place where animals are 'beaten down' or killed). This in turn went back to Vulgar Latin *\*abbattuere*, a compound verb formed from the prefix *ad-* 'completely' and *battuere* 'beat' (source of English *battle*, *combat*, etc).

▶ abate, abattoir, battle, combat

**rebel** [13] Etymologically, a *rebel* is someone who, having been defeated, 'makes war again' against his conquerors. The word comes via Old French *rebelle* from Latin *rebellis*, an adjective formed from the prefix *re-* 'again' and *bellum* 'war' (source of English *bellicose* [15] and *belligerent* [16]). The same Latin word underlies English *revel* [14]; the semantic link between these two rather unlikely relatives is the noisy disturbance or uproar that goes with a rebellion, not too dissimilar to that made by a crowd of revellers.

▶ belligerent, revel

**recalcitrant**    [19] People who are *recalcitrant* are etymologically 'kicking back' against whatever restrains or upsets them. The word was borrowed from French *récalcitrant*, a descendant of the present participle of Latin *recalcitrāre* 'kick back.' This was a compound verb formed from the prefix *re-* 'back, again' and *calcitrāre* 'kick,' which in turn was derived from Latin *calx* 'heel.'

**recap**    [20] The *-cap* of *recap* has of course no immediate connection with *cap*. The word is short for *recapitulate* [16], which etymologically denotes 'repeat the headings.' It comes from late Latin *recapitulāre*, a compound verb formed from the prefix *re-* 'again' and *capitulum* 'section of text, heading' (source of English *chapter*). *Capitulum* was a diminutive form of Latin *caput* 'head,' which may ultimately underlie English *cap* – so the two words could after all be linked.

▶ capitulate, chapter

**receive**    [13] To *receive* something is etymologically to 'take it back.' The word comes via Old French *receivre* from Latin *recipere* 'regain,' a compound verb formed from the prefix *re-*'back, again' and *capere* 'take' (source of English *capture*). Other English descendants of *recipere* are *receipt* [14] (which goes back to medieval Latin *recepta*, a noun use of the verb's feminine past participle), *receptacle* [15], *reception* [14], *recipe*, and *recipient* [16].

▶ captive, capture, receptacle, recipe

**recent**    [16] English acquired *recent* from Latin *recēns* 'new, fresh,' possibly via French *récent*. It is not clear where the Latin word came from, although some have linked it with Greek *kainós* 'new' (source of the English geological term *cainozoic* [19]) and Sanskrit *kanīna-* 'young.'

**recidivist**    [19] A *recidivist* – a 'persistent offender' – is etymologically someone who 'falls back.' The word was borrowed from French *récidiviste*, a descendant of medieval Latin *recidīvāre*. This in turn was based on the noun *recidīvus* 'falling back,' a derivative of Latin *recidere* 'fall back,' which was a compound verb formed from the prefix *re-* 'back, again' and *cadere* 'fall' (source of English *cadence, case, decadent*, etc).

▶ cadaver, cadence, case, decadent

**recipe**    [14] *Recipe* originated as the imperative form of Latin *recipere* 'receive, take' (source of English *receive*). It was commonly used in Latin, and occasionally English, lists of ingredients for medicines and dishes (as in 'Take three eggs . . . '), and by the end of the 16th century it was being applied to the medical for-

mulae themselves. Its modern gastronomic sense did not emerge until the mid-18th century.

▶ receive

**reciprocal**    [16] English adapted *reciprocal* from Latin *reciprocus* 'alternating.' This was a compound adjective based ultimately on the elements *re-* 'back, backwards' and *prō-*'for, forwards.'

**recite**    [15] *Recite* came, probably via Old French *reciter*, from Latin *recitāre* 'read out.' This was a compound verb formed from the prefix *re-* 'back, again' and *citāre* 'call, summon' (source also of English *cite, excite, incite*, etc). *Recitative* 'speech-like singing' [17] was borrowed from Italian *recitativo*.

▶ cite, excite, incite

**reckless**    [OE] The *reck-* of *reckless* is the same word as the now virtually obsolete verb *reck* 'care.' It is not clear where this ultimately came from, but the compound *reckless* itself evidently goes back to the prehistoric West Germanic period, for it also occurs in German (*ruchlos*) and Dutch (*roekeloos*).

**reckon**    [OE] *Reckon* originally meant 'give a list of, enumerate, tell.' The sense 'count' had developed by the 13th century, and 'estimate, consider' emerged in the 14th century. It comes ultimately from a prehistoric West Germanic *\*rekenōjan*, which also produced German *rechnen* 'count' and Dutch *rekenen*.

**recluse**    [13] A *recluse* is etymologically a person who is 'shut up.' The word was borrowed from *reclus*, the past participle of Old French *reclure* 'shut up.' This was descended from Latin *reclūdere*, a compound verb formed from the prefix *re-* 'again' and *claudere* 'shut' (source of English *close*) which originally, paradoxically, meant 'open' – the notion being 'reversing the process of closing.' 'Shut up' emerged in the post-classical period.

▶ close

**recognize**    [15] Latin *gnōscere* 'become acquainted' came from the same prehistoric Indo-European base, *\*gnō-*, as produced English *know*. Combination with the prefix *co-* 'with' gave *cognōscere* 'know' (source of English *cognition, quaint*, etc). And this in turn had the prefix *re-* 'again' added to it to produce *recognōscere* 'know again,' which found its way into English via *reconniss-*, the stem of Old French *reconnaistre* (the *-ize* ending is an English introduction). English has three noun derivatives of the verb: *recognition* [15], from Latin *recognitiō*; *recognizance* [14], now purely a legal term, borrowed from Old French *reconnissance* and remodelled on the basis of *recognize*; and *reconnaissance* [19], borrowed from modern French during the Napoleonic wars. *Reconnoitre* [18] comes from the now obsolete French *reconnoître*, which like its surviving variant *reconnaître* goes back to Latin *recognōscere*.

▶ cognition, know, quaint, reconnaissance, reconnoitre

**recoil** [13] *Recoil* has no connection with *coil*. In fact, etymologically it means virtually 'withdraw backside first,' for it was coined in French on the basis of *cul* 'arse, backside.' This went back to Latin *cūlus* 'arse,' which was probably related to Sanskrit *kūla-* 'rearguard.'

**recollect** [16] *Recollect* originated in Latin as *recolligere*, a compound verb formed from the prefix *re-* 'again' and *colligere* 'gather' (source of English *collect*). At first it simply meant literally 'gather again,' but in the post-classical period it was extended metaphorically to 'recall, remember.' English acquired it through its past participial stem *recollect-*.

**recondite** [17] *Recondite* 'obscure, abstruse' means etymologically 'hidden.' It comes from *reconditus*, the past participle of Latin *recondere* 'hide.' This was a compound verb formed from the prefix *re-* 'again' and *condere* 'put away, store' (ultimate source of English *condiment* [15], literally 'stored' or 'preserved' food).

▶ condiment

**reconnaissance**   see RECOGNIZE
**reconnoitre**   see RECOGNIZE

**record** [13] To *record* something is etymologically to commit it to one's 'heart.' The word comes via Old French *recorder* from Latin *recordārī* 'go over in one's mind, ponder, remember.' This was a compound verb based on Latin *cor* 'heart' (source of English *concord, cordial* [14], *courage*, etc), used metaphorically in the sense 'mind.' The notion of 'putting something down in writing or other permanent form' did not emerge until the Old French stage in the word's history. The derivative *recorder* 'woodwind instrument' [15] depends on a now obsolete sense of *record*, 'practise a tune.'

▶ concord, cordial, courage, quarry

**recourse**   see COURSE

**recover** [14] *Recover* and *recuperate* [16] are ultimately the same word. Both come from Latin *recuperāre* 'recover, regain,' a compound verb based on the stem *cup-* 'take' (a variant of which produced *capere* 'take,' source of English *captive, capture*, etc). *Recuperate* itself was acquired directly from the Latin verb's past participle, whereas *recover* was routed via Old French *recoverer*. (*Re-cover* 'cover again,' spelled similarly but pronounced differently, also dates from the 14th century.)

▶ captive, capture, recuperate

**recruit** [17] Etymologically, a *recruit* is something that 'grows again.' The word's ultimate ancestor is Latin *recrēscere* 'regrow,' a compound verb formed from the prefix *re-* 'again' and *crēscere* 'grow' (source of English *crescent, increase*, etc). This passed into French as *recroître*, whose feminine past participle in

the standard language was *recrue*. In the dialect of northeastern France, however, it was *recrute*, and it was this, used as a noun meaning 'new growth,' hence 'reinforcement of troops,' that gave English *recruit*.

▶ crescent, croissant, increase

**rector** [14] A *rector* is etymologically a 'ruler.' The word comes via Old French *rectour* from Latin *rēctor* 'governor,' a derivative of the verb *regere* 'govern, rule' (from which English gets *regent, region*, etc). It carried its original meaning with it into English, with reference both to Roman governors in the ancient world and to God as 'ruler' of the universe (Sir Matthew Hale in 1676 referred to God as the 'great dispenser or permitter and rector of all the events in the world'), but by the 18th century it had largely become restricted to the more specialized senses 'clergyman in charge of a parish' and 'head of a college.'

▶ regent, regiment, region

**rectum** [16] *Rectum* is one of a range of words bequeathed to English by Latin *rēctus* 'straight, correct' (a distant relative of English *right*). Others include *rectangle* [16], *rectify* [14], and *rectitude* [15]. *Rectum* itself is short for *rēctum intestīnum* 'straight intestine' – a term contrasting the rectum with the convolutions of the remainder of the intestines.

▶ direct, rectify, rectitude, right

**recumbent**   see INCUBATE
**recuperate**   see RECOVER
**recusant**   see REFUSE

**red** [OE] *Red* is an ancient colour-term, whose history can be traced back to prehistoric Indo-European *\*reudh-*. This also produced Greek *eruthrós* 'red' (source of English *erythrocyte* 'red blood cell' [19]) and a whole range of Latin 'red'-words, including *ruber* (source of English *rubicund* and *ruby*), *rubeus* (source of English *rouge* [15]), *russus* (source of English *rissole* and *russet*), and *rūfus* (source of English *rufous* [18]). Amongst other English words from the same Indo-European source are *robust, ruby, ruddy* [OE], and *rust*. The immediate Germanic precursor of *red* was *\*rauthaz*, which also produced German *rot*, Dutch *rood*, Swedish *röd*, and Danish *rød*.

▶ corroborate, erythrocyte, rissole, robust, rouge, ruby, ruddy, russet, rust

**redeem** [15] The *-deem* is not the same word as *deem* (which is related to *doom*). In fact, there never was a true *-deem* in it. It comes from Latin *emere* 'take, buy' (source also of English *example, prompt*, etc), which when combined with the prefix *re-* 'again, back' had a *d* grafted into it to produce *redimere* 'buy back.' English probably acquired it via French *rédimer*.

▶ example, prompt, sample

**redolent** [14] Etymologically, something that is *redolent* of something 'smells' of it. The word comes ultimately from Latin *olēre* 'smell,' which was derived from the same base as produced English *odour*. Combination with the prefix *re-* 'back' resulted in *redolēre* 'emit a smell,' from whose present participle English gets *redolent*. The Latin word was mainly used to convey the notion 'smelling *of* something,' and this lies behind the English word's metaphorical use for 'suggestive, reminiscent, evocative,' first recorded in the early 19th century.

▶ odour

**redoubt**  [17]  *Redoubt* 'stronghold' has no etymological connection with *doubt* (although *redoubtable* [14] does – it derives from the French ancestor of *doubt*, which originally meant 'fear,' and so historically denotes 'to be feared'). It was borrowed from French *redoute*, which goes back via obsolete Italian *ridotta* to medieval Latin *reductus* 'hidden place, refuge,' a noun use of the past participle of Latin *redūcere* 'bring back, withdraw' (source of English *reduce*). The *b* was inserted under the influence of *redoubtable*.

▶ reduce

**redound**  see REDUNDANT

**reduce**  [14]  'Lessen, diminish' is a comparatively recent semantic development for *reduce*. Its Latin ancestor was certainly not used in that sense. This was *redūcere*, a compound verb formed from the prefix *re-* 'back, again' and *dūcere* 'lead, bring' (source of English *duct, duke, educate*, etc). It meant literally 'bring back,' hence 'restore' and also 'withdraw.' The original 'bring back' made the journey to English, and even survived into the early 17th century ('reducing often to my memory the conceit of that Roman stoic,' Sir Henry Wotton, *Elements of Architecture* 1624). The sense 'lessen, diminish' seems to be the result of a semantic progression from 'bring back to a particular condition' via 'bring back to order' and 'bring to subjection.'

▶ duct, duke, educate, introduce, produce, redoubt

**redundant**  [17]  Etymologically, something that is *redundant* 'overflows' because there is too much of it. The word comes from the present participle of Latin *redundāre* 'flow back, overflow' (source also of English *redound* [14]). This was a compound verb formed from the prefix *re-* 'back, again' and *undāre* 'rise in waves, surge,' a derivative of *unda* 'wave' (source of English *undulate*).

▶ redound, surround, undulate

**reef**  English has two words *reef*, which both come from the same source, but have reached the language via different routes. That source was Old Norse *rif* 'rib,' a close relative of English *rib*. Amongst its metaphorical senses were 'horizontal section of sail,' which English acquired in the 14th century via Middle Dutch *rif* as *riff*, later *reef*, and 'underwater ridge of rock,' which came into English in the 16th century via Middle Low

German *ref*. The former was put to verbal use in the 17th century in the sense 'furl sails,' which may underlie *reefer* 'marijuana cigarette' [20] -perhaps a 'furled' cigarette.

▶ rib

**reek**  [OE]  *Reek* originally meant 'smoke' (Edinburgh was called *Auld* [old] *Reekie* because of its smoky chimneys, not because it smelled). The word came from a prehistoric Germanic *\*raukiz*, which also produced German *rauch*, Dutch *rook*, Swedish *rök*, and Danish *røk*, all meaning 'smoke.' It is likely that it was related to Latin *ructāre* 'spew out' (source of English *eructate* [17]), in which case the etymological notion underlying *reek* 'smoke' is of something 'belching' out. The English sense 'bad smell' emerged in the 17th century.

▶ eructate

**refer**  [14]  To *refer* something is etymologically to 'carry it back.' The word comes via Old French *referer* from Latin *referre*, a compound verb formed from the prefix *re-* 'back' and *ferre* 'carry' (source of English *fertile* and related to English *bear*). Of its derivatives, *referee* [16] is an English coinage, and *referendum* [19] is an adoption of the neuter gerundive of *referre* – literally, 'that which is to be referred.' *Relātus*, which was used as the past participle of Latin *referre*, has given English *relate*.

▶ bear, referee, referendum

**refine**  see FINE

**reflect**  [15]  To *reflect* something is etymologically to 'bend it back.' The word comes via Old French *reflecter* from Latin *reflectere* 'bend back,' a compound verb formed from the prefix *re-* 'back' and *flectere* 'bend' (source also of English *deflect* [17], *flex* [16], *flexible* [15], *inflect* [15], etc). The word's optical application is a post-Latin development.

▶ deflect, flex, flexible, inflect

**refrain**  *Refrain* 'chorus of a song' [14] and *refrain* 'desist' [14] are different words. The former comes via Old French *refrain* from Provençal *refranh*. This was a derivative of the verb *refranhar*, which went back via Vulgar Latin *\*refrangere* to Latin *refringere* 'break off' (source of English *refract* [17]). The etymological notion underlying the word is that the chorus of a song 'breaks off' and then resumes. *Refrain* 'desist' is descended from Latin *refrēnāre* 'hold back,' a compound verb formed from the prefix *re-* 'back' and *frēnum* 'bridle.' It reached English via Old French *refrener*.

▶ fraction, refract

**refuge**  [14]  A *refuge* is etymologically a place one 'flees' to in order to get away from danger. The word comes via Old French *refuge* from Latin *refugium*, a derivative of *refugere*. This was a compound verb formed from the prefix *re-* 'away' and *fugere* 'flee' (source of English *fugitive* [14] and *fugue* [16]). The derivative *refugee* [17] is an adaptation of *refugié*, the past participle of modern French *refugier* 'take refuge.'

► fugitive, refugee

## refulgent    SEE FLAME

## refuse    [14]    *Refuse* comes via Old French *refuser* from an unrecorded Vulgar Latin *\*refūsāre*. It is not altogether clear where this came from, for it has no direct Latin antecedent. One theory is that it represents a blend of Latin *recūsāre* 'refuse' (source of English *recusant* [16]), a compound verb based on *causa* 'cause,' and *refūtāre* 'rebut' (source of English *refute* [16]), a compound verb based on the element *\*fūt-*, found also in English *confute* [16]. But another long-established school of thought derives it from *refūsus*, the past participle of Latin *refundere* 'pour back' (source of English *refund* [14]) – the underlying notion being of something 'poured back' or 'rejected.' The noun *refuse* 'rubbish' [15] probably comes from Old French *refus* 'refusal,' a derivative of *refuser* 'refuse.'

## refute    SEE BEAT

## regal    [14]    *Regal* and *royal* are doublets: that is to say, they come from the same ultimate source, but have diverged over the centuries. This source was *rēgālis*, a derivative of Latin *rēx* 'king.' This came from Indo-European *\*rēg-*, which also produced the Sanskrit ancestor of English *rajah*, and was a lengthened version of *\*reg-*, source of English *rector, regiment, region, regular, reign, right, rule*, etc. *Regal* was probably borrowed direct from Latin, whereas *royal* was routed via Old French. Also from *rēx* come *regalia* [16] and *regicide* [16].

► rajah, rector, regiment, region, regular, reign, right, royal, rule

## regale    SEE GALLANT

## regard    [14]    The notions of 'looking at something, keeping it in sight' and 'guarding it' are closely linked, and often coexist in single words. *Watch* is an example, and so was Old French *garder*, ancestor of English *guard*. Addition of the prefix *re-* 'back' produced *regarder* 'look back at, keep one's eyes on,' hence simply 'look at.' The Anglo-Norman version of the word gave English *reward*.

► guard, reward, ward

## regatta    [17]    The word *regatta* originated in Italy, and at first denoted a gondola race on the Grand Canal in Venice. It appears to have been derived from a Venetian dialect verb *rigattare* 'contend, fight,' of uncertain origin. The first record of its application to a boat race in England is in June 1775, when a 'regatta' was held on the Thames: the *Public advertiser* noted that 'The Regatta will keep at home many of our Nobility and wealthy Commoners,' and Dr Johnson wrote to his friend Mrs Thrale on June 21 'I am glad you are to be at the regatta.'

## regent    [14]    *Regent* is one of a large family of English words that go back to Latin *regere* 'rule,' a descendant of the Indo-European base *reg-* 'move in a straight line,' hence 'direct, guide, rule.' Others include *correct, direct, dirge, erect, rector, régime* [18], *regimen* [14] (and its more heavily disguised twin *realm*), *regiment* [14] (which originally meant 'government'), *region* [14] (etymologically a 'governed area'), *resurrect, source*, and *surge*. *Regent* itself comes from the present participle of the Latin verb. Related words in Latin include *rēx* 'king' (source of English *regal, regalia, royal*, etc), *rēgula* 'rule' (source of English *rail* 'bar,' *regular, rule*, etc), and *rēgnum* 'kingship' (source of English *reign*); and among other English words from the same Indo-European source are *raj, rich*, and *right*.

► address, correct, direct, dirge, dress, erect, rajah, realm, rector, regiment, region, regular, reign, right, royal, rule

## register    [14]    *Register* comes via Old French *registre* from late Latin *regestum* 'list.' This was a noun use of the past participle of *regerere* 'bring back,' hence 'set down, record,' a compound verb formed from the prefix *re-* 'back, again' and *gerere* 'bring, carry' (source also of English *congest, digest, gesture, jester, suggest*, etc).

► congest, digest, gesture, jester, suggest

## regret    [14]    The origins of *regret* are not altogether clear, but it may mean etymologically 'weep over again.' It was borrowed from Old French *regreter*, which could have been based on a prehistoric Germanic verb *\*grētan* 'weep' (source of archaic English *greet* 'weep').

## regular    [14]    *Regular* 'according to a rule' is the most instantly recognizable English descendant of Latin *rēgula* 'rule' (others include *rail* 'bar' and *rule*). It goes back ultimately to the same Indo-European base as produced Latin *regere* 'rule' (source of English *rector, regent*, etc) and *rēx* 'king' (source of English *regal, royal*, etc). From it was derived the late Latin verb *rēgulāre*, which has given English *regulate* [17], and may also lie behind *rile* 'annoy' [19], a variant of an earlier *roil* which was possibly imported via Old French *ruiler* 'mix mortar.'

► rector, regent, regulate, rile, rule

## regurgitate    SEE GORGE

## rehearse    [13]    To *rehearse* something is etymologically to 'rake it over.' The word comes from Old French *rehercer* 'repeat,' a compound verb based on *hercer* 'harrow.' This was a derivative of the noun *herce* 'large agricultural rake,' from which English gets *hearse*. At first in English too *rehearse* meant simply 'say over again, repeat, recite'; not until the late 16th

century did the modern theatrical meaning begin to emerge.

▶ hearse

**reign** [13] *Reign* goes back via Old French *reignier* to Latin *rēgnāre* 'be king, rule,' a derivative of *rēgnum* 'kingship' (source of English *interregnum* [16]). This was closely related to *rēx* 'king' (source of English *regal, royal*, etc), and also to *regere* 'rule' (source of English *rector, regent*, etc).

▶ interregnum, regent

**reimburse**    see PURSE

**rein** [13] A *rein* is etymologically something that 'retains.' It goes back via Old French *rene* to Vulgar Latin *\*retina*, a descendant of the Latin verb *retinēre* 'hold back,' from which English gets *retain* and *retinue*. The *rein* for horses has no connection with the *rein-* of *reindeer* [14], incidentally; that comes from Old Norse *hreinn* 'reindeer,' which may be of Lappish origin.

▶ retain, retinue

**rejoice** [14] *Rejoice* was adapted from *rejoiss-*, the stem form of Old French *rejoir* 'be joyful.' This was a compound verb formed from the intensive prefix *re-* and *joir* 'be joyful,' which went back to Latin *gaudēre* 'rejoice,' ultimate source of English *joy*. English originally used *rejoice* for 'enjoy the possession of.' This survived until as late as the 16th century ('Many covetous men do we see . . . to whom God gives power to get riches . . . but not liberty to rejoice and use them,' Sir Geoffrey Fenton, *Golden Epistles* 1577), and may lie behind the modern use of *rejoice in* for 'possess.'

▶ joy

**relate** [16] Something that is *related* to something else is etymologically 'carried back' to it. The word is based on *relātus*, the past participle of Latin *referre* 'carry back, refer to' (source of English *refer*). (*Lātus* was not the original past participle of Latin *ferre* 'carry'; it was drafted in from *tollere* 'raise,' source of English *extol* and *tolerate*.) Derivatives in English include *relation* [14] and *relative* [14].

▶ extol, tolerate

**relax**    see RELISH

**release**    see RELISH

**relevant** [16] *Relevant* comes ultimately from the present participle of Latin *relevāre* 'raise,' source of English *relief* and *relieve*. The modern English sense 'appropriate' probably developed from a medieval application of *relevāre* to 'take up,' hence 'take possession of property,' which led to *relevant* being used as a legal term for 'connected with.'

▶ relief, relieve

**relic** [13] A *relic* is etymologically something 'left' behind. The word comes via Old French *relique* from Latin *reliquiae* 'remains, particularly of a dead

saint.' This was a noun use of the feminine plural of *reliquus* 'remaining,' an adjective formed with the prefix *re-* from the base *\*liq-* 'leave' (source also of English *delinquent* [17] – etymologically 'leaving things undone' – and *relinquish* [15], and also of *ellipse, lend*, and *loan*).

▶ delinquent, ellipse, lend, loan, relinquish

**relieve** [14] *Relieve* goes back via Old French *relever* to Latin *relevāre* 'raise again,' a compound verb formed from the prefix *re-* 'again' and *levāre* 'raise' (source of English *elevate, levy*, etc). Its metaphorical extension to 'lighten, alleviate' began in Latin. The derived noun *relief* reached English in two phases. First, in the standard sense 'easing, alleviation,' via Anglo-Norman *relef* in the 14th century; and then, in the 17th century, via French from Italian *relievo* in the sense 'raised area in a design' – a return to the etymological meaning 'raise.'

▶ elevate, levy, relevant

**religion** [12] Latin *religiō* originally meant 'obligation, bond.' It was probably derived from the verb *religāre* 'tie back, tie tight' (source of English *rely*), a compound formed from the prefix *re-* 'back' and *ligāre* 'tie' (source of English *liable, ligament*, etc). It developed the specialized sense 'bond between human beings and the gods,' and from the 5th century it came to be used for 'monastic life' – the sense in which English originally acquired it via Old French *religion*. 'Religious practices' emerged from this, but the word's standard modern meaning did not develop until as recently as the 16th century.

▶ ally, liable, ligament, ligature, rely

**relinquish**    see RELIC

**relish** [16] Ultimately, *relax* [15], *release* [13], and *relish* are all the same word. They go back to Latin *relaxāre* 'loosen,' a compound verb formed from the prefix *re-* 'back' and *laxāre*, a derivative of *laxus* 'loose' (from which English gets *languish* [13] and *lax* [14]). *Relax* was acquired from the Latin verb itself, while *release* came via Old French *relaisser* (the notion of 'loosening' having led on to 'letting go'). *Relish* came from Old French *relais*, a noun derived from *relaisser*; the sense 'taste' came from the idea of what is 'released' or 'left behind' after the food or drink has been swallowed.

▶ languish, lax, relax, release

**reluctant** [17] To be *reluctant* about doing something is etymologically to 'struggle against' it. The word comes from the present participle of Latin *reluctārī*, a compound verb formed from the prefix *re-* 'against' and *luctārī* 'struggle.' Among the first English writers to employ it was John Milton, who used it in the literal Latin sense, describing the writhing Satan: 'a monstrous serpent on his belly prone, reluctant, but in vain,' *Paradise Lost* 1667. 'Unwilling, averse,' a metaphorical extension which saw the light of day in Latin, made its debut in English at the start of the 18th century.

**rely** [14] *Rely* comes via Old French *relier* from Latin *religāre* 'tie back, tie tightly' (source also of English *religion*). It was a compound verb formed from the prefix *re-* 'back' and *ligāre* 'tie' (source of English *ally*, *liable*, *ligament*, etc). It was originally used for 'assemble,' which by the 16th century had developed via 'come together with one's friends' to 'depend.' The derivative *reliable* is first recorded in 16th-century Scottish English, but did not enter general usage until the mid 19th century.

▶ ally, liable, ligament, ligature, religion

**remain** [14] Latin *manēre* meant 'stay' (it has given English *manor*, *mansion*, *permanent* [15], etc). Combination with the prefix *re-* 'back, in place' produced *remanēre* 'stay behind, remain,' which passed into English via Old French *remanoir*. Its present participle gave English *remnant* [14]. A variant of *remanoir* was *remaindre*, which is the source of English *remainder* [15].

▶ manor, mansion, permanent, remnant

**remark** [17] *Remark* originated in French as an intensified version of *marquer*, in the sense 'observe, notice' (French had acquired *marquer* from the same Germanic source as produced English *mark*). The sense 'say something' emerged from the notion of 'making a verbal observation.' The derived *remarkable* [17] soon developed the sense 'extraordinary' from its original 'worthy of being noticed.'

▶ mark

**remedy** [13] *Remedy* is closely related to *medicine*. It comes via Anglo-Norman *remedie* from Latin *remedium* 'medicine' a noun formed from the same stem, *med-*, as produced *medērī* 'heal' (source of English *medical*, *medicine*, etc). The extension in meaning from 'medicine' to 'something that corrects a wrong' took place in Latin.

▶ medicine

**remember** [14] Latin *memor* meant 'mindful' (it gave English *memorial*, *memory*, etc, and went back ultimately to the Indo-European base *\*men-*, *\*mon-* 'think,' source of a wide range of English vocabulary from *comment* to *mind*). From it in the post-classical period was formed the verb *rememorārī* 'recall to mind,' which passed into English via Old French *remembrer*.

▶ comment, mental, mind

**remind** [17] *Remind* is an English coinage. It was formed, apparently in the 1640s, from the prefix *re-* and the verb *mind*, in the sense 'remember' (now restricted to Scottish English). It may have been modelled on the now obsolete *rememorate*, which came from the same Latin source as English *remember*. It was origi-

nally used for 'remember,' but the modern sense 'cause to remember' emerged as early as the 1660s.

**reminiscence** see MEMORY

**remnant** see REMAIN

**remonstrate** see MONSTER

**remorse** [14] *Remorse* etymologically denotes the 'biting' of conscience. The word comes ultimately from medieval Latin *remorsus* 'torment,' a derivative of Latin *remordēre* 'bite back,' hence 'torment.' This was a compound verb formed from the prefix *re-* 'back, again' and *mordēre* 'bite' (source of English *morsel*). The noun was used in the expression *remorsus conscientiae* 'torment of conscience,' which passed into Old French as *remors de conscience*. English adopted this at the end of the 14th century, and by the beginning of the 15th century *remorse* was being used on its own in the same sense.

▶ morsel

**remove** [14] The *-move* of *remove* comes from the same source as English *move* itself – Latin *movēre* 'move.' Combination with the prefix *re-* 'again, back' produced *removēre* 'move back, move away,' which reached English via Old French *removeir*. The Latin past participle *remōtus* gave English *remote* [15], etymologically 'moved away to a distant place.'

▶ move, remote

**renaissance** see NATIVE

**rend** see RENT

**render** [14] Latin *reddere* meant 'give back.' It was a compound verb formed from the prefix *re-* 'back' and *dāre* 'give' (source of English *date, donate*, etc). In Vulgar Latin this was changed to *\*rendere*, perhaps under the influence of *prendere* 'take,' which passed into English via Old French *rendre*. *Rent* 'payment' goes back to the past participle of *\*rendere*.

▶ date, donate, rent

**rendezvous** [16] *Rendezvous* was borrowed from French *rendez-vous*, a lexicalization of *rendez-vous*, the imperative plural of *se rendre*. This meant literally 'present yourself' – that is, at a particular place. English first used the word as a verb in the mid 17th century.

**renegade** [16] A *renegade* is etymologically a 'denier.' The word is an anglicization of Spanish *renegado*, a term picked up via Anglo-Hispanic contact at the end of the 16th century and itself quite commonly used in English until the 18th century. *Renegado* itself comes from medieval Latin *renegātus*, a noun use of the past participle of Latin *renegāre* 'deny' (source of English *renegue* [16]). This was a compound verb formed from the intensive prefix *re-* and *negāre* 'deny' (source of English *deny* [13] and *negative* [14]).

▶ deny, negative, renegue

**rennet** [15] *Rennet* probably goes back to an unrecorded Old English *\*rynet*. This appears to have been derived fron the verb *run*, which was used dialectally into the 20th century for 'curdle.' The underlying notion is of the solid parts of milk 'running' together and coagulating.

▶ run

**renounce** SEE PRONOUNCE

**renown** [14] To be *renowned* is etymologically to be 'named again,' and hence to be 'famous.' The word comes from Old French *renon*, a derivative of the verb *renomer* 'make famous.' This was formed from the prefix *re-* 'again' and *nomer* 'name,' a descendant of Latin *nōmināre*, from which English gets *nominate*.

▶ nominate, noun

**rent** English has two words *rent*. The one meaning 'payment' [12] comes via Old French *rente* from Vulgar Latin *\*rendita*, a noun use of the feminine past participle of *\*rendere* 'give back' (source of English *render*). *Rent* 'tear, rift' [16] comes from the verb *rend* [OE], which goes back to Old English *rendan*. Its ultimate antecedents are not known, although it may be related to Sanskrit *rándhra-* 'split.'

▶ render

**repair** *Repair* 'mend' [14] and *repair* 'go' [14] are two distinct words. The former comes via Old French *reparer* from Latin *reparāre* 'put back in order,' a compound verb formed from the prefix *re-* 'back' and *parāre* 'put in order' (source of English *prepare*). *Repair* 'go' is ultimately the same word as *repatriate* [17]. Both go back to late Latin *repatriāre* 'go home,' a compound verb based on Latin *patria* 'homeland' (a relative of English *father*, *patron*, etc). *Repatriate* was acquired direct from Latin, whereas *repair* was routed via Old French *repairer*.

▶ prepare / father, paternal, patriot, patron, repatriate

**repast** [14] The closest English relative of *repast* is not *past* but *pasture*. It was borrowed from Old French *repast*, a derivative of *repaistre* 'feed.' This in turn went back to late Latin *repascere* 'feed again,' a compound verb formed from the prefix *re-* 'again' and *pascere* 'feed' (whose past participial stem formed the basis of English *pasture*).

▶ pasture

**repeal** SEE APPEAL

**repeat** [14] The *-peat* of *repeat* comes ultimately from Latin *petere* 'go to, seek,' which has also given English *appetite*, *compete*, *impetuous*, *perpetual* [14], *petition* [14], and *petulant* [16]. Addition of the prefix *re-* 'back, again' produced *repetere* 'go back to,' which reached English via Old French *repeter*.

▶ appetite, compete, impetuous, perpetual, petition, petulant

**repel** SEE PULSE

**repertory** [16] A *repertory* is etymologically a list of things 'found.' The word was adopted from late Latin *repertōrium*, a derivative of *reperīre* 'find out.' This was formed from the base *\*per-* 'attempt,' which has also given English *experience*, *expert*, *peril*, *pirate*, etc. The sense 'list of plays, pieces of, music, etc performed' was introduced from French in the 19th century, along with the French form *repertoire*.

▶ experience, expert, peril, pirate

**replete** SEE FULL

**reply** [14] Etymologically, *reply* means 'fold back.' It comes ultimately from Latin *replicāre* 'fold back, unfold,' a compound verb formed from the prefix *re-* 'back' and *plicāre* 'fold' (source of English *ply* and related to English *fold*). This came to be used metaphorically for 'go over again, repeat' (whence English *replicate* [16]), and also as a legal term for 'respond.' In this latter sense it passed into English via Old French *replier*.

▶ fold, ply, replicate

**report** [14] To *report* something is etymologically to 'carry it back.' The word was borrowed from Old French *reporter*, which went back to Latin *reportāre*, a compound verb formed from the prefix *re-* 'back' and *portāre* 'carry' (source of English *import*, *portable*, *porter*, etc). The metaphorical application to 'bringing back news' developed in Latin.

▶ export, import, port, portable, porter

**repose** *Repose* 'rest' [15] and *repose* 'place' [15] (as in 'repose confidence in someone') are distinct words in English. The former comes via Old French *reposer* from late Latin *repausāre*, a compound verb based on *pausāre* 'rest' (source of English *pause*). The latter was an English coinage, formed from the prefix *re-* and the verb *pose* 'place.' It was modelled on Latin *repōnere* 'replace,' whose derivative *repositorium* has given English *repository* [15].

▶ pause / position, repository

**reprehensible** SEE REPRIEVE

**represent** [14] English borrowed *represent* from Latin *repraesentāre*, which meant 'present again, bring back,' hence 'show.' It was a compound verb formed from the prefix *re-* 'back, again' and *praesentāre*, source of English *present*. The notion of 'standing in the place of another' is a post-classical development.

▶ present

**repress** SEE PRESS

**reprieve** [16] *Reprieve* originally meant 'send back to prison' ('Of this treason he was found guilty, and reprieved in the Tower a long time,' Edmund Campion, *History of Ireland* 1571), but since this was often the alternative to execution, the word soon came to mean 'suspend a death sentence.' The form in which it originally occurs, at the end of the 15th century, is *repry*, and it is not clear where the *v* came from. *Repry* was borrowed from *repris*, the past participle of Old French *reprendre* 'take back.' This in turn went back to Latin *reprehendere* (source of English *reprehensible* [14]), a compound verb formed from the prefix *re-* 'back, again' and *prehendere* 'seize, take' (source of English *prison, prize, surprise*, etc). The medieval Latin derivative *reprehensālia* produced English *reprisal* [15], and the feminine past participle of Old French *reprendre* was the source of English *reprise* [14].

▸ apprehend, prison, prize, reprisal, reprise, surprise

**reproach**   [15]   The *-proach* of *reproach* is the same as that of *approach*. Both go back ultimately to Latin *prope* 'near.' From this was formed the Vulgar Latin verb *\*repropiāre* 'bring back near,' which, by the time it reached Old French as *reprochier*, had evolved metaphorically towards the notion of 'bringing somebody face to face with something for which they should be blamed.'

▸ approach

**reprobate**   [16]   The Latin prefix *re-* usually denoted 'return' or 'repetition,' but it was also used for 'reversal of a previous condition.' This usage lies behind Latin *reprobāre* (source of English *reprove* [14]), a compound verb based on *probāre* 'test, approve' (source of English *prove*). It meant 'disapprove,' and its past participle *reprobātus* was used in post-classical Latin to denote a person 'disapproved or abandoned by God' because of their wickedness.

▸ probation, probe, prove, reprove

**republic**   [17]   Latin *rēspublica* meant literally a 'public matter.' It was a compound noun formed from *rēs* 'thing, matter' (source of English *real*) and *publicus* 'public' (source of English *public*). It was used as a term for the 'state' as governed by its people, and it was first taken over in English in the sense 'state governed by elected representatives of the people, rather than by a king' in the first decade of the 17th century.

▸ public, real

**repudiate**   [16]   *Repudiate* originally meant 'divorce one's wife.' It comes from Latin *repudiāre* 'divorce, reject,' a derivative of the noun *repudium* 'divorce.' It has been suggested that the ultimate source of this may be *pēs* 'foot' (source of English *pedal*), in which case its underlying meaning would be virtually 'kick out.'

**repugnant**   see PUGNACIOUS

**request**   [14]   *Request* and *require* [14] come from the same ultimate source: Latin *requīrere*. This was a compound verb formed from the prefix *re-* 'again' and *quaerere* 'ask, search' (source of English *enquire*, *question*, etc). It originally meant 'seek again, ask for

again,' and it passed into Vulgar Latin as *\*requaerere*, whose feminine past participle *\*requaesita* has given English *request*. 'Ask for' gradually passed via 'demand' into 'need,' and it was in this sense that English acquired the verb *\*requaerere*, through Old French *requere*, as *require*. Derivatives include *requisite* [15] and *requisition* [16].

▸ enquire, inquest, query, question, requisition

**requite**   see QUIT

**rescind**   see SCISSORS

**rescue**   see QUASH

**resemble**   [14]   *Resemble* goes back ultimately to Latin *similis* 'like,' source of English *similar*. From it was formed the verb *similāre* 'imitate,' which passed into Old French as *sembler* 'be like, seem' (source of English *semblance*). Addition of the intensive prefix *re-* produced *resembler* 'be very like' – whence English *resemble*.

▸ similar

**resent**   [17]   Etymologically, to *resent* something is to 'feel it strongly.' The word was borrowed from early modern French *resentir*, a compound verb formed from the intensive prefix *re-* and *sentir* 'feel' (a relative of English *sense, sentiment*, etc). It had a range of meanings in English in the 17th and 18th centuries, including its original 'feel strongly' and also simply 'experience a particular emotion' ('God resents an infinite satisfaction in the accomplishment of his own will,' Robert Boyle, *Treatise of Seraphic Love* 1648), but gradually they all gave way to 'feel aggrieved at.'

▸ sensation, sense, sentiment

**reside**   [15]   The *-side* of *reside* has no connection with English *side*. It comes from Latin *sedēre* 'settle' (source of English *sedentary, session*, etc and related to *sit*). Combination with the prefix *re-* 'back' produced *residēre* 'settle back, remain in place, rest,' which passed into English via its present participle as *resident* 'settling permanently in a place' [14]. *Reside* is either a back-formation from this or a borrowing from French *résider*. The past participle of *residēre* was *residuus*, whose neuter form *residuum* was used as a noun meaning 'that which settles back,' hence 'that which is left behind.' It passed into English via Old French as *residue* [14].

▸ residue, sedentary, session, sit

**resign**   see SIGN

**resin**   [14]   *Resin* comes via Old French *resine* and Latin *resīna* from Greek *rhētínē* 'resin,' a word of unknown origin. A collateral form that arose in medieval Latin was *rosīna*, which has given English *rosin* [14].

▸ rosin

**resist**   see STATUE

**resolve**   see SOLVE

**resonant**   see SOUND

**resource**   see SURGE

**respect**   [14]   *Respect* and *respite* [13] are ultimately the same word. Both go back to *respectus*, the past participle of Latin *respicere* 'look back at,' hence 'look at, regard, consider.' This was a compound verb formed from the prefix *re-* 'back' and *specere* 'look' (source of English *spectacle, speculate*, etc). *Respectus* passed into English, perhaps via Old French *respect*, as *respect*, in the sense 'regard, relation' (as in *with respect to*); the key modern meaning 'deference, esteem' developed towards the end of the 16th century. An earlier borrowing of *respectus* into Old French produced *respit*, which preserved another meaning of the Latin word, 'refuge.' This was the source of English *respite*.

▶ inspect, respite, spectacle, spectator

**respire**   see SPIRIT

**resplendent**   see SPLENDID

**respond**   [16]   *Respond* comes from Latin *respondēre* 'promise in return,' a compound verb formed from the prefix *re-* 'back' and *spondēre* 'promise' (source of English *sponsor, spouse*, etc). The notion of 'obligation' survives in the derivative *responsible* [16]. The Italian descendant of *respondēre* is *rispondere*, whose feminine past participle *risposta* has given English *riposte* [18] (originally a fencing term).

▶ sponsor, spouse

**rest**   English has two words *rest* in current general use: 'repose' [OE] and 'remainder' [15]. The former is a general Germanic term, with relatives in German (*rast*) and Swedish (*rast*), but its ultimate antecedents are uncertain. The latter comes via Old French *rester* 'remain' from Latin *restāre* 'stand back,' a compound verb formed from the prefix *re-* 'back' and *stāre* 'stand' (source of English *statue, status*, etc and related to English *stand*). Amongst its derivatives is *restive* [16], which has completely reversed its meaning over the centuries. It comes from Vulgar Latin *\*restīvus* 'inclined to remain, unwilling to move,' and reached English via Old French *restif* in the sense 'inactive.' The modern meaning 'restless, uneasy' comes partly from an intermediate 'refractory, hard to control,' but also through association with the unrelated *rest* 'repose.'

▶ arrest, stand, station, statue

**restaurant**   [19]   A *restaurant* is etymologically a place where one is 'restored' or refreshed. The word was borrowed from French *restaurant*, a noun use of the present participle of *restaurer* 'restore,' whose Old French ancestor *restorer* gave English *restore* [13]. This went back to Latin *restaurāre* 'restore, repair,' a compound verb based on an earlier *instaurāre* 'restore,

renew, repeat' – a word of uncertain origin which may have been related to Greek *stavrós* 'stake, pale.'

▶ restore, store

**restitution**   see STATUE

**restive**   see REST

**restrain**   see STRAIN

**result**   [15]   Etymologically, to *result* is to 'jump backwards.' The word comes ultimately from Latin *resultāre* 'jump backwards,' hence 'rebound,' a compound verb formed from the prefix *re-* 'back' and *saltāre* 'jump' (source of English *insult, sauté*, etc). In medieval Latin it came to be used figuratively for 'happen as a consequence,' the sense in which English borrowed it. It was not used as a noun until the 17th century.

▶ assault, insult, sauté

**resurrection**   see SURGE

**retail**   [14]   *Retail* etymologically denotes the sale of 'cut-off' bits, hence sale in small quantities. It comes from Old French *retaille* 'piece cut off,' a derivative of *retaillier* 'cut up.' This was a compound verb formed from the intensive prefix *re-* and *taillier* 'cut' (source of English *tailor*). Its use in English for 'sell in small quantities' was probably inspired by the Italian *retagliare*, which has the same meaning. The figurative sense 'relate, tell' appeared at the end of the 16th century.

▶ tailor

**retaliate**   [17]   To *retaliate* is etymologically to give someone 'so much' or an equal amount in return for what they have given you. Its ultimate source is Latin *tālis* 'suchlike' (source of French *tel* 'such'). This formed the basis of a noun *tāliō* 'punishment equal in severity to the wrong that occasioned it,' which was combined with the prefix *re-* 'back' to create the verb *retaliāre* 'repay in kind' – whence English *retaliate*.

**reticent**   [19]   The ultimate source of *reticent* is Latin *tacēre* 'be silent' (source of English *tacit* and *taciturn*). Combination with the intensive prefix *re-* produced *reticēre* 'keep silent,' whose present participle gave English *reticent*. It was preceded into the language by over two hundred years by the derived noun *reticence*.

▶ tacit, taciturn

**reticule**   [18]   *Reticule* is a now superannuated term for a small handbag. It alludes to the fact that such bags were originally made from netted fabric. The Latin word for 'net' was *rēte*, whose diminutive form *rēticulum* was used for 'netted bag' – whence, via French *réticule*, English *reticule*. From *rēticulum* was derived *rēticulātus* 'having a network pattern,' which has given English *reticulated* [18] (used by Dr Johnson in his famous definition of *network*: 'any thing reticulated or decussated, at equal distances, with interstices between the intersections,' 1755). *Rēte* was also the source of medieval Latin *retina* 'inner lining of the eyeball,' borrowed by English as *retina* [14].

▶ retina

**retinue**   [14]    A *retinue* is etymologically 'that which is retained.' The word was borrowed from Old French *retenue*, the feminine past participle of *retenir* 'keep, restrain' (source of English *retain* [14]). This in turn went back via Vulgar Latin *\*retenēre* to Latin *retinēre* 'hold back,' a compound verb formed from the prefix *re-* 'back' and *tenēre* 'hold' (source of English *contain, obtain*, etc). The notion behind *retinue* is of a body of men 'retained' in one's service. Another English descendant of *retinēre* is *rein*.

▶ contain, detain, obtain, rein, retain

**retort**    see TORMENT

**retreat**   [14]    *Retreat* and *retract* [15] are ultimately the same word. Both go back to Latin *retrahere* 'draw back,' a compound verb formed from the prefix *re-* 'back' and *trahere* 'draw, pull' (source of English *tractor*). This passed into Old French as *retraire*, and its past participle *retrait* came to be used as a noun meaning 'withdrawal' – whence English *retreat*. Meanwhile the past participle of *retrahere, retractus*, had been used as the basis of a new Latin verb, *retractāre*, which passed into English via Old French *retracter* as *retract*.

▶ contract, distract, retract, tractor

**retrench**   [16]    *Retrench* originally meant literally 'dig a new trench as a second line of defence.' It was borrowed from early modern French *retrencher*, a descendant of Old French *retrenchier*. This was a compound verb formed from the prefix *re-* 'again' and *trenchier* 'cut off' (source of English *trench, trenchant*, etc).

The standard present-day sense of *retrench*, 'cut back, economize,' first recorded in the 17th century, is a return to the underlying meaning of French *retrencher*.        •

▶ trench, trenchant

**retribution**    see TRIBE

**retrieve**   [15]    To *retrieve* something is etymologically to 'refind' it. The word comes from *retreuv-*, the stem of Old French *retrover*. This was a compound verb formed from the prefix *re-* 'again' and *trover* 'find' (ancestor of modern French *trouver* and source of English *troubadour* and *trove*, as in *treasure trove*). Its original application in English was to dogs refinding game that had been temporarily lost (hence the term *retriever* [15]).

▶ troubadour, trove

**retrograde**    see GRADUAL

**return**   [14]    The origins of *return* are in Vulgar Latin. There, Latin *tornāre* (source of English *turn*), which originally meant 'turn on a lathe,' was combined with the prefix *re-* 'back' to produce *\*retornāre* 'turn back,' which passed via Old French *retorner* into English as *return*.

▶ turn

**reveal**   [14]    To *reveal* something is etymologically to 'unveil' it. The word comes via Old French *reveler* from Latin *revēlāre* 'unveil, disclose,' a compound verb formed from the prefix *re-* 'back' (in the sense 'reverting to a former condition') and *vēlum* 'veil' (source of English *veil*).

▶ veil

**reveille**    see VIGIL

**revenge**    see VINDICATE

**reverberate**   [16]    Latin *verbera* meant 'whips, rods' (it was related to Greek *rhábdos* 'stick'). From it was derived the verb *verberāre* 'whip, beat,' which with the addition of the prefix *re-* 'back' produced *reverberāre* 'beat back.' When this first arrived in English it was used literally (Thomas Coryat, for instance, in his *Crudities* 1611, wrote of 'a strong wall to repulse and reverberate the furious waves of the sea'), but it was not long before the metaphorical application to the re-echoing of sounds took over.

**revere**   [17]    *Revere* goes back ultimately to Latin *verērī* 'hold in awe or fear,' a possible distant relative of English *aware* and *beware*. Addition of the intensive prefix *re-* produced *reverērī*, which English probably acquired via French *révérer*. The derivative *reverend* [15], which comes from the Latin gerundive *reverendus* 'to be revered,' has been used from earliest times as a title of respect for clergymen. That was for long a common application of *reverent* [14] too, which came from the Latin present participial stem *reverent-*.

**reverse**    see VERSE

**revile**    see VILIFY

**revise**    see VISIT

**revive**    see VIVID

**revoke**    see VOCATION

**revolt**   [16]    Latin *volvere* meant 'roll' (it is the source of English *vault* 'jump'). Addition of the prefix *re-* 'back' produced *revolvere* 'roll back, unroll,' hence 'come to the original point, return, revolve.' English acquired this as *revolve* [14], and also took over its late Latin derivative *revolūtiō* via Old French as *revolution* [14], whose leading modern meaning 'violent overthrow of a government' emerged in the 16th century via an intermediate 'complete reversal.' The term *revolver* [19] for a pistol with a revolving chamber was apparently coined by its inventor Samuel Colt. *Revolt* itself came via French *révolter* and Italian *rivoltare* from Vulgar Latin *\*revolvitāre*, a derivative of *revolvere*.

▶ vault, volume

**reward**   [14]    *Reward* is ultimately the same word as *regard*, and indeed was originally used interchangeably with it. It came from *rewarder*, the Anglo-

Norman version of Old French *regarder*, source of English *regard*. The modern meaning of *reward*, 'recompense,' which goes back to the 14th century, presumably arose from the notion of 'regarding' someone with favour.

▶ guard, regard

**rhapsody** [16] A *rhapsody* is etymologically the product of a 'weaver of songs.' It goes back ultimately to Greek *rhapsōidíā* 'epic poem recited on a single occasion,' which was derived from *rhapsōidós* 'writer of such poems.' This was a compound formed from *rháptein* 'sew together' and *ōidé* 'song' (source of English *ode, parody, prosody*, etc). The somewhat trivialized modern meaning 'self-indulgently effusive piece of verse, music, etc' emerged in the 17th century.

▶ melody, ode, parody, prosody

**rhetoric** [14] In ancient Greece, a *rhḗtōr* was a 'public speaker,' an 'orator.' The word went back to a prehistoric Indo-European base *wer- 'speak, say,' which also produced English *verb* and *word*. From it was derived the adjective *rhētorikós*, which passed into English as a noun via Latin *rhētorica* and Old French *rethorique*.

▶ verb, word

**rheumatic** [14] Greek *rheuma* meant literally 'flow, stream' (it came ultimately from the same Indo-European base as produced English *stream*, and was a close relative of the Greek verb *rhein* 'flow,' which provides the second halves of English *catarrh* and *diarrhoea*). It was used for a 'watery discharge from the body,' and was borrowed into English (via late Latin *rheuma* and Old French *reume*) as *rheum* [14] in the sense 'mucous discharge from the eyes or nose.' Pains in the joints were in former times thought to be caused by watery secretions within the body, and so towards the end of the 17th century the term *rheumatism* was applied to them.

▶ catarrh, diarrhoea, rhyme, rhythm

**rhinoceros** [13] *Rhinoceros* means literally 'nose-horn.' The term was coined in Greek from *rhīno-*, the stem form of *rhīs* 'nose,' and *kéras* 'horn' (a distant relative of English *horn*). Greek *rhīnókerōs* reached English via Latin *rhīnocerōs*. The abbreviated form *rhino* is first recorded in the 1880s.

▶ antirrhinum, horn, keratin

**rhizome** see LIQUORICE

**rhododendron** [17] A *rhododendron* is etymologically a 'rose-tree.' The term comes from Greek *rhodódendron*, a compound formed from *rhódon* 'rose' (apparently a relative of English *rose*) and *déndron* 'tree' (source of English *dendrite* [18] and *dendrochronology* [20]). This denoted the 'oleander,' an application it retained through Latin *rhododendron* into English. The first record of its use for the plant we now

know as the rhododendron dates from the mid 17th century.

▶ rose

**rhubarb** [14] The Greeks had two words for 'rhubarb': *rhéon*, which was borrowed from Persian *rēwend*, and which evolved into Latin *rheum*, now the plant's scientific name; and *rha*, which is said to have come from *Rha*, an ancient name of the river Volga, in allusion to the fact that rhubarb was once grown on its banks (rhubarb is native to China, and was once imported to Europe via Russia). In medieval Latin rhubarb became known as *rha barbarum* 'barbarian rhubarb, foreign rhubarb,' again with reference to the plant's exotic origins; and in due course association with Latin *rheum* altered this to *rheubarbarum*. It passed into English via Vulgar Latin *rheubarbum* and Old French *reubarbe*.

▶ barbarian

**rhyme** [12] Etymologically, *rhyme* and *rhythm* are the same word. Both go back to medieval Latin *rythmus* 'rhythm,' but whereas *rhythm* has reached us almost unchanged, *rhyme* has come via a branch line. The sort of accented verse to which the medieval Latin word was applied commonly rhymed, and so when *rythmus* passed into early Old French as *ritme*, it carried connotations of 'rhyming' with it. This later developed to *rime*, and when English borrowed it as *rime*, it still contained the notion of 'rhythm'; but by the 13th century 'rhyme' was becoming its main meaning. The spelling *rhyme*, which emerged around 1600, represents a conscious partial return to the word's ultimate ancestors, Latin *rhythmus* and Greek *rhuthmós*.

▶ rhythm

**rhythm** [16] *Rhythm* goes back ultimately to Greek *rhuthmós*. This originally meant 'recurring motion,' and was related to the verb *rhein* 'flow' (source of English *catarrh* and *diarrhoea*). It was subsequently applied to 'recurrent accents in verse,' in which sense it passed into English via Latin *rhythmus*. (Later Old French alteration of the word led to English *rhyme*.)

▶ catarrh, diarrhoea, rheumatic, rhyme

**rib** [OE] *Rib* is a widespread Germanic word, which goes back to a prehistoric *rebjō*, source also of German *rippe*, Dutch *rib*, Swedish *ribba* 'lath,' etc. Its Old Norse form *rif* is the ancestor of English *reef*. Outside Germanic it is related to Russian *rebro* 'rib.'

▶ reef

**ribald** [13] *Ribald* was originally a noun, a derogatory term meaning 'retainer or dependent of low status.' It was borrowed from Old French *ribaut*, a derivative of the verb *riber* 'sleep around.' This in turn went back to Old High German *rīban* 'rub,' hence 'copulate.' It was not used as an adjective until the early 16th century.

**rice** [13] The word *rice* is presumably, like the plant it names, of oriental origin; its ancestor may well be represented in Sanskrit *vrīhi-*. It first appeared in Europe as Greek *órūza*. This passed into Latin as *oryza*, and eventually spread throughout the languages of Europe: French *riz*, Italian *riso*, Spanish *arroz*, German *reis*, Dutch *rijst*, Swedish and Russian *ris*, Welsh *reis*, Lithuanian *rysai*, English *rice*, etc.

**rich** [OE] The original meaning of *rich* was 'mighty, noble.' It goes back ultimately to the Indo-European base *\*reg-* 'move in a straight line,' hence 'direct,' hence 'rule,' source of English *right*, Latin *rēx* 'king' (ancestor of English *regal, royal*, etc), and Latin *regere* 'rule' (ancestor of English *regent, regiment*, etc). The Old Celtic equivalent of Latin *rēx* was *rīx* 'king.' This was borrowed into prehistoric Germanic, where it subsequently evolved into German *reich*, Dutch *rijk*, Swedish *rik*, Danish *rig*, and English *rich*. (It was also taken over by the Romance languages, giving French *riche*, Italian *ricco*, etc.) The sense 'mighty, noble' survived in English into the late Middle Ages, but 'wealthy' had started to develop in Germanic, and eventually saw off 'mighty.'
▶ regal, right, royal

**rid** [13] The verb *rid* was borrowed from Old Norse *rythja*, ancestor of modern Swedish *rödja*, Danish *rydde*, and Norwegian *rydja*. This in turn went back to a prehistoric Germanic *\*rudjan*. Its past participle *rid* has been used in the context *be rid of, get rid of* since the 15th century. *Riddance* is a 16th-century English coinage.

**riddle** [OE] English has two separate words *riddle*. The 'puzzling' sort of *riddle* is etymologically somthing you 'read.' For it originated as a derivative of Old English *rǣdan*, the ancestor of modern English *read*. One of its earlier meanings was 'interpret' – hence *riddle*. *Riddle* 'sieve' goes back to a prehistoric German *khrid-* 'shake,' which also produced German dialect *reiter* 'seive.' It is also related to Latin *crībrum* 'seive' and *cernere* 'separate' (source of English *decree, discern, secret*, etc).
▶ read / certain, decree, discern, secret

**ride** [OE] *Ride* is a widespread Germanic verb, with close relatives in German *reiten*, Dutch *rijden*, Swedish *rida*, and Danish *ride*. It apparently has connections in the Celtic languages – Irish *rīadaim* 'ride' and Gaulish *rēda* 'chariot,' for instance – but its ultimate provenance is unclear.
▶ raid, road

**ridge** [OE] Old English *hrycg* denoted 'the back,' as its modern Germanic relatives – German *rücken*, Dutch *rug*, Swedish *rygg*, and Danish *ryg* – still do. But a gradual semantic focussing on the 'backbone' led by the 14th century to the emergence of 'long narrow raised area,' today's main meaning. It goes back

to a prehistoric Germanic *\*khrugjaz*, which may have been related to Sanskrit *kruñc-* 'be crooked' – in which case the notion underlying the word would be of a 'bent back.'

**riding** [11] Until 1974 Yorkshire was divided for administrative purposes into three *ridings*. The word has no connection with *ride*. It means etymologically 'third part.' It was borrowed from Old Norse *thrithjungr* 'third part,' a derivative of *thrithi* 'third.' Its original English form was *\*thrithing*, later *thriding* or *triding*, and it eventually lost its initial *t* through assimilation into the *t* of the preceding *east* and *west*.
▶ three

**right** [OE] *Right* goes back ultimately to the Indo-European base *\*reg-* 'move in a straight line,' hence 'direct,' hence 'rule,' which also produced English *rich* and Latin *rēx* 'king' (source of English *regal, royal*, etc). Combination with the past participial suffix *\*-to-* resulted in Latin *rēctus* 'straight, right,' which lies behind English *rectify, rectum*, etc, and prehistoric Germanic *\*rekhtaz*, which has evolved into German and Dutch *recht*, Swedish *rätt*, Danish *ret*, and English *right*. The use of the word as the opposite of *left*, paralleled in German and Dutch but not in the Scandinavian languages, derives from the notion that the right hand is the 'correct' hand to use. (French *droit* 'right' goes back to Latin *dīrēctus*, a derivative of *rēctus*.) The derived *righteous* [OE] etymologically means 'in the right way'; it was compounded in the Old English period from *riht* 'right' and *wīs* 'way' (ancestor of the modern English suffix *-wise*).
▶ address, direct, raj, rector, regal, regiment, royal

**rigmarole** [18] *Rigmarole* is a corruption of an earlier *ragman roll*, a term first encountered in the late 13th century. It denoted a roll of parchment used in a gambling game. The roll had things written on it, such as names, with pieces of string attached to them, and participants had to select a string at random. The word *ragman* may have been a contraction of *ragged man*, perhaps in allusion to the appearance of the roll, with all its bits of string hanging from it. *Ragman roll* eventually came to be used for any 'list' or 'catalogue,' and *ragman* itself denoted a 'long rambling discourse' in 16th-century Scottish English – the meaning which had somehow transferred itself to *rigmarole* when it emerged in the early 18th century.

**rile** see REGULAR

**ring** [OE] English has two distinct words *ring*. The one meaning 'circle' goes back to a prehistoric Germanic *\*khrenggaz*, which also produced German, Dutch, Swedish, and Danish *ring* (not to mention the Finnish borrowing *rengas*). It may be related to Old Church Slavonic *kragu* 'circle.' The Germanic form was taken over by Old French as *ranc*, from which English gets *rank*, and also as *renc*, which may be the source of English *rink* [18]. *Ring* 'chime' presumably goes back to a prehistoric Germanic ancestor that imitated the sound of clanging, and also produced German and Dutch *ringen*, Swedish *ringa*, and Danish *ringe* (the suggestion that it contains some reference to the circular motion of tolling bells is attractive, but has no basis in fact).

▶ range, rank, rink

**ripe**  [OE]  *Ripe* is restricted to the West Germanic languages – it has relatives in German *reif* and Dutch *rijp*. Its antecedents are uncertain, but some have linked it with *reap* [OE], as if its underlying meaning is 'ready for harvesting.' And *reap* itself may go back to an Indo-European base *rei- 'tear, scratch,' and hence denote etymologically 'strip' the fruits, seeds, etc from plants.

**riparian**  SEE RIVER

**riposte**  SEE RESPOND

**rise**  [OE]  Not surprisingly, *rise* and *raise* are closely related. Both go back to a common prehistoric Germanic ancestor meaning 'go up.' This reached English directly as *rise*, while its causative derivative, meaning 'cause to go up,' has given English *raise*, and also *rear*. The derived *arise* is of long standing. It is not clear what the word's ultimate ancestry may be; some have linked it with Latin *rīvus* 'stream' (source of English *rivulet*), from the notion of a stream 'rising' in a particular place.

▶ raise, rear

**risk**  [17]  The ultimate origins of *risk* have never been satisfactorily explained. English acquired it via French *risque* from Italian *risco*, a derivative of the verb *riscare* 'run into danger,' but there speculation takes over. One persistant theory is that its ancestral meaning is 'sail dangerously close to rocks,' and attempts have been made to link it with Greek *rhíza* 'cliff' and Latin *resegāre* 'cut off short' (from the notion of coastal rocks being 'cut off sharply' or 'sheer'). English acquired the French past participial form *risqué* in the 19th century.

**rissole**  [18]  *Rissoles* originally got their name from their colour. The word comes via French *rissole* and Old French *ruissole* from Vulgar Latin *russeola, a shortening of *russeola pasta 'reddish pastry.' Late Latin *russeolus* 'reddish' was a derivative of Latin *russus* 'red' (source of English *russet*), and is distantly related to English *red*.

▶ red, russet, rust

**ritual**  [16]  *Ritual* was borrowed from Latin *rītuālis*, a derivative of *rītus* 'religious or other ceremony or practice' (from which, via Old French *rite*, English gets *rite* [14]). It may have been related to Sanskrit *rīti- 'going, way, custom.'

▶ rite

**rival**  [16]  A *rival* is etymologically 'someone who uses the same stream as another.' The word comes

from Latin *rīvālis*, a noun use of an adjective meaning 'of a stream,' derived from *rīvus* 'stream' (source of English *derive*). People who use or live by the same stream are neighbours and hence, human nature being as it is, are usually in competition with each other – hence *rival*.

▶ derive

**river**  [13]  Etymologically, the term *river* denotes the 'banks' of a river, rather than the water that flows between them. Its distant ancestor is Latin *rīpa* 'bank.' From this was derived the adjective *rīpārius* (source of English *riparian* 'of a river-bank' [19]), whose feminine form came to be used in Vulgar Latin as a noun, *rīpāria, denoting 'land by the water's edge.' From it evolved Italian *riviera* 'bank' (whence English *Riviera* [18]) and Old French *riviere*. This originally meant 'river-bank,' but this subsequently developed to 'river,' the sense in which English adopted the word. A heavily disguised English relative is *arrive*, which etymologically denotes 'come to the shore.'

▶ arrive, riparian, Riviera

**roach**  SEE COCKROACH

**road**  [OE]  *Road* comes from the same ultimate source as *ride* – and indeed in the Old English period it meant either simply 'riding' or 'hostile incursion on horseback' (a sense preserved in *inroads* [16] and also in *raid*, which is historically the same word as *road*). By the 14th century the sense 'sheltered anchorage' (now represented by the plural *roads*) had emerged, but the central modern meaning 'track for traffic' did not put in an appearance until the late 16th century (hitherto the main words for expressing this concept had been *way* and *street*).

▶ inroads, raid, ride

**roast**  [13]  *Roast* can be traced back ultimately to a prehistoric West Germanic term for a 'metal grid for cooking things on.' From this was derived the verb *raustjan, which evolved into German *rösten* and Dutch *roosten*. There is no trace of it in Old English, however: English got it via Old French *rostir*, which had been borrowed from Germanic. A derivative of Dutch *roosten* was *rooster* 'gridiron.' The resemblance between a gridiron pattern and lines ruled on paper led to the metaphorical use of *rooster* for 'list, table' – whence English *roster* [18].

▶ roster

**rob**  [13]  *Rob* goes back ultimately to a prehistoric Germanic *raub- 'break' (a close relative of the Latin base *rup- 'break,' which has given English *rout*, *route*, and *rupture*). This produced Old English *rēafian* 'rob,' which although it has now died out has left us its derivative *bereave* [OE], and also Middle Dutch *rōven* 'rob,' which gave English *rover* 'pirate' [14]. It was also borrowed into Old French as *robber*, which is the source of modern English *rob*. Other English descendants of the Germanic base are *robe*, *rubbish*, and *rubble*.

► bereave, corrupt, disrupt, robe, rout, route, rover, rubbish, rubble, rupture

**robe** [13] A *robe* is etymologically 'something stolen,' hence a 'looted garment,' and finally simply a '(long) garment.' The word comes ultimately from Vulgar Latin *\*rauba*, which was borrowed from the same Germanic base as produced English *bereave* and *rob*. It passed into English via Old French *robe*. This still retained the ancestral meaning 'stolen things, spoils' as well as the new 'garment,' and in that sense it has given English *rubbish* and *rubble*.

► rob

**robin** [15] *Robin* was borrowed from the French male first name *Robin*, a familiar form of *Robert*, which is first recorded as a bird-name in the 15th century. It originally appeared in English, in the mid-15th century, in the expression *robin redbreast*, and *robin* was not used on its own until about a hundred years later. Since then its has gradually ousted the native *ruddock* (a relative of *red*) as the standard term for the bird. (The name *Robert*, incidentally, is of Germanic origin, and means etymologically 'fame-bright.')

**robot** [20] *Robot* is a Czech contribution to English. It comes from *robota* 'forced labour, drudgery,' a word related to German *arbeit* 'work.' It was used by the Czech dramatist Karel Čapek in his play *R.U.R. (Rossum's Universal Robots)* 1920 for 'mechanical people constructed to do menial tasks.' English acquired it via German *robot*, and the first record of it in an English text comes from 1923.

**robust** [16] By a series of semantic twists, *robust* is related to *red*. It comes ultimately from Indo-European *\*reudh-*'red' (source of English *red*). This produced Latin *rōbus*, which was applied to a particular sort of oak tree with reddish wood. The oak being synonymous with strength, *rōbus* in due course came to mean 'strength.' This was carried over into the derived *rōbustus* 'firm, strong, solid,' from which English gets *robust*, and also into the verb *rōborāre* 'strengthen,' source of English *corroborate* [16].

► corroborate, red

**rock** English has two words *rock*, both of uncertain origin. The older, 'sway' [11], goes back to a prehistoric Germanic base *\*rukk-* 'move,' which also produced German *rücken* 'move' and Dutch *rukken* 'pull, jerk,' but beyond that its trail goes cold. *Rock* 'stone' [14] was borrowed from Old French *rocque*. This has relatives in Italian *rocca* and Spanish *roca*, but where it ultimately came from is not known. The French word is also the ultimate source of English *rococo*.

► rococo

**rocket** English has two words *rocket*. The older, and now less familiar, is the name of a plant of the cab-

bage family whose leaves are used in salads. It was inspired by the plant's downy stems, for it goes back ultimately to Latin *ērūca*, which originally meant 'hairy caterpillar.' This may have been related to *ērīcius* 'hedgehog,' from which English gets *caprice* and *urchin*. It passed into Italian as *ruca*, whose diminutive form *ruchetta* developed a variant *rochetta* – whence French *roquette* and finally English *rocket* [16]. *Rocket* 'projectile' [17] is ultimately an allusion to the shape of such objects. It comes via Old French *roquette* from Italian *rocchetto*, a diminutive form of *rocca* 'spool' – hence the application to the 'cylindrical' rocket. *Rocca* itself represents a borrowing from a prehistoric Germanic *\*rukkon*, which also lies behind English *ratchet*.

► caprice, urchin / ratchet

**rococo** [19] Old French *roque* was the source of English *rock* 'stone.' From its modern French descendant *roc* was derived *rocaille* 'decoration in the form of pebbles, shells, etc.,' which was altered to *rococo* as a term for a style characterized by convoluted ornamentation.

► rock

**rod** [12] It seems likely that *rod* is related to English *rood* [OE]. In post-Anglo-Saxon times this has mainly been used for 'cross of Christ,' and it now survives mainly in *rood screen* 'altar screen,' but in the Old English period it was also used for 'rod.' Where their Germanic ancestor, which also produced German *rute* 'rod' and Norwegian dialect *rodda* 'stake,' came from is not clear. The use of *rod* for a unit of measurement dates from the mid 15th century.

► rood

**rodent** see ROSTRUM

**rodeo** see ROTA

**roe** *Roe* the deer [OE] and *roe* 'fish eggs' [15] are distinct words. The former goes back to a prehistoric Germanic *\*raikh-*, which also produced German *reh*, Dutch *ree*, Swedish *råa*, and Danish *raa*. Its underlying meaning may be 'spotted,' an allusion to the roe deer's dappled coat. *Roe* 'fish eggs' was borrowed from Middle Dutch or Middle Low German *roge*, a word of uncertain origin.

**rogue** [16] *Rogue* originated as a thieves' slang term for a 'vagrant' in the mid-16th century. It is not clear where it came from, but one suggestion is that it was derived from the contemporary slang term *roger* 'beggar who pretended to be a poor university student in order play on people's feelings.' This was based on Latin *rogāre* 'ask,' source of English *interrogate, prerogative*, etc.

**roister** see RURAL

**roll** English has two words *roll*, both of which go back ultimately to Latin *rotulus* 'small wheel,' a diminutive form of *rota* 'wheel' (source of English *rotate*, *rotund, round*, etc). This passed via Old French *rolle* into English as *roll* 'rolled-up parchment' [13]. The modern French version of the word has given English *role* [17], whose underlying notion is of a 'rolled-up' piece of paper with the actor's lines written on it. From *rotulus* was derived the Vulgar Latin verb *\*rotulāre*, which has given English its verb *roll* [14]. *Control* comes from the same source.

▶ control, rota, rotate, round

**romance** [13] A *romance* is etymologically a story written in the language 'of Rome.' The word comes from Old French *romanz*, which denoted 'something written in French (as opposed to classical Latin).' This went back to the Vulgar Latin adverb *\*rōmānicē* 'in the local vernacular descended from Latin' (contrasted with *latinē* 'in Latin'). This in turn came from Latin *rōmānicus* 'Roman,' a derivative ultimately of *Rōma* 'Rome.' In practice, these medieval vernacular tales were usually about chivalric adventure, and that was the starting point from which the modern meaning of *romance*, and its derivative *romantic* [17], developed. The original sense survives in the linguistic term *Romance*, denoting languages such as French, Italian, Spanish, Portuguese, Rumanian, etc that have evolved from Latin.

**rondo**   see ROUND

**rood**   see ROD

**roof** [OE] The antecedents of *roof* are far from clear. Its only surviving relative seems to be Dutch *roef* 'cabin, coffin lid,' and although it also had links with Old Norse *hróf* 'boat-shed,' its ultimate origins remain a mystery.

**room** [OE] The Old English word for 'room' was *cofa* (ancestor of modern English *cove* 'sheltered bay'). At that time, *room* meant simply 'space' (as its German relative *raum* still does). Its modern sense 'chamber' did not emerge until the 15th century. It comes ultimately from the prehistoric Germanic adjective *\*rūmaz* 'spacious,' which may be related to Latin *rūs* 'country,' source of English *rural* and *rustic*. *Rummage* is a distant relative.

▶ rummage, rural

**root** *Root* of a plant [OE] and *root* 'dig with the nose' [14] are distinct words. The former was borrowed from Old Norse *rót*, which goes back ultimately to the Indo-European base *\*wrd-*. This also produced Latin *rādīx* 'root,' source of English *radical, radish*, etc. *Root* 'dig' is an alteration of an earlier *wroot*, which went back to Old English *wrōtan*. It is usually assumed that *root* 'cheer, support,' which first emerged in America in the late 19th century, is the same word.

▶ radical, radish

**rope** [OE] *Rope* is a general Germanic term, represented also by German *reif*, Dutch *reep*, Swedish *rep*,

and Danish *reb* (the German word now means 'hoop, loop'). These point to a prehistoric Germanic ancestor *\*raipaz*, whose ultimate origins are not known. A *stirrup* is etymologically a 'climbing rope.'

▶ stirrup

**rosary** [14] *Rosary* comes from Latin *rosārium* 'rose garden,' a derivative of *rosa* 'rose.' It was a common conceit in the Middle Ages to name collections of verse or similar short pieces after bunches of flowers (*anthology* comes from the Greek word for 'flower,' and a similar inspiration underlies *florilegium*, while a 13th-century volume of the collected works of the Persian poet Sa'di was called the *Rose garden*). That was the background against which a collection of Roman Catholic prayers, consisting of Aves, Paternosters, and Glorias, came to be known as a *rosary*. A string of beads of varying sizes came to be used for counting off how far one has got in saying these prayers (English *bead* itself comes from a word meaning 'prayer'), and this too was termed *rosary*.

▶ rose

**rose** [OE] *Rose* is a general European term, represented also in French, German, and Danish *rose*, Italian and Spanish *rosa*, Dutch *roos*, Swedish *ros*, Russian *roza*, etc. These all go back ultimately to Latin *rosa*, which was either borrowed from, or came from the same source as Greek *rhódon* 'rose,' a word of eastern Mediterranean origin.

▶ rhododendron

**rosemary** [15] Originally, *rosemary* had no connection with either 'roses' or 'Mary.' Etymologically it means 'sea-dew.' It comes, probably via Old French *rosmarin*, from late Latin *rōsmarīnum*. This in turn was a conflation of Latin *rōs marīnus*, *rōs* meaning 'dew' and *marīnus* 'of the sea' (an allusion to the fact that the plant grew near sea coasts). The word originally entered English in the 14th century as *rosmarine*, but association with *rose* and *Mary* (the Virgin Mary, no doubt) led to its alteration to *rosemary*.

▶ marine, mere, mermaid

**rosin**   see RESIN

**roster**   see ROAST

**rostrum** [16] Latin *rōstrum* originally meant 'beak' or 'muzzle of an animal' – it was derived from the verb *rōdere* 'gnaw' (source of English *corrode* [14], *erode* [17], and *rodent* [19]). The word was also applied metaphorically to the 'beaklike' prows of ships. In 338BC the platform for public speakers in the Forum in Rome was adorned with the prows of ships captured from Antium (modern Anzio), and so in due course all such platforms came to be known as *rostra* – whence the English word.

▶ corrode, erode, rodent

**rot** [OE] *Rot* goes back to a prehistoric Germanic *\*rutjan*, which also produced Dutch *rotten*. It may be related ultimately to Latin *rudis* 'rough,' source of English *rude*. The adjective *rotten* [13] was borrowed from Old Norse *rotinn*, which came from the same Germanic stem as produced *\*rutjan*. The mild imprecation *drat* [19] is a conflation of *God* and *rot*.

▶ rude

**rota** [17] Latin *rota* denoted 'wheel': it came ultimately from a prehistoric Indo-European base *\*reth-* meaning 'run, roll,' which also produced German *rad* 'wheel.' It was introduced into English in 1659 by the republican James Harrington as the name for a political club he founded to advocate his idea that government office should be held in rotation.

Derivatives of *rota* have contributed richly to English. Medieval Latin *rotārius* has given *rotary* [18]. From the verb *rotāre* 'revolve' have come *rotate* [19] and, via its Spanish descendant *rodear*, *rodeo* [19] (etymologically a 'rounding-up' or 'surrounding' of cattle). *Rotundus*, a derivative of *rotāre*, has produced *rotund* [18] and *round*. The diminutive form *rotulus* has given *control* and *roll*. And *roue* 'wheel,' the French descendant of *rota*, is the source of *roué* [18], etymologically someone broken on the 'wheel.'

▶ control, prune, rodeo, roll, rondo, rotate, rotund, round

**rouge** see RED

**rough** [OE] *Rough* goes back to a prehistoric West Germanic *\*rūkhwaz*, which also produced German *rauh* and Dutch *ruw*. Despite the similarity of form and sense, *ruffian* is not related, and there is no evidence that *ruffle* is either.

**round** [13] *Round* goes back ultimately to Latin *rotundus* 'round,' source of English *rotund*. In Vulgar Latin this became *\*retundus*, which passed into Old French as *reont*, later *ront*. Its stem form *rond-* gave English *round*. Derivatives to have reached English include *prune* 'cut branches,' *rondo* [18], *roundel* [13], and *roundelay* [16]; but *surround*, despite the similarity, is not related.

▶ rota, rotund

**rout** English has two words *rout*. 'Disorderly retreat' [16] comes via archaic French *route* 'dispersed group' and Italian *rotta* 'breakage' from Vulgar Latin *\*rupta*, a noun use of the past participle of Latin *rumpere* 'break' (source of English *corrupt*, *disrupt* [17], *erupt*, and *rupture* and related to English *rob*). Other English descendants of *\*rupta* are *route*, *routine*, and *rut*. *Rout* 'dig with the nose,' hence 'search, rummage' [16] is a variant form of *root*.

▶ corrupt, disrupt, erupt, rob, robe, route, routine, rupture, rut / root

**route** see RUT
**routine** see RUT
**roux** see RUSSET
**rover** see ROB
**row** There are three distinct words *row* in English. The one meaning 'use oars' [OE] goes back to a prehistoric Germanic base *\*rō-* 'steer,' which also produced Dutch *roeijen* and Swedish *ro*, not to mention English *rudder*. *Row* 'orderly line' [OE] comes from a prehistoric Germanic *\*raigwa*, and is probably related to German *reihe* 'row.' *Row* 'noisy quarrel' [18] seems to have originated in the late 18th century as a piece of Cambridge University slang, but where it came from is not known.

▶ rudder

**royal** [14] *Royal* and *regal* are ultimately the same word. Both go back to the Latin adjective *rēgālis*, a derivative of *rēx* 'king.' But whereas *regal* was probably borrowed direct from Latin, *royal* was acquired via Old French, where *rēgālis* became *roial*.

▶ regal

**rub** [14] The antecedents of *rub* are unclear. It may have been borrowed from Low German *rubben*, but since it is not known where that came from, it does not get us much further. The derivative *rubber* [16] was originally used simply for 'something for rubbing with.' But since the substance obtained from rubber trees was early on used for pencil erasers, it became known from the end of the 18th century as *rubber* (or in full *India-rubber*, from its place of origin). It is not clear whether *rubber* 'set of games' [16], which originated as a bowls term, is the same word.

▶ rubber

**rubble** [14] Old French *robe* (a relative of English *rob*) originally meant 'loot, odds and ends stolen' (its later sense 'stolen clothes' led on to English *robe*). From it was derived Anglo-Norman *\*robel* 'bits of broken stone,' which passed into English as *rubble*. The plural of *\*robel* would have been *\*robeus*, and this may have been the starting point for Anglo-Norman *rubbous*, which became English *rubbish* [14].

▶ rob, rubbish

**ruby** [14] *Ruby* goes back ultimately to Latin *ruber* 'red,' a descendant of the same Indo-European base as produced English *red*. From it was derived the medieval Latin adjective *rubīnus*, which was used in the term *lapis rubīnus* 'red stone.' In due course *rubīnus* itself came to be employed as a noun in this sense, and it passed into English via Old French *rubi*. Other English words from the same source include *rubella* [19], *rubicund* [16], *rubidium* [19], and *rubric* [14] (headings in ancient and medieval manuscripts were often written in red ink).

▶ red, rubella, rubicund, rubric

**rudder** [OE] *Rudder* comes from the same source as English *row* 'use oars' – prehistoric Germanic *\*rō-* 'steer.' Indeed it originally denoted an 'oar used for steering'; the modern application to a fixed steering surface did not emerge until the 14th century. Its west Germanic ancestor *\*rōthra-* also produced German *ruder* and Dutch *roer*.

▶ row

**ruddy** see RED

**rude** [14] *Rude* comes via Old French *rude* from Latin *rudis* 'rough, raw.' This seems originally to have denoted 'rough unpolished stone' – it was related to Latin *rūdus* 'broken stone' – but its ultimate origins are unknown. From it were derived *rudīmentum* 'beginning' (etymologically 'raw state'), which has given English *rudiment* [16], and *ērudīre* 'take the roughness out of,' hence 'polish, teach,' source of English *erudite*.

▶ erudite, rot, rudiment

**rue** *Rue* 'regret' [OE] and *rue* the plant [14] are distinct words. The former goes back to a prehistoric Germanic source, of uncertain ultimate origins, which meant 'distress,' and which also produced German *reuen* and Dutch *rouwen*. In the early Middle English period, when it still meant 'cause to feel pity' (a sense which has now died out), a noun *ruth* 'pity' was formed from it, which survives in *ruthless* [14]. And a cognate noun *rue* once existed too, meaning 'sorrow, regret,' which also lives on only in the form of a derivative: *rueful* [13]. The plant-name *rue* comes via Old French *rue* and Latin *rūta* from Greek *rhūté*.

▶ rueful, ruthless

**rufous** see RED

**rug** [16] The ancestry of *rug* is not altogether clear. It originally meant 'rough woollen cloth,' which appears to link it with words such as Swedish *rugg* 'ruffled hair' and Old Norse *rogg* 'tuft' (source of English *rag*), so it could well be a Scandinavian borrowing. It was not used for a 'mat' until the early 19th century. The original notion of 'roughness' or 'shagginess' is better preserved in *rugged* [14], which presumably comes from a related source.

**rugby** [19] Legend has it that the game of rugby football was born at Rugby School in Warwickshire in 1823 when, during an ordinary game of football, a boy called William Webb Ellis picked up the ball and ran with it. The use of the term *rugby* for the game is not recorded before 1864, and the public-school slang version *rugger* dates from the 1890s.

**ruin** [14] If something is *ruined*, etymologically it has simply 'fallen down.' The word's ultimate ancestor is Latin *ruere* 'fall, crumble' (source also of English

*congruent*). From it was derived the noun *ruīna* 'fall,' which passed into English via Old French *ruine*.

▶ congruent

**rule** [13] *Rule* is one of a largish family of English words that go back ultimately to Latin *rēgula* 'straight stick, ruler, rule, pattern' (whose close relatives *rēx* 'king' and *regere* 'rule' have also contributed royally to English vocabulary in the form of *rector, regent, regiment, royal*, etc). Derivatives have produced *regular* and *regulate*, while *rēgula* itself has given *rail* 'bar' and, via Vulgar Latin *\*regula* and Old French *reule*, *rule*.

▶ rail, raj, rector, regal, regent, regular, regulate, royal

**rummage** [16] *Rummage* is etymologically 'roomage.' It originally denoted the 'stowage of cargo in a ship's hold.' It came from Anglo-Norman *\*rumage*, a reduced form of Old French *arrumage*. This was derived from the verb *arrumer* 'stow in a hold,' which itself was based on *run* 'ship's hold.' And this in turn was borrowed from Middle Dutch *ruim* 'space,' a relative of English *room*. The verb *rummage*, derived from the noun, was also used for 'search a ship's hold,' which is where the modern notion of 'rummaging around' comes from.

▶ room

**run** [14] *Run* is quite a widespread Germanic verb, represented also by German *rennen* and Swedish *ränna*. Its ultimate ancestry is not known, although links have been suggested with Sanskrit *rnoti* 'he moves' and Greek *órnūmi* 'rouse.' The Old English verb was *rinnan*; *run*, which was originally a past form, did not begin to emerge as the infinitive until the early 14th century, and it was not common until the 16th century. *Runnel* 'brook' [OE] comes from the same Germanic source, and *rennet* may be related.

▶ rennet, runnel

**rune** [17] Old English had a word *rūn*, which appears originally to have denoted 'mystery,' and hence 'carved or written character with mysterious or magical properties.' This had died out by the end of the Middle Ages, but its Old Norse relative *\*rún* lived on to become modern Swedish *runa* and Danish *rune*, and when antiquarian interest in the ancient runic writing system developed in Britain in the 16th century, they were borrowed into English as *rune*.

**runnel** see RUN

**rupture** see CORRUPT

**rural** [15] Latin *rūs* denoted 'the country' (it came ultimately from an Indo-European ancestor meaning 'open space,' which also produced English *room*). Its stem form was *rūr-*, on which was based the adjective *rūrālis*, source of English *rural*. A related adjective, this time derived from the nominative form, was *rūsticus*, which has given English *rustic* [15], and is also the ultimate source (via Old French *rustre* 'ruffian') of English *roister* [16].

▶ roister, room, rustic

**ruse** [15] *Ruse* and *rush* 'hurry' are ultimately the same word. Both come from Old French *ruser* 'drive back, detour.' From this was derived the noun *ruse*, which brought the sense 'detour, deviation' with it into English. It was used in the context of a hunted animal dodging about and doubling back on its tracks to throw off its pursuers, and this led in the early 17th century to the emergence of the metaphorical sense 'trick, stratagem.' The precise origins of Old French *ruser* are uncertain. It is generally referred to Latin *recūsāre* 'refuse,' source of English *recusant* and possibly of *refuse*, but it has also been speculated that it came via a Vulgar Latin *\*rursāre* or *\*rusāre* from Latin *rursus* 'backwards.'

▶ rush

**rush** English has two words *rush*. The plant-name [OE] goes back to a prehistoric Germanic *\*rusk-*, which also produced German and Dutch *rusch*, and may be related to Latin *restis* 'rush.' *Rush* 'hurry' [14] goes back ultimately to Old French *ruser* 'drive back, detour,' source of English *ruse*. It reached English via Anglo-Norman *russher*, where until the 17th century it was used in its original sense 'drive back, repulse.' The sense 'hurry' developed in Anglo-Norman, presumably from some association of the sound of the word with 'hurrying.'

▶ ruse

**russet** [13] Latin *russus* 'red' went back ultimately to the prehistoric Indo-European *\*reudh-* 'red,' which also produced English *red*. From it was descended Old French *rous*, whose modern form *roux* has given English *roux* 'flour and butter mixture' [19] (it is short for *beurre roux* 'browned butter'). This formed the basis of a diminutive form *rousset*, which passed into English via Anglo-Norman *russet*. The application of the word to a red-skinned variety of apple dates from the 18th century.

▶ red, roux

**rust** [OE] Etymologically, *rust* means 'reddened.' The word goes back ultimately to the Indo-European base *\*reudh-* 'red' (source also of English *red*). This produced a prehistoric Germanic noun which has evolved into German and Swedish *rost*, Dutch *roest*, and English and Danish *rust*.

▶ red

**rut** The *rut* of deer [15] and the *rut* of a wheel [16] are not related. The latter in fact is historically the same word as *route*. Both go back ultimately to Vulgar Latin *\*rupta*, which was a noun use of the past participle of Latin *rumpere* 'break' (source also of English *rout* and *rupture*). The etymological notion underlying it is therefore of a path that has been 'broken' by constant use, a 'beaten track.' It passed into Old French as *rute* or *rote*, and it was this that gave English *rut*, which originally denoted the 'track' made by a wheel. The later French form *route* is the source of English *route* [16]. *Routine* [17] comes from a French derivative of *route*.

*Rut* 'oestrus' comes via Old French *rut* from Latin *rugītus*, a derivative of *rugīre* 'roar.'

▶ rout, rupture

# S

---

**sabbath** [OE] The *sabbath* is etymologically the day of 'rest.' The word comes ultimately from Hebrew *shabbāth*, a derivative of *shābath* 'rest.' English acquired it via Greek *sábbaton* and Latin *sabbatum*. The modern use of the derived *sabbatical* [16] for a 'period away from normal duties,' first recorded in the 19th century, evolved from its original application to the one year in seven when, according to ancient Jewish law, land had to be left fallow. French *samedi* 'Saturday' comes from the same source.
▶ sabbatical

**sable** [14] The sable, an animal like a large weasel with valuable fur, lives in northern Europe and Asia, and its name reflects where it comes from – for it is of Slavic origin, related to Russian *sóbol'*. It came west with the fur trade, and was borrowed into medieval Latin as *sabellum*. From there it made its way into English via Old French *sable*.

**sabotage** [20] The etymological idea underlying *sabotage* is of 'clattering along in noisy shoes.' For its ultimate ancestor is French *sabot*, a word of unknown origin which means 'clog.' From it was derived *saboter* 'walk along noisily in clogs,' hence (via the notion of 'clumsiness') 'do work badly,' and finally 'destroy tools, machines, etc deliberately.' This in turn formed the basis of the noun *sabotage*, which originally denoted the 'destruction of machinery, etc by factory workers,' but gradually broadened out to include any deliberate disruptive destruction. English acquired it around 1910.

**sabre** [17] Both the sabre and its name are of eastern European origin. The word comes from either Polish *szabla* or Hungarian *szablya*. It was westernized as *sabel* in German, and in the early 17th century it passed in this guise into French, where for reasons that are not altogether clear is soon evolved into *sabre* – source of the English word.

**sac** see SACHET

**saccharin** [19] Medieval Latin *saccharum* 'sugar' belonged to the same word-family as the ances-

tor of English *sugar*. Its original contribution to English was the adjective *saccharine* 'sugary' [17]; and in the late 1870s the German chemist Fahlberg used it in coining the term *saccharin* for the new sweetening substance he had invented. English borrowed it in the mid 1880s.
▶ sugar

**sachet** [19] A *sachet* is etymologically a 'little sack.' The word was borrowed from French *sachet*, a diminutive form of *sac* 'bag,' which came from the same Latin source that produced English *sack*. *Sac* itself was acquired by English as a biological term in the 18th century.
▶ sack

**sack** English has three separate words *sack*, one of them now a historical relic and the other two ultimately related. *Sack* 'large bag' [OE] was borrowed from Latin *saccus* (source also of English *sac*, *sachet*, and *satchel*). This in turn came from Greek *sákkos* 'rough cloth used for packing,' which was of Semitic origin (Hebrew has *saq* meaning both 'sack' and 'sackcloth'). The colloquial sense 'dismissal from work' (as in *get the sack*) arose in the early 19th century, perhaps from the notion of a dismissed worker going away with his tools or clothing in his bag. *Sack* 'plunder' [16] came via French *sac* from *sacco* 'bag,' the Italian descendant of Latin *saccus*. This was used in expressions like *mettere a sacco*, literally 'put in a bag,' which denoted figuratively 'plunder, pillage' (no doubt inspired by the notion of 'putting one's loot in a bag').

*Sack* 'sherry-like wine' [16] (Sir John Falstaff's favourite tipple) was an alteration of *seck*. This was short for *wine sec*, a partial translation of French *vin sec* 'dry wine' (French *sec* came from Latin *siccus* 'dry,' source of English *desiccate* [16]).
▶ sac, sachet, satchel / desiccate, sec

**sacred** [14] *Sacred* is one of a wide range of English words that go back to Latin *sacer* 'sacred, holy' (which itself came from the same base that produced Latin *sancīre* 'consecrate,' source of English *saint,* *sanctuary*, etc). Many of them come via the derived verb *sacrāre* 'consecrate.' These include *consecrate* [15], *execrate* [16], *sacrament* [12], and *sacred* itself, which was originally the past participle of the now obsolete verb *sacre* 'consecrate,' a descendant via Old French *sacrer* of Latin *sacrāre*. Amongst other relatives are *sacerdotal* [14] (from Latin *sacerdōs* 'priest,' a derivative of the same base as *sacer*), *sacrifice* [13] (from a Latin compound meaning 'make holy'), *sacrilege* [13] (from a Latin compound meaning 'steal holy things'), *sacristan* and its more heavily disguised relative *sexton*, *sacrosanct* [17] (etymologically 'consecrated with religious ceremonies'), and *sacrum* 'bottom section of the spine' [18] (short for medieval Latin *os sacrum* 'holy bone,' which was a direct translation of Greek *hieron ostéon*, an allusion to the use of the bone in sacrificial ceremonies).

▶ consecrate, execrate, sacrament, sacrifice, sacristan, saint, sanctuary, sexton

**sad** [OE] Originally, to feel *sad* was to feel that one had had 'enough.' For the word comes ultimately from the same Indo-European base that produced English *satisfy* and *saturate*. By the time it reached English (via a prehistoric Germanic *\*sathaz*) 'enough' had already become extended to 'weary,' and the modern sense 'unhappy' emerged in the 14th century. The original notion of 'sufficiency' has now died out in the case of *sad*, but it survives in the case of *sated* [17], an alteration (probably under the influence of *satiate*) of the past participle of an earlier verb *sade* 'satiate,' which was derived from *sad*.

▶ sated, satiate, satisfy, saturate

**saddle** [OE] *Saddle* comes from a prehistoric Germanic *\*sathulaz*, which also produced German *sattel*, Dutch *zadel*, and Swedish *sadel*. Etymologically it no doubt signifies something to 'sit' on, hailing ultimately from the Indo-European base *\*sed-* 'sit,' from which English gets *sit*.

▶ sit

**sadist** [19] The terms *sadist* and *sadism* commemorate the so-called Marquis de Sade (in fact he was a count), the French writer who lived between 1740 and 1815. Towards the end of the 18th century he produced several pornographic novels, whose theme of sexual gratification through (among other things) the inflicting of pain led in the late 19th century to the use of his name by psychiatrists to describe such behaviour. By the 1930s *sadism* had become a general term for 'gratuitous cruelty.'

**safe** [13] Like *save*, and indeed *salvage* and *salvation*, *safe* comes from Latin *salvus* 'uninjured.' It reached English via Old French *sauf*. *Salvus* itself went back to a prehistoric Indo-European *\*solwos* 'whole,' which came from the same base that produced English *soldier*, *solemn*, and *solid*. The noun *safe* 'strongbox'

[15] was originally *save*, a derivative of the verb, but by the late 17th century it had, under the influence of the adjective, become *safe*. The plant-name *sage* [14] comes via Old French *sauge* from Latin *salvia*, etymologically the 'healing' plant, a derivative of *salvus* (English acquired *salvia* itself in the 19th century).

▶ sage, salute, salvage, salvation, salvia, save, soldier, solemn, solid

**saffron** [13] Saffron brought its name with it along the spice route from the Middle East. It comes from Arabic *za'farān*, a word of unknown origin, and reached English via medieval Latin *safranum* and Old French *safran*. The town of Saffron Walden in Essex is so named from its once thriving saffron-growing industry.

**sag** [15] There are several Scandinavian verbs that bear a strong resemblance to *sag*, including Swedish *sacka* and Danish *sakke*, and it seems likely that one of these was borrowed into Middle Low German as *sacken* 'settle, subside,' and subsequently found its way into English as *sag* (whose original meaning was 'subside').

**saga** see SAW

**sagacious** see SEEK

**sage** see SAFE

**sago** [16] *Sago* is of Malay origin. The Portuguese were responsible for introducing the Malay term *sāgū* to English, as *sagu*; the modern form *sago*, which became established during the 17th and 18th centuries, came via Dutch.

**sail** [OE] *Sail* has numerous relatives in the other Germanic languages, among them German and Swedish *segel*, Dutch *zeil*, and Danish *sejl*. These all come from a prehistoric Germanic *\*seglam*, which some have traced back to an Indo-European *\*seklom*. This was presumably formed from the same Indo-European base (*\*sek-* 'cut') that produced English *dissect*, *saw*, *segment*, etc, and so *sail* may signify etymologically a piece of 'cut' cloth.

▶ dissect, saw, segment

**saint** [OE] Latin *sancīre* meant 'consecrate' (it was formed from the same base as produced *sacer* 'holy,' source of English *sacred*, *sacrifice*, etc). Its past participle was *sanctus*. This came to be used as an adjective meaning 'holy, sacred,' and in due course as a noun too, 'holy person.' English originally borrowed it direct from Latin, as *sanct*, but this was superseded in the 12th century by *saint*, acquired via Old French. Other English words based on the Latin stem *sanct-* include *sanction*, *sanctity*, etc, and *saunter* may be related to *saint*.

▶ sacred

**sake** English has two nouns *sake*. The older, now used only in the expression *for the sake of*, was originally an independent fully-fledged noun, with a range of meanings including 'strife,' 'guilt,' and 'lawsuit' [OE]. Its use in *for the sake of,* which emerged in the 13th century, probably arose out of its legal usage, and thus denoted originally 'on behalf of a litigant's case in a lawsuit.' The word itself came from a prehistoric Germanic *sakō* 'affair, thing, charge, accusation,' which also produced German *sache* 'affair, subject, lawsuit.' It is also represented in English *forsake* [OE], which etymologically means 'accuse, quarrel with,' hence 'decline,' and finally 'give up'; *keepsake* [18], etymologically something that is kept for the 'sake' of the giver; and *namesake* [17], which probably arose from the notion of two people being linked or associated for the 'sake' of their names. *Seek* is a distant relation.

*Sake,* or *saki,* 'rice wine' [17] was borrowed from Japanese, where it literally means 'alcohol.'

▶ forsake, keepsake, namesake, seek, seize

**salacious** see SALIENT

**salad** [15] Etymologically, a *salad* is a 'salted' dish. The word comes via Old French *salade* from Vulgar Latin *\*salāta,* a noun use of the feminine past participle of Latin *\*salāre* 'put salt on to, treat with salt.' This in turn was a derivative of *sāl* 'salt,' a relative of English *salt.* The Romans were fond of dishes of assorted raw vegetables with a dressing, and this often consisted of brine – hence the name, which is short for *herba salāta* 'salted vegetables.'

▶ salt

**salary** [14] *Salary* goes back to a Latin word that originally denoted an 'allowance given to Roman soldiers for buying salt' (salt being in former times a valued commodity, over which wars were fought, rather than taken for granted as it is today). This was *salārium,* a derivative of *sāl* 'salt.' It soon broadened out to mean 'fixed periodic payment for work done,' and passed in this sense via Anglo-Norman *salarie* into English.

▶ salt

**sale** [11] *Sale* was borrowed from Old Norse *sala.* This came from the same prehistoric Germanic base, *\*sal-,* that produced English *sell.* The word's specific application to the 'selling of goods at lower-than-normal prices' did not emerge until the 1860s.

▶ sell

**salient** [16] *Salient* is one of a large number of English words that go back ultimately to Latin *salīre* 'jump.' Others include *assail, assault, desultory, insult, sally, sauté,* and also *salacious* [17], which goes back to Latin *salāx* 'given to leaping on to females in order to copulate,' a derivative of *salīre. Salient* itself comes from the present participle *saliēns,* and was originally used as a heraldic term, meaning 'jumping'; the

metaphorical 'prominent' did not emerge until the 18th century.

▶ assail, assault, desultory, insult, result, salacious, sally, sauté

**sallow** [OE] English has two distinct words *sallow.* The adjective goes back to a prehistoric Germanic *\*salwa-,* which was also borrowed into French as *sale* 'dirty.' The underlying meaning appears to be 'dark-coloured.' Its only surviving relative among the mainstream Germanic languages is Icelandic *sölr* 'yellow.' *Sallow* 'willow' comes from a prehistoric Germanic *\*salkhaz,* which also produced French *saule* 'willow' and was distantly related to Latin *salix* 'willow.'

**sally** [16] To *sally* is etymologically to 'jump.' For the word comes ultimately from Latin *salīre* 'jump,' source also of English *assail, insult, salient,* etc. It passed into Old French as *salir,* which later became *saillir.* From this was derived a noun *saillie* 'jump,' hence 'sudden breaking out from a defended position to attack,' which English took over and soon turned into a verb. (The name *Sally,* incidentally, is an alteration of *Sarah,* by the same phonetic process that produced *Del, Hal, Moll,* and *Tel* from *Derek, Harry, Mary,* and *Terence.*)

▶ salient

**salmon** [13] The ancestral Indo-European word for 'salmon' is *lax.* It survives in numerous modern European languages, including German *lachs,* Swedish *lax* (whence English *gravlax*), Yiddish *laks* (source of English *lox* 'smoked salmon'), and Russian *losos'.* The Old English member of the family was *læx,* but in the 13th century this was replaced by *salmon,* a borrowing from Anglo-Norman *saumoun.* This in turn went back to Latin *salmō,* which some have linked with *salīre* 'jump' (source of English *assail, insult, salient,* etc) – hence the 'leaping' fish.

**saloon** [18] *Saloon* is part of a widespread western European family of words for 'large room.' They go back to a prehistoric Germanic *\*salaz,* ancestor of German *saal.* This was borrowed into Vulgar Latin as *\*sala,* whose descendants include French *salle* and Italian *sala.* A derivative of this, denoting 'large size,' was *salone,* which was borrowed into French as *salon.* English acquired this at the beginning of the 18th century in two forms: the original *salon* and the anglicized *saloon.*

**salt** [OE] *Salt* was a key element in the diet of our Indo-European ancestors, and their word for it, *\*sal-,* is the source of virtually all the modern European terms, including Russian *sol',* Polish *sól,* Serbo-Croat *so,* Irish *salann,* and Welsh *halen.* Greek *háls* has given English *halogen* [19]. And Latin *sāl,* besides evolving into French *sel,* Italian *sale,* Spanish *sal,* and Rumanian *sare,* has contributed an enormous range of vocabulary to English, including *salad, salary, saline* [15], *sauce, saucer,* and *sausage.* Its Germanic descendant was *salt-, which has produced Swedish, Danish, and English *salt* and Dutch *zout*, and also lies behind English *silt* and *souse*.

▶ halogen, salad, salary, saline, sauce, saucer, sausage, silt, souse

**saltcellar** [15] *Saltcellar* is a tautology – for etymologically it means 'saltcellar for salt.' Its second element has no connection with underground rooms. Its spelling merely disguises its origins, which are in Anglo-Norman *\*saler* 'saltcellar,' a derivative ultimately of Latin *sāl* 'salt.' This was adopted into English in the 14th century as *saler*, later *seler*, but when its etymological links with *salt* began to fade from people's awareness, *salt* was tacked on to the front to reinforce the meaning, and when they disappeared altogether in the 16th century the spelling became assimilated to that of the similar-sounding *cellar*.

**saltpetre** see PETROL

**salute** [14] *Salute* goes back ultimately to the Latin noun *salūs*, a relative of *salvus* 'safe, healthy' (source of English *safe* and *save*). This had two main strands of meaning. The primary one was 'health, wellbeing,' and in that sense it lies behind English *salubrious* [16] and *salutary* [15]. But by extension it also denoted a 'wish for someone's well-being,' hence a 'greeting,' and it is this that has given English, via its derived verb *salūtāre* 'greet,' *salute*.

▶ safe, salubrious, save

**salvage** [17] The *salvage* of a ship is etymologically simply a payment made for 'saving' it. The word comes via Old French *salvage* from medieval Latin *salvāgium*, a derivative of late Latin *salvāre* 'save' (source of English *save*). The use of English *salvage* as a verb is a comparatively recent development, dating from the 1880s.

▶ save

**salvation** see SAVE

**salve** [OE] The central semantic element of modern English *salve* is 'healing,' but its underlying etymological meaning is 'oily substance.' It goes back to a prehistoric West Germanic *\*salbō*, which had relatives in Greek *élpos* 'oil' and Sanskrit *srpras* 'greasy.' The Germanic form has evolved into German *salbe* and Dutch *zalf* as well as English *salve*.

**salver** [17] The word *salver* recalls the ancient practice of paranoid monarchs employing a special servant to taste their food before it was committed to the royal mouth, in case it was poisoned. The Spanish term for this was *salva*, a derivative of the verb *salvar* 'save,' hence 'make safe, try something out to make sure it is safe,' which in turn was descended from Latin *salvāre* 'save' (source of English *save*). By extension the Spanish noun came to be used for a tray on which the tested food was presented to the king, and it passed into

French as *salve*. When English adopted it, the ending *-er* was added, perhaps on the model of *platter*.

▶ save

**salvia** see SAFE

**salvo** [16] When English originally acquired the word *salvo*, it was in the forms *salve* or *salva*, which came respectively from French *salve* and its source, Italian *salva*. This originally meant 'salute, greeting' (it came from *salvē* 'hail,' the imperative form of Latin *salvēre* 'be in good health,' which is related to English *safe*, *salubrious*, *salute*, *save*, etc). Important personages being greeted with a volley of gunfire, *salva* soon came to be used for such a discharge of guns (the related English *salute* has developed along the same lines – as in a '21-gun salute'). The form *salvo*, which emerged in the 17th century, is an alteration of *salva*.

▶ safe, salute, save

**same** [12] *Same* comes ultimately from Indo-European *\*somós* 'same.' This also produced Greek *homós* 'same' (source of the English prefix *homo-*, as in *homosexual*), and was a variant of the base that gave Latin *similis* 'similar' (source of English *similar* and *simulate*), Latin *simul* 'at the same time' (source of English *assemble* and *simultaneous*), Latin *simplus* 'simple' (source of English *simple*), Latin *singulus* 'single' (source of English *single* and *singular*), and English *seem* and *some*. The Indo-European adjective passed into prehistoric Germanic as *\*samaz*, which in due course evolved into Old Norse *same*. The Vikings brought the word with them to England, where it gradually replaced the native terms for 'same,' *ilk* and *self*.

**sample** see EXAMPLE

**sanatorium** see SANE

**sanctity** [14] Latin *sanctus* 'holy' (source of English *saint*) originated as the past participle of *sancīre* 'consecrate,' a verb derived from the same base that produced *sacer* 'sacred' (source of English *sacred*, *sacrifice*, etc). Amongst its derivatives to have reached English are *sanctify* [14], *sanctimonious* [17], *sanctity*, *sanctuary* [14], and *sanctum* [16]. And its stem *sanct-* formed the basis of the Latin noun *sanctiō* 'ordaining of something as sacred or inviolable,' hence more broadly a 'decree, sanction,' from which English gets *sanction* [16].

▶ sacred, saint

**sand** [OE] *Sand* is a widespread Germanic word, shared by German, Swedish, and Danish (Dutch has *zand*). Its prehistoric source was *\*sandam*, which went back to an Indo-European *\*samdam*. This also produced Latin *sabulum* 'sand,' which evolved into French *sable* and Italian *sabbia* 'sand.' It probably came ultimately from a base which signified 'grind, crush.'

**sandal** [14] English acquired *sandal* from Latin *sandalium*. This in turn was borrowed from Greek *sandálion*, a diminutive form of *sándalon* 'wooden shoe,' which probably came from a western Asian language. It has no connection with the *sandal-* of *sandalwood* [16], which came via medieval Latin *sandalum* and Greek *sántalon* or *sándanon* from Sanskrit *candanah*.

**sandwich** [18] John Montagu, the fourth Earl of Sandwich (1718–92), is said to have been so addicted to the gambling table that in order to sustain him through an entire 24-hour session uninterrupted, he had a portable meal of cold beef between slices of toast brought to him. The basic idea was nothing new, of course, but the Earl's patronage ensured it a vogue, and by the early 1760s we have the first evidence of his name being attached to it: the historian Edward Gibbon in 1762 recorded in his diary how he dined at the Cocoa Tree and saw 'twenty or thirty of the best men in the kingdom ... supping at little tables ... upon a bit of cold meat, or a Sandwich.'

**sane** [17] Latin *sānus*, a word of uncertain origin, meant 'healthy' – a connotation perpetuated in its derivative *sanatorium* 'sick-room' [19]. Its use with reference to mental rather than physical health (as in the Latin tag *mēns sāna in corpore sāno* 'a healthy mind in a healthy body') led to its adoption in English for 'of sound mind, not mad.'
▶ sanatorium, sanitary

**sap** English has three distinct words *sap*. The oldest, 'plant-juice' [OE], goes back to a prehistoric Germanic *\*sappam*, which also produced German *saft* 'juice.' This in turn was a descendant of Indo-European *\*sapon-*, from which came Latin *sapa* 'new wine.' *Sap* 'undermine' [16] was borrowed via French *saper* from Italian *zappare*, which may have been ultimately of Arabic origin. Its original literal sense 'dig a trench or tunnel underneath in order to attack' has now been largely superseded by the metaphorical 'weaken,' which has been heavily influenced by *sap* 'plant-juice' (from the notion of 'draining sap from a plant'). The colloquial *sap* 'fool' [19] may be short for an earlier *sapskull*, a compound formed from *sap* in the now seldom heard sense 'sapwood' – hence 'wooden head.'

**sapient** [15] Like English *taste*, Latin *sapere* combined the notions of 'appreciating flavour' and 'fine discrimination,' and hence meant both 'taste' and 'be wise.' In the former sense it has given English *savour* and *savoury*, while the latter has fed through into English in its present participial form as *sapient*. It is also the source of Spanish *saber* 'know,' which via a West African pidgin has given English the slang term *savvy* 'understand' [18], and French *savoir* 'know,' as in English *savoir-faire* [19].
▶ savour, savoury

**sapphire** [13] *Sapphire* can be traced back through Old French *safir* and Latin *sapphīrus* to Greek

*sáppheiros* (which seems to have denoted 'lapis lazuli,' another blue stone), but beyond that its origins are uncertain. It may have been acquired via a Semitic language (Hebrew has *sappir*), but it has been suggested that its ultimate source could be Sanskrit *sanipriya*, which stood for a type of dark-coloured precious stone. It meant literally 'precious to the planet Saturn,' and was a compound of *Sani* 'Saturn' and *priya* 'precious.'

**Saracen** [13] The *Saracens* were etymologically 'people of the sunrise' – hence 'easterners.' The word comes via Old French *Saracin* and late Latin *Saracēnus* from Greek *Sarakēnós*, which was probably adapted from Arabic *sharqī* 'eastern.' This was a derivative of *sharq* 'sunrise.' *Sarsen* [17] stones, large isolated boulders found in southern England, were probably named from some fanciful association with Saracens.

**sarcasm** [16] A *sarcastic* remark is etymologically one which involves the 'rending of flesh.' Greek *sárx* meant 'flesh' (it has given English *sarcoma* [17] and *sarcophagus*), and it formed the basis of a verb *sarkázein* 'tear the flesh,' hence 'bite one's lip, gnash one's teeth,' and by further extension 'make a cutting remark.' This gave rise to the late Greek derivative *sarkasmós*, which passed into English via late Latin *sarcasmos* and French *sarcasme*.
▶ sarcoma, sarcophagus

**sarcophagus** [17] A *sarcophagus* is etymologically a 'flesh-eater': the word comes via Latin *sarcophagus* from Greek *sarkophágos*, a compound formed from *sárx* 'flesh' (source of English *sarcasm*) and *-phágos* 'eating.' This originated as the term for a particular type of limestone that in the ancient world was used for making coffins, since bodies buried in them quickly decomposed. By extension it came to be used for the coffins themselves.
▶ sarcasm

**sardonic** [17] The Greek word for 'scornful, mocking' was *sardánios*, but this came to be changed to *sardónios*, which literally meant 'Sardinian,' through association with the Latin term *herba Sardonia* 'Sardinian plant,' the name of a sort of plant which when eaten caused facial contortions that resembled a scornful grin. English acquired the word via Latin *sardonius* and French *sardonique*. The *sardine* [15] probably gets its name from Sardinia too.
▶ sardine

**sarsen** see SARACEN

**sash** The *sash* you wear [16] and the *sash* that goes in a window [17] are distinct words. The former comes from Arabic *shāsh* 'turban,' and that is exactly how English first acquired it: 'All of them wear on their heads white shashes and turbans, the badge of their religion,' George Sandys, *Travels* 1615. But the Arabic word also denoted a strip of muslin or other material from which such turbans were constructed, and it is that

application that led towards the end of the 17th century to the current sense of the English word. The altered form *sash* appeared around the same time. *Sash* 'window-frame' was originally *chassis*, an early borrowing of French *chassis* 'frame' (it was acquired again in the sense 'frame of a carriage' in the 19th century). This evolved to *shashes*, and in due course came to be regarded as a plural form, so a new singular *sash* emerged. French *chassis* itself goes back ultimately to Latin *capsa* 'box,' source of English *capsule, case*, etc.
▶ capsule, case, chassis

**sassenach** [18] *Sassenach*, the Gaelic name for the English, etymologically means 'Saxon.' Its ultimate source is probably *Saxonēs*, the Latin version of *Seaxe*, which was the Old English term for the Saxon people. The Celts of Scotland took this over as *Sasunnoch*, the Irish as *Sasanach*, and the Welsh as *Seisnig*. The English form of the word appears to have been established by Sir Walter Scott in the early 19th century.
▶ Saxon

**satchel** [14] A *satchel* is etymologically a 'small sack' or bag. The word comes via Old French *sachel* from Latin *saccellus*, a diminutive form of *saccus* 'bag' (source of English *sack*). Its specific application to a 'bag for carrying school books' emerged in the mid 16th century, and is reflected by Shakespeare in Jaques's 'Seven ages of man' speech in *As You Like It* 1600: 'And then the whining schoolboy, with his satchel and shining morning face, creeping like snail unwillingly to school.'
▶ sachet, sack

**sated** see SAD

**sateen** see SATIN

**satellite** [16] *Satellite* comes via French *satellite* from Latin *satelles* 'attendant, escort,' which itself probably went back to Etruscan *satnal*. Its use for a 'body orbiting a planet' is first recorded in English in 1665, and comes from the astronomer Johannes Kepler's application of Latin *satelles* to the moons of Jupiter.

**satiate** [16] Like *satisfy*, *satiate* comes from Latin *satis* 'enough,' a descendant of the same Indo-European base that produced English *sad* and *sated*. *Satis* formed the basis of a verb *satiāre* 'give enough or too much,' which was originally taken over by English in the former of these senses, virtually the equivalent of *satisfy*, but since the 17th century this has been gradually pushed aside by the more opprobrious 'give too much, surfeit.' From the same source come *satiable* [16] and *satiety* [16].
▶ sad, sated, satisfy

**satin** [14] Like many other fabric names, *satin* betrays the fabric's place of origin, although only after a little digging. It comes via Old French *satin* from Arabic *zaitūnī*, which denoted 'of Zaitun' – and *Zaitun* was the Arabic rendering of *Tseutung*, the former name of a port (now *Tsinkiang*) in southern China from which satin was exported. *Sateen* [19] is an alteration of *satin*, on the model of *velveteen*.

**satire** [16] A *satire* is etymologically a 'verse medley,' an 'assortment of pieces on various subjects.' The word comes via Old French *satire* from Latin *satira* 'mixture,' an alteration of an earlier *satura*. This is said to have been derived from *satus* 'full' (a relative of *satis* 'enough,' source of English *satisfy*), and the link in the semantic chain from 'full' to 'mixture' is 'plateful of assorted fruit,' the earliest recorded meaning of *satura*. By classical times, Latin *satira* had moved on from being a general literary miscellany to its now familiar role as a 'literary work ridiculing or denouncing people's follies or vices.' The word has no etymological connection, incidentally, with *satyr* 'Greek woodland god' [14], which comes ultimately from Greek *sáturos*, a word of unknown origin.

**satisfy** [15] Etymologically, *satisfy* means 'make enough.' It comes, via Old French *satisfier*, from Latin *satisfacere* 'satisfy, content,' a compound verb formed from *satis* 'enough' (a relative of English *sad, sated*, and *saturate*, and source of English *satiate*). The derived noun *satisfaction* reached English well over a century before the verb, in the specialized ecclesiastical sense 'performance of penance.'
▶ sad, sated, satiate, saturate

**saturate** [16] Latin *satur* meant 'full,' and in particular 'full of food, full up' (it was a relative of *satis* 'enough,' source of English *satiate* and *satisfy*). From it was formed a verb *saturāre* 'fill, glut, surfeit,' whose past participle has given English *saturate*. At first this was used as a synonym of *satisfy* or *satiate* ('so to saturate their insatiable hunger,' Thomas Bell, *Survey of Popery* 1596), and the modern sense 'soak' did not emerge fully until the mid 18th century.
▶ sad, sated, satisfy

**Saturday** [OE] *Saturday* is etymologically 'Saturn's day.' Old English *Sæterdæg* was short for *Sæternes dæg*, a translation of Latin *Sāturnī diēs* 'Saturn's day.' *Saturn* [OE] itself, as the name of both the god and the planet, comes from Latin *Sāturnus*, which may have been of Etruscan origin. In ancient Rome, the festival held in honour of Saturn, which took place in December, was the occasion for fairly uninhibited revelry. It was called the *Sāturnālia*, which English acquired as *saturnalia* [16]. Those born under Saturn, by contrast, were considered by ancient and medieval astrologers to be of gloomy temperament – hence the adjective *saturnine* [15].
▶ Saturn, saturnalia, saturnine

**sauce** [14] *Sauce* is one of a range of English words (others include *salad, salary*, and *sausage*) that go back ultimately to Latin *sāl* 'salt' (a relative of English *salt*). From it was formed the adjective *salsus* 'salted,' whose feminine form *salsa* was used in Vulgar Latin for a 'brine dressing or pickle.' This later evolved into Italian and Spanish *salsa* 'sauce' and French *sauce*, from which English gets *sauce*. The derivative *saucy* 'cheeky' no doubt arose from the 'piquancy' or 'tartness' of sauces.

*Saucer* [14] originally meant 'sauceboat,' and was borrowed from Old French *saussier*, a derivative of *sauce*. The modern application to a 'dish for a cup' did not evolve until the 18th century.

▶ salt, saucer

**saunter**    [15]    *Saunter*'s modern connotations of 'walking' did not emerge until the 17th century, but it is presumably the same word as Middle English *santer* 'muse.' The origins of this, however, are largely a matter of speculation. One theory is that it is connected with the 15th-century term *sawnterell* 'pretended saint, sanctimonious person,' the notion being that those who affect piety go around with a faraway mystical musing air. *Sawnterell* in turn was probably a derivative of *saint*.

▶ saint

**sausage**    [15]    A *sausage* is etymologically a dish made by 'salting.' The word comes via Old Northern French *saussiche* from late Latin *salsīcia*, a noun use of the neuter plural of *salsīcius* 'made by salting.' This in turn was based on Latin *salsus* 'salted,' a derivative of *sāl* 'salt.' The earliest record of the use of *sausage dog* for 'dachshund' (an allusion to its cylindrical shape, and also perhaps to the Germans' supposed liking for sausages) dates from the late 1930s.

▶ salt

**sauté**    [19]    If you *sauté* something, you are etymologically making it 'jump.' The word comes from the past participle of French *sauter* 'jump,' a descendant of Latin *saltāre* 'jump.' This in turn was derived from *salīre* 'jump,' which has given English *assail, insult, salacious, salient*, etc. In the cookery sense *sauter* is used causatively, to 'make something jump,' hence to 'toss' it in a frying pan.

▶ assault, insult, result, salacious, salient

**savage**    [13]    A *savage* is etymologically someone who comes from the 'woods' – woodlands being anciently viewed as places of untamed nature, beyond the pale of civilized human society. The word comes via Old French *sauvage* from Vulgar Latin *\*salvāticus*, an alteration of Latin *silvāticus* 'of the woods, wild.' This was a derivative of *silva* 'woods, forest' (source of English *sylvan* [16]), a word of uncertain origin.

▶ sylvan

**save**    English has two distinct words *save*, which come from the same ultimate source, but have entered

the language along very different routes. That source was Latin *salvus* 'unharmed,' ancestor of English *safe*. Its ablative form *salvō* was used as a virtual preposition, in the sense 'without injury to, without prejudice to,' hence 'except,' and this passed into English via Old French *sauf* as the preposition and conjunction *save* [13]. The verb *save* [13] goes back via Anglo-Norman *sauver* to late Latin *salvāre* (source also of English *salvage, salver*, and *salvation* [13]), which in turn was derived from *salvus*. The derivative *saviour* [13] comes via Old French *sauveour* from late Latin *salvātor*.

▶ safe, sage, salvation, saviour

**saveloy**    [19]    *Saveloy* 'spicy sausage' is etymologically a sausage made from 'brains.' The word is an anglicization of early modern French *cervelat*, which in turn was borrowed from Italian *cervellata*, a diminutive form of *cervello* 'brains.' This was a descendant of Latin *cerebellum* (acquired by English in the 16th century), itself a diminutive of *cerebrum* 'brain' (source of English *cerebral* [19]). And *cerebrum* is distantly related to Swedish *hjarna* and Danish *hjerne* 'brain,' all three going back ultimately to a prehistoric Indo-European base meaning 'head.'

▶ cerebral

**saviour**    see SAVE

**savoir-faire**    see SAPIENT

**savour**    [13]    Latin *sapere* meant both 'taste' and 'be wise.' In the latter sense it has given English *sapient*, but the former only was preserved in its derived noun *sapor* 'taste.' This found its way into English via Old French *savour*. The derivative *savoury* [13] originally meant 'pleasant-tasting.' Its modern use, contrasted with *sweet*, dates from the 17th century.

▶ sapient

**savvy**    see SAPIENT

**saw**    Not counting the past tense of *see*, English has two words *saw*. The one meaning 'toothed cutting tool' [OE] comes from a prehistoric Germanic *\*sagō*, a close relative of which produced German *säge* 'saw.' This in turn was descended from an Indo-European base *\*sak-*, *\*sek-* 'cut,' which also lies behind English *section, segment, sickle*, etc. The now seldom heard *saw* 'saying, adage' [OE] comes from a different prehistoric Germanic *\*sagō*, which was derived from the verb *\*sagjan* 'say' (ancestor of English *say*) and also produced Old Norse *saga* 'narrative' (source of English *saga* [18]).

▶ section, segment, sickle / saga, say

**saxifrage**    [15]    The *saxifrage* is etymologically the 'stone-breaker.' The word comes via Old French *saxifrage* from late Latin *saxifraga*, a compound formed from Latin *saxum* 'rock' and *frag-*, the stem of *frangere* 'break' (source of English *fraction, fracture*, etc). The name is an allusion to the fact that the plant grows in crevices in rock, and so gives the impression of splitting the rock.

▶ fraction, fracture, fragment

**saxophone** [19] The saxophone commemorates the name of its inventor, the Belgian musical instrument maker Adolphe Sax (1814–94) (his real Christian names were Antoine Joseph). He seems to have devised it around 1840, and the term *saxophone* first appeared in English in 1851, in the catalogue of the Great Exhibition. His father Charles Joseph Sax (1791–1865) was also an instrument maker, and similarly had an instrument of his invention named after him – the *saxhorn* [19].

**say** [OE] *Say* is part of a widespread Germanic family of 'say'-verbs, which also contains German *sagen*, Dutch *zeggen*, Swedish *säga*, and Danish *sige*. These point back to a common Germanic ancestor *sagjan*, which was descended from the Indo-European base *seq-. This originally signified 'point out,' but evolved to 'say,' and it also lies behind Lithuanian *saký-ti*, Latvian *sacīt*, Welsh *eb*, and Latin *inquit*, all of which mean 'say.'

▶ saga, saw

**scab** [13] Old English had a word *sceabb* 'scab.' This survived into modern English as *shab*, a dialectal synonym of *scab*, but it is only represented in the mainstream language by its derivative *shabby*. It is its Old Norse relative *skabbr*, borrowed in the 13th century as *scab*, which has become the general English term for a 'crust over a wound.' The derogatory sense 'strike-breaker' emerged in the 19th century from an earlier, 16th-century 'despicable person.' The word comes ultimately from the Germanic base *skab-'scratch, shave' (source also of English *shave* [OE]), which was descended from the same Indo-European base that produced Latin *scabiēs* 'itch' (source of English *scabies* [14], *scabious* [14] – a plant so called because it was supposed to cure skin diseases – and *scabrous* [17]).

▶ scabies, shabby, shave

**scabbard** [13] English acquired *scabbard* from Anglo-Norman *escaubers*. This appears to have been a compound formed from Old High German *scār*, which usually meant 'scissors' but was also used for 'sword' (it came from the same base that produced English *shear*), and the element -*berc* 'protection' (as in *hauberk* [13], which etymologically means 'neck-protection'), which was derived from *bergan* 'protect' (a relative of English *borough, borrow, bury*, etc). So essentially, a *scabbard* is 'sword-protection.'

▶ borough, borrow, bury, share, shear, shirt, short, skirt

**scabies** see SCAB

**scabrous** see SCAB

**scaffold** [14] Historically, *scaffold* and *catafalque* [17] 'coffin-stand' are virtually the same word.

*Catafalque* comes via French *catafalque* and Italian *catafalco* from Vulgar Latin *catafalcum*, a word of uncertain origin. Combination with the prefix *ex-* produced *excatafalcum*, which passed into English via Old French *eschaffaut* and Anglo-Norman *scaffaut*. The word originally denoted any sort of platform, and did not narrow down to 'platform for executions' until the 16th century. The derivative *scaffolding*, a term which originally alluded to the platforms set up around a building rather than to poles supporting them, also dates from the 14th century.

▶ catafalque

**scald** [13] *Scald* comes ultimately from Latin *calidus* 'hot' (source also of English *cauldron* and *chowder* and related to *calorie* and *nonchalant*). From it was derived the verb *excaldāre* 'wash in hot water,' which passed into English via Anglo-Norman *escalder* as *scald*.

▶ calorie, cauldron, chowder, nonchalant

**scale** English has three separate words *scale*. The oldest, 'pan of a balance' [13], was borrowed from Old Norse *skál* 'bowl, drinking cup' (ancestor of Swedish *skål*, from which English gets the toast *skol* [16]). This was descended from a Germanic base *skal-, *skel-, *skul-, denoting 'split, divide, peel,' which also produced English *scalp, shell, shelter, shield, skill*, probably *skull*, and also *scale* 'external plate on fish, etc' [14]. This second *scale* was borrowed from Old French *escale*, which itself was acquired from prehistoric Germanic *skalō* – another derivative of *skal-. Its modern German descendant, *schale*, is the probable source of English *shale* [18]. The third *scale*, which originally meant 'ladder' [15], came from Latin *scāla* 'ladder,' a descendant of the same base as Latin *scandere* 'climb,' from which English gets *ascend, descend, scan*, and *scandal*. (In modern French *scāla* has evolved to *échelle*, whose derivative *échelon* has given English *echelon* [18].) The modern meanings of the word, variations on the theme 'system of graduations used for measuring,' are metaphorical extensions of the original 'ladder, steps.' Its use as a verb, meaning 'climb,' goes back to the medieval Latin derivative *scālāre*.

▶ scalp, shell, shelter, shield, skill, skol, skull / shale / ascend, descend, echelon, scan, scandal

**scallion** see SHALLOT

**scalp** [13] *Scalp* originally meant 'top of the head, cranium'; it was not used for the 'skin on top of the head' until the 17th century. It is not altogether clear where the word came from, but its resemblance to Old Norse *skálpr* 'sheath, shell' and the fact that it first appeared in Scotland and the north of England suggest that it was borrowed from a Scandinavian language. Its ultimate ancestor was no doubt the Germanic base *skal-, *skel-, *skul-, source also of English *shell* and probably *skull*.

▶ scale, shell, skull

**scalpel** see SCULPTURE

**scan** [14] Latin *scandere* meant 'climb' (it has given English *ascend* and *descend*). In the post-classical period it was used metaphorically for 'analyse the rising and falling rhythm of poetry,' and it was in this sense that it passed into English as *scan*. It was broadened out semantically to 'examine' in the 16th century, and to 'look at widely' in the 18th century. The Latin past participle *scansus* formed the basis of the noun *scansiō*, from which English gets *scansion* [17].

▶ ascend, descend, scandal

**scandal** [16] Greek *skándalon* originally meant literally 'trap' (it came from prehistoric Indo-European *skand-* 'jump,' which also produced Latin *scandere* 'climb,' source of English *ascend*, *descend*, and *scan*). It was extended metaphorically to 'snare for the unwary, stumbling block,' and passed into late Latin as *scandalum*, which was used for 'cause of offence.' It came down to Old French as *escandle*, which was not only the source of a short-lived Middle English *scandle*, but also lies behind English *slander*. It was the later French form *scandale* that gave English *scandal*.

▶ ascend, descend, scan, slander

**scarce** [13] *Scarce* comes via Anglo-Norman *scars*, earlier *escars*, from Vulgar Latin *\*excarpsus* 'picked out,' hence 'rare.' This was the past participle of *\*excarpere*, an alteration of classical Latin *excerpere* 'pick out, select' (source of English *excerpt* [17]). And *excerpere* was a compound verb formed from the prefix *ex-* 'out' and *carpere* 'pluck' (source of English *carpet* and related to *harvest*).

▶ carpet, excerpt, harvest

**scarf** English has two words *scarf*. The older, but now less frequent, is 'joint between two pieces of wood' [14]. This may have been borrowed from an Old French *\*escarf*, which itself was possibly based ultimately on a Scandinavian source (Swedish has *skarf* 'joint between pieces of wood'). The *scarf* that is worn [16] comes from Old Northern French *escarpe*. This was equivalent to central Old French *escharpe, escherpe*, which originally denoted a 'pilgrim's bag hung round the neck.' It came via a Frankish *\*skirpja* from Latin *scirpea* 'basket made from rushes,' a derivative of *scirpus* 'rush.'

**scarlet** [13] *Scarlet* originally denoted a sumptuous sort of cloth, which came in various colours, not just red. Red was evidently the commonest colour, however, for by the 15th century we find the word *scarlet* being used for 'red.' It was borrowed from Old French *escarlate*, but where that came from is not known (some have derived it from Persian *saqalāt* 'rich cloth,' but this has not been conclusively established).

**scathe** [12] *Scathe* is now encountered virtually only in the negative form *unscathed* (first recorded in the 14th century), but originally it was a verb in its own right, meaning 'harm.' It was borrowed from Old Norse *skatha*, which was descended from a prehistoric Germanic *\*skathōjan* (source also of German and Dutch *schaden* 'harm'). This was formed from a base *\*skath-*, which has links with Irish *scathaim* 'mutilate, lame' and Greek *askēthḗs* 'unhurt.'

**scatter** [13] *Scatter* originally meant 'squander,' and appears to have started life as an alteration of *shatter*. It first appears in northern and Scottish texts, and so the change from /sh/ to /sk/ is probably due to Norse influence. The origins of *shatter* [12] itself are not known.

▶ shatter

**scavenger** [15] A *scavenger* was originally a *scavager* – the extra *n* is the same as that intruded into *messenger, passenger*, etc. This was acquired from Anglo-Norman *scawager*, and it started life as a term for an official whose job was to collect taxes levied on foreign merchants. Etymologically it denoted 'inspector,' for it was derived from the verb *escauwer* 'inspect,' which was borrowed from Flemish *scauwen* 'look at,' a relative of English *show*. By the 16th century the *scavenger* had begun to come down in the world, first to a 'street-cleaner' and finally to 'one who gathers or lives on what others have thrown away.' The verb *scavenge* was derived from it in the 17th century.

▶ show

**scene** [16] Greek *skēnḗ* originally meant 'tent' (it was related to *skiá* 'shadow,' a descendant of the same Indo-European base that produced English *shimmer* and *shine*, and so etymologically denoted 'something that gives shade'). Such tents or booths were used for presenting plays, and eventually the word *skēnḗ* came to denote the backdrop against which drama is performed. It passed into English via Latin *scaena*. The Italian version of the word, *scena* (itself borrowed into English in the 19th century), has the derivative *scenario*, which has been acquired by English on two separate occasions: first as *scenery* [18] and later as *scenario* [19].

▶ scenario, shimmer, shine

**scent** [14] *Scent* comes ultimately from the same source that gave English *sensation, sense, sentient*, and *sentiment* – namely, Latin *sentīre* 'feel, perceive.' It arrived via Old French *sentir*, and at first was *sent* in English ('Fishes lurking among the stones [the dogs] seek out with their sent,' James Dalrymple, *Leslie's history of Scotland* 1596). The modern *sc-* spelling did not begin to emerge until the 17th century. It is not known what the reason for it was, although it may have been a resolution of a possible confusion with the past form of *send*.

▶ sensation, sense, sentient, sentiment

**sceptic** [16] The Greek verb *sképtesthai* meant 'examine, consider' (it was descended from a base *\*skep-* which was related to *\*skop-*, source of English *scope*, and may have been a reversed version of *\*spek-*, from which English gets *spectator, speculate*, etc). From it was derived the adjective *skeptikós*, which was applied to various schools of philosophy (particularly that of Pyrrho of Elis) which stressed the need for careful examination of a proposition, starting from an attitude of doubt, before accepting it. The word passed via Latin *scepticus* and French *sceptique* into English as *sceptic*, by which time it had acquired broader connotations of 'initial doubt.'

▶ scope

**sceptre** see SHAFT

**schedule** [14] Late Latin *scedula* meant 'small piece of paper.' It was a diminutive form of Latin *sceda* 'papyrus leaf, piece of paper, page,' itself a borrowing from Greek *skhédē*. By the time it reached English via Old French *cedule* it had moved on semantically to 'small piece of paper with writing on it, used as a ticket or label'; and this subsequently developed through 'supplementary sheet giving a summary, list of additional points, etc' to any 'list giving details of what has been arranged.' Until around 1800 the word was pronounced /sed-/; but then in Britain, apparently under French influence, it changed to /shed-/, while Americans reverted to the original Greek with /sked-/.

**scheme** [16] Greek *skhêma* meant 'form, figure.' Latin took it over as *schēma* and used it as the equivalent of *figure* in a range of applications, such as 'figure of speech' and 'diagram,' many of which were originally taken over by English ('In the text, by a very elegant scheme of speech he does . . . once more set them at liberty,' John Tillotson, *Sermons* 1684). The modern sense 'plan,' which presumably developed out of 'diagram,' began to emerge in the mid 17th century.

**scherzo** see SCORN

**schism** [14] The Greek verb *skhízein* meant 'split' (it has given English *schizophrenia*, and a common source lies behind English *schist* [18], etymologically a 'split rock,' and *shit*). From it was derived the noun *skhísma*, literally 'split, division,' which in the Greek translation of the New Testament was applied to dissensions or discords between factions in the Church. English acquired it via late Latin *schisma* and Old French *scisme* or *sisme*.

▶ concise, decide, schist, schizophrenia, scissors, shit

**schizophrenia** [20] *Schizophrenia* means literally 'split mind.' It is a Latinized version of German *schizophrenie*, coined in 1910 by E Bleuler from Greek

*skhízein* 'split' (source of English *schism* and *schist*) and *phrén* 'mind' (source of English *frantic* and *phrenology*).

▶ frantic, phrenology, schism

**schlemiel** see SHEMOZZLE

**schlep** see SHEMOZZLE

**schlock** see SHEMOZZLE

**schmaltz** see ENAMEL

**schmuck** see SHEMOZZLE

**school** *School* for teaching [OE] and *school* of fish [14] are different words. The former was borrowed into prehistoric Germanic from medieval Latin *scōla*, and has since evolved into German *schule*, Dutch *school*, Swedish *skola*, and Danish *skole*, as well as English *school*. The medieval Latin word itself goes back via classical Latin *schola* to Greek *skholḗ*. This originally denoted 'leisure,' and only gradually developed through 'leisure used for intellectual argument or education' and 'lecture' to 'school' (in the sense 'educational assembly') and finally 'school' the building. The Latin word has spread throughout Europe, not just in the Romance languages (French *école*, Italian *scuola*, Spanish *escuela*), but also into Welsh *ysgol*, Irish *scoil*, Latvian *skuola*, Russian *shkola*, Polish *szkola*, etc. Derivatives of the Latin word in English include *scholar* [14] and *scholastic* [16].

*School* of fish was borrowed from Middle Dutch *schōle* 'troop, group.' This went back to a prehistoric West Germanic *\*skulo*, which may have been derived from the base *\*skal-, \*skel-, \*skul-* 'split, divide' (source also of English *scale, scalp, shell*, etc); if so, it would mean etymologically a 'division.'

▶ scholar, scholastic / shoal

**science** [14] Etymologically, *science* simply means 'knowledge,' for it comes via Old French *science* from Latin *scientia*, a noun formed from the present participle of the verb *scīre* 'know.' It early on passed via 'knowledge gained by study' to a 'particular branch of study,' but its modern connotations of technical, mathematical, or broadly 'non-arts' studies did not begin to emerge until the 18th century. The derivative *scientist* was coined in 1840 by William Whewell: 'We need very much a name to describe a cultivator of science in general. I should incline to call him a Scientist,' *Philosophy of the Inductive Sciences* 1840.

▶ conscious

**scintillate** see TINSEL

**scissors** [14] *Scissors* are etymologically a 'cutting' implement. The word comes via Old French *cisoires* from *cīsōria*, the plural of late Latin *cīsōrium* 'cutting implement,' which was derived from Latin *caedere* 'cut' (source of English *concise, decide, incision*, etc). The original form of the word in English was *sisoures*; the *sc-* spelling did not come on the scene until the 16th century, presumably through association with Latin *scindere* 'cut' (source of English *rescind* [17] and *scission* 'cutting' [15], and related to Greek *skhízein* 'split,' from which English gets *schism* and *schizophrenia*).

▶ concise, decide, incision, rescind, schism, shit

**sclerosis** see SKELETON

**scold** [13] *Scold* was originally a noun, denoting an argumentative or nagging woman – the sort who had a 'scold's bridle' fitted to keep her tongue quiet. It appears to have been borrowed from Old Norse *skáld* 'poet,' the semantic link perhaps being the poet's role of satirizing or poking fun at people (in Icelandic law in former times the term *skáldskapr*, literally 'poetry,' denoted 'libel in verse'). The origins of *skáld* itself are not known. *Scold* began to be used as a verb in the 14th century, at first in the sense 'argue, nag.' The modern transitive use 'reprove' is not recorded until the early 18th century.

**sconce** Effectively, English now only has one word *sconce* in general use, although others have come and gone in the past. That is the noun meaning 'candlestick' or 'wall bracket for a light' [14]. It originally denoted a 'lantern' or 'covered candlestick,' and came via Old French *esconse* from medieval Latin *absconsa*. This was short for *laterna absconsa*, literally 'hidden lantern'; *absconsa* was the feminine past participle of Latin *abscondere* 'hide' (source of English *abscond* [16]), a compound verb formed from the prefix *ab-* 'away' and *condere* 'put, stow.' It may be that *sconce* 'lantern, lamp' lay behind the now obsolete slang *sconce* 'head' [16], and there are grounds for believing that this in turn inspired the old university slang term *sconce* 'penalty of drinking a large amount of beer for a breach of the rules' [17] (the underlying notion being of a poll tax or 'head' tax). A fourth *sconce*, now altogether defunct, was a military term for a 'small fort' [16]. This was borrowed from Dutch *schans*, which came via Middle High German *schanze* from Italian *scanso* 'defence.' This in turn was a derivative of the verb *scansare* 'turn aside, ward off,' which was descended from Vulgar Latin *\*excampsāre*, a compound verb formed from the prefix *ex-* 'out' and *campsāre* 'turn round, sail by.' A memory of the word survives in English, however, in the derived verb *ensconce* [16] (etymologically 'hide behind a fortification').

▶ abscond / ensconce

**scone** [16] The word *scone* first appeared in Scottish English, and does not seem to have made any significant headway south of the border until the 19th century (helped on its way, no doubt, by that great proselytizer of Scottish vocabulary, Sir Walter Scott). It was borrowed from Dutch *schoonbrood* 'fine white bread,' a compound formed from *schoon* 'beautiful, bright, white' (first cousin to German *schön* 'beautiful'

and related to English *sheen* and *show*) and *brood* 'bread.'

▶ sheen, show

**scoop** [14] *Scoop* appears to go back ultimately to a prehistoric Germanic base *\*skap-* which originally denoted 'chop or dig out' (it was later extended metaphorically to 'form,' and in that sense has given English *shape*). It had a variant form *\*skōp-*, amongst whose derivatives was West Germanic *\*skōpō*. This evolved into Middle Dutch and Middle Low German *schōpe*, which was used for the bucket of a dredge, water-wheel, etc, and English borrowed it early in the 14th century. The journalistic sense 'story reported in advance of competitors' emerged in the USA in the 1870s.

▶ shape

**scope** [16] Greek *skopós* meant 'target.' As it passed via Italian *scopo* into English it evolved metaphorically to 'aim kept in view, goal, purpose' ('the seventh Council of Carthage and the Milevitane Council, which both tend to one end and scope, that there should be no appellations made out of Africa,' Nicholas Harpsfield, *The Pretended Divorce between Henry VIII and Catherine of Aragon* 1555), but the further step to 'range' seems to be an English development. The Greek word came from the base *\*skop-* 'look, observe,' which also produced *-skopos* 'looking' (ultimate source of English *bishop*, which etymologically denotes 'overseer') and *-skópion* 'instrument for observing' (which lies behind English *microscope, telescope*, etc). *Sceptic* comes from a variant of the same base.

▶ bishop, sceptic

**score** [11] The etymological notion underlying *score* is of 'cutting' – for it is related to English *shear*. It was borrowed from Old Norse *skor*, which went back to the same prehistoric Germanic base – *\*skur-*, *\*sker-* 'cut' – that produced *shear* (not to mention *share*, *shore*, and *short*). It had a range of meanings, from 'notch' to 'record kept by cutting notches,' but it was specifically the 'number twenty' (presumably originally 'twenty recorded by cutting notches') that English at first took over. The other senses followed, perhaps as a result of reborrowing, in the 14th century, but the main modern meaning, 'number of points made in a game' (originally as recorded by cutting notches), is a purely English development of the 18th century. Roughly contemporary is 'written music,' which is said to come from the linking together of related staves with a single common bar line or 'score' (in the sense 'mark'). The verb *score* 'mark with lines' was borrowed in the 14th century from Old Norse *skora*.

▶ share, shear, shirt, short, skirt

**scorn** [12] *Scorn* reached English via Old French, but it is ultimately of Germanic origin. Its immediate source was Old French *escharnir*, a descendant of Vulgar Latin *\*escarnīre*. This had been borrowed from a prehistoric Germanic *skarnjan 'mock, deride, make fun of.' A product of the same base was Middle High German scherz 'joke, jest,' which was borrowed into Italian as scherzo and subsequently made its way into English as the musical term scherzo 'lively passage' [19].

▶ scherzo

## scot-free   see SHOT

## scour   [13] The notion of 'cleaning' implicit in scour evolved from an earlier 'take care of.' For the word goes back ultimately to Latin cūrāre (source of English cure), which originally meant 'take care of,' and only in medieval times came to mean 'clean.' Combination with the prefix ex- 'out' produced excūrāre 'clean out,' which reached English via Old French escurer and Middle Dutch scūren. Scour 'search thoroughly' [14] (as in 'scour the countryside') is a different word, and may come from Old Norse skýra 'rush in.'

▶ cure

## scourge   [13] Scourge comes ultimately from a Latin word for a 'long strip of leather,' corrigio, which itself was borrowed from Celtic. It had a number of specific applications, including 'shoelace,' 'rein,' and 'whip,' and it was the last that formed the basis of the Vulgar Latin verb *excorrigiāre 'whip,' which passed into English via Old French escorgier and its derived noun escorge.

## scout   [14] Etymologically, a scout is someone who 'listens.' For the word goes back ultimately to Latin auscultāre 'listen,' a derivative of the same base that produced Latin auris 'ear' (source of English aural [19] and distantly related to English ear). This passed into Old French as escouter 'listen' (its modern descendant is écouter), which English adopted as the verb scout, meaning 'look about, spy.' The noun, from the French derivative escoute, followed in the 15th century.

▶ aural, ear

## scrape   [14] Scrape is certainly of Germanic origin, but it is not clear whether it was borrowed from Old Norse skrapa (ancestor of Swedish skrapa and Danish skrabe) or Middle Dutch schrapen. Either way it goes back to a prehistoric Germanic base *skrap-, source also of Old English scrapian 'scratch,' which survived into the 16th century as shrape. Scrap 'small piece' [14] was borrowed from Old Norse skrap 'remnants, trifles,' a derivative of the same base as skrapa; and scrap 'fight' [17] may have originated as a variant of scrape.

▶ scrap

## scratch   [15] Early Middle English had two words for 'scratch' – scrat and cratch; and it seems likely that scratch represents a blend of them. Where exactly they came from is not clear, although cratch is no doubt related to German kratzen 'scratch,' and both probably had their origins in imitation of the sound of scratching.

## screen   [15] Screen goes back ultimately to a Frankish *skrank 'barrier,' a distant ancestor of German schrank 'cupboard.' This was taken over into Old Northern French as escran, and it was a variant form of this, escren, that became English screen.

## screw   [15] Screw comes ultimately from a Latin word meaning 'female pig' – scrōfa (source also of English scrofula [14], a disease to which pigs were once thought to be particularly prone). By the medieval period scrōfa was being used for a 'screw,' mainly no doubt in allusion to the pig's curly, corkscrew-like tail, but also perhaps partly prompted by the resemblance to Latin scrobis 'ditch, trench,' hence 'cunt,' which was used in Vulgar Latin for the 'groove in a screw-head' (the use of the verb screw for 'copulate,' first recorded in the early 18th century, is purely coincidental). English got the word from Old French escroue, which came either directly from Latin scrōfa or via prehistoric West Germanic *scrūva (source of German schraube 'screw').

▶ scrofula

## scribe   [14] Scribe is at the centre of a large network of English words that go back to Latin scrībere 'write.' Others include ascribe [15], describe, scribble [15], and shrive, while its past participle scriptus has contributed script [14], scripture [13], and transcript [13]. Scribe itself comes from the Latin derivative scrība 'official writer.' Scrībere went back to an Indo-European base which meant 'cut, incise,' reflecting the origins of writing in carving marks on stone, wood, or clay; this was *skreibh-, an extension of *sker-, from which English gets shear, short, etc.

▶ ascribe, conscription, describe, scribble, script, share, shear, short, shrive, transcribe

## scrimmage   see SKIRMISH

## scrofula   see SCREW

## scroll   [15] Scroll has no family connection with roll, although roll is largely responsible for its present-day form. Etymologically it is actually the same word as shred. Both go back to a prehistoric Germanic *skrautha 'something cut.' This evolved in a straight line to give English shred, but it was also borrowed through medieval Latin scrōda into Old French as escroe, where its meaning 'cut piece, strip' narrowed to 'strip of parchment.' Its Anglo-Norman version escrowe was acquired by English, where it split in two. It survives in full as escrow [16], a legal term for a sort of deed, but a shortened form, scrow, also emerged, and association with roll (in the sense 'roll of parchment') led to its being altered to scrowle or scroll.

▶ escrow, shred

## scrummage   see SKIRMISH

## scruple   [16] Latin scrūpus meant 'sharp stone,' and the notion of something troubling the mind like a painful stone in the shoe led to its metaphorical

use for 'anxiety, doubt, particularly over a moral issue.' Both meanings were carried over into the diminutive form *scrūpulus*, which also came to be used for a very small unit of weight. This passed into English via French *scrupule* as *scruple*, on the way losing the literal sense 'small stone.'

**scrutinize** [17] The etymological notion underlying *scrutinize* is of ragpickers searching through piles of garbage looking for anything of use or value. For its ultimate source is Latin *scrūta* 'rubbish.' From this was formed the verb *scrūtārī* 'rummage through rubbish,' hence broadly 'search, examine.' This in turn formed the basis of the noun *scrūtinium*, source of English *scrutiny* [15], from which *scrutinize* was derived.

**scud** see SCUTTLE

**scullery** [15] A *scullery* is etymologically a place where 'dishes' are handled. For it goes back ultimately to Latin *scutra* 'wooden dish.' Its diminutive form *scutella* was used for a sort of square tray or stand for plates, glasses, vases, etc. Association with *scūtum* 'shield' led to this being changed in Vulgar Latin to *\*scūtella*, which passed into Old French as *escuele* 'dish.' Its derivative *escuelerie* 'place where dishes, plates, and other kitchen utensils are kept, cleaned, etc' passed into English via Anglo-Norman *squillerie* as *scullery*. Also descended from *scutella* are English *scuttle* and *skillet*.

**sculpture** [14] Latin *sculpere* meant 'carve, scratch' (it was a variant of *scalpere*, from which English gets *scalpel* [18]). From is past participle *sculptus* was formed the noun *sculptūra*, acquired by English as *sculpture*. The agent noun *sculptor* [17] also comes from Latin, while the verb *sculpt* [19] was borrowed from French *sculpter*.

▶ scalpel

**scum** [13] *Scum* is etymologically a 'layer on top' of something. The word's modern connotations of 'dirt' are a secondary development. It comes ultimately from prehistoric Germanic *\*skūman*, a derivative of the base *\*skū-* 'cover,' and its relatives include German *schaum* 'foam' (source of English *meerschaum* [18], literally 'sea-foam'). English *scum* originally meant 'foam' too ('Those small white Fish to Venus consecrated, though without Venus' aid they be created of th' Ocean scum,' Joshua Sylvester, *Divine Weeks and Works of Du Bartas* 1598), the notion being of a layer of froth 'covering' liquid, but by the 15th century it was broadening out to any 'film on top of liquid,' and from there it went downhill to a 'film of dirt' and then simply 'dirt.' Germanic *\*skūman* was borrowed into Old French as *escume*, and this formed the basis of a verb *escumer* 'remove the top layer,' from which English gets *skim* [15].

▶ meerschaum, skim

**scuttle** English has three distinct words *scuttle*. The oldest, 'large container' [15] (now mainly encountered in *coal-scuttle*), was borrowed from Old Norse *skutill*, which goes back ultimately to Latin *scutella* 'tray, salver' (from which English also gets *scullery* and *skillet*). *Scuttle* 'sink a ship' [17] is a verbal use of an earlier noun *scuttle* 'opening or hatch in a ship's side.' This was borrowed from early modern French *escoutille* 'hatch,' which in turn came from Spanish *escotilla*, a diminutive form of *escota* 'opening in a garment.' And *escota* was derived from *escotar* 'cut out,' a compound verb formed with the prefix *e-* 'out' from the Germanic stem *\*skaut-* (source of English *sheet*). *Scuttle* 'run' [17] is a variant of the now obsolete *scuddle*, which was derived from *scud* 'move quickly' [16]; and *scud* itself may have been an alteration of *scut* 'rabbit's tail' [15] (a word of unknown origin), the underlying meaning therefore being 'run like a rabbit.'

▶ scullery, skillet / sheet / scud, scut

**scythe** [OE] *Scythe* goes back ultimately to the Indo-European base *\*sek-* 'cut,' source also of English *section, segment, sickle*, etc. Its Germanic descendant was *\*seg-*, which produced the noun *\*segithō*, source of English *scythe* (the variant *\*sag-* lies behind English *saw*). Until the 17th century the word was generally spelled *sythe*; modern *scythe* is due to the influence of *scissors*.

▶ section, segment, sickle

**sea** [OE] *Sea* is a widespread Germanic word, related to German *see*, Dutch *zee*, Swedish *sjö*, and Danish *sø* (the Scandinavian words are now more usually used for 'lake' than 'sea'). These all point back to a prehistoric Germanic *\*saiwiz*, but it is not known where that came from.

**seal** *Seal* the animal [OE] and *seal* 'impressed mark, closure' [13] are of course different words. The former goes back to a prehistoric Germanic *\*selkhaz*, a word of unknown origin which also produced Swedish *säl* and Danish *sæl*. The latter was borrowed from Anglo-Norman *seal*, a descendant of Latin *sigillum*. This, a diminutive form of *signum* (from which English gets *sign*), meant 'little mark or picture,' and came to be used for such a mark distinctive of a particular person.

▶ sign, signal

**seam** [OE] A *seam* is etymologically a joint made by 'sewing.' The word goes back to a prehistoric Germanic *\*saumaz* (source also of German *saum*, Dutch *zoom*, Swedish *söm*, and Danish *søm*), which was derived from the base *\*sau-*, the ancestor of English *sew*.

▶ sew

**séance** see SESSION

**search** [14] Etymologically, *search* denotes 'going round in a circle' – for its ultimate source is Latin *circus* 'circle' (source of English *circle* and *circus*). From this was derived the verb *circāre* 'go round,' which by the time it had reached Old French as *cerchier* had acquired connotations of 'examining' or 'exploring.' English took it over via Anglo-Norman *sercher*. (It is no relation, incidentally, to English *seek*.)

▶ circle, circus

**season** [13]  A *season* is etymologically a time of 'sowing seeds.' The word comes via Old French *seson* from Latin *satiō* 'act of sowing,' a derivative of *satus*, the past participle of *serere* 'sow, plant' (which went back to the same Indo-European base that produced English *seed*, *semen*, and *sow*). In post-classical times 'act of sowing' evolved into 'time for sowing,' and by the time it reached Old French it had developed further to any 'suitable time.' The application to 'any of the four main divisions of the year' emerged in English in the 14th century. The use of *season* as a verb, meaning 'add flavourings to,' had its beginnings in post-classical Latin, and arose as the result of a progression from 'sow' through 'ripen' to 'cook thoroughly or well.'

▶ seed, semen, sow

**seat** [12]  *Seat* is of course a close relative of *sit* – they come from the same prehistoric Germanic base, *\*set-*. But unlike *sit*, it is not a long-established native word. It is a borrowing, from Old Norse *sáeti*. It originally meant 'act of sitting,' and was not used for 'something to sit on' until the 13th century.

▶ sit

**sebaceous**   see SUET

**secateurs**   see SECTION

**second** [13]  Latin *secundus* originally meant 'following' – it was derived from *sequī* 'follow,' source of English *sequence* – and only secondarily came to be used as the ordinal version of 'two.' English acquired it via Old French *second*, employing it to take over part of the role of *other*, which until then had denoted 'second' as well as 'other.' Its noun use for 'sixtieth of a minute,' first recorded in English in the 14th century, comes from medieval Latin *secunda minuta*, literally 'second minute' – a *minute* was a 'sixtieth part,' and so a 'second minute' was a 'sixtieth of a sixtieth.' Latin *secundus* was also used for 'favourable,' and in this sense the verb *secundāre* was formed from it, meaning 'favour.' English acquired it via French *seconder* as *second* 'support' [16]. (The differently pronounced *second* 'transfer to a different job' [19] comes from the French phrase *en second* 'in second rank.')

▶ sect, sequal, sequence, sue, suit

**secret** [14]  Etymologically, something that is *secret* is 'separated' from others, hence put out of the way, hidden. The word comes via Old French *secret* from Latin *sēcrētus*, an adjectival use of the past partici-

ple of *sēcernere* 'separate.' This was a compound verb formed from the prefix *sē-* 'apart' and *cernere* 'separate' (source also of English *certain, discern, excrement*, etc). From the 16th to the 18th centuries, *secret* was used as a verb, meaning 'hide,' but it was then altered to *secrete*, on the model of Latin *sēcrētus*. (The other verb *secrete*, 'produce fluids or other substances' [18], is a back-formation from *secretion* [17], which goes back to Latin *sēcrētiō* 'separation,' a derivative of *sēcernere*.) A *secretary* is etymologically a 'secret' or confidential helper.

▶ certain, decree, discern, excrement, secretary

**secretary** [14]  A *secretary* was originally a 'person in someone else's confidence, sharing secret or private matters with them' ('[Christ] taking with him his three special secretaries, that is to say Peter and James and John,' Nicholas Love, *Mirror of the life of Jesus Christ* 1400). The word was adapted from late Latin *sēcrētārius* 'confidential aide,' a derivative of Latin *sēcrētus* 'secret.' The notion of writing letters and performing other clerical duties developed in the Latin word, and first emerged in English in the 15th century.

▶ secret

**sect** [14]  Despite its similarity to *section* and *sector*, *sect* has nothing to do with 'cutting.' It comes via Old French *secte* from Latin *secta*, which denoted literally a 'following,' hence a 'faction of supporters' (it was a noun use of *sectus*, an archaic past participle of *sequī* 'follow,' from which English gets *sequence, sue*, etc). *Set* 'group' is ultimately the same word as *sect*.

▶ second, sequal, sequence, set, sue, suit

**section** [16]  *Section* is one of a wide range of English words that go back to Latin *secāre* 'cut.' Others include *bisect* [17], *dissect* [17], *insect, intersect* [17], *secateurs* [19], *sector* [16], and *segment* [16]. It goes back ultimately to the Indo-European base *\*sek-* 'cut,' which also produced English *saw, scythe, sedge*, and *sickle*. The immediate source of *section* itself was the Latin derivative *sectiō* 'cutting.'

▶ bisect, dissect, insect, saw, scythe, secateurs, sedge, segment, sickle

**secular** [13]  Latin *saeculum*, a word of uncertain origin, meant 'generation, age.' It was used in early Christian texts for the 'temporal world' (as opposed to the 'spiritual world'), and that was the sense in which its derived adjective *saeculāris* passed via Old French *seculer* into English. The more familiar modern English meaning 'non-religious' emerged in the 16th century.

**secure** [16]  Something that is *secure* is etymologically 'carefree.' The word was borrowed from Latin *sēcūrus*, a compound adjective formed from the prefix *sē-* 'without' and *cūra* 'care' (source of English *curate, cure*, etc). The metaphorical extension from 'free from care' to 'free from danger, safe' took place in post-Augustan Latin. *Sure* is in effect a telescoped version of *secure*.

▶ curate, cure, sure

**sedentary** see SESSION

**sedge** [OE] The *sedge* is etymologically the plant with 'cutting' leaves. The word goes back to a prehistoric Germanic *sagjaz*, which was descended from the Indo-European base *sek-* 'cut' (source also of English *saw, section, segment, sickle*, etc).

▶ section, segment

**sediment** see SESSION

**see** English has two words *see*. The older is the verb, 'perceive visually' [OE]. Like its Germanic cousins, German *sehen*, Dutch *zien*, and Swedish and Danish *se*, it goes back to a prehistoric *sekhwan*, which was descended from an Indo-European base *seq-*. This may have been the same *seq-* that produced Latin *sequī* 'follow' (source of English *sequence, sue*, etc), in which case *see* would denote etymologically 'follow with the eyes.' *See* 'diocese' [13] originally signified 'bishop's throne.' It came via Anglo-Norman *se* from Vulgar Latin *sedem* 'seat,' descendant of classical Latin *sēdem*, the accusative case of *sēdes* 'seat.' This in turn went back to the Indo-European base *sed-* 'sit,' which also produced English *sit*.

▶ sight / seat, sit

**seed** [OE] *Seed* is a general Germanic word, related to German *saat*, Dutch *zaad*, Swedish *söd*, and Danish *sæd*. Their common ancestor was Germanic *sæthiz*. This was formed from the base *sæ-*, which produced English *sow* and went back ultimately to Indo-European *sē-*, source of English *disseminate* [17], *season, semen* [18], and *seminar* [19].

▶ disseminate, season, semen, seminar

**seek** [OE] *Seek* has several Germanic relatives – German *suchen*, Swedish *söka*, Danish *søge*, etc – which point back to a prehistoric Germanic ancestor *sōkjan*. The base from which this was derived, *sōk-*, went back to an Indo-European *sāg-*, which also produced (via Latin) English *presage* [14] and *sagacious* [17]. If Old English *sēcan* had developed in the ordinary way, it would have become modern English *seech*, not *seek*. For various reasons it did not, but we can see how it would have been in its derivative *beseech* [12].

▶ beseech, presage, sagacious, sake

**seem** [12] Originally, *seem* meant 'be suitable' (a meaning preserved in the derived *seemly* [13]). It was borrowed from the Old Norse verb *soema* 'conform to, honour.' This was derived from the adjective *soemr* 'fitting,' a descendant of the prehistoric base *sōm-* (to which English *same* is distantly related). The sense 'appear to be' emerged in the early 13th century.

▶ same, seemly, soft

**seethe** [OE] *Seethe* was once the standard word for 'boil,' until it began to be overtaken by the French import *boil* in the Middle English period. In the 16th century a new meaning, 'soak,' emerged, now preserved only in the past participle *sodden*. And the modern metaphorical 'be violently agitated' came on the scene in the 17th century. The word goes back to a prehistoric Germanic *seuth-*, which also produced German *sieden* and Dutch *zieden* 'boil.' English *suds* probably comes from a variant of the same base.

▶ sodden

**segment** see SECTION

**segregate** [16] The etymological idea underlying *segregate* is of 'removal from a flock.' The word comes from Latin *sēgregāre*, a compound verb formed from the prefix *sē-* 'apart' and *grex* 'flock' (source also of English *aggregate, congregation, egregious* [16], and *gregarious* [17]).

▶ aggregate, congregation, egregious, gregarious

**seigneur** see SIR

**seize** [13] *Seize* entered English as a term in the feudal legal system, meaning 'take possession of property.' It was borrowed from Old French *seisir*, which went back via a Gallo-Latin *sacīre* 'claim' to a prehistoric Germanic *sakjan*. This in turn was derived from the base *sak-* 'process,' which also produced English *sake* (one of whose ancestral meanings was 'legal action').

▶ sake

**seldom** [OE] *Seldom* goes back to a prehistoric Germanic *selda-*, of which the underlying notion appears to have been 'strange and rare.' Its modern Germanic relatives include German *selten*, Dutch *zelten*, Swedish *sällan*, and Danish *sjelden*.

**select** [16] *Select* is one of a wide range of English words that go back ultimately to Latin *legere* 'choose' or its past participle *lectus* (others include *collect* and *elect* and, from its later extended meaning 'read,' *lectern* and *lecture*). Addition of the prefix *sē-* 'apart' produced *sēligere* 'choose out,' whose past participle *sēlectus* gave English *select*, both as adjective and verb.

▶ collect, elect, lecture, legible

**self** [OE] *Self* is a general Germanic word, closely related to German *selbe*, Dutch *zelf*, Swedish *sjelv*, and Danish *selv*. These all point back to a prehistoric Germanic *selba-*. Where this came from is not known for certain, although it seems likely to be related in some way to various pronouns denoting 'oneself,' such as German *sich* and French *se*. According to John Hacket in his *Scrinia reserata* 1693, the word *selfish* was coined in the early 1640s by the Presbyterians.

**sell** [OE] The underlying etymological meaning of *sell* is 'give up, hand over,' but gradually the notion of handing something over in exchange for something else, particularly money, led to its present-day sense. Both meanings co-existed in Old English, but the original one had largely died out by the 14th century. The word comes from a prehistoric Germanic *saljan, which also produced Swedish sälga and Danish sælge 'sell.' The noun sale is a product of the same base.

► sale

**semantic** [17] Sēma was the Greek word for 'sign.' It has been widely pressed into service in the modern European languages for coining new terms, including semaphore [19] (a borrowing from French, which etymologically means 'signal-carrier'), semasiology [19] (a German coinage), and semiology [17]. The adjective derived from sēma was semantikós which reached English via French sémantique. It was fleetingly adopted in the mid-17th century as a word for 'interpreting the 'signs' of weather,' but it did not come into its own as a linguistic term until the end of the 19th century.

► semaphore, semiology

**semblance** see SIMILAR

**semen** see SEED

**seminar** see SEED

**semolina** [18] Latin simila meant 'fine flour' (it has given English the simnel [13] of simnel cake, which originally denoted 'bread made from fine flour'). From it was descended Italian semola 'bran,' whose diminutive form semolino was adapted into English as semolina.

► simnel

**senate** [13] The Roman senate was etymologically an assembly of 'elders.' Latin senātus was a derivative of senex 'old,' which has also given English senile, senior, sir, etc. English acquired the word via Old French senat. Senator [13] comes from the Latin derivative senātor.

► senile, senior, sir

**send** [OE] English shares send with the other Germanic languages – German senden, Dutch zenden, Swedish sönda, and Danish sende. These all go back to a prehistoric ancestor *santhjan, which originated as a causative derivative of a base denoting 'go, journey' – so etymologically send means 'cause to go.'

**senior** [14] Senior was borrowed direct from Latin senior, which was the comparative form of senex 'old.' This in turn was descended from the Indo-European base *sen-, which also produced Welsh hen, Gothic sineigs, Lithuanian senas, and Armenian hin, all meaning 'old.'

English is also indebted to senex for senate and senile [17], while senior has contributed sir and the whole range of Romance terms of address, including monsieur, señor, and signor.

► senate, senior, sir

**sennight** see FORTNIGHT

**señor** see SIR

**sense** [14] Sense comes ultimately from Latin sentīre 'feel,' a prodigious contributor to English vocabulary (it is also the source of assent [13], consent, dissent [16], resent, sentence, sentient [17], and sentiment). From it was derived the noun sēnsus 'faculty of perceiving,' which was borrowed by English as sense. And sēnsus in turn spawned its own derivatives, which have given English sensation [17], sensible [14], sensitive [14], sensual [15], and sensuous [17].

► assent, consent, dissent, resent, sensible, sentence, sentiment

**sentence** [13] 'Complete grammatical unit' is a comparatively recent meaning of sentence, which only emerged in English in the 15th century. Its Latin ancestor sententia originally meant 'feeling,' for it was a derivative of sentīre 'feel' (source also of English sense, sentiment, etc). It subsequently broadened out to 'opinion, judgment,' which was the starting point for the use of English sentence for 'judicial declaration of punishment.' Sententia also came to denote 'meaning,' and hence 'meaning expressed in words' and 'maxim.' The former lies behind the grammatical sense of English sentence, while the latter survives in the derived adjective sententious [15].

► sense, sententious

**sentiment** [17] Sentiment comes via Old French sentiment from medieval Latin sentīmentum 'feeling,' a derivative of Latin sentīre 'feel' (from which English gets sensation, sense, sentence, etc). It originally meant 'feeling' and 'opinion' (the former now defunct, the latter surviving with a somewhat old-fashioned air in such expressions as 'My sentiments exactly!'). The sense '(excessively) refined feeling' did not emerge until the mid-18th century.

► sense

**sentry** [17] Sentry is probably short for the now obsolete centrinell 'sentry.' This first appeared in the 16th century as a variant of sentinel [16], which came via French sentinelle from Italian sentinella. It is not altogether clear where the Italian noun came from, but it may well have been derived from the verb sentire 'perceive, watch,' a descendant of Latin sentīre 'feel' (from which English gets sense, sentence, sentiment, etc).

► sentinel

**separate** [15] Etymologically, separate means 'arrange apart.' It comes from the past participle of Latin sēparāre, a compound verb formed from the prefix sē- 'apart' and parāre 'arrange (in advance), furnish, make ready' (source also of English *prepare*). *Sever* is essentially the same word as *separate*, in reduced form.

▶ prepare, sever

## September [11]
*September* is etymologically the 'seventh' month. The word comes from Latin *September*, a derivative of *septem* 'seven' (the Roman year started with March). Other English descendants of Latin *septem*, which is a distant relative of English *seven*, include *septet* [19] and *septuagenarian* [18].

▶ seven

## sepulchre [12]
*Sepulchre* comes ultimately from Latin *sepelīre* 'bury, inter.' From its past participle *sepultus* was derived the noun *sepulcrum* 'burying place, tomb,' which passed into English via Old French *sepulcre*. There is no etymological justification for the *ch* spelling.

## sequence [14]
*Sequence* is at the centre of a large family of English words that go back ultimately to Latin *sequī* 'follow' (others include *consecutive* [17], *consequence* [14], *ensue*, *obsequious* [15], *persecute* [15], *prosecute*, *pursue*, *second*, *sect*, *subsequent* [15], *sue*, and *suit*). *Sequence* itself comes from late Latin *sequentia*, a derivative of the present participle *sequēns*. Another Latin derivative was *sequēla* 'that which follows,' which has given English *sequal* [15]. *Sequī* came from the Indo-European base *\*seq-*, which also produced Greek *hépomai*, Irish *sechur*, Lithuanian *sekti*, and Sanskrit *sac-*, all meaning 'follow.'

▶ consecutive, consequence, ensue, obsequious, persecute, prosecute, pursue, second, sect, sequal, set, sue, suit

## seraglio    see CARAVAN

## serenade [17]
A *serenade* is strictly a 'song sung in the evening,' but in fact historically it has nothing to do with 'night' – etymologically it is a 'serene' piece of music. The word comes via French *sérénade* from Italian *serenata*, a derivative of *sereno* 'serene.' The notion of a *serenata* as a piece of 'night' music arose through association with *sera* 'evening' (a relative of French *soir* 'evening,' from which English gets *soirée* [19]). Italian *sereno* came from Latin *serēnus* 'bright, clear,' which also produced English *serene* [16].

▶ serene

## serendipity [18]
*Serendipity* – the 'faculty of making lucky discoveries' – was coined in 1754 by the British writer Horace Walpole (1717–97). He took it from *The Three Princes of Serendip*, the title of a fairy tale whose leading characters, in Walpole's words, 'were always making discoveries, by accidents and sagacity, of things they were not in quest of.' (*Serendip* is an old name for Sri Lanka.)

## serene    see SERENADE

## serge [14]
The textile term *serge* is first cousin to *silk*. It comes via Old French *sarge* from *\*sārica*, a Vulgar Latin alteration of Latin *sērica*. This was short for *lāna sērica*, which meant literally 'wool of the Seres.' *Seres* was a name given to a people living in what we would now call China, and it is also the ultimate source of the word *silk*.

▶ silk

## sergeant [12]
A *sergeant* is etymologically simply a 'servant' – and indeed that is what the word originally meant in English. It comes via Old French *sergent* from Latin *servient-*, the present participial stem of *servīre* 'serve.' It was subsequently incorporated into the terminology of the feudal system, roughly equivalent in application to *esquire*, and it was also used for various legal officers, but it does not seem to have become a specific military rank until the mid 16th century. 'Sergeant' then was a comparatively exalted position, but by the end of the century we see it settling into its modern niche as a senior noncomissioned officer.

▶ servant, serve

## series [17]
Latin *seriēs* (from which English got *series*) denoted a 'succession of things connected together.' It was derived from *serere* 'connect,' which has also given English *assert* and *insert* [16]. *Serial* [19] was coined specifically with reference to stories published in instalments.

▶ assert, insert, serial

## serious [15]
*Serious* comes ultimately from Latin *sērius* 'serious, grave.' From this was derived late Latin *sēriōsus*, which passed into English via Old French *serieux*. It is not clear where *sērius* came from, although some have linked it with German *schwer* 'heavy' ('seriousness' and 'weightiness' being semantically close).

## sermon [12]
Latin *sermō* meant simply 'talk, conversation, discourse,' but by the time it reached English via Anglo-Norman *sermun* it had narrowed down to an 'address given from a pulpit on a religious topic.' It is not clear what its ultimate ancestry is, but probably the favourite candidate as its source is the Indo-European base *\*swer-*, *\*swar-*, which gave English *answer* and *swear*.

## serpent [14]
The *serpent* is etymologically a 'crawling' animal. The word comes via Old French *serpent* from Latin *serpēns*, a noun use of the present participle of *serpere* 'crawl, creep.' This was a close relative of Greek *hérpein* 'creep,' from which English gets *herpes* [17] (etymologically the 'creeping' disease) and *herpetology* 'study of reptiles' [19].

▶ herpes

## serried [17]
The phrase *serried ranks* is first recorded in William Wilkie's *Epigoniad* 1757, but it

was clearly inspired by Milton's 'Nor serv'd it to relax their serried files' in *Paradise Lost* 1667. It means 'rows crowded close together,' and *serried* is the past participle of a now obsolete verb *serry* 'press together.' This was borrowed from *serré*, the past participle of Old French *serrer* 'close,' which went back via Vulgar Latin *serrāre* to Latin *serāre*, a derivative of the noun *sera* 'lock, bolt.'

**serve** [13] Latin *servus* 'slave' has been a rich source of English vocabulary. It is the direct ancestor of *serf* [15] (and of the second syllable of *concierge* [17]), but it is its derivatives that have made the most numerous contributions. From the verb *servīre* 'serve' come *deserve, dessert, sergeant, servant* [13], *serve*, and *serviette* [15] (but not, despite the similarity, *conserve, observe, preserve, reserve*, etc, which go back to the unrelated Latin *servāre* 'keep, protect'). *Servītium* 'slavery' has provided *service* [12] and its derivative *serviceable* [14], while from *servīlis* 'slavish' comes *servile* [14].

▶ concierge, deserve, dessert, serf, serviette, servile

**sesquipedalian** [17] *Sesquipedalian* means etymologically 'a foot and a half long.' Its use in English was inspired by the Roman poet Horace's phrase *sesquipedalia verba*, literally 'words a foot and a half long,' hence 'preposterously long words that sound pompous' – of which *sesquipedalian* itself is an appropriately good example. It is a compound word formed from the Latin prefix *sesqui-* 'half as much again' (a derivative of *sēmi-* 'half') and *pēs* 'foot.'

▶ foot, pedal

**session** [14] Etymologically, a *session* is simply a 'sitting.' The word comes via Old French *session* from Latin *sessiō*, a derivative of *sedēre* 'sit.' Its sense development reflects the symbolic association of 'sitting down' with the conducting of business, which can be seen anew in the modern English expression *get round a table*. Other English descendants of Latin *sedēre*, which is closely related to English *sit*, include *assess, assiduous* [16], *insidious* [16], *séance* [19], *sedentary* [16], *sediment* [16], *size, subsidy* [14], and *supersede*.

▶ assess, assiduous, insidious, séance, sedentary, sediment, size, subsidy, supersede

**set** English has two words *set*. The verb [OE] is simply the causative version of *sit*. That is to say, etymologically it means 'cause to sit.' It comes from a prehistoric Germanic *satjan* (source also of German *setzen*, Dutch *zetten*, Swedish *sätta*, and Danish *sætte*), which was a causative variant of *setjan*, ancestor of English *sit*. *Set* 'group' [14] is essentially the same word as *sect*. It comes via Old French *sette* from Latin *secta*, source of English *sect*. It originally meant strictly a 'group of people,' and its far broader modern application, which emerged in the 16th century, is no doubt due

to association with the verb *set* and the notion of 'setting' things together.

▶ sit / sect

**settle** [OE] Although now far less common, the noun *settle* 'bench' is older than the verb, and indeed was the source of it. It evolved (along with German *sessel*) from a prehistoric Germanic *setlaz*, which was derived from the same base that produced English *sit*. (*Saddle* comes from a variant of the same base.) In Old English times it was *setl*, and still meant simply 'seat.' This formed the basis of a verb *setlan* 'put in a position of repose,' ancestor of modern English *settle*.

▶ saddle, sit

**seven** [OE] The Indo-European term for 'seven' was *septm*. This evolved into Latin *septem* (source of English *September*), Greek *heptá* (source of English *heptathlon* [20]), and Germanic *sebun*. And *sebun* in turn has diversified into German *sieben*, Dutch *zeven*, Swedish *sju*, Danish *syv*, and English *seven*.

▶ heptathlon, September

**several** [15] Etymologically, *several* means 'separate.' It comes via Anglo-Norman *several* from medieval Latin *sēparālis*, a derivative of Latin *sēpar* 'separate.' This in turn was formed from *sēparāre* 'separate' (source of English *separate*), whose Vulgar Latin descendant *sēperāre* passed into English via Anglo-Norman *severer* as *sever* [14]. *Several*'s original sense 'separate, individual' survives in legal terminology, but it has been superseded in the general language by 'many,' which emerged in the 16th and 17th centuries via 'different, various.'

▶ prepare, separate, sever

**severe** [16] *Severe* is a descendant, via Old French *severe*, of Latin *sevērus*, a word of uncertain origin. English *asseveration* 'firm declaration' [16] comes from its Latin derivative *asseverāre* 'assert earnestly.'

▶ asseveration

**sew** [OE] *Sew* comes, with its relatives Swedish *sy* and Danish *sye*, from a prehistoric Germanic *siwjan*. This was descended from an Indo-European base *siw-*, *sju-* that also produced Latin *suere* 'sew' (source of English *suture* [16]), Greek *humén* 'membrane' (source of English *hymen* [17]), and English *seam*. It is no relation to *sow*.

▶ hymen, seam, suture

**sewer** [15] Etymologically, *sewer* denotes the 'removal of water.' The word comes via Anglo-Norman *sever* from Vulgar Latin *exaquāria*, a derivative of *exaquāre* 'remove water, drain.' This was a compound verb formed from Latin *ex-* 'out' and *aqua* 'water.' The derivatives *sewage* [19] and *sewerage* [19] are both native English formations.

▶ aquatic

**sex**   [14]   *Sex* comes via Old French *sexe* from Latin *sexus*. This has traditionally been explained as a relative of Latin *secāre* 'cut' (source of English *section, sector*, etc), as if it denoted etymologically that 'section' of the population which is male or female, but that view is no longer generally held. The use of *sex* for 'sexual intercourse' (first recorded in the works of D H Lawrence) and the derivative *sexy* are both 20th-century developments.

**sextant**   [17]   A *sextant* is etymologically an instrument based on a 'sixth' of a circle. Sextants measure off the angle between the horizon and a celestial body on a graduated scale that is marked on an arc equal to one sixth of a circle. They were first named at the beginning of the 17th century by the Danish astronomer Tycho Brahe, who used the term *sextāns* 'sixth part,' a derivative of Latin *sextus* 'sixth' (to which English *six* is closely related). The anglicized version *sextant* is first recorded in 1628.

▶ six

**sexton**   [14]   *Sexton* and *sacristan* [14] are doublets: that is to say, they started out as the same word, but have diverged over the centuries. Both come from medieval Latin *sacristānus*, a derivative of *sacrista* 'person in charge of holy vessels' (which in turn was based on Latin *sacer* 'holy,' source of English *sacred*), but whereas *sacristan* was borrowed directly from Latin, *sexton* came via the roundabout route of Anglo-Norman *segerstaine*.

▶ sacred, sacristan, saint

**shabby**   [17]   Etymologically, *shabby* means 'scabby.' It comes from a now obsolete *shab*, which denoted 'scab,' and also metaphorically 'disreputable fellow.' It was the native equivalent to Old Norse *\*skabbr* 'scab,' from which English gets *scab*.

▶ scab

**shaddock**   [17]   The shaddock is a large citrus fruit, similar to a grapefruit. Its name commemorates one Captain Shaddock, the commander of an East India Company ship who at some point in the late 17th century stopped off at Jamaica en route from the East Indies to England and left some seeds of the shaddock tree there.

**shade**   [OE]   *Shade* and *shadow* [12] are ultimately the same word. Both originated in Old English *sceadu*. *Shade* is the direct descendant of this, whereas *shadow* comes from its inflected form *sceaduwe*. *Sceadu* itself went back via prehistoric Germanic *\*skathwō* (source also of German *schatten* and Dutch *schaduw*) to Indo-European *\*skotwā* (whence also Greek *skótos* 'darkness' and Welsh *cysgod* 'shade'). *Shed* 'hut' probably originated as a variant of *shade*.

▶ shadow, shed

**shaft**   [OE]   *Shaft* is a general Germanic word, shared by German and Dutch *schaft* and Swedish and Danish *skaft*. These point back to a common prehistoric ancestor *\*skaftaz*, which may have been descended from the Indo-European base *\*scap-* 'support' (source of English *sceptre* [13]).

▶ sceptre

**shag**   [OE]   *Shag* originally meant 'rough untidy hair,' a sense now more familiar in its derivative *shaggy* [16]. Related Old Norse forms such as *skegg* 'beard,' *skagi* 'promontory,' and *skaga* 'project' suggest that its underlying meaning is 'something that sticks out.' The bird-name *shag*, which denotes a relative of the cormorant and was first recorded in the 16th century, may be an allusion to the bird's shaggy crest. The origins of the verb *shag* 'copulate with,' which dates from the late 18th century, are not known, although it may be distantly related to *shake*.

**shagreen**   see CHAGRIN

**shake**   [OE]   *Shake* is a general Germanic verb, although today its only surviving relatives are Swedish *skaka* and Norwegian *skage*. It comes from a prehistoric Germanic *\*skakan*, which goes back to the Indo-European base *\*skeg-*, *\*skek-* (source also of Sanskrit *khajati* 'agitate, churn' and Welsh *ysgogi* 'move').

**shale**   see SCALE

**shall**   [OE]   The etymological meaning of *shall* is 'owe.' It goes back to a prehistoric Germanic base *\*skal-*, *\*skul-* which also produced German *sollen* 'ought to' and *schuld* 'debt.' Its use in English as an auxiliary verb denoting future time evolved via the intermediate senses 'ought to, must' and 'be to.' The notion of obligation survives in *should*, which originated as its past tense.

▶ should

**shallot**   [17]   The *shallot* is etymologically the onion from 'Ascalon,' an ancient port in southern Palestine. The Romans called it *Ascalōnia caepa* 'Ascalonian onion,' or *ascalōnia* for short. In Vulgar Latin this became *\*escalonia*, which passed into Old French as *escaloigne* (source of English *scallion* [14], still used for 'spring onion' in America and elsewhere). The variant form *eschalotte* developed. English took this over as *eschalot* ('Eschalots are now from France become an English plant,' John Mortimer, *Whole Art of Husbandry* 1707), and soon lopped off the first syllable to produce *shallot*.

▶ scallion

**sham**   see SHAME

**shamble**   [17]   *Shamble* 'slouch' and the noun *shambles* [15] are probably related. The latter originally meant 'meat market.' It arose out of the plural of the now obsolete *shamble* 'meat stall, meat table,' which represented a semantic specialization of Old English *sceamul* 'stool, table.' This was descended from prehistoric Germanic *skamul* (source also of German *schemel* 'stool'), which in turn was borrowed from Latin *scamellum*, a diminutive form of *scamnum* 'bench.' In the 16th century, the signification of *shambles* moved on to 'slaughterhouse,' and hence metaphorically to any 'scene of bloodshed and slaughter,' but the milder modern sense 'scene of disorder or ruin' did not emerge until as recently as the early 20th century. The verb *shamble* is thought to come from the now obsolete expression *shamble legs* 'ungainly legs,' an allusion to the rickety legs of the stalls or tables in meat markets.

**shame** [OE] *Shame* is a general Germanic term, with relatives in German *scham*, Dutch *schaam*, and Swedish and Danish *skam*. Their common ancestor is a prehistoric *skamō*, a word of unknown origin. *Sham* [17] probably originated in a northern English pronunciation of *shame*.

The compound *shamefaced* [16] has no etymological connection with *face*. It is an alteration of an earlier *shamefast*, whose second element is the same word as *fast* 'firm,' and its underlying meaning is 'held firm by shame.'
▶ sham

**shank** [OE] *Shank* originally meant 'leg,' or more specifically 'shin' (Edward I of England was nicknamed 'Longshanks' on account of his long legs). The word goes back to a prehistoric West Germanic *skangkan*, which also produced Dutch *schenk* 'leg-bone' and is closely related to German *schinken* 'ham.' Its ultimate origins are not known, although it has been suggested that it arose from the notion of 'crookedness' or 'lameness' (in which case German *hinken* 'limp' may be related). The main modern meaning of *shank*, 'stem, shaft,' emerged in the 16th century.

**shanty** English has two distinct words *shanty*. The older, 'shack' [19], originated in America, and the fact that to begin with it was mainly used for the houses of Irish immigrants suggests that it may have come from Irish *sean tig* 'old house.' *Shanty* 'sailor's song' [19] probably comes from *chantez*, the imperative plural of French *chanter* 'sing.'
▶ canto, chant

**shape** [OE] *Shape* goes back ultimately to the prehistoric Germanic base *skap-* 'form, create,' which also produced German *schaffen* and Swedish *skapa* 'create, make.' 'Create' seems to have been a secondary meaning of the base, evolving out of an earlier 'chop or dig out,' which probably gave rise to English *scoop*.
▶ scoop

**share** *Share* 'plough-blade' [OE] and *share* 'portion' [14] are distinct words, but they are ultimately related. The former came from the Germanic base *skar-*, *sker-* 'cut,' which also produced English *score*, *shear*, *short*, etc. Its German relative is *schar* 'ploughshare.'

*Share* 'portion' appears to be a survival of Old English *scearu*. This is only recorded in the senses 'groin' and 'tonsure,' but they share a meaning element ('dividing' in the case of the groin, the 'forking' of the body, and 'cutting' in the case of tonsure) that leads back to Germanic *skar-*, *sker-*, and suggests that *share* 'portion' denotes etymologically something 'cut' up or divided between people.
▶ score, sharp, shear, shirt, short, skirt

**shark** [16] The origins of the word *shark* are obscure. It appears to have been introduced to English in the late 1560s by members of Sir John Hawkins' expedition (a ballad of 1569 recorded 'There is no proper name for [the fish] that I know, but that certain men of Captain Hawkins's doth call it a shark'), but it is not known where they got it from. A resemblance to Austrian dialect *schirk* 'sturgeon' has been noted. Also not clear is whether *shark* 'swindler' (first recorded in the 18th century) is the same word; an alternative possibility is that it came from German *schurke* 'scoundrel.'

**sharp** [OE] *Sharp*, together with its close relatives German *scharf*, Dutch *scherp*, and Swedish and Danish *skarp*, goes back to a prehistoric Germanic *skarpaz*. This was probably descended from an extension of the Indo-European base *sker-* 'cut' (source of English *score*, *share*, *shear*, etc). Welsh has borrowed *sharp* as *siarp*.
▶ shear

**shatter** see SCATTER

**shave** see SCAB

**shawl** [17] The shawl was originally an Oriental garment – an oblong strip of cloth worn variously over the shoulders, round the waist, or as a turban, and supposedly woven from the hair of a species of Tibetan goat. Versions of it did not begin to be worn in the West until the mid-18th century. Its name comes via Urdu from Persian *shāl*, which may be derived from *Shāliāt*, an Indian town.

**she** [12] The Old English word for 'she' was *hēo*. As this evolved during the late Old English period, its main pronunciation stress shifted from the *e* to the *o*. The *o* gradually changed to an *e* sound, while the original *e* became transmuted into a *y* sound, which eventually merged with the *h* to form *sh*. The original *h* survives in *her*.
▶ he, her, it

**shear** [OE] *Shear* is the principal English descendant of the Indo-European base *sker-* 'cut,' which has also produced English *score*, *share*, *shirt*, *short*, and *skirt*, and probably *sharp* and *shore* as well. A variant of the base without the *s* is responsible for *curt* and *curtail*. The immediate source of *shear* itself is prehistoric Germanic *skeran*, which also evolved into German and Dutch *scheren*, Swedish *skära*, and Danish *skjære*. The verb *sheer* 'swerve' [17] probably originated as a variant of *shear*, but the adjective *sheer* [16] is an entirely different word. It probably represents a survival of Old English *scīr* 'bright, shining,' which came ultimately from the Germanic base *\*ski-*, source also of English *shimmer* and *shine*.

▶ curt, curtail, score, share, sheer, shirt, short, skirt

**sheath** [OE]   A *sheath* is probably etymologically a 'split stick.' The word comes from a prehistoric Germanic *\*skaithiz*, which also produced German *scheide*, Dutch *schede*, and Danish *skede*. This seems to have been derived from the base *\*skaith* 'divide, split' (source also of English *shed* 'give off, drop' and *ski*), in which case the notion underlying it would have been of a stick split open so that a sword blade could be inserted into it.

▶ shed, ski

**shed**   English has two distinct words *shed*. The verb [OE] originally meant 'divide, separate, split' (a 14th-century religious poem paraphrased Genesis with 'the sun to shed the day from the night'), and the modern range of senses, 'give off, drop,' did not begin to emerge until the Middle English period. It goes back to a prehistoric Germanic *\*skaithan*, which also produced German and Dutch *scheiden* 'separate.' This was derived from a base *\*skaith-* 'divide, split,' source also of English *ski* and probably *sheath*. *Shed* 'hut' [15] may be an alteration of *shade* (but the *shed* of *watershed* is of course a noun use of the verb *shed*).

▶ sheath, ski / shade

**sheen** [OE]   Despite its similarity in form and meaning, *sheen* has no etymological connection with *shine*. It was originally an adjective, meaning 'beautiful, bright.' Like its relatives, German *schön* and Dutch *schoon*, it goes back to a prehistoric Germanic *\*skauniz*, which was derived from the base *\*skau-* 'see, look' (source also of English *scavenger* and *show*). It was not used as a noun until the early 17th century (it is first recorded in Shakespeare).

▶ scavenger, scone, show

**sheep** [OE]   *Sheep* is a West Germanic word, with relatives in German *schaf* and Dutch *schaap*. It is not known where it came from, although it has been speculated that it may be related to German *schaffen* 'make, create' (and hence to English *shape*), and that its underlying meaning is hence 'creature.' The derivative *sheepish* [12] originally meant simply 'sheeplike.' It had a variety of metaphorical applications in Middle English, including 'silly' and 'fearful,' but the modern 'shy' did not emerge until the late 17th century. *Shepherd* is of course based on *sheep*.

**sheer**   see SHEAR

**sheet**   *Sheet* 'cloth' [OE] and *sheet* 'rope attached to a sail' [OE] are distinct words, although they have a common ancestor. This was the Germanic base *\*skaut-*, *\*skut-* 'project,' which also produced English *scot-free*, *scuttle* 'sink a ship,' *shoot, shot, shout, shut*, and *skit*. This produced two Old English nouns, *scēte* 'cloth' and *scēata* 'sail-rope,' which have formally coalesced in modern English as *sheet*, but retained their distinctive meanings. (*Sheet* 'cloth' was not used specifically for 'bed sheet' until the 13th century.)

▶ scot-free, scuttle, shoot, shot, shout, shut, skit

**shelf** [14]   *Shelf* appears to have been borrowed from Middle Low German *schelf* 'shelf.' This may have come from the Germanic base *\*skelf-* 'split,' which also produced Old English *scylfe* 'partition,' the word's underlying meaning therefore being a 'piece of split wood used for standing things on.' The derivative *shelve* dates from the 16th century.

**shell** [OE]   *Shell* goes back ultimately to the Germanic base *\*skal-* 'divide, separate,' which also produced English *scale, scalp, school* (of fish), *shale, shelter, shield, shoal* (of fish), *skill*, and *skol*. Its underlying meaning is hence a 'covering that splits off or is peeled off.' Its immediate Germanic ancestor was *\*skaljō*, which also produced Dutch *schel* and Norwegian *skjæl*. *Shellac* [18] is a compound of *shell* and *lac* 'lacquer, varnish' (a word of Sanskrit origin, of which *lacquer* is a derivative), and is a direct translation of French *laque en écailles* 'lac (melted) in thin plates.'

▶ scale, scalp, school, shale, shelter, shield, shoal, skill, skol

**shelter** [16]   The origins of *shelter* are unclear, but the most usually accepted explanation is that it is an alteration of the now obsolete *sheltron*. This denoted a body of troops which protected itself in battle with a covering of joined shields. It was descended from Old English *scieldtruma*, a compound formed from *scield*, the ancestor of modern English *shield*, and *truma* 'troop.'

▶ shield

**shemozzle** [19]   *Shemozzle* is one of a number of Yiddish words beginning with *sh* to have found their way into English. Most are relatively recent introductions, via American English – *schlemiel* 'fool, blunderer' [19] (possibly from a Biblical character Shelumiel who came to a sticky end), *schlep* 'carry, lug' [20] (ultimately from German *schleppen* 'drag'), *schlock* 'trash' [20] (originally 'broken merchandise,' and so perhaps related to German *schlagen* 'hit'), *schmaltz* 'oversentimentality' [20] (originally 'melted fat,' and so distantly related to English *smelt*), *schmuck* 'fool, oaf' [19] (literally 'penis') – but *shemozzle* is of an earlier vintage, brought by Jewish immigrants to the East End of London. It is a compound formed from Yiddish *shlim* 'bad' and *mazel* 'luck' (as in the Yiddish greeting *mazel tov* 'good luck'), and was independently borrowed into American English as *schlimazel* 'loser, failure' [20].

**shepherd** [OE] *Shepherd* is of course a compound of *sheep* and *herd* – but not *herd* 'group of animals.' This is a different *herd*, meaning 'herdsman,' which now survives only in compounds (*cowherd* and *goatherd* are other examples). It comes from the same Germanic source as *herd* 'group of animals.'
▶ herd, sheep

**sherbet** [17] Like *syrup*, *sherbet* goes back ultimately to the Arabic verb *shariba* 'drink,' whose initial /shr/ sound was originally imitative of the sound of noisy drinking or slurping. From it was derived the noun *sharbah*, whose plural *sharbāt* passed into Turkish as *sherbet* or *shorbet*. English took over the former as *sherbet*, and originally used it for a 'cooling Middle Eastern drink, made with melted snow.' Its modern application, to a powder for making sweet fizzy drinks (or just for eating), did not emerge until the mid-19th century. Italian adopted *shorbet* as *sorbetto*, which reached English via French as *sorbet* [16].
▶ sorbet, syrup

**sheriff** [OE] A *sheriff* is etymologically a 'shire-reeve' – that is, a 'county official.' The term was compounded in the Old English period from *scīr*, ancestor of modern English *shire*, and *gerēfa* 'local official,' a word based on *rōf* 'assembly' which survives as the historical term *reeve*. It was used for the 'monarch's representative in a county.'
▶ reeve, shire

**sherpa** [19] The Sherpas are a Tibetan people who live in northern Nepal. Their name for themselves (*sharpa* in Tibetan) means literally 'dweller in an eastern country.' They act as mountain guides in the Himalayas, and since the exploits on Mount Everest of Tenzing Norgay, a Sherpa, became well known in the 1950s, *sherpa* has become a generic term for a 'Himalayan mountain guide.'

**sherry** [16] Various sorts of dryish or sweetened white wine known as *sack* (etymologically 'dry wine') were imported into England in the 16th and 17th centuries. Many came from Spain, and the sort made around Xerez (now Jerez) in southern Spain was called in English (in an approximation to the Spanish pronunciation of *Xerez*) *sherris sack*. Before the end of the 16th century this had been reduced to *sherry*, which in due course came to be applied to the fortified Spanish wine that now goes by that name.

**shibboleth** [14] Hebrew *shibbōleth* meant 'stream.' According to the Bible, the Gileadites used it as a password, for they knew their enemies the Ephraimites could not pronounce the *sh* properly ('And it was so, that when those Ephraimites which were escaped said, Let me go over; that the men of Gilead said unto him, Art thou an Ephraimite? If he said, Nay, then they said unto him, Say now Shibboleth: and he said Sibboleth: for he could not frame to pronounce it right,'

Judges 12:5–6). In 17th-century English it came to be applied generically to any word used as a test of pronunciation, particularly as a sign of belonging to a group, and hence by extension to any catchword or slogan adopted by a group, and this eventually evolved into the modern sense 'outmoded slogan, practice, etc still adhered to.'

**shield** [OE] *Shield* goes back to a prehistoric Germanic *skelduz, which also produced German and Dutch *schild*, Swedish *sköld*, and Danish *skjoldr*. This was probably derived from the Germanic base *skel- 'divide, split, separate' (source also of English *scale*, *shell*, etc), and hence denoted etymologically a 'flat piece of wood produced by splitting a log, board.' *Shelter* is probably descended from a compound formed from *shield*.
▶ scale, shell, shelter

**shift** [OE] Old English *sciftan* meant 'arrange' (it came from a prehistoric Germanic base *skip-, which also produced German *schichten* 'arrange in layers, pile up,' and traces of its original meaning survive in *makeshift* [16], denoting something arranged or contrived for lack of anything better). Its modern meaning 'move' emerged in the 14th century, via an intermediate 'change.' The notion of 'change' underlies the use of the noun *shift* for 'woman's slip,' which evolved from an earlier 'change of clothing,' and also its use for a 'particular working period,' marked by a 'change' of workers at beginning and end.

**shilling** [OE] *Shilling* has relatives in the other Germanic languages – German *schilling*, Dutch *schelling*, and Swedish and Danish *skilling* – which point back to a prehistoric Germanic *skillingaz. Where this came from, however, is a mystery. Among suggestions are that it was formed from the base *skel- 'divide, separate' (source of English *scale*, *shell*, etc), and hence denotes etymologically a 'division' of a standard unit of weight or currency; or from the base *skell- 'resound, ring' (source of Dutch *schel* 'shrill' and German *schelle* 'bell').

**shimmer** [OE] *Shimmer* goes back to a prehistoric Germanic *skim- (source also of German *schimmern* 'glitter, gleam'). This was an extension of the base *ski-, from which English gets *sheer* and *shine*.
▶ sheer, shine

**shin** [OE] *Shin* has Germanic relatives in German *schiene* 'thin plate,' Dutch *schen* 'shin,' Swedish *skena* 'shin,' and Danish *skinne* 'splint.' Its underlying meaning seems to be 'thin piece.' The first record of its use as a verb, meaning 'climb with the hands and legs,' comes from the early 19th century.

**shindy** [19] *Shindy* is an alteration of *shinty* [18], the name of a rumbustious Scottish game resembling hockey which was also used in the 19th century for a 'commotion.' *Shinty* itself appears to be a lexicalization of *shin t'ye* 'shin to you,' a cry supposedly uttered by players of the game. *Shindig* [19] is probably an alteration of *shindy*.

▶ shindig, shinty

**shine** [OE] *Shine* and its Germanic relatives, German *scheinen*, Dutch *schijnen*, Swedish *skina*, and Danish *skinne*, go back to a prehistoric *\*skīnan*. This was derived from *\*ski-*, a base which also produced English *sheer* and *shimmer* (*sheen*, despite its similarity, is not connected). Other descendants of this base were Greek *skiá* 'shadow' and *skēnḗ* 'tent' (source of English *scene*); the semantic link between the rather unlikely bedfellows 'shining' and 'shadow' is held to be 'faint light.'

▶ scene, sheer, shimmer

**shingle** English has two distinct words *shingle*. The older, 'roof tile' [12], was borrowed from Latin *scindula*, a variant of *scandula* 'roof tile.' This was probably derived from *scandere* 'ascend' (source of English *ascend, descend, scan*, etc), the underlying notion being of rows of tiles rising one above the other like steps. *Shingle* 'beach pebbles' [16] is of unknown origin; it may be related to Norwegian *singl* 'coarse sand' and North Frisian *singel* 'gravel.' *Shingles* [14], incidentally, the name of a viral infection, comes from Latin *cingulum* 'girdle,' a close relative of English *cincture* 'girdle': the disease is often characterized by skin eruptions that almost encircle the body.

▶ ascend, descend, scan / cincture

**ship** [OE] *Ship* comes from a prehistoric Germanic *\*skipam*, which also produced German *schiff*, Dutch *schip*, Swedish *skepp*, and Danish *skib*. It is not known for certain where this came from, although a link has been suggested with Latvian *shkibīt* 'cut, hew,' in which case the underlying meaning of *ship* could be 'hollowed-out log' – a 'dugout,' in other words. The Old High German form *schif* was borrowed into Italian as *schifo*, and this made its way via French *esquif* into English as *skiff* [16]. The Middle Dutch form *schip* had a derivative *schipper* 'captain of a small ship,' which has given English *skipper* [14]. And *equip* too comes from a relative of English *ship*.

▶ equip, skiff, skipper

**shire** [OE] The original meaning of *shire*, which did not survive beyond the Old English period, was 'official charge, administrative office,' and it has been suggested that the word is related ultimately to Latin *cūra* 'care, charge' (source of English *curate, cure*, etc). Already by the 9th century it was being used for an 'administrative area ruled by a governor,' and over the next hundred years the application to what is now known as a *county* emerged. (*County* itself was introduced in the 14th century, and gradually ousted *shire*.) *Sheriff* is a compound based on *shire*.

▶ sheriff

**shirt** [OE] A *shirt*, like a *skirt*, is etymologically a 'short' garment, one that stops at or just below the waist rather than reaching down to the knees or beyond. In common with Swedish *skjorta* and Danish *skjorte*, it comes from the prehistoric base *\*skurt-*, source of English *short*. *Shirty* 'angry' [19] was inspired by the now defunct expression *get one's shirt out* 'lose one's temper' (the opposite *keep one's shirt on* 'remain calm' survives).

▶ share, shear, short, skirt

**shit** [14] The verb *shit* is an alteration (due to the influence of the past participle *shitten*) of an earlier *shite* [OE]. This, like German *scheissen*, Dutch *schijten*, Swedish *skita*, and Danish *skide*, goes back to a prehistoric Germanic base *\*skīt-*, which in turn was descended from Indo-European *\*skheid-* 'split, divide, separate' (source of English *schism* and *schist*) – the underlying notion being of 'separation' from the body, and hence 'discharge' from the body. The noun *shit*, a derivative of the verb, is first recorded in the 16th century.

▶ schism, schist, schizophrenia

**shiver** *Shiver* 'tremble' [13] and *shiver* 'sliver, fragment' [12] are different words. The former was originally *chiver*, which may have been an alteration of an earlier *chevel* 'shiver.' This in turn was derived from the Old English noun *ceafl* 'jaw' (source of English *jowl*), and so etymologically denoted the 'chattering of the teeth.' *Shiver* 'fragment' may have been borrowed from Low German (Middle Low German had *schever*). It goes back ultimately to the prehistoric Germanic base *\*skif-* 'split.'

▶ jowl

**shoal** English has two distinct words *shoal*. 'Shallow area' [16] is descended from the Old English adjective *sceald* 'shallow,' which in turn came from prehistoric Germanic *\*skaldaz*. (English *shallow* [15] is related, although it is not clear precisely how.) *Shoal* of fish [16] is simply a reborrowing of Middle Dutch *schōle*, which had earlier been taken over as *school*.

▶ school

**shock** English has two words *shock* in current general usage. *Shock* 'heavy blow, unpleasant surprise' [16] was borrowed from French *choc*, a derivative of the verb *choquer* 'strike,' whose origins are unknown. *Shock* 'thick shaggy mass of hair' [19] is a nominalization of an earlier adjective *shock* 'thick and shaggy' [17], but it is not clear where this came from. It has been linked with the obsolete *shough*, which referred to a sort of dog, and another possibility is that it is connected with the now little used *shock* 'stack of sheaves of corn' [14]. This was probably borrowed from Middle Dutch or Middle Low German *schok*.

**shoe** [OE] *Shoe* is a strictly Germanic word, with no living relatives in other branches of the Indo-European language family. It comes from a prehistoric Germanic *skōkhaz, which is probably descended ultimately from the Indo-European base *skeu- 'cover.' Its cousins are German schuh, Dutch schoen, and Swedish and Danish sko. Until the early modern English period shoon vied with shoes as its plural; and the archaic past form of the verb, shod, still survives.

▶ shod

**shoot** [OE] Like sheet, shout, shut, and perhaps skit [15], shoot goes back ultimately to the prehistoric Germanic base *skeut-, *skaut-, *skut- 'project.' This formed the basis of a verb *skeutan, which evolved into German schiessen, Dutch schieten, Swedish skjuta, and Danish skyde as well as English shoot. The noun shot comes from the same source.

▶ sheet, shot, shout, shut

**shop** [13] The word shop had humble beginnings. It goes back to a prehistoric Germanic *skoppan, which denoted a small additional structure, such as a lean-to shed or a porch. There is one isolated example of an Old English descendant of this – sceoppa, which denoted a 'treasury' – but this does not appear to have survived. The modern English word was borrowed from Old French eschoppe 'booth, stall,' which in turn had got it from Middle Low German schoppe. German dialect schopf 'shed, shelter' comes from the same source. The verb shop originated in the 16th century, in the sense 'imprison' (reflecting a now obsolete slang use of the noun shop for 'prison'). This is the ancestor of modern British slang shop 'inform against.' The sense 'visit shops to buy things' emerged in the mid 18th century.

**shore** English has two words shore. The one meaning 'land at the water's edge' [14] was borrowed from Middle Dutch or Middle Low German schōre, which probably came from the Germanic base *skur- 'cut' (source also of English score, shear, etc). Shore 'support' [14], as in 'shore up,' comes from Middle Dutch schōren 'prop,' a word of unknown origin.

▶ share, shear, short

**short** [OE] Etymologically, something that is short has been 'cut off.' The word's immediate Germanic ancestor was *skurtaz, which was descended from an extension of the Indo-European base *sker- 'cut' (source also of English score, share, shear, etc). Another version of the base, without the s, was the source of Latin curtus 'short,' which has produced English curt and curtail, and also supplied the word for 'short' in the other Germanic languages (German kurz and Dutch, Swedish, and Danish kort), as well as of course as the Romance languages (French court, Italian and Spanish corto, and Rumanian scurt). The shirt and the skirt are etymologically 'short' garments.

▶ curt, curtail, score, share, shear, shore, short, skirt

**shot** [OE] Shot goes back to a prehistoric Germanic *skutaz, which was derived from the same base

that produced English shoot. It used to mean 'payment' as well as 'act of shooting,' a sense shared by its Old Norse relative skot, which provided English with the scot of scot-free [16] (etymologically 'without having to pay').

▶ scot-free, shoot

**should** [OE] Should started life as the past tense of shall. It preserves the word's original connotations of 'obligation' which have all but disappeared from shall.

▶ shall

**shoulder** [OE] Shoulder is a general West Germanic word, with relatives in German schulter and Dutch schouder (it was also borrowed into Swedish and Danish as skuldra and skulder respectively). It goes back to a prehistoric *skuldr-, but where this came from is not clear. One suggestion is that it is distantly related to English shield, and originally denoted 'shoulderblade' (the underlying meaning being 'flat piece').

**shout** [14] The origins of shout are disputed. One school of thought traces it back to the prehistoric Germanic base *skeut-, *skaut-, *skut- 'project' (source of English sheet and shoot), as if its etymological meaning were 'throw one's voice out forcibly,' while another views it as a borrowing from Old Norse skúta 'taunt,' which may be a distant relative of Greek kudázein 'abuse.'

**shove** [OE] Shove was originally a perfectly respectable, neutral verb for 'push forcefully, thrust,' but over the centuries it has come down in the world, acquiring connotations of rudeness. In common with German schieben and Dutch schuiven it goes back to a prehistoric Germanic *skeuban. This was formed from a base which also produced English scuffle [16], sheaf [OE], shuffle [16], and indeed shovel [OE] (etymologically an 'implement for shoving'), and may be distantly related to Lithuanian skubus 'quick' and Old Church Slavonic skubati 'pull.'

▶ scuffle, sheaf, shovel, shuffle

**show** [OE] Show originally meant 'look at.' Its modern senses – basically 'cause to look at' – did not begin to develop until the early Middle English period. It comes from a prehistoric West Germanic *skauwōjan, whose German descendant schauen still means 'look at' (and whose Flemish descendant scauwen gave English scavenger). This in turn was derived from the base *skau- 'see, look,' source also of English sheen and German schön 'beautiful.' And the ultimate ancestor of *skau- was an Indo-European base which also produced Greek keein 'observe' and Latin cavēre 'beware' (source of English caution [13] and caveat [16]).

▶ caution, caveat, scavenger, scone, sheen

**shower** [OE] Shower comes from a prehistoric West Germanic *skūra, which also produced German *schauer* and Dutch *schoer*. Its ultimate ancestry is uncertain.

**shrapnel** The term *shrapnel* commemorates the name of General Henry Shrapnel (1761–1842), a British artillery officer who in the course of the Peninsular War, at the beginning of the 19th century, invented an exploding shell that sent bullets flying in all directions.

**shred** [OE] A *shred* is etymologically a 'cut' piece. The word comes ultimately from the prehistoric West Germanic base *\*skraud-*, *\*skreud-*, *\*skrud-* 'cut,' source also of English *shroud*. From it was formed the noun *\*skrautha*, which has evolved into German *schrot*, Dutch *schroot*, and English *shred*, and has also, via a circuitous route, given English *scroll*.

▶ scroll, shroud

**shrewd** [14] *Shrewd* originally meant 'wicked, dangerous.' Its modern sense 'astute' did not develop (via a less approbatory 'cunning') until the 16th century. It was derived from *shrew* 'wicked man' (a sense now obsolete). This is generally assumed to be the same noun as *shrew* the animal-name [OE], a word of uncertain origin. Shrews were formerly thought to have a poisonous bite, and were held in superstitious fear – hence the term's metaphorical application. The move from 'wicked man' via 'bad-tempered abusive complainer' to 'nagging woman' began in the 14th century.

▶ shrew

**shrift** see SHRIVE

**shrimp** [14] The shrimp's name appears to echo its small size. It was probably borrowed from some Low German source, and its possible relatives include Middle Low German *schrempen* 'shrink, wrinkle' and modern German *schrumpfen* 'shrivel, shrink.' Its use for a 'tiny person' is virtually as old in English as its application to the crustacean, and probably goes right back to its original source.

**shrive** [OE] *Shrive* 'hear someone's confession' goes back ultimately to Latin *scrībere* 'write' (source of English *scribe, script*, etc). This was borrowed into prehistoric West Germanic as *\*skrīban*, whose direct descendants are German *schreiben* and Dutch *schrijven* 'write.' But it also developed a specialized sense 'prescribe penances,' and it is this that has given English *shrive*. Today the word is best known in the form of *shrove*, its past tense, which is used in *Shrove Tuesday* [15] (an allusion to the practice of going to confession at the beginning of Lent), and the derived noun *shrift* 'penance, confession' [OE] (the expression *short shrift* originally referred to the short period of time allowed to someone about to be executed to say their confession).

▶ scribe, script, shrift, shrove

**shroud** [OE] *Shroud* originally meant simply 'garment' – a sense which survived into the early mod-

ern English period ('My princely robes are laid aside, whose glittering pomp Diana's shrouds supplies,' Christopher Marlowe and Thomas Nashe, *Dido Queen of Carthage* 1594). Not until the late 16th century did the modern meaning 'winding-sheet' begin to emerge. The word derives ultimately from the prehistoric West Germanic base *\*skraud-*, *\*skreud-*, *\*skrud-* 'cut' (source also of English *shred*).

▶ shred

**Shrove Tuesday** see SHRIVE

**shut** [OE] *Shut* comes ultimately from the same prehistoric Germanic base (*\*skaut-*, *\*skeut-*, *\*skut-* 'project') that produced English *shoot*, and its underlying etymological reference is to the 'shooting' of a bolt across a door to fasten it. Its immediate West Germanic ancestor was *\*skuttjan*, which also produced Dutch *schutten* 'obstruct.' In Old English this became *scyttan*, which if it had evolved unchecked would have given modern English *shit*. For reasons of delicacy, perhaps, the West Midlands form *shut* was drafted into the general language in the 16th century.

▶ sheet, shoot, shot, shout, shuttle

**shuttle** [OE] A *shuttle* is etymologically something that is 'shot.' Indeed, the word's Old English precursor *scytel* meant 'arrow' or 'dart.' It comes ultimately from the prehistoric Germanic base *\*skaut-*, *\*skeut-*, *\*skut-* 'project,' which also produced English *shoot* and *shut*. There is a gap between the disappearance of Old English *scytel* and the emergence of *shuttle* in the 14th century, but they are presumably the same word (a shuttle being something that is thrown or 'shot' across a loom).

▶ shut

**shy** *Shy* 'timid, reserved' [OE] goes back to a prehistoric Germanic *\*skeukhwaz* 'afraid' (source also of English *eschew* and *skew*). It is generally assumed that *shy* 'throw' [18] must have come from it, but the exact nature of the relationship between the two words is not clear. The original application of the verb seems to have been specifically to the throwing of sticks at chickens, and it has been suggested, not altogether convincingly, that its use alludes to the notion of a 'shy' cockerel that refuses to fight (there was an 18th- and early 19th-century slang term *shy-cock* which meant 'cowardly person').

▶ eschew, skew

**shyster** [19] *Shyster* 'unscrupulous lawyer' originated in the USA in the 1840s. It is generally supposed to come from the name of one Scheuster, a New York lawyer of that era who was constantly being rebuked by judges for his sharp practices. An alternative explanation, however, is that it represents an alteration of German *scheisser*, literally 'shitter.'

**sick** [OE] The ultimate origins of *sick* are a mystery. It has been traced back to a hypothetical prehistoric Germanic *seukaz, but beyond that nothing certain is known. Its modern relatives are German *siech*, Dutch *ziek*, Swedish *sjuk*, and Danish *syg*.

**sickle** [OE] A *sickle* is etymologically a 'cutting' tool. Like its close relatives German *sichel* and Dutch *zikkel*, it originated in a prehistoric Germanic borrowing of Latin *secula* 'sickle.' This was a derivative of the verb *secāre* 'cut' (source of English *section*, *sector*, etc), which in turn went back to the Indo-European base *sek-* 'cut' (source also of English *scythe*).

▶ scythe, section, segment

**side** [OE] The etymological meaning of *side* appears to be the 'long' surface of something (as opposed to the *ends* or the *top* or *bottom*, which are the 'shorter' or 'narrower' surfaces). The word goes back, together with German *seite*, Dutch *zijde*, Swedish *sida*, and Danish *side*, to a prehistoric Germanic *sīthō*, which was probably derived from the adjective *sīthaz* 'long, deep, low' (source of Swedish *sid* 'long').

**sight** [OE] *Sight* is a derivative of the prehistoric Germanic base *sekh-*, which also produced English *see*. In the case of its Germanic relatives, German *gesicht*, Dutch *gezicht*, Swedish *ansikte*, and Danish *ansigt*, the notion of 'sight' has led on via 'appearance' to 'face.'

▶ see

**sign** [13] *Sign* comes via Old French *signe* from Latin *signum* 'mark.' It already had the meaning 'mark denoting something' in Latin, and it was in this sense that it entered English, gradually ousting the native word *token*. The verb *sign* goes back ultimately to the Latin derivative *signāre* 'mark.' English acquired it in the 14th century, and first used it for 'write one's name' in the 15th century. Other related forms in English include *assign* [14], *consign* [15], *design, ensign* [14], *insignia* [17], *resign* [14] (in which the prefix *re-* has the force of 'un-'), *seal* 'wax impression, fastening,' *signal, signatory* [17], *signature* [16], *signet* [14], *significant* [16], and *signify* [13]. The ultimate source of Latin *signum* is uncertain. It was once assumed to go back to the Indo-European base *sek-*'cut' (source of English *saw, section*, etc), as if it denoted etymologically a 'cut mark,' but now Indo-European *seq-* 'point out,' hence 'say, tell' (source of English *say*) is viewed as a more likely ancestor.

▶ assign, consign, design, ensign, insignia, resign, seal, signal, signature, significant

**signal** [16] Latin *signālis* meant 'of a sign' (it was derived from *signum* 'mark, token,' source of English *sign*). It came to be used as a noun, and passed via medieval Latin *signāle* into Old French as *seignal*. This was later relatinized into *signal*, in which form it was taken over by English. The adjective *signal* 'conspicuous' came from the same ultimate source, but via a more circuitous route. The Italian version of the noun *signal*

is *segnale*. From it was derived the verb *segnalare* 'make famous,' whose past participle *segnalato* gave French *signalé* – whence English *signal*.

▶ sign

**signor** see SIR

**silent** [16] *Silent* comes from the present participle of Latin *silēre* 'be silent.' It is not clear what the origins of this were, although it seems likely to be related in some way to Gothic *anasilan*, a verb which denoted the wind dying down, and also perhaps to Latin *dēsinere* 'stop' (in which case its underlying meaning would be 'stop speaking'). The Latin-derived noun *silentium* actually reached English much earlier than the adjective, as *silence* [13].

**silhouette** [18] The term *silhouette* commemorates the name of the French author and politician Étienne de Silhouette (1709–67). As finance minister in the late 1750s he gained a reputation for cheeseparing, and *silhouette* came to be used for anything skimped. One account of the application of the word to a 'simple cut-out picture' is that it carries on this notion of 'simplicity' or 'lack of finish,' but an alternative theory is that Silhouette himself was in the habit of making such pictures. The metaphorical use of the term for a 'dark image against a bright background' emerged in the mid-19th century.

**silicon** [19] *Silicon* was coined in 1817 by the British chemist Thomas Thomson. Like the slightly earlier *silica*, it was based on Latin *silex* 'flint.' From the same source comes *silicone*, which dates from the 1860s.

**silk** [OE] Like the substance itself, the word *silk* originated in the Far East, possibly in Chinese *sī* 'silk.' Its immediate ancestor is most closely represented by Manchurian *sirghe* and Mongolian *sirkek*. Silk-traders brought their term west, and the Greeks used it to coin a name for them: *Seres*, the 'silk people.' That is the source of Latin *sēricum* and Irish *sīric* 'silk,' and also of English *serge*. But there must have been another oriental form, with an *l* rather than an *r*, which made its more northerly way via the Balto-Slavic languages (leaving Russian *shelk* and Lithuanian *shilkai* 'silk') to Germanic, where it has given Swedish and Danish *silke* and English *silk*.

▶ serge

**sill** [OE] *Sill* originally denoted the 'foundation of a wall.' Not until the 15th century was it used for the 'base of a window-frame.' It is related to German *schwelle* 'threshold' and possibly also to English *sole* 'underside of the foot.'

**silly** [OE] In one of the more celebrated semantic volte-faces in the history of the English lexicon, *silly* has been transformed over the past millennium from 'blessed, happy' to 'stupid.' The word goes back ultimately to a prehistoric West Germanic *sǣliga, a derivative of *sǣli 'luck, happiness.' It reached Old English as gesǣlig, still meaning 'happy,' but as it evolved formally in Middle English through seely to silly, its meaning developed via 'blessed,' 'pious,' 'innocent, harmless,' 'pitiable,' and 'feeble' to 'feeble in mind, foolish.' The related German selig retains its original meaning 'happy, blessed.'

**silt** [15] The likelihood is that silt originally referred to the mud in salt flats by river estuaries, and that it is etymologically related to salt. It was probably borrowed from a Scandinavian word – Danish and Norwegian have the apparently related sylt 'salt marsh.'
► salt

**silver** [OE] The word silver probably originated in Asia Minor. Its unidentified source word was borrowed into prehistoric Germanic as *silubr-, which has evolved into German silber, Dutch zilver, Danish sølf, and English and Swedish silver. Borrowing of the same ancestral form into the Balto-Slavic languages produced Russian serebro, Polish and Serbo-Croat srebro, Lithuanian sidabras, and Latvian sidrabs.

**similar** [17] Similar comes via French similaire from medieval Latin *similāris, a derivative of Latin similis 'like, similar.' This or the closely related simul 'at the same time' have also given English assemble [13], dissemble [15], ensemble [15], resemble, semblance [13], similitude [14], simulate [17], and simultaneous [17]. Its ultimate source was the Indo-European base *sem-, *som-, which also lies behind English same, simple, single, and the homo- of homosexual.
► assemble, dissemble, ensemble, resemble, same, semblance, simple, simulate, simultaneous, single

**simnel** [13] Simnel, a term now used for a cake made at Easter, originally denoted 'bread made from fine flour.' It was borrowed from Old French simenel, which itself came from either Latin simila (source of English semolina) or Greek semídālis, both meaning 'fine flour.'

**simony** [13] Simony, a term which denotes the 'selling of ecclesiastical offices,' perpetuates the name of Simon Magus. He was a Samaritan who according to Acts 8:18–20 tried to buy the power of conferring the Holy Ghost on people: 'And when Simon saw that through laying on of the apostles' hands the Holy Ghost was given, he offered them money, saying, Give me also this power, that on whomsoever I lay hands, he may receive the Holy Ghost. But Peter said unto him, Thy money perish with thee, because thou hast thought that the gift of God may be purchased with money.'

**simple** [13] Etymologically, simple denotes 'same-fold' – that is, not multifarious. It goes back ultimately to a compound formed from prehistoric Indo-European *sm-, *sem-, *som-'same' (source also of English same, similar, single, etc) and *pl- 'fold'

(source of English fold, ply, etc). This passed into Latin as simplus 'single,' which found its way into English via Old French simple.
► fold, ply, same, similar

**simulate** see SIMILAR

**simultaneous** see SIMILAR

**sin** [OE] Sin comes from a prehistoric Germanic *sunjō, a close relative of which produced German sünde, Dutch zonde, and Swedish and Danish synd 'sin.' It is not altogether clear what its ultimate origins were, but it has been linked with Latin sōns 'guilty,' and also with English sooth 'truth' and Sanskrit satya- 'real, true,' as if its ancestral meaning were '(truly) guilty.'

**since** [15] Since is a contracted form of Middle English sithenes 'since.' This in turn went back (with the addition of a final -s) to Old English siththan, a compound adverb and conjunction formed from sīth 'after' (a relative of German seit 'since') and thām 'that.'

**sine** [16] As in the case of many other mathematical terms, English is indebted to Arabic for sine. But here the debt is only semantic, not formal. The word sine itself was borrowed from Latin sinus 'curve, fold, hollow' (source also of English sinuous [16] and indeed of sinus [16], whose anatomical use comes from the notion of a 'hollow' place or cavity). In post-classical times it came to denote the 'fold of a garment,' and so it was mistakenly used to translate Arabic jayb 'chord of an arc,' a doppelganger of Arabic jayb 'fold of a garment.'
► sinuous, sinus

**sinecure** [17] Sinecure means literally 'without cure.' It comes from the Latin phrase beneficium sine cūrā 'benefice without cure,' that is to say an ecclesiastical office that does not involve the cure of souls (looking after people's spiritual welfare), the usual duty of a priest. Hence it came to be applied to any appointment that involves payment for no work.

**sing** [OE] Sing is a general Germanic word, related to German singen, Dutch zingen, Swedish sjunga, and Danish synge, and of course to the noun song. It is thought that it may have distant links with Greek omphḗ 'voice' and Welsh dehongli 'explain, interpret.'
► song

**single** [14] Single comes via Old French sengle or single from Latin singulus. This was formed from sim-, the stem of simplus 'single' (which came from the same Indo-European base that produced English same and similar), together with the diminutive suffix *-go and a further element *-lo. Singlet 'vest' [18] was coined on the model of doublet, in allusion to its being an unlined garment, made from a 'single' layer of material.
► same, similar, simple

**singular** [14] *Singular* comes ultimately from Latin *singulāris* 'alone of its kind,' a derivative of *singulus* 'single.' It reached English via Old French *singuler* as *singuler* (the modern spelling *singular* is a 17th-century relatinization). The word's grammatical application, and its use for 'remarkable, extraordinary,' both developed in Latin.

▶ single

**sinister** see LEFT

**sink** [OE] *Sink* is a general Germanic verb, with relatives in German *sinken*, Dutch *zinken*, Swedish *sjunka*, and Danish *synke*. But where their common Germanic ancestor came from is not known. These days, *sink* means both 'go below water' and 'cause to go below water,' but originally it was used only for the former. There was a separate but closely related verb, *sench*, for 'cause to sink,' which died out in the 14th century. The noun *sink* [15] originally denoted a pit 'sunk' in the ground for receiving water.

**sinuous** see SINE

**sinus** see SINE

**sir** [13] In common with many other European terms of address for men (such as *monsieur* and *señor*), *sir* goes back ultimately to Latin *senior* 'older' (source also of English *senior*). This was reduced in Vulgar Latin to *\*seior*, which found its way into Old French as *\*sieire*, later *sire*. English borrowed this as *sire* [13], which in weakly-stressed positions (prefixed to names, for instance) became *sir*. Other titles based on *senior* that have found their way into English include French *monsieur* [15] (literally 'my sire'), together with its plural *messieurs* [17], abbreviated to *messrs* [18]; French *seigneur* [16]; Spanish *señor* [17]; and Italian *signor* [16].

*Surly* [16] is an alteration of an earlier *sirly* 'lordly,' a derivative of *sir*. The meaning 'grumpy' evolved via an intermediate 'haughty.'

▶ senator, senior, sire, surly

**siren** [14] The *Seirēnes* were sea nymphs who, according to Greek mythology, sat on rocks luring impressionable sailors to their doom with the sweetness of their singing. Latin took the word over as *sīrēna*, and it passed into English via Old French *sereine*. The term was applied to an acoustical instrument invented in 1819 by Cagniard de la Tour, that produced musical sounds and was used for measuring the frequency of sound waves, and it was this that formed the basis of its later use (in the 1870s) for a device for giving loud warning signals.

**sirloin** [16] One of the oldest of etymological chestnuts is that *sirloin* got its name because a particular English king found the joint of beef so excellent that he knighted it. The monarch in question has been variously identified as Henry VIII, James I, and Charles II, but while the first of these is chronologically possible, in fact the story has no truth in it at all. The more sober facts are that the word was borrowed from Old French *\*surloigne*, a compound formed from *sur* 'above' and *loigne* 'loin' (source of English *loin*). The spelling *sir-* (first recorded in the 18th century) no doubt owes something to the 'knighting' story.

▶ loin, lumbar

**sirocco** [17] The sirocco is a hot wind that blows into southern Europe from North Africa. Etymologically its name means 'east' wind. The term comes via French *sirocco* and Italian *scirocco* from Arabic *sharūq* 'east,' hence 'east wind,' a derivative of the verbal past form *sharaqa* 'rose' (the allusion being to the direction of the rising sun).

**sister** [OE] *Sister* is one of a widespread family of 'sister'-words that go back ultimately to Indo-European *\*swesor*. Amongst its other descendants are Latin *soror* (source of French *soeur*, Italian *sorella*, and Rumanian *sora*, not to mention English *sorority* [16]), Russian, Czech, and Serbo-Croat *sestra*, Polish *siostra*, Welsh *chwaer*, Breton *c'hoar*, Lithuanian *sesuo*, and Sanskrit *svasar-*. To prehistoric Germanic it contributed *\*swestr*, which has evolved into German *schwester*, Dutch *zuster*, Swedish *syster*, Danish *søster*, and English *sister*. English *cousin* goes back ultimately to a compound based on *\*swesor*, the Old Latin antecedent of *soror*.

▶ sorority

**sit** [OE] *Sit* comes from a prehistoric Germanic *\*sitjan* or *\*setjan*, which also produced German *sitzen*, Dutch *zitten*, Swedish *sitta*, and Danish *sidde*. This was derived from a base *\*set-*, source also of English *seat, set* (etymologically 'cause to sit'), and *settle*. And this in turn went back to the Indo-European base *\*sed-* 'sit,' which has contributed hugely to English vocabulary – mainly through its Latin descendant *sedēre* 'sit' (source of English *assess, insidious, séance, session, size, subsidy*, etc), but also via Welsh, in the form of *eisteddfod*. It lies in addition behind English *saddle* and *soot*, and its other progeny include Russian *sidet'*, Serbo-Croat *sjediti*, and Latvian *sēdēt* 'sit.'

▶ assess, eisteddfod, insidious, saddle, séance, seat, session, set, settle, size, subsidy

**situate** [16] *Situate*, originally an adjective, goes back to late Latin *situātus* 'placed,' a derivative of Latin *situs* 'position' (from which English gets *site* [14]). This probably originated as a noun use of *situs*, the past participle of *sinere* 'allow,' hence 'allow to stay,' hence 'put.'

▶ site

**six** [OE] The Indo-European ancestor of *six* was *\*seks*, which also produced Latin *sex* (source of English *sextant, sextuplet*, etc), Greek *héx*, Welsh *chwech*, Russian *shest'*, etc. The word's Germanic relatives include German *sechs*, Dutch *zes*, and Swedish and Danish *sex*.

▶ sextant

**size** [13]  The etymological notion underlying *size* is of 'settling' something, of fixing an amount. The word is a curtailed version of *assize*, which went back ultimately to Latin *assidēre*, literally 'sit beside someone.' By the time it reached English, via Old French, it had acquired connotations of 'sitting down to make a judgment on something,' such as a law case (hence the meaning of English *assize*). Other matters decided on in this way included the standardization of amounts (of taxes, for example, or food), and this led to the word *size* being used for 'dimension.' *Size* 'gum' [15] may be the same word, but the nature of the relationship between the two is unclear.

▶ assize, sit

**skate**  English has two words *skate*. The older is the fish-name [14], which was borrowed from Old Norse *skata*. *Skate* used for gliding over ice [17] comes from an Old French word for 'stilt' – *eschasse*. Its northern dialect form was *escase*. This was borrowed into English in the 16th century as the now obsolete *scatch* 'stilt,' and into Middle Dutch as *schaetse*, its meaning unaccountably changed to 'skate.' Its modern Dutch descendant *schaats* was borrowed into English as *scates*, which soon came to be regarded as a plural, and was 'singularized' to *skate*. *Eschasse* itself came from a Frankish *\*skakkja*, a derivative of the verb *\*skakan* 'run fast,' which in turn was descended from prehistoric Germanic *\*skakan* (source of English *shake*).

▶ shake

**skeleton** [16]  A *skeleton* is etymologically a 'dried-up' or 'withered' body. The word comes via modern Latin from Greek *skeletón*, short for *sōma skeletón* 'dried-up body.' The adjective *skeletós* was derived from *skéllein* 'dry up, wither,' and was related to *sklērós* 'dry, hard,' from which English gets *sclerosis* [14].

▶ sclerosis

**sketch** [17]  *Sketch* comes ultimately from Greek *skhédios* 'impromptu.' This reached English by a rather roundabout route: via Latin *schedius*, which led to a Vulgar Latin verb *schediāre* 'do hastily,' source of Italian *schizzare* 'make a sketch,' which in turn produced the noun *schizzo* 'sketch,' borrowed into English via German *skizze* or Dutch *schets*.

**skew**  SEE ESCHEW

**skewbald** [17]  *Skewbald*, which denotes a horse with brown and white patches, is a compound formed (on the model of *piebald*) from an earlier *skued* 'skewbald' and *bald* (in the ancestral sense 'having white patches on the coat'). It is not clear where *skued* came from. One candidate as its ancestor is Old French

*escu* 'shield,' as if it meant etymologically 'marked with shield shapes' or 'chequered,' but another possibility is Middle English *skew* '(cloudy) skies.'

**ski** [19]  A *ski* is etymologically a piece of wood 'split' from a tree trunk. The word was borrowed from Norwegian *ski*, a descendant of Old Norse *skíth* 'piece of split wood, ski.' This in turn came from the prehistoric Germanic base *\*skīth-, \*skaith-* 'divide, split,' source also of English *sheath, shed*, etc. The Norwegian word is pronounced /she/, and that is the way in which it was once often said (and indeed sometimes spelled) in English. (Old Norse *skíth* may also lie behind English *skid* [17], which originally meant 'block of wood used as a support,' hence 'wooden chock for stopping a wheel.' The modern sense only emerged in the 19th century, from the notion of a wheel slipping when it is prevented from revolving.)

▶ sheath, shed, skid

**skiff**  SEE SHIP

**skill** [12]  *Skill* etymologically denotes not a physical accomplishment, but the mental capacity to make 'distinctions.' It was borrowed from Old Norse *skil* 'distinction, discernment, knowledge,' whose relatives include Dutch *geschil* 'difference,' and which goes back ultimately to the prehistoric Germanic base *\*skel-* 'divide, separate' (source also of English *scale, shell, shield*, etc). The modern English sense emerged in the 13th century.

▶ scale, shell, shield

**skillet** [15]  *Skillet* may come ultimately from the same source as English *scuttle* 'large container' – Latin *scutella*, a diminutive form of *scutra* 'dish, platter.' This was altered in the post-classical period to *\*scūtella*, which passed into Old French as *escuele* (source of Middle English *skele* 'dish,' recorded only once). A further diminutive form *escuelete* 'small platter' emerged, which is a plausible source of English *skillet*. (An alternative possibility is that it was derived from the now virtually obsolete English *skeel* 'bucket' [14], which was borrowed from a Scandinavian source related to Old Norse *skjóla* 'bucket.')

▶ scuttle

**skim**  SEE SCUM

**skin** [11]  The ancestral English word for 'skin' is *hide*. *Skin* was borrowed at the end of the Old English period from Old Norse *skinn* (source of Swedish *skin* and Danish *skind*). The etymological notion underlying the word is of 'peeling' or 'slicing' off an outer layer (it goes back ultimately to a prehistoric Indo-European base *\*sken-* 'cut off,' which was an extension of *\*sek-* 'cut,' source of English *section, sector, sickle*, etc), and so it presumably referred originally to the pelts removed from hunted animals.

▶ section, segment, sickle

**skipper**   see SHIP

**skirmish**   [14]  English adapted *skirmish* from *eskermiss-*, the present stem of Old French *eskermir* 'fight with a sword.' This in turn went back to a Frankish *\*skirmjan*, a relative of modern German *schirmen*. A variant of *skirmish* arose with the *i* and *r* sounds reversed, giving *scrimish*, which is the source of modern English *scrimmage* [15] and also of *scrummage* [19] and its abbreviation *scrum* [19].

▶ scrimmage, scrummage

**skirt**   [13]  Essentially *skirt* is the same word as *shirt*. It was borrowed from Old Norse *skyrta* 'shirt,' which came from the same prehistoric Germanic source as English *shirt*, and likewise meant etymologically 'short garment.' It is not clear why English came to use the word for 'woman's garment hanging from the waist,' but a link may be provided by modern Icelandic *skyrta*, which denotes a sort of long shirt with full tails that come down well below the waist. Swedish *skört* and Danish *skørt* 'skirt' were borrowed from the related Middle Low German *schorte* 'apron.'

▶ shear, shirt, short

**skive**   see ESCHEW

**skol**   see SCALE

**skull**   [13]  The Old English word for 'skull' was *hēafodpanne*, literally 'head-pan.' It has never been firmly established where its Middle English replacement *skull* came from, but is seems more than likely that it was borrowed from a Scandinavian language (Swedish and Norwegian have *skalle* 'skull').

**sky**   [13]  Our Anglo-Saxon ancestors called the sky *heofon* 'heaven.' Not until the early Middle English period did *heaven* begin to be pushed aside by *sky*, a borrowing from Old Norse *ský* 'cloud.' This came ultimately from an Indo-European base meaning 'cover,' which also produced Latin *obscūrus*, source of English *obscure* [14]. (For a while English continued to use *sky* for 'cloud' as well as for 'sky': the medieval Scots poet William Dunbar wrote, 'When sable all the heaven arrays with misty vapours, clouds, and skies.')

▶ obscure

**slack**   [OE]  In common with Dutch and Swedish *slak, slack* comes from a prehistoric Germanic *\*slakaz*. This was derived from the same ultimate source that produced Latin *laxus* 'loose' (source of English *lax, relax, release*, and *relish*) and *languēre* 'languish' (source of English *languish*). The plural noun *slacks* was first used for 'trousers' in the early 19th century. (The noun *slack* 'small pieces of coal' [15] is a different word, probably borrowed from Middle Dutch *slacke* 'waste produced by smelting metal.')

▶ languish, lax, relax, release, relinquish

**slander**   [13]  *Slander* and *scandal* are ultimately the same word. Both go back to Latin *scandalum*

'cause of offence.' This passed into Old French as *escandle*, which in due course had its consonants switched round to produce *esclandre*, source of English *slander*. *Scandal* was borrowed from the later French form *scandale*.

▶ scandal

**slang**   [18]  *Slang* is a mystery word. It first appeared in underworld argot of the mid-18th century. It had a range of meanings – 'cant,' 'nonsense,' 'line of business,' and, as a verb, 'defraud.' Most of these have died out, but 'cant' is the lineal ancestor of the word's modern meaning. It is not clear where it came from, although the use of the verb *slang* for 'abuse,' and the expression *slanging match* 'abusive argument,' suggest some connection with Norwegian dialect *sleng-* 'offensive language' (found only in compounds).

**slat**   [14]  *Slat* was adapted from Old French *esclat* 'piece broken off, splinter.' This was derived from the verb *esclater* 'shatter,' a descendant of Vulgar Latin *\*esclatāre* or *\*exclatāre*. And this in turn may have been formed from a base *\*clat-* suggestive of the sound of breaking. An alternative theory, however, is that it goes back to a prehistoric Germanic *\*slaitan* 'cause to split or break,' a variant of *\*slītan* 'split, break' (from which English gets *slice* and *slit*). The feminine form of Old French *esclat* was *esclate*, which has given English *slate* [14]. And its modern descendant *éclat* was borrowed by English in the 17th century in the metaphorical sense 'brilliance.'

It has been conjectured that *esclater* may have been related to Old French *esclachier* 'break,' which could have had a variant form *\*esclaschier*. This would be a plausible candidate as a source for English *slash* [14].

▶ slate

**slaughter**   [13]  *Slaughter* was borrowed from Old Norse *\*slahtr*, which went back to the same prehistoric Germanic base (*\*slakh-* 'strike') that produced English *slay*. Old English appears to have had its own version of the word, *\*slæht*, which survived into the 17th century as *slaught*. This forms the second syllable of *onslaught* [17], where it replaced the *-slag* in the borrowing from Middle Dutch *aenslag* (literally 'on-striking').

▶ onslaught, slay

**slave**   [13]  The word *slave* commemorates the fate of the Slavic people in the past, reduced by conquest to a state of slavery. For ultimately *slave* and *Slav* are one and the same. The earliest record we have of the ethnic name is as Slavic *Sloveninu*, a word of unknown origin borrowed by Byzantine Greek as *Sklábos* and passed on to medieval Latin as *Sclavus*. It was this that was turned into a generic term *sclavus* 'slave,' which passed into English via Old French *esclave*.

**slay**   [OE]  Etymologically, *slay* means 'hit' (its German relative *schlagen* still does), but from the earliest Old English times it was also used for 'kill.' It comes from a prehistoric Germanic base *slakh-, *slag-, *slōg- 'hit,' which also produced English onslaught, slaughter, the sledge of sledgehammer, sleight, sly, and possibly slag [16] (from the notion of 'hitting' rock to produce fragments), slog, and slug 'hit.'

▶ onslaught, slaughter, sledge, sleight, sly

**sledge**    English has two words sledge. The sledge [OE] of sledgehammer [15] was once a word in its own right, meaning 'heavy hammer.' It goes back to the prehistoric Germanic base *slakh- 'hit,' source also of English slaughter, slay, etc. Sledge 'snow vehicle' [17] was borrowed from Middle Dutch sleedse. Like Dutch slee (source of English sleigh [18]) and Middle Low German sledde (source of English sled [14]), its ultimate ancestor was the prehistoric Germanic base *slid- 'slide' (source of English slide).

Sledging 'unsettling a batsman with taunts' [20], which originated in Australia in the 1970s, may have been derived from sledgehammer.

▶ slaughter, slay, sly / sled, sleigh, slide

**sleek**    [16]    Sleek originated as a variant form of slick [14], which probably went back to an unrecorded Old English *slice. It apparently has relatives in Icelandic slíkja and Norwegian slikja 'smoothen.'

▶ slick

**sleep**    [OE]    Sleep comes from a prehistoric West Germanic *slǣpan, which also produced German schlafen and Dutch slapen. Its ancestry has not been pieced together in detail, but it is related to Dutch slap 'sluggish' and German schlaff 'slack, loose,' and a link has been suggested with Lithuanian slabnas 'weak.'

**sleigh**    see SLEDGE

**sleuth**    [12]    Sleuth originally meant 'track, trail' ('John of Lorn perceived the hound had lost the sleuth,' John Barbour, The Bruce 1375). It was borrowed from Old Norse slóth 'track, trail,' which was probably also the ultimate source of English slot 'trail of an animal' [16]. In the 14th century the compound sleuth-hound 'bloodhound for tracking fugitives' was coined. This was later shortened back to sleuth, and applied in 19th-century America to a 'detective.'

▶ slot

**slice**    [14]    Slice comes from Old French esclice 'splinter,' a derivative of the verb esclicier 'reduce to splinters, shatter.' This in turn was acquired from Frankish *slītjan, a descendant of prehistoric Germanic *slītan 'slit' (source of English slit and possibly of slat and slate). English originally took over the word's French meaning, but this had died out by the end of the 16th century. The modern sense 'piece cut from something' is first recorded in the early 15th century.

▶ slit

**slick**    see SLEEK

**slide**    [OE]    Slide comes from a prehistoric Germanic *slīd- 'slide, slip,' which also produced English sled, sledge, sleigh, and slither [OE]. Its ultimate source was the Indo-European base *slei- or *lei-, a prolific source of words for 'slide.' A version with -dh- on the end lies behind slide, and is also responsible for Greek olisthánein, Lithuanian slysti, Latvian slīdēt, and probably Welsh llithro 'slide.' A version suffixed -b- produced English slip, and one ending in -g- has spread throughout the Slavic languages, giving Russian skol'zit', Czech klouznouti, etc, all meaning 'slide.'

▶ sled, sledge, sleigh, slither

**slight**    [13]    The ancestral sense of slight is 'level, even.' It goes back to a prehistoric Germanic *slekhtaz, a word of unknown origin which had that meaning, but whose descendants have diversified semantically beyond all recognition (German schlecht and Dutch slecht, for instance, now mean 'bad,' having arrived there by way of 'level, smooth' and 'simple, ordinary'). 'Smooth' was the original meaning of English slight (Miles Coverdale, in his 1535 translation of the Bible, recorded how David 'chose five slight stones out of the river' to confront Goliath with (1 Samuel 17:40), where the Authorized Version of 1611 has 'smooth stones'), and it survived dialectally into the 20th century. By the 14th century, however, it was evolving into 'slim,' and this eventually became, in the early 16th century, 'small in amount.' English acquired the adjective from Old Norse sléttr 'smooth,' and Old Norse was also the original source of a verb slight [13], meaning 'make level or smooth.' This died out in the 17th century, however, and the modern verb slight 'disdain, snub,' first recorded at the end of the 16th century, is derived from the adjective, in the sense 'of little importance.' The noun comes from the verb.

**slim**    [17]    Slim is now quite an upbeat word, but that is a comparatively new departure, for historically it has been neutral if not downright derogatory. It was borrowed from Dutch slim 'small, inferior,' which went back via Middle Dutch slim 'slanting, bad' to a prehistoric Germanic *slimbaz 'oblique, crooked' (source also of German schlimm 'bad'). It may be distantly related to Latvian slīps 'crooked, steep.'

**slime**    [OE]    Along with its relatives German schleim, Dutch slijm, and Danish slim, slime comes from a prehistoric Germanic slīm-. This probably has connections with English lime 'calcium' and Latin līmus 'mud.'

**sling**    English has at least two distinct words sling, maybe more – the picture is far from clear. The first to appear was the verb, 'throw' [13]. This was probably borrowed from Old Norse slyngva, but as it originally meant specifically 'throw with a sling' there is clearly some connection with the noun sling 'strap for throwing stones' [13], whose immediate source was perhaps Middle Low German *slinge*. *Sling* 'loop or strap for holding things' [14] may be the same word, although there is no conclusive proof for this. *Sling* 'spirit-based drink' [18] first came on the scene in America, but its origins are unknown.

**slip**   There are three separate words *slip* in English. The verb [13] was probably borrowed from Middle Low German *slippen*, a product of the prehistoric Germanic base *\*slip-*. This in turn went back to Indo-European *\*sleib-* (source also of English *lubricate* [17]), a variant of the base which gave English *slide*. *Slippery* [16] was based on an earlier and now defunct *slipper* 'slippery,' which also goes back to Germanic *\*slip-*. It may have been coined by the Bible translator Miles Coverdale, who used it in Psalm 34:6: 'Let their way be dark and slippery.' It is thought that he modelled it on German *schlipfferig* 'slippery,' used in the same passage by Martin Luther in his translation of the Bible. *Slipper* 'soft shoe' [15] was originally a shoe 'slipped' on to the foot; and someone who is *slipshod* [16] is etymologically wearing 'loose shoes.'

*Slip* 'thinned clay' [OE] is descended from Old English *slypa* 'slime,' and may be related to *slop* [14]. One of its earlier meanings was 'dung,' which is fossilized in the second element of *cowslip*.

*Slip* 'strip, piece' [15], as in a 'slip of paper,' was probably borrowed from Middle Low German or Middle Dutch *slippe* 'cut, slit, strip.'
▶ lubricate, slide / cowslip, slop

**slit**   [13]   *Slit* is not recorded in Old English, but it is assumed to have existed, as *\*slittan* (its first cousin *slītan* 'slit' survived into the 20th century in Scottish English as *slite*). It goes back ultimately to the same Germanic base that produced English *slice* and possibly also *slash, slat* and *slate*.
▶ slice

**sloe**   [OE]   Etymologically, the *sloe* is probably the 'blue-black' fruit. The word comes, along with its relatives German *schlehe*, Dutch *slee*, Swedish *slå*, and Danish *slaa*, from a prehistoric Germanic *\*slaikhwōn*, which has been linked with Latin *līvēre* 'be blue-black' (source of English *livid* [17]). Another close relative is Serbo-Croat *shljiva* 'plum,' whose derivative *shljivovica* 'plum brandy' has given English *slivovitz* [19].
▶ livid, slivovitz

**slogan**   [16]   *Slogan* is a Gaelic contribution to English. It comes from *sluaghghairm* 'war-cry,' a compound formed from *sluagh* 'army' and *ghairm* 'shout.' English at first used it in its original Gaelic sense, and the metaphorical 'catchphrase' did not emerge until the 18th century.

**slop**   see SLIP

**slope**   [15]   The noun *slope* did not emerge until the 17th century. Originally it was an adverb, short for the now defunct *aslope*. This is generally supposed to go back to an unrecorded Old English *\*āslopen*, an adverbial use of the past participle of *āslūpan* 'slip away.' Such a scenario would appear to fit in well with the colloquial *slope off* 'leave,' but in fact this usage did not emerge until the early 19th century, in America.

**slow**   [OE]   The etymological notion underlying *slow* is 'dullness, sluggishness'; 'lack of speed' is a secondary development. The word goes back to a prehistoric Germanic *\*slæwaz*, which also produced Swedish *slö* and Danish *sløv* 'dull, blunt.' The original idea of 'sluggishness' is better preserved in the derivative *sloth* [12] (etymologically 'slow-ness').
▶ sloth

**slug**   English has at least two, possibly four distinct words *slug*. The oldest, 'shell-less mollusc' [15], originally meant 'slow or lazy person.' It was not applied to the slow-moving animal until the 18th century. It was probably a borrowing from a Scandinavian source (Norwegian has a dialectal *slugg* 'large heavy body'). A similar ancestor, such as Swedish dialect *slogga* 'be lazy,' may lie behind the now obsolete English verb *slug* 'be lazy,' from which were derived *sluggard* [14] and *sluggish* [14].

*Slug* 'bullet' [17] is of uncertain origin. It may have come from *slug* 'mollusc,' in allusion to the shape of the animal, but that suggestion depends on the supposition that *slug* was being used for the mollusc at least a hundred years before our earliest written record of it. *Slug* 'swig of drink' [18] may be the same word, but it has also been speculated that it comes from Irish Gaelic *slog* 'swallow.'

*Slug* 'hit' [19] and the related *slog* [19] probably go back ultimately to the prehistoric Germanic base *\*slakh-, \*slag-, \*slōg-* 'hit' (source of English *slaughter, slay*, etc).
▶ slog

**sluice**   [14]   A *sluice* is etymologically a device for 'excluding' water. The word comes via Old French *escluse* from Gallo-Roman *\*exclūsa*, a noun use of the feminine past participle of Latin *exclūdere* 'shut out' (source of English *exclude* [14]). This was a compound verb formed from the prefix *ex-* 'out' and *claudere* 'shut' (source of English *close*).
▶ close, exclude

**slush**   [17]   Like the very similar (and perhaps ultimately identical) *slosh* [19] and *sludge* [17], *slush* probably originated in imitation of the sound of squelching or splashing. The similarity of early modern Danish *slus* 'sleet, mud' and Norwegian *slusk* 'slushy' suggests the possibility of a Scandinavian borrowing rather than a native formation. *Slush fund* [19] comes from the use of *slush* for 'grease that is a by-product of cooking in a ship's galley,' the allusion being to the 'greasing' of people's palms with money.

**sly** [12] Etymologically, *sly* means 'able to hit.' It was borrowed from Old Norse *slœgr* 'clever, cunning,' which went back ultimately to the prehistoric Germanic base *slakh-, *slag-, *slōg- 'hit' (source also of English *slaughter, slay*, etc). The word's original approbatory connotations of 'cleverness' or 'skill' survived into the 20th century in northern dialects, but elsewhere they were soon ousted by the notion of 'underhandedness.' More neutral associations linger on in *sleight* 'dexterity' [13] (as in 'sleight of hand'), which was acquired from an Old Norse derivative of *slœgr*.

▶ slaughter, slay, sleight

**smack** English has four separate words *smack*. The oldest, 'taste' [OE], is now mainly used metaphorically (as in *smack of* 'suggest'). It has relatives in German *geschmack*, Dutch *smaak*, Swedish *smak*, and Danish *smag* 'taste,' and may be distantly linked to Lithuanian *smagus* 'pleasing.'

*Smack* 'hit' [16] at first meant 'open the lips noisily,' and was borrowed from Middle Low German or Middle Dutch *smacken*, which no doubt originated in imitation of the noise made. It was not used for 'hit with the palm of the hand' until the mid 19th century. The slang use of the derivative *smacker* for 'money' originated in the USA around the end of World War I.

*Smack* 'small sailing boat' [17] was borrowed from Dutch *smak*, a word of unknown origin. And *smack* 'heroin' [20] is probably an alteration of *schmeck* 'heroin or other drug' [20], which in turn comes from Yiddish *schmeck* 'sniff.'

**small** [OE] *Small* comes from a prehistoric Germanic *smalaz*, which in turn probably goes back ultimately to *smel-*, a variant of the Indo-European base *mel-* 'grind' (source of English *meal, mill*, etc). Etymologically, therefore, it could well denote 'ground up into little bits.' Its Germanic relatives, such as German *schmal* and Dutch *smal*, have become specialized in meaning to 'narrow,' but while English did start off down this semantic path, it has long since abandoned it.

▶ meal, mill, molar

**smallpox** see POX

**smart** [OE] *Smart* originated as a verb, meaning 'be painful.' It came from a West Germanic base *smert-, *smart-* (source also of German *schmerz* and Dutch *smart* 'pain'), which may go back ultimately to the same Indo-European ancestor that produced Greek *smerdnós* 'terrible' and Latin *mordēre* 'bite' (source of English *morsel, remorse*, etc). The adjective *smart* was derived from the verb in the 11th century, and at first meant 'stinging, painful.' Its modern senses 'clever' and 'neat' emerged in the 17th and 18th centuries respectively.

▶ morsel, remorse

**smear** [OE] *Smear* comes from a prehistoric Germanic *smerwjan*, which also produced German *schmieren*, Dutch *smeren*, Swedish *smörja*, and Danish *smøre*. The Swedish and Danish words for 'butter,' *smör* and *smør*, come from the same source (the former is the first element in the compound *smörgåsbord* 'open-sandwich table,' literally 'butter goose table,' from which English gets *smorgasbord* [19]). Also closely related are Irish *smir* 'marrow' and Greek *smúris* 'polishing powder' (source of English *emery* [15]).

▶ emery, smorgasbord

**smell** [12] *Smell* is something of a mystery word. It is assumed to go back to an Old English *smiellan* or *smyllan*, but no such verb has been recorded, nor have any related forms in other languages been pinpointed for certain. One theory links it with English *smoulder* [14] and the related Dutch *smeulen* 'smoulder,' as if the notion of 'smelling' arose from the idea of breathing vapour or smoke through the nose.

**smelt** see MELT

**smile** [13] The Old English word for 'smile' was *smearcian*, ancestor of modern English *smirk*. This was descended ultimately from the Indo-European base *smei-*, which also produced Greek *meidos* 'laugh,' Sanskrit *smeras* 'smiling,' Latvian *smaidît* 'smile,' and Russian *smejat' sja* 'laugh.' *Smile*, which from the 13th century began to push *smirk* towards the more specialized sense 'smile in a self-satisfied way,' comes from the same base, and was probably borrowed from a Scandinavian source (Swedish has *smila* and Danish *smile*).

▶ smirk

**smite** [OE] Old English *smītan* meant 'smear' (it came from a prehistoric Germanic *smītan*, which also produced German *schmeissen* 'throw,' and probably went back ultimately to the Indo-European base *smēi-*, source of Greek *smékhein* 'rub, cleanse,' from which English gets *smegma* [19]). Exactly the same odd semantic development from 'smear' to 'hit,' presumably via an intervening 'stroke,' happened in the case of *strike*.

▶ smegma, smut

**smith** [OE] *Smith* is a general Germanic word, with relatives in German *schmied*, Dutch *smid*, and Swedish and Danish *smed*. These point back to a prehistoric Germanic ancestor *smithaz*. This appears to have meant simply 'worker, craftsman,' a sense which survived into Old Norse *smithr*. The specialization to 'metal-worker' is a secondary development.

**smock** [OE] *Smock* originally denoted a woman's undergarment, and etymologically it may be a garment one 'creeps' or 'burrows' into. For it may be related to Old English *smūgan* 'creep' and *smygel* 'burrow' and to Old Norse *smjúga* 'creep into, put on a garment.' The underlying comparison seems to be between pulling on a tight undershirt over one's head and burrowing into a narrow space. Low German *smukkelen* or *smuggelen*, the source of English *smuggle* [17], may come from the same source.

▶ smuggle

**smoke** [OE] *Smoke* has close relatives in German *schmauch* and Dutch *smook*, now specialized in meaning to 'thick smoke.' And more distantly it is linked to Welsh *mwg* and Breton *moged* 'smoke,' Lithuanian *smaugti* 'choke with smoke,' Greek *smugenai* 'be consumed with heat,' and Armenian *mux* 'smoke.' The use of the verb *smoke* in connection with tobacco is first recorded in 1604, in James I's *Counterblast to Tobacco*.

**smooth** [OE] *Smooth* is a mystery word, with no known relatives in any other Indo-European language. The usual term in Old English was *smēthe*, which survived into modern English dialect speech as *smeeth*. *Smooth* comes from the late Old English variant *smōth*.

**smorgasbord**   see SMEAR
**smuggle**   see SMOCK

**smut** [16] *Smut* is a member of a large but loosely-knit family of West Germanic words beginning with *sm* and ending in *t* or *d* that convey the general notion of 'putting dirt on something.' Others include German *schmutzen* 'get dirty' and English *smudge* [15], and also English *smite*, which originally meant 'smear.' *Smut* itself may have been borrowed from Low German *smutt*.

▶ smite, smudge

**snack** [15] *Snack* originally meant 'bite' ('The . . . Tuscan hound . . . with his wide chafts [jaws] at him makes a snack,' Gavin Douglas, *Æneid* 1513). It was not used for a 'quick meal' (as in 'have a bite to eat') until the 18th century. It was borrowed from Middle Dutch *snac* or *snack* 'bite,' which was closely related to *snappen* 'seize,' source of English *snap* [15]. From *snappen* was derived the noun *snaps* 'gulp, mouthful,' which was borrowed by German as *schnapps* 'gin-like drink,' source of English *schnapps* [19]. And English *snatch* [13] is probably closely related to *snack*.

▶ schnapps, snap, snatch

**snail** [OE] *Snail*, like German dialect *schnägel*, Swedish *snigel*, and Danish *snegl*, comes from a prehistoric Germanic base *\*snag-, \*sneg-* 'crawl,' which also produced German *schnecke* 'snail' and English *snake*. Lithuanian *snāke* 'snail' is a distant relative.

▶ snake

**snake** [OE] The *snake*, like the *serpent* (and indeed the *snail*) is etymologically the 'crawling' animal. Along with Swedish *snok* and Danish *snog*, it comes from a prehistoric Germanic base denoting 'crawl,' which also produced English *snail* and German dialect *schnaacken* 'crawl.'

▶ snail

**snap**   see SNACK

**snapdragon** [16] The herbalist John Gerard (no feminist, evidently) gave the reason why antirrhinums were called *snapdragons*: 'The flowers [are] fashioned like a dragon's mouth; from whence the women have taken the name Snapdragon,' *Herbal* 1597. The term was also used from the early 18th century for a party game which involved picking raisins out of a bowl of burning brandy and eating them while they were still alight – the allusion being of course to the dragon's fire-breathing habits.

**snatch**   see SNACK

**sneeze** [15] The Old English word for 'sneeze' was *fnēsan*, a distant relative of Greek *pneuma* 'breath' (source of English *pneumatic*). This survived into Middle English as *fnese*. The letters *f* and *s* were very similar in medieval script, so it could have played a part in the late 15th-century emergence of *sneeze*. *Fnese* had largely died out by the early 15th century, and it could well be that when printing got into full swing in the 1490s, with many old manuscript texts being reissued in printed form, printers unfamiliar with the old word *fnese* assumed it had the much more common initial consonant cluster *sn-*. Another factor in the equation is the now obsolete verb *neeze* 'sneeze.' This was borrowed in the 14th century from Old Norse *hnósja*, a descendant of the Indo-European base *\*ksneu-*, which also produced German *niesen*, Dutch *niezen*, Swedish *nysa*, Danish *nyse*, and Russian *chikhat'* 'sneeze.' It bridged the gap between *fnese* and *sneeze*, and the new *sneeze* no doubt struck people as a more expressive alternative to the old *neeze*. (Both *fnese* and *neeze* go back ultimately to an imitation of the sound of breathing, blowing, or sneezing.)

▶ pneumatic

**sniff**   see SNUFF
**snivel**   see SNUFF

**snob** [18] *Snob* originally meant a 'shoemaker.' Cambridge University students of the late 18th century took it over as a slang term for a 'townsman, someone not a member of the university,' and it seems to have been this usage which formed the basis in the 1830s for the emergence of the new general sense 'member of the lower orders' ('The nobs have lost their dirty seats – the honest snobs have got 'em,' proclaimed the *Lincoln Herald* on 22 July 1831, anticipating the new Reform Act). This in turn developed into 'ostentatiously vulgar person,' but it was the novelist William Thackeray who really sowed the seeds of the word's modern meaning in his *Book of Snobs* 1848, where he used it for 'someone vulgarly aping his social superiors.' It has since broadened out to include those who insist on their gentility as well as those who aspire to it. As for the origins of the word *snob* itself, they remain a mystery. An ingenious suggestion once put forward is that it came from *s. nob.*, supposedly an abbreviation for Latin *sine nobilitate* 'without nobility,' but this ignores the word's early history.

**snooker** [19] The most widely canvassed theory of the origins of the term *snooker* is that it is an adaptation of late 19th-century army slang *snooker* 'new cadet' ('These embryo generals were called by the somewhat sneering terms of 'snookers' or 'last-joined',' *Routledge's Every Boy's Annual* 1872). The game was invented, as a diversion perhaps from the monotony of billiards, by British army officers serving in India in the 1870s, and the story goes that the term *snooker* was applied to it by Colonel Sir Neville Chamberlain (1856–1944), at that time a subaltern in the Devonshire Regiment stationed in Jubbulpore, in allusion to the inept play of one of his brother officers. The ancestry of *snooker* 'new cadet,' however, remains a mystery.

**snore** [14] Like *snort* [14] (which originally meant 'snore'), *snore* goes back ultimately to a prehistoric Germanic base *\*snor-*, imitative of the sound it represents. From the same source came German *schnarchen* 'snore,' which produced the German dialect noun *schnorchel* 'snout.' The mainstream language adopted it as a term for a 'breathing tube,' and English borrowed it as *snorkel* [20].

▶ snorkel, snort

**snout** [13] *Snout* and *snot* [14] are very close etymologically. Both go back ultimately to a prehistoric Germanic base *\*snut-*or *\*snūt-*, source also of obsolete English *snite* 'wipe or pick one's nose,' German *schneuzen* 'blow one's nose,' and German *schnauze* 'snout' (whence English *schnauzer* 'German breed of dog' [20]). The colloquial *snoot* 'nose' [19] is an alteration of *snout*, and formed the basis of the adjective *snooty* [20] (the underlying idea being of holding one's 'nose' in the air in a superior way).

▶ schnauzer, snooty, snot

**snow** [OE] *Snow* is an ancient word, with relatives throughout the Indo-European languages. Its ultimate ancestor was Indo-European *\*snigwh-* or *\*snoigwho-*. This also produced Latin *nix* (source of French *neige*, Italian *neve*, and Spanish *nieve*), obsolete Welsh *nyf*, Russian *sneg*, Czech *snóh*, Latvian *sniegs*, etc. Its prehistoric Germanic descendant was *\*snaiwaz*, which has evolved into German *schnee*, Dutch *sneeuw*, Swedish *snö*, Danish *sne*, and English *snow*.

**snuff** English has three words *snuff*, all probably going back ultimately to a prehistoric Germanic base *\*snuf-*, imitative of the sound of drawing air noisily in through the nose. *Snuff* 'powdered tobacco for inhaling' [17] was borrowed from Dutch *snuf*. This was probably short for *snuftabak*, etymologically 'sniff-tobacco,' which in turn was derived from Middle Dutch *snuffen*

'sniff, snuffle,' source of English *snuff* 'sniff' [16]. That base *\*snuf-*also produced English *snuffle* [16], probably borrowed from Low German or Dutch *snuffelen*, and *snivel* [14], which may go back to an unrecorded Old English *\*snyflan*; and *sniff* [14], if not directly related, was certainly similarly inspired by the sound of sniffing.

*Snuff* 'put out a candle' was derived in the 15th century from the noun *snuff* 'burnt candlewick' [14]. The origins of this are not known, but the fact that the now obsolete verb *snot* was once used for 'put out a candle' as well as 'blow one's nose' suggests that this *snuff* too may ultimately have connections with the inner workings of the nose (possibly a perceived resemblance between an extinguished candlewick and a piece of nasal mucus), and with the base *\*snuf-*. *Snuff it* 'die' is first recorded in the late 19th century.

▶ snivel

**so** [OE] *So* is a general Germanic word, with relatives in German *so*, Dutch *zo*, Swedish *så*, and Danish *saa*. It is also distantly connected with Greek *hōs* 'as' and *hóppōs* 'how.' Far back in its history it participated in the formation of English *as* and *such*.

**soak** [OE] *Soak* and *suck* come from the same ultimate source, the prehistoric Germanic base *\*suk-*. It appears to have been a fairly late Germanic formation, for its only known immediate relative is West Frisian *soken* or *zoken* 'soak.'

▶ suck

**soap** [OE] The word *soap* is of West Germanic origin. It comes from a prehistoric *\*saipō* (source also of German *seife* and Dutch *zeep*). This may have been related to Old English *sīpian* 'drip,' suggesting that it perhaps originally referred to a stage in the manufacture of soap. The Romans, like the Greeks, used oil for cleansing the skin, not soap, and so they did not have their own native word for it. Instead they borrowed the Germanic term, as *sāpō*, which has evolved into French *savon*, Italian *sapone*, and Spanish *jabon*. Germanic *\*saipō* was also acquired by Latvian (*ziepes*), Finnish (*saippio*), and Lappish (*saipo*).

**sober** [13] *Sober* comes via Old French *sobre* from Latin *sōbrius* 'not drunk.' This was the opposite of *ēbrius* 'drunk' (source of French *ivre* 'drunk' and English *inebriate* [15]), but where *ēbrius* came from, and precisely what connection the presumably related *sōbrius* has with it, are not known.

▶ inebriate

**soccer** [19] *Soccer* was coined from *Association football*, a term introduced around 1870 for football played according to the rules of the Football Association (as opposed to *Rugby football*). The suffix *-er* was commonly used as a more-or-less meaningless addition to nouns in British public-school and university slang of the late 19th and early 20th centuries (*footer* 'football' was formed in the same way). Originally, in the 1890s, *socker* vied with *soccer* as the word's spelling.

**social** [16] Latin *socius* meant 'companion, partner.' It came ultimately from the Indo-European base *\*seq-* 'follow' (source of English *sequal, sequence*, etc). From it was derived the adjective *sociālis*, which has given English *social* (*socialism* was coined in the early 19th century). Other Latin derivatives have given English *associate, sociable* [16] and *society* [16]. *Sociology* [19] was borrowed from French *sociologie*, a term coined in 1830 by the philosopher Auguste Comte.
▶ associate, sequal, sequence, society, sue, suit

**sock** English has two distinct words *sock*. The noun 'foot covering' [OE] originally meant 'light shoe,' and went back ultimately to Greek *súkkhos*, a word perhaps borrowed from some Asiatic language. Latin took this over as *soccus*, which was then borrowed into prehistoric Germanic as *\*sok-*. And this in turn evolved into German *socke*, Dutch *zok*, Swedish *socka*, Danish *sok*, and English *sock*. The origins of *sock* 'hit' [17] are not known.

**sod** see SODOMY

**soda** [16] *Soda* comes from medieval Latin *soda*, which may have been derived from Latin *sodānum* 'samphire, glasswort' (the plant samphire was burned to obtain soda for making glass). Another of the uses of samphire was as a headache cure, and it has been speculated that *sodānum* may have come ultimately from Arabic *sudā* 'headache,' a derivative of *sada'a* 'split.' *Sodium* was coined from *soda* in 1807 by the English chemist Humphry Davy.
▶ sodium

**sodomy** [13] The term *sodomy* commemorates the ancient Palestinian city of Sodom, which according to the Bible was a hotbed of unnatural vice ('But before they lay down, the men of the city, even the men of Sodom, compassed the house round, both old and young, all the people from every quarter. And they called unto Lot, and said unto him, Where are the men which came in to thee this night? bring them out unto us, that we may know them. And Lot went out at the door unto them, and shut the door after him. And said, I pray you, brethren, do not so wickedly. Behold now, I have two daughters which have not known man; let me, I pray you, bring them out unto you, and do ye to them as is good in your eyes: only unto these men do nothing; for therefore came they under the shadow of my roof,' Genesis 19:4–8). Anal intercourse and allied practices were known in late Latin as *peccātum Sodomīticum* 'sin of Sodom,' and from this was coined the medieval Latin term *sodomia* – whence English *sodomy*. The abusive *sod* [19] is short for the related *sodomite* [14].

**soft** [OE] *Soft* goes back to a prehistoric West Germanic *\*samft-*, which also produced German *sanft* 'gentle, easy, smooth' and Dutch *zacht* 'soft.' It may go

back ultimately to the prehistoric base *\*sōm-* 'fitting, agreeable,' source of English *seem* and *seemly*.
▶ seem, seemly

**soil** *Soil* 'ground' [14] and *soil* 'make dirty' [13] are distinct words. The former comes from Anglo-Norman *soil* 'land.' This was the formal descendant of Latin *solium* 'seat,' but its use for 'land' appears to have arisen from confusion with Latin *solum* 'ground.'

Etymologically, to *soil* something virtually amounts to making a pigsty of it. The verb comes via Old French *souiller* from Vulgar Latin *\*suculāre* 'make dirty,' a derivative of Latin *suculus* 'little pig.' This was a diminutive form of *sūs* 'pig,' a relative of English *sow*. French *souiller* may also be the source of English *sully* [16].
▶ sow, sully

**soirée** see SERENADE

**sojourn** [13] To *sojourn* in a place is etymologically to 'spend the day' there. The word comes via Old French *sojorner* from Vulgar Latin *\*subdiurnāre* 'spend the day,' a compound verb formed from the Latin prefix *sub* 'under,' hence 'during,' and late Latin *diurnum* 'day' (source of English *diurnal, journey*, etc).
▶ diurnal, journey

**solace** see CONSOLE

**solar** [15] *Solar* comes from Latin *sōlāris*, a derivative of *sōl* 'sun.' This went back to the same ultimate Indo-European base, *\*su-*, that produced English *sun*. *Solarium* [19] was borrowed from another Latin derivative, *sōlārium*, which denoted a 'sundial' as well as a 'balcony, flat rooftop, or other part of a house exposed to the sun.' *Solstice* [13] means etymologically the 'sun standing still.' It comes from Latin *sōlstitium*, a compound formed from *sōl* and *stit-*, the past participial stem of *sistere* 'make stand.'
▶ solarium, solstice

**solder** [14] To *solder* something is etymologically to make it 'solid.' The word was originally acquired, as a noun, from Old French *soldure*, a derivative of the verb *solder* 'solder.' This in turn came from Latin *solidāre* 'make solid, strengthen, fasten,' a derivative of *solidus* 'solid' (source of English *solid*).
▶ soldier, solid

**soldier** [13] The etymological idea underlying the word *soldier* is the 'pay' received by mercenary soldiers. It was borrowed from Old French *soudier* or *soldier*, a derivative of *soulde* 'pay.' This in turn went back to Latin *solidus*, a term used for an ancient Roman gold coin; it was short for *nummus solidus*, literally 'solid coin.'
▶ solid

**sole** English has three separate words *sole*, two of them closely related. *Sole* 'underneath of the foot' [14] comes via Old French *sole* from Vulgar Latin *\*sola*, a descendant of Latin *solea* 'sandal, sill' (a possible relative of English *sill*). And this in turn was derived from Latin *solum* 'ground, sole of the foot' (a possible contributor to English *soil*). *Sole* 'flatfish' [14] was independently borrowed from Old French *sole* in the sense 'flatfish,' a metaphorical extension based on the similarity in shape between the fish and the sole of the foot.

*Sole* 'only' [14] comes via Old French *soul* (ancestor of modern French *seul* 'only, sole') from Latin *sōlus* 'alone, single.' The origins of this are uncertain, but it may be related to the pronoun *sē* 'oneself,' in which case it could mean etymologically 'by oneself.' Its other contributions to English include *desolate* [14], *soliloquy* [17], *solitary* [14], *solo* [17] (via Italian), and *sullen*.

▶ sill / desolate, solitary, solo, sullen

**solecism** [16] *Solecism* 'act of (grammatical) impropriety' comes via Latin *soloecismus* from Greek *soloikismós*, a derivative of *sóloikos* 'ungrammatical utterance.' This is said to have referred originally to the speech of Athenian colonists in Soloi, in ancient Cilicia, southern Turkey, held by snooty sophisticates back home in Athens to be a debased form of their own speech.

**solemn** [14] *Solemn* comes via Old French *solemne* from Latin *sollemnis* 'customary,' hence 'performed with due ceremony on a particular fixed day.' This was derived from *sollus* 'whole' (source also of English *solicit*).

▶ solicit

**sol-fa** [16] *Sol-fa* is a lexicalization of two of the syllables (*sol* and *fa*) used in the tonic sol-fa system for representing the notes of the musical scale. In Italian the combination was turned into a verb, *solfeggiare*, a derivative of which has given English *solfeggio* 'use of the sol-fa system' [18]. (Another English word based on the name of notes of the scale is *gamut*.)

**solicit** [15] The ultimate source of *solicit* is Latin *sollicitus* 'agitated,' which also gave English *solicitous* [16]. It was a compound adjective, formed from *sollus* 'whole' (source also of English *solemn*) and *citus*, the past participle of *ciēre* 'move' (source of English *cite*, *excite*, etc) – hence literally 'completely moved.' From it was formed the verb *sollicitāre* 'disturb, agitate,' which passed into English via Old French *solliciter*. By the time it arrived it had acquired the additional meaning 'manage affairs,' which lies behind the derived *solicitor* [15]; and the original 'disturb' (which has since died out) gave rise in the 16th century to 'trouble with requests.'

French *insouciant*, borrowed by English in the 19th century, goes back ultimately to Latin *sollicitāre*.

▶ cite, excite, incite, insouciant, solemn, solid

**solid** [14] *Solid* comes via Old French *solide* from Latin *solidus* 'solid, whole' (source also of Eng-

lish *solder* and *soldier* and of the French coin term *sou*). It went back to the same base (Indo-European *sol-*) that produced Latin *sollus* 'whole' (source of English *solemn* and *solicit*) and *salvus* 'unharmed' (source of English *safe*, *save*, etc).

▶ solder, soldier, solemn, solicit

**solitary**　see SOLE

**solo**　see SOLE

**solstice**　see SOLAR

**solve** [15] Etymologically, *solve* means 'release,' particularly by the payment of debt. It was borrowed from Latin *solvere* 'release, unbind, pay,' which was descended from an earlier *\*seluere*. This was a compound verb based on *luere* 'loosen, release, pay,' a descendant of the same Indo-European base that produced English *analyse, loose, lose*, etc. The notion of 'payment of debts' survives in English *solvent* [17], and a metaphorical extension of 'loosening' to 'turning a solid into a liquid' can be seen in *soluble* [14] and the derivative *dissolve* [14]. The use of *solve* for 'explain,' now the major English sense, emerged in Latin, but it was not a major feature of the Latin verb. Other related forms include *absolute, absolve*, and *resolve* [14].

▶ absolute, absolve, analyse, dissolve, loose, lose, resolve, solution

**sombre** [18] Something that is *sombre* is etymologically 'under a shadow, in the shade.' The word comes from French *sombre*, an adjective derived ultimately from Vulgar Latin *\*subombrāre* 'put in shadow, shade.' This was a compound verb formed from Latin *sub-* 'under' and *umbra* 'shade, shadow' (source of English *umbrage, umbrella*, etc). Another descendant of Vulgar Latin *\*subombrāre* is Spanish *sombra* 'shade,' from which was derived *sombrero* 'hat for giving shade,' borrowed by English in the 18th century.

▶ sombrero, umbrage, umbrella

**some** [OE] *Some* goes back ultimately to Indo-European *\*smmos*, which passed into prehistoric Germanic as *\*sumaz*. This has now died out in most Germanic languages other than English, although a few derivatives survive, such as Dutch *sommige* 'some.' The Indo-European form also produced Greek *hamos* 'somehow' and Sanskrit *samás* 'some, every,' and variants of the base from which it came have also given English *same, seem, similar*, and *simple*.

▶ same, seem, similar, simple

**somersault** [16] *Somersaults* have no connection with 'summer.' The first element of the word means etymologically 'over.' It comes from Old French *sombresault*, an alteration of an earlier *sobresault*. And this in turn was acquired from Provençal *\*sobresaut*, a compound formed from *sobre* 'over, above' (a descendant of Latin *sūpra*) and *saut* 'jump' (a descendant of

Latin *saltus*, which has close relatives in English *assault, insult, sauté*, etc).

▶ assault, insult, result, sauté

**son** [OE] *Son* is an ancient word, with relatives in several Indo-European languages: Russian, Polish, and Czech *syn*, for instance, Sanskrit *sūnús*, and Greek *huiús*. These point back to an ancestral *\*sunu-* or *\*sunyu-*. This may have been related to Sanskrit *sú-* 'bear, carry,' in which case its original meaning would have been 'birth,' which evolved via 'offspring' to 'son.' The prehistoric Germanic descendant of *\*sunu-* was *\*sunuz*, which has diversified into German *sohn*, Dutch *zoon*, Danish *søn*, and English and Swedish *son*.

**sonata** see SOUND

**song** [OE] *Song* comes from a prehistoric Germanic *\*sanggwaz*, a derivative of the same base that produced *sing*. Its Germanic relatives include German and Danish *sang*, Dutch *zang*, and Swedish *sång*.

▶ sing

**sonnet** [16] A *sonnet* is etymologically a 'little sound.' The word comes, via French *sonnet* and Italian *sonetto*, from Provençal *sonet*, a diminutive form of *son* 'song.' This in turn was descended from Latin *sonus* 'sound' (source of English *sound*).

▶ sound

**sonorous** see SOUND

**soon** [OE] In Old English times, *soon* meant 'straightaway,' but human nature being what it is, the tendency to procrastinate led over the centuries to a change in meaning to 'after a short while.' (The same thing happened to *anon*, and is in the process of happening to *directly*.) The word itself comes from a prehistoric West Germanic *\*sǣnō*, whose other descendants apart from *soon* have all but died out.

**soot** [OE] *Soot* is etymologically that which 'sits' on something – that is, a film which settles on a surface. The word comes from a prehistoric Germanic *\*sōtam*, which was descended from the Indo-European base *\*sōd-*, *\*sed-* 'sit' (source also of English *settle, sit*, etc). By the time it reached English it had become specialized in meaning to the 'fine black particles produced by burning.'

▶ settle, sit

**sooth** [OE] *Sooth* 'truth' (which now survives in current usage only in the compound *soothsayer* [14]) goes back ultimately to Indo-European *\*sntyós* (possible ancestor also of English *sin*). This was a derivative of the base *\*es-* 'be,' and hence etymologically means 'that which is.' It passed into prehistoric Germanic as the adjective *\*santhaz*. As in English, in most other Germanic languages the word has now died out, but it survives in Swedish (*sann*) and Danish (*sand*) as an adjective meaning 'true.' From the Old English form *sōth* a verb was formed, *sōthian* 'prove to be true,' which has

evolved into modern English *soothe*. Its present-day meaning did not emerge, via intermediate 'confirm' and 'please or flatter by confirming or agreeing,' until the 17th century.

▶ soothe

**sop** [OE] The word *sop* originally denoted a 'piece of bread, cake, etc dipped into water, milk, wine, or similar liquid.' The modern metaphorical meaning 'something given to gain favour, bribe' did not emerge until the mid-17th century, in allusion to the piece of bread soaked in enticing honey but spiked with a soporific drug that was given to the guard dog Cerberus to put him to sleep so that Aeneas could visit the Underworld. The word goes back ultimately to the same prehistoric Germanic base (*\*sup-*) that produced English *sip* and *sup* 'drink,' and also, via the Romance languages, *soup* and *supper*. The corresponding verb *sop* 'dip in liquid' now survives only in the present participial form *sopping* 'soaking wet' [19].

▶ sip, soup, sup, supper

**sophisticate** [14] As those who hanker for the ancestral meanings of words never tire of pointing out, *sophisticated* originally meant 'adulterated, corrupted.' The modern approbatory sense 'worldly-wise, cultured' did not emerge (via an intermediate 'lacking primitive or original naturalness or naivety') until the end of the 19th century; and 'refined and elaborate' (as in 'a sophisticated missile system') is more recent still, not being recorded until after World War II. The verb was adapted from the past participle of medieval Latin *sophisticāre*. This was derived from Latin *sophisticus*, a borrowing from Greek *sophistikós*, which in turn was derived from *sophistḗs*, a noun which meant literally 'expert, deviser,' but was also used for a school of 5th-century BC Greek philosophers (the *Sophists*) who came to be despised for their specious and intellectually dishonest reasoning (hence English *sophistry* [14]). *Sophistḗs* itself came via *sophízesthai* 'play subtle tricks' from *sophós* 'skilled, clever, wise,' a word of unknown origin.

*Sophomore* 'second-year student' [17] is an alteration of an earlier *sophumer* 'arguer,' a derivative of *sophum*, which is a now defunct variant of *sophism*.

▶ sophistry, sophomore

**soprano** see SUPER

**sorbet** see SHERBET

**sorcerer** [16] A *sorcerer* is etymologically a drawer of 'lots' – for the word comes ultimately from Latin *sors* 'lot' (source also of English *sort*). The plural *sortēs* was used for the 'responses made by oracles,' and this formed the basis of the Vulgar Latin noun *\*sortārius* 'priest of the oracle,' hence 'caster of spells.' It passed into English via Old French *sorcier* as *sorser*, which was later extended to *sorcerer*.

▶ sort

**sore** [OE] *Sore* comes from a prehistoric Germanic *sairaz* 'painful, pained,' which was related to Irish Gaelic *sāeth* 'affliction, sickness' and possibly Latin *saevus* 'fierce.' It was borrowed into Finnish as *sairas* 'ill.' The adverbial use of *sore* as an intensive (as in 'sore afraid') has now died out, but it survives in the related German *sehr* 'very.' The word's ancestral connotations were of mental as well as physical pain, and while *sore* has preserved the latter, the derivative *sorry* has kept to the former.

▶ sorry

**sorrel** SEE SOUR

**sorry** [OE] *Sorry* goes back to a prehistoric West Germanic *sairig-*, a derivative of *sairaz* (source of English *sore*). The original base denoted physical as well as mental pain, but it is the latter semantic path that has been taken by *sorry*. Despite the similarity, incidentally, *sorry* has no etymological connection with *sorrow* [OE], which comes from a prehistoric Germanic base meaning 'care,' and is related to modern German *sorge* 'worry, sorrow.'

▶ sore

**sort** [14] Latin *sors* originally denoted a 'piece of wood used for drawing lots' (it is the source of English *sorcerer*). It later developed metaphorically into 'that which is allotted to one by fate,' and hence one's 'fortune' or 'condition,' and by the time it had turned into *sorta*, in the post-Latin precursor of the Romance languages, its meaning had evolved further to 'rank, class, order.' It was this sense that reached English, via Old French *sorte*. The notion of 'arranging into classes' underlies the verb *sort*, and also the derived *assort* [15]. From the same source comes *consort* [15].

▶ assort, consort, sorcerer

**soubrette** SEE SUPER

**soul** [OE] Behind the word *soul* lies the ancient notion of the soul as something fleeting or mercurial. For its prehistoric Germanic ancestor, *saiwalō*, was related to Greek *aiólos* 'quick-moving.' Its modern Germanic cousins include German *seele*, Dutch *ziel*, Swedish *själ*, and Danish *sjœl*.

**sound** English has no fewer than four distinct words *sound*. The oldest, 'channel, strait' [OE], originally meant 'swimming.' It came from a prehistoric Germanic *sundam*, a derivative of the base *sum-*, *swem-* 'swim' (source of English *swim*). The sense 'channel' was adopted from a related Scandinavian word (such as Danish *sund*) in the 15th century. *Sound* 'undamaged' [12] is a shortened version of Old English *gesund*, which went back to prehistoric West Germanic *gasundaz*, a word of uncertain origin. Its modern relatives, German *gesund* and Dutch *gezond* 'well, healthy,' retain the ancestral prefix. *Sound* 'noise' [13] comes via Anglo-Norman *soun* from Latin *sonus*

'sound,' a relative of Sanskrit *svan-* 'make a noise.' Amongst the Latin word's many other contributions to English are *consonant, dissonant* [15], *resonant* [16], *sonata* [17] (via Italian), *sonorous* [17], and *sonnet*. *Sound* 'plumb the depths' [14] (as in *sounding line*) comes via Old French *sonder* from Vulgar Latin *subundāre*, a compound verb formed from Latin *sub-* 'under' and *unda* 'wave' (source of English *undulate*).

▶ swim / consonant, dissonant, resonant, sonata, sonnet, sonorous / surround, undulate

**soup** [17] *Soup* was borrowed from French *soupe*. This, like its English relative *sop*, originally denoted a 'piece of bread soaked in liquid.' One way of making such sops was to put them in the bottom of a bowl and pour broth over them, and eventually *soupe* came to denote the 'broth' itself – the sense in which English acquired it. The word was descended from late Latin *suppa*, a derivative of the verb *suppāre* 'soak,' which was formed from the borrowed Germanic base *sup-* (source of English *sop* and *sup* 'drink').

▶ sop, sup, supper

**sour** [OE] *Sour* is a general Germanic word, with relatives in German *sauer*, Dutch *zuur*, and Swedish and Danish *sur*. Their common ancestor was prehistoric Germanic *sūraz*, which was related to Lithuanian *sūrus* 'salty' and Old Church Slavonic *syru* 'damp, raw.' *Sorrel* [14] is etymologically the 'sour' plant: its Old French source *sorele* came ultimately from Germanic *sūraz*.

▶ sorrel

**source** [14] A *source* is etymologically something that has 'surged' up. The word comes from Old French *sourse* 'spring,' a noun use of the feminine past participle of *sourdre* 'rise, spring.' This in turn was descended from Latin *surgere* 'rise,' source of English *surge*. The notion of the 'place where a watercourse springs from the ground' led on naturally to the metaphorical 'place of origin.'

▶ surge

**souse** [14] To *souse* something is etymologically to steep it in 'salt.' The word comes via Old French *sous* from Old Saxon *sultia* or Old High German *sulza* 'brine,' descendants of the prehistoric Germanic base *salt-*, *sult-* (from which English gets *salt*). The notion of pickling something in brine soon broadened out to pickling in other liquids, such as vinegar, and by the 16th century *souse* was being used metaphorically for 'drench.'

▶ salt

**south** [OE] *South*, together with its relatives German *süd*, Dutch *zuid*, Swedish *söder*, and Danish *syd*, goes back to a prehistoric Germanic *suntha-*. This may have been derived from the base of *sunnōn* 'sun' – in which case *south* would mean etymologically 'region of the sun, side on which the sun appears.' French *sud* 'south' was borrowed from English.

**sovereign**    [13]    A *sovereign* is etymologically someone who is 'above' others. The word comes via Old French *souverein* 'ruler,' a descendant of Vulgar Latin *\*superānus*. This was derived from the Latin preposition *super* 'above.' In the 1490s the term was applied to a gold coin worth 22s 6d (£1.12½), a usage which served as a model in 1817 for its application to a gold coin worth one pound.

▶ super

**sow**    English has two words *sow*, both of which go back to the Old English period. The verb, 'put seeds in the ground,' comes from a prehistoric Germanic *\*sǣjan*, which also produced German *säen*, Dutch *zaaien*, Swedish *så*, and Danish *saa*. It was formed from the base *\*sǣ-* (source of English *seed*), which goes back ultimately to Indo-European *\*sē-* (source of English *season, semen*, etc). *Sow* 'female pig' is descended from an Indo-European base *\*su-* (possibly imitative of the noise made by a pig), which also produced Greek *hus* 'pig' (whose feminine form *húaina* is the source of English *hyena* [16]), Latin *sūs* 'pig,' German *sau* 'sow,' and English *swine*.

▶ season, seed, semen / hyena, swine

**soy**    [17]    Chinese *shi-yu* is the ultimate source of *soy* (*shi* means 'salted beans' and *yu* means 'oil'). Japanese adopted the term as *shō-yu*, whose colloquial form *soy* was borrowed by English at the end of the 17th century. Dutch acquired *shō-yu* as *soja*, from which English gets *soya* [17].

**spa**    [17]    The town of Spa, in eastern Belgium, has medicinal mineral springs. They were discovered in the 14th century, and by the early 17th century were well enough known in Britain for the town's name to be used as a generic term for 'medicinal springs.' The present-day application to a 'town containing such springs' emerged towards the end of the 18th century.

**space**    [13]    *Space* comes via Old French *espace* from Latin *spatium* 'distance, space, period,' a word of unknown origin. Its modern English application to the 'expanse in which the Universe is contained' did not emerge until the 19th century. The Latin derived adjective *spatiōsus* has given English *spacious* [14], but *spatial* [19] was coined in English directly from Latin *spatium*.

**spade**    English has two words *spade*, but they are ultimately related. *Spade* for digging [OE] comes from a Low German source, which also produced Dutch *spade*. This went back to, or shared a common source with, Greek *spáthē* 'broad blade,' which was borrowed into Latin as *spatha* 'broad flat instrument' (source of the English botanical term *spathe* [18]). This in turn

passed into Italian as *spada* 'broad sword,' whose plural *spade* gave English the playing-card symbol *spade* [16]. The corresponding French term is *épée* 'sword,' adopted by English as a fencing term in the 19th century; and its Old French precursor *espee* is the ultimate source of English *spay* [15]. The diminutive form of Latin *spatha* was *spathula*, from which English gets *spatula* [16].

▶ spathe, spatula, spay, spoon

**spaghetti**    [19]    *Spaghetti* comes from the plural of Italian *spaghetto*, a diminutive form of *spago* 'string' (a word of uncertain origin). The earliest record of its use in English is by Eliza Acton in her *Modern Cookery* 1849, but it was still sufficiently unfamiliar then for her to mis-spell it *sparghetti*.

**span**    [OE]    *Span* is of Germanic origin, with relatives in German and Dutch *spanne*, Swedish *spann*, and Danish *spand*. It originated in the notion of the distance between the tip of the thumb and the tip of the little finger. The verb *span* was derived in the 14th century from the noun. Its German relative *spannen* 'stretch, tighten' produced the derived noun *spanner*, which was borrowed by English in the 17th century.

▶ spanner

**spaniel**    [14]    The *spaniel* is etymologically the 'Spanish' dog. The word comes via Old French *espaigneul* 'Spanish' and Vulgar Latin *\*spāniōlus* from Latin *Hispāniōlus*, a derivative of *Hispānia* 'Spain.' The breed of dog was of Spanish origin.

▶ Spain

**sparse**    see SPREAD

**spasm**    [14]    A *spasm* is etymologically a sudden 'stretching' of a muscle (although in fact physiologically spasms are contractions of muscle tissue). The word comes via Old French *spasme* and Latin *spasmus* from Greek *spasmós*, a derivative of the verb *span* 'pull.' This in turn was descended from the Indo-European base *\*spə-* 'stretch.' The metaphorical notion of 'intermittence' (based on the intervals between spasms) emerged in the derived adjective *spasmodic* [17] in the 19th century.

▶ stadium

**spat**    English has three words *spat* (not counting the past form of *spit*). The oldest, 'young of an oyster or similar shellfish' [17], comes from Anglo-Norman *spat*, but the origins of that are unknown. *Spat* 'shoe-covering' [19] is short for the earlier *spatterdash* [17]. This was a compound formed from *spatter* [16] (a word based ultimately on the sound of spattering) and *dash* (used here in the now archaic sense 'splash violently'). *Spat* 'tiff' [19] originated in the USA, but its ancestry is not known.

**spathe**    see SPADE

**spatial**    see SPACE

**spatula**    see SPADE

**spawn**    [14] *Spawn* is ultimately the same word as *expand*, and etymologically it denotes the 'spreading out' of a fish's eggs by its shedding them into the water. The word comes from *espaundre*, an Anglo-Norman variant of Old French *espandre* 'spread, shed.' This was descended from Latin *expandere* 'spread out' (source of English *expand* [15]), a compound verb formed from the prefix *ex-* 'out' and *pandere* 'spread.'
▶ expand

**spay**    see SPADE

**speak**    [OE] The usual Old English word for 'speak' was *sprecan*, which has close living relatives in German *sprechen* and Dutch *spreken*. *Specan*, the ancestor of modern English *speak*, did not appear until around the year 1000, but already by the 12th century it had virtually replaced *sprecan*. It is not known how the *r*-less form (which has no surviving relatives in other Germanic languages) arose, but it is clearly a secondary development of the *r*-form. This seems to be connected with Danish *spage* 'crackle,' Lithuanian *sprageti* 'crackle,' and Sanskrit *sphūrj-* 'crackle, rustle,' suggesting that the English word's use for 'utter, say' arose via an earlier 'crackle, prattle, babble, chatter' (English 'crack on about something,' 'not what it's cracked up to be,' and 'crack a joke' are remnants of an earlier widespread use of English *crack* for 'speak').
▶ speech

**spear**    [OE] *Spear* is a general Germanic word, with relatives in German and Dutch *speer* (the Scandinavian forms have died out). Its ultimate ancestry is uncertain, although it may have distant links with English *spar* and Latin *sparus* 'hunting spear.'

**special**    [13] Latin *speciēs* originally denoted the 'outward aspect,' the 'look' of something (it was derived from *specere* 'look,' source of English *spectacle, spectator, spy*, etc). It later evolved metaphorically to 'type, kind,' and in that sense was adopted by English as *species* [16] (*spice* is ultimately the same word). From it was derived the adjective *speciālis* 'of a particular type,' which has given English *special* (*especial* [14] came via Old French *especial*). Other derivatives have given English *specific* [17], *specify* [13], *specimen* [17], and *specious* [17] (from Latin *speciōsus* 'good-looking').
▶ spectacle, spectator, spice, spy

**spectacle**    [14] *Spectacle* is one of a large family of English words that go back ultimately to Latin *specere* 'look' (a descendant of the Indo-European base *\*spek-* 'look,' of which a reversed Greek version *\*skep-* gave English *sceptic* and *scope*). Others include *special, species, spectator* [16], *spectre* [17] (etymologically an 'appearance' or 'image'), *spectrum* [17] (from Latin *spectrum* 'appearance,' ultimate source also of *spectre*, and first used for the 'band of colours' by Isaac Newton around 1671), *speculate* [16], *spite*, and *spy*, not to mention prefixed forms such as *aspect* [14], *auspice, conspicuous* [16], *espionage, expect, frontispiece, inspect* [17], *respect*, and *suspect*. *Spectacle* itself comes via Old French *spectacle* from the Latin derivative *spectāculum* 'show, sight.' The application to a 'device for seeing with,' which lies behind English *spectacles* [15] and its abbreviation *specs* [19], is a post-Latin development.
▶ auspice, conspicuous, espionage, expect, frontispiece, inspect, respect, special, species, suspect

**speech**    [OE] *Speech* originated as a derivative of the late Old English verb *specan*, ancestor of modern English *speak*. It was originally used for the 'action of speaking' in general, or for 'conversation'; the modern application to an 'address delivered to an audience' did not emerge until the 16th century.
▶ speak

**speed**    [OE] *Speed* originally meant 'success, prosperity' – and when you wish someone *Godspeed*, you are wishing them 'good fortune.' Largely, though, it is the secondary sense 'quickness,' which first emerged in the late Old English period, that has survived to the present day. It has a surviving Germanic relative in Dutch *spoed* 'quickness,' and it also has possible links with Old Church Slavonic *speti* 'succeed.' It was first used as a slang term for 'amphetamine' in the mid 1960s.

**spell**    English has three distinct words *spell*, although two of them come from the same ultimate source. *Spell* 'name the letters of a word' [13] was adapted from Old French *espeler* 'read out.' This was descended from an earlier *\*espeldre*, which was borrowed from prehistoric Germanic *\*spellōn*. And it was a noun relative of this, *\*spellam*, which gave English *spell* 'magic formula' [OE]. *Spell* 'period of time' [16] may go back ultimately to Old English *spelian* 'substitute'; its original meaning was 'replace someone else at a job,' and the main modern sense 'period of time' did not emerge, via 'period of work,' until the 18th century.

**spend**    [OE] *Spend* is a blend of verbs from two distinct sources, but both going back ultimately to Latin *pendere* 'weigh, pay.' The earlier was Latin *expendere* 'pay out' (later to give English *expend* [15]), which Old English took over as *spendan*. (It was also the source of German *spenden*.) This was later reinforced by *dispend*, a borrowing from Old French *despendre* which now survives only in *dispense*.
▶ dispense, expend, pendant, pendulum

**sperm**    [14] *Sperm* is etymologically something that is 'sown,' like 'seed.' The word comes, via late Latin *sperma*, from Greek *spérma* 'seed.' This was a derivative of the same base as produced English *diaspora, sporadic,* and *spore,* and it may ultimately be related to English *spray.*

▶ diaspora, sporadic, spore

**spew** see SPIT

**sphere** [17] *Sphere* goes back ultimately to Greek *sphaira,* a word of uncertain origin, which reached English via Latin *sphaera* or *sphēra* and Old French *espere.* Amongst the theories put forward to account for its ancestry are that it was derived from Greek *sphurás* 'fall of dung, round pellet of dung, pill,' which has relatives in Lithuanian *spira* 'sheep-dung' and modern Icelandic *sperthill* 'goat-dung'; and that it is related to Greek *spaírein* 'quiver' and Sanskrit *sphur-* 'spring, quiver, trouble.' It metaphorical use in English for 'area of activity' dates from the early 17th century.

**sphinx** [16] The original Sphinx was a monster, half woman and half lion, which terrorized the country around Thebes in ancient Greece. According to legend, it would waylay travellers and ask them a riddle; and if they could not solve it, it killed them. One of its favoured methods was strangulation, and its name supposedly means 'the strangler' – as if it were derived from Greek *sphíggein* 'bind tight' (source of English *sphincter* [16]). However, this account of its name sounds as mythological as the account of its existence, and a more likely explanation is perhaps that the word was derived from the name of Mount Phikion, not far from ancient Thebes.

One of the first yachts to carry a spinnaker sail, in the mid-1860s, was the *Sphinx,* and it has been conjectured that its name (or rather a mispronunciation /spingks/) formed the basis of the term *spinnaker* [19], perhaps as a partial blend with *spanker,* the name of another type of sail.

▶ spinnaker

**spice** [13] *Spice* is ultimately the same word as *species.* It comes via Old French *espice* from Latin *speciēs* 'appearance, kind.' In late Latin its plural came to be used for 'goods, wares,' probably from the notion of a particular 'sort' of merchandise, and by the the time the word reached English its usage had narrowed still further to 'aromatic plant substances of oriental or tropical origin, used in cooking.'

▶ special

**spick and span** see SPIKE

**spider** [OE] The *spider* is etymologically the 'spinner.' Its name goes back to a primitive Old English *\*spinthron,* a derivative of the verb *spinnan* 'spin.' The inspiration is the same, and much more obvious, behind other Germanic words for 'spider,' such as German *spinne,* Dutch *spinner,* Swedish *spindel,* and Danish *spinder.*

▶ spin

**spike** English has two etymologically distinct words *spike,* although they are so similar in meaning that they are commonly regarded as one and the same. *Spike* 'long sharp piece' [13] was probably borrowed from Middle Dutch *spiker.* It has another relative in Swedish *spik* 'nail,' and goes back ultimately to prehistoric Germanic *\*speik-, \*spaik-* (source also of English *spoke*). The *spick* of *spick and span* [17] is a variant of *spike.* The expression is an elaboration of an earlier *span-new* 'brand-new,' which was borrowed from Old Norse *spánnýr* 'as new as a new chip of wood' (*spánn* 'chip' is related to English *spoon,* which originally meant 'chip'). The *spick* was added in imitation of Dutch *spiksplinter nieuw* 'spike-splinter new.'

*Spike* 'ear of corn, arrangement of flowers on a stalk similar to this' [14] was borrowed from Latin *spīca,* a close relative of *spīna* 'thorn' (source of English *spine*). *Spīca* is also ultimately responsible for English *spigot* [14], perhaps via the diminutive *spiculum;* and it forms the first syllable of *spikenard* [14], the name of a sort of ancient aromatic ointment or of the plant that probably produced it.

▶ spick / spigot, spine, spoke

**spill** *Spill* 'let fall' [OE] and *spill* 'thin piece of wood' are distinct words. The former originally meant 'destroy, kill'; the modern sense 'allow liquid to pour out or fall,' which did not emerge until the 14th century, arose as a rather grisly metaphor based on the notion of 'shedding blood.' The ultimate origins of the word, which has relatives in Dutch *spillen* and Swedish *spilla,* are not known. *Spill* 'thin piece of wood' was probably borrowed from Middle Low German or Middle Dutch *spile* 'splinter, wooden pin, bar, etc,' which also gave English *spile* 'bung' [16]. This in turn went back to a prehistoric West Germanic *\*spinla* (source also of English *spindle*). The familiar modern use of *spill* for a 'small slip of wood, paper, etc used for carrying a flame' did not emerge until the early 19th century.

▶ spin, spindle

**spin** [OE] *Spin* is a general Germanic word, with relatives in German and Dutch *spinnen,* Swedish *spinna,* and Danish *spinde.* It goes back ultimately to a prehistoric Indo-European base *\*spen-*or *\*pen-* 'stretch' which also produced English *span,* Lithuanian *pinti* 'plait,' and Old Church Slavonic *peti* 'stretch.' English words derived from it or its immediate Germanic ancestor include *spider, spill* 'slip of wood,' *spindle* [OE], and *spinster* [14] (originally a 'female spinner,' and not used as a designation of an unmarried woman until the 17th century).

▶ spider, spill, spindle, spinster

**spinach** [16] The ultimate origin of the word *spinach* is Persian *aspanākh,* which passed via Arabic *isfināj,* medieval Latin *spinachia,* and Spanish *espinaca* into Old French as *espinache.* Middle Dutch borrowed this as *spinaetse*, the probable source of English *spinach*. It has been speculated that the change of form from Arabic to Latin may have been partly motivated by the 'spiny' seeds of certain types of spinach.

**spindle**    see SPIN

**spine**    [14]    *Spine* comes via Old French *espine* from Latin *spīna* 'thorn,' which was probably derived from the same base as *spīca* 'ear of corn' (source of English *spike* 'pointed flower head'). The metaphorical extension 'backbone' developed in Latin, perhaps via 'prickle' and 'fish bone.' A *spinney* [16] is etymologically a 'thorny thicket.' The word comes via Old French *espinei* from Vulgar Latin \**spīnēta*, an alteration of Latin *spīnētum* 'thorny hedge,' which was derived from *spīna*.

▶ spike, spinney

**spinet**    [17]    A *spinet* is a sort of small harpsichord. English acquired the term via early modern French *espinette* from Italian *spinetta*, and one version of its origin is that it came from the name of one Giovanni Spinetti, a Venetian who supposedly invented the instrument at the beginning of the 16th century. A more prosaic story is that it was a diminutive form of *spina* 'thorn' (a relative of English *spine*), the allusion being to the plucking of the strings with thornlike quills.

**spinnaker**    see SPHINX

**spinster**    see SPIN

**spiral**    [16]    *Spiral* comes via French *spiral* from medieval Latin *spīrālis* 'coiled,' a derivative of Latin *spīra*. This in turn went back to Greek *speira* 'coil.' English also acquired the noun, as *spire* [16], which is used for the 'tip of a spiral shell.' It is not the same word as the *spire* of a church [OE], which originally meant 'stalk, stem,' and may go back ultimately to the base \**spī*- (source of English *spike* 'pointed flower head' and *spine*). The *spiraea* [17] is etymologically the 'coiled' plant; and *spiraea* in turn was used to form the term *aspirin*.

▶ aspirin, spiraea

**spirit**    [13]    Latin *spīritus* originally meant 'breath': it was derived from the verb *spīrāre* 'breathe' (source of English *aspire* [15], *conspire* [14], *expire* [15], *inspire* [14], *perspire* [17], *respire* [14], *transpire* [16], etc), which probably came ultimately from the prehistoric Indo-European base \**speis*- or \**peis*-, imitative of the sound of blowing or breathing out (source also of Old Church Slavonic *piskati* 'whistle,' Serbo-Croat *pistati* 'hiss,' and Old Norse *físa* 'fart'). But in the Augustan period it gradually began to take over as the word for 'soul' from *anima* (source of English *animal, animate*, etc), which itself originally denoted 'breath,'

and in Christian Latin writings it was the standard term used.

▶ aspire, conspire, expire, inspire, perspire, respire, transpire

**spit**    English has two words *spit* in current usage. *Spit* 'eject saliva' [OE] is one of a sizable group of English words beginning *sp*- which denote 'ejecting or discharging liquid.' Others include *spew* [OE], *spout* [14], *spurt* [16], and *sputter* [16]. They all go back ultimately to an Indo-European base \**spyēu*-, \**spyū*-, etc, imitative of the sound of spitting, which also produced Latin *spuere* 'spit' (source of English *cuspidor* [18] and *sputum* [17]). The immediate source of *spit* itself was the prehistoric Germanic base \**spit*-, a variant of which, \**spāt*-, produced English *spittle* [15] (originally *spattle*, but changed through association with *spit*).

*Spit* for roasting things on [OE] comes from a prehistoric Germanic \**spituz*, which also produced German *spiess* and Dutch *spit*.

▶ cuspidor, spew, spout, spurt, sputter, sputum

**spite**    [13]    *Spite* was adapted from Old French *despit* 'scorn, ill will,' which was also borrowed intact as *despite* [13]. This came from Latin *dēspectus*, the past participle of *dēspicere* 'look down on' (source of English *despise* [13]), which was a compound verb formed from the prefix *dē*- 'down' and *specere* 'look' (source of English *spectacle, spy*, etc). The use of *in spite of* and *despite* for 'notwithstanding' goes back via an intermediate 'in defiance of' to an original 'in contempt of.'

▶ despise, species, spectator, spy

**spleen**    [13]    *Spleen* comes via Old French *esplen* and Latin *splēn* from Greek *splén*, which may have been related to Latin *liēn* 'spleen' and Greek *splágkhnon* 'entrails' (source of English *splanchnic* 'of the viscera' [17]). In medieval physiology many internal organs were held to be the seat of a particular emotion, and the spleen was no exception. It had several conflicting states of mind attributed to it, but the one which survives is 'moroseness' or 'bad temper,' in the derived adjective *splenetic* [16].

**splendid**    [17]    *Splendid* comes via French *splendide* from Latin *splendidus*, a derivative of the verb *splendēre* 'shine.' This went back ultimately to the Indo-European base \**splend*- or \**plend*- 'bright,' which also produced Old Lithuanian *splendeti* 'shine' and Welsh *llathru* 'polish.' Amongst the derivatives adopted by English are *resplendent* [15], *splediferous* [15] (from *splendiferus*, a medieval alteration of late Latin *splendō:ifer*, literally 'bearing brightness,' hence 'full of splendour' – its modern use, as a jocular alternative to *splendid*, is a 19th-century American innovation), and *splendour* [15].

▶ resplendent

**split** [16]   *Split* was borrowed from Middle Dutch *splitten*. This, like German *spleissen* 'splice' and English *splice* [16], goes back to a prehistoric base *\*spleid-*, which may have been related to *\*spel-*, the source of English *spill*.

▶ splice

**spoil** [13]   Latin *spolium* originally denoted 'skin stripped from a killed animal' (it went back ultimately to the Indo-European base *\*spel-* 'split, burst,' which also produced German *spalten* 'split,' and probably English *spill* and *split*). It broadened out metaphorically via 'weapons stripped from a fallen enemy' to 'booty' in general, which lies behind English *spoils*. The word itself was borrowed from Old French *espoille*, a derivative of the verb *espoillier*, which in turn went back to Latin *spoliāre* 'despoil' (source of English *spoliation* [14]), a derivative of *spolium*. The verb *spoil* came either from Old French *espoillier*, or is short for *despoil* [13], which went back via Old French *despoillier* to Latin *dēspoliāre*. It used to mean 'strip of possessions,' as *despoil* still does, but in the 16th century it moved across to take over the semantic territory of the similar-sounding *spill* (which once meant 'destroy, ruin').

▶ despoil, spoliation

**spoke** [OE]   Like its relatives German *speiche* and Dutch *speek, spoke* goes back to a prehistoric Germanic *\*spaikōn*. This was derived from the base *\*spaik-*, *\*speik-*, which also produced English *spike*.

▶ spike

**spoliation**   see SPOIL

**sponsor** [17]   Etymologically, a *sponsor* is someone who makes a 'solemn promise.' The word was borrowed from Latin *sponsor*, a derivative of *spondēre* 'promise solemnly,' which denoted 'someone who stands surety for another.' In the Christian era it came to be used for a 'godparent,' which was its original sense in English. From the same source come English *despond, respond, spouse*, and probably *spontaneous* [17].

▶ despond, respond, spontaneous, spouse

**spoon** [OE]   The word *spoon* originally denoted 'chip of wood.' Such chips typically being slightly concave, they could be used for conveying liquid, and by the 14th century *spoon*, through Scandinavian influence, was being used in its present-day sense. It goes back ultimately to the same prehistoric base as produced English *spade*, and its Old Norse relative *spánn* 'chip' lies behind the *span* of *spick and span*. The late 19th-century slang use 'court, make love, bill and coo' comes from a late 18th-century application of the noun to a 'shallow' or foolish person.

▶ spade

**spoonerism** [19]   The term *spoonerism* commemorates the name of the Reverend William Spooner (1844–1930), Warden of New College, Oxford, who reputedly was in the habit of producing utterances with the initial letters of words reversed, often to comic effect (as in 'hush my brat' for 'brush my hat' or 'scoop of boy trouts' for 'troop of boy scouts').

**spoor**   see SPUR

**sporadic** [17]   *Sporadic* means etymologically 'scattered like seed.' It comes via medieval Latin *sporadicus* from Greek *sporadikós*, a derivative of the adjective *sporás* 'scattered.' This was formed from the same base as produced *sporá* 'act of sowing, seed,' ancestor of English *diaspora* [19] (etymologically 'dispersal') and *spore* [19]. And both were related to *speírein* 'sow,' source of English *sperm*.

▶ diaspora, sperm, spore

**sporran** [19]   English acquired *sporran* from Gaelic, of course, but it is not ultimately of Celtic origin. It goes back to Latin *bursa* 'purse' (source of English *bursar, purse*, etc) which was early on borrowed into the Celtic languages, giving Irish *sparán* and Welsg *ysbur* as well as Gaelic *sporan*. As with so many other Scotticisms, it was Walter Scott who introduced the word to English.

▶ bursar, purse, reimburse

**sport** [14]   *Sport* is short for *disport* [14]. This came from Anglo-Norman *desporter* 'carry away,' hence 'divert,' a compound verb formed from the prefix *des-* 'apart' and *porter* 'carry.' The noun originally meant 'amusement, recreation,' and it was not used in its main modern sense 'athletic contests' until the mid 19th century.

▶ disport, port, portable

**spot** [12]   *Spot* may have been borrowed from Low German *spot* or Middle Dutch *spotte*. These point back to a prehistoric Germanic *\*sput-*, which also produced Norwegian *spott* 'speck, spot.' There may also be some connection with Old English *splott* 'spot.'

**spouse** [12]   A *spouse* is etymologically someone who has made a 'promise' to another – in this case, of marriage. The word comes via Old French *spous, spouse* from Latin *spōnsus* 'bridegroom' and *spōnsa* 'bride,' noun uses of the past participle of *spondēre* 'promise solemnly, betroth' (source of English *despondent* and *sponsor*).

▶ sponsor

**spout**   see SPIT

**sprain**   see EXPRESS

**spread** [OE]   *Spread* is a general West Germanic word, with relatives in German *spreiten* and Dutch *speiden*. These point back to a common prehistoric ancestor *\*spraidjan*. Where that came from is not clear, although it may have links with Latin *spargere* 'scatter, sprinkle' (source of English *aspersion* [16] and *sparse*

[18]) and Greek *speírein* 'sow' (a relative of English *sperm*, *spore*, etc).

**spring** [OE] The noun *spring* and the verb *spring* come from the same source: the Indo-European base *\*sprengh-*, which denoted 'rapid movement.' Of its Germanic verbal descendants, German and Dutch *springen*, like English *spring*, have moved on semantically to 'jump,' but Swedish *springa* 'run' has stayed closer to its roots. The noun *spring* in Old English times denoted the place where a stream 'rises' from the ground, which soon evolved metaphorically into 'source, origin' in general. The notion of 'rising' was also applied figuratively to the 'beginning of the day' and to the 'emergence of new growth,' and the latter led in the 16th century, via the expression *spring of the year*, to the use of *spring* for the 'season following winter' (replacing the previous term *Lent*).

**spruce** *Spruce* 'neat' [16] and *spruce* the tree [17] are completely different words, of course, but they could have a common origin – in *Spruce*, the old English name for Prussia. *Spruce* the tree was originally the *spruce fir*, literally the 'Prussian fir.' And it is thought that the adjective *spruce* may have come from the expression *spruce leather* 'Prussian leather,' which denoted a particularly fine sort of leather, used for making jackets. The word itself is an unexplained alteration of *Pruce* 'Prussia,' which was acquired via Old French from medieval Latin *Prussia*.

▶ Prussia

**spume** see FOAM

**spur** [OE] *Spur* goes back ultimately to Indo-European *\*sper-*'hit with the foot, kick' (source also of English *spurn* [OE], which originally meant literally 'hit with the foot, trip over'). From it was descended the prehistoric Germanic noun *\*spuron*, which produced German *sporn* 'spur,' Dutch *spoor* 'track' (source of English *spoor* [19]), and Swedish *sporre* 'spur' as well as English *spur*.

▶ spoor, spurn

**spurt** see SPIT

**sputter** see SPIT

**sputum** see SPIT

**spy** [13] A *spy* is etymologically someone who 'looks.' The word was adapted from Old French *espie* 'watcher, spy,' a derivative of *espier* 'watch, spy' (from which English gets the verb *spy*, and also *espy* [14] and *espionage* [18]). This in turn was formed from the borrowed Germanic base *\*spekh-* (source of German *spähen* 'reconnoitre, watch' and Swedish *speja* 'spy, scout'), which went back ultimately to Indo-European *\*spek-* 'look' (source of English *inspect*, *spectator*, etc).

▶ espionage, expect, inspect, special, spectator

**squadron** [16] A *squadron* is etymologically a 'square.' The current sense 'military group' comes from an earlier 'square formation of troops.' The word was borrowed from Italian *squadrone*, a derivative of *squadra* 'square,' which comes from the same source as English *square*. The related *squad* [17] comes from French *escouade*, an alteration of *escadre*, which was acquired from Italian *squadra*.

▶ quarter, square

**square** [13] Etymologically a *square* is a 'four'-sided figure. The word comes via Old French *esquare* or *esqire* (*squire* was the Middle English form of *square*) from Vulgar Latin *\*exquadra*, a derivative of *\*exquadrāre* 'square.' This was a compound verb formed from the intensive prefix *ex-* and Latin *quadrāre* 'square,' a derivative of the Latin stem *quat-*, *quad-* 'four,' from which English gets *quadrant*, *quarantine*, *quarter*, etc, as well as *cadre*, and, via Italian, *squad* and *squadron*. The use of the adjective *square* for 'stuffy, old-fashioned' originated in jazz circles in the USA in the 1940s.

▶ cadre, quadrant, quarter, squadron

**squash** see QUASH

**squat** [13] Someone who *squats* is etymologically 'forced together' – and indeed the verb originally meant 'squash, flatten' in English ('This stone shall fall on such men, and squat them all to powder,' John Wyclif, *Sermons* 1380). Not until the early 15th century did the modern sense (based on the notion of hunching oneself up small and low) emerge. The word was adapted from Old French *esquatir*, a compound verb formed from the intensive prefix *es-* and *quatir* 'press flat.' This in turn came from Vulgar Latin *\*coactīre* 'press together,' a verb based on Latin *coāctus*, the past participle of *cōgere* 'force together' (from which English gets *cogent* [17]). The adjectival use of *squat* for 'thickset,' which preserves some of the word's original connotations of being 'flattened,' is first recorded in 1630. *Swat* 'slap' [17] originated as a variant of *squat*.

▶ cogent, swat

**squint** [14] *Squint* is short for the now nearly defunct *asquint* [13], which may have been based on the ancestor of Dutch *schuinte* 'slope, slant,' a derivative of *schuin* 'sideways, sloping.' The origins of this are not known.

**squire** [13] A *squire* is etymologically a 'shield-carrier.' The word was adapted from Old French *esquier* (which was later reborrowed into English as *esquire* [15]). This was descended from Latin *scūtārius* 'shield-carrier,' a derivative of *scūtum* 'shield' (source also of English *escutcheon* [15]).

▶ escutcheon

**squirrel** [14] The squirrel's name means etymologically 'little shadow-tail.' It comes via Anglo-

Norman *esquirel* from Vulgar Latin *\*scūriŏlus*, a diminutive form of *\*scūrius*. This was an alteration of Latin *sciūrus* 'squirrel' (now the scientific name for the squirrel genus), which in turn came from Greek *skíouros*, a compound formed from *skiá* 'shadow' and *ourá* 'tail.'

▶ constable, establish, stand

**stable**   English has two distinct words *stable*, but both come ultimately from the same source: the Indo-European base *\*stā-* 'stand,' ancestor also of English *stand*. The adjective *stable* [13] comes via Old French *estable* from Latin *stabilis* 'standing firm,' which has also given English *establish, stability* [15], and *stabilize* [19]. It was formed from the base *\*stā-*, as was Latin *stabulum* 'standing-place,' hence 'enclosure for animals,' which English acquired via Old French *estable* as *stable* [13]. The corresponding Germanic formation, also based on *\*stā-*, is *stall*. A *constable* is etymologically an 'officer in charge of stables.'

**stadium**   [16]   Greek *stádion* denoted a 'racetrack,' particularly the one at Olympia, which was about 185 metres long. In due course the word came to be used as a term for a measure of length equal to this, and that was the sense in which English originally acquired it, via Latin *stadium*. The original 'racetrack' was introduced in the 17th century, and 'sports arena' is a modern development of this. The Greek word itself was an alteration of an earlier *spádion* 'racetrack,' a derivative of *span* 'pull' (source of English *spasm*). The change from *sp-* to *st-* was perhaps set in motion by Greek *stádios* 'fixed, firm.'

▶ spasm

**staff**   [OE]   *Staff* is a widespread Germanic word, with relatives in German *stab*, Dutch and Swedish *staf*, and Danish *stav*. These point back to a common Germanic ancestor *\*stabaz*. Its ancestral meaning is 'stick,' and its use as a collective term for 'employees,' which dates in English from the 18th century, probably originated as an allusion to the carrying of a *staff* or 'stick' of office by a person in charge of subordinates – who thus became subsumed metaphorically under the notion of his 'staff.'

**stage**   [13]   A *stage* (like a *stable*) is etymologically a 'standing-place.' The word comes via Old French *estage* from Vulgar Latin *\*staticum* 'standing-place, position,' a derivative of Latin *stāre* 'stand' (to which English *stand* is distantly related). By the time it arrived in English it had acquired the additional connotation of a 'set of positions one above the other,' and this led to its use in the more concrete senses 'storey, floor' and 'raised platform.' The specific application to a 'platform in a theatre' emerged in the mid-16th century. The sense 'section of a journey' (on which *stagecoach* [17] is based) developed at the end of the 16th century, presumably on the analogy of physical levels succeeding one another in 'steps' or 'tiers'; and the further metaphoricization to 'step in development' took place in the 19th century.

▶ stand

**staid**   see STAY

**stair**   [OE]   A *stair* is etymologically something you 'climb.' The word goes back to a prehistoric Germanic *\*staigrī* (source also of Dutch *steiger* 'scaffolding'). This was derived from the base *\*staig-, \*stig-* 'rise,' which also produced English *stile, stirrup*, and *sty* in the eye. And this in turn went back to an Indo-European *\*steigh-* 'go, rise,' source also of Greek *steíkhein* 'stride, go' and Irish *tiagu* 'go.'

▶ stile, stirrup, sty

**stake**   [OE]   *Stake* 'post' comes ultimately from the prehistoric Germanic base *\*stak-, \*stek-, \*stik-* 'pierce, prick,' which also produced English *attach, stick, stockade*, etc. It may be that *stake* 'wager' [16] is the same word, alluding to a supposed former practice of putting the object wagered (such as one's shirt) on a post before the start of the contest.

▶ attach, stick, stockade

**stalactite**   [17]   A *stalactite* is etymologically something that 'drips.' The word was coined in modern Latin as *stalactītēs*, based on Greek *stalaktós* 'dripping,' a derivative of the verb *stalássein* 'drip.' Also derived from *stalássein* was *stalagmós* 'dropping,' which formed the basis of *stalagmite* [17].

**stale**   [13]   Something that is *stale* has etymologically been allowed to 'stand' – so that it is no longer fresh. The word comes from Old French *estale* 'stationary,' a derivative of *estaler* 'halt' (from which English gets the verb *stall*). And this in turn goes back ultimately to the prehistoric Germanic base *\*sta-* 'stand.' *Stale* originally denoted wine, beer, etc that had 'stood' long enough for the sediment to clear ('If mead is well sod [boiled] and stale it is liking to the taste,' John de Trevisa, *De proprietatibus rerum* 1398), and it was not until the early 16th century that derogatory connotations of lack of freshness began to creep in.

▶ stall, stand

**stalemate**   [18]   *Stalemate* is a compound noun, based on the now obsolete *stale* 'stalemate.' And this in turn was probably borrowed from Anglo-Norman *estale* 'fixed position,' a derivative of Old French *estaler* 'halt,' which also underlies English *stale* and *stall*. So etymologically, when you reach *stalemate* in chess, you have to 'stand' or 'halt' where you are, going neither forward nor back.

**stalk**   English has two distinct words *stalk*. The noun, 'plant stem' [14], probably originated as a diminutive form of the now extinct *stale* 'long handle,' a word distantly related to Greek *steleá* 'handle.' The verb, 'track stealthily' [OE], goes back to a prehistoric Germanic *stalkōjan, which was formed from the same base as produced English *steal*. The sense 'walk haughtily,' diametrically opposed to 'track stealthily,' emerged in the 16th century.

**stall** *Stall* 'compartment, booth, etc' [OE] and *stall* 'stop' [15] are distinct words, but they have a common ancestor, in prehistoric Germanic *stal-, *stel-* 'position' (source of English *still*). This in turn was formed from the base *sta-* 'stand,' which also produced English *stand*. From *stal-* was derived the noun *stallaz* 'standing-place (for an animal),' which has given German, Swedish, and English *stall*, Dutch *stal*, and Danish *stald*. A *stallion* [14] is etymologically a horse kept in a 'stall' for breeding purposes. And *stable* represents a parallel Latin formation to the Germanic *stall* (it has become specialized to a 'building for horses,' whereas *stall* developed to 'standing-place for a single animal'). The same Germanic base produced Frankish *stal* 'position,' which formed the basis of Old French *estaler* 'halt,' source of the English verb *stall*, and also of English *stale* and *stalemate*.

▶ stale, stallion, stand, still

**stalwart** [14] The ancestor of *stalwart* was Old English *stǣlwierthe*. The second half of this compound adjective denoted 'worth, worthy,' but the precise significance of the first element is not clear. It represents Old English *stǣl* 'place,' perhaps used here in the metaphorical sense 'stead,' so that etymologically the word would mean 'able to stand someone in good stead.' But *stǣl* itself may have been a contraction of *stathol* 'foundation,' so the underlying meaning of the compound could be 'foundation-worthy,' hence 'firmly fixed' (an adjective *statholfæst* existed in Old English, meaning 'firm, stable'). South of the border it became *stalworth*, which had virtually died out by the end of the 17th century. But the Scottish variant *stalwart*, first recorded in the late 14th century, survived, and was brought into the general language by Sir Walter Scott.

**stamina** [17] Etymologically, *stamina* is the plural of *stamen* 'male reproductive part of a flower' [17]. The ultimate source of both is Latin *stāmen* 'thread of woven cloth,' which went back to Indo-European *stāmen-*, a derivative of the base *stā-* 'stand' (source also of English *stand*). The application to the plant-part appears to go back to the Roman naturalist Pliny, who used *stāmen* for the stamens of a sort of lily, which resembled threads of cloth. The Latin plural *stāmina* was borrowed into English in the metaphorical sense 'threads of human life, vital capacities,' and by the 18th century it had broadened out to 'vigour.'

▶ stamen, stand

**stammer** [OE] To *stammer* is etymologically to be 'impeded' in speech. The word comes (along with Dutch *stameren*) from a prehistoric West Germanic *stamrōjan*, which was derived from the base *stam-*,

*stum-* 'check, impede' (source also of English *stem* 'halt, check' and *stumble*).

▶ stem, stumble

**stamp** [12] *Stamp* originally meant 'crush into small pieces, pound.' The sense 'slam the foot down' did not emerge until the 14th century, and 'imprint with a design by pressure' (which forms the semantic basis of *postage stamp* [19]) is as recent as the 16th century. The word comes, probably via an unrecorded Old English *stampian*, from prehistoric Germanic *stampōjan* (source also of German *stampfen*, Dutch *stampen*, Swedish *stampa*, and Danish *stampe*). This was derived from the noun *stampaz* 'pestle,' which was formed from the base *stamp-* (a non-nasalized version of which, *stap-*, lies behind English *step*). The Germanic verb was borrowed into Vulgar Latin as *stampīre*, whose past participle has given English, via Mexican Spanish, *stampede* [19].

▶ stampede, step

**stance** see STANZA

**stand** [OE] *Stand* goes back ultimately to the prehistoric Indo-European base *stā-* 'stand.' This passed into Germanic as *sta-, *stō-*. Addition of the suffix *-nd-* produced *standan*, source of English *stand*, while past forms were created with the suffix *-t-*, which has given English *stood*. Another descendant of the Indo-European base was Latin *stāre* 'stand,' a prolific source of English words (among them *stage*, *stanza*, *state*, *station*, *statue*, etc).

▶ stable, stage, stall, stamina, stanza, state, static, station, statue, steed, stool, stud, system

**standard** *Standard* 'flag, banner' [12] denotes etymologically something that is 'extended' or unfurled. The word comes from Anglo-Norman *estaundart* 'flag displayed on a battlefield so that troops can rally to it.' This was a derivative of Old French *estendre* 'extend' (first cousin of English *extend*). The sense 'criterion, norm,' which emerged in the 15th century, is probably a metaphorical application of the notion of the 'royal standard' or banner as being the point from which authoritative commands (as of standards of weight and measurement) are issued. *Standard* 'upright object, such as a tree' [13] is probably an alteration of *stander*.

▶ extend / stand

**stanza** [16] Etymologically, a *stanza* is a place where one 'stands' or stops. The word was borrowed from Italian *stanza*, a descendant of Vulgar Latin *stantia* 'standing, stopping-place,' which in turn was derived from the present participle of Latin *stāre* 'stand' (source of English *stage, state, station*, etc). Its application to a 'verse of poetry' arose in Italian from the notion of 'stopping' at the end of a section. *Stanza* was borrowed into French as *stance*, from which English gets *stance* [16].

▶ stance, stand, state, station

**staple**   English has two distinct words *staple*, but they come from a common ancestor – prehistoric Germanic *\*stapulaz* 'pillar.' This evolved into English *staple* [OE], which at first retained its ancestral meaning 'post, pillar.' The modern sense 'U-shaped metal bar' did not emerge until the end of the 13th century, and the details of its development from 'pillar' are obscure. The Middle Low German and Middle Dutch descendant of *\*stapulaz* was *stapel*, which had the additional meaning 'market, shop' (presumably from the notion of a stall situated behind the 'pillars' of an arcade). This was borrowed into Old French as *estaple*, which in turn gave English *staple* 'market' [15], hence 'principal commercial commodity.'

**star**   [OE]   *Star* is a general Germanic word, with relatives in German *stern*, Dutch *ster*, Swedish *stjärna*, and Danish *stjerne*. These were all descended from a prehistoric Germanic base *\*ster-*, which had come down unaltered from Indo-European *\*ster-* 'star,' source also of Latin *stēlla* 'star' (from which English gets *stellar* [16]) and Greek *astér* 'star' (from which English gets *asterisk, astronomy, disaster*, etc). The ultimate source of the Indo-European base is not known for certain, but the traditional view is that it comes from the base *\*ster-* 'spread out,' the underlying notion being of the stars 'spread out' in the sky. *Sterling* 'British money' was originally named from the design of a small 'star' on a coin, but *starling* is not etymologically related. The modern sense of *star*, 'leading performer,' is first recorded in the early 19th century.

▶ asterisk, astronomy, disaster, stellar, sterling

**starboard**   [OE]   *Starboard* is etymologically 'steer-board.' The word originated as an Old English compound formed from *stēor* 'paddle, rudder' (a relative of the verb *steer*) and *bord* 'board.' The early Germanic peoples propelled and steered their boats by means of a paddle on the right-hand side of the vessel – hence the use of *starboard* as the nautical equivalent of *right*.

▶ steer

**stare**   [OE]   The etymological notion underlying *stare* is of 'fixity' or 'rigidity.' It goes back ultimately to the prehistoric Germanic base *\*star-*, *\*ster-* 'be rigid,' which also produced English *starch* [15], *stark* [OE], *starve* (originally 'be stiff,' hence 'die'), *stern* 'severe,' and *stork* (etymologically the 'stiff'-legged bird). Thus to *stare* is to 'look fixedly.' (Greek *stereós* 'solid,' source of English *stereo*, came from the same Indo-European base as produced *\*ster-*.)

▶ starch, stark, starve, stereo, stern, stork

**starling**   [OE]   *Starling* is a diminutive form. The original Old English name of the bird was *stær*,

which together with German *star*, Swedish *stare*, and Danish *stær* goes back to a prehistoric Germanic *\*staraz*. This was related to Latin *sturnus* 'starling.'

**start**   [OE]   *Start* originally meant 'jump, leap, caper' ('Him lust not [he did not like] to play nor start, nor to dance, nor to sing,' Chaucer, *Romance of the Rose* 1366). This gradually evolved via 'make a sudden movement' to 'begin a journey,' but it did not emerge as a fully-fledged synonym for 'begin' until the end of the 18th century. *Startle* [OE], which came from the same Germanic base *\*start-*, has kept more closely to the notion of 'sudden movement.'

▶ startle

**starve**   [OE]   *Starve* means etymologically 'be stiff' – it goes back to a prehistoric Germanic base *\*star-*, *\*ster-* 'be stiff,' which also produced English *starch, stare*, etc. The 'stiffness' of a corpse led to its use for 'die' – a meaning which it retains in the related German *sterben* and Dutch *sterven*. In English, however, from the 12th century onwards, *starve* gradually narrowed down in meaning to 'dying from cold' (which survived into the modern era in northern dialects) and 'dying from hunger.'

▶ starch, stare, stork

**state**   [13]   *State* comes, partly via Old French *estat* (source of English *estate*), from Latin *status* 'way of standing, condition, position,' which was formed from the same base as *stāre* 'stand' (a distant relative of English *stand*). The word's political sense, 'body politic,' first recorded in the 16th century, comes from Latin expressions such as *status rei publicae* 'condition of the republic' and *status civitatis* 'condition of the body politic.' The verb *state* originally meant 'put, place'; its modern meaning 'declare' arose from the notion of 'placing' something on record, setting it out in detail. English borrowed *status* itself in the 17th century.

▶ estate, stand, station, statistic, statue, statute

**static**   [17]   *Static* means etymologically 'causing to stand.' Its ultimate ancestor is Greek *statós* 'placed, standing,' a derivative of the base *\*sta-* 'stand' (to which English *stand* is related). From this was derived *statikós* 'causing to stand,' which passed into English via Latin *staticus*.

▶ stand

**station**   [14]   A *station* is etymologically a 'standing,' hence a 'place for standing' – a guard who takes up his 'station' outside a building goes and 'stands' there. The word comes via Old French *station* from Latin *statiō* 'standing,' a descendant of the base *\*stā-* 'stand' (to which English *stand* is related). Various metaphorical senses emerged in Latin, such as 'post, job' and 'abode, residence,' but 'stopping place for vehicles' is a post-Latin development. It came out of an earlier 'stopping place on a journey,' and is first recorded in English at the end of the 18th century, in the

USA, with reference to coach routes. The application to 'railway stations' dates from the 1830s. The notion of 'standing still' is preserved in the derived adjective *stationary* [15].

▶ constant, instant, stand, state, stationary, stationery, statue

**stationer** [15] In medeval Latin a *statiōnārius* was originally a 'trader who kept a permanent stall' (as opposed to an itinerant seller). The word was derived from Latin *statiō* 'standing, keeping still' (source of English *station*), which in the post-classical meaning evolved in meaning to 'shop.' Such permanent shops were comparatively rare in the Middle Ages. Of those that did exist, the commonest were bookshops, licensed by the universities, and so when English adopted the Latin term, it was used in the sense 'bookseller.' It has since come down in the world somewhat to 'seller of paper, pens, etc' (a sense first recorded in the mid 17th century), but the earlier application is preserved in the name of the *Stationers' Company*, a London livery company to which booksellers and publishers belong. The derivative *stationery* dates from the 18th century.

▶ station

**statistic** [18] The term *statistics* [18] etymologically denotes the 'science of the state.' It comes from *statisticus* 'of state affairs,' a modern Latin coinage based on classical Latin *status* (source of English *state*). It was the 18th-century German political scientist Aschenwall who brought it (in German *statistisch*) into general usage, in the specific sense 'of the collection and evaluation of data (particularly numerical data) relating to the study of the state and its functions and institutions.' By the 1830s it had broadened out into its modern general sense. English acquired the word from German.

▶ state

**statue** [14] A *statue* is etymologically something that has been 'set up' or 'erected.' The word comes via Old French *statue* from Latin *statua*, a derivative of *statuere* 'cause to stand, erect, establish' (source of English *constitute, destitute* [14], *institute, prostitute, restitution* [13], *statute* [13], and *substitute* [16]). This in turn was formed from *status* (source of English *state* and *status*), the past participle of Latin *stāre* 'stand' (source of English *contrast* [16], *cost, stage, station, stay*, etc). And *stāre* came ultimately from the Indo-European base *\*stā-* 'stand,' which is also the ancestor of English *stable, stand, stead, stem*, etc. Amongst the host of other English words that come from the prolific Latin *stāre* are (via its present participle *stāns*) *circumstance* [13], *constant, distant, instant, stance, stanza, substance*, etc, and (via the derivative *sistere* 'stand') *assist, consist, desist* [15], *exist, insist* [16], *persist* [16], and *resist* [14].

▶ assist, circumstance, consist, constant, contrast, cost,

desist, destitute, distant, estate, exist, insist, instant, institute, persist, prostitute, resist, restitution, stable, stance, stand, stanza, state, station, statistic, status, statute, stay, stead, stem, stoic, substance, substitute

**status**     see STATE

**statute**     see STATUE

**stay** English has three distinct words *stay*, two of them ultimately from the same source. *Stay* 'stop' [15] comes from *estai-*, the present stem of Old French *ester* 'stand, stop.' This in turn went back to Latin *stāre* 'stand' (source of English *state, statue*, etc). *Staid* [16] originated as the past participle of *stay*. *Stay* 'strong rope' [OE] comes from a prehistoric Germanic *\*staga-*. This was derived from a base *\*stagh-, \*stakh-* 'be firm,' which also produced English *steel* and (by borrowing) Old French *estayer* 'support' (source of English *stay* 'support' [16]).

▶ staid, stand, statue / steel

**stead** [OE] *Stead* 'place' comes from a prehistoric Germanic *\*stadiz*, which also produced German *statt* 'place' and *stadt* 'town.' This in turn went back to Indo-European *\*statís*, a derivative of the base *\*stə-, \*stā-* 'stand,' which also produced English *stand* and Latin *stāre* 'stand' (source of English *state, statue*, etc). The expression *in the stead of* 'in place of,' and its lexicalized form *instead*, originated in the 13th century, modelled on Old French *en lieu de*.

▶ stand, state, statue, steady

**steady** [16] *Steady* was derived from *stead* 'place,' probably on the model of Middle Low German *stēdig* 'stable.' This in turn went back to a prehistoric Germanic *\*stadigaz*, a product of the same base as produced English *stead*. Its etymological meaning is 'fixed in one place.'

▶ stead

**steal** [OE] *Steal* comes from a prehistoric Germanic base *\*stel-*. This also produced German *stehlen*, Dutch *stelen*, Swedish *stjäla*, and Danish *stjæle*, but its ultimate ancestry is unknown. The derived *stealth* [13] originally meant 'theft' ('I know my lord hath spent of Timon's wealth, and now ingratitude makes it worse than stealth,' Shakespeare, *Timon of Athens* 1607), but this has gradually been ousted by the metaphorical 'furtiveness.' *Stalk* 'follow furtively' comes from the same Germanic base.

▶ stalk, stealth

**steam** [OE] *Steam* comes from a prehistoric Germanic *\*staumaz*, a word of uncertain origin which also produced Dutch *stoom*. It originally denoted any 'vapour given off by something hot'; the specific modern sense 'vapour from boiling water' emerged in the 15th century.

**steed**   see STUD

**steel**   [OE]   *Steel* is etymologically a 'firm' substance. The word goes back to a prehistoric West Germanic *stakhlam*, which was derived from the Germanic base *stakh-, *stagh- 'be firm' (source also of English *stay* 'rope, support'). It has Germanic relatives in German *stahl* and Dutch *staal*.

▶ stay

**steep**   English has two words *steep*. The adjective, 'precipitous' [OE], originally meant 'very high.' It came from the prehistoric Germanic base *staup-, *stūp-, which also produced English *steeple* [OE] (etymologically a 'high' tower) and *stoop* [OE]. The verb *steep* 'soak' [14] probably came via an unrecorded Old English *stīepan from prehistoric Germanic *staupjan. This was formed from the base *staup-, *stup-, which also produced English *stoup* 'water vessel' [14] (a borrowing from Old Norse).

▶ steeple, stoop, stoup

**steer**   *Steer* 'control direction' [OE] and *steer* 'young ox' [OE] are quite unrelated. The latter comes from a prehistoric Germanic *(s)teuraz, which also produced German and Dutch *stier*, Swedish *tjur*, and Danish *tyr* 'bull.' It was descended from a base denoting 'strength' or 'sturdiness' (source also of Sanskrit *sthūra*- 'strong, thick'), and may be related to Latin *taurus* 'bull.' *Steer* 'control direction' comes from a prehistoric Germanic *steurjan, source also of German *steuern*, Dutch *stieren*, Swedish *styra*, and Danish *styre*. This in turn was derived from the noun *steurō 'steering,' which also lies behind English *stern* and the first syllable of *starboard*.

▶ starboard, stern

**stem**   The *stem* [OE] of a tree is etymologically the upright part, the part that 'stands' up. The word comes from prehistoric Germanic *stamniz, a derivative of the base *sta- 'stand' (which also produced English *stand*). The application to the 'front of a vessel' (as in *from stem to stern*) comes from the notion of an 'upright beam' at the prow (and originally the stern also) of a boat, which dates back to the Anglo-Saxon period. *Stem* 'stop' [13] was borrowed from Old Norse *stemma*, a descendant of prehistoric Germanic *stamjan. This was formed from the base *stam- 'stop, check,' which also produced English *stammer* and *stumble*.

▶ stand, statue / stammer, stumble

**stench**   see STINK

**stencil**   [14]   *Stencil* was originally a verb, meaning 'decorate with bright colours.' It came from Old French *estenceler* 'cause to sparkle,' a derivative of *estencele* 'spark.' This was descended from Vulgar Latin *stincilla, an alteration of Latin *scintilla* 'spark' (source of English *scintilla* 'jot' [17] and *scintillate* [17]). There are no records of this original verb beyond

the 15th century, and the noun *stencil* 'sheet with cut-out designs' did not appear until the early 18th century, but despite the long gap, they are generally assumed to be the same word.

▶ scintillate, tinsel

**stentorian**   [17]   Stentor was a Greek warrior in the Trojan war, whose abnormally loud voice earned him the job of herald (his name was derived from the Greek verb *sténein* 'groan, moan'). *Stentorian*, based on late Latin *stentoreus* or Greek *stentóreios*, commemorates his carrying tones.

**step**   [OE]   *Step*, together with its relatives German *stapfen* and Dutch *steppen*, comes from a prehistoric West Germanic base *stap- 'tread' (a nasalized version of which produced English *stamp*). (Russian *step'*, source of English *steppe* [17], is not related.) The prefix *step-* [OE], as in *stepdaughter*, *stepfather*, etc, originated in a word meaning 'orphan.' It is related to Old High German *stiufen* 'bereave.'

▶ stamp

**stereo**   [19]   Greek *stereós* meant 'solid.' The earliest English compound noun formed from it was *stereometry* [16], a mathematical term denoting the measurement of solid or three-dimensional objects. This was followed by *stereographic* [17], *stereotype* [18] (coined in French and originally used for a 'solid' printing block; the metaphorical 'unvaried or conventional image' emerged in the middle of the 19th century), *stereoscope* [19] (a viewer for producing 'solid' or three-dimensional images), and *stereophonic* 'producing three-dimensional sound' [20]. *Stereo* was used in the 19th century as an abbreviation for *stereotype* and *stereoscopic*; its use for *stereophonic* dates from the early 1950s.

▶ stare, stork

**sterile**   [16]   *Sterile* is a word of ancient ancestry, which goes right back to the prehistoric Indo-European base *ster- (source also of Greek *stériphos* and Gothic *stairō* 'infertile'). The Latin descendant of the base was *sterilis*, acquired by English via French *stérile*.

**sterling**   [13]   *Sterling* 'British money' originated as a term for an English silver penny from the 13th to the 15th centuries. The first ones struck had the design of a small star on them – hence the name *sterling* (and its now defunct variant *starling*), literally 'little star.' Two hundred and forty of such coins formed a unit of weight, known as a *pound of sterlings*. The earliest use of *sterling* as a general term for 'English currency' dates from the mid 16th century.

▶ star

**stern**   English has two distinct words *stern*. The older, the adjective 'severe' [OE], comes from a prehistoric Germanic *sternjaz, which was probably derived from the base *ster-, *star- 'be rigid' (source also of English *starch, stare, starve*, etc). *Stern* 'rear of a ves-

sel' [13] is etymologically the 'steering' end of a ship.
The word was probably borrowed from Old Norse
*stjórn* 'steering,' a derivative of the same base as produced *stýra* 'steer' (source of English *steer*).

▶ starch, stare, starve, stereo, stork / steer

**stevedore**   [18]   A *stevedore* 'docker' is etymologically a 'packer' of cargo. The word was originally borrowed into American English from Spanish
*estivador*, a derivative of *estivar* 'stow cargo.' This was
descended from Latin *stīpāre* 'press, pack' (source also
of English *constipation*).

▶ constipation, stiff

**stew**   [14]   The cooking sense of *stew* is a secondary development, first recorded in English in the 15th
century. It originally denoted 'take a steam bath.' It
came via Old French *estuver* from Vulgar Latin *\*extūfāre*. This was a compound verb formed from a probable noun *\*tūfus* 'hot vapour, steam,' a descendant of
Greek *túphos* 'smoke, steam, stupor' (source also of
English *typhus* [18] and *typhoid* [18]). *\*Extūfāre* probably lies behind English *stifle* too.

▶ stifle, stove, typhoid, typhus

**steward**   [OE]   A *steward* is etymologically
someone 'in charge of a sty.' Its Old English ancestor
*stigweard* was a compound formed from *stig* 'hall,
house' (a relative, if not the direct ancestor, of English
*sty* 'dwelling for pigs') and *weard* 'guardian, keeper' –
hence 'keeper of the hall.'

▶ guard, sty, ward

**stick**   *Stick* 'piece of wood' [OE] and *stick* 'fix, adhere' [OE] come from the same Germanic source: the
base *\*stik-*, *\*stek-*, *\*stak-* 'pierce, prick, be sharp'
(which also produced English *attach, stake, stitch,
stockade*, and *stoke*). This in turn went back to the Indo-
European base *\*stig-*, *\*steig-*, whose other descendants
include Greek *stígma* (source of English *stigma*) and
Latin *stīgāre* 'prick, incite' (source of English *instigate*
[16]) and *stinguere* 'prick' (source of English *distinct,
extinct*, and *instinct*). From the Germanic base was derived a verb, source of English *stick*, which originally
meant 'pierce.' The notion of 'piercing' led on via
'thrusting something sharp into something' and 'becoming fixed in something' to 'adhering.' The same
base produced the noun *\*stikkon*, etymologically a
'pointed' piece of wood, for piercing, which has become English *stick*. Yet another derivative of the base
was Old English *sticels* 'spine, prickle,' which forms
the first element of the fish-name *stickleback* [15] –
etymologically 'prickly back.'

▶ attach, distinct, extinct, instigate, instinct, stake, stigma, stimulate, stitch, stockade, stoke, style

**stiff**   [OE]   *Stiff* goes back to prehistoric Germanic
*\*stīfaz* 'inflexible,' source also of German *steif*, Dutch
*stijf*, Swedish *styf*, and Danish *stiv*. This in turn was descended from an Indo-European *\*stīpos*, a derivative of

the same base as produced Latin *stīpāre* 'press, pack'
(source of English *constipate* and *stevedore*), Latvian
*stipt* 'stiffen,' and Lithuanian *stiprùs* 'strong.'

▶ constipation, stevedore

**stifle**   [14]   *Stiffle* was probably adapted from Old
French *estouffer* 'choke, smother.' This in turn went
back to a Vulgar Latin *\*extuffāre*, which may have been
a blend of *\*extūfāre* 'take a steam bath' (source of English *stew*) and late Latin *stuppāre* 'stop up, plug' (source
of English *stop* and *stuff*).

▶ stew, stop, stuff

**stigma**   [16]   Greek *stígma* denoted a 'mark
made on the skin with a sharp implement,' hence a 'tattoo' or 'brand.' It was derived from the Indo-European
base *\*stig-* 'be sharp, pierce,' which also produced
English *stick, stitch*, etc. By the time it arrived in English, via Latin *stigma*, it has acquired the connotation of
a 'brand of shame,' and it was also used specifically for
the marks made on Christ's hands and feet by the nails
of the cross.

▶ stick, stitch

**stile**   [OE]   A *stile* is etymologically something
you 'climb.' The word goes back ultimately to the prehistoric Germanic base *\*stig-* 'climb' (source also of
English *stair, stirrup*, etc, and of German *steigen*
'climb, rise').

▶ stair, stirrup

**still**   The adjective *still* 'not moving' [OE] comes
from a prehistoric West Germanic *\*stillja* or *\*stellja*,
which also produced German *still* and Dutch *stil*. It was
derived from the base *\*stel-* 'fixed, not moving, standing' (a variant of which lies behind English *stalemate*
and *stall*). It was used as an adverb in the Old English
period, denoting 'not changing physical position,' and
this gradually evolved metaphorically via 'never changing or stopping, always' to (in the 16th century) 'until
now.' The noun *still* 'distilling apparatus' [16] is of
course a different word. It comes from the now defunct
verb *still* 'distil.' This was short for *distil* [14], which
came from Latin *distillāre*, a derivative ultimately of
the noun *stilla* 'drop' (source also of English *instil*
[16]).

▶ stalemate, stall / distil, instil

**stilt**   [14]   *Stilt* was probably acquired from some
Low German source – Low German and Flemish have
*stilte*. Its ultimate ancestor was a prehistoric Germanic
*\*steltjōn*, which was formed from a base meaning 'walk
stiffly, strut' (source also of German *stolz* 'proud' and
English *stout*). The derived *stilted* 'over-dignified'
dates from the early 19th century.

▶ stout

**stimulate**   [16]   Latin *stimulus* denoted a
'pointed stick for goading animals on' (it probably came
ultimately from an Indo-European base *\*sti-* 'point,
prick, pierce,' extensions of which lie behind English

*stick, stitch, style*, etc). It was used metaphorically for 'something that incites or causes a response,' and in that sense was borrowed into English as *stimulus* [17]. *Stimulate* itself comes from the past participle of the derived verb *stimulāre* 'goad on.'

▶ stick, stitch, style

**sting** [OE] *Sting* comes from a prehistoric Germanic base *\*stengg-*, which also produced Swedish *stinga* and Danish *stinge*. This denoted 'pierce with something sharp' ('He with a spear stung the proud Viking,' *Battle of Maldon* 993), a meaning which was not ousted in English by the more specialized application to insects until the late 15th century. *Stingy* [17] may be based on *stinge* 'act of stinging,' a dialectal noun derived from Old English *stingan* 'sting'; an underlying sense 'having a sting, sharp' is revealed in the dialectal sense 'bad-tempered.'

**stink** [OE] *Stink* comes from a prehistoric West Germanic *\*stingkwan*, which also produced German and Dutch *stinken*. Another form of the base, *\*stengkw-*, gave English *stench* [OE]. Its ancestral meaning is probably simply 'smell,' but it early on became specialized to 'smell bad.'

▶ stench

**stipend** [15] Latin *stīpendium* denoted a 'tax' or 'levy.' It was a compound noun formed from *stips* 'payment, donation' and *pendere* 'weigh, pay.' It subsequently shifted in meaning to 'wages, salary,' and particularly 'soldier's pay,' both of which passed into English via Old French *stipende*.

▶ pendant, pendulum, spend

**stipulate** [17] Tradition has it that the etymological notion underlying *stipulate* is an ancient custom of breaking a straw to seal a bargain. The word comes from the Latin verb *stipulārī* 'bargain, demand,' and it has been speculated that this was derived from Latin *stipula* 'straw' (source also of English *stubble* [13]). The theory has not been conclusively demonstrated, but it makes a good story. Another possibility is some connection with Old Latin *stipulus* 'firm.'

**stir** [OE] The etymological connotations of *stir* are of 'agitation' and 'disturbance'; the notion of 'mixing a liquid with circular movements of a spoon or other implement' is a secondary development. The verb goes back to a prehistoric Germanic *\*sturjan*, whose only other living descendant is Norwegian *styrja* 'make a disturbance.' It was formed from a base *\*stur-*, which was probably also responsible for English *storm*.

▶ storm

**stirrup** [OE] A *stirrup* is etymologically a 'climbing rope.' The word goes back to a prehistoric Germanic compound formed from the base *\*stig-* 'climb' (source also of English *stair* and *stile*) and

*\*raipaz* (ancestor of English *rope*). The earliest stirrups were looped pieces of rope.

▶ rope, stair, stile

**stitch** [OE] *Stitch* was originally a noun, meaning 'sting, prick' (a sense which survives in the very specialized application to a 'pain in the side, caused by exertion'). It came from a prehistoric Germanic *\*stikiz*, which was formed from the base *\*stik-* 'pierce, prick' (source also of English *stick*). Its use as a verb, denoting 'join with thread by piercing with a needle,' emerged at the beginning of the 13th century, and the sewing sense fed back into the noun.

▶ stick

**stock** [OE] The word *stock* originally denoted a 'tree-trunk.' It came from a prehistoric Germanic *\*stukkaz*, which also produced German *stock* 'stick' and Swedish *stock* 'log.' The lineal semantic descent to the *stocks* [14], a punishment device made from large pieces of wood, is clear enough, but how *stock* came to be used for a 'supply, store' (a sense first recorded in the 15th century) is more of a mystery. It may be that a trademan's supply of goods was thought of metaphorically as the trunk of a tree, from which profits grew like branches; and another possibility is that the usage was inspired by an unrecorded application of *stock* to a wooden storage chest or money box. *Stock* 'broth' was so named (in the 18th century, apparently) because one keeps a 'stock' of it on hand in the stockpot, for use at need. The original notion of a stout piece of wood is preserved in the derivative *stocky* [14], and also in *stock-still* [15] – literally 'as still as a log.'

**stocking** [16] *Stocking* is a derivative of *stock*, in the now defunct sense 'stocking.' This appears to have arisen in the 15th century from the blackly humorous comparison of the *stocks* in which one's legs are restrained as a punishment with 'leggings, hose.' Until comparatively recently *stocking* was a unisex term (as it still is in the expression *in one's stockinged feet*); the restriction to 'women's hose' is a 20th-century development.

▶ stock

**stoic** [16] The Greek philosopher Zeno (*c*334– *c*262BC), who taught that only virtue is necessarily good, and that pleasure and pain are matters of indifference, is reputed to have lectured to his followers and students in a porch or portico in Athens. The Greek word for 'porch' was *stoá* (a descendant of the Indo-European base *\*stā-*, *\*sto-* 'stand,' which also produced English *stand*), and so Zeno's teachings came to be characterized by the term *stōikós*. This passed into English via Latin *stōicus* as *stoic*, carrying with it metaphorical associations of 'impassivity' as well as the literal application to Zeno and his followers.

▶ stand, statue

**stoke** [17]   Stoke is a back-formation from stoker [17], which was borrowed from Dutch stoker. This in turn was derived from the verb stoken 'put fuel into a furnace,' a descendant of Middle Dutch stoken 'push, poke.' And stoken came from a prehistoric Germanic base *stok-, a variant of *stik-, *stek- 'pierce, prick,' from which English gets stick, stitch, etc. So the etymological meaning underlying stoke is of 'thrusting' fuel into a fire like a sharp instrument being pushed into something.
▶ stick, stitch

**stomach** [14]   Greek stómakhos was derived from stóma 'mouth,' and originally denoted the 'throat' or 'oesophagus.' It was also applied to the opening or 'mouth' of various internal organs, particularly the stomach, and eventually came to be used for the stomach itself. English acquired the word via Latin stomachus and Old French stomaque.

**stone** [OE]   Stone is a general Germanic word, with relatives in German stein, Dutch steen, and Swedish and Danish sten. These all go back to a prehistoric *stainaz, which was derived from a base denoting 'stiffness' or 'solidity' (source also of Greek stía 'pebble' and stéar 'stiff, fat,' Sanskrit styā- 'stiffen,' and Serbo-Croat stijena 'rock'). The use of the English term for a measure of weight, equal to fourteen pounds, dates from the 14th century.

**stool** [OE]   Although stools are for sitting on, the word's etymological meaning is 'stand.' It comes from a prehistoric Germanic *stōlaz, which was formed from the base *stō-, *sta- 'stand' (source of English stand) using the noun suffix *-l- (in much the same way as saddle was formed from a base meaning 'sit'). The notion of 'standing' no doubt passed into 'sitting' via an intermediate generalized 'be positioned or situated.' In the 15th century stool came to be applied specifically to a 'commode,' and this led to its use in the following century for an 'act of defecating,' and hence for a 'piece of faeces.' Stoolpigeon [19] originated in American English as a term for a decoy pigeon tied to a stool.
▶ stall, stand

**stoop** see STEEP

**stop** [14]   'Close an opening, plug' is the original meaning of stop. It comes via Old English *stoppian (recorded only in compounds) from a prehistoric Germanic *stoppōn 'plug up' (source of English stuff). The sense 'halt' emerged in Middle English from the notion of 'preventing a flow by blocking a hole.'
▶ stuff

**store** [13]   Store is a shortened version of the now defunct astor 'supplies, stock of provisions.' This was borrowed from Old French estor, a derivative of estorer 'build, restore, furnish, stock,' which in turn came from Latin instaurāre 'renew, repair, restore' (source also of

English restaurant and restore, and possible relative of Greek stavrós 'stake, pale'). The use of store for 'shop' arose in American English in the early 18th century.
▶ restaurant, restore

**storey** [14]   Storey is etymologically the same word as story. Both come ultimately from Latin historia 'story' (source also of English history). Storey itself was borrowed directly from Anglo-Latin historia, which is known to have been used for 'picture,' and may also have denoted a 'row of pictures in the form of stained glass windows or statues, telling a story,' which filled the entire wall between floor and ceiling at a given level of a building.
▶ history, story

**stork** [OE]   The stork may get its name from its rather stiff-legged gait. The word comes from a prehistoric Germanic *sturkaz, which also produced German storch and Dutch, Swedish, and Danish stork. This may have been formed from the base *sturk-, *stark-, *sterk- 'rigid,' which also produced English starch and stark.
▶ starch, stare, stark, starve, stereo

**storm** [OE]   Etymologically, a storm is probably a 'violent disturbance or agitation'; its meteorological connotations appear to be a secondary development. The word comes from a prehistoric Germanic *sturmaz (source also of German sturm and Dutch, Swedish, and Danish storm). This was probably formed from the base *stur- 'disturbance, agitation,' which also lies behind English stir.
▶ stir

**story** [13]   Story comes via Anglo-Norman estorie from Latin historia 'account of events, narrative, history' (source also of English history and storey). It originally retained the senses 'factual account of past events' and 'past events in general,' but since the 17th century these have gradually been taken over by history, and the use of story has been concentrated more on 'fictional narratives.'
▶ history, storey

**stoup** see STEEP

**stout** [14]   Stout originally meant 'proud, brave.' It came via Anglo-Norman stout from a prehistoric West Germanic *stult-(source also of German stolz 'proud'), which may have been related to the ancestor of English stilt. The notion of 'braveness' led on to that of 'physical strength' and 'powerful physique,' but the word did not go downhill to 'fat' until the end of the 18th century. The application to a sort of strong beer dates from the 17th century.
▶ stilt

**stove** [15]   Stove probably goes back ultimately to Vulgar Latin *extūfāre 'take a steam bath' (source also of English stew). From this was derived a noun denoting a 'heated room used for such baths,' which was disseminated widely throughout the Romance and Germanic languages. In its modern German and Danish descendants, *stube* and *stue*, the meaning element 'heat' has disappeared, leaving simply 'room' (Latvian *istaba*, Serbo-Croat *soba*, and Polish *izba* 'room' represent borrowings from Germanic), but in the Romance languages (Italian *stufa*, Spanish *estufa*, Rumanian *soba*) 'heated room' has shrunk to 'heated cupboard for cooking, oven.' The English word, borrowed from Middle Low German *stove*, has taken the same semantic course.

▶ stew

**straddle** see STRIDE
**straggle** see STRETCH
**straight** [14] *Straight* began life as the past participle of *stretch*. Nowadays this verb has a perfectly normal past form (*stretched*), but in Middle English it was *straught* (source of *distraught* [14], an alteration of *distract*) or *straight* – whence the adjective *straight*. The sense 'not bent or curved' derives from the notion of stretching something between two points. *Straightaway* [15] originally meant 'by a straight path'; the temporal sense 'immediately' emerged in the 16th century.

▶ distract, distraught, stretch

**strain** English has two distinct words *strain*. The older, 'line of ancestry' [OE], denotes etymologically 'something gained by accumulation.' It comes from the prehistoric base *\*streu-* 'pile up,' which was related to Latin *struere* 'build' (source of English *destroy*, *structure*, etc). In the Old English period the notion of 'gaining something' was extended metaphorically to 'producing offspring,' which formed the jumping-off point for the word's modern range of meanings. *Strain* 'pull tight, wrench' [13] was borrowed from *estreign-*, the stem form of Old French *estreindre* 'pull tight, tie.' This in turn was descended from Latin *stringere* 'pull tight, tie tight' (source also of English *strait*, *strict*, and *stringent* [17] and of a host of derived forms such as *constrain* [14], *prestige*, *restrain* [14] and *constrict*, *district*, *restrict*, etc). *Strain* 'tune' [16] is assumed to be the same word, perhaps deriving ultimately from the notion of 'stretching' the strings of a musical instrument.

▶ construct, destroy, structure / constrain, constrict, district, prestige, restrain, restrict, strait, strict, stringent

**strait** [12] *Strait* was originally an adjective and adverb, meaning 'narrow' or 'tight.' It reached English via Old French *estreit* 'narrow, tight' from Latin *strictus* (source of English *strict*). Its use as a noun, 'narrow waterway,' emerged in the 14th century, and the metaphorical *straits* 'difficulties' is a 16th-century development.

▶ strict

**strange** [13] The etymological notion underlying *strange* is of being 'beyond the usual bounds or boundaries.' This evolved into 'foreign' (which survives in the closely related French *étrange*) and 'odd.' The word came via Old French *estrange* from Latin *extrāneus* 'foreign, strange' (source of English *extraneous* [17]), an adjective based on *extrā* 'outward, outside.' *Stranger* [14] goes back to *\*extrāneārius*, a Vulgar Latin derivative of *extraneus*; and another derivative, *extrāneāre* 'alienate,' produced English *estrange* [15].

▶ estrange, extraneous

**strangle** [13] *Strangle* comes via Old French *estrangler* and Latin *strangulāre* from Greek *straggalān* 'strangle.' This was related to *straggós* 'twisted,' and has more distant links with English *string* and *strong* – the common semantic denominator being 'stiffness, tautness.'

▶ string, strong

**strata** [16] Latin *strātum* meant 'something laid down.' It was a noun use of the neuter past participle of *sternere* 'spread out, lay down, stretch out,' which also produced English *consternation* [17] and *prostrate* [14]. Its use for the abstract concept of a 'layer' (in English more usually in the plural *strata*) is a modern Latin development. Other English words from the same source include *stratify* [17], *stratosphere* [20] (the 'layer' of the atmosphere above the troposphere), *stratus* [19] (cloud in thin 'layer'-like form), and *street*.

▶ consternation, prostrate, straw, street

**strategy** [17] Etymologically, *strategy* denotes 'leading an army.' It comes ultimately from Greek *stratēgós* 'commander-in-chief, general,' a compound noun formed from *stratós* 'army' and *ágein* 'lead' (a relative of English *act*, *agent*, etc). From it was formed *stratēgíā* 'generalship,' which reached English via French *stratégie*. Another derivative was *stratēgeín* 'be a general,' which in turn spawned *stratēgēma* 'act of a general.' This passed via Latin *stratēgēma* and French *stratagème* into English as *stratagem* [15].

**straw** [OE] *Straw* is etymologically something 'strewn' on the floor. The word goes back to a prehistoric Germanic *\*strāwam* (source also of German *stroh*, Dutch *stroo*, Swedish *strå*, and Danish *straa*). This was formed from the same base as produced *strew* [OE], and goes back ultimately to Indo-European *\*ster-* 'spread,' source also of Latin *sternere* 'spread out' (from which English gets *prostrate*, *strata*, etc). Dried grain stalks were commonly scattered over floors as an ancient form of temporary carpeting, and so they came to be termed *straw*.

▶ strata, strew

**strawberry** [OE] The origins of *strawberry* have long puzzled etymologists. The two most plausible suggestions put forward are that the runners put out by strawberry plants, long trailing shoots that spread across the ground, reminded people of straws laid on the floor; and that word preserves a now defunct sense of *straw*, 'small piece of straw or chaff,' supposedly in allusion to the fruit's 'chafflike' external seeds.

**streak** [OE] *Streak* and *strike* are closely related. Both come from a prehistoric Germanic base *\*strik-*, denoting 'touch lightly.' But whereas the connotations of *strike* have become more violent, *streak* has moved semantically from the action to the effect it produced on a surface. Originally, in the Old English period, it denoted simply a 'mark,' but by the 16th century it had narrowed down to a long thin mark. The use of the verb *streak* for 'run naked through a public place' dates from the early 1970s.

▶ strike

**stream** [OE] A *stream* is etymologically something that 'flows.' The word comes from a prehistoric Germanic *\*straumaz* (source also of German *strom*, Dutch *stroom*, Swedish *ström*, and Danish *strøm*). This in turn was derived from the Indo-European base *\*sreu-* 'flow,' which has also given English *catarrh*, *diarrhoea*, and *rheumatism*. Non-Germanic relatives of *stream* include Polish *strumyk* 'brook' and Sanskrit *srotas-* 'stream.'

▶ catarrh, diarrhoea, rheumatism

**street** [OE] Etymologically, a *street* is a road that has been 'spread' – with paving stones, that is. A 'paved' road, in other words. The term was borrowed into prehistoric West Germanic from Latin *strāta*, short for *via strāta* 'paved road.' *Strāta* was the feminine form of *strātus*, the past participle of *sternere* 'spread out' (source of English *strata*, *stratify*, etc). The related Germanic forms are German *strasse* and Dutch *straat*, while the term is also preserved in the Romance languages, in Italian *strada*, which was borrowed by Rumanian as *strada*.

▶ strata

**strength** [OE] *Strength* is of course closely related to *strong*. It was formed in prehistoric Germanic (as *\*stranggithō*) from the ancestor of modern English *strong*. The verb *strengthen* was coined from it in the 13th century.

▶ string, strong

**stretch** [OE] *Stretch* comes from a prehistoric West Germanic *\*strakkjan* (source also of German *strecken* and Dutch *strekken*). This was formed from a base *\*strak-*, which probably also produced English *straggle* [14]. It is not certain where *\*strak-* came from, but probably it was an alteration of *\*stark-* 'rigid' (source of English *starch* and *stark*). Reversal of speech sounds (here *a* and *r*) is quite common; the process is known as metathesis. The notions of 'rigidity' and 'stretching' do not appear very compatible at first sight, but it is thought that the original application of *stretch* was to 'stretching the limbs,' in the sense of making

them straight or 'stiff.' *Straight* comes from a former past participle of *stretch*.

▶ straggle, straight

**strew** see STRAW

**strict** [16] *Strict* was acquired direct from *strictus*, the past participle of Latin *stringere* 'pull tight, tighten' (source also of English *prestige*, *strain*, and *stringent*). The original literal sense 'tight' survived into English ('She wildly breaketh from their strict embrace,' Shakespeare, *Venus and Adonis* 1592), but it has since given way to various metaphorical extensions. Routed via Old French, *strictus* has given English *strait*, and English is also indebted to it for *stress* [14] (via the Vulgar Latin derivative *\*strictia*) and *stricture* [14], not to mention prefixed forms such as *constrain*, *constrict* [18], *distrain*, *distress*, *district*, *restrain*, and *restrict* [16].

▶ constrain, constrict, distrain, distress, district, prestige, restrain, restrict, strain, stress, stricture, stringent

**stride** [OE] *Stride* comes from a prehistoric Germanic base *\*strīd-*, whose other descendants (German *streiten* and Dutch *strijden* 'quarrel,' Swedish and Danish *strid* 'strife, affliction') suggest a basic underlying meaning 'severity, great effort.' There may also be a link with English *strife* and *strive*. *Straddle* [16] comes from a variant of the same base. The use of the plural noun *strides* for 'trousers' dates from the late 19th century.

▶ straddle

**strident** [17] *Strident* was adopted from the present participle of Latin *strīdēre* 'make a harsh noise, creak.' This also produced English *stridulate* [19], which denotes the sound made by grasshoppers.

▶ stridulate

**strife** see STRIVE

**strike** [OE] *Strike* comes from a prehistoric Germanic base which denoted 'touch lightly' – a sense which survived into English ('That good horse blessed he then, and lovingly struck its mane,' *Sir Ferumbras* 1380). The more violent modern sense 'hit hard' did not begin to encroach until the 13th century. The related *stroke* retains the original meaning, but another relative, *streak*, has also lost it. All three go back to West Germanic *\*strīk-*, *\*straik-*, which in turn were descended from the Indo-European base *\*strig-*, *\*streig-*, *\*stroig-*, source of Latin *strigilis* 'tool for scraping the skin after a bath' (acquired by English as *strigil* [16]). The use of *strike* for 'withdraw labour' developed in the mid-18th century (it is first recorded in the *Annual Register* 1768: 'This day the hatters struck, and refused to work till their wages are raised'). It probably comes from the notion of 'downing' one's tools, as in *strike a sail* 'lower a sail.'

▶ streak, strigil, stroke

**string**   [OE]   *String* is etymologically something that has been pulled 'taut' or 'stiff.' It comes from a prehistoric Germanic base *strang-, denoting 'taut, stiff,' which also produced English *strong*.

▶ strong

**stringent**   see STRAIN

**strip**   *Strip* 'narrow piece' [15] and *strip* 'remove covering' [13] are distinct words. The former was perhaps borrowed from Middle Low German *strippe* 'strap,' and may be related to English *stripe* [17], an acquisition from Middle Dutch *strīfe*. A *stripling* [13] is etymologically someone who is as thin as a 'strip.' *Strip* 'unclothe' goes back to a prehistoric Germanic *straupjan*, which also produced German *streifen* and Dutch *stroopen*. There was once a third English word *strip*, meaning 'move quickly,' but it now survives only in the derived *outstrip* [16]; its origins are uncertain.

▶ stripe, stripling

**strive**   [13]   *Strive* was borrowed from Old French *estriver* 'quarrel, strive.' It is not certain where this came from, although it has been suggested that it was acquired from Old High German *strīt* 'contention,' a relative of English *stride*. *Strife* [13] comes from the associated Old French noun *estrif*.

▶ strife

**stroke**   The verb *stroke* [OE] and the noun *stroke* [13] are different words, but they come ultimately from the same source – the prehistoric Germanic base *strīk-, *straik- 'touch lightly' (from which English also gets *streak* and *strike*). The verb has stayed very close semantically to its source, whereas the noun has followed the same path as its corresponding verb *strike*.

▶ streak, strike

**strong**   [OE]   *Strong* comes from a prehistoric Germanic *stranggaz* (its immediate Germanic siblings have now died out, but German *streng* 'severe' is quite closely related). It went back ultimately to a base denoting 'stiffness' or 'tautness,' which also produced English *string*.

▶ string

**strontium**   [19]   The element *strontium* gets its name from the Strontian area of the Highland region of Scotland, which contains lead mines in which strontium was first discovered. Indeed, it was originally called *strontian*; the latinized version *strontium* was introduced by the chemist Sir Humphry Davy in 1808.

**structure**   [15]   *Structure* comes via Old French *structure* from Latin *structūra*, a noun derived from the past participle of *struere* 'build.' Other English words from the same source are *construct, construe, destroy, destruction, instruct*, and *obstruct* [17].

▶ construct, construe, destroy, destruction, instruct, obstruct, strain

**struthious**   see OSTRICH

**stud**   *Stud* 'place where horses are bred' and *stud* 'nail' [OE] are different words. The former (like *stable* and *stall*) denotes etymologically a place where animals 'stand,' in this case for breeding purposes. It comes from a prehistoric Germanic *stōtham*, a derivative of the base *sta-, *stō- 'stand' (source also of English *stand*, and of *steed* [OE], which originally denoted a 'male horse used for breeding'). The use of the word for a 'man who is highly active and proficient sexually' dates from the end of the 19th century. The ancestry of *stud* 'nail' is not altogether clear, although it appears to be related to German *stützen* 'support.' It originally meant 'post, support,' a sense preserved in the building term *stud* 'upright post to which boards are fixed,' and 'nail' (presumed to represent the same word) did not emerge until the 15th century.

▶ stand, steed

**study**   [13]   *Study* comes via Old French *estudie* from Latin *studium* 'eagerness, intense application,' hence 'application to learning' (English *studio* [19] comes from the same ultimate source, only via Italian). *Studium* in turn was derived from the verb *studēre* 'be eager, study' (source of English *student* [15]). This probably went back ultimately to the Indo-European base *steud-, *teud- 'hit,' which also produced Latin *tundere* 'hit' (source of English *contusion* and *obtuse*) and German *stossen* 'shove, hit' – the underlying notion of *study* thus being the 'application of extreme effort.'

▶ contusion, obtuse, student, studio

**stuff**   [14]   *Stuff* is ultimately the same word as *stop*. It comes via Old French *estoffer* and prehistoric Germanic *stopfōn*, earlier *stoppōn* (source of English *stop*), from late Latin *stuppāre* 'plug, stop up.' This originally denoted literally 'stop up a hole with a plug of coarse fibres,' for it was derived from Latin *stuppa* 'coarse fibres, tow,' a borrowing from Greek *stúppē*. The noun *stuff* comes from Old French *estoffe* 'provisions,' a derivative of *estoffer*.

▶ stop

**stumble**   [14]   *Stumble* was probably borrowed from an unrecorded Old Norse *stumla*. This would have come, along with its first cousin *stumra* 'trip,' from a prehistoric Germanic base *stum-, *stam- 'check, impede,' which also produced English *stammer* and *stem* 'halt, check.'

▶ stammer, stem

**stun**   [13]   *Stun* is virtually the same word as *astonish* and *astound*, and like them it denotes etymologically 'leave thunderstruck.' It comes via Anglo-Norman *estuner* from Vulgar Latin *extonāre* 'stupefy.' This was a compound verb, formed from the Latin intensive prefix *ex-* and *tonāre* 'thunder' (a relative of English *thunder*) and based on the model of Latin *at-*

*tonāre* 'stupefy,' similarly formed from *tonāre* but with the prefix *ad-*. The variant *\*astoner* produced English *astonish* and *astound*.

▶ astonish, astound, thunder

**stupid** [16] As the related *stupefy* [16] and *stupor* [17] still do, *stupid* originally denoted 'mental numbness'; 'lack of intelligence' is a secondary development. It comes via Old French *stupide* from Latin *stupidus*, a derivative of *stupēre* 'be stunned or numbed with shock.' This was descended from an Indo-European base *\*stup-* or *\*tup-* 'hit,' which also produced Greek *túptein* 'hit' and Sanskrit *tup-* 'harm, hurt.'

▶ stupefy, stupor

**sturdy** [13] Someone who is *sturdy* is etymologically 'as drunk as a thrush' – the ancient Roman equivalent to 'pissed as a newt.' The word comes from Old French *estourdi* 'stunned, dazed, violent,' the past participle of *estourdir*. This went back to a Vulgar Latin *\*exturdīre* 'be dazed like a drunken thrush,' a compound verb formed from the intensive prefix *ex-* and Latin *turdus* 'thrush' (the use of the thrush as a symbol of drunkenness perhaps arose from observations of the birds staggering around after feasting on stolen fermenting wine grapes). The metaphorical Old French sense 'violent, reckless' passed over into English, and by the 14th century had evolved into 'strong, vigorous, robust.'

**sty** English has two distinct words *sty*. The 'pig enclosure' [OE] is not recorded for certain as an independent word before the 13th century, but it occurs in compounds in Old English, and it is probably the same word as Old English *stig* 'hall' (source of English *steward*). It goes back ultimately to a prehistoric Germanic *\*stijam*. The *sty* on one's eye [17] denotes etymologically a 'swelling.' It comes from the now defunct *styany* 'sty.' This was misinterpreted as 'sty-on-eye,' but in fact it was a compound formed from Middle English *styan* 'swelling' (a descendant of the present participle of Old English *stīgan* 'rise,' which is related to modern English *stair* and *stirrup*) and *eye*.

▶ steward / eye, stair, stirrup

**style** [13] *Style* comes via Old French *stile* from Latin *stilus*, which denoted a 'pointed writing instrument.' It came to be used metaphorically for 'something written,' and hence for 'manner of writing.' The spelling with *y* instead of *i* arose from the misapprehension that the word was of Greek origin. It also invaded *stylus* [18], which was acquired directly from Latin.

▶ stimulate, stylus

**suave** see PERSUADE

**subdue** [14] *Subdue* denotes etymologically 'lead away.' It came via Anglo-Norman *\*subduer* from Latin *subdūcere* 'lead away, withdraw,' a compound verb formed from the prefix *sub-* 'from under, away'

and *dūcere* 'lead' (source of English *duct, duke*, etc). The sense 'conquer, subjugate, suppress' arose through association with the long defunct and quite unrelated English *subdit* 'subject,' which came from *subditus*, the past participle of Latin *subdere* 'bring under, subjugate.'

▶ duct, duke

**subject** [14] To *subject* something is etymologically to 'throw it under.' The verb comes via Old French *subjecter* from Latin *sujectāre*, which was formed from *subjectus*, the past participle of Latin *subicere* 'bring down.' This in turn was a compound verb formed from the prefix *sub-* 'under' and *jacere* 'throw' (source also of English *abject* [15], *adjacent*, *adjective, conjecture, dejected* [15], *inject* [17], *jet, jettison, jetty, reject* [15], etc). The noun *subject*, which also came from Latin *subjectus*, originally denoted a person 'subjected' to the control of another (as in 'the Queen's subjects'). The most salient modern sense, 'topic,' comes ultimately from the notion of 'that which is operated on by something else.'

▶ abject, adjacent, adjective, conjecture, dejected, inject, jet, jettison, jetty, object, reject

**subjugate** see YOKE

**sublime** [16] *Sublime* was borrowed from Latin *sublīmis* 'lofty, exalted.' This was a compound adjective formed from the prefix *sub-*'under' and probably *līmen* 'lintel, threshold' (a relative of *līmes* 'boundary,' from which English gets *limit*). *Sub-*here probably has the force of 'up to,' so that the word denotes etymologically 'as high as the top of a door.' The same elements were used in the 1880s to coin *subliminal*, as a direct rendering of the German psychological term *unter der schwelle des bewusstseins* 'below the threshold of consciousness.'

▶ limit

**submerge** see MERGE

**suborn** see ORNAMENT

**subsequent** see SEQUENCE

**subsidy** see SESSION

**substance** [13] Latin *substantia* denoted the 'essence' of something. Derived from the present participle of *substāre* 'be present,' a compound verb formed from the prefix *sub-* 'under' and *stāre* 'stand' (a relative of English *stand*), it was virtually a loan-translation of Greek *hupóstasis* 'substance, existence, essence,' which likewise was formed from elements meaning literally 'under' and 'stand.' The word's ultimate etymological meaning is thus 'that which underlies or is the essence of something.'

▶ stand, station, statue

**substitute** see STATUE

**subtle** [14] Latin *subtīlis*, the ultimate source of English *subtle*, seems to have originated as a weaving term. It probably goes back ultimately to the phrase *sub tēla* 'beneath the lengthwise threads in a loom' (*tēla*, source of English *toilet* and *toils*, was a contraction of \**texla*, a relative of English *textile*). As this was lexicalized via \**subtēlis* to *subtīlis*, it developed the meaning 'finely woven,' which subsequently broadened out to 'fine, thin.' By the time it reached English, via Old French *sutil*, it had evolved further, to 'making fine discriminations.'

▶ textile, toilet

**subtract** [16] To *subtract* something is etymologically to 'pull it away.' The word comes from *subtractus*, the past participle of Latin *subtrahere* 'pull away.' This was a compound verb formed from the prefix *sub-*, usually 'under' but here used in the sense 'away,' and *trahere* 'pull' (source of English *traction, tractor, trait*, etc). The strictly mathematical use of the word is a post-Latin development.

▶ contract, retract, traction, tractor, trait

**suburb**   see URBAN

**succeed** [15] To *succeed* someone is etymologically to 'go next to them,' hence to follow them. The word comes via Old French *succeder* from Latin *succēdere*, a compound verb formed from the prefix *sub-* 'under' (used here in the sense 'next below,' hence 'next to, after') and *cēdere* 'go' (source also of English *cede, exceed, proceed*, etc). The notion of 'getting near to something' evolved in Latin into 'doing well, prospering' – whence the other main meaning of English *succeed*.

▶ cede, excede, proceed, success

**succour** [13] If you *succour* someone, you are literally 'running under' them. The word comes via Old French *socorre* from Latin *succurrere*, a compound verb formed from the prefix *sub-* 'under' and *currere* 'run' (source of English *courier, course, current*, etc). The original sense 'run under' evolved metaphoriclly to 'run to someone's assistance,' and then to simply 'help.'

▶ courier, course, current

**succubus**   see INCUBATE

**succumb** [15] Someone who *succumbs* to something is etymologically 'lying down under' it. The word comes via Old French *succomber* from Latin *succumbere*, a compound verb formed from the prefix *sub-* 'under' and *-cumbere* 'lie.' This verbal element also produced English *incumbent* and *recumbent*, and the non-nasalized version of its stem lies behind *covey, incubate, incubus*, and *succubus*.

▶ covey, incubate, incumbent, recumbent

**such** [OE] Etymologically, *such* means 'so formed.' It comes from a prehistoric Germanic compound formed from \**swa* 'so' (ancestor of English *so*) amd \**līk-* 'form, body' (source of English *like*). This

reached Old English as *swylc*, which gradually lost its *l* and *w* and evolved into modern English *such*. Amongst its Germanic relatives are German *solch*, Dutch *zulk*, Swedish *slik*, and Danish *slig*.

▶ like, so

**suck** [OE] *Suck* is part of a widespread Indo-European family of 'suck'-words which go back to the base \**seug-*, \**seuk-*. This no doubt originated in imitation of the sound of sucking from the mother's breast. Amongst its relatives are Latin *sūgere* (whose past participle *sūctus* gave English *suction* [17]), Welsh *sugno*, German *saugen*, Dutch *zuigen*, Swedish *suga*, and Danish *suge*. *Suckle* [15] was probably a backformation from *suckling* [13], itself a derivative of *suck*. Also from *suck* comes *sucker* [14], which originally denoted a 'baby still at the breast'; its use for a 'gullible person' (that is, someone as naive as an unweaned child) originated in American English in the early 19th century.

▶ suction, suckle

**sudden** [13] The etymological notion underlying *sudden* is of something approaching stealthily or without warning, so that it takes one by surprise. It comes via Anglo-Norman *sudein* from late Latin *subitānus*, an alteration of Latin *subitāneus* 'sudden.' This was derived from *subitus* 'sudden,' an adjectival use of the past participle of *subīre* 'approach stealthily.' And *subīre* was a compound verb formed from the prefix *sub-*, used here in the sense 'secretly,' and *īre* 'go' (source of English *ambition, exit, issue*, etc).

▶ ambition, exit, issue

**suds** [16] *Suds* was probably borrowed from Middle Dutch *sudse* 'marsh, swamp' (it was used in the East Anglian dialect for 'muddy swamp water' or 'flood water,' and probably the notion of scum or flotsam on such water led on to 'floating bubbles, lather' – first recorded at the end of the 15th century). The word's ultimate source is no doubt the prehistoric Germanic base \**suth-* 'boil,' which also produced English *seethe* and *sodden*.

▶ seethe, sodden

**sue** [13] *Sue*, like its close relative *pursue*, originally meant 'follow' ('My wickednesses ever follow me, as men may see the shadow a body sue,' Thomas Hoccleve, *Complaint* 1421). It comes via Anglo-Norman *suer* from Vulgar Latin \**sequere* 'follow,' an alteration of Latin *sequī* 'follow' (source also of English *consecutive, ensue* [14], *persecute, pursue, sequence, sect, set, suit*, etc). Its legal use, which emerged in the 14th century, is based on the notion of 'following' up a matter in court (a similar inspiration underlies the related *prosecute*).

▶ consecutive, ensue, persecute, prosecute, pursue, sect, sequence, set, suit

**suet**  [14]  *Suet* goes back ultimately to Latin *sē-bum* 'tallow,' which also produced English *sebaceous* [18]. This passed into Anglo-Norman as *seu* or *sue*, of which a presumed diminutive form *\*sewet* gave English *suet*.

▶ sebaceous

**suffer**  [13]  To *suffer* something is etymologically to 'hold it up from underneath,' to 'sustain' it.' The word comes via Anglo-Norman *suffrir* from Vulgar Latin *\*sufferīre*, an alteration of Latin *sufferre* 'sustain.' This was a compound verb formed from the prefix *sub-* 'up from underneath' and *ferre* 'carry' (a relative of English *bear*). The word's modern meaning evolved from 'sustain' via 'undergo' and 'undergo something unpleasant' to 'endure.'

▶ bear

**sufficient**  [14]  *Sufficient* originated as the present participle of Latin *sufficere* 'be enough' (source also of English *suffice* [14]). This was a compound verb formed from the prefix *sub-* 'under' and *facere* 'do, make' (source of English *fact, factory*, etc). It originally meant literally 'put under,' and the notion of 'enough' evolved via 'cause to take the place of.'

▶ fact, factory, fashion

**suffix**  see FIX

**suffocate**  [16]  To *suffocate* someone is etymologically to press down their 'throat.' The word comes from the past participle of Latin *suffocāre*, a compound verb formed from the prefix *sub-* 'under, down' and *faucēs* 'throat' (source of the English technical term *faucal* 'of the throat' [19]). The origins of *faucēs* are not known.

▶ faucal

**sugar**  [13]  The ultimate source of *sugar* is Sanskrit, where the substance was named with a term that originally meant 'gravel, grit' – *sharkarā*. This was borrowed into Arabic as *sukkar*, which made its way into English via medieval Latin *succarum*, Italian *zucchero*, and Old French *sukere*. The Sanskrit word was also acquired by Greek as *sákkharon*, which passed into English through medieval Latin *saccharum* as *saccharin*.

▶ saccharin

**suggest**  [16]  To *suggest* something is etymologically to 'carry it under.' It comes from the past participle of Latin *suggerere*, a compound verb formed from the suffix *sub-* and *gerere* 'carry' (source also of English *digest, gesture*, etc). Its meaning evolved via 'heap up, build' and 'furnish a supply' to 'bring forward an idea.'

▶ congest, digest, gesture

**suit**  [13]  As in the case of its first cousins *sect* and *set*, the etymological notion underlying *suit* is 'following.' It comes via Anglo-Norman *siute* from Vulgar Latin *\*sequita*, a noun use of the feminine past participle of *\*sequere* 'follow,' which in turn was an alteration of Latin *sequī* 'follow' (source of English *consequence, persecute, sequence*, etc). It was originally used for a 'body of followers, retinue,' and it passed from this via a 'set of things in general' to (in the 15th century) a 'set of clothes or armour.' *Suite* [17] is essentially the same word, but borrowed from modern French. A *suitor* [13] is etymologically a 'follower.'

▶ sect, set, sue, suite

**sulk**  [18]  *Sulk* was a back-formation from *sulky* [18], which in turn was derived from the now obsolete *sulke* 'sluggish' [17]. It has been plausibly suggested that this may have been descended from Old English *āsolcen* 'sluggish, inactive,' an adjectival use of the past participle of *āseolcan* 'be lazy or slow.' In the mid-18th century the term *sulky* was applied to a 'single-seat carriage,' from the notion of the 'standoffishness' of a lone driver.

**sullen**  [16]  The etymological notion underlying *sullen* is of being miserable because one is 'on one's own.' The word comes from Anglo-Norman *\*solein* 'alone,' hence 'miserable,' a derivative of Old French *soul* 'alone' (source of English *sole*).

▶ sole, solo

**sully**  see SOIL

**sulphur**  [14]  The origins of Latin *sulphur* are not known, although it may have links with German *schwefel* 'sulphur.' It has spread throughout the Romance languages (French *soufre*, Italian *solfo*, and, with the addition of Arabic *al* 'the,' Spanish *azufre*), and has been borrowed into Dutch as *sulfer* and into English (where it eventually replaced the native *brimstone* [12], etymologically 'burning stone') as *sulphur*.

**sultan**  [16]  Arabic *sultān* meant 'ruler.' It was derived from Aramaic *shultānā* 'power,' which in turn was based on the verb *shəlēt* 'have power.' English acquired the word via medieval Latin *sultānus*. The Italian version of the word is *sultano*, whose feminine form has given English *sultana* 'sultan's wife' [16]. The word was applied to a variety of small raisin (originally in full *sultana raisin*) in the early 19th century.

**sum**  [13]  Latin *summus* meant 'highest' (a meaning preserved in English *summit* [15], which is ultimately derived from it); it evolved from an earlier *\*supmus*, a superlative form based on the stem of Latin *super* 'above' (source of English *super*). When the Romans counted up columns of figures they worked from the bottom upwards, and put the total on top – whence the use of the expression *rēs summa*, literally 'highest thing,' for 'total.' This was eventually shortened to *summa*, which reached English via Old French *summe*. Other derivatives in English include *consummate* [15] and *summary* [15].

▶ consummate, summary, summit

**summer** [OE] *Summer* is a general Germanic word, with relatives in German and Danish *sommer*, Dutch *zomer*, and Swedish *sommar*. It goes back ultimately to an Indo-European base *\*sem-*, which also produced Welsh *haf* 'summer' and Sanskrit *sámā* 'year, season.'

**summit** see SUM

**summon** see MONSTER

**sumptuous** [15] Etymologically, *sumptuous* denotes 'expensive, costly'; its modern connotations of 'luxury' or 'lavishness' are a secondary development. It comes via Old French *somptueux* from Latin *sumptuōsus*, a derivative of *sumptus* 'expense.' This in turn was based on the past participle of the verb *sūmere* 'spend, consume, take' (source also of English *assume* [15], *consume* [14], *presume* [14], *resume* [15], and *subsume* [16]). And *sūmere* in turn was a compound verb, formed from the prefix *sub-* 'under' and *emere* 'take' (source of English *example, redeem*, etc).

▶ assume, consume, example, presume, redeem, resume, sample, subsume

**sun** [OE] Not surprisingly, considering the central importance of the sun to human life, the word for it in the vast majority of modern European languages goes back to a common Indo-European source – *\*sāu-* or *\*su-*. These variants have however differentiated into several distinct camps. The *\*sāu-* form adopted an *-l-* suffix, and evolved into Greek *hélios* (source of English *heliotrope*), Latin *sōl* (whence French *soleil*, Italian *sole*, and Spanish *sol*, not to mention English *solar, solarium*, etc), Welsh *haul*, and Swedish and Danish *sol*. The *\*su-* form with an *-l-* ending has given Russian *solnce*, Czech *slunce*, Serbo-Croat *sunce*, etc. But the modern West Germanic languages have inherited the *\*su-* form with an *-n-* suffix, giving German *sonne*, Dutch *zon*, and English *sun*.

▶ heliotrope, solar, solarium

**Sunday** [OE] *Sunday* is part of the general system of naming days of the week after heavenly bodies inherited by the Germanic peoples from the ancient Mediterranean world. The Romans called the day *diēs sōlis* 'day of the sun,' which in translation has become German *sonntag*, Dutch *zondag*, Swedish *söndag*, Danish *søndag*, and English *sunday*. Welsh retains the term (*dydd sul*), but the Romance languages have gone over to variations on 'Lord's day' (French *dimanche*, Spanish *domingo*, etc).

**sundry** [OE] *Sundry* goes back to an Old English *syndrig* 'apart, separate.' This, like *sunder* [OE], is descended ultimately from an Indo-European base *\*su-*, denoting 'separation,' which also produced Latin *sine* 'without,' Welsh *hanner* 'half,' and German *sondern* 'but.'

**super** [17] *Super* has been used over the centuries as an abbreviated form of a variety of English words containing the Latin element *super* 'above.' Its earliest manifestation, short for the now defunct *insuper* 'balance left over,' did not last long and it was the 19th century which really saw an explosion in the use of the word. In 1807 it appeared as an abbreviation for the chemical term *supersalt*, and in the 1850s its long career as an 'extra person' (short for *supernumerary* [17]) began. Its application to *superintendant* [16], today its commonest noun usage, dates from around 1870. But it is as an adjective that it has made its greatest impact. In this context it is short for *superfine* [15], and originally, in the mid 19th century, its use was restricted to denoting the 'highest grade of goods' ('showing me a roll of cloth which he said was extra super,' Charles Dickens, *David Copperfield* 1850); not until the early 20th century did it really begin to come into its own as a general term of approval.

Amongst the more heavily disguised English descendants of Latin *super* (a relative of Latin *sub* 'below' and also of English *sum* and *supine*) are *insuperable* [14], *soprano* [18], *soubrette* [18], and *sovereign*. And *superior* [14] comes from the Latin comparative form *superior* 'higher.'

▶ insuperable, soprano, soubrette, sovereign, superb, superior, supreme

**superb** [16] Etymologically, *superb* denotes being 'above.' It comes ultimately from Latin *super* 'above, over,' which with the addition of the suffix *\*bh-* produced *superbus*. This had the sense 'superior,' and it also, from the notion of being 'above oneself,' of thinking oneself 'superior,' came to mean 'proud.' English acquired it via Old French *superbe*.

▶ super

**supercilious** [16] The etymological notion underlying *supercilious* is of raising the 'eyebrows' as a sign of haughty disdain. It comes from Latin *superciliōsus*, a derivative of *supercilium* 'eyebrow,' hence 'haughtiness.' This was a compound noun formed from the prefix *super-* 'above' and *cilium* 'eyelid' (source of the English biological term *cilium* 'hairlike process' [18], whose meaning evolved via an intermediate 'eyelash').

**superficial** [14] *Superficial* means literally 'of the surface.' It comes from Latin *superficiālis*, a derivative of *superficiēs* 'surface.' This was a compound noun formed from the prefix *super-* 'above' and *faciēs* 'face' (ancestor of English *face*). The main modern sense, 'concerned only with outward appearances,' emerged in the 16th century.

▶ face, surface

**superfluous** see FLUX

**superman** [20] The term *superman* was introduced into English in 1903 by George Bernard Shaw in his play *Man and Superman*. It was a direct translation of German *übermensch*, coined by the philosopher Friedrich Nietsche to designate a superior, highly evolved human being that transcended good and evil.

**supersede**  [15]  Etymologically, to *supersede* something is to 'sit above' it, hence to 'be above' it or 'desist' from doing it. The word comes via Old French *superseder* from Latin *supersedēre* 'desist from,' a compound verb formed from the prefix *super-* 'above' and *sedēre* 'sit' (source of English *sedentary, session*, etc). It carried the sense 'desist from' with it into English ('I could not see, but your both majesties must supersede and give place to your ardent appetites, in concluding of the said marriage,' *State Papers of Henry VIII* 1527), but this gradually evolved via 'set aside' to 'take the place of something set aside.' The word is frequently spelled *supercede*, as if it came from Latin *cēdere* 'go,' and there are long-standing historical precedents for this, going back via Old French *superceder* to medieval Latin *supercēdere*.

▶ sedentary, session

**superstition**  [15]  Etymologically, *superstition* denotes 'standing over' something. It comes via Old French *superstition* from Latin *superstitiō*, a derivative of *superstāre* 'stand over.' This was a compound verb formed from the prefix *super-* 'above' and *stāre* 'stand' (a relative of English *stand*). The sense 'irrational fear,' which evolved in Latin, may have been based on the notion of someone 'standing over' something in awe or fear.

▶ stand, station, statue

**supine**  [15]  *Supine* means literally 'lying on one's back.' It comes from Latin *supīnus*. This was derived from a prehistoric base *\*sup-* 'up' which also produced Latin *super* 'above, over' (and *summus*, source of English *sum*), so the word's etymological meaning is presumably 'with the front of one's body upwards.' The metaphorical sense 'inactive' evolved in Latin. The origins of the use of *supine* as a noun, to designate a type of 'verbal noun,' are not known.

**supper**  [13]  *Supper* started life as a verb. It was borrowed from Old French *super*, which was a noun use of the verb *super* 'eat one's evening meal' (source of English *sup* 'have supper' [13]). This in turn was formed from the Germanic base *\*sup-*, which also produced English *sip, sop,* and *sup* [OE] and Latin *\*suppāre* 'soak' (source of English *soup*).

▶ sip, sop, soup, sup

**supplant**  [13]  *Supplant* has no connection with things that grow, even though it may be related to English *plant*. Etymologically it means 'trip up.' It comes via Old French *supplanter* from Latin *supplantāre* 'trip up,' hence 'overthrow,' a compound verb formed from the prefix *sub-* 'up from under' and *planta* 'sole of the foot' (possible ancestor of English *plant*).

**supplement**  see SUPPLY

**supplicate**  [15]  Someone who *supplicates* is etymologically 'bending or folding up underneath' – hence 'kneeling down to pray.' The word comes from the past participle of Latin *supplicāre*, a compound verb formed from the prefix *sub-* 'down, underneath' and *plicāre* 'fold' (a relative of English *fold*). Also formed from *sub-* and the base *\*plic-* was Latin *supplex* 'bending under,' hence 'submissive,' from which English gets *supple* [13].

▶ complicate, fold, ply, supple

**supply**  [14]  Latin *supplēre* meant 'fill up, complete.' It was a compound verb formed from the prefix *sub-* 'under, from below,' hence 'up,' and *plēre* 'fill' (source of English *accomplish, complete*, etc). The sense 'provide' evolved via the notion of 'making good a deficiency, fulfilling a need.'

The original meaning is better preserved in *supplement* [14], whose Latin ancestor *supplēmentum* was derived from *supplēre*.

▶ accomplish, complete, full, plus, supplement, surplus

**support**  [14]  Latin *supportāre* meant 'carry, convey, bring' (it was a compound verb formed from the prefix *sub-* 'up, towards' and *portāre* 'carry,' source of English *portable, porter*, etc). The sense 'endure' (represented in English mainly by the derivative *insupportable* [16]) evolved in post-classical Latin. 'Bear the weight of' is not recorded in English until the 16th century.

▶ port, portable, porter

**suppose**  [14]  Latin *suppōnere* meant literally 'put under' (it was a compound verb formed from the prefix *sub-* 'under' and *pōnere* 'put, place,' source of English *position*, and its original meaning is best preserved in English *suppository* [14], literally 'something placed underneath'). From it was derived the noun *suppositiō*, which, on the analogy of Greek *hupóthesis* (source of English *hypothesis* [16], and itself made up of elements meaning literally 'under' and 'put'), came to be used for an 'assumption' – English gets *supposition* [15] from it. This meaning then fed back into the verb, which English acquired via Old French *supposer*.

▶ position, suppository

**suppress**  see PRESS

**suppurate**  see PUS

**supreme**  [16]  *Supreme* comes ultimately from Latin *suprā* 'above' (a close relative of *super*). From this was formed the adjective *suprēmus* 'highest,' which English adopted as *supreme*. *Supremo* is a 20th-century borrowing of the Spanish version of the word.

▶ super

**sure**  [14]  *Sure* and *secure* are doublets – that is to say, they come from the same ultimate source, but have diverged over the centuries. Latin *sēcūrus* (etymologically 'without care') was borrowed directly into English as *secure*, but in Old French it evolved into *sur*, from which English gets *sure*.

▶ secure

**surface** [17] *Surface* was coined in French on the model of Latin *superficiēs* 'surface' (source of English *superficial*). It contains the same elements: *sur*- 'above' (a descendant of Latin *super*) and *face* 'face.'

▶ face, superficial

**surge** [15] Latin *surgere* meant literally 'lead up from below,' hence 'rise' – it originated as a compound verb formed from the prefix *sub*- 'up from below' and *regere* 'rule,' hence 'lead' (source of English *regiment*, *region*, etc). English acquired it via Old Spanish *surgir* and Old French *sourgir*, by which time it had taken on watery associations, of waves heaving. *Surgere* also produced English *resource* [17], *resurrection* [13], and *source*.

▶ rector, regiment, region, resource, resurrection, source

**surgeon** [14] A *surgeon* is etymologically someone who does 'hand work' – that is, a medical practitioner who performs manual operations on the body, as opposed to administering drugs. The word comes via Anglo-Norman *surgien* from Vulgar Latin *\*chirurgiānus*, a derivative of Latin *chirurgia* 'work of a surgeon.' This was borrowed from Greek *kheirurgíā*, which in turn was derived from *kheirourgós* 'working by hand,' a compound noun formed from *kheír* 'hand' (source of English *chiropodist* [18]) and *érgon* 'work' (source of English *energy*).

▶ chiropodist, energy, work

**surplus** see FULL

**surprise** [15] To *surprise* someone is etymologically to 'overtake' them. The word comes from the past participle of Old French *surprendre* 'overtake,' a compound verb formed from the prefix *sur*- 'over' and *prendre* 'take.' By the time it reached English it was being used for 'affect suddenly, as with a particular emotion' ('He shall be so surprised with anger and furious woodness [madness],' William Caxton, *Eneydos* 1490), and this gradually evolved via 'take unawares' to, in the mid 17th century, 'astonish.'

▶ apprehend, comprehend, prison, reprehensible

**surrender** [15] To *surrender* is etymologically to 'give up.' The word was borrowed from Old French *surrendre* 'deliver over, give up,' a compound verb formed from the prefix *sur*- 'over' and *rendre* 'give, deliver' (source of English *render*).

▶ render

**surreptitious** [15] Latin *surreptītius* meant 'taken away secretly.' It was formed from the past participle of *surripere* 'take away secretly,' a compound verb formed from the prefix *sub*- 'under,' hence 'secretly,' and *rapere* 'seize' (source of English *rape, rapture,*

etc). English acquired *surreptitious* direct from the Latin adjective.

▶ rape, rapture, ravenous

**surrogate** [17] A *surrogate* is etymologically someone who has been 'asked for' to take the place of another. The word was borrowed from Latin *surrogātus*, a later form of *subrogātus*, the past participle of *subrogāre* 'nominate an alternative candidate.' This was a compound verb formed from the prefix *sub*-, used here in the sense 'instead of,' and *rogāre* 'ask for, propose' (source of English *interrogate, prerogative*, etc).

▶ interrogate, prerogative

**surround** [15] Although *surround* means 'exist round' something, it has no etymological connection with *round*. It comes via Old French *suronder* from late Latin *superundāre* 'overflow.' This was a compound verb formed from the prefix *super*- 'over' and *undāre* 'rise in waves,' a derivative of *unda* 'wave' (source of English *undulate*). English took the word over in its original sense, and this survived into the 17th century (an Act of Parliament of 1609 noted that 'the sea hath broken in . . . and hath decayed, surrounded, and drowned up much hard ground'). The modern sense 'exist round, encircle' arose in the early 17th century, presumably by association with *round*.

▶ abundant, redundant, sound, undulate

**surveillance** see VIGIL

**survey** [15] To *survey* something is etymologically to 'oversee' it. The word comes via Anglo-Norman *surveier* from medieval Latin *supervidēre*, a compound verb formed from the prefix *super*- 'over' and *vidēre* 'see' (source of English *view, vision*, etc).

▶ view, vision

**survive** see VIVID

**suspect** [14] Latin *suspicere* originally meant literally 'look up at' (it was a compound verb formed from the prefix *sub*-'up from under' and *specere* 'look at,' source of English *spectator, spy*, etc). It evolved metaphorically along two lines: 'look up to, admire,' which has since died out, and 'look at secretly,' hence 'look at distrustfully,' which has passed into English in the form of its past participial stem *suspect*-. *Suspicion* [14] comes from the medieval Latin derivative *suspectiō*.

▶ expect, inspect, spectator, spy, suspicion

**suspend** [13] To *suspend* something is etymologically to 'hang it up.' The word comes via Old French *suspendre* from Latin *suspendere* 'hang up,' a compound verb formed from the prefix *sub*- 'up from under,' hence 'up,' and *pendere* 'hang' (source of English *depend, pendent*, etc). The metaphorical sense 'delay' developed in Latin.

▶ depend, pendant, pendulum

**suture**    see SEW

**swallow**    English has two distinct words *swallow*. The verb, 'ingest' [OE], comes from a prehistoric Germanic *\*swelgan*, which also produced German *schwelgen*, Dutch *swelgen*, Swedish *svälja*, and Danish *svælge*. It was formed from a base which also gave Old Norse *svelgr* 'whirlpool, devourer.' *Swallow* the bird [OE] comes from a prehistoric Germanic *\*swalwōn*, which also produced German *schwalbe*, Dutch *zwaluw*, Swedish *svala*, and Danish *svale* and is probably related to Russian *solovej* 'nightingale.'

**swan**    [OE]    *Swan* is a general Germanic word, with relatives in German *schwan*, Dutch *zwaan*, Swedish *svan*, and Danish *svane*. These all come from a prehistoric base *\*swan-*, which may go back ultimately to Indo-European *\*swon-*, *\*swen-* 'make sound' (source of Latin *sonus* 'sound,' from which English gets *sound*). If it does, the swan was originally named for the (admittedly rather unmusical) sound it makes.

▶ sound

**swap**    [14]    *Swap* originally meant 'hit' ('With a swing of his sword [he] swapped him in the face,' *Destruction of Troy* 1400). It came from a prehistoric Germanic base denoting 'hit' (presumably imitative of the sound of hitting), which also produced German *schwappen* 'splash, whack.' The modern English sense 'exchange' emerged in the 16th century from the notion of 'striking the hands together to seal a bargain.'

**swarm**    *Swarm* 'group of insects' [OE] and *swarm* 'climb' [16] are distinct words. The former comes from a prehistoric Germanic *\*swarmaz*, which also produced German *schwarm*, and is closely related to Dutch *swerm*, Swedish *svärm*, and Danish *sværm*. It may go back ultimately to an Indo-European base which also lay behind Latin *susurrus* 'hum' and Sanskrit *svárati* 'it sounds.' The origins of *swarm* 'climb' are not known.

**swarthy**    [16]    Old English *sweart* meant 'black.' It came from a prehistoric Germanic *\*swartaz*, which also produced German *schwarz*, Dutch *zwart*, Swedish *svart*, and Danish *sort*, and may go back ultimately to the same Indo-European base as gave Latin *sordidus* 'dirty' (source of English *sordid* [16]). It survives, just, in modern English as *swart* 'dark, black.' From this in the 16th century was derived the now defunct *swarty*, of which *swarthy* is an unexplained variant.

▶ sordid

**swashbuckle**    [19]    *Swashbuckle* is a back-formation from *swashbuckler* [16], which originally denoted a warrior who struck his shield with his sword as a sign of aggression and machismo, rather like a gorilla beating its chest. It was a compound formed from *swash* 'hit' [16], a word of imitative origin which is now restricted to the sound of water splashing against a sur-

face, and *buckler* 'shield.' It was used broadly for a 'swaggering fellow,' but the word's modern associations of romantic swordplay and high adventure did not begin to emerge until the early 19th century.

**swat**    see SQUAT

**swear**    [OE]    *Swear* is a general Germanic word, with relatives in German *schwören*, Dutch *zweren*, Swedish *svärja*, and Danish *sverge*. They all go back to a prehistoric Germanic *\*swarjan*, a derivative of the base *\*swar-*, which also lies behind the second syllable of English *answer*. And this in turn may come ultimately from the same Indo-European base as produced English *sermon*. The verb's original meaning was 'take an oath'; its use for 'curse, blaspheme' dates from the 15th century.

▶ answer

**sweat**    [OE]    *Sweat* is part of a widespread family of 'sweat'-words that goes back ultimately to the prehistoric Indo-European base *\*sweid-*, *\*swoid-*. Other members include Greek *hidrōs*, Latin *sūdor* (source of English *exude* [16]), Welsh *chwys*, Latvian *sviēdri*, and Sanskrit *svédas*. Amongst its Germanic descendants was *\*swaitjan*, which evolved into German *schweissen* 'weld,' Dutch *zweeten* 'sweat,' and English *sweat*. *Swot* [19] originated as a dialectal variant of *sweat*.

▶ exude, swot

**sweep**    [13]    The Old English word for 'sweep' was *swāpan*, which evolved into Middle English *swope*. Modern English *sweep*, which began to emerge in the 13th century, probably came from the old past tense *swepe*, a descendant of Old English *swēop*. *Swāpan* itself came from a prehistoric Germanic base *\*swei-* 'swing, bend,' which also produced German *schweifen* 'wander' and English *swift*. *Swipe* [19] probably originated as a dialectal variant of *sweep*.

▶ swift, swipe

**sweet**    [OE]    *Sweet* is part of an ancient family of 'sweet'-words that goes back to the Indo-European base *\*swād-*. From this evolved Greek *hēdús* 'sweet' (and also *hēdoné* 'pleasure,' source of English *hedonism* [19]), Latin *suāvis* 'sweet, pleasant' (source of English *suave*) and *suādēre* 'advise' (source of English *dissuade* and *persuade*), and Sanskrit *svādús* 'pleasant-tasting.' Its Germanic descendant was *\*swōtja-*, which evolved into German *süss*, Dutch *zoot*, Swedish *söt*, Danish *sød*, and English *sweet*. The use of the noun *sweet* for a 'piece of confectionery' (presumably short for *sweetmeat* [15]) dates from the mid-19th century.

▶ dissuade, hedonism, persuade, suave

**sweetbread**    see PANCREAS

**swell**    [OE]    *Swell* comes from prehistoric Germanic *\*swellan*, a verb of unknown origin which also produced German *schwellen*, Dutch *zwellen*, and Swedish *svälla*. Its use as an adjective, meaning 'fine,' emerged at the beginning of the 19th century. The notion underlying it is 'suitable to a swell, a fashionable or stylish person'; and this application of the noun *swell* probably arose out of an earlier use for 'swollen' or pompous behaviour.

**swift** [OE] The etymological meaning of *swift* appears to be 'moving along a course'; 'speed' is a secondary development. It goes back ultimately to the prehistoric Germanic base *swei- 'swing, bend,' which also produced English *sweep*, *swivel* [14], and the long defunct *swive* 'copulate with' (a descendant of Old English *swīfan* 'move in a course'). Its use as a name for the fast-flying swallow-like bird dates from the 17th century.

▶ sweep, swivel

**swim** [OE] Together with German *schwimmen*, Dutch *zwemmen*, Swedish *simma*, and Danish *svømme*, *swim* goes back to a prehistoric Germanic *swemjan*, a derivative of the same base as produced Old Norse *sund* 'swimming' (source of English *sound* 'channel, strait'). A link with Welsh *chwyfio* 'stir, wave, brandish' has been suggested.

▶ sound

**swine** [OE] *Swine* is the ancestral English term for the 'pig,' and it remained the main word until *pig* began to take over from it in the early modern English period. It came from a prehistoric Germanic *swīnam*, which also produced German *schwein*, Dutch *swijn*, and Swedish and Danish *svin*. And this in turn went back to Indo-European *su-, source also of English *hyena* and *sow*.

▶ hyena, sow

**swing** [OE] *Swing* goes back ultimately to a prehistoric Germanic base *swinggw-, which denoted 'violent circulatory movement.' One of its specific applications was to the wielding of a whip, and indeed the English verb *swing* originally meant 'flog' ('They bind him and swing him and spit on his face,' *Blickling Homilies* 971). Another Old English sense was 'rush,' but the main modern meaning 'oscillate' did not emerge until as recently as the 16th century. The ancestral notion of 'flogging' or 'beating' is better preserved in the related *swinge* [16].

▶ swinge

**swipe** see SWEEP

**switch** [16] *Switch* originally denoted a 'thin flexible twig'; it may have been borrowed from Middle Dutch *swijch* 'bough, twig.' From the noun was derived the verb *switch*. This originally meant 'beat with a switch,' but in the early 19th century the sense 'bend or waggle to and fro like a flexible stick' emerged, and this led on in the middle of the century via 'divert' to 'turn off a train on to another track' (the usage developed in American English, where the apparatus used for this is still known as a *switch*, as opposed to British English

*points*). By the end of the century this had broadened out to 'connect or disconnect by pushing a contact to or fro.' The notion of 'exchanging' or 'swopping' did not emerge until as recently as the 1890s.

**swivel** see SWIFT

**sword** [OE] *Sword* comes from a prehistoric Germanic *swerþam, which also produced German *schwert*, Dutch *zwaard*, Swedish *svärd*, and Danish *sværd*. It is not known what its ultimate source was, although it has been speculated that it may have links with Old High German *swerdo* 'pain' – in which case its etymological meaning would be the 'stinger, causer of pain.'

**swot** see SWEAT

**sybarite** [16] Sybaris was an ancient Greek colony in southern Italy. It was a flourishing trading centre, and its inhabitants put their considerable wealth to the service of unrestrained self-indulgence. Their luxurious and debauched ways became a byword in the ancient world, and Greek *Subarītēs* 'inhabitant of Sybaris' came to be synonymous with 'pleasure-seeker,' and also with 'lecher' – both heterosexual and homosexual. English acquired the word via Latin *Sybarīta*, and has rather toned down its connotations.

**sycamore** [14] The *sycamore* is etymologically either the 'fig-mulberry' or the 'mulberry-mulberry.' The word came via Old French *sicamor* and Latin *sȳcomorus* from Greek *sūkómoros*. This was a compound based on *móron* 'mulberry,' its first element being either Greek *sūkon* 'fig' or an adaptation of Hebrew *shiqmāh* 'mulberry.' It was originally used in English for a type of fig tree (the *sycomores* mentioned in the Bible – as in 'The sycomores are cut down, but we will change them into cedars,' Isaiah 9:10 – are fig trees), and the modern application to a variety of maple did not emerge until the 16th century.

▶ sycophant

**sycophant** [16] *Sycophants* are etymologically 'fig-showers.' The word comes via Latin *sȳcophanta* from Greek *sūkophántēs*, a compound formed from *sūkon* 'fig' and *-phántēs* 'shower,' a derivative of *phaínein* 'show' (source of English *fancy, phantom*, etc). *Sūkon* (which probably came from a Semitic source that also produced Latin *fīcus* 'fig,' source of English *fig*) was used metaphorically for 'cunt,' and hence for an 'indecent gesture made by putting the thumb into the mouth or between two fingers.' People who grassed on criminals were said to 'show them the fig' – 'show them two fingers,' as it might be expressed in modern English. And so the term *sūkophántēs* came to be used for an 'informer,' and eventually, via 'one who ingratiates himself by informing,' for a 'flatterer' or 'toady.'

▶ fancy, phantom, sycamore

**syllable**   [14]  A *syllable* is etymologically a 'gathering together' of letters. The word comes from Anglo-Norman *sillable*, an alteration of Old French *sillabe*, which went back via Latin *syllaba* to Greek *sullabé* 'gathering, gathering together of letters, syllable.' This was a derivative of *sullambánein* 'gather together,' hence 'spell together,' a compound verb formed from the prefix *sun-* 'together' and *lambánein* 'take, grasp.'

**syllabus**   [17]  The word *syllabus* is the result of a misprint. It originated as Greek *sittúbā* 'label, table of contents,' which was borrowed into Latin as *sittyba*. However, in an early printed edition of Cicero's *Letters to Atticus*, in the 1470s, its accusative plural form *sittybas* was misprinted as *syllabos*. This was taken as representing a Greek *súllabos*, a supposed (but quite spurious) derivative of Greek *sullambánein* 'gather together' (source of English *syllable*), which was then relatinized to *syllabus*. Its earliest application to the 'contents of a course of instruction' appears to date from the late 18th century.

**syllogism**   [14]  A *syllogism* is etymologically something 'reasoned together,' hence 'inferred.' The word comes via Old French *sillogisme* and Latin *syllogismus* from Greek *sullogismós*, a derivative of *sullogízesthai* 'reason together, infer.' This was a compound verb formed from the prefix *sun-* 'together' and *logízesthai* 'reason, reckon, compute,' a derivative of *lógos* 'word, discourse, computation' (source of English *logarithm, logic*, etc).
▶ logarithm, logic

**sylvan**   see SAVAGE

**symbol**   [15]  Etymologically, a *symbol* is something 'thrown together.' The word's ultimate source is Greek *sumbállein*, a compound verb formed from the prefix *sun-* 'together' and *bállein* 'throw' (source of English *ballistic, problem*, etc). The notion of 'throwing or putting things together' led on to the notion of 'contrast,' and so *sumbállein* came to be used for 'compare.' From it was derived *súmbolon*, which denoted an 'identifying token' – because such tokens were 'compared' with a counterpart to make sure they were genuine – and hence an 'outward sign' of something.
▶ ballistic, parable, parole, problem

**sympathy**   [16]  *Sympathy* is etymologically 'feeling with' someone else. The word comes via Latin *sympathīa* from Greek *sumpátheia*, a derivative of *sumpathés* 'feeling with or similarly to someone else.' This was a compound adjective formed from the prefix *sun-* 'together, with, like' and *páthos* 'feeling' (source of English *pathetic* [16], *pathology* [17], *pathos* [17], etc).
▶ pathetic, pathology, pathos

**symphony**   [13]  *Symphony* originally meant 'harmony'; it was not used for a 'large-scale piece of orchestral music in several movements' until the late 18th century. The word came via Old French *symphonie* and Latin *symphōnia* from Greek *sumphōníā*, a derivative of *súmphōnos* 'harmonious.' This was a compound adjective formed from the prefix *sun-* 'together' and *phōné* 'sound' (source of English *phone, phonetic*, etc).
▶ phone, phonetic

**symposium**   [18]  A *symposium* is etymologically a 'get-together for a drink.' The word comes via Latin *symposium* from Greek *sumpósion*, a derivative of *sumpótēs* 'drinking companion.' This was a compound noun formed from the prefix *sun-* 'together' and the base *\*pot-* 'drink' (source of English *poison, potion*, etc). The Greeks favoured lubricating intellectual discussion with drink, and so the term *sumpósion* came to be used for a meeting which combined elements of party and intellectual interchange.
▶ poison, potable, potion

**symptom**   [16]  A *symptom* is etymologically something that 'happens' – an occurrence or phenomenon. The word's application to physiological phenomena as signs of disease is a secondary development. It comes via late Latin *symptōma* from Greek *súmptōma* 'occurrence,' a derivative of *sumpíptein* 'fall together,' hence 'fall on, happen to.' This was a compound verb formed from the prefix *sun-* 'together' and *píptein* 'fall.'

**synagogue**   [12]  A *synagogue* is etymologically an 'assembly.' The word comes via Old French *sinagoge* and late Latin *synagōga* from Greek *sunagōgé* 'meeting, assembly.' This was a derivative of *sunágein* 'bring together,' hence 'assemble,' a compound verb formed from the prefix *sun-* 'together' and *ágein* 'lead, drive.' Its specific application to an assembly for Jewish worship was introduced by early Greek translators of the Old Testament.
▶ act, agent

**syndicate**   [17]  A *syndicate* was originally a 'body of syndics' or delegates. *Syndic* [17] came via Old French *syndic* 'delegate' and late Latin *syndicus* 'delegate' from Greek *súndikos* 'assistant in a court of law, public advocate.' This was a compound noun formed from the prefix *sun-* 'with' and *díkē* 'judgment.'

**synonym**   see NAME

**syphilis**   [18]  *Syphilus* was the name of a shepherd who according to *Syphilis sive morbus Gallicus* (Syphilis or the French disease) 1530, a poem by the Veronese doctor Girolamo Fracastoro, was the first sufferer from syphilis. The word *Syphilis* in Fracastoro's title meant simply 'narrative about Syphilus'; he did not use it as a generic term for the disease until 1546, in a treatise called *De contagione* (Concerning contagious disease). It is not known where he got the name *Syphilus* from.

**syringe**   [15]   Syringes get their name from their cylindrical shape. The word comes from late Latin *syringa*, an alteration of Latin *syrinx*, which in turn went back to Greek *súrigx* 'pipe, shepherd's pipe.' The stems of both the mock orange shrub and the lilac were used for making such pipes – hence their alternative name *syringa* [17].

▶ syringa

**syrup**   [14]   *Syrup* is etymologically 'something drunk.' Like *sherbet*, it goes back ultimately to the Arabic verb *shariba* 'drink,' whose initial /shr/ sound originated in imitation of the sound of slurping. From this was derived the noun *sharāb* 'drink,' which passed into English via medieval Latin *siropus* and Old French *sirop*. Arab drinks tend to be liberally sweetened, and so when the word came west it was with the specific sense 'thick sweet liquid.'

▶ sherbet, sorbet

**system**   [17]   A *system* is etymologically something that is 'brought together.' The word comes via French *système* and late Latin *systēma* from Greek *sústēma* 'combined or organized whole, formed from many parts.' This was a derivative of *sunistánai* 'bring together, combine,' a compound verb formed from the prefix *sun-* 'together' and *histánai* 'cause to stand' (a relative of English *stand*).

▶ stand

# T

**tabby** [17] By a bizarre series of etymological twists and turns, the *tabby* cat commemorates a textile manufacturing suburb of Baghdad. This was *Al-'attābīya*, named after Prince Attāb, who lived there. The cloth made there was known as *'attābī*, and the term passed via Old French *atabis* and modern French *tabis* into English as *tabby*. This originally denoted a sort of rich silk taffeta ('This day ... put on ... my false tabby waistcoat with gold lace' noted Samuel Pepys in his diary for 13 October 1661), but since such cloth was originally usually striped, by the 1660s the word was being applied to brindled cats.

**tabernacle** SEE TAVERN

**table** [12] Latin *tabula* originally denoted a 'board' or 'plank,' and hence a 'slab for writing on' and a 'list or similar arrangement of words or figures written on such a slab' (as in a 'table of contents'). It was in the farther outposts of the Roman empire that the sense 'piece of furniture for serving meals on' emerged – possibly in Frankish, where it would have been a direct translation of the term used for 'table,' which meant literally 'serving board' (until tables with legs found their way northward from Greece and Rome, food had been served on individual trays or boards). In much of the empire it became established as the word for 'table' (and it passed into English via Old French *table*), although in Spanish the original Latin term *mensa* survived as *mesa*. Derivatives in English include *entablature* [17], *tableau* [17] (originally a French diminutive form), *tablet*, *tabloid*, and *tabular* [17].

▶ entablature, tableau, tablet, tabloid, tabular

**tabloid** [19] *Tabloid* originated as a trade-name for a brand of tablets of condensed medicine, registered in 1884 by Burroughs, Wellcome and Company. It was an alteration of *tablet* [14], which came from Old French *tablete*, a diminutive form of *table* (source of English *table*). This originally denoted a 'slab for writing on or inscribing.' Such slabs would have been flat and often quite small, and in the late 16th century the term came to be applied to a 'flat compressed piece of something' – such as soap or medicine. The notion of 'compression' or 'condensation' underlies the use of *tabloid* for newspapers of small page size and 'condensed' versions of news stories, which emerged at the beginning of the 20th century ('He advocated tabloid journalism,' *Westminster gazette* 1 January 1901).

▶ table

**tabor** SEE TAMBOURINE

**tacit** [17] *Tacit* was adapted from Latin *tacitus*, the past participle of *tacēre* 'be silent.' Another derivative of this was Latin *taciturnus*, from which English gets *taciturn* [18]; and *tacēre* also lies behind English *reticent*.

▶ reticent, taciturn

**tack** English has three distinct words *tack*. The oldest, meaning 'nail or other fastening' [14], comes from Old Northern French *taque*, a variant of Old French *tache* 'nail, fastening.' This was borrowed from prehistoric Germanic, but the nature of its connection with *attach*, if any, is not known. In the 15th century it was applied to the 'ropes, cables, etc fastening a ship's sails,' and the adjustment of these fastenings when changing direction led to the use of *tack* as a verb meaning 'change direction in a boat.' *Tacky* 'sticky,' derived from *tack* in the 18th century, also depends on the general notion of 'fastening' (the origins of the other *tacky*, 'shoddy, tasteless' [19], are not known).

*Tack* 'horse's harness and other equipment' [20] is short for *tackle* [13]. This was probably borrowed from Middle Low German *takel*, a derivative of *taken* 'seize' (to which English *take* is related). The origins of *tack* 'food' [19] (as in *hard tack*) are not known.

▶ tackle

**tact** [17] *Tact* originally denoted the 'sense of touch' (that is what Alexander Ross was referring to when he wrote 'Of all the creatures, the sense of tact is most exquisite in man,' *Arcana microcosmi* 1651). But by the end of the 18th century it had evolved semantically via 'refined faculty of perception' to 'skill in behaving or speaking with propriety or sensitivity.' It was acquired via French *tact* from Latin *tactus* 'sense of touch,' a noun use of the past participle of *tangere* 'touch' (source of English *contact, tangent, tangible*, etc). *Tactile* [17], from the Latin derivative *tactilis*, preserves the original notion of 'touching.'

▶ contact, contagion, tactile, tangent, tangible

**tactic** [17] *Tactics* denotes etymologically 'arrangement, setting in order.' It goes back ultimately to Greek *tássein* 'put in order,' hence 'arrange in battle formation.' From this was derived *taktós* 'arranged,' which formed the basis of the further adjective *taktikós* 'concerned with arrangement or (military) planning' (source of English *tactic* and *tactical* [16]). It was used in the plural, *taktiká*, for 'matters relating to arrangement,' and this served as a model for English *tactics*.

**tadpole** [15] A *tadpole* is etymologically a 'toad-head.' The word was coined from Middle English *tadde* 'toad' and *pol* 'head' (ancestor of modern English *poll* 'voting,' historically a counting of 'heads'). Tadpoles, with their moonlike faces appearing to take up about half of their small globular bodies, seem rather like animated heads.

▶ poll, toad

**tail** [OE] *Tail* comes from a prehistoric Germanic *\*taglaz*, whose other modern descendants include German *zagel* 'penis' and Swedish *tagel* 'horsehair.' This in turn went back to an Indo-European *\*doklos*, which had the general meaning 'something long and thin.'

**tailor** [13] A *tailor* is etymologically a 'cutter.' The word was acquired from Anglo-Norman *taillour*, a variant of Old French *tailleur*. This went back to Vulgar Latin *\*tāliātor* 'cutter,' a derivative of *\*tāliāre* 'cut,' which in turn was formed from Latin *tālea* 'cutting' (in the sense of a 'piece of a plant removed for grafting or regrowing'). The specific application of the word to a 'cutter or maker of clothes' was foreshadowed in medieval Latin *tāliātor vestium* and Old French *tailleur d'habits*, and by the time it reached English, the memory of its etymological connection with 'cutting' had virtually disappeared; indeed in strict technical usage *tailor* 'person who makes up clothes' contrasts with *cutter* 'person who cuts out the cloth.' Other English descendants of *tālea* include *detail, entail, retail*, and *tally* [15] (which depends on another meaning of *tālea*, 'twig,' hence 'notches cut on a stick for counting').

▶ detail, entail, retail, tally

**taint** see TINGE

**take** [12] *Take* was borrowed from Old Norse *taka*, whose modern descendents include Swedish *taga* and Danish *tage*. Now defunct relatives include Middle Dutch *tāken* 'seize' and Gothic *tekan* 'touch,' and its ancestral meaning is probably 'lay hands on,' but its ultimate origins are not known.

**tale** [OE] A *tale* is etymologically something that is 'told.' The word is descended from a prehistoric Germanic *\*talō*, a derivative of the base *\*tal-*, which also produced English *talk* and *tell*. Of its Germanic relatives, German *zahl*, Dutch *getal*, Swedish *antal*, and Danish *tal* all mean 'number,' reflecting a secondary meaning 'reckoning, enumeration' which once existed in English, perhaps as an introduction from Old Norse (it survives in the related *teller* 'counter of votes' and *all told*).

▶ talk, tell

**talent** [13] Greek *tálanton* meant 'balance, weight,' and hence 'unit of weight or money.' Latin borrowed it as *talentum*, using it metaphorically for 'mental inclination,' and it was in this sense that English originally acquired it, via Old French *talent*. 'Unit of money' did not arrive (apart from one isolated Old English instance) until the late 14th century, and it was the use of the word in the parable of the talents (Matthew 25:14–30), in which a master gave his servants talents (money), which two of them put out to interest, earning their master's approval, while the other less enterprising servant simply buried his, that led in the early 15th century to the use of the term for 'aptitude, ability.'

**talisman** [17] *Talisman*, one of the very few English nouns ending in -man which does not turn into -men in the plural (*dragoman* is another), denotes etymologically an 'object consecrated by the completion of a religious ritual.' It comes via French *talisman* from medieval Greek *télesmon*, an alteration of late Greek *télesma* 'consecrated object.' This in turn was derived from the verb *teleín* 'complete,' hence 'perform a ritual,' hence 'consecrate,' which was based on *télos* 'aim, result' (source of English *teleology* [18]).

▶ teleology, television

**talk** [13] *Talk* has only one close relative – East Frisian *talken* 'talk, chatter.' This suggests that it may first have seen the light of day just before the Anglo-Saxon peoples first crossed the North Sea to Britain – they were then in close contact with the Frisians. However, there is no record of the verb in Old English, and it first crops up in West Midland texts of the early 13th century. Its ultimate source is the prehistoric Germanic base *\*tal-*, which also produced English *tale* and *tell*.

▶ tale, tell

**tall** [14] The ancestral meaning of *tall* is 'quick.' It is a descendant of Old English *getæl* 'quick, ready,' whose relatives included Old Frisian *tel* and Old High German *gizal* 'quick,' and which may go back ultimately to the prehistoric Germanic base *\*tal-* (source of English *tale, talk*, and *tell*). By the time of its re-emergence in Middle English it was being used for 'brave, bold,' but the modern sense 'of great height' did not develop until the 16th century.

**talon**    [14]    Latin *tālus* meant 'ankle' (it was probably a borrowing from Celtic – Irish has *sal* 'talon'). From it was derived Vulgar Latin *\*tālō* 'heel, spur,' which passed into English via Old French *talon*. In English its meaning evolved via 'heel of an animal' and 'bird of prey's claw' to 'claw' in general.

**tambourine**    [16]    *Tambourine* is one of a small family of English words that go back ultimately to Persian *tabīr* 'drum.' This found its way via Provençal *tabor* and Old French *tabour* into English as *tabor* 'small drum' [13]. The Persian word was adopted into Arabic, where it was swallowed up by the similar-sounding *tambūr* 'lute' – so that *tambūr* now meant 'drum.' This was borrowed into Old French as *tambour*, and passed on to English as *tambour* [15]. *Tambourine* comes from a French diminutive form.

▶ tabor

**tame**    [OE]    *Tame* evolved from a prehistoric Germanic *\*tamaz*, which also produced German *zahm* and Dutch *tam*. This in turn was descended from the Indo-European base *\*dom-*, which also lay behind Latin *domāre* 'tame, subdue' (source of English *daunt* [13] and *indomitable* [17]) and Greek *damān* 'tame, subdue' (source of English *adamant* and *diamond*).

▶ adamant, daunt, diamond, indomitable

**tamper**    [16]    *Tamper* began life as a variant of *temper*. It originally meant 'mix clay together with water to make it suitable for use.' However, the notion of 'mixing' seems to lead on naturally to 'interference' (*meddle* originally meant 'mix'), and by the end of the 16th century we find that 'tampering with clay' had moved on to 'tampering with anything' – 'interfering' with it.

▶ temper

**tan**    [OE]    *Tan* was borrowed into late Old English from the medieval Latin verb *tannāre*. This was derived from *tannum* 'oak bark' (oak bark is used in tanning leather), which itself was probably a loan-word from Gaulish *tanno-* 'oak.' The French noun *tan* 'tan' came ultimately from the same Latin source. From it was derived *tanin*, acquired by English as *tannin* [19]; and its immediate Old French predecessor formed the basis of an adjective *tané* 'tan-coloured, dark,' whose Anglo-Norman version *tauné* gave English *tawny* [14].

▶ tannin, tawny

**tandem**    [18]    Latin *tandem* meant 'eventually, at length.' Its use for 'acting conjointly' arose from an 18th-century play on words, in which 'at length' was jocularly interpreted as 'lengthwise, in a straight line,' and the word was applied to a 'carriage drawn by two horses one behind the other in a straight line.' In the 1880s it was transferred to a 'bicycle with two seats, one behind the other.' Its more general modern use, for 'acting together,' dates from the early 20th century.

**tangerine**    [18]    The tangerine was originally exported to Britain, in the 1840s, from the Moroccan port of Tangier, and so it was called the *Tangerine orange* (*Tangerine* started life as an adjective meaning 'of Tangier': 'an old Tangerine captain with a wooden leg,' Joseph Addison, *Tatler* 1710). This was soon shortened to *tangerine*. It was first used as a colour term at the end of the 19th century.

**tangible**    [16]    *Tangible* means literally 'touchable.' It comes via French *tangible* from late Latin *tangibilis*, a derivative of Latin *tangere* 'touch.' Other English words from this source include *tangent* [16], etymologically a line 'touching' a circle. Its past participle *tactus* has contributed *contact*, *intact*, and *tact*, while the base from which it was formed, *\*tag-*, has also produced *contagion*, *contaminate*, *entire*, and *integrity*.

▶ contact, contagion, contaminate, intact, integrity, tact, task, taste, tax

**tank**    [17]    *Tank* 'water-storage container' originated in India, where it denoted a 'pond.' It was borrowed from a local word, such as Gujarati *tānkh* or Marathi *tānken* 'pond, cistern.' These in turn probably went back to Sanskrit *tadāga* 'pond, lake,' which was of Dravidian origin. The word was applied as a secret code name to the new armoured vehicle at the end of 1915, supposedly because it was thought to resemble a benzene tank.

**tannin**    see TAN

**tantalize**    [16]    The verb *tantalize* was inspired by the sad story of Tantalus, a mythical king of Phrygia in the ancient world. He had displeased the gods in some way (versions differ as to how, the commonest being that he had stolen their food), and as a punishment he was condemned to stand for ever in water up to his chin, while overhead hung boughs laden with fruit: whenever he stooped to drink, the water disappeared, and when he tried to reach the fruit, the wind blew it away. The term *tantalus*, coined in the 19th century for a lockable decanter stand whose contents can be seen but not got at, preserves the same idea.

**tantamount**    [17]    *Tantamount* means etymologically 'amounting to as much.' It comes from an earlier verb *tantamount* 'amount to as much as, be equal to,' which was a lexicalization of the Anglo-Norman expression *tant amunter* 'amount to as much.' This was made up of *tant* 'as much,' which came via Old French from Latin *tantus*, and *amunter*, ancestor of English *amount*.

▶ amount, paramount

**taper**    [OE]    *Taper* is ultimately the same word as *paper*. Both go bach to Latin *papyrus* 'papyrus.' This was used among other things for a 'candlewick made from papyrus,' and hence for a 'candle.' It seems to have been borrowed in this sense into Old English as *papur*, and by a process known as dissimilation (in which one of a pair of similar speech sounds is changed, so as to break up the pair) it became *tapur*. The verb *taper* 'become narrower,' which emerged in the 16th century, is an allusion to the shape of the candle.

▶ paper, papyrus

**tapestry** [15] The ultimate source of *tapestry* is Greek *tápēs* 'tapestry, woven carpet.' Its diminutive form *tapétion* was borrowed via late Latin *tapētium* into Old French as *tapis* 'carpet.' From this was derived the verb *tapisser* 'cover with a carpet,' and this in turn formed the basis of a noun *tapisserie* 'carpets, woven material.' English took it over and altered it to *tapestry*.

**tar** [OE] *Tar* is etymologically a substance produced from 'trees.' The word goes back via a prehistoric Germanic *terw-* (source also of German and Dutch *teer*, Swedish *tjära*, and Danish *tjære*) to Indo-European *drew-* 'tree' (source of English *tree*) – the original application of the word evidently having been to the tarry resins produced by conifers. (The *tar* [17] of *Jack tar* 'sailor' is short for *tarpaulin* [17], a compound noun probably formed from *tar* and *pall* 'covering.')

▶ tree, trough

**tarantella** [18] In the 15th century in southern Italy an epidemic of a curious nervous disorder broke out, one of whose symptoms was an uncontrollable compulsion to whirl and cavort around, as if dancing. The people attributed it to the bite of a spider, the *tarantula* [16], named after the local town and seaport of Taranto. In due course the dancing came to be rationalized as a method of counteracting the effects of the spider's bite, and it was named *tarantella*, a diminutive form of *Taranto*. The word finally came to stand for a particular type of dance.

**tardy** see BUSTARD

**tarmac** [20] The term *tarmac* commemorates the name of John Loudon McAdam (1756–1836), a Scottish civil engineer who developed a method of levelling roads and covering them with gravel. Setting the gravel in tar produced in the 1880s the term *tarmacadam*, and in 1903 the abbreviated form *tarmac* was registered as a trademark. By 1919 the word was being used in British English as a synonym for 'runway.'

**task** see TAX

**taste** [13] The origins of *taste* are not entirely clear, but what does seem certain is that it is connected in some way with Latin *tangere* 'touch'; indeed it was originally used for 'touch' in English ('With that finger he will it taste if it is rightly wrought,' *St Michael* 1290), and its French relative *tâter* denotes 'feel.' It was once generally supposed that it came from Latin *taxāre* 'feel, assess' (source of English *tax*), which was derived from *tangere*. The theory is that *taxāre* produced a Vulgar

Latin derivative *\*taxitāre*, which turned into *tastāre* – whence Old French *taster*, and eventually English *taste*. Another theory has it, however, that *\*tastāre* was a blend of *tangere* with Latin *gustāre* 'taste' (source of English *gusto*).

▶ tangent, tangible

**tattoo** English has two words *tattoo*. The older, 'military display' [17], was borrowed from a Dutch word, *taptoe*, that means literally 'tap to,' that is, 'shut the tap' – a signal to shut off the taps of the beer barrels at closing time in the taverns. By the time it reached English it was being used for a 'drum beat signalling the time for soldiers to return to their quarters at night,' and in the 18th century it was applied to a 'military display based on this.' The *tattoo* on the skin [18] was borrowed from a Polynesian language, such as Tahitian (*tatau*) or Marquesan (*ta-tu*).

▶ tap

**taunt** [16] The etymological notion underlying *taunt* is of giving someone tit for tat, of returning as much in reply as has been given. It comes from the French phrase *tant pour tant* 'so much for so much.' This was borrowed into English in the early 16th century as *taunt pour taunt* or (partially anglicized) *taunt for taunt*, which was used for a 'sarcastic rejoinder.' The first record of the use of *taunt* on its own (as a verb) dates from 1513.

**tavern** [13] *Tavern* comes via Old French *taverne* from Latin *taberna* 'hut, inn,' a word possibly of Etruscan origin. Derived from *taberna*, in the sense 'hut,' was the diminutive form *tabernāculum* 'tent,' which was borrowed into English as *tabernacle* [13]. Its original application was to the tent which according to the Bible covered the Ark of the Covenant.

▶ tabernacle

**tawdry** [17] Anna, Anglo-Saxon king of East Anglia, had a daughter called Etheldrida, who became queen of Northumbria (she died in 679). She had an inordinate fondness in her youth for fine lace neckerchiefs, and when she was later afflicted by a fatal tumour of the neck, she regarded it as divine retribution for her former extravagance. After her death she was canonized and made patron saint of Ely. In the Middle Ages fairs were held in her memory, known as 'St Audrey's fairs' (*Audry* is a conflated version of *Etheldrida*), at which lace neckties were sold. These were termed *Seynt Audries lace*, a name eventually eroded to *tawdrie lace*. They were often made from cheap gaudy material, and so by the end of the 17th century *tawdry* was being used generally for 'cheap and gaudy.'

**tawny** see TAN

**tax** [13] *Tax* originally denoted 'assess an amount to be levied'; the notion of 'imposing such a levy' is a secondary development. The word comes via Old French *taxer* from Latin *taxāre* 'touch, assess, appraise,' a derivative of *tangere* 'touch' (source of English *contact, tangible*, etc). From *taxāre* was derived the medieval Latin noun *taxa* 'tax, piece of work imposed,' which passed into English via Anglo-Norman *tasque* as *task* [13].

▸ tact, tangent, tangible, task

**taxi** [20] *Taxi* is short for *taximeter cab*, a term coined around 1890 for a cab fitted with a taximeter, a device for showing the fare to be paid. *Taximeter* [19] was borrowed from French *taximètre*, a compound noun formed from *taxe* 'charge, tariff' (a relative of English *tax*) and *mètre* 'meter.'

▸ tax

**tea** [17] English acquired *tea* via Dutch *thee* and Malay *teh* from *te*, the word for 'tea' in the Amoy dialect of Chinese, from southeast China (the Mandarin Chinese version of the word is *chá*, from which English got *cha* [17]). It was originally pronounced /tay/ as well as /tee/, but it was the latter which eventually won out.

▸ cha

**teach** [OE] To *teach* someone is etymologically to 'show' them something. The word goes back ultimately to the prehistoric Indo-European base *\*deik-* 'show,' which also produced Greek *deiknúnai* 'show' (source of English *paradigm* [15]) and Latin *dīcere* 'say' (source of English *diction, dictionary*, etc). Its Germanic descendant was *\*taik-*, which produced English *token* and German *zeigen* 'show.' From it was derived the verb *\*taikjan*, ancestor of English *teach*.

▸ diction, dictionary, paradigm, token

**team** [OE] The etymological notion underlying the word *team* is 'pulling.' It goes back ultimately to the Indo-European base *\*deuk-* 'pull,' which also produced Latin *dūcere* 'pull, lead' (source of English *abduct, duke*, etc). Its Germanic descendant was *\*taukh-*. From this was derived a noun *\*taugmaz*, whose later form *\*taumaz* gave English *team*. This originally denoted a group of animals harnessed together to 'pull' a load, but the modern sense 'group of people acting together' did not emerge from this until the 16th century. Another strand in the meaning of the base is 'giving birth, offspring' (presumably based on the notion of children being 'drawn' forth from the womb). This has now disappeared from *team*, but traces of it can still be detected in the related *teem* [OE], whose modern connotations of 'abundance' go back to an earlier 'bring forth offspring prolifically.' From the same source come English *tie* and *tow*.

▸ abduct, duct, duke, educate, teem, tie, tow

**teapoy** see FOOT

▸ lachrymose / dermatitis, epidermis, turd

**tear** English has two separate words *tear*, both of ancient ancestry. The sort of *tear* that one weeps [OE] goes back (together with its Germanic relatives German *träne*, Dutch *traan*, Swedish *tår*, and Danish *taare*) to

prehistoric Indo-European *\*dakru-*, a word of uncertain origin which also produced Welsh *deigryn* and Latin *lacrima* (source of English *lachrymal* [16] and *lachrymose* [17]).

*Tear* 'rip' [OE] comes from an Indo-European base *\*der-* 'tear,' which also produced Russian *drat* and Polish *drzeć* 'tear.' The base *\*der-* denoted the concept of 'flaying' as well as 'tearing,' in which sense it produced English *turd* and Greek *dérma* 'skin' (source of English *dermatitis, epidermis*, etc).

**tease** [OE] *Tease* originally meant 'separate the fibres of wool' (a sense still perceptible in the metaphorical *tease out* 'disentangle something complicated'). It came from a prehistoric West Germanic *\*taisjan*, whose base was also the source of English *teasel* [OE], a plant whose prickly flower heads were used for carding wool. The notion of 'irritating someone with prickles' led in the 17th century to *tease* being used for 'pester,' which gradually weakened into 'make fun of.'

**technical** [17] Greek *tékhnē* denoted 'skill, art, craft, trade' (it may have come from the Indo-European base *\*tek-* 'shape, make,' which also produced Greek *téktōn* 'carpenter, builder,' source of English *architect* and *tectonic* [17]). From it was derived the adjective *tekhnikós*, which passed into English via Latin *technicus* as *technic* (now obsolete) and *technical*. *Technique* [19] comes from a noun use of the French adjective *technique* 'technical.' From the same source come *technicolour* [20], based on the trademark *Technicolor* (registered in 1929), and *technology* [17].

▸ architect, technique, tectonic, text

**teddy** English has two words *teddy*, both of them based on affectionate alterations of male first names. The *teddy bear* [20] was named after Theodore ('Teddy') Roosevelt, president of the USA from 1901 to 1909. One of his favourite leisure pursuits was hunting bears, and early in 1906 the *New York Times* published a humorous poem about the adventures of two bears, which were named Teddy B and Teddy G in his honour. The names were then appropriated to two bears that had just been presented to the Bronx Zoo; and before the year was out, toy manufacturers with an eye for profit had put toy bears called *teddy bears* on the market.

The *teddy* of *teddy boy* [20] is short for *Edward*, an allusion to the teddy boys' preference for clothes in a style reminiscent of the Edwardian period (1901–10). The first record of the word comes from 1954.

**teem** see TEAM

**teen** [OE] The element *-teen* (as in *thirteen, fourteen*, etc) originated as an inflected form of *ten*. The noun *teen*, usually used in the expression *in one's teens* 'from the ages of thirteen to nineteen,' was derived from it in the 17th century ('Your poor young things, when they are once in the teens, think they shall never be married,' William Wycherley, *Gentleman Dancing-*

*Master* 1673). The compound *teenage* is first recorded in 1921, *teenager* in 1941.

▶ ten

**teetotal** [19] The adverb *teetotally* is first recorded in America in 1832 (James Hall, in his *Legends of West Philadelphia*, recorded a Kentucky backwoodsman as saying 'These Mingoes . . . ought to be essentially, and particularly, and tee-totally obflisticated off of the face of the whole yearth'); the *tee* represents the initial *t* of *total*, as if repeating it to give extra emphasis to the word. The application of the adjective *teetotal* to 'total abstinence from alcohol' (that is, including beer, and not just spirits) is virtually contemporary. It is credited to a certain Richard Turner, of Preston, Lancashire, who is reputed to have used it in a speech to a temperance society in September 1833.

**teleology** see TALISMAN

**television** [20] *Television* means etymologically 'far vision.' Its first element, *tele-*, comes from Greek *tḗle* 'far off,' a descendant of the same base as *télos* 'end' (source of English *talisman* and *teleology*). Other English compounds formed from it include *telegraph* [18], *telegram* [19], *telepathy* [19] (etymologically 'far feeling,' coined by the psychologist Frederic Myers in 1882), *telephone* [19], *telescope* [17] (a word of Italian origin), and *telex* [20] (a blend of *teleprinter* and *exchange*). *Television* itself was coined in French, and was borrowed into English in 1907. Of its abbreviations, *telly* dates from about 1940, *TV* from 1948.

▶ talisman, teleology

**tell** [OE] *Tell* goes back to a prehistoric Germanic *\*taljan*, a derivative of *\*talō* 'something told' (from which English gets *tale*). This in turn was formed from the base *\*tal-*, source also of English *talk*. Beside 'narrative, discourse' lies another strand of meaning, 'counting, enumeration' (pointing back to an original common denominator 'put in order'), which survives in *all told* and the derivative *teller* 'counter of votes,' and also in the related German *zählen* 'count.'

▶ tale, talk

**temerity** [15] Someone who behaves with *temerity* is etymologically acting in the 'dark.' The word was adapted from Latin *temeritās* 'rashness,' a derivative of *temere* 'blindly,' hence 'rashly.' This in turn was formed from an unrecorded *\*temus* 'darkness,' a relative of *tenebrae* 'darkness,' and hence originally denoted 'acting in the dark, so that one cannot see.'

**temper** [OE] The verb *temper* was borrowed into Old English from Latin *temperāre* 'mix, blend.' This seems originally to have meant 'mix in due proportion,' and so may have been derived from Latin *tempus* 'time, due time' (source of English *temporary*). The noun *temper* was derived from the verb in the 14th century in the sense 'mixture of elements,' and this led on in the 17th century to 'set of mental traits' (a meaning that

has now largely passed to the derivative *temperament* [15]). The modern sense 'ill humour' emerged from this in the 19th century. Another meaning of Latin *temperāre* was 'restrain oneself,' which has come through into the derivatives *temperance* [14] and *temperate* [14]. Other relatives include *distemper* and *temperature*.

*Tamper* probably originated as an alteration of *temper*.

▶ distemper, tamper, tempera, temperature

**tempera** see DISTEMPER

**temperature** [16] Like its relatives *temper* and *temperament, temperature* originally meant 'mixture' (Philemon Holland in 1601 wrote of 'a temperature of brass and iron together'). The modern sense 'degree of heat' emerged in the late 17th century, and seems to have evolved from another early and now obsolete sense, 'mild weather.' This reflected the 'restraint' strand of meaning in the word's ultimate source, Latin *temperāre*, which also survives in English *temperance* and *temperate*.

▶ temper

**tempest** [13] Latin *tempestās* started off meaning nothing more alarming than 'period of time' (it was a derivative of *tempus* 'time,' source of English *temporary*). Gradually, however, it progressed via 'weather' to 'bad weather, storm.' *Tempus* moved in to take its place in the neutral sense 'weather,' and provides the word for 'weather' in modern French (*temps*), Italian (*tempo*), Spanish (*tiempo*), and Rumanian (*timp*). Other languages whose word for 'weather' comes from a term originally denoting 'time' include Russian (*pogoda*), Polish (*czas*), Czech (*počasí*), Latvian (*laiks*), and Breton (*amzer*).

▶ temporary

**temple** *Temple* for worship [OE] and *temple* at the side of the head [14] are distinct words. The former was borrowed from Latin *templum*, which originated as a term relating to divination, used by priests in ancient times. It denoted a space marked out or 'cut' out as suitable for making observations on which auguries were based – some say a space marked out on the ground, others a section of the night sky. It probably came ultimately from the base *\*tem-* 'cut,' which also produced Greek *témein* 'cut' and the English suffix *-tomy* 'surgical cutting.' It has found its way into most western European languages, including German, Dutch, Swedish, and Danish *tempel* and Welsh *teml* as well as the Romance languages.

*Temple* 'area at the side of the head' comes via Old French *temple* from Vulgar Latin *\*tempula*, an alteration of *tempora*, the plural of Latin *tempus*. This of course originally meant 'time' (English gets *temporary* from it), and it seems that the sense 'area at the side of the head' arose via an intermediate 'appropriate time, proper period,' hence 'right place (for dealing someone a fatal blow).'

▶ tome / temporary

**temporary** [16] *Temporary* was adapted from Latin *temporārius*, a derivative of *tempus* 'time.' The origins of this are not certain, but it could go back ultimately to the prehistoric base *\*ten-* 'stretch' (source of English *tend, tense, thin*, etc), in which case it would denote etymologically a 'stretch of time.' Other English derivatives include *extempore, tempest, temple* 'side of the head,' *tempo* [18] (via Italian), *temporal* [14], and *tense* 'verb category.'

▶ extempore, tempest, temple, tempo, tense

**ten** [OE] *Ten* is part of a general European family of 'ten'-words which goes back ultimately to prehistoric Indo-European *\*dekm*. This also produced Greek *déka* (source of English *dean* and *decade* and the prefix *deca-*), Latin *decem* (source of English *December, decimal, decimate, dime*, etc), and Russian *désyat'*. Its Germanic descendant was *\*tekhan*, which has evolved into German *zehn*, Dutch *tien*, Swedish *tio*, Danish *ti*, and English *ten*. Also related are *teen* and *tithe*.

▶ dean, decade, December, decimal, decimate, dime, teen, tithe

**tenant** [14] A *tenant* is etymologically a 'holder.' The word comes from Old French *tenant*, a noun use of the present participle of *tenir* 'hold.' This in turn went back to Latin *tenēre* 'hold,' a descendant of the Indo-European base *\*ten-* 'stretch, extend' (source also of English *tend, tense, thin*, etc). Also from Latin *tenēre* come English *tenacious* [16], *tenement* [14], *tenet* [17], and *tenor*, not to mention *contain, continue, detain, maintain, obtain, retain*, etc, while French *tenir* has additionally produced *tenable* [16], *tenon* [15], *tenure* [15], and probably *tennis*.

▶ contain, continue, detain, maintain, obtain, retain, tenable, tenacious, tend, tenement, tenet, tennis, tenon, tenor, tense, tenure, thin

**tend** English has two distinct words *tend*, but they come from the same ultimate source. *Tend* 'look after' [14] is short for *attend*, which goes back to a Latin compound verb based on *tendere* 'stretch' – source of English *tend* 'have an inclination' [14]. *Tendere* itself was descended from the Indo-European base *\*ten-* 'stretch' (source also of English *tenant, tenuous, thin, tone, tune*, etc), and its other contributions to English include *contend* [15], *distend* [14], *extend, intend, portend* [15], *pretend*, and also *ostensible, tendency* [17], *tense, tension*, and *tent*.

▶ contend, distend, extend, intend, ostensible, portend, pretend, tenant, tense, tent, tenuous, thin, tone, tune

**tender** English has two distinct words *tender*, both of which go back ultimately to the Indo-European base *\*ten-* 'stretch.' The adjective, 'delicate, fragile' [13], comes via Old French *tendre* from Latin *tener*

'delicate,' a descendant of *\*ten-* and source also of English *tendril* [16] (etymologically a 'tender' shoot). The verb, 'offer' [16], comes from another Old French *tendre*, which went back to Latin *tendere* 'stretch, hold out' (source of English *tend, tendency*, etc).

▶ tenant, tend, tendril

**tenement** see TENANT

**tenet** see TENANT

**tennis** [14] The earliest recorded English forms of the word *tennis* include *tenetz, teneys*, and *tenes*. These suggest that it probably came from *tenez*, the imperative plural of Old French *tenir* 'hold,' hence 'receive,' supposedly shouted by the server to his opponent as a warning to get ready to receive the ball. The word originally referred, of course, to what is now known as *real tennis*; it was first applied to the newly invented outdoor game in 1874, in the compound *lawn tennis*, and this was soon shortened to simply *tennis*.

▶ tenant

**tenon** see TENANT

**tenor** [13] Latin *tenor* was derived from the verb *tenēre* 'hold' (source also of English *tenacious, tenant*, etc), and so etymologically denoted 'that which is held to,' hence a 'continuous course.' This evolved in due course into the 'general sense or import' of a piece of speech or writing, in which sense English acquired it via Anglo-Norman *tenur*. The musical term *tenor*, which is basically the same word, arrived in the 14th century via Italian *tenore* and Old French *tenor*. It denotes etymologically the voice that 'holds' the melodic line.

▶ tenant

**tense** English has two separate words *tense*. The older, 'verb form indicating time' [14], came via Old French *tens* from Latin *tempus* 'time' (source also of English *temporal, temporary*, etc). The original meaning 'time' survived into English, but died out in the early 16th century. The adjective *tense* [17] was adapted from *tensus*, the past participle of Latin *tendere* 'stretch' (source also of English *tend, tendency*, etc). It originally meant simply 'stretched tight,' and the metaphorical 'strained' did not emerge until the 19th century. *Tension* [16] comes from the Latin derivative *tensiō*.

▶ temporary / tend

**tent** [13] A *tent* is etymologically something that is 'stretched' – over a frame to provide shelter. The word comes via Old French *tente* from Vulgar Latin *\*tenta*, a noun derived from the past participial stem of Latin *tendere* 'stretch' (source of English *tend, tendency*, etc). It was supposedly inspired by the expression *pelles tendere*, literally 'stretch skins,' that is, 'stetch animal hides over a framework to make a tent,' which was used metaphorically for 'set up a camp.'

▶ tend

**tenth**    see TITHE

**tenuous**    [16]    *Tenuous* comes from the same ultimate ancestor as *thin*. It is an alteration of an earlier and now defunct *tenuious*, which was adapted from Latin *tenuis* 'thin.' And this went back to the Indo-European base *\*ten-* 'stretch,' a variant of which produced English *thin*.

▶ tend, thin

**tenure**    see TENANT

**tepid**    [14]    English gets *tepid* from Latin *tepidus*, a derivative of *tepēre* 'be warm.' This was descended from the Indo-European base *\*tep-* 'warm,' which also produced Russian *teplyj* 'warm,' Czech *teplý* 'warm,' and Welsh *twym* 'hot.'

**term**    [13]    The etymological notion underlying the word *term* is of a 'limit' or 'boundary,' and hence of an 'end.' It comes via Old French *terme* from Latin *terminus* 'boundary, limit,' which was also borrowed into Welsh as *terfyn* 'boundary' and directly into English in the 17th century as *terminus* 'finishing point' (it was first applied to railway stations in the 1830s). The notion of a 'time limit' led to its use for a 'period of time,' the sense in which it was first used in English; the particular application to a 'period in which a school, lawcourt, etc is in session' emerged in the mid 15th century. The sense 'word or phrase expressing a particular idea' arose (through Greek influence) in medieval Latin from the concept of 'limiting' the application of an expression. Also from Latin *terminus* come English *determine*, *exterminate* [16], *terminal* [15], *terminate* [16], and *terminology* [19].

▶ determine, exterminate, terminology, terminus

**termagent**    [13]    *Termagent* was originally the name of a blustering arrogant Muslim deity in medieval mystery plays; it was not used for a 'quarrelsome woman' until the 16th century. It was an alteration of an earlier *Tervagant*, which came via Old French *Tervagant* from Italian *Trivigante*. It is not known for certain where this came from. It has been interpreted as literally 'three-wandering,' in allusion to the moon travelling in different guises to heaven, earth, and hell, as if it were formed from Latin *tri-* 'three' and *vagārī* 'wander' (source of English *vagabond*, *vagrant*, etc); but it may simply have been borrowed from some unknown oriental language.

**terrace**    [16]    *Terrace* is one of a small family of English words that go back ultimately to Latin *terra* 'earth, land.' This was probably descended from Indo-European *\*tersā-* 'dry' (source also of English *thirst*, *torrid*, etc), in which case it denoted etymologically 'dry land,' as opposed to 'sea.' The family also includes *inter* [14] (etymologically 'put into the earth'), *terra cotta* [18] (from Italian, literally 'cooked earth'), *terra firma* [17] (literally 'firm land'), *terrain* [18], *terrestri-*

*al* [15], *terrier* [15] (etymologically a dog which is sent down burrows in the 'earth' after its quarry), *terrine, territory* [15], and *tureen*. *Terrace* itself came via Old French *terrace* from the Vulgar Latin derivative *\*terrāceus*, which denoted a 'platform made from a pile of earth or rubble.'

▶ terrain, terrestrial, terrier, terrine, territory, thirst, torrid, tureen

**terror**    [14]    To be *terrified* is etymologically to 'shake with fear.' The ultimate ancestor of Latin *terror* 'fear' (source of English *terror*) and *terrēre* 'frighten' (source of English *deter* [16], *terrible* [15], *terrific* [17], and *terrify* [16]) was the Indo-European base *\*tre-* 'shake,' which also produced English *tremble, tremor*, etc. *Terrorism* [18] and *terrorist* [18] were coined in French in the 1790s to denote the activities of the Revolutionary government during the 'Terror,' when thousands of its opponents were put to death. It broadened out towards its present-day meaning in the 19th century.

▶ deter, terrible, terrify, tremble, tremor

**terse**    [17]    *Terse* originally meant 'polished, smooth' ('This man . . . so laboured upon it that he left it smooth and terse,' Helkiah Crooke, *Description of the Body of Man* 1615). By the 18th century, however, the associated notion of 'neatness' had led on to 'neatly concise.' The word's present-day negative connotations of 'brusqueness' seem to be a comparatively recent development. It was borrowed from *tersus*, the past participle of Latin *tergēre* 'wipe' (source also of English *detergent*).

▶ detergent

**tertiary**    see THIRD

**test**    [14]    Latin *testum* denoted an 'eathenware pot.' English acquired it via Old French *test*, and used it originally for a 'pot in which metals are subjected to heat.' Among the purposes these *tests* were put to was assaying, to ascertain the quality of metal, and by the 16th century the word was being used metaphorically for an 'examination of properties or qualities.' English *testy* and French *tête* 'head' are close relatives.

▶ testy

**testament**    [13]    *Testament* is one of a range of English words that go back to Latin *testis* 'witness.' This was derived from a prehistoric Indo-European base *\*tris-* 'three,' and so denoted etymologically a 'third person,' who was not party to an agreement and thus could be a disinterested witness to it. Other English members of the *testis* family include *testicle* [15] (which etymologically 'bears witness' to a man's virility), *testify* [14], *testimony* [14], and the prefixed forms *attest* [16], *contest, detest, intestate* [14], and *protest*. The use of *testament* for 'will' was inspired by the notion of a 'witnessed' document. Its application to the two parts of the Bible arose from a mistranslation of Greek *diathḗkē*, which meant both 'covenant' and 'will, testament.' It was used for the 'covenant' between God and human beings, but Latin translators rendered it as if it were being used for 'will' rather than 'covenant.'

▶ attest, contest, detest, intestate, protest, testicle, testify, testimony, three

**testy** [14]  *Testy* means etymologically 'heady.' It was borrowed from Anglo-Norman *testif*, a derivative of Old French *teste* 'head' (ancestor of modern French *tête*). This in turn went back to Latin *testa* 'tile, earthenware pot' (a relative of *testum*, from which English gets *test*), which in the post-classical period was used humorously for 'head.' English acquired *testy* in the sense 'headstrong, impetuous,' but by the 16th century it had shifted via 'impatient' to 'irritable.'

▶ test

**text** [14]  Latin *texere* meant 'weave' (this was actually a secondary sense, its original meaning being 'build,' and it went back ultimately to the Indo-European base *tek-* 'make,' source also of English *technical*). Its past participle *textus* was used as a noun meaning 'woven material,' and hence metaphorically 'literary composition.' English acquired it via Old French *texte*. Other English words from the same source include *context* [15], *pretext* [16], *subtle, textile* [17], *texture* [15], *tissue*, and *toilet*.

▶ architect, context, pretext, subtle, technical, texture, tissue, toilet

**than** [OE]  *Than* is ultimately the same word as *then*, and the two were used interchangeably until the end of the 17th century. It is not clear how the adverb came to be used as a conjunction denoting comparison, although it is possible that the comparison implicit in expressions like 'This one is better; then there is that one' may have led on to 'This one is better than that one.'

▶ then

**thank** [OE]  The notion of 'gratitude' in modern English *thank* arose out of an earlier 'thoughtfulness.' For the word goes back ultimately to prehistoric Germanic *\*thangk-*, *\*thengk-*, which also produced English *think*, and the noun *thank* originally meant 'thought' (a 12th-century translation of the gospels has 'From the heart come evil thanks' Matthew 15:19, where the Authorized Version gives 'Out of the heart proceed evil thoughts'). The sense 'thought' graduated via 'favourable thought, good will' to 'gratitude.' It was originally singular, and the modern plural usage did not emerge until the 14th century. *Thank you* first appeared in the 15th century, short for *I thank you*.

▶ think

**that** [OE]  *That* is a very ancient word, going right back to prehistoric Indo-European *\*tad* (source also of Greek *tó* 'the' and Russian *tot'*, *ta*, *to* 'that'). Its original function in English was as the neuter form of a demon-

strative pronoun. This came to be used as the definite article (modern English *the*), but as the grammatical gender system began to break down in the early Middle English period, *that* broke away from the definite article and began to be used as a demonstrative adjective. Its use as a relative pronoun goes back to the Old English period.

▶ the

**thatch** [OE]  To *thatch* a building is etymologically to 'cover' it; the notion of 'straw' is a secondary development. The word goes back ultimately to the Indo-European base *\*tog-*, *\*teg-* 'cover' (source also of English *detect, integument, protect, tile*, and *toga*). Its Germanic descendant was *\*thak-* (source of German *dach* 'roof' and English *deck*). From this was derived *\*thakjan*, which gave English *thatch*.

▶ deck, detect, integument, protect, thug, tile, toga

**the** [OE]  The nominative forms of the Old English definite article were *se* (masculine), *sēo* (feminine), and *thæt* (neuter – ancestor of modern English *that*). In the late Old English period *se* was replaced by *the*, probably an eroded version of *that* and perhaps the same word as the Old English relative particle *the*. Its drafting in to take the place of *se* was no doubt promoted by the fact that all the inflected forms of the Old English definite article (*thone, thæm, thæs*, etc) began with *th-*. When the distinction between genders began to die out in the early Middle English period, *the* took over as the general form.

▶ that, then, there, this, though

**theatre** [14]  A *theatre* is etymologically a place for 'looking at' something. The word comes via Old French *theatre* and Latin *theātrum* from Greek *théātron*. This was derived from the verb *theãsthai* 'watch, look at,' whose base *thea-* also produced English *theory*. It was first used in English for the open-air amphitheatres of the ancient world; its application to contemporary playhouses dates from the end of the 16th century.

▶ theory

**theft**  see THIEF

**their** [12]  Like *they* and *them*, *their* was borrowed from Old Norse. Its source was *theirra*, the genitive plural form of the demonstrative adjective *sá*. The pronoun form *theirs* [13] is an English creation.

▶ them, they

**them** [12]  The Old English set of forms of the third person plural pronoun was *hīe, hiera*, and *him*. These were replaced at the end of the Old English period by *they, their*, and *them*, which came from Old Norse, but the colloquial '*em* for *them* is a lineal descendant of *him*.

▶ their, they

**theme** [13] Greek *théma* denoted etymologically 'something placed,' hence a 'proposition' (it was formed from the base *\*the-*, source also of *tithénai* 'place, put' and distant relative of English *do*). English acquired the word via Latin *thēma* and Old French *\*teme* as *teme*, but soon reverted to the Latin spelling.

▶ do

**then** [OE] *Then* was formed from the ancient demonstrative base *\*ta-*, which also underlies English *that* and *there*. Its West Germanic relatives include German *dann* and Dutch *dan*. It is ultimately the same word as *than*.

▶ than, the, there

**theology** [14] Greek *theós* meant 'god.' (Despite the more than passing similarity, it is not related to Latin *deus* 'god,' source of English *deity*. Its precise ancestry has never been determined. It may go back ultimately to the Indo-European base *\*dhē-* 'put, place,' which also produced English *do*, but it could equally well have been borrowed from a non-Indo-European source.) From it was derived *theología* 'study of divine things,' which passed into English via Latin *theologia* and Old French *theologie*, and also *apothéōsis* 'deification,' from which English gets *apotheosis* [17].

▶ apotheosis

**theory** [16] The etymological notion underlying *theory* is of 'looking'; only secondarily did it develop via 'contemplation' to 'mental conception.' It comes via late Latin *theōria* from Greek *theōría* 'contemplation, speculation, theory.' This was a derivative of *theōrós* 'spectator,' which was formed from the base *thea-* (source also of *theásthai* 'watch, look at,' from which English gets *theatre*). Also derived from *theōrós* was *theōreín* 'look at,' which formed the basis of *theōrēma* 'speculation, intuition, theory,' acquired by English via late Latin *theōrēma* as *theorem* [16]. From the same source comes *theoretical* [17].

▶ theatre

**therapy** [19] Greek *théraps* denoted an 'attendant.' From it was derived the verb *therapeúein* 'attend, administer treatment to,' which itself produced two further derivatives: *therapeía* 'treatment,' which gave English *therapy*, and *therapeutés* 'person who administers treatment,' source of the adjective *therapeutikós*, from which English gets *therapeutic* [16].

**there** [OE] *There* was formed in prehistoric Germanic from the demonstrative base *\*tha-* (which also underlies English *that* and *then*) and the suffix *-r* used in making adverbs of place (it occurs also in English *here* and *where*). Its Germanic relatives include German *da*, Dutch *daar*, and Swedish and Danish *der*.

▶ here, the, then, where

**thermometer** [17] Greek *thérmē* meant 'heat' (it came from prehistoric Indo-European

*\*ghwerm-*, *\*ghworm-*, which probably also produced English *warm*). From it was formed French *thermomètre* (first recorded in 1624), which was borrowed into English in the early 1630s. The same source produced English *therm* [19] and *thermal* [18]; and *thermos* (from the related Greek *thermós* 'hot') was registered as a trademark for a vacuum flask in 1907.

▶ warm

**thesaurus** SEE TREASURE

**these** [13] The Old English plural of *this* was *thās* or *thōs*. This evolved into *those*, which came to be used as the plural of *that*, and it was replaced as the plural of *this* by *thise*, formed from *this* with the plural ending *-e*, which in due course turned into *these*.

▶ this

**thesis** [14] Greek *thésis* meant literally a 'placing' or 'laying down' (it was derived from the verb *tithénai* 'put, place,' which also gave English *apothecary*). It evolved metaphorically to 'proposition,' and passed in this sense via late Latin *thesis* into English.

▶ apothecary, bodega, boutique

**they** [12] Like *their* and *them*, *they* was borrowed from Old Norse. Its source was *their*, the plural form of the demonstrative adjective *sá*, and it replaced the native Old English pronoun *hīe*.

▶ their, them

**thick** [OE] *Thick* comes from a prehistoric Germanic *\*thekwia-*, which also produced German *dick*, Dutch *dik*, Swedish *tjock*, and Danish *tyk*. It is related to Welsh *tew* and Breton *teo* 'thick,' but its ultimate antecedents are not known. *Thicket* [OE] is a derivative.

**thief** [OE] *Thief* goes back to a prehistoric Germanic *\*theubaz*, which also produced German *dieb*, Dutch *dief*, Swedish *tjuf*, and Danish *tyv*. It is not clear where this came from, although it might be related to Lithuanian *tupeti* 'cower, squat' and Latvian *tupt* 'squat,' in which case it would denote etymologically 'crouching, furtive person.' From *\*theubaz* was derived *\*thiūbithō*, ancestor of modern English *theft*.

▶ theft

**thigh** [OE] The *thigh* is etymologically the 'plump' part of the leg. Together with Dutch *dij*, it evolved from a prehistoric Germanic *\*theukham*. This went back to Indo-European *\*teuk-*, *\*tauk-*, *\*tuk-*, which also produced Lithuanian *táukas* 'fat.' And these in turn were extensions of the base *\*tu-* 'swell,' source of English *thousand*, *thumb*, *tumour*, etc.

▶ thousand, thumb, tumour

**thimble** [OE] A *thimble* is etymologically a 'thumb implement.' The word goes back to Old English *thȳmel*, a derivative of *thūma* 'thumb.' In Old English (where it is recorded only once) it was used for a 'fingerstall.' By the time it reappears in the 15th century we find it being applied to a 'leather finger-protector used for pushing in a needle,' and it was extended to metal thimbles, introduced in the 17th century.

▶ thumb

**thin** [OE] *Thin* denotes etymologically 'stretched.' It goes back ultimately to the Indo-European base *\*ten-* 'stretch,' which also produced Latin *tenuis* 'thin' (source of English *tenuous*) and Latin *tendere* 'stretch' (source of English *tend, tense*, etc). From this was descended prehistoric Germanic *\*thunnuz*, which has evolved into German *dünn*, Dutch *dun*, Swedish *tunn*, Danish *tynd*, and English *thin*.

▶ tend, tense, tenuous

**thing** [OE] The ancestral meaning of *thing* is 'time': it goes back to a prehistoric Germanic *\*thingam*, which was related to Gothic *theihs* 'time,' and may come ultimately from the Indo-European base *\*ten-* 'stretch' (source of English *tend, tense*, etc). In Germanic it evolved semantically via 'appointed time' to 'judicial or legislative assembly.' This was the meaning it originally had in English, and it survives in other Germanic languages (the Icelandic parliament is known as the *Althing*, literally 'general assembly'). In English, however, it moved on through 'subject for discussion at such an assembly' to 'subject in general, affair, matter' and finally 'entity, object.' (The ancient meaning 'assembly' is preserved in fossilized form in English *husting*, etymologically a 'house assembly').

▶ husting

**think** [OE] *Think* goes back to an Old English *thencan*. This was a variant of *thyncan* 'seem, appear,' which survives in the archaic *methinks* (literally 'it seems to me'), and so etymologically *think* probably carries the notion of 'causing images, reflections, etc to appear to oneself, in one's brain.' The noun *thought* comes from the same prehistoric Germanic base as produced the verb (as does English *thank*). Related Germanic forms include German and Dutch *denken*, Swedish *tänka*, and Danish *tænke*.

▶ thank, thought

**third** [OE] *Third* goes back ultimately to an Indo-European *\*tritjos*, an ordinal derivative of the base that produced English *three*. Amongst its other descendants were Greek *trítos*, Latin *tertius* (source of English *tertiary* [16]), Russian *tretij*, Polish *trzeci*, Latvian *trešais*, and Welsh *tryddydd*. In prehistoric Germanic it became *\*thrithjaz*, which has evolved into German *dritte*, Dutch *derde*, Swedish and Danish *tredje*, and English *third*.

▶ three

**thirst** [OE] The etymological notion underlying the word *thirst* is of being 'dry.' For it goes back ultimately to the Indo-European base *\*trs, \*tors-* 'dry,' which also produced Latin *torrēre* 'parch' (source of English *toast, torrid*, etc). From this was formed the prehistoric West Germanic noun *\*thurstu*, which has

evolved into German *durst*, Dutch *dorst*, and English *thirst*.

▶ terrace, toast, torrid

**this** [OE] *This* is descended from the neuter form of the Old English demonstrative adjective and pronoun whose masculine form was *thes*. It was formed in the prehistoric Germanic period from the demonstrative base *\*tha-* (source also of English *that, there*, etc) and a suffix *\*-se* which had the function of indicating a specific thing.

▶ the, those

**thong** [OE] Etymologically, a *thong* is something that 'binds' up. The word comes from a prehistoric Germanic *\*thwangg-*, which also produced German *zwang* 'constraint.' In the Old English period it was *thwong*; it began to lose its *w* in the 13th century.

**thorn** [OE] *Thorn* is an ancient word, which goes all the way back to an Indo-European *\*trnus*. The Germanic descendant of this was *\*thurnuz*, which evolved into German *dorn*, Dutch *doorn*, Swedish and Danish *torn*, and English *thorn*.

**thorough** [OE] *Thorough* is ultimately the same word as *through*. Both go back to Old English *thurh* 'through.' In its single-syllable form it has stuck to its original role as a preposition and adverb, but in the case of *thorough* this has now virtually died out, leaving only the adjective, which evolved in the 13th century from the notion of going 'through' something so as to affect every part.

▶ thrill, through

**those** [OE] Originally, *those* was the plural of *this*. It did not move across to *that* until the Middle English period, gradually replacing its previous plural *thō*. The game of musical chairs was completed by *these*, which was a new formation based on *this*.

▶ this

**though** [12] English borrowed *though* from Old Norse *thōh*, and by the end of the 15th century it had virtually wiped out the related native form, which went back to Old English *thēah*.

Both came from a prehistoric Germanic adverb formed from the demonstrative base *\*tha-* (source also of English *that, there*, etc) and a suffix meaning 'and.' Modern Germanic relatives include German and Dutch *doch*.

▶ the

**thought** [OE] *Thought* comes from a prehistoric Germanic noun *\*gathangkht-*, which was formed from the same base as produced English *think*. Its modern Germanic relatives include German *gedächtnis* 'memory' and Dutch *gedachte* 'thought.'

▶ thank, think

**thousand** [OE] *Thousand* is a compound noun of some antiquity, which seems to mean etymologically 'several hundreds.' Its first element probably comes from a base denoting 'increase' or 'multiplicity,' which also produced Latin *tumēre* 'swell' (source of English *tumour*) and Sanskrit *tuvi* 'much'; its second element is the same as the first element of English *hundred*. The combination resulted in a prehistoric Germanic *\*thusundi*, which evolved into German *tausend*, Dutch *duizend*, Swedish *tusen*, Danish *tusind*, and English *thousand*. It is shared by the Slavic languages – Russian, for instance, has *tysjacha*.

▶ hundred, thigh, thumb, tumour

**thrash**   see THRESHOLD

**thread**   [OE]   A *thread* is etymologically something 'twisted.' The word comes from a prehistoric Germanic *\*thrǣthuz*, which was derived from the base *\*thrǣ-* 'twist' (source also of English *throw*). Other descendants of *\*thrǣthuz* include Dutch *draad*, Swedish *tråd*, and Danish *traad* 'thread' and German *draht* 'wire.'

▶ throw

**threat**   [OE]   *Threat* originally meant 'trouble, oppression'; 'expression of an intention to do harm' is a secondary sense, which arose out of the notion of 'putting pressure' on someone. It came from a prehistoric base *\*thraut-*, *\*threut-*, *\*thrut-*, which probably went back to Indo-European *\*trud-* 'push, press' (source also of Latin *trūdere* 'thrust,' from which English gets *abstruse, intrude*, etc, and probably also of English *thrust*).

▶ abstruse, intrude

**three**   [OE]   *Three* goes back to a prehistoric Indo-European *\*trejes*, which also produced Greek *treis*, Latin *trēs*, Russian *tri*, Sanskrit *tráyas*, etc. Its Germanic descendant was *\*thrijiz*, which has evolved into German *drei*, Dutch *drie*, Swedish and Danish *tre*, and English *three*. Amongst *three*'s many relations in English are *treble, trellis* [14] (etymologically something made from 'three threads'), *trinity, trio* [18], *triple, tripod* [17] (etymologically something with 'three feet'), *trivial* and possibly also *travail* and *tribe*.

▶ drill, testament, third, travail, treble, trellis, tribe, trinity, trio, triple, tripod, trivet, trivial

**threshold**   [OE]   The first element of *threshold* is identical with English *thresh* [OE]. This seems to go back ultimately to a prehistoric source that denoted 'making noise' (the apparently related Old Church Slavonic *tresku* meant 'crash,' and Lithuanian has *treškéti* 'crack, rattle'). By the time it reached Germanic, as *\*thresk-*, it was probably being used for 'stamp the feet noisily,' and it is this secondary notion of 'stamping' or 'treading' that lies behind *threshold* – as being something you 'tread' on as you go through a door. *Thresh* by the time it reached English had specialized further still, to mean 'separate grains from husks by stamping,' and this later evolved to simply 'separate grains from

husks.' *Thrash* [OE], which originated as a variant of *thresh*, has taken the further semantic step to 'beat, hit.' It is not known where the second element of *threshold* came from.

▶ thrash, thresh

**thrift**   see THRIVE

**thrill**   [13]   Etymologically, *thrill* denotes 'make a hole in.' It is a Middle English alteration of Old English *thȳrlian* 'pierce,' a derivative of *thȳrl* 'hole' (source of the second syllable of *nostril*). And this in turn was formed from *thurh* 'through.' The notion of 'making a hole' led in the 16th century to the metaphorical 'pierce with emotion,' but the narrowing down of this to 'fill with pleasure' seems to be a comparatively recent development, from the late 19th century. Its earlier wider connotations are preserved in the derivative *thriller* 'exciting story' [19].

▶ nostril, through

**thrive**   [13]   *Thrive* was borrowed from Old Norse *thrífask* 'grasp for oneself,' hence 'prosper,' the reflexive form of *thrífa* 'grasp, seize' (whose origins are not known). The word's semantic development from 'grasp for oneself' to 'prosper' was presumably inspired by the notion of 'accumulating resources.' *Thrift* [13], borrowed from the Old Norse derivative *thrift*, originally meant 'thriving'; the modern sense 'frugality' evolved in the 16th century – frugality being thought of as a prerequisite for prosperity.

▶ thrift

**throat**   [OE]   *Throat* comes from a prehistoric Germanic base *\*thrut-* or *\*thrūt-*. This also produced Old English *thrūtian* 'swell,' and a related base *\*strut-* was the source of the now defunct Middle English *strouten* 'bulge, swell' (not to mention Dutch *strot* 'throat'), so it has been speculated that the underlying etymological meaning of *throat* is 'swollen part' – an allusion no doubt to the bulge of the Adam's apple. *Throttle* [14] is probably a derivative of *throat*.

▶ throttle

**throng**   [13]   The etymological notion underlying *throng* is of 'pressing together.' It was borrowed from Old Norse *throng* 'crowd,' which went back ultimately to the prehistoric Germanic base *\*thringg-* 'press' (source also of German *drang* 'crowd, pressure' and *dringen* 'press'). Amongst its non-Germanic relatives is Old Persian *thraxta-* 'closely-packed.'

**throttle**   see THROAT

**through**   [OE]   *Through* comes from a prehistoric West Germanic *\*thurkh*, which also produced German *durch* and Dutch *door*. Its ultimate source was the Indo-European base *\*tr-*, which also produced Latin *trans* 'across.' *Thorough* is historically the same word as *through*.

▶ nostril, thorough, thrill

**throw** [OE] Old English *thrāwan* meant 'twist, turn.' It came from a prehistoric Germanic *\*thrējan*, which also produced German *drehen* 'turn.' This in turn went back to the Indo-European base *\*ter-*, whose other descendants include Greek *teírein* 'wear out,' Latin *terere* 'rub' (source of English *attrition* [14], *contrition* [13], and *trite* [16]), Lithuanian *trinù* 'rub, file, saw,' Welsh *taradr* 'auger,' and English *thread* and *turn*. It is not clear how the original sense 'twist, turn' (which survives in 'throwing a pot' on a potter's wheel) evolved in English into 'project, hurl' (first recorded in the 13th century), but presumably there must have been some intermediate phase such as 'throw with a twisting action - as in throwing the discus.'

▶ attrition, contrition, thread, trite, turn

**thrush** *Thrush* the bird [OE] and *thrush* the disease [17] are presumably different words, although the origins of the latter are obscure. The bird-name goes back to a prehistoric Germanic *\*thruskjōn*, and has relatives in Latin *turdus* 'thrush' (source of English *sturdy*), German *drossel* 'thrush,' and the now archaic English *throstle* 'thrush.' The first record we have of *thrush* the disease is in Samuel Pepys's diary, for 17 June 1665: 'He hath a fever, a thrush, and a hickup.' It may have been of Scandinavian origin (Danish has *troske* for a similar disease).

**thrust** [12] *Thrust* was borrowed from Old Norse *thrýsta* 'thrust, compress.' It probably goes back ultimately to the Indo-European base *\*trud-* 'push, press,' whose other descendants include Latin *trūdere* 'thrust' (source of English *abstruse, intrude*, etc) and probably also English *threat*.

**thug** [19] Hindi *thag* means literally 'robber, cheat' (it is descended from Sanskrit *sthaga* 'robber,' a derivative of *sthagati* 'cover, hide,' which goes back ultimately to the Indo-European base *\*steg-*, *\*teg-* 'cover,' source also of English *deck, detect, integument, protect, thatch*, etc). It came to be applied to members of a band of professional thieves and murderers in India, whose preferred method of dispatching their victims was strangulation (their other name was *phansigar*, literally 'strangler'); and English took it over in the 1830s as a general term for a 'brutally violent person.'

▶ deck, detect, protect, thatch

**thumb** [OE] The *thumb* is etymologically the 'swollen' part – an allusion to its greater thickness than the other fingers. Along with its relatives German *daumen* and Dutch *duim*, it goes back to a prehistoric West Germanic *\*thūmon*. This in turn can be traced to Indo-European *\*tum-* 'swell,' which also produced English *tumour* and *tumult*. The *b* in *thumb* appeared in the early Middle English period, when it was still a two-syllable word (*thumbe*), and at first was pronounced, but it has fallen silent over the centuries.

▶ thigh, thimble, tumour, tumult

**thunder** [OE] Etymologically, *thunder* is nothing more than 'noise.' In common with German *donner*, Dutch *donder*, and Danish *torden*, it goes back to a prehistoric Germanic *\*thonara-*. This was descended from the Indo-European base *\*ton-*, *\*tn-* 'resound,' which also produced the Latin verb *tonāre* 'thunder' (source of English *astound, detonate*, and *stun*) and the Latin noun *tonitrus* 'thunder' (source of French *tonnerre* 'thunder'). *Thursday* is etymologically the 'day of thunder.'

▶ astound, detonate, stun, Thursday, tornado

**Thursday** [OE] The Romans called the fourth day of the week *diēs Iovis* 'Jupiter's day.' When the Germanic peoples took over their system of naming days after the gods, or the planets they represented, they replaced Jupiter, the Roman sky-god, with the Germanic god of thunder, Thor, whose name comes from the same source as English *thunder*. This produced a prehistoric Germanic *\*thonaras daga-*, which evolved into Old English *thunresdæg*. The modern form *Thursday* is partly due to association with Old Norse *thórsdagr*.

▶ thunder

**thus** [OE] *Thus* is something of a mystery word. It presumably belongs to the family of words (*that, there*, etc) that go back to the prehistoric Germanic demonstrative base *\*tha-*, but how its fits into the family tree is not clear. Its only close relative is Dutch *dus* 'thus.'

**thwart** [13] *Thwart* was originally an adverb and adjective, meaning 'across, crosswise.' It was however used as a verb, meaning 'obstruct' (from the metaphorical notion of 'crossing' someone) as early as the 13th century. It was borrowed from Old Norse *thvert*, the neuter form of *thverr* 'transverse.' This went back to a prehistoric Germanic *\*thwerkhwaz* (possible source also of English *queer*), which in turn was descended from Indo-European *\*twork-*, *\*twerk-* 'twist' (source also of English *torch, torment, torture*, etc). How the noun *thwart* 'seat across a boat' [18] fits into the picture is not altogether clear. Its modern meaning clearly connects it with *thwart* 'across,' but the notion of 'crosswise' may have been a secondary development. For an earlier noun *thought* 'seat in a boat' existed, which came ultimately from Old English *thofta* 'rower's bench,' and it could be that *thwart* the modern English noun represents a blending, both formal and semantic, of *thwart* 'across' with the now obsolete *thought*.

▶ queer, torch, torment, torture

**thyroid** [18] The thyroid glands are situated in the neck, and they get their name ultimately from a comparison of the shape of the large oblong cartilage in front of the throat (which includes the Adam's apple) with that of a door. The word comes via early modern French *thyroide* from Greek *thuroidés* 'door-shaped,' an alteration of *thureoeidḗs*, which was derived from *thúrā* 'door' (a relative of English *door*). The term *khóndros thureoiedḗs*, literally 'door-shaped cartilage,' was used by the Greek physician Galen for the 'cartilage in front of the throat' (now known in English as the *thyroid cartilage*).

▶ door, foreign

**tick**    English now has no fewer than four distinct words *tick* in general use. The oldest, *tick* 'mite' [OE], comes from a prehistoric West Germanic *\*tik-*, which may be related to Armenian *tiz* 'bug.' *Tick* 'sound of a clock, mark of correctness, etc' [13] originally meant broadly 'light touch, tap'; its modern uses are secondary and comparatively recent developments ('sound of a clock' appears to have evolved in the 16th century, and 'mark of correctness' did not emerge until the 19th century). *Tickle* [14] is probably a derivative. *Tick* 'mattress case' [15] was borrowed from Middle Dutch *tēke*, which went back via Latin *thēca* to Greek *thḗkē* 'cover, case.' And *tick* 'credit' [17] (as in *on tick*) is short for *ticket*.

▶ tickle / ticket

**ticket**    [16]    *Ticket* was adapted from early modern French *étiquet* 'ticket, label,' whose present-day descendant *étiquette* has given English *etiquette*. The etymological notion underlying *étiquet* was of 'sticking' a label on, for it was derived ultimately from the Old French verb *estiquier* 'stick,' a borrowing from Middle Dutch *steken* 'stick' – to which English *stick* is related.

▶ etiquette, stick

**tickle**    see TICK

**tide**    [OE]    *Tide* originally meant 'time' – as in the tautologous 'time and tide wait for no man.' Like the related German *zeit*, Dutch *tijd*, and Swedish and Danish *tid*, all of which mean 'time,' it comes from a prehistoric Germanic *\*tīdiz*. This was derived from the base *\*tī-* (source also of English *time*), which in turn went back to the Indo-European base *\*dī-* 'divide, cut up' – so etymologically the word denotes 'time cut up, portion of time.' This notion of a 'period' or 'season' is preserved in now rather archaic expression such as *Christmastide*, *Whitsuntide*, and *noontide*. The application to the rise and fall of the sea, which emerged in the 14th century, is due to the influence of the related Middle Low German *tīde* and Middle Dutch *ghetīde*, where it presumably arose from the notion of the 'fixed time' of the high and low points of the tide. *Betide* [13] was formed from the now archaic verb *tide* 'happen,' a derivative of the noun.

▶ betide, tidy, time

**tidings**    [OE]    *Tidings* is etymologically 'that which happens.' It is closely related to English *tide*, in the sense 'happen' (as in *betide*). It was adapted from Old Norse *títhendi* 'happenings, events, news,' a deriv-

ative of the adjective *títhr* 'happening.' A similar semantic development from 'events' to 'news of events' lies behind the related German *zeitung* 'newspaper.'

**tidy**    [13]    *Tidy* originally meant 'timely, seasonable' (it was a derivative of *tide*, in the now superannuated sense 'time, season'). It early on evolved metaphorically to 'good-looking,' and hence 'good,' but the modern sense 'neat' did not emerge until the 18th century. *Titivate* [19] may have been based on *tidy*.

▶ tide, titivate

**tie**    [OE]    *Tie* comes from a prehistoric Germanic *\*taugian*. This was derived from the base *\*taukh-*, *\*teuk-* 'pull' (source also of English *team* and *tug* and closely related to *tow*). And this in turn went back to Indo-European *\*deuk-*, which also produced Latin *dūcere* 'lead' (source of English *duct*, *duke*, etc). The use of the noun *tie* for a 'necktie' dates from the mid 18th century.

▶ duct, duke, educate, team, teem, tow, tug

**tiger**    [13]    English got *tiger* via Old French *tigre* and Latin *tigris* from Greek *tígris*, a word presumably of oriental origin. It was originally taken over directly from Latin in the Old English period as *tigras*, but this did not survive.

**tight**    [14]    *Tight* originally meant 'dense' ('His squire rode all night in a wood that was full tight,' *Torrent of Portugal* 1435). It appears to have been an alteration of an earlier *thight* 'dense, thickset,' which was borrowed from Old Norse *théttr* 'watertight, dense.' And this, like German and Dutch *dicht* 'dense, close,' came from a prehistoric Germanic *\*thingkhtaz*, whose other relatives include Lithuanian *tankus* 'thick, standing close together,' Irish *contēcim* 'coagulate,' and Sanskrit *tañc-* 'contract.' The sense 'firmly fixed' developed in the 16th century, 'drunk' in the 19th century.

**tilde**    see TITLE

**tile**    [OE]    A *tile* is etymologically a 'cover.' The word comes ultimately from Latin *tēgula* 'tile,' a derivative of the same Indo-European base as produced English *deck* and *thatch* and Latin *tegere* 'cover' (source of English *detect*, *protect*, etc). *Tēgula* was borrowed into prehistoric West Germanic as *\*tegala*, which evolved into German *ziegel*, Dutch *tegel*, and English *tile*.

▶ deck, detect, protect, thatch, toga

**till**    English has three distinct words *till*, but two of them are probably related. The etymological notion underlying *till* 'cultivate the soil' [OE] is of 'striving to obtain a goal.' Indeed, that is what its Old English ancestor *tilian* originally meant; 'cultivate' is a late Old English development, via an intermediate 'labour.' The verb comes from a prehistoric Germanic *\*tilōjan*, a derivative of the noun *\*tilam* 'aim, purpose' (source of German *ziel* 'goal'). This passed into Old English as *till* 'fixed point,' which seems to have been converted into a preposition meaning 'up to a particular point (originally in space, but soon also in time).' The compound *until* dates from the 13th century; its first element was borrowed from Old Norse *\*und* 'till.' The origins of *till* 'money box' [15] are uncertain.

**tiller**   see TOIL

**tilt**   [14]   *Tilt* originally meant 'fall over'; the sense 'slant' is not recorded before the 16th century. The word is probably descended from an unrecorded Old English *\*tyltan*, whose ultimate source would have been the prehistoric Germanic adjective *\*taltaz* 'unsteady' (ancestor also of Swedish *tulta* 'totter'). *Tilt* 'joust' (first recorded in the 16th century) has traditionally been regarded as the same word, based presumably on the notion of making one's opponent 'fall over,' but this is not certain.

**timber**   [OE]   *Timber* originally denoted a 'building' – the Lindisfarne Gospels of around 950 translated Mark 13:1 ('See what manner of stones and what buildings are here') as 'See what stones and what timber.' It comes from a prehistoric Germanic *\*timram*, whose German descendant *zimmer* 'room' has remained closer to its semantic roots (but German *zimmermann* means 'carpenter'). And this in turn went back to Indo- European *\*demrom*, a derivative of the base *\*dem-*, *\*dom-* 'build,' from which English also gets *dome, domestic*, etc. The sense 'building' gradually developed into 'building material,' then 'wood used for building,' and finally 'wood' in general.

▶ dome, domestic

**timbre**   see TIMPANI

**time**   [OE]   *Time* originally denoted 'delimited section of existence, period.' Its ultimate source is the Indo-European base *\*dī-* 'cut up, divide.' This passed into prehistoric Germanic as *\*tī-* (source also of English *tide*), and addition of the suffix *\*-mon-* produced *\*tīmon* – whence English *time* and Swedish *timme* 'hour.' The application of the word to the more generalized, abstract notion of 'continuous duration' dates from the 14th century.

▶ tide

**timid**   [16]   The Latin verb *timēre* meant 'fear' (its origins are not known). From it were derived the adjective *timidus* (source of English *timid*) and the noun *timor* 'fear' (whose medieval Latin descendant *timorōsus* 'fearful' gave English *timorous* [15]).

▶ timorous

**timpani**   [16]   *Timpani* was borrowed from Italian, where it is the plural of *timpano* 'kettledrum.' This in turn went back via Latin *tympanum* 'drum' (source of English *tympanum* 'ear-drum' [17]) to Greek *túmpanon* 'drum,' a close relative of the verb *túptein* 'hit.' Part of the same word-family is *timbre* 'sound-quality' [19],

whose French antecedent meant 'bell hit with a hammer.'

▶ timbre, tympanum

**tin**   [OE]   *Tin* is a general Germanic word, with relatives in German *zinn*, Dutch and Danish *tin*, and Swedish *tenn*. These point to a common ancestor *\*tinam*, but where this came from is not known. The word was first used for a 'tin can' in the early 19th century. *Tinker* may be related.

**tincture**   see TINGE

**tinder**   [OE]   *Tinder*, and its relatives German *zunder*, Dutch *tonder*, and Swedish *tunder*, go back to a prehistoric Germanic base *\*tund-* 'ignite, kindle,' which also produced German *anzünden*, Swedish *upptända*, and Danish *antænde* 'kindle.' Its ultimate origins are not known. The now clichéd *tinder-dry* is first recorded in Rudyard Kipling's *Light That Failed* 1891: 'the tinder-dry clumps of scrub.'

**tinge**   [15]   Etymologically, *tinge* denotes 'soak, moisten.' That is what its Latin source, *tingere*, originally meant. The notion of 'colour' comes from a secondary Latin sense, 'dye,' which arose from the concept of 'dipping in liquid dye.' The Latin past participle, *tinctus*, lies behind English *taint* [14], *tincture* [14], and *tint* [18].

▶ taint, tincture, tint

**tinker**   [13]   Etymologically, a *tinker* is probably a 'worker in tin.' It could well be descended from an unrecorded Old English *\*tinecere*, a plausible derivative of *tin*. There is an alternative possibility, however: it may have been derived from the now obsolete verb *tink* 'tinkle' (which, like *tinkle* [14] itself, was of imitative origin), in allusion to the metallic sounds made by tinkers repairing pots (northern and Scottish dialects had the word *tinkler* for 'tinker').

**tinsel**   [16]   *Tinsel* is etymologically something that 'sparkles.' Its ultimate source is Latin *scintilla* 'spark,' which has also given English *scintillate* [17]. This was altered in the post-classical period to *\*stincilla*, which passed into Old French as *estincele* 'spark.' From this was derived the adjective *estincelé* 'sparkling,' which was applied particularly to fabric with metallic thread woven into it. English took this over as *tinselle*, originally an adjective but soon used as a noun. Its derogatory connotations of 'gaudiness' or 'cheap glamour' began to emerge in the 17th century.

▶ scintillate, stencil

**tint**   see TINGE

**tip**   English has three distinct words *tip*, two of them possibly related. *Tip* 'extremity' [15] was probably borrowed from Old Norse *typpi*. This was descended from prehistoric Germanic *\*tupp-* 'upper extremity' (source also of English *top* and *toupee*). *Tip* 'touch lightly' [13] (as in 'tip-and-run cricket') may have been borrowed from Low German *tippen*, although it could be the same word as *tip* 'extremity' (from the notion of 'just touching something with the tip of something else'). It was used in 17th-century underworld argot for 'give' (as in 'tip someone the wink'), and this evolved in the 18th century to 'give a gratuity.' The antecedents of *tip* 'overturn' [14] (originally *tipe*) are not known, although the fact that it first appeared in northern dialects suggests that it may have been borrowed from a Scandinavian language. The derived *tipsy* [16] denotes etymologically 'liable to fall over.'

▶ top, toupee / tipsy

**tire** [OE]   *Tire* is something of a mystery word. It was relatively common in the Old English period (where it originally meant 'fail, cease, come to an end' – 'become weary' is a secondary development), but then it disappeared, to return in the 14th century. Nor is anything certain known about its pre-English ancestry, although it may go back to the Indo-European base *\*deus-* (source also of Sanskrit *dosa-* 'fault, lack'). The use of the past participle *tired* as an adjective dates from the late 14th century.

**tissue** [14]   *Tissue* is etymologically 'woven' cloth. The word was borrowed from Old French *tissu* 'fine woven cloth,' which was a noun use of the past participle of *tistre* 'weave.' This in turn was descended from Latin *texere* 'weave' (source of English *text, texture*, etc). The application of the word to 'physiological substance' dates from the early 19th century. The original notion of weaving is preserved metaphorically in expressions such as 'tissue of lies.'

▶ technical, text, texture, toilet

**tit**   English has three separate words *tit*. The oldest, 'breast' [OE], belongs to a West Germanic family of terms for 'breast' or 'nipple' that also includes German *zitze* and Dutch *tit*: it presumably originated in imitation of a baby's sucking sounds. From Germanic it was borrowed into the Romance languages, giving Italian *tetta*, Spanish *teta*, Rumanian *tata*, and French *tette*. The Old French ancestor of this, *tete*, gave English *teat* [13], which gradually replaced *tit* as the 'polite' term. (*Titillate* [17] may be ultimately related.) *Tit* the bird [18] is short for *titmouse* [14]. This in turn was formed from an earlier and now defunct *tit*, used in compounds denoting 'small things' and probably borrowed from a Scandinavian language, and Middle English *mose* 'titmouse,' which came from a prehistoric Germanic *\*maisōn* (source also of German *meise* and Dutch *mees* 'tit'). And the *tit* [16] of *tit for tat* (which produced British rhyming slang *titfer* 'hat' [20]) originally denoted a 'light blow, tap,' and was presumably of onomatopoeic origin. (The *tit-* of *titbit* [17], incidentally, is probably a different word. It was originally *tid-* – as it still is in

American English – and it may go back ultimately to Old English *tiddre* 'frail.')

▶ teat, titillate / titmouse

**titchy** [20]   *Titchy* commemorates the 'Tichborne claimant,' the title given to Arthur Orton, who, in an English *cause célèbre* of the 1860s, returned from Australia claiming to be Roger Tichborne, the heir to an English baronetcy who had supposedly been lost at sea. The diminutive music-hall comedian Harry Relph (1868–1828) bore some resemblance to Orton, and so he acquired the nickname 'Little Tich.' This in due course spread to other small people (the tiny Kent and England leg-spinner A P Freeman (1888–1965) was called 'Tich'), but it does not appear to have been until the 1950s that *tich*, or *titch*, established itself as a colloquial generic term for a 'small person.' With it came the derived adjective *titchy*.

**tithe** [OE]   Originally, *tithe* meant simply a 'tenth' – a sense that has revived somewhat in recent years. The specific application to a 'ten per-cent levy on annual production, paid to the Church' dates from the 12th century. It comes from Old English *tēotha* 'tenth' (the modern English form *tenth* arose in the 12th century, through the influence of *ten*).

▶ ten

**titillate**   see TIT

**titivate**   see TIDY

**title** [13]   *Title* comes via Old French *title* from Latin *titulus* 'inscription on a tomb or altar, label, title.' Other contributions made by the Latin word to English include *entitle* [14], *tilde* [19], *tittle* [14], and *titular* [18].

▶ entitle, tilde, tittle, titular

**titmouse**   see TIT

**to** [OE]   *To* comes from a prehistoric West Germanic *\*tō*, which also produced German *zu* and Dutch *toe*. This went back ultimately to an Indo-European *\*do*, which also produced Russian *do* 'to.' *Too* is historically the same word as *to*.

▶ too

**toad** [OE]   *Toad* is a mystery word, with no known relatives in any other Indo-European language. Of its derivatives, *toady* [19] is short for the earlier *toad eater* 'sycophant' [17]. This originated in the dubious selling methods of itinerant quack doctors. They employed an assistant who pretended to eat a toad (toads were thought to be poisonous), so that the quack could appear to effect a miraculous cure with his medicine. The toad-eating assistant came to be a byword for 'servility' or 'dependency,' and hence for 'servile flattery.' *Toadstools* [14] were named for their stool-like shape, and also because of an association between poisonous fungi and the supposedly poisonous toad.

**toast** [14]   *Toast* comes via Old French *toster* 'roast, grill' from Vulgar Latin *\*tostāre*, a derivative of the past participle of Latin *torrēre* 'parch' (source of English *torrid*). Its use as a noun, meaning 'toasted bread,' dates from the 15th century. It was common to put sippets or croutons of spiced toast into drinks to improve their flavour, and it was the custom of gallants in the 17th century, when (as they frequently did) they drank the health of ladies, to say that the name of the lady in question enhanced the flavour of their drink better than any toast. That is supposedly the origin of the use of the term *toast* for 'drinking someone's health.'

▶ thirst, torrent, torrid

**tobacco** [16]   Tobacco was introduced to Europe from the Americas, and that is where its name came from too. It originated in a Carib word, and reached English via Spanish and Portuguese *tabaco*. What precisely the Carib word meant, however, is a matter of dispute. Some say that it referred to tobacco leaves rolled up into a cylindrical shape for smoking, while others maintain that it denoted a pipe for smoking the tobacco in. The word has spread to virtually all European languages (French *tabac*, German, Dutch, Russian, and Czech *tabak*, Welsh *tybaco*, etc), and only a few remnants of alternative terms remain: Rumanian *tutun* and Polish *tytun*, for instance, borrowings from Turkish *tütün*, which originally meant 'smoke,' and Breton *butun*, which came from *petȳ*, the word for 'tobacco' in the Guarani language of South America (source also of English *petunia* [19], a close relative of the tobacco plant).

**toccata**   see TOUCH

**tocsin**   see TOUCH

**today** [OE]   *Today* is simply a compound assembled from the preposition *to* (in the now obsolete sense 'at, on') and *day*. Parallel formations are Dutch *vandaag* (literally 'from or of day') and Swedish and Danish *i dag* ('in day'). In fact virtually all the terms for 'today' in the European languages contain an element meaning 'day,' but not all of them are as obvious as *today*, *vandaag*, and *i dag*. German *heute*, for instance, comes from a prehistoric Germanic *\*hiu tagu*, which meant literally 'on this day.' Russian *segodnja* likewise denotes etymologically 'this day.' And the second syllable of Latin *hodiē* 'today' (ancestor of French *aujourd'hui*, Italian *oggi*, and Spanish *hoy*) represents an inflected form of *diēs* 'day.' *Tomorrow* and *tonight* [OE] were formed on the same basis.

**toddy** [17]   *Toddy* originally meant 'palm sap.' It was an alteration of an earlier *tarry*, which was borrowed from Hindi *tārī*. This was a derivative of *tār* 'palm tree,' a descendant of Sanskrit *tāla* or *tāra*, which in turn was probably borrowed from a Dravidian language of southern India (Kannada has *tar*, Telugu *tādu*). This palm sap was used as a drink, often in a

potently fermented form, and in the 18th century *toddy* came to denote a hot spirit-based drink.

**toe** [OE]   Many European languages use the same word for 'finger' and 'toe' (Spanish *dedo*, for example, and Russian and Polish *palec*), and English *toe* may have originated in such a dual-purpose term. Its prehistoric Germanic ancestor was *\*taikhwōn*, and it has been speculated that this may be related to Latin *digitus* 'finger, toe' (source of English *digit*). Other descendants of the Germanic form include German *zehe*, Dutch *tee*, Swedish *tåa*, and Danish *taa*.

▶ digit

**toff** [19]   *Toff* probably originated as an alteration of *tuft* [14], which was used from the 18th century as an Oxford University slang term for a 'titled undergraduate' (students who came from noble families wore a gold tassel or 'tuft' on their caps). *Tuft* itself was adapted from Old French *tofe* or *toffe* 'tuft,' a word of Germanic origin.

▶ tuft

**toffee** [19]   *Toffee* is one of the mystery words of English. It is an alteration of an earlier *taffy* [19] (still current in American English), but where that came from is not known. The early 19th-century spelling *toughy* suggests that it may have been derived from *tough*, in allusion to the sweet's texture, but it is probably only a later folk-etymologizing rationalization. Another possibility is that it came from *tafia* 'rumlike drink made from molasses' [18], an alteration of *ratafia* [17], which was of West Indian Creole origin.

**toga**   see PROTECT

**together** [OE]   The etymological notion underlying *together* is of 'gathering' things into one group. It was formed from the preposition *to* and the element *\*gad-* denoting 'association, company,' which also lies behind *gather*.

▶ gather

**toil**   English has two words *toil*, one of them now used only in the plural. *Toil* 'work' comes via Anglo-Norman *toiler* 'stir, agitate, wrangle' from Latin *tudiculāre* 'stir around.' This was derived from *tudicula* 'mill for crushing olives,' a diminutive form of *tudes* 'hammer,' which went back to the prehistoric base *\*tud-* 'hit,' source also of Latin *tundere* 'beat, crush,' which gave English *abstruse*, *protrude*, etc. *Toils* 'entanglements' represents a plural use of the now archaic *toil* 'net' [16]. This denoted etymologically 'something woven': it came via Old French *toile* from Latin *tēla*, a contraction of an earlier *\*texla*, which was derived from the base *\*tex-* 'weave' (source of English *text*, *textile*, etc). *Toilet* [16] was borrowed from French *toilette*, a diminutive form of *toile*. It originally meant 'cloth cover,' but it gradually evolved via 'cloth cover for a dressing table' to 'the act of dressing and grooming oneself.' The sense 'lavatory' emerged in mid 19th-century

America, from the now obsolete 'dressing room (with lavatory attached),' inspired no doubt by the same delicacy that produced American English *bathroom* 'lavatory.' Another member of the same word-family is *tiller* [15], which came via Anglo-Norman *telier* 'weaver's beam' from medieval Latin *tēlārium*, a derivative of *tēla*.

▶ abstruse, protrude / technical, text, textile, texture, tiller, tissue, toilet

**token** [OE] A *token* is etymologically something that 'shows' you something. It comes from a prehistoric Germanic *\*taiknam*, which also produced German *zeichen* 'sign.' This in turn was formed from a base *\*taik-* 'show,' which also produced English *teach*.

▶ teach

**tolerate** [16] To *tolerate* something is etymologically to 'bear' it. The word comes from the past participle of Latin *tolerāre* 'bear, tolerate.' This in turn was formed from a base *\*tol-* 'lift, carry,' which also underlies English *extol* [15].

▶ extol

**toll** *Toll* 'charge, payment' [OE] and *toll* 'ring a bell' [15] are distinct words. The former was borrowed into Old English from medieval Latin *tolōneum* 'place where tolls are collected,' an alteration of late Latin *telōneum*. This in turn was borrowed from Greek *telṓnion*, a derivative of *télos* 'tax.' The ancestry of *toll* 'ring a bell' is more conjectural. It may be the same word as the long-obsolete *toll* 'pull,' which went back to an Old English *\*tollian*.

**tombola** see TUMBLE

**tomboy** [16] *Tomboy* originally denoted a 'rude or boisterous boy,' but before the end of the 16th century it was being applied to a 'girl who behaves like a boisterous boy.' *Tom* (the familiar form of *Thomas*) is presumably being used to denote 'maleness' (here 'typical male aggressiveness').

**tome** [16] *Tome* comes via French *tome* and Latin *tomus* from Greek *tómos*. This originally meant 'slice, piece' (it went back to the prehistoric Indo-European base *\*tom-*, *\*tem-* 'cut,' which is also responsible for English *temple*, *tonsorial* [19], *tonsure* [14], and the surgical suffix *-tomy* 'cutting'), but it was extended metaphorically to a 'cut roll of paper' and eventually to a 'volume, book.'

▶ temple, tonsorial, tonsure

**tomorrow** [OE] *Tomorrow* was formed (following the model of *today*) from the preposition *to* (here in the sense 'at, on') and *morgenne*, the dative form of Old English *morgen* 'morning,' which has evolved into modern English *morn* and *morrow*.

▶ morning

**ton** [14] *Ton* originated as a variant of *tun* 'barrel' [OE]. At first it was used for a unit of capacity, equal to

the space occupied by a tun of wine, but by the end of the 15th century we find it being applied to a unit of weight. *Tun* itself was acquired from medieval Latin *tunna*, which was probably of Gaulish origin. Another of its descendants was Old French *tonne*, whose diminutive *tonel* was borrowed into English as *tunnel* [15]. This was originally used for a 'tubular net for catching birds,' and then for a 'chimney flue' or 'funnel.' It was not applied to an 'underground passage' until as recently as the late 18th century.

▶ tun, tunnel

**tone** [14] English acquired *tone* via Old French *ton* and Latin *tonus* from Greek *tónos* 'stretching, tension,' hence 'sound.' This in turn went back to the Indo-European base *\*ton-*, *\*ten-* 'stretch,' which also produced English *tend*, *tense*, *thin*, etc. The semantic transference from 'tension' to 'sound' may have arisen from the notion of tightening the strings of a musical instrument, but it could also be due to association with another Indo-European base *\*ton-*, meaning 'resound' (source of English *thunder*). The derivative *tonic* [17] comes ultimately from Greek *tonikós*. *Tune* is an unexplained variant of *tone*.

▶ tend, tense, tenuous, thin, tune

**tongs** [OE] The etymological notion underlying the word *tongs* is of 'biting.' It comes from a prehistoric Germanic *\*tanguz* (source also of German *zange*, Dutch and Danish *tang*, and Swedish *tång*), which went back ultimately to the Indo-European base *\*dank-* 'bite' (ancestor of Greek *dáknein* 'bite'). (*Tong* 'Chinese secret society' [19], incidentally, comes from Cantonese *tong* 'assembly hall.')

**tongue** [OE] *Tongue* is a general Germanic word, with relatives in German *zunge*, Dutch *tong*, Swedish *tonga*, and Danish *tonge*. These all evolved from a prehistoric Germanic *\*tunggōn*, whose ultimate ancestor was Indo-European *\*dnghwā-*. This also produced Latin *lingua* 'tongue, language' (source of English *language*, *linguistic*, etc), Welsh *tafod* 'tongue,' Russian *jazyk* 'tongue,' etc.

▶ language, linguistic

**tonsorial** see TOME

**tonsure** see TOME

**too** [16] *Too* is historically the same word as *to*, but the two were not differentiated orthographically until the 16th century. The sense 'also' comes from the notion of addition implicit in putting something 'to' something else; and 'addition' led on to 'excess.'

▶ to

**tool** [OE] A *tool* is etymologically an implement used to 'make' something. It came from a prehistoric Germanic *\*tōwlam*. This was derived from a base *\*tōw-*, *\*taw-*, which produced a variety of other words with the general sense 'make, prepare, do' (most of them have now died out, but survivors include Dutch *touwen* and English *taw* 'make leather').

▶ taw, tow

**tooth** [OE] Etymologically, a *tooth* is an 'eater.' Its ultimate source is the prehistoric Indo-European base *ed- 'eat,' which also lies behind English *eat* and *edible*. From this was formed the noun *dont-, *dent- 'tooth,' whose descendants include Latin *dēns* 'tooth' (source of English *dentist, indent, trident* [16], etc), Greek *odón* 'tooth' (source of English *odontology* [19]), Welsh *dant* 'tooth,' and prehistoric Germanic *tanthuz*. This evolved into German *zahn*, Dutch, Swedish, and Danish *tand*, and English *tooth*. A variant of *tanthuz* may lie behind English *tusk*.

▶ dentist, eat, edible, indent, odontology, trident, tusk

**top** English apparently has two distinct words *top*. The one meaning 'uppermost part' [OE] came from a prehistoric Germanic *toppaz*, whose original meaning seems to have been 'tuft of hair on top of the head, topknot': this sense survived into English, although it has now died out, and amongst the other descendants of *toppaz* are German *zopf* 'plait.' The Germanic word was borrowed into Old French as *top* or *toup* 'tuft of hair,' which is the ultimate source of English *toupee* [18]. And a variant of the base from which it was formed may lie behind English *tip*. *Topple* [16] is a derivative of *top*.

It is generally assumed that *top* 'spinning toy' [11] is a different word, but it is not known where it came from.

▶ tip, topple, toupée

**topic** [16] Greek *tópos* meant 'place.' From it was derived the adjective *topikós* 'of a place,' which came to mean 'commonplace.' Aristotle used it in the title of his treatise *Tà topiká*, which contains commonplace arguments, and it was with direct reference to this that the word first arrived in English (via Latin *topica*). The sense 'subject, theme' arose in the 18th century from the notion of the various heads of argument contained in *Tà topiká* and works like it. The derived *topical* [16] originally meant 'of topics'; the specialization to 'of topics of the day, of current interest' is as recent as the second half of the 19th century. The word's original notion of 'place' is preserved in *topography* [15] and *topology* [17].

The diminutive form of Greek *tópos* was *tópion* 'small place,' hence 'field.' Latin took over its plural as *topia*, and used it for 'ornamental gardening.' From it was derived the adjective *topiārius*, which forms the basis of English *topiary* [16].

▶ topiary, topography

**topple** see TOP

**torch** [13] A *torch* is etymologically something 'twisted.' The word comes via Old French *torche* from

Vulgar Latin *torca*, which was derived from the Latin verb *torquēre* 'twist' (source also of English *torment, torture*, etc). The notion underlying the word is of pieces of straw or similar material 'twisted' together and then dipped in some inflammable material. That is what it still denotes in American English, but in British English it has been reapplied to a battery-driven alternative to this.

▶ torment, torque, torture

**torment** [13] The notion underlying *torment* is of an instrument of torture worked by 'twisting.' The word was borrowed from Latin *tormentum* 'instrument of torture,' hence 'torture, great suffering.' This was a contraction of an earlier *torquementum*, a derivative of *torquēre* 'twist,' which has also given English *contort* [15], *extort* [16], *retort* [16], *torch, torque* [19], *torsion* [15], *tort* [14], *tortuous* [15], and *torture* [16] (literally 'twisting').

▶ contort, extort, retort, thwart, torch, torque, torsion, tort, torture

**tornado** [16] *Tornado* appears to denote etymologically something that 'turns,' but this is due to a piece of English folk-etymologizing. Its actual source is Spanish *tronada* 'thunderstorm,' a derivative of the verb *tronar* 'thunder' (which in turn went back to Latin *tonāre* 'thunder,' source of English *astonish, detonate*, etc). It was at first used in English for a 'violent thunderstorm,' but confusion with Spanish *tornado* 'turned' had converted *tronada* into *tornado*, and as early as the 1620s we find it being applied to a 'whirlwind.'

▶ thunder

**torpid** [17] *Torpid* was acquired from Latin *torpidus*, a derivative of *torpēre* 'be stiff, numb, inactive, etc.' Also from *torpēre* came *torpēdō*, which was applied to a type of fish capable of producing an electric shock with which it numbs its prey. English adopted the term as *torpedo* [16]. The fish is long and thin, and in the 1860s its name was applied to an underwater self-propelled missile which shares its shape, and its disconcerting effect on enemies (it had earlier, from the late 18th century, been used for a sort of underwater mine).

▶ torpedo

**torrent** [17] Despite its firm connections with 'water,' *torrent* comes from a source that meant 'scorch, parch.' This was Latin *torrēre*, which also produced English *toast* and *torrid* [16] and is related to *thirst*. Its present participle *torrēns* was used metaphorically as an adjective of streams that 'boil' or 'bubble' because of their strong current, and it was in this sense that it passed as a noun via Italian *torrente* and French *torrent* into English.

▶ thirst, toast, torrid

**torsion**    see TORMENT

**tort**    see TORMENT

**tortoise**    see TURTLE

**tortuous**    see TORMENT

**torture**    see TORMENT

**Tory**    [17]    The term *tory* originally denoted an Irish guerrilla, one of a group of Irishmen who in the 1640s were thrown off their property by the British and took to a life of harrying and plundering the British occupiers (it is an anglicization of Irish *\*tóraighe* 'pursuer,' which was derived from *tóir* 'pursue'). In the 1670s it was applied as a term of abuse to Irish Catholic royalists, and then more generally to supporters of the Catholic James II, and after 1689 it came to be used for the members of the British political party that had at first opposed the removal of James and his replacement with the Protestant William and Mary.

**total**    [14]    *Total* goes back ultimately to Latin *tōtus* 'whole' (source also of French *tout*, Italian *tutto*, and Spanish *todo* 'all'). From it was derived medieval Latin *totālis* 'of the whole,' which passed into English via Old French *total*. *Tot* [18], as in 'tot up,' is short for *total*. *Totalizator* was coined in Australia in the late 1870s, and the abbreviation *tote* started life in Australian English too.

▶ tot

**totem**    [18]    *Totem* is of native American origin, and denotes etymologically 'belonging to a family or group.' Its ultimate source is the stem *\*ōtē-* 'belong to a local group,' and it was adapted from an Ojibwa derivative formed with a possessive prefix ending in *t*, such as *otōtēman* 'his group or family,' hence 'his family mark.'

**touch**    [13]    The etymological notion underlying *touch* seems to be the 'striking of a bell.' It comes via Old French *tochier* from Vulgar Latin *\*toccāre* 'hit, knock,' which appears originally to have denoted 'make the sound *toc* by striking something, such as a bell' (as in English *tick-tock*). The connection with bells is preserved in *tocsin* 'signal given with a bell' [16], which comes via French *tocsin* from Provençal *tocasenh*, a compound formed from *tocar* 'strike' and *senh* 'bell' (a relative of English *sign*). Another member of the family is *toccata* [18], a borrowing from Italian, which etymologically denotes the 'touching' of the keys of an instrument with the fingers.

▶ toccata, tocsin

**toupée**    see TOP

**tour**    [14]    Etymologically, a *tour* is a 'circular movement.' The word comes via Old French *tour* from Latin *tornus* 'lathe,' which also produced English *turn*. It was not used for a 'journey of visits' – literally a 'circuitous journey' – until the 17th century (the term *grand tour*, denoting a lengthy journey around western

Europe formerly undertaken by fashionable young men, ostensibly for educational purposes, is first recorded in the mid-18th century, but the derivative *tourist* does not crop up until about 1800). *Tournament* [13] and *tourney* [13] both go back ultimately to a Vulgar Latin derivative of *tornus*, the underlying etymological notion being of the combatants 'turning' or wheeling round to face each other. And *tourniquet* [17] probably comes from the same source.

▶ tournament, tourniquet, turn

**tousle**    [15]    *Tousle* was derived from an earlier *touse* 'pull about, shake' (probable source also of *tussle* [15]), which went back to an Old English *\*tūsian*. Amongst its relatives is German *zausen* 'tug, tousle.'

▶ tussle

**tout**    [14]    The etymological notion underlying *tout* is of 'sticking out, projecting.' It goes back ultimately to the prehistoric Germanic base *\*tūt-* 'project,' whose other descendants include Dutch *tuit* 'spout.' It is assumed to have produced an Old English *\*tūtian*, but it does not turn up in the written record until the Middle English period, by which time the notion of 'poking out' had moved on to 'peeking' or 'peeping.' It progressed further to 'spy on,' but the modern 'look for business' did not emerge until the 18th century.

**tow**    English has two words *tow*. The older, 'pull' [OE], came from a prehistoric Germanic *\*togōjan* (source also of Norwegian *toga* 'pull'). This was derived from the base *\*tog-*, variants of which gave English *team*, *tug*, etc, and it goes back ultimately to the same Indo-European base as produced Latin *dūcere* 'pull, lead' (source of English *conduct*, *duke*, etc). *Tow* 'flax or hemp fibre' [14] was borrowed from Middle Low German *touw*. This probably went back to the prehistoric Germanic base *\*tōw-*, *\*taw-* 'make, prepare' (source also of English *tool*), in the specialized sense 'make yarn from wool, spin.'

▶ conduct, duct, duke, educate, team, teem, tie, tug / tool

**towards**    [OE]    The suffix *-ward* or *-wards*, which underlies *towards*, *forward*, and a host of other English adverbs and adjectives, comes from a prehistoric Germanic *\*-warth*. This in turn goes back to the Indo-European base *\*wert-* 'turn' (source also of English *convert*, *version*, etc) – so etymologically, *towards* denotes 'turning to' something.

▶ convert, version

**towel**    [13]    A *towel* is etymologically something for 'washing' with. The word comes from Old French *toaille*, which was a borrowing from prehistoric Germanic *\*thwakhliō*. This was derived from the verb *\*thwakhan* 'wash,' whose modern descendants include Swedish *tvätta* and Danish *tvætte* 'wash.' Another relative is Swedish *tvål* 'soap.'

**tower**    [12]    The ultimate source of *tower* is Greek *túrris*, a word probably from a pre-Indo-European language of the Mediterranean region. It passed into English via Latin *turris* and Old French *tur, tor*. *Turret* [14] comes from the Old French diminutive *turet*.

▶ turret

**town** [OE] The ancestral meaning of *town* is 'enclosed place' – amongst its relatives are German *zaun* 'hedge, fence' and Old Irish *dūn* 'fort, camp, fortified place.' Its Old English forerunner *tūn* was used for an 'enclosure' or 'yard,' and also for a 'building or set of buildings within an enclosure,' hence a 'farm.' This in due course evolved to a 'cluster of dwellings,' and by the 12th century the modern English sense of the word was in place (the standard Old English term for 'town' was *burg*, ancestor of modern English *borough*). The -*ton* ending of English place-names goes back in many cases to a time when the word meant 'farmstead.'

**toxic** [17] The etymological meaning underlying *toxic* is of 'poisoned arrows.' Its ultimate source is Greek *tóxon* 'bow,' which also gave English *toxophily* 'archery' [19]. From it was derived *toxikós* 'of bows and arrows,' which formed the basis of a noun *toxikón* 'poison for putting on arrows.' Latin took this over as *toxicum* 'poison,' and the medieval Latin derivative *toxicus* gave English *toxic*.

▶ toxophily

**toy** [14] Nothing is known for certain about the origins of *toy*. It originally meant 'amorous dalliance' ('So said he, and forbore not glance or toy, of amorous intent, well understood of Eve,' Milton, *Paradise Lost* 1667), traces of which survive in the verbal sense 'amuse oneself idly.' 'Plaything' first appeared towards the end of the 16th century.

**trace** English has two distinct words *trace*, but they come from the same ultimate ancestor. This was *tractus* (source also of English *tract, tractor, treat*, etc), the past participle of Latin *trahere* 'pull.' This passed into Old French as *trait* 'pulling, draught,' hence 'harness-strap,' from which English gets *trait* [16]. Its plural *trais* was borrowed by English as *trace* 'harness-strap' [14]. *Tractus* also formed the basis of a Vulgar Latin verb *\*tractiāre* 'drag,' which evolved into Old French *tracier* 'make one's way,' source of the English verb *trace* [14]. A noun *trace* was also derived from *tracier*, and this too was acquired by English as *trace* [13]. At first it denoted a 'path' or 'track'; the modern sense 'visible sign' did not develop until the 17th century.

▶ attract, contract, tract, tractor, trait, treat

**track** [15] *Track* was borrowed from Old French *trac* 'trail, set of footprints, etc.' This too appears to have been a loanword, from Middle Dutch *trek* 'pulling' (ultimate source of English *trek* [19], via Afrikaans), which was derived from the verb *trekken* 'pull.' The sense 'path' did not emerge until as recently as the 19th century.

▶ trek

**tracklements**        see DREDGE

**tractor** [17] *Tractor* is one of a large family of English words that come from *tractus*, the past participle of Latin *trahere* 'pull' (others include *abstract* [14], *attract, contract, detract* [15], *distract* [14], *extract* [15], *retract, subtract, trace, tract* [14], *tractable* [16], *traction* [17], *trait, treat, treatise*, and *treaty*). *Tractor* itself was originally used in English for a device, invented by the 18th-century American doctor Elisha Perkins, for 'pulling' across the surface of the skin, which was supposed to relieve rheumatic pains. It was not applied to a 'vehicle for pulling loads' until the end of the 19th century.

From Latin *trahere* itself come English *retreat* and *train*; and *drag* may go back to the same ultimate source.

▶ abstract, attract, contract, detract, distract, extract, retract, retreat, subtract, trace, tract, train, trait, treat, treaty

**trade** [14] *Trade* originally meant 'way, track.' Not until the 16th century did the modern sense 'buying and selling' emerge, via 'regular path followed by someone' and 'business pursued by someone.' Etymologically, it amounts to a 'trodden' path; for it was borrowed from Middle Low German *trade* 'track,' which goes back ultimately to the prehistoric Germanic base *\*trad-, \*tred-*, source also of English *tread* and *trot*.

▶ tread, trot

**traffic** [16] The ultimate origins of *traffic* are not known. It was acquired from French *traffique*, which in turn was borrowed from Old Italian *traffico*, a derivative of the verb *trafficare* 'trade,' but there the trail goes cold. It is generally assumed that the word's first element goes back to the Latin prefix *trāns-* 'across.'

**tragedy** [14] Etymologically, a *tragedy* is probably a 'goat-song.' The word comes via Old French *tragedie* and Latin *tragoedia* from Greek *tragōidíā*, a compound formed from *trágos* 'goat' and *ōidē* 'song' (source of English *ode, parody, rhapsody*, etc). It is thought that the underlying reference may be to a sort of ancient Greek drama in which the chorus were dressed as satyrs, goatlike woodland deities.

▶ melody, ode, parody, prosody, rhapsody

**trail**    see TRAWL

**train** [14] A *train* is etymologically something that is 'pulled' along. The word was borrowed from Old French *train*, a derivative of the verb *trahiner* 'drag.' And this in turn went back to Vulgar Latin *\*tragināre*, a derivative of Latin *\*tragere*, a variant of *trahere* 'pull.' It was first used in English for 'delay,' from the notion of being 'pulled' back, and 'part of a garment that trails behind' dates from the 15th century. When steam locomotives pulling carriages were introduced in the 1820s, the combined vehicle was called a *train of carriages*;

the simple term *train* is first recorded in 1835. The use of the verb *train* for 'instruct, school,' which dates from the 16th century, evolved from an earlier 'direct the course of growth of a plant,' which in turn went back to the original notion of 'pulling.'

▶ tractor

**trait**  see TRACE

**traitor**  [13]  *Traitor* and *tradition* [14] come from the same ultimate source: Latin *trādere*. This was a compound verb formed from the prefix *trāns*- 'across' and *dare* 'give' (source of English *data, date*, etc). It originally meant 'hand over, deliver,' and it is this sense that (via the derivative *trāditiō*) has given English *tradition* – etymologically something 'handed over' to succeeding generations. But it was also used metaphorically for 'betray,' and this meaning has passed through into English in *betray, traitor,* and *treason*.

▶ betray, tradition, traitor, treason

**tram**  [16]  *Tram* was borrowed from Middle Low German or Middle Dutch *trame* 'balk of timber, beam,' a word of unknown origin. It was originally used in English for the 'shafts' of a cart, and then for the cart itself. The track on which such carts ran in mines and similar places came to be known as *tramlines*, and this term was adopted in the 19th century for a track used for passenger road vehicles. These in turn were called *tramcars*, or *trams* for short.

**trance**  see TRANSIENT

**transcript**  see SCRIBE

**transfer**  [14]  *Transfer* comes via Old French *transferer* from Latin *trānsferre* 'carry across.' This was a compound verb formed from the prefix *trāns*- 'across' (a distant relative of English *through*) and *ferre* 'carry' (a relative of English *bear, birth, fertile,* etc). Its past participle *trānslātus* gave English *translate*.

▶ bear

**transfix**  see FIX

**transgress**  see GRADUAL

**transient**  [17]  English adapted *transient* from *trānsiēns*, the present participle of Latin *trānsīre* 'go over.' This was a compound verb formed from the prefix *trāns*- 'across, over' and *īre* 'go' (source also of English *coitus, exit, obituary,* etc). Also from *trānsīre* come English *trance* [14], *transit* [15], *transition* [16], *transitive* [16], and *transitory* [14].

▶ coitus, exit, obituary, transit, transitory

**translate**  [13]  To *translate* something is etymologically to 'carry it across' from one language into another. The word was acquired from *trānslātus*, the past participle of Latin *trānsferre* 'carry across, transfer, translate' (source of English *transfer*).

▶ extol, relate

**transparent**  [15]  Etymologically, something that is *transparent* allows the light to 'appear through' it. The word comes via Old French from medieval Latin *trānspārēns*, the present participle of *trānspārēre* 'be seen through.' This was a compound verb formed from the Latin prefix *trāns*- 'across, through' and *pārēre* 'show, appear' (source of English *appear*).

▶ appear

**transpire**  see SPIRIT

**transpose**  see POSITION

**transvestite**  see TRAVESTY

**trap**  [OE]  The precise origins of *trap* are obscure. It goes back to an Old English *træppe*, and it has various relatives in the modern Germanic and Romance languages – Flemish *trape*, French *trappe*, Portuguese *trapa*, for instance – but its ultimate ancestry has never been unravelled. Its application to a small carriage emerged in the 19th century; it may be short for *rattle-trap* 'rickety vehicle.'

**trapeze**  [19]  *Trapeze* and *quadruped* are ultimately the same word: both mean etymologically 'four feet.' *Trapeze* comes via French *trapèze* and late Latin *trapezium* (source of English *trapezium* [16]) from Greek *trapézion* 'small table.' This was a diminutive form of *trápeza* 'table,' literally 'four-footed' thing, a compound noun formed from *tetra*- 'four' and *peza* 'foot' (a relative of English *foot*). The Greek mathematician Euclid used *trapézion* for a 'table'-shaped geometrical figure, a quadrilateral. The application to the piece of gymnastic equipment, which evolved in French, alludes to the quadrilateral shape formed by the trapeze's ropes and crossbar and the roof or other support it hangs from.

▶ foot, quadruped

**trappings**  [14]  *Trappings* are etymologically 'drapery.' The word was adapted from Anglo-Norman *\*trapour*, a variant of Old French *drapure*; and this in turn was a derivative of *drap* 'cloth,' source of English *drape, drapery*, etc. It was originally used in English for an 'ornamental covering for a horse,' and its more general modern meaning did not emerge until the 16th century.

▶ drape, drapery

**travel**  [14]  *Travel* and *travail* [13] are doublets – that is to say, they have a common ancestor, but have split into separate words. Their ultimate source is medieval Latin *trepālium*, a term for an instrument of torture made of three sharp stakes. This was a compound noun formed from Latin *trēs* 'three' and *pālus* 'stake' (source of English *pale*). From it was formed a verb *\*trepāliāre* 'torture on the *trepālium*,' hence generally 'torture.' This passed into Old French as *travailler*, where its reflexive use 'put oneself to pain or trouble' evolved to 'work hard.' Its noun derivative *travail* 'painful effort, hard work' was borrowed by English as *travail*, and this quickly developed a new sense, 'journey' (presumably from the notion of a 'wearisome journey'), which came to be distinguished by the spelling *travel*.

▶ pale, three, travail

**travesty**  [17]  *Travesty* and *transvestite* [20] are first cousins. Both are compounded of the Latin elements *trāns-*'across' and *vestīre* 'clothe' (source of English *vest, vestment*, etc), but they are separate formations. *Travesty* comes ultimately from Italian *travestire* 'change clothes so as to disguise,' formed from the Italian descendants of the Latin elements. This was borrowed into French as *travestir* 'ridicule,' and its past participle *travesti* gave English *travesty*. *Transvestite* is a new formation, coined in German in the first decade of the 20th century (although there are a couple of isolated instances of a verb *transvest* 'cross-dress' from the 1650s).

▶ invest, transvestite, vest, vestment

**trawl**  [17]  *Trawl* was probably borrowed from Middle Dutch *traghelen* 'drag.' This was a derivative of *traghel* 'net pulled along behind a boat for catching fish,' which in turn came from Latin *trāgula*, a possible relative of *trahere* 'pull' (source of English *tractor, treat*, etc). *Trāgula* probably also lies behind English *trail* [14].

▶ trail

**tray**  see TREE

**treachery**  [13]  Despite the passing resemblance, *treachery* has no etymological connection with *traitor* or *treason*. In fact, its closest English relative is *trick*. The word was borrowed from Old French *trecherie*, a derivative of *trichier* 'cheat' (source of English *trick*).

▶ trick

**treacle**  [14]  *Treacle* is etymologically an 'antidote to the bite of wild animals.' The word comes via Old French *triacle* and Latin *thēriaca* from Greek *thēriakḗ*. This was short for *antídotos thēriakḗ* 'antidote to poisonous animals,' *thēriakḗ* being a derivative of *thēríon* 'wild animal, poisonous animal,' which in turn came from *thḗr* 'wild savage.' It retained its original meaning into English, but it then gradually broadened out into 'medicine,' and the practice of disguising the unpleasant taste of medicine with sugar syrup led in the 17th century to its application to 'syrup.'

**tread**  [OE]  *Tread* comes from a prehistoric Germanic *\*trethan*, which also produced German *treten*, Dutch *treden*, Swedish *träda*, and Danish *træde*. It does not appear to have any relations outside Germanic, however. *Trade* comes from the same base, and it is thought that *trot* [13] may do so too, although its immediate source was Old French *troter*.

▶ trade, trot

**treason**  [13]  *Treason* and *tradition* are doublets – they have a common source. This was Latin *trāditiō*, a derivative of *trādere* 'hand over, deliver' (source also of English *traitor*). The notion of 'handing something on to someone else' lies behind *tradition*, but *treason* (acquired via Anglo-Norman *treisoun*) gets its meaning from the metaphorically extended Latin sense 'hand over treacherously, betray.'

▶ betray, tradition, traitor

**treasure**  [12]  *Treasure* comes ultimately from Greek *thēsaurós* 'treasure,' a word of unknown origin. This was borrowed into Latin as *thēsaurus* (acquired directly by English as *thesaurus* [19] with the metaphorical sense 'treasury of knowledge, words, etc'), and it made its way into English via Vulgar Latin *\*tresaurus* and Old French *tresor*.

▶ thesaurus

**treat**  [13]  *Treat* comes ultimately from Latin *tractāre*, a derivative of *tractus* (source of English *contract, tractor*, etc), the past participle of *trahere* 'pull.' Originally *tractāre* meant 'drag,' but it branched out metaphorically to 'handle, deal with, discuss,' and it was in these senses that it reached English via Anglo-Norman *treter*. The notion of 'dealing with something by discussion' also underlies *treatise* [14] and *treaty* [14], which come from the same ultimate source.

▶ contract, tractor, treatise, treaty

**treble**  [14]  *Treble* and *triple* [15] come from the same ultimate source: Latin *triplus* 'threefold.' This in turn was borrowed from Greek *triploûs*, a compound adjective formed from *tri-* 'three' and the base *\*pl-* 'fold' (which lies behind English *ply* and is related to English *fold*). *Triplus* passed into Old French, where it split into two: *treble* and *triple*. Both were taken over into English (the former has now died out in French). The application of *treble* to the highest part in music, equivalent to *soprano*, which dates from the 14th century, probably comes from the notion of its being the 'third' part, above *bass* and *alto*.

▶ fold, ply, three, triple

**tree**  [OE]  *Tree* is part of an ancient and widespread family of 'tree'-words that goes back ultimately to Indo-European *\*deru, \*doru-*. This appears originally to have designated specifically the 'oak,' rather than 'tree' in general, an application retained by some of its descendants: Greek *drûs*, for instance (source of English *dryad* [14]), and Welsh *derwen* (a possible relative of English *druid*). From it came Germanic *\*trewam*, which has evolved into Swedish *träd*, Danish *træ*, and English *tree*. Other English words from the same source include *tray* [OE] (etymologically a 'wooden' vessel), *trough*, and possibly *tar*.

▶ druid, dryad, tar, tray, trough

**trek**   see TRACK

**trellis**   see THREE

**tremble**   [14]   *Tremble* goes back ultimately to a prehistoric base *\*trem-* 'shake,' which probably has connections with English *terrify, terror,* etc. Amongst the Latin descendants of this base were *tremor* 'shaking' (source of English *tremor* [14]), *tremere* 'tremble' (source of English *tremendous* [17]), and *tremulus* 'shaking' (source of English *tremolo* [19] and *tremulous* [17]). The last of these formed the basis of a Vulgar Latin verb *\*tremulāre*, which passed into English via Old French *trembler* as *tremble*.

▶ terrify, terror, tremendous, tremor, tremulous

**trench**   [14]   A *trench* is etymologically something 'cut' or 'sliced.' The word was borrowed from Old French *trenche* 'slice, cutting, ditch,' a derivative of *trenchier* 'cut' (from which English gets *trenchant* [14]). And this in turn went back to Latin *truncāre* 'cut, mutilate' (source of English *truncate* [15]), a derivative of *truncus* 'tree-trunk, torso' (source of English *trunk*) – the semantic link being the 'cutting' of branches from a tree or of limbs from a body. The sense 'ditch' for *trench* comes of course from the notion of 'cutting' a long narrow hole in the ground (a similar inspiration underlies *cutting* 'excavation for a railway, road, etc'). *Trencher* 'platter' [14] came from the Anglo-Norman derivative *trenchour*, and originally denoted both a board for 'cutting' food up on and a 'slice' of bread used as a plate.

▶ trenchant, trencher, truncate, trunk

**trend**   [OE]   The etymological notion underlying *trend* is of 'circularity' or 'roundness.' It comes from a prehistoric Germanic base *\*trend-, \*trund-*, which also produced Dutch *trent* 'circumference,' Swedish *trind* 'round,' and English *trundle* [16], and it was originally used in the sense 'revolve, roll.' This gradually evolved via 'turn' to, in the 16th century, 'turn in a particular direction, take a particular course.' The first record of the derivative *trendy* dates from 1962.

▶ trundle

**trepidation**   see INTREPID

**trespass**   [13]   To *trespass* is etymologically to 'pass across' something. The word was acquired from Old French *trespasser*, a descendant of medieval Latin *trānspassāre*. This was a compound verb formed from the Latin prefix *trāns-* 'across' and Vulgar Latin *\*passāre* 'pass.'

▶ pass

**trews**   see TROUSERS

**tribe**   [13]   *Tribe* comes via Old French *tribu* from Latin *tribus* 'division of the Roman people.' This was probably derived from the base *\*tri-* 'three,' and denoted etymologically the 'three original tribes of Rome' – the Tities, the Ramnes, and the Luceres. The 'head of a tribe' was known as a *tribūnus*, whence English *tribune* [14]; and the verb for 'give out amongst the tribes' was *tribuere*, source of English *contribute* [16], *distribute* [15], *retribution* [14], and *tribute* [14].

▶ contribute, distribute, retribution, three, tribune, tribute

**tribulation**   [13]   Latin *tribulum* denoted an agricultural implement consisting of a wooden board with sharp stones or metal teeth underneath, used for threshing grain (it was derived from the base *\*trī-*, a variant of *\*ter-* 'rub,' which also produced English *attrition, contrition, detriment, detritus, diatribe, tribadism* 'lesbianism' [19], and *trite*). From this was derived the verb *tribulāre* 'press,' which was used by Christian writers for 'oppress, afflict.' And this sense provoked the derivative *tribulātiō* 'affliction,' which passed into English via Old French *tribulation*.

▶ attrition, contrition, detriment, detritus, diatribe, throw, tribadism, trite

**trick**   [15]   *Trick* comes from Old French *trique*, a variant of *triche*, which was derived from the verb *trichier* 'cheat' (source of English *treachery*). And this in turn probably came from Latin *trīcarī* 'make difficulties, play tricks' (source also of English *extricate* [17] and *intricate* [15]), a derivative of *trīcae* 'difficulties, tricks,' whose origins are unknown. *Tricky* dates from the 18th century, its use for 'difficult' from the end of the 19th century.

▶ extricate, intricate, treachery

**trident**   see TOOTH

**trifle**   [13]   *Trifle* was acquired from Old French *truffle*, a derivative of *truffe* 'trickery, deceit' (it is not known where this came from; it has no connection with English *truffle*, which may come ultimately from the same source as *tuber*). The first record of its application to a 'sweet dessert confection' dates from the end of the 16th century.

**trilby**   [19]   The word *trilby* commemorates the name of Trilby O'Ferrall, the eponymous heroine of George du Maurier's novel *Trilby* 1894. She was an artist's model in Paris who fell under the spell of Svengali. In the stage version of the book the character Trilby wore a soft felt hat with an indented top, and the style soon became fashionable. The novel also dwells on the erotic qualities of Trilby's feet, and for a while in the early 20th century *trilbies* was used as a slang term for 'feet.'

**trim**   [16]   The origins of *trim* are uncertain, but it may come from an unrecorded Middle English verb *\*trimmen* 'arrange,' a descendant of Old English *trymman* or *trymian* 'make stronger or firmer.'

**trinity**   [13]   *Trinity* comes via Old French *trinite* from Latin *trīnitās* 'group of three.' This was a derivative of *trīnus* 'threefol.,' which in turn came from *tria* 'three,' a close relative of English *three*.

▶ three

**trio**   see THREE

**trip**   [14]   The original meaning of *trip* was 'move lightly or nimbly.' 'Stumble' is a secondary development, and the use of the derived noun for 'short journey' did not emerge until the late 17th century (it was apparently originally a nautical usage). The word was borrowed from Old French *tripper*, which in turn was acquired from Middle Dutch *trippen* 'hop, skip.'

**tripod**   see FOOT, THREE

**trireme**   see OAR

**trite**   see THROW

**triumph**   [14]   *Triumph* comes via Old French *triumphe* from Latin *triumphus*, which denoted a 'public celebration to welcome home a victorious general.' It was an alteration of Old Latin *triumpus*, which was probably borrowed from Greek *thríambos* 'hymn to Bacchus.' The cards term *trump* is an alteration of *triumph*.

▶ trump

**trivet**   see FOOT

**trivial**   [15]   Medieval educationists recognized seven liberal arts: the lower three, grammar, logic, and rhetoric, were known as the *trivium*, and the upper four, arithmetic, astronomy, geometry, and music, were known as the *quadrivium*. The notion of 'less important subjects' led in the 16th century to the use of the derived adjective *trivial* for 'commonplace, of little importance.' Latin *trivium* itself was a compound noun formed from the prefix *tri-* 'three' and *via* 'way, road,' and originally meant 'place where three roads meet.'

▶ three, via

**trochlea**   see TRUCKLE

**trombone**   see TRUMP

**troop**   [16]   *Troop* was borrowed from French *troupe* (acquired again as *troupe* in the 19th century). This appears to have been a back-formation from *troupeau* 'flock, herd,' a diminutive formation based on Latin *troppus*. And *troppus* itself may have been of Germanic origin. By the time the word reached English it was already being applied to a 'group of soldiers,' and its plural was being used as a collective term for 'soldiers.'

▶ troupe

**trope**   see TROUBADOUR

**trophy**   [16]   A *trophy* is etymologically something awarded to commemorate the enemy's 'turning round' and running away. The word comes via French *trophée* and Latin *trophaeum* from Greek *trópaion* 'monument to the enemy's defeat.' This was a noun use of the adjective *tropaíos* 'of turning,' a derivative of

*tropé* 'turning,' hence 'turning back the enemy' (source also of English *tropic*).

▶ tropic

**tropic**   [14]   The etymological notion underlying the word *tropic* is of 'turning,' and the reason for its application to the hot regions of the world is that the two lines of latitude which bound them (the *tropic of Cancer* and the *tropic of Capricorn*) mark the points at which the sun reaches its zenith at the solstices and then 'turns' back. The word comes via Latin *tropicus* from Greek *tropikós*, a derivative of *tropé* 'turning' (source also of English *trophy* and related to the second syllable of *contrive*).

▶ contrive, trophy, troubadour

**trot**   [13]   *Trot*'s closest English relative is probably *tread*. It was borrowed from Old French *troter*, which went back via Vulgar Latin *\*trottāre* to a Frankish *\*trottōn*. This seems to have been derived from the same Germanic base as produced English *tread*. The colloquial use of the noun for 'diarrhoea' dates from the early 19th century – originally in the singular, but since at least the early 20th century in the plural, *the trots*.

▶ tread

**troth**   see TRUE

**troubadour**   [18]   A *troubadour* is etymologically someone who 'finds' – that is, 'composes' – songs. The word comes via French *troubadour* from Provençal *trobador*, a derivative of the verb *trobar* (whose modern French equivalent is *trouver*). This seems originally to have meant 'compose,' and later to have shifted its semantic ground via 'invent' to 'find.' It is not known for certain where it came from, but one theory traces it back via a Vulgar Latin *\*tropāre* to Latin *tropus* 'figure of speech' (source of English *trope* [16]). This in turn was borrowed from Greek *trópos* 'turn,' a relative of English *trophy* and *tropic*. If this is so, its ancestral meaning would be 'use figures of speech.'

▶ tropic

**trouble**   [13]   *Trouble* is etymologically something that 'disturbs' one – indeed, the two words are related. *Trouble* was borrowed from Old French *trouble* or *tourble*, a derivative of the verb *tourbler*. This was descended from Vulgar Latin *\*turbulāre*, a derivative of *\*turbulus*, which in turn was an alteration of Latin *turbidus* 'wild, confused, muddy' (source of English *turbid* [17]). And *turbidus* itself was derived from *turba* 'disturbance, crowd' (a borrowing from Greek *túrbē* 'disorder'), which also produced the verb *turbāre* 'disturb' (source of English *disturb* [13] and *turbulent* [16]). *Turbine* too is closely related.

▶ disturb, turbid, turbine, turbulent

**trough**   [OE]   Etymologically, a *trough* is something made out of 'wood.' Its ultimate source is Indo-European *\*drukós*, a derivative of the base *\*dru-* 'wood, tree' (source also of English *tree*). This passed into prehistoric Germanic as *trugaz, which has since diversified into German and Dutch trog, Swedish tråg, Danish trug, and English trough. English trug 'shallow basket' [16] is a variant of trough.

▶ tray, tree, trug

**troupe**   see TROOP

**trousers**   [17]   Trousers is a Gaelic contribution to English vocabulary. Irish trius and Scots Gaelic triubhas (singular nouns) denote 'close-fitting shorts.' They were borrowed into English in the 16th century as trouse or trews. The latter form has survived intact, but trouse, through the influence of drawers, was expanded into trousers.

▶ trews

**trow**   see TRUE

**truant**   [13]   A truant was originally a 'beggar' or 'vagrant.' The word was borrowed from Old French truant 'vagabond,' which in turn came from Gaulish trugant- (amongst its Celtic relatives are Gaelic trudanach 'vagabond' and Welsh truan 'wretched'). The word was not applied to absconding schoolchildren until the 15th century.

**truce**   [13]   Historically, truce is simply the plural of the noun version of the adjective true. In Old English this was trēow, which meant 'faith, pledge.' It was often used in the plural with the same meaning as the singular, and this tendency increased in early Middle English to the point where the singular disappeared altogether. It had meanwhile narrowed down in meaning to a 'pledge to stop fighting.'

▶ true

**truck**   English has two distinct words truck. The earlier, 'dealings,' as in 'have no truck with,' was originally a verb, meaning 'exchange, barter' [13]. It was borrowed from Anglo-Norman *truquer, but its ultimate ancestry is unknown. Americans call a 'market garden' a truck farm, from the former practice of bartering its produce. Truck 'goods vehicle' [17] is generally assumed to be short for truckle; it was originally used for a 'small wooden wheel,' particularly one on the carriage of a naval cannon.

▶ truckle

**truckle**   [15]   A truckle is a 'small wooden wheel or caster.' The word was originally used for a 'pulley' (an application which has now largely died out), and it was borrowed from Anglo-Norman trocle. This in turn came via Latin trochlea 'system of pulleys' (source of English trochlea [17], an anatomical term for a 'structure resembling a pulley') from Greek trokhilía 'pulley, system of pulleys, roller, etc.' Truckle-bed was a term applied to a sort of low bed on casters that could be pushed under a larger bed when not in use, and the notion of sleeping in the truckle-bed, 'beneath' someone

in the higher main bed, led in the 17th century to the use of truckle as a verb meaning 'be subservient.'

▶ trochlea, truck

**true**   [OE]   The underlying etymological meaning of true is 'faithful, steadfast, firm'; 'in accordance with the facts' is a secondary development. It goes back to the prehistoric Germanic base *treww-, which also produced German treue and Dutch trouw 'faithful' and the English noun truce, and it has been speculated that it may ultimately have links with the Indo-European base *dru- 'wood, tree' (source of English tree), the semantic link being the firmness or steadfastness of oaks and suchlike trees. Truth [OE] comes from the same source, as do its derivative betroth [14], its now archaic variant troth [16], the equally dated trow [OE], and probably also trust and tryst.

▶ betroth, troth, trow, truce, trust, truth, tryst

**truffle**   [16]   English acquired truffle, probably via Dutch truffel, from early modern French truffle, a derivative of Old French truffe (which survives as the modern French term for the fungus). This in turn came via Provençal trufa from a Vulgar Latin *tūfera, an alteration of the plural of Latin tūber 'swelling, lump, tuber, truffle' (from which English gets tuber [17] and tuberculosis [19]). The term was first used for a chocolate sweet with the external appearance of a truffle in the 1920s.

▶ tuber, tuberculosis

**trump**   There are two distinct words trump in English. The now archaic term for a 'trumpet' [13] is of Germanic origin, although it and its derivatives reached English via the Romance languages. Its ultimate source was Old High German trumpa, which no doubt started life as an imitation of the sound made by the instrument it denoted. This passed into English via Old French trompe. Its diminutive trompette has given English trumpet [13], while its Italian relative trombone (literally 'big trump') is the source of English trombone. The cards term trump [16] is an alteration of triumph.

▶ drum, trombone, trumpet / triumph

**truncate**   see TRENCH

**trundle**   see TREND

**trunk**   [15]   Trunk came via Old French tronc from Latin truncus (source also of English trench and truncate). This denoted 'something with its protruding parts torn off,' hence 'something regarded separately from its protruding parts' – the stem of a tree without its branches, or a body without its limbs. The application of the English word to an 'elephant's proboscis,' which dates from the 16th century, apparently arose from some confusion with trump 'trumpet.'

▶ trench, truncate

**trust**   [13]   Trust was probably borrowed from Old Norse traust 'help, confidence, firmness.' This, together with its modern German and Dutch relatives *trost* and *troost* 'consolation,' goes back to the same prehistoric Germanic base as produced English *true* and *truth*. *Tryst* [14] is probably closely related. It was borrowed from Old French *triste* 'appointed place for positioning oneself during a hunt,' which itself was very likely acquired from a Scandinavian source connected with *traust*.

▶ true

## truth　see TRUE

## try
[13]　*Try* originally meant 'separate, sift out.' It was borrowed from Old French *trier* 'separate, sift,' and it has been speculated that this went back to a Vulgar Latin *trītāre*, formed from the past participle of Latin *terere* 'rub' (source of English *attrition, detritus, trite*, etc). The notion of 'separation' led via 'separating out the good' to 'examine, test' and, in the 14th century, 'attempt.' The derivative *trial* [16] was borrowed from Anglo-Norman after the sense 'attempt' developed for *try* in English, and so has never wholeheartedly taken over this meaning.

▶ trial

## tsar
[16]　*Caesar* was a Roman cognomen (English gets *caesarian* from it) and from the days of Augustus was used as part of the title of 'emperor.' The Germanic peoples took it over in this sense (it is the source of German *kaiser*) and passed it on to prehistoric Slavic as *tsēsari*. This has evolved into Serbo-Croat and Bulgarian *tsar* and Russian *tsar'* – source of English *tsar*.

▶ Caesar

## tube
[17]　The ultimate origins of *tube* are unclear. It comes, probably via French *tube*, from Latin *tubus* 'tube.' This was closely related to *tuba* 'war trumpet,' source of English *tuba* [19], but what their joint ancestor might be is not known.

▶ tuba

## tuber　see TRUFFLE

## tuberculosis　see TRUFFLE

## tuck　see TUG

## Tuesday
[OE]　Tiu was the Germanic god of war and the sky (his name came from the same source as produced Latin *deus* 'god,' from which English gets *deity*). When the Germanic peoples took over the Roman system of naming the days of the week after the gods, they replaced the term for the second day of the week, *diēs Martis* 'day of Mars, the war-god' (source of French *Mardi* 'Tuesday') with 'Tiu's day' – hence *Tuesday*. The Norse version of the god's name appears in Swedish *tisdag* and Danish *tirsdag*.

▶ deity

## tuft　see TOFF

## tug
[13]　*Tug* goes back to a prehistoric Germanic base *teukh-* 'pull' (source also of German *ziehen* 'pull'

and English *tuck* [14], whose original meaning was 'pull up, gather up'). This in turn was descended from Indo-European *deuk-* 'pull,' from which English gets *conduct, duke, reduce*, etc.

▶ conduct, duct, duke, educate, reduce, tie, tow

## tulip
[16]　*Tulip* and *turban* [16] are ultimately the same word. Both come from Persian *dulband*, and the name was applied to the plant because of its flower's supposed resemblance to a turban. *Dulband* was borrowed into Turkish as *tuliband*, and this made its way into English via early modern French *tulipan* and modern Latin *tulipa*, acquiring its botanical meaning along the way (relatives that preserve the link with *turban* slightly more closely include Swedish *tulpan*, Danish *tulipan*, Italian *tulipano*, and Russian *tjul'pan*). Meanwhile Turkish *tuliband* evolved to *tülbend*, and this passed into English via Italian *turbante* and French *turbant* as *turban*.

▶ turban

## tumble
[13]　*Tumble* was borrowed from Middle Low German *tummelen*, which has other relatives in modern German *tummeln* 'bustle, hurry' and *taumeln* 'reel, stagger.' All were formed from a base that also found its way into the Romance languages, producing French *tomber* 'fall' (source of English *tumbrel* [14], which in Old French denoted a 'chute' or 'cart that could be tipped up') and Italian *tombolare* 'tumble, turn somersaults' (source of English *tombola* [19]). The derivative *tumbler* [14] originally denoted an 'acrobat'; the application to a 'drinking glass,' which emerged in the mid 17th century, comes from the fact that such glasses were originally made with rounded bottoms, so that they could not be put down until they were empty.

▶ tombola

## tumour
[16]　*Tumour* is one of a small family of English words that go back ultimately to Latin *tumēre* 'swell.' Others include *contumacy, contumely, tumid* 'swollen' [16], and *tumult* [15].

▶ contumacy, contumely, thigh, thumb, tumid, tumult

## tun　see TON

## tune
[14]　*Tune* originated as a variant of *tone*, and to begin with it was used for 'sound, tone' ('He told him of the death of Brunes; then were made hideous tunes of many a gentle damsel,' *Troy book* 1400). Very quickly, however, the sense 'melody' emerged (it is not present in *tone*), and eventually took over from 'sound.' The derivative *attune* dates from the late 16th century.

▶ attune, tone

## tunnel　see TON

## turban　see TULIP

## turbid　see TROUBLE

## turbine
[19]　Latin *turbō* denoted 'whirl,' 'whirling thing,' or 'whirlwind,' and also 'spinning-top' (it was related to *turba* 'disturbance, crowd,'

source of English *disturb, trouble*, etc). From it around 1824 was coined French *turbine*, applied originally to a revolving wheel on an axis, driven by water-pressure. It was borrowed into English in the early 1840s.

▶ disturb, trouble

**turbot** [13] The *turbot* is etymologically the 'thorn-flatfish.' Its name comes via Old French *turbot* from Old Swedish *törnbut* 'turbot.' This was a compound noun formed from *törn* 'thorn' (a relative of English *thorn*) and *but* 'flatfish,' a borrowing from Middle Low German *but* which probably denoted etymologically 'stumpy,' and also supplied the final syllable of English *halibut* [15]. The name presumably alludes to the bony nodules on the fish's back.

▶ halibut, thorn

**turbulent** SEE TROUBLE

**turd** [OE] *Turd* is an ancient word, traceable right back to Indo-European *\*drtom*. This was formed from the base *\*dr-*, *\*der-* 'flay, tear' (source also of English *tear*), and so etymologically denoted that which is 'separated' from the body, like flayed skin, and hence ejected or excreted from the body. It passed into English via prehistoric Germanic *\*turdam*. A distant relative is Latvian *dirsti* 'defecate.'

▶ tear

**tureen** [18] *Tureen* and *terrine* are ultimately the same word. Both were borrowed simultaneously from French *terrine* 'deep earthenware dish' in the early 18th century, since when in its original sense 'dish' it has been contorted to *tureen* (perhaps partly through some association with *Turin*) and applied specifically to a 'soup dish,' while in the extended sense 'paté-like dish made in a terrine' it has remained as *terrine*. The French word originated as a noun use of the feminine form of Old French *terrin* 'earthen,' which went back ultimately to Latin *terra* 'earth' (source of English *terrace, terrain*, etc).

▶ terrine

**turf** [OE] *Turf* is a general Germanic word. It goes back to a prehistoric Germanic *\*turb-*, which also produced German *torf* 'peat,' Dutch *turf*, Swedish *torf*, and Danish *tørv*, and was borrowed into the Romance languages, giving French *tourbe*, Italian *torba*, and Spanish *turba*. Its ultimate source was the Indo-European base *\*drbh-*.

**turkey** [16] The term *turkey* was originally applied to the 'guinea-fowl,' apparently because the bird was imported into Europe from Africa by the Portuguese through Turkish territory. When the American bird we now know as the *turkey* was introduced to the British in the mid 16th century, it seems to have reminded them of the guinea fowl, for they transferred the guinea fowl's name *turkey* to it.

**turn** [OE] The ultimate source of *turn* is Greek *tórnos* 'lathe,' which was probably related to Latin *terere* 'rub' (source of English *attrition, detritus, trite*, etc). Latin took this over as *tornus* and formed a verb from it, *tornāre* 'turn on a lathe,' hence 'round off, make smooth.' Old English borrowed *tornāre* as *turnian*, which was later reinforced by Old French *turner*. To the same word family belong *tour* and *tournament*.

▶ attrition, detriment, detritus, tour, tournament, trite

**turnip** [16] Etymologically, a *turnip* may be a 'turned neep' – that is, a neep, or turnip, that has been 'turned' on a lathe, so as to be round (the turnip is a roughly spherical vegetable). Its second syllable, *-nip*, goes back ultimately to Latin *nāpus* 'turnip,' which was adopted by Old English as *næp*. It survives in Scottish English as *neep*, which is used for 'swedes' as well as 'turnips.' The linking of the first syllable with *turn* is purely conjectural, and has never been definitely established.

▶ neep

**turpentine** [14] *Turpentine* is nowadays used for an oil obtained from pine trees, but it originally denoted the 'resin of the terebinth,' a small European tree of the sumach family. The name of the terebinth is probably of non-Indo-European origin. It was borrowed into Greek as *térbinthos*, which made its way into Latin as *terbinthus*. Its resin was called *terbenthina rēsīna*. The adjective *terbenthina* came to be used as a noun, and this passed into English via Old French *terbentine*.

**turquoise** [14] *Turquoise* is etymologically the 'Turkish' stone. The word was borrowed from Old French *turqueise*, short for *pierre turqueise* 'Turkish stone.' The stone was so called because it was first found in Turkestan. The present-day form of the word, which dates from the 16th century, is due to the influence of modern French *turquoise*. It was first used as a colour adjective in the late 16th century.

**turret** SEE TOWER

**turtle** *Turtle* the dove [OE] and *turtle* the marine reptile [17] are different words. The former was borrowed from Latin *turtur*, which no doubt originated in imitation of the bird's cooing. It is now encountered only in the compound *turtledove*, first recorded in the 13th century. *Turtle* the reptile is more of a mystery. It is generally assumed to be an alteration of French *tortue* 'tortoise' (source of English *tortoise* [15]), but since it is not known where that came from, it does not get us much further. The expression *turn turtle* (which dates from the 19th century) alludes to the practice of sailors turning turtles over on to their backs, like beetles, so that they were helpless and could be easily captured.

▶ tortoise

**tussle**    see TOUSLE

**tutor**    [14]   A *tutor* is etymologically someone who 'looks after' another – indeed, it was originally used for a 'guardian' or 'protector': 'The king ... behested himself to be a tutor and defender of him and of his,' *Foundation of St Bartholomew's church* 1425. The word's educational connotations are a secondary development. It comes via Anglo-Norman *tutour* from Latin *tūtor*, a derivative of *tuērī* 'look after, protect.' From the same source comes English *tuition* [15], and also *tutelage* [17], which retains its original sense of 'guardianship.'

▶ tuition, tutelage

**twain**    see TWO

**twat**    see TWIT

**tweak**    see TWIG

**tweed**    [19]   The story attached to the origin of *tweed* is that it resulted from a misreading of *tweel*, or perhaps more plausibly the past form *tweeled*, Scottish variants of *twill* or *twilled*, under the influence of the name of the Scottish river *Tweed*. Early accounts date its coinage to 1831, and ascribe it to the London cloth merchant James Locke (although Locke himself in his book *Tweed and Don* 1860 does not make any such claim). The term was in general use by 1850, and it was registered as a trademark. (*Twill* itself is etymologically 'two-threaded' cloth; it is a compound formed from *twi-* 'two' and Latin *līcium* 'thread.')

**twelve**    [OE]   Etymologically, *twelve* probably means 'two over' (just as *eleven* means 'one over'). It appears to go back to a prehistoric Germanic compound formed from *\*twa-* 'two' and *\*lif-* (a relative of English *leave*), which also produced German *zwölf*, Dutch *twaalf*, Swedish *tolf*, and Danish *tolv*. If so, its underlying meaning is 'two left (over ten),' hence 'ten plus two.'

▶ leave, two

**twenty**    [OE]   *Twenty* is etymologically 'two tens.' The second syllable, *-ty*, is related to *ten*, and *twen-* goes back to the same source as *two*, although its precise ancestry is not clear.

▶ ten, two

**twice**    [12]   *Twice* was formed from Old English *twige* 'twice' (itself based on *twi-*, the combining form of *two*) and the genitive ending *-s*, which was used for creating adverbs, such as *always, nowadays, once, thrice,* etc.

▶ two

**twig**    English has two separate words *twig*. The older, 'small branch' [OE], which has relatives in German *zweig* and Dutch *tijg*, appears to have been formed from the Germanic base *\*twi-* 'two,' and so etymologically it presumably denotes a 'forked branch.' The origins of *twig* 'catch on, understand' [18] are uncertain. It may be

the same word as the contemporary but now defunct *twig* 'pull.' This was presumably related to *tweak* [17] and *twitch* [12], which go back to a prehistoric Germanic base *\*twik-*.

▶ tweak, twitch, two

**twilight**    [15]   *Twilight* is etymologically 'light between day and night.' The word was compounded from the prefix *twi-* 'two,' apparently used here in the sense 'between' (*between* itself comes from the same ultimate source as *two*) and *light*. German has the parallel *zwielicht*.

▶ two

**twill**    see DRILL

**twin**    [OE]   *Twin* originally meant simply 'double,' but the specific application to 'two people born at the same birth' had already evolved by the end of the Old English period. The word goes back via prehistoric Germanic *\*twisnaz* to Indo-European *\*dwisno-*, a derivative of the base *\*dwi-* 'double' (other derivatives formed with the same *-n* suffix include English *between* and *twine* [OE] – etymologically thread of 'two' strands).

▶ between, twine, two

**twist**    [OE]   *Twist* appears to come ultimately from prehistoric Germanic base *\*twi-* 'double,' which also underlies English *twice, twig, twin,* etc. In Old English it is found only in compound words, denoting such things as 'rope' (presumably originally made from 'two' strands) and 'forked objects.' It does not appear as an independent word until the 14th century, by which time its association with 'rope' had given it the sense 'wrench, wind.'

▶ two

**twit**    *Twit* was originally, and still is, a verb, meaning 'taunt' [16]. It is a shortened version of the now defunct *atwite*. This went back to Old English *ǣtwītan*, a compound verb formed from the prefix *ǣt-*, denoting 'opposition,' and *wītan* 'reproach.' It is not altogether clear whether the noun *twit* 'fool' is the same word. There is an isolated example of what could be *twit* 'fool' recorded from the early 18th century, but it did not really begin to proliferate as a mild term of abuse until the 1950s. Semantically, the connection is plausible – a 'fool' could be a 'person who is taunted' (presumably for being foolish) – but an alternative theory is that it is an alteration of *twat* [17]. This originally meant 'cunt,' and is not recorded as a term of abuse until the 1920s. It is not known where it came from. (It was, incidentally, the object of one of the more ludicrous misapprehensions in English literature. There is a passage in *Vanity of Vanities* 1660 that reads 'They talked of his having a cardinal's hat, they'd send him as soon an old nun's twat.' Robert Browning took 'twat' as meaning some item of nun's clothing, and so wrote in his *Pippa Passes* 1841 'Sing to the bats' sleek sisterhoods full complines with gallantry: Then, owls and bats, cowls and twats, monks and nuns, in a cloister's moods, adjourn to the oak-stump pantry!')

**twitch**   see TWIG

**two**   [OE]   *Two* is an ancient word, traceable right back to Indo-European *\*duwo*. Amongst its other descendants were Greek *dúo*, Latin *duo* (source of English *deuce, double, dual, duet, duo*, etc), Russian *dva*, and Welsh *dau*. In the Germanic languages, aside from English, it has evolved into German *zwei*, Dutch *twee*, Swedish *två*, and Danish *to*. *Two* represents the Old English feminine and neuter forms *twā*; the masculine *twegen* has become *twain*.

▶ between, deuce, double, dual, duet, duo, twain, twelve, twenty, twice, twig, twilight, twin, twist

**tycoon**   [19]   Japanese *taikun* was a title used for the military commander or shogun of Japan, particularly by his supporters when addressing foreigners, in the attempt to convey the impression that he was more powerful and important than the emperor. For it meant literally 'great prince, emperor.' It was borrowed from ancient Chinese *t'ai kiuən* 'emperor,' a compound formed from *t'ai* 'great' and *kiuən* 'prince.' English acquired it in the 1850s, and it began to be used more generally for a 'high-ranking personage' in the USA soon afterwards. The specific application to businessmen seems to have evolved after World War I.

**type**   [15]   The etymological notion underlying the word *type* is of making an impression by 'striking.' It comes via Latin *typus* from Greek *túpos* 'blow, impres-

sion,' a derivative of *túptein* 'hit.' In post-classical Latin the meaning 'form, sort' evolved (in much the same way as it did in the case of *stamp*). The more concrete metaphorical attachment to 'making a mark by stamping' had already been made in the classical period, and this eventually led in the 18th century to the use of English *type* for a 'printing block with a letter on it.'

**typhoid**   see STEW

**typhoon**   [16]   A *typhoon* is etymologically a 'great wind.' The word was adapted from Cantonese Chinese *daai feng* 'great wind,' its form no doubt influenced by Greek *Tūphón*, father of the winds in Greek mythology (his name was derived from the verb *túphein* 'smoke,' which also produced *túphos* 'smoke,' hence 'fever causing delusion,' source of English *stew*, *typhoid*, and *typhus*).

**typhus**   see STEW

**tyre**   [15]   The word *tyre* was originally used for a protective covering of metal plates put round the rim of a wooden wheel. It is thought that it was short for *attire* [13] (a borrowing from Old French, but ultimately of unknown origin), the notion being of 'attiring' the wheels in their covering. At first the word was spelled *tire* or *tyre* indiscriminately. By the 18th century *tire* had become the standard form, and it remains so in American English, but when rubber wheel cushions were introduced in the 19th century, British English took to spelling them *tyre*.

▶ attire

# U

**ubiquitous** [19] Latin *ubīque* meant 'everywhere' (it was formed from *ubī* 'where' and a generalizing particle *-que*). From it was derived the modern Latin noun *ubīquitās* 'quality of being everywhere.' This was adopted into English as *ubiquity* [16], which later formed the basis of *ubiquitous*.

**udder** [OE] *Udder* goes back ultimately to prehistoric Indo-European *\*ūdhr-*. This, or variants of it, produced the word for 'udder' in the majority of Indo-European languages: Greek *oúthar*, Latin *über* (source of English *exuberant*), Sanskrit *ūdhar*, Russian *vymja*, German *euter*, Dutch *uier*, Swedish *juver*, and Danish *yver* for instance, as well as English *udder*.
▶ exuberant

**ugly** [13] *Ugly* originally meant 'horrible, frightening'; 'offensive to the sight' is a secondary development, first recorded in the 14th century. The word was borrowed from Old Norse *uggligr*, a derivative of the verb *ugga* 'fear.' In the early 1930s it was applied, in the altered spelling *ugli*, to a new sort of citrus fruit, a hybrid of the grapefruit and the tangerine; the reference is to the fruit's unprepossessing knobbly skin.

**ullage** [15] *Ullage* denotes the amount of unfilled space in a wine bottle or barrel. It goes back ultimately to Latin *oculus* 'eye' (a distant relative of English *eye*), in the metaphorical sense 'bung-hole of a barrel.' As the word passed into Old French as *oeil*, this meaning followed it, and it formed the basis of a varb *ouiller* 'fill up a barrel to the bung-hole.' From this was derived *ouillage*, which English acquired via Anglo-Norman *ulliage* as *ullage*.
▶ eye, ocular

**ulterior** [17] *Ulterior* goes back to an unrecorded Latin *\*ulter* 'distant' (a relative of *ultrā* 'beyond,' source of the English prefix *ultra-*). Its comparative form was *ulterior*, which meant literally 'more distant.' Its superlative form was *ultimus*, which lies behind English *ultimate* [17] and *ultimatum* [18] (etymologically the 'farthest' or last point).
▶ ultimate, ultimatum

**ultramarine** [16] *Ultramarine* originally denoted a blue pigment made from the stone lapis lazuli. This was imported in the Middle Ages from Asia by sea, and so it was termed in medieval Latin *ultrāmarīnus*, literally 'beyond the seas.' This was a compound adjective formed from the prefix *ultrā-* 'beyond' and *marīnus* 'of the sea' (source of English *marine*).
▶ marine, mere, mermaid

**umbilical** [16] *Umbilical* was borrowed from medieval Latin *umbilīcālis*, a derivative of Latin *umbilīcus* 'navel.' This went back ultimately to the Indo-European base *\*onobh-*, a variant of which, *\*nobh-*, produced English *navel* [OE].
▶ navel

**umbrage** [15] *Umbrage* is one of a group of English words that go back ultimately to Latin *umbra* 'shadow.' Indeed, it was originally used for 'shade, shadow' in English: 'the light, and also . . . the false umbrage which the moon doth show forth,' Betham, *Precepts of War* 1544. The expression *take umbrage* 'take offence' arises from a metaphorical extension of 'shadow' to 'suspicion,' which took place in French. The word itself reached English via Old French *umbrage* from Vulgar Latin *\*umbrāticum*, a noun use of the neuter form of Latin *umbrāticus* 'shadowy,' which was derived from *umbra*. Other English words from the same source include *adumbrate* [16], *penumbra* [17], *sombre, sombrero, umbel* [16], and *umbrella*.
▶ adumbrate, penumbra, sombre, sombrero, umbel, umbrella

**umbrella** [17] Etymologically, an *umbrella* is a 'little shadow.' The word was borrowed from Italian *ombrella*, a diminutive form of *ombra* 'shade, shadow.' This in turn went back to Latin *umbra*, source of English *sombre, umbrage*, etc. It originally denoted a 'sunshade,' and that meaning followed it into English, but it was not long before the vagaries of the British climate saw it being applied to a 'protector against rain.'
▶ umbrage

**umpire** [15] An *umpire* is etymologically someone who is 'not the equal' of others, and is therefore neutral between them. The word's ultimate source is Old French *nomper*, a compound noun formed from the prefix *non-* 'not' and *per* 'equal' (source of English *peer*). This was borrowed into English in the 14th century as *noumpere*, but soon misdivision of *a noumpere* as *an oumpere* led to *umpire* (the same process produced *adder* from an original *nadder*).

▶ peer

**umpteen** [20] *Umpteen* was derived from an earlier *umpty*. This began life as a signallers' slang term for a 'dash' in morse code (like its companion *iddy* for 'dot,' it was purely fanciful in origin). Its similarity to *twenty*, *thirty*, etc led to its being used for an 'indefinitely large number,' and *umpteen* simply replaced the *-ty* suffix with *-teen*.

**unanimous** [17] *Unanimous* means etymologically 'of a single mind,' hence 'sharing the same opinion.' It comes from Latin *ūnanimus* 'of one mind,' a compound adjective formed from *ūnus* 'one' and *animus* 'mind, spirit' (a relative of English *animal, animate*, etc).

▶ animal, animate

**uncle** [13] *Uncle* comes via Anglo-Norman *uncle* and late Latin *auunculus* from Latin *avunculus* 'mother's brother, maternal uncle' (source also of English *avuncular* [19]). This was a diminutive noun derived from the prehistoric base *\*aw-* 'grandparent,' and it has relatives in Latin *avus* 'grandfather,' Welsh *ewythr* 'uncle,' Polish *wuj* 'uncle,' Armenian *hav* 'uncle,' etc.

▶ avuncular

**uncouth** [OE] *Uncouth* originally meant 'unknown' or 'unfamiliar' – a sense which survived into the 17th century ('Now the whole superficies of the earth as well uncouth as discovered, is but a little point,' John Boys, *Works* 1616). 'Crude, awkward' is a secondary development, first recorded in the 16th century. The word was formed in the prehistoric Germanic period fron the prefix *un-* 'not' and the past participle of *\*kunnan* 'know' (whose closest living English relative is *could*).

▶ could

**unction** [14] *Unction* was borrowed from Latin *unctiō*, a derivative of *unguere* 'anoint' (source also of English *unguent* [15]). This was descended from the same prehistoric ancestor as produced Welsh *ymenyn* 'butter.' *Unctuous* [14], from the medieval Latin derivative *unctuōsus*, originally meant literally 'oily, greasy,' but has since moved into more metaphorical areas.

▶ unctuous, unguent

**under** [OE] *Under* originated as a comparative form. It has been traced back to a prehistoric Indo-European *\*ndhero-*, which meant 'lower,' and is also the ultimate source of English *inferior* [15]. This passed into Germanic as *\*unther-*, which has evolved into German *unter*, Dutch *onder*, and Swedish, Danish, and English *under*.

▶ inferior

**understand** [OE] The compound verb *understand* was formed in the centuries immediately preceding the Anglo-Saxon invasions of Britain. It is composed, of course, of *under* and *stand*, and the semantic link between 'standing under' something and 'knowing about' it may be 'being close to' it.

**undulate** [17] *Undulate* goes back ultimately to Latin *unda* 'wave,' source also of English *inundate* [17], *redundant*, and *surround*. This in turn was descended from the Indo-European base *\*ud-*, which also produced Greek *húdōr* 'water' (source of the English prefix *hydro-*), and variants of which lie behind English *vodka, water*, and *wet*.

▶ abound, inundate, redundant, sound, surround

**ungulate** see NAIL

**unicorn** [13] Legends of a one-horned beast abounded in ancient times, perhaps inspired by the rhinoceros, or a sideways view of an antelope. When the early Greek translators of the Hebrew Bible came across the word *re'em*, which seems to have denoted a sort of wild ox, they rendered it *monókerōs* (literally 'one-horn'), perhaps identifying it with the rhinoceros. The Vulgate turned this into Latin as *unicornis*, a noun use of an already existant Latin adjective meaning 'one-horned,' formed from *ūnus* 'one' and *cornū* 'horn' (a relative of English *horn*).

▶ horn

**uniform** [16] Something that is *uniform* has literally only 'one form,' the same throughout. The word comes, probably via French *uniforme*, from Latin *ūniformis*, a compound adjective formed from *ūnus* 'one' and *forma* 'form.' Its use as a noun, for a 'set of identical clothes worn by everyone,' dates from the 18th century, and was inspired by French.

▶ form

**union** [15] *Union* is one of a range of English words that go back to Latin *ūnus* 'one.' This in turn was descended from a prehistoric Indo-European *\*oinos*, which also produced English *one*. Other members of the family include *inch, ounce, unique, unite* [15], etc. As for *union* itself, its immediate ancestor was *ūniō*, a derivative of *ūnus* which denoted 'unity' or 'the number one.' The application of the English word to an 'association of workers' dates from the early 19th century (a somewhat earlier term was *combination*).

▶ inch, one, ounce, unique, unite

**unique** [17] *Unique* comes via French *unique* from Latin *ūnicus* 'only, sole.' This was derived from *ūnus* 'one,' a distant relative of English *one*. It originally meant simply 'single, sole' in English, and the extended sense 'unequalled, unparalleled,' which has often drawn the hostile criticism of purists (particularly when accompanied by qualifiers such as *very* or *completely*), did not emerge until the late 18th century, under French influence.

▶ one, union

**unison** [16] *Unison* originated as a musical term, denoting 'of the same sound.' It comes via Old French *unison* from late Latin *ūnisonus*, a compound adjective formed from *ūnus* 'one' and *sonus* 'sound' (source of English *sound*). The metaphorical sense 'agreement, concord' emerged in the 17th century.

▶ sound

**unit** [16] The term *unit* was given general currency by the 16th-century English mathematician, astrologer, and magician John Dee. It was formed from Latin *ūnus*, probably on the analogy of *digit*, and used as a mathematical term to replace *unity* as a translation of Euclid's *monás* 'indivisible number.' In a comment added to his introduction to Sir Henry Billingsley's translation of Euclid, Dee wrote 'Note the word *unit* to express the Greek *monas*, and not *unity*: as we have all commonly until now used.'

**unite** see UNION

**universe** [14] *Universe* denotes etymologically 'turned into one,' hence 'whole, indivisible.' It goes back ultimately to Latin *ūniversus* 'whole, entire,' a compound adjective formed from *ūnus* 'one' and *versus*, the past participle of *vertere* 'turn.' Its neuter form, *ūniversum*, was used as a noun meaning the 'whole world' (based on the model of Greek *to hólon* 'the whole'), and this passed into English via Old French *univers*. The Latin derivative *ūniversālis* gave English *universal* [14].

▶ convert, version

**university** [14] The etymological notion underlying a *university* is that it denotes the 'whole' number of those belonging to it. The word comes via Old French *universite* from Latin *ūniversitās*, which was derived from *ūniversus* (source of English *universe*). This originally meant the 'whole,' but in the post-classical period it was applied to guilds and other such associations, referring to the 'totality' of their membership. These included societies of teachers and students, from which the modern meaning of *university* emerged.

▶ universe

**unkempt** [15] *Unkempt* means literally 'uncombed.' It was coined from the prefix *un-* 'not' and the past participle of the now defunct verb *kemb* 'comb.' This came from a prehistoric Germanic *\*kambjan*, a derivative of *\*kambaz* 'comb' (ancestor of the English

noun *comb*). It began to be replaced by the new verb *comb* in the 14th century.

▶ comb

**until** see TILL

**unwieldy** [14] *Unwieldy* originally meant 'weak, feeble' ('a toothless, old, impotent, and unwieldy woman,' Reginald Scot, *Discovery of Witchcraft* 1584). The meaning 'awkward to handle' developed in the 16th century. The word was based on the now seldom encountered *wieldy*, which evolved from Old English *wielde* 'active, vigorous.' This in turn went back to the Germanic base *\*walth-* 'have power,' source also of English *herald* and *wield*.

▶ herald, wield

**up** [OE] *Up* is part of a widespread family of Germanic adverbs which also includes German *auf*, Dutch and Danish *op*, and Swedish *upp*. It goes back ultimately to Indo-European *\*up-*, which also produced English *over* and the prefixes *hyper-* and *super-* and may lie behind English *evil*. To *open* something is etymologically to put it 'up.'

▶ open, over

**upbraid** [OE] *Upbraid* originally meant 'throw something up against someone as a fault.' It was formed from *up* and the ancestor of modern English *braid*, which used to mean 'throw,' amongst other things. The object of the verb was originally the 'fault'; the shift of focus to the 'person blamed' began in the 13th century.

▶ braid

**upholster** [19] *Upholster* has no etymological connection with *holsters*. It is a back-formation from *upholsterer* [17], which itself was derived from an earlier but now obsolete *upholster* 'person who deals in or repairs small articles.' This was an agent noun formed from the verb *uphold* [13] (a compound of *up* and *hold*), in the now defunct sense 'repair.'

▶ hold

**uproar** [16] *Uproar* has no direct etymological connection with *roar*. It originally meant 'uprising, insurrection,' and was borrowed from Dutch *oproer*. This is a compound formed from *op* 'up' and *roer* 'movement.' It was first used in English by William Tindale, in his 1526 translation of the Bible (for Acts 21:38 he has 'that Egyptian which made an uproar, and led out into the wilderness about four thousand men'). The sense 'loud outcry,' which was inspired of course by the similarity of *roar*, emerged as early as the 1540s.

**upstart** [16] An *upstart* is etymologically simply someone who has 'started up' – but *start* in its early sense 'jump, spring, rise.' *Start-up* was an early alternative version of the word ('That young start-up hath all the glory of my overthrow,' says Don John in Shakespeare's *Much Ado About Nothing* 1599), but it did not survive the 17th century.

**uranium** [18] *Ouranós* was an ancient sky god in Greek mythology, consort of Gaea and father of Cronos and the Titans (his name was a personification of Greek *ouranós* 'heaven'). The Romans called him *Ūranus*, and the name soon came to be applied to the seventh planet from the sun after it was discovered in 1781. The term *uranium* was derived from it in 1789 by the German chemist Martin Klaproth, and is first recorded in English in 1797.

**urban** [17] *Urban* comes from Latin *urbānus*, a derivative of *urbs* 'city' (a word of unknown origin). It was preceded into English by *urbane* [16], which is essentially the same word, but came via Old French *urbaine*. It was originally used as *urban* is now, but after *urban* arrived it gradually took the metaphorical path to 'smooth, sophisticated.' The derivatives *suburb* and *suburban* date from the 14th and 17th centuries respectively; and *suburbia* was coined in the 1890s.
▶ suburban, urbane

**urchin** [13] *Urchin* originally meant 'hedgehog.' It was borrowed from Old Northern French *herichon*, which came via Vulgar Latin *\*hēriciō* from Latin *hērīcius* or *ērīcius* 'hedgehog,' a derivative of *ēr* 'hedgehog.' This ancestral sense now survives only dialectally, but its spiny connotations are preserved in *sea urchin*, which dates from the late 16th century. The metaphorical 'dirty scruffy child, brat' emerged in the 16th century too. The second syllable of *caprice* goes back to Latin *ērīcius*.
▶ caprice

**Urdu** see HOARD

**urge** [16] *Urge* was borrowed from Latin *urgēre* 'push, press, compel.' Its present participle gave English *urgent* [15], which thus means etymologically 'pressing.'
▶ urgent

**urine** [14] *Urine* comes via Old French *urine* from Latin *ūrīna*, which may be related to Greek *oûron* 'urine' (source of English *urea* [19], *ureter* [16], *urethra* [17], and *uric* [18]) and Sanskrit *varsa-* 'rain.' *Urinal* [13] comes from the late Latin derivative *ūrīnālis*.

**us** [OE] *Us* can be traced back ultimately to Indo-European *\*ns*. This passed into prehistoric Germanic as *uns*, which has evolved into German *uns*, Dutch *ons*, Swedish and Danish *os*, and English *us*. Latin *nōs* 'we' (source of French *nous*) is distantly related.
▶ our, we

**use** [13] The verb *use* comes via Old French *user* from Vulgar Latin *\*ūsāre*. This was derived from *ūsus*, the past participle of Latin *ūtī* 'use' (source also of English *utensil*, *utility* [14], *utilize* [19], etc). Latin *ūsus* was also used as a noun, meaning 'use, usage,' and this has given English the noun *use* [13] and the derivatives *usage* [13] (an Old French formation), *usual*, *usurp*, and *usury*. *Abuse* [14] and *peruse* [15] (etymologically 'use up') go back to the same Latin roots.
▶ abuse, peruse, usual, usurp, usury, utensil, utilize

**usher** [14] An *usher* is etymologically a 'doorkeeper.' The word comes via Anglo-Norman *usser* from medieval Latin *ūstārius*, an alteration of classical Latin *ōstārius* 'door-keeper.' This was derived from *ōstium* 'door,' which in turn was based on *ōs* 'mouth' (source of English *oral*). The *usher*'s job-description gradually broadened out from standing at the door to accompanying visitors inside and showing them to their places, which led in the 16th century to the emergence of the verb *usher*.
▶ oral

**usual** [14] That which is *usual* is etymologically that which is commonly 'used' or employed, or which commonly obtains. The word was acquired, probably via Old French *usual*, from late Latin *ūsuālis*, a derivative of Latin *ūsus* (source of the English noun *use*).
▶ use

**usurp** [14] Etymologically, to *usurp* something is probably to 'seize it for one's own use.' The word comes via Old French *usurper* from Latin *ūsūrpāre*, which may have been formed from the noun *ūsus* 'use' (source of English *use*) and *rapere* 'seize' (source of English *rape, rapture, ravish*, etc).
▶ rape, rapture, ravish, use

**usury** [14] *Usury* is etymologically 'use' of money lent. The term comes via Anglo-Norman *\*usurie* from medieval Latin *ūsūria*, an alteration of classical Latin *ūsūra* 'use of money lent,' hence 'interest.' This in turn was derived from *ūsus* 'use,' source also of English *use* and *usage*.
▶ use

**utensil** [14] Latin *ūtēnsilis* meant 'usable, useful.' It was derived from the verb *ūtī* 'use' (source also of English *use, utility, utilize*, etc). In the Middle Ages it was adapted into a noun, *ūtēnsilia*, meaning 'things for use, implements.' This passed into English via Old French *utensile* as *utensil*, still a collective noun, but by the 15th century it was being used for an individual 'implement.'
▶ use

**uterus** [17] Latin *uterus* 'belly, womb' goes back ultimately to an Indo-European *\*udero-* or *\*wedero-*, which also produced Sanskrit *udáram* 'belly,' Latvian *vēders* 'belly,' and possibly Greek *hustérā* 'womb' (source of English *hysteria*). It was first used in English by Helkiah Crooke in his *Description of the Body of Man* 1615.
▶ hysteria

**utility** see USE

**utopia** [16] *Utopia* means etymologically 'no-place.' It was coined by the English statesman and scholar Sir Thomas More from Greek *ou* 'not' and *tópos* 'place' (source of English *topic*). He used it as the name of an imaginary island whose inhabitants had organized their society along the lines of what he regarded as a theoretically ideal commonwealth, which he described in his book *Utopia* 1516. The word was first used as a more general term for an 'ideal place' in the early 17th century.

▶ topic

**utter**   English has two distinct words *utter*, but they come from the same ultimate source – *out*. The older, 'complete, thorough-going' [OE] originated as a comparative form of *out* (or *ūt*, as it was in the Old English period), and so morphologically is the same word as outer. It did not begin to be used as an intensive adjective until the 15th century. *Utter* 'express openly, say' [14] was borrowed from Middle Dutch *ūteren* 'drive out, announce, speak,' a derivative of Old Low German *ūt* 'out.'

▶ out

**uvula**   [14]   The uvula, a small globular mass of tissue suspended from the rear of the roof of the mouth, reminded the Romans of a small grape. They therefore called it *uva*, which meant literally 'grape' (it is not known where this ultimately came from, but it may be distantly related to Russian *jagoda* 'berry'). In postclassical times the diminutive form *uvula* took over in this sense.

# V

**vacant** [13] Latin *vacāre* meant 'be empty.' Its present participle *vacāns* has provided English with *vacant*, while its past participle lies behind English *vacate* [17] and *vacation* [14]. It also formed the basis of an adjective *vacuus* 'empty,' from which English gets *vacuous* [17] and *vacuum* [16] (the term *vacuum cleaner* is first recorded in 1903, and the consequent verb *vacuum* in 1922). English *avoid* and *void* come from a variant of Latin *vacāre*.
▶ vacate, vacuum

**vaccine** [18] *Vaccine* was adapted from Latin *vaccīnus*, which means literally 'of a cow' (it was a derivative of *vacca* 'cow,' source of French *vache*). It was used by the British physician Edward Jenner at the end of the 18th century in the terms *vaccine disease* for 'cowpox,' and hence *vaccine inoculation* for the technique he developed of preventing smallpox by injecting people with cowpox virus. The verb *vaccinate* was coined from it at the beginning of the 19th century, but *vaccine* itself was not used as a noun, meaning 'inoculated material,' until the 1840s.

**vagabond** [15] A *vagabond* is etymologically a 'wanderer.' The word comes via Old French *vagabond* from Latin *vagābundus*, which was derived from *vagārī* 'wander' (source also of English *termagant*, *vagary* [16], and *vagrant* [15]). And *vagārī* in turn was based on *vagus* 'wandering, undecided' (source also of English *vague* [16]).
▶ termagant, vagary, vagrant, vague

**vagina** see VANILLA

**vain** [13] Latin *vānus* meant 'empty' (it was related to *vacuus* 'empty,' source of English *vacuum*). It passed into English via Old French *vain* in the sense 'worthless,' and the main modern meaning 'conceited' did not develop until the 17th century. Also from *vānus* come English *evanescent*, *vanish*, *vanity* [13], and *vaunt* [14], and *wane*, *want*, etc go back to the same ultimate Indo-European base.
▶ evanescent, vanish, vanity, vaunt, wane, want

**vainglorious** see GLORY
**vale** see VALLEY
**valency** see VALUE
**valet** see VARLET
**valiant** see VALUE
**valid** [16] Something that is *valid* is etymologically 'strong,' and hence 'effective.' The word comes via French *valide* from Latin *validus* 'strong, effective,' which was derived from the verb *valēre* 'be strong' (source also of English *valiant*, *valour*, *value*, etc). The negative form *invalid* [16] also goes back to Latin, but its specific application to infirm people, differentiated with a distinct pronunciation, was introduced from French in the 17th century.
▶ valiant, valour, value

**valley** [13] *Valley* comes via Anglo-Norman *valey* from *\*vallāta*, a Vulgar Latin derivative of Latin *vallis* 'valley,' whose origins are uncertain. A more direct English descendant of *vallis* is *vale* [13].
▶ vale

**value** [14] To have *value* is etymologically to be 'strong' or 'effective,' and hence to have 'worth.' The word was borrowed from Old French *value*, a noun use of the feminine past participle of *valoir* 'be worth.' This was descended from Latin *valēre* 'be strong, be of value,' which also produced English *avail* [13], *available* [15] (which originally meant 'advantageous,' and was not used for 'accessible for use' until as recently as the 19th century), *convalesce* [15], *valency* [19], *valiant* [14], *valid*, and *valour* [14].
▶ available, convalesce, valency, valiant, valid, valour

**valve** [14] The etymological notion underlying *valve* is of a door opening and closing. The word was adapted from Latin *valva*, which denoted one of the sections of a folding or revolving door, and may have had links with *volvere* 'roll' (source of English *revolve*). It carried its original meaning with it into English, but it was not used at all widely until various metaphorical senses, such as 'flap controlling the flow of a fluid' and 'half of a shell,' evolved. The electronic *valve* is so called because current can flow in only one direction through it; the usage dates from the early 20th century.

**vamp**　English has two distinct words *vamp*. The now dated slang term for a 'seductive woman' [20] is short for *vampire*. The other *vamp*, 'extemporize on the piano,' was originally a noun meaning the 'part of a stocking that covers the foot and ankle' [13]. It was borrowed from Anglo-Norman *\*vaumpé*, a reduced form of Old French *avantpié*. This was a compound noun formed from *avant* 'in front' and *pié* 'foot.' From it in the 16th century was derived a verb *vamp*, meaning 'provide a stocking with a new vamp,' and this evolved semantically via 'patch up, repair' to, in the 18th century, 'extemporize.'

▶ vampire / foot, pedal

**vampire**　[18]　*Vampire* probably goes back ultimately to *ubyr*, a word for 'witch' in the Kazan Tatar language of an area to the east of Moscow. This was borrowed into Russian as *upyr'*, and from there probably found its way into Hungarian as *vampir*. English acquired it via French *vampire* or German *vampir*. The application of the word to a type of blood-sucking bat was introduced by the 18th-century French biologist Buffon.

**van**　see CARAVAN

**vandal**　[17]　The term *vandal* commemorates a Germanic tribe, the Vandals, who sacked Rome in 455AD, and thereby earned themselves a reputation as destroyers of civilization. Their name for themselves was *\*Wandal-*, which etymologically means 'wanderer.'

**vane**　[15]　*Vane* is an alteration of an earlier *fane* 'flag, weather-cock,' which was descended from Old English *fana*. This in turn came from a prehistoric Germanic *\*fanon*. The change from *fane* to *vane* took place in southwest England, where initial *f* and *s* have a tendency to become *v* and *z* (as in *zyder* for *cyder*).

**vanguard**　[15]　*Vanguards* have nothing to do with guarding vans. The word denotes etymologically an 'advance guard.' It is short for the long defunct *avantgard*, which was borrowed from Old French *avant-garde*, a compound formed from *avant* 'in front' and *garde* 'guard.' (Its modern French descendant was reborrowed into English as *avant-garde* [20].)

▶ avant-garde, guard

**vanilla**　[17]　A *vanilla* pod is etymologically a 'little vagina.' The word was borrowed from Spanish *vainilla*, a diminutive form of *vaina* 'sheath' (the pod was so named because of its sheath-like shape). *Vaina* was descended from Latin *vāgīna* 'sheath,' which came to be jokingly applied to the 'female reproductive passage' – hence English *vagina* [17].

▶ vagina

**vanish**　[14]　To *vanish* is etymologically to 'become empty.' The word comes via Old French *esvanir* 'disappear' from Vulgar Latin *\*exvānīre*, a variant of Latin *ēvānēscere* 'disappear' (source also of English *evanescent* [18]). This was a compound verb formed from the prefix *ex-* 'out' and *vānus* 'empty' (source of English *vain, vanity, vaunt*, etc.).

▶ evanescent, vain, vanity, vaunt

**vanity**　see VAIN

**vanquish**　[14]　*Vanquish* was adapted from *vainquiss-*, the stem form of Old French *vainquir* 'defeat.' This was derived from *vaintre* 'defeat,' a descendant of Latin *vincere* 'defeat' (source also of English *convince, invincible* [15], *victory*, etc.).

▶ convince, invincible, victory

**vapour**　[14]　Latin *vapor* meant 'steam, heat.' English acquired it via Old French *vapour*. The now archaic use of the plural, *vapours*, for a 'fit of fainting, hysteria, etc.,' which dates from the 17th century, was inspired by the notion that exhalations from the stomach and other internal organs affected the brain. *Vapid* [17] comes from Latin *vapidus* 'insipid,' which may have been related to *vapor*.

▶ vapid

**varlet**　[15]　*Varlet* and *valet* [16] are doublets – they come from the same ultimate source. This was Vulgar Latin *\*vassus*, a borrowing from Old Celtic *\*wasso-* 'young man, squire.' From *\*vassus* were derived two medieval Latin diminutive forms: *vassallus*, which has given English *vassal* [14], and *\*vassellitus*. This passed into Old French as *vaslet*, which diversified into *valet* (source of English *valet*) and *varlet* (source of English *varlet*). Both to begin with retained their original connotations of a 'young man in service to a knight,' and hence by extension any 'feudal retainer or servant,' but while *valet* still denotes a 'servant,' *varlet* went down in the world in the 16th century to 'knave.'

▶ valet, vassal

**varnish**　[14]　*Varnish* may come ultimately from *Berenice* (Greek *Bereníkē*), the name of a city in Cyrenaica, Libya, which was credited with the first use of varnishes. *Bereníkē* became a generic term in medieval Greek, and is thought to lie behind medieval Latin *veronix* 'resin used in varnishes,' which passed into English via Old French *vernis*.

**vary**　[14]　Latin *varius* meant 'speckled, variegated, changeable' (it gave English *various* [16], and may have been related to Latin *vārus* 'bent, crooked, knock-kneed,' source of English *prevaricate*). It had a range of derivatives, which have given English *variable* [14], *variance* [14], *variant* [14], *variegate* [17], *variety* [16], *variola* 'smallpox' [18] (which retains the original notion of 'speckling'), and *vary*.

▶ prevaricate, variegate, variety, variola, various

**vase** [17] Latin *vās* meant a 'dish' or 'vessel' (its diminutive forms *vāsculum* and *vāscellum* have given English *vascular* [17] and *vessel* respectively). It passed into English via French *vase*, and at first was pronounced to rhyme with *base*. This pronunciation survives in American English, but in Britain since the 19th century *vase* has been rhymed with *bores* (now defunct) and *bars* (the present-day way of saying the word).

▶ vascular, vessel

**vaseline** [19] The term *vaseline* was coined around 1872 as a trade name for a sort of petroleum jelly newly brought out by the Chesebrough Manufacturing Company. The first syllable, *vas-*, comes from an anglicized spelling of German *wasser* 'water'; the second represents the *el-* of Greek *élaion* 'oil'; and the third is the scientific-sounding suffix *-ine*.

▶ water

**vassal** see VARLET

**vast** [16] Latin *vastus* originally meant 'empty, unoccupied, deserted.' The sense 'huge,' in which English borrowed it, is a secondary semantic development. Another metaphorical route took it to 'ravaged, destroyed,' in which sense it lies behind English *devastate* and *waste*.

▶ devastate, waste

**vat** [13] *Vat* comes from a prehistoric Germanic *\*fatam* 'vessel, barrel,' which also produced German *fass*, Dutch *vat*, Swedish *fat*, and Danish *fad*. It passed into Old English as *fæt*, whose direct descendant, *fat*, had largely died out by the end of the 19th century; *vat* represents a southwestern dialect form.

**vaudeville** [18] In 15th-century France there was a fashion for songs from the valley of the Vire, in the Calvados region of Normandy (particularly popular, apparently, were the satirical songs composed by a local fuller, Olivier Basselin). They were known as *chansons du Vau de Vire* 'songs of the valley of the Vire,' which became shortened to *vaudevire*, and this was later altered to *vaudeville*. It was originally used in English for a 'popular song'; the application to 'light variety entertainment' did not emerge until the early 19th century.

**vault** *Vault* 'arched roof' [14] and *vault* 'jump' [16] are distinct words, although they share a common ancestor: Latin *volvere* 'roll, turn' (source also of English *involve, revolve*, etc). Its feminine past participle *volūta* evolved in Vulgar Latin into *\*volta*, which was used as a noun meaning 'turn,' hence 'curved roof.' English acquired it via Old French *voute* or *vaute*. The use of vaulted ceilings in underground rooms led in the 16th century to the application of *vault* to 'burial chamber.'

Also from *volvere* came Vulgar Latin *\*volvitāre*

'turn a horse,' hence 'leap, gambol.' This passed via Italian *voltare* and French *volter* into English as *vault*.

▶ involve, revolve, volume

**vaunt** see VAIN

**veal** [14] The Latin word for 'calf' was *vitulus* (it appears originally to have denoted 'yearling,' for it is probably related to Greek *étos* 'year'). Its diminutive form *vitellus* passed into English via Anglo-Norman *veel*, in the sense 'calf-meat.' Its Old French cousin, *veel*, formed the basis of a derivative *velin* 'calfskin for writing on,' which English adopted and adapted into *vellum* [15].

▶ vellum

**vector** see VEHICLE

**vegetable** [14] Latin *vegēre* meant 'be active' (it was formed from the same Indo-European base as lies behind English *vigil, vigour*, and *wake*). From it was derived *vegetus* 'active,' which in turn formed the basis of *vegetāre* 'enliven, animate.' From this again came late Latin *vegetābilis* 'enlivening,' which came to be applied specifically to plant growth. It was in this sense that the word entered English (via Old French *vegetable*), and it was not further narrowed down to 'plant grown for food' until the 18th century. Its semantic descent from its original links with 'life, liveliness' was completed in the early 20th century, when *vegetable* came to be used for an 'inactive person.' The derivative *vegetarian* was formed in the early 1840s, and *vegan* was coined from this around 1944.

▶ vigil, vigour, wake

**vehicle** [17] A *vehicle* is etymologically something that 'carries.' The word comes via French *véhicule* from Latin *vehiculum*, a derivative of *vehere* 'carry.' This also gave English *convex, inveigh, vector* [18] (etymologically a 'carrier'), and *vex* [15], and it came ultimately from a prehistoric Indo-European base *\*wegh-*, ancestor also of English *waggon, way, weigh*, etc.

▶ convex, inveigh, vector, vex, waggon, way, weigh

**veil** [13] The ultimate source of *veil* is Latin *vēlum* 'sail, curtain, veil,' and English acquired it via Anglo-Norman *veile*. To *reveal* something is etymologically to 'remove a veil' from it.

▶ reveal

**vein** [13] *Vein* comes via Old French *veine* from Latin *vēna* 'blood vessel,' a word of uncertain origin. Acquired directly from Latin were the derivatives *venose* [17] and *venous* [17].

**veld** see FIELD

**vellum** see VEAL

**velvet** [14] *Velvet* is etymologically a 'hairy' or 'downy' fabric. Its ultimate ancestor is Latin *villus* 'hair, down,' which also produced English *velours* [18]. From it was derived medieval Latin *villūtus* 'shaggy,' which passed into Old French as *velu* 'velvety.' And this in turn formed the basis of a noun *veluotte*, from which English got *velvet*. The derivative *velveteen* dates from the 18th century.

▶ velours

**vend** [17] Latin *vēndere* meant 'sell': it was a compound verb formed from *vēnum* 'sale' (source of English *venal* 'corrupt, bribable' [17]) and *dare* 'give' (source of English *data*). English acquired the word via French *vendre*, but it was preceded into the language by the derivative *vendor* [16].

▶ data, date, donate, venal

**vendetta** see VINDICATE

**veneer** [17] *Veneer* is ultimately the same word as *furnish*. Both come from Old French *fournir*, but *veneer* was routed via German, which borrowed *fournir* as *furniren*. The verbal noun derived from this, *furnirung*, was borrowed into English as *faneering* in the highly specialized sense 'provision of a thin surface layer of fine wood.' The noun *veneer* was a back-formation from this.

▶ furnish

**venereal** [15] Latin *venus* meant 'love, charm' (it came ultimately from the same Indo-European base as produced English *wish* and *winsome* and Sanskrit *vāñchā* 'wish'). It was not that common as a generic term, its most familiar role being as the name of the Roman goddess of love. From it was derived *venereus* 'of sexual love or sexual intercourse,' which English borrowed and adapted as *venereal*. The term *venereal disease* dates from the mid 17th century. Other contributions made by Latin *venus* to English include *venerable* [15] and *venerate* [17] (from Latin *venerārī* 'revere,' a derivative of *venus*), *venial* [13], and possibly *venom*.

▶ venerate, venial, Venus, winsome, wish

**vengeance** see VINDICATE

**venison** [13] Latin *vēnātiō* meant 'hunting,' hence 'hunted animals, game' (it was derived from *vēnārī* 'hunt,' which may be distantly related to English *win*). English acquired it via Old French *venison* in the sense 'flesh of hunted animals used for food,' and the modern specialization to 'deer-meat' did not begin to emerge until the 18th century.

**venom** [13] *Venom* comes via Old French *venim* from Vulgar Latin *\*venīmen*, an alteration of Latin *venēnum* 'drug, poison.' It has been speculated that this was derived ultimately from *venus* 'love' (source of English *venerate, venereal*, etc), in which case its ancestral sense would presumably have been 'love-potion.'

**vent** English has two words *vent*. The verb, 'provide with an outlet' [14], came via Old French *esventer* from Vulgar Latin *\*exventāre* 'let out air.' This was a compound verb formed from the Latin prefix *ex-* 'out' and *ventum* 'wind' (source also of English *ventilate* [15] and distantly related to English *wind*). *Vent* 'slit in the back of a garment' [15] goes back via Old French *fente* to Vulgar Latin *\*findita* 'slit,' a noun use of the feminine past participle of Latin *findere* 'split' (source also of English *fission* [19] and *fissure* [14]).

▶ ventilate, wind / fission, fissure

**ventriloquist** [17] A *ventriloquist* is etymologically a 'stomach-speaker.' The word is an anglicization of late Latin *ventriloquus*, a compound formed from Latin *venter* 'stomach' (source also of English *ventral* [18] and *ventricle* [14]) and *loquī* 'speak' (source of English *colloquial* [18], *elocution* [15], *eloquent* [14], *loquacious* [17], etc). The ultimate model for this was Greek *eggastrímuthos* 'speaking in the stomach.' The term was originally a literal one; it referred to the supposed phenomenon of speaking from the stomach or abdomen, particularly as a sign of possession by an evil spirit. It was not used for the trick of throwing one's voice until the end of the 18th century.

▶ colloquial, elocution, eloquent, locution, loquatious, ventral, ventricle

**verb** [14] Latin *verbum* originally meant simply 'word' (a sense preserved in English *verbal* [15], *verbiage* [18], and *verbose* [17]); the specific application to a 'word expressing action or occurrence,' which passed into English via Old French *verbe*, is a secondary development. *Verbum* goes back ultimately to the Indo-European base *\*wer-*, which also produced English *word*. English *verve* [17] comes ultimately from the Latin plural *verba*.

▶ verbose, verve, word

**verdict** [13] A *verdict* is etymologically a 'true saying.' The word was borrowed from *verdit*, the Anglo-Norman variant of Old French *veirdit*. This was a compound term formed from *veir* 'true' (a descendant of Latin *vērum* and relative of English *very*) and *dit* 'saying, speech,' which came from Latin *dictum*. The partial latinization of *verdit* to *verdict* took place in the 16th century.

▶ diction, dictionary, very

**verdigris** [14] Etymologically, *verdigris* means 'green of Greece.' It comes from Old French *vertegrez*, a conflation of *vert de Grece* 'green of Greece' (*vert* came from Latin *viridis* 'green,' which also gave English *verdant* [16] and *verdure* [14] and may be related to Old English *wīse* 'sprout, stalk,' Old Norse *vísir* 'bud, sprout,' and Lithuanian *veisti* 'propagate'). The reason for the application of the term to the patina on copper is not known.

▶ verdant, verdure

**verge** English has two words *verge*. The noun [14], which now means 'edge,' was originally used in English for 'penis' (it is to this day a technical term for the male reproductive organ of invertebrate animals). It comes via Old French *verge* from Latin *virga* 'rod' (source also of English *virgule* [19]), and the sense 'edge' emerged in the 15th century from the notion of the limits of territorial jurisdiction of the Lord High Steward, as symbolized by his 'rod' of office. A *verger* is likewise etymologically someone who carries an official 'rod.' The verb *verge* [17] comes from Latin *vergere* 'bend, incline,' which also gave English *converge* [17] and *diverge* [17].

▶ verger, virgule / converge, diverge

**verify**    see VERY

**veritable**    see VERY

**vermilion**    [13]  Etymologically, *vermilion* is 'worm'-coloured. The word comes from Old French *vermeillon*, a derivative of *vermeil* 'vermilion.' This in turn came from Latin *vermiculus* 'little worm,' a diminutive form of *vermis* 'worm' (source of English *vermicelli, vermin*, etc and related to English *worm*). The link between 'worms' and 'red' is that in the post-classical period, Latin *vermiculus* was used for the 'kermes,' a sort of scale insect from which red dye was obtained.

▶ vermin

**vermin**    [13]  *Vermin* comes via Old French *vermin* from Vulgar Latin *\*vermīnum* 'noxious animals,' a derivative of Latin *vermis* 'worm.' This came ultimately from Indo-European *\*wrmi-*, which also produced English *worm*, and among the other contributions it has made to English are *vermicelli* [17] (from an Italian diminutive meaning 'little worms'), *vermicular* [17], *vermiculite* [19] (so called because when heated it produces wormlike projections), *vermifuge* [17], and *vermilion*.

▶ vermicelli, vermilion, worm

**vermouth**    [19]  *Vermouth* gets its name from its being originally flavoured with wormwood, a bitter-tasting plant. The German term for the plant, and the drink, is *wermut*, a word of unknown origin, and this passed into English via French *vermout*. (The corresponding Old English name for the plant, incidentally, was *wermōd*, and this was later altered to *wormwood* from the use of the plant as a cure for intestinal worms.)

**verse**    [OE]  *Verse* is one of a large family of English words that come ultimately from the Latin verb *vertere* or its past participial stem *vers-*. Others include *versatile* [17], *version* [16], *versus* [15], *vertebra, vertical*, and *vertigo*, as well as prefixed forms such as *controversy* [14], *conversation, convert, diverse, invert* [16], *pervert* [14], and *reverse* [14]. Latin *vertere* itself came from the Indo-European base *\*wert-*, which also produced English *weird* and the suffix *-ward*. *Verse* was borrowed from the Latin derivative *versus* 'turning, turning of the plough,' hence 'furrow,' and by further metaphorical extension 'line, line of poetry.'

▶ controversy, conversation, convert, diverse, invert,

pervert, reverse, subvert, versatile, version, versus, vertebra, vertical, vertigo, weird

**vertebra**    [17]  A *vertebra* is etymologically a bony pivot, a bone on which other bones 'turn.' The word's Latin source, *vertebra*, was derived from the verb *vertere* 'turn' (source also of English *verse, version*, etc).

▶ verse

**vertical**    [16]  Latin *vertex* originally meant 'whirl' (it was derived from *vertere* 'turn,' source also of English *verse, version*, etc, and was itself borrowed into English in the 16th century). It came to be applied metaphorically to the 'spiral of hair on top of the head,' and was then extended further to 'highest point.' From it was derived late Latin *verticālis*, which passed into English via French *vertical*. It originally denoted 'of the highest point in the sky, the zenith,' and since this is directly overhead, by the 18th century *vertical* had come to be used for 'perpendicular.' Also from *vertere* came Latin *vertīgō* 'whirling,' borrowed into English as *vertigo* 'dizziness' [16].

▶ verse

**verve**    see VERB

**very**    [13]  Latin *vērus* meant 'true' (it came ultimately from Indo-European *\*wēros*, source also of German *wahr* 'true,' and it has also given English *verdict, verify* [14], *verisimilitude* [17], and *veritable* [15]). From it was derived Vulgar Latin *\*vērāius*, which passed into English via Old French *verai*. *Very* was originally exclusively an adjective, meaning 'true.' It was not used as an adverb, meaning 'truly,' until the 14th century, and its modern role as an intensifier did not begin to emerge until the 15th century.

▶ verdict, verify

**vespers**    [17]  Latin *vesper* meant 'evening,' and like Greek *hésperos* it went back ultimately to Indo-European *\*wespero-*. This was formed from a base *\*we-* which denoted 'down' and also produced English *west*, so etymologically *vesper* signified 'time when the sun goes down.' (Russian *vecher* 'evening' comes from another version of the same base.) English *vespers* itself goes back via Old French *vespres* to the plural of the variant Latin form *vespera*.

▶ west

**vessel**    [13]  Latin *vascellum* meant 'small dish or utensil.' It was a diminutive form of *vas* 'dish, vessel' (source of English *vase*). It passed into English via Old French *vaissel* and Anglo-Norman *vessel*, on the way acquiring the additional meaning 'ship.'

▶ vase

**vest**    [17]  *Vest* was originally used fairly generally for a 'robe' or 'gown.' Its earliest specific application was to a 'sleeveless jacket worn under an outer coat.' It was Charles II of England who introduced the fashion, and the first reference to *vest* in this sense is in Samuel Pepys's diary for 8 October 1666: 'The King hath yesterday, in Council, declared his resolution for setting a fashion in clothes . . . It will be a vest, I know not well how; but it is to teach the nobility thrift.' The direct descendant of this is American English *vest* for 'waistcoat.' The British application of the word to an undergarment for the upper part of the body did not emerge until the 19th century. The word came via French *veste* and Italian *veste* from Latin *vestis* 'clothing, garment.' This went back to the Indo-European base *wes-, which also produced English *wear*. The derived Latin verb *vestīre* originally meant 'clothe,' and hence 'induct into an office by dressing in the appropriate garments.' It has given English its verb *vest* [15], as well as *divest* [17] and *invest*. Other English words from the same source include *travesty, vestment* [13], *vestry* [14], and *vesture* [14].

▶ divest, invest, travesty, vestry, wear

**vestige**    [17]    *Vestige* comes via French *vestige* from Latin *vestīgium* 'footprint, trace,' a word of uncertain origin. From it was derived *vestīgāre* 'track, trace,' which has given English *investigate*.

▶ investigate

**vestment**    see VEST

**vestry**    see VEST

**vet**    [19]    *Vet* is short for *veterinary surgeon*. As a verb, it was originally used (in the 1890s) for 'examine an animal medically,' but before the end of the 19th century this had broadened out to 'investigate, screen.' *Veterinary* [18] itself came from Latin *veterīnārius*, a derivative of *veterīnus* 'of cattle and similar domestic animals.'

**veteran**    [16]    *Veteran* comes via French *vétéran* from Latin *veterānus* 'old.' This was a derivative of *vetus* 'old,' which is the ancestor of French *vieux*, Italian *vecchio*, and Spanish *viejo*. It went back ultimately to Indo-European *wetus- (source also of Latvian *vecs* 'old'). This may be related to Greek *étos* 'year,' in which case 'old' could derive from an ancestral meaning 'full of years.'

**veto**    [17]    Latin *vetō* meant 'I forbid' (it was the first person present singular of *vetāre* 'forbid,' a verb of uncertain origin which may be related to Welsh *gwadu* 'deny'). It was used in the Roman senate by tribunes of the people as a formula for objecting to proposals, and it was originally introduced into English as part of the terminology of parliamentary procedure.

**vex**    see VEHICLE

**via**    see VOYAGE

**viable**    see VITAL

**vibrate**    [17]    *Vibrate* comes from Latin *vibrāre* 'move quickly to and fro, shake.' This went back ultimately to a prehistoric Indo-European base *wib-,

*weib- 'move quickly to and fro,' which also produced English *weave* 'move to and fro' (as in 'weave through the traffic'), *whip*, and *wipe*.

▶ weave, whip, wipe

**vicar**    [13]    A *vicar* is etymologically a 'substitute' for or 'representative' of someone else: thus the pope is the *vicar* of God on Earth, and the *vicar* of a parish was originally someone who stood in for the parson or rector. The word comes via Old French *vicaire* from Latin *vicārius* 'substitute, deputy.' This was a noun use of the adjective *vicārius* 'substituting' (source of English *vicarious* [17], which more closely preserves the meaning of its Latin original). And *vicārius* in turn was derived from *vicis* 'change, turn, office,' source also of English *vicissitude* [16] and the prefix *vice-*.

▶ vicarious, vicissitude

**vice**    Including the prefix *vice-*, English has three distinct words *vice*. The oldest, 'wickedness' [13], comes via Old French *vice* from Latin *vitium* 'defect, offence,' which also gave English *vicious* [14], *vitiate* [16], and *vituperate* [16]. *Vice* 'tool for holding' [14] was acquired via Old French *viz* from Latin *vītis*. This came to denote 'vine' (in which sense it gave English *viticulture* 'vine-growing' [19]), but originally it signified 'tendril,' and it was this that lay behind the original meanings of English *vice*: 'winding staircase' and 'screw.' Its modern application began to emerge in the 15th century, and derived from the notion of jaws being opened and closed by means of a 'screw.' The prefix *vice-* [15] comes from Latin *vice* 'in place of,' the ablative case of *vicis* 'change' (source of English *vicar, vicissitude*, etc).

▶ vicious, vitiate, vituperate / viticulture

**vicinity**    [16]    Latin *vīcus* meant 'group of houses, village' (it is related to the *-wich* or *-wick* of English place-names, which originally meant 'hamlet, town'). From it was derived *vīcīnus* 'neighbouring,' which in turn produced *vīcīnitās* 'neighbourhood,' source of English *vicinity*.

**vicissitude**    see VICAR

**victim**    [15]    *Victim* originally denoted a 'person or animal killed as a sacrifice'; the more general notion of 'someone who suffers from or is killed by something' is a secondary development. The word was borrowed from Latin *victima*, which may be related to German *weihen* 'consecrate.'

**victory**    [14]    Latin *vincere* meant 'defeat' (it has given English *convince, evince, invincible*, and *vanquish*). Its past participle was *victus*, from which English gets *convict, evict, victor* [14] (etymologically a 'defeater, conqueror'), and *victory*.

▶ convict, convince, evict, evince, invincible, vanquish

**victuals**    [14]    *Victuals* are etymologically something you eat to stay 'alive.' The word came from late Latin *vĭctūālia* 'provisions,' a noun use of the plural of *vĭctūālis* 'of nourishment.' This in turn was derived from *vĭctus* 'livelihood,' which was formed from the same base as *vivere* 'live' (source of English *convivial*, *revive*, *survive*, *viper*, *vivacious*, *vivid*, etc, as well as of a range of words descended from its derivative *vīta* 'life,' such as *vital* and *vitamin*). The pronunciation of the word, /vitəlz/, reflects the form in which it was originally acquired, via Old French *vitaille*, but its spelling represents a return to its Latin original.

▶ convivial, revive, survive, viper, vivacious, vivid

**video**    see VISIT

**vie**   [15]   *Vie* is ultimately the same word as *invite*. It is a shortened version of the now defunct *envie* 'make a challenge,' which came via Old French *envier* from Latin *invītāre* (source of English *invite*), a word of uncertain origin which meant 'challenge' as well as 'invite.'

▶ invite

**view**   [15]   Etymologically, a *view* is simply something 'seen.' The word was borrowed from Old French *veue*, a noun use of the feminine past participle of *veoir* 'see.' This was descended from Latin *vidēre* 'see' (source of English *vision*, *visit*, etc).

▶ vision

**vigil**   [13]   Etymologically, to take part in a *vigil*, you have to be 'alert' and 'awake.' The word comes via Old French *vigile* from Latin *vigilia*, which was derived from the adjective *vigil* 'awake, alert,' so the notion underlying it is of staying awake to keep watch. Another derivative of the Latin adjective was *vigilāre* 'keep watch,' which lies behind English *reveille* [17], *surveillance* [19], *vigilant* [15], and *vigilante* [19] (via Spanish). It came ultimately from the Indo-European base *wog-*, *weg-* 'be lively or active,' which also produced English *vigour*, *wake* and *watch*.

▶ reveille, surveillance, vigilante, vigour, wake, watch

**vignette**   [18]   A *vignette* is etymologically a picture with a border of 'vine' tendrils, leaves, etc round it. The word comes from Old French *vignette*, a diminutive form of *vigne* 'vine' (source of English *vine* and related to English *wine*). It was originally applied to decorations in medieval manuscripts, but it was then transferred to the border around pictures, and finally to the pictures themselves. The conscious link with 'vines' now became broken, and in the 19th century the term moved on to a 'head-and-shoulders photograph' and (metaphorically) a 'short verbal description.'

▶ vine, wine

**vigour**   [14]   Latin *vigēre* meant 'be lively, flourish' (it came from the Indo-European base *wog-*, *weg-* 'be lively or active,' which also produced English *vigil*, *wake* and *watch*). From it was derived the noun *vigor* 'liveliness,' which passed into English via

Old French *vigour*. From the same source come *vigorous* [14] and *invigorate* [17].

▶ invigorate, vigil

**viking**   [19]   There are two competing theories as to the origin of the word *viking*. If its ancestry is genuinely Scandinavian (and Old Norse *víkingr* is first recorded in the 10th century), then it was presumably based on Old Norse *vík* 'inlet,' and it would denote etymologically 'person who lives by the fjords' – a logical enough notion. However, earlier traces of the word have been found in Old English and Old Frisian, from around the 8th century, which suggests the alternative theory that it may have been coined from Old English *wīc* 'camp' (ancestor of the *-wick*, *-wich* of English place-names). On this view, the term originated as a word used by the Anglo-Saxons for the Norse raiders, who made temporary camps while they attacked and plundered the local populace. It was introduced into modern English at the start of the 19th century as an antiquarian's or historian's term.

**vile**   [13]   The ancestral meaning of *vile* is 'of low status, quality, or price, cheap, common'; its use as a general epithet of 'horribleness' is a secondary development. It comes via Old French *vil* from Latin *vīlis*, a word of uncertain origin. The same source has given English *revile* [14] and *vilify* [15].

▶ revile, vilify

**villa**   [17]   Latin *vīlla* denoted a 'country house.' It was a condensation of an earlier *\*wīcslā*, which in turn was derived from *\*wīcus* 'group of houses, camp, village, etc' (source of the *-wick*, *-wich* of English place-names). And *\*wīcus* was descended from Indo-European *\*weik-*, *\*wik-*, *\*woik-*, which also produced Greek *oíkos* 'house' (source of English *economy*). To the same family belong *village* [14], a derivative of Old French *ville* in its extended sense 'town,' and *villain* [14], which came via Old French *vilain* from Vulgar Latin *\*vīllānus*, literally 'dweller in a villa,' and originally denoted 'feudal serf' (now usually spelled *villein*, to distinguish it from the metaphorical 'scoundrel, criminal').

▶ economy, village, villain

**vindicate**   [16]   Latin *vindex* meant 'claimant, defender, avenger.' From it was derived *vindicāre* 'claim, defend, revenge,' which gave English *vindicate*, as well as (via French) *avenge* [14], *revenge* [14], and *vengeance* [13]. *Vindicāre* in turn formed the basis of *vindicta* 'vengeance,' from which English gets *vindictive* [17] and (via Italian) *vendetta* [19].

▶ avenge, revenge, vendetta, vengeance, vindictive

**vine**    see WINE

**vinegar**   [13]   Etymologically, *vinegar* is 'sour wine.' The term was borrowed from Old French *vyn egre*, whose elements went back respectively to Latin *vīnum* 'wine' (source of English *wine*) and *acer* 'sharp, pungent' (source of English *eager*). In modern French, *vyn egre* became *vinaigre*, and its diminutive form has given English *vinaigrette* [17]. This originally denoted a sort of small French carriage, which supposedly resembled a vinegar-seller's cart; the modern application to an 'oil-and-vinegar dressing' is not recorded in English until the end of the 19th century.

▶ acid, acrid, eager, wine

**vintage**   [15]   The *vintage* is etymologically the 'taking away of wine.' The word's ultimate source is Latin *vindēmia* 'grape gathering,' a compound noun formed from *vīnum* 'wine' (source of English *wine*) and *dēmere* 'take away, take off' (which in turn was a compound verb based on *emere* 'buy, take'). This passed into English via Old French *vendange* as *vendage*, which by association with *vintner* [15] (another derivative ultimately of Latin *vīnum*) soon changed to *vintage*. It continued at first to be restricted to the general sense 'grape crop.' The specific application to the crop of a particular year did not begin to emerge until the 18th century, and this led at the end of the 19th century to the broad use of the word for 'year when something was produced.' Connotations of 'oldness' were encouraged by its application to 'vintage cars,' first recorded in 1928.

▶ vine, vintner, wine

**violate**   [15]   Latin *violāre* 'treat with violence' was derived from the noun *vīs* 'force, energy' (whose accusative form, *vim*, is probably the source of English *vim* [19]). Its past participle gave English *violate*, while its present participle is ultimately responsible for English *violent* [14].

▶ vim, violent

**violet**   [14]   *Violet* was borrowed from Old French *violete*, a diminutive form of *viole* 'violet.' This in turn went back to Latin *viola* 'violet,' itself acquired by English in the 15th century. The word probably originated in a pre-Indo-European Mediterranean language, which also produced Greek *íon* 'violet' (source of English *iodine*). Its primary application is as a plant-name; its use as a colour term is a secondary application.

▶ iodine

**violin**   [16]   *Violin* has been traced back to Vulgar Latin *\*vītula* 'stringed instrument,' which was based ultimately on the name of *Vītula*, a Roman goddess of joy and victory (and has also, via a prehistoric Germanic borrowing, given English *fiddle*). The Vulgar Latin term passed via Provençal *viola* and Old French *viole* into English as *viol* [15], which survives as the name of an early form of stringed instrument. Its Italian counterpart is *viola*, which has given English *viola* [18], and its diminutive form *violino* is the source of *violin*.

▶ fiddle, viola

**viper**   [16]   A *viper* is etymologically a creature that 'gives birth to live young.' The word comes via Old

French *vipere* from Latin *vīpera* 'snake.' This was a contraction of an earlier *\*vīvipera*, a compound noun formed from *vīvus* 'alive' (source of English *vivacious, vivid*, etc) and *parere* 'give birth' (source of English *parent, parturition*, etc) – in former times it was thought that snakes gave birth to live young. Latin *vīpera* is also the ancestor of English *wyvern* 'dragon-like creature' [17] and possibly of *weever* [17], the name of a type of fish with poisonous spines; and the elements from which it was formed also of course underlie the English adjective *viviparous*.

▶ parent, vivid, viviparous

**virago**   see VIRTUE

**virgin**   [13]   *Virgin* comes via Old French *virgine* from Latin *virgō*, a word of uncertain origin. The *virginals* [16], a form of small harpsichord, were so called because they were intended for playing by girls or young women.

**virgule**   see VERGE

**virtue**   [13]   Latin *virtūs* 'bravery, strength, capacity, skill, merit' was derived from *vir* 'man' (source also of English *virago* 'manlike woman' [14] and *virile* [15]), and so etymologically it denoted 'manliness.' It passed into English via Old French *vertu*. Derivatives include *virtual* [14] which, preserving another semantic aspect of its source, originally meant 'having power, in effect,' but by the 17th century had evolved into its modern sense 'so in effect or in essence'; and *virtuoso* [17], which was borrowed from Italian and goes back to the ancestral sense 'skill.'

▶ virago, virile, virtual, virtuoso

**visa**   [19]   A *visa* is etymologically something 'seen.' The word comes via French *visa* from Latin *vīsa*, literally 'things seen,' a noun use of the neuter plural form of the past participle of *vidēre* 'see' (source of English *vision, visit*, etc). The notion underlying the word is that a *visa* is a note or other mark made on a passport to signify that it has been officially 'seen' or examined.

▶ visit, vision

**visit**   [13]   *Visit* is one of a large family of English words that go back to Latin *vidēre* 'see.' This in turn was descended from the Indo-European base *\*woid-, \*weid-, \*wid-*, which also produced English *wise* and *wit*. Other members of the family include *envy, revise* [16], *survey, video* [20], *view, visa, visage, visible* [14], *vision* [13], *visor, vista* [17], and *visual* [15]. *Visit* itself comes from the Latin derivative *visitāre*, which meant literally 'go to see.'

▶ envy, revise, survey, video, view, visa, visible, vision, visor, vista, visual, wise, wit

**visor**   [14]   A *visor* is etymologically something that covers the 'face.' The word was borrowed from Anglo-Norman *viser*, a derivative of Old French *vis* 'face.' This in turn was descended from Latin *vīsus* 'sight, appearance' (a noun use of the past participle of *vidēre* 'see,' source of English *vision, visit,* etc), which in post-classical times was used for 'face.' Another derivative of Old French *vis* was *visage* 'face,' from which English got *visage* [13].

▶ visit, vision

**vista**   see VISIT

**visual**   see VISIT

**vital**   [14]   *Vital* comes via Old French *vital* from Latin *vītālis*. This was a derivative of *vīta* 'life.' And *vīta* went back ultimately to Latin *vīvus* 'living,' source of English *vivacious, vivid,* etc. *Viable* [19] is also descended from *vīta*, and etymologically means 'capable of life.'

▶ viable, vitamin, vivid

**vitamin**   [20]   The word *vitamin* was originally coined in German around 1912 by the biochemist Casimir Funk as *Vitamine*. He formed it from Latin *vīta* 'life' and *amine* 'amine,' because he thought that vitamins contained amino acids. When this was shown not to be the case, the spelling was altered to *vitamin*.

▶ amine, vital

**vitreous**   [17]   Latin *vitrum* meant 'glass' (it may be the same word as *vitrum* 'woad, plant producing blue dye,' the link being the bluish-green colour of glass, and it might even be distantly related to English *woad* itself). From it was derived *vitreus* 'clear, transparent,' which gave English *vitreous*. The sulphates of various metals have a glassy appearance, and so in medieval Latin the term *vitriolum* (a derivative of *vitrum*) was applied to them – whence English *vitriol* [14].

▶ vitriol

**vivacious**   see VICTUAL

**vivid**   [17]   *Vivid* was acquired from Latin *vīvidus* 'full of life, lively.' This was derived from *vīvere* 'live,' which in turn went back to the Indo-European base *gwei-*, source also of English *biology, quick,* and *zoo*. To the same immediate word-family belong *convivial* [17], *revive* [15], *survive* [15], *victuals, viper, vital, vitamin, vivacious* [17], and *vivisection* [18].

▶ biology, convivial, quick, revive, survive, victuals, viper, vital, vitamin, vivacious, vivisection, zoo

**viviparous**   see PARENT

**vixen**   [15]   The only Old English word on record for a 'female fox' is *fyxe*. *Fixene* first appears in the late Middle English period. It was formed using the suffix *-en*, denoting 'female.' This was once quite common – Old English had *biren* 'female bear,' for instance, and *gyden* 'goddess' – but it now survives only in *vixen*. (Its German counterpart, *-in*, is still a live suffix.) The initial *v* of *vixen* comes from southwestern England.

▶ fox

**vocation**   [15]   A *vocation* is etymologically a 'calling.' The word comes via Old French *vocation* from Latin *vocātiō*. This was derived from the verb *vocāre* 'call,' which came from the same base as *vōx* 'voice' (source of English *vocal, voice,* etc). Also from *vocāre* come *convoke* [16], *evoke* [17], *invoke* [15], *provoke* [15], *revoke* [16], *vocabulary* [16], *vocative* [15], and *vouch*.

▶ convoke, evoke, invoke, provoke, revoke, vocabulary, voice, vouch

**vodka**   [19]   *Vodka* denotes etymologically 'little water.' The word was borrowed at the beginning of the 19th century from Russian *vodka*, which is a diminutive form of *voda* 'water.' And *voda* came from the same Indo-European source (*wedōr*, *wodōr*) as produced English *water*. The euphemistic application of the term *water* to distilled spirits is also responsible for *eau de vie* and *whisky*, both of which mean literally 'water of life.'

▶ water

**vogue**   [16]   The etymological notion underlying the word *vogue* is of being borne along on the 'waves' of fashion. Its immediate source was French *vogue*. This was originally used for 'rowing,' but was subsequently extended metaphorically via 'smooth easy course' and 'successful course' to 'fashionable course.' French *vogue* itself, though, was of Germanic origin. It was a derivative of the verb *voguer* 'row, go along smoothly,' which was probably borrowed from Old Low German *wogon* 'float on the waves' (a relative of English *waggon, way,* etc).

▶ waggon, way

**voice**   [13]   *Voice* comes via Old French *vois* from Latin *vōx* 'voice,' whose other contributions to English include *vocal* [14], *vociferous* [17], and *vowel*. Its ultimate source is the Indo-European base *wek-* 'speak, say,' which also produced Latin *vocāre* 'call,' ancestor of English *vocabulary, vocation,* etc.

▶ vocal, vocation, vociferous, vowel

**void**   see AVOID

**volatile**   see VOLLEY

**volcano**   [17]   *Volcanoes* get their name from Vulcan, the Roman god of fire. His name in Latin was *Volcānus*, and it was the Italian descendant of this, *volcano*, that was originally adapted as a term for 'fire-emitting mountain.' English borrowed the word from Italian. Also commemorating Vulcan is the *vulcanizion* [19] of rubber. The term appears to have been coined around 1845 by a certain Mr Brockedon, a friend of the English chemist Thomas Hancock (1786–1865), an early pioneer of the process. Latin *Volcānus* itself may be related to Cretan *Welkhanoc*, which came from Hittite *Valhannasses*.

▶ vulcanization

**vole** [19]  A *vole* is etymologically a 'fieldmouse.' The word is short for an earlier *volemouse*, which is assumed to have been borrowed from an unrecorded Norwegian compound *\*vollmus*. The first element of this, *voll* 'field,' was descended from Old Norse *völlr* 'field,' which in turn went back to prehistoric Germanic *\*walthus* (source also of English *weald* [OE] and *wold* [OE] and German *wald* 'forest'). It may be related ultimately to *wild*. The second element, *mus*, is the same word as English *mouse*.

▶ weald, wold

**volition** [17]  *Volition* comes via French *volition* from medieval Latin *volitiō*, a noun derived from Latin *volō* 'I will.' Together with English *will*, this went back ultimately to Indo-European *\*wel-*, *\*wol-* 'be pleasing,' which also produced English *volunteer* and *voluptuous*.

▶ voluntary, volunteer, voluptuous, will

**volley** [16]  A *volley* is etymologically a 'flight' of something, such as missiles. The word comes via Old French *volee* from Vulgar Latin *\*volāta* 'flight,' which was a noun use of the feminine past participle of Latin *volāre* 'fly' (source also of English *volatile* [17]). The origins of this are not certain, although it may be distantly related to Sanskrit *garutmant-* 'bird.' The use of *volley* as a sporting term for a 'shot hit before the ball bounces' dates from the 19th century.

▶ volatile

**volume** [14]  *Volume* is one of a sizeable family of English words that go back to Latin *volvere* 'roll, turn.' Others include *convolution* [16], *convolvulus* [16], *devolution* [16], *evolution* [14], *involve* [14], *revolt*, *revolve*, *vault*, *volte-face* [19], and *voluble* [16]. *Volume* itself comes via Old French *volum* from Latin *volūmen*, a derivative of *volvere*. The sense 'book' evolved from the notion of a 'roll' of parchment. The word came to have connotations of a 'big' book, and this gave rise in the 16th century to the sense 'size of a book.' By the 17th century this had broadened out to 'size' in general, but the modern sense 'size of sound' did not emerge until the early 19th century. Latin *volvere* itself came ultimately from the Indo-European base *\*wol-*, *\*wel-* 'turn,' which also produced English *wallow*.

▶ convolution, convolvulus, devolution, evolution, involve, revolt, revolution, revolve, vault, volte-face, voluble, wallow

**volunteer** [17]  *Volunteer* comes via French *volontaire* from Latin *voluntārius*, a noun use of the adjective which gave English *voluntary* [14]. This was derived from the noun *voluntās* 'will, free will,' which itself was based on *volō* 'I will' (source also of English *volition*).

▶ volition

**voluptuous** [14]  *Voluptuous* goes back ultimately to the Indo-European base *\*wol-*, *\*wel-* 'be pleasing,' which also produced English *volunteer* and *will*. From it was descended the Latin adverb *volup* 'agreeably,' from which were derived in turn the noun *voluptās* 'pleasure' and the adjective *voluptuōsus* 'giving pleasure.' In its transmission via Old French *voluptueux* to English, it acquired additional connotations of 'sensual pleasure.'

▶ volition

**vomit** [14]  *Vomit* comes from *vomitus*, the past participle of Latin *vomere* 'vomit.' This was descended from the prehistoric Indo-European base *\*wem-*, which also produced Greek *emeín* 'vomit' (source of English *emetic* [17]).

▶ emetic

**vote** [15]  *Vote* goes back ultimately to Latin *vovēre* 'promise solemnly, wish for.' Its past participle was *vōtus*, which fed directly into English as the verb *vote*; the noun *vote* comes from the Latin derivative *vōtum*. The modern English meaning of the word comes from the notion of expressing one's 'wishes' by means of casting a ballot. 'Wishing, desiring' was a secondary semantic development of the Latin verb; its original meaning, 'promise solemnly,' is preserved in English *vow* [13], which comes via Anglo-Norman *vou* from Latin *vōtum*.

▶ vow

**vouch** [14]  *Vouch* originally meant 'call as a witness'; 'guarantee' is a 16th-century development. The word was borrowed from Old French *voucher* 'summon,' which in turn appears to have evolved from Latin *vocāre* 'call' (source of English *vocation, vocative*, etc). Anglo-Norman used the Old French infinitive verb as a noun, meaning 'summons,' from which English gets *voucher* [16]. *Vouchsafe* [14] originated as a compound of *vouch* 'guarantee' and *safe*.

▶ vocation

**vow**  see VOTE

**vowel** [14]  A *vowel* is etymologically a 'vocal' sound – that is, one made by vibrating the vocal chords. The word comes via Old French *vouel* from Latin *vōcālis*. This was short for *littera vōcālis* 'vocal letter, letter that sounds,' *sonus vōcālis* 'vocal sound,' etc. *Vōcālis* (source of English *vocal*) was derived from *vōx* 'voice' (source of English *voice*).

▶ voice

**voyage** [13]  *Voyage* goes back ultimately to Latin *via* 'way' (source also of the English preposition *via* [18]). From it was derived *viāticum*, which originally meant 'provisions for a journey,' but in post-classical times was used for simply 'journey.' English acquired it via Old French *veiyage* and Anglo-Norman *voiage*.

▶ via

**vulcanization**   see VOLCANO

**vulgar**   [14]   Latin *vulgus*, a word of uncertain origin, denoted the 'common people.' From it was derived the adjective *vulgāris*, from which English gets *vulgar*. The *Vulgate* [17], a version of the Bible translated into Latin in the 4th century, was so called because it made the text available to the 'common people.' *Divulge* comes from the same source, and means etymologically 'make known to the common people.'

▶ divulge

**vulture**   [14]   The origins of Latin *vultur* 'vulture' are uncertain, although it may be related to Latin *vellere* 'pluck, tear.' English acquired it not directly, but by way of its derived adjective *vulturius*, which produced the Old French noun *voltour*. This passed into English via Anglo-Norman *vultur*.

# W

**wafer** [14] *Wafer* and *waffle* [18] are essentially the same word. Both come ultimately from a Low German term whose underlying etymological meaning was of a 'honeycomb'-patterned cake or biscuit – a sense *wafer* has since lost. The ancestral form was *wāfel*, which seems to have come from the prehistoric Germanic base *\*wab-, \*web-* (source of English *weave*) and is probably related to German *wabe* 'honeycomb.' Old French borrowed Middle Low German *wāfel* as *gaufre* (which is where English got *goffer* 'crimp' [18] from). The Anglo-Norman version of this was *wafre* – whence English *wafer*. *Waffle* was borrowed direct into American English from Dutch *wafel*. (The verb *waffle* 'speak verbosely' [19], incidentally, is not the same word. It is a derivative of an earlier *waff* [17], used for the sounds a dog makes, which like *woof* was of imitative origin.)

▶ goffer, waffle, weave, web

**waft** [16] A *wafter* was an 'armed ship used for convoying others' (the word was borrowed from Middle Dutch *wachter* 'guard,' which came from the same prehistoric Germanic base as English *wait, wake,* and *watch*). The verb *waft* was derived from it by back-formation, and at first was used for 'convey by water, convoy' ('Because certain pirates . . . were lurking at the Thames mouth . . . Thomas Lord Camoys with certain ships of war was appointed to waft over the king,' Edward Hall, *Chronicle* 1548). The change from 'conveyance by water' to 'conveyance through the air' began in the 17th century.

▶ wait, wake, watch

**wag** [13] *Wag* was derived from the Middle English descendant of Old English *wagian* 'totter,' a word related to English *wave* of the sea. *Waggle* [15] was based on it. The noun *wag* 'comical fellow,' first recorded in the 16th century, is generally taken to be short for *waghalter*, literally 'someone who swings to and fro in a noose,' hence 'someone destined for the gallows.'

▶ waggle

**wage** [14] *Wage* and *gage* (as in *engage*) are doublets – that is to say, they come from the same ultimate source, but have drifted apart over the centuries. The source in this case was prehistoric Germanic *\*wathjam* 'pledge,' which is also the ancestor of English *wedding*. It was borrowed into Old French as *gage*, which is where English gets *gage* from; but its Anglo-Norman form was *wage*, which accounts for English *wage*. *Gage, engage,* and the derivative *wager* [14] all preserve to some degree the original notion of 'giving a pledge or security,' but *wage* has moved on via 'payment' to 'payment for work done.'

▶ engage, gage, wager, wedding

**waggon** [16] *Waggon* was borrowed from Dutch *wagen*. It has gradually replaced the native English form *wain* 'waggon' [OE]. Both words go back via prehistoric Germanic *\*wagnaz, \*wegnaz* to Indo-European *\*woghnos, \*weghnos*, a derivative of the base *\*wogh-, \*wegh-* 'carry' (which also produced English *vehicle, way, weigh*, etc).

▶ vehicle, vex, wain, wainscot, way, weigh

**wainscot** [14] *Wainscot* was borrowed from Middle Low German *wagenschot*. It is not altogether clear what the origins of this were, but the generally accepted theory is that it is a compound of *wagen* 'waggon' and *schot* 'planks, boards,' and that it therefore originally meant 'planks used for making waggons.' To begin with it was applied in English to 'high-grade oak imported from Russia, Germany, and Holland.' Such wood was used mainly for panelling rooms, and by the 16th century *wainscot* had come to signify 'wood panelling.'

▶ waggon, wain

**waist** [14] *Waist* is something of a mystery word, but it is generally taken to denote etymologically 'girth to which one has grown.' It is probably descended from an unrecorded Old English *\*wæst*, which would have gone back to prehistoric Germanic *\*wakhs-* 'grow,' source of English *wax* 'grow' (as in *wax and wane*). Related forms which support this hypothesis include Icelandic *vöxstr* and Gothic *wahstus*, which mean 'growth, size.'

**wait** [12] *Wait* originally meant 'look, spy.' But the notion of remaining in hiding, keeping a watch on one's enemies' movements led via the sense 'remain, stay (in expectation)' to, in the 17th century, 'defer action.' The word was borrowed from Old Northern French *waitier*, which was itself a loanword from prehistoric Germanic *wakhtan* (ultimate source also of English *waft*). This in turn was formed from the base *wak-*, which also produced English *wake, watch*, etc. The sense 'serve food at table' emerged in the 16th century from an earlier 'attend on.'

▶ waft, wake, watch

**waive** [13] To *waive* something is etymologically to make a 'waif' of it. The word comes from Anglo-Norman *weyver*, a derivative of the noun *weif* (source of English *waif* [14]). This originally meant 'ownerless property,' and so the verb came to be used for 'abandon.' Its specific application in English to 'relinquishing a right' emerged in English in the 15th century. Anglo-Norman *weif* itself was ultimately of Scandinavian origin.

▶ waif

**wake** English has two distinct words *wake*. The older, 'not sleep' [OE], goes back ultimately to the prolific Indo-European base *wog-*, *weg-* 'be active or lively.' This proliferated semantically in many directions, including 'growth' (in which it gave English *vegetable*) and 'staying awake,' which developed into 'watching' and from there into 'guarding' (all three preserved in *vigil*). The original sense 'liveliness' is represented in *vigour*. The prehistoric Germanic base *wak-* took over the 'not sleep, watch' group of senses. From it was derived the verb *wakōjan*, which subsequently split into two in English, producing *wake* and *watch*. The noun *wake*, which (unlike the verb) preserves the 'watch' strand of meaning (now specialized to 'watching over a dead body'), comes from the same base. *Waken* [12] was borrowed from the related Old Norse *vakna*.

*Wake* 'track of a boat' [16] probably came via Middle Low German *wake* from Old Norse *vök* 'hole in the ice.'

▶ vegetable, vigil, vigour, waft, wait, watch

**walk** [OE] *Walk* originally meant 'roll about, toss' (an 11th-century Anglo-Saxon glossary translated Latin *ferventis oceani* as 'walking sea'). This gradually broadened out via 'move about' to 'go on a journey,' but the specific application to 'travelling on foot' did not emerge until the 13th century. The verb came from a prehistoric Germanic *walkan*, which also produced Dutch *walken* 'make felt by beating' and French *gauchir* 'turn aside, detour' (source of English *gauche* [18]). It is ultimately related to Sanskrit *valgati* 'hops.'

▶ gauche

**wall** [OE] *Wall* was borrowed into Old English from Latin *vallum* 'rampart.' This originally denoted a 'stockade made of stakes,' and it was derived from *vallus* 'stake.' German *wall*, Dutch *wal*, and Swedish *vall*, also borrowings from Latin, preserve its meaning 'rampart, embankment,' but English *wall* has become considerably wider in its application. An *interval* is etymologically a space 'between ramparts.'

▶ interval

**wallet** [19] Etymologically, a *wallet* may be something 'rolled' up. The word originally denoted a 'traveller's pack'; its application to a 'small flat case for money and papers' arose in 19th-century American English. It was probably borrowed from an Anglo-Norman *walet*, which could have been formed from the prehistoric Germanic base *wal-* 'roll' (source also of English *wallow*).

**wallop** [14] *Wallop* and *gallop* are doublets – that is to say, they began life as the same word, but have gradually drifted apart. Their ultimate common source was Frankish *walahlaupan* 'jump well.' This was a compound verb formed from *wala* 'well' and *hlaupan* 'jump,' a relative of English *leap*. This was borrowed into Old French as *galoper*, which gave English *gallop*. But the northern dialect of Old French took it over as *waloper*, which is where English *wallop* comes from. This was originally used for 'gallop' ('Came there king Charlemagne, as fast as his horse might wallop,' William Caxton, *Four Sons of Aymon* 1489), but after the acquisition of *gallop* it began to go steadily downhill semantically, helped on its way perhaps by its sound, suggestive of hitting.

▶ gallop

**wallow** [OE] To *wallow* is etymologically to 'roll' about. The word goes back ultimately to the Indo-European base *wol-*, *wel-* 'roll,' which also produced English *helix, involve, vault, volume*, etc. From this was descended prehistoric Germanic *wal-*, *wel-* (source of English *waltz, welter*, etc, and possibly of *wallet*). The extended form *walw-* produced West Germanic *walwōjan*, which evolved into English *wallow*.

▶ involve, revolve, volume, waltz, welter

**walnut** [OE] A *walnut* is etymologically a 'foreign nut.' Its name alludes to the fact that the nut was regarded by the Germanic peoples as an exotic import from southern Europe, land of Romans and Celts (their own native nut was the hazel). Prehistoric Germanic *walkhaz* originally meant 'Celtic' (it was borrowed from Latin *Volcae*, the name of a Celtic people), but it soon broadened out to include anyone or anything foreign (including the Romans) within its scope. Its original Celtic connotations survive, however, in *Welsh* and *Walloon* (the name of a people of Gaulish origin), both of which go back to *walkhaz*. English shares the formation *walnut* with its Germanic neighbours – German *walnuss*, Dutch *walnoot*, Swedish *valnöt*, and Danish *valnød*.

▶ Walloon, Welsh

**walrus** [17] Etymologically, a *walrus* is probably a 'whale-horse.' The word seems to have been borrowed from Dutch *walrus*, which was an inversion of a presumed prehistoric Germanic compound represented by Old English *horschwæl* and Old Norse *hrosshvalr*. (The inversion may have been due to the influence of Dutch *walvisch* 'whale' – literally 'whale-fish' – but it could also owe something to French influence, since French noun compounds of this sort are often in the reverse order to corresponding Germanic ones.) The element *wal-* is clearly the same word as *whale*, and *-rus* is generally assumed to be *horse*. It has, however, been suggested that the *horsc-* of the Old English term was an alteration of *morsa*, a name for the walrus of Lappish origin which is also the source of French *morse* 'walrus.'

▶ horse, whale

**waltz** [18] To *waltz* is etymologically to 'roll.' The word was adapted from German *walzen*. This meant literally 'roll, revolve.' Its application to a dance that involves spinning round is a secondary development. It came from the prehistoric Germanic base *\*wal-*, *\*wel-* 'roll,' which also produced English *wallow*, *welter*, etc, and it is ultimately related to English *involve*, *volume*, etc.

▶ wallow

**wand** [12] A *wand* is etymologically a 'bendable' stick. The word was borrowed from Old Norse *vöndr* 'thin straight stick.' This in turn went back to a prehistoric Germanic *\*wanduz*, which was derived from *\*wand-*, *\*wend-* 'turn' (source also of English *wander*, *went*, etc). A stick that can be 'turned' is one that can be 'bent,' hence a 'flexible stick.' The earliest record of the word's use for a 'stick with magic powers' comes from the 15th century.

▶ wander, went

**wander** [OE] To *wander* is etymologically to 'turn' off the correct path. The word comes, together with German *wandern*, from a prehistoric West Germanic *\*wandrōjan*, which was derived from the base *\*wand-*, *\*wend-* 'turn' (source also of English *wand*, *went*, etc). The German compound *wanderlust*, literally 'travel-desire,' was borrowed into English at the beginning of the 20th century.

▶ wand, went

**wane** [OE] *Wane* and Norwegian *vana* 'spoil, waste' are the only survivors of a family of Germanic verbs that goes back to a prehistoric *\*wanōjan*. This was derived from the base *\*wan-* 'lacking,' which also produced English *want*. The related but now defunct

English adjective *wane* 'lacking' is represented in the first syllable of *wanton*.

▶ want, wanton

**want** [12] Etymologically, to *want* something is to 'lack' it (a sense still intact in the noun *want*); 'wishing to have' is a secondary extension of this. The word was borrowed from Old Norse *vanta* 'be lacking.' This in turn was descended from a prehistoric Germanic *\*wanatōn*, which was formed from the base *\*wan-* 'lacking' (source also of English *wane*).

▶ wane

**wanton** [13] Someone who is *wanton* is etymologically 'lacking in proper upbringing or discipline.' The word was formed from the Middle English prefix *wan-* 'un-' (a reduced form of the adjective *wane* 'lacking,' which is related to the modern English verb *wane*) and *towen*, a descendant of Old English *togen*, the past participle of *tēon* 'pull,' hence 'bring up, train, discipline.'

▶ wane

**war** [12] The word *war* was acquired from *werre*, the northern dialect form of Old French *guerre*. This in turn came from prehistoric Germanic *\*werra* 'strife,' which was formed from the base *\*wers-* (source also of English *worse* and German *wirren* 'confuse'). *Warrior* [13] is from the Old Northern French derivative *werreieor*. The diminutive of *guerra*, the Spanish equivalent of French *guerre*, gave English *guerilla*.

▶ guerilla

**warble** [14] The etymological notion underlying the word *warble* is of 'whirling around'; its application to sounds, originally in the sense 'whirl of notes, trill,' is a secondary development. It was borrowed from Old Northern French *werbler*, a derivative of the noun *werble* 'trill, melody.' And this in turn came from Frankish *\*hwirbilōn* 'whirl, trill,' which is distantly related to English *whirl*. (*Warble* 'swelling on an animal's back caused by insect larva' [16] is a completely different word. It may have been borrowed from the now obsolete Swedish compound *varbulde*, literally 'pustumour,' or a related Scandinavian word.)

**ward** [OE] *Ward* and *guard* are ultimately the same word. Both go back to a prehistoric West Germanic *\*wartho* 'watching over.' But whereas *guard* reached English via Old French, *ward* is a lineal descendant of the Germanic word. The noun originally meant 'watching, guarding'; its application to an individual room of an institution where people are guarded or looked after (at first including prisons as well as hospitals) dates from the 16th century. The verb *ward* (now mainly encountered in *ward off*) comes from the Germanic derivative *\*warthōjan*. The early sense 'guardianship, custody' is preserved in such expressions as *ward of court*, and also in *warden* [13] (from the Old Northern French derivative *wardein*, corresponding to the central

French form *guardien* 'guardian') and *warder* [14], from Anglo-Norman *wardere*. The word's ultimate source is the base *\*war-* 'watch, be on one's guard, take care' (source also of English *aware, beware, warn, wary*, etc).

▶ aware, beware, guard, warn, wary

**wardrobe** [14] A *wardrobe* was originally a room in which clothes were kept. It did not shrink to a cupboard until the 18th century. The word was borrowed from Old Northern French *warderobe*, a compound formed from *warder* 'look after, keep' (a relative of English *ward*) and *robe* 'garment.'

▶ robe, ward

**ware** English has two distinct words *ware*, but the likelihood is that both come from the same ultimate source – the prehistoric Germanic base *\*war-, \*wer-*. This denoted 'watch, be on one's guard, take care,' and also produced English *ward* and *warn*. It may have had links with Latin *vērērī* 'fear' (source of English *revere*). From it was formed the adjective *\*waraz*, which evolved into English *ware* [OE] – now virtually obsolete except in the derived forms *aware* [13], *beware* [13], and *wary* [16]. It is thought that *ware* 'article for sale' [OE] could also come from the base *\*war-* – its etymological meaning thus being 'something one takes care of.' Borrowed into French, *\*war-* produced *garage*, subsequently acquired by English.

▶ aware, beware, garage, guard, ward, warn, warrant, wary

**warlock** [OE] Etymologically, a *warlock* is a 'liar on oath,' and hence a 'traitor' or 'deceiver.' Indeed, the word originally meant 'traitor' in English. It soon broadened out into a general term of abuse, and it was also used as an epithet for the 'Devil,' but the modern sense 'evil sorcerer' did not emerge until the 14th century. It started life as a compound noun formed from *wǣr* 'faith, pledge' (a relative of English *very* and German *wahr* 'true') and *-loga* 'liar' (a derivative of *lēogan*, the ancestor of modern English *lie*).

▶ lie, very

**warm** [OE] English, German, and Dutch *warm* and Swedish and Danish *varm* go back to a common prehistoric source, *\*warmaz*. This in turn was descended from Indo-European *\*ghworm-, \*ghwerm-*, which also produced Greek *thermós* 'hot' (source of English *thermal, thermometer*, etc), Latin *formus* 'warm' and *fornus* 'oven' (source of English *fornication* and *furnace*), and Armenian *jerm* 'warm.'

▶ fornication, furnace, thermal

**warn** [OE] *Warn*, and its German relative *warnen*, go back to a prehistoric West Germanic *\*warnōjan*. This was formed from the base *\*war-* 'watch, be on one's guard, take care,' which also produced English *ward, ware, wary*, etc. Germanic *\*warnjan*, which evidently had close links with

*\*warnōjan*, was borrowed into French, and surfaced in English as *garnish*.

▶ garnish, ward, ware, wary

**warp** [OE] *Warp* originally meant 'throw' ('Saint Paul's head after his decease in a deep vewar [fishpond] warped was,' *Scottish Legends of the Saints* 1375). The notion of 'bending' or 'twisting' is a secondary development (first recorded in the 14th century). Its immediate inspiration may have been the related Old Norse past participle *orpinn* 'warped,' but the underlying motivation was no doubt a conceptual link between 'throwing' and 'twisting,' presumably via 'throw with a twisting action' (it is probably no coincidence that English *throw* originally meant 'twist'). The word came from a prehistoric Germanic base *\*werb-*, which also produced German *werfen* and Dutch *werpan* 'throw.' This was probably descended from Indo-European *\*wer-*, source also of Latin *vertere* 'turn,' from which English gets *revert, version*, etc.

▶ convert, revert, version, wharf

**warrant** [13] *Warrant* probably goes back ultimately to *werenti* 'protector,' a noun use of the present participle of Old High German *werren* 'protect,' which in turn was formed from the base *\*wer-* 'watch, be on one's guard, take care' (source of English *ward, wary*, etc). This was borrowed into medieval Latin as *warantus*, and passed into English via Old Northern French *warant*. The central Old French form of the word was *garant*, which passed into English via Spanish as *guarantee*.

▶ guarantee, ware

**warren** [14] A *warren* is etymologically a 'fenced-off' area. The word was acquired from *warenne*, the Anglo-Norman version of Old French *garenne* 'game-park.' This in turn came from Gaulish *\*varrenna* 'area bounded by a fence,' which was derived from *\*varros* 'post.' The specific link with rabbits (originally as a reserve set aside for breeding rabbits, now an area where wild rabbits live) is a secondary development.

**warrior** see WAR

**wary** see WARE

**wash** [OE] Etymologically, to *wash* something is probably to clean it with 'water.' Like German *waschen*, Dutch *wasschen*, and Swedish *vaska*, it goes back to a prehistoric Germanic *\*waskan*, which seems to have been derived from *\*wat-*, the base which produced English *water*. (*Washer* 'small disc with a hole' [14] is usually assumed to come from the same source, but its semantic link with *wash* has never been satisfactorily explained.)

▶ water

**wasp** [OE] Etymologically, the *wasp* may be the 'weaver.' The word comes ultimately from Indo-European *wobhes- or *wops-, which was probably derived from the base *webh-, *wobh- 'weave' (source of English weave, web, etc); the allusion is presumably to the papery nest which many species construct. West Germanic took this over as *wabis- or *waps-, and the process of metathesis (reversal of sounds) produced English wasp and German wespe. From the same Indo-European ancestor come Latin vespa (source of French guêpe, Italian vespa, and Spanish avispa) and Russian osa.

▶ weave, web

**wassail** [13] Wassail was borrowed from Old Norse ves heill, literally 'be healthy.' This was a toast or salutation given when about to drink (much like English good health!). Ves was the imperative singular of vesa or vera 'be' (a relative of English was and were) and heill is essentially the same word as English hale and whole, and related to healthy.

▶ hale, healthy, whole

**waste** [12] The etymological notions underlying waste are 'emptiness' and 'desolation.' Its main modern sense, 'squander,' is a comparatively recent development, first recorded in English in the 14th century. Its ultimate source is Latin vāstus 'empty,' which has also given English devastate and vast. From this was formed the verb vāstāre 'devastate, lay waste,' which passed into English via Old Northern French waster. The derivative wastrel dates from the 16th century.

▶ devastate, vast

**watch** [OE] Ultimately, watch and wake are the same word. The two verbs share a common ancestor (prehistoric Germanic *wakōjan), and to begin with watch was used for 'be awake' ('He sleepeth on the day and watcheth all the night,' John Lydgate, 1430). The notion of being 'alert and vigilant,' of being 'on the look-out,' is implicit in that of being 'awake' (indeed, vigil and vigilant are members of the same word family), but watch did not develop fully into 'observe, look at closely' until the 14th century. The sort of watch that tells the time is probably so called not because you look at it to see what the time is, but because originally it woke you up. The earliest records of the noun's application to a timepiece (in the 15th century) refer to an 'alarm clock'; it was not used for what we would today recognize as a 'watch' until the end of the 16th century.

▶ vegetable, vigil, vigour, waft, wait, wake

**water** [OE] Water is an ancient and widespread word, which goes back ultimately to prehistoric Indo-European *wodōr. Its relatives include Greek húdōr 'water' (source of the English prefix hydro-), Latin unda 'wave' (source of English redundant, surround, undulate, etc), Russian voda 'water' (source of English vodka), Gaelic uisge 'water' (source of English whisky), Lithuanian vanduō 'water,' Latvian ūdens

'water,' Sanskrit udán 'water,' and Hittite watar 'water.' In the Germanic languages it has become German wasser (source of English vaseline), Dutch and English water, Swedish vatten, and Danish vand. Otter comes from a variant of the same Indo-European base, as may winter, and wet is closely related.

▶ abound, hydro-, otter, redundant, surround, undulate, vaseline, vodka, wet, whisky

**Waterloo** [19] The decisive battle at which the army of Napoleon was finally defeated by British, Dutch, and Prussian forces was fought just outside the village of Waterloo, near Brussels in Belgium, on 18 June 1815. The word Waterloo soon came to be used metaphorically for a 'final and crushing defeat, something that puts one hors de combat for ever.' The first record of this new application comes in a letter written in 1816 by Lord Byron to his friend Thomas Moore: 'It [Armenian] is . . . a Waterloo of an Alphabet.'

**wave** English has two words wave, distinct in origin, which have grown to resemble each other over the centuries. The verb, 'move to and fro' [OE], goes back to a prehistoric Germanic base *wab-, which also produced English waver [14] (borrowed from Old Norse vafra 'move unsteadily') and wobble [17]. The noun wave 'movement of the sea' [16] seems to be an alteration (under the influence of the verb wave) of an earlier wawe 'wave.' This in turn probably went back to Old English wǣg 'motion, wave,' a derivative of the verb which produced modern English wag.

▶ waver, wobble / wag

**wax** Wax 'soft oily substance' [OE] and the now archaic wax 'grow, become' [OE] are distinct words. The former comes (together with German wachs, Dutch was, Swedish vax, and Danish vox) from a prehistoric Germanic *wakhsam. This in turn was descended from the Indo-European *weg- 'weave' (source also of English veil). Wax originally referred specifically to 'beeswax,' and the word's underlying etymological reference is to the combs 'woven' from wax by bees. Russian and Czech vosk 'wax' come from the same ultimate source. The verb wax goes back to the Indo-European base *woks-, a variant of which has given English auction and augment. Although it has largely died out in English, its relatives in the other Germanic languages (meaning 'grow') are still very much alive: German wachsen, Dutch wassen, Swedish växa, and Danish vokse.

▶ veil / auction, augment

**way** [OE] In common with German and Dutch weg, Swedish väg, and Danish vej, way goes back to a prehistoric Germanic *wegaz. This was formed from the base *weg- 'move, carry' (source also of English waggon, wee, and weigh), which in turn was descended from Indo-European *wegh-. This also produced English *vector, vehicle*, etc, and a variant of it is responsible for English *wag* and *wave* of the sea.

▶ vehicle, vogue, wag, waggon, wave, wee, weigh

**we** [OE] *We* goes back ultimately to Indo-European *\*wei*, which also produced Sanskrit *vayám* 'we.' The precise process by which this evolved into German *wir*, Dutch *wij*, Swedish and Danish *vi*, and English *we* has never been unravelled.

**weak** [13] Etymologically, something that is *weak* is 'bendable.' The word was borrowed from Old Norse *veikr*. This was descended from prehistoric Germanic *\*waikwaz*, which also produced German *weich* and Dutch *week* 'soft.' And this in turn was formed from *\*waikw-*, *\*wikw-* 'give way, yield,' a derivative of the base *\*wik-* 'bend,' which also produced the *witch* of English *witch hazel* [16] (etymologically the hazel with 'bendy' branches) and possibly English *week*.

**wealth** [13] The now virtually defunct *weal* [OE] meant 'welfare,' and also 'riches'; it was descended from prehistoric West Germanic *\*welon*, a derivative of the same base as produced English *well*. The abstract-noun suffix *-th* was added to it in early Middle English to produce *wealth*. This also originally meant 'welfare, well-being' as well as 'riches,' a sense which now survives only in the compound *commonwealth* [15].

▶ well

**wean** [OE] The etymological notion underlying *wean* is of 'becoming accustomed.' The specialization to 'making accustomed to food other than mother's milk' is a secondary development. The word comes from a prehistoric Germanic *\*wanjan* (source also of German *gewöhnen* 'accustom'). This was derived from the adjective *\*wanaz* 'accustomed,' which in turn was formed from the base *\*wan-*, *\*wen-*, *\*wun-*(source also of English *winsome*, *wish*, and *wont* 'accustomed' [OE]).

▶ winsome, wish, wont

**weapon** [OE] *Weapon* comes from a prehistoric Germanic *\*wæpnam*, a source it shares with German *waffe*, Dutch *wapen*, Swedish *vapen*, and Danish *vaaben*. But of the ancestry of the Germanic form nothing certain is known.

**wear** [OE] *Wear* goes back to a prehistoric Germanic *\*wazjan*, of whose other descendants only the Icelandic past participle *varinn* 'clad' survives. This was formed from the base *\*was-*, which in turn was descended from Indo-European *\*wes-*, source of Latin *vestis* 'clothing,' from which English gets *vest, vestment*, etc.

▶ vest

**weary** [OE] *Weary* is descended from a West Germanic *\*wōriga*, whose other offspring have all died out. It was formed from the base *\*wōr-*, which also pro-

duced Old English *wōrian* 'wander, totter' and Old Norse *ōrr* 'mad,' but its ultimate ancestry is uncertain.

**weather** [OE] *Weather* goes back ultimately to the Indo-European base *\*we-* 'blow,' which also produced English *ventilate* and *wind*. From it were formed two nouns, *\*wedhrom* (source of Russian *vedro* 'good weather') and *\*wetróm* (source of Lithuanian *vétra* 'storm'). One or other of these became prehistoric Germanic *\*wethram*, which evolved into German *wetter*, Dutch *weer*, Swedish *väder*, Danish *vejr*, and English *weather*. *Wither* [14] may have originated as a variant of *weather*, in the sense 'show the effects of being exposed to the elements.'

▶ ventilate, wind

**weave** English has two distinct verbs *weave*, but they have grown to resemble each other closely over the centuries. *Weave* 'make cloth' [OE] goes back to a prehistoric Germanic *\*weben*, which also produced German *weben*, Dutch *weven*, Swedish *väva*, and Danish *væve*. It was formed from the base *\*web-*, *\*wab-*(source also of English *wafer, web*, and *weft* [OE]), which in turn went back to Indo-European *\*webh-*, *\*wobh-*, probable source of English *wasp*. *Weave* 'take a zigzag course' [13] was probably borrowed from Old Norse *veifa*. This was descended from prehistoric Germanic *\*weibjan*, which came from the Indo-European base *\*weib-*, *\*wib-* 'move quickly' (source also of English *vibrate, whip*, and *wipe*). At first it meant 'move about, travel' ('Then the evil ghost fares out of the man and weaves wide . . . seeking rest,' 11th-century English poem). The notion of 'moving from side to side, threading one's way' did not emerge until the 16th century, presumably through the influence of the other verb *weave*.

▶ wafer, wasp, web, weft / vibrate, whip, wipe

**web** [OE] A *web* is etymologically something 'woven.' In common with Dutch *web*, Swedish *väf*, and Danish *væv*, the word goes back to a prehistoric Germanic *\*wabjam*. This was derived from the base *\*wab-*, *\*web-*, which also produced English *weave* 'make cloth.' The derivative *webster* [OE] originally denoted a 'female weaver,' but it now survives only as a surname.

▶ weave

**wedding** [OE] A *wedding* is etymologically a ceremony at which people 'promise' to marry each other. The word's source, the verb *wed* [OE], goes back to prehistoric Germanic *\*wathjōjan* (source also of German *wetten* 'wager'). This in turn was derived from the noun *\*wathjam* 'pledge,' which also produced English *engage, wage*, and *wager*.

▶ engage, wage, wager

**Wednesday** [OE] The Romans called the middle day of the week *Mercurii diēs* 'Mercury's day' (source of French *mercredi*, Italian *mercoledì*, and

Spanish *miercoles*). The Germanic peoples equated Mercury with their own god Woden or Odin (whose name may etymologically mean the 'inspired or mad one'), and they translated the Latin term accordingly, giving Dutch *woensdag*, Swedish and Danish *onsdag*, and English *Wednesday*.

**wee** English has two words *wee*. The older, 'small' [OE], was originally a noun, Old English *wēg* or *wēge*. This meant 'weight,' and is closely related to English *weigh*. Its use in contexts such as *a little wee*, literally 'a small weight,' meant that by the 13th century it had shifted semantically to 'small amount,' but it did not become an adjective until the 15th century. *Weeny* was derived from it in the 18th century. *Wee* 'urine, urinate' [20] and its reduplication *wee-wee* [20] are nursery words, and no doubt originated in some sort of fanciful imitation of the sound of urinating.

▶ weigh

**week** [OE] *Week* evolved from a prehistoric Germanic *\*wikōn*, which also produced German *woche*, Dutch *week*, Swedish *vecka*, and Danish *uge*. This was probably derived from the base *\*wik-* 'bend, turn, change' (source also of English *weak*), and it is thought that it may originally have denoted 'time-change,' perhaps with specific reference to the change of phase of the moon.

**ween** see WISH

**weep** [OE] *Weep* goes back to prehistoric Germanic *\*wōpjan*, which probably originated in imitation of the sound of wailing or lamentation. Most of its Germanic relatives have long since died out, but Icelandic still has *æpa* 'cry out, scream.'

**weever** see VIPER

**weevil** [15] Old English had a word *wifel* 'beetle,' but this appears to have died out, and *weevil* was probably borrowed from Middle Low German *wevel*. Both words had the same ultimate origin, however: prehistoric Germanic *\*webilaz*. It is not clear whether this was derived from the base *\*web-*, *\*wab-* 'weave' (source of English *weave* 'make cloth' and *web*), in which case the *weevil* would be the 'weaving' creature; or from the base *\*web-* 'move quickly' (source of English *weave* 'move in a zigzag way,' *whip*, etc), in which case it would be the 'quick mover.'

**weft** see WEAVE

**weigh** [OE] The etymological notion underlying *weigh* is 'carrying': for it comes ultimately from the Indo-European base *\*wegh-*, which also produced Latin *vehere* 'carry' (source of English *vector, vehicle*, etc). The idea of 'heaviness' is a secondary development. The word's immediate source was prehistoric Germanic *\*wegan*, which also produced Dutch *wegen*, Swedish *väga*, and Danish *veie* 'weigh' and German

*bewegen* 'move.' The derivative *weight* [OE] also goes back to prehistoric Germanic.

▶ vehicle, waggon, wee

**weir** [OE] A *weir* is etymologically a structure for 'hindering' the flow of water. The word's Old English ancestor was derived from the verb *werian* 'defend, protect,' also 'hinder,' and hence by extension 'dam up,' which was distantly related to Sanskrit *vr* 'cover' and *vāraya* 'stop, hinder,' and came ultimately from the Indo-European base *\*wer-* 'cover, shut.'

**weird** [OE] Originally, *weird* was a noun, meaning 'fate, destiny.' Etymologically it denoted 'that which comes about': for it was derived from the same base which produced the now obsolete English verb *worth* 'come to be, become' (a relative of German *werden* 'become'). It was used adjectivally in Middle English in the sense 'having power to control fate' (which is where the *weird sisters* who confronted Macbeth come in), but the modern sense 'uncanny' did not emerge until the early 19th century, inspired by, but taking semantic liberties with, Shakespeare's use of the word.

▶ verse

**welcome** [12] Old English had the greeting *wilcume*, which was a compound word formed from *wil-* 'pleasure' (ancestor of modern English *will*) and *cume*, a derivative of *cuman* 'come.' From it was formed the verb *wilcumian* 'welcome.' (German has the parallel *wilkommen*.) Then in the early Middle English period, due to the similarity of *well* and the influence of the parallel Old French greeting *bienvenu* (literally 'well come'), it changed to *welcome*.

▶ come, will

**weld** [16] *Weld* is ultimately the same verb as *well* (as in 'The tears welled up in his eyes'). This originally meant 'boil, melt,' but in the 15th century (perhaps under the influence of Swedish *välla* 'gush, weld') it began to be used for 'fuse metal by heating.' *Weld* itself presumably arose from the use of the past form *welled* as a present form.

▶ well

**well** English has two distinct words *well*, both of ancient ancestry. The adverb, 'satisfactorily' [OE], has relatives throughout the Germanic languages (German *wohl*, Dutch *wel*, Swedish *väl*, and Danish *vel*), and probably goes back ultimately to the Indo-European base *\*wel-*, *\*wol-*, which also gave English *voluntary, wealth*, and *will*. It was not used as an adjective until the 13th century. *Well* 'water-hole' [OE] is descended from the Germanic base *\*wal-*, *\*wel-* 'roll' (source also of English *wallet, wallow, waltz, welter*, etc), and so etymologically denotes a place where water 'bubbles' up. This original notion of turbulent overflowing liquid is better preserved in the related verb *well* 'gush' [OE], which to begin with meant 'boil,' and hence 'melt metal' ('He made him drink welled lead,' *Holy Rood* 1300), and produced English *weld*.

▶ voluntary, wealth, will / volume, wallow, waltz, weld, welter

**wellington** [19] The first duke of Wellington (1769–1852) was perhaps the best-known figure in British public life during the first half of the 19th century, having won considerable prestige for his military campaigns during the Napoleonic wars, and (in what amounted virtually to the first instance of personally endorsed clothing) several types of garment worn by or associated with him were named after him – among them the *Wellington coat*, the *Wellington hat*, and the *Wellington trousers*. It was, however, the *Wellington boot* (first recorded in 1817) that carried his name down to posterity. The abbreviation *welly* is first recorded in 1961, and its use as a verb meaning 'kick' dates from the mid 1960s. The duke is also commemorated by the *wellingtonia* [19], a large Californian conifer.

**Welsh rabbit** [18] Despite the proverbial liking of the Welsh for cheese, there is no known connection between Wales and the *Welsh rabbit*; it is thought the epithet may reflect an earlier humorous use of *Welsh* for inferior things or substitutes for the real thing (the use of one's hand to comb one's hair used to be known as the *Welsh comb*, for instance). But if the *Welsh* part of the compound is dubious, the *rabbit* part is downright impenetrable. All that can be said with reasonable certainty is that *it* is the original form (first recorded in 1725), and that *rarebit* (first recorded in 1785) is a later perversion by those who found *rabbit* a little vulgar.

**welter** [13] *Welter* was originally a verb, meaning 'roll about' (borrowed probably from Middle Dutch *welteren*, it came ultimately from the Germanic base *\*wal-*, *\*wel-* 'roll,' source also of English *wallet, wallow, waltz*, etc, and is distantly related to English *involve, revolve*, etc). It was first used as a noun in the 16th century, in the sense 'confusion, turmoil,' but the modern sense 'confused mass, jumble' did not emerge fully until the mid 19th century. The *welter* of *welterweight* [19], which originally meant 'heavyweight horseman or boxer,' may be the same word, but it is perhaps more likely to have been derived from the verb *welt* in the sense 'hit, thrash.' This originally meant 'provide a shoe with a welt or strip of leather,' and was derived from the noun *welt* [15], a word of uncertain origin.

▶ involve, revolve, volume, wallow, waltz, weld, well

**wend** [OE] *Wend* comes from the prehistoric Germanic base *\*wand-*, *\*wend-* 'turn,' which also produced German and Dutch *wenden*, Swedish *vända*, and Danish *vende* 'turn' (and English *wand* and *wander*). It started off meaning 'turn' in English too, but it soon broadened out to 'go,' and from the end of the 15th cen-

tury its past form *went* has been used as the past tense of *go*.

▶ wand, wander, wind

**werewolf** [OE] Etymologically, a *werewolf* is probably a 'man-wolf.' Its first element, *were-*, is generally assumed to be the same word as the long obsolete Old English noun *wer* 'man' (a relative of Latin *vir* 'man,' from which English gets *virile*).

▶ virile, world

**west** [OE] Etymologically, the *west* may be the direction in which the sun goes 'down.' Together with German and Dutch *west*, Swedish *väster*, and Danish *vest*, it comes from a prehistoric Germanic *\*westaz*. This in turn was descended from the Indo-European base *\*wes-*, which also produced Latin *vesper* (source of English *vespers*) and Greek *hésperos* 'evening' and was related to Sanskrit *avas* 'down.' French *ouest* and Spanish *oeste* were borrowed from English *west*, Rumanian *vest* from German *west*.

▶ vespers

**wet** [OE] *Wet* is closely related to *water*. Together with Swedish *våt*, Danish *vaad*, Norwegian *vaat*, Icelandic *votur*, and Frisian *wiet, wiat*, it was formed from the same prehistoric base as produced English *water*.

▶ water

**whale** [OE] *Whale* comes from a prehistoric Germanic *\*khwal-*, which also produced Swedish and Danish *hval* and the *wal-* of German *walfisch* 'whale.' The expression *a whale of*, meaning 'no end of,' originated in the USA towards the end of the 19th century.

**wharf** [OE] *Wharf* has relatives in German *werft* 'wharf, shipyard' and Dutch *werf* 'shipyard.' All three appear to go back to a prehistoric Germanic base *\*(kh)werb-*, *\*(kh)warb-* 'turn,' which also produced German *werfen* 'throw' and English *warp*.

▶ version, warp

**what** [OE] *What* traces its history right back to Indo-European *\*qwod*, which also produced Latin *quod* 'what.' The Germanic descendant of this was *\*khwat*, which has evolved into German *was*, Dutch *wat*, Swedish *vad*, Danish *hvad*, and English *what*.

**wheat** [OE] *Wheat* is etymologically the 'white' grain. The word comes from prehistoric Germanic *\*khvaitjaz* (source also of German *weizen*, Dutch *weit*, Swedish *hvete*, and Danish *hvede*), which was derived from a variant of the base *\*khwīt-*, source of English *white*. It alludes to the 'white' flour produced by grinding the grain.

▶ white

**wheatear** [16] The *wheatear* is etymologically the 'white-arsed' bird. The word is a back-formation from an earlier *wheatears*, a singular form which came to be regarded as plural. And *wheatears* in turn was an alteration (due no doubt to confusion with *wheat*) of *whiteeres*, a compound formed from *white* and *arse*. Like the parallel French term *culblanc*, it alludes to the white feathers on the bird's rump.

▶ arse, white

**wheel** [OE] A *wheel* is etymologically simply something that 'goes round.' It is a member of a large family of words that goes back to Indo-European *\*qweqwlo-*, which was derived from *\*qwelo-*'go round.' Other members include Greek *kúklos* 'circle' (source of English *cycle*), Sanskrit *cakrá-* 'circle, wheel' (source of English *chukker*), Serbo-Croat and Czech *kolo* 'wheel,' and Russian *koleso* 'wheel.' Its prehistoric Germanic descendant was *\*khwekhula*, which evolved into Dutch *wiel*, Swedish and Danish *hjul*, and English *wheel*.

▶ chukker, cycle, encyclopedia

**when** [OE] *When* was formed from the ancient interrogative base *\*qwo-* (source also of English *what, who*, etc) and a nasal suffix which also appears in *then*. From the same ancestor, but with an additional dental suffix, came Latin *quando* 'when,' source of English *quandary*.

▶ quandary

**where** [OE] *Where* is an ancient Indo-European formation derived from the interrogative base *\*qwo-* (source also of English *what, who*, etc). In Germanic (where its relatives include Dutch *waar*, Swedish *var*, Danish *hvor*, and the *war-* of German *warum* 'why') it has largely become limited in its application to 'place,' but in other branches of the Indo-European language family it performs other interrogative functions: Latin *cūr* 'why,' for instance, Welsh *pyr* 'why,' and Sanskrit *kárhi-* 'when,' beside Lithuanian *kur* 'where.'

**whether** [OE] *Whether* was formed in the prehistoric Germanic period from the interrogative base *\*khwa-, \*khwe-* (source of English *what, who*, etc) and the comparative suffix *\*-theraz*, which also occurs in English *other*. Its Germanic relatives include German *weder* 'neither' and Swedish *hvar* 'each.' English *either* goes back to a Germanic compound formed from the ancestors of *ay* and *whether*.

▶ either, other

**which** [OE] Etymologically, *which* means 'what like, of what form or sort?' The word was formed in the prehistoric Germanic period from the interrogative base *\*khwa-, \*khwe-* (source of English *what, who*, etc) and *\*līka-* 'body, form' (source of English *like* and also incorporated into English *each* and *such*). Its Germanic relatives include German *welch* and Dutch *welk* 'which.'

▶ like

**Whig** [17] *Whig* appears to be short for the now obsolete Scottish term *whiggamaire*. This presumably originally meant 'horse-driver' (it is assumed to have been formed from the Scottish verb *whig* 'drive,' whose origins are not known, and *maire*, a Scottish form of *mare* 'female horse'), but its earliest recorded application was to Presbyterian supporters in Scotland. It was later adopted as a name for those who opposed the succession of the Catholic James II, and by 1689 it had established itself as the title of one of the two main British political parties, opposed to the Tories.

**while** [OE] *While* comes via prehistoric Germanic *\*khwīlō* from the Indo-European base *\*qwi-*. This denoted 'rest,' and its meaning was carried through into Latin *quiēs* (source of English *quiet*) and *tranquillus* (source of English *tranquil*) and Swedish *hvila* and Danish *hvile* 'repose, refreshment.' In English, however, and the other Germanic languages (German *weile* and Dutch *wijl*), the notion of 'rest' has passed, presumably via 'period of rest,' to 'period of time.' English *while* was first used as a conjunction in the 12th century.

▶ quiet, tranquil

**whin** SEE GORSE

**whip** [13] *Whip* was originally a verb, meaning 'move quickly.' It was probably borrowed from Middle Low German or Middle Dutch *wippen* 'vacillate, swing,' which in turn went back to the prehistoric Germanic base *\*wip-* 'move quickly' (source also of English *wipe*). And *\*wip-* itself was descended from Indo-European *\*wib-*, from which English gets *vibrate*. *Wafer, weave, web*, etc come from variants of the same base. The application of *whip* to a 'flexible implement for lashing' is first recorded in the 14th century.

▶ vibrate, weave, wipe

**whisk** SEE WHIST

**whisky** [18] *Whisky* denotes etymologically 'water of life.' The word is short for an earlier *whiskybae*, which was an alteration of *usquebaugh*; and this in turn was an anglicization of Gaelic *uisge beatha* 'water of life' (Gaelic *uisge* 'water' comes from the same Indo-European source as English *water*, and *beatha* 'life' is related to Latin *vīta* 'life' and English *vital*). The distinction in spelling between Scotch *whisky* and American and Irish *whiskey* goes back no further than the 19th century. French *eau de vie* 'brandy,' literally 'water of life,' is semantically identical.

▶ vital, water

**whisper** [OE] *Whisper* comes ultimately from the prehistoric Germanic base *\*khwis-*, which imitated a sort of hissing sound. This also produced German *wispeln* and *wispern* 'whisper,' and with a different suffix it gave English *whistle*.

▶ whistle

**whist** [17] The game of *whist* was originally called *whisk*, and it is generally assumed that the name came from the 'whisking' away of the cards after the tricks had been taken (*whisk* [14] itself was borrowed from a Scandinavian source that went back ultimately to the prehistoric Germanic base *\*wisk-* 'move quickly'). Charles Cotton, however, in his *Complete Gamester* 1680, said that it was 'called Whist from the silence that is to be observed in the play' (*whist* is also a now archaic exclamation meaning 'be quiet!').

**whistle** [OE] Like *whisper*, *whistle* goes back ultimately to the prehistoric Germanic base *\*khwis-*, which denoted a 'hissing' sound. Related forms include Swedish *vissla* 'whistle' and Danish *hvisle* 'hiss.'

▶ whisper

**white** [OE] *White* goes back ultimately to Indo-European *\*kwitnos* or *\*kwidnos*, which was formed from the same base as produced Sanskrit *sveta-* 'white' and Russian *svet* 'light.' It passed into prehistoric Germanic as *\*khwītaz*, which has since evolved into German *weiss*, Swedish *vit*, Danish *hvid*, and English *white* (Dutch *wit* comes from a variant of the same Germanic source). *Wheat* is etymologically the 'white' grain.

▶ wheat, Whitsun

**whitlow**   see FLAKE

**Whitsun** [OE] *Whitsun* is etymologically 'white Sunday.' The name comes from the ancient tradition of clothing newly baptized people in white on the feast of Pentecost. The abbreviated form *Whit* began to be used with other days of the week (such as *Whit Monday*) in the 16th century, but its broader modern usage (as in *Whit week*, *Whit bank holiday*, etc) did not emerge until the end of the 19th century.

▶ Sunday, white

**who** [OE] *Who* goes right back to Indo-European *\*qwos*, *\*qwes* (source also of Russian *kto* 'who'), whose neuter form *\*qwod* gave English *what*. Its prehistoric Germanic descendant was *\*khwaz*, *\*khwez*, which has evolved into German *wer*, Dutch *wie*, Danish *hvo*, and English *who*. *Whom* comes from the Old English dative form *hwǣm*.

**whole** [OE] *Whole* is at the centre of a tightly-knit family of English words descended from prehistoric Germanic *\*khailaz* 'undamaged' (the other members – *hail* 'salute,' *hale*, *hallow*, *heal*, *health*, and *holy* – have branched off in different semantic directions, but *whole* has stayed fairly close to its source). The Germanic form, which also produced German *heil*, Dutch *heel*, and Swedish and Danish *hel*, went back to an Indo-European *\*qoilos*, source also of Russian *celyj* 'whole' and Welsh *coel* 'good omen.' *Hale* [13] originated as a northern variant of *whole* (whose *wh-* spelling emerged in the 16th century). The compound *wholesome* was probably formed in Old English, but it is not recorded until the 12th century.

▶ hail, hale, hallow, heal, health, holy

**whore** [OE] A *whore* is etymologically a 'lover.' The word goes back ultimately to the Indo-European base *\*qār-*, which also produced Latin *cārus* 'dear' (source of English *caress* and *charity*), Old Irish *caraim* 'I love,' and Latvian *kārs* 'randy, greedy.' It gave prehistoric Germanic *\*khōrōn*, which evolved into German *hure*, Dutch *hoer*, Swedish *hora*, Danish *hore*, and English *whore* (whose *wh-* spelling first appeared in the 16th century).

▶ caress, charity

**why** [OE] *Why* goes back to Indo-European *\*qwei*, the locative case of the interrogative base *\*qwo-* (source of English *what* and *who*). This passed into prehistoric Germanic as *\*khwī*, which has since died out in all the Germanic languages apart from Danish (*hvi*) and English (*why*).

**wick** [OE] *Wick* 'burning fibre in a candle or lamp' has West Germanic relatives in German *wieche* and Dutch *wiek*, but its ultimate ancestry is uncertain (a connection has been suggested with Old Irish *figim* 'I weave'). The *wick* of *get on someone's wick* 'annoy someone,' incidentally (first recorded in 1945), is probably a different word. It appears to be short for *Hampton Wick*, rhyming slang for 'prick, penis' (Hampton Wick is a district in southwest London; its *wick* means historically 'village, town,' and is the same word ultimately as the *-wich*, *-wick* of English place-names).

**wicked** [13] *Wicked* and *witch* are closely related. *Wicked* is an extension, using the suffix *-ed*, of the now obsolete adjective *wick* 'wicked.' And this in turn originated as an adjectival use of Old English *wicca* 'wizard,' whose feminine form is the ancestor of modern English *witch*.

▶ witch

**wicket** [13] A *wicket* was originally a 'small gate,' and etymologically the word appears to denote something that 'turns' – presumably on a hinge in opening and closing. It was borrowed from Old Northern French *wiket*, which in turn came from a Germanic source represented also by modern Swedish *vika* 'fold, turn.' The set of stumps originally used for cricket resembled a gate – indeed the game's first batsmen may have defended an actual gate in a sheep pen – and so it came to be known as a *wicket*. This was in the 18th century; the extension of the term to the 'pitch' dates from the mid 19th century.

**wide** [OE] *Wide* is a general Germanic word, with relatives in German *weit*, Dutch *wijd*, and Swedish and Danish *vid*. All are descended from prehistoric Germanic *\*wīdaz*, which may go back ultimately to the Indo-European base *\*wi-* 'apart, away' (source also of Sanskrit *vitarám* 'further'). *Width* was coined in the early 17th century, probably on the analogy of *breadth*.

**widow** [OE] A *widow* is etymologically a woman who has been 'separated,' left 'solitary.' The word goes back ultimately to Indo-European *\*widhewo*, an adjective formed from the base *\*weidh-* 'separate' (source also of English *divide* and Sanskrit *vidhu-* 'solitary'). This produced a large number of words for 'widow' in the Indo-European languages, including Latin *vidua* (source of French *veuve*, Italian *vedova*, and Spanish *viuda*), Russian and Czech *vdova*, and Welsh *gweddr*. To the Germanic languages it has given German *witwe* and Dutch *weduwe* as well as English *widow*. *Widower* was coined in the 14th century.

▶ divide, individual

**width** see WIDE

**wield** [OE] To *wield* something is etymologically to 'command' or 'rule' it. Indeed, that is what the word originally meant in English. 'Handle, use' is a secondary development. It goes back to a prehistoric base *\*wald-*, which also produced German *walten*, Lithuanian *valdyti*, Czech *vládnouti*, and Polish *wɫadać* 'rule, govern' and Russian *vladet'* 'possess, own.' And this in turn was probably an extension of Indo-European *\*wal-*, source also of Latin *valēre* 'be strong,' from which English gets *valid, value*, etc.

▶ valid, value

**wife** [OE] *Wife* originally meant simply 'woman,' but the semantic restriction to 'married woman' began in the Old English period and has become more and more firmly established as the centuries have passed. Of the word's Germanic relatives, German *weib* has largely been replaced by *frau*, and Dutch *wijf*, Swedish *vif*, and Danish *viv* are no longer front-line words. It is not known what its ultimate source was. A *woman* is etymologically a 'wife-man,' that is, a 'woman-person,' a 'female-person.'

**wig** [17] *Wig* is short for *periwig* [16], which in turn is an alteration of *perwike*, a now defunct variant of *peruke* [16]; and *peruke* came via French *perruque* from Italian *perrucca*, a word of unknown origin. *Wigging* 'scolding,' first recorded at the beginning of the 19th century, may have been inspired by the notion of being told off by a *bigwig* [18], etymologically a 'high-ranking bewigged dignitary.'

▶ periwig, peruke

**wiggle** see EARWIG

**wild** [OE] *Wild* is a general Germanic word, shared by German and Dutch (*wild*) and Swedish and Danish (*vild*). All go back to a prehistoric ancestor *\*wilthijaz*, which in turn was probably descended from Indo-European *\*ghwelt-* (source of Welsh *gwyllt* 'wild'). The derivative *wilderness* [OE] etymologically denotes the 'condition of being a wild animal.' It originated as an abstract noun formed from Old English *wild dēor* 'wild animal.' But by the time it appears in texts, the modern sense 'wild land' is complete. The noun is thought to have been the source of the now defunct verb *wilder*, which probably served as the basis of *bewilder* [17]. *Wildebeest* [19] was acquired from Afrikaans.

▶ bewilder, wilderness

**will** *Will* the noun [OE] and the two verbs *will* [OE] all go back ultimately to the Indo-European base *\*wel-*, *\*wol-*'be pleasing,' which also produced English *voluntary, voluptuous, wealth, well* 'satisfactorily,' etc. From it was derived a noun, *\*weljon*, which evolved into English *will*, and also German *wille*, Dutch *wil*, Swedish *vilja*, and Danish *vilje*. The verb *will* 'decide on or resolve by force of the will' was formed in the prehistoric Germanic period from the noun. The auxiliary verb *will*, expressing intention or future time, comes from a prehistoric Germanic *\*weljan*. *Would* evolved from its original Old English past form *wolde*.

▶ voluntary, voluptuous, wealth, will, would

**willy-nilly** [17] *Willy-nilly* originated in the expression *will I, nill I*, literally 'whether I wish it or do not wish it' (*nill* 'be unwilling,' long defunct as an independent verb, was formed from *will* and the negative prefix *ne-*).

**wimp** [20] The first record of the word *wimp* 'feeble ineffectual person' is from as long ago as 1920, but it was not used at all widely until the early 1960s. Its origins have never been satisfactorily explained. Perhaps the least unlikely suggestion is that it is short for *whimper*. No connection with the now obsolete slang *wimp* 'woman' [20] (perhaps an alteration of *women*) has ever been demonstrated. In the 1980s WIMP was used as an acronym for 'weakly interacting massive particle' and for 'windows/icon/mouse/pointer,' a computer term.

**win** [OE] *Win* probably goes back ultimately to the Indo-European base *\*van-* 'overcome, conquer,' which also produced Sanskrit *van-* 'gain, acquire.' Its Germanic relatives include German *gewinnen* 'gain' and Swedish *vinna* 'win.'

**wind** English has three distinct words *wind*. The noun, 'moving air' [OE], came from a prehistoric Germanic *\*windaz*, which also produced German and Dutch *wind* and Swedish and Danish *vind*. This in turn went back to Indo-European *\*went-*, whose other descendants include Latin *ventus* (source of English *vent, ventilate*, etc) and Welsh *gwynt*. And *\*went-* itself was derived from the base *\*we-* 'blow,' source also of Greek *aétēs* 'wind' and *áēr* 'air' (from which English gets *air*), Sanskrit *vátas* 'wind,' and Russian *vejat* 'blow.' The now archaic verb *wind* 'blow a horn' [16], for all that it rhymes with *wind* 'wrap round,' was derived from the noun *wind*. *Wind* 'wrap round' [OE] originally meant 'go in a particular direction'; 'wrap' did not emerge until the 14th century, via an intermediate 'go in a circle.'

It came from a prehistoric Germanic *windan (source also of German and Dutch winden, Swedish vinda, and Danish vinde), which was formed from a variant of the base which produced English wand, wander, and wend.

► air, vent, ventilate, weather, winnow / wand, wander, went

**window** [13] A window is etymologically a 'wind-eye' – that is, an 'eye'-like opening for admitting the air. The word was borrowed from Old Norse vindauga, a compound noun formed from vindr 'wind' and auga 'eye.' Danish vindue is descended from the Old Norse form, which was also taken over by Irish as fuinneog.

► eye, wind

**wine** [OE] Wine comes from Latin vīnum. This was borrowed into prehistoric Germanic as *wīnam, which subsequently evolved into German wein, Dutch wijn, Swedish and Danish vin, and English wine. It also gave French vin and Italian and Spanish vino, and was extensively acquired by other Indo-European languages, including Russian and Serbo-Croat vino, Polish wino, Lithuanian vỹnas, and Welsh gwin. The Latin word itself came from an ancient Mediterranean source, possibly non-Indo-European, which also produced Greek oínos 'wine' (source of English oenology [19]), Albanian vēne 'wine,' and Armenian gini 'wine.' The same ancestral term also fed into the Semitic languages, giving Arabic wain, Hebrew yayin, and Assyrian īnn 'wine.' Latin vīnum additionally gave English vintage and vintner, and its derivative vīnea 'vineyard, vine' produced English vine [13].

► oenology, vine, vintage, vintner

**wing** [12] Wing was borrowed from Old Norse vængir, source also of Swedish and Danish vinge and Norwegian veng. This came ultimately from the Indo-European base *we- 'blow,' and the missing semantic link with 'wing' may be 'flutter.'

**winnow** [OE] Etymologically, to winnow grain is to separate it from the chaff by means of the 'wind.' The verb was coined in the Old English period from wind. The same notion underlay Latin ventilāre 'winnow' (source of English ventilate), which was derived from ventus 'wind' (a relative of English wind).

► wind

**winsome** see WISH

**winter** [OE] Winter is a general Germanic word (German and Dutch spell it the same, Swedish and Danish have vinter). Its prehistoric ancestor was *wentrus, but the ultimate source of this is uncertain. It could well go back to a nasalized version of the Indo-European base *wed-, *wod-, *ud- 'wet' (source also of English otter, water and wet), in which case winter would be etymologically the 'wet' season. But an alternative theory traces it back to Indo-European *wind- 'white' (source of Breton gwenn, Welsh gwyn – which may un-

derlie English penguin – and Irish fionn 'white'), in which case it would denote the 'white' season.

**wire** [OE] Wire probably goes back ultimately to the Indo-European base *wi- 'plait.' Related forms in other Germanic languages have now largely died out. The adjective wireless is first recorded in 1894 (in the term wireless telephone); its use as a noun dates from around 1903.

**wise** English has two distinct words wise, but they come from the same ultimate source: the Indo-European base *woid-, *weid-, *wid-. This denoted 'see,' and hence 'know,' and it also produced English idea, vision, and wit. From it was formed the past participial adjective *wīttos, which passed into prehistoric Germanic as *wīsaz 'knowing things, learned.' And this has since evolved into German weise, Dutch wijs, Swedish and Danish vis, and English wise. Wisdom [OE] and wizard are derivatives. Meanwhile, another derivative of the same prehistoric base was the Germanic noun *wīsōn, *wīsō, whose original meaning 'appearance' (going back to the ancestral 'see' of the base) had developed via 'for, shape' and 'kind, sort' to 'way, manner.' This produced German weise, Dutch wijze, Swedish and Danish vis (used largely in compounds and phrases), and English wise (similarly nowadays restricted mainly to compounds, such as likewise and otherwise). Guise is ultimately the same word, filtered through Old French.

► guise, idea, vision, wit, wizard

**wiseacre** [16] Wiseacre has no etymological connection with acres. The word's ancestral meaning is 'person who sees or knows things, prophet.' It was borrowed from Middle Dutch wijsseggher, which denoted 'soothsayer' (with no derogatory connotations). And this in turn came from Old High German wīssago, an alteration (due to the similarity of wīs 'wise' and sagen 'say') of wīzago 'prophet,' which was derived from the prehistoric Germanic base *wīt- 'know' (source of English wise and wit).

**wish** [OE] Wish comes from a prehistoric Germanic *wunskjan, which also produced German wünschen, Swedish önska, and Danish ønske. Its ultimate ancestor is the Indo-European base *wun-, *wen-, *won-, source also of English wean, ween 'think, suppose' [OE] (now archaic except in the derivative overweening [14]), the win- of winsome [OE], and wont 'accustomed,' and of German wonne 'joy.'

► overweening, wean, winsome, wont

**wit** Both the noun wit [OE] and the verb [OE] go back ultimately to the Indo-European base *woid-, *weid-, *wid-. This originally meant 'see,' in which sense it has given English visible, vision, etc, but it developed metaphorically to 'know,' and it is this sense that lies behind English wit. The noun to begin with denoted 'mind, understanding, judgement, sense' (a meaning preserved in expressions such as 'keep one's wits about one' and 'slow-witted'), and the modern sense 'clever humourousness' did not begin to emerge until the 16th century. The verb has now virtually died out, except in the expression *to wit*. *Witness* is etymologically the state of 'knowing.' Other English words that come from the same Indo-European base or its Germanic descendant include *guide, history, idea, story*, and *twit*.

▶ guide, guise, history, idea, story, twit, vision, wise, witness

**witch** [OE] The close Germanic relatives of *witch* have died out, but it seems that it may be related to German *weihen* 'consecrate' and even, distantly, to English *victim* (etymologically 'someone killed in a religious ritual'), so the word's underlying signification is of a 'priestess.' *Wicked* was derived from Old English *wicca* 'wizard,' the masculine form of *wicce*, ancestor of modern English *witch*.

▶ wicked

**with** [OE] The ancestral meaning of *with* is 'against' (retained by its German relative *wider*). It goes back ultimately to the Indo-European base *wi-*, which denoted 'separation.' The notion of 'accompaniment' is a secondary development, albeit an ancient one, and the idea of 'instrumentality' did not emerge until the 12th century.

**wither** see WEATHER

**witness** [OE] *Witness* originally meant 'knowledge' or 'wisdom'; it was simply an abstract noun formed from *wit*. This was extended via 'knowledge gained by observation' to 'testimony' in the Old English period, and by the beginning of the Middle English period 'person who gives testimony' was well established.

▶ wit

**wizard** [15] A *wizard* is etymologically a 'wise' man – indeed originally the word was used for 'philosopher' or 'sage,' without any suggestion of magical practices. It was derived from *wise*. The distinction between philosophy and magic was sufficiently blurred in the Middle Ages for the sense 'magician' to emerge in the 16th century, and that is the one which has prevailed.

▶ wise

**wobble** see WAVE

**wog** see GOLLYWOG

**wolf** [OE] *Wolf* is an ancient word, which has been traced back to Indo-European *wlqwos*. This, or its variant *lukwos*, also produced Greek *lúkos* (source of English *lycanthropy* '(delusion of) turning into a wolf' [16]), Latin *lupus* (source of French *loup*, Italian *lupo*, and Spanish *lobo*, and probably also of English *lupin* [14]), Sanskrit *vrkas*, Russian *volk*, Polish *wilk*,

Czech *vlk*, Serbo-Croat *vuk*, Lithuanian *vilkas*, Latvian *vilks*, Albanian *u'lk*, and Armenian *gail*. In prehistoric Germanic it gave *wulfaz*, which has evolved into German, Dutch, and English *wolf* and Swedish and Danish *ulv*.

▶ lupin, lycanthropy

**woman** [OE] A *woman* is etymologically a 'wife-man' – that is to say, a 'female person.' The word was compounded in the Old English period from *wīf* 'woman' (source of modern English *wife*) and *man* 'person' (source of modern English *man*). Already by the end of the Old English period the *f* of *wifman* was disappearing, giving *wiman*, and the influence of the *w* sound started to turn this into *woman* in the 13th century. *Woman* did not finally oust the two more ancient words for 'female person,' *wife* and the now obsolete *quean*, until the end of the Middle English period.

▶ man, wife

**wonder** [OE] *Wonder* is something of a mystery word. It is widespread in the Germanic languages (German has *wunder*, Dutch *wonder*, Swedish *undran*, and Danish *undren*), but its ultimate ancestry is unknown.

**wont** see WEAN

**wood** [OE] The ancestral meaning of *wood* is probably 'collection of trees, forest'; 'tree' (now obsolete) and 'substance from which trees are made' are secondary developments. The word goes back to prehistoric Germanic *widuz*, which also produced Swedish and Danish *ved* 'firewood,' and it has Celtic relatives in Gaelic *fiodh* 'wood, woods,' Welsh *gwydd* 'trees,' and Breton *gwez* 'trees.' Its ultimate source is not known for certain, although it has been suggested that it may go back to the Indo-European base *weidh-* 'separate' (source also of English *divide* and *widow*). According to this theory, it would originally have denoted a 'separated' or 'remote' piece of territory, near the outer edge or borders of known land; and since such remote, uninhabited areas were usually wooded, it came to denote 'forest' (*forest* itself may mean etymologically 'outside area,' and the Old Norse word for 'forest,' *mork*, originally signified 'border area').

**wool** [OE] *Wool* goes back to Indo-European *wlnā*, which also produced Latin *lāna* (source of English *lanolin* [19]), Czech *vlna*, Polish *we†na*, and Welsh *gwlān* (probable source of English *flannel*). In prehistoric Germanic it had become *wullō*, which evolved into German *wolle*, Dutch *wol*, Swedish *ull*, Danish *uld*, and English *wool*.

▶ flannel, lanolin

**word** [OE] *Word* and *verb* are closely related. Both go back ultimately to the Indo-European base *wer-* 'speak, say,' which also produced Greek *rhétōr* 'public speaker' (source of English *rhetoric*), Latvian *vārds* 'word,' and Lithuanian *vardas* 'name.' Its prehistoric Germanic descendant was *wordam*, which has given German *wort*, Dutch *woord*, Swedish and Danish *ord*, and English *word*.

▶ verb

**work** [OE] *Work* is at the centre of a small family of English words that go back ultimately to Indo-European *werg-*, *worg-* 'do, work' (other members include *energy, organ*, and *orgy*). From this base was formed the noun *wergon*, which passed into prehistoric Germanic as *werkam*, and evolved from there into German and Dutch *werk*, Swedish *verk*, and English *work*. *Wright* 'craftsman' [OE] (which now survives only in compounds) comes from the same source (with the transposition of *r* and the vowel), as does *wrought*, originally the past participle of the verb *work*.

▶ energy, organ, orgy, wright, wrought

**world** [OE] Etymologically, *world* means 'age of man.' That is the basis of its earliest recorded sense, 'earthly existence, human life.' But already by the 9th century it was being used for the 'earth' itself. It is a compound noun formed in the prehistoric Germanic period from *weraz* 'man' (probable source of the *were-* of English *werewolf* and related to *virile*) and *ald-* 'age' (ancestor of English *old*), and its relatives include German *welt*, Dutch *wereld*, Swedish *verld*, and Danish *verden*.

▶ old, virile, werewolf

**worm** [OE] The ancestral meaning of *worm* appears to be 'snake'; its application to smaller limbless creatures is a secondary development. It comes from a prehistoric Germanic *wurmiz*, *wurmaz*, which also produced German *wurm*, Dutch *worm*, and Danish *orm* 'worm' and Swedish *orm* 'snake.' And this in turn went back to Indo-European *wrmi-*, *wrmo-* (source also of Latin *vermis*, from which English gets *vermilion* and *vermin*), a possible derivative of the base *wer-* 'turn, twist' (source of English *convert, reverse*, etc) – in which case the *worm* would be etymologically the 'twisting' or 'winding' creature.

▶ vermilion, vermin

**wormwood** see VERMOUTH

**worry** [OE] *Worry* originally meant 'strangle.' It comes from a prehistoric West Germanic *wurgjan*, which also produced German *würgen* 'choke, strangle.' The sense 'harass physically' (as in 'dogs worrying sheep') emerged in the 16th century, via an intermediate 'seize by the throat,' and the modern sense 'vex, disturb' came on the scene in the 17th century, but the verb was not used intransitively until the mid-19th century.

**worse** [OE] *Worse* goes back to prehistoric Germanic *wersizon*. This was a comparative formation based on *wers-*, which also produced English *war* and German *wirren* 'confuse.' The superlative *worst* [OE] came from the same base.

**worship** [OE] *Worship* began life as a compound noun meaning virtually 'worthiness.' It was formed from the adjective *worth* and the noun suffix *-ship* 'state, condition,' and at first was used for 'distinction, credit, dignity.' This soon passed into 'respect, reverence,' but it was not used in specifically religious contexts until the 13th century. The verb dates from the 12th century.

▶ worth

**worth** [OE] *Worth* is a general Germanic adjective, with relatives in German *wert*, Dutch *waard*, Swedish *värd*, and Danish *værd* (*worth* 'value' [OE] is a noun use of the adjective). Its ultimate ancestry is uncertain, although it has been speculated that it may go back to the Indo-European base *wer-* 'turn,' which also produced Latin *vertere* (source of English *convert, version*, etc), German *werden* 'become,' and the now obsolete English verb *worth* 'become,' not to mention English *weird* and possibly *worm*. Derived from *worth* are *worship* and *worthy* [13].

▶ worship, worthy

**would** [OE] *Would* goes back to *wold-*, the Old English past tense of *will*. Its vowel is inherited from the Indo-European variant *wol-* (as in German *wollen* 'will, want'), rather than the *wel-* that produced the English present form *will*. Its use as an auxiliary to form the conditional dates back to the Old English period.

▶ will

**wound** [OE] *Wound* is a widespread Germanic word, with relatives in German *wunde*, Dutch *wond*, and Icelandic *und* (Danish *vunde* is a reborrowing from Low German). Its ultimate origins are uncertain, but it has been speculated that it may go back to an Indo-European base *wen-*, which also produced Welsh *gwanu* 'stab.'

**wrangle** see WRONG

**wrap** [14] The antecedents of *wrap* are a mystery. It has no known Germanic relatives, although it is similar to North Frisian *wrappe* 'stop up' and Danish dialect *vrappe* 'stuff.' A possible connection has been suggested with Greek *ráptein* 'sew, patch' and Lithuanian *verpti* 'spin.'

**wreath** see WRIST

**wreck** [13] *Wreck* goes back ultimately to the Indo-European base *wreg-*, a variant of which may be responsible for English *urge*. Its Germanic descendant *wrek-* formed the basis of a verb *wrekan* 'drive.' The native English descendant of this is *wreak* [OE], which originally meant 'drive out,' and developed its modern meaning via 'give vent to anger or other violent emotions.' *Wreck* itself was acquired via Old Norse *wrek* and Anglo-Norman *wrec*, and etymologically it denotes a ship that has been 'driven' on to the shore. A variant of the same base, *wrak-*, lies behind English *wretch* [OE] (etymologically someone 'driven' out, an 'exile') and also possibly French *garçon* 'boy.'

▸ urge, wreak, wretch

**wriggle**   see WRY

**wright**   see WORK

**wring**   see WRONG

**wrist**   [OE] The *wrist* is etymologically the 'twisting' joint. The word goes back to prehistoric Germanic *\*wristiz*, which also produced German *rist* 'instep, wrist' and Swedish *vrist* 'instep, ankle.' This was derived from the base *\*writh-*, whose *wr-* sound seems originally to have been symbolic of the action of twisting. Variants of the base lie behind English *wreath* [OE], *wrest* [OE], and *writhe* [OE]; and *gaiter* may be related.

▸ wreath, wrest, writhe

**write**   [OE] The etymological notion underlying *write* is of 'cutting' or 'scratching' (it is related to German *reissen* 'tear'). The earliest form of writing involved cutting marks on stone, wood, etc, and the same word was carried over when the technology of writing moved on to pen and ink. It comes from a prehistoric Germanic *\*wrītan*, but its ultimate origins are not known. The noun *writ* [OE] goes back to the same Germanic base.

▸ writ

**writhe**   see WRIST

**wrong**   [OE] Etymologically, *wrong* probably means 'twisted.' It was borrowed into late Old English from Old Norse *\*vrangr* 'awry' (*rangr* is the recorded form), which was descended from prehistoric Germanic *\*wrangg-* (source also of English *wrangle* [14]). A variant of the same base, *\*wrengg-*, produced English *wring* [OE].

▸ wrangle, wring

**wrought**   see WORK

**wry**   [16] *Wry* means literally 'twisted' (many other English words beginning with *wr-*, such as *wrist* and *writhe*, share the same basic meaning). It comes from the now obsolete verb *wry* 'deviate, twist,' which was descended from Old English *wrīgian* 'turn, tend in a particular direction.' *Wriggle* [15] is probably related.

▸ wriggle

**wyvern**   see VIPER

# X

**xenon** [19] *Xenon* is etymologically the 'strange' gas. It was named in 1898 by its discoverer, the British chemist Sir William Ramsay. He adapted the term from the neuter form of Greek *xénos* 'strange,' which may be a distant relative of English *guest, hospital, host*, etc, and is also the source of English *xenophobia* 'fear of foreigners' [19].

▶ guest, hospital, host, xenophobia

**xerox** [20] Greek *xērós* meant 'dry' (it may be the ultimate source of English *elixir*, and is perhaps distantly related to English *serene* and *serenade*). From it was derived in the 1940s the term *xerography*, which denotes a process of photographic reproduction that does not involve the use of liquid developers. And *xerography* in turn formed the basis of *xerox*, which was registered as a trademark for the process in 1952 by the Haloid Company of Rochester, New York (later renamed the Xerox Corporation).

▶ elixir, serenade, serene

**xylophone** [19] Etymologically, a *xylophone* makes 'sounds' from 'wood.' The term was coined in the 1860s from Greek *xúlon* 'wood' (an allusion to the instrument's tuned wooden bars) and the combining form *-phone* 'sound.'

# Y

**yacht** [16] A *yacht* is etymologically a boat for 'chasing' others. The word was borrowed from early modern Dutch *jaghte*. This was short for *jaghtschip*, literally 'chase ship,' a compound noun formed from *jaght*, a derivative of the verb *jagen* 'hunt, chase,' and *schip* 'ship.' The Dutch word (whose present-day form is *jacht*) has been borrowed into many other European languages, including French and German *jacht* and Russian *jakhta*.

**Yankee** [17] *Yankee* appears to have started life as a nickname for Dutchmen, and it is thought that it may represent Dutch *Janke*, a diminutive form of the common Dutch forename *Jan*. It was first used as a term for inhabitants of New England (where of course there were many early Dutch settlers) in the mid-18th century, and its application gradually spread to cover all the northern states and (more loosely, by non-American speakers) the whole of the USA.

**yard** *Yard* 'enclosed area' [OE] and *yard* 'three feet' [OE] are distinct words, both of ancient ancestry. The former probably goes back ultimately to Indo-European *\*ghorto-*, which also produced Latin *cohors* 'court' (source of English *cohort* and *court*) and *hortus* 'garden' (source of English *horticulture*) and Russian *gorod* 'town' (as in *Leningrad*). Its prehistoric Germanic descendant was *\*gard-*, which, as well as providing English with *yard*, has produced *garden*, *garth* [14] (via Old Norse), and the second syllable of *orchard*.

*Yard* 'three feet' originally meant 'stick, rod' (a sense preserved nautically, as in *yardarm* [16]). It goes back ultimately to prehistoric Germanic *\*gazdaz* 'pointed stick' (source of the *gad* of *gadfly* [16], etymologically the fly with the 'sting'). From this was derived West Germanic *\*gazdjō*, which evolved into German *gerte* 'sapling, riding cane,' Dutch *gard* 'twig, rod,' and English *yard*. The Anglo-Saxons used the term as a unit of measurement of land, equal to about five metres (what later became known as a *rod, pole,* or *perch*), but its

modern use for 'three feet' did not emerge until the 14th century.
► cohort, court, garden, garth, horticulture, orchard / gadfly

**yarn** [OE] *Yarn* comes from prehistoric Germanic *\*garn-*, which also produced German, Swedish, and Danish *garn* and Dutch *garen*. This in turn went back to an Indo-European base whose other descendants include Greek *khordḗ* 'string' (source of English *chord, cord*). The sailors' expression *spin a yarn* 'tell a story' led in the 19th century to the use of *yarn* for 'story, tale.'
► chord, cord

**yawn** [OE] *Yawn* goes back ultimately to the Indo-European base *\*ghei-, \*ghi-*, which also produced Greek *kháskein* 'gape' (a close relative of English *chasm* [17]) and Latin *hiāre* 'gape, yawn' (source of English *hiatus* [16]). The base passed into prehistoric Germanic as *\*gai-, \*gi-*, whose surviving descendants are German *gähnen*, Dutch *geeuwen*, and English *yawn*. English *gap* and *gape* probably come from an extension of the same Indo-European base.
► chasm, gap, gape, hiatus

**year** [OE] *Year* is part of a widespread European family of 'time'-words that goes back ultimately to Indo-European *\*jēr-, \*jōr-*. This also produced Greek *hṓrā* 'season' (ultimate source of English *hour*), Czech *jaro* 'spring,' and Avestan (the ancient Persian sacred language) *yāre* 'year.' From it was descended prehistoric Germanic *\*jǣram*, which has evolved into German *jahr*, Dutch *jaar*, Swedish *år*, Dutch *aar*, and English *year*. It has been speculated that the Indo-European forms themselves may have been derived from a base meaning 'go,' in which case the etymological notion underlying the word would be of time proceeding.
► hour

**yearn** SEE EUCHARIST

**yeast** [OE] *Yeast* is etymologically a substance that causes 'fermentation.' For its ultimate source is the Indo-European base *\*jes-* 'boil, foam, froth,' which also produced Greek *zeín* 'boil' (source of English *eczema*) and Welsh *iās* 'seething.' Its Germanic descendant produced German *gischt* 'yeast, froth,' Dutch *gist, gest* 'yeast,' and English *yeast*.

▶ eczema

## yell   see NIGHTINGALE

## yellow
[OE]   *Yellow* is a member of an ancient and widespread family of European colour-terms descended from Indo-European *\*ghel-, \*ghol-*, which denoted both 'yellow' and 'green.' From it were descended Latin *helvus* 'yellowish' and possibly *galbus* 'greenish-yellow' (source of French *jaune* 'yellow' and English *jaundice*), Greek *kholé* 'bile' (source of English *choleric, melancholy*, etc), Russian *zheltyj* 'yellow,' Lithuanian *geltonas* 'yellow,' and English *gall* and *gold*. In the Germanic languages it has produced German *gelb*, Dutch *gel*, Swedish and Danish *gul*, and English *yellow*. A *yolk* [OE] is etymologically a 'yellow' substance.

▶ choleric, gall, gold, jaundice, melancholy, yolk

## yeoman
[14]   Etymologically, a *yeoman* is probably simply a 'young man'; indeed originally the word denoted a 'junior household servant,' between a squire and a page in rank. It started life as *yongman*, a compound of Middle English *yong* 'young' and *man*, and was gradually eroded to *yeoman*. The modern sense 'freeholding farmer,' and its metaphorical extensions, emerged in the 15th century.

▶ man, young

## yes
[OE]   *Yes* is descended from Old English *gese*. It is thought that this was a compound formed from *gēa* 'yes' (ancestor of archaic English *yea* and related to German and Dutch *ja* 'yes') and *sīe*, the third-person present singular subjunctive of *be*, and that it therefore originally meant literally 'yes, may it be so.' It was at first used as a response to negative questions, while *yea* was used for positive questions, but around the end of the 16th century this distinction began to disappear, and *yea* has since died out.

▶ yea

## yesterday
[OE]   The *yester-* of *yesterday* (and of *yesteryear* [19], coined by Dante Gabriel Rossetti) was originally a free-standing word, meaning 'yesterday,' but by the time records of it in Old English begin it was already locked into a collocation with *day*. Its ultimate source is Indo-European *\*ghes*, which also produced Latin *herī* (source of French *hier*, Italian and Rumanian *ieri*, and Spanish *ayer*), Welsh *doe*, German *gestern*, and Dutch *gisteren*.

## yet
[OE]   *Yet* is one of the mystery words of English. It seems to have emerged from the Anglo-Frisian group of dialects in northeastern Europe before the Angles and Saxons crossed the Channel (Old Frisian had *iēta*), but its ultimate source is unknown.

## yield
[OE]   *Yield* is descended from prehistoric Germanic *\*gelthan* 'pay,' which also produced German *gelten* 'pay' (German *geld* 'money' comes from the same base). It originally meant 'pay' in English too, and it seems the sense 'surrender,' which emerged in the 13th century, may be due to the influence of French *rendre* 'give,' which is used reflexively for 'surrender.'

## yoghurt
[17]   It has taken a long time for *yoghurt* to settle down orthographically, and the process is not yet complete. It was originally acquired (from Turkish *yoghurt*) in the 1620s as *yoghurd*, and since then spellings such as *yaghourt, yooghort, yughard, yohourth*, and *yaourt* (reflecting the fact that Turkish *gh* is silent) have been tried. *Yoghurt* still vies with *yogurt*.

## yoke
[OE]   The etymological idea underlying *yoke* is of 'joining' – here, of joining two animals together. The word came ultimately from Indo-European *\*jugom*, which also produced Latin *jugum* 'yoke' (source of English *conjugal, jugular* [16], and *subjugate* [15]), Welsh *iau* 'yoke,' Czech *jho* 'yoke,' Sanskrit *yugám* 'yoke,' etc. The prehistoric Germanic descendant of this was *\*jukam* (borrowed into Finnish as *juko*), which evolved into German *joch*, Dutch *juk*, Swedish *ok*, Danish *aag*, and English *yoke*. The Indo-European form itself was derived from the base *\*jug-, \*jeug-, \*joug-* 'join,' which also produced Latin *jungere* 'join' (source of English *join, junction*, etc) and Sanskrit *yoga* 'union' (acquired by English via Hindi as *yoga* [19], which literally denotes 'union with the universal spirit').

▶ conjugate, join, jugular, junction, subjugate, yoga

## yolk   see YELLOW

## you
[OE]   *You* was originally the accusative and dative form of *ye* 'you,' but it began to take over as the nominative form in the 15th century, and at the same time was in the process of ousting the singular *thou* to become the general second-person pronoun. Its West Germanic ancestor *\*iwwiz*, which also produced German *euch* and Dutch *u*, went back ultimately to Indo-European *\*ju* (source also of Greek *úmme*, Sanskrit *yūyám*, and Lithuanian *jūs*). *Your* [OE] comes from the same source, with the genitive ending *-er*.

## young
[OE]   *Young* is part of a widespread family of words that go back to Indo-European *\*juwngkós* 'young' (others include Welsh *ieuanc*, Irish *ōg*, and Sanskrit *juvacás*). And this in turn was derived from *\*juwen-*, which produced Latin *juvenis* (source of English *junior, juvenile*, etc), Lithuanian *jaunas*, Russian *junyj*, Bulgarian *jun*, etc. The Indo-European adjective passed into prehistoric Germanic as *\*juwunggaz*. This was later contracted to *\*junggaz*, which evolved into German *jung*, Dutch *jong*, Swedish and Danish *ung*, and English *young*. *Youth* [OE], and its relatives German *Jugend* and Dutch *jeugd*, go back to prehistoric

West Germanic *jugunth-, an alteration of *juwunth-, which was derived from *juwunggaz 'young.'

▶ junior, juvenile, yeoman, youth

**your** see YOU

**Yule** [OE] Old English gēol, the ancestor of modern English Yule, was originally the name of a pre-Christian mid-winter festival, but it later came to be applied to 'Christmas.' It was related to Old Norse jól 'mid-winter festival' (possible source of English jolly), but where it ultimately came from is not known. It has been speculated that it may be descended from the Indo-European base *qwelo- 'go round' (source of English cycle and wheel), in which case it would denote etymologically the 'turn' of the year.

**yuppie** [20] Yuppie is an acronym, formed in the USA from the initial letters of 'young urban professional.' It came on the scene in 1984, and at first competed with yumpie (formed from 'young upwardly mobile people'). It was yuppie which won out, and indeed has thrived to such an extent as to produce a whole range of (more or less ephemeral) clones such as buppie 'black yuppie,' guppie 'green [ecologically concerned] yuppie,' and Juppie 'Japanese yuppie.'

# Z

---

**zany** [16] *Zany* originated as the name of a character in the old Italian commedia dell'arte, who tried, rather feebly, to mimic the antics of the clown. It came from Italian *Zanni*, a Venetian and Lombardic variant of *Gianni*, the pet form of *Giovanni* (the Italian equivalent of English *John*). Its meaning was broadened out to 'buffoon' in the 17th century, but it does not seem to have really established itself as an adjective until the mid 19th century.
▶ John

**zeal** [14] *Zeal* is closely related to *jealousy*. It comes via late Latin *zēlus* from Greek *zḗlos* 'fervour, jealousy.' The medieval Latin derivative *zēlōsus* has left English a double legacy: *zealous* [16] and (via Old French) *jealous*.
▶ jealous

**zenana** SEE GYNAECOLOGY

**zenith** [14] Arabic *samt arrās* means literally 'path over the head.' *Samt* 'path, road' made its way via Old Spanish *zenit* and Old French *cenit* into English as *zenith*, bringing with it the metaphorical application to the 'point in the sky directly overhead.' The plural of *samt*, *sumūt*, is the ultimate source of English *azimuth* [14].
▶ azimuth

**zero** [17] In common with many other English mathematical terms, *zero* comes ultimately from Arabic. Its distant ancestor is Arabic *sifr*, a noun use of an adjective meaning 'empty,' which also produced English *cipher*. It passed into English via Old Spanish *zero* and French *zéro*.
▶ cipher

**zither** SEE GUITAR

**zodiac** [14] The *zodiac* is etymologically a circle of 'little animals.' Greek *zṓidion* originally denoted a 'carved figure of an animal' (it was a diminutive of *zṓion* 'animal,' a relative of English *zoo*). From it was derived the adjective *zōidiakós*, which was used in the expression *zōidiakós kúklos* 'circle of carved figures,' denoting the twelve figures or signs representing the divisions of a band around the celestial sphere. *Zōidiakós* became a noun in its own right, and passed into English via Latin *zōdiacus* and French *zodiaque*.
▶ zoo

**zombie** [19] *Zombie* was originally the name of a snake-god in the voodoo cult of West Africa, and later of the Caribbean, and it comes from a West African language (it is related to Kongo *nzambi* 'god' and *zumbi* 'fetish'). It was later applied to a reanimated corpse in the voodoo cult, and a ghoulish sense of humour transferred the English word in the 1930s to a 'catatonically slow-witted person.'

**zoo** [19] Greek *zṓion* meant 'animal' (it came from the Indo-European base *\*gwei-*, which also lies behind English *biology*, *quick*, and *vital*). From it was formed modern Latin *zōologia* 'study of animals,' which English adapted as *zoology* [17]. *Zoological* was derived from this in the 19th century, and when the Zoological Society of London opened their exhibition of live wild animals in Regent's Park in 1829, they called it the *Zoological Gardens*. This was soon abbreviated to 'the Zoological,' and by the mid 1840s it had shrunk further to *zoo*.
▶ biology, quick, vital